C0-DBT-221

Jeffrey D. Allred, Deseret News

Conference-goers file into the Conference Center prior to the Saturday Morning session in October.

BX
8606
D47
2012
GTU

GTU

Deseret News

President
Clark Gilbert

Managing editor
Richard Hall

Church News editor
Gerry Avant

Almanac editor
Shaun Stahle

Almanac assistant
Dell Van Orden

Church News staff
Marianne Holman
Ryan Morgenegg
R. Scott Lloyd
Jason Swensen
Sarah Jane Weaver
Jerry Wellman

Church News artist
Aaron Thorup

LDS Church graphics/maps
Gary Christensen

Church History Department
Church Historian and Recorder
and Executive Director
Elder Marlin K. Jensen

Assistant Executive Director
Elder Paul K. Sybrowsky

Assistant Church Historian/
Recorder
Richard E. Turley Jr.

Almanac chairman
Grant A. Anderson

Staff contributors
Jeff Anderson
Mary Teresa Anderson
Mel Bashore
Jay Burrup
Clint Christensen
Scott Christensen
Marie Erickson
Matt Heiss
Gordon Irving
Mike Landon
Christine Marin
Blake Miller
Brian Reeves
William W. Slaughter
Sarah Sorenson
Jennifer A. St. Clair

TABLE OF CONTENTS

6 1156 1920

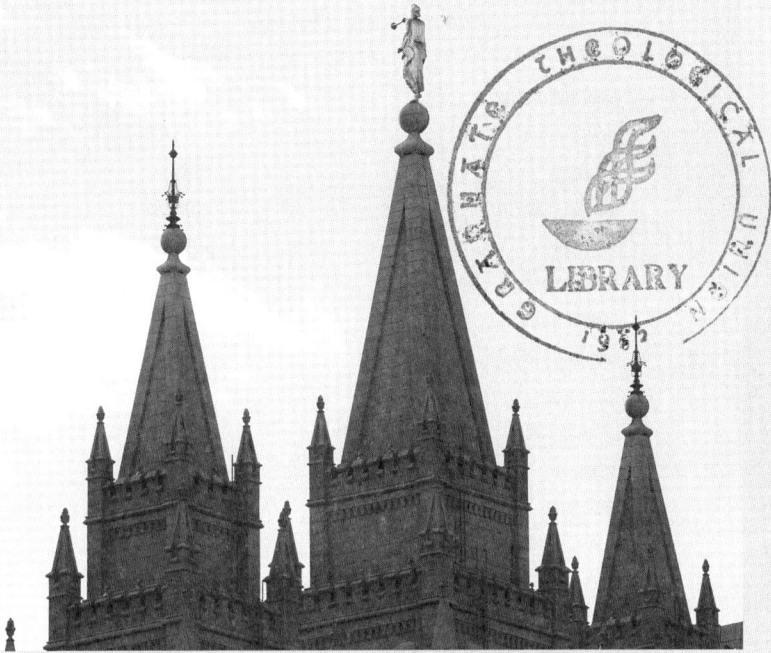

Scott G Winterton, Deseret News

The magnificent spires of the Salt Lake Temple cast against the October sky.

Foreword

By definition, the 2012 Church News almanac is thin on plot, but thick on substance.

We invite you to peruse the statistics, the histories, the biographies. In the course of some thoughtful reflection, you'll gain a sensation of the Church in motion. You'll sense a steady cadence to it's growth.

And then you'll marvel how faith continues to increase in a world overwhelmed with problems.

How to contact us

The Deseret News Church Almanac is prepared and edited by the staff of the Church News, a section of the Deseret News, with the assistance of the Church History Department of The Church of Jesus Christ of Latter-day Saints.

Copyright Deseret News 2012

Deseret News, 50 South 300 West, Salt Lake City, UT 84111

Mailing address, P.O. Box 1257, Salt Lake City, UT 84110

E-mail address: churchnews@desnews.com

Visit Church News online

www.ldschurch.com

NEWS
IN REVIEW

GENERAL
AUTHORITIES

CHURCH
STATISTICS
MAPS

TEMPLE
FACTS

CHURCH
HISTORIES

INDEX

STATISTICAL PROFILE

Membership by Areas of the Church

For more statistical information about the Church, see pages 195-209

Africa Southeast Area	150,266
Africa West Area	175,039
Asia Area	155,173
Asia North Area	216,895
Brazil Area	1,138,473
Caribbean Area	177,654
Central America Area	637,905
Chile Area	563,671
Europe Area	449,582
Europe East Area	41,171
Idaho Area	379,761
Mexico Area	1,234,545
Middle East/Africa North Area	3,795
North America Central Area	564,978
North America Northeast Area	581,721
North America Northwest Area	487,626
North America Southeast Area	509,454
North America Southwest Area	1,017,008
North America West Area	826,178
Pacific Area	463,498
Philippines Area	645,776
South America Northwest Area	1,184,962
South America South Area	565,925
Utah North Area	542,093
Utah Salt Lake City Area	685,742
Utah South Area	732,576

TOTAL CHURCH MEMBERSHIP

14,131,467

As of 1 January 2011.
Total includes additional membership not assigned
to an area of the Church.

New children of record *in 2010*	120,528
Convert baptisms *in 2010*	272,814

STATISTICAL PROFILE

STAKES

2,896
As of 1 January 2011

New stakes created since October 2010

Daru Papua New Guinea
Kananga DR Congo
Gweru Zimbabwe
Luputa DR Congo
Jakarta Indonesia
Navarrete Dominican Republic
Casa Grande Peru
Assin Foso Ghana
Huaraz Peru
Paniqui Philippines
Moscow Russia
Macae Brazil
Castanhal Brazil
Barrigada Guam
West Haven Utah
Pacajus Brazil
Fortaleza Brazil Benfica
High Point North Carolina
Waco Texas
Arlington Washington
Alphaville Brazil
San Francisco Venezuela
Belem Brazil Icoaraci
Belem Brazil Entroncamento
Alvarenga Brazil
Lincoln California
Conyers Georgia
Riverton Utah Harvest Park
Antananarivo Madagascar Ivandry
Prescott Valley Arizona
Martinez de la Torre Mexico
Sonzacate El Salvador
Tegucigalpa Honduras Loarque
San Cristobal Venezuela Pirineos
Sumare Brazil
Punaauia Tahiti
Parker Colorado South
Pasco Washington North
Centurion South Africa
Alpine Utah YSA
Lehi Utah YSA
Layton Utah Legacy
Makati Philippines East
Clinton Utah West
Syracuse Utah Lake View YSA
Layton Utah YSA
West Jordan Utah YSA
Taylorsville Utah YSA
Draper Utah YSA
Sandy Utah YSA
Sao Paulo Brazil Ferriera
Rio de Janeiro Brazil Engenho de Dentro
Bountiful Utah YSA
Murray Utah YSA
Lagos Nigeria South
Cumaná Venezuela
Enoch Utah West
Cagua Venezuela
Star Idaho
Buenos Aires Argentina Ramos Mejia
Rexburg Idaho YSA 4th

WARDS/BRANCHES

28,660
As of 1 January 2011

MISSIONS

340
As of 1 October 2011

New missions created in 2011

Zambia Lusaka

Benin Cotonou

Mexico Mexico City Southeast

Peru Chiclayo

Philippines Quezon City North

MISSIONARIES

52,225
*total full-time missionaries
serving as of 1 January 2011*

**Missionaries who began service,
by year**

2000	34,503
2001	34,684
2002	36,196
2003	30,467
2004	29,548
2005	30,587
2006	30,653
2007	30,384
2008	30,312
2009	29,168
2010	30,563

TEMPLES

135
As of 1 October 2011

Temples dedicated in 2011

San Salvador El Salvador
21 August 2011

Quetzaltenango Guatemala
11 December 2011

BOOK OF MORMON

150 million
copies published as of April 23, 2011

Quick Facts

82
Full language translations

25
Partial language translations

FAMILYSEARCH.ORG

15 billion hits
since the site was launched in 1999

Quick Facts

Hits per day: **10 million**

Visitors per month: **3 million**

Pages viewed per day: **1 million**

Registered users: **1 million**

Hits since launch: **15 billion**

Visitors since launch: **150 million**

COUNTRIES WHERE CHURCH IS ORGANIZED

185
As of 1 October 2011

FIRST STAKES ORGANIZED IN COUNTRIES
in 2010-11

Barrigada Guam Stake
12 December 2010

Jakarta Indonesia Stake
22 May 2011

Moscow Russia Stake
5 June 2011

Courtesy Africa Southeawst Area public affairs

Elder Jeffrey R. Holland, center, and Elder Steven E. Snow meet with missionaries in the Democratic Republic of Congo Lubumbashi Mission. Two countries, Angola and Burundi, were dedicated for the preaching of the gospel.

OCTOBER 2010

Apostles bless two African nations during lengthy tour

Two African countries – Angola and Burundi – and their people were blessed by two apostles in October.

On Oct. 19, Elder Jeffrey R. Holland of the Quorum of the Twelve – on a hill overlooking Bujumbura, the capital of Burundi – pronounced a blessing on the country and its people, dedicating the country for missionary work. He encouraged those present to dedicate their lives as he dedicated the land.

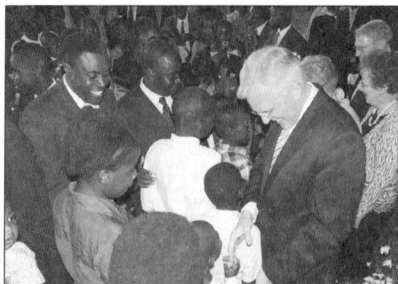

Courtesy Africa Southeawst Area public affairs

Elder D. Todd Christofferson greets Church members in Zimbabwe during his apostolic visit.

The next day, on Oct. 20, Elder Elder D. Todd Christofferson, also of the Quorum of the Twelve, and a small group of Church leaders and members gathered at the base of a large, several-hundred-year-old baobab tree on a quiet hill overlooking the capital city of Luanda to the north and the Atlantic Ocean to the west. There, Elder Christofferson pronounced a blessing on Angola and formally opened the country to missionary work.

During their two-week visit in southeast Africa, Elder Holland also visited two areas in South Africa, and Elder Christofferson also visited the Democratic Republic of Congo and Zimbabwe. The two apostles traveled a combined distance of 120,000 miles – 34,000 of them in Africa. They held a number of meetings, including nine member meetings, four priesthood leadership meetings, eight missionary meetings and four young single adult devotionals. They concluded their Africa visit on Oct. 27.

ALSO IN THE NEWS IN OCTOBER 2010

Oct. 13-15: Fifty-three new temple presidents and matrons received instruction, training and counsel from President Thomas S. Monson and his counselors and other General Authorities, at the 2010 Seminar for New Temple Presidents, held in the Salt Lake Temple. The new temple presidents and matrons began their service in November, 2010.

Oct. 15: Elder Russell M. Nelson of the Quorum of the Twelve rededicated the newly renovated visitors center adjacent to the Los Angeles California Temple. Included in the center is a 16-foot reproduction of Bertel Thorvaldsen's marble sculpture, "The Christus."

Oct. 23: President Thomas S. Monson broke ground for the Rome Italy Temple

Jason Swensen/Church News

President Thomas S. Monson speaks during ground breaking of the Rome Italy Temple.

IRI

The Rome Italy Temple will be part of a complex of other Church building.

and dedicated the site for the temple in the "Eternal City." After the groundbreaking ceremony, President Monson said, "This is one of the greatest blessings that has ever come to Italy."

Oct. 25: Church members in Indonesia assembled relief kits, including blankets, hygiene items and food for victims of two major disasters that struck the country – the eruption of Mount Merapi and the tsunami that followed. The volcano erupted again on Nov. 3. Almost 500 people were killed and more than 15,000 were displaced after the tsunami struck the Mentawai Islands.

Oct. 27: The Church announced it had donated $927,400 to Operation Smile, an international children's medical charity, to help change the lives of 3,864 children born with cleft lips and cleft palates in Kenya, Ethiopia, Egypt and Jordan. In addition to the donation, the Church also announced it would help identify Latter-day Saints who have specific medical and dental expertise who could volunteer their time with the organization.

Oct. 30: Elder Neil L. Andersen of the Quorum of the Twelve broke ground and dedicated the site for the Cordoba Argentina Temple. Located in northern Argentina, the Cordoba temple, when completed, will be the second temple in the country.

Oct. 31: At a fireside for LDS military personnel, President Dieter F. Uchtdorf, second counselor in the First Presidency, addressed more than 1,000 men, women and family members from four branches of the U.S. military at the Draper Utah Stake Center. By way of a Skype service Internet connection, about two dozen members of the Utah National Guard's 19th Special Forces Group (Airborne) and the 141st Military Intelligence Battalion deployed in Iraq viewed the fireside proceedings.

IRI

Elder Dallin H. Oaks of the Quorum of the Twelve displays Handbook 2 during the Worldwide leadership training.

NOVEMBER 2010

'A treasure'

Two new administrative handbooks — described by President Thomas S. Monson as "an invaluable resource" and "a treasure" — were introduced to local Church leaders at the 2010 Worldwide Leadership Training meeting that was broadcast Nov. 13. The special pre-recorded training meeting originated from Church headquarters in Salt Lake City and broadcast during the course of the day to 95 countries in every time zone and in 22 languages.

Handbook 1 is primarily for bishops and stake presidents and has relatively few changes. Handbook 2, which contains chapters necessary to administer the Church in bishoprics, branch presidencies, quorums and auxiliary organizations, has the vast majority of revisions.

In his remarks, President Monson said it would be nearly impossible to maintain the integrity of the policies, procedures and programs of the Church without handbooks, which are available to Church leaders everywhere in every language they represent.

He further said if local leaders are not familiar with policies and procedures,

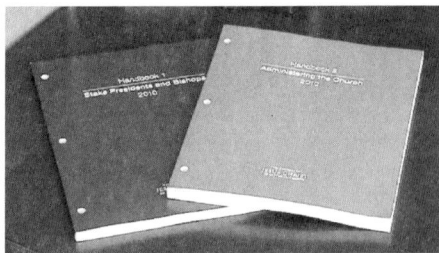

IRI

The new handbooks of instructions.

aberrations can creep into programs of the Church. "In almost all cases, if leaders would only read, understand and follow the handbook, such problems would not occur," President Monson said.

President Boyd K. Packer, president of the Quorum of the Twelve, gave the concluding address at the training meeting and said the new handbooks provide for simplification and flexibility. Elders Dallin H. Oaks, M. Russell Ballard, Jeffrey R. Holland, David A. Bednar, and Quentin L. Cook, all of the Quorum of the Twelve; Elder Walter F. Gonzalez of the Presidency of the Seventy; and Julie B. Beck, general president of the Relief Society, also participated.

ALSO IN THE NEWS IN NOVEMBER 2010

Nov. 8: The refurbished Los Angeles Family History Library — one of the Church's flagship facilities for family history — was reopened after undergoing extensive renovation and electronic upgrades.

Nov. 12: The BYU Museum of Art opened a six-month exhibit of paintings by renowned Danish artist Carl Heinrich Bloch, who lived in the 1800s and is well known today for his artwork of the Savior used in Church books and materials, and LDS meetinghouses and temples around the world. More than 230,000 people viewed the exhibit before it closed on May 7, 2011.

Nov. 13: Ground for the Gilbert Arizona Temple in the Salt River Valley was broken by Elder Claudio R.M. Costa of the Presidency of the Seventy, who also dedicated the site for Arizona's fourth temple. More than 7,500 people attended the groundbreaking ceremony.

Nov. 16: Three key leaders of the Boy Scouts of America — Rex W. Tillerson, national president; Tico Perez, national commissioner; and Robert J. Mazzuva, chief Scout executive - met with the First Presidency and other Church leaders, including the general presidencies of Young Men and Primary. Purpose of the meeting was to establish communication with the leaders of the Church and to share BSA strategic plans with Church leaders. President Thomas S. Monson is no stranger to the BSA leaders. He has served on the BSA Executive Board for 40 years, longer than any other member.

Nov. 19-20: In Hawaii for the rededication of the Laie Hawaii Temple, President Thomas S. Monson received a grand welcome Nov. 19 at the Polynesian Cultural Center, where he toured villages, attended the night show, and interacted with performers and tourists. The next evening, on Nov. 20, he attended a youth cultural celebration, titled "The Gathering Place," in the Cannon Activities Center on the BYU-Hawaii campus. More than 2,000 youth portrayed significant events in Hawaiian Church history and the history of the Laie temple. A large replica of the temple was featured in the center of the arena. President Monson told the youth that the temple "shines as a beacon of righteousness to all who will follow its light."

Nov. 21: President Monson rededicated the Laie Hawaii Temple in three sessions, saying it was a privilege to be in the historic House of the Lord that had been renewed. The temple, originally dedicated in 1919, was closed in December 2008 for extensive remodeling and refurbishing.

Nov. 24: In response to a major cholera outbreak in Papua New Guinea, the Church sent 25 tons of emergency food and medical supplies to the affected region. The first shipment, which included food, antibacterial soap and cooking oil, arrived on the tiny island of Daru, Papua New Guinea, on Nov. 24. The devastating cholera outbreak claimed the lives of more than 300 people, including 76 Church members in four branches.

Gerry Avant, Church News

President Thomas S. Monson, center, rededicated the Laie Hawaii Temple. He is accompanied by, from left, Elder William R. Walker, President Henry B. Eyring and his wife, Kathleen; Elder Quentin L. Cook and his wife, Mary.

Partaking of gospel peace

S peaking at the annual First Presidency Christmas devotional on Dec. 5, President Thomas S. Monson said the Christmas season brings to all people a measure of happiness that corresponds to the degree to which they have turned their minds, feelings and actions to the Savior.

Addressing thousands in the Conference Center in Salt Lake City and to hundreds of thousands around the world over the Church's satellite system and through live streaming on lds.org, President Monson said, "There is no better time than now, this very Christmas season, for all of us to rededicate ourselves to the principles taught by Jesus the Christ."

Also speaking at the devotional were President Henry B. Eyring, first counselor in the First Presidency, and President Dieter F. Uchtdorf, second counselor in the First Presidency.

President Eyring said the greatest gift Church members can offer during the Christmas season is to point those they love and serve toward the Savior Jesus Christ, the only source of eternal life. President Uchtdorf said, "While it's true we can find materialism and anxiety in Christmas, it is also true that if we have eyes to see, we can experience the powerful message of the birth of the Son of God and feel the hope and peace He brings to the world."

Music for the program was provided by the Mormon Tabernacle Choir and the Orchestra at Temple Square.

"May the spirit of love which comes at Christmas time fill our homes and our lives and linger there long after the tree is down and the lights are put away for another year."
— President Monson

President Thomas S. Monson delivers a message during the First Presidency Christmas Devotional focused on the spirit of giving, of forgetting self and finding time for others.

Scott G. Winterton, Deseret News

December: At least 27 LDS families from four stakes and two districts in northern Venezuela were displaced by widespread flooding caused by torrential rains during the first week of December. Seven meetinghouses were damaged. The Church provided food, water, clothing, blankets and other relief supplies to members and community residents who were displaced.

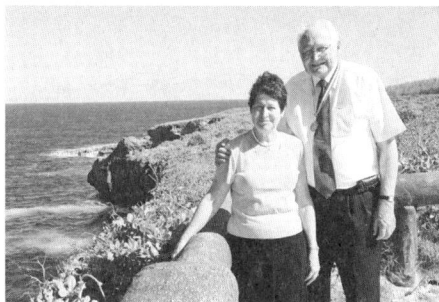

Courtesy Michael Dowdle

Elder L. Tom Perry and his wife, Sister Barbara Perry, visited the island of Guam to organize the first stake.

Dec. 12: The first stake in Guam, the largest of the Mariana Islands in the Pacific, was created from the Guam District by Elder L. Tom Perry of the Quorum of the Twelve. The Barrigada Guam Stake has five wards, including one on the island of Saipan, where members participated in the special occasion by tele-conference.

Dec. 14: Citing a longtime presence in Switzerland, the Church in a statement expressed hope that the Swiss government will continue to allow missionaries to continue their work in the nation despite a new policy that would ban all missionaries from non-European Union countries beginning in 2012.

Dec. 17: President Henry B. Eyring dedicated the new BYU-Idaho Center at the Church-owned school in Rexburg, Idaho. The center's auditorium, which seats 15,000, resembles the Conference Center adjacent to Temple Square. The dedication also included the newly remodeled and enlarged Manwaring Center. President Eyring, first counselor in the First Presidency, served as president of Ricks College – the predecessor to BYU-Idaho – from 1971-77,

Dec. 17: Elder L. Tom Perry of the Quorum of the Twelve addressed graduates at commencement services at BYU-Hawaii in Laie, Oahu, saying that through building friendships individuals are bringing each other closer to Christ.

Dec. 17: The historic Provo, Utah, tabernacle, which was built in 1883, was gutted by a four-alarm fire, leaving only its fortress-like walls standing.

Dec. 18: Elder Marlin K. Jensen of the Seventy addressed the largest fall graduating class in the history of BYU-Idaho, telling the 1,482 graduates of many important events in life that lead individuals down the path of discipleship. Elder Paul V. Johnson, also of the Seventy and commissioner of Church Education, also spoke to the graduates.

Courtesy Michael Lewis

President Henry B. Eyring dedicated the new BYU-Idaho Center which seats 15,000.

Tom Smart, Deseret News

President Dieter F. Uchtdorf addresses seminary and institute employees during the annual "Evening with a General Authority." He spoke of the great responsibility teachers have in raising the rising generation.

JANUARY 2011

Sacred call to teach

"The call is teach is an opportunity to follow Jesus Christ, the Master Teacher," President Dieter F. Uchtdorf, second counselor in the First Presidency, told thousands of LDS religion instructors on Jan. 28 in a televised meeting that was transmitted in 23 languages to more than 150 countries around the world.

"The positive impact ... might not be readily apparent. Nevertheless, don't underestimate what the Lord is doing through you."
— President Uchtdorf

President Uchtdorf spoke to seminary, institute, BYU, BYU-Idaho, BYU-Hawaii and LDS College teachers gathered in the Tabernacle on Temple Square in Salt Lake City, as well as an audience of more than 42,000 volunteers throughout the world via satellite telecast. He addressed the great responsibility that seminary, institute and religion instructors have in teaching the rising generation.

In his speech, President Uchtdorf gave five guidelines to help teachers touch the hearts of their students: Follow the Master Teacher, teach the truth with courage and clarity, teach by the spirit, teach from the heart, and testify.

ALSO IN THE NEWS IN JANUARY 2011

January: Some 125 members of the Church lost their homes to flooding and landslides in areas around Rio de Janeiro and Sao Paulo in what was called Brazil's worst natural disaster in the past half century. The Church sent some 52 tons of emergency provisions to hardest hit areas, and members in the 39 stakes in San Paulo donated 50 boxes of food, per stake, to the relief effort. An LDS meetinghouse in Nova Friburgo was seriously damaged.

Courtesy Central America Area

Elder M. Russell Ballard, left, visits with Guatemalan President Alvaro Colom, right. He is accompanied by Elder Don R. Clarke of the Seventy.

• Elder M. Russell Ballard of the Quorum of the Twelve — during a 10-day trip to Central America, from Jan. 14-23, where he conducted Church business and held priesthood leadership meetings — met with Alvaro Colom, president of Guatemala.

Jan. 10: Weeks of flooding in the Australian state of Queensland turned into a larger storm that resulted in 22 member families being displaced due to the flooding, with 15 of those losing everything. Like the flooding in Brazil, the Australian flooding was said to be the worst flooding in half a century.

Jan. 11-13: New presidents of Missionary Training Centers and visitors center directors and their wives gathered for three days of instruction by General Authorities at the Missionary Training Center in Provo and at Church headquarters in Salt Lake City. Focus of the seminar was inviting others to come unto Christ by helping them receive the restored gospel through faith in Him and His Atonement.

Elder David A. Bednar, with his wife, Susan, greet members during their visit to the Marshall Islands.

Jan. 24: During a 13-day trip to the Pacific Area, from Jan. 12-25, Elder David A. Bednar of the Quorum of the Twelve became the first apostle to visit the Marshall Islands, which are made up of two atoll chains in the Pacific, Majuro and Christmas Island. During his visit, Elder Bednar met with the acting president of the Marshall Islands, Jack Ading, minister of finance, on Jan. 24.

Jan. 24: Conversing in French, Elder Neil L. Andersen of the Quorum of the Twelve met with the president of French Polynesia, Gaston Tong Sang on Jan. 24 during a visit to Tahiti as part of a 12-day trip from Jan. 12-25 to the Pacific Area. Among other items, they discussed the importance of the Church in French Polynesia and the role of the family.

Church News

FamilySearch.org is easily one of the most popular genealogy websites in the world. More than 15 billion hits have been received since the site was launched in 1999. More than 1 billion names are contained in the records.

FEBRUARY 2011

FamilySearch receives 10 million hits a day

The Church's free website, FamilySearch.org, receives more than 10 million hits a day and since it was launched in 1999, the site has had some 15 billion hits, the Feb. 26 Church News reported . FamilySearch.org is the No. 1 non-paid search result on Google for the search term "genealogy research," making it one of the most popular genealogy websites in the world. Three million visitors visit the site each month and more than 150 million people have visited the site since it was launched.

The site contains a billion names in searchable records, many of them indexed by some 125,000 volunteers from around the world who process a million names a day. The website also has research helps, guides and advice from FamilySearch experts. People can also share their own family history knowledge with others.

The No. 1 non-paid search result on Google for the search term "genealogy research" is FamilySearch.org.

Feb. 4: The Mormon Tabernacle Choir and Orchestra at Temple Square performed in concert at Dixie State College in St. George Utah, commemorating the 150th anniversary of the city and the 100th anniversary of the college.

Feb. 5: Speaking at Chapman University Law School in Orange, Calif., Elder Dallin H. Oaks of the Quorum of the Twelve said religious freedom is one of the U.S. Constitution's supremely important founding principles. However, he said, the constitutional guarantee of free exercise of religion "is weakening in its effects and in public esteem" that can be attributed "to the ascendancy of moral relativism."

Feb. 12: For the second time in four months, the Church broadcast a worldwide leadership training meeting to assist local priesthood and auxiliary leaders in using the new administrative handbooks. Purpose of the meeting was to reaffirm the content of the worldwide leadership training broadcast of Nov. 13, 2010, when the handbooks were introduced. President Henry B. Eyring, first counselor in the First Presidency, in addressing the meeting, said, "When you see the joy which the gospel brings to those you serve and feel the loving appreciation from the Savior, you will come to love the handbook for what it helped you feel and do."

Feb. 20: President Boyd K. Packer, president of the Quorum of the Twelve, addressed the Southern Chile Stake Conference that was broadcast over the Church satellite system to Church buildings in 40 stakes and 16 districts throughout southern Chile. President Packer, speaking from a studio in the Conference Center in Salt Lake City, spoke about the Prophet Joseph Smith. Also participating in the conference were Elder D. Todd Christofferson of the Quorum of the Twelve, Elder Richard J. Maynes of the Seventy, and Elaine S. Dalton, Young Women general president.

Feb. 20: Presiding Bishop H. David Burton represented the Church in hosting the annual Interfaith Musical Tribute in the Salt Lake Tabernacle that brought together many religious groups that participated in a concert, themed "Many Faiths, One Family." The concert celebrated Utah's religious diversity and promoted unity.

IRI

President Henry B. Eyring addresses Church leaders during the 2011 Worldwide Leadership Training.

Feb. 22: The homes of 17 LDS families from four wards in Christchurch, New Zealand, were destroyed in a 6.3 magnitude earthquake that killed more than 100 people. The Church donated $25,000 to help victims of the quake, which followed a 7.2 magnitude earthquake that struck the area in September 2010.

Feb. 26: Thousands of Relief Society sisters and priesthood leaders from more than 40 stakes in southeastern Idaho gathered on the BYU-Idaho campus to hear Julie B. Beck, Relief Society general president, speak of the need for Relief Society sisters to join in doing the Lord's work. She also opened for a question-and-answer session during the two meetings that were held, one in the BYU-Idaho Center and one in the Hart Auditorium.

Feb. 27: President Dieter F. Uchtforf, second counselor in the First Presidency, returned to Big Spring, Texas, after 50 years to rededicate the first phase chapel in Big Spring, which he help build in the 1960s when he was stationed at nearby Webb Air Force Base as a member of the German Air Force sent to the U.S. to train as a fighter pilot. He also dedicated the final phase of the Big Spring Ward meetinghouse.

Church News

Three months after a devastating earthquake and tsunami destroyed Kesennuma, Japan, Yumiko Yoshiki, a member of the Church in Japan, tells how Church members survived the disaster and are rebuilding their homes.

MARCH 2011

Church responds with 'love and support' to Japan

A 9.0-magnitude earthquake, the largest earthquake to ever hit Japan — and a powerful tsunami that followed — devastated northern Japan on March 11, leaving more than 15,500 people dead, including two Latter-day Saints, and destroying more than 550,000 homes. Upwards to 60 member families lost their homes in the tsunami, and 23 meetinghouses sustained varying degrees of damage. The earthquake also damaged the cooling functions at key nuclear plants in northern Japan, triggering fire and radiation leaks. The earthquake and tsunami caused destruction over 300 miles.

Shortly after the disaster the First Presidency issued a statement, saying, "We express our love and support to the people of Japan as they deal with this terrible tragedy. Our prayers, and the prayers of millions of Latter-day Saints across the world, are with them as they begin to recover from this disaster." President Thomas S. Monson, in his opening address at general conference on April 2, referred to the Japan disaster when he said, "The Church continues to provide humanitarian aid in times of disaster. Most recently our hearts and our help have gone out to Japan following the devastating earthquake and tsunami and the resultant nuclear challenges.... Our help will be ongoing in Japan and in any other areas where there is a need."

In the days and weeks after the Japan disaster, the Church distributed more than 200 tons of goods, including food, water, blankets, bedding, clothing, fuel, and hygiene supplies, and cash donations. A total of 30,000 hygiene kits were assembled by 1,800 members in Tokyo and Nagoya. More than 150,000 hours of service were donated by 16,000 Church volunteers.

ALSO IN THE NEWS IN MARCH 2011

IRI

President Thomas S. Monson studies a painting by Michael Malm, "Of Such is the Kingdom of Heaven," after cutting the ribbon on two new exhibits in the LDS Church History Museum showcasing member talent.

March: The second volume of the "Revelations and Translations" series of the Joseph Smith Papers was published. The new volume includes photos of each page of the 1833 Book of Commandments and of the first edition of the Doctrine and Covenants, published in 1835, as well as selections from the 1844 edition of the Doctrine and Covenants and photos and/or transcripts of several other related documents.

March 10: President Thomas S. Monson cut ribbons to open two new exhibits at the Church History Museum, located across the street west of Temple Square. One new exhibit showcases the work of some of the Church's outstanding artists; the other, an eclectic display of quilts symbolizes the global reach and history of Latter-day Saints and their faith.

IRI

Elder Jeffrey R. Holland and Elder David F. Evans meet with members of the media to explain the Church's relief efforts in Japan following the March 11 disaster.

March 15: In response to the radiation danger created on March 11 when the 9.0-magnitude earthquake in northern Japan damaged the cooling functions of key nuclear plants, the Church announced it would evacuate 200 missionaries in the Japan Tokyo and Japan Sendai missions to other missions in Japan. The missionaries later returned to the Tokyo and Sendai missions. Forty-five missionaries were given early releases and returned home.

March 21: Dixie State College officials in St. George, Utah, broke ground for a new 170,000-square-foot, five-story building that will bear the name of Elder Jeffrey R. Holland. Elder Holland of the Quorum of the Twelve and a 1963 graduate of college attended the groundbreaking ceremony. The Jeffrey R. Holland Centennial Commons Building, the keystone of Dixie's overall campus master plan to accommodate recent growth, is scheduled for completion in late May 2012.

March 21: The South America South Area presidency – Elders Mervyn B. Arnold, Marcos A. Aidukaitis and Bradley D. Foster — called on the former president of Uruguay, Dr. Tabaré Vásquez, at his home in Montevideo and thanked him for some decisions he made during his administration on different matters that coincided with Church issues. Dr. Vásquez served as president of Uruguay until March 1, 2010.

March 26: Young women are the "bright hope of the Lord's Church," President Henry B. Eyring, first counselor in the First Presidency, told a capacity congregation in the Conference Center in Salt Lake City at the General Young Women Meeting. Elaine S. Dalton, general president of the Young Women, and her counselor Mary N. Cook and Ann M. Dibb, also spoke. The meeting was translated and broadcast to meetinghouses throughout the world.

March 31: President Dieter F. Uchtdorf, second counselor in the First Presidency, spoke at a dinner program in Salt Lake City, held in conjunction with the spring meeting of Collegium Aesculapium, a non-profit organization of LDS physician and health professionals. He spoke on the Church's welfare program, saying "we are anxiously engaged in relieving suffering among all people in every corner of the world."

Mike Terry, Deseret News

Women participating in the annual BYU Women's Conference sing a closing hymn in the Marriott Center.

APRIL 2010

Bringing about great things

More than 15,000 women from throughout the world gathered April 28-29, on the BYU campus for the annual Women's Conference to receive instruction and give service. Theme for this year's conference was from Alma 37:6-7 in the Book of Mormon: "By small and simple things are great things brought to pass."

Co-sponsored by BYU and the Relief Society organization, more than 100 classes – six in Spanish – were available, in addition to organized humanitarian projects. The classes covered a wide variety of topics.

Among speakers at the conference were Elder David A. Bednar of the Quorum of the Twelve and Julie B. Beck, general Relief Society president.

"We should find great comfort in the fact that ordinary people who faithfully, diligently and consistently do simple things that are right before God will bring forth extraordinary results," Elder Bednar told conference-goers. Sister Beck spoke of the divine identity of women and said, "We have non-negotiable responsibilities. ... We do not get a pass from the responsibilities we are given. We cannot give them away. They are our sacred duties and we fulfill them under covenant."

> *"We should find great comfort in the fact that ordinary people who faithfully, diligently and consistently do simple things that are right before God will bring forth extraordinary results." — Elder Bednar*

President Thomas S. Monson and his wife, Frances, acknowledge the congregation in Conference Center.

April 2: President Thomas S. Monson opened the 181st Annual General Conference of the Church by announcing plans to build temples in Fort Collins, Colo.; Meridian, Idaho, and Winnipeg, Manitoba., bringing the total of operating temples and temples announced or under construction to 160. More than 100,000 Church members gathered in the Conference Center April 2-3 to hear President Monson and other Church leaders offer counsel and direction.

Also announced during the conference was the calling of seven members to the First Quorum of the Seventy, four to the Second Quorum of Seventy, and 41 as Area Seventies. The conference was translated into 90 languages and broadcast to more than 170 countries and territories.

April 9: Elder Russell M. Nelson of the Quorum of the Twelve addressed graduates at commencement services at BYU-Hawaii, saying prophetic visions are gifts from Heavenly Father to guide His faithful children. He then cited prophetic visions of the past and present and said with the blessings of past and present prophetic visions, individuals are more prepared for the future.

April 9: Elder Steven L. Snow of the Presidency of the Seventy shared with BYU-Idaho graduates ways to avoid stumbling blocks as they make their way in the world. He listed four stumbling blocks individuals should watch out for: pride, excessive debt, career over family and the downsides of technology.

April 14: Addressing 480 graduates of LDS Business College from 70 countries in the Tabernacle on Temple Square during the school's commencement services, Elder Russell M. Nelson of the Quorum of the Twelve spoke on the importance of goal setting in establishing priorities in life. During the services, Elder Nelson received the college's Distinguished Alumnus Award, the highest honor given by the school.

April 15: In a letter to Church leaders, the First Presidency announced plans for a historic site in the township once known as Harmony in northeast Pennsylvania (now Oakland Township) where the Prophet Joseph Smith translated much of the Book of Mormon and where the priesthood was restored in 1829. Groundbreaking for the project, which will include reconstruction of historical buildings, construction of a combination meetinghouse and visitors center, and monuments commemorating the restoration of the Aaronic and Melchizedek priesthoods, is expected to take place in 2012.

April 16: President Dieter F. Uchtdorf, second counselor in the First Presidency, addressed the BYU Management Society's annual awards dinner in Washington, D.C., which was attended by business, government, diplomatic and political leaders, as well as diplomats from Africa, Asia, Latin America and Europe. President Uchtdorf, who spoke on "The Church in a Global World," received the society's Distinguished Public Service Award for his humanitarian service.

April 21: Elder Richard G. Scott of the Quorum of the Twelve addressed more than 6,000 BYU graduates in commencement services, telling them, "This world is in serious trouble. The fundamental values of this nation are being undermined." However, he said, despite the difficulties in the world, a solid foundation of faith, character and integrity will help individuals find peace, joy and purpose in life.

April 23: The150th millionth copy of the Book of Mormon was recently published, the *Church News* reported. To date, the book has been fully translated into 82 languages and partially translated in 25 more.

April 27: Some 150 tornadoes touched down across six states in the U.S. South, carving a path of death and destruction. More than 300 people in Alabama, Mississippi, Tennessee, Georgia and Virginia were killed in what was called the largest and most damaging tornado outbreak in U.S. history. No missionaries or members were injured, but several member families lost their homes entirely or their homes were badly damaged. On May 7-8, about 3,000 members of the Church, dressed in yellow "Helping Hands" T-shirts from 23 stakes in four Southern states, participated in clean-up and relief projects in areas impacted by the tornadoes.

April 30: The evening before the Atlanta Georgia Temple was rededicated May 1 by President Thomas S. Monson, 2,700 young men and women from throughout the temple district presented a youth cultural celebration. The program, held in downtown Atlanta's Civic Center and titled "Southern Lights," recapped highlights of U.S., Georgia and Church history in the state. Before the program began, President Monson addressed the nearly 3,000 people who attended the celebration, directing his remarks to the youth.

Courtesy Carmen Borup

Church members, including this young man, aided in the clean up after a tornado destroyed much of Joplin, Mo.

MAY 2011

Members fill 7,400 work orders after tornado

A tornado – said to be the United States' deadliest tornado in more than 50 years – ripped through Joplin, a community of 50,000 people in southwest Missouri on May 22, leaving 130 people dead, more than 750 injured, and some 25 percent of the buildings in town destroyed or significantly damaged. Included among the buildings destroyed was the Joplin Missouri Stake Center. In addition, 27 homes of Latter-day Saints were destroyed and another 41 member homes were severely damaged.

"There is an energetic and motivated effort to move forward and rebuild our lives and our community."
– President Montague

Because the stake center was destroyed, Church leaders set up an LDS command center in a 5,000-square-foot warehouse, located four miles north of the tornado's path

President Matthew G. Montague, first counselor in the Joplin stake presidency, said the damage in the city was "incomprehensible," and noted that many areas were simply unrecognizable.

On May 28, more than 550 Church members from the Rogers Arkansas and Springfield Missouri stakes, clad in yellow "Mormon Helping Hands" T-shirts converged on the city to help in cleanup efforts, completing 7,400 work orders. Member-volunteer help in the recovery effort continued every weekend for the next couple of months.

ALSO IN THE NEWS IN MAY 2011

Gerry Avant, Church News

President Thomas S. Monson greets Vivian Frost following the rededication of the Atlanta Georgia Temple.

May 1: Only days after deadly tornados swept through the southern United States on April 27, President Thomas S. Monson rededicated the Atlanta Georgia Temple, bringing comfort and reassurance to storm-weary members of the Church. During the temple's open house April 9-23, 2011, some 57,000 people toured the sacred edifice, which was originally dedicated in 1983.

Kristin Murphy, Deseret News

Scott Simmers prepares to throw a dodge ball during a Young Single Adult ward activity in Draper, Utah.

May 1: In an effort to increase accountability and foster activity for young single adults 18-30 years old, student wards in Salt Lake and Davis counties in Utah were eliminated and replaced by young single adult wards and stakes. Changes in Utah County came later. The change from student units to YSA wards and stakes began in April 2010 in other parts of Utah.

May 6: President Thomas S. Monson, in delivering the Centennial Commencement address at Dixie State College in St. George, Utah, spoke of three "bridges" to help the more than 1,500 graduates safely cross the "deep and wide" chasms of life": the bridge of attitude, the bridge of integrity and the bridge of service. President Monson was awarded an honorary doctorate of humanities by the college. (See Awards and Honors on page 37)

May 10: FamilySearch, the Church's free family history website announced at the National Genealogical Society conference the release of millions of online records, which include service records for both the Confederate and Union armies, as well as enlistment and pension records. Some of the records were previously available but were added to familysearch.org/civilwar as part of the project.

May 15: The branch meetinghouse and 10 member homes in the northern Alberta community of Slave Lake were destroyed by a forest fire that was fueled by strong winds.

May 22: The first stake in Indonesia, the Jakarta Indonesia Stake, was created from the Jakarta Indonesia District by Elder David A. Bednar of the Quorum of the Twelve. The new stake includes eight wards.

May 26: President Dieter F. Uchtdorf , second counselor in the First Presidency, addressed some 800 community, business and religious leaders at the Los Angeles World Affairs Council, a nonpartisan organization dedicated to furthering brotherhood and understanding between opposing cultures, beliefs, religions and world views.

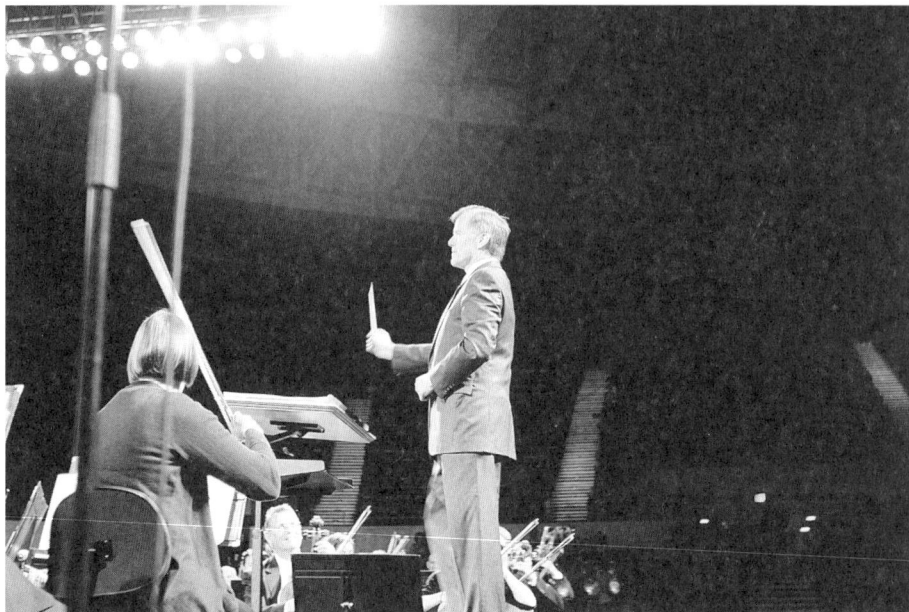

Gerry Avant, Church News

Virginia Gov. Robert McDonell leads the Mormon Tabernacle Choir during a concert in Norfolk, Va., on June 20.

JUNE 2011

'No finer choir'

President Thomas S. Monson said "there is no finer choir in the entire world," and the governor of Virginia, Robert McDonnell, described the choir as "300-plus best vocalists in all of America."

Both were referring to the Mormon Tabernacle Choir, which performed seven concerts in five cities in the eastern United States and Canada during its week-long 2011 summer tour from June 20-27.

President Monson attended the final concert of the tour on June 27 in Toronto, Ontario. It was the sixth time the choir had performed in Toronto, where two performances were held in Roy Thomson Hall. President Monson spoke at a reception prior to the final concert, saying, "I do not hesitate to profess that there is no finer choir in the entire world, and in combination with the Orchestra at Temple Square, their music is magnificent. Until you've experienced a live concert, however, you cannot appreciate all that they have to offer," he declared.

The first concert of the tour was in Norfolk, Va., on June 20. Gov. McDonnell was among the 7,500 people who attended the concert in Scope Arena. He mounted the conductor's podium to lead the choir and orchestra in "This Land Is Your Land," which was performed as an encore. Two days later, on June 22, in Wolf Trap in Vienna, Va., near Washington, D.C., U.S. Sen. Mark R. Warner, D-Va., directed the choir in the same encore number at the conclusion of the concert.

Other performances of the choir and orchestra were held in Philadelphia, Pa., on June 23; and in Chautauqua, N.Y., where two performances were held, on June 25.

On June 21, the choir and orchestra visited Colonial Williamsburg in Virginia, and while mingling with some 4,000 spectators, burst into song in a "flash mob" performance which started out with just three male singers and eventually involved the full choir singing. The choir and orchestra also made a brief stop in Palmyra, N.Y. on June 24, where they visited the Sacred Grove and the Hill Cumorah.

ALSO IN THE NEWS IN JUNE 2011

June 4: Ground for the Phoenix Arizona Temple – the fifth temple in Arizona – was broken and the site dedicated by Elder Ronald A. Rasband of the Presidency of the Seventy. The groundbreaking service was broadcast live to meetinghouses throughout the temple district.

June 5: The Moscow Russia Stake – the first stake in Russia and the second stake in the former Soviet Union – was created by Elder Russell M. Nelson of the Quorum of the Twelve. More than 1,100 members gathered in Moscow's Plaza Auditorium for the creation of the stake, which has six wards and three branches. The first stake created in the former Soviet Union was the Kyiv Ukraine Stake, organized in 2004. (See feature articles on Russia's first stake beginning on page 41.)

June 8: President Henry B. Eyring, first counselor in the First Presidency, dedicated the new Sugar House Utah Welfare Center. The 65,000-square-foot facility in southeast Salt Lake City includes a Deseret Industries thrift store, and LDS Employment and LDS Family Services centers.

R. Scott Lloyd, Church News

President Thomas S. Monson cuts the ribbon to begin the Centennial Celebration of the Hotel Utah/Joseph Smith Memorial Building June 9 before a capacity crowd.

June 9-10: President Thomas S. Monson cut a ribbon on June 9, opening up a celebration commemorating the 100th anniversary of what was formerly the Hotel Utah in downtown Salt Lake City, now renewed and re-purposed as the Joseph Smith Memorial Building. The Mormon Tabernacle Choir serenaded the gathered crowd with "It's a Grand Night for Singing," "Happy Birthday" and the hymn "Praise to the Man" in honor of the Prophet Joseph Smith. On June 10, President Monson addressed a dinner audience that filled the building's lobby and several adjacent dining halls. An exhibit of memorabilia and artifacts from the hotel's glory days was on display through the first week in October.

June 14: President Thomas S. Monson joined government and education leaders to break ground for the Beverley Taylor Sorenson Arts and Education Center at the University of Utah, named after the complex's key benefactor.

June 15: Presiding Bishop H. David Burton traveled

to Japan to survey the destruction left by the March 11, 2011, earthquake and tsunami and to view some of the many Church relief efforts being undertaken in areas impacted most by the disaster. Indicative of the Church's humanitarian efforts is a donation of ice and refrigeration equipment and supplies to a Japanese fisherman's union whose members were unable to work since the disaster. Helping the disaster victims in Japan through the Church's humanitarian fund is a priority, Bishop Burton said.

June 18: Elder Walter F. González of the Presidency of the Seventy broke ground and dedicated the site for the Ft. Lauderdale temple, which, when built, will serve some 25,000 members in Florida. Proceedings of the groundbreaking service were telecast via satellite to 25 meetinghouses in South Florida.

June 19: President Henry B. Eyring, first counselor in the First Presidency, rededicated the rebuilt Longfellow Park meetinghouse in Cambridge, Mass., that was originally dedicated in 1956 by President David O. McKay, but was destroyed by a fire in 2009 that was caused by an electrical malfunction. For six decades the meetinghouse had served thousands of Church members who went to Cambridge to pursue higher education. President Boyd K. Packer, president of the Quorum of the Twelve, also spoke at the services, which were broadcast to four other chapels in the Cambridge Massachusetts Stake.

June 23: Giving the opening address at the 2011 Seminar for New Mission Presidents, President Thomas S. Monson focused his talk on motivating missionaries. He told the 128 new mission presidents and their wives that missionaries are a precious commodity entrusted to their care. During the four-day seminar, President Monson's counselors, President Henry B. Eyring and President Dieter F. Uchtdorf, also spoke, as did President Boyd K. Packer and other General Authorities.

June 24: About 75 member homes were completely inundated and many other member home were partially flooded in Minot, N.D., after heavy rains and the melting of a record snow-pack combined to create record-breaking floods. More than 1,200 residents were displaced.

June 25-26: While in eastern Canada, President Thomas S. Monson dedicated a camp bearing his name on June 25. Located near Peterborough about 120 miles east of Toronto, the Thomas S. Monson Camp serves members of the Ottawa, Oshawa, Brampton, Mississauga, Hamilton, Kitchener and London stakes and the Kingston District. The camp covers 400 acres of which 15 acres have been developed; the rest remain as natural habitat. The next day, on June 26, President Monson spoke in a combined sacrament meeting of the Etobicoke and Churchville Young Single Adult wards, where he talked about choices and consequences.

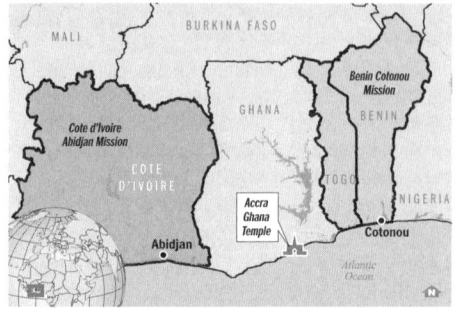

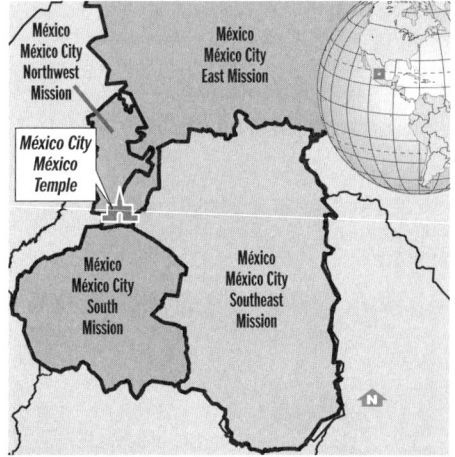

Deseret News graphics

Five new missions added

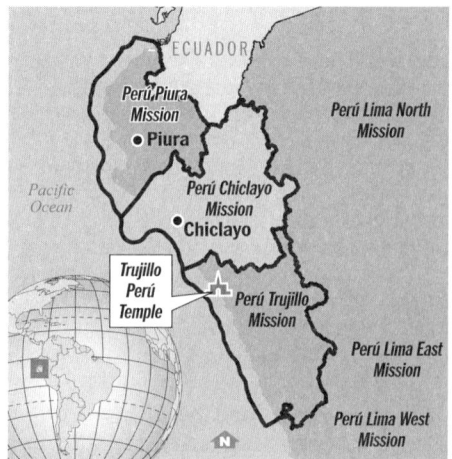

Five new missions of the Church were created in Africa, Latin America and the Philippines and five missions in Europe and North America were combined with neighboring missions. The changes were effective in July with the changes in mission leadership.

The new missions are the Zambia Lusaka Mission, created in a division of the Zimbabwe Harare Mission; the Benin Cotonou Mission, created in a division of the Ivory Coast Abidjan Mission; the Mexico Mexico City Southeast Mission, created by realigning the Mexico Mexico City East, Mexico Mexico City Northwest and Mexico Mexico City South missions; the Peru Chiclayo Mission, created by dividing the Peru Pirua and Peru Trujillo missions; and the Philippines Quezon City North Mission, created by dividing the Philippines Manila and Philip-

pines Quezon City missions.

The missions in Europe combined with

other missions are the Portugal Porto Mission, which became part of the Portugal Lisbon Mission; the Switzerland Geneva Mission, which became part of the France Paris and France Toulouse missions. The headquarters of the Toulouse Mission was moved to Lyon, and the mission was renamed by France Lyon Mission.

Mission changes in North America include the combining of Canada Toronto East and West missions, with the resulting mission renamed the Canada Toronto Mission. Also the Connecticut Hartford Mission became part of the Massachusetts Boston Mission, and the Georgia Macon Mission became part of a realignment of the Georgia Atlanta, Florida Jacksonville, Florida Tallahassee, and South Carolina Columbia missions.

ALSO IN THE NEWS IN JULY 2011

July 22: Elder Paul K. Sybrowsky of the Seventy addressed more than 1,400 graduates at commencement exercises at BYU-Idaho — the most any spring BYU-Idaho class has ever had — and counseled them if they remember their principles and purposes in life, they will always be guided to make right decisions.

July 28-30: More than 2,000 participants from around the country attended the BYU-Idaho annual education conference. "Where Can I Turn for Peace" was the theme of this year's conference, which offered more than 400 classes on a variety of topics. Elder Paul V. Johnson of the Seventy addressed a devotional assembly on July 29 and spoke of the peace that comes from following the Prince of Peace.

July 30: Approximately 120,000 Latter-day Saints, dressed in familiar yellow Mormon Helping Hands vests, participated in the "National Day of Voluntary Action – A Solidarity Saturday" in Brazil. They performed various service projects throughout the Federal District, 26 state capitals, and 180 cities.

Courtesy of BYU-Idaho

More than 1,400 graduates attend commencement exercises at BYU-Idaho, the largest class of spring graduates.

Jessica Black, Church News

The BYU-Idaho education conference is growing with participants attending from around the country.

Courtesy of Africa Southeast Area

To strengthen families and build communities, members in the Africa Southeast Area cleaned and beautified.

AUGUST 2011

To strengthen families and build communities

Donning yellow vests, thousands of members of the Church in Africa participated Aug. 20 in the Fifth Annual All-Africa Mormon Helping Hands service project, helping to clean up and improve communities throughout the continent.

In the Africa West Area, more than 10,000 members of the Church from 59 stakes and districts in Nigeria, Ghana, Sierra Leone, Liberia, Ivory Coast, Togo, and Benin joined with members of other faiths, the media, private business, government officials and tribal chiefs in performing service in the seven countries. In the Africa Southeast Area, members participated in a wide range of projects from Accra, Ghana, to Cape Town, South Africa.

The continent-wide day of service was themed

"Strengthening families, building communities," and projects ranged from planting and painting to cleaning and clearing.

Asare Dediako, an assembly member in Ghana, summed up the day of service when he said, "Worshipping of the Lord will not be completed if service to humanity is not part of it. The service rendered today will go a long way to set an example for others to follow."

Aug. 11: Elder Craig C. Christensen of the Seventy addressed graduates at BYU's summer commencement exercises, and shared three steps to take daily in order to ensure long-term happiness and ultimate success: Seek spiritual experiences every day, work productively every day with purpose and balance, and find ways to daily serve others. The 2,342 graduates came from 49 states, 44 countries and four territories.

Aug. 12: President Henry B. Eyring, first counselor in the First Presidency, dedicate two new buildings at BYU: The state-of-the-art, 100,000-square-foot BYU Broadcasting Building on campus, which houses TV and radio production studios, video editing facilities and executive offices, and the Information Technology Building on University Avenue in Provo. "These buildings have been built to take advantage of the wonderful and miraculous technology that will enable the university and the Church to reach the hearts and minds of members and friends around the globe," President Eyring said.

Aug. 15-19: Twenty thousand people from 49 states and 14 other countries participated in this year's BYU Campus Education Week, attending more than 1,000 classes by 233 presenters. The theme for the week was "That all may be edified." (D&C 88:122). Elder Jay E. Jensen of the Presidency of the Seventy spoke at the Education Week devotional on Aug. 16 and shared ways in which individuals can improve their teaching and learning.

Aug. 20: In El Salvador to dedicate the San Salvador temple, President Henry B. Eyring, first counselor in the First Presidency, met with the president of the country,

Mauricio Funes, in his presidential palace. The visit was the first time a member of the First Presidency had met with a president of El Salvador. Among items they discussed were the Church's humanitarian efforts in the country and the LDS tradition of service and self-reliance. President Eyring was accompanied by Elder D. Todd Christofferson of the Quorum of the Twelve; Elder William R. Walker and Elder Enrique R. Falabella, both of the Seventy; and Elder Carlos Rivas, an Area Seventy.

Aug. 20: The evening before the dedication of the San Salvador El Salvador Temple, more than 3,000 youth from the country's 16 stakes performed in a cultural celebration in San Salvador's National Gymnasium, featuring song and dance in tribute to their rich cultural history, and to their country, faith and the temple.

Aug. 21: President Henry B. Eyring, first counselor in the First Presidency, dedicated the San Salvador El Salvador Temple. Dedicated in three sessions, the temple is the fourth temple in Central America and the 135th operating temple in the Church.

Aug. 24: The Church announced plans to construct a new state-of-the-art building at the Missionary Training Center in Provo, Utah, to replace the Melvin J. Ballard Building, which will be demolished as part of the construction process in early 2012. The new building is scheduled to be completed by the fall of 2013.

Aug. 27-29: Powerful Atlantic Hurricane Irene swept through the Caribbean, eastern United States, and into Canada, leaving a path of death and destruction. Thousands of LDS volunteers turned out to help in recovery efforts.

Jason Swensen, Church News

President Henry B. Eyring, center right, meets with El Salvador's President Mauricio Funes and first lady Vanda Pignato, left. Elders D. Todd Christofferson, right, attended with Carlos Rivas, William R. Walker and Enrique R. Falabella.

Mike Segar, Associated Press

A flower lied on the wall of one of the pools at the 9/11 memorial plaza in the World Trade Center site in New York.

SEPTEMBER 2011

Pres. Monson is invited to address the nation

President Thomas S. Monson was invited by the Washington Post to address the issue of faith after 9/11.

In connection with the 10-year observance of the Sept. 11, 2001, attacks on America, President Thomas S. Monson was among 10 opinion leaders invited by *The Washington Post* to address a topic for publication in the newspaper's Sept. 8, 2011, online blog "On Faith: A Conversation of Religion and Politics." Heading the blog were the questions: "What have we learned about religion in the past 10 years? What was the spiritual impact of 9/11?"

President Monson wrote in his response: "If there is a spiritual lesson to be learned from our experience on that fateful day, it may be that we owe to God the same faithfulness that He gives to us.

"We should strive for steadiness, and for a commitment that does not ebb and flow with the years or the crisis of our lives.

"It should not require tragedy for us to remember Him, and we should not be compelled to humility before giving Him our faith and trust. We ... should be with Him in every season.

"The way to be with God in every season is to strive to be near Him every week and each day. We truly "need Him every hour," not just in hours of devastation. We must speak to Him, listen to Him, and serve Him. If we wish to serve Him, we should serve our fellow men. We will mourn the lives we lost, but we should also fix the lives that can be mended and heal the hearts that may yet be healed.

"It is constancy that God would have from us. Tragedies are not merely opportunities to give Him a fleeting thought, or for momentary insight to His plan for our happiness. Destruction allows us to rebuild our lives in the way He teaches us, and to become something different than we were. We can make Him the center of our thoughts and His Son, Jesus Christ, the pattern for our behavior. We may not only find faith in God in our sorrow. We may also become faithful to Him in times of calm."

Deb Gehris, LDS Church

Veteran newsman Tom Brokaw joined the Mormon Tabernacle Choir to present a special national 9/11 broadcast.

ALSO IN THE NEWS IN SEPTEMBER 2011

Sept. 3: Three hundred LDS volunteers, wearing yellow "Mormon Helping Hands" T-shirts, performed more than 1,800 hours of service in North Carolina, which was among the states hardest hit by Hurricane Irene on Aug. 27. In addition to the service performed by the volunteers, two tractor-trailers from the Church Bishops' storehouse in Tucker, Ga., delivered food, water, tarps, generators, chain saws, and hygiene kits to the affected areas.

Sept. 11: During their weekly nationwide television and radio broadcast "Music and the Spoken Word," the Mormon Tabernacle Choir and Orchestra at Temple Square presented a special memorial performance on the 10th anniversary of the Sept. 11, 2001, attacks on America. Guest narrator for the broadcast, titled "9/11: Rising Above," was Tom Brokaw, the former "NBC Nightly News" anchor, who had pre-recorded his segments.

Sept. 13: The Church donated a parcel of land in downtown Salt Lake City to the American Cancer Society, which will become the site of the society's newest Hope Lodge. The old 13th Ward meetinghouse, built in 1951, is currently on the 2.2-acre site at 100 South and 400 East but it has not be used for four years.

Sept. 14: Ground for the Trujillo Peru Temple was broken and the site was dedicated by Elder Rafael E. Pino of the Seventy. The temple, when completed, will be the second temple in Peru.

Sept. 17: President Henry B. Eyring, first counselor in the First Presidency, broke ground and dedicated the site for the Philadelphia Pennsylvania Temple, which when completed will serve members from eight stakes in Pennsylvania, New Jersey and Delaware.

Sept. 21: LDS Business College celebrated its 125th anniversary at its Triad Campus in downtown Salt Lake City with students, faculty and community members singing "Happy Birthday" and participating in games and activities.

Sept. 24: Speaking at the General Relief Society Meeting in the Conference Center, President Dieter F. Uchtdorf, second counselor in the First Presidency, used the forget-me-not flower, which has five petals, as a metaphor to illustrate five things he would like the women of the Church to remember: forget not to be patient with yourself, forget not the difference between a good sacrifice and a foolish sacrifice, forget not to be happy now, forget not the "why" of the gospel, and forget not that the Lord loves you. The general Relief Society president, Julie B. Beck, and her counselors, Silvia H. Allred and Barbara Thompson, also spoke at the meeting.

A view of the conference center from behind the podium during the 181st semiannual general conference.

IRI

OCTOBER 2011

Church continues to expand

At the opening session of the 181st Semiannual Conference of the Church on Oct. 1, President Thomas S. Monson announced six new temples, including a second temple in Provo, Utah. The temple will be converted from the rebuilt Provo Tabernacle, which was destroyed by a four-alarm fire on Dec. 17, 2010, leaving only its walls standing. President Monson said the current Provo Temple is among the busiest temples in the Church, and the new temple will take some of the pressure off the existing temple in Provo.

Other temples announced by President Monson will be in Paris, France; Kinshasa, Democratic Republic of the Congo; Durban, South Africa; Barranquilla, Colombia; and Star Valley, Wyo. The announcement brings the total number of

President Monson greets members of the Quorum of the Twelve.

temples worldwide to 166, with 135 in operation and 31 under construction or in various stages of planning.

During the Saturday afternoon session of conference, five members of the First Quorum of the Seventy were released and given emeritus status. They were Elders Gary J. Coleman, Richard G. Hinckley, Yoshihiko Kikuchi, Carl B. Pratt, and Cecil O.

Six new temples announced, proceedings translated into 93 languages.

Samuelson (who will continue to serve as president of BYU).

Also three members of the Second Quorum of the Seventy, Elders Won Yong Ko, Lowell M. Snow, and Paul K. Sybrowsky, were released.

The conference was translated into more than 93 languages and broadcast to more than 170 countries and territories.

ALSO IN THE NEWS IN OCTOBER 2011

Scott G Winterton, Deseret News

Elder Dallin H. Oaks with deacons from the Payson area turn dirt to break ground on the Payson temple.

Oct. 8: Ground for the Payson Utah Temple was broken and the site dedicated by Elder Dallin H. Oaks of the Quorum of the Twelve.

IRI

Under rainy skies members in Sapporo, Japan, join in the groundbreaking ceremonies of the temple Oct. 22.

Oct. 22: Ground was broken for the Sapporo Japan Temple by Elder Gary E. Stevenson of the Seventy. This will be the third temple in Japan.

Changes in General Church leadership

Presidency of the Seventy

• **ELDER TAD R. CALLISTER** of the Second Quorum of the Seventy was called to the Presidency of the Seventy, effective Aug. 1, 2011, and sustained Oct. 1, 2011, to fill a vacancy created by the call of **ELDER CLAUDIO R.M. COSTA** as president of the Brazil Area. Elder Costa had served in the presidency since 2007.

Elder Tad R.
Callister

First Quorum of the Seventy

• Seven new members of the First Quorum of the Seventy were sustained April 2, 2011. They are **ELDERS JOSÉ L. ALONSO, IAN S. ARDERN, DON R. CLARKE, CARL B. COOK, LEGRAND R. CURTIS JR., W. CHRISTOPHER WADDELL,** and **KAZUHIKO YAMASHITA.** Elder Clarke previously served in the Second Quorum of the Seventy.

Elder José L.
Alonso

Elder Ian S.
Ardern

Elder Don R.
Clarke

Elder Carl B.
Cook

Elder LeGrand R.
Curtis Jr.

Elder W. Christopher
Waddell

Elder Kazuhiko
Yamashita

• Five members of the First Quorum of the Seventy were granted emeritus status Oct. 1, 2011. They were **GARY J. COLEMAN, RICHARD G. HINCKLEY, YOSHIHIKO KIKUCHI, CARL B. PRATT,** and **CECIL O. SAMUELSON.**

Elder Gary J.
Coleman

Elder Richard G.
Hinckley

Elder Yoshihiko
Kikuchi

Elder Carl B.
Pratt

Elder Cecil O.
Samuelson

Second Quorum of the Seventy

• Four new members of the Second Quorum of the Seventy were sustained April 2, 2011. They are **ELDERS RANDALL K. BENNETT, J. DEVN CORNISH, O. VINCENT HALECK,** and **LARRY Y. WILSON.**

• Three members of the Second Quorum of the Seventy were released Oct. 1, 2011. They were **WON YONG KO, LOWELL M. SNOW,** and **PAUL K. SYBROWSKY.**

Elder Randall K.
Bennett

Elder J. Devn
Cornish

Elder O. Vincent
Haleck

Elder Larry Y.
Wilson

Elder Won
Yong Ko

Elder Lowell M.
Snow

Elder Paul K.
Sybrowsky

Administrative and Policy Announcements

• The Church issued an official statement regarding immigration on June 10, 2011. The statement said:

"Around the world, debate on the immigration question has become intense. This is especially so in the United States. Most Americans agree that the federal government of the United States should secure its borders and sharply reduce or eliminate the flow of undocumented immigrants. Unchecked and unregulated, such a flow may destabilize society and ultimately become unsustainable.

"As a matter of policy, The Church of Jesus Christ of Latter-day Saints discourages its members from entering any country without legal documentation and from deliberately overstaying legal travel visas.

"What to do with the estimated 12 million undocumented immigrants now residing in various states within the United States is the biggest challenge in the immigration debate. The bedrock moral issue for The Church of Jesus Christ of Latter-day Saints is how we treat each other as children of God.

"The history of mass expulsion or mistreatment of individuals or families is cause for concern especially where race, culture, or religion are involved. This should give pause to any policy that contemplates targeting any one group, particularly if that group comes mostly from one heritage.

"As those on all sides of the immigration debate in the United States have noted, this issue is one that must ultimately be resolved by the federal government.

"The Church of Jesus Christ of Latter-day Saints is concerned that any state legislation that only contains enforcement provisions is likely to fall short of the high moral standard of treating each other as children of God.

"The Church supports an approach where undocumented immigrants are allowed to square themselves with the law and continue to work without this necessarily leading to citizenship.

"In furtherance of needed immigration reform in the United States, The Church of Jesus Christ of Latter-day Saints supports a balanced and civil approach to a challenging problem, fully consistent with its tradition of compassion, its reverence for family, and its commitment to law." (*LDS Church News,* June 18, p. 2)

• The First Presidency and the Quorum of the Twelve approved changes affecting the length of service and transportation and housing costs for senior missionaries. The changes went into effect Sept. 1, 2011.

Under the old policy, senior couples serving a mission outside of their country of residence served for at least 18 months, and transportation to and from the field was paid by the Church. Under the new policy, senior couples may serve a mission outside their country of residence for 6 or 12 months, but must pay for transportation costs to and from the field. Transportation costs for terms of 18 or 23 months continue to be paid by the Church.

Housing costs (including rent, utilities and furnishings) under the old policy were paid completely by the missionary couple. Under the new policy, local leaders responsible for senior missionaries secure housing and pay all housing costs, and then missionary couples from the United States, Canada, western Europe, Japan and Australia reimburse the housing costs, up to a cap of $1,400 a month. Missionary couples from all other countries reimburse up to their individual ability to pay, but not to exceed $1,400.

All couples continue to pay for food and other personal expenses.

Jason Swensen, Church News

President Thomas S. Monson offers closing remarks while presiding at the groundbreaking ceremony for the Rome Italy Temple on Oct. 23, 2010.

Rome Italy Temple rendering.

Temple News

Courtesy of Elder Neil L. Andersen

Elder Neil L. Andersen presides over the ground-breaking of the Cordoba Argentina Temple.

Scott P. Adair

Elder Claudio R.M. Costa breaks ground for the Gilbert Arizona Temple Nov. 13, 2010.

IRI

Members gather outside Laie Hawaii Temple for rededication on Sunday, Nov. 21, 2010.

• President Thomas S. Monson broke ground and dedicated the site for the **Rome Italy Temple** on Oct. 23, 2010. "This is one of the greatest blessings that has ever come to Italy," said President Monson, who announced the temple in the "Eternal City" during general conference on Oct. 4, 2008.

• Ground was broken and the site dedicated for the **Cordoba Argentina Temple** on Oct. 30, 2010, by Elder Neil L. Andersen of the Quorum of the Twelve. Some 500 members gathered at the temple site for the groundbreaking services. When completed, the sacred edifice, located in northern Argentina, will be the second temple in the country.

• In groundbreaking services on Nov. 13, 2010, Elder Claudio R.M. Costa of the Presidency of the Seventy broke ground and dedicated the site for the **Gilbert Arizona Temple** in Arizona's Salt River Valley. More than 7,500 people attended the services, with many more watching a broadcast of the proceedings at local stake centers.

• President Thomas S. Monson rededicated the **Laie Hawaii Temple** in three sessions on Nov. 21, 2010. The temple, which was originally dedicated in 1919 as the fifth temple in the Church, was closed in December 2008 for extensive remodeling and refurbishing.

• President Thomas S. Monson opened the 181st Annual General Conference of the Church on April 2, 2011, by announcing plans to build temples in **Fort Collins, Colo.; Meridian, Idaho;** and **Winnipeg, Manitoba.**

• The **Ogden Utah Temple** on April 2, 2011, was closed for extensive renovation. Following the renovation, the temple, which was originally dedicated in 1972 as the14th operating temple in the Church, will be rededicated.

• After extensive refurbishing, the **Atlanta Georgia Temple** was rededicated in two sessions on May 1, 2011, by President Thomas S. Monson. The temple

Gerry Avant, Church News
The Atlanta Georgia Temple was rededicated on Sunday, May 1, 2011, by President Thomas S. Monson.

Jill Adair
Church leaders break ground for the Phoenix Arizona Temple on June 4, 2011.

Fermin Acevedo
Elders M. Anthony Burns and William R. Walker unveil a rendering of the Ft. Lauderdale Temple.

Jason Swensen, Church News
Crowds watch President Henry B. Eyring during the cornerstone ceremony of the El Salvador temple.

was closed July 1, 2009, when the refurbishing work began.

• In a letter to local priesthood leaders, dated May 10, 2011, the First Presidency announced that, beginning July 11, 2011, the **Boise Idaho Temple** would be closed for extensive renovation.

• Ground for the fifth temple in Arizona – the **Phoenix Arizona Temple** – was broken and the site dedicated by Elder Ronald A. Rasband of the Presidency of the Seventy on June 4, 2011.

• Ground was broken and the site dedicated for the **Fort Lauderdale Florida Temple** on June 18, 2011, by Elder Walter F. González of the Presidency of the Seventy.

• A gold-leafed statue of the Angel Moroni was placed atop the east spire of the **Brigham City Utah Temple** on July 12, 2011. Construction of the temple, which was announced at general conference on Oct. 3, 2009, began in July 2010.

• The **San Salvador El Salvador Temple**, the 135th operating temple in the Church and the fourth in Central America, was dedicated Aug. 21, 2011, in three sessions, by President Henry B. Eyring, first counselor in the First Presidency.

• On Sept. 17, 2011, President Henry B. Eyring, first counselor in the First Presidency, broke ground and dedicated the site for the **Philadelphia Pennsylvania Temple,** which will serve members from eight stakes in Pennsylvania, New Jersey and Delaware. The groundbreaking ceremony was broadcast to each meetinghouse in the temple district.

• Ground for the second temple in Peru – the **Trujillo Peru Temple** – was broken and the site dedicated on Sept. 14, 2011, by Elder Rafael E. Pino of the Seventy

• Elder Dallin H. Oaks of the Quorum of the Twelve broke ground and dedicated the site for

the **Payson Utah Temple** on Oct. 8, 2011.

• Elder Gary E. Stevenson presided over the groundbreaking and site dedication of the **Sapporo Japan Temple** on Oct. 22, the third temple in Japan.

President Thomas S. Monson announced six new temples in October general conference, including a second temple in Provo, Utah. The temple will be converted from the rebuilt **Provo Tabernacle,** which was destroyed by a four-alarm fire on Dec. 17, 2010. Other temples announced by President Monson will be in **Paris, France; Kinshasa, Democratic Republic of the Congo; Durban, South Africa; Barranquilla, Colombia;** and **Star Valley, Wyo.**

Awards and Honors

- The Mormon Tabernacle Choir's program **"Music and the Spoken Word"** – the longest-running, uninterrupted network broadcast in history, which began July 15, 1929 – was inducted into the National Radio Hall of Fame in ceremonies on Nov. 6, 2010, that was broadcast from Chicago.

- The National Military Family Association honored the **Joe** and **Tawny Campbell family** – members of the Church stationed in Landstuhl, Germany – as the Army Family of the Year for 2010, an award that recognizes families from each of the branches of the military for, among other criteria, service to their nation.

- **Fred Riley,** manager of special projects for Church Humanitarian Services, was inducted into the National Council for Adoption's Hall of Fame, the Dec. 4, 2010, *LDS Church News* reported.

- For the second consecutive year, **President Thomas S. Monson** was named the top octogenarian in the United States by Slate, an online current affairs and culture magazine, reported the Dec. 11, 2010, *LDS Church News.* Ranking "80 people over the age of 80" according to "their power and importance, with extra credit given for energetic achievements," Slate stated that President Monson "stands atop the list."

K. David Scott

Mack Wilberg, left, and Lloyd Newell represented the Tabernacle Choir when the "Music and the Spoken Word" was inducted into National Radio Hall of Fame.

- **Elder D. Todd Christofferson** of the Quorum of the Twelve received the J.Reuben Clark Law Society Distinguished Service Award Feb. 4, 2011, for his contributions over many years in the field of law. His speech to the society in the Conference Center Little Theater in Salt Lake City was carried via broadcast to chapters throughout the world.

- For his ongoing service and contributions to the Utah community, **Presiding Bishop H. David Burton** was named "A Giant in Our City" March 16, 2011, by the Salt Lake Chamber. The award is one of the business community's most prestigious honors.

- **President Dieter F. Uchtdorf,** second counselor in the First Presidency, was honored March 31, 2011, by the Collegium Aesculapium, a non-profit organization of LDS physicians and health professionals, for his contributions in humanitarian aid.

- In a ceremony in the Church Administration Building in Salt Lake City, **President Thomas S. Monson** received the Silver Fox Award on April 1, 2011, from Scouts Canada which honors "those deemed to have contributed service of the most exceptional character to Scouting in the international field, performed by persons who are not members of Scout Canada."

- Honored for his efforts to build people "economically, socially and spiritually," **President Dieter F. Uchtdorf,** second counselor in the First Presidency, received the

2011 Legacy of Life award on April 7, 2011, from the Deseret Foundation's Heart and Lung Research Foundation.

• **Elder Russell M. Nelson** of the Quorum of the Twelve, who addressed graduates of LDS Business College on April 14, 2011, received the college's Distinguished Alumnus Award.

• **Jimmer Fredette,** BYU's star basketball player, became the first consensus national player of the year in school history by sweeping all of the major national player of the year awards. On April 8, 2011, he was given the prestigious John R. Wooden national player of the year award. Previously, he won the Naismith, Oscar Robertson, Adolph Rupp, Association of Basketball Coaches, and Associated Press national player of the year awards.

Scott G. Winterton, Deseret News

President Dieter F. Uchtdorf is presented with the Legacy of Life award by Johnny Cook M.D. on March 31, 2011, during the National LDS physicians conference.

• **President Dieter F. Uchtdorf,** second counselor in the First Presidency, who spoke at the BYU Management Society's annual awards dinner in Washington, D.C., on April 16, 2011, received the society's Distinguished Public Service Award for humanitarian service.

• For his "extraordinary commitment to defending human rights and advancing democratic principles of government," **Stephen Beecroft,** U.S. ambassador to Jordan and a 1983 graduate of BYU, received the Diplomacy for Human Rights Awards from the U.S. Department on State of April 21, 2011, in Washington, D.C.

• The American Mothers, Inc., named **Shawnalee "Shawni" Eyre Pothier** the National Young Mother of the Year for 2011during its annual national convention in Salt Lake City on April 30, 2011. She was Arizona's Young Mother of the Year representative.

• **President Thomas S. Monson** was awarded an honorary doctorate of humanities May 6, 2011, by Dixie State College in St. George, Utah, where he delivered the Centennial Commencement address to more than 1,500 graduates.

• **John Rosenberg,** dean of the College of Humanities at BYU, was given the Officer's Cross of the Order of Civil Merit by D. Jorge Dezcallar de Mazarredo, Spain's ambassador to the United States, on behalf of King Juan Carlos I and the Spanish government.

Jason Swensen, Church News

Dixie State College of Utah President Stephen D. Nadauld, right, presents President Thomas S. Monson with an honorary doctorate. State Regent Jerry C. Atkin is at left.

• During its Centennial Gala in the Salt Palace ballroom on Sept. 20, 2011, Salt Lake City's Rotary Club presented **President Thomas S. Monson** and five others the "Service Above Self" award – the highest award given by the Rotary Club. President Monson was recognized for the depth and breadth of his personal ministry beyond his official ministry as president of the Church.

Deaths

- **Vivian Paulsen,** 68, who served as managing editor of *The Friend* magazine, from 1982-2008, died Oct. 2, 2010, in Salt Lake City, Utah.

- **Richard T. Wootton,** 92, who served as president of the Church College of Hawaii (now BYU-Hawaii) from 1959-64, died Nov. 2, 2010, in Mesa, Ariz.

- **Elder Jermaine Luther Walker,** a missionary serving in the Jamaica Kingston Mission, died Jan. 17, 2011, after he was accidentally shot by a stray bullet in a crossfire between local police and another vehicle while he was riding in a van with other missionaries who were returning to their apartment in Kingston.

- **Ruth Hardy Funk,** 93, who served as general president of the Young Women from 1972-78, died Feb. 5, 2011, in Salt Lake City, Utah.

- **Carlos J. Garcia,** 74, who served as an Area Seventy from 2001-2007, died Feb. 26, 2011, in Chino, Calif.

- **J. Elliott Cameron,** 88, who served as president of Snow College in Ephraim, Utah, from 1956-58, as president of BYU-Hawaii from 1980-86, and as commissioner of education for the Church from 1986-89, died Feb. 27, 2011, in Provo, Utah. He also served as president of the Provo Utah Temple from 1989-92.

- **Wendell M. Smoot Jr.,** 90, president of the Mormon Tabernacle Choir, from 1984 to 2000, died July 3, 2011. During his tenure, he provided ecclesiastical and administrative leadership for the choir as it gave some 850 performances. He assisted in negotiations for recording contracts and arranged choir tours to destinations in the United States, Europe, Asia, the South Pacific, and the Middle East.

- **Beverly Joy Frewin Evans,** 85, who served as first counselor in the general Relief Society presidency from 1984 to 1990, died July 5, 2011.

- **J Malan Heslop,** 88, former editor of the *Church News* and *Deseret News* managing editor, died July 29, 2011, in Salt Lake City, Utah.

- **Colleen Monson Bangerter,** 76, who served as the first lady when her husband, Norman H. Bangerter, was governor of Utah from 1985-1993, died July 29, 2011, in South Jordan, Utah.

- **Chieko N. Okazaki,** 84, who served as first counselor in the Relief Society general presidency, from 1990-1997, died Aug. 1, 2011, in Salt Lake City, Utah.

- U.S. Navy Petty Officer First Class **Jason Workman,** 33, a member of the elite SEAL Team 6 who grew up in Blanding, Utah, was among 31 Americans killed Aug. 5, 2011, when their helicopter was shot down by insurgents in Afghanistan's Maidan Wardak province.

- **Sister Vanessa Bentley,** 22, a missionary from Tucson, Ariz., serving in the New York Utica Mission, died Aug. 30, 2011, in a two-car collision in upstate New York.

- **Sister Ann Baker Jones,** 69, a senior missionary from Taylorsville, Utah, serving in the Texas San Antonio Mission, died Sept. 23, 2011, after suffering severe burns in a fire caused by a gas leak in a kitchen stove in the mobile home in which they were living.

Deaths of General Authorities

• **Elder Hans B. Ringger,** 84, who served in the First Quorum of the Seventy from April 6, 1985, until he was granted emeritus status on Sept. 30, 1995, died Oct. 18, 2010, in Basel, Switzerland.

• **Elder LeGrand R. Curtis Sr.,** 86, who was called to the Second Quorum of the Seventy on March 31, 1990, and served until his release on Sept. 30, 1995, died Dec. 19, 2010, in Cottonwood Heights, Utah.

• **Elder Adney Y. Komatsu,** 87, the first member of the Church of Japanese descent to be called as a General Authority, died Feb. 23, 2011, in Honolulu, Hawaii. He was called as an Assistant to the Twelve on April 4, 1975, and to the First Quorum of the Seventy on Oct. 1, 1976, serving until Oct. 2, 1993, when he was granted emeritus status.

• **Elder Richard B. Wirthlin,** 80, who served in the Second Quorum of the Seventy from April 6, 1996, until his release on Oct. 6, 2001, died March 16, 2011, in Holladay, Utah. Before his call as a General Authority, he was a renowned pollster and a close adviser to U.S. President Ronald Reagan and served as his political strategist and pollster.

• **Elder Jack H Goaslind Jr.,** 83, who served 20 years in the First Quorum of the Seventy, from Sept. 30, 1978, until he was granted emeritus status on Oct. 3, 1998, died April 27, 2011, in Salt Lake City, Utah. He served twice as a member of the Presidency of the Seventy, from Oct. 6, 1985, to Aug. 15, 1987, and again from Aug. 15, 1995, to Aug. 15, 1998.

• **Elder Marion D. Hanks,** 89, who served 39 years as a General Authority, died August 5, 2011, in Salt Lake City, Utah. He was called to the First Council of Seventy on Oct. 4, 1953, and served in that capacity until April 6, 1968, when he was sustained as an Assistant to the Twelve. On Oct. 1, 1976, he was called to the First Quorum of the Seventy and served twice in the Presidency of the Seventy, from Oct. 1, 1976 to April 5, 1980, and again from Oct. 6, 1984 to Aug. 15, 1992. He was granted emeritus status on Oct. 3, 1992.

• **Elder Monte J. Brough,** 72, who served 18 years as a General Authority, died Sept. 20, 2011, in Kaysville, Utah. He was called to the Second Quorum of the Seventy on Oct. 1, 1989, and served in that quorum until April 6, 1991, when he was called to the First Quorum of the Seventy. He served in the Presidency of the Seventy from Aug. 15, 1993, until Aug. 15, 1998, and was granted emeritus status on Oct. 6, 2007.

Members of the Quorum of the Twelve Apostles are President Boyd K. Packer, L. Tom Perry, Russell M. Nelson, Dallin H. Oaks, M. Russell Ballard, back row: Richard G. Scott, Robert D. Hales, Jeffrey R. Holland, David A. Bednar, Quentin L. Cook, D. Todd Christofferson, Neil L. Andersen.

IRI

Courtesy Europe East Area

Elder Russel M. Nelson, center, shakes hands with members of the newly formed Moscow Russia Stake, the country's first stake. Elder Gregory A. Schwitzer of the Seventy and Sister Wendy Nelson are also in the line.

Long-awaited, eagerly anticipated

First stake organized in 'that vast empire'

By Jason Swensen Church News staff writer

The Church's history in Russia stretches back almost 170 years when the Prophet Joseph Smith called Orson Hyde of the Quorum of the Twelve and George J. Adams as the first two missionaries "to that vast empire" of Russia, to which, the Prophet stated, "is attached some of the most important things concerning the advancement and building

"To that vast empire is attached some of the most important things concerning the advancement and building up of the kingdom of God in the last days"

up of the kingdom of God in the last days" (History of the Church, 6:41).

Recently one of Elder Hyde's apostolic successors, Elder Russell M. Nelson, presided over another historic moment in Russia — the organization of the nation's first stake.

On June 5, more than 1,100 people gathered inside Moscow's Amber Plaza Auditorium to participate in the organization of the Moscow Russia Stake. The new unit includes six wards and three branches. Yakov Mikhaylovich Boyko was called to preside over the stake, with Vladimir Nikolaievich Astashov and Viktor Mikhaylovich Kremenchuk serving as first and second counselor, respectively. Vyacheslav Viktorovich Protopopov was ordained as stake patriarch.

In an email to the *Church News* dispatched from Russia, Elder Nelson rejoiced in the creation of Russia's first stake.

"On this historic occasion, my feelings are those of heartfelt gratitude to our Heavenly Father," he wrote. "He loves His children and wants them to find joy and peace. He is helping His children in Russia to find their faith, to desire to repent, be baptized and keep His commandments. They are developing a deep desire to return to Him, endowed and sealed to their families."

Elder Nelson added that he witnessed scores of "dear people" weep for joy when their stake was organized.

"I thought of the leaders, missionaries and members on both sides of the veil whose efforts have helped to make this possible. I remembered in the early 1990s when food was scarce, dear Russian members waited in long lines for food for missionaries so that they could teach their friends and families."

Elder Nelson was accompanied at the stake organization meeting by his wife, Sister Wendy Nelson. They were joined by his son, Russell M. Nelson Jr., who served among the early group of missionaries to Russia in 1991-93.

Elder Gregory A. Schwitzer of the Seventy and president of the East Europe Area and his wife, Sister JoAnn

"On this historic occasion, my feelings are those of heartfelt gratitude to our Heavenly Father. He loves His children and wants them to find joy and peace. He is helping His children in Russia to find their faith, to desire to repent, be baptized and keep His commandments. They are developing a deep desire to return to Him, endowed and sealed to their families," Elder Nelson wrote.

Schwitzer, also participated in the stake conference. A special participant at the event was Elder Dennis B. Neuenschwander, an emeritus Seventy who has played an instrumental role in the organization and growth of the Church in Russia.

During the meeting, Elder Nelson counseled the members of the new stake to find unity in their faith. "Pray for your new leaders. They will need your prayers," he counseled. "Be valiant in every possible way to live the gospel, especially in teaching your children as your read the scriptures together."

There are more than 21,000 Latter-day Saints in Russia, worshipping in 116 congregations. The Church's interest in this European nation goes back to 1843 when Joseph Smith called Elder Hyde and Brother Adams to serve as missionaries in Russia.

That mission was never fulfilled because of the martyrdom of the Prophet and the Church's departure from Nauvoo. Sixty years later, in early August of 1903, Elder Francis M. Lyman of the Quorum of the Twelve offered prayers of dedication in the Russian cities of St. Petersburg and Moscow. Missionaries arrived in Leningrad, now St. Petersburg, in the early days of 1990. Announcement that the Church was formally recognized in Russia by the Soviet government was made on June 24, 1991, coincident with the concert of the Mormon Tabernacle Choir at the Bolshoi Theater in Moscow.

In 2002, President Gordon B. Hinckley became the first Church president to visit Russia, where he spoke to a gathering of 2,300 members. President Hinckley returned to Russia three years later.

Elder Nelson is, himself, no stranger to Russia. He made his first visit in 1966 — decades before the fall of the Soviet Union — with a small team of doctors representing the American Heart Association to teach Russian doctors. He returned to medical meetings in 1971. Years later, in 1990, as an ordained apostle, Elder Nelson offered prayers of rededication in Leningrad and Moscow.

The Church's interest in this European nation goes back to 1843 when Joseph Smith called Elder Orson Hyde and Brother George J. Adam to serve as missionaries in Russia.
That mission was never fulfilled because of the martyrdom of the Prophet and the Church's departure from Nauvoo. Sixty years later, in early August of 1903, Elder Francis M. Lyman of the Quorum of the Twelve offered prayers of dedication in the Russian cities of St. Petersburg and Moscow. Missionaries arrived in Leningrad, now St. Petersburg, in the early days of 1990.

Courtesy Europe East Area

Young Russian members gather in the Amber Plaza Auditorium in Moscow to participate in the organization of the country's first stake. More than 1,000 members attended to witness the historic event.

Courtesy Europe East Area

A spirit of jubilation attended the long-awaited event. What seemed nearly impossible to early members of the Church came to fruition as Elder Russell M. Nelson created the Moscow Russia Stake on June 5, 2011.

Long-awaited, eagerly anticipated

With a new stake, members step into a new Russia

By Jason Swensen Church News staff writer

Members and missionaries in Moscow, Russia, were correct in feeling optimistic last summer when a temple was dedicated in neighboring Ukraine.

The opening of the Kyiv Ukraine Temple in 2010 was a monumental event for Latter-day Saints who have lived and labored in Moscow. Local Latter-day Saints would no longer have to travel, at significant expense, to Finland or Sweden to claim their temple blessings. A temple was just an overnight train ride away.

But the opening of the Ukraine temple was also a symbolic blessing for Moscow members. It was a reassuring confirmation that, indeed, the Church was growing in the former Soviet Union. A short time after the dedication, Moscow member Vladimir Kabanovy told the *Deseret News* that "the Church will continue to grow — I envision the stakes of Zion here."

Brother Kabanovy's dream for a stake in Russia was realized June 5 when Elder Russell M. Nelson of the Quorum of the Twelve organized the Moscow Russia Stake.

More than 1,000 people witnessed that event, signaling a new day and new opportunities for Latter-day Saints living in the Russian capital.

"We are very happy to have the stake in Moscow, it's a

The opening of the Ukraine temple was a symbolic blessing for Moscow members. It was a reassuring confirmation that, indeed, the Church was growing in the former Soviet Union. More than 1,000 people witnessed the creation of Russia's first stake, signaling a new day and new opportunities for Latter-day Saints living in the Russian capital.

historical event," wrote Brother Kabanovy in an e-mail.

His sentiments were echoed by others who have come to love Moscow and the promise found in its faithful "pioneer" members.

Elder Dennis B. Neuenschwander, now an emeritus Seventy, was presiding over the Austria Vienna East Mission in 1990 when he accompanied the first missionaries to enter Ukraine. Later he served in the presidency of the East Europe Area, which is now headquartered in Moscow, and played an instrumental role in the development of the missionary work in Moscow and its surrounding regions.

From the first days of his service in Russia and Eastern Europe, Elder Neuenschwander taught the importance of local members taking responsibility for the Church in their own cities and communities. That teaching, he said, assumed new meaning with the recent organization of Russia's first stake.

"The Saints in Russia, but most particularly those in Moscow, stepped into a new Russia with the formation of this stake," he noted in an e-mail to the Church News. "Until the [organization of the stake], the directing keys of the priesthood had resided exclusively with the mission presidents, almost all of whom were foreigners. If, for some reason, the mission presidents would have left Russia, the priesthood keys would have gone with them."

That all changed with the calling of local member Yakov Mikhaylovich Boyko to preside over the Moscow Russia Stake.

"The keys of the priesthood are in Russia to stay — nothing can remove them," he wrote. "There is such a feeling of relief in my heart over this matter."

A few weeks ago, Elder Neuenschwander and his wife, Sister Joni Neuenschwander, were asked to participate in a stake conference in Kyiv. While sitting on the stand, he felt overwhelmed by the spiritual maturity of the Ukrainian members.

"I had that same confirming feeling about the Saints in the Moscow stake. This is only the beginning, but

"The Saints in Russia, but most particularly those in Moscow, stepped into a new Russia with the formation of this stake. … The keys of the priesthood are in Russia to stay — nothing can remove them. There is such a feeling of relief in my heart over this matter," said Elder Dennis B. Neuenschwander, now an emeritus Seventy

how spiritually significant it is."

Ralph and Julie Ann Moffat are serving a full-time mission in Russia. The Moffats echoed Elder Neuenschwander's sentiment that the Moscow members have a call of responsibility in their own city. Families will play a pivotal role in the stability of the new stake, said Elder Moffat.

"The focus on families will strengthen the growth of the Church in this marvelous part of the world," he added. "We need to internalize the sweetness of the gift of a stake and do all we can, member by member and family by family, to teach by what we live so that we may, individual by individual and family by family, receive the fullness of the great blessings that the gospel of Jesus Christ can bring to all nations and people."

In his counsel to the Moscow members, East Europe Area President Gregory A. Schwitzer of the Seventy said the new stake is synonymous with spiritual safety and protection.

"Where is a stake born?" he asked. "It is born within each of us."

"Where is a stake born? It is born within each of us," said Elder Gregory A. Schwitzer of the Seventy, counseling the Moscow members that a new stake is synonymous with spiritual safety and protection.

Courtesy Europe East Area

Elder Russell M. Nelson greets local members of the newly organization Moscow Russia Stake.

Courtesy of Europe East Area

On a sunny spring day, members of the Church arrive early at Moscow's Amber Plaza Auditorium on June 5, 2011. Some came great distances, all came eager to participate in the organization of the Moscow Russia Stake.

Long-awaited, eagerly anticipated

Church's pioneers in Eastern Europe played pivotal role

By Jason Swensen Church News staff writer

The Church is experiencing exciting, historical moments in the Europe East Area. Last summer, President Thomas S. Monson dedicated the area's first temple with the opening of the Kyiv Ukraine Temple. Then a few months later on June 5, 2011, Elder Russell M. Nelson of the Quorum of the Twelve organized the Russia Moscow Stake, the nation's first.

But even as the tens of thousands of members in the Europe East Area celebrate recent milestones, there is much to be learned from the region's LDS history. During his recent visit to the area, Elder Nelson took a few moments to pay tribute to the Church's pioneer past in eastern Europe. Such pioneers — including many who are still alive and laboring faithfully in the congregations and communities — played pivotal roles in helping the Church take its maiden steps in this area of the world.

After organizing the new stake, Elder Nelson traveled to St. Petersburg to preside over a district conference and meet with missionaries. While speaking to some 500 people in attendance at the district conference, the Apostle spoke of the Russian "pioneers" and their priceless, essential service and contributions. He recalled the joy he and other Church leaders felt in 1995 when Vyacheslav I. Efimov became the first Russian native to be called as a mission president, serving in the Russia

The Apostle spoke of the Russian "pioneers" and their priceless, essential service and contributions. He recalled the joy he and other Church leaders felt in 1995 when Vyacheslav I. Efimov became the first Russian native to be called as a mission president.

Yekaterinburg Mission.

Elder Nelson met with President Efimov and his wife, Galina, when the couple traveled to Utah to participate in the new mission president's training seminar before they began their calling.

"We showed them the page proofs of the Doctrine and Covenants in the Russian language," said Elder Nelson. "President Efimov had never seen the Doctrine and Covenants in Russian, and when he saw it for the first time in page proof form, he and his wife wept for joy."

President Efimov died unexpectedly at a young age after fulfilling his mission. His passing saddened Elder Nelson and many others who had high hopes for President Efimov's continued Church service in Russia. The Apostle found comfort in knowing he was likely performing missionary work on the other side of the veil.

Elder Nelson then asked if Sister Efimov was in attendance at the St. Petersburg district conference. "And way in the back, there she was." He invited her to come forward and share her thoughts and testimony.

"Sister Efimov talked about how she and her husband are partners in missionary work," said Elder Nelson. "President Efimov is working on the other side of the veil, and she's working on this side of the veil. They are still united in missionary service."

As Sister Efimov shared her testimony, "there was not a dry eye in the place."

St. Petersburg is a special place for Elder Nelson. His granddaughter, Sister Lindsay Irion, is serving in the Russia St. Petersburg Mission — a mission presided over by native Ukrainian, President Gennady Podvodov. The Apostle — who has participated in the Church in Russia since it's beginnings — takes pleasure in knowing his own granddaughter is serving in a mission presided over by a Russian-speaking priesthood leader.

"The dear Russian people who love the Lord can finally hear the truth of the restoration of the gospel in its fullness and receive the blessings of eternal glory in the celestial kingdom with our Heavenly Father," he said.

"We showed them the page proofs of the Doctrine and Covenants in the Russian language," said Elder Nelson. "President Efimov had never seen the Doctrine and Covenants in Russian, and when he saw it for the first time in page proof form, he and his wife wept for joy."

While in Russia, Elder Nelson also presided over an annual review of the Europe East Area. He was joined in his review by Elder L. Whitney Clayton of the Presidency of the Seventy. They were joined in their travels by their wives, Sister Wendy Nelson and Sister Kathy Ann Clayton.

The Brethren reviewed the affairs of the Church in the area with members of the Europe Area Presidency, Elder Gregory A. Schwitzer and Elder Larry R. Lawrence of the Seventy and many of their associates. The third member of the area presidency, Elder Aleksandr N. Manzhos, an Area Seventy, was excused to participate in the marriage of his daughter in the Kyiv Ukraine Temple.

"The area presidency is doing a fantastic job managing the affairs of the Church," said Elder Nelson. "They are responsible for more than 40,000 members, 14 missions, two stakes, 25 mission districts, and deal with 10 different languages."

Elder Nelson returned to Church headquarters hopeful for the coming days and years for the Church in Russia and eastern Europe. "They are good missionaries. They joyfully share the gospel with their friends and family because they know what it's like to be without it. They enjoy great missionary opportunities."

> *"The area presidency is doing a fantastic job managing the affairs of the Church," said Elder Nelson. "They are responsible for more than 40,000 members, 14 missions, two stakes, 25 mission districts, and deal with 10 different languages."*

Young women and Young single adults sing in the choir of the newly organized Moscow Russia Stake on June 5, 2011.

Courtesy Europe East Area

Thomas S. Monson
PRESIDENT

President Thomas S. Monson has been on the Lord's errand all his life, from serving as president of his ward's teachers quorum in his teens, to serving as bishop in his early 20s, to presiding over a mission in his early 30s, to becoming a member of the Quorum of the Twelve at age 36.

For the 22 years prior to being set apart as 16th president of the Church on Feb. 3, 2008, President Monson served as counselor to three presidents: second counselor to President Ezra Taft Benson and President Howard W. Hunter and, for nearly 13 years, first counselor to President Gordon B. Hinckley.

Five years after his call to the Twelve, he was given a special assignment for the work of the Church in Europe, requiring many visits with members behind the Iron Curtain in the German Democratic Republic, Czechoslovakia, Poland and Hungary. He had a key role in gaining permission from the East German government to build the Freiberg Germany Temple, which was dedicated in 1985, and in advancing the work of the Lord in other eastern European countries that were part of the communist bloc.

His life is associated with benevolence and compassion, serving others with a desire to nourish the weak and strengthen the weary. His role in the Church's welfare program has been characterized by one-on-one service.

Thomas S. Monson

He remembers how his father never spoke ill of another and would leave the room when others spoke disrespectfully or negatively. He often speaks of his mother, who taught him compassion by her acts of service to others, particularly those who were hungry or in need.

On one occasion, on a cold winter's night, a knock came at Bishop Monson's door. A German man living in Ogden, Utah, began to weep as he told how his brother, a faithful member in Germany during World War II, and his family were moving from Germany to an apartment in Bishop Monson's ward. Then-Bishop Monson visited the apartment and found it woefully inadequate. The next morning during a ward welfare committee meeting, he described the challenge. Members offered their skills and services. When the family arrived three weeks later, they found new carpet and paint, adequate lighting and full cupboards. "The father ... buried his head in my shoulder and repeated the words, 'Mein Bruder, mein Bruder, mein Bruder.' "

BIOGRAPHY

FAMILY: Born Aug. 21, 1927, in Salt Lake City to G. Spencer and Gladys Condie Monson; two brothers and three sisters; married Frances Beverly Johnson in the Salt Lake Temple on Oct. 7, 1948; three children: two sons, Tom and Clark; one daughter, Ann Dibb; eight grandchildren and seven great-grandchildren.

CHURCH SERVICE: Called at age 22 as bishop of the Sixth-Seventh Ward in Salt Lake City, with some 1,080 members, including about 84 widows; called as counselor in a stake presidency at age 27; called as president of the Canadian Mission at age 31; served on several Church committees, including the Adult Correlation Committee, and helped pioneer the home teaching program of the Church; sustained on Oct. 4, 1963, at age 36 to the Quorum of the Twelve, and ordained an apostle on Oct. 10, 1963. As a member of the Quorum of the Twelve, he supervised the missions in western America, the South Pacific, Mexico, Central America and Europe. After a number of years and following the policy of rotation, the European missions were transferred to another member of the Twelve; however, Elder Monson retained responsibility for all countries behind the Iron Curtain. He was instrumental in obtaining government approval for the construction of the Freiberg Germany Temple, served as chairman of the Scriptures Publication Committee and supervised the process which resulted in new editions of the Standard Works of the Church. Called on Nov. 10, 1985, as second counselor to President Ezra Taft Benson; called in 1994 as second counselor to President Howard W. Hunter and in 1995 as first counselor to President Gordon B. Hinckley; ordained and set apart on Feb. 3, 2008, as president of The Church of Jesus Christ of Latter-day Saints.

EDUCATION: Graduated with honors from the University of Utah in 1948 with a degree in business; received an MBA from Brigham Young University, and received honorary Doctor of Laws degree from BYU, honorary Doctor of Humane Letters from Salt Lake Community College, honorary Doctor of Business from the University of Utah, honorary Doctor of Communication from Utah Valley University, honorary Doctor of Public Service from Southern Utah University, honorary Doctorate of humanities from Weber State University, and honorary Doctor of Humanities degree from Dixie State College of Utah.

EMPLOYMENT: Began working for Deseret News in 1948 as assistant classified advertising manager; shortly thereafter he became classified advertising manager; he became an officer of Newspaper Agency Corporation in 1952, became sales manager of Deseret News Press in 1953, and later became assistant general manager; served as president of the Printing Industry of Utah and later served as a director of the Printing Industries of America; named general manager of Deseret Press upon returning home from serving as a mission president in Canada; chairman of the Deseret News board of directors for 19 years.

CIVIC: Has served more than four decades on the National Executive Board of Boy Scouts of America; received Scouting's Silver Beaver and Silver Buffalo awards, International Scouting's highest award, the Bronze Wolf, and Scouts Canada's Silver Fox Award. In December 1981, he was appointed by U.S. President Ronald Reagan to serve on the President's Task Force for Private Sector Initiatives. He served in this capacity from December 1981 to December 1982 when the work of the task force was completed.

The joy in their faces of the First Presidency reflects the joy in their lives.

IRI

Henry B. Eyring

FIRST COUNSELOR IN FIRST PRESIDENCY

President Henry B. Eyring was set apart Feb. 3, 2008, as first counselor in the First Presidency to President Thomas S. Monson, and sustained April 5, 2008, in the solemn assembly of general conference.

He was sustained Oct. 6, 2007, and set apart Oct. 11, 2007, as second counselor in the First Presidency to President Gordon B. Hinckley.

He was sustained to the Quorum of the Twelve April 1, 1995, and ordained an apostle April 6, 1995, at age 61.

He was sustained to the First Quorum of the Seventy Oct. 3, 1992, and as first counselor in the Presiding Bishopric April 6, 1985.

Before being called as a General Authority he served as a regional representative, member of the Sunday School general board, and bishop.

Born May 31, 1933, in Princeton, N.J., to Henry and Mildred Bennion Eyring.

He received a bachelor's degree in physics from the University of Utah, and master's and doctoral degrees from Harvard University in business administration. He became an assistant professor and associate professor at the Stanford Graduate School of Business in Palo Alto, Calif.

Henry B. Eyring

He served as the president of Ricks College, 1971-77, before being called as deputy commissioner, and then commissioner of Church Education.

He and his wife, Kathleen Johnson Eyring, are parents of six children and have 28 grandchildren.

President Eyring was reared by parents who valued education. His father was a chemistry professor at Princeton University and dean of the graduate school at the University of Utah. His mother had been a professor at the University of Utah and a doctoral candidate at the University of Wisconsin when she met and married her husband.

The Eyring home was a learning laboratory — filled with discussion about "deep, serious things" — where President Eyring learned to cherish religion and appreciate science and to respect others. Once President Eyring asked his father why he asked the gas station attendants questions. "Dad said, 'I never met a man I couldn't learn something from.' "

Dieter F. Uchtdorf

SECOND COUNSELOR IN FIRST PRESIDENCY

President Dieter F. Uchtdorf was set apart Feb. 3, 2008, as second counselor in the First Presidency to President Thomas S. Monson, and sustained April 5, 2008, in the solemn assembly in general conference.

He was sustained to the Quorum of the Twelve Oct. 2, 2004, and ordained an apostle Oct. 7, 2004, at age 63.

He was called to the Presidency of the Seventy Aug. 15, 2002, and sustained Oct. 5, 2002.

He was sustained to the First Quorum of the Seventy April 6, 1996.

He was sustained to the Second Quorum of the Seventy April 2, 1994.

Prior to being called as a General Authority, he served twice as stake president.

Born Nov. 6, 1940, in Ostrava, in the former Czechoslovakia, to Karl Albert and Hilde Else Opelt Uchtdorf, he grew up in Germany.

He received an education in engineering, business administration and international management.

President Uchtdorf served in the German Air Force for six years. He earned his wings as a fighter pilot in the U.S. and German Air Forces.

In 1965, President Uchtdorf joined Lufthansa German Airlines as a pilot. He worked as an airline captain from 1970 to 1996, flying multiple types of airplanes and completing his career flying the B-747. He held several executive positions, including head of the airline pilot school, director of in-flight services, and head of cockpit crews. At the time of his call as a General Authority, he was the senior vice president of flight operations and chief pilot of Lufthansa German Airlines. He was also chairman of the Flight Operations Committee of the International Air Transport Association. He has served as a board member for several government and business executive committees.

President Uchtdorf married Harriet Reich in 1962. They are the parents of two children and have six grandchildren. Since his call as an apostle, President and Sister Uchtdorf now have their permanent home in the United States.

His family joined the Church as a result of a missionary-minded, elderly woman who invited his grandmother to Church in East Germany. He was baptized two years after his family, when he turned 8 years old.

The Uchtdorfs are grateful for the gospel principle that families can be together forever.

Dieter F. Uchtdorf

THE QUORUM OF TWELVE APOSTLES

Boyd K. Packer

Set apart as president of the Quorum of the Twelve on Feb. 3, 2008. Previously set apart as acting president of the Quorum of the Twelve on June 5, 1994, and again March 12, 1995. Sustained as an Assistant to the Twelve Sept. 30, 1961; sustained to the Quorum of the Twelve April 6, 1970, and ordained an apostle April 9, 1970, at age 45. Former supervisor of Seminaries and Institutes of Religion; former president of the New England States Mission. Received bachelor's and master's degrees from Utah State University, and Ed.D. in educational administration from BYU. Pilot in the Pacific Theater during World War II. Born Sept. 10, 1924, in Brigham City, Utah, a son of Ira Wight and Emma Jensen Packer. Wife, Donna Smith; parents of 10 children.

L. Tom Perry

Sustained as an Assistant to the Twelve Oct. 6, 1972; sustained to the Quorum of the Twelve on April 6, 1974, and ordained an apostle April 11, 1974, at age 51. Served in the Marines in the Pacific during World War II. Graduated from Utah State University with a B.S. degree in finance; was controller, vice president and treasurer of department store organizations in Idaho, California and Boston, Mass. Former president of the Boston Stake and served as counselor in other stake presidencies and bishoprics. Born Aug. 5, 1922, in Logan, Utah, to L. Tom and Nora Sonne Perry. Wife, Virginia Lee; parents of three children. She died in 1974. Married Barbara Dayton in 1976.

Russell M. Nelson

Sustained to the Quorum of the Twelve April 7, 1984, and ordained an apostle April 12, 1984, at age 59. Former Sunday School general president, regional representative, and stake president. Renowned surgeon and medical researcher. Received B.A. and M.D. degrees from University of Utah, and Ph.D. from University of Minnesota. Former president of the Utah Medical Association Society for Vascular Surgery and former chairman of the Council on Cardiovascular Surgery for the American Heart Association. Born Sept. 9, 1924, in Salt Lake City, Utah, to Marion C. and Edna Anderson Nelson. Wife, Dantzel White Nelson; parents of 10 children. She died Feb. 12, 2005. Married Wendy Watson on April 6, 2006.

Dallin H. Oaks

Sustained to the Quorum of the Twelve April 7, 1984, and ordained an apostle May 3, 1984, at age 51. Graduate of BYU in accounting; J.D. cum laude the University of Chicago Law School; law clerk to U.S. Supreme Court Chief Justice Earl Warren; practiced law in Chicago; professor of law at the University of Chicago; nine years as BYU president; three-and-one-half years as a justice of the Utah Supreme Court; and five years as chairman of the board of the Public Broadcasting Service. Former regional representative and counselor in stake presidency. Born Aug. 12, 1932, in Provo, Utah, a son of Dr. Lloyd E. and Stella Harris Oaks. Wife, June Dixon Oaks died July 21, 1998; parents of six children. Married Kristen Meredith McMain on Aug. 25, 2000.

M. Russell Ballard

S ustained to the First Quorum of the Seventy April 3, 1976; called to the presidency of the quorum Feb. 21, 1980 and sustained April 5, 1980. Sustained to the Quorum of the Twelve Oct. 6, 1985, and ordained an apostle Oct. 10, 1985, at age 57. Much of his ministry has focused on missionary work. Served on several community and national boards. Prior to his call to the Seventy, he organized and directed several business and civic enterprises. Served as a counselor to his mission president, bishop twice, and presided over the Canada Toronto Mission. Born Oct. 8, 1928, in Salt Lake City, Utah, to Melvin Russell Sr. and Geraldine Smith Ballard. Wife, Barbara Bowen; parents of seven children.

Richard G. Scott

S ustained to the First Quorum of the Seventy April 2, 1977, and to the quorum presidency Oct. 1, 1983; sustained to the Quorum of the Twelve Oct. 1, 1988, and ordained apostle Oct. 6, 1988, at age 59. Received B.S. degree in mechanical engineering from George Washington University, completed post-graduate work in nuclear engineering at Oak Ridge, Tenn. Worked on the staff of Adm. Hyman Rickover, developing military and private nuclear power reactors; was consultant to nuclear power industry. Former president of Argentina North Mission, regional representative, and counselor in the Washington D.C. Stake presidency. Born Nov. 7, 1928, in Pocatello, Idaho, to Kenneth Leroy and Mary Eliza Whittle Scott. Wife, Jeanene Watkins; parents of seven children. She died May 15, 1995.

Robert D. Hales

Sustained as an Assistant to the Twelve April 4, 1975, and to the First Quorum of the Seventy Oct. 1, 1976; sustained as Presiding Bishop April 6, 1985; sustained to the Quorum of the Twelve April 2, 1994, and ordained an apostle April 7, 1994, at age 61. Former first counselor in the Sunday School general presidency, president of the England London Mission, regional representative, stake president's counselor, served as a branch president and bishop. Earned bachelor's degree from the University of Utah and master's degree in business administration from Harvard; served in the U.S. Air Force as jet fighter pilot; was an executive with four major national companies. Born Aug. 24, 1932, in New York City, N.Y., to John Rulon and Vera Marie Holbrook Hales. Wife, Mary Elene Crandall; parents of two children.

Jeffrey R. Holland

Ordained an apostle June 23, 1994, at age 53, and sustained to the Quorum of the Twelve Oct. 1, 1994. Sustained to the First Quorum of the Seventy on April 1, 1989, while serving as president of Brigham Young University. Former Church Commissioner of Education, 1976-80; BYU president from 1980-89, former dean of College of Religion at BYU. Received bachelor's degree in English, and master's degree in religious education from BYU, and master's degree and doctorate in American studies from Yale University. Former regional representative, counselor in stake presidency, and bishop. Born Dec. 3, 1940, in St. George, Utah, to Frank D. and Alice Bentley Holland. Wife, Patricia Terry; parents of three children.

David A. Bednar

Sustained to the Quorum of the Twelve Oct. 2, 2004; ordained an apostle Oct. 7, 2004, at age 52. Former Area Seventy, Area Authority, regional representative, stake president and bishop. Received bachelor's degree and master's degree from BYU, and doctorate from Purdue University. Professor of business management at Texas Tech University and at University of Arkansas. President of Brigham Young University-Idaho from 1997-2004. Born June 15, 1952, in Oakland, Calif., to Anthony G. and Lavina Whitney Bednar. Wife, Susan Kae Robinson; parents of three sons.

Quentin L. Cook

Sustained to the Second Quorum of the Seventy April 6, 1996; sustained to the First Quorum of the Seventy April 5, 1998; called to the Presidency of the Seventy Aug. 1, 2007; sustained to the Quorum of the Twelve Oct. 6, 2007, ordained an apostle Oct. 11, 2007, at age 67. Former Area Authority in the North America West Area, regional representative, president of the San Francisco California Stake, stake president's counselor and bishop. Former managing partner of a law firm and president and CEO of a California healthcare system. Received bachelor's degree from Utah State University and juris doctorate from Stanford University. Born Sept. 8, 1940, in Logan, Utah, to J. Vernon and Bernice Kimball Cook. Wife, Mary Gaddie; parents of three children.

D. Todd Christofferson

Sustained to the First Quorum of the Seventy April 3, 1993; called to the Presidency of the Seventy Aug. 15, 1998, and sustained Oct. 3, 1998; sustained to the Quorum of the Twelve April 5, 2008, ordained an apostle April 10, 2008, at age 63. Former regional representative, stake president, stake president's counselor, bishop and missionary in the Argentina North Mission. Received bachelor's degree in English/international relations from BYU; juris doctorate from Duke University. Former associate general counsel of NationsBank Corp., (now Bank of America) in Charlotte, N.C.; practiced law in Washington, D.C., Tennessee and North Carolina, and was law clerk to John J. Sirica, U.S. District Court for the District of Columbia, 1972-74. Born Jan. 24, 1945, in American Fork, Utah, to Paul V. and Jeanne Swenson Christofferson. Wife, Katherine Jacob; parents of five children.

Neil L. Andersen

Sustained to the First Quorum of the Seventy April 3, 1993, at age 41; called to the Presidency of the Seventy Aug. 15, 2005, sustained Oct. 1, 2005, and was serving as the senior president when he was sustained to the Quorum of the Twelve April 4, 2009; ordained an apostle April 9, 2009, at age 57. Former president of the France Bordeaux Mission and president of the Tampa Florida Stake. Served 10 years in Europe and South America areas. Received a bachelor's degree from BYU, received master's degree in business from Harvard University. His business interests included advertising, real estate development and health care, all based in Florida. Speaks French, Portuguese and Spanish. Born Aug. 9, 1951, in Logan, Utah, to Lyle P. and Kathryn Andersen. Wife, Kathy Sue Williams; parents of four children.

PRESIDENCY OF THE SEVENTY

Ronald A. Rasband

Sustained to the First Quorum of the Seventy April 1, 2000, at age 49; called to the Presidency of the Seventy Aug. 15, 2005, and sustained Oct. 1, 2005. Former president of New York New York North Mission, high councilor and bishop. Was self-employed businessman and previously was president and chief operations officer of Huntsman Chemical Corporation. Attended University of Utah and received an honorary doctorate of business and commerce from Utah Valley State College in Orem, Utah. Born Feb. 6, 1951, in Salt Lake City, Utah, to Rulon Hawkins and Verda Anderson Rasband. Wife, Melanie Twitchell Rasband; parents of five children.

Steven E. Snow

Sustained to the First Quorum of the Seventy March 31, 2001, at age 51; called to the Presidency of the Seventy Aug. 1, 2007, and sustained Oct. 6, 2007. Former Area Authority Seventy in the Utah South Area, president of the California San Fernando Mission, stake president and bishop. Received bachelor's degree in accounting from Utah State University and juris doctorate from Brigham Young University. Was senior partner in law firm of Snow Nuffer and formerly deputy county attorney for Washington County, Utah. Born Nov. 23, 1949, in St. George, Utah, to Gregg E. and Viola Jean Goates Snow. Wife, Phyllis Squire Snow; parents of four sons.

Walter F. Gonzalez

Sustained to the First Quorum of the Seventy March 31, 2001, at age 48; sustained to the Presidency of the Seventy Oct. 6, 2007. Former Area Authority Seventy, serving as second counselor in the South America North Area presidency, and was previously regional representative, president of the Guayaquil Ecuador South Mission, 1989-92, stake president and area public affairs director. Received bachelor's degree at Indiana University and a technician's certificate at CEMLAD Institute. Formerly Church Educational System director for South America North Area and a CES employee. Born Nov. 18, 1952, in Montevideo, Uruguay, to Fermin Gabino and Victoria Dolores Nunez Gonzalez. Wife, Zulma Anahir Nunez Gonzalez; parents of four children.

L. Whitney Clayton

Sustained to the First Quorum of the Seventy March 31, 2001, at age 51; sustained to the Presidency of the Seventy April 5, 2008. Former Area Authority Seventy in the North America West Area, regional representative, mission president's counselor, high councilor, and bishop. Received bachelor's degree in finance from the University of Utah and law degree from the University of Pacific. Was an attorney and shareholder with Call, Clayton, and Jensen, a California law firm. Born Feb. 24, 1950, in Salt Lake City, Utah, to L. Whitney and Elizabeth Graham Touchstone Clayton. Wife, Kathy Ann Kipp Clayton; parents of seven children.

Jay E. Jensen

Called to the Second Quorum of the Seventy June 6, 1992, at age 50, and sustained Oct. 3, 1992. Sustained to the First Quorum of the Seventy April 1, 1995. Called to the Presidency of the Seventy Aug. 1, 2008, and sustained Oct. 4, 2008. Former president of the Colombia Cali Mission, stake president's counselor and bishop. Former director of CES curriculum, and later director of scripture coordination for the Church Curriculum Department. Received bachelor's, master's, and doctoral degrees in Spanish and history, Church history and doctrine, and education, respectively, from BYU. Born Feb. 5, 1942, in Payson, Utah, to Ruel W. and Ethel Otte Jensen. Wife, Lona Lee Child Jensen; parents of six children.

Donald L. Hallstrom

Sustained to the First Quorum of the Seventy April 1, 2000, at age 50; sustained to the Presidency of the Seventy April 4, 2009. Former Area Authority Seventy, regional representative, stake president, and bishop. Former president and owner of real estate economics company. Received bachelor's degree in economics from BYU. Born July 27, 1949, in Honolulu, Hawaii, to James E. and Betty Jo Lambert Hallstrom. Wife, Diane Clifton Hallstrom; parents of four children.

PRESIDENCY OF THE SEVENTY

Tad R. Callister

Sustained to the Second Quorum of the Seventy April 5, 2008, at age 62. Called to the Presidency of the Seventy Aug. 15, 2011, and sustained Oct. 1, 2011. Former Area Seventy, regional representative, president of Canada Toronto East Mission and mission president's counselor, temple ordinance worker, stake president and counselor, bishop, and stake mission president. Was president of a Boy Scout Council. Former attorney. Received bachelor's degree in accounting from BYU, juris doctorate from UCLA, master's degree in tax law from New York University Law School. Born Dec. 17, 1945, in Glendale, Calif., to Reed and Norinne Richards Callister. Wife, Kathryn Saporiti Callister; parents of six children.

FIRST QUORUM OF THE SEVENTY

Marcos A. Aidukaitis

Sustained to the First Quorum of the Seventy April 5, 2008, at age 48. Former Area Seventy in Brazil South Area, president of Brazil Brasilia Mission and stake president. Was partner at MAV Distribution. Received bachelor's degree in mechanical engineering from BYU, master's degree of business administration from BYU's Marriott School of Management. Born Aug. 30, 1959, in Porto Alegre, Brazil, to Antony and Maria Dittrich Aidukaitis. Wife, Luisa Englert Aidukaitis; parents of five children.

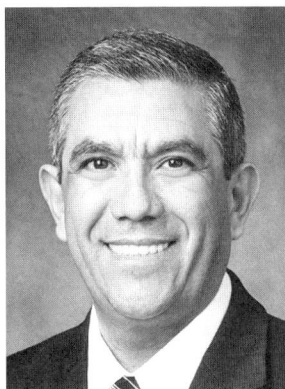

José L. Alonso

Sustained to the First Quorum of the Seventy April 2, 2011, at age 52. Former Area Seventy, counselor in Mexico North Area presidency, president of Mexico Tijuana Mission, mission president's counselor, stake president, and bishop. Received medical degree as homeopathic physician and surgeon from Escuela de Homeopatia de Mexico and a degree in pediatric development from National Institute of Pediatrics. In addition to his medical career, he also served as an institute director with the Church Educational System. Born in November 1958 in Mexico City, Mexico, to Luis Juan Alonso Jimenez and Maria De la Luz Trejo Quiroz. Wife, Rebecca Salazar Ramirez Alonso; parents of two sons.

Carlos H. Amado

Sustained to the Second Quorum of the Seventy April 1, 1989, at age 44; sustained to the First Quorum Oct. 3, 1992. Former president of the Guatemala Guatemala City Mission, where he was assigned to reopen the El Salvador San Salvador Mission, chairman of the Guatemala City Temple Committee, regional representative, stake president and counselor, bishop, and branch president. Received degree from the Technical Vocational Institute of Guatemala City; former technical draftsman, and later, area director for the Church Educational System. Born Sept. 25, 1944, in Guatemala City, Guatemala, to Carlos and Rosario Funes de Amado. Wife, Mayavel Pineda Amado; parents of five children.

Ian S. Ardern

Sustained to the First Quorum of the Seventy April 2, 2011, at age 57. Former Area Seventy, president of Fiji Suva Mission, stake president's counselor, stake Young Men president, high councilor, and bishop. Received bachelor's and master's degrees in education, both from University of Waikato in Hamilton, New Zealand. Formerly Pacific Area director for Church Educational System, also was institute director and seminary coordinator in New Zealand and principal of Church College of New Zealand. Born in February 1954, in Te Aroha, New Zealand, to Harry Wiltshire and Gwladys Marjorie Arden. Wife, Paula Ann Judd Andern; parents of four children.

Mervyn B. Arnold

Sustained to the Second Quorum of the Seventy April 5, 2003, at age 54; sustained to First Quorum of the Seventy April 4, 2009. Former president of the Costa Rica San Jose Mission, counselor in stake presidency, high councilor and bishop. Received bachelor's degree in business and master's degree in public administration, both from BYU. Founder and co-owner of a building and development company. Following retirement from business, became director of Training and Field Services in the Church Missionary Department. Born July 19, 1948, in Salt Lake City, Utah, to John E.S. and Jasmine Bennion Arnold. Wife, Devonna Kress Arnold; parents of six children.

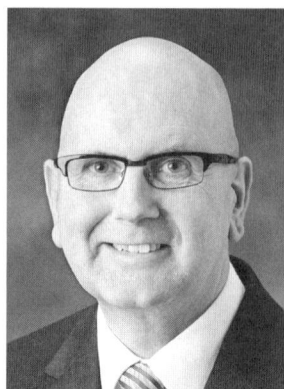

David S. Baxter

Sustained to the First Quorum of the Seventy April 1, 2006, at age 51. Former Area Seventy and second counselor in the Europe West Area presidency, mission president's counselor, stake president and bishop. Received bachelor of science degree in business management from the University of Wales; was senior executive for British Telecom. Born Feb. 7, 1955, in Stirling, Scotland, to Allan D. and Ellen S. Steel Baxter. Wife, Dianne Lewars Baxter; parents of four children.

Shayne M. Bowen

Sustained to the First Quorum of the Seventy April 1, 2006, at age 51. Former Area Seventy in the Idaho Area, president of Spain Barcelona Mission, stake president, high councilor, bishop, high priests group instructor, and elders quorum president. Received bachelor's degree in English from BYU, chartered underwriter and chartered financial consultant from American College; was owner of an insurance agency. Born Aug. 29, 1954, in Rigby, Idaho, to Lyle and Jacqueline Neeley Bowen. Wife, Lynette Mortensen Bowen; parents of seven children.

Gérald Caussé

Sustained to the First Quorum of the Seventy April 5, 2008, at age 44. Former Area Seventy in Europe West Area, stake president and counselor, and high priests group leader. Was general manager for Pomona, France's largest food distributor. Received equivalent of a master's degree in business administration from ESSEC Business School in Paris with emphasis in finance and marketing. Served in military in a NATO Agency. Born May 20, 1963, in Bordeaux, France, to Jean and Marie Blanche Bonnet Caussé. Wife, Valérie Babin Caussé; parents of five children.

Yoon Hwan Choi

Sustained to the First Quorum of the Seventy April 4, 2009, at age 51. Former Area Seventy in the Asia North Area, stake president and counselor, high councilor, mission president's counselor, stake mission president, bishop and counselor and temple ordinance worker. Received bachelor's degree in business information management from BYU-Hawaii, master's degree in business information systems and education from Utah State University. Formerly, regional manager for temporal affairs for the Church in Korea. Was staff sergeant in South Korean Army. Born May 18, 1957, in Seoul, Korea, to Dong Hun and Jeong Soon Lee Choi. Wife, Bon Kyung Koo Choi; parents of three children.

Craig C. Christensen

Sustained to the Second Quorum of the Seventy Oct. 5, 2002, at age 46; sustained to the First Quorum of the Seventy April 5, 2008. Former Area Authority Seventy, president of the Mexico Mexico City East Mission from 1995-98, high councilor, bishop and missionary in Chile. Received a bachelor's degree in accounting from Brigham Young University and an MBA from the University of Washington; real estate developer and franchised automobile dealer. Born March 18, 1956, in Salt Lake City, Utah, to Sheron Glen and Colleen Cloward Christensen. Wife, Debora Bliss Jones Christensen, parents of four children.

Don R. Clarke

Sustained to the Second Quorum of the Seventy April 1, 2006, at age 60; sustained to First Quorum of the Seventy April 2, 2011. Former president of Bolivia Santa Cruz Mission, stake president, assistant director of Church hosting, high councilor, stake Young Men president and bishop, Received associate degree from Ricks College, bachelor's degree in business from BYU, and MBA from Washington State University. Held senior executive positions and CEO in several companies. Born Dec. 11, 1945, in Rexburg, Idaho, to Raymond Ernest and Gladys Lydia Larsen Clarke. Wife, Mary Anne Jackson Clarke; parents of six children.

Carl B. Cook

Sustained to the First Quorum of the Seventy April 2, 2011, at age 53. Former Area Seventy, president of New Zealand Auckland Mission, stake president and counselor and bishop. Received bachelor of arts degree in business marketing from Weber State College and master's degree in business administration from Utah State University. Worked in real estate development. Born in October 1957, in Ogden, Utah, to Bert E. Cook and Ramona Cook Barker. Wife, Lynette Hansen Cook; parents of five children.

Lawrence E. Corbridge

Sustained to the First Quorum of the Seventy April 5, 2008, at age 58. Former president of the Chile Santiago North Mission, stake president, high councilor and bishop. Was partner and senior attorney in Salt Lake City law firm. Received bachelor's degree in business management and finance from BYU, and juris doctorate from BYU's J. Reuben Clark Law School. Born April 6, 1949, in Moscow, Idaho, to Ivan and Agnes Howe Corbridge. Wife, Jacquelyn Gayle Shamo Corbridge; parents of five children.

Claudio R.M. Costa

Sustained to the Second Quorum of the Seventy April 2, 1994, at age 45; sustained to the First Quorum of the Seventy March 31, 2001; called to the Presidency of the Seventy Aug. 1, 2007, and sustained Oct. 6, 2007. Served in the presidency until Oct. 1, 2011. Former president of the Brazil Manaus Mission, regional representative, stake president's counselor and bishop. Graduated from Colegio Pio XII, attended Paulista School of Marketing, Paulista Institute of Gems and Precious Metals. Former CES associate area director, diamond cutter and finance director of Diversified Almeida Prado Co. Born March 25, 1949, in Santos, Brazil, to Nelson Mendes and Luzia Tassar Simoes Costa. Wife, Margareth Fernandes Morgado Mendes Costa; parents of four children.

LeGrand R. Curtis Jr.

Sustained to the First Quorum of the Seventy April 2, 2011, at age 58. Former Area Seventy, president of Italy Padova Mission, stake president and counselor, and bishop. Received bachelor of arts degree in economics from BYU and juris doctorate from University of Michigan. Was attorney, and adjunct professor of law at BYU. Born in August 1952, in Ogden, Utah, to LeGrand R. Sr. and Patricia Glade Curtis. Wife Jane Cowan Curtis; parents of five children.

Benjamin De Hoyos

Sustained to the First Quorum of the Seventy April 2, 2005, at age 52. Former Area Seventy in the Mexico South Area, president of Mexico Tuxtla Gutierrez Mission, stake president and counselor, high councilor, and branch president. Received bachelor's degree in education from Normal Superior Benavente, master's degree in business management from Chapultepec University. Was Church Educational System director of Mexico. Born Feb. 20, 1953 in Monterrey, N.L., Mexico, to Alfredo and Sara Estrada de De Hoyos. Wife, Evelia Genesta De Hoyos; parents of six children.

John B. Dickson

Called to the Second Quorum of the Seventy June 6, 1992, at age 48, and sustained Oct. 3, 1992. Sustained to the First Quorum of the Seventy April 1, 1995. Former president of the Mexico Mexico City North Mission, stake president, and stake president's counselor. Was vice president of sawmill and timber company. Received bachelor's degree from Brigham Young University in business administration. Born July 12, 1943, in Tacoma, Wash., to John H. and Helen Bassett Dickson. Wife, Delores Jones Dickson; parents of eight children.

Kevin R. Duncan

Sustained to the First Quorum of the Seventy April 3, 2010, at age 49. Former Area Seventy in the Utah South Area, president of the Chile Santiago North Mission, Church-service missionary as associate international legal counsel in South America, high councilor, bishop's counselor, ward executive secretary and ward mission leader. Received bachelor of science degree in accounting, master's degree in taxation, and juris doctorate from BYU; was attorney and founded a corporation, from which he retired in 2005. Born in October 1960, in Ogden, Utah, reared by his mother LaRene Cook and his step-father, David Cook. Married Wendy Wallentine in 1982, she died in 1984; married Nancy Elizabeth Smart in 1986; parents of five children.

David F. Evans

Sustained to the First Quorum of the Seventy April 2, 2005, at age 53. Former president of Japan Nagoya Mission, stake president and counselor, bishop and bishop's counselor, stake Young Men president. Received bachelor's degree in community health education from the University of Utah and juris doctorate from BYU. Was partner and practicing attorney with Durham, Jones and Pinegar law firm, and an executive in investment banking business. Born Aug. 11, 1951, in Salt Lake City, Utah, to David C. and Joy Frewin Evans. Wife, Mary Dee Shepherd Evans; parents of eight children.

Enrique R. Falabella

Sustained to the First Quorum of the Seventy March 31, 2007, at age 56. Former Area Seventy in the Central America Area, regional representative, stake president, bishop and stake mission president. Received degree in agronomy from the University of San Carlos in Guatemala and studied marketing at the University of Costa Rica. Formerly agronomical engineer for Bayer. Born May 9, 1950, in Guatemala City, Guatemala, to Udine and Leonor Arellano Falabella. Wife, Blanca Lidia Sanchez Falabella; parents of five children.

Eduardo Gavarret

Sustained to the First Quorum of the Seventy April 5, 2008, at age 51. Former president of Paraguay Asuncion Mission, Area Authority Seventy, regional representative, stake president and bishop. Former employment included pharmaceutical sales and management in several South American countries. Graduated from the Escuela Superior de Administracion Empresas in business administration, and received master of business administration degree in marketing from Instituto Nacional de Pos-graduacão in Brazil. Born May 11, 1956, in Minas, Uruguay, to Juan and Elsa Inzaurralde Gaverret. Wife, Norma Gorgorso Gavarrei; parents of three children.

Carlos A. Godoy

Sustained to the First Quorum of the Seventy April 5, 2008, at age 47. Former Area Seventy in the Brazil Area, president of Brazil Belem Mission, high councilor, bishop and regional welfare agent. Employed in various business positions before starting his own company as a business consultant in organizational change management. Received bachelor's degree in economics and political science from Pontificia Universidade Católica and master's degree in organizational behavior from BYU. Served in Brazilian army. Born Feb. 4, 1961, in Porto Alegre, Brazil, to Moacir and Ivone Poersch Godoy. Wife, Mônica Soares Brandao Godoy; parents of four children.

Christoffel Golden Jr.

Sustained to the First Quorum of the Seventy March 31, 2001, at age 48. Former Area Authority Seventy in the Africa Southeast Area, stake president and counselor, and bishop. Received bachelor's degree in political science and post graduate honors degree in international politics from the University of South Africa. After a long and varied business career, served as Church Educational System director for Africa Southeast Area. Born June 1, 1952, in Johannesburg, South Africa, to Christoffel and Maria S. Oosthuisen Golden. Wife, Diane Norma Hulbert Golden; parents of four children.

Gerrit W. Gong

Sustained to the First Quorum of the Seventy April 3, 2010, at age 56. Former Area Seventy in the Utah South Area, stake president, high councilor, stake mission president, bishop and counselor, high priest group leader and seminary teacher. Received bachelor's degree in university studies and Asian studies from BYU, master's degree and doctorate in international relations from Oxford University; was assistant to the president for planning and assessment at BYU and had served as special assistant to the Undersecretary of State at the U.S. State Department and to the U.S. ambassador in Beijing. Born in Redwood City, Calif., to Walter A. and Jean C. Gong. Wife, Susan Lindsay Gong; parents of four children.

C. Scott Grow

Sustained to the First Quorum of the Seventy April 2, 2005, at age 56. Former Area Seventy in the North America Northwest and Idaho Areas, president of Uruguay Montevideo Mission, stake president and counselor, high councilor Young Men president, and bishop's counselor. Received bachelor's degree in accounting from BYU. Worked at major accounting and business consulting firms before establishing his own accounting partnership. Born May 5, 1948, in Moscow, Idaho, to Cecil W. and Elsie Mae Lee Grow. Wife, Rhonda Lee Patten Grow; parents of eight children.

James J. Hamula

Sustained to the First Quorum of the Seventy April 5, 2008, at age 50. Former Area Seventy in the North America Southwest Area, president of the Washington D.C. South Mission, stake president and bishop. Was attorney and shareholder in an Arizona law firm. Received bachelor's and master's degrees in political science/philosophy from BYU, and juris doctorate from BYU. Born Nov. 20, 1957, in Long Beach, Calif., to Joseph Frank and Joyce Evelyn Jacobs Hamula. Wife, Joyce Anderson Hamula; parents of six children.

Keith K. Hilbig

Sustained to the Second Quorum of the Seventy March 31, 2001, at age 59; sustained to the First Quorum of the Seventy April 1, 2006. Former Area Authority Seventy, regional representative, president of Switzerland Zurich Mission, stake president, bishop, temple ordinance worker and Europe East and North America Northwest Area presidencies. Received bachelor's degree in European history from Princeton University and law degree from Duke University. Formerly international legal counsel for the Church in Europe. Born March 13, 1942, in Milwaukee, Wis., to Karl Herbert and Mildred Bower Hilbig. Wife, Susan Rae Logie Hilbig; parents of six children.

Marlin K. Jensen

Church Historian and Recorder, was sustained to the First Quorum of the Seventy April 1, 1989, at age 46; served in the Presidency of the Seventy from Aug. 15, 1998, to Aug. 15, 2001. Was general president of the Sunday School from Oct. 7, 2000, to Oct. 6, 2001. Former president of the New York Rochester Mission, regional representative, stake president, and bishop. Received bachelor's degree in German from Brigham Young University and juris doctorate from University of Utah; was attorney specializing in business and estate planning. Born May 18, 1942, in Ogden, Utah, to Keith G. and Lula Hill Jensen. Wife, Kathleen Bushnell Jensen; parents of eight children.

Daniel L. Johnson

Sustained to the First Quorum of the Seventy April 1, 2006, at age 59. Former Area Seventy in the Mexico North Area, president of Ecuador Guayaquil North Mission, counselor to mission president and stake president, and bishop. Received bachelor's degree in accounting and economics from BYU; former executive in international companies, as well as holding Church and family farming positions throughout the United States and Latin America. Born Dec. 15, 1946, in Colonia Juarez, Mexico, to Leroy and Rita Skousen Johnson. Wife, LeAnn Holman Johnson; parents of six children.

Paul V. Johnson

Sustained to the First Quorum of the Seventy April 2, 2005, at age 50. Former Area Seventy In the Utah Salt Lake City Area, counselor in stake presidency, high councilor, bishop, and ward Young Men president. Received bachelor's degree in zoology and master's degree in counseling and guidance from BYU, and doctorate in instructional technology from Utah State University. Formerly Church Educational System administrator of Religious Education and Elementary and Secondary Education. Born June 24, 1954, in Gainesville, Fla., to Vere Hodges and Winifred Amacher Johnson. Wife, Leslie Jill Washburn Johnson; parents of nine children.

Patrick Kearon

Sustained to the First Quorum of the Seventy April 3, 2010, at age 48. Former Area Seventy in the Europe West Area, stake president, counselor in bishopric, ward Young Men president and branch president. Attended schools in Saudi Arabia and England; formerly owner with his wife of Kearon Hulme Communications, a public affairs consultancy, had worked in the United Kingdom, Saudi Arabia and United States in the health care, food, automotive and transportation industries. Born in July 1961, in Carlisle, England, to Paddy and Patricia Kearon. Wife, Jennifer Carole Hulme Kearon; parents of four children.

Paul E. Koelliker

Sustained to the First Quorum of the Seventy April 2, 2005, at age 62. Former temple sealer, stake president, high councilor, bishop, high priests group assistant, elders quorum counselor, and counselor in ward Young Men presidency. Received bachelor's degree in business administration from University of Utah. Formerly managing director of Church Temple Department, as well as working in senior managerial positions for the Church. Born March 12, 1943, in Pittsburg, Calif., to Edward Conrad and Lois Bernice Olson Koelliker. Wife, Freda Ann Neilson Koelliker; parents of seven children.

Erich W. Kopischke

Sustained to the First Quorum of the Seventy March 31, 2007, at age 50. Former Area Seventy in the Europe Central Area, president of the Germany Berlin Mission, stake president, district president, high councilor, bishop's counselor and branch president. Served in German military, 1977-1978. Attended vocational school. Was Church Educational System coordinator in Germany. Born Oct. 20, 1956, in Elmshom, Germany, to Kurt and Helga Haupt Kopischke. Wife, Christiane Glück Kopischke; parents of seven children.

Richard J. Maynes

Sustained to the Second Quorum of the Seventy April 5, 1997, at age 46; sustained to the First Quorum of the Seventy March 31, 2001. Former president of the Mexico Monterrey Mission. Received bachelor's degree from Brigham Young University, and MBA degree from the American Graduate School of International Management. Was owner and president of Raymond Production Systems Inc. Born Oct. 29, 1950, in Berkeley, Calif., to Stan and Betty Maynes. Wife, Nancy J. Purrington Maynes; parents of four children.

Marcus B. Nash

Sustained to the First Quorum of the Seventy April 1, 2006, at age 49. Former Area Seventy in the North America Northwest Area, stake president, bishop, Young Men president and elders quorum president. Received bachelor's degree in international relations and law degree, both from BYU. Was partner in a major law firm in Seattle, Wash. Born March 26, 1957, in Seattle, Wash., to Brent and Beverly Bell Nash. Wife, Shelley Hatch Nash; parents of five children.

Brent H. Nielson

Sustained to the First Quorum of the Seventy April 4, 2009, at age 54. Former Area Seventy in the Idaho Area, chairman of the Twin Falls Temple committee, stake president and counselor, high councilor, bishop and ward Young Men president. Received bachelor's degree in English from BYU, juris doctorate from University of Utah. Formerly, attorney/partner in law firm in Idaho. Born Dec. 8, 1954, in Burley, Idaho, to Norman and Lucille Hatch Nielsen. Wife, Marcia Ann Bradford Nielson; parents of six children.

Allan F. Packer

Sustained to the First Quorum of the Seventy April 5, 2008, at age 59. Former president of Spain Málaga Mission, member of Young Men general board, stake president's counselor, bishop and counselor, and Young Men president. Was in-field representative for the Church's Missionary Department and vice president of various companies. Received bachelor's degree in electronic engineering technology from BYU. Born July 7, 1948, in Brigham City, Utah, to Boyd K. and Donna Smith Packer. Wife, Terri Anne Bennett Packer; parents of eight children.

Kevin W. Pearson

Sustained to the First Quorum of the Seventy April 5, 2008, at age 51. Former president of Washington Tacoma Mission, bishop, bishop's counselor, elder's quorum president and Young Men president. Was CEO of a health care information company. Received bachelor's degree in finance from University of Utah, master's degree in business administration and corporate finance from Harvard Business School. Born April 10, 1957, to Wayne F. and Velda Labrum Pearson. Wife, June Langeland Pearson; parents of six children.

Anthony D. Perkins

Sustained to the First Quorum of the Seventy April 1, 2006, at age 45. Former president of the Taiwan Taipei Mission, counselor in district presidency, counselor in branch presidency and elders quorum president. Received bachelor's degree in finance from BYU, MBA from the University of Pennsylvania's Wharton School, and master's degree in international studies from University of Pennsylvania. Was senior partner in a management consulting firm. Born July 22, 1960, in Cortez, Colo., to Larry Lazelle and Sunny Kimballa Luther Perkins. Wife, Christine Abbott Perkins; parents of six children.

Paul B. Pieper

Sustained to the First Quorum of the Seventy April 2, 2005, at age 47. Former president of Russia St. Petersburg Mission, counselor in stake presidency, high councilor and branch president. Studied international relations at BYU, then received bachelor's degree in political science and juris doctorate, both from University of Utah. Was attorney and international development consultant. Born Oct. 7, 1957, in Pocatello, Idaho, to Dee M. and Norma Bowen Pieper. Wife, Melissa Tuttle Pieper; parents of six children.

Rafael E. Pino

Sustained to the First Quorum of the Seventy April 5, 2008, at age 52. Former Area Seventy in the South America North Area, president of the Argentina Rosario Mission, stake president, high councilor and bishop. Worked for the Church in a variety of capacities, including Member and Statistical Records Division and Temporal Affairs. Received a certificate in administration in Caracas, Venezuela. Born Oct. 27, 1955, in Valencia, Venezuela, to Arturo and Josefina Gimenez Pino. Wife, Patricia Monica Dassler Pino; parents of three children.

Bruce D. Porter

Sustained to the Second Quorum of the Seventy April 1, 1995, at age 42; sustained to the First Quorum of the Seventy April 5, 2003. Former stake president's counselor, stake mission president, bishop and branch president. Was a professor of political science at BYU and former executive director of the U.S. Board for International Broadcasting; was research fellow at Harvard University, and served as a corporate analyst for the Northrop Corporation and a staff member of the U.S. Senate Armed Services Committee. Graduated from BYU and earned M.A. and Ph.D. degrees from Harvard University. Born in Albuquerque, N.M., Sept. 18, 1952, to Lyle Kay and Wilma Holmes Porter. Wife, Susan Elizabeth Holland Porter; parents of four children.

Dale G. Renlund

Sustained to the First Quorum of the Seventy April 4, 2009, at age 56. Former Area Seventy in the Utah Salt Lake City and Utah North areas, stake president, high councilor, bishop and ward mission leader. Received bachelor's degree in chemistry from University of Utah, doctorate in medicine from University of Utah, and training in internal medicine and cardiovascular diseases at Johns Hopkins Hospital, Baltimore, Md. He is an emeritus professor of medicine at the University of Utah, and former cardiologist specializing in heart failure and heart transplantation. Born Nov. 13, 1952, in Salt Lake City, Utah, to Mats Ake and Mariana Andersson Renlund. Wife, Ruth Lybbert Renlund; parents of one daughter.

Michael T. Ringwood

Sustained to the First Quorum of the Seventy April 4, 2009, at age 51. Former president of the Korea Seoul West Mission, stake president and counselor, bishop, elders quorum president and ward Young Men president. Received bachelor of arts degree in accounting from BYU; was member of board of advisers at BYU School of Accountancy. Formerly, executive for several corporations. Born Feb. 14, 1958, in Provo, Utah, to Howard Lee and Sharon Burt Ringwood. Wife, Rosalie Nelson Ringwood; parents of five children.

Lynn G. Robbins

Sustained to the Second Quorum of the Seventy April 5, 1997, at age 44; sustained to the First Quorum of the Seventy April 1, 2000. Former president of the Uruguay Montevideo Mission, high councilor, bishop and bishop's counselor. Was co-founder and former senior vice president of Franklin Quest. Received bachelor's degree from Utah State University and master's degree from American Graduate School of International Management. Born Oct. 27, 1952, to Joshua Grant and Evelyn Reed Robbins; raised in Springville, Utah. Wife, Jan Neilson Robbins; parents of seven children.

Joseph W. Sitati

Sustained to the First Quorum of the Seventy April 4, 2009, at age 56. Former Area Seventy, president of the Nigeria Calabar Mission, stake president, mission president's counselor, district president and branch president. Received bachelor's degree in mechanical engineering from University of Nairobi and diploma in accounting and finance from Association of Certified Accountants. Formerly, Church's international director of Public Affairs in Africa. Born May 16, 1952, in Bungoma, Kenya, to Nathan Barasa and Lenah Naliaka Mwasme Sitati. Wife, Gladys Nangoni Sitati; parents of five children.

Ulisses Soares

Sustained to the First Quorum of the Seventy April 2, 2005, at age 46. Former president of the Portugal Porto Mission, regional welfare agent, stake president, high councilor, stake executive secretary, bishop's counselor, and elders quorum president. Received bachelor's degree in accounting and economics from Pontificia Catholic University, master's degree in business administration from National Institute of Post Graduate Study. Was director of temporal affairs for the Church in Brazil. Born Oct. 2, 1958, in Sao Paulo, Brazil, to Apparecido and Mercedes Carecho Soares. Wife, Rosana Fernandes Morgado Soares; parents of three children.

Gary E. Stevenson

Sustained to the First Quorum of the Seventy April 5, 2008, at age 52. Former president of the Japan Nagoya Mission, counselor in stake presidency, and bishop and counselor. Was chief operating officer of Icon Health and Fitness Inc. Received bachelor's degree in business administration from Utah State University. Served on BYU Marriott School of Business National Advisory Council and Utah State University Foundation Board. Born Aug. 6, 1955, in Ogden, Utah, to Evan Noel and Vera Jean Hall Stevenson. Wife, Lesa Jean Higley Stevenson; parents of four children.

Michael J. Teh

Sustained to the First Quorum of the Seventy March 31, 2007, at age 41. Former Area Seventy in the Philippines Area, mission president's counselor, stake president's counselor, high councilor, stake clerk, bishop and bishop's counselor. Received bachelor's degree in business administration from De La Salle University in Manila. Was recorder at Manila Philippines Temple. Born June 25, 1965, in Davao City, Philippines, to Martin and Norma Uy Teh. Wife, Grace May Weedon Teh; parents of three children.

José A Teixeira

Sustained to the First Quorum of the Seventy April 5, 2008, at age 47. Former Area Seventy in Portugal, president of Brazil Sao Paulo South Mission, stake president and counselor, bishop's counselor, district president, and high priest group leader. Former area finance manager and later international controller for the Church in Europe and Africa. Attended IAT Technical Improvement Institute in Lisbon, Portugal. Served in the Portuguese Air Force. Born Feb. 24, 1961, in Vila Real, Portugal, to Fernando and Benilde Teixeira. Wife, Maria Filomena Lopes Teles Grilo Teixeira; parents of three children.

Octaviano Tenorio

Sustained to the First Quorum of the Seventy March 31, 2007, at age 64. Former Area Seventy in the Mexico South Area, president of the Mexico Tuxtla Gutierrez Mission, regional representative, stake president, stake president's counselor and branch president. Received certificate in finance from the Academia Practica de Comercio. Former Mexico City Mexico Temple recorder. Born Oct. 31, 1942, in Tilapan, Veracruz, Mexico, to Octaviano and Flora Dominguez Tenorio. Wife, Rosa Elva ValenzuelaTenorio; parents of five children.

Juan A. Uceda

Sustained to the First Quorum of the Seventy April 3, 2010, at age 56. Former Area Seventy, president of the Peru Lima North Mission, stake president and counselor, and bishop. Received bachelor's degree in public relations from San Luis Gonzaga Univeristy; was Church Educational System area director for Peru and Bolivia, owned and operated a school in New Jersey. Born in July 1953, in Lima, Peru, to Juan Jose and Ines Uceda. Wife, Maria Isabel Bendezu Uceda; parents of five children.

Francisco J. Viñas

Sustained to the Second Quorum of the Seventy April 6, 1996, at age 49; sustained to the First Quorum of the Seventy April 4, 1998. Former Area Authority Seventy in the Europe West Area, president of Argentina Salta Mission, regional representative, stake president, counselor, bishop, and branch president. Was Church Educational System director and coordinator for Uruguay and Spain. Born Dec. 28, 1946, in Seville, Spain, to Rafael and Sacramento Serrano de Viñas. Wife, Cristina Helenas Gaminara de Vinas; parents of three children.

W. Christopher Waddell

Sustained to the First Quorum of the Seventy April 2, 2011, at age 51. Former Area Seventy, president of Spain Barcelona Mission, mission president's counselor, stake president and counselor, high councilor, and bishop and counselor. Received bachelor's degree in history from San Diego State University and did graduate work in BYU executive MBA program. Formerly first vice president of investments at Merrill Lynch, working in international division with clients primarily in Mexico. Born in June 1959 in Los Angeles, Calif., to Wayne and Joann Waddell. Wife, Carol Stansel Waddell; parents of four children.

William R. Walker

Sustained to the Second Quorum of the Seventy April 6, 2002, at age 57; sustained to the First Quorum of the Seventy April 5, 2008. Former president of the Japan Tokyo South Mission, stake president and bishop. Received bachelor's degree in international relations from Brigham Young University. Formerly held a number of executive positions in investment banking and other business fields. Born May 25, 1944, to J. Harris and Beth Russell Walker; raised in Raymond, Alberta, Canada. Wife, Vicki Van Wagenen Walker; parents of five children.

F. Michael Watson

Sustained to the First Quorum of the Seventy April 5, 2008, at age 65. Former sealer in Bountiful Utah Temple, stake president, stake mission president, bishop, branch president, and elders quorum president. Served as assistant secretary and secretary to the First Presidency, assistant secretary and secretary to the Quorum of the Twelve. Received bachelor's degree in business and office administration from Utah State University. Served three years in U.S. Army. Born March 9, 1943, in Spring City, Utah, to Frank C. and Genniel Baxter Watson. Wife, Jolene Mann Watson; parents of 12 children.

Kazuhiko Yamashita

Sustained to the First Quorum of the Seventy April 2, 2011, at age 57. Former Area Seventy, mission president's counselor, stake president, stake mission president, high councilor, and bishop and counselor. Received bachelor's degree in education from Saitama University and master's degree in sports science from Tsukuba University. Was assistant professor at Tsukuba University and a professor at Fukuoka University. Born in September 1953, in Tokyo, Japan, to Sadae Nakazawa and Kiyoshi Yamashita. Wife, Tazuko Tashiro Yamashita; parents of six children.

Jorge F. Zeballos

Sustained to the First Quorum of the Seventy April 5, 2008, at age 52. Former Area Seventy, president of Chile Concepcion South Mission, regional representative, stake president and bishop. Former mining engineer and manager of corporate affairs of large Chilean mining company. Receive bachelor's degree in civil engineering from Santa Maria University, master's degree in business administration from BYU. Born July 19, 1955, in Ovalle, Chile, to Alberto and Ines Zeballos. Wife, Carmen Gloria Valenzuela Zeballos; parents of five children.

Claudio D. Zivic

Sustained to the First Quorum of the Seventy March 31, 2007, at age 58. Former Area Seventy in the South America South Area, president of the Spain Bilbao Mission, regional representative, temple ordinance worker, stake president's counselor, high councilor, bishop and bishop's counselor. Received a degree in accounting from the University of Buenos Aires. Was CPA, working in manufacturing and marketing fields. Born Dec. 19, 1948, in Buenos Aires, Argentina, to Sergio Zivic and Eleonora Zalewski de Zivic. Wife, Dina Noemi Alvarez Zivic; parents of five children.

W. Craig Zwick

Sustained to the First Quorum of the Seventy April 1, 1995, at age 47. Former president of the Chile Santiago South Mission, stake Young Men president, stake mission president's counselor, high councilor, and bishop's counselor. Was executive director of the Utah Department of Transportation, former building contractor. Received bachelor of science degree in business management from the University of Utah. Born June 30, 1947, in Salt Lake City, Utah, to William E. and Audrey McDonough Zwick. Wife, Janet Johnson Zwick; parents of four children.

THE SECOND QUORUM OF THE SEVENTY

Wilford W. Andersen

Sustained to the Second Quorum of the Seventy April 4, 2009, at age 59. Former Area Seventy in the North America Southwest Area, president of Mexico Guadalajara Mission, temple ordinance worker, stake president and counselor, high councilor, stake executive secretary, bishop and counselor, and institute teacher. Received bachelor's degree in business management and juris doctorate, both from BYU. Formerly managing partner of a real estate investment firm. Born Aug. 22, 1949, in Mesa, Ariz., to Darl and Erma Farnsworth Andersen. Wife, Kathleen Bennion Andersen; parents of nine children.

Koichi Aoyagi

Sustained to the Second Quorum of the Seventy April 4, 2009, at age 64. Former Area Seventy in the Asia North Area, president of the Tokyo Japan Missionary Training Center, president of Japan Sendai Mission, regional representative, stake president, high councilor and branch president. Studied foreign trading at Kanagawa University, earned a real estate license from Japan Real Estate Academy. Formerly real estate and construction manager for the Asia North Area, assistant recorder in the Tokyo Japan Temple. Born March 24, 1945, in Matsumoto, Nagano, Japan, to Sueno Aoyagi and Mitsuo Yagasaki. Wife, Shiroko Momose Aoyagi; parents of four children.

Randall K. Bennett

Sustained to the Second Quorum of the Seventy April 2, 2011, at age 55. Former president of Russia Samara Mission, high councilor, Provo Missionary Training Center branch president and counselor, counselor in bishopric, and Young Men president. Received bachelor of science degree and DDS degree, both from University of Alberta, and master of science degree in orthodontics from Loma Linda University in California. Was orthodontist. Born in June 1955 in Magrath, Alberta, to Donald K. and Anne Darlene Long Bennett. Wife, Shelley Dianne Watchman Bennett; parents of four children.

Craig A. Cardon

Sustained to the Second Quorum of the Seventy April 1, 2006, at age 57. Former president of Italy Rome Mission, stake president and counselor, high councilor and bishop. Received bachelor's degree in accounting from Arizona State University, master's degree in public administration from Harvard University; was co-owner of family business, primarily in real estate development. Born Dec. 30, 1948, in Mesa, Ariz., to Wilford Pratt and Vilate Allen Cardon. Wife, Deborah Dana Cardon; parents of eight children.

Bruce A. Carlson

Sustained to the Second Quorum of the Seventy April 4, 2009, at age 59. Former member of Church Military Advisory Committee, temple ordinance worker, high councilor and bishop. Received bachelor of arts degree from University of Minnesota, master of arts degree from Webster University; graduated from U.S. Air Force Fighter Weapons School and earned distinguished graduate award for a master of arts degree from the Naval War College. Formerly a general in the U.S. Air Force, flew fighter aircraft and served in senior staff positions at the Pentagon. Born Oct. 3, 1949, in Hibbing, Minn., to Clifford and Helen Spencer Carlson. Wife, Vicki Lynn Martens Carlson; parents of three children.

J. Devn Cornish

Sustained to the Second Quorum of the Seventy April 2, 2011, at age 59. Former Area Seventy, president of the Dominican Republic Santiago Mission, stake president, high councilor, bishop, high priests group leader, elders quorum president, ward Young Men president and ward executive secretary. Received bachelor of science and medical degrees from Johns Hopkins University. Was medical doctor specializing in newborn intensive care; was a major in the U.S. Air Force Medical Corps. Born in April 1951 in Salt Lake City, Utah, to George O. and Naomi Black Cornish. Wife, Elaine Simmons Cornish; parents of six children.

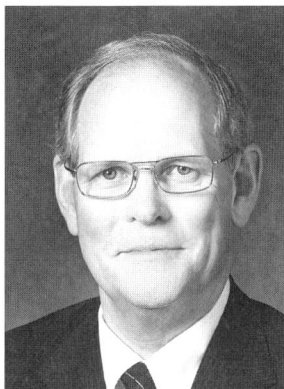

Keith R. Edwards

Sustained to the Second Quorum of the Seventy April 1, 2006, at age 64. Former Area Seventy in the North America Southwest Area, president of Zimbabwe Harare Mission, stake president and counselor, high councilor, bishop and counselor, regional welfare director, assistant temple recorder and temple ordinance worker. Received bachelor's degree in political science from BYU and juris doctorate from University of Utah. Was senior partner in law firm. Born March 16, 1942, in Boulder City, Nev., to Elbert Bird and Mary Reid Edwards. Wife, Judith Higgins Edwards; parents of seven children.

Stanley G. Ellis

Sustained to the Second Quorum of the Seventy April 1, 2006, at age 59. Former Area Seventy in the North America Southwest Area, president of Brazil Sao Paulo North Mission, stake president and counselor, high councilor, bishop's counselor and elders quorum president. Received bachelor's degree in government studies from Harvard University and juris doctorate from BYU. Was financial consultant. Born Jan. 22, 1947, in Burley, Idaho, to Stephen B. and Hazel Taylor Ellis. Wife, Kathryn Kloepfer Ellis; parents of nine children.

Bradley D. Foster

Sustained to the Second Quorum of the Seventy April 4, 2009, at age 60. Former president of California Arcadia Mission, stake president, high councilor, bishop, stake mission president and elders quorum president. Attended Ricks College, focusing on pre-veterinary studies. Formerly, owner of Foster Agribusiness, a producer of Idaho potatoes, beef and fertilizer; was a member of the Idaho Potato Commission and on the President's Advancement Council at BYU-Idaho. Born March 5, 1949, in Idaho Falls, Idaho, to Dewain and Melba Sauer Foster. Wife, Sharol Lynn Anderson Foster; parents of four children.

Larry W. Gibbons

Sustained to the Second Quorum of the Seventy April 1, 2006, at age 63. Former Area Seventy, regional representative and stake president and counselor.

Was a major in U.S. Army. Attended Stanford University, received medical degree from University of Utah., and master's degree in public health from Harvard University. Former president and medical director of medical clinic in Dallas, Texas. Born July 30, 1942, in Logan, Utah, to Andrew H. and Lola Heaton Gibbons. Wife, LaDawn Anderson Gibbons; parents of two children.

O. Vincent Haleck

Sustained to the Second Quorum of the Seventy April 2, 2011, at age 62. Former president of the Samoa Apia Mission, stake president, patriarch, high councilor, and bishop. Received bachelor's degree in advertising and marketing from BYU. Operated family-owned food services business in America Samoa. Born in January 1949, in Utulei, America Samoa, to Otto Vincent and Dorothy Swan Haleck. Wife, Peggy Ann Cameron Haleck; parents of three children.

Larry R. Lawrence

Sustained to the Second Quorum of the Seventy April 3, 2010, at age 62. Former Area Seventy in the North America West Area, president of the Russia Novosibirsk Mission, stake president and counselor, high councilor, stake mission president, bishop and elders quorum president. Received bachelor of science degree in agricultural biochemistry and doctorate in medicine both from the University of Arizona; was an ophthalmologist. Born in August 1947, in Cheverly, Md., to Argil and Mary Lawrence. Wife, Laurel Stott Lawrence; parents of six children.

Per G. Malm

Sustained to the Second Quorum of the Seventy April 3, 2010, at age 61. Former Area Seventy in Europe Area, president of Norway Oslo Mission, counselor in mission presidency, public affairs director for Sweden, stake president and counselor, high councilor, branch president and stake mission president. Received master's degree in business and public law from University of Göteborg and Swedish law degree from University of Lund, both in Sweden; was business consultant and former director for temporal affairs for the Church in Europe. Born in September 1948, in Jönköping, Sweden, to Gösta I. and Anna-Greta Malm. Wife, Ingrid Agneta Karlsson Malm; parents of eight children.

James B. Martino

Sustained to the Second Quorum of the Seventy April 4, 2009, at age 58. Former Area Seventy in the North America Southwest Area, president of Venezuela Maracaibo Mission, stake president, stake executive secretary, high councilor, stake Young Men president, mission president's counselor and bishop. Received bachelor of science degree in business from BYU. Formerly, chairman, president and chief executive officer of a family business. Born March 28, 1951, in Denton, Texas, to Frank Nilson and Betty Jean Newman Martino. Wife, Jennie Marie Barron Martino; parents of five children.

Jairo Mazzagardi

Sustained to the Second Quorum of the Seventy April 3, 2010, at age 62. Former Area Seventy, president of Sao Paulo Brazil Temple, counselor in the Campinas Brazil Temple, temple sealer, president of Brazil Salvador Mission, regional representative, stake president and counselor, high councilor and bishop's counselor. Former owner of a real estate company. Born in April 1947 in Itu, Brazil, to Antonio and Margarida Massagardi. Wife, Elizabeth Lenne Mazzagardi; parents of three children.

Kent F. Richards

Sustained to the Second Quorum of the Seventy April 4, 2009, at age 63. Former president of Texas San Antonio Mission, stake president, high councilor, bishop, elders quorum president, and Scoutmaster. Received bachelor of science degree in medical biology and doctor of medicine degree, both from the University of Utah. Was a general surgeon, chairman of the department of surgery at LDS Hospital and senior vice president and member of the board of trustees of a health care organization. Born Feb. 25, 1946, in Salt Lake City, Utah, to C. Elliott and Margaret Farnsworth Richards. Wife, Marsha Gurr Richards parents of eight children.

Gregory A. Schwitzer

Sustained to the Second Quorum of the Seventy April 4, 2009, at age 61. Former president of Russian Yekaterinburg Mission, stake president and counselor, high councilor, bishop's counselor, and temple sealer. Received bachelor of arts degree in biology and medical degree, both from University of Utah. Formerly, vice president of clinical programs at Intermountain Health Care; served five years in the U.S. Army Medical Corps. Born April 2, 1948, in Ogden, Utah, to Harvey R. and Gloria Jane Spiers Schwitzer. Wife, Jo Ann Elizabeth Rawsthorne Schwitzer; parents of five children.

Kent D. Watson

Sustained to the Second Quorum of the Seventy April 5, 2008, at age 64. Former president of Taiwan Taichung Mission, interim president of Taiwan Kaohsiung Mission, stake president's counselor, bishop, branch president, ward clerk and Scoutmaster. Was chief executive officer of an international accounting firm. Received bachelor's and master's degrees in accounting from BYU. Born May 8, 1943, in Cedar City, Utah, to L. Dee and Joyce Judd Watson. Wife, Connie Lingmann Watson; parents of five children.

Larry Y. Wilson

Sustained to the Second Quorum of the Seventy April 2, 2011, at age 61. Former Area Seventy, stake president and bishop. Received bachelor of arts degree in English and American literature from Harvard University; master's degree in business administration from Stanford Graduate School of Business. Was senior vice president of financial and strategic planning for Kaiser Foundation Health Plan in Oakland, Calif. Born in December 1949, in Salt Lake City, Utah, to George W. and Ida Young Wilson. Wife, Lynda Mackey Wilson; parents for four children.

AREA SEVENTIES
(As of October 2011)

THE THIRD QUORUM OF THE SEVENTY
Area Seventies residing in Africa Southeast, Africa West, Europe, Europe East and Middle East/Africa North Areas comprise the Third Quorum of the Seventy

AFRICA SOUTHEAST AREA
Colin H. Bricknell, Garith C. Hill, Kapumba T. Kola, Alfred Kyungu, T. Jackson Mkhabela, Hesbon O. Usi

AFRICA WEST AREA
Richard K. Ahadjie, Ini B. Ekong, Declan O. Madu, Freebody A. Mensah, Adesina J. Olukanni, Norbert K. Ounleu

EUROPE AREA
Hans T. Boom, Patrick M. Boutoille, George R. Donaldson, Christian H. Fingerle, Alfredo L. Gessati, Matti T. Jouttenus, Stephen C. Kerr, Faustino López, R. Ingvar Olsson, José L. Reina, Fernando A.R. Da Rocha, Manfred Schütze, Louis Weidmann, Craig T. Wright

EUROPE EAST AREA
Dmitry V. Marchenko, Sergiy N. Mikulin, Arayik V. Minasyan, Anatoly K. Reshetnikov, Gvido Senkans

MIDDLE EAST/AFRICA NORTH AREA
Larry S. Kacher

THE FOURTH QUORUM OF THE SEVENTY
Area Seventies residing in the Caribbean, Central America, Mexico and South America Northwest Areas comprise the Fourth Quorum of the Seventy

CARIBBEAN
Jorge S. Dominguez, Hugo E. Martinez, Fouchard Pierre-Nau

CENTRAL AMERICA AREA
Pedro E. Abularach, Carlos L. Astorga, Rafael E. Castro, Luis G. Duarte, German Laboriel, Cesar A. Morales, Carlos F. Rivas, Ricardo Valladares

MEXICO AREA
Sergio M. Anaya, Hector Avila, David Cabrera, Mario L. Carlos, Mosiah S. Delgado, Julio C. González, Luis S. Hernandez, Miguel Hidalgo, Lester F. Johnson, Glendon Lyons, Abraham Martinez, Ismael Mendoza, Abelardo Morales, Ernesto R. Toris, Arnulfo Valenzuela, Emer Villalobos, Omar Villalobos

SOUTH AMERICA NORTHWEST AREA
Winsor, Balderrama Sejas, René J. Cabrera, César A. Dávila, César H. Hooker, Javier Ibañez, Alexander T. Mestre, Enrique J. Montoya, Gamaliel Osorno, Carlos Solis, Ruben D. Torres, Fabian I. Vallejo, Richard C. Zambrano

THE FIFTH QUORUM OF THE SEVENTY

Area Seventies residing in the Idaho, North America Northwest, North America West, Utah North, Utah Salt Lake City, and Utah South Areas make up the Fifth Quorum of the Seventy

IDAHO AREA

Kent J. Allen, Robert E. Chambers, Kim B. Clark, K. Brett Nattress, J. Craig Rowe, Alan J. Webb

NORTH AMERICA NORTHWEST AREA

Marvin T. Brinkerhoff, Philip K. Bussey, Paul D. M. Christensen, R. Bruce Merrell, Brad K. Risenmay

NORTH AMERICA WEST AREA

Nelson D. Córdova, Jerryl L. Garns, Allen D. Haynie, Douglas F. Higham, Robert N. Packer, William F. Reynolds, Frank V. Trythall, Scott D. Whiting

UTAH NORTH AREA

Thomas M. Cherrington, Wynn R. Dewsnup, Craig G. Fisher, J. Roger Fluhman, Gary B. Porter, Lynn L. Summerhays

UTAH SALT LAKE CITY AREA

Stephen B. Allen, Samuel W. Clark, Gary L. Crittenden, Rodolfo C. Franco, Patrick H. Price, Warren G. Tate

UTAH SOUTH AREA

Dennis C. Brimhall, Gary B. Doxey, Von G. Keetch, Dane O. Leavitt, Steven J. Lund, Christopher B. Munday, Craig B. Terry, Terry L. Wade, Richard W. Wheeler, Randy W. Wilkinson, Kevin J. Worthen

THE SIXTH QUORUM OF THE SEVENTY

Area Seventies residing in the, North America Central, North America Northeast, North America Southeast and North America Southwest Areas comprise the Sixth Quorum of the Seventy

NORTH AMERICA CENTRAL AREA

Donald D. Deshler, Brent J. Hillier, Richard K. Melchin, Nathaniel R. Payne, Michael J. Reall, George F. Rhodes Jr., Terrence C. Smith, Jack D. Ward

NORTH AMERICA NORTHEAST AREA

Nolan D. Archibald, David L. Cook, Matthew J. Eyring, Jack N. Gerard, J. Christopher Lansing, W.T. David Murray, Jeffery E. Olson, Walter C. Selden, Robert B. Smith

NORTH AMERICA SOUTHEAST AREA

R. Randall Bluth, M. Anthony Burns, Robert C. Gay, M. Keith Giddens, Robert W. Hymas, David H. Ingram, Rulon D. Munns

NORTH AMERICA SOUTHWEST AREA

Stephen L. Fluckiger, James B. Gibson, George M. Keele, David E. LeSueur, S. Gifford Nielsen, Michael D. Pickerd, Jonathan C. Roberts, J. Romeo Villarreal, Perry M. Webb, Jim L. Wright

THE SEVENTH QUORUM OF THE SEVENTY

Area Seventies residing in Brazil, Chile and South America South Areas comprise the Seventh Quorum of the Seventy

BRAZIL AREA

Climato C.A.Almeida, Fernando J.D. Araújo, Victor A. Asconavieta, Milton Camargo, Renato Capelletti, Rogério G. R. Cruz, David G. Fernandes, Paulo H. Itinose, Mauro Junot De Maria, Joni L. Koch, Paulo C. Loureiro, Renato M. Petla, Marcos A. Prieto, Paulo R. Puerta, Edson D. G. Ribeiro, A. Ricardo Sant'Ana, Mozart B. Soares, Norland Souza, Natã C. Tobias, Carlos A.C. Villanova

CHILE AREA

Juan C. Barros, Hernán D. Ferreira, G. Guillermo Garcia, Richardo P. Giménez, Mario E. Guerra, Hernan I. Herrera, Valentin F. Nuñez, Wenceslao H. Svec, Gerardo J. Wilhelm

SOUTH AMERICA SOUTH AREA

Rubén V. Alliaud, Juan C. Avila, Marcelo F. Chappe, Nicolas L. Di Giovanni, Juan A. Etchegaray, Daniel A. Moreno, Alejandro S. Patanía, Esteban G. Resek, Rubén L. Spitale

THE EIGHTH QUORUM OF THE SEVENTY

Area Seventies residing in Asia, Asia North, Pacific and the Philippines Areas make up the Eighth Quorum of the Seventy

ASIA AREA

Victor Kah Keng Chen, Kuo Chiang Chung, Jui Chang Juan, Joshua Subandriyo, Stanley Wan, Chi Hong (Sam) Wong

ASIA NORTH AREA

Duck Soo Bae, Tetsuji Ishii, Chang Ho Kim, Katsumi Kusume, Hirofumi Nakatsuka, Satoshi Nishihara, Hee Keun Oh, Chikao Oishi, Kouzou Tashiro

PACIFIC AREA

Jeffrey D. Cummings, Sione M. Fineanganofo, David J. Hoare, Douglas W. Jessop, Peter F. Meurs, Michael A. Roberts, T. Marama Tarati, David J. Thomson, Terence M. Vinson, Taniela B. Wakolo

PHILIPPINES AREA

Manuel M. Agustin, Eleazer S. Collado, Jovencio A. Guanzon, Remegio E. Meim, Benson E. Misalucha, Ramon C. Nobleza, Abenir V. Pajaro, Cesar A. Perez Jr., Fabian L. Sinamban, Miguel R. Valdez

THE PRESIDING BISHOPRIC

Richard C. Edgley

Called as first counselor in the Presiding Bishopric Dec. 27, 1995; sustained April 6, 1996. Sustained as second counselor to Presiding Bishop Robert D. Hales on Oct. 3, 1992, at age 56, and as second counselor to Presiding Bishop Merrill J. Bateman on April 2, 1994. Former stake president and bishop. Was managing director of the Church's Finance and Records Department, board member of various Church-related corporations. Received bachelor's degree in political science from BYU and master's degree in business administration from Indiana University. Born Feb. 6, 1936, in Preston, Idaho, to Phenoi Harrison and Ona Crockett Edgley. Wife, Pauline Nielson Edgley; parents of six children.

H. David Burton

Called as Presiding Bishop Dec. 27, 1995; sustained April 6, 1996. Sustained as first counselor to Presiding Bishop Robert D. Hales on Oct. 3, 1992, at age 54, and first counselor to Presiding Bishop Merrill J. Bateman on April 2, 1994. Former stake president and temple sealer. Former secretary to the Presiding Bishopric for 14 years. Received bachelor's degree in economics from the University of Utah and master's degree from University of Michigan in business administration. Born April 26, 1938, in Salt Lake City, Utah, to Harold Nelson and Blanche Mabel Swanson Burton. Wife, Barbara Matheson Burton; parents of five children.

Keith B. McMullin

Called as second counselor in the Presiding Bishopric Dec. 27, 1995, at age 54; sustained April 6, 1996. Former president of Germany Frankfurt Mission, stake president, bishop and counselor, and high councilor. Was managing director of Church Welfare Services. Received bachelor's degree in banking and finance from University of Utah. Born Aug. 18, 1941, in St. George, Utah, to Lawrence and Margaret Savage McMullin. Wife, Carolyn Jean Gibbs McMullin; parents of eight children.

HISTORICAL LISTING OF GENERAL AUTHORITIES
PRESIDENTS OF THE CHURCH

1. JOSEPH SMITH JR. – Born December 23, 1805, in Sharon, Windsor, Co., Vermont, Joseph Smith Jr. was the fifth of eleven children of Joseph Smith and Lucy Mack. He worked on the family farm in Vermont and later in western New York.

Married Emma Hale Jan. 18, 1827; they had seven children. Received the Melchizedek Priesthood (ordained apostle) in May-June 1829 by Peter, James, and John (D&C 20:2, 27:12); sustained as First Elder of the Church April 6, 1830, at age 24; ordained high priest June 3, 1831, by Lyman Wight, sustained as president of the High Priesthood Jan. 25, 1832, at age 26 at a conference at Amherst, Lorain Co., Ohio.

A series of remarkable spiritual experiences prepared him for his prophetic calling. Beginning in 1820 at Palmyra, New York, Joseph Smith saw God the Father and Jesus Christ in vision. Through revelation, he translated and published the Book of Mormon, organized The Church of Jesus Christ of Latter-day Saints on April 6, 1830, and received revelations to guide the Church. By inspiration, he called apostles and other Church leaders, defined doctrines, and taught the principles and ordinances that lead to exaltation. Under his leadership, Latter-day Saints founded communities in Ohio, Missouri, and Illinois.

On June 27, 1844, at Carthage, Illinois, Joseph Smith died a martyr, at age 38.

2. BRIGHAM YOUNG – Born June 1, 1801, at Whitingham, Windham Co., Vermont, to John Young and Abigail Howe.

On Feb. 14, 1835, three years after he joined the Church, he was called to the Quorum of the Twelve Apostles, at age 33, by the Three Witnesses to the Book of Mormon: Oliver Cowdery, David Whitmer, and Martin Harris. He was sustained as president of the Quorum of the Twelve Apostles April 14, 1840.

As successor to Joseph Smith, he led the migration west in 1846–47 to the Rocky Mountains and founded Salt Lake City. He was sustained as president of the Church on December 27, 1847. As Church president and territorial governor of Utah, he established Latter-day Saint settlements in Utah and throughout the American West. Under his direction, construction commenced on the Salt Lake, St. George, Logan and Manti temples.

He brought the telegraph and the railroad to Utah and encouraged cooperative industry among Latter-day Saints, and he encouraged excellence and refinement in every aspect of life.

He died Aug. 29, 1877, in Salt Lake City at age 76 after nearly 30 years as Church president.

3. JOHN TAYLOR – Born November 1, 1808, in Milnthorpe, Westmorland, England. An 1832 immigrant to Toronto, Ontario, Canada, he was a cooper and part-time Methodist minister. He and his wife, Leonora, joined the Church in 1836. Two years later, on Dec. 19, 1838, he became an apostle under the hands of Brigham Young and Heber C. Kimball, at age 30. He was sustained as president of the Quorum of the Twelve Apostles Oct. 6, 1877.

He enjoyed close association with Joseph Smith and Brigham Young. He accompanied Joseph Smith to Carthage, Illinois, in June 1844, and was seriously wounded when Joseph Smith was killed. He was sustained as president of the Church on October 10, 1880, during one of the most challenging periods in Church history.

The Church was persecuted for the practice of plural marriage and many Latter-day Saints were being fined, imprisoned and denied the vote due to their beliefs and practices. He organized members to meet this trial of their faith and for the last 2 1/2 years of his life administered the affairs of the Church from seclusion resulting from anti-polygamy legislation. After seven eventful years as president, he died July 25, 1887, in Kaysville, Utah, at age 78.

4. WILFORD WOODRUFF – Born March 1, 1807, at Avon (Farmington), Hartford Co., Connecticut, to Aphek Woodruff and Beulah Thompson.

A miller by trade, he joined the Church in 1833 and served two missions before being ordained an apostle on April 26, 1839, by Brigham Young, at age 32. As a member of the Quorum of the Twelve Apostles, he completed four additional missions, presided over the temple in St. George, Utah, and served six years as Church historian. He was sustained as Church president on April 7, 1889, at age 82.

As president of the Church, he dedicated temples in Salt Lake City and Manti, Utah, oversaw the organization of the Genealogical Society, and re-emphasized the value of historical record-keeping. After much pondering and prayer, he received a revelation that the Latter-day Saints should cease the practice of plural marriage.

In 1890, he wrote the Manifesto, testifying that the Church had ceased teaching the practice of plural marriage. In addition to being the Lord's mouthpiece for that revelation, President Woodruff also left a legacy that emphasized missionary and temple work. He died in San Francisco, Calif., on Sept. 2, 1898, at age 91.

5. LORENZO SNOW – Born April 3, 1814, at Mantua, Portage Co., Ohio, to Oliver Snow and Rosetta Leonora Pettibone. As a youth, he preferred academic study to an apprenticeship. Study of Hebrew and theology led to his conversion to the Church in 1836. He spent the rest of his life in service as a missionary, apostle and Church president.

He was ordained apostle Feb. 12, 1849, by Heber C. Kimball, at age 34; sustained as counselor to President Brigham Young April 8, 1873; sustained as assistant counselor to President Brigham Young May 9, 1874; sustained as president of the Quorum of the Twelve Apostles April 7, 1889; began serving as president of the Church Sept. 13, 1898, at age 84.

He helped the Church recover from the challenges of the previous decades. He stabilized Church finances as he encouraged members to pay their tithes and offerings, promising them that the "windows of heaven would be opened." He expanded Church missionary efforts. He opened a new era in Latter-day Saint history in the 20th Century.

He died in Salt Lake City on Oct. 10, 1901, at age 87.

6. JOSEPH FIELDING SMITH – Born Nov. 13, 1838, in Far West, Caldwell, Co., Missouri, to Hyrum Smith and Mary Fielding.

In 1844, his father was martyred along with his uncle, the Prophet Joseph Smith. Young Joseph F. Smith helped his mother migrate to Utah in 1848 and establish a house in Salt Lake City. After she died in 1852, he began a life of service to the Church, and in Utah's territorial legislature from 1865 to 1874.

He was ordained apostle by Brigham Young and named counselor to the First Presidency July 1, 1866, at age 27; set apart as a member of the Quorum of the Twelve Apostles Oct. 8, 1867; released as counselor to the First Presidency at the death of President Young Aug. 29, 1877; sustained as second counselor to President John Taylor Oct. 10, 1880; released at the death of President Taylor July 25, 1887; sustained as second counselor to President Wilford Woodruff April 7, 1889; sustained as second counselor to President Lorenzo Snow Sept. 13, 1898; sustained as first counselor to Lorenzo Snow Oct. 6, 1901, not set apart to this position; released at the death of President Snow

Oct. 10, 1901. He became president of the Church on Oct. 17, 1901.

While ushering the Church into the 20th Century, Joseph F. Smith brought Latter-day Saints to a better appreciation of early Church history. He worked to improve the public image of the Church by developing important Church historical sites in New York, Missouri, and Illinois, building a visitors' bureau, and expanding Church missionary and educational systems. He clarified important doctrines, served numerous missions, and directed the construction of a new headquarters complex for an expanding Church.

After 17 years as Church president, Joseph F. Smith died on Nov. 19, 1918, in Salt Lake City, at age 80.

7. HEBER JEDDY GRANT — Born Nov. 22, 1856, in Salt Lake City, Utah, to Jedediah Morgan Grant and Rachel Ridgeway Ivins. He was raised by his widowed mother. By the time he was 15, he had begun a successful business career and had been ordained to the office of seventy. Ten years later, he was ordained to the Quorum of the Twelve Apostles on Oct. 16, 1882, at age 25, where he served for 37 years. He became president of the Quorum of the Twelve Nov. 23, 1916.

After becoming Church president on Nov. 23, 1918, at age 62, he dedicated three new temples, developed the Welfare Program, and helped Latter-day Saints cope with the tragedy of World War II. His business experience enabled him to modernize Church organizations and procedures. His missionary efforts, including extensive speaking engagements and friendships with national business leaders, brought the Church to the attention of the nation.

After 27 years as president, he died in Salt Lake City, Utah, on May 14, 1945, at age 88.

8. GEORGE ALBERT SMITH — Born April 4, 1870, in Salt Lake City, Utah, to John Henry Smith and Sarah Farr. Married Lucy Emily Woodruff May 25, 1892 (she died Nov. 5, 1937); they had three children.

His father and grandfather, George A. Smith, were counselors to Church presidents. While employed in the Federal Land Office for Utah, he was called to the Quorum of the Twelve Apostles on Oct. 8, 1903, at age 33, by Joseph F. Smith. He was sustained as president of the Quorum of the Twelve July 1, 1943.

Despite fragile health and impaired eyesight, he had a distinguished career as a Church leader. He became president of the Church on May 21, 1945, at age 75. He organized the Church's massive welfare assistance to Europe following World War II. He also championed Scouting among Latter-day Saints. Through numerous other civic and Church responsibilities, President Smith lived that portion of his personal creed that declared, "I would be a friend to the friendless and find joy in ministering to the needs of the poor" (Improvement Era Mar. 1932, 295).

After six years as president, he died in Salt Lake City on his 81st birthday, April 4, 1951.

9. DAVID OMAN McKAY — Born in Huntsville, Weber Co., Utah on Sept. 8, 1873, to David McKay and Jennette Eveline Evans, he studied at the Weber Stake Academy and the University of Utah to prepare for a career in education. After completing formal schooling and a mission, he married his college sweetheart, Emma Ray Riggs, Jan. 2, 1901. She died Nov. 14, 1970.

Five years after their marriage, on April 9, 1906, he was called as an apostle, at age 32, beginning a life of service in the Church's highest councils. He was sustained as second counselor to President Heber J. Grant Oct. 6, 1934; sustained as second counselor to President George Albert Smith May 21, 1945; and sustained as president of the Quorum of the Twelve Apostles Sept. 30, 1950.

He was sustained president of the Church on April 9, 1951, at age 77. He expanded the vision of the Church's worldwide mission, and under his administration, the first non-English speaking stakes outside of the United States were created. He also strengthened Church membership with a renewed emphasis on the value of family life and education.

After 44 years in the Quorum of the Twelve, and 19 years as president of the Church, he died on Jan. 18, 1970, in Salt Lake City, Utah, at age 96.

10. JOSEPH FIELDING SMITH – Born July 19, 1876, in Salt Lake City, Utah, to Joseph F. Smith and Julina Lambson. He spent his entire life in Church service. During nearly three-quarters of a century, he was a missionary, Church historian, president of the Genealogical Society and of the Salt Lake Temple, an apostle, and Church president. In addition, he supervised the evacuation of LDS missionaries from Europe prior to World War II, dedicated four countries in the Far East for missionary work, and inaugurated the first area conference of the Church in 1971 in England.

He married Louie E. Shurtliff April 26, 1898 (she died March 30, 1908); they had two children. Married Ethel G. Reynolds Nov. 2, 1908 (she died Aug. 26, 1937); they had nine children. Married Jessie Ella Evans April 12, 1938 (she died Aug. 3, 1971).

He was ordained apostle April 7, 1910, by Joseph F. Smith, at age 33; sustained as acting president of the Quorum of the Twelve Apostles Sept. 30, 1950; sustained as president of the Quorum of the Twelve Apostles April 9, 1951; sustained as counselor in the First Presidency Oct. 29, 1965.

He became president of the Church on Jan. 23, 1970, at age 93. As one of the Church's most prolific writers, Joseph Fielding Smith's numerous books and articles helped educate generations of Latter-day Saints about the history and doctrine of the Church. Under President Smith's administration, missionary work continued to grow, the Ogden and Provo temples were dedicated, several Church departments were restructured, and the Church magazines were consolidated.

On July 2, 1972, President Smith died quietly at his home in Salt Lake City, at age 95.

11. HAROLD BINGHAM LEE – Born on March 28, 1899, in Clifton, Oneida Co., Idaho, to Samuel M. Lee and Louisa Bingham. In Idaho, and later in Utah, he developed careers in education, business, and government. As president of the Salt Lake Pioneer Stake during the Great Depression, he initiated a program of self-help and relief that grew into the welfare system of the Church.

He married Fern Lucinda Tanner Nov. 14, 1923 (she died Sept. 24, 1962); they had two children. Married Freda Joan Jensen June 17, 1963.

After his call to the Quorum of the Twelve Apostles on April 10, 1941, by Heber J. Grant, at age 42, he continued to work with the welfare program, which served needy individuals and communities in many countries. He initiated organizational changes to improve the coordination of efforts at Church headquarters and among all Latter-day Saint congregations. These helped the Church prepare for its rapid expansion of members, activities, and influence of the decades that followed.

He was sustained as president of the Quorum of the Twelve Jan. 23, 1970; sustained as first counselor to President Joseph Fielding Smith Jan. 23, 1970.

He became president of the Church on July 7, 1972, at age 73. As Church president, he traveled often and frequently addressed the youth of the Church.

After only 18 months as Church president, he died on Dec. 26, 1973, in Salt Lake City, at age 74.

12. SPENCER WOOLLEY KIMBALL – Born March 28, 1895, in Salt Lake City, Utah, to Andrew Kimball and Olive Woolley, Spencer W. Kimball grew up in Thatcher, Ariz. After completing a mission and marrying Camilla Eyring on Nov. 16, 1917, they settled in Safford, Ariz., to raise their family and run an insurance business. They had four children. Years of Church and community leadership preceded his calling as an apostle when he was ordained by Heber J. Grant on Oct. 7, 1943, at age 48. He was set apart as acting president of the Quorum of the Twelve Apostles Jan. 23, 1970; set apart as president of the Quorum of the Twelve July 7, 1972. Overcoming severe health problems, he became Church president on Dec. 30, 1973, at the age of 78. He led the Church with spiritual power and energetic determination during a period of dramatic vitality and growth. His administration produced significant advances in doctrinal understanding, member unity, and gospel expansion worldwide. In the 12 years of his presidency, the number of operating temples doubled, the number of missionaries increased by 50 percent, and the priesthood was extended to all worthy male members.

He died in Salt Lake City on Nov. 5, 1985, at age 90.

13. EZRA TAFT BENSON – Born Aug. 4, 1899, in Whitney, Franklin Co., Idaho, to George T. Benson and Sarah Dunkley, he learned early the principle of hard work on the family farm. He served a mission to Great Britain and after his return was married to his sweetheart, Flora Amussen, on Sept. 10, 1926; they had six children. He received his education in agriculture and went on to hold many important positions within the industry.

He was ordained an apostle on Oct. 7, 1943, by President Heber J. Grant, at age 44, after having been president of two stakes. From 1953 to 1961, he served as Secretary of Agriculture in the cabinet of U. S. President Dwight D. Eisenhower. He was set apart as president of the Quorum of the Twelve Apostles Dec. 30, 1973.

On Nov. 10, 1985, he became president of the Church, at age 86. Having a resolute testimony of the power of the Book of Mormon, he emphasized the importance of it in daily scripture study, missionary efforts, and gospel teaching. His love of freedom, home, and family were also evident in his addresses and counsel to Church members. Despite his failing health, the Church continued to grow under his administration, temples were dedicated, and missionary work expanded around the world, particularly in eastern Europe.

He died in Salt Lake City, Utah, on May 30, 1994, at age 94.

14. HOWARD WILLIAM HUNTER – Born Nov. 14, 1907, in Boise, Ada Co., Idaho, to John William Hunter and Nellie Marie Rasmussen.

He had a love for music in his youth. After high school, his band, 'Hunter's Croonaders,' toured for five months on the SS President Jackson, which gave him the opportunity to see many exotic sites in Asia.

He married Clara May (Claire) Jeffs June 10, 1931, she died Oct. 9, 1983; they had three children (one died in infancy). He married Inis Bernice Egan on April 12, 1990.

Upon his marriage to Clara May Jeffs in 1931, he gave up his music career in favor of a stable family life. He studied law and became a successful lawyer in California. Various positions of priesthood leadership prepared him for his call to the apostleship in 1959. He was ordained an apostle Oct. 15, 1959, by David O. McKay, and set apart as acting president of the Quorum of the Twelve Nov. 10, 1985, and as president of the Quorum of the Twelve on June 2, 1988.

After 35 years as an apostle, he became president of the Church on June 5, 1994, at age 86. During his short presidency, he challenged all members of the Church to become temple worthy, prior to a decade of increased temple building, and invited members who had become offended to come back to the Church. He traveled as often as his health permitted, dedicating two temples and commemorating the 150th anniversary of the martyrdom of Joseph and Hyrum Smith in Nauvoo and Carthage, Ill.

He died March 3, 1995, in Salt Lake City, Utah, at age 87.

15. GORDON BITNER HINCKLEY –

Born June 23, 1910, in Salt Lake City, Utah, to Bryant S. and Ada Bitner Hinckley. As a young man, he earned a reputation as an outstanding writer and speaker because of his ability with words. After graduating from the University of Utah in 1932 with a major in English, he served a mission in the British Isles from 1933-1935.

Upon his return home, he reported to the First Presidency in an interview that led to employment with the Church as secretary of the then-recently formed Radio, Publicity, and Mission Literature Committee. Except for a short period during World War II, he worked for the Church for nearly 25 years, where he pioneered the adaptation of Church materials, particularly historical, for radio and later television programming and prepared various materials for missionaries. In 1951, he was called as executive secretary of the General Missionary Committee.

On April 29, 1937, he married Marjorie Pay in the Salt Lake Temple. They had five children. She died April 6, 2004. Prior to being called as a General Authority, he was a third-generation stake president and served on the Sunday School General Board.

He was sustained as an Assistant to the Twelve April 6, 1958. Three-and-a-half years later, on Sept. 30, 1961, he was sustained a member of the Quorum of the Twelve and was ordained an apostle on Oct. 5, 1961, at age 51. He served in the Twelve for 20 years and then served 14 years as a counselor to three Church presidents: Presidents Spencer W. Kimball, from 1981-1985; Ezra Taft Benson, from 1985-1994; and Howard W. Hunter, from 1994-1995. He was ordained and set apart as the 15th president of the Church on March 12, 1995, at age 84.

As president of the Church, President Hinckley had a strong desire to be out among the people and during his presidency he traveled more than a million miles and spoke to hundreds of thousands of members in more than 60 nations in Africa, Asia, the Pacific, Europe, and North, Central and South America. He was the first Church president to visit mainland China, West Africa, Russia and Ukraine.

A man of wit and wisdom, President Hinckley left behind a rich legacy. He envisioned the concept of small temples – perhaps the hallmark of his presidency – which helped fulfill his desire to provide temples close to members wherever they were. During the 12 years of his presidency, 79 new temples were announced worldwide. He dedicated 63 of the 77 temples that were dedicated during the same period. During the time he served in the First Presidency, he dedicated or rededicated 95 of the 124 temples then in operation. His leadership advanced the Church on every front, and construction of the massive Conference Center in Salt Lake City will forever be linked with his legacy.

He was awarded 10 honorary degrees, and in 2004, was given the United States' highest civil award, the Presidential Medal of Freedom, by President George Bush.

He died Jan. 27, 2008, at age 97, after a long life of dedicated service to God and his fellowman. He had the distinction of being the longest-lived president of the Church.

16. THOMAS SPENCER MONSON – See current FIRST PRESIDENCY.

ASSISTANT PRESIDENTS OF THE CHURCH

1. OLIVER COWDERY – Born Oct. 3, 1806, at Wells, Rutland Co., Vermont, to William Cowdery and Rebecca Fuller. Received Melchizedek Priesthood (ordained apostle) in May-June 1829, by Peter, James and John (D&C 20:2, 27:12); sustained as Second Elder of the Church April 6, 1830, at age 23; ordained high priest Aug. 28, 1831, by Sidney Rigdon; ordained assistant president of the High Priesthood Dec. 5, 1834, at age 28; sustained as assistant counselor to the First Presidency Sept. 3, 1837; excommunicated April 11, 1838; rebaptized Nov. 12, 1848; died March 3, 1850, at Richmond, Ray Co., Missouri, at age 43.

2. HYRUM SMITH – Born Feb. 9, 1800, at Tunbridge, Orange Co., Vermont, to Joseph Smith Sr. and Lucy Mack. Ordained high priest in June 1831 by Joseph Smith; sustained as assistant counselor to the First Presidency Sept. 3, 1837, at age 37; sustained as second counselor to President Joseph Smith Nov. 7, 1837; given all the priesthood formerly held by Oliver Cowdery (including apostle); ordained Patriarch to the Church and assistant president Jan. 24, 1841, by Joseph Smith, at age 40; martyred June 27, 1844, at Carthage Jail, Carthage, Hancock Co., Illinois, at age 44.

FIRST COUNSELORS IN THE FIRST PRESIDENCY

1. SIDNEY RIGDON – Born Feb. 19, 1793, at Saint Clair Township, Allegheny Co., Pennsylvania, to William Rigdon and Nancy Bryant. Ordained high priest in June 1831 by Lyman Wight; set apart as a counselor to President Joseph Smith on March 8, 1832, sustained as first counselor on March 18, 1833, at age 40; excommunicated Sept. 8, 1844; died July 14, 1876, at Friendship, Allegany Co., New York, at age 83.

2. HEBER CHASE KIMBALL – Born June 14, 1801, at Sheldon, Franklin Co., Vermont, to Solomon Farnham Kimball and Anna Spaulding. Ordained apostle Feb. 14, 1835, under the hands of Oliver Cowdery, David Whitmer, and Martin Harris, at age 33; sustained as first counselor to President Brigham Young Dec. 27, 1847, at age 46; died June 22, 1868, at Salt Lake City, Salt Lake Co., Utah, at age 67.

3. GEORGE ALBERT SMITH – Born June 26, 1817, at Potsdam, Saint Lawrence Co., New York, to John Smith and Clarissa Lyman. Ordained apostle April 26, 1839, by Heber C. Kimball at age 21; sustained as first counselor to President Brigham Young Oct. 7, 1868, at age 51; died Sept. 1, 1875, at Salt Lake City, Salt Lake Co., Utah, at age 58.

4. JOHN WILLARD YOUNG – Born Oct. 1, 1844, at Nauvoo, Hancock Co., Illinois, to Brigham Young and Mary Ann Angell. Ordained apostle Feb. 4, 1864, by Brigham Young. Sustained as counselor to President Brigham Young April 8, 1873, at age 28; sustained as assistant counselor to President Young May 9, 1874; sustained as first counselor to President Young Oct. 7, 1876, at age 32; released at death of President Young Aug. 29, 1877; sustained as a counselor to the Twelve Apostles Oct. 6, 1877; released Oct. 6, 1891; died Feb. 11, 1924, at New York City, New York, at age 79.

5. GEORGE QUAYLE CANNON – Born Jan. 11, 1827, at Liverpool, Lancashire Co., England, to George Cannon and Ann Quayle. Ordained an apostle Aug. 26, 1860, by Brigham Young, at age 33; sustained as counselor to President Young April 8, 1873, at age 46; sustained as assistant counselor to President Young May 9, 1874; released at death of President Young Aug. 29, 1877; sustained as

first counselor to President John Taylor Oct. 10, 1880; released at death of President Taylor July 25, 1887; sustained as first counselor to President Wilford Woodruff April 7, 1889; sustained as first counselor to President Lorenzo Snow Sept. 13, 1898; died April 12, 1901, at Monterey, Monterey Co., California, at age 74.

6. JOSEPH FIELDING SMITH – See PRESIDENTS OF THE CHURCH, No. 6.

7. JOHN REX WINDER – Born Dec. 11, 1821, at Biddenden, Kent Co., England, to Richard Winder and Sophia Collins. Ordained high priest March 4, 1872, by Edward Hunter; sustained as second counselor to Presiding Bishop William B. Preston April 8, 1887, at age 65; sustained as first counselor to President Joseph F. Smith Oct. 17, 1901, at age 79; died March 27, 1910, at Salt Lake City, Salt Lake Co., Utah, at 88.

8. ANTHON HENRIK LUND – Born May 15, 1844, at Aalborg, Jutland, Denmark, to Henrik Lund and Anne C. Andersen. Ordained apostle Oct. 7, 1889, by George Q. Cannon, at age 45; sustained as second counselor to President Joseph F. Smith Oct. 17, 1901, at age 57; sustained as first counselor to President Smith April 7, 1910; sustained as first counselor to President Heber J. Grant Nov. 23, 1918; died March 2, 1921, at Salt Lake City, Salt Lake Co., Utah, at age 76.

9. CHARLES WILLIAM PENROSE – Born Feb. 4, 1832, at London, Surrey Co., England, to Richard Penrose and Matilda Sims. Ordained apostle July 7, 1904, by Joseph F. Smith, at age 72; sustained as second counselor to President Smith Dec. 7, 1911, at age 79; sustained as second counselor to President Heber J. Grant Nov. 23, 1918; sustained as first counselor to President Grant March 10, 1921; died May 15, 1925, at Salt Lake City, Salt Lake Co., Utah, at age 93.

10. ANTHONY WOODWARD IVINS – Born Sept. 16, 1852, at Toms River, Ocean Co., New Jersey, to Israel Ivins and Anna Lowrie. Ordained apostle Oct. 6, 1907, by Joseph F. Smith, at age 55; sustained as second counselor to President Heber J. Grant March 10, 1921, at age 68; sustained as first counselor to President Grant May 28, 1925; died Sept. 23, 1934, at Salt Lake City, Salt Lake Co., Utah, at age 82.

11. JOSHUA REUBEN CLARK JR. – Born Sept. 1, 1871, at Grantsville, Tooele Co., Utah, to Joshua Reuben Clark and Mary Louise Woolley. Sustained as second counselor to President Heber J. Grant, April 6, 1933, at age 61; sustained as first counselor to President Grant, Oct. 6, 1934; ordained apostle Oct. 11, 1934, at age 63, by President Grant; sustained as first counselor to President George Albert Smith May 21, 1945; sustained as second counselor to President David O. McKay April 9, 1951; sustained as first counselor to President McKay June 12, 1959; died Oct. 6, 1961, at Salt Lake City, Salt Lake Co., Utah, at age 90.

12. STEPHEN L RICHARDS – Born June 18, 1879, at Mendon, Cache Co., Utah, to Stephen Longstroth Richards and Emma Louise Stayner. Ordained apostle Jan. 18, 1917, by Joseph F. Smith, at age 37; sustained as first counselor to President David O. McKay April 9, 1951, at age 71; died May 19, 1959, at Salt Lake City, Salt Lake Co., Utah, at age 79.

13. JOSHUA REUBEN CLARK JR. – See No. 11 above.

14. HENRY DINWOODEY MOYLE – Born April 22, 1889, at Salt Lake City, Salt Lake Co., Utah, to James H. Moyle and Alice E. Dinwoodey. Ordained apostle April 10, 1947, by George Albert Smith, at age 57; sustained as second counselor to President David O. McKay June 12, 1959, at age 70; sustained as first counselor to President McKay Oct. 12, 1961; died Sept. 18, 1963, at Deer Park, Osceola Co., Florida, at age 74.

15. HUGH BROWN BROWN – Born Oct. 24, 1883, at Granger, Salt Lake Co., Utah, to Homer Manly Brown and Lydia Jane Brown. Sustained as Assistant to the Twelve Oct. 4, 1953, at age 69; ordained an apostle April 10, 1958, by David O. McKay, at age 74; sustained as counselor in the First Presidency June 22, 1961; sustained as second counselor to President McKay Oct. 12, 1961; sustained as first counselor to President McKay Oct. 4, 1963; released at death of President McKay Jan. 18, 1970, and resumed position in the Quorum of the Twelve Apostles; died Dec. 2, 1975, at Salt Lake City, Salt Lake Co., Utah, at age 92.

16. HAROLD BINGHAM LEE – See PRESIDENTS OF THE CHURCH, No. 11.

17. NATHAN ELDON TANNER – Born May 9, 1898, at Salt Lake City, Salt Lake Co., Utah, to Nathan William Tanner and Sarah Edna Brown. Sustained as Assistant to the Twelve Oct. 8, 1960, at age 62; ordained apostle Oct. 11, 1962, at age 64; sustained as second counselor to President David O. McKay Oct. 4, 1963; sustained as second counselor to President Joseph Fielding Smith Jan. 23, 1970; sustained as first counselor to President Harold B. Lee July 7, 1972; sustained as first counselor to President Spencer W. Kimball Dec. 30, 1973; died Nov. 27, 1982, at Salt Lake City, Salt Lake Co., Utah, at age 84.

18. MARION GEORGE ROMNEY – Born Sept. 19, 1897, in Colonia Juarez, Mexico, to George Samuel Romney and Teressa Artemesia Redd. Sustained as Church's first Assistant to the Twelve April 6, 1941, at age 43; ordained apostle Oct. 11, 1951, at age 54; sustained as second counselor to President Harold B. Lee July 7, 1972; sustained as second counselor to President Spencer W. Kimball Dec. 30, 1973; sustained as first counselor to President Kimball Dec. 2, 1982; released at the death of President Kimball Nov. 5, 1985, and resumed position in the Quorum of Twelve Apostle; became president of the Quorum of the Twelve Nov. 10, 1985; died May 20, 1988, at Salt Lake City, Salt Lake Co., Utah, at age 90.

19. GORDON BITNER HINCKLEY - See PRESIDENTS OF THE CHURCH, No. 15.

20. THOMAS SPENCER MONSON – See current FIRST PRESIDENCY.

21. HENRY BENNION EYRING - See current FIRST PRESIDENCY.

SECOND COUNSELORS IN THE FIRST PRESIDENCY

1. FREDERICK GRANGER WILLIAMS – Born Oct. 28, 1787, at Suffield, Hartford, Co., Connecticut, to William Wheeler Williams and Ruth Granger. Called by revelation March 1832 to be a high priest and counselor to President Joseph Smith (D&C 81:1); ordained high priest by Miles H. Jones; set apart as second counselor to President Smith March 18, 1833, at age 45; rejected Nov. 7, 1837; excommunicated March 17, 1839; restored to fellowship April 8, 1840; died Oct. 10, 1842, at Quincy, Adams Co., Illinois, at age 54.

2. HYRUM SMITH – See ASSISTANT PRESIDENTS OF THE CHURCH, No. 2.

3. WILLIAM LAW – Born Sept. 8, 1809, at Tyrone Co., North Ireland. Set apart as second counselor to President Joseph Smith Jan. 24, 1841, at age 31; excommunicated April 18, 1844; died Jan. 19, 1892, at Shullsburg, Lafayette Co., Wisconsin, at age 82.

4. WILLARD RICHARDS – Born June 24, 1804, at Hopkinton, Middlesex Co., Massachusetts, to Joseph Richards and Rhoda Howe. Ordained apostle April 14, 1840, by Brigham Young, at age 35; sustained as second counselor to President Young Dec. 27, 1847, at age 43; died March 11, 1854, at Salt Lake City, Salt Lake Co., Utah, at age 49.

5. JEDEDIAH MORGAN GRANT – Born Feb. 21, 1816, at Windsor, Broome Co., New York, to Joshua Grant and Athalia Howard. Set apart as one of the First Seven Presidents of the Seventy Dec. 2, 1845, at age 29; ordained apostle April 7, 1854, by Brigham Young, at age 38; sustained as second counselor to President Young April 7, 1854; died Dec. 1, 1856, at Salt Lake City, Salt Lake Co., Utah, at age 40.

6. DANIEL HANMER WELLS – Born Oct. 27, 1814, at Trenton, (now Barnveld) Oneida Co., New Jersey, to Daniel Wells and Catherine Chapin. Set apart as second counselor to President Young Jan. 4, 1857, at age 42; released at death of President Young Aug. 29, 1877; sustained as a counselor to the Twelve Apostles Oct. 6, 1877; died March 24, 1891, at Salt Lake City, Salt Lake Co., Utah, at age 76.

7. JOSEPH FIELDING SMITH – See PRESIDENTS OF THE CHURCH, No. 6.

8. RUDGER CLAWSON – Born March 12, 1857, at Salt Lake City, Salt Lake Co., Utah, to Hiram Bradley Clawson and Margaret Gay Judd. Ordained apostle Oct. 10, 1898, by Lorenzo Snow, at age 41; sustained as second counselor to President Snow Oct. 6, 1901, at age 44, not set apart to this position; released at death of President Snow Oct. 10, 1901, and resumed position in the Quorum of the Twelve Apostles; sustained as president of the Quorum of the Twelve Apostles March 17, 1921; died June 21, 1943, in Salt Lake City, Salt Lake Co., Utah at age 86.

9. ANTHON HENRIK LUND – See FIRST COUNSELORS IN THE FIRST PRESIDENCY, No. 8.

10. JOHN HENRY SMITH – Born Sept. 18, 1848, at Carbunca (now part of Council Bluffs), Pottawattamie Co., Iowa, to George Albert Smith and Sarah Ann Libby. Ordained apostle Oct. 27, 1880, by Wilford Woodruff, at age 32; sustained as second counselor to President Joseph F. Smith April 7, 1910, at age 61; died Oct. 13, 1911, at Salt Lake City, Salt Lake Co., Utah, at 63.

11. CHARLES WILLIAM PENROSE – See FIRST COUNSELORS IN THE FIRST PRESIDENCY, No. 9.

12. ANTHONY WOODWARD IVINS – See FIRST COUNSELORS IN THE FIRST PRESIDENCY, No. 10.

13. CHARLES WILSON NIBLEY – Born Feb. 5, 1849, at Hunterfield, Midlothian Region, Scotland, to James Nibley and Jane Wilson. Ordained high priest June 9, 1901, by Joseph F. Smith; sustained as Presiding Bishop of the Church Dec. 4, 1907, at age 58;

sustained as second counselor to President Heber J. Grant, May 28, 1925, at age 76; died Dec. 11, 1931, at Salt Lake City, Salt Lake Co., Utah, at age 82.

14. JOSHUA REUBEN CLARK JR. – See FIRST COUNSELORS IN THE FIRST PRESIDENCY, No. 11.

15. DAVID OMAN MCKAY – See PRESIDENTS OF CHURCH, No. 9.

16. JOSHUA REUBEN CLARK JR. – See FIRST COUNSELORS IN THE FIRST PRESIDENCY, No. 11.

17. HENRY DINWOODEY MOYLE – See FIRST COUNSELORS IN THE FIRST PRESIDENCY, No. 14.

18. HUGH BROWN BROWN – See FIRST COUNSELORS IN THE FIRST PRESIDENCY, No. 15.

19. NATHAN ELDON TANNER – See FIRST COUNSELORS IN THE FIRST PRESIDENCY, No. 17.

20. MARION GEORGE ROMNEY – See FIRST COUNSELORS IN THE FIRST PRESIDENCY, No. 18.

21. GORDON BITNER HINCKLEY - See PRESIDENTS OF THE CHURCH, No. 15.

22. THOMAS SPENCER MONSON – See current FIRST PRESIDENCY.

23. JAMES ESDRAS FAUST - Born July 31, 1920, in Delta, Millard Co., Utah, to George A. Faust and Amy Finlinson. Sustained an Assistant to the Twelve Oct. 6, 1972, at age 52, and to the Presidency of the Seventy Oct. 1, 1976; sustained to the Quorum of the Twelve Sept. 30, 1978, ordained apostle Oct. 1, 1978, at age 58; sustained as second counselor to President Gordon B. Hinckley March 12, 1995; died Aug. 10, 2007, at Salt Lake City, Salt Lake Co., Utah, at age 87.

24. HENRY BENNION EYRING - See current FIRST PRESIDENCY.

25. DIETER FRIEDRICH UCHTDORF - See current FIRST PRESIDENCY.

OTHER COUNSELORS IN THE FIRST PRESIDENCY

1. JESSE GAUSE – Born about 1784 at East Marlborough, Chester Co., Virginia, to William and Mary Beverly Gause. Converted from the Shaker sect, he was baptized about the end of 1831. Set apart as counselor to Joseph Smith March 8, 1832; sent on a mission Aug. 1, 1832. Excommunicated Dec. 3, 1832. Died about 1836.

2. JOHN COOK BENNETT – Born Aug. 3, 1804, at Fair Haven, Bristol Co., Massachusetts, to J. and N. Bennett. Presented as assistant president with the First Presidency April 8, 1841, at age 36 (See History of the Church 4:341); disfellowshipped May 25, 1842; excommunicated latter part of 1842; died Aug. 5, 1867, in Polk City, Polk Co., Iowa at age 63.

3. AMASA MASON LYMAN – Born March 30, 1813, at Lyman, Crafton Co., New Hampshire, to Roswell Lyman and Martha Mason. Ordained apostle Aug. 20, 1842, by Brigham Young, at age 29; replaced in the

Quorum of the Twelve Apostles Jan. 20, 1843, due to reinstatement of Orson Pratt; appointed counselor to the First Presidency about Feb. 4, 1843; retired from the First Presidency with death of Joseph Smith June 27, 1844; returned to the Quorum of the Twelve Apostles Aug. 12, 1844; deprived of apostleship Oct. 6, 1867; excommunicated May 12, 1870; died Feb. 4, 1877, at Fillmore, Millard Co., Utah, at age 63. Blessings restored after death on Jan. 12, 1909.

4. JOSEPH FIELDING SMITH – See PRESIDENTS OF CHURCH, No. 6.

5. LORENZO SNOW – See PRESIDENTS OF CHURCH, No. 5.

6. BRIGHAM YOUNG JR. – Born Dec. 18, 1836, at Kirtland, Geauga Co., Ohio, to Brigham Young and Mary Ann Angell. Ordained apostle Feb. 4, 1864, by Brigham

Young, at age 27; sustained to the Quorum of the Twelve Apostles Oct. 9, 1868; sustained as counselor to President Young April 8, 1873, at age 36; sustained as assistant counselor to President Young May 9, 1874; released at President Young's death Aug. 29, 1877, and resumed position in the Quorum of the Twelve Apostles; sustained as president of the Quorum of the Twelve Apostles Oct. 17, 1901; died April 11, 1903, in Salt Lake City, Salt Lake Co., Utah, at age 66.

7. ALBERT CARRINGTON – Born Jan. 8, 1813, at Royalton, Windsor Co., Vermont, to Daniel Van Carrington and Isabella Bowman. Ordained apostle July 3, 1870, by Brigham Young, at age 57; sustained as counselor to President Young April 8, 1873, at age 60; sustained as assistant counselor to President Young May 9, 1874; released at death of President Young Aug. 29, 1877; excommunicated Nov. 7, 1885; rebaptized Nov. 1, 1887; died Sept. 19, 1889, at Salt Lake City, Salt Lake Co., Utah, at age 76.

8. JOHN WILLARD YOUNG – See FIRST COUNSELORS IN THE FIRST PRESIDENCY, No. 4.

9. GEORGE QUAYLE CANNON – See FIRST COUNSELORS IN THE FIRST PRESIDENCY, No. 5.

10. HUGH BROWN BROWN – See FIRST COUNSELORS IN THE FIRST PRESIDENCY, No. 15.

11. JOSEPH FIELDING SMITH – See PRESIDENTS OF THE CHURCH, No. 10.

12. HENRY THORPE BEAL ISAACSON – Born Sept. 6, 1898, at Ephraim, Sanpete Co., Utah, to Martin Isaacson and Mary Jemima Beal. Ordained high priest Oct. 1, 1941, by Charles A. Callis; sustained as second counselor to Presiding Bishop LeGrand Richards Dec. 12, 1946, at age 48; sustained as first counselor to Presiding Bishop Joseph L. Wirthlin April 6, 1952; sustained as Assistant to the Twelve Sept. 30, 1961; sustained as counselor in the First Presidency Oct. 28, 1965, at age 67; released at death of President David O. McKay Jan. 18, 1970; resumed position as Assistant to the Twelve Apostles Jan. 23, 1970; died Nov. 9, 1970, at Salt Lake City, Salt Lake Co., Utah, at age 72.

13. ALVIN RULON DYER – Born Jan. 1, 1903, at Salt Lake City, Salt Lake Co., Utah, to Alfred R. Dyer and Harriet Walsh. Ordained high priest Oct. 2, 1927, by Joseph Fielding Smith; sustained an Assistant to the Twelve Oct. 11, 1958, at age 55; ordained apostle Oct. 5, 1967, by David O. McKay, at age 64; sustained as counselor in the First Presidency April 6, 1968; released at death of President McKay Jan. 18, 1970; resumed position as Assistant to the Twelve Apostles Jan. 23, 1970; sustained a member of First Quorum of the Seventy Oct. 1, 1976; died March 6, 1977, at Salt Lake City, Salt Lake Co., Utah, at age 74.

14. GORDON BITNER HINCKLEY - See PRESIDENTS OF THE CHURCH, No. 15.

ASSISTANT COUNSELORS IN THE FIRST PRESIDENCY

1. OLIVER COWDERY – See ASSISTANT PRESIDENTS OF THE CHURCH, No. 1.

2. JOSEPH SMITH SR. – Born July 12, 1771, at Topsfield, Essex Co., Massachusetts, to Asael Smith and Mary Duty. Ordained high priest June 3, 1831, by Lyman Wight; ordained Patriarch to the Church Dec. 18, 1833, at age 62; sustained as assistant counselor to the First Presidency Sept. 3, 1837, at age 66; died Sept. 14, 1840, at Nauvoo, Hancock Co., Illinois, at age 69.

3. HYRUM SMITH – See ASSISTANT PRESIDENTS OF THE CHURCH, No. 2.

4. JOHN SMITH – Born July 16, 1781, at Derryfield, Hillsboro Co., New Hampshire, to Asael Smith and Mary Duty. Ordained high priest June 3, 1833, by Lyman Wight; sustained as assistant counselor to the First Presidency Sept. 3, 1837, at age 56; released at the death of Joseph Smith June 27, 1844; ordained Patriarch to the Church Jan. 1, 1849, at age 67; died May 23, 1854, at Salt Lake City, Salt Lake Co., Utah, at age 72.

5. LORENZO SNOW – See PRESIDENTS OF THE CHURCH, No. 5.

6. BRIGHAM YOUNG JR. – See OTHER COUNSELORS IN THE FIRST PRESIDENCY, No. 6.

7. ALBERT CARRINGTON – See OTHER COUNSELORS IN THE FIRST PRESIDENCY, No. 7.

8. JOHN WILLARD YOUNG – See FIRST COUNSELORS IN THE FIRST PRESIDENCY, No. 4.

9. GEORGE QUAYLE CANNON – See FIRST COUNSELORS IN THE FIRST PRESIDENCY, No. 5.

QUORUM OF THE TWELVE APOSTLES

1. THOMAS BALDWIN MARSH – Born Nov. 1, 1800, at Acton, Middlesex Co., Massachusetts, to James Marsh and Molly Law. Ordained apostle April 25, 1835, under the hands of Oliver Cowdery, David Whitmer, and Martin Harris, at Kirtland, Ohio, at age 35; sustained as president of the Quorum of the Twelve Apostles May 2, 1835; excommunicated March 17, 1839; rebaptized July 16, 1857; died January 1866, at Ogden, Weber Co., Utah, at age 66.

2. DAVID WYMAN PATTEN – Born Nov. 14, 1799, at Theresa, Jefferson Co., New York, to Benenio Patten and Abigail Cole. Ordained apostle Feb. 15, 1835, under the hands of Oliver Cowdery, David Whitmer, and Martin Harris, at Kirtland, Ohio, at age 35; killed Oct. 25, 1838, at the Battle of Crooked River, Missouri, at age 38.

Note: David Patten was actually older than Thomas B. Marsh when called to the Twelve, but he did not know his age at that time. Subsequent records showed he was actually older by almost a year.

3. BRIGHAM YOUNG – See PRESIDENTS OF THE CHURCH, No. 2.

4. HEBER CHASE KIMBALL – See FIRST COUNSELORS IN THE FIRST PRESIDENCY, No. 2.

5. ORSON HYDE – Born Jan. 8, 1805, at Oxford, New Haven Co., Connecticut, to Nathan Hyde and Sally Thorp. Ordained apostle Feb. 15, 1835, under the hands of Oliver Cowdery, David Whitmer, and Martin Harris, at Kirtland, Ohio, at age 30; dropped from Quorum May 4, 1839; restored to Quorum June 27, 1839; sustained as president of the Quorum of the Twelve Apostles Dec. 27, 1847; Brigham Young, on April 10, 1875, took Hyde from his original position in the quorum and placed him in the order he would have been in when he was restored to fellowship had he come into the quorum at that time (See "Succession in the Priesthood" by John Taylor, p. 16.); died Nov. 28, 1878, at Spring City, Sanpete Co., Utah, at age 73.

6. WILLIAM E. MCLELLIN – Born Jan. 18, 1806, in Smith Co., Tenn. Ordained apostle Feb. 15, 1835, under the hands of Oliver Cowdery, David Whitmer,

and Martin Harris, at Kirtland, Ohio, at age 29; excommunicated May 11, 1838; died April 24, 1883, at Independence, Jackson Co., Missouri, at age 77.

7. PARLEY PARKER PRATT – Born April 12, 1807, at Burlington, Otsego Co., New York, to Jared Pratt and Charity Dickinson. Ordained apostle Feb. 21, 1835, under the hands of Joseph Smith, Oliver Cowdery, and David Whitmer, at Kirtland, Ohio, at age 27; assassinated May 13, 1857, near Van Buren, Crawford Co., Arkansas, at age 50.

8. LUKE JOHNSON – Born Nov. 3, 1807, at Pomfret, Windsor Co., Vermont, to John Johnson and Elsa Jacobs. Ordained apostle Feb. 15, 1835, by Oliver Cowdery, David Whitmer, and Martin Harris, at Kirtland, Ohio, at age 27; excommunicated April 13, 1838; rebaptized in 1846 at Nauvoo, Illinois; died Dec. 9, 1861, at Salt Lake City, Salt Lake Co., Utah, at age 54.

9. WILLIAM B. SMITH – Born March 13, 1811, at Royalton, Windsor Co., Vermont, to Joseph Smith Sr. and Lucy Mack. Ordained apostle Feb. 15, 1835, under the hands of Oliver Cowdery, David Whitmer, and Martin Harris, at Kirtland, Ohio, at age 23; dropped from the quorum May 4, 1839; restored to quorum May 25, 1839; dropped from the quorum Oct. 6, 1845; excommunicated Oct. 19, 1845; died Nov. 13, 1893, at Osterdock, Clayton Co., Iowa, at age 82.

10. ORSON PRATT – Born Sept. 19, 1811, at Hartford, Washington, Co., New York, to Jared Pratt and Charity Dickinson. Ordained apostle April 26, 1835, under the hands of Oliver Cowdery, David Whitmer, and Martin Harris, at Kirtland, Ohio, at age 23; excommunicated Aug. 20, 1842; rebaptized Jan. 20, 1843, and ordained to former office in the Quorum of the Twelve Apostles. Brigham Young

took him from his original position in the quorum in 1875 and placed him in the order he would have been in when he was restored to fellowship had he come into the quorum at that time; died Oct. 3, 1881, at Salt Lake City, Salt Lake Co., Utah, at age 70.

11. JOHN FARNHAM BOYNTON – Born Sept. 20, 1811, at Bradford, Essex Co., Massachusetts, to Eliphalet Boynton and Susannah Nichols. Ordained apostle Feb. 15, 1835, under the hands of Oliver Cowdery, David Whitmer and Martin Harris, at Kirtland, Ohio, at age 23; disfellowshipped Sept. 3, 1837; excommunicated 1837; died Oct. 20, 1890, at Syracuse, Onondaga Co., New York, at age 79.

12. LYMAN EUGENE JOHNSON – Born Oct. 24, 1811, at Pomfret, Windsor Co., Vermont, to John Johnson and Elsa Jacobs. Ordained apostle Feb. 14, 1835, under the hands of Oliver Cowdery, David Whitmer and Martin Harris, at Kirtland, Ohio, at age 23; excommunicated April 13, 1838; died Dec. 20, 1859, at Prairie du Chien, Crawford Co., Wisconsin, at age 45.

13. JOHN EDWARD PAGE – Born Feb. 25, 1799, at Trenton Township, Oneida Co., New York, to Ebenezer and Rachel Page. Ordained apostle Dec. 19, 1838, under the hands of Brigham Young and Heber C. Kimball at Far West, Missouri, at age 39; disfellowshipped Feb. 9, 1846; excommunicated June 27, 1846; died Oct. 14, 1867, at De Kalb Co., Illinois, at age 68.

14. JOHN TAYLOR – See PRESIDENTS OF THE CHURCH, No. 3.

15. WILFORD WOODRUFF – See PRESIDENTS OF THE CHURCH, No. 4.

16. GEORGE ALBERT SMITH – See FIRST COUNSELORS IN THE FIRST PRESIDENCY, No. 3.

17. WILLARD RICHARDS – See SECOND COUNSELORS IN THE FIRST PRESIDENCY, No. 4.

18. LYMAN WIGHT – Born May 9, 1796, at Fairfield, Herkimer Co., New York, to Levi Wight and Sarah Corbin. Ordained apostle April 8, 1841, by Joseph Smith, at Nauvoo, Illinois, at age 44; excommunicated

Dec. 3, 1848; died March 31, 1858, in Dexter, Texas, at age 63.

19. AMASA MASON LYMAN – See OTHER COUNSELORS IN THE FIRST PRESIDENCY, No. 3.

20. EZRA TAFT BENSON – Born Feb. 22, 1811, at Mendon, Worcester Co., Massachusetts, to John Benson and Chloe Taft. Ordained apostle July 16, 1846, by Brigham Young at Council Bluffs, Iowa, at age 35; died Sept. 3, 1869, at Ogden, Weber Co., Utah, at age 58.

21. CHARLES COULSEN RICH – Born Aug. 21, 1809, near Big Bone, Boone Co., Kentucky, to Joseph Rich and Nancy O. Neal. Ordained apostle Feb. 12, 1849, by Brigham Young, at Salt Lake City, Utah, at age 39; died Nov. 17, 1883, at Paris, Bear Lake Co., Idaho, at age 74.

22. LORENZO SNOW – See PRESIDENTS OF THE CHURCH, No. 5.

23. ERASTUS SNOW – Born Nov. 9, 1818, at Saint Johnsbury, Caledonia Co., Vermont, to Levi Snow and Lucina Streeter. Ordained apostle Feb. 12, 1849, by Brigham Young, at age 30; died May 27, 1888, at Salt Lake City, Salt Lake Co., Utah, at age 69.

24. FRANKLIN DEWEY RICHARDS – Born April 2, 1821, at Richmond, Berkshire Co., Massachusetts, to Phinehas Richards and Wealthy Dewey. Ordained apostle Feb. 12, 1849, by Heber C. Kimball, at age 27; sustained as president of the Quorum of the Twelve Apostles Sept. 13, 1898; died Dec. 9, 1899, at Ogden, Weber Co., Utah, at age 78.

25. GEORGE QUAYLE CANNON – See FIRST COUNSELORS IN THE FIRST PRESIDENCY, No. 5.

26. JOSEPH FIELDING SMITH – See PRESIDENTS OF THE CHURCH, No. 6.

27. BRIGHAM YOUNG JR. – See OTHER COUNSELORS IN THE FIRST PRESIDENCY, No. 6.

28. ALBERT CARRINGTON – See OTHER

COUNSELORS IN THE FIRST PRESIDENCY, No. 7.

29. MOSES THATCHER – Born Feb. 2, 1842, at Springfield Sangamon Co., Ill., to Hezekiah Thatcher and Alley Kitchen. Ordained apostle April 7, 1879, by John Taylor, at age 37; dropped from the Quorum of the Twelve Apostles April 6, 1896; died Aug. 21, 1909, at Logan, Cache Co., Utah, at age 67.

30. FRANCIS MARION LYMAN – Born Jan. 12, 1840, at Good Hope, McDonough Co., Illinois, to Amasa Mason Lyman and Maria Louisa Tanner. Ordained apostle Oct. 27, 1880, by John Taylor, at age 40; sustained as president of the Quorum of the Twelve Apostles Oct. 6, 1903; died Nov. 18, 1916, at Salt Lake City, Salt Lake Co., Utah, at age 76.

31. JOHN HENRY SMITH – See SECOND COUNSELORS IN THE FIRST PRESIDENCY, No. 10.

32. GEORGE TEASDALE – Born Dec. 8, 1831, at London, Middlesex Co., England, to William Russell Teasdale and Harriett H. Tidey. Ordained apostle Oct. 16, 1882, by John Taylor, at age 50; died June 9, 1907, at Salt Lake City, Salt Lake Co., Utah, at age 75.

33. HEBER JEDDY GRANT – See PRESIDENTS OF THE CHURCH, No. 7.

34. JOHN WHITTAKER TAYLOR – Born May 15, 1858, at Provo, Utah Co., Utah, to John Taylor and Sophia Whittaker. Ordained apostle April 9, 1884, by John Taylor, at age 25; resigned Oct. 28, 1905; excommunicated March 28, 1911; died Oct. 10, 1916, at Salt Lake City, Salt Lake Co., Utah, at age 58. Blessings restored May 21, 1965.

35. MARRINER WOOD MERRILL – Born Sept. 25, 1832, at Sackville, Westmoreland Co., New Brunswick, Canada, to Nathan Alexander Merrill and Sarah Ann

Reynolds. Ordained apostle Oct. 7, 1889, by Wilford Woodruff, at age 57; died Feb. 6, 1906, at Richmond, Cache Co., Utah, at age 73.

36. ANTHON HENRIK LUND – See FIRST COUNSELORS IN THE FIRST PRESIDENCY, No. 8.

37. ABRAHAM HOAGLAND CANNON – Born March 12, 1859, at Salt Lake City, Salt Lake Co., Utah, to George Quayle Cannon and Elizabeth Hoagland. Sustained as one of the First Seven Presidents of the Seventy Oct. 8, 1882, at age 23; ordained apostle Oct. 7, 1889, by Joseph F. Smith, at age 30; died July 19, 1896, at Salt Lake City, Salt Lake Co., Utah, at age 37.

38. MATTHIAS FOSS COWLEY – Born Aug. 25, 1858, at Salt Lake City, Salt Lake Co., Utah, to Matthias Cowley and Sarah Elizabeth Foss. Ordained apostle Oct. 7, 1897, by George Q. Cannon, at age 39; resigned Oct. 28, 1905; priesthood suspended May 11, 1911; restored to full membership April 3, 1936; died June 16, 1940, at Salt Lake City, Salt Lake Co., Utah, at age 81.

39. ABRAHAM OWEN WOODRUFF – Born Nov. 23, 1872, at Salt Lake City, Salt Lake Co., Utah, to Wilford Woodruff and Emma Smith. Ordained apostle Oct. 7, 1897, by Wilford Woodruff, at age 24; died June 20, 1904, at El Paso, El Paso Co., Texas, at age 31.

40. RUDGER CLAWSON – See SECOND COUNSELORS IN THE FIRST PRESIDENCY, No. 8.

41. REED SMOOT – Born Jan. 10, 1862, at Salt Lake City, Salt Lake Co., Utah, to Abraham Owen Smoot and Anne Kestine Morrison. Ordained apostle April 8, 1900, by Lorenzo Snow, at age 38; served in the U.S. Senate, 1903-32; died Feb. 9, 1941, at St. Petersburg, Pinellas Co., Florida, at age 79.

42. HYRUM MACK SMITH – Born March 21, 1872, at Salt Lake City, Salt Lake Co., Utah, to Joseph Fielding Smith and Edna Lambson. Ordained apostle Oct. 24, 1901, by Joseph F. Smith, at age 29; died Jan. 23, 1918, at Salt Lake City, Salt Lake Co., Utah, at age 45.

43. GEORGE ALBERT SMITH – See PRESIDENTS OF THE CHURCH, No. 8.

44. CHARLES WILLIAM PENROSE – See FIRST COUNSELORS IN THE FIRST PRESIDENCY, No. 9.

45. GEORGE FRANKLIN RICHARDS – Born Feb. 23, 1861, at Farmington, Davis Co., Utah, to Franklin Dewey Richards and Nanny Longstroth. Ordained apostle April 9, 1906, by Joseph F. Smith, at age 45; sustained as acting Patriarch to the Church Oct. 8, 1937; released from this position Oct. 3, 1942; sustained as president of the Quorum of the Twelve Apostles May 21, 1945; died Aug. 8, 1950, at Salt Lake City, Salt Lake Co., Utah, at age 89.

46. ORSON FERGUSON WHITNEY – Born July 1, 1855, at Salt Lake City, Salt Lake Co., Utah, to Horace Kimball Whitney and Helen Mar Kimball. Ordained apostle April 9, 1906, by Joseph F. Smith, at age 50; died May 16, 1931, at Salt Lake City, Salt Lake Co., Utah, at age 75.

47. DAVID OMAN MCKAY – See PRESIDENTS OF THE CHURCH, No. 9.

48. ANTHONY WOODWARD IVINS – See FIRST COUNSELORS IN THE FIRST PRESIDENCY, No. 10.

49. JOSEPH FIELDING SMITH – See PRESIDENTS OF THE CHURCH, No. 10.

50. JAMES EDWARD TALMAGE – Born Sept. 21, 1862, at Hungerford, Berkshire Co., England, to James J. Talmage and Susannah Preater. Ordained apostle Dec. 8, 1911, by Joseph F. Smith, at age 49; died July 27, 1933, at Salt Lake City, Salt Lake Co., Utah, at age 70.

51. STEPHEN L RICHARDS – See FIRST COUNSELORS IN THE FIRST PRESIDENCY, No. 12.

52. RICHARD ROSWELL LYMAN – Born Nov. 23, 1870, at Fillmore, Millard Co., Utah, to Francis Marion

Lyman and Clara Caroline Callister. Ordained apostle April 7, 1918, by Joseph F. Smith, at age 47; excommunicated Nov. 12, 1943; rebaptized Oct. 27, 1954; died Dec. 31, 1963, at Salt Lake City, Salt Lake Co., Utah, at age 93.

53. MELVIN JOSEPH BALLARD – Born Feb. 9, 1873, at Logan, Cache Co., Utah, to Henry Ballard and Margaret Reid McNeil. Ordained apostle Jan. 7, 1919, by Heber J. Grant, at age 45; died July 30, 1939, at Salt Lake City, Salt Lake Co., Utah, at age 66.

54. JOHN ANDREAS WIDTSOE – Born Jan. 31, 1872, at Daloe, Island of Froyen, Trondhjem, Norway, to John A. Widtsoe and Anna Karine Gaarden. Ordained apostle March 17, 1921, by Heber J. Grant, at age 49; died Nov. 29, 1952, at Salt Lake City, Salt Lake Co., Utah, at age 80.

55. JOSEPH FRANCIS MERRILL – Born Aug. 24, 1868, at Richmond, Cache Co., Utah, to Marriner Wood Merrill and Mariah Loenza Kingsbury. Ordained apostle Oct. 8, 1931, by Heber J. Grant, at age 63; died Feb. 3, 1952, at Salt Lake City, Salt Lake Co., Utah, at age 83.

56. CHARLES ALBERT CALLIS – Born May 4, 1865, at Dublin, Dublin Co., Ireland, to John Callis and Susanna Charlotte Quillam. Ordained apostle Oct. 12, 1933, by Heber J. Grant, at age 68; died Jan. 21, 1947, in Jacksonville, Duval Co., Florida, at age 81.

57. JOSHUA REUBEN CLARK JR. – See FIRST COUNSELORS IN THE FIRST PRESIDENCY, No. 11.

58. ALONZO ARZA HINCKLEY – Born April 23, 1870, at Cove Fort, Millard Co., Utah, to Ira Nathaniel Hinckley and Angeline Wilcox Noble. Ordained apostle Oct. 11,

1934, by Heber J. Grant, at age 64; died Dec. 22, 1936, at Salt Lake City, Salt Lake Co., Utah, at age 66.

59. ALBERT ERNEST BOWEN – Born Oct. 31, 1875, at Henderson Creek, Oneida Co., Idaho, to David Bowen and Annie Schackelton. Ordained apostle April 8, 1937, by Heber J. Grant, at age 61; died July 15, 1953, at Salt Lake City, Salt Lake Co., Utah, at age 77.

60. SYLVESTER QUAYLE CANNON – Born June 10, 1877, at Salt Lake City, Salt Lake Co., Utah, to George Quayle Cannon and Elizabeth Hoagland. Sustained as Presiding Bishop of the Church June 4, 1925, at age 47; sustained as Associate to the Quorum of the Twelve Apostles April 6, 1938; ordained apostle April 14, 1938, by Heber J. Grant; sustained as a member of the Quorum of the Twelve Apostles Oct. 6, 1939, at age 62; died May 29, 1943, at Salt Lake City, Salt Lake Co., Utah, at age 65.

61. HAROLD BINGHAM LEE – See PRESIDENTS OF THE CHURCH, No. 11.

62. SPENCER WOOLLEY KIMBALL – See PRESIDENTS OF THE CHURCH, No. 12.

63. EZRA TAFT BENSON – See PRESIDENTS OF THE CHURCH, No. 13.

64. MARK EDWARD PETERSEN – Born Nov. 7, 1900, at Salt Lake City, Salt Lake Co., Utah, to Christian Petersen and Christine M. Andersen. Ordained apostle April 20, 1944, by Heber J. Grant, at age 43; died Jan. 11, 1984, at Salt Lake City, Salt Lake Co., Utah, at age 83.

65. MATTHEW COWLEY – Born Aug. 2, 1897, at Preston, Franklin Co., Idaho, to Matthias Foss Cowley and Abbie Hyde. Ordained apostle Oct. 11, 1945, by George Albert Smith, at age 48; died Dec. 13, 1953, at Los Angeles, Los Angeles Co., California, at age 56.

66. HENRY DINWOODEY MOYLE – See FIRST COUNSELORS IN THE FIRST PRESIDENCY, No. 14.

67. DELBERT LEON STAPLEY – Born Dec. 11, 1896, at Mesa, Maricopa Co., Arizona, to Orley S. Stapley and Polly M. Hunsaker. Ordained apostle Oct. 5, 1950, by George Albert Smith, at age 53; died Aug. 19, 1978, at Salt Lake City, Salt Lake Co., Utah, at age 81.

68. MARION GEORGE ROMNEY – See FIRST COUNSELORS IN THE FIRST PRESIDENCY, No. 18.

69. LEGRAND RICHARDS – Born Feb. 6, 1886, at Farmington, Davis Co., Utah, to George Franklin Richards and Alice Almira Robinson. Sustained Presiding Bishop of the Church April 6, 1938, at age 52; ordained apostle April 10, 1952, by David O. McKay, at age 66; died Jan. 11, 1983, at Salt Lake City, Salt Lake Co., Utah, at age 96.

70. ADAM SAMUEL BENNION – Born Dec. 2, 1886, at Taylorsville, Salt Lake Co., Utah, to Joseph Bennion and Mary A. Sharp. Ordained apostle April 9, 1953, by David O. McKay, at age 66; died Feb. 11, 1958, at Salt Lake City, Salt Lake Co., Utah, at 71.

71. RICHARD LOUIS EVANS – Born March 23, 1906, at Salt Lake City, Salt Lake Co., Utah, to John A. Evans and Florence Neslen. Sustained as member of the First Council of the Seventy Oct. 7, 1938, at age 32; ordained apostle Oct. 8, 1953, by David O. McKay, at age 47; died Nov. 1, 1971, at Salt Lake City, Salt Lake Co., Utah, at age 65.

72. GEORGE QUAYLE MORRIS – Born Feb. 20, 1874, at Salt Lake City, Salt Lake Co., Utah, to Elias Morris and Mary L. Walker. Sustained as Assistant to the Quorum of the Twelve Apostles Oct. 6, 1951, at age 77; ordained apostle April 8, 1954, by David O. Mc-Kay, at age 80; died April 23, 1962, at Salt Lake City, Salt Lake Co., Utah, at age 88.

73. HUGH BROWN BROWN – See FIRST COUNSELORS IN THE FIRST PRESIDENCY, No. 15.

74. HOWARD WILLIAM HUNTER – See PRESIDENTS OF THE CHURCH, No. 14.

75. GORDON BITNER HINCKLEY - See PRESIDENTS OF THE CHURCH, No. 15.

76. NATHAN ELDON TANNER – See FIRST COUNSELORS IN THE FIRST PRESIDENCY, No. 17.

77. THOMAS SPENCER MONSON – See current FIRST PRESIDENCY.

78. BOYD KENNETH PACKER – See current QUORUM OF THE TWELVE.

79. MARVIN JEREMY ASHTON – Born May 6, 1915, in Salt Lake City, Salt Lake Co., Utah, to Marvin O. Ashton and Rachel Jeremy. Sustained Assistant to the Twelve Apostles Oct. 3, 1969, at age 54; ordained apostle on Dec. 2, 1971, by Harold B. Lee at age 56; died Feb. 25, 1994, at Salt Lake City, Salt Lake Co., Utah, at age 78.

80. BRUCE REDD MCCONKIE – Born July 29, 1915, at Ann Arbor, Washtenaw Co., Michigan, to Oscar Walter McConkie and Vivian Redd. Sustained to First Council of the Seventy Oct. 6, 1946, at age 31; ordained apostle Oct. 12, 1972, by Harold B. Lee, at age 57; died April 19, 1985, at Salt Lake City, Salt Lake Co., Utah, at age 69.

81. LOWELL TOM PERRY – See current QUORUM OF THE TWELVE.

82. DAVID BRUCE HAIGHT – Born Sept. 2, 1906, in Oakley, Idaho, to Hector C. Haight and Clara Tuttle. Sustained as Assistant to the Quorum of the Twelve Apostles April 6, 1970, at age 63; ordained apostle Jan 8, 1976, by Spencer W. Kimball, at age 69; sustained to the Quorum of the Twelve April 3, 1976; died July 31, 2004, at Salt Lake City, Salt Lake Co., Utah, at age 97.

83. JAMES ESDRAS FAUST - See SECOND COUNSELORS IN THE FIRST PRESIDENCY, NO. 23.

84. NEAL ASH MAXWELL – Born July 6, 1926, in Salt Lake City, Utah, to Clarence H. Maxwell and Emma Ash. Sustained as Assistant to the Quorum of the Twelve Apostles April 6, 1974, at age 47; to the Presidency of the Seventy, Oct. 1, 1976; and ordained apostle July 23, 1981, by Nathan Eldon Tanner, at age 55; sustained to the Quorum of the Twelve Oct. 3, 1981; died July 21, 2004, at Salt Lake City, Salt Lake Co., Utah, at age 78.

85. RUSSELL MARION NELSON – See current QUORUM OF THE TWELVE.

86. DALLIN HARRIS OAKS – See current QUORUM OF THE TWELVE.

87. MELVIN RUSSELL BALLARD JR. – See current QUORUM OF THE TWELVE.

88. JOSEPH BITNER WIRTHLIN – Born June 11, 1917, in Salt Lake City, Salt Lake Co., to Joseph L. Wirthlin and Madeline Bitner. Sustained as Assistant to the Quorum of the Twelve April 4, 1975, at age 57; sustained to the First Quorum of the Seventy Oct. 1, 1976, and called to the Presidency of the Seventy Aug. 28, 1986; sustained to the Quorum of the Twelve Oct. 4, 1986, and ordained an apostle Oct. 9, 1986, at age 69; died Dec. 1, 2008, at Salt Lake City, Utah, at age 91.

89. RICHARD GORDON SCOTT – See current QUORUM OF THE TWELVE.

90. ROBERT DEAN HALES – See current QUORUM OF THE TWELVE.

91. JEFFREY ROY HOLLAND – See current QUORUM OF THE TWELVE.

92. HENRY BENNION EYRING - See current FIRST PRESIDENCY.

93. DIETER FRIEDRICH UCHTDORF - See current FIRST PRESIDENCY.

94. DAVID ALLAN BEDNAR – See current QUORUM OF THE TWELVE.

95. QUENTIN LAMAR COOK – See current QUORUM OF THE TWELVE.

96. DAVID TODD CHRISTOFFERSON - See current QUORUM OF THE TWELVE.

97. NEIL LINDEN ANDERSEN - See current QUORUM OF THE TWELVE.

OTHER APOSTLES

1. JOSEPH SMITH JR. – See PRESIDENTS OF THE CHURCH, No. 1.

2. OLIVER COWDERY – See ASSISTANT PRESIDENTS OF THE CHURCH, No. 1.

3. HYRUM SMITH – See ASSISTANT PRESIDENTS OF THE CHURCH, No. 2.

4. AMASA MASON LYMAN – See OTHER COUNSELORS IN THE FIRST PRESIDENCY, No. 3.

5. JEDEDIAH MORGAN GRANT – See SECOND COUNSELORS IN THE FIRST PRESIDENCY, No. 5.

6. JOHN WILLARD YOUNG – See FIRST COUNSELORS IN THE FIRST PRESIDENCY, No. 4.

7. DANIEL HANMER WELLS – See SECOND COUNSELORS IN THE FIRST PRESIDENCY, No. 6.

8. JOSEPH ANGELL YOUNG – Born Oct. 14, 1834, in Kirtland, Geauga Co., Ohio, to Brigham Young and Mary Ann Angell. Ordained apostle Feb. 4, 1864, by Brigham Young, at age 29; died Aug. 5, 1875, at Manti, Sanpete Co., Utah, at age 40.

9. BRIGHAM YOUNG JR. – See OTHER COUNSELORS IN THE FIRST PRESIDENCY, No. 6.

10. JOSEPH FIELDING SMITH – See PRESIDENTS OF THE CHURCH, No. 6.

11. SYLVESTER QUAYLE CANNON – See QUORUM OF THE TWELVE, No. 60.

12. ALVIN RULON DYER – See OTHER COUNSELORS IN THE FIRST PRESIDENCY, No. 13.

PATRIARCHS TO THE CHURCH

1. JOSEPH SMITH SR. – See ASSISTANT COUNSELORS IN THE FIRST PRESIDENCY, No. 2.

2. HYRUM SMITH – See ASSISTANT PRESIDENTS OF THE CHURCH, No. 2.

WILLIAM SMITH – See QUORUM OF THE TWELVE, No. 9. Ordained Patriarch to the Church May 24, 1845, by the Quorum of the Twelve and then gave patriarchal blessings, but was rejected by the Church membership at the General Conference held Oct. 6, 1845. There was no patriarch until the ordination of John Smith, uncle of Joseph Smith, on Jan. 1, 1849.

3. JOHN SMITH – See ASSISTANT COUNSELORS IN THE FIRST PRESIDENCY, No. 4.

4. JOHN SMITH – Born Sept. 22, 1832, at Kirtland, Geauga Co., Ohio, the eldest son of Hyrum Smith and Jerusha Barden, nephew of Joseph Smith. Ordained Patriarch to the Church Feb. 18, 1855, by Brigham Young, at age 22; died Nov. 5, 1911, at Salt Lake City, Salt Lake Co., Utah, at age 79.

5. HYRUM GIBBS SMITH – Born July 8, 1879, at South Jordan, Salt Lake Co., Utah, the eldest son of Hyrum Fisher Smith and Annie Maria Gibbs. Ordained high priest and Patriarch to the Church May 9, 1912, by Joseph F. Smith, at age 32; died Feb. 4, 1932, at Salt Lake City, Salt Lake Co., Utah, at age 52.

(From 1932 to 1937, no Patriarch to the Church was sustained.)

GEORGE FRANKLIN RICHARDS – See QUORUM OF THE TWELVE, No. 45. (Served as acting Patriarch.)

6. JOSEPH FIELDING SMITH – Born Jan. 30, 1899, at Salt Lake City, Salt Lake Co., Utah, the eldest son of Hyrum Mack Smith and Ida E. Bowman. Ordained high priest and Patriarch to the Church Oct. 8, 1942, by Heber J. Grant, at age 43; released Oct. 6, 1946, due to ill health; died Aug. 29, 1964, in Salt Lake City, Salt Lake Co., Utah, at age 65.

7. ELDRED GEE SMITH – Born Jan. 9, 1907, at Lehi, Utah Co., Utah, the eldest son of Hyrum Gibbs Smith and Martha Electa Gee. Ordained high priest May 23, 1938, by J. Reuben Clark Jr.; ordained Patriarch to the Church April 10, 1947, by George Albert Smith, at age 40; named emeritus General Authority Oct. 6, 1979.

(No Patriarch to the Church has been sustained since Oct. 6, 1979.)

FIRST COUNCIL OF THE SEVENTY
(Functioned from February 1835 to October 1976)

1. HAZEN ALDRICH – Chosen and ordained one of the First Seven Presidents Feb. 28, 1835; released April 6, 1837, having previously been ordained high priest.

2. JOSEPH YOUNG – Born April 7, 1797, at Hopkinton, Middlesex Co., Massachusetts, to John Young and Abigail Howe. Ordained seventy Feb. 28, 1835, under the hands of Joseph Smith, Sidney Rigdon, and Frederick G. Williams; chosen and ordained one of the First Seven Presidents Feb. 28, 1835, at age 37; died July 16, 1881, at Salt Lake City, Salt Lake Co., Utah, at age 84.

3. LEVI WARD HANCOCK – Born April 7, 1803, at Springfield, Hampden, Co., Massachusetts, to Thomas Hancock and Amy Ward. Ordained seventy Feb. 28, 1835, under the hands of Joseph Smith, Sidney Rigdon, and Frederick G. Williams; chosen and ordained one of the First Seven Presidents Feb. 28, 1835, at age 31; released April 6, 1837, having supposedly previously been ordained high priest; restored to former place in the First Council Sept. 3, 1837, as he had not been ordained high priest; died June 10, 1882, at Washington, Washington Co., Utah, at age 79.

4. LEONARD RICH – Chosen and ordained one of the First Seven Presidents Feb. 28, 1835; released April 6, 1837, having previously been ordained high priest.

5. ZEBEDEE COLTRIN – Born Sept. 7, 1804, at Ovid, Seneca Co., New York, to John Coltrin Jr. and Sarah Graham. Chosen and ordained one of the First Seven Presidents Feb. 28, 1835, at age 30; released April 6, 1837, having previously been ordained high priest; died July 21, 1887, at Spanish Fork, Utah Co., Utah, at age 82.

6. LYMAN ROYAL SHERMAN – Born May 22, 1804, at Salem, Essex Co., Massachusetts, to Elkanah Sherman and Asenath Hulbert. Chosen and ordained one of the First Seven Presidents Feb. 28, 1835, at age 30; released April 6, 1837, having previously been ordained high priest; died Jan. 27, 1839, at age 34.

7. SYLVESTER SMITH – Chosen and ordained one of the First Seven Presidents Feb. 28, 1835; released April 6, 1837, having previously been ordained high priest.

8. JOHN GOULD – Born May 11, 1808. Ordained seventy and set apart as one of the First Seven Presidents April 6, 1837, by Sidney Rigdon and Hyrum Smith, at age 28; released Sept. 3, 1837, to be ordained high priest. Died May 9, 1851, at age 42.

9. JAMES FOSTER – Born April 1, 1775, at Morgan Co., New Hampshire. Ordained seventy April 6, 1837, under the hands of Sidney Rigdon and Hyrum Smith; set apart as one of the First Seven Presidents April 6, 1837, at age 62; died Dec. 21, 1841, at Morgan Co., Illinois, at age 66.

10. DANIEL SANBORN MILES – Born July 23, 1772, at Sanbornton, Belknap Co., New Hampshire, to Josiah Miles and Marah Sanborn. Ordained seventy April 6, 1837, by Hazen Aldrich; set apart as one of the First Seven Presidents April 6, 1837, by Sidney Rigdon and Hyrum Smith, at age 64; died in autumn of 1845, at Hancock Co., Illinois, at age 73.

11. JOSIAH BUTTERFIELD – Born March 13 or 18, 1795, at Saco, York Co., Maine, to Abel and Mary or Mercy Butterfield. Ordained seventy April 6, 1837, under the hands of Sidney Rigdon and Hyrum Smith; set apart as one of the First Seven Presidents April 6, 1837, at age 42; excommunicated Oct. 7, 1844; died in April 1871 at Monterey Co., California, at age 76.

12. SALMON GEE – Born Oct. 16, 1792, at Lyme, New London Co., Connecticut, to Zopher Gee and Esther Beckwith. Ordained seventy April 6, 1837, under the hands of Sidney Rigdon and Hyrum Smith; set apart as one of the First Seven Presidents April 6, 1837, at age 44; fellowship withdrawn March 6, 1838; died Sept. 13, 1845, at Ambrosia, Lee Co., Iowa, at age 52; posthumously reinstated Sept. 14, 1967.

13. JOHN GAYLORD – Born July 12, 1797, in Pennsylvania, to Chauncey Gaylord. Ordained seventy Dec. 20, 1836, by Hazen Aldrich; set apart as one of the First Seven Presidents April 6, 1837, at age 39, by Sidney Rigdon and others; excommunicated Jan. 13, 1838; rejoined the Church at Nauvoo, Illinois, Oct. 5,

1839; died July 17, 1878, at age 81.

14. HENRY HARRIMAN – Born June 9, 1804, at Rowley, Essex Co., Massachusetts, to Enoch Harriman and Sarah Brocklebank. Ordained seventy March 1835, under the hands of Joseph Smith and Sidney Rigdon; set apart as one of the First Seven Presidents Feb. 6, 1838, by Joseph Young and others, at age 33; died May 17, 1891, at Huntington, Emery Co., Utah, at 86.

15. ZERA PULSIPHER – Born June 24, 1789, at Rockingham, Windham Co., Vermont, to John Pulsipher and Elizabeth Dutton. Ordained seventy March 6, 1838, under the hands of Joseph Young and James Foster; set apart as one of the First Seven Presidents March 6, 1838, at age 48; released April 12, 1862; died Jan. 1, 1872, at Hebron, Washington Co., Utah, at age 82.

Roger Orton was excommunicated Nov. 30, 1837; returned to the Church; sustained as one of the First Seven Presidents April 7, 1845, but was never set apart and did not function; dropped from this position Oct. 6, 1845.

16. ALBERT PERRY ROCKWOOD – Born June 5, 1805, at Holliston, Middlesex Co., Massachusetts, to Luther Rockwood and Ruth Perry. Ordained seventy Jan. 5, 1839, under the hands of Joseph Young, Henry Harriman, and Zera Pulsipher; set apart as one of the First Seven Presidents Dec. 2, 1845, by Brigham Young and others, at age 40; died Nov. 26, 1879, at Sugar House, Salt Lake Co., Utah, at age 74.

17. BENJAMIN LYNN CLAPP – Born Aug. 19, 1814, at West Huntsville, Madison Co., Alabama, to Ludwig Lewis Clapp and Margaret Ann Loy. Ordained seventy Oct. 20, 1844, under the hands of Joseph Young and Levi W. Hancock; set apart as one of the First Seven Presidents Dec. 2, 1845, by Brigham Young and others, at age 31; excommunicated April 7, 1859; died Oct. 31, 1865 in Woodbridge, Calif., at age 51.

18. JEDEDIAH MORGAN GRANT – See SECOND COUNSELORS IN THE FIRST PRESIDENCY, No. 5.

19. HORACE SUNDERLIN ELDREDGE – Born Feb. 6, 1816, at Brutus, Cayuga Co., New York, to Alanson Eldredge and Esther Sunderlin. Ordained seventy Oct. 13, 1844, by Joseph Young; sustained as one of the First Seven Presidents Oct. 7, 1854, at age 38; died Sept. 6, 1888, at Salt Lake City, Salt Lake Co., Utah, at age 72.

20. JACOB GATES – Born March 9, 1811, at Saint Johnsbury, Caledonia Co., Vermont, to Thomas Gates and Patty Plumley. Ordained seventy Dec. 19, 1838, under the hands of Joseph Smith and Sidney Rigdon; sustained as one of the First Seven Presidents April 6, 1860, at age 49; set apart Oct. 8, 1862, by Orson Hyde; died April 14, 1892, at Provo, Utah Co., Utah, at age 81.

21. JOHN VAN COTT – Born Sept. 7, 1814, at Canaan, Columbia Co., New York, to Losee Van Cott and Lovinia Pratt. Ordained seventy Feb. 25, 1847, by Joseph Young; sustained as one of the First Seven Presidents Oct. 8, 1862, at age 48; set apart by John Taylor; died Feb. 18, 1883, at Salt Lake City, Salt Lake Co., Utah, at age 68.

22. WILLIAM WHITTAKER TAYLOR – Born Sept. 11, 1853, at Salt Lake City, Salt Lake Co., Utah, to John Taylor and Harriet Whittaker. Ordained seventy Oct. 11, 1875, by Orson Pratt; sustained as one of the First Seven Presidents April 7, 1880, at age 26; set apart by John Taylor; died Aug. 1, 1884, at Salt Lake City, Salt Lake Co., Utah, at age 30.

23. ABRAHAM HOAGLAND CANNON – See QUORUM OF THE TWELVE, No. 37.

THEODORE BELDEN LEWIS – Born Nov. 18, 1843, at St. Louis, St. Louis Co., Missouri, to Thomas Anderson Lewis and Martha J. O. Belden. Ordained high priest at Nephi, Utah (date not known); sustained as one of the First Seven Presidents Oct. 8, 1882, at age 38; on Oct. 9, when he was to be set apart, he reported that he was already a high priest, so he was not set apart and did not function in this position.

24. SEYMOUR BICKNELL YOUNG – Born Oct. 3, 1837, at Kirtland, Geauga Co., Ohio, to Joseph Young and Jane Adeline Bicknell. Ordained seventy Feb. 18, 1857, by Edmund Ellsworth; set apart by Franklin D. Richards as one of the First Seven Presidents Oct. 14, 1882, at age 45; sustained April 8, 1883; died Dec. 15, 1924, at Salt Lake City, Salt Lake Co., Utah, at age 87.

25. CHRISTIAN DANIEL FJELSTED – Born Feb. 20, 1829, at Amagar, Sundbyvester Co., Denmark, to Hendrick Ludvig Fjelsted and Ann Catrine Hendriksen. Ordained seventy Feb. 5, 1859, by William H. Walker; sustained as one of the First Seven Presidents April 6, 1884, at age 55; set apart by Wilford Woodruff; died Dec. 23, 1905, at Salt Lake City, Salt Lake Co., Utah, at age 76.

26. JOHN MORGAN – Born Aug. 8, 1842, at Greensburg, Decatur Co., Indiana, to Gerrard Morgan and Ann Eliza Hamilton. Ordained seventy Oct. 8, 1875, by Joseph Young; sustained as one of the First Seven Presidents Oct. 5, 1884, at age 42; set apart by Wilford Woodruff; died Aug. 14, 1894, at Preston, Franklin Co., Idaho, at 52.

27. BRIGHAM HENRY ROBERTS – Born March 13, 1857, at Warrington, Lancashire Co., England, to Benjamin Roberts and Ann Everington. Ordained seventy March 8, 1877, by Nathan T. Porter. Sustained as one of the First Seven Presidents Oct. 7, 1888, at age 31; set apart by Lorenzo Snow; died Sept. 27, 1933, at Salt Lake City, Salt Lake Co., Utah, at age 76.

28. GEORGE REYNOLDS – Born Jan. 1, 1842, at Marylebone, London Co., London, England, to George Reynolds and Julia Ann Tautz. Ordained seventy March 18, 1866, by Israel Barlow; sustained as one of the First Seven Presidents April 5, 1890, at age 48; set apart by Lorenzo Snow; died Aug. 9, 1909, at Salt Lake City, Salt Lake Co., Utah, at age 67.

29. JONATHAN GOLDEN KIMBALL – Born June 9, 1853, at Salt Lake City, Salt Lake Co., Utah, to Heber Chase Kimball and Christeen Golden. Ordained seventy July 21, 1886, by William M. Allred; sustained as one of the First Seven Presidents April 5, 1892, at age 38; set apart by Francis M. Lyman; died in an automobile accident Sept. 2, 1938, near Reno, Nevada, at age 85.

30. RULON SEYMOUR WELLS – Born July 7, 1854, at Salt Lake City, Salt Lake Co., Utah, to Daniel Hanmer Wells and Louisa Free. Ordained seventy Oct. 22, 1875, by Brigham Young; sustained as one of the First Seven Presidents April 5, 1893, at age 38; set apart by George Q. Cannon; died May 7, 1941, at Salt Lake City, Salt Lake Co., Utah, at age 86.

31. EDWARD STEVENSON – Born May 1, 1820, at Gibraltar, England, to Joseph Stevenson and Elizabeth Stevens. Ordained seventy May 1, 1844, by Joseph Young; sustained as one of the First Seven Presidents Oct. 7, 1894, at age 74; set apart by Brigham Young Jr.; died Jan. 27, 1897, at Salt Lake City, Salt Lake Co., Utah, at age 76.

32. JOSEPH WILLIAM MCMURRIN – Born Sept. 5, 1858, at Tooele, Tooele Co., Utah, to Joseph McMurrin and Margaret Leaning. Ordained seventy April 21, 1884, by Royal Barney; sustained as one of the First Seven Presidents Oct. 5, 1897, at age 39; set apart Jan. 21, 1898, by Anthon H. Lund; died Oct. 24, 1932, at Los Angeles, Los

Angeles Co., California, at age 74.

33. CHARLES HENRY HART – Born July 5, 1866, at Bloomington, Bear Lake Co., Idaho, to James Henry Hart and Sabina Scheib. Ordained seventy Aug. 10, 1890, by John Henry Smith; sustained as one of the First Seven Presidents April 9, 1906, at age 39; set apart by Joseph F. Smith; died Sept. 29, 1934, at Salt Lake Co., Utah, at age 68.

34. LEVI EDGAR YOUNG – Born Feb. 2, 1874, at Salt Lake City, Salt Lake Co., Utah, to Seymour Bicknell Young and Ann Elizabeth Riter. Ordained seventy June 18, 1897, by Seymour B. Young; sustained as one of the First Seven Presidents Oct. 6, 1909, at age 35; set apart Jan. 23, 1910, by John Henry Smith; died Dec. 13, 1963, at Salt Lake City, Salt Lake Co., Utah, at age 89.

35. REY LUCERO PRATT – Born Oct. 11, 1878, at Salt Lake City, Salt Lake Co., Utah, to Helaman Pratt and Emeline Victoria Billingsley. Ordained seventy Sept. 23, 1911, by Rulon S. Wells; sustained as one of the First Seven Presidents Jan. 29, 1925, at age 46; set apart April 7, 1925, by Anthony W. Ivins; died April 14, 1931, at Salt Lake City, Salt Lake Co., Utah at age 52.

36. ANTOINE RIDGEWAY IVINS – Born May 11, 1881, at St. George, Washington Co., Utah, to Anthony Woodward Ivins and Elizabeth A. Snow. Ordained seventy Dec. 28, 1913, by Fred E. Barker; sustained as one of the First Seven Presidents Oct. 4, 1931, at age 50; ordained high priest June 11, 1961, by David O. McKay; died Oct. 18, 1967, at Salt Lake City, Salt Lake Co., Utah, at age 86.

37. SAMUEL OTIS BENNION – Born June 9, 1874, at Taylorsville, Salt Lake Co., Utah, to John Rowland Bennion and Emma Jane Terry. Ordained seventy March 14, 1904,

by Samuel Gerrard; sustained as one of the First Seven Presidents April 6, 1933, at age 58; set apart by Heber J. Grant; died March 8, 1945, at Salt Lake City, Salt Lake Co., Utah, at age 70.

38. JOHN HARRIS TAYLOR – Born June 28, 1875, at Salt Lake City, Salt Lake Co., Utah, to Thomas E. Taylor and Emma L. Harris. Ordained seventy Jan. 24, 1896, by Heber J. Grant; sustained as one of the First Seven Presidents Oct. 6, 1933, at age 58; set apart by Heber J. Grant; died May 28, 1946, at Salt Lake City, Salt Lake Co., Utah, at age 70.

39. RUFUS KAY HARDY – Born May 28, 1878, at Salt Lake City, Salt Lake Co., Utah, to Rufus H. Hardy and Annie Kay. Ordained seventy July 2, 1897, by John Henry Smith; sustained to the First Council of the Seventy Oct. 6, 1934, at age 56; set apart Feb. 7, 1935, by Heber J. Grant; died March 7, 1945, at Salt Lake City, Salt Lake Co., Utah, at age 66.

40. RICHARD LOUIS EVANS – See QUORUM OF THE TWELVE, No. 71.

41. OSCAR AMMON KIRKHAM – Born Jan. 22, 1880, at Lehi, Utah Co., Utah, to James Kirkham and Martha Mercer. Ordained seventy Feb. 26, 1905, by Joseph W. McMurrin; sustained to the First Council of the Seventy Oct. 5, 1941, at age 61; set apart by Heber J. Grant; died March 10, 1958, at Salt Lake City, Salt Lake Co., Utah, at 78.

42. SEYMOUR DILWORTH YOUNG – See FIRST QUORUM OF THE SEVENTY, No. 24.

43. MILTON REED HUNTER – Born Oct. 25, 1902, at Holden, Millard Co., Utah, to John E. Hunter and Margaret Teeples. Ordained seventy Aug. 31, 1928, by Rulon S. Wells; sustained to the First Council of the Seventy April 6, 1945, at age 42; ordained high priest June 11, 1961, by David O. McKay; died June 27, 1975, at Salt Lake City, Salt Lake Co., Utah, at age 72.

44. BRUCE REDD MCCONKIE – See QUORUM OF THE

TWELVE, No. 80.

45. MARION DUFF HANKS – See PRESIDENCY OF THE SEVENTY, No. 6.

46. ALBERT THEODORE TUTTLE – See PRESIDENCY OF THE SEVENTY, No. 4.

47. PAUL HAROLD DUNN – See PRESIDENCY OF THE SEVENTY, No. 7.

48. HARTMAN RECTOR JR. – See FIRST QUORUM OF THE SEVENTY, No. 25.

49. LOREN CHARLES DUNN – See FIRST QUORUM OF SEVENTY, No. 26.

50. REX DEE PINEGAR – See PRESIDENCY OF THE SEVENTY, No. 23.

51. GENE RAYMOND COOK – See FIRST QUORUM OF THE SEVENTY, NO. 28.

On Oct. 3, 1975, the First Quorum of the Seventy was reconstituted with the sustaining of three members, Elders Charles Didier, William R. Bradford, and George P. Lee. Four additional members, Elders Carlos E. Asay, M. Russell Ballard, John H. Groberg, and Jacob de Jager, were sustained April 3, 1976. On Oct. 1, 1976, the members of the First Council of the Seventy and the Assistants to the Quorum of the Twelve Apostles were released and sustained to the First Quorum of the Seventy. A Presidency of the First Quorum of the Seventy was sustained.

ASSISTANTS TO THE TWELVE
(Functioned from April 1941 to October 1976)

1. MARION GEORGE ROMNEY – See FIRST COUNSELORS IN THE FIRST PRESIDENCY, No. 18.

2. THOMAS EVANS MCKAY – Born Oct. 29, 1875, at Huntsville, Weber Co., Utah, to David McKay and Jennette Eveline Evans. Sustained as Assistant to the Quorum of the Twelve Apostles April 6, 1941, and set apart May 23, 1941, by Heber J. Grant, at age 65; died Jan. 15, 1958, at Salt Lake City, Salt Lake Co., Utah, at age 82.

3. CLIFFORD EARL YOUNG – Born Dec. 7, 1883, at Salt Lake City, Salt Lake Co., Utah, to Seymour Bicknell Young and Ann Elizabeth Riter. Sustained as Assistant to the Quorum of the Twelve Apostles April 6, 1941, and set apart May 23, 1941, by President Grant, at age 57; died Aug. 21, 1958, at Salt Lake City, Salt Lake Co., Utah, at age 74.

4. ALMA SONNE – See FIRST QUORUM OF THE SEVENTY, No. 8.

5. NICHOLAS GROESBECK SMITH – Born June 20, 1881, at Salt Lake City, Salt Lake Co., Utah, to John Henry Smith and Josephine Groesbeck. Sustained an Assistant to the Quorum of the Twelve

Apostles April 6, 1941; set apart Oct. 1, 1941, by Heber J. Grant, at age 60; died Oct. 27, 1945, at Salt Lake City, Salt Lake Co., Utah, at age 64.

6. GEORGE QUAYLE MORRIS — See QUORUM OF THE TWELVE, No. 72.

7. STAYNER RICHARDS – Born Dec. 20, 1885, at Salt Lake City, Salt Lake Co., Utah, to Stephen Longstroth Richards and Emma Louise Stayner. Sustained as Assistant to the Quorum of the Twelve Apostles Oct. 6, 1951, and set apart Oct. 11, 1951, by David O. McKay, at age 65; died May 28, 1953, at Salt Lake City, Salt Lake Co., Utah, at age 67.

8. EL RAY LAVAR CHRISTIANSEN – Born July 13, 1897, at Mayfield, Sanpete Co., Utah, to Parley Christiansen and Dorthea C. Jensen. Sustained as Assistant to the Quorum of the Twelve Apostles Oct. 6, 1951, and set apart Oct. 11, 1951, by Stephen L Richards, at age 54; died Dec. 2, 1975, at Salt Lake City, Salt Lake Co., Utah, at age 78.

9. JOHN LONGDEN – Born Nov. 4, 1898, at Oldham, Lancashire Co., England, to Thomas Johnson Longden and Lizetta Taylor. Sustained as Assistant to the Quorum of the Twelve Apostles Oct. 6, 1951, and set apart Oct. 11, 1951, by J.

Reuben Clark Jr., at age 52; died Aug. 30, 1969, at Salt Lake City, Salt Lake Co., Utah, at age 70.

10. HUGH BROWN BROWN – See FIRST COUNSELORS IN THE FIRST PRESIDENCY, No. 15.

11. STERLING WELLING SILL – See FIRST QUORUM OF THE SEVENTY, No. 9.

12. GORDON BITNER HINCKLEY - See PRESIDENTS OF THE CHURCH, No. 15.

13. HENRY DIXON TAYLOR – See FIRST QUORUM OF THE SEVENTY, No. 10.

14. WILLIAM JAMES CRITCHLOW JR. – Born Aug. 21, 1892, at Brigham City, Box Elder Co., Utah, to William James Critchlow and Anna C. Gregerson. Sustained as Assistant to the Quorum of the Twelve Apostles Oct. 11, 1958, and set apart Oct. 16, 1958, by David O. McKay, at age 66; died Aug. 29, 1968, at Ogden, Weber Co., Utah, at age 76.

15. ALVIN RULON DYER – See OTHER COUNSELORS IN THE FIRST PRESIDENCY, No. 13.

16. NATHAN ELDON TANNER – See FIRST COUNSELORS IN THE FIRST PRESIDENCY, No. 17.

17. FRANKLIN DEWEY RICHARDS – See PRESIDENCY OF THE SEVENTY, No. 1.

18. THEODORE MOYLE BURTON – See FIRST QUORUM OF THE SEVENTY, No. 12.

19. HENRY THORPE BEAL ISAACSON – See OTHER COUNSELORS IN THE FIRST PRESIDENCY, No. 12.

20. BOYD KENNETH PACKER – See current QUORUM OF THE TWELVE.

21. BERNARD PARK BROCKBANK – See FIRST QUORUM OF SEVENTY, No. 13.

22. JAMES ALFRED CULLIMORE – See FIRST QUORUM OF THE SEVENTY, No. 14.

23. MARION DUFF HANKS – See PRESIDENCY OF THE SEVENTY, No. 6.

24. MARVIN JEREMY ASHTON – See QUORUM OF THE TWELVE, No. 79.

25. JOSEPH ANDERSON – See FIRST QUORUM OF THE SEVENTY, No. 15.

26. DAVID BRUCE HAIGHT – See QUORUM OF THE TWELVE, No. 82.

27. WILLIAM HUNTER BENNETT – See FIRST QUORUM OF SEVENTY, No. 16.

28. JOHN HENRY VANDENBERG – See PRESIDING BISHOPS, No. 9.

29. ROBERT LEATHAM SIMPSON – See FIRST QUORUM OF THE SEVENTY, No. 18.

30. OSCAR LESLIE STONE – See FIRST QUORUM OF THE SEVENTY, No. 19.

31. JAMES ESDRAS FAUST - See SECOND COUNSELORS IN THE FIRST PRESIDENCY, NO. 23.

32. LOWELL TOM PERRY – See current QUORUM OF THE TWELVE.

33. JOHN THOMAS FYANS – See PRESIDENCY OF THE SEVENTY, No. 3.

34. NEAL ASH MAXWELL – See QUORUM OF THE TWELVE, No. 84.

35. WILLIAM GRANT BANGERTER – See PRESIDENCY OF SEVENTY, No. 8.

36. ROBERT DEAN HALES – See current QUORUM OF THE TWELVE.

37. ADNEY YOSHIO KOMATSU – See FIRST QUORUM OF SEVENTY, No. 22.

38. JOSEPH BITNER WIRTHLIN – See QUORUM OF THE TWELVE, No. 88.

On Oct. 1, 1976, the Assistants to the Quorum of the Twelve were released and sustained to the First Quorum of the Seventy.

PRESIDENCY OF THE SEVENTY

(From Oct. 3, 1975, to April 1, 1989, served as the Presidency of the First Quorum of the Seventy; from April 1, 1989, to April 1997, served as the Presidency of both the First and Second Quorums of the Seventy; since April 1997, serves as the Presidency of all Quorums of the Seventy.)

1. FRANKLIN DEWEY RICHARDS – Born Nov. 17, 1900, in Ogden, Weber Co., Utah, to Charles C. Richards and Louisa L. Peery. Sustained as Assistant to the Quorum of the Twelve Apostles Oct. 8, 1960, at age 59; sustained to First Quorum of the Seventy Oct. 1, 1976; served in Presidency of the First Quorum of the Seventy, Oct. 1, 1976, to Oct. 1, 1983; died Nov. 13, 1987, at Salt Lake City, Salt Lake Co., Utah, at age 86.

2. JAMES ESDRAS FAUST - See SECOND COUNSELORS IN THE FIRST PRESIDENCY, NO. 23.

3. JOHN THOMAS FYANS – Born May 17, 1918, in Moreland, Bingham Co., Idaho, to Joseph Fyans and Mae Farnsworth. Sustained as Assistant to the Quorum of the Twelve Apostles April 6, 1974, at age 55; sustained to First Quorum of the Seventy Oct. 1, 1976; served in Presidency of the First Quorum of the Seventy, Oct. 1, 1976, to Oct. 6, 1985; named emeritus General Authority Sept. 30, 1989; died May 18, 2008, at Sandy, Salt Lake Co., Utah, at age 90.

4. ALBERT THEODORE TUTTLE – Born March 2, 1919, in Manti, Sanpete Co., Utah, to Albert M. Tuttle and Clarice Beal. Sustained to First Council of the Seventy April 6, 1958, at age 39; sustained to First Quorum of the Seventy Oct. 1, 1976; served in Presidency of the First Quorum of the Seventy, Oct. 1, 1976, to Feb. 22, 1980; died Nov. 28, 1986, at Salt Lake City, Salt Lake Co., Utah, at age 67.

5. NEAL ASH MAXWELL – See QUORUM OF THE TWELVE, No. 84.

6. MARION DUFF HANKS – Born Oct. 13, 1921, in Salt Lake City, Salt Lake Co., Utah, to Stanley Alonzo Hanks and Maude Frame. Sustained to First Council of the Seventy Oct. 4, 1953, at age 31, and as Assistant to the Quorum of the Twelve Apostles April 6, 1968; sustained to the First Quorum of the Seventy Oct. 1, 1976; served in the Presidency of the First Quorum of the Seventy from Oct. 1, 1976-April 5, 1980, and from Oct. 6, 1984-Aug. 15, 1992; named emeritus General Authority Oct. 3, 1992; died Aug. 5, 2011, at Salt Lake City, Salt Lake Co., Utah, at age 89.

7. PAUL HAROLD DUNN – Born April 24, 1924, in Provo, Utah Co., Utah, to Joshua Harold Dunn and Geneve Roberts. Sustained to First Council of the Seventy April 6, 1964, at age 39; sustained to First Quorum of the Seventy Oct. 1, 1976; served in Presidency of the First Quorum of the Seventy, Oct. 1, 1976, to Feb. 22, 1980; named emeritus General Authority Sept. 30, 1989; died Jan. 9, 1998, at Salt Lake City, Salt Lake Co., Utah, at age 73.

8. WILLIAM GRANT BANGERTER – Born June 8, 1918, in Granger, Salt Lake Co., Utah, to William Henry Bangerter and Isabelle Bawden. Sustained as Assistant to the Quorum of the Twelve Apostles April 4, 1975, at age 56; sustained to First Quorum of the Seventy Oct. 1, 1976; served in Presidency of the First Quorum of the Seventy from Sept. 30, 1978, to April 5, 1980, and from Feb. 17, 1985, to Sept. 30, 1989; named emeritus General Authority Sept. 30, 1989; died April 18, 2010, in Provo, Utah Co., Utah, at age 91.

9. CARLOS EGAN ASAY – Born June 12, 1926, in Sutherland, Millard Co., Utah, to A.E. Lyle Asay and Elsie Egan. Sustained to the First Quorum of the Seventy April 3, 1976, at age 49; served in Presidency of the Seventy from Feb. 22, 1980, to Aug. 15, 1986, and from Oct. 1, 1989, to Aug. 15, 1996; named emeritus General Authority Oct. 5, 1996; died April 10, 1999, in Bountiful, Davis Co., Utah, at age 72.

10. MELVIN RUSSELL BALLARD JR. – See current QUORUM OF THE TWELVE.

11. DEAN LEROY LARSEN – Born March 24, 1927, in

Hyrum, Cache Co., Utah, to Edgar Niels Larsen and Gertrude Prouse. Sustained to First Quorum of the Seventy Oct. 1, 1976, at age 49; served in Presidency of the Seventy, Feb. 22, 1980, to Aug. 15, 1993; named emeritus General Authority Oct. 4, 1997.

12. ROYDEN GLADE DERRICK – Born Sept. 7, 1915, in Salt Lake City, Salt Lake Co., Utah, to Hyrum H. Derrick and Margaret Glade. Sustained to First Quorum of the Seventy Oct. 1, 1976, at age 61; served in Presidency of the First Quorum of the Seventy, April 5, 1980, to Oct. 6, 1984; named emeritus General Authority Sept. 30, 1989; died Dec. 7, 2009, in Salt Lake City, Salt Lake Co., Utah, at age 94.

13. GEORGE HOMER DURHAM – Born Feb. 4, 1911, in Parowan, Iron Co., Utah, to George H. Durham and Mary Ellen Marsden. Sustained to First Quorum of the Seventy April 2, 1977, at age 66; served in Presidency of the First Quorum of the Seventy, Oct. 1, 1981, until his death Jan. 10, 1985, at Salt Lake City, Salt Lake Co., Utah, at age 73.

14. RICHARD GORDON SCOTT – See current QUORUM OF THE TWELVE.

15. MARION DUFF HANKS – See PRESIDENCY OF THE SEVENTY, No. 6.

16. WILLIAM GRANT BANGERTER – See PRESIDENCY OF THE SEVENTY, No. 8.

17. JACK H GOASLIND JR. – Born April 18, 1928, in Salt Lake City, Utah, to Jack H. Goaslind and Anita Jack. Sustained to the First Quorum of the Seventy Sept. 30, 1978, at age 50; served in the Presidency of the Seventy, Oct. 6, 1985, to Aug. 15, 1987, and from Aug. 15, 1995, to Aug. 15, 1998; named emeritus General Authority Oct. 3, 1998 ; died April 27, 2011, at Salt Lake City, Salt Lake Co., Utah, at age 83.

18. ROBERT LEGRAND BACKMAN – Born March 22, 1922, in Salt Lake City, Salt Lake Co., Utah, to LeGrand P. Backman and Edith

Price. Sustained to the First Quorum of the Seventy April 1, 1978, at age 56; served in the Presidency of the Seventy, Oct. 6, 1985, to Aug. 15, 1992; named emeritus General Authority Oct. 3, 1992.

19. JOSEPH BITNER WIRTHLIN – See QUORUM OF THE TWELVE, No. 88.

20. HUGH WALLACE PINNOCK – Born Jan. 15, 1934, in Salt Lake City, Salt Lake Co., Utah, to Lawrence Sylvester Pinnock and Florence Boden. Sustained to the First Quorum of the Seventy Oct. 1, 1977, at age 43; served in the Presidency of the Seventy, Oct. 4, 1986, to Oct. 1, 1989; died Dec. 15, 2000, in Salt Lake City, Salt Lake Co., Utah, at age 66.

21. JAMES MARTIN PARAMORE – Born May 6, 1928, in Salt Lake City, Salt Lake Co., Utah, to James F. Paramore and Ruth C. Martin. Sustained to First Quorum of the Seventy April 2, 1977, at age 48, and served in the Presidency of the Seventy, Aug. 15, 1987, to Aug. 15, 1993; named emeritus General Authority Oct. 3, 1998.

22. JOHN RICHARD CLARKE – Born April 4, 1927, in Rexburg, Madison Co., Idaho, to John Roland Clarke and Nora L. Redford. Sustained as second counselor in Presiding Bishopric Oct. 1, 1976, at age 49, and to the First Quorum of the Seventy, April 6, 1985; served in the Presidency of the Seventy, Oct. 1, 1988, to Aug. 15, 1993; named emeritus General Authority Oct. 4, 1997.

23. REX DEE PINEGAR – Born Sept. 18, 1931, in Orem, Utah Co., Utah, to John E. Pinegar and Grace Murl Ellis. Sustained to the First Council of the Seventy Oct. 6, 1972, at age 41; sustained to First Quorum of the Seventy Oct. 1, 1976; served in the Presidency of the Seventy, Sept. 30, 1989, to Aug. 15, 1995; named emeritus General Authority Oct. 6, 2001.

24. CARLOS EGAN ASAY – See PRESIDENCY OF THE SEVENTY, No. 9.

25. CHARLES AMAND ANDRE DIDIER – Born Oct. 5, 1935, in Ixelles, Belgium, to Andre Didier and

Gabrielle Colpaert. Sustained to the First Quorum of the Seventy Oct. 3, 1975, at age 39; served in the Presidency of the Seventy Aug. 15, 1992, to Aug. 15, 1995; called to the presidency for the second time Aug. 15, 2001, and served until Aug. 1, 2007; named emeritus General Authority Oct. 3, 2009.

26. LLOYD ALDIN PORTER – Born June 30, 1931, in Salt Lake City, Salt Lake Co., Utah, to J. Lloyd Porter and Revon Hayward. Sustained to the First Quorum of the Seventy April 4, 1987, at age 55; sustained to the Second Quorum of the Seventy April 1, 1989; sustained to the First Quorum of the Seventy April 6, 1991; served in the Presidency of the Seventy, Aug. 15, 1992, to Aug. 15, 2001; named emeritus General Authority Oct. 6, 2001

27. JOE JUNIOR CHRISTENSEN – Born July 21, 1929, in Banida, Franklin Co., Idaho, to Joseph A. Christensen and Goldie Miles. Sustained to First Quorum of the Seventy April 1, 1989, at age 59; served in the Presidency of the Seventy, Aug. 15, 1993, to Aug. 15, 1999; named emeritus General Authority Oct. 2, 1999.

28. MONTE JAMES BROUGH – Born June 11, 1939, in Randolph, Rich Co., Utah, to Richard Muir Brough and Gwendolyn Kearl. Sustained to the Second Quorum of the Seventy Oct. 1, 1989, at age 49; sustained to the First Quorum of the Seventy April 6, 1991; served in the Presidency of the Seventy from Aug. 15, 1993, to Aug. 15, 1998; named emeritus General Authority Oct. 6, 2007; died Sept. 20, 2011, at Kaysville, Davis Co., at age 72.

29. WARREN EUGENE HANSEN – Born Aug. 23, 1928, in Tremonton, Box Elder Co., Utah, to Warren E. Hansen and Ruth Steed. Sustained to the First Quorum of the Seventy April 1, 1989, at age 60; served in the Presidency of the Seventy, Aug. 15, 1993, to Aug. 15, 1998; named emeritus General Authority Oct. 3, 1998.

30. JACK H GOASLIND JR. – See PRESIDENCY OF THE SEVENTY, No. 17.

31. HAROLD GORDON HILLAM - Born Sept. 1, 1934, in Sugar City, Madison Co., Idaho, to Gordon R. Hillam and Florence Evelyn Skidmore. Sustained to the Second Quorum of the Seventy March 31, 1990, at age 54; sustained to the First Quorum of the Seventy April 6, 1991; served in the Presidency of the Seventy from Aug. 15, 1995, to Aug. 15, 2000; named emeritus General Authority Oct. 1, 2005.

32. EARL CARR TINGEY - Born June 11, 1934, in Bountiful, Davis Co., Utah, to William W. Tingey and Sylvia Carr. Called to the First Quorum of the Seventy Dec. 5, 1990, at age 56, and sustained April 6, 1991; served in the Presidency of the Seventy from Aug. 15, 1996, to Aug. 1, 2008; named emeritus General Authority Oct. 4, 2008.

33. DAVID TODD CHRISTOFFERSON - See current QUORUM OF THE TWELVE.

34. MARLIN KEITH JENSEN – See current FIRST QUORUM OF THE SEVENTY.

35. DAVID EUGENE SORENSEN - Born June 29, 1933, in Aurora, Millard Co., Utah, to Alma Sorensen and Metta Amelia Helquist. Called to the Second Quorum of the Seventy June 6, 1992, at age 58, and sustained Oct. 3, 1992; sustained to the First Quorum of the Seventy April 1, 1995; served in the Presidency of the Seventy from Aug. 15, 1998, to Aug. 15, 2005; named emeritus General Authority Oct. 1, 2005.

36. BENJAMIN BERRY BANKS – Born April 4, 1932, in Murray, Salt Lake Co., Utah, to Ben F. Banks and Samantha Berry. Sustained to the Second Quorum of the Seventy April 1, 1989, at age 56; called to the First Quorum of the Seventy June 6, 1992, and sustained Oct. 3, 1992; served in the Presidency of the Seventy, Aug. 15, 1999, to Aug. 15, 2002; named emeritus General Authority Oct. 5, 2002.

37. DENNIS BRAMWELL NEUENSCHWANDER – Born Oct. 6, 1939, in Salt Lake City, Salt Lake Co., Utah, to George Henry Neuenschwander and Genevieve Bramwell. Sustained to the Second Quorum of the Seventy April 6, 1991, at age 59; sustained to the First Quorum of the Seventy Oct. 1, 1994; served in the Presidency of the Seventy Aug. 15, 2000, to April 3, 2004; named emeritus General Authority Oct. 3, 2009.

38. CHARLES AMAND ANDRE DIDIER - See PRESIDENCY OF THE SEVENTY, No. 25.

39. CECIL OSBORN SAMUELSON JR. - See current FIRST QUORUM OF THE SEVENTY.

40. DIETER FRIEDRICH UCHTDORF - See current FIRST PRESIDENCY.

41. MERRILL JOSEPH BATEMAN - Born June 19, 1936, in Lehi, Utah Co., Utah, to Joseph Frederic Bateman and Belva Smith. Called to the Second Quorum of the Seventy June 6, 1992, at age 55, and sustained Oct. 3, 1992; sustained as Presiding Bishop April 2, 1994, and served until Nov. 2, 1995; when he was named president of BYU; called to the First Quorum of the Seventy Nov. 2, 1995, and sustained April 6, 1996; served in the Presidency of the Seventy from April 5, 2003, after being released as president of BYU, to Aug. 1, 2007; named emeritus General Authority Oct. 6, 2007.

42. JOHN HOLBROOK GROBERG - Born June 17, 1934, in Idaho Falls, Bonneville Co., Idaho, to Delbert V. Groberg and Jennie Holbrook. Sustained to the First Quorum of the Seventy April 3, 1976, at age 41; sustained to the Presidency of the Seventy, April 3, 2004, and served until Aug. 15, 2005; named emeritus General Authority Oct. 1, 2005.

43. ROBERT CHARLES OAKS - Born Feb.14, 1936, in Los Angeles, Los Angeles Co., Calif., to Charles E. Oaks and Ann Bonnett. Sustained to the Second Quorum of the Seventy April 1, 2000, at age 64; served in the Presidency of the Seventy from Oct. 2, 2004, to Aug. 1, 2007; released Oct. 3, 2009.

44. NEIL LINDEN ANDERSEN - See current QUORUM OF THE TWELVE.

45. RONALD A RASBAND - See current PRESIDENCY OF THE SEVENTY.

46. QUENTIN LAMAR COOK - See current QUORUM OF THE TWELVE.

47. CLAUDIO ROBERTO MENDEZ COSTA - See current FIRST QUORUM OF THE SEVENTY..

48. STEVEN ERASTUS SNOW – See current PRESIDENCY OF THE SEVENTY.

49. WALTER FERMIN GONZALEZ – See current PRESIDENCY OF THE SEVENTY.

50. LYNDON WHITNEY CLAYTON – See current PRESIDENCY OF THE SEVENTY.

51. JAY EDWIN JENSEN – See current PRESIDENCY OF THE SEVENTY.

52. DONALD LARRY HALLSTROM – See current PRESIDENCY OF THE SEVENTY.

53. TAD RICHARDS CALLISTER – See current PRESIDENCY OF THE SEVENTY.

FIRST QUORUM OF THE SEVENTY

The organization of the First Quorum of the Seventy was announced Oct. 3, 1975, and the first members of the quorum were sustained in general conference.

The following year, on Oct. 1, 1976, members of the First Council of the Seventy and the Assistants to the Twelve were released in general conference and called to the First Quorum of the Seventy.

1. FRANKLIN DEWEY RICHARDS – See PRESIDENCY OF THE SEVENTY, No. 1.

2. JAMES ESDRAS FAUST - See SECOND COUNSELORS IN THE FIRST PRESIDENCY, NO. 23.

3. JOHN THOMAS FYANS – See PRESIDENCY OF THE SEVENTY, No. 3.

4. ALBERT THEODORE TUTTLE – See PRESIDENCY OF THE SEVENTY, No. 4.

5. NEAL ASH MAXWELL – See QUORUM OF THE TWELVE, No. 84.

6. MARION DUFF HANKS – See PRESIDENCY OF THE SEVENTY, No. 6.

7. PAUL HAROLD DUNN – See PRESIDENCY OF THE SEVENTY, No. 7.

8. ALMA SONNE – Born March 5, 1884, at Logan, Cache Co., Utah, to Niels C. Sonne and Elisa Peterson. Sustained as Assistant to the Quorum of the Twelve Apostles April 6, 1941, at age 57; sustained to First Quorum of the Seventy Oct. 1, 1976; died Nov. 27, 1977, at Logan, Cache Co., Utah, at age 93.

9. STERLING WELLING SILL – Born March 31, 1903, at Layton, Davis Co., Utah, to Joseph Albert Sill and Marietta Welling. Sustained as Assistant to the Quorum of the Twelve Apostles April 6, 1954, at age 51; sustained to First Quorum of the Seventy Oct. 1, 1976; named emeritus General Authority Dec. 31, 1978; died May 25, 1994, in Salt Lake Co., Utah, at age 91.

10. HENRY DIXON TAYLOR – Born Nov. 22, 1903, in Provo, Utah Co., Utah, to Arthur N. Taylor and Maria Dixon. Sustained as Assistant to the Quorum of the Twelve Apostles April 6, 1958, at age 54; sustained to First Quorum of the Seventy Oct. 1, 1976; named emeritus General Authority Sept. 30, 1978; died Feb. 24, 1987, at Salt Lake City, Salt Lake Co., Utah, at age 83.

11. ALVIN RULON DYER – See OTHER COUNSELORS IN THE FIRST PRESIDENCY, No. 13.

12. THEODORE MOYLE BURTON – Born March 27, 1907, at Salt Lake City, Salt Lake Co., Utah, to Theodore T. Burton and Florence Moyle. Sustained as Assistant to the Quorum of the Twelve Apostles Oct. 8, 1960, at age 53; sustained to First Quorum of the Seventy Oct. 1, 1976; named emeritus General Authority Sept. 30, 1989; died Dec. 22, 1989, at Salt Lake City, Salt Lake Co., Utah, at age 82.

13. BERNARD PARK BROCKBANK – Born May 24, 1909, at Salt Lake City, Salt Lake Co., Utah, to Taylor P. Brockbank and Sarah LeCheminant. Sustained as Assistant to the Quorum of the Twelve Apostles Oct. 6, 1962, at age 53; sustained to First Quorum of the Seventy Oct. 1, 1976; named emeritus General Authority Oct. 4, 1980; died Oct. 11, 2000, at Holladay, Salt Lake Co., Utah at age 91.

14. JAMES ALFRED CULLIMORE – Born Jan. 17, 1906, at Lindon, Utah Co., Utah, to Albert Lorenzo Cullimore and Luella Keetch. Sustained an Assistant to the Quorum of the Twelve Apostles April 6, 1966, at age 60; sustained to First Quorum of the Seventy Oct. 1, 1976; named emeritus General Authority Sept. 30, 1978; died June 14, 1986, at Salt Lake City, Salt Lake Co., Utah, at age 80.

15. JOSEPH ANDERSON – Born Nov. 20, 1889, at Salt Lake City, Salt Lake Co., Utah, to George Anderson and Isabella Watson. Sustained as Assistant to the Quorum of the Twelve Apostles April 6, 1970, at age 80; sustained to First Quorum of the Seventy Oct. 1, 1976; named emeritus General Authority Dec. 31, 1978; died March 13, 1992, at Salt Lake City,

Salt Lake Co., Utah, at age 102.

16. WILLIAM HUNTER BENNETT – Born Nov. 5, 1910, at Taber, Alberta, Canada, to William Alvin Bennett and Mary Walker. Sustained as Assistant to the Quorum of the Twelve Apostles April 6, 1970, at age 59; sustained to First Quorum of the Seventy Oct. 1, 1976; named emeritus General Authority Dec. 31, 1978; died July 23, 1980, at Bountiful, Davis Co., Utah, at age 69.

17. JOHN HENRY VANDENBERG – See PRESIDING BISHOPS, No. 9.

18. ROBERT LEATHAM SIMPSON – Born Aug. 8, 1915, at Salt Lake City, Salt Lake Co., Utah, to Heber C. Simpson and Lillian Leatham. Sus-tained as first counselor to Presiding Bishop John H. Vandenberg Sept. 30, 1961, at age 46; sustained as Assistant to the Quorum of the Twelve Apostles April 6, 1972; sustained to First Quorum of the Seventy Oct. 1, 1976; named emeritus General Authority Oct. 1, 1989; died April 15, 2003, at St. George, Washington Co., Utah, at age 87.

19. OSCAR LESLIE STONE – Born May 28, 1903, at Chapin, Idaho, to Frank J. Stone and Mable Crandall. Sustained as Assistant to the Quorum of the Twelve Apostles, Oct. 6, 1972, at age 69; sustained to First Quorum of the Seventy, Oct. 1, 1976; named emeritus General Authority Oct. 4, 1980; died April 26, 1986, at Salt Lake City, Salt Lake Co., Utah, at age 82.

20. WILLIAM GRANT BANGERTER – See PRESIDENCY OF THE SEVENTY, No. 8.

21. ROBERT DEAN HALES – See current QUORUM OF THE TWELVE.

22. ADNEY YOSHIO KOMATSU – Born Aug. 2, 1923, at Honolulu, Honolulu Co., Oahu, Hawaii, to Jizaemon Komatsu and Misao Tabata. Sustained as Assistant to the Quorum of the Twelve Apostles, April 4,1975, at age 51; sustained to the First Quorum of the Seventy Oct. 1, 1976; named emeritus General

Authority Oct. 2, 1993 ; died Feb. 23, 2011, at Honolulu, Honolulu Co., Hawaii, at age 87.

23. JOSEPH BITNER WIRTHLIN – See QUORUM OF THE TWELVE, No. 88.

24. SEYMOUR DILWORTH YOUNG – Born Sept. 7, 1897, at Salt Lake City, Salt Lake Co., Utah, to Seymour Bicknell Young Jr. and Carlie Louine Clawson. Sustained to the First Council of the Seventy April 6, 1945, at age 47; sustained to the First Quorum of the Seventy Oct. 1, 1976; named emeritus General Authority Sept. 30, 1978; died July 9, 1981, at Salt Lake City, Salt Lake Co., Utah, at age 83.

25. HARTMAN RECTOR JR. – Born Aug. 20, 1924, at Moberly, Randolph Co., Missouri, to Hartman Rector and Vivian Fay Garvin. Sustained to the First Council of the Seventy April 6, 1968, at age 43; sustained to the First Quorum of the Seventy Oct. 1, 1976; named emeritus General Authority Oct. 1, 1994.

26. LOREN CHARLES DUNN – Born June 12, 1930, in Tooele, Tooele Co., Utah, to Alex F. Dunn and Carol Horsfall. Sustained to the First Council of the Seventy April 6, 1968, at age 37, and to the First Quorum of the Seventy Oct. 1, 1976; named emeritus General Authority Oct. 7, 2000; died May 16, 2001, at Boston, Suffolk Co., Mass., at age 70.

27. REX DEE PINEGAR – See PRESIDENCY OF THE SEVENTY, No. 23.

28. GENE RAYMOND COOK - Born Sept. 1, 1941, in Lehi, Utah Co., Utah, to Clarence H. Cook and Cora Myrl Thornton. Sustained to the First Council of the Seventy Oct. 3, 1975, at age 34; sustained to the First Quorum of the Seventy Oct. 1, 1976; named emeritus General Authority Oct. 6, 2007.

29. CHARLES AMAND ANDRE DIDIER - See PRESIDENCY OF THE SEVENTY, No. 25.

30. WILLIAM RAWSEL BRADFORD - Born Oct. 25, 1933, in Springville, Utah Co., to Rawsel W. Bradford and Mary Waddoups. Sustained to First Quorum of the Seventy Oct. 3, 1975, at age 41; named emeritus General Authority Oct. 4, 2003.

31. GEORGE PATRICK LEE - Born March 23, 1943, at Towaoc, Ute Mountain Indian Reservation, Colorado, to Pete Lee and Mae K. Asdzaatchii. Sustained to First Quorum of the Seventy Oct. 3, 1975, at age 32; excommunicated Sept. 1, 1989 ; died July 28, 2010, in Provo, Utah Co., Utah, at age 67.

32. CARLOS EGAN ASAY - See PRESIDENCY OF THE SEVENTY, No. 9.

33. MELVIN RUSSELL BALLARD JR. - See current QUORUM OF THE TWELVE.

34. JOHN HOLBROOK GROBERG - See PRESIDENCY OF THE SEVENTY, No. 42.

35. JACOB DE JAGER - Born Jan. 16, 1923, at The Hague, South Holland, Netherlands, to Alexander Philippis de Jager and Maria Jacoba Cornelia Scheele. Sustained to the First Quorum of the Seventy April 3, 1976, at age 53; named emeritus General Authority Oct. 2, 1993; died Feb. 25, 2004, in Salt Lake City, Salt Lake Co., Utah, at age 81.

36. VAUGHN J FEATHERSTONE - Born March 26, 1931, in Stockton, Tooele Co., Utah, to Stephen E. Featherstone and Emma M. Johnson. Sustained as second counselor in the Presiding Bishopric April 6, 1972, at age 41; sustained to the First Quorum of the Seventy Oct. 1, 1976; named emeritus General Authority Oct. 6, 2001.

37. DEAN LEROY LARSEN - See PRESIDENCY OF THE SEVENTY, No. 11.

38. ROYDEN GLADE DERRICK - See PRESIDENCY OF THE SEVENTY, No. 12.

39. ROBERT EARL WELLS - Born Dec. 28, 1927, in Las Vegas, Clark Co., Nevada, to Robert Stephen Wells and Zella Verona Earl. Sustained to the First Quorum of the Seventy Oct. 1, 1976, at age 48; named emeritus General Authority Oct. 4, 1997.

40. GEORGE HOMER DURHAM - See PRESIDENCY OF THE SEVENTY, No. 13.

41. JAMES MARTIN PARAMORE - See PRESIDENCY OF THE SEVENTY, No. 21.

42. RICHARD GORDON SCOTT - See current QUORUM OF THE TWELVE.

43. HUGH WALLACE PINNOCK - See PRESIDENCY OF THE SEVENTY, No. 20.

44. FRIEDRICH ENZIO BUSCHE - Born April 5, 1930, in Dortmund, Germany, to Friedrich Busche and Anna Weber. Sustained to the First Quorum of the Seventy Oct. 1, 1977, at age 47; named emeritus General Authority Oct, 7, 2000.

45. YOSHIHIKO KIKUCHI - Born July 25, 1941, in Hokkaido, Japan, to Hatsuo and Koyo Ikeda Kikuchi. Sustained to the First Quorum of the Seventy Oct. 1, 1977, at age 36; named emeritus General Authority Oct. 1, 2011.

46. RONALD EUGENE POELMAN - Born May 10, 1928, in Salt Lake City, Salt Lake Co., Utah, to Hendrick Poelman and Ella May Perkins. Sustained to the First Quorum of the Seventy April 1, 1978, at age 49; named emeritus General Authority Oct. 3, 1998.

47. DEREK ALFRED CUTHBERT - Born Oct. 5, 1926, at Nottingham, Derbyshire Co., England, to Harry Cuthbert and Hilda May Freck. Sustained to the First Quorum of the Seventy April 1, 1978, at age 51; died April 7, 1991, at Salt Lake City, Salt Lake Co., Utah, at age 64.

48. ROBERT LEGRAND BACKMAN - See PRESIDENCY OF THE SEVENTY, No. 18.

49. REX CROPPER REEVE SR. – Born Nov. 23, 1914, at Hinckley, Millard Co., Utah, to Arthur H. Reeve and Mary A. Cropper. Sustained to First Quorum of the Seventy April 1, 1978, at age 63; named emeritus General Authority Sept. 30, 1989; died July 18, 2005, in Murray, Salt Lake Co., at age 90.

50. FRED BURTON HOWARD – Born March 24, 1933, in Logan, Cache Co., to Fred P. Howard and Beatrice Ward. Sustained to the First Quorum of the Seventy Sept. 30, 1978, at age 45; named emeritus General Authority Oct. 1, 2005.

51. TEDDY EUGENE BREWERTON – Born March 30, 1925, at Raymond, Alberta, Canada, to Lee Brewerton and Jane Fisher. Sustained to the First Quorum of the Seventy, Sept. 30, 1978, at age 53; named emeritus General Authority Sept. 30, 1995.

52. JACK H GOASLIND JR. – See PRESIDENCY OF THE SEVENTY, No. 17.

53. ANGEL ABREA – Born Sept. 13, 1933, in Buenos Aires, Argentina, to Edealo Abrea and Zulema Estrada. Sustained to First Quorum of the Seventy April 4, 1981, at age 47; named emeritus General Authority Oct. 4, 2003.

54. JOHN KAY CARMACK – Born May 10, 1931, in Winslow, Navajo Co., Ariz., to Cecil E. Carmack and Gladys Bushman. Sustained to the First Quorum of the Seventy April 7, 1984, at age 52; named emeritus General Authority Oct. 6, 2001.

55. RUSSELL CARL TAYLOR – Born Nov. 25, 1925, at Red Mesa, Conejos Co., Colorado, to Leo Sanford Taylor and Florence Stella Dean. Sustained to First Quorum of the Seventy April 7, 1984, at age 58; sustained to Second Quorum of the Seventy April 1, 1989; released Sept. 30, 1989.

56. ROBERT B HARBERTSON – Born April 19, 1932, at Ogden, Weber Co. Utah, to Brigham Y. Harbertson and Gladys Venice Lewis. Sustained to First Quorum of the Seventy April 7, 1984, at age 51; sustained to Second Quorum of the Seventy April 1, 1989; released Sept. 30, 1989.

57. DEVERE HARRIS – Born May 30, 1916, at Portage, Box Elder Co. Utah, to Robert Crumbell Harris and Sylvia Green. Sustained to First Quorum of the Seventy April 7, 1984, at age 67; sustained to Second Quorum of the Seventy April 1, 1989; released Sept. 30, 1989; died July 6, 2006, in Logan, Cache Co., Utah, at age 90.

58. SPENCER HAMLIN OSBORN – Born July 8, 1921, at Salt Lake City, Salt Lake Co., Utah, to William W. Osborn and Alice M. Hamlin. Sustained to First Quorum of the Seventy April 7, 1984, at age 62; sustained to Second Quorum of the Seventy April 1, 1989; released Sept. 30, 1989; died May 1, 2006, in Salt Lake City, Salt Lake Co., Utah, at age 84.

59. PHILLIP TADJE SONNTAG – Born July 13, 1921, at Salt Lake City, Salt Lake Co., Utah, to Richard Peter Sonntag and Lena Emma Tadje. Sustained to First Quorum of the Seventy April 7, 1984, at age 62; sustained to Second Quorum of the Seventy April 1, 1989; released Sept. 30, 1989.

60. JOHN SONNENBERG – Born April 11, 1922, at Schneidemuhle, Germany, to Otto Paul Sonnenberg and Lucille Mielke. Sustained to First Quorum of the Seventy Oct. 6, 1984, at age 62; sustained to Second Quorum of the Seventy April 1, 1989; released Sept. 30, 1989.

61. FERRIL ARTHUR KAY – Born July 15, 1916, at Annabella, Sevier Co., Utah, to Samuel Arthur Kay and Medora Hooper. Sustained to First Quorum of the Seventy Oct. 6, 1984, at age 68; sustained to Second Quorum of the Seventy April 1, 1989; released Sept. 30, 1989; died Dec. 13, 2005, in Kirkland, King Co., Wash., at age 89.

62. KEITH WILSON WILCOX – Born May 15, 1921, at Hyrum, Cache Co., Utah, to Irving C. Wilcox and Nancy Mary Wilson. Sustained to First Quorum of the Seventy Oct. 6, 1984, at age 63; sustained to Second Quorum of the Seventy April 1, 1989; released Sept. 30, 1989.

63. VICTOR LEE BROWN – See PRESIDING BISHOPS, No. 10.

64. HAROLD BURKE PETERSON – Born Sept. 19, 1923, in Salt Lake City, Salt Lake Co., Utah, to Harold A. Peterson and Juna Tye. Sustained as first counselor in Presiding Bishopric April 6, 1972, at age 48; sustained to the First Quorum of the Seventy April 6, 1985; named emeritus General Authority Oct. 2, 1993.

65. JOHN RICHARD CLARKE – See PRESIDENCY OF THE SEVENTY, No. 22.

66. HANS BENJAMIN RINGGER – Born Nov. 2, 1925, in Zurich, Switzerland, to Carl Ringger and Maria Reif. Sustained to the First Quorum of the Seventy April 6, 1985, at age 59; named emeritus General Authority Sept. 30, 1995; died Oct. 18, 2010, at Basil, Switzerland, at age 84.

67. WALDO PRATT CALL – Born Feb. 5, 1928, at Colonia Juarez, Chihuahua, Mexico, to Charles Helaman Call and Hannah Skousen. Sustained to First Quorum of the Seventy April 6, 1985, at age 57; sustained to Second Quorum of the Seventy April 1, 1989; released Oct. 6, 1990.

68. HELIO DA ROCHA CAMARGO – Born Feb. 1, 1926, at Resende, Rio de Janeiro, Brazil, to Jose Medeiros de Camargo and Else Ferreira da Rocha. Sustained to First Quorum of the Seventy April 6, 1985, at age 59; sustained to Second Quorum of the Seventy April 1, 1989; released Oct. 6, 1990.

69. HANS VERLAN ANDERSEN – Born Nov. 6, 1914, in Logan, Cache Co., Utah, to Hans Andersen and Mynoa Richardson. Sustained to the First Quorum of the Seventy April 6, 1986, at age 71; sustained to the Second Quorum of the Seventy April 1, 1989; released Oct. 5, 1991; died July 16, 1992, at Orem, Utah Co., Utah, at age 77.

70. GEORGE IVINS CANNON – Born March 9, 1920, in Salt Lake City, Salt Lake Co., Utah, to George J. Cannon and Lucy Grant. Sustained to the First Quorum of the Seventy April 6, 1986, at age 66; sustained to the Second Quorum of the Seventy April 1, 1989; released Oct. 5, 1991; died Aug. 4, 2009, in Salt Lake City, Salt Lake Co., Utah, at age 89.

71. FRANCIS MARION GIBBONS – Born April 10, 1921, in St. Johns, Apache Co., Arizona, to Andrew S. Gibbons and Adeline Christensen. Sustained to the First Quorum of the Seventy April 6, 1986, at age 64; sustained to the Second Quorum of the Seventy April 1, 1989; released Oct. 5, 1991.

72. GARDNER HALE RUSSELL – Born Aug. 12, 1920, in Salt Lake City, Salt Lake Co., Utah, to Harry J. Russell and Agnes Gardner. Sustained to the First Quorum of the Seventy April 6, 1986, at age 65; sustained to the Second Quorum of the Seventy April 1, 1989; released Oct. 5, 1991.

73. GEORGE RICHARD HILL III –
Born Nov. 24, 1921, in Ogden,
Weber Co., Utah, to George
Richard Hill Jr. and Elizabeth O.
McKay. Sustained to the First
Quorum of the Seventy April 4,
1987, at age 65; sustained to the
Second Quorum of the Seventy
April 1, 1989; released Oct. 3, 1992; died April 22,
2001, at Salt Lake City, Salt Lake Co., Utah, at age
79.

74. JOHN ROGER LASATER – Born
Dec. 8, 1931, in Farmington,
Davis Co., Utah, to Robert B.
Lasater and Rowena Saunders.
Sustained to the First Quorum of
the Seventy April 4, 1987, at age
55; sustained to the Second
Quorum of the Seventy April 1,
1989; released Oct. 3, 1992.

75. DOUGLAS JAMES MARTIN – Born
April 20, 1927, in Hastings, New
Zealand, to George Martin and
Jesse Jamieson. Sustained to the
First Quorum of the Seventy April
4, 1987, at age 59; sustained to the
Second Quorum of the Seventy
April 1, 1989; released Oct. 3,
1992 ; died Jan. 23, 2010, in Hamilton, New
Zealand, at age 82.

76. ALEXANDER BAILLIE MORRISON
– Born Dec. 22, 1930, in
Edmonton, Alberta, Canada, to
Alexander S. Morrison and
Christina Wilson. Sustained to
the First Quorum of the Seventy
April 4, 1987, at age 56;
sustained to the Second Quorum
of the Seventy April 1, 1989; sustained to the First
Quorum of the Seventy April 6, 1991; named
emeritus Oct. 7, 2000.

77. LLOYD ALDIN PORTER – See PRESIDENCY OF
THE SEVENTY, No. 26.

78. GLEN LARKIN RUDD – Born
May 18, 1918, in Salt Lake City,
Salt Lake Co., Utah, to Charles
P. Rudd and Gladys Harman.
Sustained to First Quorum of the
Seventy April 4, 1987, at age 68;
sustained to the Second Quorum
of the Seventy April 1, 1989;

released Oct. 3, 1992.

79. DOUGLAS HILL SMITH – Born
May 11, 1921, in Salt Lake City,
Salt Lake Co., Utah, to Virgil H.
Smith and Winifred Pearl Hill.
Sustained to the First Quorum
of the Seventy April 4, 1987, at
age 65; sustained to the Second
Quorum of the Seventy April 1,
1989; released Oct. 3, 1992; died Jan. 29, 2009, in
Salt Lake City, Salt Lake Co., Utah, at age 87.

80. LYNN ANDREW SORENSEN –
Born Sept. 25, 1919, in Salt Lake
City, Salt Lake Co., Utah, to Ulric
Andrew Sorensen and Ferny
Boam. Sustained to the First
Quorum of the Seventy April 4,
1987, at age 67; sustained to the
Second Quorum of the Seventy
April 1, 1989; released Oct. 3, 1992.

81. ROBERT EDWARD SACKLEY –
Born Dec. 17, 1922, in Lismore,
New South Wales, Australia, to
Cecil James Sackley and Mary
Duncan. Sustained to the First
Quorum of the Seventy April 2,
1988, at age 65; sustained to the
Second Quorum of the Seventy
April 1, 1989; died Feb. 22, 1993, near Brisbane,
Australia, at age 70.

82. LARRY LIONEL KENDRICK –
Born Sept. 19, 1931, in Baton
Rouge, East Baton Rouge Parish,
La., to Bonnie Delen Kendrick
and Edna Campbell Forbes.
Sustained to the First Quorum
of the Seventy April 2, 1988, at
age 56; sustained to the Second
Quorum of the Seventy April 1, 1989; sustained to
the First Quorum of the Seventy April 6, 1991;
named emeritus General Authority Oct. 6, 2001.

83. MONTE JAMES BROUGH - See PRESIDENCY OF
THE SEVENTY, No. 28.

84. ALBERT CHOULES JR. – Born
Feb. 15, 1926, in Driggs, Teton
Co., Idaho, to Albert Choules
and Rula Wilson. Sustained to
the First Quorum of the Seventy
Oct. 1, 1988, at age 62;
sustained to the Second Quorum
of the Seventy April 1, 1989; released Oct. 1, 1994.

85. LLOYD PREAL GEORGE JR. –
Born Sept. 17, 1920, in Kanosh,
Millard Co., Utah, to Preal
George and Artemesia Palmer.
Sustained to the First Quorum
of the Seventy Oct. 1, 1988, at
age 68; sustained to the Second
Quorum of the Seventy April 1,
1989; released Oct. 1, 1994; died
May 13, 1996, at Salt Lake City, Salt Lake Co.,
Utah, at age 75.

86. GERALD ELDON MELCHIN – Born
May 24, 1921, in Kitchener,
Ontario, Can-ada, to Arthur
Melchin and Rosetta Willis.
Sustained to the First Quorum of
the Seventy on Oct. 1, 1988, at
age 67; sustained to the Second
Quorum of the Seventy April 1,
1989; released Oct. 1, 1994.

87. JOE JUNIOR CHRISTENSEN – See PRESIDENCY
OF THE SEVENTY, No. 27.

88. WARREN EUGENE HANSEN JR. – See
PRESIDENCY OF THE SEVENTY, No. 29.

89. JEFFREY ROY HOLLAND — See current QUORUM
OF THE TWELVE.

90. MARLIN KEITH JENSEN – See current FIRST
QUORUM OF THE SEVENTY.

91. EARL CARR TINGEY – See PRESIDENCY OF
THE SEVENTY, No. 32.

92. HAROLD GORDON HILLAM – See PRESIDENCY
OF THE SEVENTY, No. 31.

93. CARLOS HUMBERTO AMADO – See current FIRST
QUORUM OF THE SEVENTY.

94. BENJAMIN BERRY BANKS – See PRESIDENCY
OF THE SEVENTY, NO. 36.

95. SPENCER JOEL CONDIE – Born
Aug. 27, 1940, in Preston,
Franklin Co., Idaho, to Spencer
C. Condie and Josie Peterson.
Sustained to the Second Quorum
of the Seventy April 1, 1989, at
age 48; sustained to the First
Quorum of the Seventy Oct. 3,
1992; named emeritus General Authority Oct. 2,
2010.

96. ROBERT KENT DELLENBACH –
Born May 10, 1937, in Salt Lake
City, Salt Lake Co., Utah, to
Frank Dellenbach and Leona
Conshafter. Sustained to the
Second Quorum of the Seventy
March 31, 1990, at age 52; called
to the First Quorum of the
Seventy June 6, 1992, and sustained Oct. 3, 1992;
named emeritus General Authority Oct. 6, 2007.

97. HENRY BENNION EYRING – See current FIRST
PRESIDENCY.

98. GLENN LEROY PACE – Born
March 21, 1940, in Provo, Utah
Co., Utah, to Kenneth LeRoy
Pace and Elizabeth A. Wilde.
Sustained as second counselor in
the Presiding Bishopric April 6,
1985, at age 45; sustained to the
First Quorum of the Seventy Oct. 3, 1992; named
emeritus General Authority Oct. 2, 2010.

99. FLOYD MELVIN HAMMOND –
Born Dec. 19, 1933, in Blackfoot,
Bingham Co., Idaho, to Floyd
Milton Hammond and Ruby Hoge.
Sustained to the Second Quorum
of the Seventy April 1, 1989, at
age 55; sustained to the First
Quorum of the Seventy April 3,
1993; named emeritus General Authority Oct. 1,
2005.

100. KENNETH JOHNSON – Born
July 5, 1940, in Norwich,
England, to Bertie A.M. Johnson
and Ada Hutson. Sustained to the
Second Quorum of the Seventy
March 31, 1990, at age 49;
sustained to the First Quorum of
the Seventy April 3, 1993; named
emeritus General Authority Oct. 2, 2010.

101. LYNN ALVIN MICKELSEN –
Born July 21, 1935, in Idaho
Falls, Bonneville Co., Idaho, to
Lloyd P. Mickelsen and Reva Faye
Willmore. Sustained to the
Second Quorum of the Seventy
March 31, 1990, at age 54;
sustained to the First Quorum of
the Seventy April 3, 1993; named emeritus General
Authority Oct. 3, 2009.

102. NEIL LINDEN ANDERSEN - See current QUORUM OF THE TWELVE.

103. DAVID TODD CHRISTOFFERSON – See current QUORUM OF THE TWELVE.

104. CREE-L KOFFORD - Born July 11, 1933, in Santaquin, Utah Co., Utah, to Cree Clarence Kofford and Melba Nelson. Sustained to Second Quorum of the Seventy April 6, 1991, at age 57; sustained to First Quorum of the Seventy April 2, 1994; named emeritus General Authority Oct. 4, 2003.

105. DENNIS BRAMWELL NEUENSCHWANDER - See PRESIDENCY OF THE SEVENTY, No. 37.

106. ANDREW WAYNE PETERSON – Born June 8, 1947, in San Francisco, San Francisco Co., Calif., to Wayne Leo Peterson and Virginia Parker. Sustained to First Quorum of the Seventy Oct. 1, 1994, at age 47; named emeritus General Authority Oct. 2, 1999; died Dec. 31, 2003, in Salt Lake City, Salt Lake Co., Utah, at age 56.

107. CECIL OSBORN SAMUELSON JR. - Born Aug. 1, 1941, in Salt Lake City, in Salt Lake Co., Utah, to Cecil Osborn Samuelson Sr. and Janet Brazier Mitchell. Sustained to the First Quorum of the Seventy Oct. 1, 1994, at age 53; named emeritus General Authority Oct. 1, 2011.

108. JOHN BAIRD DICKSON – See current FIRST QUORUM OF THE SEVENTY.

109. JAY EDWIN JENSEN - See current PRESIDENCY OF THE SEVENTY.

110. DAVID EUGENE SORENSEN - See PRESIDENCY OF THE SEVENTY, No. 35.

111. WILLIAM CRAIG ZWICK – See current FIRST QUORUM OF THE SEVENTY.

112. MERRILL JOSEPH BATEMAN - See PRESIDENCY OF THE SEVENTY, No. 41.

113. DALLAS NIELSEN ARCHIBALD – Born July 24, 1938, in Logan, Cache Co., Utah, to Ezra Wilson Archibald and Marguerite Nielsen. Called to the Second Quorum of the Seventy June 6, 1992, at age 53, and sustained Oct. 3, 1992; sustained to First Quorum of the Seventy April 6, 1996; drowned in a boating accident Dec. 14, 1998, near Concepcion, Chile, at age 60.

114. DIETER FRIEDRICH UCHTDORF - See current FIRST PRESIDENCY.

115. BRUCE CLARK HAFEN – Born Oct. 30, 1940, in St. George, Washington Co., Utah, to Orval Hafen and Ruth Clark. Sustained to the First Quorum of the Seventy April 6, 1996, at age 55; named emeritus General Authority Oct. 2, 2010.

116. GARY JEROME COLEMAN – Born Sept. 18, 1941, in Wenatchee, Chelan Co., Wash., to Benton Joseph Coleman and Evalin Barrett. Called to the Second Quorum of the Seventy June 6, 1992, at age 50 and sustained Oct. 3, 1992; sustained to the First Quorum of the Seventy April 5, 1997; named emeritus General Authority Oct. 1, 2011.

117. JOHN MAX MADSEN – Born April 24, 1939, in Washington, D.C., to Louis L. Madsen and Edith Louise Gundersen. Called to Second Quorum of Seventy June 6, 1992, at age 53, and sustained Oct. 3, 1992; sustained to First Quorum April 5, 1997; named emeritus General Authority Oct. 3, 2009.

118. WM. ROLFE KERR - Born June 29, 1935, in Tremonton, Box Elder Co., Utah , to Clifton G.M. Kerr and Irene Pack. Sustained to the Second Quorum of the Seventy April 6, 1996, at age 60; sustained to the First Quorum of the Seventy April 5, 1997; named emeritus General Authority Oct. 6, 2007.

119. CARL BARTON PRATT – Born Oct. 30, 1941, in Monterrey, Mexico, to Carl Barton Pratt and LaVern Whetten. Sustained to the First Quorum of the Seventy April 5, 1997, at age 55; named emeritus General Authority Oct. 1, 2011.

120. SHELDON FAY CHILD - Born May 8, 1938, in Ogden, Weber Co., Utah, to Mark Fay Child and Viola Criddle. Sustained to the Second Quorum of the Seventy April 6, 1996, at age 57; sustained to the First Quorum of the Seventy April 5, 1998; named emeritus General Authority Oct. 4, 2008.

121. QUENTIN LAMAR COOK - See current QUORUM OF THE TWELVE.

122. FRANCISCO JOSE VINAS - See current FIRST QUORUM OF THE SEVENTY.

123. LANCE BRADLEY WICKMAN – Born Nov. 11, 1940, in Seattle, King Co., Wash., to Alton C. Wickman and Irene Marilyn Carlson. Sustained to the Second Quorum of the Seventy April 2, 1994, at age 53; sustained to the First Quorum of the Seventy April 1, 2000; named emeritus General Authority Oct. 2, 2010.

124. LYNN GRANT ROBBINS – See current FIRST QUORUM OF THE SEVENTY.

125. DONALD LARRY HALLSTROM – See current PRESIDENCY OF THE SEVENTY.

126. RONALD A RASBAND - See current PRESIDENCY OF THE SEVENTY.

127. CLAUDIO ROBERTO MENDEZ COSTA - See current FIRST QUORUM OF THE SEVENTY.

128. RICHARD JOHN MAYNES – See current FIRST QUORUM OF THE SEVENTY.

129. LYNDON WHITNEY CLAYTON - See current PRESIDENCY OF THE SEVENTY.

130. CHRISTOFFEL GOLDEN JR. – See current FIRST QUORUM OF THE SEVENTY.

131. WALTER FERMIN GONZALEZ - See current PRESIDENCY OF THE SEVENTY.

132. STEVEN ERASTUS SNOW – See current PRESIDENCY OF THE SEVENTY.

133. BRUCE DOUGLAS PORTER - See current FIRST QUORUM OF THE SEVENTY.

134. BENJAMIN DE HOYOS - See current FIRST QUORUM OF THE SEVENTY.

135. DAVID FREWIN EVANS - See current FIRST QUORUM OF THE SEVENTY.

136. CECIL SCOTT GROW - See current FIRST QUORUM OF THE SEVENTY.

137. RICHARD GORDON HINCKLEY - Born May 2, 1941, in Salt Lake City, Salt Lake Co., Utah, to Gordon Bitner Hinckley and Marjorie Pay. Sustained to the First Quorum of the Seventy April 2, 2005, at age 63; named emeritus General Authority Oct. 1, 2011.

138. PAUL VERE JOHNSON - See current FIRST QUORUM OF THE SEVENTY.

139. PAUL EDWARD KOELLIKER - See current FIRST QUORUM OF THE SEVENTY.

140. PAUL BOWEN PIEPER - See current FIRST QUORUM OF THE SEVENTY.

141. ULISSES SOARES - See current FIRST QUORUM OF THE SEVENTY.

142. KEITH KARLTON HILBIG - See current FIRST QUORUM OF THE SEVENTY.

143. DAVID STEWARD BAXTER - See current FIRST QUORUM OF THE SEVENTY.

144. SHAYNE MARTELL BOWEN - See current FIRST QUORUM OF THE SEVENTY.

145. DANIEL LEROY JOHNSON - See current FIRST QUORUM OF THE SEVENTY.

146. MARCUS BELL NASH - See current FIRST QUORUM OF THE SEVENTY.

147. ANTHONY DUANE PERKINS - See current FIRST QUORUM OF THE SEVENTY.

148. ENRIQUE RIENZI SALVATORE FALABELLA - See current FIRST QUORUM OF THE SEVENTY.

149. ERICH WILLI HORST KOPISCHKE - See current FIRST QUORUM OF THE SEVENTY.

150. MICHAEL JOHN UY TEH - See current FIRST QUORUM OF THE SEVENTY.

151. OCTAVIANO TENORIO - See current FIRST QUORUM OF THE SEVENTY.

152. CLAUDIO DANIEL ZIVIC - See current FIRST QUORUM OF THE SEVENTY.

153. CRAIG CLOWARD CHRISTENSEN - See current FIRST QUORUM OF THE SEVENTY

154. WILLIAM RUSSELL WALKER – See current FIRST QUORUM OF THE SEVENTY

155. MARCUS ANTONY AIDUKAITIS - See current FIRST QUORUM OF THE SEVENTY.

156. GÉRALD JEAN CAUSSÉ - See current FIRST QUORUM OF THE SEVENTY.

157. LAWRENCE EDWARD CORBRIDGE - See current FIRST QUORUM OF THE SEVENTY.

158. EDUARDO GAVARRET – See current FIRST QUORUM OF THE SEVENTY.

159. CARLOS AUGUSTO GODOY – See current FIRST QUORUM OF THE SEVENTY.

160. JAMES JOSEPH HAMULA – See current FIRST QUORUM OF THE SEVENTY.

161. ALLAN FORREST PACKER – See current FIRST QUORUM OF THE SEVENTY.

162. KEVIN WAYNE PEARSON – See current FIRST QUORUM OF THE SEVENTY.

163. RAFAEL EDUARDO PINO – See current FIRST QUORUM OF THE SEVENTY.

164. GARY EVAN STEVENSON – See current FIRST QUORUM OF THE SEVENTY.

165. JOSÉ AUGUSTO TEIXEIRA – See current FIRST QUORUM OF THE SEVENTY.

166. FRANK MICHAEL WATSON – See current FIRST QUORUM OF THE SEVENTY.

167. JORGE FERNANDO ZEBALLOS – See current FIRST QUORUM OF THE SEVENTY.

168. MERVYN BENNION ARNOLD – See current FIRST QUORUM OF THE SEVENTY.

169. YOON HWAN CHOI – See current FIRST QUORUM OF THE SEVENTY.

170. BRENT HATCH NIELSON – See current FIRST QUORUM OF THE SEVENTY.

171. DALE GUNNAR RENLUND – See current FIRST QUORUM OF THE SEVENTY.

172. MICHAEL TALLY RINGWOOD – See current FIRST QUORUM OF THE SEVENTY.

173. JOSEPH WAFULA SITATI – See current FIRST QUORUM OF THE SEVENTY.

174. KEVIN READ DUNCAN – See current FIRST QUORUM OF THE SEVENTY.

175. GERRIT WALTER GONG – See current FIRST QUORUM OF THE SEVENTY.

176. PATRICK ROBERT DAVID KEARNON – See current FIRST QUORUM OF THE SEVENTY.

177. JUAN ALBERTO UCEDA – See current FIRST QUORUM OF THE SEVENTY.

178. JOSÉ LUIS ALONSO – See current FIRST QUORUM OF THE SEVENTY.

179. IAN SIDNEY ARDERN – See current FIRST QUORUM OF THE SEVENTY.

180. DON RAY CLARKE – See current FIRST QUORUM OF THE SEVENTY.

181. CARL BERT COOK – See current FIRST QUORUM OF THE SEVENTY.

182. LE GRAND RAINE CURTIS JR. – See current FIRST QUORUM OF THE SEVENTY.

183. WAYNE CHRISTOPHER WADDELL – See current FIRST QUORUM OF THE SEVENTY.

184. KAZUHIKO YAMASHITA – See current FIRST QUORUM OF THE SEVENTY.

SECOND QUORUM OF THE SEVENTY

The Second Quorum of the Seventy was created April 1, 1989, in response to the "continued rapid growth of the Church." (Church News, April 8, 1989.)

The initial members of the Second Quorum were those General Authorities serving under a five-year call (called from April 1984 to October 1988) in the First Quorum of the Seventy. General Authorities in the Second Quorum are now generally called for six years.

1. RUSSELL CARL TAYLOR – See FIRST QUORUM OF THE SEVENTY, No. 55.

2. ROBERT B HARBERTSON – See FIRST QUORUM OF THE SEVENTY, No. 56.

3. DEVERE HARRIS – See FIRST QUORUM OF THE SEVENTY, No. 57.

4. SPENCER HAMLIN OSBORN – See FIRST QUORUM OF THE SEVENTY, No. 58.

5. PHILIP TADJE SONNTAG – See FIRST QUORUM OF THE SEVENTY, No. 59.

6. JOHN SONNENBERG – See FIRST QUORUM OF THE SEVENTY, No. 60.

7. FERRIL ARTHUR KAY – See FIRST QUORUM OF THE SEVENTY, No. 61.

8. KEITH WILSON WILCOX – See FIRST QUORUM OF THE SEVENTY, No. 62.

9. WALDO PRATT CALL – See FIRST QUORUM OF THE SEVENTY, No. 67.

10. HELIO DA ROCHA CAMARGO – See FIRST QUORUM OF THE SEVENTY, No. 68.

11. HANS VERLAN ANDERSEN – See FIRST QUORUM OF THE SEVENTY, No. 69.

12. GEORGE IVINS CANNON – See FIRST QUORUM OF THE SEVENTY, No. 70.

13. FRANCIS MARION GIBBONS – See FIRST QUORUM OF THE SEVENTY, No. 71.

14. GARDNER HALE RUSSELL – See FIRST QUORUM OF THE SEVENTY, No. 72.

15. GEORGE RICHARD HILL III – See FIRST QUORUM OF THE SEVENTY, No. 73.

16. JOHN ROGER LASATER – See FIRST QUORUM OF THE SEVENTY, No. 74.

17. DOUGLAS JAMES MARTIN – See FIRST QUORUM OF THE SEVENTY, No. 75.

18. ALEXANDER BAILLIE MORRISON – See FIRST QUORUM OF THE SEVENTY, No. 76.

19. LLOYD ALDIN PORTER – See PRESIDENCY OF THE SEVENTY, NO. 26.

20. GLEN LARKIN RUDD – See FIRST QUORUM OF THE SEVENTY, No. 78.

21. DOUGLAS HILL SMITH – See FIRST QUORUM OF THE SEVENTY, No. 79.

22. LYNN ANDREW SORENSEN – See FIRST QUORUM OF THE SEVENTY, No. 80.

23. ROBERT EDWARD SACKLEY – See FIRST QUORUM OF THE SEVENTY, No. 81.

24. LARRY LIONEL KENDRICK – See FIRST QUORUM OF THE SEVENTY, No. 82.

25. MONTE JAMES BROUGH – See PRESIDENCY OF THE SEVENTY, No. 28.

26. ALBERT CHOULES JR. – See FIRST QUORUM OF THE SEVENTY, No. 84.

27. LLOYD PREAL GEORGE JR. – See FIRST QUORUM OF THE SEVENTY, No. 85.

28. GERALD ELDON MELCHIN – See FIRST QUORUM OF THE SEVENTY, No. 86.

29. CARLOS HUMBERTO AMADO – See current FIRST QUORUM OF THE SEVENTY.

30. BENJAMIN BERRY BANKS – See PRESIDENCY OF THE SEVENTY, No. 36.

31. SPENCER JOEL CONDIE – See FIRST QUORUM OF THE SEVENTY, NO. 95.

32. FLOYD MELVIN HAMMOND - See FIRST QUORUM OF THE SEVENTY, No. 99.

33. MALCOLM SETH JEPPSEN – Born Nov. 1, 1924, in Mantua, Box Elder Co., Utah, to Conrad Jeppsen and Laurine Nielsen. Sustained to the Second Quorum of the Seventy April 1, 1989, at age 64; released Oct. 1, 1994.

34. RICHARD POWELL LINDSAY – Born March 18, 1926, in Salt Lake City, Salt Lake Co., Utah, to Samuel Bennion Lindsay and Mary Alice Powell. Sustained to the Second Quorum of the Seventy April 1, 1989, at age 63; released Oct. 1, 1994 ; died June

4, 2010, in Salt Lake City, Salt Lake Co., Utah, at age 84.

35. MERLIN REX LYBBERT – Born Jan. 31, 1926, in Cardston, Alberta, Canada, to Charles Lester Lybbert and Delvia Reed. Sustained to the Second Quorum of the Seventy April 1, 1989, at age 63; released Oct. 1, 1994; died July 6, 2001, at Salt Lake City, Salt Lake Co., Utah, at age 75.

36. HORACIO ANTONIO TENORIO – Born March 6, 1935, in Mexico City, Distrito Federal, Mexico, to Leopoldo Horacio Tenorio and Blanca Otilia Oriza Arenas. Sustained to the Second Quorum of the Seventy April 1, 1989, at age 54; released Oct. 1, 1994.

37. EDUARDO AYALA – Born May 3, 1937, in Coronel, Chile, to Magdonio Ayala and Maria Aburto. Sustained to the Second Quorum of the Seventy March 31, 1990, at age 52; released Sept. 30, 1995.

38. LEGRAND RAINE CURTIS SR. – Born May 22, 1924, in Salt Lake City, Salt Lake Co., Utah, to Alexander R. Curtis and Genevieve Raine. Sustained to the Second Quorum of the Seventy March 31, 1990, at age 66; released Sept. 30, 1995; died Dec. 19, 2010, at Cottonwood Heights, Salt Lake Co., Utah, at age 86.

39. CLINTON LOUIS CUTLER – Born Dec. 27, 1929, in Salt Lake City, Salt Lake Co., Utah, to Benjamin Lewis Cutler and Hellie Helena Sharp. Sustained to the Second Quorum of the Seventy March 31, 1990, at age 60; died April 9, 1994, at South Jordan, Salt Lake Co., Utah, at age 64.

40. ROBERT KENT DELLENBACH – See FIRST QUORUM OF THE SEVENTY, No. 96.

41. HAROLD GORDON HILLAM - See PRESIDENCY OF THE SEVENTY, No. 31.

42. KENNETH JOHNSON – See FIRST QUORUM OF THE SEVENTY, NO. 100.

43. HELVECIO MARTINS – Born July 27, 1930, in Rio de Janeiro, Brazil, to Honorio Martins and Benedicta Francisca. Sustained to the Second Quorum of the Seventy March 31, 1990, at age 59; released Sept. 30, 1995, died May 14, 2005.

44. LYNN ALVIN MICKELSEN – See FIRST QUORUM OF THE SEVENTY, No. 101.

45. J BALLARD WASHBURN – Born Jan. 18, 1929, in Blanding, San Juan Co., Utah, to Alvin Lavell Washburn and Wasel Black. Sustained to the Second Quorum of the Seventy March 31, 1990, at age 61; released Sept. 30, 1995.

46. DURREL ARDEN WOOLSEY – Born June 12, 1926, at Escalante, Garfield Co., Utah, to Willis A. Woolsey and Ruby Riddle. Sustained to the Second Quorum of the Seventy March 31, 1990, at age 63; released Sept. 30, 1995.

47. RULON GERALD CRAVEN – Born Nov. 11, 1924, in Murray, Salt Lake Co., Utah, to Gerald and Susie Craven. Called to the Second Quorum of the Seventy Dec. 5, 1990, at age 66, and sustained April 6, 1991; released Oct. 5, 1996.

48. WILLIAM MCKENZIE LAWRENCE – Born Oct. 28, 1926, in Salt Lake City, Salt Lake Co., Utah, to Richard Sterling Lawrence and Thelma McKenzie. Called to the Second Quorum of the Seventy Jan. 1, 1991, at age 64, and sustained April 6, 1991; released Oct. 5, 1996.

49. JULIO ENRIQUE DAVILA – Born
May 23, 1932, in Bucaramunga,
Colombia, to Julio E. Davila
Villamicar and Rita Penalosa de
Davila. Sustained to the Second
Quorum of the Seventy April 6,
1991, at age 58; released Oct. 5,
1996.

50. GRAHAM WATSON DOXEY –
Born March 30, 1927, in Salt
Lake City, Salt Lake Co., Utah,
to Graham H. Doxey and Leone
Watson. Sustained to the Second
Quorum of the Seventy April 6,
1991, at age 64; released Oct. 5,
1996.

51. CREE-L KOFFORD - See FIRST QUORUM OF
THE SEVENTY, No. 104.

52. JOSEPH CARL MUREN – Born
Feb. 5, 1936, in Richmond,
Contra Costa Co., California, to
Joseph S. Muren and Alba Maria
Cairo. Sustained to the Second
Quorum of the Seventy April 6,
1991, at age 55; released Oct. 5,
1996; died July 27, 2009, at
Layton, Davis Co., Utah, at age 73.

53. DENNIS BRAMWELL NEUENSCHWANDER - See
PRESIDENCY OF THE SEVENTY, No. 37.

54. JORGE ALFONSO ROJAS – Born
Sept. 27, 1940, in Delicias,
Chihuahua, Mexico, to Rodolfo
Rojas and Hilaria Ornelas.
Sustained to the Second Quorum
of the Seventy April 6, 1991, at
age 50; released Oct. 5, 1996.

55. HAN IN SANG – Born Dec. 10,
1938, in Seoul, Korea, to Han
Chang Soo and Lee Do Ho.
Called to the Second Quorum of
the Seventy June 1, 1991, at age
52, and sustained Oct. 5, 1991;
released Oct. 5, 1996.

56. STEPHEN DOUGLAS NADAULD –
Born May 31, 1942, in Idaho
Falls, Bonneville Co., Idaho, to
Sterling Dwaine Nadauld and
Lois Madsen. Called to the
Second Quorum of the Seventy

June 1, 1991, at age 49, and sustained Oct. 5, 1991;
released Oct. 5, 1996.

57. SAM KOYEI SHIMABUKURO –
Born June 7, 1925, in Waipahu,
Honolulu Co., Oahu, Hawaii, to
Kame Shimabukuro and Ushi
Nakasone. Called to the Second
Quorum of the Seventy July 13,
1991, at age 66, and sustained
Oct. 5, 1991; released Oct. 5,
1996.

58. LINO ALVAREZ – Born July 18,
1944, in Arteaga, Coahuila,
Mexico, to Lino Alvarez and
Margarita Vasquez. Called to the
Second Quorum of the Seventy
June 6, 1992, at age 47, and
sustained Oct. 3, 1992; released
Oct. 4, 1997.

59. DALLAS NIELSEN ARCHIBALD – See FIRST
QUORUM OF THE SEVENTY, No. 113.

60. MERRILL JOSEPH BATEMAN - See PRESIDENCY
OF THE SEVENTY, No. 41.

61. CHELLUS MAX CALDWELL –
Born Dec. 4, 1933, in Salt Lake
City, Salt Lake Co., to Chellus M.
and Electa J. Caldwell. Called to
the Second Quorum of the
Seventy June 6, 1992, at age 58,
and sustained Oct. 3, 1992;
released Oct. 4, 1997.

62. GARY JEROME COLEMAN – See current FIRST
QUORUM OF THE SEVENTY, No. 116.

63. JOHN BAIRD DICKSON – See current FIRST
QUORUM OF THE SEVENTY.

64. JOHN EMERSON FOWLER –
Born Nov. 10, 1944, in Redding,
Shasta Co., California, to R.
Walter Fowler and Lois Manita
Clayton. Called to the Second
Quorum of the Seventy June 6,
1992, at age 47, and sustained
Oct. 3, 1992; released Oct. 4,
1997.

65. JAY EDWIN JENSEN – See current PRESIDENCY
OF THE SEVENTY.

66. AUGUSTO ALANDY LIM – Born May 4, 1934, in Santa Cruz, Philippines, to Leon B. Lim and Beatriz R. Alandy. Called to the Second Quorum of the Seventy June 6, 1992, at age 58, and sustained Oct. 3, 1992; released Oct. 4, 1997.

67. JOHN MAX MADSEN – See FIRST QUORUM OF THE SEVENTY, No. 117.

68. VICTOR DALLAS MERRELL – Born Jan. 25, 1936, in Basalt, Bingham Co., Idaho, to Victor Lybbert Merrell and Beatrice Jensen. Called to the Second Quorum of the Seventy June 6, 1992, at age 56, and sustained Oct. 3, 1992; released Oct. 4, 1997.

69. DAVID EUGENE SORENSEN – See PRESIDENCY OF THE SEVENTY, No. 35.

70. FRANK DAVID STANLEY – Born Sept. 11, 1935, in Salt Lake City, Salt Lake Co., Utah, to O. Frank Stanley and Winifred Parker. Called to the Second Quorum of the Seventy June 6, 1992, at age 56, and sustained Oct. 3, 1992; released Oct. 4, 1997.

71. KWOK YUEN TAI – Born June 30, 1941, in Hong Kong, to Lung Hing Tai and Yau Yin Chu. Sustained to the Second Quorum of the Seventy June 6, 1992, at age 50, and sustained Oct. 3, 1992; released Oct. 4, 1997.

72. LOWELL DALE WOOD – Born Jan. 23, 1933, in Cardston, Alberta, Canada, to Wm. Dale Wood and Donna Wolf. Called to the Second Quorum of the Seventy June 6, 1992, at age 59, and sustained Oct. 3, 1992; died March 7, 1997, in Apia, Samoa, at age 64.

73. CLAUDIO ROBERTO MENDES COSTA – See current FIRST QUORUM OF THE SEVENTY.

74. WILLIAM DON LADD – Born July 14, 1933, in San Mateo, Putnam Co., Fla., to Joseph Donald Ladd and Phyllis Rose Anderson. Sustained to the Second Quorum of the Seventy April 2, 1994, at age 60; released Oct. 7, 2000; died Oct. 6, 2009, in Snellville, Gwinnett Co., Ga., at age 76.

75. JAMES OSTERMANN MASON – Born June 19, 1930, in Salt Lake City, Salt Lake Co., Utah, to A. Stanton Mason and Neoma Thorup. Sustained to the Second Quorum of the Seventy April 2, 1994, at age 63; released Oct. 7, 2000.

76. DIETER FRIEDRICH UCHTDORF - See current FIRST PRESIDENCY.

77. LANCE BRADLEY WICKMAN – See FIRST QUORUM OF THE SEVENTY, NO. 123.

78. BRUCE DOUGLAS PORTER - See current FIRST QUORUM OF THE SEVENTY.

79. LOWELL EDWARD BROWN – Born June 18, 1937, In P reston, Franklin Co., Idaho, to Lowell Brown and Helen Peterson. Sustained to the Second Quorum of the Seventy April 6, 1996, at age 58; released Oct. 5, 2002.

80. SHELDON FAY CHILD - See FIRST QUORUM OF THE SEVENTY, No. 120.

81. QUENTIN LAMAR COOK – See current QUORUM OF THE TWELVE.

82. WM. ROLFE KERR - See FIRST QUORUM OF THE SEVENTY, No. 118.

83. DENNIS ERICKSEN SIMMONS – Born June 27, 1934, in Beaver Dam, Box Elder Co., Utah, to Thomas Yates Simmons and Sylvia Ericksen. Sustained to the Second Quorum of the Seventy April 6, 1996, at age 61; released Oct. 1, 2005.

84. JERALD LYNN TAYLOR – Born March 22, 1937, in Colonia Dublan, Mexico, to Loren LeRoy Taylor and Lillian Hatch. Sustained to the Second Quorum of the Seventy April 6, 1996, at age 59; released Oct. 5, 2002.

85. FRANCISCO JOSE VINAS – See current FIRST QUORUM OF THE SEVENTY.

86. RICHARD BITNER WIRTHLIN – Born March 15, 1931, in Salt Lake City, Salt Lake Co., Utah, to Joseph L. Wirthlin and Madeline Bitner. Sustained to the Second Quorum of the Seventy April 6, 1996, at age 65; released Oct. 6, 2001; died March 16, 2011, at Holladay, Salt Lake Co., Utah, at age 80.

87. RICHARD DAVID ALLRED – Born Aug. 3, 1932, in Salt Lake City, Salt Lake Co., Utah, to Elwood B. Allred and Glendora Malcom. Sustained to the Second Quorum of the Seventy April 5, 1997, at age 64; released Oct. 5, 2002.

88. ERAN ABEGG CALL – Born Dec. 2, 1929, in Colonia Dublan, Mexico, to Anson Bowen Call and Julie Sarah Abegg. Sustained to the Second Quorum of the Seventy April 5, 1997, at age 67; released Oct. 7, 2000.

89. RICHARD ERNEST COOK – Born Sept. 7, 1930, in Pleasant Grove, Utah Co., Utah, to Ernest William Cook and Clara Blackhurst. Sustained to the Second Quorum of the Seventy April 5, 1997, at age 66; released Oct. 6, 2001.

90. DUANE BIRD GERRARD - Born April 22, 1938, in Murray, Salt Lake Co., Utah, to Leonard Gerrard and Mildred Bird. Sustained to Second Quorum of the Seventy April 5, 1997, at age 58; released Oct. 4, 2003.

91. WAYNE MITCHELL HANCOCK – Born July 16, 1931, in Safford, Graham Co., Ariz., to Wayne M.P. Hancock and Phyllis Lines. Sustained to the Second Quorum of the Seventy April 5, 1997, at age 65; released Oct. 6, 2001.

92. JOSEPH KENT JOLLEY - Born Dec. 30, 1933, in Rexburg, Madison Co., Idaho, to William Afton Jolley and Mildred Mangum. Sustained to Second Quorum of the Seventy April 5, 1997, at age 63; released Oct. 4, 2003.

93. RICHARD JOHN MAYNES – See current FIRST QUORUM OF THE SEVENTY.

94. DALE EMERSON MILLER – Born April 2, 1936, in Los Angeles, Los Angeles Co., Calif., to Wade Elliott Miller and Romania Davis. Sustained to the Second Quorum of the Seventy April 5, 1997, at age 61; released Sept. 30, 2006.

95. LYNN GRANT ROBBINS – See current FIRST QUORUM OF THE SEVENTY.

96. DONALD LAFAYETTE STAHELI – Born Oct.19, 1931, in St. George, Washington Co., Utah, to Lafayette Staheli and Grace Sullivan. Sustained to the Second Quorum of the Seventy April 5, 1997, at age 65; released Sept. 30, 2006 ; died May 29, 2010, in St. George, Washington Co., Utah, at age 78.

97. RICHARD EYRING TURLEY SR. – Born Dec. 29, 1930, in El Paso, El Paso Co., Texas, to Edward Vernon Turley and Winifred Louise Roche. Sustained to the Second Quorum of the Seventy April 5, 1997, at age 66; released Oct. 7, 2000.

98. ATHOS MARQUES AMORIM – Born June 14, 1932, in Rio de Janeiro, Brazil, to Antonio Marques Amorim and Maria Carlota Martins Ferreira. Sustained to the Second Quorum

of the Seventy April 4, 1998, at age 65; released Oct. 5, 2002.

99. E RAY BATEMAN - Born Oct. 20, 1937, in Sandy, Salt Lake Co., Utah, to Marlon Samuel Bateman and Mary Armstrong. Sustained to the Second Quorum of the Seventy April 4, 1998, at age 60; released Oct. 2, 2004.

100. VAL RIGBY CHRISTENSEN - Born Sept. 27, 1935, in Hooper, Weber Co., Utah, to Leonard Christensen and Jennie Lowe Rigby. Sustained to the Second Quorum of the Seventy April 4, 1998, at age 62; released Oct. 2, 2004.

101. RONALD TOMLINSON HALVERSON - Born Dec. 18, 1936, in Ogden, Weber Co., Utah, to Marlow Halverson and Hilda Tomlinson. Sustained to the Second Quorum of the Seventy April 4, 1998, at age 61; released Sept. 30, 2006.

102. EARL MERRILL MONSON - Born July 26, 1932, in Salt Lake City, Salt Lake Co., Utah, to Charles Horald Monson and Ortencia Hendricks Merrill. Sustained to the Second Quorum of the Seventy April 4, 1998, at age 65; released Oct. 5, 2002.

103. MERRILL CLAYTON OAKS - Born Jan. 12, 1936, in Twin Falls, Twin Falls Co., Idaho, to Lloyd E. Oaks and Stella Harris. Sustained to the Second Quorum of the Seventy April 4, 1998, at age 62; released Oct. 2, 2004.

104. HORACE BRYAN RICHARDS - Born March 18, 1934, in Salt Lake City, Salt Lake Co., Utah, to Horace B. Richards and LynnAnne Taylor. Sustained to the Second Quorum of the Seventy April 4, 1998, at age 64; released Sept. 30, 2006.

105. NED BARDEANE ROUECHE - Born Aug. 5, 1934, in Salt Lake City, Salt Lake Co., to Leonard C. Roueche and Ruth Lee. Sustained to the Second Quorum of the Seventy April 4, 1998, at age 63; released Oct. 1, 2005.

106. DON LEE TOBLER - Born July 25, 1933, in Provo, Utah Co., Utah, to Donald Tobler and Louise Shoell. Sustained to Second Quorum of the Seventy April 4, 1998, at age 64; released Oct. 4, 2003.

107. GORDON TAYLOR WATTS - Born Feb. 23, 1935, in South Weber, Davis Co., Utah, to Elwood Taylor Watts and Edna Davis. Sustained to the Second Quorum of the Seventy April 4, 1998, at age 63; released Oct. 2, 2004.

108. STEPHEN ALLAN WEST - Born March 23, 1935, in Salt Lake City, Salt Lake Co., Utah, to Allan Morrell West and Ferne Page. Sustained to the Second Quorum of the Seventy April 4, 1998, at age 63; released Oct. 2, 2004.

109. ROBERT JAY WHETTEN - Born April 12, 1943, in Chuichupa, Chihuahua, Mexico, to Glen A. Whetten and Ada May Judd. Sustained to the Second Quorum of the Seventy April 4, 1998, at age 54; released Sept. 30, 2006.

110. RAPHAEL HUNTER WOOD - Born July 11, 1931, in Salt Lake City, Salt Lake Co., Utah, to Ray G. Wood and Mary Hunter. Sustained to the Second Quorum of the Seventy April 4, 1998, at age 66; released Oct. 6, 2001.

111. ADHEMAR DAMIANI – Born Dec. 18, 1939, in Sao Paulo, Sao Paulo State, Brazil, to Antonio and Maria Damiani. Sustained to the Second Quorum of the Seventy April 3, 1999, at age 59; released Oct. 1, 2005.

112. STEPHEN BERG OVESON – Born July 9, 1936, in Grass Valley, Sherman Co., Ore., to Merrill M. Oveson and Mal Berg. Sustained to the Second Quorum of the Seventy April 3, 1999, at age 62; released Oct. 1, 2005.

113. DAVID RODGER STONE – Born June 16, 1936, in Buenos Aires, Argentina, to Hubert J. Stone and Ethel R. Grant. Sustained to the Second Quorum of the Seventy April 3, 1999, at age 62; released Sept. 30, 2006.

114. HARVEY BRUCE STUCKI – Born Dec. 1, 1937, in St. George, Washington Co., Utah, to Harvey Stucki and Anna Hilda Wittwer. Sustained to the Second Quorum of the Seventy April 3, 1999, at age 61; released Sept. 30, 2006.

115. RICHARD HENRY WINKEL – Born May 17, 1942, in Oakland, Almeda Co., Calif., to Francis Benjamin Winkel and Karen Hart. Sustained to the Second Quorum of the Seventy April 3, 1999, at age 56; released Sept. 30, 2006.

116. ROBERT STEPHEN WOOD – Born Dec. 25, 1936, in Idaho Falls, Bonneville Co., Idaho, to John Albert (Jack) Wood and Blanche Wood. Sustained to the Second Quorum of the Seventy April 3, 1999, at age 62, released Oct. 3, 2009.

117. DOUGLAS LANE CALLISTER – Born Feb. 17, 1939, in Glendale, Los Angeles Co., Calif., to Reed Eddington Callister and Norinne Richards. Sustained to the Second

Quorum of the Seventy April 1, 2000, at age 61; released Oct. 3, 2009.

118. DARWIN B. CHRISTENSON – Born Aug. 11, 1935, in Firth, Bingham Co., Idaho, to Lars H. Christenson and Olive Brough. Sustained to the Second Quorum of the Seventy April 1, 2000, at age 64; released Oct. 1, 2005.

119. KEITH CROCKETT - Born Jan. 15, 1934, in Pima, Graham Co., Ariz., to Wilford Woodruff Crockett III and Jacy Boggs. Sustained to the Second Quorum of the Seventy April 1, 2000, at age 66; released Oct. 2, 2004.

120. HIMAN ALDRIDGE GILLESPIE – Born May 22, 1935, in Riverside, Riverside Co., Calif., to Lionel Aldridge Gillespie and Amelia Eileen Baird. Sustained to the Second Quorum of the Seventy April 1, 2000, at age 64; released Oct. 1, 2005.

121. ROBERT CHARLES OAKS – See PRESIDENCY OF THE SEVENTY, No.43.

122. KEITH KARLTON HILBIG – See current FIRST QUORUM OF THE SEVENTY.

123. ROBERT FRANK ORTON – Born Aug. 24, 1936, in Reno, Washoe Co., Nev., to H. Frank Orton and Gwen Riggs. Sustained to the Second Quorum of the Seventy March 31, 2001, at age 64; released Oct. 6, 2007.

124. WAYNE SKEEN PETERSON – Born Oct. 6, 1939, in Ogden, Weber Co., Utah, to Rulon P. Peterson and Naomi Skeen. Sustained to the Second Quorum of the Seventy March 31, 2001, at age 61; released Oct. 6, 2007.

125. RALPH CONRAD SCHULTZ – Born March 11, 1938, in North Bend, Coos Co., Ore., to Ralph C. Schultz and Dorothy Bushong. Sustained to the Second Quorum of the Seventy March 31, 2001, at age 63;

released Oct. 6, 2007.

126. ROBERT RICKY STEUER - Born Dec. 6, 1943, in Milwaukee, Milwaukee Co., Wisc., to Fritz Steuer and Hulda Hanel. Sustained to the Second Quorum of the Seventy March 31, 2001, at age 57; released Oct. 4, 2008.

127. HARLEY ROSS WORKMAN – Born Dec. 31, 1940, in Salt Lake City, Salt Lake Co., Utah, to Harley Workman and Lucille Ramsey. Sustained to the Second Quorum of the Seventy March 31, 2001, at age 60; released Oct. 6, 2007.

128. GERALD NIELS LUND - Born Sept. 12, 1939, in Fountain Green, Sanpete Co., Utah, to Jewell G. Lund and Evelyn Mortensen. Sustained to the Second Quorum of the Seventy April 6, 2002, at age 62; released Oct. 4, 2008.

129. WILLIAM RUSSELL WALKER – See current FIRST QUORUM OF THE SEVENTY.

130. CRAIG CLOWARD CHRISTENSEN – See current FIRST QUORUM OF THE SEVENTY.

131. JAMES MEYERS DUNN – Born April 16, 1940, in Pocatello, Bannock Co., Idaho, to Bill E. Dunn and Melba Meyers. Sustained to the Second Quorum of the Seventy Oct. 5, 2002, at age 62; released Oct. 3, 2009.

132. DONALD REX GERRATT – Born April 9, 1936, in Heyburn, Minidoka Co., Idaho., to Donald Wayne Gerratt and Ann Bailey. Sustained to the Second Quorum of the Seventy Oct. 5, 2002, at age 66; released Oct. 6, 2007.

133. DARYL HODGES GARN – Born Dec. 28, 1938, in Tremonton, Box Elder Co., Utah, to Uel A. Garn and Lolita Hodges. Sustained to the Second Quorum of the Seventy Oct. 5, 2002, at age 63; released Oct. 3, 2009.

134. SPENCER VIRGIL JONES – Born Sept. 17, 1945, in Safford, Graham Co., Ariz., to Virgil Worth Jones and Nellie Mae Baker. Sustained to the Second Quorum of the Seventy Oct. 5, 2002, at age 57; released Oct. 2, 2010.

135. MERVYN BENNION ARNOLD – See current FIRST QUORUM OF THE SEVENTY.

136. SHIRLEY DEAN CHRISTENSEN – Born Jan. 8, 1939, in Preston, Franklin Co., Idaho, to LaGrand Christensen and Blanche Naef. Sustained to the Second Quorum of the Seventy April 5, 2003, at age 64; released Oct. 3, 2009.

137. CLATE WHEELER MASK JR. – Born Aug. 20, 1942, in El Paso, El Paso Co., Texas, to Clate W. Mask and Marva Gonzalez. Sustained to the Second Quorum of the Seventy April 5, 2003, at age 60; released Oct. 3, 2009.

138. WILLIAM WATTS PARMLEY – Born Jan. 22, 1936, in Salt Lake City, Salt Lake Co., Utah, to Thomas Jennison Parmley and Martha LaVern Watts. Sustained to the Second Quorum of the Seventy April 5, 2003, at age 67; released Oct. 3, 2009.

139. WILFORD DOUGLAS SHUMWAY – Born May 8, 1940, in St. Johns, Apache Co., Ariz., to Wilford Shumway and Mabel Shumway. Sustained to the Second Quorum of the Seventy April 5, 2003, at age 62; released Oct. 3, 2009.

140. WON YONG KO - Born Oct. 15, 1945, in Pusan, South Korea, to Chang Soo and Sang Soon Lee Kim. Sustained to the Second Quorum of the Seventy April 2, 2005, at age 59; released Oct. 1, 2011.

141. WOLFGANG HEINZ JÜRGEN PAUL - Born Feb. 28, 1940, in Munster, Germany, to Johann Paul and Berta Starbati. Sustained to the Second Quorum of the Seventy April 2, 2005; released Oct. 2, 2010.

142. LOWELL MILLER SNOW - Born Jan. 2, 1944, in St. George, Washington Co., Utah, to Rulon Snow and Marian Miller. Sustained to the Second Quorum of the Seventy April 2, 2005, at age 61; released Oct. 1, 2011.

143. PAUL KAY SYBROWSKY - Born Aug. 22, 1944, in Salt Lake City, Salt Lake Co., Utah, to Paul H. and Betty Ann Sybrowsky. Sustained to the Second Quorum of the Seventy April 2, 2005, at age 60; released Oct. 1, 2011.

144. CRAIG ALLEN CARDON - See current SECOND QUORUM OF THE SEVENTY.

145. DON RAY CLARKE - See current FIRST QUORUM OF THE SEVENTY.

146. KEITH REID EDWARDS - See current FIRST QUORUM OF THE SEVENTY.

147. STANLEY GARELD ELLIS - See current SECOND QUORUM OF THE SEVENTY.

148. LARRY WAYNE GIBBONS - See current SECOND QUORUM OF THE SEVENTY.

149. TAD RICHARDS CALLISTER - See current PRESIDENCY OF THE SEVENTY.

150. KENT DEE WATSON - See current SECOND QUORUM OF THE SEVENTY.

151. WILFORD WAYNE ANDERSEN – See current SECOND QUORUM OF THE SEVENTY.

152. KOICHI AOYAGI – See current SECOND QUORUM OF THE SEVENTY.

153. BRUCE ALLEN CARLSON – See current SECOND QUORUM OF THE SEVENTY.

154. BRADLEY DUANE FOSTER – See current SECOND QUORUM OF THE SEVENTY.

155. JAMES BOYD MARTINO – See current SECOND QUORUM OF THE SEVENTY.

156. KENT FARNSWORTH RICHARDS – See current SECOND QUORUM OF THE SEVENTY.

157. GREGORY ALLAN SCHWITZER – See current SECOND QUORUM OF THE SEVENTY.

158. LARRY RAY LAWRENCE - See current SECOND QUORUM OF THE SEVENTY.

159. PER GÖSTA MALM - See current SECOND QUORUM OF THE SEVENTY.

160. JAIRO MAZZAGARDI - See current SECOND QUORUM OF THE SEVENTY.

161. RANDALL KAY BENNETT – See current SECOND QUORUM OF THE SEVENTY.

162. JOHN DEVN CORNISH – See current SECOND QUORUM OF THE SEVENTY.

163. OTTO VINCENT HALECK – See current SECOND QUORUM OF THE SEVENTY.

164. LARRY YOUNG WILSON – See current SECOND QUORUM OF THE SEVENTY.

PRESIDING BISHOPS

1. EDWARD PARTRIDGE — Born Aug. 27, 1793, at Pittsfield, Berkshire Co., Massachusetts, to William Partridge and Jemima Bidwell. Called by revelation to be the First Bishop of the Church Feb. 4, 1831, at age 37 (D&C 41:9); died May 27, 1840, at Nauvoo, Hancock Co., Illinois, at age 46.

2. NEWEL KIMBALL WHITNEY — Born Feb. 5, 1795, at Marlborough, Windham Co., Vermont, to Samuel Whitney and Susanna Kimball. Called by revelation to be the First Bishop of Kirtland (D&C 72:8); sustained as First Bishop of the Church Oct. 7, 1844, at age 49; sustained as Presiding Bishop of the Church April 6, 1847; died Sept. 23, 1850, at Salt Lake City, Salt Lake Co., Utah, at age 55.

GEORGE MILLER — Born Nov. 25, 1794, at Orange Co., Virginia, to John Miller and Margaret Pfeiffer. Sustained as Second Bishop of the Church Oct. 7, 1844, at age 49; dropped prior to 1847; disfellowshipped Oct. 20, 1848.

3. EDWARD HUNTER — Born June 22, 1793, at Newton, Delaware Co., Pennsylvania, to Edward Hunter and Hannah Maris. Sustained as Presiding Bishop of the Church April 7, 1851, at age 57; died Oct. 16, 1883, at Salt Lake City, Salt Lake Co., Utah, at age 90.

4. WILLIAM BOWKER PRESTON — Born Nov. 24, 1830, at Halifax, Franklin Co., Virginia, to Christopher Preston and Martha Mitchell Clayton. Sustained as Presiding Bishop of the Church April 6, 1884, at age 53; released due to ill health Dec. 4, 1907; died Aug. 2, 1908, at Salt Lake City, Salt Lake Co., Utah, at age 77.

5. CHARLES WILSON NIBLEY — See SECOND COUNSELORS IN THE FIRST PRESIDENCY, No. 13.

6. SYLVESTER QUAYLE CANNON — See QUORUM OF THE TWELVE, No. 60.

7. LeGrand Richards — See QUORUM OF THE TWELVE, No. 69.

8. JOSEPH LEOPOLD WIRTHLIN — Born Aug. 14, 1893, at Salt Lake City, Salt Lake Co., Utah, to Joseph Wirthlin and Emma Hillstead. Sustained as second counselor to Presiding Bishop LeGrand Richards April 6, 1938, at age 44; sustained as first counselor to Bishop Richards Dec. 12, 1946; sustained as Presiding Bishop of the Church April 6, 1952, at age 58; released Sept. 30, 1961; died Jan. 25, 1963, at Salt Lake City, Salt Lake Co., Utah, at age 69.

9. JOHN HENRY VANDENBERG — Born Dec. 18, 1904, at Ogden, Weber Co., Utah, to Dirk Vandenberg and Maria Alkema. Sustained as Presiding Bishop of the Church Sept. 30, 1961, at age 56; sustained as Assistant to the Quorum of the Twelve Apostles April 6, 1972; sustained to First Quorum of the Seventy Oct. 1, 1976; named emeritus General Authority Dec. 31, 1978; died June 3, 1992, at Sandy, Salt Lake Co., Utah, at age 87.

10. VICTOR LEE BROWN — Born July 31, 1914, at Cardston, Alberta, Canada, to Gerald Stephen Brown and Maggie Calder Lee. Sustained as second counselor to Presiding Bishop John H. Vandenberg Sept. 30, 1961, at age 47; sustained as Presiding Bishop of the Church April 6, 1972; sustained to First Quorum of the Seventy April 6, 1985; named emeritus General Authority Sept. 30, 1989; died March 26, 1996, at Salt Lake City, Salt Lake Co., Utah at age 81.

11. ROBERT DEAN HALES — See current QUORUM OF THE TWELVE.

12. MERRILL JOSEPH BATEMAN — See PRESIDENCY OF THE SEVENTY, No. 41.

13. HAROLD DAVID BURTON — See current PRESIDING BISHOPRIC.

FIRST COUNSELORS TO PRESIDING BISHOPS

1. ISAAC MORLEY – Born March 11, 1786, at Montague, Hampshire Co., Massachusetts, to Thomas Morley and Editha Marsh. Set apart as first counselor to Presiding Bishop Edward Partridge June 6, 1831, at age 45; released at the death of Bishop Partridge May 27, 1840; died June 24, 1865, at Fairview, Sanpete Co., Utah, at age 79.

2. LEONARD WILFORD HARDY – Born Dec. 31, 1805, at Bradford, Essex Co., Massachusetts, to Simon Hardy and Rhoda Hardy. Sustained as first counselor to Presiding Bishop Edward Hunter Oct. 6, 1856, at age 50; died July 31, 1884, at Salt Lake City, Salt Lake Co., Utah, at age 78.

3. ROBERT TAYLOR BURTON – Born Oct. 25, 1821, at Amhertsburg, Ontario, Canada, to Samuel Burton and Hannah Shipley. Sustained as second counselor to Presiding Bishop Edward Hunter Oct. 9, 1874, at age 52; sustained as first counselor to Presiding Bishop William B. Preston Oct. 5, 1884; died Nov. 11, 1907, at Salt Lake City, Salt Lake Co., Utah, at age 86.

4. ORRIN PORTER MILLER – Born Sept. 11, 1858, at Mill Creek, Salt Lake Co., Utah, to Reuben G. Miller and Ann Craynor. Sustained as second counselor to Presiding Bishop William B. Preston Oct. 24, 1901, at age 43; sustained as first counselor to Presiding Bishop Charles W. Nibley Dec. 4, 1907, at age 49; died July 7, 1918, at Salt Lake City, Salt Lake Co., Utah at age 59.

5. DAVID ASAEL SMITH – Born May 24, 1879, at Salt Lake City, Salt Lake Co., Utah, to Joseph Fielding Smith and Julina Lambson. Sustained as second counselor to Presiding Bishop Charles W. Nibley Dec. 4, 1907, at age 28; sustained as first counselor to Bishop Nibley July 18, 1918; sustained as first counselor to Presiding Bishop Sylvester Q. Cannon June 4, 1925; released April 6, 1938; died April 6, 1952, at Salt Lake City, Salt Lake Co., Utah, at age 72.

6. MARVIN OWEN ASHTON – Born April 8, 1883, at Salt Lake City, Salt Lake Co., Utah, to Edward T. Ashton and Effie W. Morris. Sustained as first counselor to Presiding Bishop LeGrand Richards April 6, 1938, at age 54; died Oct. 7, 1946, at Salt Lake City, Salt Lake Co., Utah, at age 63.

7. JOSEPH LEOPOLD WIRTHLIN – See PRESIDING BISHOPS, No., 8.

8. HENRY THORPE BEAL ISAACSON – See OTHER COUNSELORS IN THE FIRST PRESIDENCY, No. 12.

9. ROBERT LEATHAM SIMPSON – See FIRST QUORUM OF THE SEVENTY, No. 18.

10. HAROLD BURKE PETERSON – See FIRST QUORUM OF THE SEVENTY, No. 64.

11. HENRY BENNION EYRING – See current FIRST PRESIDENCY.

12. HAROLD DAVID BURTON – See current PRESIDING BISHOPRIC.

13. RICHARD CROCKETT EDGLEY – See current PRESIDING BISHOPRIC.

SECOND COUNSELORS TO PRESIDING BISHOPS

1. JOHN CORRILL – Born Sept. 17, 1794, at Worcester Co., Massachusetts. Set apart as second counselor to Presiding Bishop Edward Partridge June 6, 1831, at age 36; released Aug. 1, 1837; excommunicated March 17, 1839.

2. TITUS BILLINGS – Born March 25, 1793, at Greenfield, Franklin Co., Massachusetts, to Ebenezer Billings and Esther Joyce. Set apart as second counselor to Presiding Bishop Edward Partridge Aug. 1, 1837, at age 44; released at the death of Bishop Partridge May 27, 1840; died Feb. 6, 1866, at Provo, Utah Co., Utah, at age 72.

3. JESSE CARTER LITTLE – Born Sept. 26, 1815, at Belmont, Waldo Co., Maine, to Thomas Little and Relief White. Sustained as second counselor to Presiding Bishop Edward Hunter Oct. 6, 1856, at age 41; resigned summer of 1874; died Dec. 26, 1893, at Salt Lake City, Salt Lake Co., Utah, at age 78.

4. ROBERT TAYLOR BURTON – See FIRST COUNSELORS IN THE PRESIDING BISHOPRIC, No. 3.

5. JOHN QUAYLE CANNON – Born April 19, 1857, at San Francisco, San Francisco Co., California, to George Quayle Cannon and Elizabeth Hoagland. Sustained as second counselor to Presiding Bishop William B. Preston Oct. 5, 1884, at age 27; excommunicated Sept. 5, 1886; rebaptized May 6, 1888; died Jan. 14, 1931, at Salt Lake City, Salt Lake Co., Utah, at 73.

6. JOHN REX WINDER – See FIRST COUNSELORS IN THE FIRST PRESIDENCY, No. 7.

7. ORRIN PORTER MILLER – See FIRST COUNSELORS IN THE PRESIDING BISHOPRIC, No. 4.

8. DAVID ASAEL SMITH – See FIRST COUNSELORS IN THE PRESIDING BISHOPRIC, No. 5.

9. JOHN WELLS – Born Sept. 16, 1864, at Carlton, Nottinghamshire, England, to Thomas Potter Wells and Sarah Cook. Sustained as second counselor to Presiding Bishop Charles W. Nibley July 18, 1918, at age 53; sustained as second counselor to Presiding Bishop Sylvester Q. Cannon June 4, 1925; released April 6, 1938, when Bishop Cannon was released; died April 18, 1941, at Salt Lake City, Salt Lake Co., Utah, at age 76.

10. JOSEPH LEOPOLD WIRTHLIN – See PRESIDING BISHOPS, No. 8.

11. HENRY THORPE BEAL ISAACSON – See OTHER COUNSELORS IN THE FIRST PRESIDENCY, No. 12.

12. CARL WILLIAM BUEHNER – Born Dec. 27, 1898, at Stuttgart, Wuerttemberg, Germany, to Carl F. Buehner and Anna B. Geigle. Sustained as second counselor to Presiding Bishop Joseph L. Wirthlin April 6, 1952, at age 53; released Sept. 30, 1961; died Nov. 18, 1974, at Salt Lake City, Salt Lake Co., Utah, at age 75.

13. VICTOR LEE BROWN – See PRESIDING BISHOPS, No. 10.

14. VAUGHN J FEATHERSTONE – See FIRST QUORUM OF THE SEVENTY, No. 36.

15. JOHN RICHARD CLARKE – See PRESIDENCY OF THE SEVENTY, No. 22.

16. GLENN LEROY PACE – See current FIRST QUORUM OF THE SEVENTY.

17. RICHARD CROCKETT EDGLEY – See current PRESIDING BISHOPRIC.

18. KEITH B. MCMULLIN – See current PRESIDING BISHOPRIC.

Scott Abbott, Deseret News

Conference-goers fill the grounds as they leave the Conference Center following Sunday morning session.

LENGTH OF SERVICE
IN FIRST PRESIDENCY AND QUORUM OF THE TWELVE

(As of October 2011)

Name	Date of service, (Age at time)	Length of service	†Total Years as General Authority
David O. McKay	Apr 1906 (32) - Jan 1970 (96)	63 yrs 9 mos	
Heber J. Grant	Oct 1882 (25) - May 1945 (88)	62 yrs 7 mos	
Joseph Fielding Smith	Apr 1910 (33) - Jul 1972 (95)	62 yrs 3 mos	
Wilford Woodruff	Apr 1839 (32) - Sep 1898 (91)	59 yrs 5 mos	
*Lorenzo Snow	Feb 1849 (34) - Oct 1901 (87)	52 yrs 8 mos	
Joseph F. Smith	Jul 1866 (27) - Nov 1918 (80)	52 yrs 4 mos	
Franklin D. Richards	Feb 1849 (27) - Dec 1899 (78)	50 yrs 10 mos	
Ezra Taft Benson	Oct 1943 (44) - May 1994 (94)	50 yrs 7 mos	
John Taylor	Dec 1838 (30) - Jul 1887 (78)	48 yrs 7 mos	
• Thomas S. Monson	Oct 1963 (36) - present	48 yrs	
George Albert Smith	Oct 1903 (33) - Apr 1951 (81)	47 yrs 6 mos	
Gordon B. Hinckley	Oct 1961 (51) - Jan 2008 (97)	46 yrs 3 mos	49 yrs 9 mos
Orson Pratt	Apr 1835 (23) - Aug 1842		
	Jan 1843 - Oct 1881 (70)	46 yrs 1 mo	
Rudger Clawson	Oct 1898 (41) - Jun 1943 (86)	44 yrs 8 mos	
George F. Richards	Apr 1906 (45) - Aug 1950 (89)	44 yrs 4 mos	
Orson Hyde	Feb 1835 (30) - May 1839		
	Jun 1839 - Nov 1878 (73)	43 yrs 8 mos	
Brigham Young	Feb 1835 (33) - Aug 1877 (76)	42 yrs 6 mos	
Stephen L Richards	Jan 1917 (37) - May 1959 (79)	42 yrs 4 mos	
Spencer W. Kimball	Oct 1943 (48) - Nov 1985 (90)	42 yrs 1 mo	
• Boyd K. Packer	Apr 1970 (45) - present	41 yrs 6 mos	50 yrs
Reed Smoot	Apr 1900 (38) - Feb 1941 (79)	40 yrs 10 mos	
*George Q. Cannon	Aug 1860 (33) - Apr 1901 (74)	40 yrs 8 mos	
Mark E. Petersen	Apr 1944 (43) - Jan 1984 (83)	39 yrs 9 mos	
Erastus Snow	Feb 1849 (30) - May 1888 (69)	39 yrs 3 mos	
• L. Tom Perry	Apr 1974 (51) - present	37 yrs 6 mos	39 yrs
Marion G. Romney	Oct 1951 (54) - May 1988 (90)	36 yrs 7 mos	47 yrs 1 mo
George A. Smith	Apr 1839 (21) - Sep 1875 (58)	36 yrs 5 mos	
Francis M. Lyman	Oct 1880 (40) - Nov 1916 (76)	36 yrs 1 mo	
Howard W. Hunter	Oct 1959 (51) - Mar 1995 (87)	35 yrs 5 mo	
Charles C. Rich	Feb 1849 (39) - Nov 1883 (74)	34 yrs 9 mos	
*Brigham Young Jr.	Oct 1868 (31) - Apr 1903 (66)	34 yrs 6 mos	
Heber C. Kimball	Feb 1835 (33) - Jun 1868 (67)	33 yrs 4 mos	
Harold B. Lee	Apr 1941 (42) - Dec 1973 (74)	32 yrs 8 mos	
John A. Widtsoe	Mar 1921 (49) - Nov 1952 (80)	31 yrs 8 mos	
Anthon H. Lund	Oct 1889 (45) - Mar 1921 (76)	31 yrs 5 mos	
John Henry Smith	Oct 1880 (32) - Oct 1911 (63)	31 yrs	
LeGrand Richards	Apr 1952 (66) - Jan 1983 (96)	30 yrs 9 mos	44 yrs 9 mos

James E. Faust	Oct 1978 (58) - Aug 2007 (87)	28 yrs 10 mos	34 yrs 10 mos
David B. Haight	Jan 1976 (69) - Jul 2004 (97)	28 yrs 6 mos	34 yrs 3 mos
J. Reuben Clark Jr.	Apr 1933 (61) - Oct 1961 (90)	28 yrs 6 mos	
Delbert L. Stapley	Oct 1950 (53) - Aug 1978 (81)	27 yrs 10 mos	
• Russell M. Nelson	Apr 1984 (59) - present	27 yrs 6 mos	
• Dallin H. Oaks	Apr 1984 (51) - present	27 yrs 6 mos	
Anthony W. Ivins	Oct 1907 (55) - Sep 1934 (82)	26 yrs 11 mos	
• M. Russell Ballard	Oct 1985 (57) - present	26 yrs	35 yrs 6 mos
Richard R. Lyman	Apr 1918 (47) - Nov 1943 (72)	25 yrs 7 mos	
Amasa M. Lyman	Aug 1842 (29) - Oct 1867 (54)	25 yrs 2 mos	
Orson F. Whitney	Apr 1906 (50) - May 1931 (75)	25 yrs 1 mo	
George Teasdale	Oct 1882 (50) - Jun 1907 (75)	24 yrs 8 mo	
Ezra T. Benson	Jul 1846 (35) - Sep 1869 (58)	23 yrs 2 mos	
• Richard G. Scott	Oct 1988 (59) - present	23 yrs	34 yrs 6 mos
Neal A. Maxwell	Jul 1981 (55) - Jul 2004 (78)	23 yrs	30 yrs 3 mos
Parley P. Pratt	Feb 1835 (27) - May 1857 (50)	22 yrs 3 mos	
Joseph B. Wirthlin	Oct 1986 (69) - Dec 2008 (91)	22 yrs 2 mos	33 yrs 8 mos
Marvin J. Ashton	Dec 1971 (56) - Feb 1994 (78)	22 yrs 2 mos	24 yrs 4 mos
James E. Talmage	Dec 1911 (49) - Jul 1933 (70)	21 yrs 7 mos	
John W. Taylor	Apr 1884 (25) - Oct 1905 (47)	21 yrs 6 mos	
Charles W. Penrose	Jul 1904 (72) - May 1925 (93)	20 yrs 10 mos	
#Daniel H. Wells	Jan 1857 (42) - Aug 1877 (62)	20 yrs 7 mos	34 yrs 2 mos
Melvin J. Ballard	Jan 1919 (45) - Jul 1939 (66)	20 yrs 6 mos	
Joseph F. Merrill	Oct 1931 (63) - Feb 1952 (83)	20 yrs 4 mos	
N. Eldon Tanner	Oct 1962 (64) - Nov 1982 (84)	20 yrs 1 mo	22 yrs 1 mo
Richard L. Evans	Oct 1953 (47) - Nov 1971 (65)	18 yrs 1 mo	33 yrs 1 mo
Hugh B. Brown	Apr 1958 (74) - Dec 1975 (92)	17 yrs 8 mos	22 yrs 2 mos
• Robert D. Hales	Apr 1994 (61) - present	17 yrs 6 mos	36 yrs 6 mos
• Jeffrey R. Holland	Jun 1994 (53) - present	17 yrs 4 mos	22 yrs 4 mos
Moses Thatcher	Apr 1879 (37) - Apr 1896 (54)	17 yrs	
• Henry B. Eyring	Apr 1995 (61) - present	16 yrs 6 mos	26 yrs 6 mos
Henry D. Moyle	Apr 1947 (57) - Sep 1963 (74)	16 yrs 5 mos	
Marriner W. Merrill	Oct 1889 (57) - Feb 1906 (73)	16 yrs 4 mos	
Hyrum Mack Smith	Oct 1901 (29) - Jan 1918 (45)	16 yrs 3 mos	
Albert E. Bowen	Apr 1937 (61) - Jul 1953 (77)	16 yrs 3 mos	
* Albert Carrington	Jul 1870 (57) - Nov 1885 (72)	15 yrs 4 mos	
Joseph Smith	Apr 1830 (24) - Jun 1844 (38)	14 yrs 2 mos	
Willard Richards	Apr 1840 (35) - Mar 1854 (49)	13 yrs 11 mos	
Charles A. Callis	Oct 1933 (68) - Jan 1947 (81)	13 yrs 3 mos	
Bruce R. McConkie	Oct 1972 (57) - Apr 1985 (69)	12 yrs 6 mos	38 yrs 6 mos
Sidney Rigdon	Mar 1833 (40) - Jun 1844 (51)	11 yrs 3 mos	
William Smith	Feb 1835 (23) - Oct 1845 (34)	10 yrs 8 mos	
John R. Winder	Oct 1901 (79) - Mar 1910 (88)	8 yrs 5 mos	22 yrs 11 mos
Matthew Cowley	Oct 1945 (48) - Dec 1953 (56)	8 yrs 2 mos	
George Q. Morris	Apr 1954 (80) - Apr 1962 (88)	8 yrs	10 yrs 6 mos
Matthias F. Cowley	Oct 1897 (39) - Oct 1905 (47)	8 yrs	
*+Oliver Cowdery	Apr 1830 (23) - Apr 1838 (31)	8 yrs	
Lyman Wight	Apr 1841 (44) - Dec 1848 (52)	7 yrs 8 mos	

Name	Dates		
John E. Page	Dec 1838 (39) - Feb 1846 (47)	7 yrs 2 mos	
• Dieter F. Uchtdorf	Oct 2004 (63) - present	7 yrs	17 yrs 6 mos
• David A. Bednar	Oct 2004 (52) - present	7 yrs	
Abraham H. Cannon	Oct 1889 (30) - Jul 1896 (37)	6 yrs 9 mos	13 yrs 9 mos
*+Hyrum Smith	Sep 1837 (37) - Jun 1844 (44)	6 yrs 9 mos	
*John Smith	Sep 1837 (56) - Jun 1844 (62)	6 yrs 9 mos	
Abraham O. Woodruff	Oct 1897 (24) - Jun 1904 (31)	6 yrs 8 mos	
Charles W. Nibley	May 1925 (76) - Dec 1931 (82)	6 yrs 7 mos	24 yrs
Sylvester Q. Cannon	Apr 1938 (60) - May 1943 (65)	5 yrs 1 mo	18 yrs
Adam S. Bennion	Apr 1953 (66) - Feb 1958 (71)	4 yrs 10 mos	
Frederick G. Williams	Mar 1833 (45) - Nov 1837 (50)	4 yrs 8 mos	
*#John Willard Young	Apr 1873 (28) - Aug 1877 (32)	4 yrs 4 mos	18 yrs 6 mos
Thorpe B. Isaacson	Oct 1965 (67) - Jan 1970 (71)	4 yrs 3 mos	23 yrs 1 mo
• Quentin L. Cook	Oct 2007 (67) - present	4 yrs	15 yrs 6 mos
Thomas B. Marsh	Apr 1835 (35) - Mar 1839 (39)	3 yrs 11 mos	
David W. Patten	Feb 1835 (35) - Oct 1838 (38)	3 yrs 8 mos	
• D. Todd Christofferson	Apr 2008 (63) - present	3 yr 6 mos	18 yrs 6 mos William
E. M'Lellin	Feb 1835 (29) - May 1838 (32)	3 yrs 3 mos	
William Law	Jan 1841 (31) - Apr 1844 (34)	3 yrs 3 mos	
Luke Johnson	Feb 1835 (27) - Apr 1838 (30)	3 yrs 2 mos	
Lyman E. Johnson	Feb 1835 (23) - Apr 1838 (26)	3 yrs 2 mos	
*Joseph Smith Sr.	Sep 1837 (66) - Sep 1840 (69)	3 yrs	6 yrs 9 mos
Jedediah M. Grant	Apr 1854 (38) - Dec 1856 (40)	2 yrs 8 mos	11 yrs
John F. Boynton	Feb 1835 (23) - Sep 1837 (25)	2 yrs 7 mos	
• Neil L. Andersen	Apr 2009 (57) - present	2 yr 6 mos	18 yrs 6 mos
Alonzo A. Hinckley	Oct 1934 (64) - Dec 1936 (66)	2 yrs 2 mos	
Alvin R. Dyer	Apr 1968 (65) - Jan 1970 (67)	1 yr 9 mos	18 yrs 5 mos

Bold Face denotes Church president.

• Currently serving.

†Includes service in the First Council of the Seventy, Assistants to the Twelve, First and Second Quorums of the Seventy, Presiding Bishopric, or as Church Patriarch.

* Served as assistant counselor in the First Presidency.

Served in the First Presidency as counselor to Brigham Young; after President Young's death sustained as counselor to Twelve Apostles.

+ Served as Assistant President of the Church

General Officers of the Church

Primary General Presidency

As of October 2011

Jean A. Stevens
First Counselor

Service began April 3, 2010 to present. Born in Salt Lake City, Utah, to O. Claron and Helen Alldredge; attended BYU, graduated from the University of Utah with a degree in mathematics and a teaching certificate and has been a PTA and education volunteer; former Primary general board member, ward Relief Society president, Young Women president, Primary counselor and gospel doctrine teacher; married Mark W. Stevens; parents of five children.

Rosemary M. Wixom
President

Service began April 3, 2010 to present. Born in Ogden, Utah, to Robert Wayne and Mary Cannon Mix; received bachelor's degree in elementary education from Utah State University; former member of the general boards of the Young Women and Primary, stake Young Women president, stake Primary president, Lamba Delta Sigma adviser at the University of Utah Institute, and served with husband when he was president of the Washington D.C. South Mission; married Blaine Jackson "Jack" Wixom Jr.; parents of six children.

Cheryl A. Esplin
Second Counselor

Service began April 3, 2010 to present. Born in Lovell, Wyo., to Orson Harris and Mildred Sylvia Stahle Asay; graduated from BYU with a degree in elementary education; former Primary general board member, stake Relief Society president, ward Young Women president, Primary counselor, and served with husband when he was president of the North Carolina Raleigh Mission; married Max Esplin; parents of five children.

Primary history

Noting the rough and careless behavior of the boys in her Farmington, Utah, neighborhood, Aurelia Spencer Rogers asked, "What will our girls do for good husbands, if this state of things continues?" Then she asked, "Could there not be an organization for little boys, and have them trained to make better men?"

The answer was, "Yes." With the approval of President John Taylor, the encouragement of Relief Society general president Eliza R. Snow, and after receiving a calling from her bishop, Sister Rogers began planning for the first meeting of the Primary Association, and it was an overwhelming success. On Sunday, Aug. 25, 1878, she stood at the entrance to the meetinghouse and welcomed 224 boys and girls to Primary. Girls were invited because Sister Rogers thought they could help with the singing that she believed necessary. During the first meeting, Sister Rogers instructed the children to be obedient and to be kind to one another.

During the next decade, the Primary Association was organized in almost every LDS settlement. During one trip through Southern Utah, Sister Snow and her first counselor in the Relief Society presidency, Zina Young, organized 35 Primaries.

From its beginning, Primary included songs, poetry, and activities. The boys wore uniforms to the meetings. All the children met together during the first 10 years. After that, they were divided into age groups.

Sister Louie B. Felt was called as the first general president of the Primary in 1880, but the Relief Society continued to take the responsibility for organizing Primaries. Sister Felt and other general officers began taking more responsibility for Primary development after 1890.

Serving as Primary general president for 45 years, Sister Felt oversaw many developments in the organization. In 1902, publication of the Children's Friend magazine began. In 1913, the Primary began contributing to pediatric hospital care. That program was culminated in 1952 with the completion of the Primary Children's Hospital in Salt Lake City. Contributions from Primary children helped support the hospital.

Beginning in 1929 when the Primary took over more responsibility for the spiritual training of children, lessons were planned for three weeks of the month and an activity on the fourth week. The Cub Scout program became the responsibility of the Primary in 1952.

Primary meetings were held midweek until the Church instituted the consolidated meeting plan in 1980. Then it replaced Junior Sunday School for providing Sunday religious instruction for children ages 3 to 11. The Primary meets for one hour and forty minutes of the three-hour meeting block, dividing the time between group meetings, classroom instruction, and sharing time. Athough women continue to serve exclusively in Primary presidencies, men are also called to teach classes. Weekday activities are held on a quarterly basis.

Yearly, usually in September or October, ward and branch Primaries throughout the Church present the Children's Sacrament Meeting Presentation, during which the children share, through song and the spoken word, what they have learned during the year.

In April 2003, the First Presidency announced a new Faith in God for Girls and Faith in God for Boys program. The program, for children ages 8 through 11, was implemented in the United States and Canada July 1, 2003, and implemented internationally in 2004.

The new program replaces the Gospel in Action award and Achievement Days and alters what has been known as the Cub Scout Faith in God Award. As part of the program, the Church published Faith in God guidebooks for boys and girls, which are designed to help boys prepare for the Aaronic Priesthood and girls to become righteous young women.

Sources: Sisters and Little Saints, by Carol Cornwall Madsen and Susan Oman; Encyclopedia of Mormonism; Church News.

HISTORICAL LISTING OF GENERAL PRESIDENCIES
OF THE PRIMARY ASSOCIATION

(Presidents pictured)

1. President, LOUIE BOUTON FELT, 19 Jun 1880-6 Oct 1925.

First Counselors, Matilda Morehouse W. Barratt - 19 Jun 1880-Oct 1888; Lillie Tuckett Freeze - Oct 1888-8 Dec 1905; May Anderson - 29 Dec 1905-6 Oct 1925.

Second Counselors, Clare Cordelia Moses Cannon - 19 Jun 1880-4 Oct 1895; Josephine Richards West - 15 Dec 1896-24 Nov 1905; Clara Woodruff Beebe - 29 Dec 1905-6 Oct 1925.

2. President, MAY ANDERSON - 6 Oct 1925-31 Dec 1939.

First Counselors, Sadie Grant Pack - 6 Oct 1925-11 Sep 1929; Isabelle Salmon Ross - 11 Sep 1929-31 Dec 1939.

Second Counselors, Isabelle Salmon Ross - 6 Oct 1925-11 Sep 1929; Edna Harker Thomas - 11 Sep 1929-11 Dec 1933; Edith Hunter Lambert - 11 Dec 1933-31 Dec 1939.

3. President, MAY GREEN HINCKLEY - 1 Jan 1940-2 May 1943.

First Counselor, Adele Cannon Howells - 1 Jan 1940-2 May 1943.

Second Counselors, Janet Murdock Thompson - 1 Jan 1940-May 1942; LaVern Watts Parmley - May 1942-2 May 1943.

4. President, ADELE CANNON HOWELLS - 20 Jul 1943-14 Apr 1951.

First Counselor, La-Vern Watts Parmley - 20 Jul 1943-14 Apr 1951.

Second Counselor, Dessie Grant Boyle - 20 Jul 1943-14 Apr 1951.

5. President, LAVERN WATTS PARMLEY - 16 May 1951-5 Oct 1974.

First Counselors, Arta Matthews Hale - 16 May 1951-6 Apr 1962; Leone Watson Doxey - 6 Apr 1962-23 Oct 1969; Lucile Cardon Reading - 8 Jan 1970-6 Aug 1970; Naomi Ward Randall - 4 Oct 1970-5 Oct 1974.

Second Counselors, Florence Holbrook Richards - 15 May 1951-11 Jun 1953; Leone Watson Doxey - 10 Sep 1953-6 Apr 1962; Eileen Robinson Dunyon - 6 Apr 1962-3 Jun 1963; Lucile Cardon Reading - 23 Jul 1963-8 Jan 1970; Florence Reece Lane - 8 Jan 1970-5 Oct 1974.

6. President, NAOMI MAXFIELD SHUMWAY - 5 Oct 1974-5 Apr 1980.

First Counselors, Sarah Broadbent Paulsen - 5 Oct 1974-2 Apr 1977; Colleen Bushman Lemmon - 2 Apr 1977-5 Apr 1980.

Second Counselors, Colleen Bushman Lemmon - 5 Oct 1974-2 Apr 1977; Dorthea Christiansen Murdock - 2 Apr 1977-5 Apr 1980.

7. President, DWAN JACOBSEN YOUNG - 5 Apr 1980-2 Apr 1988.

First Counselor, Virginia Beesley Cannon - 5 Apr 1980-2 Apr 1988.

Second Counselor, Michaelene Packer Grassli - 5 Apr 1980-2 Apr 1988.

8. President, MICHAELENE PACKER GRASSLI - 2 Apr 1988-1 Oct 1994.

First Counselor, Betty Jo Nelson Jepsen - 2 Apr 1988-1 Oct 1994.

Second Counselor, Ruth Broadbent Wright - 2 Apr 1988-1 Oct 1994.

9. President, PATRICIA P. PINEGAR - 1 Oct 1994 - 2 Oct 1999.

First Counselor, Anne G. Wirthlin, 1 Oct 1994-2 Oct 1999.

Second Counselor, Susan L. Warner, 10 Oct 1994-2 Oct 1999.

10. President, COLEEN K. MENLOVE – 2 Oct 1999 – 2 April 2005.

First Counselor, Sydney S. Reynolds – 2 Oct 1999 – 2 April 2005.

Second Counselor, Gayle M. Clegg – 2 Oct 1999 – 2 April 2005.

11. President, CHERYL C. LANT – April 2, 2005 – 3 April 2010.

First Counselor, Margaret S. Lifferth – April 2, 2005 – 3 April 2010.

Second Counselor, Vicki F. Matsumori – April 2, 2005 – 3 April 2010.

Relief Society Presidency

As of October 2011

Silvia H. Allred
First Counselor

Julie B. Beck
President

Barbara Thompson
Second Counselor

Silvia Henriquez Allred, March 31, 2007 to present. Born in San Salvador, El Salvador, to Carlos Florentino and Hilda Alvarenga Henriquez. Received teaching certificate in El Salvador, attended BYU and University of Arizona. Served with husband when he was president of the Dominican Republic Missionary Training Center and president of the Paraguay Asuncion Mission; former member of Young Women general board, stake Relief Society president and stake Primary president; PTA president in Argentina. Married Jeffry A. Allred; parents of eight children.

Julie B. Beck, March 31, 2007 to present. Born in Salt Lake City, Utah, to Wm. Grant and Geraldine Hamblin Bangerter. Received bachelor's degree in family science from BYU; former first counselor in the Young Women general presidency; Young Women general board member; ward Young Women president, counselor and adviser; Primary president, counselor and teacher; stake Relief Society president's counselor; ward Relief Society teacher; PTA president and officer. Married Ramon P. Beck; parents of three children.

Barbara Thompson, March 31, 2007 to present. Born in San Luis Obispo, Calif., to Wesley Peter and Fern Rymer Thompson. Received bachelor's degree in social work from BYU; master's degree from the University of Utah; former member of Relief Society general board, ward Young Women president, Relief Society counselor, Laurel and Beehive adviser, gospel doctrine teacher, and ward activities committee chairwoman. Serves as an official with Christmas Box International, a charity focused on abused and neglected children; executive director of an international assessment center for abused and neglected children.

Relief Society history

In 1842, a small group of women met at the home of Sarah M. Kimball in Nauvoo, Ill., to organize a sewing society to aid Nauvoo Temple workmen. They sought the endorsement of the Prophet Joseph Smith, who praised their efforts but said the Lord had something better in mind for them. It would be an organization under the priesthood after the pattern of the priesthood. He organized the Female Relief Society on March 17, 1842. The Prophet said that the restored Church could not be perfect or complete without it. He charged members with the responsibility to save souls and taught them principles of the gospel. The women elected Emma Smith as their president, and she selected two counselors.

From that original organization stemmed what is now the Relief Society, the official adult women's organization of the Church. Its motto, "Charity Never Faileth," states what has been the objective of society members from the first: to love and nurture one another and minister to the needs of Church members and others. The Female Relief Society of Nauvoo contributed to the Nauvoo Temple and supported moral reform. Members were primarily concerned with helping the poor. In July 1843, a visiting committee of four was appointed in each ward to assess needs and distribute necessities, the beginning of the visiting teaching effort that has been a part of Relief Society since then. By 1844, the society had 1,341 members. The Female Relief Society of Nauvoo ceased to function after March 1844 amid increasing tension.

Although women carried out charitable works and a few meetings were conducted at Winter Quarters, Neb., there was no formal Relief Society during the Saints' westward trek or for several years thereafter.

In February 1854, 16 women responded to an exhortation of President Brigham Young to form a society of females to make clothing for Indian women and children. This "Indian Relief Society" met until June 1854, when President Young encouraged such organizations in individual wards. In 1866, President Young reorganized the Relief Society Churchwide, appointing Eliza R. Snow to assist bishops in establishing the organization in each ward. By 1880, there was a local unit of the Relief Society in each of 300 wards, caring for the needy within its ward boundaries and using visiting teachers to collect and distribute donations. Ward Relief Societies managed their own finances and many built their own meeting halls. In line with the Church's move for self-sufficiency, the Relief Society sponsored cooperative economic enterprises in the late 1800s, such as making and marketing homemade goods, raising silk worms, storing grain, and financing the medical training of midwives and female doctors. The Relief Society also promoted women's right to vote and helped organize and nurture the Young Ladies' Retrenchment Association (forerunner to the Young Women) and the Primary.

By the turn of the 20th century, needs of women were changing, and the format of lessons was adapted and standardized to meet the needs. The Relief Society Magazine, introduced in 1915, contained lessons for each month on theological, cultural, and homemaking topics. The monthly format of rotating topics has remained since then, with various subject matter.

Beginning in 1921, concern over high maternal and infant mortality led to the establishment of health clinics and two stake Relief Society maternity hospitals, one operated in the Snowflake (Arizona) Stake and another in the Cottonwood (Utah) Stake. In 1944, visiting teachers ceased collecting charitable funds. After September 1971, all LDS women were automatically included as members of the Relief Society, rather than paying dues.

In 1956, the Relief Society Building in Salt Lake City, built from contributions from LDS women and funds from the Church, was dedicated. In the latter 20th Century, Relief Society became more fully coordinated under the larger Church structure.

The ward Relief Society president, under the direction of the bishop, has been responsible since 1921 for assessing needs and distributing relief to the needy. Ward Relief Society presidents supervise other charitable work such as caring for the sick, called "compassionate service" to distinguish it from "welfare service."

The Relief Society promoted scholarly study of women's concerns by helping establish the Women's Research Center at BYU, rallied members to contribute to the Monument to Women at Nauvoo, Ill., in 1978, and celebrated its sesquicentennial in 1992. A literacy effort, implemented in January 1993, was to teach basic gospel literacy skills.

Sources: Encyclopedia of Mormonism; Women of Covenant: The Story of Relief Society, by Jill Mulvay Derr, Janath Russell Cannon, and Maureen Ursenbach Beecher, Deseret Book, 1992; Church News, Jan. 30, 1993; "Strengthening the Work of Melchizedek Priesthood Quorums and Relief Society," Church News, Nov. 1, 1997; Church News, Oct. 1, 1999.

HISTORICAL LISTING OF GENERAL PRESIDENCIES OF THE RELIEF SOCIETIES

(Presidents pictured)

1. President, EMMA HALE SMITH - 17 Mar 1842-16 Mar 1844.

First Counselor, Sarah Marietta Kingsley Cleveland - 17 Mar 1842-16 Mar 1844.

Second Counselor, Elizabeth Ann Smith Whitney - 17 Mar 1842-16 Mar 1844.

2. President, ELIZA ROXCY SNOW - 1866-5 Dec 1887.

First Counselor, Zina Diantha Huntington Young - 19 Jun 1880-8 Apr 1888.

Second Counselor, Elizabeth Ann Smith Whitney - 19 Jun 1880-15 Feb 1882.

3. President, ZINA DIANTHA HUNTINGTON YOUNG - 8 Apr 1888-28 Aug 1901.

First Counselor, Jane Snyder Richards - 11 Oct 1888-10 Nov 1901.

Second Counselor, Bathsheba Wilson Smith - 11 Oct 1888-10 Nov 1901.

4. President, BATHSHEBA WILSON SMITH - 10 Nov 1901-20 Sep 1910.

First Counselor, Annie Taylor Hyde - 10 Nov 1901-2 Mar 1909.

Second Counselor, Ida Smoot Dusenberry, 10 Nov 1901-20 Sep 1910.

5. President, EMMELINE WOODWARD B. WELLS - 3 Oct 1910-2 Apr 1921.

First Counselor, Clarissa Smith Williams - 3 Oct 1910-2 Apr 1921.

Second Counselor, Julina Lambson Smith - 3 Oct 1910-2 Apr 1921.

6. President, CLARISSA SMITH WILLIAMS - 2 Apr 1921-7 Oct 1928.

First Counselor, Jennie Brimhall Knight - 2 Apr 1921-7 Oct 1928.

Second Counselor, Louise Yates Robison - 2 Apr 1921-7 Oct 1928.

7. President, LOUISE YATES ROBISON - 7 Oct 1928-Dec 1939.

First Counselor, Amy Brown Lyman - 7 Oct 1928-Dec 1939.

Second Counselors, Julia Alleman Child - 7 Oct 1928-23 Jan 1935; Kate Montgomery Barker - 3 Apr 1935-31 Dec 1939.

8. President, AMY BROWN LYMAN - 1 Jan 1940-6 Apr 1945.

First Counselor, Marcia Knowlton Howells - Apr 1940-6 Apr 1945.

Second Counselors, Donna Durrant Sorensen, Apr 1940-12 Oct 1942; Belle Smith Spafford, 12 Oct 1942-6 Apr 1945.

9. President, BELLE SMITH SPAFFORD - 6 Apr 1945-3 Oct 1974.

First Counselor, Marianne Clark Sharp - 6 Apr 1945-3 Oct 1974.

Second Counselor, Gertrude Ryberg Garff - 6 Apr 1945-30 Sep 1947; Velma Nebeker Simonsen - 3 Oct 1947-17 Dec 1956; Helen Woodruff Anderson - Jan 1957-Aug 1958; Louise Wallace Madsen - Aug 1958-3 Oct 1974.

10. President, BARBARA BRADSHAW SMITH - 3 Oct 1974-7 Apr 1984.

First Counselors, Janath Russell Cannon - 3 Oct 1974-28 Nov 1978; Marian Richards Boyer - 28 Nov 1978-7 Apr 1984.

Second Counselors, Marian Richards Boyer - 3 Oct 1974-28 Nov 1978; Shirley Wilkes Thomas - 28 Nov 1978-24 Jun 1983; Ann Stoddard Reese, 1 Oct 1983-7 Apr 1984.

11. President, BARBARA WOODHEAD WINDER - 7 Apr 1984-31 Mar 1990.

First Counselor, Joy Frewin Evans - 21 May 1984-31 Mar 1990.

Second Counselor, Joanne Bushman Doxey - 21 May 1984-31 Mar 1990.

12. President, ELAINE LOW JACK - 31 Mar 1990-5 Apr 1997.

First Counselor, Chieko Nishimura Okazaki - 31 Mar 1990-5 Apr 1997.

Second Counselor, Aileen Hales Clyde - 31 Mar 1990-5 Apr 1997.

13. President, MARY ELLEN WOOD SMOOT - 5 Apr 1997-6 Apr 2002.

First Counselor, Virginia Urry Jensen - 5 Apr 1997-6 Apr 2002.

Second Counselor, Sheri L. Dew - 5 Apr 1997-6 Apr 2002.

14. President, BONNIE DANSIE PARKIN - 6 Apr 2002-31 Mar 2007.

First Counselor, Kathleen Hurst Hughes, 6 Apr 2002-31 Mar 2007.

Second Counselor, Anne Clark Pingree, 6 Apr 2002-31 Mar 2007

Sunday School Presidency

As of October 2011

David M. McConkie
First Counselor

Russell T. Osguthorpe
President

Mathew O. Richardson
Second Counselor

David M. McConkie, 4 Apr 2009 to present. Salt Lake City attorney; born in Salt Lake City, Utah, to F. Briton and Beth Merrill McConkie; formerly stake president and counselor, high councilor, stake Young Men president, and bishop; was a staff sergeant in the Utah Air National Guard; received bachelor's degree in history and juris doctorate, both from the University of Utah; wife, JoAnne Albrecht McConkie; parents of seven children.

Russell T. Osguthorpe, 4 Apr 2009 to present. BYU professor of instructional psychology and technology and director of the Center for Teaching and Learning; born in Salt Lake City, Utah, to Wesley Trenton and Iva Russell Osguthorpe; served as an Area Seventy, president of the South Dakota Rapid City Mission, stake president, stake Young Men president, bishop's counselor and branch president, and member of the Mormon Tabernacle Choir; was a captain and chaplain in the U.S. Army Reserve Signal Corps; received bachelor's degree in psychology, master's degree in school psychology, doctorate in instructional psychology, all from BYU; wife, Lola Sedgwick Osguthorpe; parents of five children.

Matthew O. Richardson, 4 Apr 2009 to present. BYU professor of Church history and doctrine and former associate dean of religious education at BYU; born in Salt Lake City, Utah, to Edward M. and Andrea Ottesen Richardson; former bishop, member of elders quorum presidencies, ward Young Men president and ward mission leader; received bachelor's degree in communications, master's degree and doctorate in education, all from BYU; wife, Lisa Jackson Richardson; parents of four children.

Sunday School history

Though a few small Sunday School groups met regularly in Latter-day Saint communities before the Saints' westward exodus, Sunday School did not begin as a Church institution until after their arrival in the Salt Lake Valley in 1847.

Richard Ballantyne was a convert to the Church who, as a Presbyterian in his native Scotland, had organized a Sunday School. In Salt Lake City, disturbed by observing the children at play on the Sabbath day, he saw the need for a Sunday School.

In May 1849, he began plans to start a Sunday School. He built a structure on the northeast corner of 100 West and 300 South streets in Salt Lake City to serve both as his home and a place to hold a Sunday School. A monument on that corner today (now 200 West) commemorates the location of the first Sunday School, which was held Dec. 9, 1849, and involved 50 children. The following year, a meetinghouse was built for the Salt Lake 14th Ward, in which Brother Ballantyne was second counselor in the bishopric. An expanded Sunday School was moved into the new building and divided into a number of smaller classes, with additional teachers and two assistant superintendents.

Other wards in the valley and elsewhere followed the example of Brother Ballantyne and started Sunday Schools. They were somewhat autonomous, devising their own curricula and having their own administration, but functioning under the direction of the ward bishop.

With the coming of Johnston's Army to Utah, the Sunday School movement was suspended as many of the Saints moved south, but with the lessening of tensions in 1860, the Sunday School was resumed. By 1870, more than 200 Sunday Schools had been formed.

On Nov. 11, 1867, the Deseret Sunday School Union was organized by interested Church leaders, including President Brigham Young. Elder George Q. Cannon of the Quorum of the Twelve became the first general superintendent of the Sunday School. Its functions were to determine lesson topics and source materials and to address topics of punctuality, grading, prizes and rewards, recording and increasing attendance, music, elementary catechism, and libraries. The general Sunday School fostered uniformity in the theretofore disparate and independent Sunday Schools in the Church.

In 1866, prior to formation of the general Sunday School, a publication called the Juvenile Instructor was founded privately by Elder Cannon who also served as editor. It featured material on the scriptures, musical compositions and aids to gospel instruction. The publication became the official voice of the Deseret Sunday School Union, which purchased it from the Cannon family in January 1901. In 1929, the name was changed to the Instructor. It was discontinued in 1970 when the Church magazine structure was changed.

In early 1877, the sacrament was instituted as part of Sunday School. The practice continued until 1980, when Sunday meetings were consolidated into a three-hour block, with sacrament administered only during sacrament meeting.

The Deseret Sunday School Union continued to grow through the 1900s. Stake Sunday School superintendencies were designated to supervise ward Sunday Schools. General meetings of the Sunday School were held twice a year in connection with general conference. Five new classes for older children and youth were added in the early 1900s, followed shortly by the introduction of adult classes.

A Sunday School general board was introduced in the 1870s. In the 1900s, it was expanded and members traveled extensively to provide advice and support for local programs.

An effort in 1971 to correlate all Church functions under priesthood leadership affected the Sunday School. Dynamic changes followed, including centralized curriculum planning and writing, and an eight-year cycle of scripture instruction (later shortened to four years) for adult classes, focusing in turn on the Old Testament and Pearl of Great Price, the New Testament, the Book of Mormon, and the Doctrine and Covenants and Church History. Later, the size of the general board was reduced, and stake boards were discontinued.

On June 25, 1972, with Russell M. Nelson as presiding officer of the Sunday School, the title was changed from superintendent to president, and the title of assistants to counselors.

With the introduction of the consolidated meeting schedule in 1980, children's Sunday School classes were discontinued, that function being filled by the Primary. In recent years, Sunday School curriculum for adults has included a Gospel Doctrine class and additional classes on Gospel Essentials, family history, and family relations.

A modified Church curriculum implemented Jan. 1, 1995, provided that classes for youth ages 14-18 study the scriptures using the Gospel Principles or Gospel Doctrine courses of study. Under the modified plan, youth ages 12-13 on alternate years study presidents of the Church and preparing for exaltation.

Throughout 1999, the Church observed the sesquicentennial of the Sunday School program by opening the 1949 centennial box and putting together a bicentennial box, the latter representative of a global Sunday School program. The new bicentennial box will be opened in 2049. The Museum of Church History and Art held a yearlong exhibit, "Sunday School: 150 Years of Teaching the Gospel," which opened July 6, 1998. Attending the reception were former members of the 1949 Deseret Sunday School Union General Board who had watched the centennial box closed 50 years earlier.

An administrative change in the general presidency of the Sunday School was announced at general conference April 3, 2004. Members of the Seventy were relieved from the responsibility of serving in auxiliary presidencies, and a new Sunday School general presidency, composed of non-General Authorities, was called. Members of the Seventy had served in the Sunday School general presidency since Oct. 6, 1979.

Sources: Encyclopedia of Mormonism; Jubilee History of Latter-day Saints Sunday Schools, published by the Deseret Sunday School Union; *Church News,* July 1, 1972; First Presidency letter to General Authorities and priesthood leaders, April 21, 1994; "Exhibit serves as beginning of Sunday School celebration," by Sarah Jane Weaver, *Church News,* July 11, 1998.

HISTORICAL LISTING OF GENERAL SUPERINTENDENCIES AND PRESIDENCIES OF THE SUNDAY SCHOOL

(Presidents, superintendents pictured)

1. Superintendent, GEORGE Q. CANNON (as apostle, counselor in First Presidency) - Nov 1867-Apr 1901. See photo, FIRST COUNSELORS IN THE FIRST PRESIDENCY, No. 5.

First Assistants, George Goddard - Jun 1872-Jan 1899; Karl G. Maeser - Jan 1899-Feb 1901.

Second Assistants, John Morgan - Jun 1883-Jul 1894; Karl G. Maeser - Jul 1894-Jan 1899; George Reynolds - Jan 1899-May 1901.

2. Superintendent, LORENZO SNOW (as president of the Church) - May 1901-Oct 1901. See photo, PRESIDENTS OF THE CHURCH, No. 5.

First Assistant, George Reynolds - May 1901-Oct 1901.

Second Assistant, Jay M. Tanner - May 1901-Oct 1901.

3. Superintendent, JOSEPH F. SMITH (as president of the Church) - Nov 1901-Nov 1918. See photo, PRESIDENTS OF THE CHURCH, No. 6.

First Assistants, George Reynolds - Nov 1901-May 1909, David O. McKay (as apostle) - May 1909-Nov 1918.

Second Assistants, Jay M. Tanner - Nov 1901-April 1906; David O. McKay(as apostle) - Jan 1907-May 1909, Stephen L Richards - May 1909-Nov 1918.

4. Superintendent, DAVID O. MCKAY (as apostle) - Dec 1918-Oct 1934. See photo, PRESIDENTS OF THE CHURCH, No. 9.

First Assistant, Stephen L Richards (as apostle) - Dec 1918-Oct 1934.

Second Assistant, George D. Pyper - Dec 1918-Oct 1934.

5. Superintendent, GEORGE D. PYPER - Oct 1934-Jan 1943.

First Assistant, Milton Bennion - Oct 1934-May 1943.

Second Assistant, George R. Hill - Oct 1934-May 1943.

6. Superintendent, MILTON BENNION - May 1943-Sep 1949.

First Assistant, George R. Hill - May 1943-Sep 1949.

Second Assistant, Albert Hamer Reiser - May 1943-Sep 1949.

7. Superintendent, GEORGE R. HILL - Sep 1949-Nov 1966.

First Assistants, Albert Hamer Reiser - Sep 1949-Oct 1952; David Lawrence McKay - Oct 1952-Nov 1966.

Second Assistants, David Lawrence McKay - Sep 1949-Oct 1952; Lynn S. Richards - Oct 1952-Nov 1966.

8. Superintendent, DAVID LAWRENCE MCKAY - Nov 1966-Jun 1971.

First Assistant, Lynn S. Richards - Nov 1966-Jun 1971.

Second Assistant, Royden G. Derrick - Nov. 1966-Jun 1971.

9. President, RUSSELL M. NELSON - Jun 1971-Oct 1979. See photo, current QUORUM OF THE TWELVE. (Note: titles changed from superintendent to president, and from assistants to counselors on June 25, 1972.)

First Counselors, Joseph B. Wirthlin - Jun 1971-Apr 1975, B. Lloyd Poelman - Apr 1975-Mar 1978; Joe J. Christensen - Mar 1978-Aug 1979; William D. Oswald - Aug 1979-Oct 1979.

Second Counselors, Richard L. Warner - Jun 1971-Apr 1975; Joe J. Christensen - Apr 1975-Mar 1978; William D. Oswald - May 1978-Aug 1979; J. Hugh Baird - Aug 1979-Oct 1979.

(From Oct. 6, 1979, to April 3, 2004, the general presidency of the Sunday School was composed of members of the Seventy.)

10. President, HUGH W. PINNOCK - Oct 1979-Aug 1986. See photo, PRESIDENCY OF THE SEVENTY, No. 20.

First Counselors, Ronald E. Poelman - Oct 1979-Jul 1981; Robert D. Hales - Jul 1981-Jul 1985; Adney Y. Komatsu - Jul 1985-Aug 1986.

Second Counselors, Jack H Goaslind Jr. - Oct 1979-Jul 1981; James M. Paramore - Jul 1981-Jan 1983; Loren C. Dunn - Jan 1983-Jul 1985; Ronald E. Poelman - Jul 1985-Aug 1986.

11. President, ROBERT L. SIMPSON - Aug 1986-30 Sep 1989. See photo, FIRST QUORUM OF THE SEVENTY, No. 18.

First Counselors, Adney Y. Komatsu - Aug 1986-Aug. 1987; Devere Harris - Aug 1987-30 Sep 1989.

Second Counselors, A. Theodore Tuttle - Aug 1986-Nov 1986; Devere Harris - Jan 1987-Aug 1987; Phillip T. Sonntag - Aug 1987-Aug 1988; Derek A. Cuthbert - Aug 1988-30 Sep 1989.

12. President, HUGH W. PINNOCK - 30 Sep 1989-15 Aug 1992. See photo, PRESIDENCY OF THE SEVENTY, No. 20.

First Counselors, Derek A. Cuthbert - 15 Aug 1988-1 Jan 1991; H. Verlan Andersen - 1 Jan 1991-5 Oct 1991; Hartman Rector Jr. - 5 Oct 1991-15 Aug 1992.

Second Counselors, Ted E. Brewerton - 30 Sep 1989-1 Oct 1990; H. Verlan Andersen - 6 Oct 1990-1 Jan 1991; Rulon G. Craven - 1 Jan 1991-5 Oct 1991; Clinton L. Cutler - 5 Oct 1991-15 Aug 1992.

13. President, MERLIN R. LYBBERT, - 15 Aug 1992-15 Aug 1994. See photo, SECOND QUORUM OF THE SEVENTY, No. 35.

First Counselor, Clinton L. Cutler - 15 Aug 1992-April 9, 1994.

Second Counselor, Ronald E. Poelman - 15 Aug 1992-15 Aug 1994.

14. President, CHARLES DIDIER, 15 Aug 1994 – 30 Sep 1995. See photo, current FIRST QUORUM OF THE SEVENTY.

First Counselor, J Ballard Washburn - 15 Aug 1994-30 Sep 1995.

Second Counselor, F. Burton Howard - 15 Aug 1994-30 Sep 1995.

15. President, HAROLD G. HILLAM, 30 Sep 1995 – 7 Oct 2000. See photo, PRESIDENCY OF THE SEVENTY, No. 31.

First Counselors, F. Burton Howard, 30 Sep 1995 - 4 Oct 1997; Glenn L. Pace, 4 Oct 1997 - 3 Oct 1998; Neil L. Andersen, 3 Oct 1998 - 7 Oct 2000.

Second Counselors, Glenn L. Pace, 30 Sep 1995 - 4 Oct 1997; Neil L. Andersen, 4 Oct 1997 - 3 Oct 1998; John H. Groberg, 3 Oct 1998 - 7 Oct 2000.

16. President, MARLIN K. JENSEN - 7 Oct 2000-6 Oct 2001. See photo, current FIRST QUORUM OF THE SEVENTY.

First Counselor, Neil L. Andersen - 7 Oct 2000-6 Oct 2001.

Second Counselor, John H. Groberg - 7 Oct 2000-6 Oct 2001.

17. President, CECIL O. SAMUELSON - 6 Oct 2001-5 Apr 2003. See photo, current FIRST QUORUM OF THE SEVENTY.

First Counselor, John H. Groberg - 6 Oct 2001 - 5 Apr 2003.

Second Counselor, Richard J. Maynes - 6 Oct 2001 - 5 Oct 2002; Val R. Christensen - 5 Oct 2002 - 5 Apr 2003.

18. President, MERRILL J. BATEMAN, 5 Apr 2003-3 Apr 2004. See photo, PRESIDENCY OF THE SEVENTY, NO. 41.

First Counselor, John H. Groberg - 5 Apr 2003 - 3 Apr 2004.

Second Counselor, Val R. Christensen, 5 Apr 2003 - 3 Apr 2004.

19. President, A. ROGER MERRILL, 3 Apr 2004 – 4 Apr 2009.

First Counselor, Daniel K. Judd, 3 Apr 2004 – 4 Apr 2009.

Second Counselor, William D. Oswald, 3 Apr 2004 – 4 Apr 2009.

Young Men Presidency

As of October 2011

Larry M. Gibson
First Counselor

Larry M. Gibson, 4 April 2009 to present. Executive vice president and CTO for a Fortune 500 company; born in Boulder City, Nev., to Robert Owen and Thais Miner Gibson; formerly stake president and counselor, high councilor, bishop, and stake and ward Young Men president; received bachelor's degree in computer science and business and master's degree in information science, both from BYU; wife, Shirley Barton Gibson; parents of six children.

David L. Beck
President

David L. Beck, 4 April 2009 to present. An executive with a manufacturing and distribution company and serves on the board of a technical college; born in Salt Lake City, Utah, to Wayne and Evelyn Moon Beck; formerly president of the Brazil Rio de Janeiro North Mission, stake president, high councilor, bishop and counselor, and elders quorum president; received bachelor's degree in electrical engineering and master's degree in engineering administration, both from University of Utah; wife, Robyn Ericksen Beck; parents of four children.

Adrian Ochoa
Second Counselor

Adrian Ochoa, 4 April 2009 to present. Has worked in advertising and film production in the United States and Mexico, and developed multiple marketing campaigns for some 500 companies in the world; born in San Francisco, Calif., to Eduardo and Consuelo Ochoa; formerly Area Seventy, area public affairs director, president of Honduras San Pedro Sula Mission, stake president, and high priests group leader; received bachelor's degree in communication, master's degree in business and marketing; wife, Nancy Villareal Ochoa; parents of five children.

Young Men history

The Young Men organization has been significantly streamlined and simplified since its inception in 1875 as the Young Men's Mutual Improvement Association. The YMMIA was established by President Brigham Young, who called Junius F. Wells to organize Mutual Improvement Associations in wards throughout the Church, under the direction of ward superintendencies. It was intended that the YMMIA help young men develop spiritually and intellectually and provide supervised recreational opportunities. Today, its primary purpose is furthering the work of the Aaronic Priesthood.

On June 10, 1875, Brother Wells called a meeting in the 13th Ward chapel in Salt Lake City and the first ward YMMIA was organized.

In the fall of 1875, John Henry Smith, Milton H. Hardy, and B. Morris Young were called by the First Presidency to assist Brother Wells in visiting the settlements of the Saints and promoting the YMMIA. By April 1876, there were 57 ward YMMIAs in existence with a membership of about 1,200 youth. That same year, a YMMIA central committee was formed with Brother Wells as president. The committee later became the General Board of the YMMIA, which has continued through the years and is now known as the Young Men General Board.

From 1876 to 1905, young men were called to serve YMMIA missions to increase membership and assist local superintendencies. Initially, all of the young men met together regardless of age. Later, the YMMIA adopted four grades or classes: Scouts (ages

12-14), Vanguards (15-16), M Men (17-23), and Adults. As the programs developed and as needs of the youth changed, further refinements were made to the class structure. Today, Young Men classes correspond with the deacons, teachers, and priests quorums in the Aaronic Priesthood.

In October 1879, the monthly Contributor was launched with Brother Wells as editor. It served as the publication of the YM-MIA until October 1899, at which time the publication of the Improvement Era was begun by the General Board.

The YMMIA met separately from the Young Women's Mutual Improvement Association (YWMIA) until around 1900 when the two joined to form the Mutual Improvement Association (called MIA or Mutual).

In 1913, the Church formed a formal partnership with Boy Scouts of America and was granted a national charter on May 21 of that year. Scouting exists today as a major component of the Young Men organization to help accomplish the purposes of the Aaronic Priesthood and to complement Sunday quorum instruction. Besides its partnership with BSA, the Church has established affiliations with other national Scouting organizations throughout the world whose programs, values, goals, and ideals are compatible with those of the Church.

In addition to Scouting, YMMIA activities in the early and mid-1900s included sports, dance, drama, and music. Athletics became a major part of the program, and stake tournament winners progressed to the All-Church tournaments in Salt Lake City, which were discontinued in the early 1970s.

In the mid-1900s, the general-level organization consisted of a superintendency of five men and a general board of 60 to 70 men. The general level was supported by a general fund, paid into by stakes based on YMMIA membership, sale of YMMIA materials, and investments. Besides planning and organizing major sports and cultural events, general board members would regularly travel with General Authorities and provide training for local YMMIA leaders.

In the 1960s under priesthood correlation, responsibility for training shifted to local priesthood leaders, the general fund was discontinued, production and sale of materials were centralized, and the size and scope of the general superintendency and board were greatly reduced.

On June 25, 1972, the title of the presiding officers of the YMMIA and Sunday School were changed from superintendent to president, and the title of assistants to counselors "to more closely define the relationship between the two auxiliaries with the functions of the priesthood," according to President Harold B. Lee, then first counselor in the First Presidency.

The Aaronic Priesthood-MIA was organized Nov. 9, 1972, with efforts centering more fully around the Aaronic Priesthood quorums. In June 1974, the name Aaronic Priesthood-MIA was shortened to Aaronic Priesthood and conducted under the direction of the Presiding Bishopric. In May 1977, the name was changed to Young Men and a general presidency was reinstated. In October 1979, it was announced that the Young Men general presidency would be comprised of three members of the Seventy. Since 1989, the general board has been comprised of less than a dozen men who continue to assist the presidency with curriculum development and Aaronic Priesthood and Scouting training.

On Sept. 28, 2001, the First Presidency announced a new program, "Aaronic Priesthood: Fulfilling Our Duty to God," for which were introduced three guidebooks, one each for deacons, teachers and priests, that explain the program and outline steps to earning the Duty to God Award. The Aaronic Priesthood Duty to God program, implemented in the United States and Canada in January 2002, is designed to help young men prepare for the Melchizedek Priesthood, the temple endowment, a full-time mission, marriage and fatherhood. At the same time, the First Presidency also announced an updated, simplified Young Women Personal Progress Program, which mirrors the values of the new Duty to God program. Both programs are based on standards set forth in an updated For the Strength of Youth guidebook.

An administrative change in the general presidency of the Young Men was announced at general conference April 3, 2004. Members of the Seventy were relieved from the responsibility of serving in auxiliary presidencies, and a new Young Men general presidency, composed of non-General Authorities, was called. Members of the Seventy had served in the Young Men general presidency since Oct. 6, 1979.

Sources: Encyclopedia of Mormonism; Encyclopedic History of the Church by Andrew Jenson, p. 969; Church News, July 1, 1972, May 3, 1997; "Program will improve their lives," by Jason Swensen, Church News, Oct. 27, 2001.

HISTORICAL LISTING OF GENERAL SUPERINTENDENCIES AND PRESIDENCIES OF THE YOUNG MEN IMPROVEMENT ASSOCIATION AND YOUNG MEN

(Presidents, superintendents pictured)

1. Superintendent, JUNIUS F. WELLS - 1876-1880.

First Counselor, M. H. Hardy.

Second Counselor, Rodney C. Badger.

2. Superintendent, WILFORD WOODRUFF (as apostle, president of the Church) - 1880-1898. See photo, PRESIDENTS OF THE CHURCH, No. 4.

First Assistant, Joseph F. Smith.

Second Assistant, Moses Thatcher.

3. Superintendent, LORENZO SNOW (as president of the Church) - 1898-1901. See photo, PRESIDENTS OF THE CHURCH, No. 5.

First Assistant, Joseph F. Smith.

Second Assistant, Heber J. Grant.

Assistant, B. H. Roberts.

4. Superintendent, JOSEPH F. SMITH (as president of the Church) - 1901-1918. See photo, PRESIDENTS OF THE CHURCH, No. 6.

First Assistant, Heber J. Grant.

Second Assistant, B. H. Roberts.

5. Superintendent, ANTHONY W. IVINS (as apostle) - 1918-1921. See photo, FIRST COUNSELORS IN THE FIRST PRESIDENCY, No. 10.

First Assistant, B. H. Roberts

Second Assistant, Richard R. Lyman.

6. Superintendent, GEORGE ALBERT SMITH (as apostle — 1921-1935. See photo, PRESIDENTS OF THE CHURCH, No. 8.

First Assistant, B. H. Roberts.

Second Assistants, Richard R. Lyman; Melvin J. Ballard.

7. Superintendent, ALBERT E. BOWEN - 1935-1937. See photo, QUORUM OF THE TWELVE, No. 59.

First Assistant, George Q. Morris.

Second Assistant, Franklin West.

8. Superintendent, GEORGE Q. MORRIS - 1937-1948. See photo, QUORUM OF THE TWELVE, No. 72.

First Assistants, Joseph J. Cannon; John D. Giles.

Second Assistants, Burton K. Farnsworth; Lorenzo H. Hatch.

9. Superintendent, ELBERT R. CURTIS - 1948-1958.

First Assistant, A. Walter Stevenson.

Second Assistants, Ralph W. Hardy; David S. King.

10. Superintendent, JOSEPH T. BENTLEY - 2 Jul 1958-6 Oct 1962.

First Assistants, Alvin R. Dyer - 2 Jul 1958-6 Dec 1958; G. Carlos Smith - 6 Dec 1958-9 Jun 1961; Marvin J. Ashton, 9 Jun 1961-6 Oct 1962.

Second Assistants, Marvin J. Ashton - 6 Dec 1958-9 Jun 1961; Verl F. Scott, 9 Jun 1961-4 Oct 1961; Carl W. Buehner, 25 Oct 1961-Oct 1962.

11. Superintendent, G. CARLOS SMITH - 6 Oct 1962-17 Sep 1969.

First Assistant, Marvin J. Ashton - 6 Oct 1962-17 Sep 1969.

Second Assistants, Carl W. Beuhner - 6 Oct 1962-Oct 1967; George R. Hill - 6 Oct 1967-17 Sep 1969.

12. Superintendent, W. JAY ELDREDGE - 17 Sep 1969-25 Jun 1972.

First Assistants, George R. Hill - 17 Sep 1969-24 Jun 1972.

Second Assistant, George I. Cannon - 17 Sep 1969-25 Jun 1972.

13. President, W. JAY ELDREDGE - 25 Jun 1972-9 Nov 1972 (see photo above).

First Counselor, George I. Cannon - 25 Jun 1972-9 Nov 1972.

Second Counselor, Robert L. Backman, 25 Jun 1972-9 Nov 1972.

AARONIC PRIESTHOOD MIA

14. President, ROBERT L. BACKMAN - 9 Nov 1972-23 Jun 1974. See photo, PRESIDENCY OF THE SEVENTY, No. 18.

First Counselor, LeGrand R. Curtis - 9 Nov 1972-23 Jun 1974.

Second Counselor, Jack H Goaslind Jr. - 9 Nov 1972-23 Jun 1974.

Note: On June 23, 1974, the Aaronic Priesthood MIA was dissolved and was replaced by the Aaronic Priesthood and the Young Women directly under the stewardship of the Presiding Bishop. In April 1977, it was renamed the Young Men, and both it and the Young Women came under the direction of the Priesthood Department.

YOUNG MEN

15. President, NEIL D. SCHAERRER - 7 Apr 1977-Oct 1979.

First Counselor, Graham W. Doxey - 7 Apr 1977-Oct 1979.

Second Counselor, Quinn G. McKay - 7 Apr 1977-Oct 1979

From Oct. 6, 1979, to April 3, 2004, the general presidency of the Young Men was composed of members of the Seventy.

16. President, ROBERT L. BACKMAN - Oct 1979-Nov 1985. See photo, PRESIDENCY OF THE SEVENTY, No. 18.

First Counselor, Vaughn J Featherstone - Oct 1979-Nov 1985.

Second Counselor, Rex D. Pinegar - Oct 1979-Nov 1985.

17. President, VAUGHN J FEATHERSTONE - Nov 1985-6 Oct 1990. See photo, FIRST QUORUM OF THE SEVENTY, No. 36.

First Counselors, Rex D. Pinegar - Nov 1985-30 Sep 1989; Jeffrey R. Holland - 30 Sep 1989-6 Oct 1990.

Second Counselors, Robert L. Simpson - Nov 1985-15 Aug 1986; Hartman Rector Jr. - 15 Aug 1986-Oct 1988; Robert B Harbertson, Oct 1988-30 Sep 1989; Monte J. Brough, 30 Sep 1989-6 Oct 1990.

18. President, JACK H GOASLIND - 6 Oct 1990-3 Oct 1998. See photo, PRESIDENCY OF THE SEVENTY, No. 17.

First Counselors, LeGrand R. Curtis -6 Oct 1990-5 Oct 1991; Robert K. Dellenbach - 5 Oct 1991-3 Oct 1992; Stephen D. Nadauld - 3 Oct 1992-5 Oct 1996; Vaughn J Featherstone - 5 Oct 1996-17 May 1997; F. David Stanley - 17 May 1997-4 Oct 1997; Robert K. Dellenbach - 4 Oct 1997-3 Oct 1998.

Second Counselors, Robert K. Dellenbach, 6 Oct 1990-5 Oct 1991; Stephen D. Nadauld - 5 Oct 1991-30 Oct 1992; L. Lionel Kendrick - 3 Oct 1992-15 Aug 1993; Vaughn J Featherstone -15 Aug 1993-5 Oct 1996; F. David Stanley - 5 Oct 1996-17 May 1997; Robert K. Dellenbach - 17 May 1997-4 Oct 1997; F. Melvin Hammond - 4 Oct 1997-3 Oct 1998.

19. President, ROBERT K. DELLENBACH – 3 Oct 1998 – 6 Oct 2001. See photo, FIRST QUORUM OF THE SEVENTY, No. 96.

First Counselor, F. Melvin Hammond - 3 Oct 1998-6 Oct 2001.

Second Counselor, John M. Madsen - 3 Oct 1998-6 Oct 2001.

20. President, F. MELVIN HAMMOND – 6 Oct 2001 – 3 Apr 2004. See photo, FIRST QUORUM OF THE SEVENTY, No. 99.

First Counselor, Glenn L. Pace - 6 Oct 2001 - 4 Oct 2003; Lynn G. Robbins - 4 Oct 2003 - 3 Apr 2004.

Second Counselor, Spencer J. Condie - 6 Oct 2001 - 4 Oct 2003; Donald L Hallstrom - 4 Oct 2003 - 3 Apr 2004.

21. President, CHARLES W. DAHLQUIST II – 3 Apr 2004 – 4 Apr 2009.

First Counselor, Dean R. Burgess, — 3 Apr 2004 – 4 Apr 2009.

Second Counselor, Michael A; Neider, — 3 Apr 2004 – 4 Apr 2009.

Young Women General Presidency
As of October 2011

Mary N. Cook
First Counselor

Began serving on April 5, 2008 to present; previously served as second counselor from March 31, 2007, to April 5, 2008. Born in Salt Lake City, Utah, to Kenneth N. and Fern Swan Nielsen; received bachelor's and master's degree in speech pathology and audiology, and Ed.S. degree from BYU; former member of Young Women general board, Relief Society president, Primary counselor. She is a former special education teacher, administrator and elementary school principal in Jordan (Utah) School District; married Richard E. Cook; he and his first wife, Clea, who died in 1984, had four children.

Elaine S. Dalton
President

Began serving on April 5, 2008 to present; previously served as first counselor from March 31,2007, to April 5, 2008, and second counselor from Oct. 5, 2002, to March 31, 2007. Born in Ogden, Utah, to Melvin L. and Emma Martin Schwartz; received bachelor's degree in English from BYU; served as second counselor in Young Women general presidency until being sustained as first counselor March 31, 2007; former Young Women general board member, stake Young Women president, counselor and adviser; Young Single Adult Relief Society adviser and Relief Society instructor; married Stephen E. Dalton; parents of six children.

Ann M. Dibb
Second Counselor

Began serving on April 5, 2008 to present. Born in Salt Lake City, Utah, to Thomas S. and Frances Johnson Monson; received bachelor's degree from BYU in elementary education; former Young Women general board member, Primary president, Young Women president, Relief Society counselor, and counselor in stake Young Women presidency; married Roger A. Dibb; parents of four children.

Young Women History

President Brigham Young organized the Young Ladies Department of the Cooperative Retrenchment Association — predecessor to the Young Women program — on the evening of Nov. 28, 1869, in the parlor of the Lion House in Salt Lake City. He encouraged his older daughters, who were the charter members, to "retrench in your dress, in your tables, in your speech, wherein you have been guilty of silly, extravagant speeches and light-mindedness of thought. Retrench in everything that is bad and worthless, and improve in everything that is good and beautiful."

Thus, the Retrenchment Association was organized. Relief Society Gen. Pres. Eliza R. Snow supervised the association; Ella Young Empey was named as president.

News of the organization spread quickly. By the end of 1870, retrenchment associations had been established in several Mormon settlements. In addition, the organization had divided into senior and junior associations.

Not long after the creation of the Young Men's Mutual Improvement Association in 1875, President Young approved a name change to "Young Ladies National Mutual Improvement Association" to correspond to the young men's organization. The two organizations began holding monthly meetings together. In 1904, the word "National" was dropped since the Young Ladies' organization had become international in scope. Throughout the early years of the association's existence, the YLNMIA was directed through local ward efforts. The first stake board was organized in 1878 in the Salt Lake Stake, antedating the appointment of a general board. In 1880, Elmina S. Taylor was called as the first general president. She called as her counselors Margaret (Maggie) Y. Taylor and Martha (Mattie) Horne, with Louie Wells as secretary and Fanny Y. Thatcher as treasurer. That same year, Pres. Taylor presided over the first general conference of the YLNMIA.

Under the new general presidency's direction, the association encouraged the study of gospel principles, development of individual talents, and service to those in need. General, stake, and ward boards were subsequently appointed, lesson manuals were produced, and joint activities were established with the YMMIA. The *Young Woman's Journal* began in 1889 and began printing a series of lessons.

In 1888, the first annual June Conference for young women and young men was held. Leaders provided special training in physical activity, story-telling, and music and class instruction.

Four decades later, in 1929, a new summer camping program was announced at June Conference, and the *Young Woman's Journal* and *The Improvement Era* merged with the November issue. During the 1930s, MIA leaders gave new emphasis to music, dance, and the performing arts, with an annual June Conference dance festival being held.

In the late 1940s and the 1950s, the First Presidency turned over to the YWMIA leaders a girls enrollment incentive program, previously administered by the Presiding Bishopric. It was designed to increase attendance at Church meetings.

In the early 1970s, President Harold B. Lee introduced a correlation program designed to integrate Church programs for youth. From this effort eventually came the Personal Progress program and the Young Womanhood Achievement Awards. During the 1980s, Sunday Young Women classes began meeting at the same time as priesthood meeting for Young Men.

During the tenure of general Pres. Ardeth G. Kapp, who served from 1984-1992, the Young Women motto, "Stand for Truth and Righteousness," was introduced, along with the Young Women logo, represented by a torch with the profile of the face of a young woman. The torch represents the light of Christ.

During Pres. Kapp's administration, the Young Women theme and values were also introduced. The values are faith, divine nature, individual worth, knowledge, choice and accountability, good works, and integrity.

A memorable event for the program is the Young Women Worldwide Celebration, held every three years. Another Young Women Worldwide Celebration was held in the year 2000, two years after the 1998 celebration, rather than the usual three years between celebrations. An exception was made for 2000 because it was the bimillennial commemoration of the Savior's birth.

An updated, simplified Young Women Personal Progress Program, which mirrors the values of the new Aaronic Priesthood Duty to God program, was implemented in the United States and Canada in January 2002. On Sept. 28, 2001, the First Presidency announced the updated Personal Progress Program, along with the new Duty to God program. Both programs are based on standards set forth in an updated For the Strength of Youth guidebook. The Young Women Personal Progress Program is designed to help girls prepare for the Young Womanhood Recognition Award. The Young Womanhood Recognition medallion was also updated to feature spires of the Salt Lake Temple in gold or silver.

The First Presidency, in a letter to priesthood leaders dated Nov. 28, 2008, announced the addition of virtue to the Young Women theme and values, to go with the organization's other values of faith, divine nature, individual worth, knowledge, choice and accountability, good works and integrity.

Sources: *Encyclopedia of Mormonism*, vols. 3-4; *A Century of Sisterhood; History of the YWMIA*, by Marba C. Josephson; *Deseret News 1993-1994 Church Almanac; Church News*, Jan. 24, 1998, April 4, 1998;; "Stand as a witness," by Julie Dockstader Heaps, Church News, Dec. 2, 2000; "Personal Progress: temple preparation," by Julie Dockstader Heaps, *Church News*, Oct. 27, 2001.

HISTORICAL LISTING OF GENERAL PRESIDENCIES OF YOUNG WOMEN MUTUAL IMPROVEMENT ASSOCIATION AND YOUNG WOMEN

(Presidents pictured)

1. President, ELMINA SHEPHERD TAYLOR - 19 Jun 1880-6 Dec 1904.

First Counselors, Margaret Young Taylor - 19 Jun 1880-1887; Maria Young Dougall - 1887-6 Dec 1904.

Second Counselor, Martha Horne Tingey - 19 Jun 1880-6 Dec 1904.

2. President, MARTHA HORNE TINGEY - 5 Apr 1905-28 Mar 1929.

First Counselor, Ruth May Fox - 5 Apr 1905-28 Mar 1929.

Second Counselors, Mae Taylor Nystrom - 5 Apr 1905-15 Jul 1923; Lucy Grant Cannon, 15 Jul 1923-28 Mar 1929.

3. President, RUTH MAY FOX - 28 Mar 1929-Oct 1937.

First Counselor, Lucy Grant Cannon - 28 Mar 1929-Oct 1937.

Second Counselor, Clarissa A. Beesley - 30 Mar 1929-Oct 1937.

4. President, LUCY GRANT CANNON - Nov 1937-6 Apr 1948.

First Counselors, Helen Spencer Williams - Nov 1937-17 May 1944; Verna Wright Goddard - Jul 1944-6 Apr 1948.

Second Counselors, Verna Wright Goddard - Nov 1937-Jul 1944; Lucy T. Anderson - 6 Jul 1944-6 Apr 1948.

5. President, BERTHA STONE REEDER - 6 Apr 1948-30 Sep 1961.

First Counselor, Emily Higgs Bennett - 13 Jun 1948-30 Sep 1961.

Second Counselor, LaRue Carr Longden - 13 Jun 1948-30 Sep 1961.

6. President, FLORENCE SMITH JACOBSEN - 30 Sep 1961-9 Nov 1972.

First Counselor, Margaret R. Jackson - 30 Sep 1961-9 Nov 1972.

Second Counselor, Dorothy Porter Holt - 30 Sep 1961-9 Nov 1972.

AARONIC PRIESTHOOD MIA (YOUNG WOMEN)

7. President, RUTH HARDY FUNK - 9 Nov 1972-23 Jun 1974.

First Counselor, Hortense Hogan Child - 9 Nov 1972-23 Jun 1974.

Second Counselor, Ardeth Greene Kapp - 9 Nov 1972-23 Jun 1974.

YOUNG WOMEN

8. President, RUTH HARDY FUNK - 23 Jun 1974-12 Jul 1978.

First Counselor, Hortense Hogan Child - 23 Jun 1974-12 Jul 1978.

Second Counselor, Ardeth Greene Kapp - 23 Jun 1974-12 Jul 1978.

9. President, ELAINE ANDERSON CANNON - 12 Jul 1978-7 Apr 1984.

First Counselor, Arlene Barlow Darger - 12 Jul 1978-7 Apr 1984.

Second Counselor, Norma Broadbent Smith - 12 Jul 1978-7 Apr 1984.

10. President, ARDETH GREENE KAPP - 7 Apr 1984-4 Apr 1992.

First Counselors, Patricia Terry Holland - 11 May 1984-6 Apr 1986; Maurine Johnson Turley - 6 Apr 1986-4 Apr 1987; Jayne Broadbent Malan - 4 Apr 1987-4 Apr 1992.

Second Counselors, Maurine Johnson Turley - 11 May 1984-6 Apr 1986; Jayne Broadbent Malan - 6 Apr 1986-4 Apr 1987; Elaine Low Jack - 4 Apr 1987-31 Mar 1990; Janette Callister Hales - 31 Mar 1990-4 Apr 1992.

11. President, JANETTE HALES BECKHAM - 4 Apr 1992-4 Oct 1997.

First Counselor, Virginia Hinckley Pearce - 4 Apr 1992-4 Oct 1997.

Second Counselors, Patricia Peterson Pinegar - 4 Apr 1992-1 Oct 1994; Bonnie Dansie Parkin - 1 Oct 1994-5 Apr 1997; Carol Burdett Thomas - 5 Apr 1997-4 Oct 1997.

12. President, MARGARET DYRENG NADAULD - 4 Oct 1997- 5 Oct 2002.

First Counselor, Carol Burdett Thomas - 4 Oct 1997- 5 Oct 2002.

Second Counselor, Sharon Greene Larson, - 4 Oct 1997- 5 Oct 2002.

13. President, SUSAN WINDER TANNER - 5 Oct 2002 – 5 Apr 2008.

First Counselor, Julie Bangerter Beck – 5 Oct 2002 – 31 Mar 2007; Elaine Schwartz Dalton – 31 Mar 2007 – 5 Apr 2008.

Second Counselor, Elaine Schwartz Dalton – 5 Oct 2002 – 31 Mar 2007; Mary Nielsen Cook – 31 Mar 2007 – 5 Apr 2008.

WORLDWIDE CHURCH

AREAS OF THE WORLD
Temples depicted

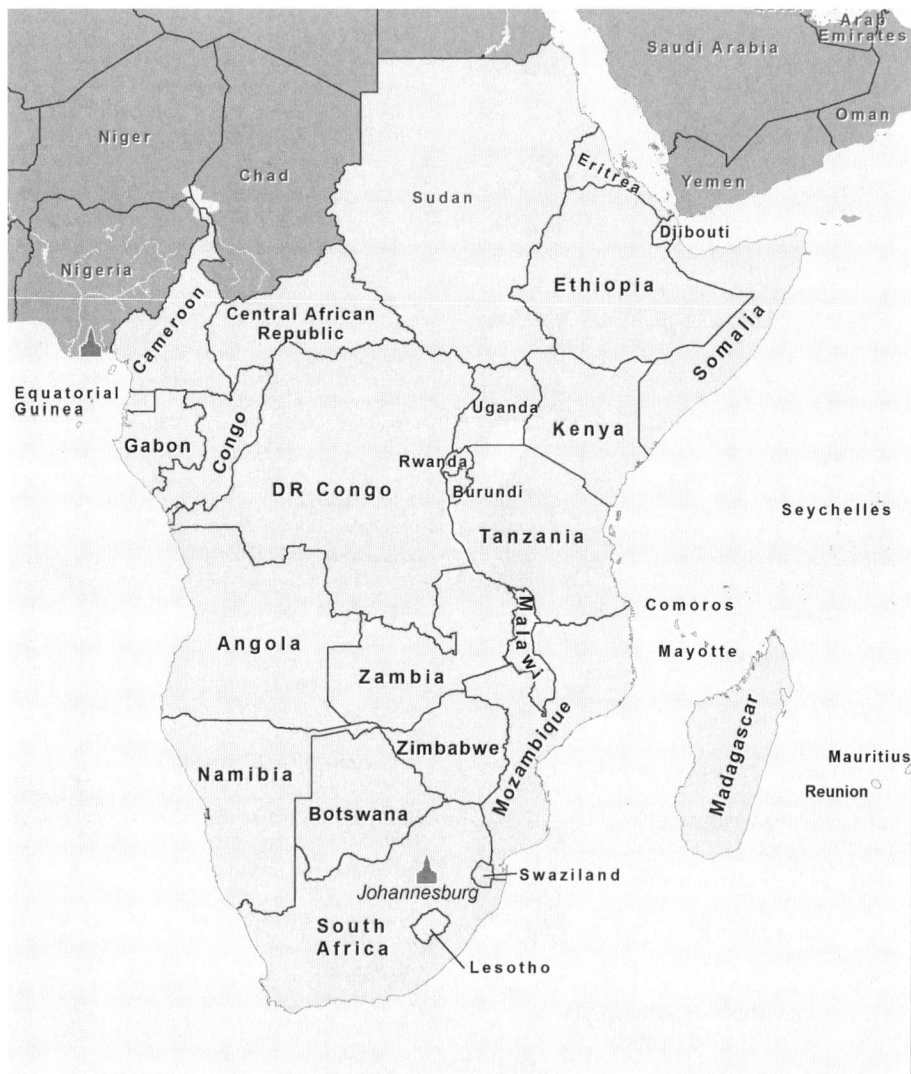

Africa Southeast Area
As of 1 January 2011

Membership: 150,266; Stakes: 25; Wards: 178; Missions: 10; Districts: 23; Branches: 278; Temples: 1; two announced: Kinshasa DR Congo, Durban South Africa. Headquarters: Johannesburg, South Africa.

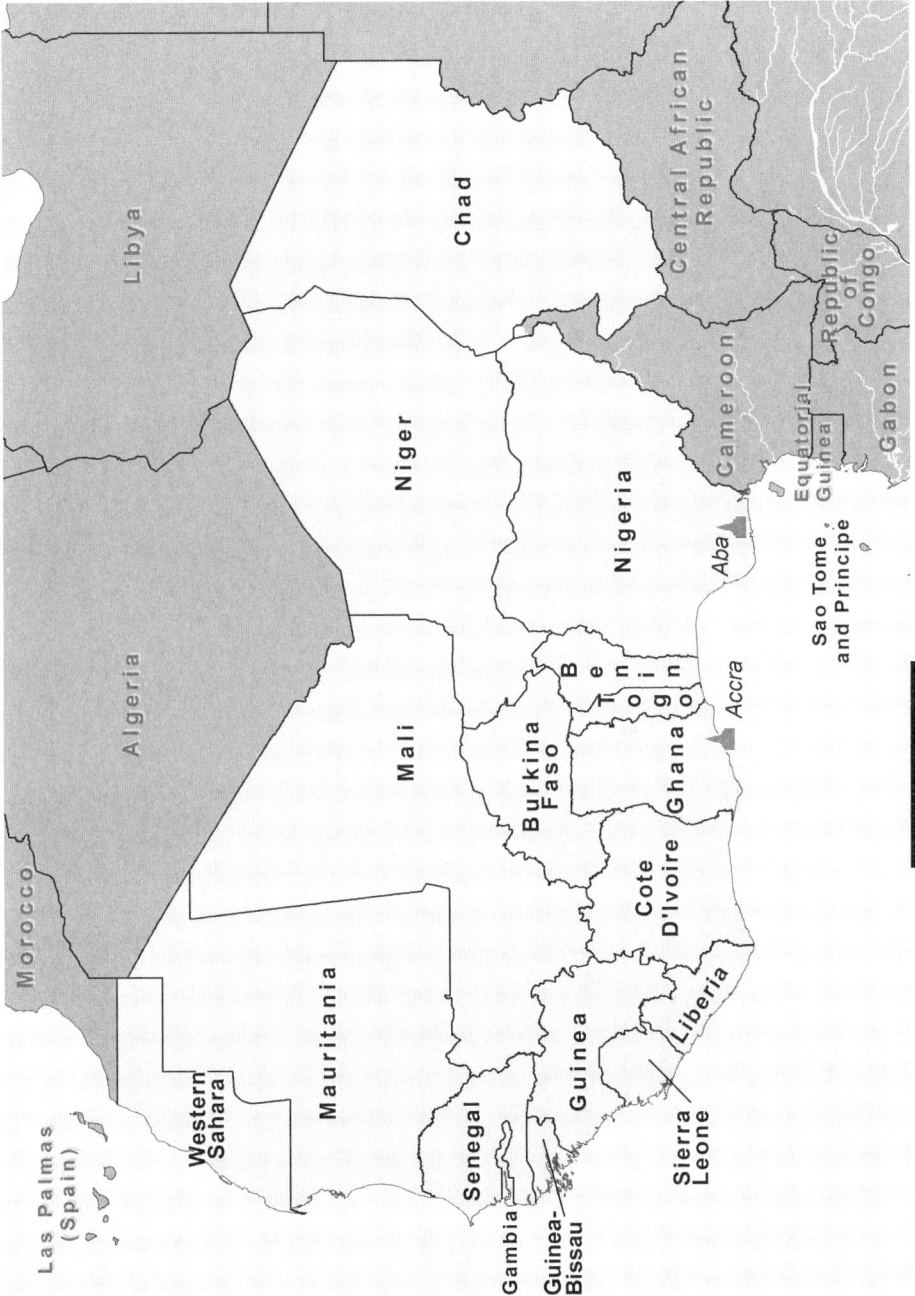

Africa West Area

As of 1 January 2011

Membership: 175,039; Stakes: 27; Wards: 227; Missions: 8; Districts: 33;
Branches: 286; Temples: 2; Headquarters: Accra, Ghana.

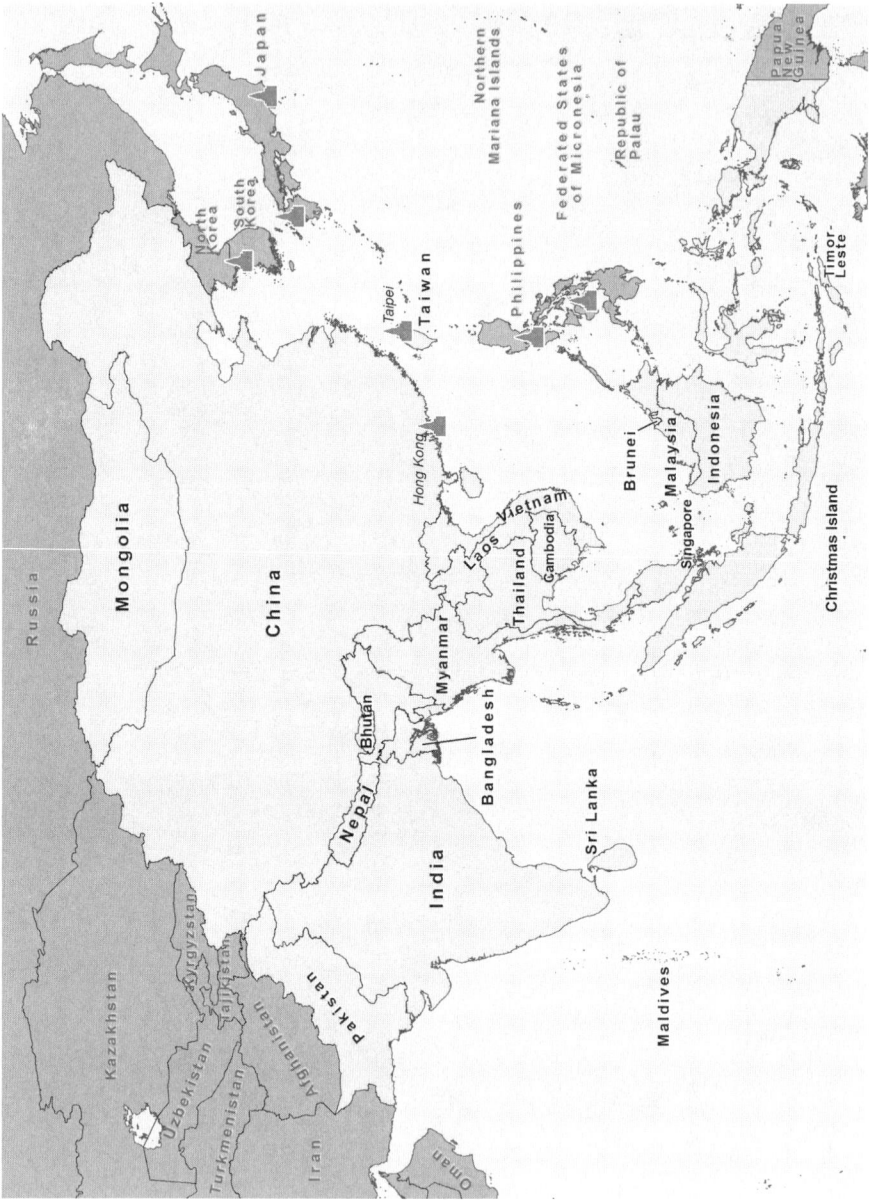

Asia Area

As of 1 January 2011

Membership: 155,173; Stakes: 18; Wards: 127; Missions: 10; Districts: 43; Branches: 267; Temples: 2; Headquarters: Hong Kong, China.

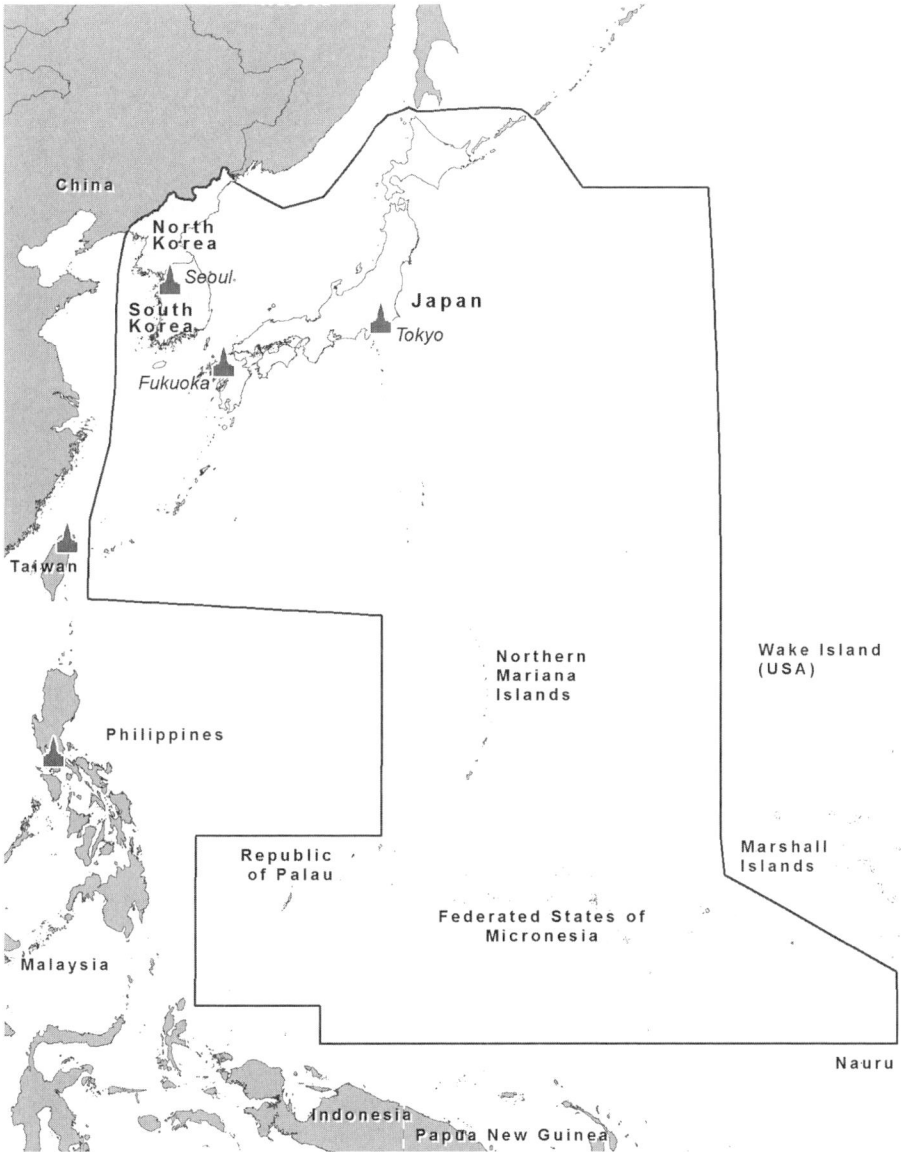

Asia North Area

As of 1 January 2011

Membership: 216,895; Stakes: 46; Wards: 258; Missions: 10; Districts: 25;
Branches: 193; Temples: 3, Sapporo announced; Headquarters: Tokyo, Japan.

Philippines Area

As of 1 January 2011

Membership: 645,776: Stakes: 80; Wards: 500; Missions: 16; Districts: 85;
Branches: 600; Temples: 2; one announced in Urdaneta.
Headquarters: Manila, Philippines.

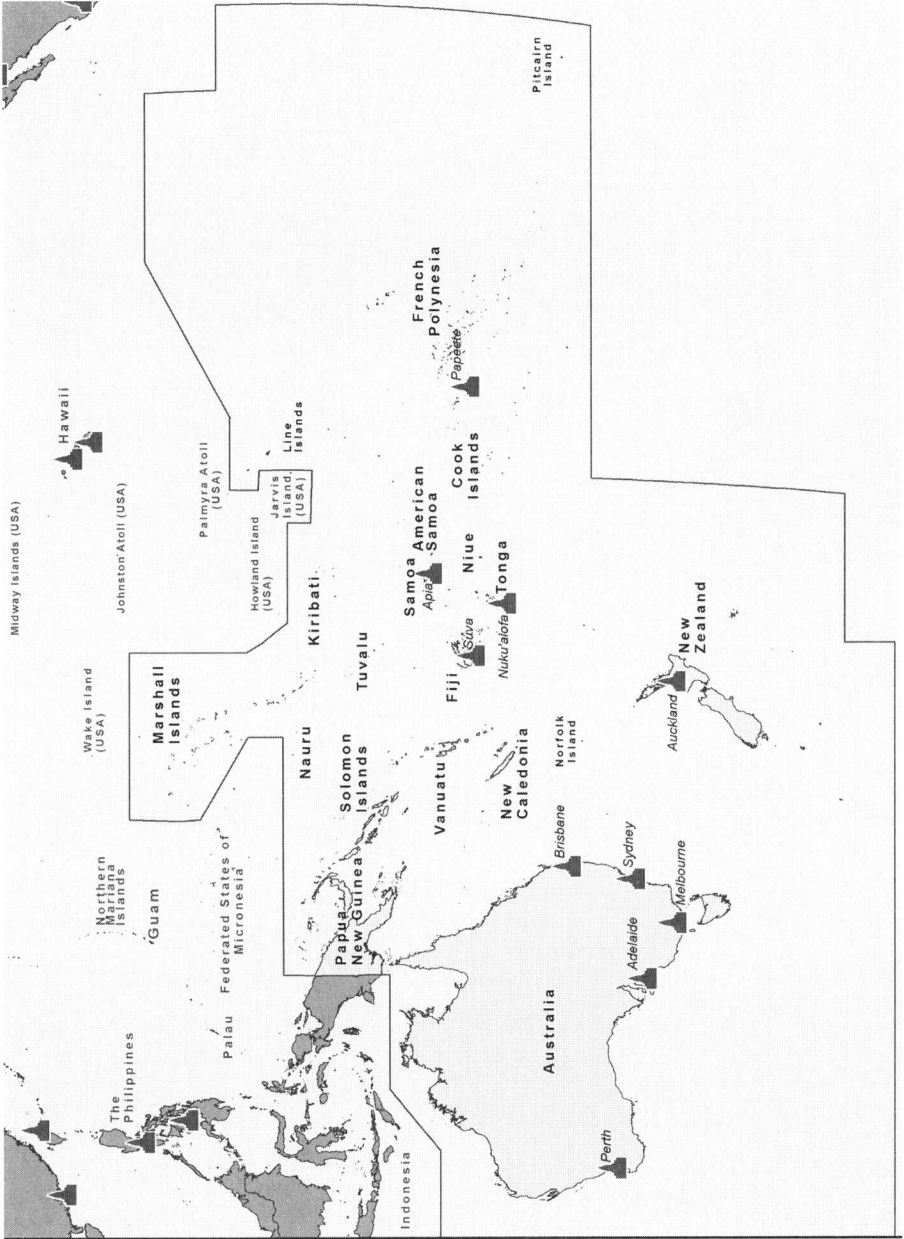

Pacific Area

As of 1 January 2011

Membership: 463,498; Stakes: 109; Wards: 735; Missions: 13;
Districts: 32; Branches: 366; Temples: 10;
Headquarters: Auckland, New Zealand.

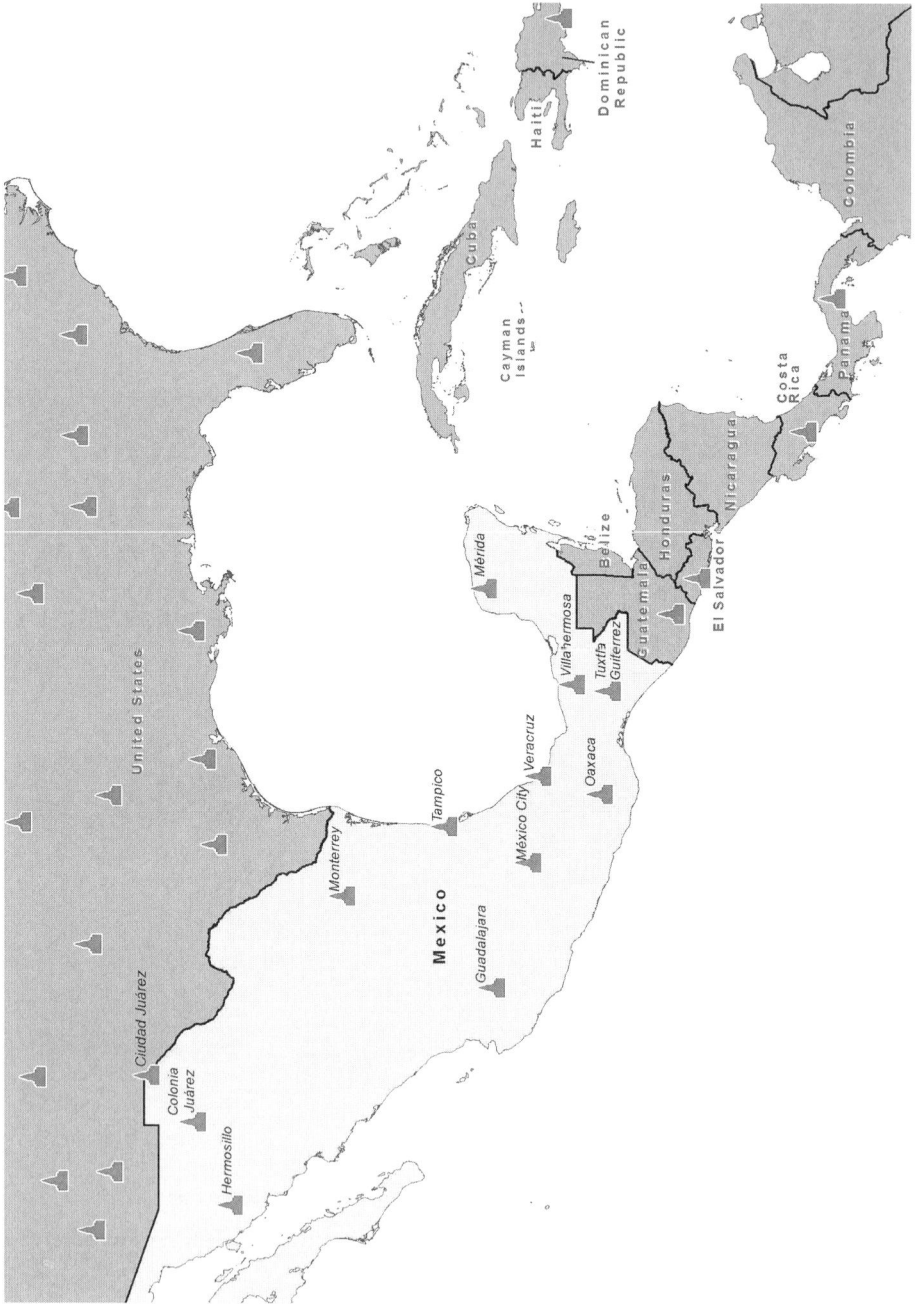

Mexico Area

As of 1 January 2011

Membership: 1,234,545; Stakes: 221; Wards: 1,544; Missions: 23; Districts: 34;
Branches: 465; Temples: 12, one announced Tijuana.
Headquarters: Mexico City, Mexico.

Haiti

Jamaica

Colombia

Panama
City

Panama

San
Jose

Costa
Rica

Nicaragua

Honduras

Belize

San
Salvador

El Salvador

Guatemala

Guatemala
City

Mexico

Central America Area
As of 1 January 2011
Membership: 637,905; Stakes: 98; Wards: 631; Missions: 14; Districts: 46;
Branches: 433; Temples: 4; two announced, Quetzaltenango Guatemala,
Tegucigalpa Honduras. Headquarters: Guatemala City, Guatemala.

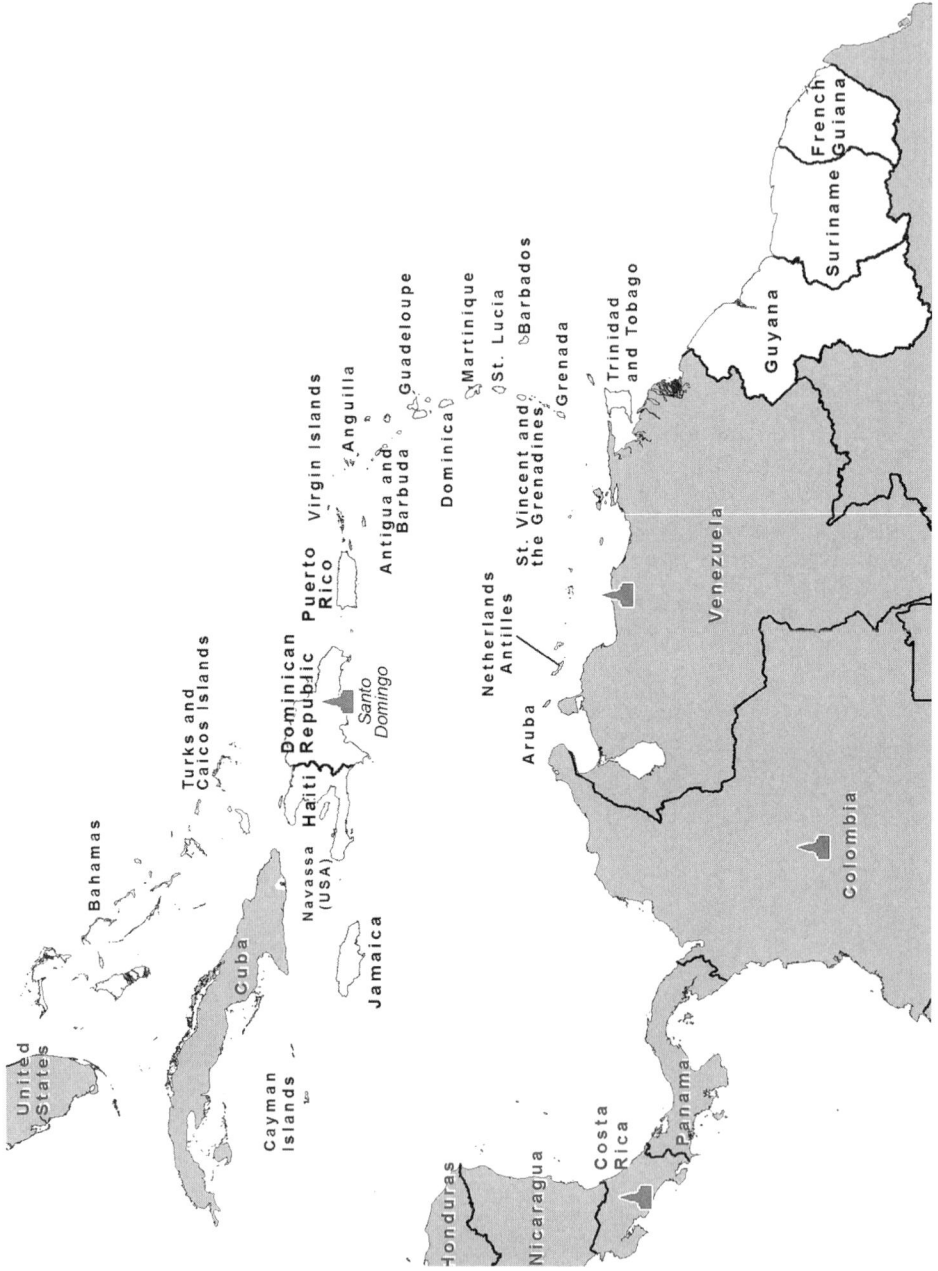

Caribbean
As of 1 January 2011

Membership: 177,654; Stakes: 26; Wards: 166; Missions: 7; Districts: 20; Branches: 198; Temples: 1;
Headquarters: Santo Domingo, Dominican Republic

Brazil Area
As of 1 January 2011

Membership: 1,138,473; Stakes: 239; Wards: 1,457; Missions: 27; Districts: 49; Branches: 467; Temples: 5, two announced, Fontaleza Brazil and Manaus Brazil; Headquarters: Sao Paulo, Brazil.

South America South Area

As of 1 January 2011

Membership: 565,925; Stakes: 96;
Wards: 651; Missions: 14; Districts: 52; Branches: 502; Temples: 3; one announced,
Cordoba Argentina; Headquarters: Buenos Aires, Argentina.

Chile Area

As of 1 January 2011
Membership: 563,671; Stakes: 74;
Wards: 421; Missions: 9; Districts: 23; Branches: 198;
Temples: 1, one announced, Concepción Chile; Headquarters: Santiago, Chile.

South America Northwest Area

As of 1 January 2011

Membership: 1,184,962; Stakes: 209; Wards: 1,359; Missions: 23; Districts: 63; Branches: 517; Temples: 5; two announced: Trujillo Peru, Barranquilla Colombia. Headquarters: Bogota, Colombia.

Ireland

Denmark

Estonia

Latvia

Lithuania

U.K.

Neth.

Germany

Belarus

Poland

Czech
Republic

France

Switz.

Austria

Ukraine

Croatia

Romania

Portugal

Italy

Serbia

Spain

Bulgaria

Greece

Tur

Morocco

Malta

Cyprus

Tunisia

L∈

Israel

Algeria

Libya

Egypt

Mali

Niger

Burkina
Faso

Chad

Benin

Sudan

Togo

Nigeria

Middle East/Africa North Area
As of 1 January 2011

Membership: 3,795; Stakes: 1; Wards; 8; Missions: 0; Districts: 4;
Branches: 29; Headquarters: Salt Lake City, Utah.

Church units in these countries are principally comprised of members
of the Church from other countries who are serving their native governments
or working for international companies as expatriates.

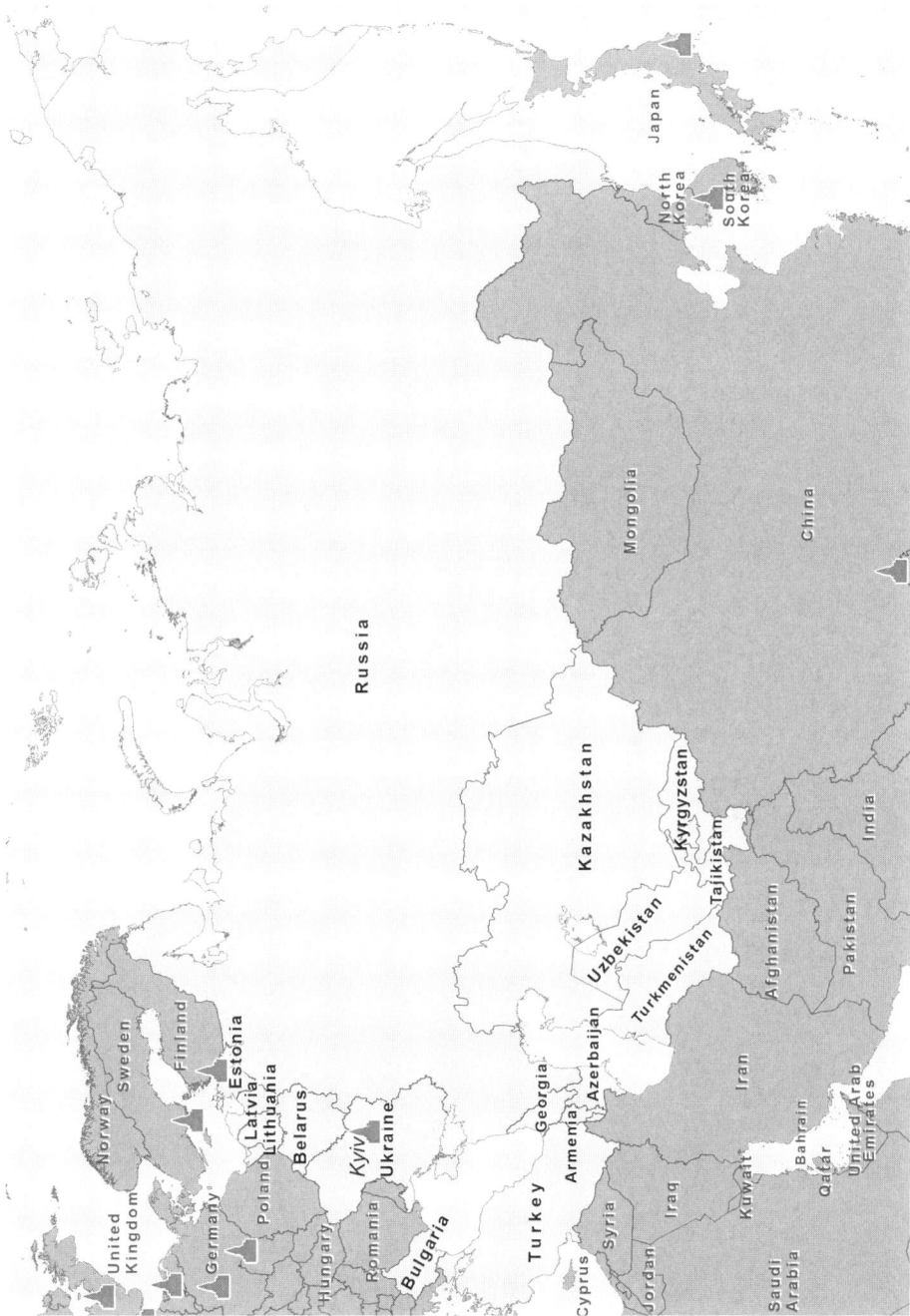

Europe East Area

As of 1 January 2011

Membership: 41,171; Stakes: 1; Wards; 8; Missions: 14; Districts: 25;
Branches: 228; Temples: 1;
Headquarters: Moscow, Russia.

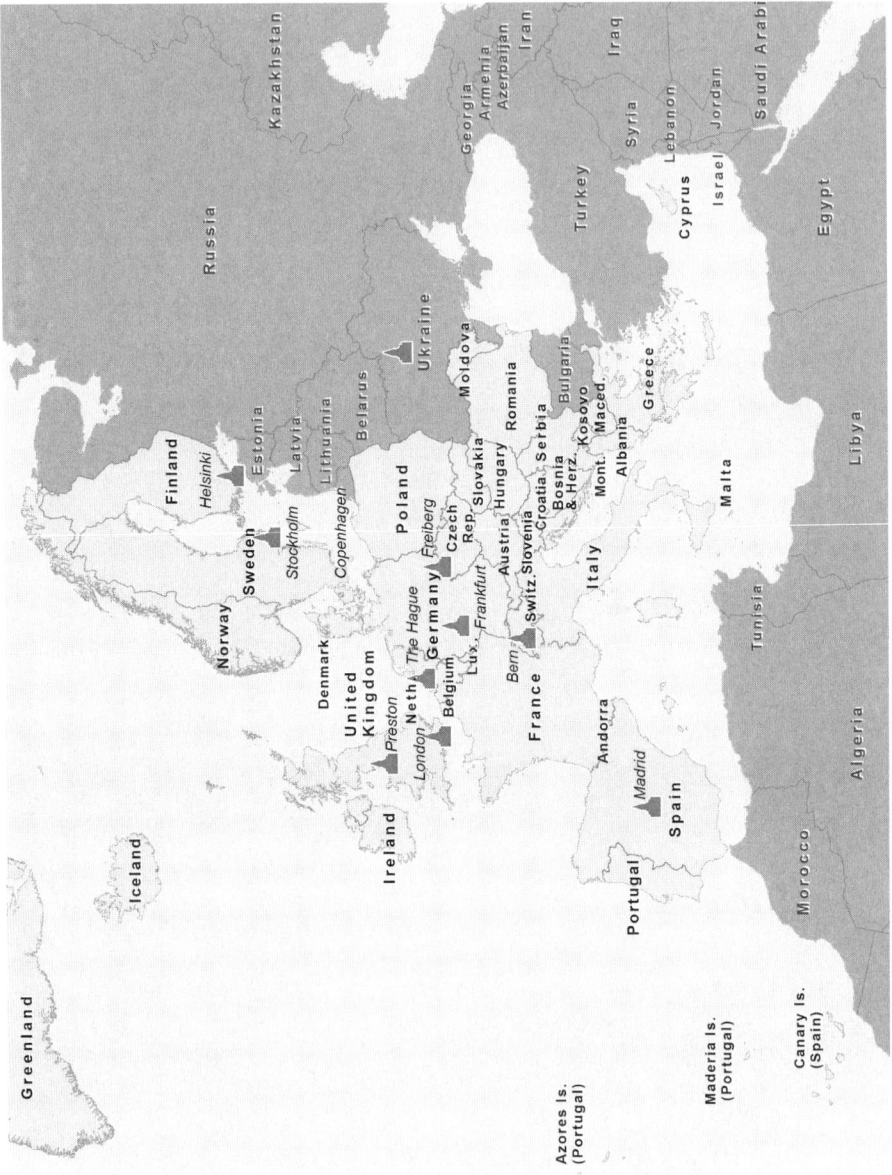

Europe Area

As of 1 January 2011

Membership: 449,582; Stakes: 114; Wards: 708; Missions: 32; Districts: 42; Branches: 573; Temples: 10; three announced: Rome Italy, Lisbon Portugal, Paris France. Headquarters: Frankfurt, Germany.

North America Northwest Area

As of 1 January 2011

Membership: 487,626; Stakes: 108; Wards: 824; Missions: 9; Districts: 1;
Branches: 176; Temples: 7; Headquarters: Salt Lake City, Utah.

Oregon

Idaho

Nevada

Sacramento

Oakland

California

Fresno

Hawaii

Laie

Los Angeles

Redlands

Newport Beach

Kailua-Kona

San Diego

North America West Area
As of 1 January 2011
Membership: 826,178; Stakes: 171; Wards: 1,300; Missions: 17;
Branches: 176; Temples: 9; Headquarters: Salt Lake City, Utah.

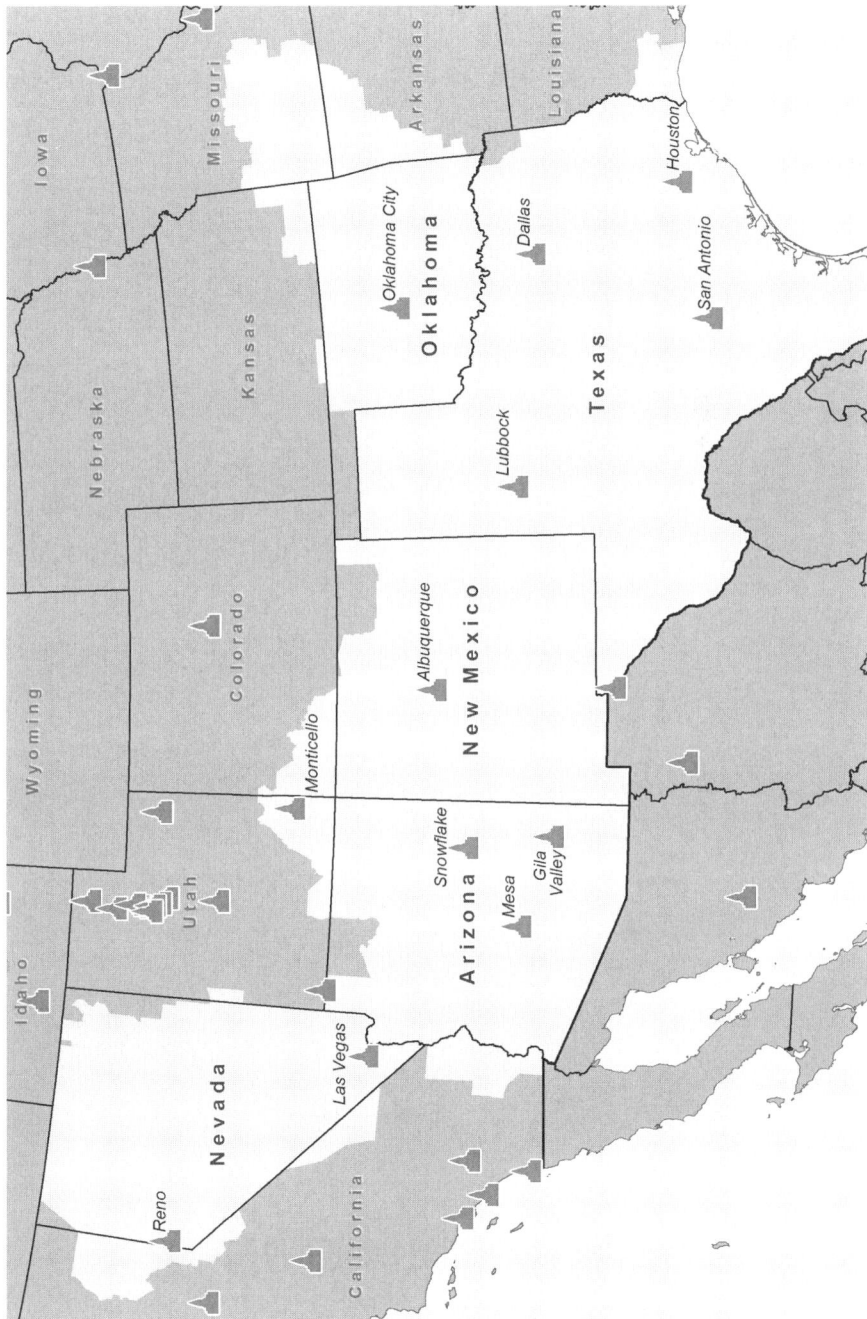

Iowa
Missouri
Arkansas
Louisiana
Oklahoma City
Oklahoma
Dallas
Houston
San Antonio
Kansas
Texas
Nebraska
Lubbock
Colorado
Albuquerque
New Mexico
Wyoming
Monticello
Snowflake
Arizona
Mesa
Gila Valley
Utah
Idaho
Nevada
Las Vegas
Reno
California

North America Southwest Area

As of 1 January 2011
Membership: 1,017,008; Stakes: 213; Wards: 1,682; Missions: 18;
Districts: 3; Branches: 346; Temples: 12; two announced, Gilbert Arizona and
Phoenix Arizona; Headquarters: Salt Lake City, Utah.

North America Central Area

As of 1 January 2011

Membership: 564,978; Stakes: 133; Wards: 1,008; Missions: 16; Districts: 2; Branches: 370; Temples: 11; four announced: Calgary Alberta, Kansas City Missouri, Fort Collins Colorado, Winnepeg Manitoba. Headquarters: Salt Lake City, Utah.

Newfoundland and Labrador

Québec

Prince Edward Is.

New Brunswick

Ontario

Halifax

ME

Nova Scotia

Montreal

VT NH

Toronto NY *Boston*

Palmyra MA

MI CT

Detroit RI

PA *Manhattan*

OH NJ

MD

IN *Columbus* DC

WV *Washington DC*

KY VA

TN NC

Bermuda

North America Northeast Area

As of 1 January 2011

Membership: 581,721; Stakes: 119; Wards: 873; Missions: 24; Districts: 8;
Branches: 399; Temples: 9, three announced, Philadelphia Pennsylvania,
Indianapolis Indiana and Hartford Connecticut;
Headquarters: Salt Lake City, Utah.

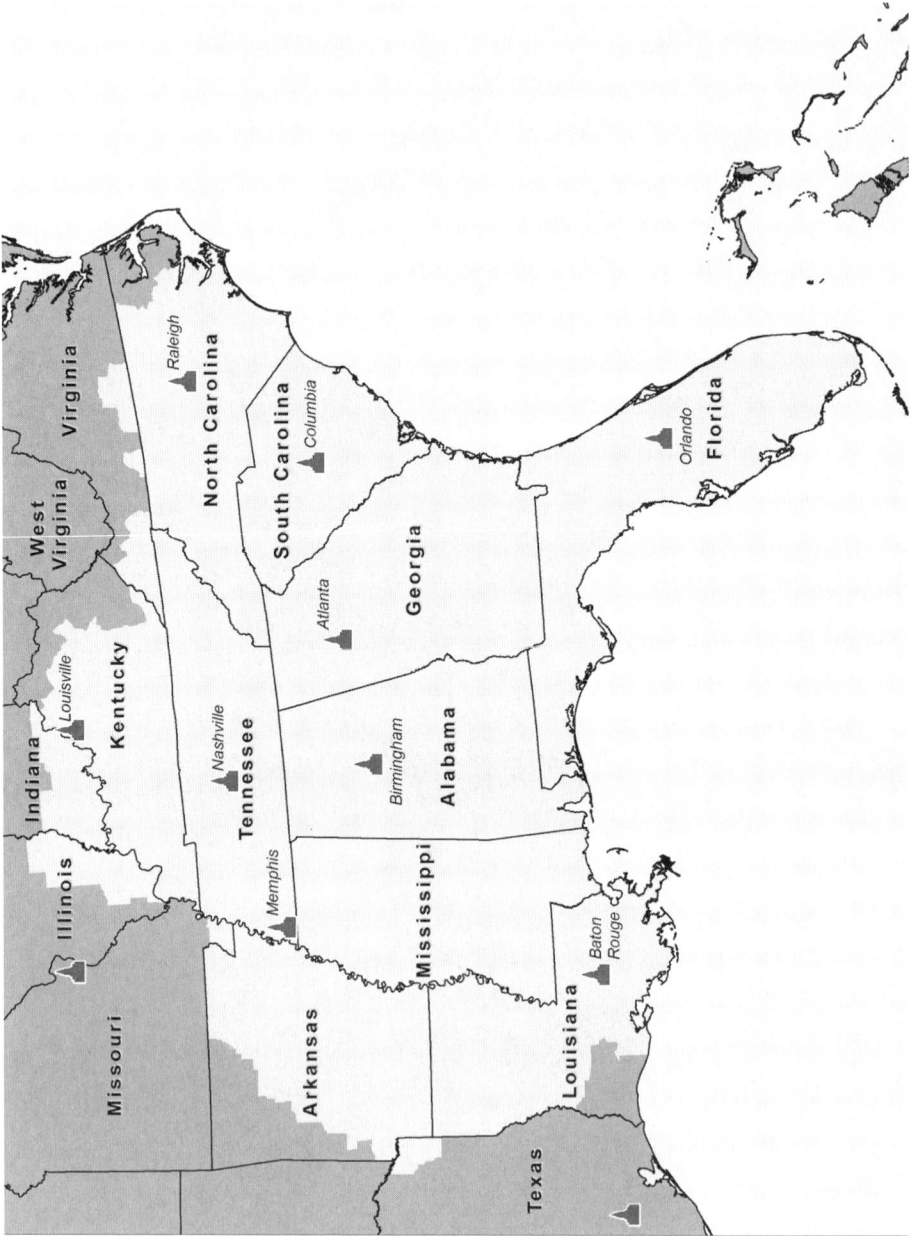

North America Southeast Area

As of 1 January 2011

Membership: 509,454; Stakes: 99; Wards: 695; Missions: 18; Districts: 0;
Branches: 291; Temples: 9, one announced, Fort Lauderdale Florida;
Headquarters: Salt Lake City, Utah.

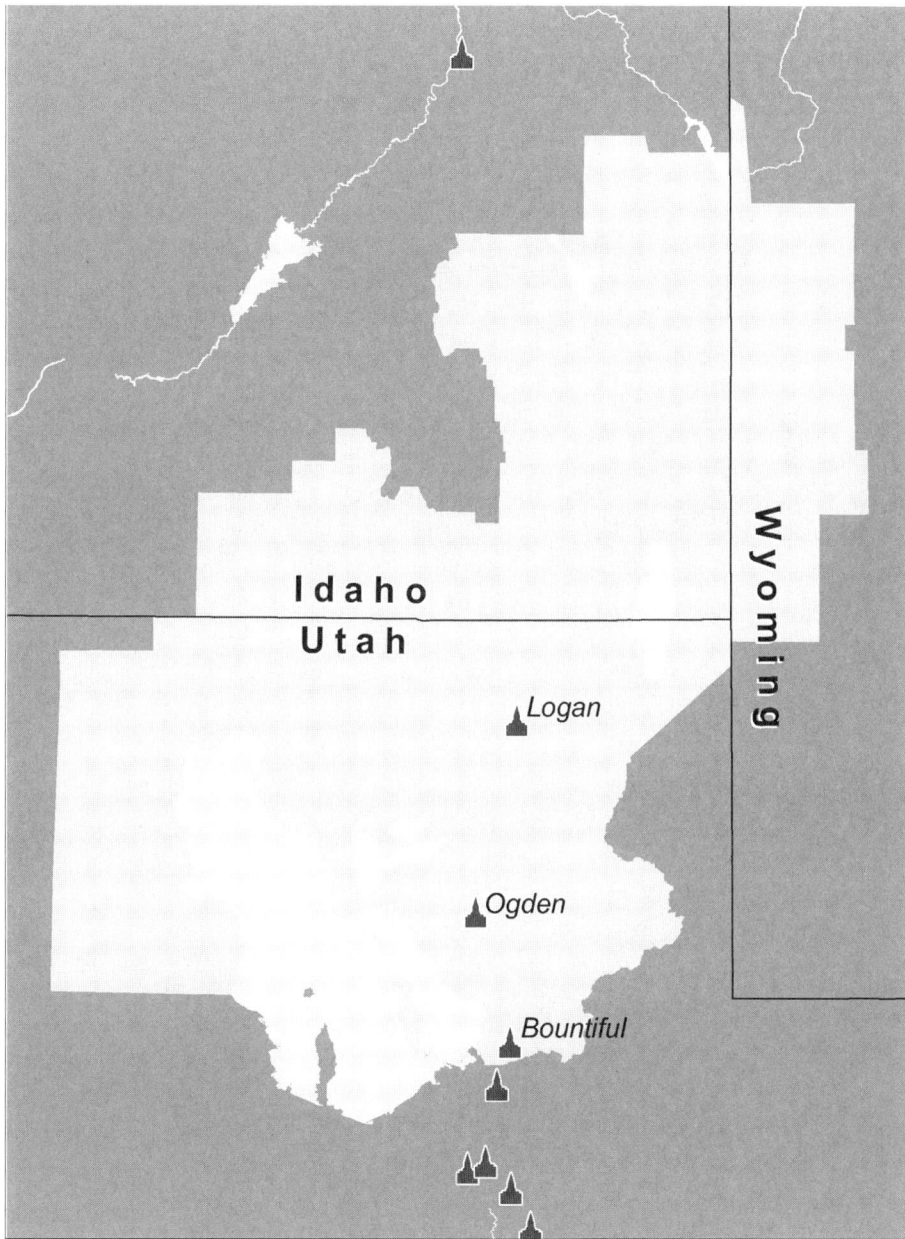

Utah North Area

As of 1 January 2011

Membership: 542,093; Stakes: 154; Wards: 1,283; Missions: 1; Branches: 83;
Temples: 3; two announced: Brigham City Utah, Star Valley Wyoming.
Headquarters: Salt Lake City, Utah

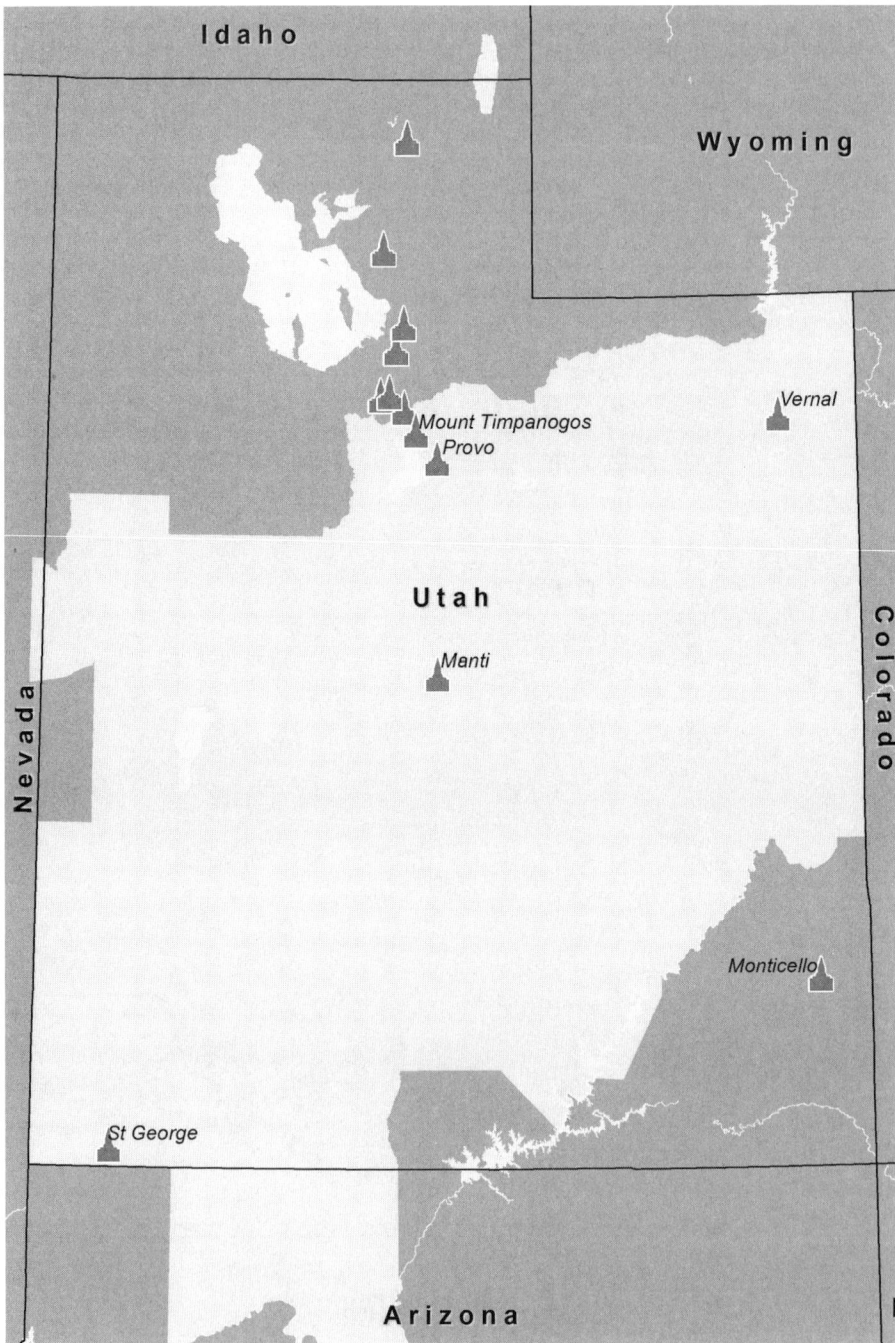

Utah South Area

As of 1 January 2011

Membership: 732,576; Stakes: 219; Wards: 1,894; Missions: 2;
Branches: 126; Temples: 5; two announced Payson Utah, Provo Utah Tabernacle.
Headquarters: Salt Lake City, Utah.

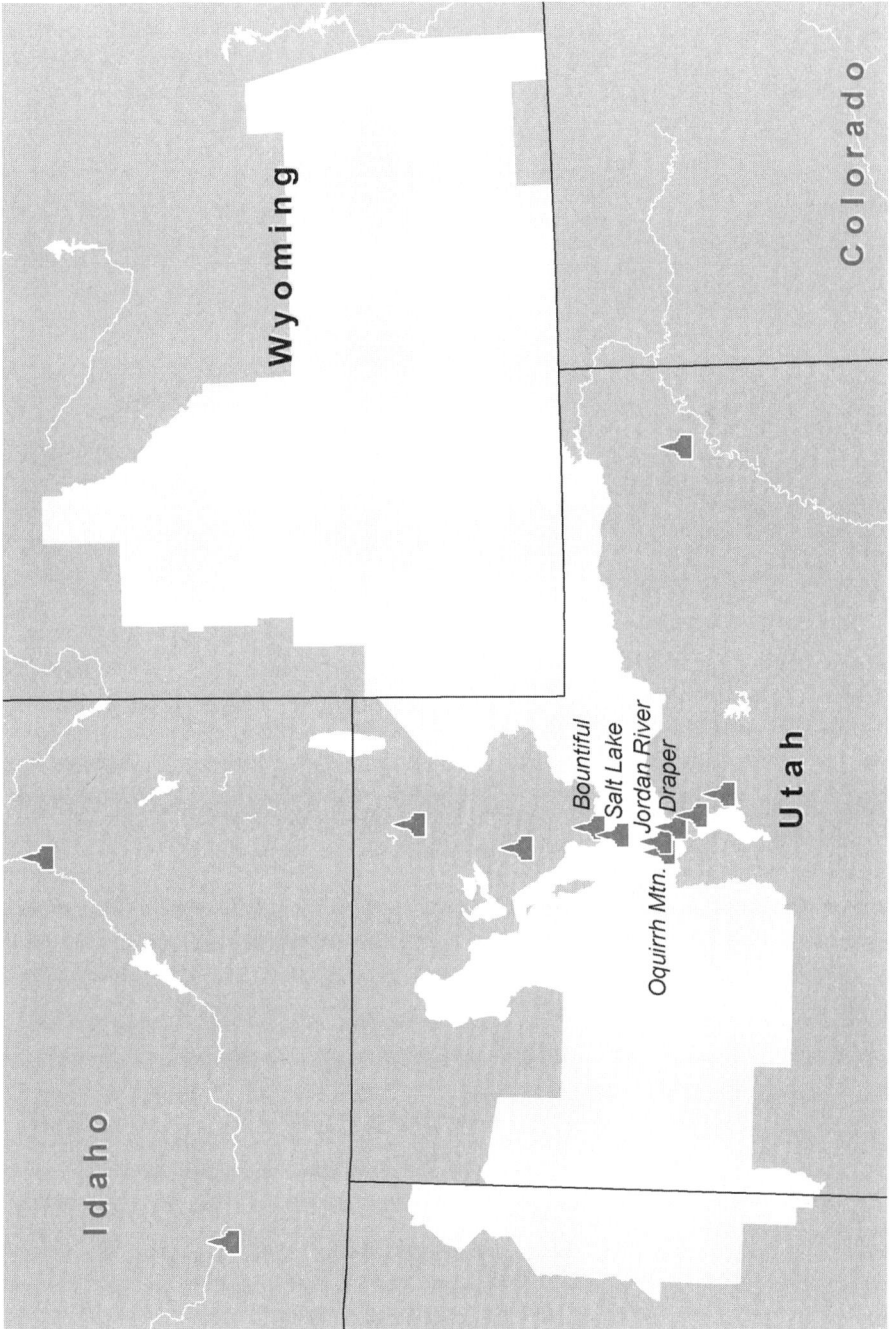

Utah Salt Lake City Area

As of 1 January 2011

Membership: 685,742; Stakes: 187; Wards: 1,421; Missions: 3; Districts: 1;
Branches: 148; Temples: 4; Headquarters: Salt Lake City, Utah.

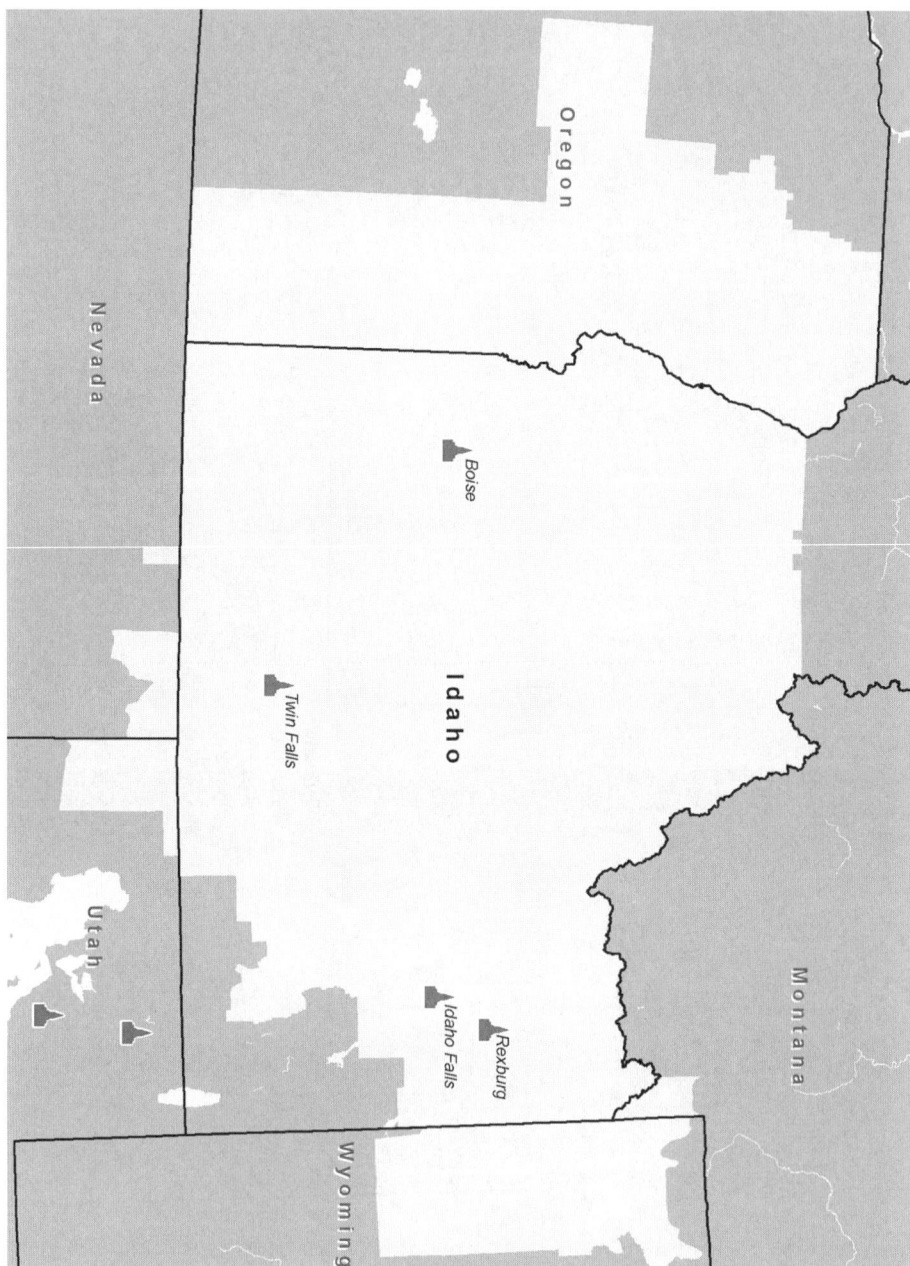

Idaho Area

As of 1 January 2011

Membership: 379,761; Stakes: 109; Wards: 896; Missions: 2;
Branches: 91; Temples: 4; one announced: Meridian Idaho.
Headquarters: Salt Lake City, Utah.

2011 MEMBERSHIP STATISTICS

As of 1 January 2011

Membership and units by Church area. area boundaries do not necessarily follow country, state or province boundaries.

Area	Membership	Stakes	Wards	Branches in stakes	Missions	Districts	Branches in missions	Total wards, branches
AFRICA SOUTHEAST	150,266	25	178	73	10	23	205	456
AFRICA WEST	175,039	27	227	40	8	33	246	513
ASIA	155,173	18	127	19	10	43	248	394
ASIA NORTH	216,895	46	258	79	10	25	114	451
BRAZIL	1,138,473	239	1,457	210	27	49	257	1,924
CARIBBEAN	177,654	26	166	46	7	20	152	364
CENTRAL AMERICA	637,905	98	631	166	14	46	267	1,064
CHILE	563,671	74	421	69	9	23	129	619
EUROPE	449,582	114	708	290	32	42	283	1,281
EUROPE EAST	41,171	1	8	3	14	25	225	236
IDAHO	379,761	109	896	91	2	0	0	987
MEXICO	1,234,545	221	1,544	237	23	34	228	2,009
MIDDLE EAST / NORTH AFRICA	3,795	1	8	9	0	4	20	37
NORTH AMERICA CENTRAL	564,978	133	1,008	352	16	2	18	1,378
NORTH AMERICA NORTHEAST	581,721	119	873	347	24	8	52	1,272
NORTH AMERICA NORTHWEST	487,626	108	824	172	9	1	4	1,000
NORTH AMERICA SOUTHEAST	509,454	99	695	291	18	0	0	986
NORTH AMERICA SOUTHWEST	1,017,008	213	1,682	333	18	3	13	2,028
NORTH AMERICA WEST	826,178	171	1,300	176	17	0	0	1,476
PACIFIC	463,498	109	735	137	13	32	229	1,101
PHILIPPINES	645,776	80	500	138	16	85	462	1,100
SOUTH AMERICA NORTHWEST	1,184,962	209	1,359	189	23	63	328	1,876
SOUTH AMERICA SOUTH	565,925	96	651	221	14	52	281	1,153
UTAH NORTH	542,093	154	1,283	83	1	0	0	1,366
UTAH SALT LAKE CITY	685,742	187	1,421	143	3	1	5	1,569
UTAH SOUTH	732,576	219	1,894	126	2	0	0	2,020
TOTALS	14,131,467	2,896	20,854	4,040	340	614	3,766	28,660

2011 Membership by Countries

Country	Membership	Stakes	Wards	Branches in stakes	Missions	Districts	Branches in missions	Total wards, branches
AFRICA								
ANGOLA	932	0	0	0	0	0	3	3
BENIN	229	0	0	0	0	0	1	1
BOTSWANA	1,331	0	2	1	0	0	1	4
CAMEROON	1,003	0	0	0	0	0	5	5
CAPE VERDE	7,456	0	0	0	1	3	18	18
CENTRAL AFRICAN REPUBLIC	427	0	0	0	0	0	1	1
COTE D'IVOIRE / IVORY COAST	15,638	4	30	2	1	1	12	44
DEMOCRATIC REPUBLIC OF CONGO	27,058	7	55	5	2	5	34	94
ETHIOPIA	1,125	0	0	0	0	1	4	4
GHANA	45,094	7	58	15	2	6	48	121
KENYA	10,270	1	5	3	1	1	28	36
LESOTHO	747	0	0	0	0	0	2	2
LIBERIA	5,447	0	0	0	0	2	13	13
MADAGASCAR	6,736	1	12	2	1	2	14	28
MALAWI	925	0	0	0	0	0	3	3
MAURITIUS	406	0	0	0	0	0	2	2
MOZAMBIQUE	5,392	0	0	0	1	2	18	18
NAMIBIA	686	0	0	0	0	0	2	2
NIGERIA	98,359	16	139	23	4	21	144	306
REPUBLIC OF CONGO	4,799	1	8	4	0	0	3	15
REUNION	851	0	0	0	0	1	4	4
SIERRA LEONE	8,907	0	0	0	1	2	23	23
SOUTH AFRICA	54,996	11	72	44	3	4	31	147
SWAZILAND	1,287	0	0	0	0	1	4	4
TANZANIA	1,007	0	0	0	0	1	5	5
TOGO	1,246	0	0	0	0	1	5	5
UGANDA	9,024	1	6	5	1	1	7	18
ZAMBIA	2,587	0	0	0	0	2	10	10
ZIMBABWE	18,549	3	18	9	1	2	21	48
AFRICA TOTALS	**332,725**	**52**	**405**	**113**	**19**	**59**	**467**	**985**
ASIA								
ARMENIA	2,888	0	0	0	1	2	15	15
BAHRAIN	134	1	0	1	0	0	0	1
CAMBODIA	10,530	0	0	0	1	5	24	24
CHINA, HONG KONG	24,425	4	23	1	1	1	8	32
CYPRUS	381	0	0	0	0	1	4	4
GEORGIA	208	0	0	0	0	0	2	2
INDIA	9,188	0	0	0	2	6	36	36
INDONESIA	6,683	0	0	0	1	3	21	21
ISRAEL	286	0	0	0	0	1	4	4
JAPAN	125,107	28	160	57	6	15	69	286
KAZAKHSTAN	162	0	0	0	0	0	1	1
MACAU	673	0	0	0	0	0	2	2

Country	Membership	Stakes	Wards	Branches in stakes	Missions	Districts	Branches in missions	Total wards, branches
MALAYSIA	7,314	0	0	1	0	6	27	28
MONGOLIA	9,896	1	6	0	1	2	17	23
PHILIPPINES	645,776	80	500	138	16	85	462	1,100
SINGAPORE	3,337	1	8	0	1	0	1	9
SOUTH KOREA	84,380	17	93	22	3	6	24	139
SRI LANKA	1,294	0	0	0	0	1	3	3
TAIWAN	53,111	11	83	11	2	1	6	100
THAILAND	16,331	1	7	6	1	5	24	37
TURKEY	254	0	0	0	0	0	4	4
UNITED ARAB EMIRATES	906	0	3	2	0	0	0	5
ASIA TOTALS	**1,003,972**	**144**	**885**	**241**	**36**	**140**	**754**	**1,880**

NORTH AMERICA

Country	Membership	Stakes	Wards	Branches in stakes	Missions	Districts	Branches in missions	Total wards, branches
ANTIGUA AND BARBUDA	189	0	0	0	0	0	1	1
ARUBA	489	0	0	0	0	0	2	2
BAHAMAS	917	0	0	0	0	0	3	3
BARBADOS	733	0	0	0	0	1	4	4
BELIZE	3,852	0	0	0	0	2	11	11
BERMUDA	140	0	0	0	0	0	1	1
CANADA								
ALBERTA	76,669	22	173	33	2	0	0	206
BRITISH COLUMBIA	29,273	8	49	25	1	1	4	78
MANITOBA	4,600	1	7	5	1	0	0	12
NEW BRUNSWICK	2,944	1	5	1	0	0	0	6
NEWFOUNDLAND	731	0	0	0	0	0	3	3
NORTHWEST TERRITORIES	128	0	0	0	0	0	1	1
NOVA SCOTIA	4,886	1	6	6	1	1	6	18
ONTARIO	45,969	9	59	29	2	2	12	100
PRINCE EDWARD ISLAND	440	0	0	0	0	0	3	3
QUEBEC	10,956	3	18	13	1	1	4	35
SASKATCHEWAN	5,554	2	8	9	0	0	0	17
YUKON	265	0	0	1	0	0	0	1
CANADA TOTALS	**182,415**	**47**	**325**	**122**	**8**	**5**	**33**	**480**
CAYMAN ISLAND	203	0	0	0	0	0	1	1
COSTA RICA	38,337	5	44	10	1	5	23	77
DOMINICA	128	0	0	0	0	0	1	1
DOMINICAN REPUBLIC	118,557	18	118	29	3	10	54	201
EL SALVADOR	109,118	17	115	29	2	2	17	161
GRENADA	230	0	0	0	0	0	1	1
GUADELOUPE	423	0	0	0	0	1	4	4
GUATEMALA	226,027	39	235	68	5	19	112	415
HAITI	16,902	2	16	0	1	2	16	32
HONDURAS	142,258	20	137	37	3	6	45	219
JAMAICA	5,721	0	0	0	1	2	20	20
MARTINIQUE	203	0	0	0	0	0	2	2
MEXICO	1,234,545	221	1,544	237	23	34	228	2,009

Country	Membership	Stakes	Wards	Branches in stakes	Missions	Districts	Branches in missions	Total wards, branches
NETHERLANDS ANTILLES								
BONAIRE	108	0	0	0	0	0	1	1
CURACAO	560	0	0	0	0	0	1	1
SAINT MAARTEN	159	0	0	0	0	0	0	1
TOTALS	827	0	0	0	0	0	3	3
NICARAGUA	71,888	9	58	10	2	7	35	103
PANAMA	46,425	8	42	12	1	5	24	78
PUERTO RICO	20,785	5	27	14	1	0	0	41
SAINT KITTS-NEVIS	197	0	0	0	0	0	1	1
SAINT LUCIA	217	0	0	0	0	0	2	2
SAINT MARTIN	75	0	0	0	0	0	1	1
SAINT VINCENT / GRENADINES	493	0	0	0	0	0	2	2
TRINIDAD & TOBAGO	2,885	1	5	3	1	0	3	11
UNITED STATES								
ALABAMA	34,725	6	41	33	1	0	0	74
ALASKA	32,170	7	50	30	1	0	0	80
ARIZONA	387,950	90	713	88	4	0	0	801
ARKANSAS	27,559	5	35	27	1	0	0	62
CALIFORNIA	763,370	157	1,187	174	16	0	0	1,361
COLORADO	142,473	30	257	32	3	0	0	289
CONNECTICUT	14,990	4	27	5	1	0	0	32
DELAWARE	5,184	1	10	3	0	0	0	13
DISTRICT OF COLUMBIA	2,382	0	2	1	0	0	0	3
FLORIDA	136,549	26	184	50	5	0	0	234
GEORGIA	77,948	15	112	39	3	0	0	151
HAWAII	69,872	15	124	10	1	0	0	134
IDAHO	414,182	121	979	98	2	0	0	1,077
ILLINOIS	55,750	12	94	34	2	0	0	128
INDIANA	41,290	11	68	31	1	0	0	99
IOWA	24,614	7	37	32	1	0	0	69
KANSAS	34,190	7	53	21	0	0	0	74
KENTUCKY	32,261	7	42	34	1	0	0	76
LOUISIANA	28,567	6	32	19	1	0	0	51
MAINE	10,684	2	16	12	0	0	0	28
MARYLAND	40,854	8	65	13	2	0	0	78
MASSACHUSETTS	24,965	4	38	13	1	0	0	51
MICHIGAN	42,319	8	66	30	2	1	9	105
MINNESOTA	30,603	8	54	25	1	0	1	80
MISSISSIPPI	21,217	4	29	14	1	0	0	43
MISSOURI	66,071	14	108	37	2	0	0	145
MONTANA	46,484	11	78	42	1	0	0	120
NEBRASKA	23,133	4	41	19	1	0	1	61
NEVADA	175,149	35	293	29	2	0	1	323
NEW HAMPSHIRE	8,231	3	16	5	1	0	0	21
NEW JERSEY	31,673	5	36	20	1	1	3	59
NEW MEXICO	67,637	13	89	46	2	0	0	135

Country	Membership	Stakes	Wards	Branches in stakes	Missions	Districts	Branches in missions	Total wards, branches
NEW YORK	78,031	14	88	48	4	3	15	151
NORTH CAROLINA	76,865	16	114	40	2	0	0	154
NORTH DAKOTA	6,930	2	7	9	0	0	0	16
OHIO	58,436	13	96	32	2	0	0	128
OKLAHOMA	43,033	7	58	25	2	0	0	83
OREGON	147,965	36	253	51	2	0	0	304
PENNSYLVANIA	49,743	10	75	32	2	0	7	107
RHODE ISLAND	3,833	0	6	1	0	0	0	7
SOUTH CAROLINA	36,947	6	49	13	1	0	0	62
SOUTH DAKOTA	9,812	2	10	12	1	1	11	33
TENNESSEE	45,574	10	69	29	2	0	0	98
TEXAS	296,141	56	451	113	8	3	13	577
UTAH	1,910,343	546	4,479	351	6	1	4	4,834
VERMONT	4,384	1	7	5	0	0	0	12
VIRGINIA	89,297	19	153	42	2	0	0	195
WASHINGTON	267,927	55	459	63	5	0	0	522
WEST VIRGINIA	16,710	4	26	12	1	0	0	38
WISCONSIN	24,496	6	42	27	1	0	0	69
WYOMING	63,069	16	133	21	0	0	0	154
U. S. TOTALS	6,144,582	1,465	11,551	1,992	102	10	58	13,601
VIRGIN ISLANDS	570	0	0	0	0	0	2	2
VIRGIN ISLANDS, British	142	0	0	0	0	0	1	1
NORTH AMERICA TOTALS	8,370,578	1,857	14,217	2,563	154	111	714	17,494

EUROPE

Country	Membership	Stakes	Wards	Branches in stakes	Missions	Districts	Branches in missions	Total wards, branches
ALBANIA	1,984	0	0	0	1	1	11	11
ANDORRA	69	0	0	0	0	0	1	1
AUSTRIA	4,294	2	12	5	0	0	0	17
BELGIUM	6,019	2	9	8	1	0	0	17
BULGARIA	2,206	0	0	0	1	2	13	13
CROATIA	532	0	0	0	0	1	6	6
CZECH REPUBLIC	2,282	0	0	0	1	2	14	14
DENMARK	4,378	2	13	9	1	0	1	23
ESTONIA	1,043	0	0	0	0	1	5	5
FINLAND	4,629	2	15	4	1	2	11	30
FRANCE (includes Corsica)	35,960	9	57	39	2	2	15	111
GERMANY	38,257	14	89	62	3	3	22	173
GREECE	735	0	0	0	1	0	4	4
GUERNSEY	48	0	0	1	0	0	0	1
HUNGARY	4,738	1	5	5	1	2	12	22
ICELAND	246	0	0	0	0	0	2	2
IRELAND	2,890	1	4	4	0	1	5	13
ISLE OF MAN	283	0	1	0	0	0	0	1
ITALY	23,976	7	43	29	2	5	27	99
JERSEY	288	0	1	0	0	0	0	1
LATVIA	1,102	0	0	0	1	1	7	7
LITHUANIA	894	0	0	0	0	1	5	5
LUXEMBOURG	296	0	1	0	0	0	0	1

Country	Membership	Stakes	Wards	Branches in stakes	Missions	Districts	Branches in missions	Total wards, branches
MALTA	146	0	0	0	0	0	1	1
MOLDOVA	321	0	0	0	0	1	2	2
NETHERLANDS	9,052	3	20	13	0	0	0	33
NORWAY	4,361	1	7	2	1	1	14	23
POLAND	1,648	0	0	0	1	2	13	13
PORTUGAL	39,031	6	33	14	2	4	21	68
ROMANIA	2,905	0	0	0	1	2	17	17
RUSSIA	21,023	0	0	0	8	13	116	116
SERBIA	307	0	0	0	0	1	3	3
SLOVAKIA	193	0	0	0	0	0	4	4
SLOVENIA	385	0	0	0	1	1	4	4
SPAIN	47,337	10	67	26	3	6	40	133
SWEDEN	9,206	4	24	11	1	1	5	40
SWITZERLAND	8,092	5	26	10	1	0	0	36
UKRAINE	10,880	1	8	3	3	4	51	62
UNITED KINGDOM								
ENGLAND	145,294	36	228	30	5	0	0	258
NORTHERN IRELAND	5,351	1	8	3	0	0	0	11
SCOTLAND	26,826	5	27	9	1	0	4	40
WALES	9,343	3	18	6	0	0	0	24
TOTALS	186,814	45	281	48	6	0	4	333
EUROPE TOTALS	478,866	115	716	293	44	60	456	1,465

SOUTH AMERICA

Country	Membership	Stakes	Wards	Branches in stakes	Missions	Districts	Branches in missions	Total wards, branches
ARGENTINA	389,393	70	481	165	10	37	195	841
BOLIVIA	172,640	24	172	26	3	10	55	253
BRAZIL	1,138,740	239	1,457	210	27	49	258	1,925
CHILE	563,689	74	421	69	9	23	130	620
COLOMBIA	172,534	28	175	26	4	12	71	272
ECUADOR	195,941	34	224	29	3	9	47	300
FRENCH GUIANA	368	0	0	0	0	1	3	3
GUYANA	5,016	0	0	0	0	2	15	15
PARAGUAY	80,788	10	63	28	2	11	58	149
PERU	493,563	94	596	72	9	24	108	776
SURINAME	1,233	0	0	0	0	1	6	6
URUGUAY	95,726	16	107	28	2	4	27	162
VENEZUELA	150,017	29	192	36	4	8	46	274
SO. AMERICA TOTALS	3,459,658	618	3,888	689	73	191	1,020	5,597

PACIFIC

Country	Membership	Stakes	Wards	Branches in stakes	Missions	Districts	Branches in missions	Total wards, branches
AMERICAN SAMOA	15,159	4	31	5	0	0	1	37
AUSTRALIA	129,744	33	203	28	5	9	53	284
COOK ISLANDS	1,853	0	0	0	0	1	5	5
FIJI	15,897	4	25	9	1	1	12	46
FRENCH POLYNESIA	21,245	6	53	5	1	3	24	82
GUAM	2,140	1	4	0	1	0	0	4
KIRIBATI	14,927	2	11	6	0	0	8	25
MARSHALL ISLANDS	5,093	1	6	1	1	1	5	12
MICRONESIA	4,193	0	0	0	0	4	20	20

Country	Membership	Stakes	Wards	Branches in stakes	Missions	Districts	Branches in missions	Total wards, branches
NAURU	96	0	0	0	0	0	1	1
NEW CALEDONIA	1,949	0	0	0	0	1	8	8
NEW ZEALAND	104,115	25	154	39	2	3	14	207
NIUE	284	0	0	0	0	0	2	2
NORTHERN MARIANA ISLANDS	632	0	1	0	0	0	0	1
PALAU	443	0	0	0	0	0	1	1
PAPUA NEW GUINEA	18,336	1	5	3	1	9	57	65
SAMOA	71,272	16	118	15	1	0	1	134
SOLOMON ISLANDS	234	0	0	0	0	0	1	1
TONGA	58,805	17	129	26	1	2	10	165
TUVALU ISLANDS	135	0	0	0	0	0	1	1
VANUATU	4,354	0	0	0	0	2	26	26
PACIFIC TOTALS	470,906	110	740	137	14	36	250	1,127

MISSIONARY STATISTICS

Year	Missionaries called	Year	Missionaries called	Year	Missionaries called	Year	Missionaries called
1830	16	1877	154	1924	867	1971	8,344
1831	58	1878	152	1925	1,131	1972	7,874
1832	72	1879	179	1926	1,236	1973	9,471
1833	41	1880	219	1927	1,017	1974	9,811
1834	111	1881	199	1928	1,193	1975	14,446
1835	84	1882	237	1929	1,058	1976	13,928
1836	80	1883	248	1930	896	1977	14,561
1837	52	1884	205	1931	678	1978	15,860
1838	16	1885	235	1932	399	1979	16,590
1839	67	1886	209	1933	525	1980	16,600
1840	80	1887	282	1934	843	1981	17,800
1841	100	1888	242	1935	960	1982	18,260
1842	45	1889	249	1936	899	1983	19,450
1843	374	1890	283	1937	1,079	1984	19,720
1844	586	1891	331	1938	1,146	1985	19,890
1845	84	1892	324	1939	1,088	1986	20,798
1846	32	1893	317	1940	1,194	1987	21,001
1847	40	1894	162	1941	1,257	1988	22,619
1848	55	1895	526	1942	629	1989	25,609
1849	58	1896	746	1943	261	1990	26,255
1850	50	1897	922	1944	427	1991	24,861
1851	44	1898	943	1945	400	1992	28,716
1852	158	1899	1,059	1946	2,297	1993	28,774
1853	33	1900	796	1947	2,132	1994	27,912
1854	119	1901	522	1948	2,161	1995	29,015
1855	65	1902	848	1949	2,363	1996	31,227
1856	130	1903	658	1950	3,015	1997	33,726
1857	88	1904	699	1951	1,801	1998	33,229
1858	0	1905	716	1952	872	1999	33,915
1859	18	1906	1,015	1953	1,750	2000	34,503
1860	96	1907	930	1954	2,022	2001	34,684
1861	19	1908	919	1955	2,414	2002	36,196
1862	27	1909	1,014	1956	2,572	2003	30,467
1863	50	1910	933	1957	2,518	2004	29,548
1864	52	1911	822	1958	2,778	2005	30,587
1865	71	1912	769	1959	2,847	2006	30,653
1866	32	1913	858	1960	4,706	2007	30,384
1867	133	1914	684	1961	5,793	2008	30,312
1868	32	1915	621	1962	5,630	2009	29,168
1869	250	1916	722	1963	5,781	2010	30,563
1870	46	1917	543	1964	5,886		
1871	167	1918	245	1965	7,139		
1872	132	1919	1,211	1966	7,021		
1873	35	1920	889	1967	6,475		
1874	98	1921	880	1968	7,178		
1875	197	1922	886	1969	6,967		
1876	211	1923	812	1970	7,590		

CHURCH STATISTICS

	Total Members	Stakes	Stake wards and branches	Missions	Mission branches	Total wards and branches
Apr. 6, 1830	6	0	0	0	0	0
Dec. 31	280	0	0	0	0	4
1831	680	0	0	0	0	6
1832	2,661	0	0	0	0	33
1833	3,140	0	0	0	0	40
1834	4,372	2	22	0	18	40
1835	8,835	2	22	0	26	48
1836	13,293	2	25	0	29	54
1837	16,282	2	25	1	42	67
1838	17,881	2	26	1	65	91
1839	16,460	3	16	2	70	86
1840	16,865	3	18	2	69	87
1841	19,856	2	19	2	84	103
1842	23,564	2	26	2	199	225
1843	25,980	2	31	2	238	269
1844	26,146	2	33	3	239	272
1845	30,332	1	34	4	277	311
1846	33,993	0	30	5	311	341
1847	34,694	1	48	5	357	405
1848	40,477	1	55	5	426	481
1849	48,160	1	75	5	515	590
1850	51,839	1	61	9	637	698
1851	52,165	4	60	11	717	777
1852	52,640	5	65	13	795	860
1853	64,154	5	75	14	885	960
1854	68,429	6	79	13	859	938
1855	63,974	6	99	14	858	957
1856	63,881	7	124	12	841	965
1857	55,236	6	77	12	742	819
1858	55,755	4	81	9	661	742
1859	57,038	4	98	9	635	733
1860	61,082	4	110	8	611	721
1861	66,211	4	126	7	588	714
1862	68,780	4	135	7	563	698
1863	71,770	4	143	7	524	667
1864	74,348	4	161	8	471	632
1865	76,771	4	164	8	436	600
1866	77,884	4	167	8	420	587
1867	81,124	4	175	8	407	582
1868	84,622	5	178	8	385	563
1869	88,432	9	187	7	383	570
1870	90,130	9	195	7	363	558
1871	95,596	9	200	7	342	542
1872	98,152	9	206	7	347	553
1873	101,538	9	213	7	348	561
1874	103,916	10	216	7	309	525
1875	107,167	10	222	7	302	524
1876	111,111	10	230	8	307	537
1877	115,065	20	252	8	285	537
1878	125,046	21	254	9	272	526
1879	128,386	22	263	10	289	552
1880	133,628	23	272	10	287	559
1881	140,733	23	283	10	293	576
1882	145,604	24	292	10	291	583
1883	151,593	27	317	11	292	609
1884	158,242	29	340	13	296	636
1885	164,130	29	348	12	311	659
1886	166,653	30	342	12	315	657
1887	173,029	31	360	12	326	686
1888	180,294	32	373	13	336	709

	Total Members	Stakes	Stake wards and branches	Missions	Mission branches	Total wards and branches
1889	183,144	32	388	12	339	727
1890	188,263	32	395	12	330	725
1891	195,445	32	409	12	332	741
1892	200,961	33	439	14	350	789
1893	214,534	34	451	15	356	807
1894	222,369	34	457	15	356	813
1895	231,116	37	479	15	356	835
1896	241,427	37	489	17	348	837
1897	255,736	37	493	18	374	867
1898	267,251	40	516	20	401	917
1899	271,681	40	506	20	412	918
1900	283,765	43	529	20	438	967
1901	292,931	50	577	21	442	1,019
1902	299,105	50	595	22	481	1,076
1903	304,901	51	612	23	477	1,089
1904	324,289	55	619	21	475	1,094
1905	332,048	55	627	22	514	1,141
1906	345,014	55	636	22	541	1,177
1907	357,913	55	634	22	558	1,192
1908	371,472	59	666	22	595	1,261
1909	377,279	60	684	21	590	1,274
1910	398,478	62	699	21	611	1,310
1911	407,291	62	706	21	632	1,338
1912	417,555	65	716	22	647	1,363
1913	431,607	66	749	22	650	1,399
1914	454,718	68	772	21	601	1,373
1915	466,238	72	783	21	608	1,391
1916	477,321	73	808	22	559	1,367
1917	488,038	75	875	22	578	1,453
1918	495,962	75	893	22	559	1,452
1919	507,961	79	888	23	554	1,442
1920	525,987	83	904	24	623	1,527
1921	548,803	86	933	25	665	1,598
1922	566,358	87	946	25	661	1,607
1923	575,896	90	962	26	697	1,659
1924	597.861	94	969	25	716	1,685
1925	613,572	94	985	28	720	1,705
1926	623,909	96	992	28	739	1,731
1927	644,745	99	1,005	28	758	1,763
1928	655,686	101	1,004	29	813	1,817
1929	663,652	104	1,004	30	823	1,827
1930	670,017	104	1,000	30	868	1,868
1931	688,435	104	1,004	31	861	1,865
1932	703,949	104	1,012	31	867	1,879
1933	717,619	105	1,014	31	875	1,889
1934	730,738	110	1,035	31	892	1,927
1935	746,384	115	1,064	32	900	1,964
1936	760,690	118	1,081	33	933	2,014
1937	767,752	118	1,101	35	951	2,052
1938	784,764	126	1,137	36	947	2,084
1939	803,528	129	1,154	35	1,002	2,156
1940	862,664	134	1,191	35	728	1,919
1941	892,080	139	1,224	36	757	1,981
1942	917,715	143	1,242	37	776	2,018
1943	937,050	146	1,261	38	807	2,068
1944	954,004	148	1,273	38	773	2,046
1945	979,454	153	1,295	38	909	2,204
1946	996,505	161	1,340	39	959	2,299
1947	1,016,170	169	1,425	43	1,149	2,574
1948	1,041,970	172	1,451	44	1,323	2,774
1949	1,078,671	175	1,501	46	1,327	2,828
1950	1,111,314	180	1,541	43	1,370	2,911

	Total Members	Stakes	Stake wards and branches	Missions	Mission branches	Total wards and branches
1951	1,147,157	191	1,666	42	1,414	3,080
1952	1,189,053	202	1,767	43	1,551	3,318
1953	1,246,362	211	1,884	42	1,399	3,283
1954	1,302,240	219	1,993	42	1,476	3,469
1955	1,357,274	224	2,082	44	1,471	3,553
1956	1,416,731	239	2,210	45	1,854	4,064
1957	1,488,314	251	2,362	45	1,740	4,102
1958	1,555,799	273	2,513	47	1,757	4,270
1959	1,616,088	290	2,614	50	1,895	4,509
1960	1,693,180	319	2,882	58	1,811	4,693
1961	1,823,661	345	3,143	67	1,872	5,015
1962	1,965,786	364	3,423	74	1,802	5,225
1963	2,117,451	389	3,615	77	1,782	5,397
1964	2,234,916	400	3,749	79	2,016	5,765
1965	2,395,932	412	3,897	76	2,137	6,034
1966	2,480,899	425	4,022	75	2,053	6,075
1967	2,614,340	448	4,166	77	1,987	6,153
1968	2,684,073	473	4,385	83	2,112	6,497
1969	2,807,456	496	4,592	88	2,016	6,608
1970	2,930,810	537	4,922	92	1,943	6,865
1971	3,090,953	562	5,135	98	1,942	7,077
1972	3,218,908	592	5,394	101	1,891	7,285
1973	3,306,658	630	5,707	108	1,817	7,524
1974	3,409,987	675	5,951	113	1,822	7,773
1975	3,572,202	737	6,390	134	1,761	8,151
1976	3,742,749	798	6,903	148	1,422	8,325
1977	3,969,220	885	7,466	157	1,694	9,180
1978	4,166,854	990	8,064	166	1,790	9,854
1979	4,404,121	1,092	9,365	175	1,121	10,486
1980	4,639,822	1,218	10,324	188	2,267	12,591
1981	4,920,449	1,321	11,063	186	2,030	13,093
1982	5,162,619	1,392	11,492	180	1,979	13,471
1983	5,351,724	1,458	11,953	177	1,991	13,943
1984	5,641,054	1,507	12,422	180	2,046	14,468
1985	5,919,483	1,582	12,939	188	2,068	15,007
1986	6,166,974	1,622	13,318	193	2,064	15,382
1987	6,394,314	1,666	13,727	205	2,307	16,034
1988	6,721,210	1,707	14,069	222	2,470	16,539
1989	7,308,444	1,739	14,533	228	2,751	17,284
1990	7,761,207	1,784	15,003	256	3,079	18,082
1991	8,089,848	1,837	15,513	267	3,325	18,838
1992	8,404,087	1,919	16,292	276	3,819	20,112
1993	8,689,168	1,968	17,048	295	4,051	21,099
1994	9,024,368	2,008	17,521	303	4,311	21,832
1995	9,338,397	2,150	18,396	307	4,277	22,673
1996	9,692,441	2,296	19,522	309	3,994	23,516
1997	10,071,783	2,424	20,776	318	3,923	24,697
1998	10,404,448	2,505	21,649	331	3,904	25,553
1999	10,752,984	2,542	21,897	333	3,896	25,793
2000	11,068,861	2,581	22,071	334	3,844	25,915
2001	11,394,518	2,607	22,249	333	3,835	26,084
2002	11,721,548	2,602	22,231	335	3,912	26,143
2003	11,985,254	2,624	22,418	337	3,819	26,237
2004	12,275,822	2,665	22,886	338	3,784	26,670
2005	12,560,869	2,701	23,307	341	3,780	27,087
2006	12,868,606	2,745	23,703	344	3,772	27,475
2007	13,193,999	2,790	24,076	348	3,751	27,827
2008	13,508,509	2,818	24,308	348	3,801	28,109
2009	13,824,854	2,865	24,329	344	3,794	28,424
2010	14,131,467	2,896	24,894	340	3,766	28,660

FIRST STAKE ORGANIZED IN COUNTRIES OF THE WORLD

COUNTRY	NAME OF STAKE	DATE ORGANIZED	CURRENT NAME
AMERICAN SAMOA	Pago Pago (488)	15 Jun 1969	Pago Pago Samoa
ARGENTINA	Buenos Aires (423)	20 Nov 1966	Buenos Aires Argentina East
AUSTRALIA	Sydney (293)	27 Mar 1960	Sydney Australia Greenwich
AUSTRIA	Vienna Austria (1126)	20 Apr 1980	Same
BELGIUM	Brussels Belgium (813)	20 Feb 1977	Same
BOLIVIA	Santa Cruz Bolivia (993)	14 Jan 1979	Santa Cruz Bolivia Cantoto
BRAZIL	Sao Paulo (417)	1 May 1966	Sao Paulo Brazil
CANADA	Alberta (35)	9 Jun 1895	Cardston Alberta
CHILE	Santiago (590)	19 Nov 1972	Santi. Chile Quinta Normal
CHINA	Hong Kong (756)	25 Apr 1976	Hong Kong Island
COLUMBIA	Bogota Colombia (805)	23 Jan 1977	Same
COSTA RICA	San Jose Costa Rica (803)	20 Jan 1977	Same
DR CONGA	Kinshasa Zaire (2258)	3 Nov 1996	Kinshasa Dem. Rep. Congo
DENMARK	Copenhagen Denmark (648)	16 Jun 1974	Same
DOMINICAN REPUBLIC	Santo Domingo DR (1593)	23 Mar 1986	Same
ECUADOR	Guayaquil Ecuador (939)	11 Jun 1978	Guayaquil Ecuador West
EL SALVADOR	San Salvador (618)	3 Jun 1978	San Salvador El Salvador
ENGLAND	Manchester (294)	27 Mar 1960	Manchester England
FIJI	Suya Fiji (1428)	12 Jun 1983	Same
FINLAND	Helsinki Finland (865)	16 Oct 1977	Same
FRANCE	Paris France (731)	16 Nov 1975	Same
GERMANY	Berlin (334)	10 Sept 1961	Berlin Germany
GHANA	Accra Ghana (1791)	21 May 1967	Same
GUAM	Barrigada Guam Stake	12 Dec 2010	Same
GUATEMALA	Guatemala City (436)	21 May 1967	Guatemala City Guatemala
HAITI	Port-au-Prince Haiti (2399)	21 Sep 1977	Same
HONDURAS	San Pedro Sula Honduras (820)	10 Apr 1977	Same
HUNGARY	Budapest Hungary (2724)	4 Jun 2006	Same
INDONESIA	Jakarta Indonesia Stake	22 May 2011	Same
IRELAND	Dublin Ireland (2034)	12 Mar 1995	Same
ITALY	Milan Italy (1274)	7 Jun 1981	Same
IVORY COAST	Abidjan Ivory Coast (2387)	17 Aug 1997	Same
JAPAN	Tokyo (505)	15 Mar 1970	Tokyo Japan
KOREA	Seoul (604)	8 Mar 1973	Seoul Korea
KENYA	Nairobi Kenya (2600b)	9 Sep 2001	Same
KIRIBATI	Tarawa Kiribati (2215)	8 Aug 1996	Same
LIBERIA	Monrovia Liberia (2562)	11 Jun 2000	Same
MADAGASCAR	Antanarivo Madagascar	17 Sep 2000	Same

MARSHALL ISLANDS	Majuro Marshall Islands (2837)	14 Jun 2009	Same
MEXICO	Juarez (37)	9 Dec 1895	Colonia Juarez Mexico
MONGOLIA	Ulaanbaatar Mongolia (2832)	7 Jun 2009	Same
NETHERLANDS	Holland (326)	12 Mar 1961	The Hague Netherlands
NEW ZEALAND	Auckland (264)	18 May 1958	Auckland N.Z. Mt. Roskill
NICARAGUA	Managua Nicaragua (1246)	22 Mar 1981	‡15 Oct 1989; Reinstated 21 Jun 1998
NIGERIA	Aba Nigeria (1695)	15 May 1988	Same
NORTHERN IRELAND	Belfast Ireland (647)	9 Jun 1974	Belfast Northern Ireland
NORWAY	Oslo Norway (835)	22 May 1988	Same
PANAMA	Panama City Panama (1081)	11 Nov 1979	Same
PAPUA NEW GUINEA	Port Moresby Papua New Guinea (2109)	22 Oct 1995	Same
PARAGUAY	Asuncion Paraguay (1002)	25 Feb 1979	Same
PERU	Lima (503)	22 Feb 1970	Lima Peru Limatambo
PHILIPPINES	Manila (613)	20 May 1973	Manila Philippines
PORTUGAL	Lisbon Portugal (1276)	10 Jun 1981	Same
PUERTO RICO	San Juan Puerto Rico (1215)	14 Dec 1980	Same
RUSSIA	Moscow Russia	5 June 2011	Same
SAMOA	Apia (353)	18 Mar 1962	Apia Samoa
SCOTLAND	Glasgow (356)	26 Aug 1962	Glasgow Scotland
SINGAPORE	Singapore Singapore (2025)	26 Feb 1995	Same
SOUTH AFRICA	Transvaal (506)	22 March 1970	Johannesburg South Africa
SPAIN	Madrid Spain (1327)	14 Mar 1982	Same
SWEDEN	Stockholm Sweden (691)	20 Apr 1975	Same
SWITZERLAND	Swiss (341)	28 Oct 1961	Zurich Switzerland
TAHITI	Tahiti (573)	14 May 1972	Papeete Tahiti
TAIWAN	Taipei Taiwan (755)	22 Apr 1976	Taipei Taiwan West
THAILAND	Bangkok Thailand (2064)	18 Jun 1995	Same
TONGA	Nuku'alofa (463)	5 Sep 1968	Nuku'alofa Tonga
TRINIDAD AND TOBAGO	Port of Spain Trinidad (2820)	1 Mar 2009	Same
UGANDA	Kampala Uganda (2868)	17 Jan 2010	Same
UKRAINE	Kyiv Ukraine (2637)	30 May 2004	Same
UNITED STATES	*Kirtland (1a)	17 Feb 1834	‡24 May 1841
	Salt Lake (1)	3 Oct 1847	Same
URUGUAY	Montevideo (444)	12 Nov 1967	Montevideo Uruguay West
VENEZUELA	Caracas Venezuela (827)	15 May 1977	Same
WALES	Merthyr Tydfil Wales (676)	12 Jan 1975	Same
ZIMBABWE	Harare Zimbabwe (2541)	12 Dec 1999	Same

() Chronological number of stake; ‡Discontinued; *First permanent stake

FIRST STAKE IN EACH STATE OF THE UNITED STATES

STATE	NAME OF STAKE	DATE ORGANIZED	CURRENT NAME
ALABAMA	Alabama (452)	3 Mar 1968	Huntsville Alabama
ALASKA	Alaska (331)	13 Aug 1961	Anchorage Alaska
ARIZONA	Little Colorado (21)	27 Jan 1878	‡18 Dec 1887
	*Maricopa (24)	10 Dec 1882	Mesa Arizona Maricopa
ARKANSAS	Arkansas (484)	1 Jun 1969	Little Rock Arkansas
CALIFORNIA	San Bernardino (4)	6 Jul 1851	‡By 1857
	*Hollywood (98)	22 May 1927	Los Angeles California
COLORADO	San Luis (26)	10 Jun 1883	Manassa Colorado
CONNECTICUT	Hartford (421)	18 Sep 1966	Hartford Connecticut
DELAWARE	Wilmington Delaware (673)	8 Dec 1975	Same
DIST. OF COLUMBIA	Washington (131)	30 Jun 1940	Washington D.C.
FLORIDA	Florida (163)	19 Jan 1947	Jacksonville Florida West
GEORGIA	Atlanta (241)	5 May 1957	Tucker Georgia
HAWAII	Oahu (113)	30 Jun 1935	Laie Hawaii
IDAHO	Bear Lake (8a)	20 Jun 1869	Paris Idaho
ILLINOIS	Nauvoo (3a)	5 Oct 1839	‡By 1846
	*Chicago (118)	29 Nov 1936	Wilmette Illinois
INDIANA	Indianapolis (283)	17 May 1959	Indianapolis Indiana
IOWA	Iowa (4a)	5 Oct 1839	‡By 6 Jan 1842
	*Cedar Rapids (419)	29 May 1966	Cedar Rapids Iowa
KANSAS	Wichita (355)	24 Jun 1962	Wichita Kansas
KENTUCKY	Louisville (540)	17 Jan 1971	Louisville Kentucky
LOUISIANA	New Orleans (221)	19 June 1955	New Orleans Louisiana
MAINE	Maine (461)	23 Jun 1968	Augusta Maine
MARYLAND	Chesapeake (526)	13 Sep 1970	Silver Spring Maryland
MASSACHUSETTS	Boston (354)	20 May 1962	Boston Massachusetts
MICHIGAN	Detroit (197)	9 Nov 1952	Bloomfield Hills Michigan
MINNESOTA	Minnesota (317)	29 Nov 1960	Minneapolis Minnesota
MISSISSIPPI	Jackson (404)	2 May 1965	Jackson Mississippi
MISSOURI	Clay-Caldwell (2a)	3 Jul 1834	‡By 1839
	*Kansas City (234)	21 Oct 1956	Kansas City Missouri
MONTANA	Butte (208)	28 Jun 1953	Butte Montana
NEBRASKA	Winter Quarters (318)	11 Dec 1960	Omaha Nebraska
NEVADA	Carson Valley (7)	4 Oct 1856	‡By 1858
	*Moapa (64)	9 Jun 1912	Logandale Nevada
NEW HAMPSHIRE	Merrimack (507)	22 Mar 1970	Nashua New Hampshire
NEW JERSEY	New Jersey (292)	28 Feb 1960	Morristown New Jersey
NEW MEXICO	Young (63)	21 May 1912	Farmington New Mexico

NEW YORK	New York (110)	9 Dec 1934	New York New York
NORTH CAROLINA	North Carolina (332)	27 Aug 1961	Kinston North Carolina
NORTH DAKOTA	Fargo North Dakota (852)	7 Aug 1977	Same
OHIO	Kirtland (1a)	17 Feb 1834	‡24 May 1841
	*Cincinnati (270)	23 Nov 1958	Cincinnati Ohio
OKLAHOMA	Tulsa (298)	1 May 1960	Tulsa Oklahoma
OREGON	Union (49)	9 Jun 1901	La Grande Oregon
PENNSYLVANIA	Philadelphia (304)	16 Oct 1960	Philadelphia Pennsylvania
SOUTH CAROLINA	South Carolina (169)	19 Oct 1947	Columbia South Carolina
SOUTH DAKOTA	Rapid City (592)	10 Dec 1972	Rapid City South Dakota
TENNESSEE	Memphis (403)	18 Apr 1965	Memphis Tennessee
TEXAS	El Paso (194)	21 Sep 1952	El Paso Texas
UTAH	Salt Lake (1)	3 Oct 1847	Same
VERMONT	Montpelier Vermont (753)	11 Apr 1976	Same
VIRGINIA	Virginia (245)	30 Jun 1957	Richmond Virginia
WASHINGTON	Seattle (124)	31 Jul 1938	Seattle Washington
WEST VIRGINIA	West Virginia (522)	23 Aug 1970	Charleston West Virginia
WISCONSIN	Milwaukee (367)	3 Feb 1963	Milwaukee Wisconsin
WYOMING	Star Valley (33)	14 Aug 1892	Afton Wyoming

() Chronological number of stake; ‡ Discontinued; *First permanent stake; (a) denotes stakes organized prior to 1844, all were discontinued by the time the early saints came West. Numbering begins with the creation of the Salt Lake Stake.

Rendering of the new Philadelphia Pennsylvania Temple in an historic setting. Ground was broken Sept. 17, 2011, by President Henry B. Eyring of the First Presidency.

Temples
of the world

TEMPLES OF THE CHURCH

Listed in order of completion

	TEMPLE	LOCATION	DEDICATED	BY WHOM
	Kirtland*	Kirtland, Ohio	27 Mar 1836	Joseph Smith
	Nauvoo**	Nauvoo, Ill.	30 Apr 1846	Joseph Young (private)
			1 May 1846	Orson Hyde (public)
1	St. George Utah	St. George, Utah	6 Apr 1877	Daniel H. Wells
	Rededicated after remodeling		11 Nov 1975	Spencer W. Kimball
2	Logan Utah	Logan, Utah	17 May 1884	John Taylor
	Rededicated after remodeling		13 Mar 1979	Spencer W. Kimball
3	Manti Utah	Manti, Utah	17 May 1888	Wilford Woodruff (private)
			21 May 1888	(Prayer read by
				Lorenzo Snow; public)
	Rededicated after remodeling		14 Jun 1985	Gordon B. Hinckley
4	Salt Lake	Salt Lake City, Utah	6 Apr 1893	Wilford Woodruff
5	Laie Hawaii	Laie, Oahu, Hawaii	27 Nov 1919	Heber J. Grant
	Rededicated after remodeling		13 Jun 1978	Spencer W. Kimball
	Rededicated after remodeling		21 Nov 2010	Thomas S. Monson
6	Cardston Alberta	Cardston, Alberta	26 Aug 1923	Heber J. Grant
	Rededicated after remodeling		2 Jul 1962	Hugh B. Brown
	Rededication after remodeling		22 Jun 1991	Gordon B. Hinckley
7	Mesa Arizona	Mesa, Ariz.	23 Oct 1927	Heber J. Grant
	Rededicated after remodeling		15 Apr 1975	Spencer W. Kimball
8	Idaho Falls Idaho	Idaho Falls, Idaho	23 Sep 1945	George Albert Smith
9	Bern Switzerland	Zollikofen, Switzerland	11 Sep 1955	David O. McKay
	Rededicated after remodeling		23 Oct 1992	Gordon B. Hinckley
10	Los Angeles California	Los Angeles, Calif.	11 Mar 1956	David O. McKay
11	Hamilton New Zealand	Hamilton, New Zealand	20 Apr 1958	David O. McKay
12	London England	Newchapel, Surrey,	7 Sep 1958	David O. McKay
	Rededicated after remodeling		18 Oct 1992	Gordon B. Hinckley
13	Oakland California	Oakland, Calif.	17 Nov 1964	David O. McKay
14	Ogden Utah	Ogden, Utah	18 Jan 1972	Joseph Fielding Smith
15	Provo Utah	Provo, Utah	9 Feb 1972	Joseph Fielding Smith
				(Prayer read by Harold B. Lee)
16	Washington D.C.	Kensington, Md.	19 Nov 1974	Spencer W. Kimball
17	São Paulo Brazil	Sao Paulo, Brazil	30 Oct 1978	Spencer W. Kimball
	Rededicated after remodeling		22 Feb 2004	Gordon B. Hinckley
18	Tokyo Japan	Tokyo, Japan	27 Oct 1980	Spencer W. Kimball
19	Seattle Washington	Bellevue, Wash.	17 Nov 1980	Spencer W. Kimball
20	Jordan River Utah	South Jordan, Utah	16 Nov 1981	Marion G. Romney
21	Atlanta Georgia	Sandy Springs, Ga.	1 Jun 1983	Gordon B. Hinckley
	Rededicated after remodeling		14 Nov 1997	Gordon B. Hinckley
	Rededicated after refurbishing		1 May 2011	Thomas S. Monson
22	Apia Samoa	Apia, Western Samoa	5 Aug 1983	Gordon B. Hinckley
	Destroyed by fire July 9, 2003.			
	Dedicated after rebuilding		4 Sep 2005	Gordon B. Hinckley
23	Nuku'alofa Tonga	Nuku'alofa, Tonga	9 Aug 1983	Gordon B. Hinckley
	Rededicated after remodeling		4 Nov 2007	Russell M. Nelson
24	Santiago Chile	Santiago, Chile	15 Sep 1983	Gordon B. Hinckley
	Rededicated after remodeling		12 Mar 2006	Gordon B. Hinckley
25	Papeete Tahiti	Pirae, Tahiti	27 Oct 1983	Gordon B. Hinckley
	Rededicated after remodeling		12 Nov 2006	L. Tom Perry
26	Mexico City Mexico	Mexico City, Mexico	2 Dec 1983	Gordon B. Hinckley
	Rededicated after remodeling		16 Nov 2008	Thomas S. Monson
27	Boise Idaho	Boise, Idaho	25 May 1984	Gordon B. Hinckley
	Rededicated after remodeling		29 May 1987	James E. Faust
28	Sydney Australia	Carlingford, Australia	20 Sep 1984	Gordon B. Hinckley
29	Manila Philippines	Quezon City, Philippines	25 Sep 1984	Gordon B. Hinckley
30	Dallas Texas	Dallas, Texas	19 Oct 1984	Gordon B. Hinckley
	Rededicated after remodeling		5 Mar 1987	Gordon B. Hinckley
31	Taipei Taiwan	Taipei, Taiwan	17 Nov 1984	Gordon B. Hinckley

32	Guatemala City Guatemala	Guatemala City, Guat.	14 Dec 1984	Gordon B. Hinckley
33	Freiberg Germany	Freiberg, Germany	29 Jun 1985	Gordon B. Hinckley
	Rededicated after remodeling		7 Sep 2002	Gordon B. Hinckley
34	Stockholm Sweden	Västerhaninge, Sweden	2 Jul 1985	Gordon B. Hinckley
35	Chicago Illinois	Glenview, Ill.	9 Aug 1985	Gordon B. Hinckley
	Rededicated after remodeling		8 Oct 1989	Gordon B. Hinckley
36	Johannesburg South Africa	Johannesburg, SA	24 Aug 1985	Gordon B. Hinckley
37	Seoul Korea	Seoul, Korea	14 Dec 1985	Gordon B. Hinckley
38	Lima Peru	Lima, Peru	10 Jan 1986	Gordon B. Hinckley
39	Buenos Aires Argentina	Buenos Aires, Argentina	17 Jan 1986	Thomas S. Monson
40	Denver Colorado	Littleton, Colo.	24 Oct 1986	Ezra Taft Benson
41	Frankfurt Germany	Friedrichsdorf, Germany	28 Aug 1987	Ezra Taft Benson
42	Portland Oregon	Lake Oswego, Ore.	19 Aug, 1989	Gordon B. Hinckley
43	Las Vegas Nevada	Las Vegas, Nev.	16 Dec 1989	Gordon B. Hinckley
44	Toronto Ontario	Brampton, Ontario,	25 Aug 1990	Gordon B. Hinckley
45	San Diego California	San Diego, Calif.	25 Apr 1993	Gordon B. Hinckley
46	Orlando Florida	Windermere, Fla.	9 Oct 1994	Howard W. Hunter
47	Bountiful Utah	Bountiful, Utah	8 Jan 1995	Howard W. Hunter
48	Hong Kong China	Hong Kong	26 May 1996	Gordon B. Hinckley
49	Mount Timpanogos Utah	American Fork, Utah	13 Oct 1996	Gordon B. Hinckley
50	St. Louis Missouri	Town and Country, Mo.	1 Jun 1997	Gordon B. Hinckley
51	Vernal Utah	Vernal, Utah	2 Nov 1997	Gordon B. Hinckley
52	Preston England	Chorley, England	7 Jun 1998	Gordon B. Hinckley
53	Monticello Utah	Monticello, Utah	26 Jul 1998	Gordon B. Hinckley
	Rededicated after remodeling		17 Nov 2002	Gordon B. Hinckley
54	Anchorage Alaska	Anchorage, Alaska	9 Jan 1999	Gordon B. Hinckley
	Rededicated after remodeling		8 Feb 2004	Gordon B. Hinckley
55	Colonia Juárez Chihuahua Mexico	Colonia Juarez, Mexico	6 Mar 1999	Gordon B. Hinckley
56	Madrid Spain	Moratalaz, Spain	19 Mar 1999	Gordon B. Hinckley
57	Bogotá Colombia	Bogota, Colombia	24 Apr 1999	Gordon B. Hinckley
58	Guayaquil Ecuador	Guayaquil, Ecuador	1 Aug 1999	Gordon B. Hinckley
59	Spokane Washington	Spokane, Wash.	21 Aug 1999	Gordon B. Hinckley
60	Columbus Ohio	Columbus, Ohio	4 Sept 1999	Gordon B. Hinckley
61	Bismarck North Dakota	Bismarck, N.D.	19 Sep 1999	Gordon B. Hinckley
62	Columbia South Carolina	Columbia, S.C.	16 Oct. 1999	Gordon B. Hinckley
63	Detroit Michigan	Bloomfield Hills, Mich.	23 Oct 1999	Gordon B. Hinckley
64	Halifax Nova Scotia	Dartmouth, Nova Scotia	14 Nov 1999	Gordon B. Hinckley
65	Regina Saskatchewan	Regina, Saskatchewan	14 Nov 1999	Boyd K. Packer
66	Billings Montana	Billings, Mont.	20 Nov 1999	Gordon B. Hinckley
67	Edmonton Alberta	Edmonton, Alberta	11 Dec 1999	Gordon B. Hinckley
68	Raleigh North Carolina	Apex, N.C.	18 Dec 1999	Gordon B. Hinckley
69	St. Paul Minnesota	Oakdale, Minn.	9 Jan 2000	Gordon B. Hinckley
70	Kona Hawaii	Kailua-Kona, Hawaii	23 Jan 2000	Gordon B. Hinckley
71	Ciudad Juárez Mexico	Ciudad Juarez, Mexico	26 Feb 2000	Gordon B. Hinckley
72	Hermosillo Sonora Mexico	Hermosillo, Mexico	27 Feb 2000	Gordon B. Hinckley
73	Albuquerque New Mexico	Albuquerque, N. M.	5 Mar 2000	Gordon B. Hinckley
74	Oaxaca Mexico	Oaxaca, Mexico	11Mar 2000	James E. Faust
75	Tuxtla Gutiérrez Mexico	Tuxtla Gutierrez, Mexico	12 Mar 2000	James E. Faust
76	Louisville Kentucky	Crestwood, Ky.	19 Mar 2000	Thomas S. Monson
77	Palmyra New York	Palmyra Village, N. Y.	6 Apr 2000	Gordon B. Hinckley
78	Fresno California	Fresno, Calif.	9 Apr 2000	Gordon B. Hinckley
79	Medford Oregon	Central Point, Ore.	16 Apr 2000	James E. Faust
80	Memphis Tennessee	Bartlett, Tenn.	23 Apr 2000	James E. Faust
81	Reno Nevada	Reno, Nev.	23 Apr 2000	Thomas S. Monson
82	Cochabamba Bolivia	Cochabamba, Bolivia	30 Apr 2000	Gordon B. Hinckley
83	Tampico Mexico	Ciudad Madero, Mexico	20 May 2000	Thomas S. Monson
84	Nashville Tennessee	Franklin, Tenn.	21 May 2000	James E. Faust
85	Villahermosa Mexico	Villahermosa, Mexico	21 May 2000	Thomas S. Monson
86	Montreal Quebec	Longueuil, Quebec	4 Jun 2000	Gordon B. Hinckley
87	San José Costa Rica	San Antonio, Costa Rica	4 Jun 2000	James E. Faust
88	Fukuoka Japan	Fukuoka, Japan	11 Jun 2000	Gordon B. Hinckley
89	Adelaide Australia	Marden, South Australia	15 Jun 2000	Gordon B. Hinckley
90	Melbourne Australia	Wantirna, Victoria, Aus.	16 Jun 2000	Gordon B. Hinckley
91	Suva Fiji	Suva, Fiji	18 Jun 2000	Gordon B. Hinckley

92	Mérida Mexico	Merida, Mexico	8 Jul 2000	Thomas S. Monson
93	Veracruz Mexico	Veracruz, Mexico	9 Jul 2000	Thomas S. Monson
94	Baton Rouge Louisiana	Baton Rouge, La.	16 Jul 2000	Gordon B. Hinckley
95	Oklahoma City Oklahoma	Yukon, Okla.	30 Jul 2000	James E. Faust
96	Caracas Venezuela	Caracas, Venezuela	20 Aug 2000	Gordon B. Hinckley
97	Houston Texas	Klein, Texas	26 Aug 2000	Gordon B. Hinckley
98	Birmingham Alabama	Gardendale, Ala.	3 Sep 2000	Gordon B. Hinckley
99	Santo Domingo Dominican Republic	Santo Domingo, Dominican Republic	17 Sep 2000	Gordon B. Hinckley
100	Boston Massachusetts	Belmont, Mass.	1 Oct 2000	Gordon B. Hinckley
101	Recife Brazil	Recife, Brazil	15 Dec 2000	Gordon B. Hinckley
102	Porto Alegre Brazil	Porto Alegre, Brazil	17 Dec 2000	Gordon B. Hinckley
103	Montevideo Uruguay	Montevideo, Uruguay	18 Mar 2001	Gordon B. Hinckley
104	Winter Quarters Nebraska	Omaha, Neb.	22 Apr 2001	Gordon B. Hinckley
105	Guadalajara Mexico	Guadalajara, Mexico	29 Apr 2001	Gordon B. Hinckley
106	Perth Australia	Yokine, Australia	20 May 2001	Gordon B. Hinckley
107	Columbia River Washington	Richland, Wash.	18 Nov 2001	Gordon B. Hinckley
108	Snowflake Arizona	Snowflake, Ariz.	3 Mar 2002	Gordon B. Hinckley
109	Lubbock Texas	Lubbock, Texas	21 Apr 2002	Gordon B. Hinckley
110	Monterrey Mexico	Monterrey, Mexico	28 Apr 2002	Gordon B. Hinckley
111	Campinas Brazil	Campinas, Brazil	17 May 2002	Gordon B. Hinckley
112	Asunción Paraguay	Asuncion, Paraguay	19 May 2002	Gordon B. Hinckley
113	Nauvoo Illinois	Nauvoo, Ill.	27 Jun 2002	Gordon B. Hinckley
114	The Hague Netherlands	Zoetermeer, Netherlands	8 Sept. 2002	Gordon B. Hinckley
115	Brisbane Australia	Kangaroo Point, Queensland	15 Jun 2003	Gordon B. Hinckley
116	Redlands California	Redlands, Calif.	14 Sep 2003	Gordon B. Hinckley
117	Accra Ghana	Accra, Ghana	11 Jan. 2004	Gordon B. Hinckley
118	Copenhagen Denmark	Copenhagen, Denmark	23 May 2004	Gordon B. Hinckley
119	Manhattan New York	New York City, New York	13 June 2004	Gordon B. Hinckley
120	San Antonio Texas	San Antonio, Texas	22 May 2005	Gordon B. Hinckley
121	Aba Nigeria	Aba, Nigeria	7 Aug 2005	Gordon B. Hinckley
122	Newport Beach California	Newport, California	28 Aug 2005	Gordon B. Hinckley
123	Sacramento California	Sacramento, California	3 Sept 2006	Gordon B. Hinckley
124	Helsinki Finland	Helsinki, Finland	22 Oct 2006	Gordon B. Hinckley
125	Rexburg Idaho	Rexburg, Idaho	10 Feb 2008	Thomas S. Monson
126	Curitiba Brazil	Curitiba, Brazil	1 June 2008	Thomas S. Monson
127	Panama City Panama	Panama City, Panama	10 August 2008	Thomas S. Monson
128	Twin Falls Idaho	Twin Falls, Idaho	24 August 2008	Thomas S. Monson
129	Draper Utah	Draper, Utah	20 March 2009	Thomas S. Monson
130	Oquirrh Mountain Utah	South Jordan, Utah	21 August 2009	Thomas S. Monson
131	Vancouver British Columbia	Langley, Vancouver	8 May 2010	Thomas S. Monson
132	The Gila Valley Arizona	Central, Arizona	23 May 2010	Thomas S. Monson
133	Cebu Philippines	Cebu City, Philippines	13 June 2010	Thomas S. Monson
134	Kyiv Ukraine	Kyiv, Ukraine	29 Aug 2010	Thomas S. Monson
135	San Salvador El Salvador	San Salvador, El Salvador	21 Aug 2011	Henry B. Eyring
136	Quetzaltenango Guatemala	Quetzaltenango, Guatemala	11 Dec 2011	

* No longer in use by the Church   **Original destroyed; rebuilt in 2002, see No. 113

Temples announced

135 temples in operation. 30 temples announced or under construction as of October 2011.

- Barranquilla Colombia
- Brigham City Utah
- Calgary Alberta
- Concepción Chile
- Córdoba Argentina
- Durban South Africa
- Fortaleza Brazil
- Fort Collins Colorado
- Fort Lauderdale Florida
- Gilbert Arizona
- Hartford Connecticut
- Indianapolis Indiana
- Kansas City Missouri
- Kinshasa DR Congo
- Lisbon Portugal
- Manaus Brazil
- Meridian Idaho
- Paris France
- Payson Utah
- Philadelphia Pennsylvania
- Phoenix Arizona
- Provo Utah Tabernacle
- Quetzaltenango Guatemala
- Rome Italy
- Sapporo Japan
- Star Valley Wyoming
- Tegucigalpa Honduras
- Tijuana Mexico
- Trujillo Peru
- Urdaneta Philippines
- Winnipeg Manitoba

TEMPLES OF THE CHURCH

Listed alphabetically as of October 2011

Temples announced during the April 2011 General Conference

Fort Collins Colorado
Announced: April 2, 2011.
Status: In planning stages.

Meridian Idaho
Announced: April 2, 2011.
Status: In planning stages.

Winnipeg Manitoba
Announced: April 2, 2011.
Status: In planning stages.

Temples announced during the October 2011 General Conference

Provo Utah Tabernacle
Announced: Oct. 1, 2011.
Status: In planning stages.

Paris France
Announced: Oct. 1, 2011.
Status: In planning stages.

Kinshasa DR Congo
Announced: Oct. 1, 2011.
Status: In planning stages.

Durban South Africa
Announced: Oct. 1, 2011.
Status: In planning stages.

Barranquilla Colombia
Announced: Oct. 1, 2011.
Status: In planning stages.

Star Valley Wyoming
Announced: Oct. 1, 2011.
Status: In planning stages.

Aba Nigeria

Announced: April 2, 2000.
Location: Okup-Umodba Road, off Aba-Owerri Road at Union Bank, Aba. Abia State, Nigeria; phone (234) 82-239-010.
Site: 6.3 acres.
Exterior finish: Namibian pearl granite.
Temple design: Classic modern.
Architects and contractors: Adeniyi Coker Architects Ltd., Marlum Nigeria Ltd.
Project manager: Russell S. Tanner.
Rooms: Celestial room, two endowment rooms, two sealing rooms and baptistry.
Total Floor area: 11,500 square feet.
Dimensions: About 147-feet by 77-feet.
District: 15 stakes, 11 districts in Nigeria, and 2 branches in Cameroon.
Groundbreaking, site dedication: Feb. 23, 2002, by Elder H. Bruce Stucki of the Seventy.
Dedication: Aug. 7, 2005, by President Gordon B. Hinckley; four sessions.
Dedicatory prayer excerpt: *Bless this nation that it may rise in strength and freedom among the nations of Africa. Bless its leaders that they may look with favor upon Thy Saints and safeguard their rights, property, and privileges.*

Accra Ghana

Announced: Feb. 16, 1998.

Location: 57 Independence Ave., North Ridge, Accra, Ghana

Site: 6 acres.

Exterior finish: Granite quarried in Namibia, Africa, called Namibia Pearl.

Temple design: Traditional, built in third generation of small temples.

Architects: ARUP

Project manager: Russ Tanner.

Contractor: Taysec Construction Limited

Rooms: Celestial room, two endowment rooms, two sealing rooms and baptristy.

Total floor area: 17,500 square feet.

Dimensions: 190 feet by 147 feet.

District: Countries in western Africa, including Nigeria, Ghana, Ivory Coast, Sierra Leone, Liberia, Benin, Togo.

Groundbreaking, site dedication: Nov. 16, 2001, by Elder Russell M. Nelson of the Quorum of the Twelve.

Dedication: Jan. 11, 2004, by President Gordon B. Hinckley; three sessions.

Dedicatory prayer excerpt: *We thank Thee for the brotherhood that exists among us, that neither color of skin nor land of birth can separate us as Thy sons and daughters who have taken upon us sacred and binding covenants.*

Adelaide Australia

Announced: March 17, 1999.

Location: 53-59 Lower Portrush Road, Marden, South Australia 5070,

Phone: (61) 8-8363-8000; no clothing rental.

Site: 6.94 acres.

Exterior finish: Snow white granite

Temple design: Traditional.

Architects: Simon Drew.

Project manager: Graham Sully.

Contractor: Balderstone-Hornibrook.

Rooms: Celestial room, two endowment rooms, two sealing rooms and baptistry.

Total floor area: 10,700 square feet.

Dimensions: 149 feet by 77 feet.

District: Three stakes and three districts in south Australia.

Groundbreaking, site dedication: May 29, 1999, by Elder Vaughn J. Featherstone of the Seventy and president of the Australia/New Zealand Area.

Dedication: June 15, 2000, by President Gordon B. Hinckley; 4 sessions.

Dedicatory prayer excerpt: *We are grateful for this nation of Australia, where there is freedom of worship, freedom of assembly, and freedom to take upon ourselves the name of our Divine Redeemer and to keep sacred the covenants which we make with Him.*

Albuquerque New Mexico

Announced: April 4, 1997.

Location: 10301 San Francisco Dr. NE, Albuquerque, N.M. 87122-3437; phone (505) 822-5110.

Site: 8.5 acres.

Exterior finish: Cast stone/granite.

Temple design: Classic modern.

Architects: Fanning Bard & Tatum.

Project manager: James Aulestia and Lloyd Hess.

Contractor: Okland Construction Co.

Rooms: Celestial room, baptistry, three sealing rooms, two ordinance rooms.

Total floor area: 34,000 square feet.

Dimensions of building: 145 feet by 134 feet.

District: 14 stakes and one district in New Mexico, part of Arizona and Colorado.

Groundbreaking, site dedication: June 20, 1998, by Elder Lynn A. Mickelsen of the Seventy and president of the North America Southwest Area.

Dedication: March 5, 2000, by President Gordon B. Hinckley; 4 sessions.

Dedicatory prayer excerpt: *Let it be a sanctuary of peace, a refuge from the noise of the world. May it be a house of quiet contemplation concerning the eternal nature of life and of Thy divine plan for Thy sons and daughters as they walk the road of immortality and eternal life.*

Anchorage Alaska

Announced: Oct. 4, 1997.

Location: 13161 Brayton Drive, Anchorage, AK 99516; phone: (907) 348-7890; no clothing rental.

Site: 5.54 acres, including adjoining meetinghouse.

Exterior finish: Granite.

Temple design: Classic modern.

Architects: McCool, Carlson & Green Architects and Church A&E Services.

Project manager: Cory Karl.

Contractor: H. Watt & Scott.

Rooms: Baptistry, celestial room, one ordinance room, one sealing room.

Total floor area: Originally 6,800 square feet; 11,937 square feet after remodeling.

Dimensions: 79 feet by 108 feet.

District: Six stakes, one district in Alaska and Yukon.

Groundbreaking, site dedication: April 17, 1998, by Elder F. Melvin Hammond of the Seventy and president of the North America Northwest Area.

Dedication: Jan. 9, 1999, by President Gordon B. Hinckley; 7 sessions. Rededicated after remodeling Feb. 8, 2004, by President Hinckley; one session,

Dedicatory prayer excerpt: *May this great work of temple building go forward across the earth to bless Thy people wherever they may be found. May all who come with hope and high expectation, leave with satisfaction and gratitude.*

Apia Samoa (rebuilt)

Announced: The First Presidency announced on July 16, 2003, that the Apia Samoa Temple, which was destroyed by fire on July 9, 2003, would be rebuilt.

Location: On site of original temple, near the school and mission home in Pesega.

Site: 2 acres.

Exterior finish: Granite.

Temple design: Reflects original design.

Architect: Naylor, Wentworth, Lund.

Project manager: William Naylor.

Contractor: Bud Bailey Construction/Jacobsen Construction.

Rooms: Celestial room, baptistry, two ordinance rooms, two sealing rooms.

Total floor area: 18,691 square feet.

Dimensions: 108 feet by 197 feet.

District: 20 stakes in Samoa and American Samoa.

Groundbreaking, site dedication: Oct. 19, 2003, by Elder Dennis E. Simmons of the Seventy.

Dedication: Sept. 4, 2005, by President Gordon B. Hinckley; two sessions.

Dedicatory prayer excerpt: *We pray that Thou wilt watch over this sacred structure and preserve it from the kind of destructve force which destroyed its predecessor building.*

Apia Samoa (original)

Destroyed by fire July 9, 2003.

Announced: Oct. 15, 1977; plans revised April 2, 1980.

Location: Near the school and mission home in Pesega.

Site: 1.7 acres.

Exterior finish: "R-wall" exterior finish and insulation system on concrete block; split cedar shake shingles on roof.

Temple design: Modern.

Architect: Emil B. Fetzer, Church architect.

Construction advisers: Dale Cook and Richard Rowley.

Contractor: Utah Construction and Development.

Rooms: Baptistry, celestial room, three sealing rooms, two ordinance rooms.

Total floor area: 14,560 square feet.

Dimensions: 142.88 feet by 115.32 feet; statue of Angel Moroni on top spire, 78 feet high.

District: 20 stakes and one district in Western Samoa and American Samoa.

Groundbreaking, site dedication: Feb. 19, 1981, by President Spencer W. Kimball, assisted by the head of state, Malieotoa Tanumafil II. Nearly 4,000 people attended.

Dedication: Aug. 5-7, 1983, by President Gordon B. Hinckley; 7 sessions.

Dedicatory prayer excerpt: *We pray for Thy blessings upon those who govern these islands and the people who dwell here that principles of peace and equity may prevail and that the citizens of these islands may have cause to rejoice in the liberty that is theirs.*

Asunción Paraguay

Announced: April 2, 2000.

Location: Esquina Espana y Brasilia streets, Asuncion, Paraguay; phone: (595) 21-230-035. No clothing rental.

Site: 7 acres including stake center.

Exterior finish: Light gray Asa Branca Brazilian granite.

Temple design: Traditional

Architect: Eduardo Signorelli.

Project manager: Javier Mendieta.

Contractor: Temple Construction Department, with Gonzalez, Acosta & Wood S.A. as construction managers.

Rooms: Celestial room, two ordinance rooms, two sealing rooms, baptistry.

Total floor area: 10,700 square feet.

Dimensions: 149 feet by 77 feet.

District: 10 stakes and 19 districts in Paraguay and several Argentine provinces.

Groundbreaking, site dedication: Feb. 3, 2001, by Elder Jay E. Jensen of the Seventy.

Dedication: May 19, 2002, by President Gordon B. Hinckley, 4 sessions.

Dedicatory prayer excerpts: *We are grateful that this Thy house has been constructed in this nation of Paraguay. Marvelous has been the growth of Thy work in this part of Thy vineyard. ... May this temple stand as a crowning jewel to Thy work in this nation. May Thy Saints throughout the land look to this Thy holy house as a sanctuary to which they may come to make sacred covenants with Thee and partake of the great blessings which Thou hast prepared for Thy faithful children.*

Atlanta Georgia

Announced: April 2, 1980.

Location: In Sandy Springs, on the northeastern outskirts of Atlanta; 6450 Barfield Rd., Atlanta, GA 30328-4283; phone, (770) 393-3698.

Site: 9.6 acres.

Exterior finish: Pre-cast stone walls, built-up roof.

Temple design: Modern.

Architect: Emil B. Fetzer, Church architect; HKS Architects Inc.

Construction adviser: Michael Enfield and Ronald Prince.

Contractor: Cube Construction Company.
Contractor for 2011 renovations: Jacobsen Construction of Salt Lake City, and Hardin Construction, Atlanta, Ga.

Rooms: Baptistry, celestial room, four sealing rooms, four ordinance rooms.

Total floor area: 34,500 square feet.

Dimensions: 198 feet by 212 feet; statue of Angel Moroni on top spire, 92 feet high.

District: 13 stakes in Georgia, and a small part of Tennessee, Alabama and North Carolina.

Groundbreaking, site dedication: March 7, 1981, by President Spencer W. Kimball.

Dedication: June 1-4, 1983, by President Gordon B. Hinckley; 11 sessions. Re-dedication of baptistry Nov. 1997 by President Gordon B. Hinckley.

Rededicated: May 1, 2011, by President Thomas S. Monson after extensive renovation.

Dedicatory prayer excerpt: *May the very presence of this temple in the midst of Thy people become a reminder of the sacred and eternal covenants made with Thee. May they strive more diligently to banish from their lives those elements which are inconsistent with the covenants they have made with Thee.*

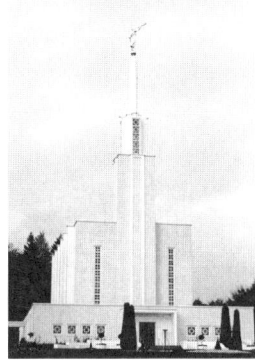

Baton Rouge Louisiana

Announced: Oct. 14, 1998.

Location: 10339 Highland Road, Baton Rouge, LA. 70810; phone, (225) 769-1197; no clothing rental.

Site: 6.3 acres, including adjoining meetinghouse.

Exterior finish: Imperial Danby White marble.

Temple design: Classic modern.

Architect: Paul Tessier of Paul Tessier & Associates, and Church A&E Services.

Project manager: Leon Rowley.

Contractor: Layton Construction Co., Construction Management Co.; Cangelosi Ward, general contractor.

Rooms: Celestial room, baptistry, two ordinance rooms, two sealing rooms.

Total floor area: 10,700 square feet.

Dimensions: 149 feet by 77 feet.

District: Nine stakes in Louisiana and Mississippi.

Groundbreaking, site dedication: May 8, 1999, by Elder Monte J. Brough of the Seventy and president of the North America Southeast Area.

Dedication: July 16, 2000, by President Gordon B. Hinckley; 4 sessions.

Dedicatory prayer excerpt: *We thank Thee for this nation in which this temple stands. It was established by men whom Thou didst raise up unto this very purpose. Thou hast spoken concerning the Constitution of its government. Surely it is a choice land and a favored nation.*

Bern Switzerland

Location: In a northern suburb of Bern in a setting with the Alps on the south, and the Jura Mountains on the west and north; Tempelstrasse 2, CH - 3052, Zollikofen, Switzerland; phone: (41) 31-915-5252.

Site: 7 acres, selected July 1952, by President David O. McKay and President Samuel E. Bringhurst of the Swiss-Austrian Mission.

Exterior finish: Reinforced concrete with a creamish gray terra cotta facing trimmed in white. Tower is white base and spire is gold-colored.

Temple design: Modern-contemporary, but similar to lines of early Church temples.

Architect: Edward O. Anderson, Church architect. Re-drawn into German specifications by Wilhelm Zimmer of Bercher and Zimmer Architects.

Contractor: Hans Jordi of Bern.

Rooms: Baptistry, celestial room, four ordinance rooms, seven sealing rooms.

Total floor area: 39,457 square feet; after remodeling, 39,063 square feet.

Dimensions: 152 feet by 84 feet; top of tower rises 140 feet.

District: 10 stakes and 21 districts in Switzerland, Austria, France, Italy, Albania and Israel (for expatriates).

Groundbreaking, site dedication: Aug. 5, 1953, by President David O. McKay.

Dedication: Sept. 11-15, 1955, by President David O. McKay; 10 sessions. Rededicated Oct. 23-25, 1992, by President Gordon B. Hinckley; 10 sessions.

Dedicatory prayer excerpt: *Increase our desire, O Father, to put forth even greater effort towards the consummation of Thy purpose to bring to pass the immortality and eternal life of all thy children.*

Billings Montana

Announced: Aug. 16, 1996.

Location: 3100 Rim Point Drive, Billings, MT, 59106; phone: (406) 655-0607.

Site: 10 acres.

Exterior finish: Wyoming white dolomite precast concrete.

Temple design: Classic modern.

Architects: CTA Architects Engineers.

Project manager: Cory Karl.

Contractor: Jacobson Construction Inc.

Rooms: Baptistry, celestial room, two ordinance rooms, three sealing rooms.

Total floor area: 33,800 square feet.

Dimensions: 183 feet by 212 feet.

District: 13 stakes in Montana and Wyoming.

Groundbreaking, site dedication: March 28, 1998, by Elder Hugh W. Pinnock of the Seventy and president of the North America Central Area.

Dedication: Nov. 20, 1999, by President Gordon B. Hinckley; 8 sessions.

Dedicatory prayer excerpt: *Those of this area who are called to teach the gospel to the world will first come here to be endowed with power from on high. Lead them in their ministry to those who will accept their testimony of the divinity of Thy restored work.*

Birmingham Alabama

Announced: Sept. 11. 1998.

Location: 1927 Mount Olive Blvd., Gardendale, AL 35071; phone: (205) 631-3444; no clothing rental.

Site: 5.6 acres, including adjoining meetinghouse.

Exterior finish: Imperial Danby White Marble.

Temple design: Classic modern

Architects: Robert Waldrip of Joyce, Prout and Associates, and Church A&E Services.

Project manager: Leon Rowley.

Contractor: Layton Construction Co., Construction Management Co., Gary C. Wyatt, Inc., general contractor.

Rooms: Celestial room, baptistry, two ordinance rooms; two sealing rooms.

Total floor area: 10,700 square feet.

Dimensions: 149 feet by 77 feet.

District: Seven stakes in Alabama, Florida.

Groundbreaking, site dedication: Oct. 9, 1999, by Elder Stephen A. West of the Seventy and second counselor in the North America Southeast Area presidency.

Dedication: Sept. 3, 2000, by President Gordon B. Hinckley: 4 sessions.

Dedicatory prayer excerpt: *May the influence of this Thy house be felt throughout this great temple district. May the Church grow and prosper here. May those in government be friendly to Thy people.*

Bismarck North Dakota

Announced: July 29, 1998.

Location: 2930 Cody Drive in northwest Bismarck, ND 58503-0116; phone (701)258-9590; no clothing rental.

Site: 1.6 acres.

Exterior finish: White marble.

Temple design: Classic modern.

Architects: Ritterbush-Ellig-Hulsing and Church A&E Services.

Project manager: Cory Karl.

Contractor: Capital City Construction.

Rooms: Celestial room, two ordinance rooms, two sealing rooms, baptistry.

Total floor area: 10,700 square feet.

Dimensions: 149 feet by 77 feet.

District: Three stakes and one district in North Dakota and South Dakota.

Groundbreaking, site dedication: Oct. 17, 1998; Elder Kenneth Johnson of the Seventy and first counselor in the North America Central Area.

Dedication: Sept. 19, 1999, by President Gordon B. Hinckley; 3 sessions.

Dedicatory prayer excerpt: *We thank Thee for the faith of Thy sons and daughters in the vast area of this temple district, men and women who love Thee and love their Redeemer, and have stood steadfast as Thy people. They have felt much alone. They are out on the frontier of the Church. Their numbers are still not large. But they are entitled to every blessing which the Church has to offer.*

Bogotá Colombia

Announced: April 7, 1984.

Location: Carrera 37 No. 125A-65, Bogota D.C., Colombia; phone: (57) 1-625-8000.

Site: 3.71 acres.

Exterior finish: granite, Asa Branca.

Temple design: Classic modern.

Architects: Cuellar, Cerrano y Gomez, S.A. and Church A&E Services.

Project manager: Cesar Davila.

Contractor: Cuellar, Cerrano y Gomez, S.A.

Rooms: Celestial room, baptistry, four ordinance rooms and three sealing rooms.

Total floor area: 53,500 square feet.

Dimensions: 76 feet by 186 feet.; spire, 124 feet high.

District: 44 stakes and districts in Colombia.

Groundbreaking, site dedication: June 26, 1993, by Elder William R. Bradford of the Seventy and president South America North Area.

Dedication: April 24, 1999, by President Gordon B. Hinckley; 11 sessions.

Dedicatory prayer excerpt: *The faithful saints of Colombia have given generously of their means to this cause.*

Boise Idaho

Status: Under renovation.

Announced: March 31, 1982.

Location: Just off Interstate 84 at 1211 S. Cole Road, Boise, ID 83709-1871; phone: (208) 322-4422.

Site: 4.83 acres.

Exterior finish: Faced with light colored marble with a slate roof. It is surrounded by three detached towers on each end; 8-foot statue of the Angel Moroni tops highest spire.

Temple design: Modern adaptation of six-spire design.

Architects: Church architectural staff, with assistance from Ron Thurber & Associates of Boise.

Construction adviser: Jerry Sears.

Contractor: Comtrol Inc. of Midvale, Utah.

Rooms: Baptistry, celestial room, four ordinance rooms, three sealing rooms.

Total floor area: 35,868 square feet after 1987 addition.

Dimensions: 236 feet by 78 feet; statue of Angel Moroni 112 feet high.

District: 35 stakes in western Idaho and two in eastern Oregon.

Groundbreaking, site dedication: Dec. 18, 1982, by Elder Mark E. Petersen of the Quorum of the Twelve.

Dedication: May 25-30, 1984, by President Gordon B. Hinckley; 24 sessions. Remodeled facilities dedicated by Elder James E. Faust Feb. 14, 1987; new baptistry dedicated by Elder Faust May 29, 1987.

Dedicatory prayer excerpt: *May Thy faithful Saints of this and future generations look to this beautiful structure as a house to which they will be made welcome ... for the making of eternal covenants with Thee, for inspiration and sanctification, as they serve unselfishly.*

Boston Massachusetts

Announced: Sept. 30, 1995.

Location: 86 Frontage Rd., Belmont, MA 02478-2135; phone: (617) 993-9993.

Site: 8 acres.

Exterior finish: Granite.

Temple design: Classic Modern.

Architect: Tsoi/Kobus & Associates and Church A&E Services.

Project manager: William Treu.

Contractor: Barr & Barr.

Rooms: Baptistry, celestial room, four sealing rooms, four ordinance rooms.

Total floor area: 69,000 square feet.

Dimensions: 90 feet by 190 feet.

District: 19 stakes, 3 districts in Connecticut, Maine, New Hampshire, Rhode Island, Massachusetts, Maine, and New York.

Groundbreaking, site dedication: June 13, 1997, by Elder Richard G. Scott of the Quorum of the Twelve.

Dedication: Oct. 1, 2000, by President Gordon B. Hinckley, 4 sessions.

Dedicatory prayer excerpt: *We are assembled to dedicate this Thy holy house. It is a special occasion. This temple becomes the 100th operating temple of Thy Church.*

We have looked forward to this occasion. We have prayed for this day....

To us it is indeed a miracle. The ground on which it stands, the circumstances of its preservation for this use, and the decision to build it here — all are miracles unto those who have been a part of this process.

Artist rendering

Bountiful Utah

Announced: May 28, 1988.

Location: In the Bountiful foothills on east bench (at 1650 East), 640 S. Bountiful Blvd, Bountiful, UT 84010-1394; phone: (801) 296-2100.

Site: 11 acres.

Exterior finish: Bethel white granite.

Temple design: Modern, with single spire.

Architect: Allen Ereckson, architect of record; Keith Stepan, project architect; and Church architectural staff.

Contractor: Okland Construction Co.

Project manager: Jerry Sears.

Construction adviser: Michael Enfield.

Rooms: Baptistry, celestial room, four endowment rooms, eight sealing rooms.

Total floor area: 104,000 square feet.

Dimensions: 145 feet by 198 feet; statue of Angel Moroni on top spire; 176 feet high.

District: 30 stakes in Central and south Davis County, Utah.

Groundbreaking, site dedication: May 2, 1992, by President Ezra Taft Benson.

Dedication: Jan. 8-14, 1995, by President Howard W. Hunter; 28 sessions.

Dedicatory prayer excerpt: *May this house provide a spirit of peace to all who observe its majesty, and especially to those who enter for their own sacred ordinances and to perform the work for their loved ones beyond the veil. Let them feel of Thy divine love and mercy. May they be privileged to say, as did the Psalmist of old, 'We took sweet counsel together, and walked unto the house of God in company.'*

Brigham City Utah

Announced: Oct. 3, 2009.

Location: 250 S. Main St., Brigham City, Utah

Groundbreaking, site dedication: Ground broken July 31, 2010, by President Boyd K. Packer of the Quorum of the Twelve.

Status: Under construction.

Brisbane Australia

Announced: July 20, 1998.

Location: 200 River Terrace; Kangaroo Point, QLD 4169, Australia; phone: (01161) 73 240-3600; no clothing rental.

Site: .86 acres

Exterior finish: Light gray granite.

Temple design: Traditional.

Architects: Phillips, Smith, Conwell Architects.

Project manager: Graham Sully

Contractor: John Holland Pty., Ltd.

Rooms: Celestial room, two ordinances rooms, two sealing rooms, baptistry.

Total floor area: 10,700 square feet.

Dimensions: 149 feet by 72 feet; statue of Angel Moroni on top spire; 71 feet high.

District: Queensland and northern areas of New South Wales.

Groundbreaking: May 26, 2001, by Elder Kenneth Johnson of the Seventy and president of the Australia/New Zealand Area,

Dedication: June 15, 2003, by President Gordon B. Hinckley in 4 sessions.

Dedicatory prayer excerpt: *We thank Thee for the strength of Thy work in this good land. We thank Thee for other houses of the Lord on the soil of this nation and are grateful to now have this beautiful structure in this great city of Brisbane together with the accompanying chapel and other facilities. On this Sabbath morning our hearts reach up to Thee in gratitude and love.*

Buenos Aires Argentina

Status: Under renovation.

Announced: April 2, 1980.

Location: On southwest outskirts of Buenos Aires; Autopista Richieri y Puente 13, B1778 dua Ciudad Evita, Buenos Aires, Argentina. Telephone: (54) 11-4 487-1520.

Site: 3.73 acres.

Exterior finish: Light gray native granite.

Temple design: Modern adaptation of earlier six-spire design.

Architects: Church architectural staff; local architect Ramon Paez.

Construction adviser: Gary Holland.

Contractor: Benito Roggio and Sons.

Rooms: Baptistry, celestial room, four ordinance rooms, three sealing rooms.

Total floor area: 17,687 square feet.

Dimensions: 178 feet by 71 feet. Angel Moroni statue is atop tallest spire, 112 feet.

District: 65 stakes, 36 districts in Argentina.

Groundbreaking, site dedication: April 20, 1983, by Elder Bruce R. McConkie of the Quorum of the Twelve.

Dedication: Jan. 17-19, 1986, by President Thomas S. Monson of the First Presidency; 11 sessions.

Dedicatory prayer excerpt: *We remember that it was in this very city of Buenos Aires, on Christmas Day in the year 1925, just 60 years ago, that Elder Melvin J. Ballard, an apostle of the Lord, dedicated all of South America for the preaching of the gospel.*

Artist rendering

Calgary Alberta

Announced: Oct. 4, 2008.

Location: Next to an existing meetinghouse at Rocky Ridge Road and Royal Oak Road.

Groundbreaking, site dedication: May 15, 2010, by Elder Donald L. Hallstrom of the Presidency of the Seventy.

Status: Under construction.

Campinas Brazil

Announced: April 3, 1997.

Location: Rodovia Heitor Penteado Kn 4,3 Distrito Souzas, Campinas, SP 13092-543 Brazil; phone: ((55) 19-3258-5470.

Site: 6.18 acres.

Exterior finish: Light gray Asa Branca granite from the state of Ceara.

Temple design: Classic modern.

Architect: JCL Arquitetos Ltd., and Church A&E Services.

Project manager: Raul Lins.

Contractor: Ernesto Woebcke.

Rooms: Four ordinance rooms, three sealing rooms, celestial room, baptistry.

Total floor area: 49,100 square feet.

Dimensions: 142 feet by 163 feet.

District: 36 stakes and six districts in the states of Sao Paulo, Rio de Janeiro and Minas Gerais.

Groundbreaking, site dedication: May 1, 1998, by President James E. Faust, second counselor in the First Presidency.

Dedication: May 17, 2002, by President Gordon B. Hinckley in 4 sessions.

Dedicatory prayer excerpt: *Here will occur a great and dedicated service in behalf of those who have passed beyond the veil of death that they might be freed from the prison-house in which they have been held, many of them for centuries. Here a selfless work of love will take place. We thank Thee for every blessing, for every opportunity which will be offered here.*

Caracas Venezuela

Announced: Sept. 30, 1995.

Location: Avenida C Con Calle C-1, Urb. Caurimare, Caracas D.F. 1062-A, Venezuela; phone: (58) 212-985-9123; no clothing rental.

Site: .5 acre.

Exterior finish: Granite.

Temple design: Classic modern.

Architect: Taller de Arquitectura and Church A&E Services.

Project manager: Duane Cheney.

Contractor: Jahn

Rooms: Two ordinance rooms, two sealing rooms, celestial room, baptistry.

Total floor area: 15,332 square feet.

Dimensions: 78 feet by 115 feet.

District: Venezuela, Trinidad and Tabago.

Groundbreaking, site dedication: Jan. 10, 1999, by Elder Francisco J. Viñas of the Seventy and president of the South America North Area.

Dedication: Aug. 20, 2000, by President Gordon B. Hinckley; 4 sessions.

Dedicatory prayer excerpt: *We pray for this great nation of Venezuela. May it hold its place among the sovereign nations of the earth. May its people be blessed and prospered. May they enjoy freedom to worship Thee without molestation of any kind. Bless the leaders of the nation with wisdom and understanding, and a great desire to serve the needs of the people.*

Cardston Alberta

Location: Cardston, about 140 miles south of Calgary in southern Alberta; 348 3rd St. West, Cardston, AB T0K 0K0 ; phone: (403) 653-3552.

Site: In 1887, eight-acre site laid out and given to the Church by Charles Ora Card. It was then called the Tabernacle Block.

Exterior finish: White granite quarried near Kootenai Lakes in Nelson, B. C. Each stone was hand-hewn at the quarry or temple site. Additions of artificial precast granite.

Temple design: Octagonal design has Grecian massiveness and a Peruvian touch of Aztec influence with pyramid silhouette.

Architects: Hyrum C. Pope and Harold W. Burton of Salt Lake City.

Rooms: Approximately 40 in original structure; now 80, including baptistry, celestial, four ordinance, five sealing.

Total floor area: Originally 29,471 square feet, 81,700 square feet after remodeling.

Dimensions: 118 feet square, height, 85 feet; footprint 165 feet by 311 feet.

District: 21 stakes in Central and southern Alberta, southeastern British Columbia, northern Montana.

Groundbreaking, site dedication: July 27, 1913, President Joseph F. Smith dedicated site . Ground broken Nov. 9, 1913, by Daniel Kent Greene of Glenwood, Alberta.

Dedication: Aug. 26-29, 1923, by President Heber J. Grant; 11 sessions. Rededicated after remodeling July 2, 1962, by President Hugh B. Brown of the First Presidency; Rededicated by President Gordon B. Hinckley June 22-24, 1991; 12 sessions.

Re-dedicatory prayer excerpt: *Bless the Latter-day Saints of Canada that they may be good citizens of the nation, men and women of integrity worthy of the respect of the people of this nation, and contributing of their talents and strength to its well-being.*

Cebu City Philippines

Announced: April 18, 2006.

Location: Gorordo Avenue, Lahug, Cebu City, Philippines.

Site: 11.6 acres.

Exterior finish: Mountain grey granite from China.

Architects: Architectural Nexus, Salt Lake City, Utah. Recio & Casa Architects, Makati City, Philippines.

Project manager: Knut Klavenes

Contractor: DDT Konstract, Inc., Philippines.

Rooms: Two ordinance rooms, two sealing rooms, celestial room, baptistry.

Total floor area: 29,556 square feet

District: More than 200,000 members living in the Visayas and Mindanao regions.

Groundbreaking, site dedication: Nov. 14, 2007, by Elder Dallin H. Oaks of the Quorum of the Twelve.

Dedication: June 13, 2010, by President Thomas S. Monson, 3 sessions.

Dedicatory prayer excerpt: *"We are in a nation of many islands, whose people love truth and whose hearts are responsive to the message of the eternal gospel. We thank Thee for their faith. We thank Thee for their spirit of sacrifice. Bless them that neither they nor the generations which follow them will go hungry or be without shelter from the storms that beat about them."*

Chicago Illinois

Announced: April 1, 1981.

Location: 20 miles north of Chicago; 4151 West Lake Ave., Glenview, IL 60025-1240; phone: (847) 299-6500.

Site: 13 acres.

Exterior finish: Gray buff marble, gray slate roof.

Temple design: Modern adaptation of earlier six-spire design.

Architects: Church architectural staff; local architect, Wight & Co.

Construction adviser: Virgil Roberts.

Contractor: Pora Construction Co., Des Plaines, Ill., with Utah Construction and Development Co.

Rooms: Baptistry, celestial room, five ordinance rooms, three sealing rooms.

Total floor area: Originally 17,850 square feet; 37,062 square feet following addition.

Dimensions: 236 feet by 78 feet; seven-foot-tall Angel Moroni statue is 112 feet high.

District: 20 stakes in Illnois, Iowa, Wisconsin, Indiana, Michigan.

Groundbreaking, site dedication: Aug. 13, 1983, by President Gordon B. Hinckley.

Dedication: Aug. 9-13, 1985, by President Gordon B. Hinckley; 19 sessions. Addition dedicated by Pres. Hinckley Oct. 8, 1989.

Dedicatory prayer excerpt: *We are mindful that Thy Prophet Joseph and his brother Hyrum were martyred in Carthage, Ill., at a time of terrible conflict and persecution.*

Ciudad Juárez Mexico

Announced: May 7, 1998.

Location: Calle Paraguay 290, Esq Jose Borunda, Col. Partido Romero, Ciudad Juarez, Mexico; phone:(52) 656-611-5146; ; no clothing rental.

Site: 1.63 acres.

Exterior finish: White marble veneer.

Temple design: Traditional Spanish.

Architect: Alvaro Iñigo and Church A&E Services.

Project manager: David Wills.

Contractor: Granay Montero/Jacobsen Construction.

Rooms: Two ordinance rooms, two sealing rooms, celestial room, baptistry.

Total floor area: 10,700 square feet.

Dimensions: 77 feet by 149 feet.

District: 10 stakes, one district in northern Chihuahua, El Paso, Texas.

Groundbreaking, site dedication: Jan. 9, 1999, by Elder Eran A. Call of the Seventy and president of the Mexico North Area.

Dedication: Feb. 26-27, 2000, by President Gordon B. Hinckley; 6 sessions.

Dedicatory prayer excerpt: *Bless this great nation of Mexico that it may rise and shine among the nations of the earth. Lift the burden of poverty from the backs of the people. Bless the leaders of government that they may welcome Thy servants, and may the message brought by Thy servants take root in the hearts of many souls.*

Cochabamba Bolivia

Announced: Jan. 13, 1995.

Location: northern side of Cochabamba at Av. Melchor Urquidi, 1500, Alto Queru Quero, Cochabamba, Bolivia; phone: (591) 4-42-93161.

Site: 6.51 acres.

Exterior finish: Blend of hand-hewn Comanche granite and plaster.

Temple design: Classic modern.

Architects: BSW and Church A&E Services.

Project manager: Javier Mendieta.

Contractor: CBI.

Rooms: Two ordinance rooms, three sealing rooms, celestial room, baptistry.

Total floor area: 33,000 square feet.

Dimensions: 128 feet by 145 feet.

District: 21 stakes, 9 districts in Bolivia.

Groundbreaking, site dedication: Nov. 10, 1996, by President Gordon B. Hinckley.

Dedication: April 30, 2000, by President Gordon B. Hinckley; 4 sessions.

Dedicatory prayer excerpt: *Our hearts are filled with thanksgiving on this historic day when we meet to dedicate this Thy holy house in Bolivia. How thankful we are for it. It is the fulfillment of our dreams, our hopes, our prayers, our faith.*

Colonia Juárez Chihuahua Mexico

Announced: Oct. 4, 1997.

Location: Calle Chihuahua y Diaz, Colonia Juarez, Chihuahua 31857, Mexico; phone: (52) -636-695-0144; no clothing rental.

Site: 1 acre.

Exterior finish: White marble.

Temple design: Classic modern.

Architects: Alvaro Iñigo and Church A&E Services.

Project manager: David Wills.

Contractor: Jacobsen Construction Co.

Rooms: Baptistry, celestial room, one ordinance room, one sealing room.

Total floor area: 6,800 square feet.

Dimensions: 102 feet by 76 feet.

District: Two stakes, two districts.

Groundbreaking, site dedication: March 7, 1998, by Elder Eran A. Call of the Seventy and president of the Mexico North Area.

Dedication: March 6, 1999, by President Gordon B. Hinckley; 4 sessions.

Dedicatory prayer excerpt: *It was here in Northern Mexico that Thou didst reveal the idea and the plan of a smaller temple, complete in every necessary detail, but suited in size to the needs and circumstances of the Church membership in this area of Thy vineyard. That revelation came of a desire and a prayer to help Thy people of these colonies who have been true and loyal during the century and more that they have lived here. They are deserving of this sacred edifice in which to labor for themselves and their forebears.*

Columbia River Washington

Announced: April 2, 2000.

Location: 969 Gage Blvd., Richland, WA 99352; phone: (509) 628-0990; no clothing rental

Site: 2.88 acres.

Exterior finish: Bethel white granite from Vermont and Italy.

Temple design: Traditional.

Architect: Architectural & Engineering Services/ Temple Construction Dept.

Project manager: Bill Naylor

Contractor: Vitus Construction, Medford, Ore.

Rooms: Celestial room, two ordinance rooms, two sealing rooms, baptistry and eating area.

Total floor area: 16,880 square feet.

Dimensions: 196 feet by 106 feet.

District: 12 stakes in southeast Washington and one stake in Oregon.

Groundbreaking, site dedication: Oct. 28, 2000, by Elder Stephen A. West of the Seventy and second counselor in the North America Northwest Area Presidency.

Dedication: Nov. 18, 2001, by President Gordon B. Hinckley; 4 sessions.

Dedicatory excerpt: *We pray that Thou wilt smile upon Thy people and their families. Open the windows of heaven and shower down blessings upon the faithful who contribute of their time and resources according to Thy will and law. May the whole earth become as Zion as Thy work spreads among the nations.*

Columbia South Carolina

Announced: Sept. 11, 1998.

Location: Corner of Trotter Road and Caughman Road in Hopkins, SC 29061-9573; phone: (803) 647-9472; no clothing rental.

Site: 3.6 acres.

Exterior finish: Imperial Danby Vermont marble.

Temple design: Traditional.

Architects: Mike Watson of Watson-Tate Architects Inc.

Project manager: Bruce Catanzaro.

Contractor: Walbridge Aldinger.

Rooms: Celestial room, two ordinance rooms, two sealing rooms and baptistry.

Total floor area: 10,700 square feet.

Dimensions: 149 feet by 77 feet.

District: 11 stakes in South Carolina, North Carolina, Georgia and Tennessee.

Groundbreaking, site dedication: Dec. 5, 1998, by Elder Gordon T. Watts of the Seventy and first counselor in the North America Southeast Area presidency.

Dedication: Oct. 16-17, 1999, by President Gordon B. Hinckley; 6 sessions.

Dedicatory prayer excerpt: *We rejoice in the presence of this house in this great state of South Carolina which has hosted Thy messengers of eternal truth. They have been coming here for generations, and there has been established a great body of faithful Latter-day Saints. We pray that the very presence of this Thy house will have a sanctifying influence upon the people of this area, and particularly upon those who enter its portals.*

Columbus Ohio

Announced: April 25, 1998.

Location: 3870 Gateway Blvd., Columbus, OH 43228; phone: (614) 351-5001; no clothing rental.

Site: 2.2 acres.

Exterior finish: Imperial Danby Vermont marble.

Temple design: Traditional.

Architects: Firestone Jaros Mullin.

Project manager: Bruce Catanzaro.

Contractor: Corna/Kokosing Construction Co.

Rooms: Celestial room, baptistry, two ordinance rooms, two sealing rooms.

Total floor area: 10,700 square feet.

Dimensions: 149 feet by 77 feet.

District: 11 stakes in northern and central Ohio, western West Virginia.

Groundbreaking, site dedication: Sept. 12, 1998, by Elder John K. Carmack of the Seventy and president of North America East Area.

Dedication: Sept. 4, 1999, by President Gordon B. Hinckley; 6 sessions.

Dedicatory prayer excerpt: *We are assembled to dedicate this Thy house. It is now 163 years since a temple was dedicated in the State of Ohio. We are reminded today of the dedication of the Kirtland Temple and of the prayer given on that occasion which Thy prophet declared was revealed unto him.*

We, too, as Saints of this day, seek Thine inspiration in the words which we direct in prayer to Thee, our Father and our God.

No artist rendering available

Concepión Chile

Announced: Oct. 3, 2009.

Status: In planning stages.

Copenhagen Denmark

Announced: March 17, 1999.

Location: Priorvej 12, 2000 Frederiksberg, Denmark; near "Old Copenhagen."

Site: Less than one acre.

Exterior finish: Original brick and columns.

Temple design: Neo-classical style of original meetinghouse.

Architects and contractors: Arcito.

Project manager: Carl Champagnie.

Rooms: Celestial room, two endowment rooms, two sealing rooms and baptistry with font resting on 12 fiberglass oxen.

Total floor area: Approximately 25,000 square feet.

Dimensions: 45 feet by 120 feet.

District: Stakes in Aarhus and Copenhagen, Denmark; Goteborg and Malmo, Sweden; and Iceland District.

Groundbreaking, site dedicated: Priorvej Chapel originally dedicated June 14, 1931. Later remodeled to become the Copenhagen Denmark Temple. Temple site dedicated April 24, 1999, by Elder Spencer J. Condie of the Seventy and president of the Europe North Area.

Dedication: May 23, 2004, by President Gordon B. Hinckley in four sessions.

Dedicatory prayer excerpt: *We thank Thee for this land, where the restored gospel was first preached more than a century and a half ago. We thank Thee for Thy faithful servants who have come here as teachers of Thy divine truth. We express our gratitude for the many thousands who have responded to their message over the years.*

Artist rendering

Córdoba Argentina

Announced: Oct. 4, 2008.

Groundbreaking: October 30, 2010, by Elder Neil L. Andersen of the Quorum of the Twelve.

The temple in Córdoba, Argentina, will be situated on the Belgrano meetinghouse site, next to the present mission home of the Church.

Status: Under construction.

Curitiba Brazil

Announced: Aug. 23, 2002

Location: Rua Deputado Heitor Alencar Furtado, 3641 — Massungue suburb, Curitiba, Parana, Brazil.

Site: 8.15 acres

Exterior features: Reinforced concrete cast onsite, with facade of sienna white granite native to the state of Espirito Santo, Brazil. Thirty art-glass window panes complete the facade exterior.

Architects: Jeronimo da Cunha Lima, Brazil; GSBS, United States.

Contractor: LDS Church Temple Construction Department of Brazil.

Rooms: Baptistry, celestial room, two ordinance rooms, two sealing rooms.

Total floor area: 27,850 square feet

Dimensions: 125 feet, 2 inches to the top of the Angel Moroni statue (the statue is 14 feet, 2 inches tall).

District: Stakes and mission districts in the Brazilian state of Parana and a portion of the state of Santa Catarina.

Groundbreaking: March 10, 2005

Dedication: June 1, 2008, by President Thomas S. Monson; four sessions.

Dedicatory prayer excerpt: *The Atonement wrought by Thy Son gives purpose to our being and turns our thoughts heavenward.*

Dallas Texas

Announced: April 1, 1981.

Location: 12 miles north of the downtown area, at 6363 Willow Lane, Dallas, TX 75230-2227; phone: (972) 991-1273.

Site: 6 acres.

Exterior finish: Light-colored marble tile walls, dark gray slate roof.

Temple design: Modern adaptation of earlier six-spire design.

Architects: Church architectural staff, with assistance from West & Humphries of Dallas.

Construction adviser: Virgil Roberts.

Contractor: Comtrol Inc. of Midvale, Utah.

Rooms: Baptistry, celestial room, five ordinance rooms, three sealing rooms.

Total floor area: Originally 17,850 square feet; 44,207 square feet following addition.

Dimensions: 236 feet by 78 feet; tower, 95 feet; statue of Angel Moroni on top spire.

District: 16 east Texas stakes and one Louisiana stake.

Groundbreaking, site dedication: Jan. 22, 1983, by President Gordon B. Hinckley.

Dedication: Oct. 19-24, 1984, by President Gordon B. Hinckley; 23 sessions. Rededicated March 5, 1989 by President Gordon B. Hinckley.

Dedicatory prayer excerpt: *May this beautiful temple, standing in this community, become a declaration to all who shall look upon it of the faith of thy Saints in the revealed things of eternity, and may they be led to respect that which is sacred unto us.*

Denver Colorado

Announced: March 31, 1982.

Location: In Littleton, about 20 miles south of Denver, at County Line Road and South University Boulevard; 2001 E. Phillips Circle, Centennial, CO., 80122-3264. Phone (303) 730-0220.

Site: 7.56 acres.

Exterior finish: Modern design; precast stone walls and built-up roof.

Temple design: Modern.

Architects: Church architectural staff.

Supervising architect: Local architect, Bobby R. Thomas.

Construction adviser: Michael Enfield.

Contractor: Langley Constructors.

Rooms: Baptistry, celestial room, four ordinance rooms, six sealing rooms.

Total floor area: 27,006 square feet.

Dimensions: 184 feet by 192 feet; single 90-foot spire capped with statue of Angel Moroni.

District: 25 stakes, one district in Colorado, eastern Wyoming, western Kansas.

Groundbreaking, site dedication: May 19, 1984, by President Gordon B. Hinckley.

Dedication: Oct. 24-28, 1986, by President Ezra Taft Benson; 19 sessions.

Dedicatory prayer excerpt: *Touch the hearts of Thy people that they may look to this temple as a refuge from the evil and turmoil of the world. May they ever live worthy of the blessings here to be found. May they be prompted to seek the records of their forebears and to serve here in their behalf, under that plan which Thou hast revealed for the salvation and exaltation of Thy children of all generations.*

Detroit Michigan

Announced: Aug. 10, 1998.

Location: 37425 N. Woodward Ave., in Bloomfield Hills, MI 48304; phone (248) 593-0690; no clothing rental.

Site: 3.1 acres.

Exterior finish: Imperial Danby Vermont marble.

Temple design: Traditional.

Architect: John Coakley of Bernath-Bernath-Coakley Associates.

Project manager: Bruce Catanzaro.

Contractor: Walbridge-Aldinger.

Rooms: Celestial room, baptistry, two ordinance rooms, two sealing rooms.

Total floor area: 10,700 square feet.

Dimensions: 149 feet by 77 feet.

District: Seven stakes, two districts in Michigan.

Groundbreaking, site dedication: Oct. 10, 1998, by Elder Jay E. Jensen of the First Quorum of the Seventy and president of the North America Northeast Area.

Dedication: Oct. 23, 1999, by President Gordon B. Hinckley; 6 sessions.

Dedicatory prayer excerpt: *May the work that will go forward in this sacred edifice please Thee and bring untold blessings to Thy sons and daughters on both sides of the veil.*

Draper Utah

Announced: Oct. 2, 2004; city announced Nov. 21, 2004.

Location: 14065 Canyon Vista Lane, Draper, Utah, 84020.

Site: Approximately 12 acres, including adjacent meetinghouse.

Exterior features: Temple white granite from China.

Temple design: Center spire.

Architects: FFKR Architects.

Project manager: Evan Nelson.

Contractor: Okland Construction.

Rooms: Baptistry, celestial room, two sets of two ordinance rooms, five sealing rooms.

Total floor area: 58,300 square feet.

District: More than 60,000 members of the 25 stakes in the Draper area.

Groundbreaking, site dedication: Aug. 5, 2006, by President Gordon B. Hinckley, with his counselors President Thomas S. Monson and President James E. Faust.

Dedication: March 20-22, 2009, by President Thomas S. Monson; 12 sessions.

Dedicatory prayer excerpt: *May this House provide a spirit of peace to all who observe its majesty, and especially to those who enter for their own sacred ordinances and to perform the work for those beyond the veil. Let them feel of Thy divine love and mercy.*

No rendering available

Edmonton Alberta

Announced: Aug. 11, 1998.

Location: 14325 53rd Ave. NW, Edmonton, Alberta T6H 5G6; phone: (780) 434-7436; no clothing rental.

Site: 1 acre.

Exterior finish: Light gray granite quarried in Quebec.

Temple design: Classic modern.

Architect: Robert Bennett of Bennett Architect, Inc. and Church A&E Services.

Project manager: Cory Karl.

Contractor: Binder Construction Limited.

Rooms: Baptistry, celestial room, two ordinance rooms, two sealing rooms.

Total floor area: 10,700 square feet.

Dimensions: 149 by 77 feet.

District: Six Edmonton area stakes.

Groundbreaking, site dedication: Feb. 27, 1999, by Elder Yoshihiko Kikuchi of the Seventy and second counselor in the North America Central Area presidency.

Dedication: Dec. 11-12, 1999, by President Gordon B. Hinckley; 7 sessions.

Dedicatory prayer excerpt: *Let Thy providence be felt in this great nation of Canada that it shall continue to be a land where Thy sons and daughters enjoy the precious boon of freedom of assembly and worship. Bless those who govern that they shall look with favor upon Thy people, and may Thy work grow in numbers, in majesty, and in strength in this good land.*

Fortaleza Brazil

Announced: Oct. 3, 2009.

Status: In planning stages.

No rendering available

Fort Collins Colorado

Announced: April 2, 2011.

Location: Southeast corner of the intersection at Trilby Road and Timberline Road in Fort Collins, Colo.

Status: In planning stages.

Artist rendering

Fort Lauderdale Florida

Announced: Oct. 3, 2009.

Location: Davie, Fla.

Groundbreaking, site dedication: June 18, 2011, by Elder Walter F. Gonzalez of the Presidency of the Seventy.

Status: Under construction.

The temple will serve approximately 25,000 Church members from congregations in the area of the Florida Keys and the Bahamas.

Frankfurt Germany

Announced: April 1, 1981.

Location: In the center of Friedrichsdorf, a small town nine miles north of Frankfurt; Talstrasse #10, D-61381 Friedrichsdorf/TS, Germany; phone (49) 6172-59000.

Site: 5.2 acres.

Exterior finish: White granite, copper roof.

Architects: Church architectural staff; local architect, Borchers-Metzner-Kramer; project architect, Hanno Luschin.

Construction adviser: Henry Haurand.

Contractor: Hochtief AG.

Rooms: Baptistry, celestial room, four ordinance rooms, five sealing rooms.

Total floor area: 24,170 square feet.

Dimensions: 93 feet by 232 feet; statue of Angel Moroni on top spire, 82 feet high.

District: 10 stakes, 4 districts in Luxembourg, northern France, Germany, Yugoslavia, Slovenia.

Groundbreaking, site dedication: July 1, 1985, by President Gordon B. Hinckley.

Dedication: Aug. 28-30, 1987, by President Ezra Taft Benson; 11 sessions.

Dedicatory prayer excerpt: *The presence of this house, on the soil of this nation, is an answer to the prayers of Thy people, and a fulfillment of the words of Thy prophets.*

Freiberg Germany

Announced: Oct. 9, 1982.

Location: In Freiberg, Hainichener Strasse 64, D09599 Freiberg, Germany; phone: (49) 3731-35960.

Site: 1 acre.

Exterior finish: Exterior white German stucco over 24-inch thick brick walls, blue gray slate stone slab roof.

Temple design: Modern design with German influence; two high arches, reminicent of Gothic style, are parallel with front of building and bisected by two similar arches to form a single spire.

Architect: Emil B. Fetzer, original; Rolf Metzner, contractor/architect of addition.

Government construction adviser: Dr. Dieter Hantzche, architect director of Bauakademie of Dresden.

Rooms: Celestial room, one ordinance room, two sealing rooms, baptistry.

Total floor area: originally 7,840 square feet; 13,500 square feet after remodeling.

Dimensions: Originally 94 feet by 75 feet; 94 feet by 112 feet after remodeling.

District: Three stakes, 15 districts in Eastern Germany, Czech Republic, Hungary.

Groundbreaking, site dedication: April 23, 1983, by Elder Thomas S. Monson of the Quorum of the Twelve.

Dedication: June 29, 1985, by President Gordon B. Hinckley; 7 sessions.

Rededication: Sept. 7, 2002, by President Gordon B. Hinckley, in one session.

Dedicatory prayer excerpt: *We thank Thee for all who have made possible its building and all who have made possible this glorious day of dedication.*

Fresno California

Announced: Jan. 8, 1999.

Location: Northwest Fresno near intersection of Valentine and Sierra avenues, 6290 N. Valentine, Fresno, CA 93711; phone: (559) 437-9451; no clothing rental.

Site: 2.2 acres.

Exterior finish: Sierra white granite

Temple design: Traditional.

Architects: Paul Stommel.

Project manager: Amos and Gloria Wright.

Contractor: Jacobsen Construction Co.

Rooms: Celestial room, baptistry, two ordinance rooms, two sealing rooms.

Total floor area: 10,700 square feet.

Dimensions: 149 feet by 77 feet.

District: Eight stakes in central California.

Groundbreaking, site dedication: March 20, 1999, by Elder John B. Dickson of the Seventy and president of the North America West Area.

Dedication: April 9, 2000, by President Gordon B. Hinckley; 4 sessions.

Dedicatory prayer excerpt: *May the work in this house unlock the prison doors beyond the veil that those who there receive the gospel may rejoice in the vicarious work performed here in their behalf.*

Fukuoka Japan

Announced: May 7, 1998.

Location: 46 Hirao Josui-Machi, Chuo-Ku, Fukuoka-shi, Fukuoka-ken 810-0029, Japan; phone: (81) 92-525-8255.

Site: .5 acres.

Exterior finish: Two granites: Empress White and Majestic Grey granite from China.

Temple design: Traditional.

Architect: Kanji Moriya and Church A&E Services.

Project manager: Jerry Sears.

Contractor: Taisei Construction Co.

Rooms: Celestial room, two endowment rooms, two sealing rooms and a baptistry.

Total floor area: 10,700 square feet.

Dimensions: 149 feet by 77 feet.

District: Four stakes, five districts in southern Japan.

Groundbreaking, site dedication: March 20, 1999, by Elder L. Lionel Kendrick of the Seventy, president of the Asia North Area.

Dedication: June 11, 2000, by President Gordon B. Hinckley; 4 sessions.

Dedicatory prayer excerpt: *Bless Thy Saints of this great nation. Magnify them, inspire them, bless them among the millions of this land that by the virtue of their lives they may stand as a city upon a hill whose light cannot be hid. Prosper them in their labors. May they never lack for food upon their tables or clothing on their backs or a shelter over their heads.*

Artist rendering

Gilbert Arizona

Announced: April 26, 2008.

Location: Southwest corner of Pecos and Greenfield roads in Gilbert, Ariz.

Groundbreaking, site dedication: Nov. 13, 2010, by Elder Claudio R.M. Costa of the Presidency of the Seventy. More than 7,500 members gathered on a clear, warm morning to witness proceedings.

Status: Under construction.

Guadalajara Mexico

Announced: April 14, 1999.

Location: Avenida Patria 879; Fraccionamiento Jardines Tepeyac, Zapopan, Jalisco 45030, Mexico; phone: 52 - 333-125- 1283; no clothing rental.

Site: 2.69 acres

Exterior finish: Blanco Guardiano white marble from Torreon, Mexico.

Temple design: Traditional.

Architect: Alvaro Iñigo.

Project manager: John Webster

Contractor: Impulsa Construction.

Rooms: Celestial room, two ordinances rooms, two sealing rooms, baptistry.

Total floor area: 10,700 square feet.

Dimensions: 77 feet x 149 feet.

District: 18 stakes and eight districts in Durango, Guadalajara, Aguascalientes, Irapuato, Leon, Mazatlan, Tepic, Xamora and Zacatecas.

Groundbreaking, site dedication: June 12, 1999, by Elder Eran A. Call of the Seventy and president of the Mexico North Area.

Dedication: April 29, 2001, by President Gordon B. Hinckley, 4 sessions.

Dedicatory prayer excerpt: *We thank Thee for the progress of Thy work in this great nation of Mexico. Move it forward, dear Father. Touch the lives and hearts of great numbers of people who will hearken to the message of truth and come into the fold of Christ. Bring about the miracle of conversion among the great and good people of this land.*

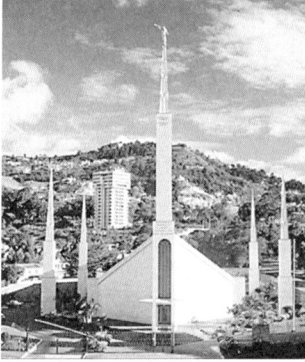

Guatemala City Guatemala

Announced: April 1, 1981.

Location: At the base of hills in southeastern Guatemala City; 24 Avenida 2-20, Zona 15, Vista Hermosa 1, Guatemala City, Guatemala; phone: (502)369-3426.

Site: 1.43 acres.

Exterior finish: Natural white Guatemala marble.

Temple design: Modern adaptation of earlier six-spire design.

Architects: Church architectural staff, assisted by Jose Asturias, Guatemala City.

Construction adviser: David Judd.

Contractor: Isa Constructors Aires Y Cia Ltd.

Rooms: Baptistry, celestial room, four ordinance rooms, three sealing rooms.

Total floor area: 17,609 square feet.

Dimensions: 178 feet by 72 feet, six spires; statue of Angel Moroni tops 126-foot spire.

District: 124 stakes and districts in Guatemala, Honduras, Belize.

Groundbreaking, site dedication: Sept. 12, 1982, by Elder Richard G. Scott of the First Quorum of the Seventy.

Dedication: Dec. 14-16, 1984, by President Gordon B. Hinckley; 10 sessions.

Dedicatory prayer excerpt: *Bless our land, O Father, this nation of Guatemala where now stands Thy holy house. May those who govern do so in righteousness. Bless them as they act to preserve the liberties ... and enhance the prosperity of the people. May there be peace in the land.*

Guayaquil Ecuador

Announced: March 31, 1982.

Location: El Principado de Las Lomas de Urdesa North in Guayaquil; Calle 6ta y Av Rodrigo Chavez Gonzalez, Principado de Las Lomas, Urdessa Norte, Guayaquil, Ecuador; phone: (593) 42-889-388.

Site: 6.25 acres.

Exterior finish: Granite (Asa Branca).

Temple design: Classic modern.

Architects: Rafael Velez Calisto, Architects & Consultants and Church A&E Services.

Project manager: Roger Sears.

Contractor: Inmomariuxi.

Rooms: Celestial room, baptistry, four ordinance rooms, three sealing rooms.

Total floor area: 70,884 square feet.

Dimensions: 154 feet by 76 feet.

District: 50 stakes and districts in Ecuador.

Groundbreaking, site dedication: Aug. 10, 1996, by Elder Richard G. Scott of the Quorum of the Twelve.

Dedication: Aug. 1, 1999, by President Gordon B. Hinckley; 8 sessions.

Dedicatory prayer excerpt: *We thank Thee for the inspiration given Thy servant in selecting this property on which to construct this sacred building. Thy guiding hand was evident in the circumstances when this site was found and determined upon.*

Halifax Nova Scotia

Announced: May 7, 1998.

Location: 44 Cumberland Drive, Dartmouth, Nova Scotia B2V 2C7; phone: (902) 434-6920; no clothing rental.

Site: 1 acre.

Exterior finish: White Bethel Granite.

Temple design: Classic modern.

Architects: L.A. Beaubien and Associates, and Church A&E Services.

Project manager: William Treu.

Contractor: Dineen Construction.

Rooms: Two ordinance rooms, two sealing rooms; celestial room, baptistry.

Total floor area: 10,700 square feet.

Dimensions: 149 feet by 77 feet.

District: Two stakes, one district in Nova Scotia, New Brunswick.

Groundbreaking, site dedication: Oct. 12, 1998, by Elder Jay E. Jensen of the Seventy.

Dedication: Nov. 14, 1999, by President Gordon B. Hinckley; 3 sessions.

Dedicatory prayer excerpt: *We dedicate the ground which surrounds this temple and upon which it stands. In the season of summer it will be beautiful with Thy wondrous creations.*

Hamilton New Zealand

Announced: Feb. 17, 1955.

Location: At site of Church College of New Zealand in Temple View, outside of Hamilton; 509 Tuhikaramea Rd., Temple View, New Zealand; phone: (64) 7-846-2750.

Site: 35 acres.

Exterior finish: Reinforced concrete block, manufactured at site, structural steel; painted white.

Temple design: Modern-contemporary.

Architect: Edward O. Anderson, Church architect.

Construction chairman: Wendell B. Mendenhall.

Construction supervisor: E. Albert Rosenvall and George R. Biesinger.

Rooms: Baptistry, celestial room, one ordinance room, three sealing rooms.

Total floor area: 42,304 square feet.

Dimensions: 159 feet by 84 feet; height of tower, 157 feet.

District: 25 stakes, 7 districts in New Zealand, Cook Islands.

Groundbreaking, site dedication: Dec. 21, 1955. First sod turned by Ariel Ballif, Wendell B. Mendenhall, and George R. Biesinger.

Dedication: April 20, 1958, by President David O. McKay; eight sessions.

Dedicatory prayer excerpt: *We invoke Thy blessing particularly upon the men and women who have so willingly and generously contributed their means, time and effort to the completion of this imposing and impressive structure. Especially we mention all those who have accepted calls as labor missionaries and literally consecrated their all upon the altar of service.*

Helsinki Finland

Announced: April 2, 2000.

Location: Leppäsillantie 3, 02620 Espoo, Finland.

Exterior finish: Light gray Italian granite; stone walls surrounding temple made of Finnish brown granite.

Temple design: classic elegance

Site: 7.4 acres

Architects: Evata Architects, Helsinki, Finland.

Project manager: Hanno Luschin.

Contractor: NCC Rakennus OY, Helsinki, Finland.

Rooms: Celestial room, baptistry, two ordinance rooms, two sealing rooms.

Total floor area: 16,350 square feet.

Dimensions: 212-feet by 103-feet by 139-feet

District: Members in Finland and Eastern Europe countries of Russia and Baltic countries.

Groundbreaking, site dedication: March 29, 2003, by Elder D. Lee Tobler of the Seventy.

Dedication: Oct. 22, 2006, by President Gordon B. Hinckley; four sessions.

Dedicatory prayer excerpt: *O God, we are so deeply grateful to those who have come to this land as Thy servants to preach the everlasting gospel. . . . We pray for this great nation of Finland. May it ever be respected and honored among the nations of the earth.*

Hermosillo Sonora Mexico

Announced: July 20, 1998.

Location: General Pedro Garcia Conde No. 303; Esq. con Juan Jose Rios, Colonia Pitic, Hermosillo, Sonora CP 83150, Mexico; phone (52) 662-210-5660; no clothing rental.

Site: 2.07 acres.

Exterior finish: White marble veneer.

Temple design: Classic modern.

Architect: Alvaro Iñigo and Church A&E Services.

Project manager: David Wills.

Contractor: Grana y Montero / Jacobsen Construction Co.

Rooms: Two ordinance rooms, two sealing rooms, celestial room, baptistry.

Total floor area: 10,700 square feet.

Dimensions: 77 feet by 149 feet.

District: 11 stakes and six districts in surrounding area.

Groundbreaking, site dedication: Dec. 5, 1998, by Elder Eran A. Call of the Seventy and counselor in the Mexico South Area presidency.

Dedication: Feb. 27, 2000, by President Gordon B. Hinckley, 4 sessions.

Dedicatory prayer excerpt: *May [this temple] be a structure of beauty, a crowning gem in this great city. We are grateful that the officials of government have permitted its construction and that it is now completed.*

Hong Kong China

Announced: Oct. 3, 1992.

Location: 2 Cornwall Street, Kowloon Tong Kowloon, Hong Kong; phone: (852) 2339-8100. First temple from existing building, comprising basement and upper floors.

Site: .3 acres.

Exterior finish: Polished granite.

Temple design: Hong Kong colonial.

Architects: Liang Peddle Thorpe Architects.

Rooms: Baptistry, celestial room, two ordinance rooms, two sealing rooms.

Total floor area: 21,744 square feet.

Dimensions of building: 70 feet by 92 feet; Angel statue is 135 feet above main floor.

District: Six stakes, four districts in China, Singapore, Mongolia.

Groundbreaking, site dedication: Jan. 22, 1994, by Elder John K. Carmack of the First Quorum of the Seventy and Asia Area president.

Dedication: May 26-27, 1996; by President Gordon B. Hinckley; 7 sessions.

Dedicatory prayer excerpt: *Thy Church in this area now comes to full maturity with the dedication of this sacred temple. We pray that this harvest of souls may continue, that in the future as in the present, Thy people may be free and secure in their worship and that none shall hinder the service of missionaries called to this area. We pray that Thy work may grow and prosper in the great Chinese realm, and may those who govern be ever receptive to those called and sent as messengers of revealed truth.*

Houston Texas

Announced: Sept. 30, 1997.

Location: 15725 Champion Forest Drive, Klein, TX 77379-7036; phone (281) 376-6804.

Site: 10.35 acres.

Exterior finish: Cast stone/granite.

Temple design: Classic modern.

Architect: Spencer Partnership Architects and Church A&E Services.

Project manager: Leon Rowley.

Contractor: SpawGlass Const.

Rooms: Two ordinance rooms, three sealing rooms, celestial room, baptistry.

Total floor area: 33,970 square feet.

Dimensions: 145 feet by 136 feet; spire 159 feet high.

District: 22 area stakes and two districts in Texas.

Groundbreaking, site dedication: June 13, 1998, by Elder Lynn A. Mickelsen of the Seventy and president of the North America Southwest Area.

Dedication: Aug. 26-27, 2000, by President Gordon B. Hinckley; 8 sessions.

Dedicatory prayer excerpt: *How glorious and complete is Thy plan for the salvation and exaltation of Thy children of all generations. How tremendous is our obligation to carry forward this great vicarious work in their behalf.*

No artist rendering available

Idaho Falls Idaho

Announced: March 3, 1937.

Location: In northwestern Idaho Falls on the banks of the Snake River; 1000 Memorial Drive, Idaho Falls, ID 83402-3497; phone: (208) 522-7669.

Site: 7 acres.

Exterior finish: Built of reinforced concrete. A mixture of white quartz aggregate and white cement called cast stone covers the 16-inch thick exterior walls in slabs two inches thick.

Temple design: Modern-contemporary.

Architects: Church board of temple architects: Edward O. Anderson, Georgius Y. Cannon, Ramm Hansen, John Fetzer, Hyrum C. Pope, Lorenzo S. Young.

Construction adviser: Arthur Price.

Contractor: Birdwell Finlayson of Pocatello, Idaho.

Rooms: Baptistry, celestial room, four ordinance rooms, nine sealing rooms.

Total floor area: 92,177 square feet.

Dimensions: 192 feet by 234 feet; tower 148 feet high. Two annexes added 7,700 square feet. A 12-foot statue of Angel Moroni was added to the tower Sept. 5, 1983.

District: 58 stakes in eastern Idaho, western Wyoming.

Groundbreaking, site dedication: Dec. 19, 1939, ground broken by David Smith, North Idaho Falls Stake president. Site dedicated Oct. 19, 1940, by President David O. McKay of the First Presidency.

Dedication: Sept. 23, 1945, by President George Albert Smith, 8 dedicatory sessions.

Dedicatory prayer excerpt: *We pray that Thou wilt accept this temple as a freewill offering from Thy children, that it will be sacred unto Thee.*

Indianapolis Indiana

Announced: Oct. 2, 2010.

Location: On the southwest corner of intersection of W 116th and Spring Mill Road in the city of Carmel, a suburb of Indianapolis.

Status: In planning stages.

Johannesburg South Africa

Announced: April 1, 1981.

Location: 2 miles north of city center; 7 Jubilee Rd., Parktown, Johannesburg 2193, South Africa; phone, (27) 11-645-1540.

Site: One acre.

Exterior finish: Masonry exterior.

Temple design: Modern adaptation of earlier six-spire design.

Architects: Church architectural staff; local architect, Halford & Halford.

Construction adviser: Stanley G. Smith.

Contractor: Tiber Bonvac.

Rooms: Baptistry, celestial room, four ordinance rooms, three sealing rooms.

Total floor area: 19,184 square feet.

Dimensions: 178 feet by 71 feet; Angel Moroni statue is atop tallest spire at 112 feet.

District: 29 stakes and districts in southern Africa.

Groundbreaking, site dedication: Nov. 27, 1982, by Elder Marvin J. Ashton of the Quorum of the Twelve.

Dedication: Aug. 24-25, 1985, by President Gordon B. Hinckley; 4 sessions.

Dedicatory prayer excerpt: *Almighty God, wilt Thou overrule for the blessing and safety of Thy faithful Saints. We pray for peace in this troubled land. Bless this nation which has befriended Thy servants. May those who rule in the offices of government be inspired to find a basis for reconciliation among those who now are in conflict one with another. May the presence of Thy house on the soil of this land bring blessings to the entire nation.*

Jordan River Utah

Announced: Feb. 3, 1978.

Location: About 15 miles south of Salt Lake City in South Jordan; 10200 South 1300 West, South Jordan, UT 84095-8814; phone: (801) 254-3003.

Site: 15 acres.

Exterior finish: Cast stone containing white marble chips. Tower appears same as the rest of the building, but in order to reduce weight it contains fiberglass in a product called cemlite.

Temple design: Modern.

Architect: Emil B. Fetzer, Church architect.

Resident project inspector: Jerry Sears.

Construction superintendent: Lawrence O. Dansie for Layton Construction Co.

Rooms: Baptistry, celestial room, six ordinance rooms, 17 sealing rooms.

Total floor area: 148,236 square feet.

Dimensions: Basement and main floor, 211 feet by 218 feet; two upper levels, 140 by 166 feet. Height to square is 58 feet, to top of tower, 219 feet, including a 20-foot statue of the Angel Moroni.

District: Southern Salt Lake County, Utah.

Groundbreaking, site dedication: June 9, 1979, by President Spencer W. Kimball.

Dedication: Nov. 16-20, 1981, by President Marion G. Romney; 15 sessions.

Dedicatory prayer excerpt: *May all who enter have clean hands and pure hearts, and may they participate with faith in the ordinances to be given herein.*

Artist rendering

Kansas City Missouri

Announced: Oct. 4, 2008.

Status: Under construction.

For the temple serving the greater Kansas City area, the site will be in Clay County, Missouri, on residential land within the Kansas City limits that is already being developed by the Church. The development is known as Shoal Creek.

Kirtland

*No longer owned by the Church.

Location: Kirtland, Ohio, 25 miles east of Cleveland, on a hill west of Chagrin River.

Site: Selected March 1833; deed recorded Aug. 4, 1834.

Exterior finish: Sandstone covered with stuccoed plaster.

Temple design: Adaptation of Federal Georgian and New England Colonial.

Architect: Joseph Smith.

Building committee: Hyrum Smith, Reynolds Cahoon and Jared Carter.

Master builder: Artemis Millett.

Rooms: Originally 15.

Total floor area: Approximately 15,000 square feet.

Dimensions: 79 feet by 59 feet; walls 50 feet high; tower height above ground, 110 feet.

Start of work: Hauling of sandstone to site began June 5, 1833.

Cornerstones: July 23, 1833.

Dedication: March 27 and 31, 1836, by President Joseph Smith. (DHC II:433)

Dedicatory prayer excerpt: *And we ask Thee, Holy Father, that Thy servants may go forth from this house, armed with Thy power and that Thy name may be upon them.*

Kona Hawaii

Announced: May 7, 1998.

Location: 75-230 Kalani Street; Kailua-Kona, HI 96740-1833; phone: (808) 331-8504; no clothing rental.

Site: 4 acres.

Exterior finish: White marble veneer.

Temple design: Traditional.

Architect: Jon Pharis of Pharis & Associates.

Project manager: Jerry Sears.

Contractor: Bud Bailey Construction.

Rooms: Celestial room, baptistry, two ordinance rooms, two sealing rooms.

Total floor area: 10,700 square feet.

Dimensions: 149 feet by 77 feet.

District: Kona, Hilo and Kahului Hawaii stakes on the islands of Maui, Molokai and Lanai.

Groundbreaking, site dedication: March 13, 1999, by Elder John B. Dickson of the Seventy and president of the North America West Area.

Dedication: Jan. 23, 2000, by President Gordon B. Hinckley; 4 sessions.

Dedicatory prayer excerpt: *Now we have this second temple here on the big island. May the work increase. May there come into the hearts of the people a growing desire to come to the House of the Lord, here to taste the sweet refreshment of the Holy Spirit.*

Kyiv Ukraine

Announced: July 20, 1998

Location: 1 Yabluneva Street, Sofiivska Borshagivka Village, Kyiv, Ukraine

Site: 50,000 square meters (about 12.4 acres).

Exterior finish: Amarelo Macieira granite with quartzite crystals which reflects sunlight.

Architects: MHTN of Salt Lake City, Utah, USA, and Strabag AG, Stuttgart, Germany

Contractor: Strabag AG, Vienna, Austria

Project manager: Hanno Luschin

Rooms: baptistry, two ordinance rooms, two sealing rooms, celestial room.

Total Floor area: 2,061 square meters (about 22,000 square feet).

Dimensions: 42 meters (about 138 feet) high, crowned with a gilded Angel Moroni statue.

District: Serving some 31,000 members living in nine Eastern European countries.

Groundbreaking: June 23, 2007, by Elder Paul B. Pieper of the Seventy and president of the Europe East Area.

Dedication: Aug. 29, 2010, by President Thomas S. Monson in three sessions.

Dedicatory prayer excerpt: *May this House provide a spirit of peace to all who observe its majesty, and especially to those who enter for their own sacred ordinances and to perform the work for their loved ones beyond the veil. Let them feel of Thy divine love and mercy.*

Laie Hawaii

Announced: Oct. 3, 1915.

Location: In Laie, on the northeast side of the island of Oahu, near BYU-Hawaii and the Polynesian Cultural Center.

Site: 11.4 acres, a portion of original property purchased by Church.

Exterior finish: Concrete made of the crushed lava rock of the area and tooled to a white cream finish.

Temple design: Suggestive of the ancient temples found in South America.

Architects: Hyrum C. Pope and Harold W. Burton.

General superintendent: Samuel E. Woolley. Polynesian Saints did much of the work.

Contractor: Jacobsen Construction Co., for 2010 renovation

Project manager: John Stoddard for 2010 renovation.

Rooms: Baptistry, celestial room, three ordinance rooms, six sealing rooms.

Total floor area: 10,500 square feet originally; approximately 47,224 square feet after 1978 remodeling.

Dimensions of building: 157 feet by 283 feet.

District: 12 stakes in Hawaii, one stake and one mission district in the Marshall ISlands.

Site dedication: June 1, 1915, site dedicated by Pres. Joseph F. Smith.

Dedication: Thanksgiving Day, Nov. 27, 1919, by President Heber J. Grant; five sessions.

Rededicated: June 13-15, 1978, by President Spencer W. Kimball after extensive remodeling; nine sessions.

Rededicated: November 21, 2010, by President Thomas S. Monson after extensive renovation, just a few days prior to its 91-year anniversary of the original dedication, three sessions.

Dedicatory prayer excerpt: *This beautiful temple has been a haven of peace. It has been the House of the Lord to all who have entered and have felt of its spirit and partaken of the blessings found here. ... I has served well.*

Las Vegas Nevada

Announced: April 7, 1984.

Location: On the east side of Las Vegas on the slope of Frenchman Mountain, 827 Temple View Drive; Las Vegas, NV 89110-2920; phone: (702) 452-5011.

Temple design: Six spires

Site: 10.3 acres.

Exterior finish: White precast stone walls and copper roof and detailing.

Architects: Tate & Snyder.

Construction adviser: Gary Holland

Contractor: Hogan & Tingey.

Rooms: Baptistry, celestial room, four ordinance rooms, six sealing rooms.

Total floor area: 80,350 square feet.

Dimensions: 195 feet by 260 feet; statue of Angel Moroni on top spire 137 feet high.

District: 19 southern Nevada stakes, two Arizona and one California stakes.

Groundbreaking, site dedication: Nov. 30, 1985, by President Gordon B. Hinckley.

Dedication: Dec. 16-18, 1989, by President Gordon B. Hinckley; 11 sessions.

Dedicatory prayer excerpt: *Within its walls are to be tasted the refreshing waters of living and eternal truth. For all who enter the portals of Thy house may this be an oasis of peace and life and light, in contrast with the clamor and evil and darkness of the world.*

Lima Peru

Announced: April 1, 1981.

Location: Southwest part of Lima, in the Molina district; Prolg. Av. Javier Prado Este 6420, La Molina, Lima 12, Peru; phone: (51) 1 348-0418.

Site: 4.5 acres.

Exterior finish: Local granite, Oriental design.

Temple design: Modern adaptation of earlier six-spire design.

Architects: Church architectural staff; local architect Jose Asturias.

Construction adviser: Sergio Gomez.

Rooms: Baptistry, celestial room, four ordinance rooms, three sealing rooms.

Total floor area: 9,600 square feet.

Dimensions: 178 feet by 71 feet. Angel Moroni statue is atop tallest spire at 112 feet.

District: 80 stakes and 32 districts in Peru.

Groundbreaking, site dedication: Sept. 11, 1982, by Elder Boyd K. Packer of the Quorum of the Twelve.

Dedication: Jan. 10-12, 1986, by President Gordon B. Hinckley; 11 sessions.

Dedicatory prayer excerpt: *We are particularly mindful this day of the sons and daughters of Lehi. They have known so much of suffering and sorrow in their many generations. They have walked in darkness and in servitude. Now thou hast touched them by the light of the everlasting gospel. The shackles of darkness are falling from their eyes as they embrace the truths of thy great work.*

Logan Utah

Location: On eastern bench overlooking Cache Valley; 175 N. 300 East, Logan, UT.

Site: 9 acres, selected by Brigham Young, May 18, 1877.

Exterior finish: Dark-colored, siliceous limestone used for the major portion of the temple. Buff-colored limestone, more easily carved, used for intricate shaping.

Temple design: Castellated style.

Architect: Truman O. Angell.

Construction heads: Superintendent of construction, Charles O. Card; master mason, John Parry; plastering foreman, William Davis. More than 25,000 people worked on temple.

Rooms: Baptistry, celestial room, four ordinance rooms, 11 sealing rooms; five stories.

Total floor area: Originally 59,130 square feet; 115,507 square feet after remodeling.

Dimensions: 168 feet by 224 feet; 86 feet high. The east tower is 170 feet high; west tower, 165 feet high; four octagonal towers, each 100 feet high.

District: 44 stakes in northern Utah, southeastern Idaho.

Groundbreaking, site dedication: May 17, 1877; site dedicated by Elder Orson Pratt, ground broken by President John W. Young of the First Presidency.

Dedication: May 17-19, 1884, by President John Taylor; 3 sessions.

On March 13-15, 1979, after extensive remodeling, the temple was rededicated by President Spencer W. Kimball; 9 sessions.

Dedicatory prayer excerpt: *And, as all wisdom dwells with Thee, and, as all light, truth and intelligence.... We ask that in this house a more full knowledge of Thee and Thy laws may be developed.*

London England

Location: 25 miles south of London, formerly an Elizabethan farm at Newchapel near Lingfield; Surrey RH7 6HW, United Kingdom; phone: (44) 1342-832759.

Site: Selected in June 1952 by President David O. McKay and Elder Stayner Richards. Purchased in 1953; 32 acres.

Exterior finish: Concrete and steel structure, brick masonry walls faced with cut Portland limestone. Spire sheathed in copper.

Temple design: Modern-contemporary.

Architect: Edward O. Anderson.

Supervising architects: T.T. Bennett and Son, London.

Contractor: Kirk and Kirk, Ltd., London.

Rooms: Baptistry, celestial room, four ordinance rooms, seven sealing rooms.

Total floor area: Originally 34,000 square feet; 42,775 square feet after remodeling.

Dimensions: 84 feet wide, 159 feet long, 56 feet to the square. The tower rises 156 feet inches from ground level, spire 33 feet above that.

District: 20 stakes in England and two in Wales.

Groundbreaking, site dedication: Aug. 10, 1953; site dedicated by David O. McKay, who broke ground on Aug. 27, 1955.

Dedication: Sept. 7-9, 1958, by President David O. McKay; 6 sessions. Rededicated Oct. 18-20, 1992, by President Gordon B. Hinckley; 10 sessions.

Dedicatory prayer excerpt: *With humility and deep gratitude we acknowledge Thy nearness, Thy divine guidance and inspiration. Help us, we pray Thee, to become even more susceptible in our spiritual response to Thee.*

Los Angeles California

Location: Atop a hill near Westwood Village, two miles west of Beverly Hills,10777 Santa Monica Blvd.; Los Angeles, CA 90025-4718; phone: (310) 474-5569.

Site: On 13 of the original 24.23 acres purchased from the Harold Lloyd Motion Picture Company on March 23, 1937, by President Heber J. Grant.

Exterior finish: The exterior is covered with 146,000 square feet of Mo-Sai stone facing, a mixture of crushed quartz and white Portland cement quarried in Utah and Nevada. Wainscot around exterior is Rockville granite from Minnesota.

Temple design: Modern.

Architect: Edward O. Anderson, Church architect. (Millard F. Malin, sculptor of 15-foot statue of Angel Moroni on spire.)

Superintendent: Vern Loder.

Contractor: Soren N. Jacobsen.

Rooms: Baptistry, celestial room, four ordinance rooms, 10 sealing rooms.

Total floor area: 190,614 square feet, or approximately 4.5 acres.

Dimensions: 269 feet by 369 feet; overall height is 257 feet .

District: 44 stakes in Southern California.

Groundbreaking, site dedication: Sept. 22, 1951, by President David O. McKay.

Dedication: March 11-14, 1956, by President David O. McKay; 8 sessions.

Dedicatory prayer excerpt: *May all who come within these sacred walls feel a peaceful, hallowed influence. Cause, O Lord, that even people who pass the grounds, or view the temple from afar, may lift their eyes from the groveling things of sordid life and look up to Thee and Thy providence.*

Louisville Kentucky

Announced: March 17, 1999.

Location: 7116 W. Highway 22, Crestwood, KY 40014; phone: (502) 241-4115; no clothing rental.

Site: 1.1 acres.

Exterior finish: Danby Vermont marble.

Temple design: Traditional.

Architects: Firestone Jaros Mullin — Mike Karpinski Architect.

Project manager: Bruce Catanzaro.

Contractor: Corna/Kokosing Construction Co.

Rooms: Celestial room, baptistry, two ordinance rooms, two sealing rooms.

Total floor area: 10,700 square feet.

Dimensions: 149 feet by 77 feet.

District: 10 stakes in Kentucky, Indiana and Ohio.

Groundbreaking, site dedication: May 29, 1999, by Elder John K. Carmack of the Seventy and president of the North America East Area.

Dedication: March 19, 2000, by President Thomas S. Monson first counselor in the First Presidency; 4 sessions.

Dedicatory prayer excerpt: *May those in the life beyond who are helpless to move forward rejoice in the completion of this sacred building.*

Lubbock Texas

Announced: April 2, 2000.

Location: 7016 Frankford Ave., Lubbock, TX 79424; phone: (806) 794-0774; no clothing rental.

Site: 2.67-acre site shared with a stake center.

Exterior finish: Light colored granite.

Temple design: Traditional.

Architect: Tisdel Minckler and Associates.

Project manager: Leon Rowley.

Contractor: SpawGlass Construction.

Rooms: Celestial room, two ordinance rooms, two sealing rooms, baptistry, chapel, offices and waiting area.

Total floor area: 16,498 square feet.

Dimensions: 188 feet x 98 feet.

District: Five stakes in west Texas and one district in eastern New Mexico.

Groundbreaking, site dedication: Nov. 4, 2000, by Elder Rex D. Pinegar of the Seventy;

Dedication: April 21, 2002, by President Gordon B. Hinckley, 4 sessions.

Dedicatory prayer excerpt: *Bless all who serve in Thy work throughout the earth. Grant unto them great joy. May the assurance of Thy love crown their lives and bring into their hearts peace and gladness. . . . We invoke Thy blessings upon this community, upon this state, upon this nation. Bless this chosen land that it may remain forever free, that peace and liberty may bless the lives of its people, and that righteousness may reign in the land.*

Artist rendering

Madrid Spain

Announced: Country announced April 4, 1993, city announced Oct. 9, 1994.

Location: Barrio de Moratalaz, corner of Hacienda de Pavones and Valdebernando, Calle del Temple No. 2; E-28030 Madrid, Spain; phone: (34) 913-017-607.

Site: 3.5 acres.

Exterior finish: Camaro Marble from Italy.

Temple design: Modern Classic.

Architects: Arquitechior Langdon, SA.

Project manager: Ralph Cluff.

Contractor: JOSTSA Construction Co.

Rooms: Baptistry, celestial room, four ordinance rooms, four sealing rooms.

Total floor area: 45,800 square feet.

Dimensions: 116 feet by 138 feet.

District: 49 stakes and districts in Spain, Portugal, Canary Islands, Cape Verde, France.

Groundbreaking, site dedication: June 11, 1996, by President Gordon B. Hinckley.

Dedication: March 19-21, 1999, by President Gordon B. Hinckley; 10 sessions.

Dedicatory prayer excerpt: *We thank Thee for this great kingdom of Spain which has been hospitable to Thy Saints. Bless this land. We are mindful that it was from these shores that Columbus sailed to discover America as foretold in the Book of Mormon.*

Manaus Brazil

Announced: May 23, 2007.

Groundbreaking, site dedication: June 20, 2008, by Elder Charles Didier of the Seventy and president of the Brazil Area.

Status: Under construction.

Manhattan New York

Announced: Aug. 7, 2002.

Location: Near Lincoln Center, 125 Columbus Ave., New York City, N.Y. 10023; between 65th and 66th. Temple comprises first, second, fifth and sixth floors; meetinghouse comprises third and fourth floors.

Site: Area occupied by former stake center.

Exterior finish: Light, variegated granite.

Architects: Frank Fernandez.

Contractors: East Coast Construction Group.

Project manager: Cory Karl.

Rooms: Two ordinance rooms, two sealing rooms, celestial room and baptistry.

Total floor area: 20,630 square feet.

District: Parts of New York, New Jersey and Connecticut.

Groundbreaking and site dedication: Building originally dedicated in 1975 by Elder Spencer W. Kimball.

Dedication: June 13, 2004, by President Gordon B. Hinckley; four sessions.

Dedicatory prayer excerpt: *May this temple be a place of quiet refuge in the midst of this great and noisy metropolis. May all who enter its portals feel they have stepped from the world into a place of thy divine presence.*

Manila Philippines

Announced: April 1, 1981.

Location: In Quezon City; 13 Temple Drive, Greenmeadows Subdivision, 1110 Quezon City, Metro Manila, Philippines.

Site: About 3.5 acres.

Exterior finish: Ceramic tile.

Temple design: Six-spire design.

Architect: Church staff, with assistance from Felipe M. Mendoza & Partners, Manila.

Construction adviser: Wayne Tuttle.

Contractor: A. C. K. Construction.

Rooms: Baptistry, celestial room, four ordinance rooms, three sealing rooms.

Total floor area: 26,683 square feet.

Dimensions: 200 feet by 75 feet, six spires; statue of Angel Moroni is 115 feet high.

District: Stakes and districts in Philippines, Indonesia, Singapore, Thailand, India, Sri Lanka, Malaysia, Cambodia, Burma and Micronesia: Majuro, Kosrae, Chuuk, Phonpei, Yap, Guam, Kwajalein.

Groundbreaking, site dedication: Aug. 25, 1982, by President Gordon B. Hinckley.

Dedication: Sept. 25-27, 1984, by President Gordon B. Hinckley; 9 sessions.

Dedicatory prayer excerpt: *Lift the blight of poverty from which so many suffer. Particularly bless Thy faithful Saints who live honestly with Thee in the payment of their tithes and offerings. Bless them that neither they nor their generations after them will go hungry, nor naked, nor without shelter from the storms that beat about them.*

Manti Utah

Location: Hill above U.S. Highway 89 in Sanpete Valley in Manti, Utah.

Site: 27 acres. "Manti Stone Quarry" had been prophesied as site for a temple since area's settlement in 1849.

Exterior finish: Cream-colored oolite limestone from quarries on which temple is built.

Temple design: The castellated style reflecting influence of Gothic Revival, French Renaissance Revival, French Second Empire and colonial architecture.

Architect: William H. Folsom.

Construction heads: William H. Folsom from Oct. 15, 1877, to Aug. 7, 1888, when Daniel H. Wells took his place as supervisor; master mason, Edward L. Parry.

Rooms: Four ordinance rooms and eight sealing rooms; baptistry, celestial room.

Total floor area: 74,792 square feet.

Dimensions of building: 178 feet by 244 feet; 86 feet high. East tower is 179 feet high, west tower 169 feet high, building at ground level is 60 feet above highway below.

District: 26 stakes in Central Utah.

Groundbreaking, site dedication: April 25, 1877, by President Brigham Young.

Dedication: May 17, 1888, private dedication held; dedicated by President Wilford Woodruff of the Quorum of the Twelve. Three public dedicatory services held May 21-23, 1888; Elder Lorenzo Snow read the prayer.

Rededicated: June 14-16, 1985, by President Gordon B. Hinckley; 9 sessions.

Dedicatory prayer excerpt: *May this holy temple be to them as one of the gates of heaven, opening into the straight and narrow path that leads to endless lives and eternal dominion.*

Medford Oregon

Announced: March 17, 1999.

Location: 3900 Grant Road, in Central Point, OR 97502; phone: (541) 664-2050; no clothing rental.

Site: 2 acres.

Exterior finish: Granite.

Temple design: Traditional.

Architects: Dan Park and Church A&E Services.

Project manager: Amos and Gloria Wright.

Contractor: Corey Vitas Construction.

Rooms: Celestial room, baptistry, two ordinance rooms, two sealing rooms.

Total floor area: 10,700 square feet.

Dimensions: 149 feet by 77 feet.

District: Eight stakes in southern Oregon and northern California.

Groundbreaking, site dedication: May 20, 1999, by Elder D. Lee Tobler of the Seventy and first counselor in the North America Northwest Area presidency.

Dedication: April 16, 2000, by President James E. Faust, second counselor in the First Presidency; 4 sessions.

Dedicatory prayer excerpt: *Bless the youth of the Church, dear Father. Lead them in paths of righteousness and truth. Protect them from the alluring and seductive calls of the adversary.*

Melbourne Australia

Announced: Oct. 30, 1998.

Location: Corner of Cathies Lane and Pumps Lane; 76 Cathies Lane, Wantirna South, VIC 3152, Australia; phone: (61) 3-9881-9700; no clothing rental.

Site: 5.98 acres, including adjoining meetinghouse.

Exterior finish: Snow white granite.

Temple design: Traditional.

Architect: Warwick Tempany and Church A&E Services.

Project manager: Graham Sully.

Contractor: Probuild.

Rooms: Celestial room, two ordinance rooms, two sealing rooms and a baptistry.

Total floor area: 10,700 square feet.

Dimensions: 149 feet by 77 feet.

District: Melbourne, Hobart, Devonport stakes and Albury districts.

Groundbreaking, site dedication: March 20, 1999, by Elder P. Bruce Mitchell, Area Authority Seventy and second counselor in the Australia/New Zealand Area presidency.

Dedication: June 16, 2000, by President Gordon B. Hinckley; 4 sessions.

Dedicatory prayer excerpt: *We are grateful for this nation of Australia, where we may worship Thee in peace, without molestation or fear or threat. Bless this land that it may remain ever strong, a nation of peace and progress among the nations of the earth.*

Memphis Tennessee

Announced: Sept. 17, 1998.

Location: 4199 Kirby-Whitten Parkway, Bartlett, TN 38135; phone: (901) 379-0202; no clothing rental.

Site: 6.35 acres, including adjoining meetinghouse.

Exterior finish: Imperial Danby White marble.

Temple design: Classic modern.

Architect: Dusty Driver of Bounds & Gillespie Architects and Church A&E Services.

Project manager: Leon Rowley.

Contractor: Layton Construction Co., Construction Management Company; Rentenbach Construction, general contractor.

Rooms: Celestial room, baptistry, two ordinance rooms, two sealing rooms.

Total floor area: 10,700 square feet.

Dimensions: 149 feet by 77 feet.

District: Five stakes in Memphis, Tenn., and Little Rock, Ark., and Tupelo, Miss.

Groundbreaking, site dedication: Jan. 16, 1999, by Elder Gordon T. Watts of the Seventy and first counselor in the North America Southeast Area presidency.

Dedication: April 23, 2000, by President James E. Faust, second counselor in First Presidency; 4 sessions.

Dedicatory prayer excerpt: *We are grateful for this nation whose Constitution and laws protect us in our worship. May these precious liberties never be lost to the people. May they be safeguarded and kept secure from those who would destroy the precious boon of freedom of worship.*

No artist rendering available

Mérida Mexico

Announced: Sept. 25, 1998.

Location: Calle 70 #527, Esq. 65 y 67; Col. Centro, Merida, Yucatan CP 97000, Mexico; phone: (52) 999-928-1643; no clothing rental.

Site: 1.31 acres.

Exterior finish: Guardiano white marble.

Temple design: Classic modern.

Architect: Alvaro Iñigo and Church A&E Services.

Project manager: Dean Fife.

Contractor: PyCSA / Okland Construction Co.

Rooms: Celestial room, baptistry, two ordinance rooms, two sealing rooms.

Total floor area: 10,700 square feet.

Dimensions: 77 feet by 149 feet.

District: Nine stakes, two districts and three branches on Yucatan Peninsula.

Groundbreaking, site dedication: Jan. 16, 1999, by Carl B. Pratt of the Seventy and president of the Mexico South Area.

Dedication: July 8, 2000, by Thomas S. Monson, first counselor in the First Presidency; 4 sessions.

Dedicatory prayer excerpt: *Help us this day to rededicate our lives to the advancement of Thy cause and kingdom.*

Meridian Idaho

Announced: April 2, 2011.

Status: In planning stages.

Mesa Arizona

Location: In Mesa, 16 miles east of Phoenix, in central Arizona's Valley of the Sun.

Site: 20-acre site selected Feb. 1, 1920, by President Heber J. Grant, Apostles David O. McKay and George F. Richards. Purchased in 1921.

Exterior finish: Concrete reinforced with steel. Exterior is faced with a terra cotta glaze that is egg-shell in color and tile-like in finish.

Temple design: Modification of the classic style, suggestive of pre-Columbian temples and even the Temple of Herod.

Architects: Don C. Young and Ramm Hansen.

Construction supervisor: Arthur Price.

Construction chairman: J.W. LeSueur, O.S. Stapley, John Cummard, Andrew Kimball.

Rooms: Baptistry, celestial room, four ordinance, nine sealing rooms.

Total floor area: 113,916 square feet.

Dimensions: 220 feet by 243 feet, and 50 feet in height above the foundation.

District: Stakes in southern Arizona.

Site dedication, groundbreaking: Site dedicated Nov. 28, 1921; ground broken April 25, 1922, by President Heber J. Grant.

Dedication: Oct. 23, 1927, by President Heber J. Grant, broadcast by radio. Rededicated after extensive remodeling April 15-16, 1975, by President Spencer W. Kimball; 7 sessions.

Dedicatory prayer excerpt: *Accept the dedication of this house and these grounds, which we have dedicated unto thee by virtue of the Priesthood of the Living God which we hold.*

Mexico City Mexico

Announced: April 3, 1976.

Location: Near Aragon public park and zoological gardens, bounded by Calle Ignacio Allende and Calle Emiliano Zapata; Avenida 510 #90, Col. San Juan de Aragon, Mexico D.F. 07950; phone: (52) 555-747-4861.

Site: 7 acres.

Exterior finish: White cast stone, ornate with adaptations of ancient Mayan designs, especially on upper portion of the structure.

Temple design: Modern adaptation of ancient Mayan architecture.

Architect: Emil B. Fetzer, Church architect.

Resident inspector: Ricardo Espiriti.

Construction superintendent: Jose Ortiz for Urbec Construction Co.

Rooms: Baptistry, celestial room, four ordinance rooms, 11 sealing rooms.

Total floor area: 116,642 square feet.

Dimensions: 178 feet by 214.5 feet; two upper levels, 119.5 feet by 157 feet. Height to square, 70 feet; to top of tower with Statue of Angel Moroni, 152 feet.

District: 109 Stakes, districts in central Mexico.

Groundbreaking, site dedication: Nov. 25, 1979, by Elder Boyd K. Packer of the Quorum of the Twelve.

Dedication: Dec. 2-4, 1983, by President Gordon B. Hinckley; 9 sessions. Rededicated Nov. 16, 2008.

Dedicatory prayer excerpt: *Bless Thy Saints in this great land and those from other lands who will use this temple. Most have in their veins the blood of Father Lehi. Thou hast kept Thine ancient promise.*

Monterrey Mexico

Announced: Dec. 27, 1995.

Location: Avenida Eugenio Garza Sada, Esq. Privada Valle de la Estansuela Colonia Valle Alto, Monterrey, Nuevo Leon 64989, Mexico; phone: (52) 806-794-0774; no clothing rental.

Site: 8.2 acres on site shared with a stake center.

Exterior finish: White marble.

Temple design: Traditional.

Architect: Alvaro Iñigo.

Project manager: William Treu.

Contractor: Okland Constructcion Co. Impulsa.

Rooms: Celestial room, two ordinance rooms, two sealing rooms, baptistry.

Total floor area: 16,017 square feet.

Dimensions: 98 feet by 188 feet.

District: 25 stakes and 7 districts in Monterrey area of northern central Mexico.

Groundbreaking, site dedication: Nov. 4, 2000, by Elder Lynn A. Mickelsen.

Dedication: April 28, 2002, by President Gordon B. Hinckley; 4 sessions.

Dedicatory prayer excerpt: *We express appreciation for the many missionaries who have labored in this great nation in teaching the eternal truths of Thy gospel. They have served with such devotion that today hundreds of thousands of Thy sons and daughters have entered the waters of baptism and have thereafter walked in faith before Thee.*

Montevideo Uruguay

Announced: Nov. 2, 1998.

Location: Calle San Carlos de Bolivar, entre Horacio Quiroga; Bolonia 1722, entre Horacio Quiroga y Bologna, Montevideo, Uruguay; phone: (598) 2-604-2212; no clothing rental.

Site: 1.59 acres.

Exterior finish: Granite.

Temple design: Classic modern.

Architect: Edvardo Signorelli.

Project manager: Javier Mendieta.

Contractor: Luis Maranges S.A.

Rooms: Two ordinance, two sealing, celestial room, baptistry.

Total floor area: 10,700 square feet.

Dimensions of building: 149 feet by 77 feet.

District: 15 Stakes and 6 districts in Uruguay.

Groundbreaking, site dedication: April 27, 1999, by Elder Richard G. Scott of the Quorum of the Twelve.

Dedication: March 18, 2001, by President Gordon B. Hinckley; 4 sessions.

Dedicatory prayer excerpt: *Dear Father, wilt Thou accept this temple as the gift of Thy sons and daughters. It has come through the faithful payment of tithing by Thy Saints across the world. May it grace this land. May the nation of Uruguay be blessed because of its presence on this soil.*

Monticello Utah

Announced: Oct. 4, 1997.

Location: 397 No. 200 West, Monticello, UT 84535; phone: (435) 587-3500; no rental clothng..

Site: 1.33 acres.

Exterior finish: White marble.

Temple design: Classic modern.

Architects: Church Architectural Services. Construction advisers: Bob Dewey, Ron Prince.

Contractor: Jacobsen Construction Co.

Rooms: Celestial room, baptistry; originally one ordinance room, one sealing room; one ordinance room and one sealing room added in remodeling.

Size: Originally 7,000 square fee; increased to 11,225 square feet in remodeling.

Dimensions: 79 feet by 108 feet, 66 feet high to statue of Angel Moroni.

District: Five stakes in southeastern Utah and southwestern Colorado.

Groundbreaking, site dedication: Nov. 17, 1997, by Elder Ben B. Banks of the Seventy and president of the Utah South Area.

Dedication: July 26-27, 1998, by President Gordon B. Hinckley; 8 sessions; rededicated Nov. 17, 2002, one session by President Gordon B. Hinckley.

Dedicatory prayer excerpt: *Bless the children that there may grow in their hearts a desire to serve Thee all the days of their lives.*

Montreal Quebec

Announced: Aug. 6, 1998.

Location: on the south shore of the St. Lawrence River across from Montreal; 1450 Boulevard Marie-Victorin, Longueuil, Quebec J4G 1A4; phone: (450) 646-5775; no clothing rental.

Site: .75 acres.

Exterior finish: Bethel white granite.

Temple design: Classic modern.

Architect: Andrij Serbyn, Sichten Soiferman and Church A&E Services.

Project manager: William Treu.

Contractor: Opron Inc.

Rooms: Celestial room, baptistry, two ordinance rooms, two sealing rooms.

Total floor area: 10,700 square feet.

Dimensions: 149 feet by 77 feet.

District: Five stakes and a district in Quebec , Ontario and Vermont.

Groundbreaking, site dedication: April 9, 1999, by Elder Gary J. Coleman of the Seventy.

Dedication: June 4, 2000, by President Gordon B. Hinckley; 4 sessions.

Dedicatory prayer excerpt: *On this historic day we sing Thy praises, dear Father. We speak words of thanksgiving.... May all who enter the portals of Thy house be worthy to come as Thy guests and enjoy Thy rich and bounteous blessings. This is a house of salvation and exaltation for the living and the dead, made possible through the Atonement of the Savior of the world. Every ordinance performed herein, every blessing granted will be eternal in its consequences.*

Mount Timpanogos Utah

Announced: Oct. 3, 1992.

Location: 742 North 900 East, American Fork, UT 84003-9124; phone: (801) 763-4540.

Site: 16.7 acres, part of a larger parcel of land that was once a welfare farm.

Exterior finish: Sierra white granite, art glass windows and bronze doors.

Temple design: Traditional, with a single spire.

Architects: Allen Erekson, architect of record; Keith Stepan, project architect; and Church architectural staff.

Contractor: Okland Construction Co.

Project manager: Jerry Sears.

Operation adviser: Michael Enfield.

Rooms: Celestial room, baptistry, four ordinance rooms, eight sealing rooms.

Total floor area: 104,000 square feet.

Dimensions: 145 feet by 198 feet; 190 foot spire, including statue of Angel Moroni.

District: 49 stakes in northern Utah County and Wasatch County.

Groundbreaking, site dedication: Oct. 9, 1993, by President Gordon B. Hinckley.

Dedication: Oct. 13-19 1996, by President Gordon B. Hinckley; 27 sessions.

Dedicatory prayer excerpt: *May it be a beacon of peace and a refuge to the troubled. May it be an holy sanctuary to those whose burdens are heavy and who seek Thy consoling comfort.*

Nashville Tennessee

Announced: Originally announced Nov. 9, 1994. Revised plans announced April 25, 1998.

Location: Franklin, about 15 miles south of Nashville, at 1100 Gray Fox Lane near Mack Hatcher Parkway; Franklin TN 37069-6501; phone: (615) 791-8668.

Site: 6.86 acres, including adjoining meetinghouse.

Exterior finish: White Imperial Danby marble.

Temple design: Classic modern.

Architect: Robert Waldrip of Joyce Prout & Associates and Church A&E Services.

Project manager: Leon Rowley.

Contractor: Layton Construction Co., construction management company; MPact Construction Group, general contractor.

Rooms: Celestial room, baptistry, two ordinance rooms, two sealing rooms.

Total floor area: 10,700 square feet.

Dimensions: 149 feet by 77 feet.

District: Seven stakes in Kentucky and Tennessee.

Groundbreaking, site dedication: March 13, 1999, by Elder John K. Carmack of the Seventy and president of the North America East Area.

Dedication: May 21, 2000, by President James E. Faust, second counselor in the First Presidency; 4 sessions.

Dedicatory prayer excerpt: *Bless all who come into the Church that they may look forward with eagerness to the day when they may enter this Thy holy house and receive the higher ordinances of the gospel.*

Nauvoo

Original no longer stands; burned by arson fire in 1848. Rebuilt 2002; see Nauvoo Illinois Temple.

Announced: Aug. 1, 1840.

Location: In Nauvoo, Ill., on a high bluff on the east side of the Mississippi River. Temple block bounded by Woodruff, Mulholland, Knight and Wells streets.

Site: Selected in October 1840 by Joseph Smith on property known as the Wells addition, slightly less than four acres.

Exterior finish: Light gray limestone quarried to the north and south of the city.

Temple design: Incorporated several types of architecture, no single style dominating.

Architect: William Weeks.

Temple building committee: Alpheus Cutler, Elias Higbee and Reynolds Cahoon. After the death of Elias Higbee in 1843, Hyrum Smith replaced him until his own death.

Rooms: Approximately 60.

Total floor area: Approximately 50,000 square feet.

Dimensions: Approximately 128 feet by 88 feet; 65 feet high, with the tower and spire reaching to 165 feet.

Groundbreaking: Feb. 18, 1841.

Cornerstones: April 6, 1841, President Joseph Smith presiding.

Dedication: Portions of the temple were dedicated and used as soon as completed. To avoid possible violence, a private dedication was held April 30, 1846, with Orson Hyde and Joseph Young officiating. The temple was dedicated publicly May 1-3, 1846; dedicatory prayer was given by Orson Hyde.

Dedicatory prayer excerpt: *We thank Thee that Thou hast given us strength to accomplish the charges delivered by Thee. Thou hast seen our labors and exertions to accomplish this purpose. By the authority of the Holy Priesthood now we offer this building as a sanctuary to Thy worthy name.*

Nauvoo Illinois

Announced: April 4, 1999.

Location: 50 North Wells, Nauvoo, Ill. 62354-0310; (217) 453-6252.

Site: About 4 acres.

Exterior finish: Limestone quarried in Alabama, a near duplicate of the original stone.

Temple design: Several styles.

Architect: FFKR Architecture of Salt Lake City, Utah.

Project director: Stephen Jacobsen.

Project manager: Gale Mair.

Project superintendent: Richard Holbrook.

Contractor: Legacy Constructors of Salt Lake City, Utah.

Rooms: Assembly room, baptistry, chapel, five progressive instruction rooms and celestial room, and six sealing rooms.

Total floor area: 47,000 square feet.

Dimensions: 128 feet by 88 feet; 150 feet high.

District: Five stakes in western Illinois and eastern Iowa.

Groundbreaking, site dedication: Oct. 24, 1999, by President Gordon B. Hinckley; cornerstone laying Nov. 5, 2000.

Dedication: June 27-30, 2002, by President Gordon B. Hinckley in 13 sessions transmitted by satellite to members around the world, including Europe East and Asia areas.

Dedicatory prayer excerpts: *On this same site in the year 1841, Thy people, under the direction of the Prophet Joseph Smith, and in obedience to revelation from Thee, began construction of a temple to the Most High.*

May this sacred house stand as a memorial to him who lived here and was buried here, Joseph Smith, the great prophet of this dispensation, and his brother Hyrum, whom he loved.

Newport Beach California

Announced: April 20, 2001.

Location: 2300 Bonita Canyon Drive, Newport Beach, Calif. (949) 729-9148.

Site: 8.8 acres.

Exterior finish: Salisbury pink granite.

Temple design: Southern California traditional.

Architects: Lloyd Platt & Associates, Lloyd Platt architect of record, Allen Erekson, project architect.

Project manager: Vern Hancock.

Contractor: Jacobsen Construction.

Rooms: Celestial room, baptistry, two ordinance rooms, three sealing rooms.

Total floor area: 17,800 square feet.

Dimensions: 200-feet by 98-feet.

District: Nearly 50,000 members from 16 stakes in Orange County, Calif.

Groundbreaking, site dedication: Aug. 15, 2003, by Elder Duane B. Gerrard of the Seventy.

Dedication: Aug. 28, 2005, by President Gordon B. Hinckley; four sessions.

Dedicatory prayer excerpt: *We thank Thee that Thy Church has come out of obscurity and darkness and now shines forth before the world.... May it continue to roll forth in majesty and power to fill the whole earth.*

Nuku'alofa Tonga

Announced: April 2, 1980.

Location: At site of Church's Liahona College; Loto Rd., Tongatapu, Nuku'alofa, Tonga.

Site: 1.2 acres.

Exterior finish: "R-wall" exterior finish and insulation system on concrete block.

Temple design: Modern.

Architect: Emil B. Fetzer, Church architect. Renovation Architect; Naylor Whenton Lund Architects.

Construction adviser: Richard Westover and Richard Rowley. Renovation adviser: Alan Rudolf.

Contractor: Utah Construction & Development. Renovation contractor: Cabella Construction, John Cabella.

Rooms: Baptistry, celestial room, three sealing rooms, two ordinance rooms.

Floor area: 14,572 square feet. Renovated floor area: 21,184 square feet.

Dimensions: 142 feet by 115 feet. Renovated dimensions: 200 feet by 115 feet.

District: 16 stakes, two districts in Tongan islands.

Groundbreaking, site dedication: Feb. 18, 1981, by President Spencer W. Kimball with Tonga's King Taufa'ahau Tupou IV.

Original dedication: Aug. 9-11, 1983, by President Gordon B. Hinckley; seven sessions. **Rededicated** Nov. 4, 2007, by Elder Russell M. Nelson, two sessions.

Dedicatory prayer excerpt: *We ask that Thou wilt accept this temple as the gift of Thy people presented unto Thee with love for the accomplishments of Thy holy purposes with reference to Thy children. It is Thy house. It is the house of Thy Son.*

Oakland California

Location: On hill overlooking San Francisco Bay, near intersection of Lincoln Avenue and Monterey Blvd.; 4770 Lincoln Ave., Oakland, CA 94602-2535; phone: (510) 531-3200.

Site: Inspected and approved by President David O. McKay in 1942; 14.5 acres purchased Jan. 28, 1943; additional land acquired later to make 18.3 acres.

Exterior finish: Reinforced concrete faced with Sierra white granite from Raymond, Calif.

Temple design: Modern, with an Oriental motif.

Architect: Harold W. Burton. Resident architect supervisor, Arthur Price.

Construction chairman: W. B. Mendenhall.

Construction supervisor: Robert C. Loder.

Contractors: Leon M. Wheatley Co., Palo Alto, Calif., and Jacobsen Construction Co., Salt Lake City.

Rooms: Baptistry, celestial room, four ordinance rooms, 7 sealing rooms.

Total floor area: 95,000 square feet.

Dimensions: Temple proper, 210 feet by 302 feet with a central tower rising 170 feet.

District: 31 stakes in northern California.

Groundbreaking, site dedication: May 26, 1962, by President David O. McKay.

Dedication: Nov. 17-19, 1964, by President David O. McKay, 6 sessions.

Dedicatory prayer excerpt: *This temple is a monument testifying to the faith and loyalty of the members of thy Church in the payment of their tithes and offerings. We thank Thee for every effort that has been put forth by the members.*

Oaxaca Mexico

Announced: Feb. 23, 1999.

Location: Avenida Universidad and Esq. Hacienda de Candiani; Fraccionamiento Real de Candiani, Oaxaca, Oaxaca 68130, Mexico; phone: (52) 951-516-9588; no clothing rental.

Site: 1.87 acres, including adjoining meetinghouse.

Exterior finish: White marble.

Temple design: Classic modern.

Architects: Alvaro Iñigo and Church A&E Services.

Project manager: Jay Erekson.

Contractor: Impulsa/Okland Construction Co.

Rooms: Celestial room, baptistry, two ordinance rooms, two sealing rooms.

Total floor area: 10,700 square feet.

Dimensions: 77 feet by 149 feet.

District: 10 stakes, one district, four branches in southern Mexico.

Groundbreaking, site dedication: March 13, 1999, by Elder Carl B. Pratt of the Seventy and president of the Mexico South Area.

Dedication: March 11, 2000, by President James E. Faust, second counselor in the First Presidency; 4 sessions.

Dedicatory prayer excerpt: *We pray for this nation of Mexico that its people may be blessed of Thee, that the poverty of the past may be lifted from their shoulders, that freedom and peace and prosperity might be enjoyed.*

Artist rendering

Ogden Utah

Announced: Aug. 24, 1967.

Location: In downtown Ogden, between Grant Avenue and Washington Boulevard; 350 22nd Street, Ogden, UT 84401-1487; phone: (801) 621-6880.

Site: 10 acres.

Exterior finish: White cast stone with a fluted appearance, gold anodized aluminum grillwork, gold directional glass windows.

Temple design: Modern and functional.

Architect: Emil B. Fetzer, Church architect.

Construction chairman: Mark B. Garff, with Fred A. Baker, vice chairman.

Contractor: Okland Construction Co.

Rooms: Baptistry, celestial room, six ordinance rooms, 11 sealing rooms, four floors.

Total floor area: 131,000 square feet.

Dimensions: 200 feet by 184 feet; tower 180 feet above ground level; single tower of 180 feet.

District: 71 Stakes in northeastern Utah, southwestern Wyoming.

Groundbreaking, site dedication: Sept. 8, 1969, President N. Eldon Tanner conducted; prayers given by President Alvin R. Dyer and President Joseph Fielding Smith; ground broken by President Hugh B. Brown.

Dedication: Jan. 18-20, 1972, by President Joseph Fielding Smith; 6 sessions.

Dedicatory prayer excerpt: *It has been our privilege, as guided by the whisperings of Thy Spirit, to build unto Thee this temple, which we now present unto Thee as another of Thy holy houses.*

Oklahoma City Oklahoma

Announced: March 14, 1999.

Location: 12030 North Mustang Road, Yukon, OK 73099-9801; phone: (405) 373-2309; no clothing rental.

Site: 1.05 acres.

Exterior finish: Imperial Danby White Marble.

Temple design: Classic modern.

Architects: Richard Lueb of the Architectural Partnership and Church A&E Services.

Project manager: Leon Rowley.

Contractor: Arnell-West Inc.

Rooms: Celestial room, baptistry, two ordinance rooms, two sealing rooms.

Total floor area: 10,769 square feet.

Dimensions: 149 feet by 77 feet.

District: 12 stakes Oklahoma, Kansas, Arkansas and Missouri.

Groundbreaking, site dedication: July 3, 1999, by Elder Rex D. Pinegar of the Seventy and president of the North America Southwest Area.

Dedication: July 30, 2000, by President James E. Faust, second counselor in the First Presidency; 4 sessions.

Dedicatory prayer excerpt: *We pray for Thy cause and kingdom, that it may grow ever stronger in this community. May all who have favored Thy cause be blessed for that which they have done. May many continue to seek for knowledge concerning Thy work until they have embraced Thy restored gospel.*

Oquirrh Mountain Utah

Announced: On Oct. 1, 2005, President Gordon B. Hinckley announced plans for a fourth temple in the southwest area of the Salt Lake Valley.

Location: 11022 S. 4000 West in South Jordan, Utah. Originally named the South Jordan Utah Temple, it was changed on Dec. 16, 2006, to avoid confusion with the Jordan River Utah Temple, also in South Jordan.

Site: 11 acres.

Exterior finish: Uinta gold granite from the Quanzhou/Xiamen area, China.

Temple design: End spire.

Architect: Naylor Wentworth Lund Architects, Salt Lake City, Utah.

Project manager: Russell S. Tanner.

Contractor: Okland Construction Co., Salt Lake City, Utah.

Rooms: Four ordinance rooms, six sealing rooms, baptistry, celestial room.

Total floor area: 60,000 square feet.

Dimensions: 108 feet by 209 feet. Height is 183 feet to top of angel statue.

District: 26 stakes in the west portion of the Salt Lake Valley.

Groundbreaking, site dedication: Dec. 16, 2006, by President Gordon B. Hinckley.

Dedication: Aug. 21-23, 2009, by President Thomas S. Monson, 9 sessions.

Dedicatory prayer excerpt: *The Plan of Salvation taught in the temple with simplicity, yet with power, will be as a never-ending beacon of divine light to guide our footsteps and keep them constantly on the pathway of eternal life.*

Orlando Florida

Announced: Feb. 17, 1990.

Location: On a knoll overlooking Butler chain of lakes at Apopka-Vineland Road on the edge of Orlando suburb of Windermere, five miles southwest of Orlando near Florida Turnpike and Interstate 4; 9000 Windy Ridge Road, Windermere, FL 34786-8347; phone: (407) 876-0022.

Site: 13 acres.

Exterior finish: White precast concrete with marble chips.

Temple design: Classic modern with one spire.

Architects: Scott Partnership Architects.

Church project manager: Ralph Cluff.

Contractor: Brice Building Company.

Rooms: Baptistry, celestial room, four ordinance rooms, five sealing rooms.

Total floor area: 69,000 square feet.

Dimensions: 216 feet by 252 feet; tower with statue of Angel Moroni is 165 feet high.

District: 23 stakes, 3 districts in Florida, Georgia, Jamaica, Puerto Rico.

Groundbreaking, site dedication: June 20, 1992, by Elder James E. Faust of the Quorum of the Twelve.

Dedication: Oct. 9-11, 1994, by President Howard W. Hunter; 12 sessions.

Dedicatory prayer excerpt: *To all who look upon it, including those who reside in this area, may it ever present a picture of peace and beauty, a structure partaking of Thy divine nature.*

Palmyra New York

Announced: Feb. 9, 1999, the 100th temple to be announced.

Location: 2720 Temple Road, Palmyra, NY 14522; phone: (315) 597-6001; no clothing rental.

Site: 5 acres; 48.7 combined with meetinghouse.

Exterior finish: Bethel White granite.

Temple design: Classic modern.

Architects: Dave A. Richards and Church A&E Services.

Project manager: William Treu.

Contractor: Okland Construction Co.

Rooms: Celestial room, baptistry, two ordinance rooms, two sealing rooms.

Total floor area: 10,700 square feet.

Dimensions: 149 feet by 77 feet.

District: Seven stakes and one district in upper New York.

Groundbreaking, site dedication: May 25, 1999, by President Gordon B. Hinckley.

Dedication: April 6, 2000, by President Gordon B. Hinckley, exactly 170 years after the organization of the Church by Joseph Smith in nearby Fayette, N. Y.; 4 sessions. First session transmitted by satellite to members around the world.

Dedicatory prayer excerpts: *It was here, on this land which the Smiths once farmed, it was here in the Grove below and to the west that Thou, the Almighty God of the universe, and Thy Beloved Son, the resurrected Lord, appeared to the boy Joseph Smith. This wondrous event parted the curtain that had been closed for centuries.*

Panama City Panama

Announced: Aug. 23, 2002.

Location: Cardenas, Corozal, Corregimiento de Ancon, entering through the Ministerio De Education, Panama City, Panama.

Site: 6.96 acres.

Exterior finish: China stone and art-glass windows.

Temple design: Classical.

Architect: Mallol & Mallol of Panama City and Naylor Wentworth Lund of Salt Lake City.

Construction adviser: Duane Cheney.

Contractor: Diaz and Guardia Panama.

Rooms: Celestial room, baptistry, two ordinance rooms, two sealing rooms.

Total floor area: 18,943 square feet.

Dimensions: 90-feet by 103-feet, height of spire 111 feet.

District: Eight stakes and six districts in Panama.

Groundbreaking, site dedication: Oct. 20, 2005, by Elder Spencer V. Jones of the Seventy.

Dedication: August 10, 2008, by President Thomas S. Monson; 4 sessions.

Dedicatory prayer excerpts: *We are grateful for the completion of this, Thy Holy House. We ask that Thou wilt bless those faithful members here and throughout the world who have contributed their tithes, making possible this magnificent edifice for the blessing of all who enter herein.*

Artist rendering

Papeete Tahiti

Announced: April 2, 1980.

Location: Route de Fautaua; Pateete, Tahiti; French Polynesia; phone: (689) 503-939.

Site: 1.7; 5 acres with meetinghouse.

Exterior finish: Stucco, using imported white sand.

Temple design: Shows some European elements of French influence as well as Polynesian culture.

Architect: Emil B. Fetzer, Church architect; upgrade, Naylor Wentworth Lund Architects.

Construction adviser: George Bonnet; upgrade, Alan Rudolph.

Contractor: Comtrol Inc., a Midvale, Utah, construction firm.

Rooms: Baptistry, celestial room, two ordinance rooms, two sealing rooms; upgrade, enlarged baptistry, additional sealing room.

Total floor area: 9,936 square feet; after remodeling, 12,150 square feet.

Dimensions: 125 feet by 105 feet, with an eight-foot statue of Angel Moroni on a 66-foot spire.

District: Six stakes and three districts in French Polynesia and the Cook Islands.

Groundbreaking, site dedication: Feb. 13, 1981, by President Spencer W. Kimball.

Dedication: Oct. 27-29, 1983, by President Gordon B. Hinckley; 6 sessions. Rededicated Nov. 12, 2006, by Elder L. Tom Perry of the Quorum of the Twelve.

Dedicatory prayer excerpt: *We ask that Thou wilt preserve [the temple] as Thy house. May it be protected by Thy power from any who would defile it. May it stand against the winds and the rains.*

Payson Utah

Announced: Jan. 25, 2010.

Location: 930 W. 1590 South, Payson, Utah.

Groundbreaking, site dedication: Oct. 8, 2011, by Elder Dallin H. Oaks of the Quorum of the Twelve.

Status: Under construction.

Artist rendering

Perth Australia

Announced: June 11, 1999.

Location: 163-173 Wordsworth Ave., Yokine, W.A. 6080, Australia; phone: (61) 89 276-0000; no clothing rental.

Site: 2.76 with meetinghouse.

Exterior finish: Olympic White Granite.

Temple design: Classic modern

Architect: Christou Cassella & JEC.

Contractor: Doric Building PTY LTD.

Rooms: Celestial room, two ordinances rooms, two sealing rooms, baptistry.

Total floor area: 10,700 square feet.

Dimensions: 149 feet by 77 feet.

District: Four Perth stakes.

Groundbreaking, site dedication: Nov. 20, 1999, by Elder Kenneth Johnson of the Seventy and first counselor in the Australia/New Zealand Area Presidency.

Dedication: May 20, 2001, by President Gordon B. Hinckley; 4 sessions.

Dedicatory prayer excerpt: *Thou hast made us partakers of Thy divine love that we may reap wondrous blessings in our own behalf and also in behalf of those who have gone before us.*

Thou hast commanded us to build sacred temples wherein these holy ordinances may be administered. In obedience to that command, we present to Thee this day another house of the Lord and dedicate it to Thy holy purposes.

Philadelphia Pennsylvania

Announced: Oct. 4, 2008.

Location: 1739 Vine St., adjacent to the Vine Street Expressway, Philadelphia, Pa.

Groundbreaking, site dedication: Sept. 17, 2011, by President Henry B. Eyring, second counselor in the First Presidency.

Status: Under construction.

Artist rendering

Phoenix Arizona

Announced: May 24, 2008.

Location: 5220 E. Pinnacle Peak Road.

Groundbreaking, site dedication: June 4, 2011, by Elder Ronald A. Rasband of the Presidency of the Seventy.

Status: Under construction.

Portland Oregon

Announced: April 7, 1984.

Location: In a wooded suburb about 10 miles south-west of downtown Portland, in the northwest corner of Oswego, adjacent to Interstate 5, 13600 SW Kruse Oaks Blvd.; Lake Oswego, OR 97035-8602; phone: (503) 639-7066.

Site: The land was purchased by the Church in mid-1960s for a junior college, but 7.3 acres was later chosen as a temple site.

Exterior finish: White marble walls and slate roof.

Temple design: Six spires.

Architects: Leland A. Gray, architect; Lee/Ruff/Waddle, site and local architects.

Construction adviser: Michael Enfield.

Contractor: Zwick Construction Co.

Rooms: Baptistry, celestial room, four ordinance, fourteen sealing rooms.

Total floor area: 80,500 square feet.

Dimensions: 267 feet by 180 feet, four towers 124 feet tall; statue of Angel Moroni on east spire, 181 feet tall.

District: 30 stakes in Oregon and parts of Washington.

Groundbreaking, site dedication: Sept. 20, 1986, by President Gordon B. Hinckley.

Dedication: Aug. 19-21, 1989, by President Gordon B. Hinckley; 11 sessions.

Dedicatory prayer excerpt: *May a spirit of solemnity rest upon all who enter herein. Open to their vision a glimpse of Thy great and everlasting designs.*

Porto Alegre Brazil

Announced: Oct 4, 1997.

Location: Northern zone of Porto Alegre, Chacara das Pedras, Rua General Salvador Pinheiro, 50-Vila Jardim, Porto Alegre RS CEP 91320-240, Brazil; phone: (55) 51-3338-0400; no clothing rental.

Site: 2 acres.

Exterior finish: Cotton white granite from Ceara State of Brazil.

Temple design: Classic modern.

Architects: Andre Belo de Faria and Church A&E Services.

Project manager: Raul Lins.

Contractor: Ernesto Woebcke.

Rooms: Two ordinance rooms, two sealing rooms, celestial room, baptistry.

Total floor area: 10,700 square feet.

Dimensions: 149 feet by 77 feet.

District: 27 stakes and four districts in southern Brazil.

Groundbreaking, site dedication: May 2, 1998, by President James E. Faust, second counselor in the First Presidency.

Dedication: Dec. 17, 2000 by President Gordon B. Hinckley; 4 sessions.

Dedicatory prayer excerpt: *We invoke Thy blessings on this great nation of Brazil that it may always be hospitable toward the missionaries who are assigned here. May the people reach out with friendly hands and have ears to listen, that Thy work may continue to grow in this part of the earth.*

Preston England

Announced: Oct. 19,1992.

Location: A6/M61 Link road, Hartwood Green; Chorley, Lancashire PR6 7EQ United Kingdom; Phone (44) 1257-226100.

Site: 15 acres (6 hectares).

Exterior finish: Olympia white granite from Sardinia.

Temple design: Modern.

Architects: Church physical facilities staff.

Project manager: Hanno Luschin.

Contractor: John Laing Construction, Ltd.

Rooms: Baptistry, celestial room, four ordinance rooms; four sealing rooms.

Total floor area: 60,000 square feet (6482.53 square meters).

Dimensions: 102 feet by 174 feet (31 meters by 53 meters); 155 foot high spire (47 meters), including statue of Angel Moroni 159 feet high.

District: 23 stakes, one district in Northern England, Scotland, Ireland, and Northern Ireland.

Groundbreaking, site dedication: June 12, 1994, by President Gordon B. Hinckley.

Dedication: June 7-10, 1998, by President Gordon B. Hinckley; 15 sessions.

Dedicatory prayer excerpt: *This magnificent temple has been reared in this beautiful area where Thy chosen servants, in the days of their deep poverty and great sacrifice, first preached the restored gospel. Through 161 years of history this land of England, together with Scotland, Wales, and Ireland, has yielded a harvest of converts who have blessed and strengthened Thy Church.*

Artist rendering

Provo Utah

Announced: Aug. 14, 1967.

Location: At the entrance of Rock Canyon on the east bench of Provo; 2200 Temple Hill Drive, Provo, UT 84604; phone; (801) 375-5775.

Site: 17 acres.

Exterior finish: White cast stone, gold anodized aluminum grills, bronze glass panels, and single spire finished in gold and anodized aluminum; similar to Ogden Temple.

Temple design: Modern and functional.

Architect: Emil B. Fetzer, Church architect.

Construction chairman: Mark B. Garff, with Fred A. Baker, vice chairman.

Construction supervisor: Hogan and Tingey, general contractors.

Rooms: Baptistry, celestial room, six ordinance rooms, 12 sealing rooms.

Total floor area: 130,825 square feet.

Dimensions: 200 feet by 184 feet; 175 feet high with a 118-foot spire on top of the building.

District: 64 stakes in Central, eastern Utah.

Groundbreaking, site dedication: Sept. 15, 1969, ground broken by President Hugh B. Brown.

Dedication: Feb. 9, 1972; dedicatory prayer written by President Joseph Fielding Smith and read by President Harold B. Lee; 2 sessions.

Dedicatory prayer excerpt: *We dedicate this temple to Thee, the Lord. We dedicate it as a house of baptism, a house of endowment, a house of marriage, a house of righteousness for the living and the dead.*

Quetzaltenango Guatemala

Announced: Dec. 16, 2006.

Groundbreaking, site dedication: March 14, 2009, by Elder Don R. Clarke of the Seventy and president of the Central America Area.

Dedication: Dec. 11, 2011, in three sessions.

Raleigh North Carolina

Announced: Sept. 3, 1998.

Location: Off State Highway 55 about 10 miles SW of Raleigh; 574 Bryan Dr., Apex, NC 27502; phone: (919) 362-4135; no clothing rental.

Site: 3.4 acres.

Exterior finish: Danby white marble with art glass windows.

Temple design: Traditional.

Architects: Dan Dills of Dills and Ainscuff.

Project manager: Bruce Catanzaro.

Contractor: Walbridge Aldinger.

Rooms: Celestial room, baptistry, two ordinance rooms, two sealing rooms.

Total floor area: 10,700 square feet

Dimensions: 149 feet by 77 feet.

District: Eight stakes in North Carolina.

Groundbreaking, site dedication: Feb. 6, 1999, by Elder Loren C. Dunn of the Seventy, first counselor in the North America East Area.

Dedication: Dec. 18, 1999, by President Gordon B. Hinckley; 7 sessions.

Dedicatory prayer excerpt: *May all who come as patrons to this temple know that they are dealing with the things of eternity, and that the relationships here entered into are everlasting.*

Recife Brazil

Announced: Jan. 13, 1995.

Location: Rua Dr. Jose de Goes 284; Parnamirim 52.060- 380 Recife - PE, Brazil; phone: (55) 81-3267 4300.

Site: 5.59 acres.

Exterior finish: Asa Branca granite from state of Ceara.

Temple design: Classic modern.

Architects: J&P Arquitetos Ltd. and Church A&E Services.

Project manager: Raul Lins.

Contractor: Hochtief do Brasil SA.

Rooms: Celestial room, baptistry, two ordinance rooms and three sealing rooms.

Total floor area: 37,200 square feet.

Dimensions: 114 feet by 158 feet.

District: 39 stakes and five districts in northern Brazil.

Groundbreaking, site dedication: Nov. 15, 1996, by President Gordon B. Hinckley.

Dedication: Dec. 15, 2000, by President Gordon B. Hinckley, 4 sessions.

Dedicatory prayer excerpts: *We are met to dedicate this beautiful temple which has been erected in honor to Thee and Thy Beloved Son, our Redeemer. Our hearts are full on this occasion for which we have longed and prayed. We are grateful to have in our midst a House of the Lord to which we may come frequently and with convenience. We thank Thee, Father, for this wonderful blessing.*

Redlands California

Announced: April 20, 2001.

Location: Corner of Wabash and Fifth Ave., (1761 Fifth Ave.) Redlands, CA.

Site: 4.55 acres.

Exterior finish: Light gray granite.

Temple design: Southern California traditional.

Architects: Lloyd Platt & Associates, with associate firm of Higginson & Cartozian.

Project manager: Jerry Sears.

Contractor: Layton Construction Co.

Rooms: Celestial room, baptistry, two ordinance rooms, three sealing rooms.

Total floor area: 17,279 square feet.

Dimensions: 200 feet by 98 feet.

District: 21 stakes in San Bernardino and Riverside counties.

Groundbreaking, site dedication: Dec. 1, 2001 by Elder Dieter F. Uchtdorf.

Dedication: Sept. 14, 2003, by President Gordon B. Hinckley; 4 sessions

Dedicatory prayer excerpt: *Father, our people are not strangers to this area. Not long after settling the Salt Lake Valley, some of them came to this region to establish an outpost of Thy Church. Thy work has more recently been firmly planted here. Wilt Thou cause it to grow and flourish and touch many hearts that they may turn to Thee and learn of Thy ways and do Thy will and bidding.*

Regina Saskatchewan

Announced: Aug. 3, 1998.

Location: 111 Wascana Gate North; Regina, Saskatchewan S4V 2J6, Canada; phone: (306) 545-8194; no clothing rental.

Site: 1 acre.

Exterior finish: Light gray granite.

Temple design: Classic modern.

Architect: Roger B. Mitchell of Banadyga Mitchell Partnership and Church A&E Services.

Project manager: Cory Karl.

Contractor: Graham Construction and Engineering, Ltd.

Rooms: Celestial room, baptistry, two ordinance rooms, two sealing rooms.

Total floor area: 10,700 square feet.

Dimensions: 149 feet by 77 feet.

District: Two stakes and one district in Saskatchewan and Manitoba.

Groundbreaking, site dedication: Nov. 14, 1998, by Elder Hugh W. Pinnock of the Seventy and president of the North America Central Area.

Dedication: Nov. 14, 1999, by President Boyd K. Packer, acting president of the Quorum of the Twelve; 3 sessions.

Dedicatory prayer excerpt: *May all who come within these walls be clean of hands and pure of mind as they engage in Thy sacred work. Bless them with joy in this service.*

Reno Nevada

Announced: April 12, 1999.

Location: 2000 Beaumont Parkway, Reno, NV 89503; phone: (775) 747-6688; no clothing rental.

Site: 1.2 acres.

Exterior finish: Granite.

Temple design: Traditional.

Architects: Church A&E Services.

Project manager: Amos and Gloria Wright

Contractor: Jacobsen Construction Co.

Rooms: Celestial room, baptistry, two ordinance rooms, two sealing rooms.

Total floor area: 10,700 square feet.

Dimensions: 149 feet by 77 feet.

District: Eight stakes in western Nevada and eastern California.

Groundbreaking, site dedication: July 24, 1999, by Elder Rex D. Pinegar of the Seventy and president of the North America Southwest Area.

Dedication: April 23, 2000, by President Thomas S. Monson, first counselor in the First Presidency; four sessions.

Dedicatory prayer excerpt: *Bless all who enter the portals of this structure that they may be worthy to come here as Thy Saints. May they do so with reverence and with a desire to promote Thy work in behalf of Thy children of all generations.*

Rexburg Idaho

Announced: Dec. 12, 2003

Location: 750 South 2nd East, Rexburg, Idaho

Site: 10 acres

Exterior finish: Precast concrete with a quartz rock finish, 700 art-glass windowpanes

Temple design: Classic modern.

Architects: Architectural Nexus; Bob Petroff

Project manager: Vern Martindale.

Contractor: Jacobsen Construction Co.

Rooms: Baptistry, celestial room, four ordinance rooms, five sealing rooms.

Total floor area: 57,504 square feet

Dimensions: 85-feet wide by 190-feet long by 169 feet high.

District: Stakes in eastern Idaho, including BYU-Idaho stakes.

Groundbreaking: July 30, 2005, by Elder John H. Groberg, of the Presidency of the Seventy.

Dedication: Feb. 10, 2008, by President Thomas S. Monson; four sessions.

Dedicatory prayer excerpt: *May Thy faithful saints of this and future generations look to this temple as a sanctuary and a place of service to Thee and to Thy children.*

Artist rendering

Rome Italy

Announced: Oct. 4, 2008.

Location: Part of a 15-acre Church-owned site near the ring road skirting the northeast section of Rome.

Groundbreaking, site dedication: Oct. 23, 2010 by President Thomas S. Monson.

Status: Under construction.

Sacramento California

Announced: April 20, 2001.

Location: 2110 California Circle, Rancho Cordova, CA 95742-6402. (916) 357-5870.

Exterior finish: Temple white granite from Fuzhou, China.

Temple design: Classic elegance

Site: 47 acres.

Architects: Brian Everett and Maury Maher of Nichols, Melburg & Rossetto of Fair Oaks, Calif.

Project manager: Vern Hancock.

Contractor: Okland Construction of Salt Lake City, Utah.

Rooms: Celestial room, baptistry, two ordinance rooms, four sealing rooms.

Total floor area: 19,500 square feet.

Dimensions: 220-feet by 120-feet by 131-feet.

District: 21 stakes in northern California.

Groundbreaking, site dedication: Aug. 22, 2004, by President Gordon B. Hinckley.

Dedication: Sept. 3, 2006, by President Gordon B. Hinckley; four sessions.

Dedicatory prayer excerpt: *We pray for this nation of which we are citizens, that the liberties and freedoms of the people may be preserved, that righteousness may reign, and peace may prevail. Take from our hearts all bitterness and hatred, and end the conflicts which rage in many quarters.*

Salt Lake

Announced: July 28, 1847.

Location: On Temple Square in the center of Salt Lake City; 50 W. North Temple St., Salt Lake City, UT 84150; phone: (801) 240-2640.

Site: 10 acres. Selected by Brigham Young.

Exterior finish: Granite from Little Cottonwood Canyon, 20 miles southeast.

Temple design: Suggestive of Gothic and other classical styles.

Architect: Truman O. Angell, Church architect, worked out plans under direction of Brigham Young. During Angell's illness, William Folsom temporarily filled his post. After Angell's death in 1887, Don Carlos Young completed work on the temple.

Construction supervisor: Daniel H. Wells supervised construction.

Rooms: Baptistry, celestial room, four progressive instruction rooms, eight sealing rooms; 562 rooms in total.

Total floor area: 382,207 square feet in the temple, including the annex.

Dimensions: 117 feet by 184 feet. At east end of the building, the height of the center pinnacle is 210 feet. The center of the three towers on the west end is 204 feet high.

District: Stakes in Salt Lake, Tooele and eastern Nevada.

Groundbreaking, site dedication: Feb. 14, 1853, President Brigham Young broke ground and Heber C. Kimball dedicated the site.

Dedication: April 6-24, 1893, by President Wilford Woodruff; 31 sessions.

Dedicatory prayer excerpt: *When Thy people. . . are oppressed and in trouble . . . we beseech Thee to look down from Thy holy habitation in mercy and tender compassion.*

San Antonio Texas

Announced: June 24, 2001; site announced Aug. 19, 2002.

Location: 20080 Stone Oak Parkway at Hardy Oak Boulevard, San Antonio, Texas 78258.

Site: About 5.5 acres

Exterior finish: Granite.

Temple design: Traditional.

Architects: Rehler, Vaughn & Koone

Project manager: Vern Martindale.

Contractor: Jacobsen Construction.

Rooms: Celestial room, two endowment rooms, two sealing rooms and baptistry.

Total floor area: Approximately 16,800 square feet.

Dimensions: 97-feet by 191-feet; height to top of statue is 115 feet.

District: Southwest Texas.

Groundbreaking, site dedication: March 29, 2003, by Elder J. Bruce Stucki of the Seventy.

Dedication: May 22, 2005, by President Gordon B. Hinckley; four sessions.

Dedicatory prayer excerpt: *We invoke Thy blessings upon the citizens of this community and state and pray that Thou wilt bless this nation of which we are all a part. May it ever remain free from bondage and be recognized as an ensign of peace and strength before the entire world. Prosper its people as they walk in righteousness before Thee.*

San Diego California

Announced: Apr. 7, 1984.

Location: In the northern part of city of San Diego near the suburb of La Jolla on a ridge above the San Diego Freeway; 7474 Charmant Dr., San Diego, CA 92122-5000.

Site: 7.2 acres.

Exterior finish: Marble chips in plaster.

Temple design: Modern, with two major towers.

Architects: Deems, Lewis & McKinnley-William Lewis, and Hyndman & Hyndman.

Project representative: Stanley G. Smith.

Contractor: Okland Construction Co.

Rooms: Baptistry, celestial room, four ordinance and eight sealing rooms.

Total floor area: 72,000 square feet.

Dimensions: 165 feet by 194 feet; roof 62 feet high; statue of Angel Moroni on top spire, 200 feet high.

District: Stakes in San Diego area and northwestern Mexico.

Groundbreaking, site dedication: Ground broken Feb. 27, 1988, by President Ezra Taft Benson; site dedicated the same day by President Thomas S. Monson.

Dedicated: April 25-30, 1993, by President Gordon B. Hinckley; 23 sessions.

Dedicatory prayer excerpt: *We thank Thee that hundreds of thousands of men and women of various faiths and philosophies have had the opportunity of walking through this sacred house prior to this time of dedication. May an attitude of respect and reverence grow within them. May very many of them be stirred to seek and learn the truths of Thy restored work.*

San José Costa Rica

Announced: March 17, 1999.

Location: Del Hotel Marriott, 600 metros oeste, Ribera de Belen, San Jose, Costa Rica.

Site: 2 acres.

Exterior finish: Blanco Guardiano white marble.

Temple design: Classic modern.

Architect: Alvaro Iñigo and Church A&E Services.

Project manager: Duane Cheney.

Contractor: Galvez y Volio.

Rooms: Celestial room, two endowment rooms, two sealing rooms, baptistry.

Total floor area: 10,700 square feet.

Dimensions: 149 feet by 77 feet.

District: 5 stakes and 6 districts in Costa Rica and Nicaragua.

Groundbreaking, site dedication: April 24, 1999, by Elder Lynn G. Robbins of the Seventy and first counselor in the Central America Area presidency.

Dedication: June 4, 2000, by President James E. Faust, second counselor in the First Presidency; 3 sessions.

Dedicatory prayer excerpt: *We thank Thee for him through whom Thou hast revealed the ordinances of this house, even the Prophet Joseph Smith. May we ever hold him in sacred remembrance as Thy servant in initiating Thy work in this season when Thou hast moved again to build Thy kingdom.*

San Salvador El Salvador

Announced: Nov. 18, 2007.

Location: Avenida el Espino, Colonia, San Benito, Frente al Redondel Roberto, D'Abuisson, Antiguo Cascatlan, San Salvador, El Salvador.

Site: 6.5 acres.

Exterior finish: Branco Sienna Granite from Brazil.

Architect: VCBO Architecture, Salt Lake City.

Contractor: Castaneda Ingenierous, San Salvador.

Rooms: Two ordinance rooms, two sealing rooms, baptistry, celestial room, brides room.

Total floor area: 27,986 square feet

District: 19 stakes and two districts in El Salvador, Nicaragua, part of Honduras and Belize.

Dimensions: 113 feet x 94 feet

Groundbreaking, site dedication: Sept. 20, 2008, with Elder Don R. Clarke of the Seventy and president of the Central America Area.

Dedication: Aug. 21, 2011, by President Henry B. Eyring, first counselor in the First Presidency.

Dedicatory prayer excerpt: *We pray for Thy blessings to rest upon this nation of El Salvador. Touch the hearts of those who govern, that the people may be blessed with freedom and opportunity. May peace reign in the land.*

Santiago Chile

Announced: April 2, 1980.

Location: At former Church school. Pocuro #1940 Providencia, 6641404 Santiago, Chile; phone: (56) 2 340 5070.

Site: 2.61 acres.

Exterior finish: Stucco on concrete block.

Temple design: Modern.

Architect: Emil B. Fetzer, Church architect.

Construction adviser: Gary Holland.

Contractor: H. Briones Y Cia & The Church of Jesus Christ of Latter-day Saints.

Rooms: Baptistry, celestial room, two ordinance rooms, three sealing rooms.

Total floor area: Original 14,572 square feet; after remodeling, 20,831 square feet.

Dimensions: 178.6 feet by 112.5 feet; statue of Angel Moroni on top spire, 76 feet high.

District: 74 stakes and 25 districts in Chile, plus three stakes and two districts in Argentina.

Groundbreaking, site dedication: May 30, 1981, by President Spencer W. Kimball, in a cold rain, attended by 6,000 members.

Dedication: Sept. 15-17, 1983, by President Gordon B. Hinckley; 10 sessions. Rededicated after renovation and enlarging March 12, 2006, by President Hinckley; two sessions.

Dedicatory prayer excerpt: *Bless Thy work in this great nation of Chile. May its citizens enjoy the blessings of freedom and liberty. May Thy work grow in strength and power, in size and dimension. . . . We remember before Thee Thy servant who is with us this day. He has grown old in years. Strengthen him in his body and in his mind.*

Santo Domingo Dominican Republic

Announced: Nov. 16, 1993.

Location: Avenida Bolivar and and Avenida Genesis; Avenida Bolivar No. 825, Los Robles, Santo Domingo, Dominican Republic; phone: (809) 731-2000.

Site: 6.42 acres.

Exterior finish: Granite, regina white.

Temple design: Classic modern.

Architects: Scott Partnership and Church A&E Services.

Project manager: Robert Prina.

Contractor: Caralva.

Rooms: Four ordinance rooms and four sealing rooms, celestial room, baptistry.

Total floor area: 67,000 square feet.

Dimensions: 88 feet by 190 feet.

District: 14 stakes and 17 districts in the Caribbean.

Groundbreaking, site dedication: Aug. 18, 1996, by Elder Richard G. Scott of the Quorum of the Twelve.

Dedication: Sept. 17, 2000, by Gordon B. Hinckley; 4 sessions.

Dedicatory prayer excerpt: *Dear Father, please look down with love upon Thy sons and daughters in this island nation and in surrounding lands. Prosper them in their labors that they may have food upon their tables and shelter over their heads. As they look to Thee, reward their faith and open Thy hand of providence toward them. May they find peace in the midst of conflict.*

São Paulo Brazil

Announced: March 1, 1975.

Location: In the Butanta section of Sao Paulo; Av. Prof. Francisco Morato 2390, Caxingui, 05512-300 Sao Paulo-SP, Brazil; phone, (55) 11-3721-9622.

Exterior finish: Reinforced concrete faced with quartz and marble aggregates.

Site: 1.85 acres.

Temple design: Modern design with Spanish influence.

Architect: Emil B. Fetzer, Church architect.

Construction chairman: Christiani Nielsen, general contractor.

Construction supervisor: Ross Jensen and James Magleby.

Rooms: Baptistry, celestial room, two ordinance rooms, four sealing rooms.

Total floor area: Originally 51,279 square feet; 55,000 square feet after remodeling.

Dimensions: 116 feet by 256 feet.

District: 154 stakes and districts in Brazil .

Groundbreaking, site dedication: March 20, 1976, by Elder James E. Faust, then an Assistant to the Twelve.

Dedication: Oct. 30-Nov. 2, 1978, by President Spencer W. Kimball; 10 sessions. Rededicated after remodeling Feb. 22, 2004, by President Gordon B. Hinckley; one session.

Dedicatory prayer excerpt: *Our Father, may peace abide in all the homes of Thy saints. May holy angels guard them. May prosperity shine upon them and sickness and disease be rebuked from their midst. May their land be made fruitful. May the waters be pure and the climate tempered to the comfort and well-being of Thy people.*

Artist rendering

Sapporo Japan

Announced: Oct. 3, 2009.

Groundbreaking, site dedication: Oct. 22, 2011, by Elder Gary E. Stevenson of the Seventy.

Status: Under construction.

Seattle Washington

Announced: Nov. 15, 1975.

Location: Across from Bellevue Community College, near the Eastgate Interchange on Interstate 90 at 2808 148th Ave. SE; Bellevue, WA 98007-6453; phone: (425) 643-5144.

Site: 18.5 acres, selected June 1975.

Exterior finish: Reinforced concrete faced with white marble aggregate and cast stone.

Temple design: Modern.

Architect: Emil B. Fetzer, Church architect.

Project representative: Michael Enfield.

Construction superintendent: Kent Carter for Jacobsen Construction Co.

Rooms: Baptistry, celestial room, four ordinance rooms, 12 sealing rooms.

Total floor area: 110,000 square feet.

Dimensions: Ground level is 141 feet by 193 feet; upper levels are 117 feet by 163 feet. Height to square is 70 feet; to top of the Angel Moroni, 179 feet.

District: Stakes in western Washington.

Groundbreaking, site dedication: May 27, 1978, by President Marion G. Romney of the First Presidency. Dedication: Nov. 17-21, 1980, by President Spencer W. Kimball; 13 sessions.

Dedicatory prayer excerpt: *Bless, we pray Thee, the presidency of this temple and the matron and all the officiators herein. Help them to create a sublime and holy atmosphere so that all ordinances may be performed with love and a sweet, spiritual tone that will cause the members to greatly desire to be here, and to return again and again.*

Seoul Korea

Announced: April 1, 1981.

Location: 500-23 Changcheon-dong, Seodaemun-ku, Seoul-shi 120-836, South Korea; phone: (82) 2-334-9100

Site: 1 acre.

Exterior finish: Granite exterior.

Temple design: Modern adaptation of earlier six-spire design.

Dimensions: 178 feet by 71 feet; Angel Moroni statue is atop tallest spire at 112 feet.

Architects: Church architectural staff; local architect, Komerican Architects.

Construction adviser: Calvin Wardell.

Contractor: Woo Chang.

Rooms: Baptistry, celestial room, four ordinance rooms, three sealing rooms.

Total floor area: 28,057 square feet.

District: 16 stakes and seven districts in South Korea.

Groundbreaking, site dedication: May 9, 1983, by Elder Marvin J. Ashton of the Quorum of the Twelve.

Dedication: Dec. 14-15, 1985, by President Gordon B. Hinckley; 6 sessions.

Dedicatory prayer excerpt: *This is the first such house of the Lord ever constructed on the mainland of Asia, this vast continent where through the generations of the past have lived unnumbered hosts whose lives have not been touched by the saving principles of the gospel.*

Snowflake Arizona

Announced: April 2, 2000.

Location: About 150 miles northeast of Phoenix; 1875 West Canyon Drive, Snowflake, AZ 85937; phone, (928) 536-6626; no clothing rental.

Site: 7.5 acre site

Exterior finish: Two tones of imported polished granite.

Temple design: Traditional.

Architect: Trest Polina of Fanning Bard Tatum Architects.

Project manager: Leon Rowley.

Contractor: Okland Construction Co. of Tempe, Ariz.

Rooms: Baptistry, celestial room, two ordinance rooms, two sealing rooms.

Total floor area: 16,567 square feet.

Dimensions: 91 feet by 149 feet, two stories.

District: 11 stakes in northeastern Arizona and a small portion of western New Mexico.

Groundbreaking, site dedication: Sept. 23, 2000, by Elder Rex D. Pinegar of the Seventy,

Dedication: March 3, 2002, by President Hinckley, 4 sessions.

Dedicatory prayer excerpts: *We are grateful that this Thy house will be available to the sons and daughters of Lehi who live nearby. Let the scales of darkness fall from their eyes and bring a fulfillment of the ancient promises made concerning them. May this house become a hallowed sanctuary for many of these, our brothers and sisters.*

Spokane Washington

Announced: Aug. 13, 1998.

Location: 13710 East 40th Ave., Spokane, WA 99214-1420; phone: (509) 926-2824.

Site: 4.2 acres.

Exterior finish: Granite.

Temple design: Traditional.

Architect: Church A&E Services.

Contractor: Arnell-West Inc.

Rooms: Baptistry, celestial room, two ordinance rooms, two sealing rooms.

Total floor area: 10,700 square feet.

Dimensions: 149 feet by 77 feet

District: 12 stakes in eastern Washington and parts of northern Idaho and western Montana.

Groundbreaking, site dedication: Oct. 10, 1998, by F. Melvin Hammond of the Seventy and president of the North America Northwest Area.

Dedication: Aug. 21, 1999, by President Gordon B. Hinckley; 11 sessions.

Dedicatory prayer excerpt: *Touch the hearts of the people in this temple district that the spirit of Elijah may rest upon them, that their hearts may turn to their fathers, and that they may be motivated to search out their forebears and do a great vicarious work.*

St. George Utah

Announced: May 1861.

Location: near the center of St. George; 250 E. 400 South, St. George, UT 84770-3699; phone: (435) 673-3533.

Site: 6 acres, selected by Brigham Young in 1871.

Exterior finish: Native red sandstone quarried north of the city; then plastered white.

Temple design: Castellated Gothic style.

Architect: Truman O. Angell.

Construction superintendent: Miles P. Romney; Edward L. Parry, head stone mason.

Rooms: Baptistry, celestial room, three ordinance rooms; eight sealing rooms, 64 rooms in original structure.

Total floor area: 56,062 square feet in original building; 108,536 square feet after remodeling completed in 1975.

Dimensions: 142 feet by 96 feet; to top of buttresses, 80 feet; after remodeling 249 feet by 282 feet.

District: Stakes in southwestern Utah, small part of Nevada and Arizona.

Groundbreaking, site dedication: Nov. 9, 1871, by President Brigham Young; site dedication prayer by George A. Smith.

Dedication: Jan. 1, 1877, completed portions were dedicated. Final dedication, April 6-8, 1877, President Brigham Young presiding, and Daniel H. Wells offered prayer.

On Nov. 11-12, 1975, after extensive remodeling, the temple was rededicated by President Spencer W. Kimball; 5 sessions.

Dedicatory prayer excerpt: *We implore Thy blessings upon the various congregations of Thy people who may assemble in this house from time to time.*

St. Louis Missouri

Announced: Dec. 18, 1990.

Location: 12555 North Outer Forty Drive, Town and Country, MO 63141-8620; phone: (314) 514-1122.

Exterior finish: Cast stone and Bethal white granite with thermal finish.

Temple design: Modern.

Site: 13 acres.

Architects: Chiodini Associates.

Project manager: Gary Holland.

Contractor: BSI Constructors Inc.

Rooms: Baptistry, celestial room, four ordinance rooms, four sealing rooms.

Total floor area: 60,085 square feet.

Dimensions: 88 feet by 190 feet; angel statue, 150 feet high.

District: 17 Stakes in Missouri, Illinois, Iowa, Kansas.

Groundbreaking, site dedication: Oct. 30, 1993, by President Gordon B. Hinckley.

Dedication: June 1-5, 1997, by President Gordon B. Hinckley; 19 sessions.

Dedicatory prayer excerpt: *Today Thy Church basks in the sunlight of good will. Hundreds of thousands of visitors have come to view this Thy holy house. They have left with respect and appreciation.*

St. Paul Minnesota

Announced: July 29, 1998.

Location: 2150 N. Hadley Ave., Oakdale, MN 55128; phone: (651) 748-5910; no clothing rental.

Site: 7.5 acres, including adjoining meetinghouse.

Exterior finish: Light gray granite veneer.

Temple design: Classic modern.

Architect: Ed Kodet, Jr. of Kodet Architect Group Ltd., and Church A&E Services.

Project manager: Cory Karl.

Contractor: Walbridge Aldinger.

Rooms: Celestial room, baptistry, two ordinance rooms, two sealing rooms.

Total floor area: 10,700 square feet.

Dimensions: 149 feet by 77 feet.

District: Nine stakes in Minnesota, parts of Wisconson and Manitoba.

Groundbreaking, site dedication: Sept. 26, 1998, by Elder Hugh W. Pinnock of the Seventy and president of the North America Central Area.

Dedication: Jan. 9, 2000, by President Gordon B. Hinckley; 4 sessions.

Dedicatory prayer excerpt: *And that all people who should enter upon the threshold of the Lord's house may feel Thy power, and feel constrained to acknowledge that Thou hast sanctified it, and that it is Thy house.*

Stockholm Sweden

Announced: April 1, 1981.

Location: Västerhaninge, 13 miles southeast of Stockholm; Tempelvägen 5, SE-137 41, Väster-haninge, Sweden; phone: (46) 8-500-65500.

Exterior finish: Masonry exterior, copper roof.

Temple design: Modern adaptation of earlier six-spire design.

Site: 4.47 acres.

Architects: Church architectural staff; local architect, John Sjöström.

Construction adviser: Henry Haurand.

Contractor: Johnson Construction Co.

Rooms: Baptistry, celestial room, four ordinance rooms; three sealing rooms.

Total floor area: 16,366 square feet.

Dimensions: 178 feet by 71 feet; Angel Moroni statue is atop tallest spire at 112 feet.

District: 38 stakes and districts in Sweden, Finland, Norway, Russia, Latvia, Lithuania, Belarus, Armenia, Ukraine and Estonia.

Groundbreaking, site dedication: March 17, 1984, by Elder Thomas S. Monson of the Quorum of the Twelve.

Dedication: July 2-4, 1985, by President Gordon B. Hinckley; 11 sessions.

Dedicatory prayer excerpt: *Bless this nation where is found Thy temple and its sister nations. ... Save these nations from war and oppression, and may their people look to Thee and open their doors and hearts to Thy messengers of eternal truth.*

Suva Fiji

Announced: May 7, 1998.

Location: Corner of Princess Road and Lakeba Street, Suva, Fiji; phone (679) 380-565; no clothing rental.

Site: 10 acres.

Exterior finish: Granite.

Temple design: Traditional.

Architects: Conway Beg of Architects Pacific.

Project manager: Jerry Sears.

Contractor: Fletcher Construction Co.

Rooms: Celestial room, two endowment rooms, two sealing rooms, baptistry.

Total floor area: 10,700 square feet.

Dimensions: 149 feet by 77 feet.

District: Five stakes and six districts in Fiji, Kiribati, Vanuatu, New Caledonia.

Groundbreaking, site dedication: May 8, 1999, by Elder Earl M. Monson of the Seventy and second counselor in the Pacific Islands Area presidency.

Dedication: June 18, 2000, by President Gordon B. Hinckley; 1 session.

Dedicatory prayer excerpt: *We are grateful ... that Thou hast favored us with a temple in this island nation. No longer will we have to travel far across the seas to do that work which Thou hast established as sacred and necessary.*

Sydney Australia

Announced: April 2, 1980.

Location: In suburban Carlingford, 15 miles northwest of downtown Sydney; 756 Pennant Hills Road, Carlingford, NSW 2118; Australia; phone: (61) 2-9841-5471.

Site: 3.06 acres.

Exterior finish: Precast panels, white quartz finish, terra cotta roof tiles.

Temple design: Modern.

Architect: Emil B. Fetzer, Church architect, and R. Lindsay Little.

Construction adviser: D. Crosbie and Richard Rowley.

Contractor: J.P. Cordukes Pty. Ltd.

Rooms: Baptistry, celestial room, three sealing rooms, two ordinance rooms.

Total floor area: 30,067 square feet.

Dimensions: 145 feet by 115 feet; statue of Angel Moroni added to top spire.

District: 11 stakes and 11 districts in Southern Australia and Papua New Guinea.

Groundbreaking, site dedication: Aug. 13, 1982, by Elder Bruce R. McConkie of the Quorum of the Twelve.

Dedication: Sept. 20-23, 1984, by President Gordon B. Hinckley; 14 sessions.

Dedicatory prayer excerpt: *May this temple with its grounds be a place of beauty to all who look upon it. May they be touched by Thy Spirit.*

Taipei Taiwan

Announced: March 31, 1982.

Location: In the Taipei business district; 256 Ai Kuo East Road, Taipei, Taiwan, R.O.C.; (886) 2 2351 0218

Site: 0.48 acres.

Exterior finish: White ceramic tile.

Temple design: Modern adaptation of earlier six-spire design.

Architect: Church architectural staff with assistance from Philip Fei & Associates of Taipei.

Construction adviser: Harold Smith.

Contractor: I. Cheng Construction & Development Corp.

Rooms: Baptistry, celestial room, four ordinance rooms, three sealing rooms.

Total floor area: 9,945 square feet.

Dimensions: 178 feet by 72 feet, six spires; statue of Angel Moroni rises to height of 126 feet.

District: Seven stakes, five districts in Taiwan.

Groundbreaking, site dedication: Aug. 26, 1982, by President Gordon B. Hinckley.

Dedication: Nov. 17-18, 1984, by President Gordon B. Hinckley; 5 sessions.

Dedicatory prayer excerpt: *We thank Thee for the firm foundation on which Thy Church is now established in this part of the earth. We thank Thee for this day when those who will use this temple may turn their hearts to their fathers, participating in this Thy holy house in those ordinances which will make it possible for their deceased forebears to move forward.*

Artist rendering

Tampico Mexico

Announced: July 20, 1998.

Location: Av. Ejercito Mexicano 74, Colonia Lomas del Gallo, Ciudad Madero, Tamaulipas 89480, Mexico; phone: (52) 833-216-9660; no clothing rental.

Site: 3.73 acres, including adjoining meetinghouse.

Exterior finish: Blanco Guardiano white marble.

Temple design: Classic modern.

Architects: Alvaro Iñigo and Church A&E Services.

Project manager: Rodolfo Avalos.

Contractor: PyCSA / Okland Const. Co.

Rooms: Celestial room, baptistry, two ordinance rooms, two sealing rooms.

Total floor area: 10,700 square feet.

Dimensions: 77 feet by 149 feet.

District: Nine stakes and three districts in northeastern Mexico.

Groundbreaking, site dedication: Nov. 28, 1998, by Elder Eran A. Call of the Seventy and counselor in the Mexico South Area presidency.

Dedication: May 20, 2000, by President Thomas S. Monson, first counselor in the First Presidency; 4 sessions.

Dedicatory prayer excerpt: *On this historic day, may a new sense of dedication come into our hearts that we may serve Thee more diligently and walk before Thee more faithfully.*

Tegucigalpa Honduras

Announced: June 9, 2006.

Location: Boulevard Suyapa, Calle acceso al Anillo Periférico, Honduras.

Groundbreaking: Sept. 12, 2009 by Elder Spencer V. Jones of the Seventy and president of the Central American Area.

Status: Construction began March 2010.

The Gila Valley Arizona

Announced: April 26, 2008.

Location: 5291 W. Highway 70 in Central, Ariz., located between Pima and Thatcher.

Site: Approximately 17 acres, including the adjacent Church meetinghouse.

Exterior finish: Architectural pre-cast concrete.

Architect: Architectural Nexus.

Project manager: Kerry B. Nielsen.

Contractor: Jacobsen Construction.

Rooms: Celestial room, two ordinance rooms, two sealing rooms, baptistry.

Total floor area: 18,561 square feet.

Dimensions: 27 feet by 104 feet.

District: Seven stakes in southeast Arizona and southwest New Mexico.

Groundbreaking, site dedication: Feb. 14, 2009, by Elder Neil L. Andersen, then of the Presidency of the Seventy

Dedication: May 23, 2010, by President Thomas S. Monson, three sessions.

Dedicatory prayer excerpt: *Because of these revelations, there will be carried forward in this house a great work of redemption in behalf of those who have passed from this life, many of whom have waited long for these saving ordinances. May this be a day of rejoicing on both sides of the veil.*

The Hague Netherlands

Announced: Aug. 16, 1999.

Location: On the outskirts of The Hague; Osijlaan 2, 2722 CV Zoetermeer, The Netherlands; phone: (31) 79-3435-318; no clothing rental.

Exterior finish: polished granite.

Temple design: Classic design.

Architect: Albert van Eerde

Project manager: Hanno Luschin.

Contractor: H BG Construction, Holland.

Rooms: Celestial room, two ordinance rooms, two sealing rooms, baptistry.

Total floor area: 14,477 square feet.

Dimensions: 81-feet by 154-feet.

District: Five stakes and one district in The Netherlands, Belgium and part of France.

Groundbreaking, site dedication: Aug. 26, 1999, by Elder John K. Carmack of the Seventy.

Dedication: Sept. 8, 2002, by President Gordon B. Hinckley; 4 sessions.

Dedicatory prayer excerpts: *Dear Father, we plead with Thee that this day of dedication may herald a new day in this great nation. Touch the hearts and the minds of the people of the land. Lead them from the pursuit of the things of the world to a new yearning for knowledge of Thee and for things divine and eternal. . . . May there be a great flowering of Thy work in this nation and in all of the lands of Europe. . . . May strong leaders rise up in ever increasing numbers.*

Tokyo Japan

Announced: Aug. 9, 1975.

Location: Opposite the Arisugawa Park; 5-8-10 Minami Azabu, Minato-Ku, Tokyo 106-0047, Japan; phone: (81) 3-3442-8171.

Site: 18,000 square feet (about 0.46 acres).

Exterior finish: Structural steel and reinforced concrete faced with 289 panels of precast stone, having the appearance of light gray granite.

Architect: Emil B. Fetzer, Church architect. Architect's local representative, Masao Shiina.

Resident engineer: Sadao Nagata.

Construction superintendent: Yuji Morimura for the Kajima Corporation.

Rooms: Baptistry, celestial room, two ordinance rooms, five sealing rooms.

Total floor area: 52,590 square feet.

Dimensions: Ground floor is 103 feet by 134 feet; upper levels are 103 by 105 feet. Height to square is 70.5 feet, to top of tower, 178 feet.

Design: Modern, one spire.

District: 45 stakes and districts in northern Japan and Vladivostok, Russia.

Groundbreaking, site dedication: Neither was held.

Dedication: Oct. 27-29, 1980, by President Spencer W. Kimball; 7 sessions.

Dedicatory prayer excerpt: *Kind Father, bless all those who come to this temple, that they may do so with humble hearts, in cleanliness, and honor, and integrity. We are grateful for these Saints, for their devotion and their faith, for their worthiness.*

Toronto Ontario

Announced: April 7, 1984.

Location: On the outskirts of Brampton, about 20 miles west of Toronto; 10060 Bramalea Rd, Brampton, Ontario, Canada L6R 1A1; phone: (905) 799-1122.

Site: Announced April 15, 1984; 14 acres.

Exterior finish: White cast stone.

Temple design: Modern.

Architects: Allward-Gouinlock Inc.

Supervising architects: Alfred T. West Jr. and Dagmar Wertheim.

Construction adviser: Jerry Sears.

Contractor: Milne & Nicholls Ltd.

Rooms: Baptistry, celestial room, four ordinance rooms, six sealing rooms.

Total floor area: 57,982 square feet.

Dimensions: 154 feet by 208 feet; spire, 171 feet high with 11-foot statue of Angel Moroni.

District: Nine stakes in Ontario.

Groundbreaking, site dedication: Oct. 10, 1987, by President Thomas S. Monson of the First Presidency.

Dedication: Aug. 25-27, 1990, by President Gordon B. Hinckley; 11 sessions.

Dedicatory prayer excerpt: *This nation has become a gathering place for people from scores of other lands. In their veins flows the blood of Israel. Many have hearkened to the testimony of Thy servants and have been favored with a knowledge of the principles and ordinances of Thine everlasting gospel.*

Artist rendering

Trujillo Peru

Announced: Dec. 13, 2008.

Groundbreaking, site dedication: Sept. 14, 2011, by Elder Rafael E. Pino of the Seventy.

Status: Under construction.

Tuxtla Gutiérrez Mexico

Announced: Feb. 25, 1999.

Location: Carretera a Chicoasen, km. 1,4; Esq. Paseo de la Roseta, Fraccionamiento San Jose Chapultepec, Tuxtla Guiterrez, Chiapas 29047, Mexico; phone: (52)961 615-8287; no clothing rental.

Site: 1.77 acres, including adjoining meetinghouse.

Exterior finish: White marble.

Temple design: Classic modern.

Architects: Alvaro Iñigo and Church A&E Services

Project manager: Bryan Hutchings and John Webster.

Contractor: Impulsa/Okland Construction Co.

Rooms: Celestial room, baptistry, two ordinance rooms, two sealing rooms.

Total floor area: 10,700 square feet.

Dimensions: 77 feet by 149 feet.

District: Five stakes one district in Chiapas, near the border of Guatemala.

Groundbreaking, site dedication: March 20, 1999, by Elder Richard E. Turley Sr. of the Seventy.

Dedication: March 12, 2000, by President James E. Faust, second counselor in the First Presidency; 4 sessions.

Dedicatory prayer excerpt: *We invoke Thy blessings upon this nation of Mexico where so many of the sons and daughters of Father Lehi dwell. Bless these Thy children. Lift them out of the depths of poverty. Bring new light and understanding into their minds. Cause them to rejoice at Thy watchcare over them.*

Twin Falls Idaho

Announced: Oct. 2, 2004.

Location: 1405 Eastland Drive North, Twin Falls, ID 83301.

Site: 5.10 acres.

Exterior finish: Concrete panels with quartz rock finish.

Temple design: Classic modern.

Architects: MHTN Architects, Inc.

Project manager: Greg Rasmussen

Contractor: Big D Construction.

Rooms: Baptistry, celestial room, four ordinance rooms, five sealing rooms.

Total floor area: 31,245 square feet

Dimensions: 152-feet 10-inches high by 178-feet 10-inches long by 87-feet 10-inches wide.

District: Southern Idaho communities of Twin Falls, Jerome, Burley, Rupert, Ketchum and Hailey.

Groundbreaking, site dedication: April 15, 2006; by Elder Neil L. Andersen of the Presidency of the Seventy.

Dedication: August 24, 2008, by President Thomas S. Monson; 4 sessions.

Dedicatory prayer excerpt: *The Plan of Salvation, taught in the temple with simplicity, yet with power, will be as a never-failing beacon of divine light to guide our footsteps and keep them constantly on the pathway of eternal life.*

Vancouver British Columbia

Announced: May 25, 2006.

Location: 20370 82nd Ave., Langley, British Columbia, Canada.

Site: 11.6 acres

Exterior finish: Branco Siena granite from Brazil.

Temple design: Classic modern.

Architects: Abbarch Architecture and GSBS of Salt Lake City, Utah.

Project manager: Alan Rudolf.

Contractor: Dominion Fairmile Construction.

Rooms: Baptistry, celestial room, two ordinance rooms, two sealing rooms.

Total floor area: 28,165 square feet.

Dimensions: 87 feet x 165 feet.

District: British Columbia and the northern portion of the state of Washington.

Groundbreaking, site dedication: Aug. 4, 2007, by Elder Ronald A. Rasband of the Presidency of the Seventy.

Dedication: May 2, 2010, by President Thomas S. Monson; 3 sessions.

Dedicatory prayer excerpt: *Our Father, we seek to be like Thee. We seek to pattern our lives after the life of Thy Son, our Savior and Redeemer, who 'went about doing good' and who set for us the perfect example. We desire righteousness for ourselves and for our children and our children's children.*

Veracruz Mexico

Announced: April 14, 1999.

Location: Av. Ejercito Mexicano, Esq. Michoacan, Boca del Rio, Veracruz 94290, Vera-cruz, Mexico; (52) 229-922-9621; no clothing rental

Site: 3.37 acres, including future meetinghouse site.

Exterior finish: Blanco Guardiano white marble.

Temple design: Classic modern.

Architect: Alvaro Iñigo and Church A&E Services.

Project manager: Rodolfo Avalvos.

Contractor: Impulsa / Okland Const. Co.

Rooms: Celestial room, baptistry, two ordinance rooms, two sealing rooms.

Total floor area: 10,700 square feet.

Dimensions: 77 feet by 149 feet.

District: Nine stakes, two districts and two unaffiliated branches in Veracruz, on eastern central coast of Mexico.

Groundbreaking: May 29, 1999, by Elder Carl B. Pratt of the Seventy and president of the Mexico South Area.

Dedication: July 9, 2000, by President Thomas S. Monson, first counselor in the First Presidency; 4 sessions.

Dedicatory prayer excerpt: *Bless the youth of the land, the young men and the young women, that they may grow up in righteousness before Thee. Bless them with love for the Savior of the world, our Lord and Master, that they may pattern their lives after [Him].*

Vernal Utah

Announced: Feb. 13, 1994.

Location: The temple is the remodeled 1905 Tabernacle at 170 So. 400 West; Vernal, UT 84078-2536; phone (435) 789-3220.

Site: 1.6 acres.

Exterior finish: Face brick.

Temple design: Adaptation of Uintah Stake Tabernacle.

Architects: FFKR Architects of Salt Lake City, Utah.

Project manager: Lloyd Hess.

Contractor: McCullough Engineering and Construction.

Rooms: Baptistry, celestial room, two ordinance rooms, three sealing rooms.

Total floor area: 33,400 square feet.

Dimensions: 175 feet by 210 feet.

District: Nine stakes in East central Utah, three in Colorado and two in Wyoming.

Groundbreaking, site dedication: May 13, 1995, by President Gordon B. Hinckley.

Dedication: Nov. 2-4, 1997, by President Gordon B. Hinckley; 11 sessions.

Dedicatory prayer excerpt: *We are grateful for this beautiful new structure which utilizes the historic tabernacle built by Thy people nearly a century ago.... Now that old and much-loved building has become the center-piece of a new and beautiful House of the Lord. It has a quiet luster all its own. We thank Thee for the use to which it has been put.*

Villahermosa Mexico

Announced: Oct. 30, 1998.

Location: In center of Villahermosa; Av 27 de Febrero # 1802; Colonia Atasta de Serra, Villahermosa, Tabasco 86100, Mexico; phone: (52) 993-352-2028; no clothing rental.

Site: 1.73 acres.

Exterior finish: Blanco Guardiano white marble.

Temple Design: Classic modern.

Architects: Alvaro Iñigo and Church A&E Services.

Project manager: John Webster and Dean Fife.

Contractor: PyCSA / Okland Construction Co.

Rooms: Celestial room, baptistry, two ordinance rooms, two sealing rooms.

Total floor area: 10,700 square feet.

Dimensions: 77 feet by 149 feet.

District: Eight stakes and two districts in Tabasco, on the east coast before the Yucatan Peninsula.

Groundbreaking: Jan. 9, 1999, by Elder Richard E. Turley Sr. of the Seventy and first counselor in the Mexico South Area.

Dedication: May 21, 2000, by President Thomas S. Monson, first counselor in the First Presidency; 4 sessions.

Dedicatory prayer excerpt: *May Thy Holy Spirit touch the hearts of all who enter these portals. May they do so with reverence and respect. May this Thy house stand as an expression of the covenant between Thee and Thy children, and wilt Thou be constrained to look with favor upon Thy people and open the windows of heaven and shower down blessings upon them.*

Washington D.C.

Announced: Nov. 15, 1968.

Location: Wooded site in Kensington, Md., near Exit 33 of the Capital Beltway (Interstate 495); 9900 Stoneybrook Dr., Kensington, MD (301) 588-0650.

Site: Selected in 1962; 52 acres.

Exterior finish: Alabama white marble.

Temple design: Design portrays the Church as "a light to the world," with three towers to the east representing the Melchizedek Priesthood leadership, and those to the west, the Aaronic Priesthood leadership.

Architects: Fred L. Markham, Henry P. Fetzer, Harold K. Beecher, Keith W. Wilcox, under general direction of Church architect Emil B. Fetzer.

Contractor: Jacobsen, Okland, and Sidney Foulger construction companies.

Rooms: Baptistry, celestial room, six ordinance rooms, 12 sealing rooms; seven floors.

Total floor area: 160,000 square feet.

Dimensions of building: 240 feet long, 136 feet wide, not including annex or bridge to temple proper.

District: 40 stakes and districts in Washington D.C., Pennsylvania, Virginia, West Virginia, Maryland, Delaware and New Jersey.

Groundbreaking, site dedication: Dec. 7, 1968, by President Hugh B. Brown.

Dedication: Nov. 19-22, 1974, by President Spencer W. Kimball; 10 sessions.

Dedicatory prayer excerpt: *We are so grateful, our Father, that Thy Son has thrown wide open the doors of the prisons for the multitudes who are waiting in the spirit world.*

No artist rendering available

Winnipeg Manitoba

Announced: April 2, 2011.

Status: In planning stages.

Winter Quarters Nebraska

Announced: June 14, 1999.

Location: adjacent to Mormon Pioneer Cemetery and across from Mormon Trail Center; 8283 North 34th Street, Omaha, NE 68112; phone: (402) 453-3406; no clothing rental.

Site: 1.92 acre site.

Exterior finish: Bethel white granite.

Temple design: Traditional design.

Architect: Dan Reinhardt of Reinhardt & Associates.

Project manager: Bill Naylor

Contractor: Lund-Ross Constructors, Inc.

Rooms: Celestial room, two ordinances rooms, two sealing rooms, baptistry.

Total floor area: 10,700 square.

Dimensions: 149 feet by 77 feet; 86 feet high.

District: 12 stakes in Nebraska, Iowa, South Dakota and Kansas.

Groundbreaking, site dedication: Nov. 28, 1999, by Elder Hugh W. Pinnock of the Seventy and president of the North America Central Area.

Dedication: April 22, 2001, by President Gordon B. Hinckley, 4 sessions. First session transmitted by satellite worldwide.

Dedicatory prayer excerpt: *As we meet together, we envision the wagons and the boats pulling in from the East and the South, while others were leaving these grounds to make the long march up the Elk Horn, along the waters of the Platte, up the valley of the Sweet Water, over the Continental Divide, and finally to the valley of the Great Salt Lake. . . . There was, at times, much of levity here. There was also much of sorrow.*

HISTORICAL CHRONOLOGY OF THE CHURCH

This chronology gives a selected listing of important dates in Church history. Among items excluded are many that can be found elsewhere in this Almanac, including information on General Authorities and the establishment of stakes and missions.

1820 **Spring** — In Joseph Smith's First Vision, in answer to his prayer that was motivated by his reading of James 1:5, Joseph was visited by the Father and the Son in what is now known as the Sacred Grove near his home in upstate New York. Jesus answered his question about which church to join, opening the door to the restoration of the gospel.

1823 **Sept. 21-22** — In five visits with Joseph Smith, the resurrected Moroni revealed the existence of ancient gold plates, from which the Book of Mormon was translated, and instructed him on his role in restoring the gospel.

1827 **Sept. 22** — Joseph Smith received the gold plates from the Angel Moroni at the Hill Cumorah in upstate New York. He also received the Urim and Thummim, which was used in translating the Book of Mormon.

1828 **February** — Martin Harris took a transcript and partial translation of the Book of Mormon to Professor Charles Anthon of Columbia College and to Dr. Samuel L. Mitchell of New York. In June, Harris borrowed and lost 116 manuscript pages.

1829 **May 15** — Joseph Smith and Oliver Cowdery received the Aaronic Priesthood from John the Baptist along the banks of the Susquehanna River, near Harmony, Pa. (See D&C 13.) The two baptized one another, as instructed.

May or June — Peter, James and John conferred the Melchizedek Priesthood upon Joseph Smith and Oliver Cowdery near the Susquehanna River between Harmony, Pa., and Colesville, N.Y.

June — The Book of Mormon translation was completed, and the three witnesses — Oliver Cowdery, David Whitmer and Martin Harris — were shown the plates by a heavenly messenger. (See D&C 17). Soon afterward, the plates were shown to eight other witnesses.

1830 **March 26** — Five thousand copies of the Book of Mormon were published by Joseph Smith and printed in Palmyra, N.Y., by E.B. Grandin at a cost of $3,000.

April 6 — Joseph Smith organized the "Church of Christ" at the Peter Whitmer Sr. home in Fayette, N.Y., with six incorporators as required by law — Joseph Smith, Oliver Cowdery, Hyrum Smith, Peter Whitmer Jr., David Whitmer and Samuel H. Smith.

June 30 — Samuel H. Smith left on a mission to neighboring villages, including Mendon, N.Y., where the Young and Kimball families resided.

Oct. 17 — Following a revelation received by the Prophet Joseph Smith (see D&C 32), Parley P. Pratt, Oliver Cowdery, Peter Whitmer Jr., and Ziba Peterson began a mission to the Lamanites, leaving copies of the Book of Mormon with the Cattaraugus Indians in New York, the Wyandots in Ohio, and the Shawnees and Delawares on the Missouri frontier. They stopped en route to teach and baptize Sidney Rigdon and a congregation of his followers in the Kirtland, Ohio, area.

Dec. 30 — The Saints were commanded in a revelation (see D&C 37) to gather in Ohio, the first commandment concerning a gathering in this dispensation.

1831 **Feb. 4** — Edward Partridge was named "bishop unto the Church." (See D&C 41.) This was the first revelation given through the Prophet Joseph Smith at Kirtland, Ohio.

July 20 — Independence, Jackson County, Mo., was designated the center place for Zion. (See D&C 57).

Aug. 2 — During a ceremony in Kaw Township, 12 miles west of Independence in Jackson County, Mo., Sidney Rigdon dedicated the Land of Zion for the gathering of the Saints. The next day, on Aug. 3, Joseph Smith dedicated a temple site at Independence, Mo.

1832 **Jan. 25** — Joseph Smith was sustained president of the high priesthood at a conference at Amherst, Ohio. Sidney Rigdon and Jesse Gause were named counselors in March 1832.

Feb. 16 — While working on the inspired revision of the Bible, Joseph Smith and Sidney Rigdon received a vision in Hiram, Ohio, of the three degrees of glory. (See D&C 76.)

March 24-25 — The Prophet Joseph Smith was residing with his family in the farm home of John Johnson in Hiram, Ohio, when a mob broke in to drag him from the side of his ailing son, Joseph. After being beaten, the Prophet regained strength and returned home to spend the night picking and scrubbing tar and feathers from his skin. On this day, he preached from the front steps of the farm home to a congregation assembled outside the door that included members of the mob that had attacked him the night before. Later that day, Joseph baptized three people.

June — Elders began teaching the restored gospel in Canada, the first missionary effort outside the United States.

1833

Jan. 22-23 — School of the Prophets began in Kirtland, Ohio.

Feb. 27 — The revelation known as the "Word of Wisdom" (D&C 89) was received by the Prophet Joseph Smith at Kirtland, Ohio.

March 18 — The First Presidency was organized when Sidney Rigdon and Frederick G. Williams were set apart by Joseph Smith to be his counselors, to which they had previously been called.

May 6 — The Saints were commanded by revelation to build a House of the Lord at Kirtland. (See D&C 94.) Further instructions were given by revelation on June 1. (See D&C 95.)

July 2 — The Prophet Joseph Smith finished the translation of the New Testament.

July 20 — A mob destroyed the Evening and Morning Star printing office in Independence, Mo., interrupting the printing of the Book of Commandments.

November — The Saints fled Jackson County, Mo., in response to mob threats and attacks and took refuge in neighboring counties, particularly Clay County.

1834

Feb. 17 — The first stake in the Church was created in Kirtland, Ohio, with Joseph Smith as president, and on the same day the first high council of the Church was organized. (See D&C 102.) A similar organization was created in Clay-Caldwell counties in Missouri on July 3, 1834, with David Whitmer as president.

May 8 — Zion's Camp began its march from New Portage, Ohio, to Clay County, Mo., to assist the exiled Missouri Saints. The camp dispersed June 30.

1835

The Church published a collection of hymns and sacred songs selected by Emma Smith. She had been appointed to the work in July 1830 (see D&C 25), but destruction of the Independence, Mo., printing press by a mob in 1833 had delayed publication.

Feb. 14 — The Quorum of the Twelve was organized after the three witnesses to the Book of Mormon, as directed by revelation (see D&C 18), selected 12 apostles at a meeting of the members of Zion's Camp in Kirtland, Ohio.

Feb. 28 — The First Quorum of the Seventy was organized in Kirtland, and its first seven presidents, who were also selected from members of Zion's Camp, were named.

March 28 — A revelation in which various priesthood offices and powers were defined (see D&C 107) was received during a meeting of the First Presidency and Quorum of the Twelve in Kirtland.

May 4 — Members of the Quroum of the Twelve left Kirtland for the eastern states on their first mission as apostles.

1836

March 27 — The Kirtland Temple, the first temple built in this dispensation, was dedicated after being under construction for nearly three years.

April 3 — The Savior and also Moses, Elias and Elijah appeared in the Kirtland Temple and committed the keys of their respective dispensations to Joseph Smith and Oliver Cowdery. (See D&C 110.)

June 29 — A mass meeting of citizens at Liberty, Mo., passed a resolution to expel the Saints from Clay County. By December many had relocated on Shoal Creek (later known as Far West) in the newly established Caldwell County, located northeast of Clay County.

1837

July 20 — The first mission in the Church — the British Mission — was organized. Apostles Heber C. Kimball and Orson Hyde and Elders Willard Richards and Joseph Fielding had left Kirtland, Ohio, June 13 for England, opening up missionary work outside North America.

July 30 — Nine persons were baptized in the River Ribble at Preston, England, the first converts to the Church in Great Britain. By December, there were 1,000 LDS members in England.

1838

March 14 — Headquarters of the Church was established in Far West, Caldwell County, Mo.

April 26 — Name of the Church — The Church of Jesus Christ of Latter-day Saints — was given by revelation. (See D&C 115).

May 19 — Joseph Smith and others visited a place on Grand River, in Missouri, about 25 miles north of Far West, called Spring Hill by the Saints, which by revelation was named Adam-ondi-Ahman because "it is the place where Adam shall come to visit his people, or the Ancient of Days shall sit, as spoken of by Daniel the prophet." (See D&C 116, Dan. 7:9-14.)

July 6 — The exodus from Kirtland, Ohio, began under the direction of the First Council of the Seventy as planned three months earlier.

July 8 — Revelation on the law of tithing (see D&C 119) was given at Far West, Mo.

Aug. 6 — A scuffle at the polls at Gallatin, Daviess County, Mo., intensified the mounting tension between Latter-day Saints and other area settlers.

Oct. 27 — Acting upon false reports of rebellion among the Mormons, Gov. Lilburn W. Boggs issued an order to exterminate or expel the Saints from Missouri.

Oct. 30 — Seventeen Latter-day Saints were killed and 12 severely wounded in the Haun's Mill Massacre at a small settlement on Shoal Creek, 12 miles east of Far West, Mo.

Oct. 31 — Joseph Smith and others were made

prisoners of the militia. The next day a court-martial ordered the Prophet and the others shot, but Brig. Gen. A.W. Doniphan refused to carry out the order.

Nov. 9 — Joseph Smith and the other prisoners arrived in Richmond, Mo., where they were put in chains and suffered much abuse by the guards. An arraignment and a two-week trial followed, resulting in their being sent Nov. 28 to the Liberty Jail in Liberty, Mo., where they were imprisoned about Dec. 1.

1839 March 20 — While in Liberty Jail, Joseph Smith wrote an epistle to the Saints, which contained fervent pleadings with the Lord regarding the suffering of the Saints and words of prophecy. (See D&C 121.) A few days later, he continued the epistle, parts of which became Sections 122 and 123 of the Doctrine and Covenants.

April 16 — Joseph Smith and four other prisoners were allowed to escape while being transferred from Daviess to Boone counties in Missouri under a change of venue in their case.

April 20 — The last of the Saints left Far West, Mo. A whole community, numbering about 15,000, had been expelled from their homes on account of their religion.

April 25 — Commerce, Ill., was selected as a gathering place for the Church. On May 1, two farms were purchased by Joseph Smith and others, the first land purchased in what later became Nauvoo.

Summer — Members of the Quorum of the Twelve, as their circumstances permitted, departed from Nauvoo, Ill., for their missions to England. (See D&C 118).

Oct. 29 — Joseph Smith left Illinois for Washington, D.C., to seek redress from the president of the United States for wrongs suffered by the Saints in Missouri.

Nov. 29 — In a meeting with U.S. President Martin Van Buren in Washington, D.C., Joseph Smith was told by the president that he [Van Buren] could do nothing to relieve the oppressions in Missouri.

1840 June 6 — Forty-one members of the Church sailed for the United States from Liverpool, England, on the ship Britannia, being the first Saints to gather from a foreign land. By 1890, some 85,000 LDS emigrants had crossed the Atlantic Ocean in about 280 voyages.

1841 Jan. 19 — A revelation (see D&C 124) given at Nauvoo, Ill., outlined instructions for building a temple in Nauvoo. Baptism for the dead was introduced.

Feb. 4 — The Nauvoo Legion was organized with Joseph Smith as lieutenant general.

Oct. 24 — At a site on the Mount of Olives in Jerusalem, Orson Hyde dedicated Palestine for the gathering of the Jews.

1842 March 1 — The Articles of Faith were published for the first time in the Times and Seasons in Nauvoo, Ill. Joseph Smith, in response to a request from John Wentworth, editor of the Chicago Democrat.

March 17 — Joseph Smith organized the Female Relief Society of Nauvoo, with Emma Smith, Sarah M. Cleveland and Elizabeth Ann Whitney as its presidency, to look after the poor and sick.

Aug. 6 — Joseph Smith prophesied that the Saints would be driven to the Rocky Mountains, but that he would not go with them.

1843 June 21 — Illinois agents, armed with a warrant from Gov. Thomas Ford, arrested Joseph Smith at Dixon, Lee County, Ill. He was released July 1, 1843.

July 12 — A revelation received in Nauvoo, Ill., on the "Eternity of the Marriage Covenant and Plural Marriage" (see D&C 132) was recorded, giving fuller meaning to the "new and everlasting covenant."

1844 Jan. 29 — A political convention in Nauvoo nominated Joseph Smith as a candidate for president of United States.

April 30 — Addison Pratt landed on Tubuai, the first missionary to begin work in the South Pacific.

June 11 — Joseph Smith and the city council were charged with riot in the destruction of the Expositor press. A Nauvoo court absolved them of the charge, but the complainant asked for the issue to be examined by the Carthage court.

June 27 — Joseph and Hyrum Smith were killed by a mob that rushed the Carthage Jail in Carthage, Ill. John Taylor was injured in the attack; Willard Richards escaped injury.

Aug. 8 — At a meeting designated for the appointment of a guardian, Rigdon stated his views, after which Brigham Young announced an afternoon meeting. During the latter session, Young claimed the right of the Twelve Apostles to lead the Church and was sustained by a vote of the Church.

1845 January — The Illinois Legislature repealed the city charter of Nauvoo.
May — The nine accused murderers of Joseph and Hyrum Smith were acquitted upon instructions of the court.

Sept. 22 — Citizens at a mass meeting in Quincy, Ill., endorsed a proposal requesting that the Saints leave Illinois as quickly as possible. The Twelve's reply reiterated the Latter-day Saints' intention to move to a remote area and asked for cooperation and an end of harassment in order to prepare for the move early the following summer.

Dec. 10, 1845-Feb. 7, 1846 — Some 5,000 members received their endowments in the yet-to-be-finished Nauvoo Temple prior to their exodus from

Nauvoo.

1846

Feb. 4 — The Mormon migration from Nauvoo began. The same day the ship Brooklyn left New York for California under the direction of Samuel Brannan.

April 24 — A temporary settlement of the westward-moving Saints was established at Garden Grove, Iowa. Other camps were established at Mount Pisgah, Iowa, on May 16; at Kanesville (Council Bluffs), Iowa, on June 14; and at Winter Quarters, Neb., in September.

May 1 — The Nauvoo Temple was dedicated in public services by Apostle Orson Hyde

July 13 — The first of the volunteer companies of the Mormon Battalion was enlisted in response to a request delivered to Brigham Young two weeks earlier by Capt. James Allen of the United States Army. The battalion left Kanesville, Iowa, for Fort Leavenworth, Kan., on July 20.

July 31 — The ship Brooklyn arrived in Yerba Buena (now San Francisco), California.

Sept. 17 — The remaining Saints in Nauvoo were driven from the city in violation of a "treaty of surrender" worked out with a citizens' committee from Quincy, Ill. The siege became known as the Battle of Nauvoo.

1847

Jan. 14 — Brigham Young presented "the word and will of the Lord" (see D&C 136) concerning the westward trek, including the pattern for organizing the wagon companies and the conduct of the participants, based on gospel principles.

Jan. 27 — The Mormon Battalion, completing its march across the Southwest, arrived at San Luis Rey, Calif., near San Diego, within view of the Pacific Ocean.

April 5 — The first pioneer company, numbering 143 men, 3 women and 2 children, left Winter Quarters, Neb., for the West, under the leadership of Brigham Young.

July 16 — Members of the Mormon Battalion were discharged at Los Angeles, Calif.

July 22-24 — Brigham Young's pioneer company arrived in the Great Salt Lake Valley. Eleven companies arrived in the valley in 1847.

July 28 — Brigham Young selected a site for the Salt Lake Temple and instructed surveyors to lay out a city on a grid pattern aligned to the compass.

Dec. 5 — The First Presidency was reorganized by the Quorum of the Twelve in Kanesville, Iowa, with Brigham Young sustained as president, and Heber C. Kimball and Willard Richards as counselors.

1848

Jan. 24 — Nine members of the discharged Mormon Battalion were at Sutter's Mill in California when gold was discovered.

The millrace, or canal to the millwheel, was dug by members of the battalion. Battalion member Henry Bigler was given credit for recording in his journal the date of discovery.

May — Millions of crickets descended into Salt Lake Valley and devoured the crops of the pioneers. The "miracle of the sea gulls" saved what was left of the crops by devouring the crickets.

Aug. 13 — A conference in Manchester, England, was attended by more than 17,000 members of the British Mission.

1849

Jan. 1 — The first $1 denomination of "valley currency" was issued and signed by Brigham Young, Heber C. Kimball and Thomas Bullock. It was the first printing in the Salt Lake Valley.

Feb. 14 — Great Salt Lake City was divided into 19 wards of nine blocks each.

March 5 — A provisional State of Deseret was established and appeals were made to the federal government for self-government.

October — A Perpetual Emigrating Fund to assist the poor to immigrate to the Salt Lake Valley was established during general conference. The system, which was incorporated a year later, continued until it was disincorporated by the Edmunds-Tucker Act in 1887.

Dec. 9 — The Sunday School was started by Richard Ballantyne in Salt Lake City. George Q. Cannon became the first general superintendent in November 1867.

1850

Missionary work took on a wider scope as missions were opened overseas in Scandinavia, France, Italy, Switzerland and Hawaii; most, however, were discontinued after a few years.

June 15 — The first edition of the Deseret News was published in Salt Lake City.

1851

Jan. 26 — The second stake in the Church and the first outside the Salt Lake Valley — since the pioneers arrived in Utah — was the Weber Stake, created by Brigham Young with headquarters in Ogden. Within the next six months, two other stakes were created, in Provo, Utah, on March 19, and in San Bernardino, Calif., on July 6.

March 24 — A company of 500 settlers called to settle in California departed from Payson, Utah. The group settled in San Bernardino, Calif., which became the first Mormon colony outside the Great Basin since the arrival of the pioneers in 1847.

May — The Book of Mormon was published in Copenhagen, Denmark, in Danish, the first language other than English in which the book was printed.

Nov. 11 — The University of the State of Deseret

(now the University of Utah) in Salt Lake City was begun.

1852 During the year, areas that were opened up to missionary work included India, China, Siam, Cape of Good Hope, Prussia, Gilbraltar and the West Indies.

April 6 — An adobe tabernacle, built on the southwest corner of the Temple Block where the Assembly Hall now stands, was dedicated.

Aug. 28-29 — At a special conference in Salt Lake City, the doctrine of plural marriage was first publicly announced, although several of the leading brethren of the Church had been practicing the principle privately since it had been taught to them by Joseph Smith.

Oct. 9 — Members, meeting in conference in the tabernacle, unanimously voted to build the Salt Lake Temple.

1853 Feb. 14 — President Brigham Young broke ground for the Salt Lake Temple and President Heber C. Kimball dedicated the site. Excavation began that day.

April 6 — The four cornerstones of the Salt Lake Temple were laid.

July 18 — The so-called "Walker War" began near Payson, Utah. This was one of several incidents of tension between Mormons and Indians in the Utah Territory. The war ended in May 1854.

1854 Jan. 19 — The official announcement adopting the Deseret Alphabet was made in the Deseret News.

Dec. 31 — It was reported that 32,627 members lived in countries comprising the European missions, of which 29,441 were in Great Britain.

1855 May 5 — The two-story adobe Endowment House in Salt Lake City was dedicated and remained in use until 1889, when it was torn down.

July 23 — The foundation of the Salt Lake Temple was finished.

Oct. 4 — The bark Julia Ann carrying 28 emigrating Church members from Australia ran aground on shoals near the Scilly Islands. Five were drowned.

Oct. 29 — In a general epistle, the First Presidency proposed that Perpetual Emigrating Fund immigrants cross the plains by handcart.

1856 During the year, a general "reformation" took place throughout the Church, in which Church members were admonished strongly from the pulpit to reform their lives and rededicate themselves to the service of the Lord. As a symbol of renewed dedication, many members renewed their covenants by rebaptism. The reformation movement continued into 1857.

June 9 — The first handcart company left Iowa

City, Iowa. Later that year, two handcart companies, captained by James G. Willie and Edward Martin, suffered tragedy due to an early winter. More than 200 in the two companies died along the trail.

1857 March 30 — Territorial Judge W.W. Drummond, who had earlier left the Territory of Utah, wrote a letter to the Attorney General of the United States, charging Mormon leaders with various crimes.

May 13 — Elder Parley P. Pratt of the Quorum of the Twelve was assassinated while on a mission in Arkansas.

May 28 — Under instructions from President James Buchanan, the United States War Department issued orders for an army to assemble at Fort Leavenworth, Kan., to march to Utah. It was assumed that the people of Utah were in rebellion against the United States. This was the beginning of the so-called "Utah War."

July 24 — While participating in the 10th anniversary celebration in Big Cottonwood Canyon of the arrival of the Pioneers, Brigham Young received word that the army, under the command of Col. Albert S. Johnston, was approaching Utah.

Sept. 7-11 — The Mountain Meadows Massacre took place, in which Arkansas immigrants on their way to California were killed in Southern Utah. Twenty years later John D. Lee was executed for his part in the crime.

Sept. 15 — Brigham Young declared Utah to be under martial law and forbade the approaching troops to enter the Salt Lake Valley. An armed militia was ordered to go to various points to harass the soldiers and prevent their entry. Brigham Young also called the elders home from foreign missions and advised the Saints in many outlying settlements in the West to return to places nearer the headquarters of the Church.

1858 Feb. 24 — Col. Thomas L. Kane, a friend of the Mormons, voluntarily arrived in Salt Lake City to try to bring about a peaceful solution to the difficulties between the federal government and the Church. After meeting with President Brigham Young, he went to Ft. Scott (near Ft. Bridger) in Wyoming and met with the incoming governor of Utah, Alfred Cummings.

June 26 — After having been stopped for the winter by the delaying tactics of the Mormons, Col. Johnston's army finally — and peacefully — entered the Salt Lake Valley. The army's encampment, until 1861, was at Camp Floyd in Cedar Valley in Utah County. Most of the Saints north of Utah County had moved south, and they only returned to their homes when peace seemed assured.

Aug. 5 — The first transatlantic telegraph cable was completed between the United States and Great

Britain.

1859 July 13 — Horace Greeley, founder and editor of the New York Tribune, had a two-hour interview with President Brigham Young, covering a variety of subjects from infant baptism to plurality of wives. The substance of his interview was published a year later in Greeley's Overland Journey from New York to San Francisco.

1860 April 3 — The Pony Express mail service began. A number of young Mormons were among the riders.

Sept. 16 — At a meeting in the bowery on the Temple Block, President Brigham Young condemned the practice of missionaries asking members in the mission field for support and, instead, said that missionary service should be financed by members at home.

Sept. 24 — The last of 10 groups of pioneers to cross the plains by handcarts arrived in Salt Lake City.

1861 March 2 — A bill was approved by U.S. President James Buchanan that provided for the organization of the Nevada Territory out of the western portions of Utah.

April 12 — The Civil War began as Confederate forces fired on Ft. Sumter in South Carolina.

April 23 — The first of several Church wagon trains left the Salt Lake Valley with provisions for incoming Saints, whom they would meet at the Missouri River. This was the beginning of a new program to help immigrating Saints that lasted until the railroad came in 1869.

Oct. 1 — The first baptisms in the Netherlands took place near the village of Broek-Akkerwoude in the northern province of Friesland. A monument marking the site was erected in 1936.

Oct. 18 — President Brigham Young sent the first telegram over the just-completed overland telegraph line.

1862 March 6 — The Salt Lake Theater, which became an important cultural center for Mormon people in the area, was dedicated. It was opened to the public two days later.

May — The Church sent 262 wagons, 292 men, 2,880 oxen and 143,315 pounds of flour to the Missouri River to assist poor immigrants from Europe on their trek to the Great Basin.

July 8 — A federal law was passed and approved by President Abraham Lincoln, defining plural marriage as bigamy and declaring it a crime. Mormons considered the law unconstitutional and refused to honor it.

1863 March 10 — President Brigham Young was arrested on a charge of bigamy and placed under a $2,000 bond by Judge

Kinney. He was never brought to trial, however.

1864 April 5 — A small group of Saints bound for Utah sailed from Port Elizabeth, South Africa. Five days later another group set sail for Utah from South Africa.

1865 A war with the Indians began in central Utah, known as the Black Hawk War. It lasted until 1867.

Jan. 18 — Orson Pratt and William W. Ritter arrived in Austria. They were soon banished.

Feb. 1 — Abraham Lincoln signed the document abolishing slavery in the United States. After ratification by 27 states. The measure became the 13th Amendment to the Constitution on Dec. 18, 1865.

April 10 — In a special conference, the Church agreed to build a telegraph line connecting the settlements in Utah. The line was completed in 1867.

April 14 — U.S. President Abraham Lincoln was assassinated by John Wilkes Booth in Ford's Theatre in Washington, D.C., while watching a performance of "Our American Cousin."

1866 Jan. 1 — The first edition of the Juvenile Instructor, the official organ of the Sunday School, was published. Its name was changed to the Instructor in 1930, and it continued publication until 1970.

1867 Oct. 6 — The first conference to be conducted in the newly completed Tabernacle on Temple Square in Salt Lake City began. The building was dedicated eight years later on Oct. 9, 1875.

Dec. 8 — Brigham Young requested that bishops reorganize Relief Societies within their wards. The societies had been disbanded during the Utah War.

1868 Jan. 29 — The name Great Salt Lake City was changed to simply Salt Lake City.

1869 March 1 — The Church-owned ZCMI opened for business. It was the forerunner of several cooperative business ventures in Utah territory.

May 10 — The transcontinental railroad was completed with the joining of the rails at Promontory Summit, Utah. The railroad had great impact on immigration policy and on the general economy of the Church in Utah.

Nov. 28 — The Young Ladies' Retrenchment Association, later renamed the Young Women's Mutual Improvement Association, was organized by Brigham Young in the Lion House in Salt Lake City. The first president, called June 19, 1880, was Elmina Shepherd Taylor. This was the forerunner of today's Young Women organization.

1870

Jan. 13 — A large mass meeting was held by the women of Salt Lake City in protest against certain anti-Mormon legislation pending in Congress. This and other such meetings demonstrated that, contrary to anti-Mormon claims, Mormon women were not antagonistic to the ecclesiastical leadership in Utah.

February — The "Liberal Party" was formed in Utah, which generally came to represent the anti-Mormon political interests, as opposed to the "People's Party," which generally represented Church interests until the end of the 19th century.

Feb. 12 — An act of the Territorial Legislature giving the elective franchise to the women of Utah was signed into law. Utah became one of the first American states or territories to grant women the right to vote.

1871

February — Judge James B. McKean, who had arrived in Utah in August 1870, made several rulings that began a bitter and antagonistic relationship between himself and Church members.

Oct. 2 — President Brigham Young was arrested on a charge of unlawful cohabitation. Various legal proceedings in the court of Judge James B. McKean lasted until April 25, 1872, during which time President Young was sometimes kept in custody in his own home. The case was dropped, however, due to a U.S. Supreme Court decision that overturned various judicial proceedings in Utah for the previous 18 months.

1872

June — The first issue of the Woman's Exponent, a paper owned and edited by Mormon women, was published. This periodical continued until 1914.

1873

April 8 — Due to failing health, President Brigham Young called five additional counselors in the First Presidency.

1874

May 9 — At general conference, which began on this date, the principal subject discussed was the "United Order." This resulted in the establishment of several cooperative economic ventures, the most notable of which were communities such as Orderville, Utah, where the residents owned no private property but held all property in common.

June 23 — The Poland Bill became a federal law. It had the effect of limiting the jurisdiction of probate courts in Utah. These courts had been authorized to conduct all civil and criminal cases and were generally favorable toward members of the Church, but now Mormons accused of crimes had to be tried in federal courts.

1875

March 18 — Judge James B. McKean, with whom the Mormons had been unhappy, was removed from office by U.S. President Ulysses S. Grant.

June 10 — The first Young Men's Mutual Improvement Association was organized in the Thirteenth Ward in Salt Lake City. On Dec. 8, 1876, a central committee was formed to coordinate all such associations. Junius F. Wells was the first superintendent. This was the forerunner of today's Young Men organization.

Oct. 16 — Brigham Young Academy, later to become Brigham Young University, was founded in Provo, Utah.

1876

March 7 — The patent was issued for Alexander Graham Bell's telephone.

March 23 — Advance companies of Saints from Utah who were called to settle in Arizona arrived at the Little Colorado. This was the beginning of Mormon colonization in Arizona.

1877

April 6 — The St. George Temple was dedicated by President Daniel H. Wells in connection with the 47th Annual Conference of the Church that was held in St. George. This was the first temple to be completed in Utah. The lower portion of the temple had been dedicated earlier, on Jan. 1, 1877, and ordinances for the dead had commenced.

Aug. 29 — President Brigham Young died at his home in Salt Lake City at age 76.

Sept. 4 — The Quorum of the Twelve, with John Taylor as president, publicly assumed its position as the head of the Church.

1878

May 19 — The Church had previously provided for the purchase of land in Conejos County, Colo., for settlements of Saints from the Southern States. On this date the first settlers arrived, thus opening Mormon settlements in Colorado.

Aug. 25 — The Primary, founded by Aurelia Rogers, held its first meeting at Farmington, Utah. The movement spread rapidly and on June 19, 1880, a Churchwide organization was established, with Louie B. Felt as the first president.

1879

Jan. 6 — The Supreme Court of the United States, in the important Reynolds case, upheld the previous conviction of George Reynolds under the 1862 anti-bigamy law. With the ruling, the court paved the way for more intense and effective prosecution of the Mormons in the 1880s.

Oct. 4 — The first edition of the Contributor, which became the official publication of the Young Men's Mutual Improvement Association, was issued. It was published until 1896.

Oct. 21 — Thomas Edison tested an electric incandescent light bulb in Menlo Park, N.J., that burned for 13 1/2 hours, marking the beginning of a new era of electric lighting.

1880 April 6 — At general conference, a special jubilee year celebration was inaugurated. Charitable actions, reminiscent of Old Testament jubilee celebrations, included rescinding half the debt owed to the Perpetual Emigrating Fund Company, distribution of cows and sheep among the needy, and advice to the Saints to forgive the worthy poor of their debts.

Oct. 10 — The First Presidency was reorganized with President John Taylor sustained as third president of the Church, with Presidents George Q. Cannon and Joseph F. Smith as counselors.

1881 Oct. 18 — Ngataki was the first Maori baptized in New Zealand.

1882 Jan. 8 — The Assembly Hall on Temple Square in Salt Lake City, completed in 1880 from left-over stones from the Salt Lake Temple construction, was dedicated.

March 22 — The Edmunds Anti-Polygamy bill became law when U.S. President Chester A. Arthur added his approval to that of the Senate and House of Representatives. Serious prosecution under this law began in 1884.

July 17 — The Deseret Hospital, the second hospital in Utah and the first Church hospital, was opened by the Relief Society in Salt Lake City.

Aug. 18 — The Utah Commission, authorized in the Edmunds law, arrived in the territory. The five members of the commission, appointed by the U.S. president, had responsibility of supervising election procedures in Utah. Since the result of its activities was to enforce the disenfranchisement of much of the Mormon population, Church members considered its work unfair.

1883 June 21 — The Council House, the first public building erected in Salt Lake City, was destroyed by fire. The structure was completed in December 1850 and was designed as a "general council house" for the Church, but was also used by the provisional State of Deseret as a statehouse. It also housed the University of Deseret for a number of years.

Aug. 26 — The first permanent branch of the Church among the Maoris in New Zealand was organized at Papawai, Wairarapa Valley, on the North Island.

Dec. 26 — Thomas L. Kane, long a friend of the Church and a champion for Mormon people, died in Philadelphia, Pa.

1884 May 17 — The Logan Temple, the second temple constructed after the Saints came west, was dedicated by President John Taylor.

June 9 — The building known as the "Cock Pit," in Preston, England, in which the first Mormon missionaries to England held meetings in 1837, tumbled down.

1885 Extensive prosecution under the Edmunds Law continued in both Utah and Idaho. Many who practiced polygamy were imprisoned, while others fled into exile, some to Mexico in 1885 and to Canada in 1887. Many Church leaders involved in plural marriage went into hiding, which was referred to as the "underground." Similar conditions continued for the next few years. These years are sometimes called the years of the "Crusade."

Feb. 1 — President John Taylor delivered his last public sermon in the Tabernacle in Salt Lake City. It was also his last appearance in public before he went to the "underground."

Feb. 3 — An Idaho law was approved by the governor that prohibited all Mormons from voting through the device of a "test oath." The Idaho "test oath" was upheld five years later by the U.S. Supreme Court on Feb. 3, 1890.

March 22 — The U.S. Supreme Court annulled the "test oath" formulated by the Utah Commission, thus restoring the right to vote to Saints in the territory.

May 13 — A delegation, appointed by a mass meeting held in the Tabernacle in Salt Lake City on May 2, met with U.S. President Grover Cleveland in the White House in Washington, D.C. They presented to the president a "Statement of Grievances and Protest" concerning injustices brought about because of the Edmunds law.

1886 Jan. 31 — The first Church meeting was held in the first meetinghouse built in Mexico on the Piedras Verdes River in the settlement of Colonia Juarez in northern Mexico.

March 6 — A mass meeting of 2,000 LDS women assembled in the Salt Lake Theater to protest the abuse heaped upon them by the federal courts and to protest the loss of their vote.

Oct. 28 — The Statue of Liberty, a gift from the French people symbolizing the friendship between the United States and France, was dedicated in New York Harbor.

1887 Feb. 17-18 — The Edmunds-Tucker Act passed Congress, and it became law without the signature of U.S. President Grover Cleveland. Among other stringent provisions, the law disincorporated the Church, dissolved the Perpetual Emigrating Fund Company and escheated its property to the government, abolished female suffrage, and provided for the confiscation of practically all the property of the Church.

June 3 — Charles O. Card, leading a contingent of eight families, pitched camp on Lee's Creek in southern Alberta, marking the beginning of the Mormon settlements in Canada. Under instructions from President John Taylor, a gathering place for Latter-day Saints in Canada was selected, and on June 17 a site was chosen for what later became Cardston.

July 25 — President John Taylor died while in "exile" at Kaysville, Utah, at age 78. The Quorum of Twelve Apostles assumed leadership of the Church until 1889.

July 30 — Under provisions of the Edmunds-Tucker Act, suits were filed against the Church and the Perpetual Emigrating Fund Company, and Church property was confiscated. A receiver for the property was appointed in November 1887, but the government allowed the Church to rent and occupy certain offices and the temple block.

1888
May 17 — The Manti Temple was dedicated in a private service by President Wilford Woodruff of the Quorum of the Twelve; a public service was held May 21.

June 8 — The Church General Board of Education sent a letter instructing each stake to establish an academy for secondary education. From 1888 to 1909, 35 academies were established in Utah, Idaho, Wyoming, Arizona, Mexico and Canada. The academy in Rexburg, Idaho, later became Ricks College and then BYU-Idaho.

1889
April 6 — The first Relief Society general conference was held in the Assembly Hall in Salt Lake City. Twenty stakes were represented.

April 7 — President Wilford Woodruff was sustained as fourth president of the Church, with Presidents George Q. Cannon and Joseph F. Smith as counselors.

October — The Young Woman's Journal, official organ of the Young Ladies' Mutual Improvement Association, began publication. It was merged with the Improvement Era in 1929.

November — The Endowment House in Salt Lake City was torn down.

1890
Sept. 24 — President Wilford Woodruff issued the "Manifesto," now included in the Doctrine and Covenants as Official Declaration — 1, that declared that no new plural marriages had been entered into with Church approval in the past year, denied that plural marriage had been taught during that time, declared the intent of the president of the Church to submit to the constitutional law of the land, and advised members of the Church to refrain from contracting any marriage forbidden by law.

Oct. 6 — The "Manifesto" was unanimously accepted by vote in general conference. This marked the beginning of reconciliation between the Church and the United States, which effectively paved the way to statehood for Utah a little more than five years

later.

Oct. 25 — The First Presidency sent a letter to stake presidents and bishops directing that a week-day religious education program be established in every ward where there was not a Church school. It was recommended that classes be taught, under the direction of the Church's General Board of Education, after school hours or on Saturdays .

1891
March — At the first triennial meeting of the National Council of Women of the United States, the Relief Society attended and became a charter member of that council.

1892
Jan. 4 — The new Brigham Young Academy building at Provo, Utah, was dedicated.

Oct. 12 — Articles of incorporation for the Relief Society were filed, after which it became known as the National Women's Relief Society. The name was again changed in 1945 to Relief Society of The Church of Jesus Christ of Latter-day Saints.

1893
Jan. 4 — The President of the United States, Benjamin Harrison, issued a proclamation of amnesty to all polygamists who had entered into that relationship before Nov. 1, 1890. The Utah Commission soon ruled that voting restrictions in the territory should be removed.

April 6 — The Salt Lake Temple was dedicated by President Wilford Woodruff. The dedicatory services were repeated almost daily until April 24 with a total of 31 services held.

May 23 — The first ordinance work, baptisms for the dead, was performed in the Salt Lake Temple. On May 24, the first endowment work and sealings were performed.

Sept. 8 — The Salt Lake Tabernacle Choir, while competing in the choral contest at the Chicago World's Fair, won second prize ($1,000). While on this tour, the choir also held concerts at Denver, Colo.; Independence, Kansas City and St. Louis, Mo.; and Omaha, Neb. The First Presidency, consisting of Wilford Woodruff, George Q. Cannon and Joseph F. Smith, accompanied the choir.

Oct. 25 — President Grover Cleveland signed a resolution, passed by Congress, for the return of the personal property of the Church. Three years later, on March 28, 1896, a memorial passed by Congress and approved by the president provided for the restoration of the Church's real estate.

1894
January — The railroad age continued with railroad building by far the nation's single largest economic enterprise.

April — President Wilford Woodruff announced in general conference that he had received a revelation that ended the law of adoption. The law of adoption was the custom of being sealed to prominent Church leaders instead of direct ancestors. He re-emphasized the need for genealogical research and sealings along natural family lines. With the termination of this type of sealings, genealogical work to trace direct ancestry increased among the members of the Church.

July 14 — President Grover Cleveland signed an act that provided for statehood for Utah. This culminated 47 years of effort on the part of Mormons in Utah to achieve this status.

Aug. 27 — President Grover Cleveland issued a proclamation granting pardons and restoring civil rights to those who had been disfranchised under anti-polygamy laws.

Nov. 13 — The genealogical society of the Church, known as the Genealogical Society of Utah, was organized.

1895
March 4 — The Utah Constitutional Convention met in Salt Lake City. John Henry Smith, a member of the Quorum of the Twelve, was elected president of that convention.

June 9 — The first stake outside the United States was created in Canada in Cardston, Alberta.

June 11 — Johan and Alma Lindelof were baptized in St. Petersburg, Russia.

Nov. 5 — By a vote of 31,305 to 7,687, the people of Utah ratified the constitution and approved statehood. The documents were later hand-delivered to President Grover Cleveland.

Dec. 9 — The first stake in Mexico, the Juarez Stake, was organized in the English-speaking Mormon colonies in northern Mexico.

1896
Jan. 4 — President Grover Cleveland signed the proclamation that admitted Utah to the Union as the 45th state. Until statehood, the affairs of the Church in the Utah Territory had been closely associated with the affairs of the civil government. With statehood and the rights of self-government secured to the people, the Church could become separate from political struggles.

Nov. 5 — The First Presidency issued a formal letter of instruction directing that the first Sunday in each month be observed as fast day, rather than the first Thursday, which had been observed as fast day since the early days of the Church in the Utah Territory.

1897
June 4 — Historian Andrew Jenson returned to Salt Lake City after circling the world obtaining information for Church history.

July 20-25 — The jubilee anniversary of the arrival of the Pioneers into the Salt Lake Valley was held in Salt Lake City for six days. The celebration began with the dedication by President Wilford

Woodruff of the Brigham Young statue that would later stand at the intersection of Main and South Temple streets on July 20, and ended with a celebration for the Pioneers in the Tabernacle on July 24 and memorial services honoring all deceased Pioneers on July 25.

November — The Improvement Era began publication as the official organ of the Young Men's Mutual Improvement Association. Other Church organizations later joined in sponsoring the monthly magazine, which continued as the official voice of the Church until 1970. It was replaced by the Ensign magazine.

1898
Jan. 24 — Four aged members of the Mormon Battalion took part in the 50th anniversary of the discovery of gold in California, which they had witnessed.

April 1 — Sisters Inez Knight and Lucy Brimhall were set apart to be missionaries in England, the first single, official, proselyting sister missionaries in the Church.

April 28 — A First Presidency statement encouraged Latter-day Saint youth to support the American effort in the Spanish-American War. This placed the Church firmly on the side of the war declarations of constituted governments and ended a policy of selective pacifism.

Sept. 2 — President Wilford Woodruff died at age 91 in San Francisco, Calif., where he had gone to seek relief from his asthma problems.

Sept. 13 — President Lorenzo Snow became fifth president of the Church. He chose Presidents George Q. Cannon and Joseph F. Smith as counselors. Both had served as counselors to President Brigham Young, President John Taylor and President Wilford Woodruff.

Oct. 15 — President Lorenzo Snow announced that the Church would issue bonds to lighten the burden of its indebtedness.

1899
May 8 — President Lorenzo Snow announced a renewed emphasis concerning the payment of tithing, which members had been neglecting for some time, at a conference in St. George, Utah.

July 2 — A solemn assembly was held in the Salt Lake Temple, attended by the Church's 26 General Authorities, presidencies of the 40 stakes, and bishops of the 478 wards of the Church. The assembly accepted the resolution that tithing is the "word and will of the Lord unto us."

Aug. 19 — Utah volunteers serving in the Philippines in the Spanish-American War returned to an enthusiastic reception from the citizens.

1900
Jan. 8 — President Lorenzo Snow issued an official statement reaffirming the Church's ban on polygamy.

Jan. 21, 28 — The mammoth Salt Lake Stake, comprised of 55 wards throughout the Salt Lake Valley, was divided and the Jordan and Granite stakes were created. It was the first stake division in the valley since the stake was created in 1847.

Jan. 25 — The U.S. House of Representatives voted to deny Utahn B.H. Roberts of the First Council of the Seventy his seat in Congress, following an investigation of the right of polygamists to hold office under the Constitution.

July 24 — Final unveiling of Brigham Young Monument at South Temple and Main in Salt Lake City was held.

1901 **May 4** — Reconstruction of the Tabernacle organ was completed by the Kimball Organ Co., making the instrument one of the finest pipe organs in the world.

Aug. 12 — Elder Heber J. Grant of the Quorum of the Twelve dedicated Japan and opened a mission there as a first step in renewed emphasis on preaching the gospel in all the world.

Oct. 10 — President Lorenzo Snow died at his home in the Beehive House in Salt Lake City at age 87.

Oct. 17 — President Joseph F. Smith was ordained and set apart as the sixth president of the Church, with Presidents John R. Winder and Anthon H. Lund as counselors. They were sustained by Church members at a special conference on Nov. 10.

1902 The Church published in book form the first volume of Joseph Smith's History of the Church, edited by B.H. Roberts. Publication continued over the next decades, with a seventh volume added in 1932.

January — The Children's Friend began publication for Primary Association teachers. The magazine later widened its audience to include children, then eliminated the teachers' departments. It was published until 1970 when it was replaced by the Friend magazine.

Aug. 4 — The First Council of the Seventy opened a Bureau of Information and Church Literature in a small octagonal booth on Temple Square. It was replaced by a larger building in March 1904 and by the present visitors centers in 1966 and 1978.

1903 **Nov. 5** — The Carthage Jail was purchased by the Church as a historic site for $4,000.

Dec. 17 — Orville and Wilbur Wright became the first men to fly when they managed to get their powered airplane off the ground near Kitty Hawk, N.C., for 12 seconds. They made four flights that day, the longest lasting for 59 seconds.

1904 **April 5** — President Joseph F. Smith issued an official statement upholding provisions of the 1890 Manifesto and invoking

excommunication against persons violating the "law of the land" by contracting new plural marriages.

1905 **Jan. 1** — The Dr. William H. Groves Latter-day Saints Hospital opened in Salt Lake City and was dedicated three days later, the first in the Church hospital system. In 1975 the Church divested itself of its hospitals and turned them over to a private organization.

Oct. 28 — Elders John W. Taylor and Matthias F. Cowley, finding themselves out of harmony with Church policy on plural marriage, submitted resignations from the Quorum of the Twelve that were announced to the Church April 6, 1906.

Dec. 23 — President Joseph F. Smith dedicated the Joseph Smith Memorial Cottage and Monument at Sharon, Windsor County, Vt., the site of the Prophet's birth 100 years earlier. The property had been purchased by the Church earlier in the year.

1906 The Sunday School introduced a Churchwide parents' class as part of an increased emphasis on the importance of the home and of the parents' role in teaching their children the gospel.

Summer — President Joseph F. Smith traveled to Europe, the first such visit of a Church president to the area. President Smith also visited Hawaii, Canada and Mexico during his presidency.

1907 The Church purchased the 100-acre Smith farm near Palmyra, N.Y., including the Sacred Grove.

Jan. 10 — President Joseph F. Smith announced that the Church was entirely free of debt, with the payment of the last two $500,000 bond issues sold by President Lorenzo Snow in December 1899 to fund the debt. The first had been paid in 1903. Retiring the debt was largely due to the renewed emphasis in the Church on tithing.

February — The United States Senate agreed to seat Utah Sen. Reed Smoot, a member of the Quorum of the Twelve, who was elected and sworn in March 5, 1903. The vote culminated a three-year investigation, during which Church officials testified concerning polygamy and Church involvement in politics.

April 5 — A vote of the general conference approved the First Presidency's 16-page summary statement of the Church position in the Smoot hearings.

Dec. 14 — The First Presidency issued the first of four letters to urge European members to not immigrate to the United States, but to remain and build up the Church in their own countries. Subsequent letters urging members not to immigrate were issued April 28, 1921, Aug. 2, 1921, and Oct. 18, 1929.

1908 Presiding Bishop Charles W. Nibley moved the Church to an all-cash basis and no longer issued tithing scrip.

April 8 — The First Presidency created a General Priesthood Committee on Outlines, which served until 1922. The committee created definite age groupings for priesthood offices (deacons at 12, teachers at 15, priests at 18, and elders at 21), provided systematic programs for year-round priesthood meetings, and in other ways reformed, reactivated and systematized priesthood work.

Oct. 1 — Henry Ford introduced his famous Model-T Ford automobile.

1909
April 6 — The North Pole was discovered by an expedition led by Robert E. Peary.

Sept. 26 — U.S. President William Howard Taft visited Salt Lake City en route to California and spoke in the Tabernacle.

November — As the debate on Darwinism and evolution continued in the national press, the First Presidency issued an official statement on the origin of man.

1910
The Bishop's Building, an office building for the Presiding Bishopric and auxiliary organizations of the Church at 50 N. Main St., opened. It was used for more than 50 years.

January — The first issue of the Utah Genealogical and Historical Magazine was published. This quarterly publication served as the voice of the Genealogical Society of Utah. It was discontinued in October 1940.

1911
The Church adopted the Boy Scout program and has since become one of the leading sponsors of this organization for young men.

April 15 — Collier's magazine published a letter from Theodore Roosevelt refuting many charges made against Utah Sen. Reed Smoot and the Church. This action helped defuse an anti-Mormon propaganda surge of 1910-11.

1912
The Church colonists in northern Mexico exited the country due to unsettled conditions during the revolution.

September — The Church's first seminary began at Granite High School in Salt Lake City, marking the beginning of a released-time weekday education program for young Latter-day Saints. As the seminary program grew, the Church phased out its involvement in academies, which were Church-sponsored high schools or junior colleges. By 1924, only the Juarez Academy in Mexico remained.

Nov. 8 — The First Presidency created a Correlation Committee, headed by Elder David O. McKay of the Quorum of the Twelve, and asked it to coordinate scheduling and prevent unnecessary duplication in programs of Church auxiliaries.

1913
The Church established the Maori Agricultural College in New Zealand. It was destroyed by an earthquake in 1931 and was never rebuilt.

May 21 — The Boy Scout program was officially adopted by the Young Men's Mutual Improvement Association and became the activity program for boys of the Church.

1914
January — *The Relief Society Magazine* appeared as a monthly publication containing lesson material for use in the women's auxiliary of the Church. The magazine carried stories, poetry, articles, homemaking helps, news and lesson material until it ceased publication in December 1970, when the Ensign magazine became the magazine for adults in the Church.

Dec. 19 — Under the pall of war, missionaries were removed from France, Germany, Switzerland and Belgium, prior to World War I.

1915
April 27 — The First Presidency inaugurated the "Home Evening" program, inviting all families to participate.

September — James E. Talmage's influential book *Jesus the Christ* was published.

Fall — The first college classes were taught at Ricks College, which had been Ricks Academy.

1916
Feb. 21 — The longest and bloodiest battle of World War I, the Battle of Verdun, began in France, resulting in the death of 1 million soldiers.

June 30 — The First Presidency and Quorum of the Twelve issued a doctrinal exposition clarifying the use of the title "Father" as it is applied to Jesus Christ.

1917
April 6 — On the opening day of the 87th Annual General Conference of the Church, the United States entered World War I as it declared war against Germany.

Oct. 2 — The Church Administration Building at 47 E. South Temple was completed.

1918
May — To alleviate shortages during World War I, the Relief Society, which had been gathering and storing wheat since 1876, sold 205,518 bushels of wheat to the U.S. government at a government price, with approval of the First Presidency and the Presiding Bishopric.

Oct. 3 — While contemplating the meaning of Christ's atonement, President Joseph F. Smith received a manifestation on the salvation of the dead and the visit of the Savior to the spirit world after His crucifixion. A report of the experience was published in December and was added first to the Pearl of Great Price and then to the Doctrine and Covenants June 6, 1979, as Section 138.

Nov. 11 — World War I ended, as Germany signed

an armistice with the Allies.

Nov. 19 — President Joseph F. Smith died six days after his 80th birthday. Because of an epidemic of influenza, no public funeral was held for the Church president.

Nov. 23 — President Heber J. Grant was ordained and set apart as the seventh president of the Church during a meeting of the Twelve in the Salt Lake Temple. He selected Presidents Anthon H. Lund and Charles W. Penrose as counselors.

1919 **April** — The April general conference of the Church was postponed due to the nationwide influenza epidemic. The conference was held June 1-3.

Oct. 10 — King Albert and Queen Elizabeth of Belgium attended a recital on Temple Square in Salt Lake City to hear the Tabernacle organ.

Nov. 27 — President Heber J. Grant dedicated the temple at Laie, Hawaii, the first temple outside the continental United States. Construction had begun soon after the site was dedicated in June 1915.

1920 In response to Church growth and need for a more cost-effective use of building funds, an "authentic form of LDS architecture" was developed. that structurally joined the previously separate chapel and classrooms with the recreational or cultural hall through a connecting foyer/office/classroom complex.

1921 Elder David O. McKay of the Quorum of the Twelve and President Hugh J. Cannon of the Liberty Stake in Salt Lake City traveled 55,896 miles in a world survey of Church missions for the First Presidency. The pair visited the Saints in the Pacific Islands, New Zealand, Australia and Asia and then made stops in India, Egypt, and Palestine before visiting the missions of Europe.

1922 May — Primary Children's Hospital opened in Salt Lake City.

1923 The Church purchased a part of the Hill Cumorah. Additional acquisitions in 1928 gave the Church possession of the entire hill and adjacent lands.

Jan. 21 — The first stake outside the traditional Mormon cultural area was created in Los Angeles, Calif.

Aug. 26 — President Heber J. Grant dedicated the Alberta Temple in Cardston, Alberta, Canada, which had been under construction for nearly a decade.

1924 March 21 — A First Presidency statement answered criticism of unauthorized plural marriages by once again confirming the Church's policy against the practice. Polygamists within the Church were excommunicated when discovered.

Oct. 3 — Radio broadcast of general conference began on KSL in Salt Lake City, the Church-owned station. Coverage was expanded into Idaho in 1941.

1925 Feb. 3 — President Heber J. Grant dedicated a remodeled home at 31 N. State St. in Salt Lake City as the Church's missionary home, offering the first organized training for missionaries in gospel topics, Church procedures, personal health and proper manners.

July 24 — In the famous "Scopes Monkey Trial," John T. Scopes, a Tennessee school teacher, was found guilty of teaching evolution in a public school.

September — The First Presidency issued a statement, " 'Mormon' View of Evolution," which, in part, stated: "The Church of Jesus Christ of Latter-day Saints, basing its belief on divine revelation, ancient and modern, declares man to be the direct and lineal offspring of Deity."

Dec. 6 — Elder Melvin J. Ballard of the Quorum of the Twelve established a mission in South America with headquarters in Buenos Aires, Argentina, opening the Church's official work in South America, which he dedicated for the preaching of the gospel on Dec. 25.

1927 May 21 — Charles Lindbergh, aboard his "Spirit of St. Louis" monoplane, completed the first transatlantic solo flight from New York City to Paris, a distance of 3,610 miles, in 33 1/2 hours.

Oct. 23 — President Heber J. Grant dedicated the Arizona Temple at Mesa, completing a project begun six years before. Dedicatory services were broadcast by radio.

1928 The Church purchased Hill Cumorah in western New York.

January — The Church published its first Melchizedek Priesthood handbook.

• The YMMIA introduced a Vanguard program for 15- and 16-year-old boys. After the National Boy Scout organization created the Explorer program in 1933, patterned in part after the Vanguards, the Church adopted Explorer Scouting.

• Priesthood quorums began meeting during the Sunday School hour for gospel instruction under a correlated experiment lasting 10 years. This priesthood Sunday School experiment included classes for all age groups, with Tuesday evening reserved as an activity night for both priesthood and young women.

1929 July 15 — The Tabernacle Choir started a weekly network radio broadcast on NBC. Richard L. Evans joined the program with his sermonettes in June 1930. "Music and the Spoken Word" eventually switched to KSL Radio on the CBS network, and has since become the longest continuing network radio broadcast in history.

Oct. 29 — The New York Stock Market collapsed in frantic trading, a dramatic beginning of the Great Depression.

November — The official publication of the Sunday School began publishing under the name of The Instructor. From 1877 until 1929, the publication was The Juvenile Instructor. The name change reflected the growing use of articles on teaching methods and gospel subjects to be used by the several Church organizations.

1930 **April 6** — The centennial of the Church's organization was observed at general conference in the Tabernacle in Salt Lake City. B.H. Roberts prepared his Comprehensive History of The Church of Jesus Christ of Latter-day Saints as a centennial memorial.

1931 **March 21** — A 10-reel film of the history of the Church was completed.

April 6 — The first edition of the Church News was printed by the Church's Deseret News.

1932 **Jan. 10** — The first missionary training classes began, which were to be organized in every ward throughout the Church.

February — The Lion House, home of Brigham Young and a noted landmark of Salt Lake City, was turned over to the Young Ladies Mutual Improvement Association by the Church for a social center for women and young ladies. Another of Brigham Young's homes, the Beehive House, was previously placed under the direction of the YLMIA as a girls' home.

1933 **Jan. 30** — Adolf Hitler was named chancellor of Germany, capping a 10-year rise to power.

Feb. 21 — The Church began a six-day commemoration of the 100th anniversary of the Word of Wisdom revelation with special observances in every ward.

June 1 — The Church opened a 500-foot exhibit in the Hall of Religions at the Century of Progress World's Fair in Chicago, Ill. The exhibit was prepared by famed LDS sculptor Avard Fairbanks.

July 26 — The first effort to mark the historic sites in Nauvoo, Ill., was made by the Relief Society when it placed a monument at the site of its organization in 1842 in Joseph Smith's store.

Nov. 5 — The First Presidency and four members of the Quorum of the Twelve participated in the dedication of the Washington, D.C., meetinghouse, which was adorned by a statue of the Angel Moroni atop its 165-foot spire.

1934 The general board of the Sunday School officially recognized the Junior Sunday School, which had been part of some ward programs for many years.

Jan. 17 — New headquarters of the Genealogical Society of Utah, located in the Joseph F. Smith Memorial Building on North Main Street in Salt Lake City, was formally opened. The building previously was part of the campus of the LDS College.

Aug. 2 — Adolf Hitler took control of Germany after the death of President Paul von Hindenburg.

1935 **Jan. 10** — In a change of policy, members of the Quorum of the Twelve were released from auxiliary leadership positions as presiding officers and general board members.

July 21 — President Heber J. Grant dedicated the Hill Cumorah Monument near Palmyra, N.Y.

1936 A separate Aaronic Priesthood program for adults, recommended by the General Priesthood Committee on Outlines 20 years earlier, was introduced.

April — The Church introduced a formal welfare program to assist in emergency situations of needy Church members and those unemployed. Called the Church Security Program at first, it was renamed the Church Welfare Program in 1938. Later it expanded its services with the addition of local production programs.

1937 **January** — The First Presidency officially adopted the practice widely utilized over several preceding decades of ordaining worthy young men in the Aaronic Priesthood at specific ages. The recommended ages for advancement from deacon to teacher to priest to elder have changed from time to time since 1937.

Feb. 20 — A portion of the Nauvoo Temple lot in Nauvoo, Ill., returned to Church ownership when Wilford C. Wood, representing the Church, purchased the property.

July — The Hill Cumorah pageant, "America's Witness for Christ," began on an outdoor stage on the side of the Hill Cumorah in New York.

Sept. 12 — President Heber J. Grant returned to Salt Lake City after a three-month tour of Europe, where he visited with Church members and missionaries in 11 countries. He dedicated nine meetinghouses and gave some 55 addresses, including the principal address at the British Mission Centennial Conference at Rochdale, England, on Aug. 1.

1938 **Aug. 14** — The first Deseret Industries store opened in Salt Lake City to provide work opportunities for the elderly and handicapped. Part of the Welfare Program, a growing network of stores still offers used furniture, clothing and other items.

November — The Genealogical Society of Utah had its own camera and began microfilming baptism and sealing records of the Salt Lake, Logan, Manti and St. George temples.

1939 June 19 — Wilford Wood purchased the Liberty Jail in Missouri on behalf of the Church.

Aug. 24 — The First Presidency directed all missionaries in Germany to move to neutral countries. Later the missionaries were instructed to leave Europe and return to the United States. The last group arrived in New York Nov. 6, 1939.

Sept. 1 — World War II began when Nazi Germany invaded Poland. Britain and France declared war on Germany two days later.

Oct. 6 — The First Presidency message on world peace was delivered in general conference by President Heber J. Grant.

1940 Jan. 28 — The Mormon Battalion Monument was dedicated in San Diego, Calif.

1941 The Presiding Bishopric inaugurated a new membership record system.

April 6 — In general conference, the First Presidency announced the new position of Assistant to the Twelve, and the first five Assistants were called and sustained.

Dec. 7 — The Japanese bombed Pearl Harbor in Hawaii, killing 2,403 Americans and wounding 1,178. The next day, President Franklin D. Roosevelt asked Congress for a declaration of war against Japan. Four days later, Germany and Italy declared war on the United States, and on the same day the U.S. declared war on the European dictatorships.

1942 Jan. 4 — The Church observed a special fast Sunday in conjunction with a national day of prayer called by President Franklin D. Roosevelt.

Feb. 28 — It was announced that due to World War II, the Relief Society general conference scheduled for April, which had been planned to commemorate the centennial anniversary of the founding of the Relief Society, along with centennial celebrations in the stakes, would not be held. Rather, celebrations were to be held on the ward and branch level.

March 23 — The First Presidency announced that for the duration of World War II it would call only older men who had been ordained high priests or seventies on full-time missions.

April 4-6 — Because of limitations on travel, the annual April general conference was closed to the general Church membership and confined to General Authorities and presidencies of the 141 stakes. The First Presidency on April 5, 1942, closed the Tabernacle for the duration of the war. Conference sessions were held in the Assembly Hall on Temple Square and in the assembly room of the Salt Lake Temple.

April 18 — May Green Hinckley, general president of the Primary Association, announced that the presiding officers of the Primary on all levels would henceforth be known as "presidents" rather than "superintendents."

July — Church Welfare leaders urged members to plant gardens, to bottle as many fruits and vegetables as they could utilize, and to store coal.

Aug. 17 — The USS Brigham Young, a Liberty class ship, was christened.

1943 March 7 — The Navajo-Zuni Mission was formed, the first mission designated only for Indians.

May 22 — USS Joseph Smith, a Liberty class ship, was launched in Richmond, Calif. Ceremonies included a tribute to Joseph Smith and a description of the Church's part in the war effort.

July 24 — The MIA completed a war service project to purchase aircraft rescue boats by purchasing war bonds. The project began May 11 and ended with 87 stakes raising a total of $3.1 million, enough to purchase 52 boats, which cost $60,000 each.

Sept. 9 — United States troops invaded Italy.

1944 March — The Church announced the purchase of Spring Hill in Missouri, known in Church history as Adam-ondi-Ahman. (See D&C 116.). Final deeds for the purchase were dated June 27, 1944, the 100th anniversary of the martyrdom of the Prophet Joseph Smith. The deed to the land was passed on to the Church by Eugene Johnson, whose family had been in possession of the property for a century.

May 15 — A 12-page monthly Church News for the 70,000 LDS servicemen was inaugurated by the First Presidency in order to keep more closely in touch with the servicemen.

June 6 — Allied forces, numbering 130,000 men, invaded Europe at Normandy, France, on "D-Day" breaking the Nazi stranglehold on the Continent and leading to the eventual surrender of Germany.

June 25 — Memorial services were held in each ward to commemorate the 100th anniversary of the martyrdom of the Prophet Joseph Smith and Hyrum Smith. Special services were also held in Carthage Jail on June 27.

July — The Church organized the Committee on Publications comprised of General Authorities to supervise the preparation and publication of all Church literature.

November — The name of the Genealogical Society of Utah was changed to the Genealogical Society of The Church of Jesus Christ of Latter-day Saints.

Nov. 28 — Young Women's Mutual Improvement Association celebrated its 75th anniversary. A plaque was dedicated by President Heber J. Grant and placed in the Lion House where the initial organization had taken place.

1945

May 14 — President Heber J. Grant died in Salt Lake City at age 88.

May 21 — At a special meeting of the Quorum of the Twelve in the Salt Lake Temple, the First Presidency was reorganized with President George Albert Smith ordained and set apart as the eighth president of the Church. Presidents J. Reuben Clark Jr. and David O. McKay, counselors to President Grant, were called also as counselors to President Smith.

July 16 — The First Presidency authorized monthly priesthood and auxiliary leadership meetings if they could be held without violating government restrictions concerning use of gas and rubber.

September — The First Presidency began calling mission presidents for areas vacated during the war. This process continued through 1946. The sending of missionaries soon followed the appointment of mission presidents. By the end of 1946, 3,000 missionaries were in the field.

Also, the Tabernacle was opened to the general public for the first time since March 1942.

Sept. 2 — Formal ceremonies of surrender, ending World War II — history's deadliest and most far-reaching conflict — were held aboard the battleship Missouri in Tokyo Bay. Japan had surrendered on Aug. 14 (V-J Day); Germany on May 8 (V-E Day).

Sept. 23 — The Idaho Falls Temple was dedicated by President George Albert Smith.

Oct. 5-7 — The first general, unrestricted conference of the Church in four years was held in the Tabernacle in Salt Lake City. (During World War II, general conferences were limited to general, stake, and ward priesthood leaders.)

Nov. 3 — President George Albert Smith met with U.S. President Harry S. Truman in the White House and presented the Church's plans to use its welfare facilities to help relieve the suffering of Latter-day Saints in Europe.

1946

January — The Church began sending supplies to the Saints in Europe. This continued for the next several years.

Feb. 4 — Elder Ezra Taft Benson of the Quorum of the Twelve, newly called as president of the European Mission, left New York for Europe to administer to the physical and spiritual needs of members there. He traveled throughout Europe for most of the year, visiting Saints who had been isolated by the war, distributing Church welfare supplies, and setting the branches of the Church in order.

May — President George Albert Smith became the first president of the Church to visit Mexico. While in the country, he met with Manuel Avila Camacho,

president of Mexico.

May 2 — The First Presidency instructed local Church leaders that in meetings where the sacrament is passed, it should be passed to the presiding officer first.

1947

The Church reached the 1 million-member mark.

May — The vast project of revising early scripture translations and translating the scriptures into additional languages was begun by the Church offices.

July 22 — A caravan of wagon-canopied automobiles of the same number of people as the original pioneer company, arrived in Salt Lake City after following the Mormon Pioneer Trail.

July 24 — Church members celebrated the 100th anniversary of the Pioneers' arrival in Salt Lake Valley. The "This Is the Place" monument was dedicated by President George Albert Smith.

November — Some 75 tons of potatoes, raised and donated by Dutch members, were delivered to needy families in Germany. A year later, the German Saints harvested their own crop of potatoes.

December — Fast day was set aside for the relief of those in need in Europe. About $210,000 was collected and then distributed to Europeans of all faiths by an agency not connected with the Church.

Also in December, more than one million people visited Temple Square in one year for the first time.

Dec. 1 — An ambitious project to microfilm European records was started by the Genealogical Society.

Dec. 20 — President George Albert Smith announced that following the end of World War II, the Church had the responsibility to carry the gospel to the people at home and abroad, a missionary posture leading to the internationalization of the Church.

1948

April — Mission presidents from around the world reported increasing numbers of baptisms. An expanded building program was started.

June — It was announced that Ricks College in Rexburg, Idaho, would become a four-year college in the 1949-50 school year.

Oct. 17 — The Tabernacle Choir performed its 1,000th national broadcast over radio.

December — Significant increases were made among the Indian membership in the Southwest states.

1949

April 5 — At a special welfare meeting held in conjunction with general conference, the Welfare Program was declared a permanent program of the Church.

A film made by the Church in Hollywood, The Lord's Way, was introduced.

October — For the first time, general conference was broadcast publicly over KSL television in Salt Lake City, although since April 1948 it had been carried by closed-circuit television to other buildings on Temple Square.

1950 **Feb. 24** — The last two missionaries of the Czechoslovakian Mission were released from prison after 27 days and expelled from communist Czechoslovakia.

Feb. 25 — Missionaries returned to Hong Kong for the first time since 1853.

March — The Tahitian mission purchased an 81-foot yacht for mission travel.

June 1 — President George Albert Smith dedicated a statue of Brigham Young at the nation's Capitol.

July 1 — The responsibility of the LDS girls' program was transferred from the Presiding Bishopric to the Young Women's Mutual Improvement Association, where it remained until 1974.

September — Early morning seminaries were inaugurated in Southern California. This was the beginning of a movement that spread seminary throughout the Church on an early morning, nonreleased-time basis.

1951 **April 4** — President George Albert Smith died in Salt Lake City at age 81.
April 9 — President David O. McKay was sustained as ninth president of the Church, with Presidents Stephen L Richards and J. Reuben Clark Jr. as counselors.

July 20 — Because the Korean War reduced the number of young elders being called as missionaries, the First Presidency issued a call for seventies to help fill the need. Many married men subsequently served full-time missions.

1952 A Systematic Program for Teaching the Gospel was published for use by the missionaries of the Church. This inaugurated the use of a standard plan of missionary work throughout the Church, although the specific format of the various lessons was modified from time to time.

March 2 — The new Primary Children's Hospital in Salt Lake City was dedicated. Half the cost of the building had been raised by children of the Church through the continuing Primary penny drive.

April 5 — The Church began carrying the priesthood session of general conference by direct telephone wire to buildings beyond Temple Square.

June — President David O. McKay made a six-week tour of European missions and branches in Holland, Denmark, Sweden, Norway, Finland, Germany, Switzerland, Wales, Scotland and France. During this trip he announced Bern, Switzerland, as site of the first European temple.

Oct. 6 — A letter from the Presiding Bishopric introduced a new Senior Aaronic Priesthood program, with men over 21 years of age organized into separate Aaronic Priesthood quorums. Subsequently, special weekday classes were encouraged in each stake to prepare these brethren for the Melchizedek Priesthood and temple ordinances.

Nov. 25 — Elder Ezra Taft Benson of the Quorum of the Twelve was chosen Secretary of Agriculture by Dwight D. Eisenhower, newly elected president of the United States. Elder Benson served in that capacity for eight years.

Dec. 31 — A letter from the First Presidency announced that the Primary Association had been assigned the duty of establishing the Cub Scout program of the Boy Scouts of America for boys of the Church.

1953 **March 25** — The First Presidency announced that returning missionaries would no longer report directly to General Authorities but, rather, to their stake presidency and high council.

July 9 — Organization of the United Church School System, with Ernest L. Wilkinson as administrator, was publicly announced.

October — The semiannual conference of the Church was broadcast by television for the first time outside the Intermountain area.

1954 **Jan. 2** — President David O. McKay left Salt Lake City on a trip to London, England; South Africa; and South and Central America. He returned in mid-February, and at that point had visited every existing mission of the Church. He was the first president of the Church to visit the South African Mission.

July — The Church announced the inauguration of the Indian Placement Program, whereby Indian students of elementary- and secondary-school age could be placed in foster homes during the school year in order for them to take advantage of better educational opportunities.

July 21 — The First Presidency announced the establishment of the Church College of Hawaii. The college commenced operation Sept. 26, 1955.

Aug. 31 — The First Presidency approved a plan to ordain young men of the Aaronic Priesthood to the office of teacher at age 14 and priest at age 16. The previous ages were 15 and 17.

1955 A special program of missionary work among the Jewish people was organized. It continued until 1959.

January-February — President David O. McKay took a trip covering more than 45,000 miles to the missions of the South Pacific, selected a site for the New Zealand Temple and discussed plans for the building of a Church college in New Zealand.

July — The Church Building Committee was organized to supervise the vast building program of the Church throughout the world.

August-September — The Tabernacle Choir made a major concert tour of Europe.

Sept. 11 — The Swiss Temple, near Bern, was dedicated by President David O. McKay.

Sept. 26 — The Church College of Hawaii, now BYU-Hawaii, was opened.

Dec. 27 — A letter from the Presiding Bishopric announced that students at BYU would be organized into campus wards and stakes beginning Jan. 8, 1956. This move set the pattern for student wards to be organized at Church colleges and institutes of religion wherever their numbers warranted it.

1956
Jan. 1 — Frederick S. Williams, former mission president in Argentina and Uruguay, moved with his family to Peru and contacted Church headquarters for permission to organize a branch and begin missionary work. First missionaries arrived Aug. 7, 1956.

Jan. 8 — The first campus wards and stakes in the Church were organized at BYU.

March 11 — President David O. McKay dedicated the Los Angeles Temple.

Oct. 3 — The new Relief Society Building in Salt Lake City was dedicated.

1957
July — The Pacific Board of Education was organized to supervise all Church schools in the Pacific area.

October — The semiannual general conference was canceled due to a flu epidemic.

1958
A new program for convert integration was adopted during the year, having been previously tried on a pilot basis in several stakes.

April 20 — The New Zealand Temple was dedicated by President David O. McKay.

Sept. 7 — The London Temple was dedicated by President David O. McKay.

Dec. 17 — The Church College of Hawaii in Laie, Hawaii, was dedicated by President David O. McKay.

1959
April 6 — President David O. McKay issued his famous "Every member a missionary" slogan.

Nov. 29 — The Tabernacle Choir received a Grammy award for its recording of the "Battle Hymn of the Republic" at the first television awards show of the National Academy of Recording Arts and Sciences in Los Angeles, Calif.

1960
Jan. 3 — The First Presidency inaugurated a three-month series of weekly Sunday evening fireside programs for youth. President David O. McKay addressed an estimated 200,000 youth at the opening fireside, carried by direct telephone wire to 290 stake centers in the United States, western Canada, and Hawaii.

Also in January, the Church began setting up the administrative framework for a large building program in Europe. By early 1961, administrative building areas outside North America had been established for all parts of the world where the Church existed, and the labor missionary program, which originated in the South Pacific in the early 1950s, was utilized in each area.

March — The First Presidency requested the General Priesthood Committee, with Elder Harold B. Lee of the Quorum of the Twelve as chairman, to make a study of Church programs and curriculum with the object of providing for better "correlation."

July 21 — First Presidency issues statement allowing young men to serve missions at age 19, even though they had not met educational and military qualifications previously required.

1961
March 12 — The first non-English-speaking stake of the Church was organized at The Hague in The Netherlands.

June-July — A number of significant developments took place that revamped the missionary program. The first seminar for all mission presidents was held June 26-July 27 in Salt Lake City, at which new programs were outlined. Also, a new teaching plan of six lessons to be used in every mission of the Church was officially presented, as was the "every member a missionary" program. The missions of the world were divided into nine areas, and a General Authority was called to administer each area.

November — A Language Training Institute was established at Brigham Young University for missionaries called to foreign countries. In 1963, it became the Language Training Mission.

Dec. 3 — The first Spanish-speaking stake in the Church was created in Mexico City.

1962
Feb. 20 — John Glenn became the first American to orbit the earth, a feat he accomplished in one hour and 37 minutes aboard the Friendship 7 space capsule.

April — At the 132nd Annual Conference, the first seminar of General Authorities and presidents of stakes outside North America was held.

Oct. 10 — The Church purchased a shortwave radio station, WRUL, with a transmitter in Boston and studios in New York City. It was subsequently used to transmit Church broadcasts to Europe and South America.

1963 Oct. 12 — The Polynesian Cultural Center, located near the Church College of Hawaii and the temple in Laie, Hawaii, was dedicated.

December — Church storage vaults for records in Little Cottonwood Canyon were completed. They were dedicated on June 22, 1966.

1964 January — A new program of home teaching, replacing ward teaching, was officially inaugurated throughout the Church after having been presented in stake conferences during the last half of 1963.

Jan. 28 — Temple Square and the Lion House in Salt Lake City were recognized as National Historic Landmarks by the federal government.

March — Two LDS schools were opened in Chile, one in Santiago and the other in Vina del Mar. During the early 1970s, the Church opened an elementary school in Paraguay, one in Bolivia and one in Peru.

April — The Mormon Pavilion opened at the New York World's Fair. The Church also built elaborate pavilions for subsequent expositions in San Antonio, Texas (1968); Japan (1970); and Spokane, Wash. (1974).

April 26 — The first meetinghouse In Asia was dedicated for the Tokyo North Branch in Japan.

Nov. 17 — The Oakland Temple was dedicated by President David O. McKay.

1965 January — The family home evening program was inaugurated and wards had a choice of which night in the week to hold home evenings. A weekly home evening had been encouraged before by Church leaders, but now the Church published a formal family home evening manual, which was placed in every LDS home.

Jan. 18 — The Tabernacle Choir sang at the inauguration of U.S. President Lyndon B. Johnson in Washington, D.C.

February — The Italian government gave permission for LDS missionaries to proselyte in the country. No missionary work had been done there since 1862.

September — Because of the war in Vietnam, a missionary quota of two per ward was established within the United States to comply with Selective Service requests.

October — With the appointment of President Joseph Fielding Smith and Elder Thorpe B. Isaacson as counselors, President David O. McKay announced that the First Presidency would be increased to five, instead of three members.

1966 May 1 — The first stake in South America was organized at Sao Paulo, Brazil.

August — A new visitors center on Temple Square

was opened to tourists. While this would be the most elaborate center, it represented a trend of building visitors centers at historic sites and temples and at various other locations during the 1960s and 1970s.

1967 April — For the first time, seven Mexican television and radio stations carried a session of general conference.

June 10 — The Six-Day War in the Middle East ended with Israel holding conquered Arab territory four times its own size.

Sept. 29 — The new administrative position of regional representative of the Twelve was announced, and the first 69 regional representatives were called and given their initial training.

1968 Feb. 2 — Six missionaries from the Taiwan and Hong Kong zones of the Southern Far East Mission were transferred to Thailand to begin missionary work.

Oct. 22 — The Church received official recognition in Spain. The first missionaries arrived in June, 1969.

1969 January — Two-month language training missions began. Language training for missionaries prior to their departure to their mission field first began during the early 1960s for Spanish, Portuguese and German language missions.

Jan. 20 — The Tabernacle Choir sang at U.S. President Richard M. Nixon's inauguration in Washington, D.C.

July 20 — U.S. astronaut Neil Armstrong became the first man to walk on the moon when he descended from the lunar module Eagle; he was followed 18 minutes later by Edwin Aldrin, pilot of the lunar module.

Nov. 1 — The Southeast Asia Mission formally opened with headquarters in Singapore. In January 1970, the first missionaries were sent to Indonesia, which was part of the mission.

1970 January — A computerized system for recording and reporting Church contributions went into operation.

Jan. 18 — President David O. McKay died in Salt Lake City at age 96.

Jan. 23 — President Joseph Fielding Smith was ordained and set apart as the 10th president of the Church and chose Presidents Harold B. Lee and N. Eldon Tanner as counselors.

March 15 — The first stake in Asia was organized in Tokyo, Japan.

March 22 — The first stake in Africa was organized in Transvaal, South Africa.

October — Monday was designated for family home evening throughout the Church; no other Church activity was to be scheduled during that time.

1971

January — Publication of new Church magazines began: the Ensign for adults, the New Era for youth and the Friend for children.

Aug. 27-29 — The first area conference of the Church was held in Manchester, England. Before the program of holding large area conferences ended in 1980, 63 were held throughout the world.

September — All LDS women were automatically enrolled as members of the Relief Society; dues were eliminated.

1972

Church sports tournaments and dance festivals were directed to be held on a regional basis instead of an all-Church basis.

Jan. 14 — The Church Historical Department was formed in a reorganization of the Church Historian's Office. Church library, archives, and history divisions were created within the new department.

Jan. 18 — The Ogden Temple was dedicated by President Joseph Fielding Smith.

Feb. 9 — The Provo Temple was dedicated by President Smith.

July 2 — President Smith died in Salt Lake City at age 95.

July 7 — President Harold B. Lee was ordained and set apart as the 11th president of the Church, with Presidents N. Eldon Tanner and Marion G. Romney as counselors.

November — The MIA was realigned into the Aaronic Priesthood and Melchizedek Priesthood MIA and was placed directly under priesthood leadership.

1973

A new set of missionary lessons was completed for use in all missions. It was the first change in missionary lessons since 1961.

February — The first Church agricultural missionaries to leave the United States were sent to the Guatemala-El Salvador Mission.

Feb. 4 — The Marriott Activities Center at BYU was dedicated. Seating 22,000, it was the largest such arena on any university campus in the United States.

March 8 — The first stake on mainland Asia was organized in Seoul, Korea.

April 7 — The creation of the Welfare Services Department was announced in general conference. The new organization brought the three welfare units — health services, social services and welfare — into full correlation.

Dec. 26 — President Harold B. Lee died in Salt Lake City at age 74.

Dec. 30 — President Spencer W. Kimball was ordained and set apart as the 12th president of the Church, with Presidents N. Eldon Tanner and Marion G. Romney as counselors.

1974

March 23 — In an exchange of pioneer homes, the Church traded the Brigham Young Forest Farm home in Salt Lake City to the state of Utah for use in the state's Pioneer State Park. The Church acquired the Brigham Young winter home in St. George and the Jacob Hamblin home in nearby Santa Clara, Utah, for use as visitor and information centers.

June 23 — MIA was dropped from the name of Church youth programs.

Sept. 1 — Church College of Hawaii became a branch of Brigham Young University and was renamed Brigham Young University-Hawaii Campus.

Sept. 6 — The First Presidency announced that the Church was divesting itself of its 15 hospitals in three western states and turning them over to a non-Church, non-profit organization, Intermountain Health Care. The Church completed the legal steps for divesting the hospitals on March 21, 1975.

Oct. 3 — Seventies quorums were authorized in all stakes and all quorums in the Church were renamed after the stake.

Nov. 19 — President Spencer W. Kimball dedicated the Washington Temple at Kensington, Md. Visitors during pre-dedication tours September through November totaled 758,327, topping the previous record of 662,401 at the Los Angeles Temple in 1956.

1975

May 3 — Citing accelerated growth of the Church worldwide, the First Presidency announced the creation of an area supervisory program and the assignment of six Assistants to the Twelve to oversee Church activities while residing outside the United States and Canada. The number of these foreign areas was increased to eight later in the year.

May 17 — A supervisory program for missions in the United States and Canada was announced, along with the assignment of members of the Quorum of the Twelve as advisers and other General Authorities as supervisors of the 12 areas.

June 27 — The end of auxiliary conferences was announced during the opening session of the 1975 June Conference. These conferences would be replaced with annual regional meetings for priesthood and auxiliary leaders.

July 24 — The 28-story Church Office Building in Salt Lake City was dedicated by President Spencer W. Kimball.

Aug. 8-17 — President Kimball spoke to a total of 44,500 members at five area conferences in the Far East, Japan, the Philippines, Hong Kong, Taiwan and Korea

Oct. 3 — President Kimball announced in general conference the organization of the First Quorum of the Seventy, and the first three members of the quorum were sustained.

Oct. 6-11 — Brigham Young University observed its 100th anniversary during homecoming week.

Nov. 7-9 — Incident to the rapid growth of the Church in Mexico, 15 stakes were created in Mexico City in one weekend.

Nov. 18 — The Church Genealogical Department was organized with five divisions, two of which were formerly known as the Genealogical Society.

1976 Feb. 15- March 2 — A total of
53,000 members in the South Pacific attended nine area conferences in American Samoa, Western Samoa, New Zealand, Fiji, Tonga, Tahiti, and Australia to hear counsel from President Spencer W. Kimball and other General Authorities.

April 3 — Members attending general conference accepted Joseph Smith's Vision of the Celestial Kingdom and Joseph F. Smith's Vision of the Redemption of the Dead for addition to the Pearl of Great Price. These scriptures became part of the Doctrine and Covenants on June 6, 1979.

June 5 — The Teton Dam in southeastern Idaho burst, sending a wall of water, between 12 and 20 feet high, onto the mostly LDS towns below. About 40,000 people, most of them members of the Church, were driven from their homes.

June 18-22 — President Kimball spoke at three area conferences in England and Scotland, which were attended by more than a total of 17,000 members.

June 25 — Missouri Gov. Christopher S. Bond signed an executive order rescinding the extermination order issued in 1838 by Gov. Lilburn W. Boggs.

July 4 — President Kimball spoke at a Church-sponsored U.S. Bicentennial devotional attended by more than 23,000 people at the Capitol Centre in Landover, Md. Numerous additional activities involved Church members in the United States during the year-long Bicentennial observance.

July 31- Aug. 8 — President Kimball addressed a total of 25,000 members from 12 countries in Europe at five area conferences in France, Finland, Denmark, The Netherlands and Germany.

Oct. 1 – Members of the First Council of the Seventy and the Assistants to the Twelve were released in general conference and called to the new First Quorum of the Seventy. Franklin D. Richards was named the first senior president.

1977 Jan. 1 — The First Presidency
announced a new format for general conferences. General sessions would be held on the first Sunday of each April and October and the preceding Saturday. Regional representative seminars would be held on the preceding Friday.

Feb. 5 — The First Presidency announced that the Quorum of the Twelve would oversee ecclesiastical matters and the Presiding Bishopric would have responsibility for temporal programs.

May 14 — A bishops central storehouse, the second in the Church and first outside of Salt Lake City, opened at Colton, Calif. Also, the Young Men program was restructured.

May 22 — Formation of a new Church Activities Committee, with responsibility for coordinating cultural arts and physical activities, was announced.

May 30 — Poland granted legal status to the Church.

July 1 — In response to continued growth in membership worldwide, the geographic subdivisions of the Church, previously known as areas, were renamed zones, and the 11 zones were subdivided into areas. Members of the First Quorum of the Seventy were assigned as zone advisers and area supervisors.

Aug 7 — North Dakota became the final state of the United States to have a stake organized and headquartered within its boundaries when the Fargo North Dakota stake was created.

Oct. 1 — The Church published A Topical Guide to the Scriptures of The Church of Jesus Christ of Latter-day Saints, the first product of a continuing scriptural-aids project established by the First Presidency.

1978 March 31 — President Spencer W.
Kimball announced that semiannual rather than quarterly stake conferences would be held starting in 1979.

April 1 — President Kimball emphasized the four-generation program, which later became the basis for the Church's computerized Ancestral File.

June 9 — In a letter dated June 8 and made public the following day, the First Presidency announced the revelation that worthy men of all races would be eligible to receive the priesthood. On Sept. 30, members accepted the revelation by a sustaining vote at general conference. The First Presidency's announcement is now Official Declaration - 2 in the Doctrine and Covenants.

July 1 — The Relief Society Monument to Women was dedicated in Nauvoo, Ill., by President Kimball.

Sept. 9 — A new missionary training program was announced: Missionaries to English-speaking missions would receive four weeks training while those learning other languages would continue to receive eight weeks training at the new Missionary Training Center in Provo, Utah, which replaced the Language Training Mission and the Mission Home in Salt Lake City.

Sept. 16 — Women and girls 12 years of age and over gathered for a first-ever special closed-circuit audio conference, similar to general conference priesthood broadcasts.

Sept. 30 — A new special emeritus status for General Authorities was announced in general conference, and seven members of the First Quorum of the Seventy were so designated.

Oct. 26 — The Missionary Training Center in Provo, Utah, previously the Language Training Mission constructed in 1976, began training all missionaries.

Nov. 9 — Elder and Sister Rendell N. Mabey and Elder and Sister Edwin Q. Cannon arrived in Nigeria as special representatives of the Church to open missionary work in West Africa.

1979
Feb. 3 — The Church Genealogical Department announced a new "family entry system" to allow submissions of names of deceased ancestors for temple work whose birthplaces and birthdates are unknown.

Feb. 18 — The Church's 1,000th stake was created at Nauvoo, Ill., by President Ezra Taft Benson of the Quorum of the Twelve.

June 6 — Joseph Smith's Vision of the Celestial Kingdom and Joseph F. Smith's Vision of the Redemption of the Dead were transferred from the Pearl of Great Price to the Doctrine and Covenants, becoming Sections 137 and 138, respectively.

Sept. 12-14 — The Tabernacle Choir, which celebrated the golden anniversary of its nationally broadcast radio program in July, toured Japan and Korea.

Sept. 29 — A new 2,400-page edition of the King James version of the Bible, with many special features, including a topical guide, a Bible dictionary, and a revolutionary footnote system, was published by the Church.

Oct. 29 — The first two converts of eastern Africa were baptized in Kenya.

Oct. 24 — President Spencer W. Kimball, on a tour of the Middle East, dedicated the Orson Hyde Memorial Gardens on the Mount of Olives in Jerusalem.

1980
Feb. 22 — The Presidency of the First Quorum of the Seventy was reorganized to strengthen the lines of administration at Church headquarters. The executive directors of the Missionary, Curriculum, Priesthood and Genealogy departments became members of the presidency.

March 2 — U.S. and Canadian members began a new consolidated meeting schedule that put priesthood, sacrament, and auxiliary meetings into one three-hour time block on Sundays.

April 6 — Celebrating the Church's 150th anniversary, President Spencer W. Kimball conducted part of general conference from the newly restored Peter Whitmer farmhouse at Fayette, N.Y., the site where the Church was organized. The proceedings in Fayette were linked with the congregation in the Tabernacle in Salt Lake City via satellite, the first time a satellite was used in the Church for transmitting broadcasts of general conference.

May — Missionary work opened in Haiti and Belize.

Oct. 18-Nov. 1 — The last of a series of large area conferences, presided over by the president of the Church, was held in six major cities in the Far East: Manila, Philippines; Hong Kong; Taipei, Taiwan; Seoul, Korea; and Tokyo and Osaka, Japan.

1981
Jan. 20 — The Tabernacle Choir participated in the inaugural festivities for President Ronald Reagan.

April 1 — Plans to build nine smaller temples in the United States, Central America, Asia, Africa and Europe were announced by President Spencer W. Kimball: Chicago, Ill.; Dallas, Texas; Guatemala City, Guatemala; Lima, Peru; Frankfurt, Germany; Stockholm, Sweden; Seoul, Korea; Manila, Philippines; and Johannesburg, South Africa.

April 3 — At the regional representatives meeting, President Spencer W. Kimball outlined three responsibilities to carry out the mission of the Church: Proclaim the gospel, perfect the saints and redeem the dead.

May 5 — The First Presidency publicly voiced its opposition to the proposed basing of the MX missile system in the Utah-Nevada desert.

July 23 — Elder Gordon B. Hinckley was called as a counselor in the First Presidency, the first time since the administration of President David O. McKay that a president had more than two counselors.

Sept. 12 — A smaller, less-expensive ward meetinghouse, called the Sage Plan, was announced by the First Presidency.

Sept. 26 — The first copies of a new version of the Triple Combination (Book of Mormon, Doctrine and Covenants and Pearl of Great Price), with extensive scripture helps, were made available to the public.

Oct. 3 — A network of 500 satellite dishes for stake centers outside Utah was announced.

1982
March 18 — Three Church executive councils were created: the Missionary Executive Council, the Priesthood Executive Council, and the Temple and Genealogy Executive Council.

April 1 — It was announced that Church membership had reached the 5-million member mark.

April 2 — At general conference, major changes in financing Church meetinghouses were announced, shifting construction costs to general Church funds and utility costs to local units. Also, the term of service for single elders serving full-time missions was reduced from two years to 18 months.

Sept. 5 — The Mormon Tabernacle Choir celebrated 50 years of continuous weekly broadcasts over the CBS radio network.

Sept. 10 — U.S. President Ronald Reagan visited Utah to tour a Church cannery and see the Church Welfare Program in action.

Oct. 3 — Elder Boyd K. Packer of the Quorum of the Twelve and a member of the Scriptures Publication Committee announced that a subtitle was being added to the Book of Mormon: "Another Testament of Jesus Christ."

Oct. 30 — A visitors center and historic site opened its doors in the three-story Grandin printing building in Palmyra, N.Y., where the first copies of the Book of Mormon were printed in 1830.

1983
Aug. 5, 9 — For the first time in Church history, two temples were dedicated within a week's time: the Apia Samoa Temple on Aug. 5 and the Nuku'alofa Tonga Temple on Aug. 9; both by President Gordon B. Hinckley.

Oct. 16 — The first of a series of multi-stake (later known as regional) conferences was held in London, England.

1984
Jan. 7 — Premier Zhao Ziyang of the People's Republic of China visited the BYU-Hawaii campus and the adjacent Polynesian Cultural Center during the first visit of a Chinese premier to the United States since the People's Republic of China was formed in 1949.

March 25 — A new program — the Four-Phase Genealogical Facilities Program — was announced, enabling wards and branches to establish genealogical facilities in their meetinghouses.

April 7 — The first members of the First Quorum of the Seventy called for temporary three- to five-year terms were sustained. They were later sustained to the Second Quorum of the Seventy, created in 1989.

June 24 — Members of the First Quorum of the Seventy were appointed to serve as area presidencies in 13 major geographical areas of the Church — seven in the United States and Canada and six in other parts of the world.

Oct. 28 — The Church's 1,500th stake was created 150 years after the first stake was organized in Kirtland, Ohio. The landmark stake was the Ciudad Obregon Mexico Yaqui Stake.

Nov. 26 — The First Presidency announced that, beginning Jan. 1, the term of full-time missionary service for single elders would again be 24 months. It had been shortened from two years to 18 months in April 1982.

1985
Jan. 27 — Latter-day Saints in the United States and Canada

participated in a special fast to benefit victims of famine in Africa and other parts of the world. The fast raised more than $6 million.

June 29 — The Freiberg Temple, located in the German Democratic Republic, then communist-controlled, was dedicated by President Gordon B. Hinckley.

Aug. 2 — A new LDS hymnbook, the first revision in 37 years, came off the presses.

Aug. 24 — The Johannesburg South Africa Temple was dedicated by President Hinckley. With the dedication of this building, there was now a temple on every continent except Antarctica.

Oct. 23 — The Church Genealogical Library in Salt Lake City was dedicated by President Hinckley.

Nov. 5 — President Spencer W. Kimball died in Salt Lake City at age 90.

Nov. 10 — President Ezra Taft Benson was ordained and set apart as the 13th president of the Church, with President Hinckley and President Thomas S. Monson as counselors.

1986
April 30 — Church membership was estimated to have reached the 6-million member milestone.

June 22 — The 1,600th stake of the Church was created by President Monson in Kitchener, Ontario.

July 6 — New missionary discussions, which focus on "teaching from the heart," were approved for use in all English-speaking missions.

Oct. 4 — Seventies quorums in stakes throughout the Church were discontinued.

Oct. 11 — In the first Churchwide Young Women activity, an estimated 300,000 gathered at sites around the world to release helium-filled balloons containing personal messages from the young women.

1987
Feb. 15 — The Tabernacle Choir marked its 3,000th radio broadcast in a series that had become the longest-running network program in the free world.

March 12 — It was announced that the Church-owned Hotel Utah, a landmark in downtown Salt Lake City for 76 years, would close as a hotel Aug. 31 and be renovated as a meetinghouse and office building.

July 15 — The Genealogical Library celebrated the conversion of the last card from its card catalog to computer.

July 24-26 — Church members throughout Britain commemorated the 150th anniversary of the first missionary work in Great Britain. Thirteen General Authorities, including President Ezra Taft Benson and President Gordon B. Hinckley, attended various events, which included dedication of historical sites, firesides and conferences.

Aug. 15 — The Church's Genealogical Department was renamed the Family History Department.

Sept. 4 — A letter from the First Presidency announced the discontinuance of the International Mission. Responsibility for its areas reverted to the respective area presidencies of the Church.

1988
Jan. 30-31 — Seven stakes were created in one weekend in Lima, Peru, by Elder Charles Didier of the Seventy.

May 15 — Elder Neal A. Maxwell of the Quorum of the Twelve organized the Aba Nigeria Stake, the first Church stake in West Africa.

May 28 — The First Presidency issued a statement on the subject of AIDS, stressing chastity before marriage, fidelity in marriage, and abstinence from homosexual behavior, yet extending sympathy to those who have contracted the disease.

June 1 — The Church was granted legal recognition in Hungary, the first of several such steps in Eastern European nations during the next two years.

August — The Church reached the milestone of having completed 100 million endowments for the dead.

The BYU Folk Dancers were the only North American dance company to perform at opening ceremonies of the 1988 Olympic Games in Seoul, Korea, viewed by an estimated 1 billion people worldwide.

Oct. 16 — Elder David B. Haight created the 1,700th stake of the Church. The new stake was in Manaus, Brazil, a city of 1.5 million in the heart of the Amazon jungle.

Oct. 24-28 — President Thomas S. Monson led a delegation of Church leaders that met with the German Democratic Republic's top government officials. It was announced Nov. 12 that the Church had been granted rights to send missionaries to the DDR and for LDS members from the DDR to serve as missionaries in other countries.

1989
El Salvador reached self-sufficiency in local full-time missionaries.
Jan. 28 — Elders Russell M. Nelson and Dallin H. Oaks of the Quorum of the Twelve completed an eight-day visit to China and were assured by high-level Chinese leaders that people are free to practice religious beliefs in that country.

April 1-2 — The Second Quorum of the Seventy was created and all General Authorities serving under a five-year call were sustained as members, along with another eight newly called General Authorities.

May 16 — The BYU Jerusalem Center for Near Eastern Studies was dedicated by President Howard W. Hunter of the Quorum of the Twelve.

June 14 — LDS missionaries and those of the Jehovah's Witnesses were expelled from Ghana, a western Africa nation where 6,000 Church members live. The Church had no advance notice of the ban. The LDS missionaries were able to return to Ghana in 1990.

June 15 — Ground was broken for the first LDS meetinghouse in Poland.

June 25 — The 100th stake in Mexico was created in Tecalco. Mexico became the first country outside the United States with 100 or more stakes.

June 27 — The renovated Carthage Jail complex in Illinois, where the Prophet Joseph Smith was martyred, was dedicated by President Gordon B. Hinckley, highlighting activities commemorating the 150th anniversary of the Mormon settlement of Nauvoo, Ill.

Oct. 17 — The first LDS meetinghouse in the Republic of Hungary, located in the capital city of Budapest, was dedicated by President Thomas S. Monson.

Nov. 9 — The Berlin Wall came down, paving the way for eventual unification of East and West Germany.

Nov. 25 — A major change in policy for financing local Church units in the United States and Canada was announced by the First Presidency. Ward members would no longer have stake and ward budget assessments.

1990
Feb. 25 — The Church was officially recognized in Kenya.

April 2 — A new Church software package called FamilySearch, designed to simplify the task of family history research, was released by the Church.

May 21 — The U.S. Supreme Court handed down a unanimous decision that money given directly to missionaries was not a deductible donation under federal tax law. The Church encouraged members to follow established procedures of contributing through their wards.

July — New missions in the Eastern European countries of Czechoslovakia, Hungary, and Poland highlighted the record 29 missions created in 1990.

Sept. 13 — Registration of the Leningrad Branch of the Church was approved by the Council on Religious Affairs of the Council of Ministers in the Soviet Union.

November — The First Presidency announced in November a new policy for United States and Canada, effective Jan. 1, 1991, that would equalize contributions required to maintain a full-time missionary.

Nov. 30 — The government of Ghana gave permission for the Church to resume activities in that West African country.

1991

April 19 — Recognition of the Church in the Ivory Coast, the center of French West Africa, was announced at a special meeting of Church members in Abidjan.

April 27 — Fifty years after the Church began keeping individual membership records, it completed computerizing membership records worldwide.

May 1 — The 500,000th full-time missionary in this dispensation was called.

May 26 — The 1,800th stake in the Church, the San Francisco de Macoris Dominican Republic Stake, was created.

June 8 — The Tabernacle Choir embarked on a 21-day tour of eight European countries, including five countries in which the choir had not performed before: Hungary, Austria, Czechoslovakia, Poland and the Soviet Union.

June 24 — The Russian Republic, the largest in the Soviet Union, granted formal recognition to the Church following the Tabernacle Choir's concert in Moscow's Bolshoi Theater.

Sept. 1 — Membership in the Church reached 8 million, about two years after membership hit the 7 million mark in December 1989.

1992

Aug. 15 — Commemorating the "second rescue" of the ill-fated Willie and Martin handcart pioneers, President Hinckley dedicated three monuments in central Wyoming. The Riverton Wyoming Stake researched family histories and performed temple ordinances for those pioneers whose work was not previously done.

Aug. 30 — The Church's 1,900th stake, the Orlando Florida South Stake, was organized by Elder Neal A. Maxwell of the Quorum of the Twelve.

Sept. 26 — The First Presidency authorized the use of humanitarian relief funds to be sent to Somalia and other African nations in the grip of the drought of the century. In an initial response, one million pounds of food was shipped.

Oct. 8 — The Church was legally recognized in Tanzania.

Dec. 6 — The Church reached a milestone of 20,000 wards and branches with the creation of the Harvest Park Ward in the Salt Lake Granger South Stake.

Dec. 15 — A gospel literacy effort sponsored by the Relief Society to help increase literacy throughout the Church was announced in a letter from the First Presidency to priesthood and Relief Society leaders.

Dec. 26 — The Tabernacle Choir left on a tour of the Holy Land. Concerts were later held in Jerusalem, Tel Aviv and Haifa.

1993

The Church received legal recognition in Italy, Madagascar, Cameroon and Ethiopia.

Jan. 6 — Four Church-service missionaries entered Hanoi, Vietnam, to give humanitarian service, teaching English to doctors and staff at a children's hospital and to teachers, staff and children at a school for young children.

April 6 — The centennial of the Salt Lake Temple was observed at a Tabernacle Choir special program, and a special mural was placed in the temple.

June 27 — After being refurbished and remodeled, the former Hotel Utah was rededicated and renamed the Joseph Smith Memorial Building, housing office and meeting facilities for the Church and a theater showing the new film "Legacy."

June 29 — The government of Mexico formally registered the LDS Church, grant-ing it all the rights of a religious organization, including the right to own property.

1994

Feb. 13 — The First Presidency announced that the 87-year-old Uintah Stake Tabernacle in Vernal, Utah, would be renovated and dedicated as Utah's 10th temple. It was the first existing building to be renovated into a temple.

May 30 — President Ezra Taft Benson, 94, president of the Church for 8 1/2 years, died in Salt Lake City.

June 5 — President Howard W. Hunter was ordained and set apart as the 14th president of the Church. Set apart as his counselors were President Gordon B. Hinckley and President Thomas S. Monson.

Aug. 6 — One-third of the population of the United States has been visited by Church representatives, and 36 percent have friends or relatives who are LDS, the Missionary Department announced.

1995

Jan. 21 — The Church reached 9 million members.

March 3 — President Hunter died at his Salt Lake City home after serving as Church president for less than nine months, the shortest tenure of any president.

March 12 — President Gordon B. Hinckley was ordained and set apart as the 15th president of the Church. Set apart as his counselors were President Thomas S. Monson, first counselor, and President James E. Faust, second counselor.

April 1 — A new administrative position, Area Authority, was announced by President Hinckley during the priesthood session of general conference. The position of regional representative was discontinued after 28 years.

June 16 — The International Olympic Committee announced that the site for the 2002 Winter Olympics would be in Salt Lake City.

Sept. 23 — At the annual General Relief Society Meeting, the First Presidency and Quorum of the Twelve issued a Proclamation to the World on the Family, reaffirming that "the family is central to the Creator's plan for the eternal destiny of His children."

Dec. 18 — President Hinckley was interviewed by CBS television host Mike Wallace on the show 60 Minutes. The show was broadcast in April 1996.

1996
Feb. 28 — A milestone was reached as a majority of members, 4,720,000, lived outside the United States, compared to 4,719,000 living within.

April 6 — President Gordon B. Hinckley announced at general conference that a new assembly hall four times the size of the Tabernacle would be built.

May 27-28 — President Hinckley, on a tour of the Orient, became the first Church president ever to visit mainland China. He also visited, from May 17 to June 1, Japan, Korea, Hong Kong, Cambodia, Vietnam, the Philippines and Saipan.

June 17-July 12 — A commemorative wagon train crossed Iowa, retracing the path of the 1846 exodus from Nauvoo, Ill.

Nov. 2 The First Presidency announced the establishment of Latter-day Saint Charities, a charitable, nonprofit corporation designed to help the Church deliver humanitarian aid to the poor and needy of the world.

Nov. 8-16 — President Hinckley spoke to gatherings of Church members and missionaries in Colombia, Peru, Bolivia, Chile, Argentina and Brazil, and broke ground for temples in Bolivia and Brazil.

Nov. 18 — Elder Joseph B. Wirthlin of the Quorum of the Twelve became the first apostle to address Latter-day Saints in Far East Russia when he spoke in Vladivostok, Russia, in the region of Siberia.

1997
January — The Church in Africa reached a milestone when the 100,000th member on the continent was baptized. The milestone marked the almost doubling of the membership in Africa in six years.

March 9 — Chile became the fourth nation in the world to have 100 or more stakes, with the creation of the Puerto Varas Chile Stake.

April 5 — During general conference, the organization of the Third, Fourth and Fifth Quorums of the Seventy was announced. Area Authorities were then ordained as Seventies, and their titled changed to Area Authority Seventy.

April 19-21 — The commemorative Mormon Trail Wagon Train, which the worldwide public would view as the centerpiece of the sesquicentennial observance of the Mormon Pioneer trek, left from two locations, Council Bluffs, Iowa, on April 19, and

Winter Quarters (Omaha), Neb., on April 21. The two contingents would later merge.

May 8-17 — President Hinckley toured the South Pacific nations of New Zealand and Australia, speaking 15 times in seven cities to a total of more than 55,000 members.

June 1 — A letter from the First Presidency announced significant modifications to the curriculum and gospel study program for the Melchizedek Priesthood and Relief Society, providing a similar meeting and instruction schedule for both organizations.

June 15 — The 100th stake in the Church's Pacific Area, the Suva Fiji North Stake, was created.

July 22 — After 93 days on the trail, the commemorative Mormon Trail Wagon Train from Winter Quarters, Neb., entered Salt Lake City, where they were greeted by about 50,000 cheering people at This Is the Place State Park. There, they heard an address by President Hinckley.

Aug. 7-14 — President Hinckley delivered 12 addresses to about 56,000 people in four nations of South America: Paraguay, Ecuador, Venezuela and Uruguay.

Oct. 4 — It was announced in general conference by President Hinckley that the Church would construct temples in remote areas of the Church that have small LDS populations. The first were to be built in Anchorage, Alaska; in the LDS colonies of northern Mexico; and in Monticello, Utah.

Oct. 10-17 — President. Hinckley addressed a total of 52,500 members in eight islands of the Pacific: Samoa, Hawaii, American Samoa, Tonga, Fiji and Tahiti.

November — Sometime during the first week of November, the Church reached 10 million members, according to Church estimates.

Nov. 8-13 — President Hinckley addressed 42,000 Church members in Mexico City and an additional 12,000 in Puebla, Mexico. On the trip, he met with Mexico's president, Dr. Ernesto Zedillo.

1998
Feb. 14-22 — President Gordon B. Hinckley became the first Church president ever to visit West Africa during a nine-day tour of Nigeria, Ghana, Kenya, Zimbabwe and South Africa. On Feb. 16, he announced plans for the first temple to be built in West Africa, in Ghana.

March 9-15 — President Hinckley addressed more than 53,000 members in 10 cities of northern Mexico: Hermosillo, Ciudad Obregon, Culiacan, Guadalajara, Torreon, Leon, Ciudad Victoria, Monterrey, Chihuahua and Ciudad Juarez.

March 26 — The replica of the Joseph Smith Sr. family log home near Palmyra, N.Y., was dedicated by President Hinckley. The home was the location where the Prophet Joseph Smith was visited in his youth by the Angel Moroni.

March 27 — After 2 1/2 years of reconstruction, the Egbert B. Grandin Building, in Palmyra, N.Y., where the Book of Mormon was published in 1829, was dedicated as a Church historic site by President Hinckley.

April 4 — President Hinckley announced in general conference that the Church would construct an additional 30 smaller temples that would bring the total number of operating temples in the Church to 100 by the year 2000.

July 26 — The Monticello Utah Temple, the prototype for a new generation of small temples in less-populous areas of the Church, was dedicated in southeast Utah by President Hinckley.

Nov. 19-21 — President Hinckley toured areas devastated caused by Hurricane Mitch in Nicaragua and Honduras and spoke to 19,000 members. In all, the Church sent 840,000 pounds of relief supplies to the affected areas.

1999
Feb. 20 — The First Presidency made a landmark announcement that a temple would be built in Palmyra, N.Y.

April 1 — The city of Omaha, Neb., deeded to the Church the pioneer cemetery at historic Winter Quarters, where some 600 Latter-day Saints are buried.

April 4 — In his closing remarks at general conference, President Hinckley made the surprise announcement that the historic Nauvoo Temple would be rebuilt.

May 24 — The FamilySearch Internet Genealogy Service, which promised to be the greatest boon to family research since the invention of the microfilm, was officially launched by President Hinckley.

June 1 — The Mormon Youth Chorus and Symphony was disbanded, and the chorus, renamed the Temple Square Chorale, became a training choir for the Tabernacle Choir. The symphony orchestra was reorganized under a new name, the Orchestra at Temple Square.

Oct. 2-3 — The last general conference in the Tabernacle on Temple Square — the site of general conferences since 1867 — was held. Future general conferences would be held in the new Conference Center.

Nov. 14 — For the first time in the history of the Church, two temples, both in Canada, were dedicated on the same day. The Halifax Nova Scotia Temple was dedicated by President Hinckley and the Regina Saskatchewan Temple was dedicated by President Boyd K. Packer, acting president of the Quorum of the Twelve.

2000
Jan. 1 — The First Presidency and the Quorum of the Twelve issued

their testimonies of the Savior in a document titled "The Living Christ."

Late February or early March — The 100 millionth copy of the Book of Mormon, since it was first published in 1830 was printed. Another milestone was reached in 2000 when the Book of Mormon was printed in its 100th language.

April 1-2 — The first general conference to be held in the new Conference Center convened, with more than 400,000 requests for free tickets, far exceeding the 21,000-seat capacity of the hall.

April 6 — The Palmyra New York Temple, located on what was once the 100-acre Joseph Smith Sr. farm and overlooking the Sacred Grove, was dedicated by President Hinckley. An estimated 1.3 million members participated in the first session, via the Church satellite system.

April 23 — The rebuilt Gadfield Elm Chapel, the oldest LDS chapel in England that was constructed in 1836 by members of the United Brethren and given to the Church four years later after 600 members of that faith joined the Church en masse, was rededicated by Elder Jeffrey R. Holland of the Quorum of the Twelve.

May 20-21 — Three temples were dedicated in two days, the first time in the history of the Church that had occurred. They were the Tampico Mexico Temple on May 20, and the Villahermosa Mexico and the Nashville Tennessee temples, both on May 21.

September — The Church reached 11 million members and, for the first time in its 170-year history, it had more non-English-speaking members than English-speaking.

Oct. 1 — The 100th operating temple in the Church, the Boston Massachusetts Temple, was dedicated by President Hinckley.

Oct. 7-8 — The new 21,000-seat Conference Center, across the street north of Temple Square, was dedicated during general conference by President Hinckley.

Nov. 5 — Following a procedure established by the Prophet Joseph Smith for the cornerstone laying of the original Nauvoo Temple April 6, 1841, President Hinckley presided over the dedication of the four cornerstones of the Nauvoo Illinois Temple.

Dec. 19 — The government of Kazakhstan, one of the former republics of what was once the Soviet Union, granted the Church official recognition.

2001
Jan. 20 – At the inauguration of U.S. President George W. Bush, the Mormon Tabernacle Choir sang in the inaugural parade in Washington, D.C., the sixth time the choir has participated in presidential inauguration festivities.

Feb. 15 – The First Presidency and Quorum of the Twelve approved a series of guidelines to reaffirm the centrality of the Savior in the name of the Church.

Church members, news organizations and others were asked to use the full and correct name of the Church – The Church of Jesus Christ of Latter-day Saints – and to avoid use of the term "Mormon Church."

March 31 – A worldwide Perpetual Education Fund, based on principles similar to those underlying the Perpetual Emigration Fund of the 1800s, was announced by President Gordon B. Hinckley.

Aug. 7 – Sea Trek 2001, an epic voyage of eight tall sailing ships commemorating the 19th century gathering of European converts to Zion, departed from Esbjerg, Denmark, on the first leg of its 59-day journey, which concluded Oct. 4 in New York City.

Aug. 10 — Ricks College in Rexburg, Idaho, was officially renamed Brigham Young University-Idaho and became a four-year university.

Sept. 7-8 — The first two meetinghouses built by the Church in the Ukraine Kiev Mission were dedicated on consecutive dates in the districts of Livoberezhny and Svyatoshinsky.

Sept. 20 — President Hinckley was among 26 religious leaders who met at the White House in Washington, D.C., with U.S. President George W. Bush regarding the terrorist attacks in New York City and Washington D.C., on Sept. 11, 2001.

Nov. 11 — The first meetinghouse built by the Church in the Czech Republic was dedicated in Brno.

Dec. 2 — The first meetinghouse in Sri Lanka was dedicated in the capital city of Colombo.

Dec. 17 — After a 32-month absence of proselytizing missionaries in the Republic of Serbia, six missionaries from the Bulgaria Sofia Mission returned to Serbia. Missionaries were withdrawn from the country in March 1999 because of conflict in the region.

2002 **Jan. 19** – The first meetinghouse in Serbia was dedicated in Belgrade. Feb. 2 – The first meetinghouse in India, the Rajahmundry Branch, was dedicated.

Feb. 8-24 – Salt Lake City hosted the 2002 Winter Olympics, with the Tabernacle Choir performing in the opening ceremonies to an estimated TV viewing audience of 3.5 billion people.

Some 10,000-20,000 Olympic visitors from many nations visited Temple Square each day.

Feb. 8 – During his brief visit to Salt Lake City to formally open the Winter Oympics, U.S. President George W. Bush and his wife, Laura, visited with the First Presidency.

May 22 – The first missionary training center in Africa opened its doors in Tema, Ghana, the 16th missionary training center throughout the world.

June 9 — The first branch of the Church in the Republic of Georgia was formed in Tbilisi.

June 27 – On the 158th anniversary of the martyrdom of the Prophet Joseph Smith and his brother, Hyrum, the rebuilt Nauvoo Illinois Temple was dedicated by President Hinckley.

Sept. 9-10 – President Hinckley became the first Church president to visit Russia and Ukraine.

2003 **Jan. 11** — The first-ever global leadership training meeting in the Church by satellite transmission was held for priesthood leaders and transmitted in 56 languages to more than 97 percent of the Church's priesthood leaders.

March 7 — The Church was granted legal recognition by government officials in Benin, a French-speaking West African coastal nation between Togo and Nigeria.

March 15 — The first meetinghouse in Guyana, an English-speaking Caribbean nation, was dedicated in Georgetown, the capital city.

July 9 — The Apia Samoa Temple was destroyed by fire, marking the first time in Church history an operational temple has burned. The First Presidency announced July 16 that the temple would be rebuilt.

Nov. 30 — The first meetinghouse of the Church in Ethiopia was dedicated in the nation's capital of Addis Ababa.

2004 **Jan. 25** – The first meetinghouse of the Church in Cambodia, a two-story structure in Phnom Penh, was dedicated.

Late January – Membership in the Church passed the 12 million mark.

April 3 – The Sixth Quorum of the Seventy was created in a division of the Fifth Quorum of the Seventy

Aug. 1 – Mexico became the first nation, outside the United States, to reach one million members of the Church.

November – The First Presidency and Quorum of the Twelve introduce "Preach My Gospel," a comprehensive and far-reaching program designed to prepare and strengthen missionaries. The 230-page booklet addresses every aspect of missionary service and is considered the most complete, orchestrated effort in the history of the Church to unify the missionary effort.

2005 During 2005, tens of thousands of Latter-day Saint youth participated in commemorative cultural events across the globe in a worldwide commemoration honoring the 200th anniversary of the birth of the Prophet Joseph Smith and the 175th anniversary of the organization of the Church.

April 19 – Two new quorums of the Seventy were announced. The Seventh Quorum was created in a division of the Fourth Quorum and the Eighth Quorum was organized by dividing the Third Quorum.

July 3 – The first meetinghouse in the southeastern African nation of Malawi, a country of 12 million people, was dedicated in the city of Blantyre.

July 31-Aug. 9 – President Hinckley traveled 24,995 miles on a seven-nation tour of Asia and Africa, holding meetings in Russia, Korea, Taiwan, China, India, Kenya and Nigeria, where he also dedicated the Aba Nigeria Temple. He was the first Church president to visit India.

Oct. 7 – The First Presidency broke ground for a five-story state-of-the-art Church History Library at a site across the street east of the Conference Center in Salt Lake City.

Nov. 12 – The first Church meetinghouse on Kiritimati Atoll, a 248-square-mile coral atoll in the Pacific Ocean, which is part of the Republic of Kiribati and also known as Christmas Island, was dedicated.

Dec. 23 – Culminating a yearlong celebration of the 200th anniversary of the birth of the Prophet Joseph Smith, the Church held a commemorative satellite broadcast that featured segments from the prophet's birthplace in Vermont, as well as from the Conference Center in Salt Lake City. The commemorative program was telecast to 161 countries by satellite and worldwide by Internet, with the proceedings translated into 81 languages.

2006 **Jan. 3** – The six-year legal battle over the Church Plaza, located between the Salt Lake Temple and the Church Office Building in Salt Lake City, ended when the deadline passed for the ACLU and its plaintiffs to appeal a decision by the 10th U.S. Circuit Court of Appeals in Denver, Colo. The appeals court on Oct. 3, 2005, upheld the sale of one block of Main Street to the Church.

March 19 – The first meetinghouse constructed by the Church in Malaysia was dedicated in Miri, Sarawak.

April 30 – The Mormon Tabernacle Choir reached a milestone when it aired the 4,000th consecutive network broadcast of its weekly "Music and Spoken Word" program.

Oct. 14 – Ground was broken in Ljubljana, the capital of Slovenia, for the first meetinghouse in the country that will serve the three branches in Slovenia, which was once part of the former country of Yugoslavia.

Oct. 18 – Official recognition of the Church in the central European country of Slovakia was granted by government officials after missionaries gathered the required 20,000 signatures necessary for a new religion to be recognized. Slovakia was once part of Czechoslovakia, but after the Berlin Wall fell in 1989, the country was divided into its two traditional ethnic groups of Czechs and Slovaks. The Czech Republic granted recognition of the Church in 1990.

Nov. 2 – President Hinckley, at 96 years and 133 days, became the longest-lived Church president, a distinction previously held by President David O. McKay.

Nov. 19 – The Mormon Tabernacle Choir was honored as a Laureate of the 2006 Mother Teresa Award for "edifying the world through inspirational choral performances and recordings."

December – The Prophet Joseph Smith and President Brigham Young were included on a list of the top 100 "Most influential figures in American history," printed in the December issue of Atlantic magazine.

2007 **March 31** – The 140th-year-old Salt Lake Tabernacle on Temple Square, closed since January 2005 for extensive renovation and remodeling, was rededicated by President Hinckley. During the renovation, the pillars were strengthened and fortified to meet seismic code, and the roof was strengthened with the addition of steel trusses. Seating capacity in the building was reduced about 1,000 to 3,456.

June 21 – The Mormon Tabernacle Choir embarked on a tour of the eastern United States and Canada, performing before a total of 50,000 people in nine concerts in seven cities. The choir returned to Salt Lake City July 3.

June 24 – Church membership has reached 13 million members, President Hinckley announced to 118 mission presidents and their wives during the New Mission Presidents Seminar at the Missionary Training Center in Provo, Utah. He also announced that since the organization of the Church in 1830, an estimated one million missionaries have served throughout the world.

December: Three years after a devastating tsunami, triggered by a 9.0-magnitude earthquake that resulted in the deaths of more than 220,000 people in a dozen countries, the Church Humanitarian Services completed its humanitarian projects in the region. In partnership with other international organizations, the Church, among other projects, constructed 902 homes, 15 schools, three health clinics, 24 village water systems and three community centers.

2008 **Jan. 27** – President Gordon B. Hinckley, the longest-lived president in the history of the Church who served as president for nearly 13 years, died in Salt Lake City at age 97.

Feb. 3 – President Thomas S. Monson, a counselor to Presidents Ezra Taft Benson, Howard W. Hunter and Gordon B. Hinckley, was ordained and set apart as the 16th president of the Church. Set apart as his counselors were President Henry B. Eyring and President Dieter F. Uchtdorf.

Aug. 11 – President Monson paid a visit to

Panama's president, Martin Torrijos and his wife, First Lady Vivian Fernandez de Torrijos. The occasion marked the first time a Church president had met with a Panamanian president.

Aug. 28 – The Church announced that more than 140 million copies of the Book of Mormon, published in 107 languages, had been distributed since its publication in 1830. Seven major editions of the book had been published up to this time.

Sept. 20 – More than 75,000 Church members in Africa united in a massive day of service that extended across 30 countries to complete more than 200 "Helping Hands" projects, designed for "Bringing Relief and Building Hope," the service day's theme.

Nov. 24 – The first volume in the Joseph Smith Papers Project – called "the single most significant historical project of our generation" by Elder Marlin K. Jensen of the Seventy and Church historian and recorder – was released as the inaugural product under the new Church Historian's Press imprint. When completed, the project will include 30 volumes in six series.

2009

June 18 – The Mormon Tabernacle Choir and Orchestra at Temple Square began a 3,700-mile, 13-day concert tour to seven U.S. cities from Ohio to Colorado, performing in Cincinnati Ohio; St. Louis, Mo.; Des Moines, Iowa; Omaha, Neb.; Kansas City, Mo.; Norman, Okla.; and Denver, Colo.

June 20 – After four years of construction, the 230,000-square-foot, 600,000-document state-of-the-art Church History Library, housing the Church's historical collections gathered over 180 years, was dedicated by President Thomas S. Monson. A stainless steel time capsule, containing an assortment of historical items, had previously been placed in an interior wall of the building on March 25.

July 20 – President Thomas S. Monson and Elder Dallin H. Oaks of the Quorum of the Twelve met with U.S. President Barack Obama in the White House, and presented the nation's leader with five large leather-bound volumes of his family history going back through several generations and covering hundreds of years.

Sept. 13 – The First Presidency announced publication of the LDS edition of the Bible in Spanish, which President Thomas S. Monson called "the finest Spanish Bible in all the world." The new edition is based on the 1909 edition of the Reina-Valera Bible.

2010

Jan. 17 – The first stake in Uganda, a small semi-tropical country in East Africa, was created in the capital city of Kampala by Elder Paul E. Koelliker of the Seventy.

April 27 – Presiding Bishop H. David Burton and his first counselor, Bishop Richard C. Edgley, unveiled to the media the first solar-powered LDS meetinghouse in North America at a new stake center in Farmington, Utah. The building is a prototype designed to evaluate the feasibility of solar power in Church meetinghouses.

June 10 – The Mormon Tabernacle Choir celebrated 100 years of musical recording with the release of a new album of recordings – a three-disc set, "100: Celebrating a Century of Recording Excellence." The first Tabernacle Choir recording was made on Sept. 1, 1910, when recording technology was still in its infancy.

June 21 – A new, 10,000-square-foot, high-tech family history library, which replaced 24 smaller, limited-use family history centers previously housed in local meetinghouses that had served some 90 stakes in the Salt Lake Valley, opened in Riverton, Utah

Aug. 29 – A new chapter in the history of the Church was opened when the first temple built in a nation of the former Soviet Union – the Kyiv Ukraine Temple that will serve nine Eastern Europe countries – was dedicated by President Thomas S. Monson.

WORLDWIDE CHURCH

Editor's note: Information in this section has been gathered from a variety of sources and is believed to be the best available at the time of publication. Corrections, additional information and further country or state histories will be appreciated. Those with comments or information may write to: Church Almanac Histories, P.O. Box 1257, Salt Lake City, UT 84110, or email: shaun@desnews.com.

UNITED STATES OF AMERICA

Jan. 1, 2011: Est. population, 304,060,000; Members, 6,058,907; Stakes, 1,451; Wards, 11,401; Branches, 2,073; Districts, 12; Missions, 104; Temples in use, 63; under construction or announced, 6; Percent LDS, 2, or one in 51.

A few stakes and missions have headquarters in states other than that for which they are named. To simplify this listing, these stakes and missions are listed in the states for which they are named.

Numbers preceding stakes and missions are their chronological numbers assigned at the time of creation. Letters are added if number has been used previously.

* Stake name changed 14 Jan 1974 or as indicated otherwise

‡ Original name

† Transferred to

Alabama

Jan. 1, 2011: Population, 4,662,000; Members, 34,725; Stakes, 6; Wards, 41; Branches, 33; Missions, 1; Temples, 1; Percent LDS, 0.7 or one in 137.

The first known missionary to visit Alabama was Lysander Davis, who preached on the Montgomery County courthouse steps on 7 October 1839. Benjamin L. Clapp, a native of Alabama, baptized a relative, Samuel Turnbow, on 2 March 1840. The first concerted missionary work began on 24 April 1842, when James Brown and John U. Eldridge were sent to do missionary work there. Brown organized branches in Tuscaloosa and Perry counties in August 1842. Brown is credited with baptizing some of the first African-Americans into the Church, including two men named Hagar and Jack, on 24 October 1843. Eldridge baptized his brother, wife and mother-in-law, probably in early spring 1842. On 10 April 1843, Benjamin L. Clapp, John Blair, Wilkinson Hewitt and Lyman Omer Littlefield were sent to labor in Alabama by Joseph Smith.

John Brown, among the early missionaries dressed in ragged clothing and looking younger than his 22 years, visited an inn at Tuscumbria on 27 August 1843. When he asked for lodging as a preacher, he was thought to be a common cotton picker. His host gathered a small group to be entertained at the expense of hearing a supposed cotton picker preach. After he began, however, "they were as motionless as statues of marble." None was baptized, but the young preacher was well-treated afterward.

A slave, Samuel D. Chambers was baptized at age 13 in 1844. Though unable to read or write and without Church direction for more than 26 years, Chambers and his wife, Amanda Leggroan, eventually joined the main body of Saints in Utah. They saved for five years after receiving their freedom at the end of the Civil War, and arrived in Utah on 27 April 1870, where they became prosperous vegetable farmers.

Most early members migrated to the West to join the body of the saints and to avoid persecution. Some Alabama members were among the group of "Mississippi Saints" that emigrated under the leadership of John Brown and William Crosby, departing Mississippi on 8 April 1846.

Missionary work resumed in the South after the Civil War with the creation of the Southern States Mission. However, persecution was widespread during the 1880s. As early as 1880, some residents asked the governor of Alabama to force missionaries from the state. By 1894, the persecution subsided to some extent.

By 29 April 1896, there were five Sunday Schools organized. On 19 December 1897, the first known branch was organized in Deer Springs. A Sunday School was organized on 22 August 1911 in Montgomery. In the early days, converts were baptized in the Alabama River. In 1930, membership in the state was 2,516, with branches in Bradleyton and Lamison, and Sunday Schools in Bessemer, Birmingham, Camden, Clayton, Decatur, Dothan, Elmont, McCalla, Mobile, Pine Hill, Selma and Sneed.

Missionary Theron W. Borup recalled that in the mid-1930s, Sunday School groups existed in Elkmont (which had a small chapel), Gadsen, Birmingham, McCalla, and Montgomery. Branches were eventually organized from these Sunday Schools. On 23 September 1937, an east-west boundary was drawn through the Alabama District, dividing it into the Alabama and North Alabama districts.

During this period, attitudes held by many people against the Church softened. In 1940, the Montgomery Branch staged a pioneer parade that attracted thousands.

On 24 November 1941, Elder George Albert Smith of the Quorum of the Twelve spoke at the Alabama district conference in Birmingham. Elder Ezra Taft Benson of the Quorum of the Twelve visited in Mobile on 28 November - 2 December 1951 and spoke at the Alabama district conference.

Many Latter-day Saint servicemen were stationed in the state during World War II, and helped strengthen the branches. After the war, the branches began to grow. A chapel was completed on 30 May 1954 in Montgomery. Alabama's first stake was created in Huntsville on 3 March 1968. The military and the space industry brought in an influx of members during this period. One of the speakers at the commemoration of the 150th anniversary of the Church in Alabama was Chief Justice Ernest C. "Sonny" Hornsby of the Alabama Supreme Court.

The Alabama Birmingham Mission was created on 1 January 1979. In the 1990s, members served their neighbors in the aftermath of hurricane Opal, and helped rebuild community chapels burned by arsonists. A temple in Birmingham was dedicated on 3 September 2000 by President Gordon B. Hinckley.

In 2002, membership reached 28,808.

Sources: Andrew Jenson, Encyclopedic History of the Church, 1941; LaMar C. Berrett, History of the Southern States Mission, 1831-1861, thesis 1960; Frank W. Riggs III, Sesquicentennial Star, 1989; Lee Warnick, "Alabama: The Northern Saints of a Southern State," Church News, 9 April 1988; "Members Rally to Help Hurricane Victims," Church News, 12 August 1995; R. Scott Lloyd, "LDS Render Service in Wake of Opal's Rage," Church News, 14 October 1995; "Helping Rebuild Burned Chapels," Church News, 9 Nov. 1996; Church News, 18 April 1998; Julie A. Dockstader, "God is Smiling Down on Us," Church News, 9 Sept. 2000, Southern States Mission, Manuscript history and historical reports, Church Archives.

Stakes — 6
(Listed alphabetically as of Oct. 1, 2011.)

No.	NameOrganized	First President
North America Southeast Area		
1362	Bessemer Alabama	12 Sep 1982 Robert Henry Shepherdson
678	Birmingham Alabama	2 Feb 1975 Fred M. Washburn
1588	Dothan Alabama	2 Mar 1986 Ned Philip Jenne
452	*Huntsville Alabama	
	‡Alabama	3 Mar 1968 Raymond D. McCurdy
964	Mobile Alabama	8 Oct 1978 Dean Arthur Rains
717	Montgomery Alabama	2 Nov 1975 Gayle Dorwin Heckel

Mission — 1
(As of Oct. 1, 2011; shown with historical number. See MISSIONS.)

(166a) ALABAMA BIRMINGHAM MISSION
3100 Lorna Road, Ste 101
Birmingham, AL 35216

Alaska

Jan. 1, 2011: Est. population, 686,000; Members, 32,170; Stakes, 7; Wards, 50; Branches, 30; Missions, 1; Districts, 0; Temples, 1; Percent LDS; 4.4, or one in 23.

The first known visit by Church members to Alaska occurred in July 1895 when President Wilford Woodruff and his counselors, George Q. Cannon and Joseph F. Smith, and their families toured Juneau and the southern portion of Alaska via steamship.

The gold rush of 1898 drew a few Latter-day Saints to Alaska, among them John Bigelow and Edward G. Cannon. Little is known of Bigelow, but Cannon, a 79-year-old who had been converted in 1871, maintained a "tabernacle which he moved about on wheels from settlement to settlement" in the Seward Peninsula and Nome area.

On 25 June 1902, Cannon baptized Kedzie Noble Winnie near Nome. Winnie reported in 1907 that gospel meetings were being held and quite a number of people were interested, including Eskimos, as well as miners and others. Cannon and Winnie worked together until Cannon's death in 1910.

In 1913, a year after Alaska became a territory of the United States, the first two missionaries, Horton E. Fackrell and William F. Webster, arrived in Juneau where they worked for a few weeks. No other known missionary work was done until Heber J. Meeks, Alvin Englestead, James Judd and Lowell T. Plowman, arrived in Alaska in 1928, under the direction of Northwestern States Mission President William R. Sloan. During the next year, the elders held 105 meetings and placed more than 1,300 copies of the Book of Mormon. They also dealt with a widespread rumor that the Church planned to colonize Alaska. Few people, however, joined the Church, and membership consisted only of a few scattered Latter-day Saints.

During the mid to late1930s, a few Latter-day Saint families had moved to Fairbanks and the first branch of the Church in Alaska was organized on 10 July 1938. The branch consisted of the Peterson, Oldroyd and Shields families with Murray Shields as president. By 1941, membership in the territory had reached 300. During the next 20 years Church membership grew due mostly to Latter-day Saints moving to Alaska with some growth due to convert baptisms. By 1961, membership was 3,051 with three branches in Anchorage and additional branches in Fairbanks, Palmer and Juneau. The Alaskan-Canadian Mission was created on 1 January 1961 (reorganized as the Alaska-British Columbia Mission in 1970) and the first stake in Alaska, the Alaska Stake, was organized 13 August 1961 with headquarters in Anchorage.

A massive earthquake struck Alaska on 27 March 1964. Among those killed were six members of the Valdez Branch. As the area was rebuilt after the earthquake, the construction effort led to a building boom that brought additional members to the state. A new stake center was dedicated in Anchorage in 1966. In 1970, membership was 6,744.

The Alaskan-British Columbia Mission was renamed the Canada Vancouver Mission on 1 July 1974 and a few months later the Alaska Anchorage Mission was created on 15 October 1974. Discovery of oil in Prudhoe Bay in 1968 and the construction of the trans-Alaska oil pipeline in the mid 1970s accelerated growth in Alaska and in the Church, but membership dropped after the pipeline was completed. Under the leadership of mission President Douglas T. Snarr, special meetinghouses designed for the Arctic were built in 1981 in many of the smaller branches. Membership in 1980 had grown to 14,414, and by 1990 had reached 21,410.

In the 1990s, members took part in community service projects that helped improve relationships for the Church. For example, when the most destructive forest fire in Alaska history took place in June 1996 near Wasilla, the Wasilla Stake center was used as a drop off center for emergency supplies and stake members worked around the clock sorting and organizing clothing and supplies to help the fire victims.

From 17-23 June 1995, President Gordon B. Hinckley visited members of the Church in Alaska, speaking at a regional conference, meeting with missionaries of the Alaska Anchorage Mission, and speaking at firesides.

The Anchorage Alaska Temple was dedicated by President Hinckley on 9 January 1999. Five years later, the temple was enlarged and rededicated by President Hinckley on 8 February 2004.

In 2002, membership reached 27,189.

Sources: Scott Kenney, ed., Wilford Woodruff's Journal, 1833-1898 1985; Andrew Jenson, Encyclopedic History of the Church, 1941; Barbara Jean Walther Adams, The History of the Mormons in Alaska, 1972, Church Archives; Patricia B. Jasper and Daine Lommel, A Gathering of Saints in Alaska, 1999; Oregon Portland Mission (Northwestern States Mission), Manuscript history and historical reports, Church Archives; Alaska Anchorage Mission; Manuscript history and historical reports, Church Archives; "Alaskan LDS Welcome Pres. Hinckley," Church News, 1 July 1995; Julie A. Dockstader, "Northernmost Temple Dedicated," Church News, 16 January 1999.

Stakes — 7
(Listed alphabetically as of Oct. 1, 2011.)

No.	Name	Organized	First President
North America Northwest Area			
331	*Anchorage Alaska		
	‡Alaska	13 Aug 1961	Orson P. Millett
2603b	Anchorage Alaska Chugach	24 Nov 2002	Ralph Lloyd VanOrden
962	Anchorage Alaska North	17 Sep 1978	Wesley R. Grover
1033	Fairbanks Alaska	27 May 1979	Dennis E. Cook
2102	Juneau Alaska	8 Oct 1995	Melvin R. Perkins
1507	Soldotna Alaska	9 Dec 1984	Merrill D. Briggs
1456	Wasilla Alaska	13 Nov 1983	Elbert Thomas Pettijohn

Mission — 1
(As of Oct. 1, 2011; shown with historical number. See MISSIONS.)
(114) ALASKA ANCHORAGE MISSION
12350 Industry Way, Suite 218
Anchorage, AK 99515

Arizona

Jan. 1, 2011: Est. population, 6,500,000; Members, 387,950; Stakes, 90; Wards, 713; Branches, 88; Missions, 4; Temples, 3, announced, 2; Percent LDS, 5.8, or one in 17.

The Mormon Battalion marched through the area that is now Arizona in 1846 on its way to California. The next time Church members entered the area was in 1858 and 1859, when Jacob Hamblin and his companions camped at Pipe Spring in the northwestern part of Arizona while journeying to and from their missions among the Moqui (Hopi) Indians east of the Colorado River. During the 1860s and 1870s, Church parties explored portions of the area searching for possible settlement sites. Also during this period, isolated ranches and small Mormon settlements were established at Short Creek (now Colorado City), Pipe Spring, Beaver Dams (now Littlefield), and Lee's Ferry, all in the area between the Utah border and the Grand Canyon known as the Arizona Strip.

The first effort at large-scale colonization by the Church in Arizona came in March of 1873 when a group of saints was sent from Utah to the Little Colorado River drainage under the direction of Horton D. Haight. The colonizers turned back, discouraged by the poor prospects, but a few returned the following year and began farming among the Indians at Moencopi, including John L. Blythe. Local hostilities forced the colonists to leave again after only one month. A year later, James S. Brown led another small colonizing group that successfully settled at Moencopi, then began exploring the surrounding area. Following these explorations, a large group of pioneers arrived in the spring of 1876 and established four settlements on the Little Colorado, which they called Ballenger's Camp (later renamed Brigham City), Sunset, Obed and Allen City (later renamed St. Joseph, then still later Joseph City).

Two years after the initial settlement, on 27 January 1878, the Little Colorado Stake, the first in Arizona, was established at these settlements. The first school in Arizona sponsored by the Church was also begun at this time at Obed. Although Joseph City is the only one of the original four settlements remaining, several other communities grew and flourished in the area as more colonists arrived during the ensuing decades and spread throughout the Little Colorado drainage.

During 1877, Jonesville (later renamed Lehi) in the Salt River Valley was established, along with St. David on the San Pedro River. The following year saw the creation of another settlement on the Salt River at Mesa. Then, beginning in 1879, several pioneer families settled at Pima on the Gila River. The next few years also saw the establishment of Thatcher in that same area.

Eventually, more than 30 Mormon colonies were started in Arizona and some of the pioneers also helped establish colonies in northern Mexico. These hardy pioneers overcame severe hardships in the early years, including drought, crop failures, difficulties with neighbors and floods. At Woodruff on the Little Colorado River, for example, members built 17 successive dams after each was destroyed by flash floods.

Over the years, members gained prominence and were involved in the progress of the state. They earned a good reputation for their industry and integrity.

On 23 October 1927, the first Arizona temple was dedicated in Mesa. Until that time, members had traveled to the St. George Temple. In fact, because of all of the bridal parties that traversed the trail during the early years, the wagon road between St. George and the Arizona settlements became known as the Honeymoon Trail. The temple at Mesa was also the first temple in the Church to be rededicated – on 15 April 1975 – after extensive remodeling and enlarging to accommodate increased attendance. A second Arizona temple was dedicated in Snowflake on 3 March 2002.

During the colonization period, many of the settlers shared the gospel with the Native Americans near their settlements. In fact, some of the earliest settlements were purposely established in or near concentrations of the Hopi people to make missionary work easier. The formation of regular missions in Arizona did not begin, however, until later in the 20th century with the establishment of the Arizona Mission (now Arizona Tempe) in 1969, followed by the Arizona Holbrook Mission in 1974, which was discontinued in 1984 when the Arizona Phoenix Mission was created. The Arizona Tucson Mission was organized in 1990. The fourth mission in Arizona, the Arizona Mesa Mission, was established in March 2002.

President Spencer W. Kimball, who served as president of the Church from 1973-1985, was reared in Thatcher and served as the first president of the Mt. Graham Stake.

Membership in 1930 totaled 18,732 members. By 1980, membership reached 171,880. By 1990, membership was 241,000, and 305,000 by 1999. In 2002, membership was 330,972 with 78 stakes.

On 14 September 1997, President Gordon B. Hinckley spoke to about 5,000 Native Americans at Window Rock on the Navajo Reservation, the first Church president to speak in the Navajo capital. Later that same year, on 13 December, the Casa Grande Arizona Stake presented a plaque to officials of the Gila River Indian Community in honor of the kindness shown to the Mormon Battalion by the Pima Indians 150 years earlier.

In June 2002, the worst forest fire in Arizona's history burned nearly a half million acres and threatened many of the towns in eastern Arizona that had been established by Mormon pioneers. The fire destroyed 467 homes and forced the evacuation of 35,000 people, including 14,000 Church members. The Church sent food, tents, sleeping bags and emergency power-generation equipment. In addition, the Church donated $125,000 for food and other supplies in the needed areas.

Membership in 2003 was 339,891.

The Gila Valley Arizona Temple was dedicated on 29 May 2010, in Central, Ariz. It became the third temple in Arizona, and the 132nd temple in the Church.

On 13 November 2010 ground was broken for the Gilbert Arizona Temple, the fourth in Arizona. More than 7,500 members and dignitaries gathered on a clear, warm morning as Elder Claudio R.M. Costa of the Presidency of the Seventy offered the dedicatory prayer. The 81,000-square-foot structure is located on the corner of Pecos and Greenfield roads in Gilbert, which is southeast of Phoenix. The area has experienced tremendous growth in membership. Since the first stake was organized in 1975 six more were organized in Gilbert by the time of the groundbreaking. The temple district will also include the five stakes in Queen Creek, the four stakes in Chandler and the four in Tempe.

On 4 June 2011 ground was broken for the Phoenix Arizona Temple, the fifth in Arizona. Hundreds gathered in triple digit heat, while many others watched proceedings in meetinghouses, as Elder Ronald A. Rasband of the Presidency of the Seventy blessed the site and broke ground. The temple is located adjacent to an 8-year-old meetinghouse.

Sources: Littlefield Ward manuscript history and historical reports, Church Archives; Lehi Ward manuscript history and historical reports, Church Archives; Mesa Ward manuscript history and historical reports, Church Archives; Thatcher Ward manuscript history and historical reports, Church Archives; Pima Ward manuscript history and historical reports, Church Archives; Southwest Indian Mission manuscript history and historical reports, Church Archives; Jenson, Andrew, Encyclopedic History of the Church of Jesus Christ of Latter-day Saints, 1941; Updike, Paul, "Early History of Arizona," The Pioneer, January 1981; Kate B. Carter, Heart Throbs of the West; Thomas Edwin Farrish, "Mormons in Arizona," reprinted in the Deseret News, 31 August 1918, section 4, 1; "President Kimball Rededicates Arizona Temple," Ensign, June 1975, p. 76; "Native Americans remembered for help to Mormon Battalion," Church News, 20 December 1997, 3; "5,000 Native Americans gather to hear prophet," Church News, 20 September 1997, 6; "Temple fulfills old prophecies," Church News, 9 March 2002, 3; "Members respond to evacuees' needs during Arizona's Rodeo-Chediski fire," Church News, 6 July 2002, 6; BYU Department of Church History and Doctrine, Regional studies in Latter-day Saint church history, 1989; Jack Cary, "St. David on the San Pedro," Arizona Highways, August 1956; McKoy, Kathleen L. Pipe Spring, Cultures at a Crossroads: An Administrative History, 2001. Gilbert Arizona Temple, Church News, Nov. 20, 2010; Church News, Phoenix temple 'divinely chosen site,' 11 June 2011, Jill B. Adair.

Stakes — 90
(Listed alphabetically as of Oct. 1, 2011.)

No.	Name	Organized	First President
North America Southwest Area			
1616	Apache Junction Arizona	16 Nov 1986	Charles Wray Squires
1666	Buckeye Arizona	13 Dec 1987	Charles Roy Rucker
1819	Casa Grande Arizona	13 Oct 1991	Scott J. McEuen
988	Chandler Arizona	3 Dec 1978	Elone Evans Farnsworth
1513	Chandler Arizona Alma	24 Feb 1985	Martin H. Durrant
2732	Chandler Arizona East	17 Sep 2006	Scott R Palmer
2255	Chandler Arizona West	20 Oct 1996	Donald Lynn Jones
1773	Chinle Arizona	30 Sep 1990	Edwin I. Tano
888	*Cottonwood Arizona		
	†Camp Verde Arizona	22 Jan 1978	John Edward Eagar
963	Duncan Arizona	24 Sep 1978	Earl Adair Merrell
1627	Eagar Arizona	25 Jan 1987	Charles D. Martin
232	*Flagstaff Arizona		
	‡Flagstaff	23 Sep 1956	Burton R. Smith
2358	Gilbert Arizona	18 May 1997	John Wootton Lewis
703	*Gilbert Arizona Greenfield	11 Oct 1981	
	‡Gilbert Arizona	24 Aug 1975	Newell A. Barney
2282	Gilbert Arizona Highland	24 Nov 1996	David E. Lesueur
2657	Gilbert Arizona Higley	31 Oct 2004	Mark Dee Pugmire
2578	Gilbert Arizona San Tan	3 Dec 2000	Mark Dee Pugmire
1295	Gilbert Arizona Stapley	11 Oct 1981	Wilburn James Brown
1661	Gilbert Arizona Val Vista	22 Nov 1987	Craig Allen Cardon
612	*Glendale Arizona		
	‡Glendale	6 May 1973	Melvin L. Huber
1236	Glendale Arizona North	15 Feb 1981	Richard Johnson Barrett
650	Globe Arizona	16 Jun 1974	Bennie Joe Cecil
2789	Goodyear Arizona	9 Dec 2007	John Clarence Hayes
536	*Holbrook Arizona		
	‡Holbrook	22 Nov 1970	Jay Barder Williams
1436	Kingman Arizona	21 Aug 1983	Louis George Sorensen
750	*Lake Havasu City Arizona	11 Feb 1997	
	‡Blythe California	14 Mar 1976	Jerry Dean Mortensen
2790	Maricopa Arizona	9 Dec 2007	Malin Walter Lewis

161	*Mesa Arizona		
	‡Mesa	8 Dec 1946	L.M. Mecham Jr.
2517	Mesa Arizona Alta Mesa	14 Mar 1999	Donald Milford Erickson
2539	Mesa Arizona Boulder Creek	5 Dec 1999	Russell David Thornock
1265	Mesa Arizona Central	10 May 1981	Clayton H. Hakes
1904	*Mesa Arizona Citrus Heights	7 May 1999	
	‡Mesa Ariz Red Mountain	20 Sep 1992	James Joseph Hamula
2625	Mesa Arizona Desert Ridge	18 Jan 2004	James Bryant Reeder
224	*Mesa Arizona East		
	*Mesa East	29 May 1970	
	‡East Mesa	20 Nov 1955	Donald Ellsworth
2777	Mesa Arizona Hermosa Vista	21 Oct 2007	Creg Donald Ostler
1087	Mesa Arizona Kimball	25 Nov 1979	Allen Smith Farnsworth
1741	Mesa Arizona Kimball East	14 Jan 1990	Wayne D. Crismon
1026	Mesa Arizona Lehi	6 May 1979	Otto Stronach Shill Jr.
24	*Mesa Arizona Maricopa		
	‡Maricopa	10 Dec 1882	Alexander F. MacDonald
2544	Mesa Arizona Maricopa North	27 Feb 2000	Jim L. Wright
1628	Mesa Arizona Mountain View	25 Jan 1987	James R. Adair
558	*Mesa Arizona North	27 Feb 2000	
	*Mesa Arizona Maricopa North	15 Mar 1978	
	*Mesa Maricopa North		
	‡Maricopa North	7 Nov 1971	Raymond L. Russell
1479	Mesa Arizona Pueblo	10 Jun 1984	E. Clark Huber
745	Mesa Arizona Salt River	15 Feb 1976	Elden S. Porter
2593	Mesa Arizona Skyline	3 Jun 2001	Kevin Fenwick Smith
362	*Mesa Arizona South		
	‡Mesa South	18 Nov 1962	Stanley F. Turley
555	*Mesa Arizona West		
	‡Mesa West	10 Oct 1971	Weymouth D. Pew
633	Page Arizona	10 Mar 1974	J Ballard Washburn
1061	Paradise Valley Arizona	9 Sep 1979	James David King
2552	Payson Arizona Stake	9 Apr 2000	J. Fred Hollobaugh
1631	Peoria Arizona	22 Feb 1987	Thomas G. Jones
2545	Peoria Arizona North	27 Jan 2000	Lloyd S. Price
121	*Phoenix Arizona		
	‡Phoenix	27 Feb 1938	James Robert Price
1233	Phoenix Arizona Deer Valley	8 Feb 1981	E. Wayne Pratt
212	*Phoenix Arizona East		
	*Phoenix East	29 May 1970	
	‡East Phoenix	28 Feb 1954	Junius E. Driggs
253	*Phoenix Arizona North		
	‡Phoenix North	19 Jan 1958	Rudger G. Smith
896	*Phoenix Arizona West Maricopa	18 May 1978	
	‡West Maricopa Arizona	5 Mar 1978	DeNelson Jones
1830	Pima Arizona	17 Nov 1991	Stephen Lavar John
2039	Pinetop-Lakeside Arizona	26 Mar 1995	Chester Trent Adams
517	*Prescott Arizona		
	‡Prescott	7 Jun 1970	Edward A. Dalton
2907	Prescott Valley Arizona	13 Mar 2011	Brent C Montierth
2609b	Queen Creek Arizona	27 Oct 2002	Russell L. Richardson
2792	Queen Creek Arizona Chandler Heights	17 Feb 2008	Russell Lyle Richardson
2656	Queen Creek Arizona East	31 Oct 2004	Brian Val Solomon
2793	Queen Creek Arizona North	17 Feb 2008	Alyn Michael McClure
2690	Queen Creek Arizona South	30 Oct 2005	Ernest Lawes
137	*St. David Arizona		
	*Arizona South	29 May 1970	
	‡Southern Arizona	2 Mar 1941	A.B. Ballantyne
31	*St. Johns Arizona		
	‡St. Johns(Arizona, N.M.)	23 Jul 1887	David K. Udall
120	*Safford Arizona		
	‡Mount Graham		
	(Arizona, N.M.)	20 Feb 1938	Spencer W. Kimball
2840	Sahuarita Arizona	21 Jun 2009	Thayne W. Hardy
1248	*Scottsdale Arizona Camelback	4 Oct 1994	
	‡Phoenix Arizona Camelback	22 Mar 1981	Ernest Widtsoe Shumway
364	Scottsdale Arizona North	4 Oct 1994	
	*Scottsdale Arizona		
	‡Scottsdale	9 Dec 1962	Junius E. Driggs
668	Show Low Arizona	24 Nov 1974	Elbert J. Lewis
1348	Sierra Vista Arizona	6 Jun 1982	C. Lavell Haymore
31a	*Snowflake Arizona		
	‡Snowflake	18 Dec 1887	Jesse N. Smith
2667	Surprise Arizona	16 Jan 2005	Alvin Bennett Hancock
2850	Surprise Arizona North	16 Aug 2009	Alvin B. Hancock
1212	Taylor Arizona	30 Nov 1980	Peter Delos Shumway
391	*Tempe Arizona		
	‡Tempe	2 Feb 1964	George Isaac Dana
738	Tempe Arizona South	18 Jan 1976	Fred Dale Markham
1708	Tempe Arizona West	8 Jan 1989	Kent M. Christiansen
2585	Tempe Arizona University	21 Jan 2001	David K. Udall
	Originally created on 12 Dec 1971		Leo Rae Huish;
	Discontinued 28 Apr 1974 †13 Salt River Valley stakes		

25	*Thatcher Arizona		
	‡Saint Joseph	25 Feb 1883	Christopher Layton
2068	Tuba City Arizona	25 June 1995	Edwin I. Tano
238	*Tucson Arizona		
	‡Tucson	2 Dec 1956	Leslie Odell Brewer
878	Tucson Arizona East	6 Nov 1977	Paul Eugene Dahl
477	*Tucson Arizona North		
	‡Tucson North	2 Feb 1969	Don Hakan Peterson
1517	Tucson Arizona Rincon	3 Mar 1985	Ernest G. Blain
2281	Tucson Arizona West	24 Nov 1996	Reed A. Hancock
959	Winslow Arizona	17 Sep 1978	Thomas A. Whipple
263	*Yuma Arizona		
	‡Yuma (Arizona, California)	27 Apr 1958	Marion Turley

		Stakes discontinued	
22	Eastern Arizona	29 Jun 1879	Jesse N. Smith
	(Arizona, N.M.)		
	Discontinued 18 Dec 1887 †St. Johns (31), Snowflake (31a)		
21	Little Colorado (Ariz., Colo.)	27 Jan 1878	Lot Smith
	Discontinued 18 Dec 1887 †Snowflake (31a)		
380	*Phoenix Arizona West		
	‡Phoenix West	1 Sep 1963	Keith W. Hubbard
	Discontinued 16 Sep 2006		

Missions — 4
(As of Oct. 1, 2011; shown with historical number. See MISSIONS.)

(179c) ARIZONA PHOENIX MISSION
18001 N 79th Ave Bldg C Ste 50
Glendale, AZ 85308-8388

(87) ARIZONA TEMPE MISSION
1871 East Del Rio Drive
Tempe, AZ 85282-2822

(231) ARIZONA TUCSON MISSION
1840 East River Road, #102
Tucson, AZ 85718

(329a) ARIZONA MESA MISSION
6265 N 82nd St.
Scottsdale AZ 85250

Arkansas

Jan. 1, 2011: Est. population, 2,855,000; Members, 27,559; Stakes, 5; Wards, 35; Branches, 27; Missions, 1; Percent LDS, 0.9, or one in 110.

Located due south of Missouri, Arkansas enjoyed an early Church presence in this dispensation as missionary efforts extended from Latter-day Saint communities to the north. Wilford Woodruff, then a priest and serving the first of his numerous missions, left Clay County, Mo., and began preaching the gospel in Arkansas. Together with Henry Brown, they arrived in Bentonville on 28 January 1835. Preaching the first sermon four days later, they met with opposition from an apostate member, Alexander Akeman. Prophetically warned in a dream of this opposition, Woodruff bore powerful testimony to the truthfulness of the restored gospel, whereupon, according to his account, Akeman fell dead. This event, together with Wilford's influential teaching, led to the baptism of a Mr. and Mrs. Jonathan Hubbel, the first converts in Arkansas, on 22 February 1835.

When Woodruff focused his missionary efforts in Tennessee, Church influence dwindled in Arkansas. Elder Abraham O. Smoot returned to the area three years later, laboring for five months. Church authorities also assigned Andrew A. Timmons, John A McIntosh, Darwin Chase, and Nathaniel Levett to serve a political mission to the state in 1844 as part of the presidential campaign of Joseph Smith. But by 1846, the events of the martyrdom and subsequent preparation for the exodus west ended missionary activities throughout the South.

The year 1857 marked a tragic era in Church history in Arkansas. Hounded in his journeys in the area by Hector H. McLean, the ex-husband of Apostle Parley P. Pratt's plural wife, Eleanor, Elder Pratt was acquitted of charges. Following him to the town of Van Buren, McLean murdered Elder Pratt on 13 May 1857. Today, a monument in the local cemetery marks his grave. Later the same year, a party of Arkansas immigrants heading for California were killed by a group of Latter-day Saints and Indians in southern Utah at Mountain Meadows. Negative feelings, and later the U.S. Civil War, kept the Church from the area for the next two decades.

After the war, the Church sent missionaries again to Arkansas in 1876. Elders Henry G. Boyle and John D. H. McAllister first preached in the state, establishing a branch in Des Arc. By 1877, 27 families totaling 125 converts emigrated west from this branch.

Arkansas converts continued to join the main body of the saints in Utah during the 1880's, but eventually a permanent presence was established. Construction on the first Latter-day Saint meetinghouse was completed in White County on 30 May 1890. Benjamin Franklin Baker, an early influential convert, helped establish the Barney Branch in 1914 with over 100 members. By 1930, Arkansas had three organized branches (Barney, El Dorado, and Little Rock) and a total membership of 944.

During these years, Arkansas formed part of several Church missions. Originally a conference of the Southern States Mission, it later became part of the Indian Territory Mission, Southwestern States Mission, Central States Mission, Texas-Louisiana Mission, Gulf States Mission, and ultimately the Arkansas Little Rock Mission, formed in 1975 with Richard M. Richards as president.

As missionary efforts increased, so did the formal Church structure in Arkansas. Elder Harold B. Lee of the Quorum of the Twelve formed the first stake in Little Rock on 1 July 1969, with Dean C. Andrew as president. Shortly thereafter, a second stake was organized in Fort Smith on 30 April 1978, under the direction of Arthur Donald Browne. Church membership continued to grow, reaching 9,878 in 1980. This growth led to the creation of a third stake, the Jacksonville Arkansas Stake on 19 June 1983, presided over by Robert Michael McChesney. A fourth stake, the Rogers Arkansas Stake was formed on 11 August 1991 with David A. Bednar as president. By the year 2000, Church membership passed 20,000.

The increased growth has led to an increased public presence in local communities by members of the Church. The first institute building, adjacent to the University of Arkansas, was dedicated in the fall of 1999. Members are also frequently recognized by media and government officials for their volunteer service.

Membership in 2003 was 21,954.

Sources: Ted S. Anderson, The Southern States Mission: 1898-1971, 1973; LaMar C. Berrett, History of the Southern States Mission, 1960; Thomas Luther Brown, History of the Church in Arkansas, Church Archives; Andrew Jenson, Encyclopedic History of the Church, 1941; Emogene Tindall, History and Genealogy of the Early Mormon Church in Arkansas: 1897-1975, 1983; George W. Rea, "The Arkansas Chapter of the Mountain Meadow Massacre," The Arkansas Historical Quarterly, Winter, 1954, vol. 13, no. 4; Southern States Mission, Manuscript history and historical reports, Church Archives; Central States Mission, Manuscript history and historical reports, Church Archives; Little Rock Arkansas Stake, Manuscript history and historical reports, Church Archives; Dorothy Maxwell and Don L. Brugger, "Little Rock Saints' Foundation of Faith," Ensign, Apr. 1995; Bruce D. Blumell, "Exodus from the South," Church News, 21 May 1977; Sarah Jane Weaver, "'Unsung Heroes' in Storms' Aftermath," Church News, 8 March 1997; C. Alan Gauldin, "Arkansas Institute Building Dedicated," Church News, 13 November 1999; "A Great Missionary," Church News, 8 March 2005.

Stakes — 5
(Listed alphabetically by area As of Oct. 1, 2011.)

No.	Name	Organized	First President
North America Southeast Area — 3			
2723	Springdale Arkansas	4 Jun 2006	Thomas Hal Bradford
484	*Little Rock Arkansas		
	‡Arkansas	1 Jun 1969	Dean C. Andrew
1432	*North Little Rock Arkansas	8 Jun 1993	
	‡Jacksonville Arkansas	19 Jun 1983	Robert Michael McChesney
North America Southwest Area — 2			
911	Fort Smith Arkansas	30 Apr 1978	Arthur Donald Browne
1807	Rogers Arkansas	11 Aug 1991	David Allen Bednar

Mission — 1
(As of Oct. 1, 2011; shown with historical number. See MISSIONS.)

(116) ARKANSAS LITTLE ROCK MISSION
905 Kierre Drive
North Little Rock, AR 72116-3709

California

Jan. 1, 2011: Est. population, 36,757,000; Members, 763,370; Stakes, 157; Wards, 1,187; Branches, 174; Missions, 16; Temples, 7; Percent LDS, 2.1, or one in 49.

A Mormon immigrant company under direction of Samuel Brannan departed on the ship Brooklyn from New York on 4 February 1846 en route to the Great Salt Lake valley via California. The group under the direction of Brannan navigated the southern tip of South America around Cape Horn and arrived at Yerba Buena on 31 July 1846. The company of around 230 people were the first known Latter-day Saints to set foot in California. Their numbers tripled the population of tiny Yerba Buena. They soon helped build it into the prosperous city of San Francisco. While there, Brannan and other Saints began publication of one of California's first English-language newspapers, the California Star, in October 1846. One of the Brooklyn saints, Angeline Lovett, set up a school in the old Franciscan Dolores Mission, the first English-language school in California.

During the early autumn of 1846 Brannan led 20 men to the San Joaquin Valley, about 70 miles east of San Francisco where they founded a Mormon farming village named New Hope Colony. It soon failed as heavy seasonal storms flooded the valley, destroying their crops. Most of the Brooklyn saints left California for Salt Lake City in 1848. On their way, they carved an emigrant road that would be used by thousands of westward bound travelers including the gold rush "Forty-Niners."

In January 1847, the Mormon Battalion arrived in San Diego. Battalion members helped construct a number of buildings and public works in San Diego. They then traveled to Los Angeles where they built a fort and raised the first American flag. Six discharged battalion members were at Sutter's Mill in northern California when gold was discovered there on 24 January 1848. The diary of battalion veteran Henry W. Bigler is used by historians to determine the details of the discovery of gold in California.

In February 1856, George Q. Cannon began publication in San Francisco of the Western Standard, a weekly periodical supportive of the Church.

The first colonization from Utah to California came in 1851 when a company of about 450 Saints under direction of Elders Amasa M. Lyman and Charles C. Rich of the Quorum of the Twelve Apostles settled at what is now San Bernardino. The colony was the final settlement in a string of Mormon communities extending 800 miles from Salt Lake City. The community thrived, and on 6 July 1851 the San Bernardino Stake, California's first, was organized. Faithful members in this colony were eventually outnumbered by less-committed members who created considerable dissension. When the troubled colony was dissolved by the Church at the advance of Johnston's Army toward Salt Lake City in 1857, about 1,400 — fewer than half the total — returned to Utah to colonize other areas. With the departure in 1857 the San Bernardino Stake was dissolved, and for a period of 35 years, the Church did not have formally organized ecclesiastical units in the state.

Missionary work was conducted in California from 1849-1858. It was discontinued when missionaries were recalled to Utah during the Utah War. The work remained dormant until 1892 when missionary activities were resumed by Luther Dalton who began missionary labors in San Francisco and Oakland. In 1894, Karl G. Maeser relocated to California to direct the Utah exhibit of the California's mid-winter fair and to serve as president of the newly re-established California Mission.

The Los Angeles Branch was created on 20 August 1895, and a year later, the Northern California and Southern California conferences were organized. The Sacramento Conference was added in 1898. Most missionary work in California before the turn of the century took place in the larger population centers.

In the 1920s, a number of talented Church members immigrated to California. Many of them and their descendants became noted leaders, including two California governors, a Church president, and internationally recognized figures in science, business, education, sports, and the arts. Since the immigration to California of the 1920s, nearly 10 percent of the membership of the Church has lived in the Golden State.

The first stake created in the state in the 20th century was the Los Angeles Stake, organized on 21 January 1923. On 22 May 1927, the Los Angeles Stake was divided to form the Los Angeles and Hollywood stakes. Shortly afterwards, on 10 July 1927, the San Francisco Stake was established.

By 1930, Church members in California numbered 21,254.

On the opening day of the San Francisco World's Fair on 18 February 1939, some 1,400 people visited the Church's exhibit, a visitors center portraying a reduced-size Salt Lake Tabernacle.

Eight California stakes were created in the 1930s, five in the 1940s, and 30 in the 1950s.

Land for California's first temple was purchased in 1937 in Los Angeles. The temple, the second largest in the Church, was dedicated in 1956. A second temple was dedicated in Oakland in 1964, followed by others dedicated in San Diego in 1993, Fresno in 2000, and Redlands in 2003. Temples are now under construction in Newport Beach and Sacramento.

The Church has a strong presence among minority groups. There are over 200 Church ethnic units and six ethnic stakes in California.

President Spencer W. Kimball spoke to a Los Angeles Area Conference in the Rose Bowl on 17-18 May 1980, drawing an estimated 75,000 members. Conference talks were simultaneously translated into seven languages. This is believed to be the largest number of members ever gathered for a Church meeting anywhere in the world.

By 1980, membership in the state totaled 541,000. From 1991 to 1993, because of an out- migration of members, membership dropped from 721,000 to 719,000. However, from 1993 to 1995, membership rose to 725,690. The Church is now the second largest religious denomination in California, with a membership of more than 740,000 in 1999.

In July 1996, the sesquicentennial of the arrival of the ship Brooklyn was celebrated through the re-enactment of the event on a replica ship that sailed into San Francisco Bay. Members throughout the state commemorated the milestone anniversary.

In San Diego's Old Town on 18 January 1997, some 2,400 members re-enacted the arrival of the Mormon Battalion in California 150 years earlier. Other Mormon Battalion celebrations along the coast followed on respective anniversaries. On 6 March 1997, President Gordon B. Hinckley spoke to a record audience of the Los Angeles World Affairs Council, and on 19 March, he addressed the World Forum of Silicon Valley. He also spoke at various Church events during the year. A Church-produced video depicting the discovery of gold at Sutter's Mill was donated to the state of California to be shown continuously at Marshall Gold Discovery State Park in Coloma.

At the beginning of the year 2000, California had 17 missions, more than any other state in the United States. In the state's major cities, many minority converts have been taught the gospel in their own language. With significant immigration to California from Latin America, five Spanish-speaking stakes have been organized, two since 1992. Various Asian and Polynesian wards function as well, and a Tongan stake was created in San Francisco in 1992.

In 2002, membership reached 765,883.

In May 2003, hundreds of Los Angeles-area Muslims and members of the Pasadena California Stake joined in preparing emergency supplies for Iraqi families. With conflicts of the war with Iraq completed, a humanitarian aid day was set for 10 May 2003 where hygiene kits for some 10,000 families were completed and added to a $650,000 shipment of medical supplies and blankets donated by the Church.

President Hinckley attended the rededication of the historic Hollywood (now Los Angeles California California) Stake tabernacle on 8 June 2003.

Membership in 2003 was 770,885.

President Hinckley dedicated the Newport Beach Temple on 28 August 2005, the sixth temple in California, and the 122nd in the Church. The 17,800 square-foot edifice, built on fertile soil once occupied by orange groves, served 47,000 members in 16 stakes.

President Hinckley returned to California on 3 September 2006 to dedicate the Sacramento California Temple, the seventh temple in California and the 123rd in the Church. It serves a district of 80,000 members.

Sources: Andrew Jenson, Encyclopedic History of the Church, 1941; Richard O. Cowan and William E. Homer, California Saints: A 150-year Legacy in the Golden State, 1996; Chad M. Orton, More Faith than Fear, the Los Angeles Stake Story, 1987; Richard O. Cowan, "It Started in Yerba Buena," Instructor, June 1961; Albert L. Zobell, "The Church in Early California," Improvement Era, May 1964; Edward Leo Lyman, "The Rise and Decline of Mormon San Bernardino," BYU Studies, Fall 1989; Daniel H. Ludlow, ed., Encyclopedia of Mormonism, 1992; Julie A. Dockstader, "Spanish Spoken Here," Church News, 15 May 1993; Ana Gabriel, "Exhibit Honors LDS Settlers in California," Church News, 6 July 1996; Gerry Avant, "The Sesquicentennial of the Mormon Battalion," and "Men of Mormon Battalion: 'No Ordinary Men,'" Church News, 25 January 1997; "Church to Create Eight New Missions," Church News, 1 March 1997; Ana Gabriel, "California Leader Accepts LDS Film For State Park," Church News, 31 January 1998; Julie A. Dockstader, "Video Tells Battalion's Part In California Gold Discovery," Church News, 31 January 1998; R. Scott Lloyd, "Symbol of Growth in Fertile San Joaquin," Church News, 22 April 2000; "3 New Temples to be Built in California," Church News, 28 April 2001; Last is Hardest: Wagons Pull Safely Over Cajon Pass," Church News, 27 October 2001; "Arrival in San Bernardino," 3 November 2001; Sonja Eddings Brown, "Hygiene Kits To Help 10,000 Iraqi Families," Church News, 17 May 2003; Lincoln Hubbard, "Unique Building Restored, Rededicated," Church News, 14 June 2003; "Ground Broken for Newport Beach Temple," Church News, 23 August 2003; Greg Hill, "Redlands Temple in Inland Empire," Church News, 20 September 2003; "Gospel blossoming in land of fertile testimonies," Church News, 3 September 2005; Greg Hill "Adding a new treasure to '49 gold rush country," Church News, 9 September 2006.

No.	Name	Organized	First President
	North America West Area — 156		
402	*Anaheim California		
	‡Anaheim	14 Mar 1965	Max V. Eliason
1514	Anaheim California East	24 Feb 1985	William E. Perron
1042	Anderson California	10 Jun 1979	Richard Miller Ericson
1263	Antioch California	3 May 1981	Clifford Spence Munns
2729	Apple Valley California	10 Sep 2006	Craig C. Garrick
864	Arcadia California	9 Oct 1977	Cree-L Kofford
1691	Antelope California	6 Mar 1988	Roger William Mack
	‡Sacramento California Antelope		
1032	Auburn California	27 May 1979	David Oliver Montague
186	*Bakersfield California		
	‡Bakersfield	27 May 1951	E. Alan Pettit
944	Bakersfield California East	18 Jun 1978	William Horsley Davies
1622	Bakersfield California South	14 Dec 1986	Jack Ray Zimmerman
763	Camarillo California	8 Aug 1976	Victor Glenn Johnson
337	*Canoga Park California		
	*Los Angeles California Canoga Park		
	‡Canoga Park	8 Oct 1961	Collins E. Jones
309	*Carlsbad California		
	‡Palomar	6 Nov 1960	Wallace F. Gray
1505	Carmichael California	25 Nov 1984	Marc Earl Hall
269	*Cerritos California		
	‡Norwalk	26 Oct 1958	Lewis Milton Jones
565	*Chico California		
	‡Chico	6 Feb 1972	Lloyd Johnson Cope
1072	Chino California	14 Oct 1979	Allen Clare Christensen
770	Chula Vista California	19 Sep 1976	Robert Eugene Floto
1150	Citrus Heights California	22 Jun 1980	James Barnes
378	*Concord California		
	‡Concord	23 Jun 1963	Ted Eugene Madsen
983	Corona California	19 Nov 1978	Darvil David McBride
226	*Covina California (Spanish)		
	‡Covina	26 Feb 1956	Elden I. Ord
502	*Cypress California		
	‡Anaheim West	15 Feb 1970	Hugh J. Sorensen
229	*Danville California	19 Jun 1989	William W. Parmley
	*Walnut Creek California		
	‡Walnut Creek	26 Aug 1956	Emery R. Ranker
1151	Davis California	22 Jun 1980	Peter Glen Kenner
1740	Del Mar California	7 Jan 1990	Robert Geoffrey Dyer
279	*Downey California	18 Feb 1986	
	*Huntington Park California		
	‡Huntington Park	19 Apr 1959	Clifford B. Wright
179	*East Los Angeles California (Spanish)	27 Jun 1993	
	*Los Angeles California East		
	*Los Angeles East	29 May 1970	
	‡East Los Angeles (California)	26 Feb 1950	Fauntleroy Hunsaker
261	*El Cajon California	30 Nov 1975	
	*San Diego California El Cajon		
	‡San Diego East	20 Apr 1958	Cecil I. Burningham
1119	*El Centro California Imperial Valley	18 Mar 1997	
	‡El Centro California	16 Mar 1980	Robert Lamoreaux
984	El Dorado California	19 Nov 1978	Harold George Sellers
487	*Elk Grove California	30 Sep 1993	
	*Sacramento California South		
	‡Sacramento South (California)	15 Jun 1969	John Henry Huber
588	*Escondido California		
	‡Escondido	24 Sep 1972	Donald R. McArthur
1847	Escondido California South	9 Feb 1992	Louis L. Rothey
338	*Eureka California		
	‡Redwood		
	(California, Oregon)	22 Oct 1961	D. DeVar Felshaw
428	Folsom California	12 Feb 1967	Harvey Stansell Greer
	*Fair Oaks California		
	‡Fair Oaks		
682	Fairfield California	16 Feb 1975	Byron Gale Wilson
1602	Fontana California	22 Jun 1986	Wayne Hall Bringhurst
425	*Fremont California		
	‡Fremont	11 Dec 1966	Francis B. Winkel
185	*Fresno California		
	‡Fresno	20 May 1951	Alwyn C. Sessions
381	*Fresno California East		
	‡Fresno East	15 Sep 1963	Melvin P. Leavitt
1463	Fresno California North	12 Feb 1984	Stephen L. Christensen
1464	Fresno California West	12 Feb 1984	Gary R. Fogg
707	Fullerton California	21 Sep 1975	Leon Tad Ballard
330	*Garden Grove California		
	‡Garden Grove	25 Jun 1961	James Malan Hobbs

786	Glendora California	14 Nov 1976	William Marshall Raymond
116	*Granada Hills California	8 Apr 1997	
	*Van Nuys California		
	*San Fernando	15 Oct 1939	
	‡Pasadena	19 Apr 1936	David H. Cannon
107	*Gridley California		
	‡Gridley	4 Nov 1934	John C. Todd
442	*Hacienda Heights California	15 Jan 1978	
	*El Monte California		
	‡El Monte	17 Sep 1967	James Cyril Brown
948	Hanford California	6 Aug 1978	Gerald Leo Thompson
228a	*Hayward California		
	‡Hayward	26 Aug 1956	Milton P. Ream
961	Hemet California	17 Sep 1978	Darrel D. Lee
1632	Hesperia California	22 Feb 1987	Larry Dale Skinner
420	*Huntington Beach California		
	‡Huntington Beach	5 Jun 1966	Conway W. Nielsen
802	Huntington Beach	16 Jan 1977	Wesley Charles Woodhouse
	California North		
1477	Huntington Park California West (Sp)	3 Jun 1984	Rafael Nestor Seminario
129	*Inglewood California	21 Feb 1993	
	*Los Angeles California Inglewood		
	‡Inglewood	26 Nov 1939	Alfred E. Rohner
1633a	Irvine California	12 Apr 1987	Jack L. Rushton Jr.
1784	Jurupa California	9 Dec 1990	Lester C. Lauritzen
518	*La Crescenta California		
	‡La Canada	7 Jun 1970	Robert C. Seamons
347	*La Verne California		
	‡Pomona	21 Jan 1962	Vern R. Peel
1354	Laguna Niguel California	20 Jun 1982	Donald H. Sedgwick
794	Lancaster California	28 Nov 1976	Stephen N. Hull
1798	Lancaster California East	19 May 1991	John Milloy Martz
2900	Lincoln California	30 Jan 2011	Mark S. Perez
1654	Livermore California	13 Sep 1987	Willis Arthur Sandholtz
822	*Lodi California	3 May 1981	
	‡Stockton California East	10 Apr 1977	Robert Graham Wade
117	*Long Beach California		
	‡Long Beach	3 May 1936	John W. Jones
177	*Long Beach California East		
	*Long Beach East	29 May 1970	
	‡East Long Beach	12 Feb 1950	John C. Dalton
704	Los Altos California	24 Aug 1975	W. Kay Williams
98	*Los Angeles California		
	*Los Angeles	19 Nov 1939	
	‡Hollywood	22 May 1927	George W. McCune
188	*Los Angeles California Santa Monica		
	‡Santa Monica (California)	1 Jul 1951	E. Garrett Barlow
1249	Manteca California	22 Mar 1981	David Leon Ward
2108	Menifee California	15 Oct 1995	Timothy Rudd
156	*Menlo Park California		
	‡Palo Alto	23 Jun 1946	Claude B. Petersen
659	Merced California	15 Sep 1974	Robert D. Rowan
826	Mission Viejo California	8 May 1977	Nolan C. Draney
399	*Modesto California		
	‡Modesto	7 Jun 1964	Clifton A. Rooker
716	Modesto California North	26 Oct 1975	Charles Elwin Boice
258	*Monterey California		
	‡Monterey Bay	2 Mar 1958	James N. Wallace Jr.
1656	Moreno Valley California	27 Sep 1987	David Lowell Briggs
831	Morgan Hill California	15 May 1977	Donald Russell Lundell
1693	Murrieta California	20 Mar 1988	Ronald Miguel Peterson
297	*Napa California		
	‡Napa	17 Apr 1960	Harry S. Cargun
652	Newbury Park California	18 Aug 1974	Lavar M. Butler
453	*Newport Beach California		
	‡Newport Beach	31 Mar 1968	Ferren L. Christensen
231	*North Hollywood California	6 Dec 1992	
	*Los Angeles California North Hollywood		
	‡Burbank (California)	16 Sep 1956	James D. Pratt
227a	*Oakland California		
	‡Oakland-Berkeley	26 Aug 1956	O. Leslie Stone
2752	Oakland California East (Tongan)	17 Feb 2007	Tevita Manuevaha Lauti
1092	Ontario California	9 Dec 1979	Seth C. Baker
251a	*Orange California		
	‡Santa Ana	8 Dec 1957	Karl C. Durham
441	*Palm Desert California		
	‡Palm Springs	27 Aug 1967	Quinten Hunsaker
459	*Palmdale California		
	‡Antelope Valley	12 May 1968	Sterling A. Johnson
739	Palos Verdes California	18 Jan 1976	Merrill Bickmore
128	*Pasadena California		
	‡Pasadena	1 Oct 1939	Bertram M. Jones
1608	Penasquitos California	21 Sep 1986	Michael Lee Jensen

215	*Placentia California		
	*Fullerton	14 Mar 1965	
	‡Orange County	27 Jun 1954	John C. Dalton
675	Pleasanton California	8 Dec 1974	Dale Edwin Nielsen
2202	Porterville California	16 Jun 1996	Steven E. Tree
1056	Poway California	26 Aug 1979	Paul B. Richardson
1648	Rancho Cucamonga California	13 Aug 1987	
	‡Cucamonga California	28 Jun 1987	Steven Thomas Escher
319	*Redding California		
	‡Redding	13 Dec 1960	Albert C. Peterson
938	*Redlands California	5 May 1987	
	‡San Bernardino California East	4 Jun 1978	Donald L. Hansen
415	*Rialto California		
	‡Rialto	20 Mar 1966	Wayne A. Reeves
521	*Ridgecrest California		
	‡Mount Whitney	16 Aug 1970	AlDean Washburn
196	*Riverside California		
	‡Mount Rubidoux	26 Oct 1952	Vern Robert Peel
1854	Rocklin California	19 Apr 1992	Jay Robert Jibson Jr.
515	*Roseville California		
	‡Roseville	17 May 1970	S. Lloyd Hamilton
108	*Sacramento California		
	‡Sacramento	4 Nov 1934	Mark W. Cram
1152	*Sacramento California Cordova	11 Jan 1994	
	*Sacramento California Rancho Cordova	17 Sep 1985	
	‡Sacramento California Cordova	22 Jun 1980	Richard W. Montgomery
290	*Sacramento California East		
	‡American River	6 Dec 1959	Austin G. Hunt
219	*Sacramento California North		
	*Sacramento North	30 Sep 1969	
	‡North Sacramento	12 Dec 1954	Austin G. Hunt
2642	San Clemente California	13 June 2004	Curtis Denzil Reese
111	*San Bernardino California		
	‡San Bernardino	3 Feb 1935	Albert Lyndon Larson
136	*San Diego California		
	‡San Diego	9 Feb 1941	Wallace W. Johnson
736	San Diego California East	30 Nov 1975	Philip Alma Petersen
489	*San Diego California North		
	‡San Diego North	22 Jun 1969	Ray Michael Brown
360	*San Diego California Sweetwater	30 Aug 1988	
	*Lemon Grove California	16 Aug 1983	
	*San Diego California South		
	‡San Diego South	21 Oct 1962	Cecil I. Burningham
1915a	San Fernando California (Spanish)	6 Dec 1992	Jose Gerardo Lombardo
99	*San Francisco California		
	‡San Francisco	10 Jul 1927	W. Aird Macdonald
1863	San Francisco California East (Tongan)	10 May 1992	Sione Fangu
1515	San Francisco California West	24 Feb 1985	Jeremiah I. Alip
202	*San Jose California		
	‡San Jose	30 Nov 1952	Vernard L. Beckstrand
450	*San Jose California South		
	‡San Jose South (California)	11 Feb 1968	DeBoyd L. Smith
329	*San Leandro California		
	‡San Leandro	21 May 1961	Milton R. Ream
248	*San Luis Obispo California		
	‡San Luis Obispo	22 Sep 1957	Arthur J. Godfrey
462	*San Rafael California		
	‡Marin	23 Jun 1968	Weston L. Roe
1838	Santa Ana California South (Spanish)	5 Jan 1992	Renan Ramos Disner
184	*Santa Barbara California		
	‡Santa Barbara	18 Mar 1951	Arthur J. Godfrey
642	*Santa Clarita California	2 Feb 1992	
	‡Los Angeles California Santa Clarita	19 May 1974	Norman D. Stevensen
823	Santa Cruz California	24 Apr 1977	Edwin Reese Davis
1920	Santa Margarita California	17 Jan 1993	David Michael Daly
384	*Santa Maria California		
	‡Santa Maria	20 Oct 1963	Clayton K. Call
181	*Santa Rosa California		
	‡Santa Rosa	7 Jan 1951	J. LeRoy Murdock
1582	Santee California	8 Dec 1985	Robert Earl Harper
387	*Saratoga California		
	‡San Jose West	10 Nov 1963	Louis W. Latimer
448	*Simi Valley California		
	‡Simi	10 Dec 1967	John Lyman Ballif III
171	*Stockton California		
	‡San Joaquin	25 Apr 1948	Wendell B. Mendenhall
2613a	Temecula California	27 Apr 2003	Kevin G. Osborne
1624	Thousand Oaks California	11 Jan 1987	Grant R. Brimhall

282	*Torrance California		
	‡Torrance	3 May 1959	Roland Earl Gagon
220	*Torrance California North		
	‡Redondo	29 May 1955	Leslie L. Prestwich
1591	Turlock California	23 Mar 1986	Robert Peebles Baker
877	Ukiah California	30 Oct 1977	Robert Vernon Knudsen
583	*Upland California		
	‡Upland	13 Aug 1972	Frank E. Finlayson
1801	Vacaville California	26 May 1991	Edwin Gordon Wells Jr.
1845	Valencia California	2 Feb 1992	Reed E. Halladay
548	*Ventura California		
	‡Ventura	30 May 1971	Joseph F. Chapman
1397	Victorville California	30 Jan 1983	Owen Dean Call
492	*Visalia California		
	‡Visalia	24 Aug 1969	Alva D. Blackburn
967	Vista California	8 Oct 1978	Jack Robert Jones
1587a	*Walnut Creek California	17 May 1992	
	‡Walnut Creek California East	16 Feb 1986	Williams F. Matthews
280	*Whittier California		
	‡Whittier	26 Apr 1959	John Collings
1079	Yuba City California	4 Nov 1979	Lowell R. Tingey
2631	Yucaipa California	25 April 2004	Kevin Koy Miskin
1969	Yucca Valley California	9 Jan 1994	Kipton Paul Madsen

North America Southwest Area — 1

1073	Quincy California	14 Oct 1979	Floyd Eugene Warren

Stakes discontinued

288	*Barstow California		
	‡Mojave	16 Aug 1959	Sterling A. Johnson
	Discontinued 24 August 2008		
159	Berkeley	13 Oct 1946	W. Glenn Harmon
	Discontinued 26 Aug 1956 †Oakland-Berkeley (227a)		
656	Cerritos California West	8 Sep 1974	Kenneth Laurence Davis
	Discontinued 19 May 1996		
806	Concord California East	23 Jan 1977	Vern W. Clark
	Discontinued 16 Feb 1986 †Walnut Creek California East (1587)		
1107	Lawndale California	17 Feb 1980	Silvon Foster Engilman
	Discontinued 21 Feb 1993		
1683	Long Beach California North	31 Jan 1988	V. Jay Spongberg
	Discontinued 7 Nov 1993		
817	Los Angeles California	13 Mar 1977	Clark Spendlove
	Granada Hills 6 Dec 1992		
88	*Los Angeles South 29 May 1970		
	Discontinued 12 Aug 1973 †Huntington Park (279)		
	*South Los Angeles 19 Nov 1939		
	‡Los Angeles	21 Jan 1923	George W. McCune
109	Oakland	2 Dec 1934	W. Aird Macdonald
	Discontinued 26 Aug 1956 †Oakland-Berkeley (227a)		
247	*Pacifica California		
	Discontinued 21 Feb 1982 †San Francisco California (99)		
	‡San Mateo	15 Sep 1957	Melvin P. Pickering
230	Reseda (California)	16 Sep 1956	Hugh C. Smith
	*Los Angeles California Chatsworth		
	Discontinued 6 Dec 1992		
787	Santa Ana California	14 Nov 1976	Wilbur Orion Jensen
	Discontinued 10 Nov 1996		
4a	San Bernardino	6 Jul 1851	David Seely
	Discontinued 1857		
585	San Jose North (California)	20 Aug 1972	Lloyd M. Gustaveson
	Discontinued 10 May 1992		
	*Santa Clara California		
1584	Fremont California South	12 Jan 1986	Jerry Valient Kirk
	Discontinued 11 Jun 2000		
1926	Highland California	14 Mar 1993	Dennis Alvin Barlow
	Discontinued	6 Mar 2005	
1649	Lompoc California	23 Aug 1987	Billy Ray Williams
	Discontinued	13 Mar 2005	
175	*Glendale California		
	‡Glendale	4 Dec 1949	Edwin Smith Dibble
	Discontinued 2 June 2007		
430	*Riverside California West		
	‡Arlington	23 Apr 1967	Clarence Leon Sirrine
	Discontinued 16 Jun 2007		
693	San Jose California East	4 May 1975	Leo E. Haney
	Discontinued	8 Sep 2007	
281	*Walnut California	23 July 1985	
	*La Puente California		
	‡West Covina	3 May 1959	Mark W. Smith
	Discontinued	8 June 2008	

(73a) CALIFORNIA ANAHEIM MISSION
501 N. Brookhurst, Ste. 100
Anaheim, CA 92801

(86) CALIFORNIA ARCADIA MISSION
170 West Duarte Road
Arcadia, CA 91007

(283) CALIFORNIA CARLSBAD MISSION
785 Grand Ave., Ste. 202
Carlsbad, CA 92008

(118) CALIFORNIA FRESNO MISSION
1814 N. Echo Ave.
Fresno, CA 93704

(324)CALIFORNIA LONG BEACH MISSION
2501 Cherry Ave, Ste 255
Signal Hill, CA. 90755-2042

(5) CALIFORNIA LOS ANGELES MISSION
1591 E. Temple Way
Los Angeles, CA 90024-5801

(85)CALIFORNIA OAKLAND/SAN FRANCISCO MISSION
4945 Lincoln Way
Oakland, CA 94602

(235) CALIFORNIA RIVERSIDE MISSION
5900 Grand Ave.
Riverside, CA 92504-1328

(284) CALIFORNIA ROSEVILLE
8331 Sierra College Blvd., Ste. 208
Roseville, CA 95661

(37) CALIFORNIA SACRAMENTO MISSION
9480 Madison Ave., Ste. 4
Orangevale, CA 95662

(182) CALIFORNIA SAN BERNARDINO
8280 Utica Ave, Ste. 150
Rancho Cucamonga, CA 91730

(113) CALIFORNIA SAN DIEGO MISSION
7404 Armstrong Pl
San Diego, CA 92111-4912

(297) CALIFORNIA SAN FERNANDO
23504 Lyons Ave., Ste. 107
Santa Clarita, CA 91321

(159) CALIFORNIA VENTURA MISSION
260 Maple Ct., Ste. 120
Ventura, CA 93003-3692

(158a) CALIFORNIA SAN JOSE MISSION
3975 McLaughlin Ave Ste A
San Jose, CA 95121-2631

(187a) CALIFORNIA SANTA ROSA MISSION
3510 Unocal Place, Ste. 302
Santa Rosa, CA 95403

Colorado

Jan. 1, 2010: Est. population, 4,939,000; Members, 142,473; Stakes, 30; Wards, 257; Branches, 32; Missions, 3; Temples, 1; Percent LDS, 2.8, or one in 36.

The first Latter-day Saints in the area that is now Colorado arrived in 1846. A company of 43 emigrants from Mississippi who were trying to meet Brigham Young's pioneer company along the Platte River discovered that he had been forced to wait at Winter Quarters. The Mississippi saints, already in western Nebraska and needing a place to camp for the winter, consulted a fur trapper who recommended Fort Pueblo near the headwaters of the Arkansas River. In August of 1846, they arrived in the vicinity of the fort and began building cabins and other necessary structures.

The following month, a detachment of Mormon Battalion family members who had accompanied the soldiers was sent to the Pueblo settlement to spend the winter. By year's end, two other groups from the Battalion consisting of the laundresses and men too sick to continue on to California had also arrived at Pueblo.

In June of 1847, a number of the saints who had spent the winter at Pueblo met Brigham Young's company at Fort Laramie and accompanied them into the Salt Lake Valley. Later that year, Elder Amasa Lyman of the Quorum of the Twelve was assigned to go to Pueblo to bring the remainder of the saints who had been waiting there to go to the Salt Lake Valley, effectively ending the presence of the Church in Colorado.

The next appearance of Church members in Colorado was in October of 1858. A Latter-day Saint family by the name of Rooker, interested in reports of gold in the area, became the first Anglo family to settle on Cherry Creek in the area that became Denver.

In 1875, Lawrence M. Petersen of Las Tijeras in southern Colorado traveled to Manti, Utah, to visit his brother. The two had been separated when Lawrence had wandered away from a Mormon train near Kansas City, Mo., in 1854 and never returned. The pioneers gave him up for lost and went on without him. He was picked up by some traders, who persuaded him to accompany them to New Mexico. He started a new life there and eventually settled in southern Colorado. When he learned many years later that his family was in Utah, he visited them and accepted the gospel. After returning to his home in Colorado, Petersen preached the gospel to the Spanish settlers and baptized about 40 of them. In April of 1877, Petersen and his group of converts were forced by opposition to move away from Las Tijeras. They subsequently settled in northern New Mexico.

President John Morgan of the Southern States Mission arrived at Pueblo at the head of a company of 70 converts from the south on 24 November 1877, with instructions to establish a permanent colony in southern Colorado. A few weeks later, Church leaders asked Lawrence Petersen for advice concerning a site for the new colony, somewhere on or near the headwaters of the Rio Grande. He suggested the Conejos River in the San Luis Valley and plans were formulated to settle the saints there the following spring.

On 24 March 1878, led by Elder James Z. Stewart, arrived at Pueblo. Stewart and President Morgan then traveled to the Conejos River, where two small ranches were purchased as a site for the new settlement. During May, Petersen and his group moved to the new settlement in New Mexico, along with a portion of those waiting at Pueblo. Later that year, in October, the rest of the Pueblo group moved to the Conejos and a group that had been called from among the Sanpete Valley settlers arrived to help establish the settlement. Upon the arrival of the latter group, the Conejos Branch was organized with Hans Jensen, brother of Lawrence Petersen, as the bishop.

In the spring of 1879, the branch was moved about three miles to the site of present-day Manassa, Colo. As the membership in the area grew, the settlers spread out and established other branches of the Church in the San Luis Valley. On 9 June 1883 the first stake in Colorado, the San Luis Stake, was formed from the Conejos settlements with Silas S. Smith as president.

While the Church was growing steadily in the San Luis Valley, John I. Hart received an assignment to take a company of saints and establish a permanent settlement at Pueblo. He and his group arrived in the summer of 1896 and reintroduced the Church in that community. Also in 1896, Apostle John W. Taylor traveled to Denver and officially established the Colorado Mission, which at the time included only Colorado. By 1907, the mission had grown to include several neighboring states and was consequently renamed the Western States Mission. This brought continued growth for the Church in the Denver area and on 30 June 1940, the Denver Stake was organized. The same day the dependent branch at Fort Collins attained independent status. The branch had been established in 1931 with the arrival of a number of Latter-day Saint faculty members and their families at Colorado State University.

By the last two decades of the 20th century, the Church had begun to mature in Colorado. That period saw the establishment in the early 1980s at Colorado Springs of the first-released time seminary program east of the Rocky Mountains and the dedication of the Denver Colorado Temple on 24 October 1986.

On 23 February 1990, the Denver area public affairs council arranged with the Denver Nuggets of the National Basketball Association for the first "Family Night With the Denver Nuggets" at McNichols Arena. The following month, on 11 March 1990, Colorado Gov. Roy Romer spoke in behalf of strong families at a Church fireside in Willow Springs.

Church members gave hundreds of hours of volunteer service during the visit of Pope John Paul II to Denver in August of 1993. That same year, on 1 July, the mission was divided into the Colorado Denver North Mission, successor to the original Colorado Mission, and the new Colorado Denver South Mission.

President Gordon B. Hinckley spoke to thousands of young people in Colorado Springs and Denver on 14 April 1996 and met again with Church members in Denver on 13 September 1997 to celebrate the 100th anniversary of the first branch of the Church in that city. On 31 July 1999, members of 19 Colorado stakes performed dozens of separate service projects as part of a state-wide "day of service" instituted by Church leaders in Colorado under the direction of Gov. Bill Owens.

As the Church in Colorado moved into the 21st century, the mission alignment was again changed with the creation of the Colorado Colorado Springs Mission on 1 July 2002, making three missions headquartered in the state. The following year, on 22 April 2003, as part of a lecture series on values, President B. Hinckley spoke to more than 6,000 people at the University of Denver about the importance the family.

Growth of membership has been steady since World War II. By 1950, membership was nearly 10,000. It increased to nearly 20,000 in 1960, and nearly 40,000 by 1970. By 1980, it was 69,000.

In 1999, membership was 112,232; and by 2002, membership reached 121,279 members organized in 29 stakes.

Sources: Manassa Colorado Stake, Manuscript history and historical reports, Church Archives; Denver Colorado Stake, Manuscript history and historical reports, Church Archives; Fort Collins Ward, Fort Collins Stake manuscript history and historical reports, Church Archives; Pueblo Branch, Manuscript history and historical reports, Church Archives; Sanford Ward, Manuscript history and historical reports, Church Archives; Manassa Branch, Manuscript history and historical reports, Church Archives; Richfield Ward, Manuscript history and historical reports, Church Archives; Colorado Denver South Mission, Manuscript history and historical reports, Church Archives; San Luis Stake, History of the organization of the Relief Society, 1884, Church Archives; Leonard Arrington, "Mississippi Mormons," Ensign, June 1997; "News of the Church," Ensign, November 1997; "News of the Church," Ensign, June 1996; "News of the Church," Ensign, June 2002; Conejos Branch, General minutes, Church Archives; Gail McHardy, A Look at the History of the Church of Jesus Christ of Latter-day Saints (Mormon) in Pueblo, Colorado, 1988; Ann Wainstein Bond, Pueblo on the Arkansas River Crossroads of Southern Colorado, 1992; "Mormon Battalion . . . and Mormon Pioneers . . .," Colorado Magazine, Summer 1970; "Denver Saints Claim Spiritual Blessings," Ensign, November 1986; "The Church in South Central Colorado," Church News, 24 August 1986; "Basketball Night Sponsored," Church News, 24 March 1990; "LDS Among Volunteers for Papal Visit," Church News, 21 August 1993; "Strong Families Build Bridges to Future," Church News, 26 April 2003; "Colorado's Governor Calls for Strong Families," Church News, 7 August 1999; "Denver Temple Dedicated," Ensign, January 1987.

Stakes — 30
(Listed alphabetically as of Oct. 1, 2011.)

No.	Name	Organized	First President
North America Central Area — 29			
1425	Alamosa Colorado	29 May 1983	Gary Reese Shawcroft
1655	Arapahoe Colorado	27 Sep 1987	Lawry Evans Doxey
287	*Arvada Colorado		
	‡Denver West	21 Jun 1959	Thomas L. Kimball
1318	Aurora Colorado	6 Dec 1981	Lawry Evans Doxey
595	*Boulder Colorado		
	‡Boulder	28 Jan 1973	C. Rodney Claridge
2630	Castle Rock Colorado	7 Mar 2004	Douglas L. Polson
301	*Colorado Springs Colorado		
	‡Pikes Peak		
	(Colorado, New Mexico)	11 Sep 1960	Ralph M. Gardner
1770	Colorado Springs Colorado East	26 Aug 1990	Jack Harmon Dunn
1134	Colorado Springs Colorado North	18 May 1980	Richard Larry Williams
1214	Columbine Colorado	7 Dec 1980	David M. Brown
132	*Denver Colorado		
	‡Denver	30 Jun 1940	Douglas M. Todd Jr.
596	*Denver Colorado North		
	‡Denver North	28 Jan 1973	Gus. F. Ranzenberger
470	*Fort Collins Colorado		
	‡Fort Collins	1 Dec 1968	Raymond Price

2542	Fountain Colorado	12 Dec 1999	Larry M. Lewis
1452	Golden Colorado	6 Nov 1983	John Marshall Simcox
223	*Grand Junction Colorado		
	‡Grand Junction	16 Oct 1955	Loyal B. Cook
1415	Grand Junction Colorado West	24 Apr 1983	Andrew H. Christensen
1528	Greeley Colorado	28 Apr 1985	Gilbert I. Sandberg
1534	*Highlands Ranch Colorado	21 Aug 1998	
	‡Willow Creek Colorado	19 May 1985	Robert K. Bills
394	*Lakewood Colorado		
	‡Denver South	19 Apr 1964	R. Raymond Barnes
625	*Littleton Colorado		
	‡Littleton	2 Sep 1973	Clinton L. Cutler
1778	Longmont Colorado	11 Nov 1990	Lynn Snarr Hutchings
2562	Loveland Colorado	18 Jun 2000	Alan J. Baker
26	*Manassa Colorado	31 May 1983	
	*La Jara Colorado		
	‡San Luis (Colorado, New Mexico)	10 Jun 1883	Silas S. Smith
320	Meeker Colorado		
	‡Craig	15 Jan 1961	Loyal B. Cook
977	Montrose Colorado	5 Nov 1978	Robert M. Esplin
2236	Parker Colorado	15 Sep 1996	William Kenneth Thiess
2906	Parker Colorado South	13 Mar 2011	Dale N. Lyman
632	Pueblo Colorado	3 Mar 1974	Louis Edward Butler
2346	Westminster Colorado	27 Apr 1997	David B. Parker

North America Southwest Area — 1

557	*Durango Colorado		
	‡Mesa Verde	7 Nov 1971	Del A. Talley Sr.

Stakes discontinued

21	Little Colorado	27 Jan 1878	Lot Smith

Discontinued (Colo., Ariz.) 18 Dec 1887 †Snowflake (31a)

Missions — 3
(As of Oct. 1, 2011; shown with historical number. See MISSIONS.)

(331a) COLORADO COLORADO SPRINGS MIS.
4090 Center Park Dr.
Colorado Springs, CO 80916

(286) COLORADO DENVER NORTH MISSION
11172 North Huron, Suite 21
Northglenn, CO 80234

(17) COLORADO DENVER SOUTH MISSION
2001 E. Easter Ave. Ste 303
Littleton, CO 80122

Connecticut

Jan. 1, 2011: Est. population, 3,501,000; Members, 14,990; Stakes, 4; Wards, 27; Branches, 5; Missions, 1; Percent LDS, 0.4, or one in 240.

Orson Hyde and Samuel H. Smith began missionary work in Connecticut in June 1832 by visiting Litchfield and Hartford counties. The first baptisms came two months later, after Orson Pratt and Lyman Sherman converted 11 in Madison and Killingworth.

During the next quarter century, LDS missionaries crisscrossed the state visiting branches and preaching to all who would hear. Among the elders was Connecticut native Wilford Woodruff, who, in July 1838, held a meeting of which he wrote, "Distress overwhelmed the whole household, and all were tempted to reject the work. . . . Filled with the power of God, I stood in the midst of the congregation and preached unto the people in great plainness the gospel of Jesus Christ." He afterward baptized his father, stepmother, sister and three others and organized a small branch in Farmington.

Early branches remained small because most Connecticut Latter-day Saints relocated to Kirtland, Nauvoo and later to Utah. As was true elsewhere in the eastern United States, missionary work was sporadic in Connecticut between the Utah War of 1857 and the reopening of the Eastern States Mission in 1893. Even after missionaries were assigned on a regular basis in the early 20th century, Church growth in the state was slow, with only 53 members in 1916, and 154 a decade later. By 1930, the Connecticut District consisted of branches in Hartford and New Haven and nearby Springfield, Mass. With the disruptions to missionary work brought on by the Great Depression and World War II, Church membership in Connecticut rose only to 184 by 1940 and 308 by the end of 1950.

During this era of limited numerical growth, the New England Mission was created in 1937, with headquarters at Cambridge, Mass., and a remodeled home was dedicated at Bridgeport in June 1944 as a branch meetinghouse. In September 1952, the first meetinghouse built by the Church in New England was dedicated for use by the Hartford Branch. By that time there were branches in Hartford, New Haven, New London, and Bridgeport, with another 83 Church members scattered throughout the state not part of any organized branch.

The 1950s saw a quadrupling of Connecticut's LDS membership, which stood at nearly 1,200 at the end of 1960. Bridgeport became a ward in the nearby New York Stake earlier that year, forging a Church link between the southwestern part of the state and the New York metropolitan area that continues to the present — Connecticut in 2004 was home to eight of the nine wards and branches of the Yorktown New York Stake.

Although Connecticut wards and branches were geographically large and a substantial share of Latter-day Saints had to travel many miles to Church meetings, membership growth continued at a relatively rapid rate during the 1960s. Membership nearly tripled during the decade, rising to 3,368 at the end of 1970, in part because of the increased unity that came as local members built several new meetinghouses, and in part because of the leadership of lifetime Church members from the western United States whose employment brought them to Connecticut.

Such growth made possible the creation of Connecticut's first stake in September 1966, with wards at Hartford, Manchester, New Haven, New London and Southington, and branches at Madison and Torrington, although three Massachusetts branches were also drawn in to provide sufficient numbers for a stake. By this time there were also wards of the New York Stake in Bridgeport and Danbury, Conn.

LDS membership in Connecticut almost doubled again during the 1970s, rising to 6,300 at the end of 1980. Partly in recognition of such growth, Connecticut's first mission was established in July 1979 with headquarters in the Hartford suburb of Bloomfield. By 1980 Latter-day Saints in Connecticut were organized into 14 wards and branches, many of them taking in as many as 20 to 25 towns. Church membership in Connecticut doubled again by 2000. Even so, Latter-day Saints continue to represent only a very small share of the state's population.

A temple was announced for Hartford in October 1992, but three years later President Gordon B. Hinckley announced that a suitable site had not been found and the First Presidency had determined instead that two temples would be built, which were eventually erected in New York City and Boston, Mass.

As of 2004 Connecticut's wards and branches belonged to the Hartford Connecticut, New Haven Connecticut, Providence Rhode Island and Yorktown New York stakes. Southwestern Connecticut's Church units include Spanish-speaking branches in Trumbull, Norwalk and Stamford, reflecting the spillover of the New York metropolitan area's Latino population into the Connecticut commuter towns

Membership was 13,714 in 2003. By 2005, membership reached 14,191.

The Connecticut Hartford Mission was consolidated with the Massachusetts Boston Mission on 1 July 2011.

Sources: Andrew Jenson, "Connecticut Conference," Encyclopedic History of the Church (1941); Earle L. Stone, "The Mormons in Connecticut, 1832-1952," master's thesis, 1980; General mission annual reports and stake and mission statistical recaps, 1940-1970, Church Archives; Directory of General Authorities and Officers, 2004; Telephone conversation with former Hartford Stake president Hugh S. West, May 2004; "Four Chapels Dedicated in New England Mission," Church News, 22 July 1944; "Chapels Needed in New England Mission," Church News, 4 October 1952; "New Stake Is Formed; Changes in 3 Others," Church News, 24 September 1966; "Nine new missions created," Church News, 10 March 1979; "Plans Are Announced for 3 More Temples," Church News, 10 October 1992; "2 Temples to Be Built in Eastern U.S.," Church News, 7 October 1995.

Stakes — 4
(Listed alphabetically as of Oct. 1, 2011.)

No.	Name	Organized	First President
North America Northeast Area			
421	*Hartford Connecticut		
	‡Hartford (Conn., Mass.)	18 Sep 1966	Hugh S. West
1288	New Haven Connecticut	30 Aug 1981	Steven Douglas Colson

Delaware

Jan. 1, 2011: Est. population, 873,000; Members, 5,184; Stakes, 1; Wards, 10; Branches, 3; Percent LDS: 0.5, or one in 185.

Jedediah M. Grant in 1837 was among the first to begin LDS missionary work in Delaware. Local missionary William I. Appleby, a resident of nearby New Jersey, preached in Wilmington in January 1841 and attended a conference of the Wilmington Branch in November of that year. Appleby also recorded in his journal that he made a number of visits to Delaware in 1843, where he held a debate in Wilmington and preached in that city and surrounding areas. Heber C. Kimball and Lyman Wight of the Quorum of the Twelve presided at a June 1844 conference in Wilmington attended by about 100 people, where the Latter-day Saints voted unanimously to follow the First Presidency and the Twelve to whatever gathering place they might select in the western United States.

In the years that followed, Delaware Latter-day Saints followed through on that commitment, either by moving to Nauvoo or later to Utah, with some of them possibly among the 70 who left Philadelphia, Pa., in April 1849 for the West with William Appleby. During the next half century, there is no evidence of missionary work or other Church activity in Delaware.

Church representatives labored sporadically in Delaware during the first four decades of the 20th century. In 1901, missionary John E. Baird left Brooklyn, N.Y., to visit missionaries in several eastern cities, including Wilmington. In 1914, Stanley A. Lawrence and Alphonso W. Taylor reported teaching a Delaware woman who had gained a testimony of the Book of Mormon. Two years later a pair of elders reported renting a hall in Wilmington where meetings were held during the winter of 1916-1917. Other meetings were held in members' homes and some of the Church's auxiliary organizations were established and held classes and activities during the 1920s and 1930s. Latter-day Saints in Wilmington asked the Eastern States Mission for help, and missionaries again worked in the area for a while during the late 1930s. Meeting attendances varied between 10 and 20, without the group developing a self-sustaining nucleus of Church membership.

In the late 1920s, what local historian Helen Stark called "a reversal of migration, this time from West to East" began to take place as Latter-day Saints from Utah and other western states came to Wilmington seeking employment. Delaware was re-opened to missionary work in April 1940, and the Church's presence in the state has been continuous since then. A branch was organized in Wilmington in September 1941 that became part of the district based in Philadelphia. Initially, the Wilmington Branch stretched some 200 miles to the south, but as members reached out to Latter-day Saints living outside of Wilmington, a group was organized at Salisbury, Md., — about 10 miles south of the Delaware state line — which became a branch in June 1953. Although it involved a 300-mile round trip, for a time Saints from Wilmington visited the new branch two Sundays a month to give aid to their fellow Church members. Later in the decade, another branch was established in Dover, the state capital.

There were approximately 100 members of the Church in Delaware in 1950. The next year the Wilmington Branch began raising money to build a meetinghouse, but it was 1955 before they succeeded in acquiring a site on which neighbors were willing to allow an LDS building to be erected. Ground was broken in 1958 and the branch moved into Delaware's first Church-built facility in May 1960, although it was another six years before the local saints could fully pay for the building so it could be dedicated. In the fall of 1960, the Philadelphia Stake was organized, including wards and branches in eastern Pennsylvania, southern New Jersey, the Wilmington Ward in Delaware, and the branches in Dover, Del., and Salisbury, Md. Of the new stake's 2,000 members, some 400 lived in Delaware.

Missionary work accelerated during the 1960s and, although no new Church units were formed in Delaware, by 1970 the membership of the Philadelphia Stake had risen to 4,600, with nearly 1,100 of them residing in the two Delaware units and the Salisbury Branch. Continuing growth during the 1970s led to a division of the stake in December 1974, with the new Wilmington Delaware Stake taking in all of Delaware, the southern part of New Jersey, the Salisbury Branch in Maryland, and several communities in southeastern Pennsylvania that were part of the Wilmington Ward. Five years later, in November 1979, the New Jersey wards and branches of the stake in Wilmington were organized as the Pitman New Jersey Stake. By August 2001, all the Pennsylvania territory of the Wilmington Delaware Stake had been transferred to stakes based in Pennsylvania. At the end of 1980, Church membership in Delaware was 1,410, with another 716 members of the stake living in Maryland.

Church growth has been the greatest in recent years in the Wilmington metropolitan area, where there has been an influx of Latter-day Saints from other states not only to work for several large chemical companies but also in the banking industry. Southern Delaware is less industrialized and most members living there have joined the Church in that area.

With the Delaware economy growing rapidly and new housing developments springing up on the western edge of the Wilmington metropolitan area, a new stake center was built at Newark in 1989 and ward and branch boundaries in northern Delaware and Maryland were realigned to shorten the distances members traveled to weekly meetings. By 2004, the Wilmington Delaware Stake was composed of eight wards in Delaware, the Salisbury Ward in Maryland, branches that met in Cambridge and North East, Maryland, and a Spanish branch that held its services in Dover, Del.

Membership reached 4,073 in 2003. By 2005, membership reached 4,279.

Sources: Andrew Jenson, "Delaware," Encyclopedic History of the Church, 1941; General mission annual reports and stake statistical recaps, 1950-1980, Church Archives; Helen Candland Stark, The L.D.S. Church in Delaware: A Book of Remembrance, 1966 (quotation is from p. 19); Afton Hepworth Hobbs, Reflections on the Salisbury Branch: A history of the early growth of The Church of Jesus Christ of Latter-day Saints on the lower Delmarva Peninsula, 1989; Susan Buhler Taber, Mormon Lives: A Year in the Elkton Ward, 1993; Kevin Stoker, "Church grows larger in 2nd smallest state," Church News, 3 December 1988; "Setting a worthy example among friends," Church News, 9 May 1998; Sharon Lance Sundelin, "The Wilmington Delaware Stake: No Small Wonder," Ensign, March 2001.

Stake — 1
(Listed alphabetically as of Oct. 1, 2011.)

No.	Name	Organized	First President
North America Northeast Area			
673	Wilmington Delaware	8 Dec 1974	Rulon Edward Johnson Jr

District of Columbia

Jan. 1, 2011: Est. population, 592,000; Members, 2,382; Stakes, 0; Wards, 2; Branches, 1; Missions, 0; Percent LDS, 0.37, or one in 269.

During the 19th century, LDS leaders were regularly in the nation's capital on behalf of the Church. The first to come was the Prophet Joseph Smith, who, with Elias Higbee, spent part of the winter of 1839-1840 seeking redress of the grievances suffered by the Saints in Missouri. While there, the two presented a lengthy petition to Congress and met with President Martin Van Buren, who infamously told the Church leaders, "Your cause is just, but I can do nothing for you." The same year Parley P. Pratt published an address in Washington setting forth the principles of the gospel and saw that a copy was presented to the President and each Cabinet member.

In 1844, Orson Hyde and Orson Pratt of the Quorum of the Twelve, later joined by fellow apostles Heber C. Kimball, William Smith and Lyman Wight, represented the cause of the Saints to President John Tyler. Elder Jesse C. Little, president of the Eastern States Mission, was the Church's representative in Washington in 1846 and negotiated the raising of a 500-man Mormon battalion as part of the United States Army of the West during the Mexican War. A few years later, Orson Pratt again visited the seat of government, where he, together with Jedediah M. Grant, met with President Millard Fillmore. While there, for about 18 months in 1853-1854, Elders Pratt and Grant published a monthly periodical, The Seer, named in memory of Joseph Smith.

After arriving in the Great Basin, Church leaders petitioned Congress for a state government, but Utah was instead granted territorial status. While pursuing statehood over the next 45 years, Latter-day Saints serving as Utah's territorial delegates to Congress lived in Washington and sought to advance the interests of Utah and the Church.

In 1903, Elder Reed Smoot of the Quorum of the Twelve was elected to represent Utah in the U. S. Senate and took up residence in Washington where he spent the next 30 years. Desiring to share the gospel with LDS students attending area universities, as well as with Church members from the West who were employed by the federal government, Sen. Smoot hosted sacrament meetings in his home from December 1909 until May 1920. Similar meetings had previously been held in the home of Utah Congressman Joseph Howell from 1904 to 1907. During this same period a small branch also functioned briefly in nearby Capitol Heights, Md., where a one-story frame meetinghouse was built by 1918.

To meet the needs of the influx of Latter-day Saints in government employment during World War I who then remained in the nation's capital, the Washington Branch was organized in June 1920. With the growth of the federal government during the New Deal era, many additional Latter-day Saints came to the area seeking employment. By 1937, there were 1,800 members of the Church in the Washington area.

Church leaders in Salt Lake City authorized the acquisition in 1924 of a building site at Sixteenth Street and Columbia

Road N. W. The seller of the property insisted that an impressive building be constructed in what was then an exclusive neighborhood. Utah architect Don Carlos Young designed a stone structure whose spire was crowned with a golden statue of the Angel Moroni similar to the one atop the Salt Lake Temple.

Ground was broken for the Washington Chapel in 1930 and was dedicated in November 1933 by President Heber J. Grant, who was accompanied for the occasion by both of his counselors in the First Presidency and five members of the Twelve.

The Washington Chapel quickly became a show place for introducing people to the Church and gave rise to regular tours of the building, organ concerts and other musical programs and the organization in 1935 of the first seventies quorum in the Eastern United States.

With missionary work accelerating, coupled with the continuing influx of Church members from Utah and elsewhere, additional branches were organized in 1938 in Arlington, Va., and Chevy Chase, Md. This was soon followed by the creation of the Capitol District, which included the Washington Branch, the two new branches, and additional branches in Baltimore and Greenbelt, Md, and Waynesboro, Pa.

In June 1940, the district became the Washington Stake, only the second stake organized in the Eastern United States since the exodus from Nauvoo. Idaho native Ezra Taft Benson served as president of the new stake, a position he held until March 1944 when he was released because of his call several months earlier to the Quorum of the Twelve.

During World War II and the ensuing years, growing numbers of Latter-day Saints came to Washington seeking education and employment or through assignment to the many nearby military installations. During the later 1940s and the 1950s, Church members increasingly established residences in the Maryland and Virginia suburbs and commuted to the District of Columbia to work.

Numerous new wards and branches were created and many meetinghouses were built to serve their needs. By 1963, the Washington metropolitan area was home to some 8,000 Church members, leading to the creation that year of the Potomac Stake, which took in the Washington Stake's Virginia and southeastern Maryland wards. In 1970, two more stakes were created in greater Washington — the Mount Vernon Stake in Virginia and the Chesapeake Stake in Maryland — with another stake being organized in Baltimore in 1974.

When the Washington Chapel was sold in 1975 — due to the deterioration of the surrounding neighborhood and the need for major repairs to the building — and the Washington Ward was discontinued, all the wards and stakes of the Washington D. C. Stake were located in Maryland.

For the next several years the Church's presence in the nation's capital was only symbolic until a singles ward and a Spanish-speaking branch were established in 1981. In 1987, the Washington D. C. 2nd Ward was organized to meet the needs of inner-city residents. These and other Church units created in subsequent years became part of the District of Columbia District in 1994. In 2004, the district consisted of seven branches, four of which held meetings in Chevy Chase or Suitland, Md., just outside the boundaries of Washington proper.

With the mid-1970s departure of the Church from the District of Columbia, the LDS focus in the greater Washington area shifted to the Washington Temple in nearby Kensington, Md. Washington Stake president J. Willard Marriott Sr. had recommended to the First Presidency in March 1954 that the Church build a temple in his community to meet the needs of the thousands of Latter-day Saints living east of the Mississippi River. Church leaders advised President Marriott that "the matter would be taken up in due time."

Seven years later the First Presidency authorized the establishment of a temple site committee, which in November 1968 recommended building on a 57-acre plot in Kensington that had been purchased in 1962. Ground was broken less than a month later, construction began in the spring of 1971. President Spencer W. Kimball dedicated the temple in November 1974.

The new structure, prominently situated near the beltway surrounding Washington, quickly became a dynamic symbol of the Church and many were eager to know more about it. The increased visibility of the Latter-day Saints in greater Washington was evidenced by the fact that more than 750,000 people toured the temple during the six-week open house prior to its dedication.

Interest continued so strong that a major visitors center was erected adjacent to the temple, with that facility being dedicated by President Kimball in July 1976 in connection with the Tabernacle Choir's participation in the celebration of the U. S. Bicentennial. By 2004, four million visitors have since toured the center.

The temple complex was only one facet of the Church's higher profile in the nation's capital during the final decades of the 20th century. Beginning with the 1953 appointment of Elder Ezra Taft Benson as Secretary of Agriculture in the Eisenhower administration, several Latter-day Saints have served in the Cabinet, while a growing number of Church members have been elected to Congress. The Tabernacle Choir was invited to perform at the inaugurations of U. S. presidents Lyndon B. Johnson in 1965, Richard M. Nixon in 1969, Ronald Reagan in 1981, George H. W. Bush in 1989, and George W. Bush in 2001.

Following the organization of the Public Communications Council of Washington, D. C. in 1974, Church-service and professional public relations personnel worked to keep the Church and its activities constantly before the public. This effort was aided by the fact that the Washington metropolitan area was home by 1985 to 63,000 Church members in 19 stakes and more than 100 wards and branches, giving the area the highest concentration of Latter-day Saints on the Eastern Seaboard. The ethnically diverse LDS population included substantial numbers of Asians, Hispanics and African-Americans, as well as those of many other countries.

As official spokeswoman for the Church in the greater Washington area, Beverly Campbell joined her efforts with those of local LDS leaders to make the Church even better known. Two of the resulting programs have enjoyed considerable visibility. Since 1978, annual Christmas lighting ceremonies have been held on the grounds of the Washington D. C. Temple. In recent years, Washington's diplomatic corps has been invited to attend these ceremonies and each year an ambassador from one of the countries participates, along with a General Authority, in switching on the lights. With the full-time Public Affairs office seeking to enhance international contacts for the Church, a Western Family Picnic has also been held each year since 1991 at the Marriott Farm in rural Hume, Va., for ambassadors and embassy officials to acquaint them and their families with the Church's values and history.

On 1 July 1986 the Washington D.C. Mission was reorganized into the Washington D.C. North and Washington D.C. South missions.

Sources: Andrew Jenson, "Washington," Encyclopedic History of the Church, 1941; Julian C. Lowe and Florian H. Thayn, History of the Mormons in the Greater Washington Area: Members of the Church of Jesus Christ of Latter-day Saints in the Washington, D. C. Area, 1839-1991, 1991; Lee H. Burke, History of the Washington D.C. LDS Ward: From Beginnings (1839) to Dissolution (1975), 1990; Mary L. Bradford, "From Colony to Community: the Washington, D. C., Saints," Ensign, August 1974; Jesse R. Smith, History of the Washington Temple, 1983; Lois Blake, "The Church in Washington: LDS / DC," This People, August-September 1984; "Membership triples in Nation's Capital," Church News, 2 December 1989; Lee Davidson, "Christmas Lighting Illuminates Friendly Ties," Church News, 12 December 1992; Alysa Hatch Whitlock, "Ambassadors' Families Welcomed at Annual Picnic," Ensign, February 1996; "Visitors center, new theater dedicated in Washington, D. C.," Church News, 2 December 2000; "LDS Number 16 in 106th Congress," Church News, 14 November 1998.

Stake — 1

(As of Oct. 1, 2009. To simplify listing, the stake and missions in the Washington, D.C., area that carry the name of Washington, D.C., are listed in the District of Columbia rather than the state where the mission offices are located.)

No.	Name	Organized	First President
North America East Area			
131	*Washington D.C.		
	‡Washington (D.C., Pa., Md.)	30 Jun 1940	Ezra Taft Benson

Missions — 2

(As of Oct. 1, 2011; shown with historical number. See MISSIONS.)

(188b) WASHINGTON D.C. NORTH MISSION
11700 Falls Rd.
Potomac, MD 20854-2823

(54) WASHINGTON D.C. SOUTH MISSION
5631 Burke Centre Parkway, Suite H
Burke, VA 22015

Florida

Jan. 1, 2011: Est. population, 18,328,000; Members 136,549; Stakes 26; Wards 184; Branches, 50; Missions 5; Temples 1; Percent LDS, 0.7, or one in 139.

William Brown and Daniel Cathcart were called by Joseph Smith to serve a mission to Pensacola in April 1843, but no record exists of them fulfilling the calling. Between April and June 1854, Phineas Young visited the Indian chiefs in Florida and distributed copies of the Book of Mormon. John Morgan, Southern States Mission president, visited Florida in 1885 but long-term missionary work did not begin until the state became part of the mission on 1 March 1894.

Missionaries began preaching in Pensacola in January 1895 and started a number of Sunday Schools, the first was in Coe Mills in May 1895. The first branch, known as the Hassell Branch, was created in Jefferson County on 9 May 1897 and in September of that year the Sanderson Branch was organized. George P. Canova, a well-to-do landowner and chairman of the Baker County Commission, became the Sanderson branch president in January 1898. However, five months later, following threats of violence, Canova was killed as he returned home from a Church meeting.

In 1906, Charles A. Callis, a later mission president and a member of the Quorum of the Twelve, became president of the Florida Conference. That same year, a meetinghouse was dedicated in Jacksonville and a year later, another meetinghouse was completed in Oak Grove.

In 1909, missionaries began working in Miami during the winter months. Five years later, Julius C. Neubeck of Miami was called on a seven-month mission by Charles A. Callis and became the first missionary from that city. Following Neubeck's mission he became the presiding elder of the Church in Miami.

By 1925, branches or Sunday Schools existed in Jacksonville, Sanderson, Tampa, Miami and in other places throughout the state. In February and March 1925, President Heber J. Grant visited Jacksonville and held public meetings. Ten years later the Florida District had 22 branches, and the West Florida District had another 13 branches.

The first stake in Florida and in the South was created in Jacksonville on 19 January 1947, by Charles A. Callis of the Quorum of the Twelve. Alvin C. Chace, a grandson of early leader George P. Canova, was called as the first president.

In 1950, the Church purchased more than 50,000 acres near Orlando, now known as Deseret Ranch. The initial purchase has grown into a 300,000-acre ranch in Central Florida. Deseret Ranch has the largest cow-calf operation in the United States with 44,000 head of cattle. It also includes various cattle enterprises, orchards and other agribusiness projects.

Membership increased rapidly as members from the West moved into the state, drawn by commerce and the aerospace industry. When the Florida Mission was created in 1960, four stakes had been organized.

Membership in Florida in 1977 was 30,000, increasing four times in less than 30 years.

Beginning in 1978 the Florida Fort Lauderdale Mission was pivotal in taking the gospel to the islands of the Caribbean and also teaching the Spanish and Creole-speaking people in southern Florida. Creation of the first Spanish-speaking stake in the Southeast in Miami on 16 January 1994 reflected the increase in membership among Cuban, Latin American and Caribbean immigrants. Another Spanish-speaking stake was created in Hialeah Gardens in 1998.

The Orlando Florida Temple was dedicated 9 October 1994 by President Howard W. Hunter. President Gordon B. Hinckley on 19 January 1997, addressed more than 5,000 members at a conference in Jacksonville, commemorating the stake's 50th anniversary.

Membership reached 122,909 in 2003. By 2005, membership reached 125,830.

Plans to construct the Ft. Lauderdale temple were announced by President Thomas S. Monson on Oct. 3, 2009. Ground was broken for the second temple in Florida on June 18, 2011, by Elder Walter F. Gonzalez of the Presidency of the Seventy. The Church purchased 32 acres of land, with 12 acres for the temple. Membership in 2010 was 136,549.

Sources: LaViece Moore-Fraser Smallwood, Salt of the South: The LDS Trail Blazers, 1997; Andrew Jenson, Encyclopedic History of the Church, 1941; LaMar C. Berrett, History of the Southern States Mission, thesis, July 1960; "New Florida Stake is No. 163 in Church," Church News, 25 January 1947; James E. Hill, "Pres. McKay Dedicates New Florida Stakehouse," Church News, 1 December 1956; "Southern States Division Set in October," Church News, 8 October 1960; Carma Wadley, "Florida's Oldest Chapel," Church News, 6 March 1976; Gordon Irving, "Early Days in Florida," Church News, 2 July 1977; Kathleen Ryan, "The First Spanish-speaking Stake in Southeast is Created in Florida," Church News, 19 February 1994; Gerry Avant, "Temple is Dedicated in Sunshine State, 20,670 Attend Sessions," Church News, 15 October 1994; Marian Bond, "Florida Stake Was First in the South," Church News, 25 January 1997; Gerry Avant, "Tabernacle Choir Brings Spiritual Enrichment on Southern U.S. Tour," Church News, 7 July 2001; Groundbreaking for Ft. Lauderdale temple, Church News, June 25, 2011.

Stakes — 26

(Listed alphabetically as of Oct. 1, 2011.)

No.	Name	Organized	First President
North America Southeast Area			
2828	Bradenton Florida	17 May 2009	Robert William Clover Sr.
1898	Brandon Florida	23 Aug 1992	James Franklin Henry
879	Cocoa Florida	13 Nov 1977	Cleavy Eugene Waters
2494	Deland Florida	20 Sep 1998	David Jay Norby
530	*Fort Lauderdale Florida		
	‡Fort Lauderdale	18 Oct 1970	Stanley C. Johnson
1472	Fort Myers Florida	13 May 1984	John M. Cyrocki
2151	Fort Walton Beach Florida	07 Jan 1996	Charles E. Atkinson Jr.
746	Gainesville Florida	29 Feb 1976	James R. Christianson
1842	*Homestead Florida	16 Jan 1994	
	‡South Miami Florida	19 Jan 1992	Dean Michael Madsen
465	*Jacksonville Florida East		
	‡Jacksonville	15 Sep 1968	Louis B. Vorwaller
163	*Jacksonville Florida West		
	‡Florida (Florida, Georgia)	19 Jan 1947	Alvin C. Chace
2844	Jacksonville Florida South	21 Jun 2009	Gene Renford Patch
1590	Lake City Florida	16 Mar 1986	Ernest Robert Peacock
1153	*Lakeland Florida	27 Aug 2000	
	*Winter Haven Florida	10 Oct 1991	
	‡Lakeland Florida	27 Jun 1980	Waymon E. Meadows
1380	* Leesburg Florida		
	*Lake Mary Florida	27 Oct 1987	
	‡Deland Florida	14 Nov 1982	Marvin Knowles
2432	Miami Lakes Florida	25 Jan 1998	Mario B. Ayaviri
	‡Hialeah Gardens Florida (Spanish)		
257	*Orlando Florida		
	‡Orlando	23 Feb 1958	W. Leonard Duggar
1900	Orlando Florida South	30 Aug 1992	Carl E. Reynolds Jr.
2692	Orlando Florida Hunters Creek	6 Nov 2005	Allan Thomas Pratt
732	*Panama City Florida	4 Feb 1986	
	‡Marianna Florida	16 Nov 1975	Riley Malone Peddie
486	*Pensacola Florida		
	‡Pensacola	15 Jun 1969	S. Elroy Stapleton
1970	Pompano Beach Florida	16 Jan 1994	Richard Merlin Smith
651	St. Petersburg Florida	18 Aug 1974	Bruce Earl Belnap
1190	*Stuart Florida	16 Jan 1994	
	‡West Palm Beach Florida	12 Oct 1980	Donald Wayne Carson
594	*Tallahassee Florida		
	‡Tallahassee	21 Jan 1973	Jay Nicholas Lybbert
289	*Tampa Florida		
	‡Tampa	25 Oct 1959	Edwin H.White
	Stakes discontinued		
311	*Miami Florida (Spanish)		
	‡Miami	13 Nov 1960	Paul R. Cheesman
	Discontinued 7 Sept 2008		

Missions — 5

(As of Oct. 1, 2011; shown with historical number. See MISSIONS.)

(178b) FLORIDA FORT LAUDERDALE MISSION
7951 SW 6th St., Ste. 110
Ft. Lauderdale, FL 33324-3211

(197) FLORIDA JACKSONVILLE MISSION
8663 Baypine Road suite 102
Jacksonville, FL 32256

(326) FLORIDA ORLANDO MISSION
10502 Satellite Blvd. Ste E
Orlando, FL 32837-8426

(96) FLORIDA TALLAHASSEE MISSION
1535 Killearn Center Blvd., Suite C-4
Tallahassee, FL 32309

(139) FLORIDA TAMPA MISSION
13153 N. Dale Mabry, Ste. 109
Tampa, FL 33618

Georgia

Jan. 1, 2011: Est. population, 9,686,000; Members 77,948; Stakes 15; Wards 112; Branches 39; Missions, 3; Temples, 1; Percent LDS, 0.77, or one in 130.

Early efforts at missionary work in Georgia began with John U. Eldredge in 1843, who preached in Georgia as he traveled

Deseret News 2012 Church News Almanac   **343**

from Alabama to North Carolina. No other work was in Georgia until 1876 with the arrival of John Morgan, who in fulfillment of a dream 10 years earlier, converted many people in Haywood Valley and organized a branch there in 1876. Haywood was located in northwestern Georgia and was near Rome, a city 60 miles north of Atlanta. In 1879, it became Southern States Mission headquarters.

In November 1877, about 80 Church members left Georgia and moved to San Luis Valley, Colo. Another group of Georgian Saints moved to Colorado in 1884. Until the end of the 19th century, groups of Church members from the South continued to migrate westward.

Missionaries were initially treated well in the South, but before long, their successes led to violent opposition. Joseph Standing was killed by a mob near Varnell's Station on 21 July 1879. His companion, Rudger Clawson, later president of the Quorum of the Twelve, escaped serious injury.

Notwithstanding the threats of mobs to missionaries, some pioneer member families joined, stayed in Georgia, and built up the Church. One prominent convert, Judge Wyatt N. Williams was baptized in Buchanan in July 1879, a few days after Standing's murder. Williams subsequently donated land and built a chapel in Haralson County at a place called "Mormon Springs," near his mill and cotton gin. Because of persecution, a branch was not initially organized but many families joined the Church in Buchanan.

In the early 1900s, Southern States Mission presidents directed that missionaries begin focusing their work more in the cities during the winter and less in the countryside. The first convert in Savannah was Julia Mozell Love, baptized in 1901. The first Sunday School in Savannah was created 26 March 1922, in the home of Arthur B. and Annie Laura Davis. A small meetinghouse, known as the "Little White Chapel," was completed in 1929.

In 1908, a branch was organized and a meetinghouse constructed in Atlanta. It was replaced in 1915 with a larger building. Heber J. Grant, then of the Quorum of the Twelve, visited Atlanta in 1911 and addressed an overflow congregation in a local Universalist church. A new meetinghouse was erected there in 1925.

One of the prominent pioneer leaders in Atlanta was Homer Yarn. In 1916, he became the first local leader of a Sunday School in Atlanta and served as Atlanta Branch president from 1923 to 1937. When the Georgia District was organized in 1937, he was called as district president. He also served as counselor in the mission presidency from 1939-57.

On 5 May 1957, Elders Mark E. Petersen and LeGrand Richards of the Quorum of the Twelve organized the first stake in Georgia, the Atlanta Stake (later changed to Tucker Stake) with William L. Nichols as president. The stake boundaries covered the northern two-thirds of the state and had 3,000 members in wards in Atlanta (2), Columbus, Macon, and Empire, and branches in Buchanan, Athens, Givson, Milledgeville and Palmetto. In June 1971, the Southern States Mission was renamed the Georgia-South Carolina Mission, then later the Georgia Atlanta Mission. In July 2003, it was divided, creating the Georgia Atlanta North Mission.

In 1983, the Atlanta Temple was completed and dedicated by President Gordon B. Hinckley, then second counselor in the First Presidency. It was the first temple built in the South.

Under the direction of Elder Alexander B. Morrison of the Seventy, the Church made strides into the inner city of Atlanta in the late 1980s and early 1990s. Five branches were established in the central sections of Atlanta among minorities, including Asian and Hispanic people. The Atlanta Georgia District functioned from 1991 to 1996 until the units were absorbed into surrounding stakes.

The year 1996 brought the Centennial Olympic Summer Games to Atlanta and hundreds of Church members volunteered during the games. President Hinckley visited Atlanta 17 May 1998 and spoke to more than 13,000 members.

In 2002, membership reached 62,301. In 2005, membership reached 69,441.

The Georgia Macon Mission was consolidated with four neighboring missions on 1 July 2011.

Sources: Andrew Jenson, Encyclopedic History of the Church, 1941; Arthur M. Richardson and Nicholas G. Morgan, Sr., The Life and Ministry of John Morgan, 1965; "William L. Nichols to Preside Over New Altanta Stake," Church News, 11 May 1957; LaMar C. Berrett, History of the Southern States Mission, thesis, July 1960; Vera Edna Browning Kimball, The Southern Miracle, 1984; Gerry Avant, "Georgia Enters Era of Temples," Church News, 24 April 1983; Mike Cannon, "Inner-city District Gathers Many of Diverse Cultures into 'Gospel Net,'" Church News, 29 May 1993; Sarah Jane Weaver, "Through Service, Members Find, Share Olympic Spirit," Church News, 27 July 1996; Richard D. Hall, "LDS Display Touches Olympic Visitors," Church News, 3 August 1996; Gerry Avant, "Savannah," Church News, 5 May 1998; Gerry Avant, "A Higher Place: Choir Lifts Audiences," Church News, 23 May 1998; Gerry Avant, "'We Are Biblical Church,' Atlanta Members Told," Church News, 23 May 1998; Gerry Avant, "A Higher Place: Choir Lifts Audiences," Church News, 30 June 2001.

Stakes — 16
(Listed alphabetically as of Oct. 1, 2011.)

No.	Name	Organized	First President
North America Southeast Area			
2218	Albany Georgia	11 Aug 1996	Gregory Wayne Widman
2632	Athens Georgia	2 May 2004	David Webb Bradley
2203	Atlanta Georgia	23 Jun 1996	John Devin Cornish
889	*Augusta Georgia	21 Aug 1988	
	‡West Columbia South Carolina	5 Feb 1978	George A. Huff Sr.
2713	Cartersville Georgia	19 Mar 2006	Marion Keith Giddens
886	Columbus Georgia	15 Jan 1978	William F. Meadows Jr.
2902	Conyers Georgia	6 Mar 2011	R. Scott Johnson
715	Douglas Georgia	26 Oct 1975	Roswald Mancil
921	*Jonesboro Georgia	29 Jan 1991	
	‡Atlanta Georgia	14 May 1978	Warren Richard Jones
1660	*Kingsland Georgia	13 May 1997	
	‡Jacksonville Florida North	15 Nov 1987	Robert Edwin Bone
241	*Lilburn Georgia	23 Jun 1996	
	*Tucker Georgia	1 Sep 1974	
	*Atlanta Georgia		
	‡Atlanta (Georgia)	5 May 1957	William L. Nicholls
373	*Macon Georgia		
	‡Macon (Georgia, Alabama)	10 Mar 1963	Rayford L. Henderson
1643	Marietta Georgia East	21 Jun 1987	Paul A. Snow

1208	*Powder Springs Georgia	10 Sep 1991	
	‡Marietta Georgia	23 Nov 1980	William K. Farrar Jr.
640	*Roswell Georgia	21 Jun 1987	
	*Sandy Springs Georgia	1 Sep 1974	
	‡Tucker Georgia	12 May 1974	Richard Parry Winder
916	Savannah Georgia	7 May 1978	Robert W. Cowart
1799	Sugar Hill Georgia	26 May 1991	Donald Arthur Cazier

Missions — 2
(As of Oct. 1, 2011; shown with historical number. See MISSIONS.)

(8b) GEORGIA ATLANTA MISSION
112 Governors Square Ste A
Fayetteville, GA 30215

(336) GEORGIA ATLANTA NORTH MISSION
1150 Cole Dr. SW
Lilburn, GA 30047

Hawaii

Jan. 1, 2011: Est. population, 1,288,000; Members, 69,872; Stakes, 15; Wards, 124; Branches, 10; Missions, 1; Temples, 2; Percent LDS: 5.3, or one in 19.

Four missionaries were called in 1843 to go to the Sandwich Islands, as they were then known. They stopped instead at Tubuai, one of the southern islands of French Polynesia. In 1846, Sam Brannan and his party of Mormon immigrants aboard the ship Brooklyn stopped in Hawaii, en route to California and the Great Basin.

In 1850, gold-mining elders serving in northern California were called to open a mission in Polynesia. They landed in Honolulu 12 Dec. 1850, under the direction of Hiram Clark. On 10 Feb. 1851, Clark baptized a 16-year-old Hawaiian man, the first convert in Hawaii. Some missionaries were not as successful and returned discouraged to the mainland. But George Q. Cannon, James Keeler, William Farrer, Henry W. Bigler, and James Hawkins remained and converted a number of people. Cannon baptized three well-educated Hawaiians, Jonathan Napela, Uaua, and Kaleohano, who later became prominent missionaries for the Church.

On 6 Aug. 1851, the Kula Branch was organized in the village of Kealakou on the island of Maui. At a conference on 18 August, four more branches were organized in Keanae, Wailua, Wainau and Nonomanu. During that year membership reached 220. The first meetinghouse on the islands was built in 1852 in Pulehu on the island of Maui. It still stands. By 1854, a colony and plantation were started at Lanai as a place of refuge from persecution from other religious groups.

Perhaps the best known missionary to the Sandwich Islands was a future Church president, Joseph F. Smith, who began his first mission when he was 15-years-old. Arriving in 1854, he worked in the islands for three years, serving as conference president on Maui, Hawaii and Molokai. He eventually served three missions to Hawaii. President Smith was so beloved by Hawaiian saints that immigrants from Hawaii to Utah named their settlement in Tooele County, "Iosepa," as he was known in Hawaiian.

The Book of Mormon was published in Hawaiian in 1855. In 1857 and 1858, missionaries left for the mainland because of the Utah War. No missionaries returned until July 1861, when Walter Murray Gibson arrived. He was a recent convert called on a mission to the South Pacific. He soon usurped Church leadership and took over the Church organization and property. Leading Hawaiian elders notified the Church of Gibson's actions and Brigham Young sent Elder Ezra T. Benson and Lorenzo Snow of the Quorum of the Twelve to investigate. Soon after their arrival they excommunicated Gibson. Elders Benson and Snow also took measures to resume active missionary work under the direction of Joseph F. Smith.

Defrauded by Gibson of its property in Lanai, the Church purchased 6,000 acres at Laie, on the island of Oahu, on 26 Jan. 1865. Soon thereafter, a colony, school and sugar factory were started.

Sunday School was introduced to the islands in 1871, YMMIA in 1872, Relief Society in 1875, and Primary in 1883. In 1877, Church leaders were given permission by the Hawaiian government to perform marriages. This came in part due to better relations with the Hawaiian government after visits by the King and Queen to the colony at Laie in 1872.

Later, many of the Hawaiians wanted to gather to Utah to receive their temple blessings, so the Church purchased a ranch in Skull Valley, near Tooele, Utah, and the Hawaiian Saints founded the colony of Iosepa in 1889. By 1910 the colony was disbanded and the colonists returned to Hawaii.

The Church built a temple in Laie, which was dedicated 27 Nov. 1919. The temple was extensively remodeled in the 1970s and rededicated on 13 June 1978.

The Oahu Stake, the first in Hawaii, and the first outside of North America, was created 30 June 1935, by Heber J. Grant. While visiting there, the former missionary to Japan felt a need for a mission to the many Japanese people in Hawaii. On 24 Feb. 1937, the Japanese Mission (later called the Central Pacific Mission) was organized in Hawaii. Over the next dozen years, nearly 700 Japanese-Americans were converted. Many of the missionaries and converts helped open and continue missionary work in Japan after World War II. Hawaiian members also opened the door for missionary work in many South Pacific islands. The Central Pacific Mission was merged with the Hawaiian mission in 1950.

Taking advantage of a law allowing one hour per week from school for students to study religion, classes were started in the school year 1938-1939 for young Latter-day Saints to study their faith. With that success, formal seminary classes were introduced in 1941. Those classes were discontinued in 1948 when a Supreme Court ruling prohibited churches using school facilities as classrooms. Early-morning seminary was introduced in 1953.

During World War II most young men of missionary age were called into the service and missionary work was dramatically reduced. After the attack on Pearl Harbor, Church services were discontinued between December 1941 and October 1942 due to the danger that armed attacks might pose to large groups meeting together. During the war, to compensate for the loss of missionaries, many servicemen were assigned to do part-time missionary work on the islands.

The Church College of Hawaii opened in Laie on 26 Sept. 1955 in temporary buildings. Formal dedication of the new campus was held on 17 Dec. 1958. Many members from the South Pacific and Asia have been educated there. On 1 July 1974 the college came under the direction of BYU and had its name changed to BYU-Hawaii. On 12 Oct. 1963, the Polynesian Cultural Center, a cluster of villages representing various South Pacific cultures, was opened. It quickly became one of Hawaii's most popular tourist attractions.

A small temple in Kailua-Kona on the island of Hawaii, was dedicated 23 Jan. 2000, the sesquicentennial year of the establishment of the Church in the Hawaiian Islands.

Membership reached 61,715 in 2003.

President Thomas S. Monson, first counselor in the First Presidency, joined students, faculty and alumni in a weeklong celebration of the 50th anniversary of Brigham Young University-Hawaii held Oct 16-23, 2005. He recounted an experience of Elder David O. McKay, then of the Quorum of the Twelve. During a visit 84 years earlier, Elder McKay envisioned a Church school of higher learning for Laie, to complement the then recently dedicated Hawaii Temple. Years later, in February 1955, as president of the Church, President McKay presided over the groundbreaking. Classes commenced in September of that year with 153 students. By 2005, there were 2,400 students from Asia, the Pacific Islands, the United States and many other parts of the world.

In 2004, membership reached 64,608. In 2005, membership reached 65,447.

Sources: Andrew Jenson, Encyclopedic History of the Church, 1941; R. Lanier Britsch, Moramona: The Mormons in Hawaii, 1989; Margaret Comfort Bock, The Church of Jesus Christ in the Hawaiian Islands," thesis, 1941; Julie A. Dockstader, "Second sacred edifice in Hawaiian Islands," Church News, 29 January 2000; Richard C. Harvey, "The development of The Church of Jesus Christ of Latter-day Saints in Hawaii," thesis, 1974; Gerry Avant, "Hawaiian jubilee," Church News, 29 October 2005.

Stakes — 15
(Listed alphabetically as of Oct. 1, 2011.)

No.	Name	Organized	First President
North America West Area			
807	*BYU-Hawaii 1st	22 Nov 1981	
	‡BYU-Hawaii	23 Jan 1977	Eric B. Shumway
1313	BYU-Hawaii 2nd	22 Nov 1981	Herbert Kamaka Sproat
2654	BYU-Hawaii 3rd	24 Oct 2004	Von Dean Orgill
473	*Hilo Hawaii		
	‡Hilo	15 Dec 1968	Rex Alton Cheney
222	*Honolulu Hawaii		
	‡Honolulu (Hawaii, Guam)	28 Aug 1955	J. A. Quealy Jr.
348	*Honolulu Hawaii West		
	‡Pearl Harbor (Hawaii)	4 Feb 1962	George Q. Cannon
729	Kahului Hawaii	9 Nov 1975	Evan Allan Larsen
560	*Kaneohe Hawaii		
	‡Kaneohe (Hawaii)	21 Nov 1971	Robert H. Finlayson
851	Kauai Hawaii	24 Jul 1977	Garner Dalton Wood
669	Kona Hawaii	24 Nov 1974	Haven J. Stringham
113	*Laie Hawaii		
	‡Oahu	30 Jun 1935	Ralph E. Wooley
1395	Laie Hawaii North	16 Jan 1983	Willard Kaaihue Kekauoha
2291	Makakilo Hawaii	8 Dec 1996	Ruben J. K. Paet
1103	Mililani Hawaii	3 Feb 1980	Kotaro Koizumi
566	*Waipahu Hawaii		
	‡Pearl Harbor West (Hawaii)	20 Feb 1972	William E. Fuhrmann

Mission — 1
(As of Oct. 1, 2011; shown with historical number. See MISSIONS.)

(9) HAWAII HONOLULU MISSION
1500 S. Beretania St., Suite 416
Honolulu, HI 96826

Idaho

Jan. 1, 2011: Est. population, 1,524,000; Members, 414,182; Stakes, 121; Wards 979; Branches, 98; Missions, 2; Temples, 4; Percent LDS, 27, or one in 4.

Latter-day Saints first attempted settlement in what is now Idaho at Fort Limhi (later spelled Lemhi) on 15 June 1855. Its name was borrowed from a prominent Book of Mormon figure. At the time, Fort Lemhi was included in Oregon Territory. Thomas Sasson Smith was chosen to supervise the colonization. Church leaders encouraged the settlers to establish ties with local Native Americans, conduct missionary work among them, and teach them farming methods. President Brigham Young and a large traveling contingent, including Native American Chief Arapeen, and possibly Chief Kanosh, visited the settlement in May 1857. Subsequent hostilities developed between the settlers and local natives, and Ft. Lemhi was abandoned in late March 1858.

A second LDS colonization effort began in 1859 when a group of Utah saints began claiming and improving land near

Franklin. The town was officially settled on 14 April 1860. The settlers assumed they were residing in Utah Territory, but an 1872 boundary survey determined they had located about a mile inside Idaho Territory. The community was named for Elder Franklin D. Richards of the Quorum of the Twelve and is noted as Idaho's first permanent Anglo-Saxon settlement. Preston Thomas was called to serve as Franklin's first bishop.

The Bear River Massacre, reputedly the worst one-day killing of Native Americans in U.S. history, took place several miles northwest of Franklin on 29 January 1863. Responding to complaints regarding Indian attacks on emigrants, settlers, miners and cattle, federal troops from Fort Douglas in Salt Lake City killed about 300 natives in an early morning attack. Residents of Franklin nursed the troops' wounds as they returned to Fort Douglas. A few settlers were permitted to return to the massacre site and rescue surviving adult Natives and three small children.

Idaho Territory was created from Oregon Territory on 4 March 1863. The following September Charles C. Rich, of the Quorum of Twelve Apostles, led a colonizing party to what is now Paris, Idaho. In 1864, the communities of Bloomington, St. Charles, Ovid, Montpelier, Fish Haven, Liberty, and Bennington were founded. Also that year, Church members established settlements and ranches farther west in Oxford, Malad City, and Marsh Valley (near Downey).

Bear Lake Stake, the first in Idaho, was organized on 20 June 1869 with David Patten Kimball as president. Brigham Young directed the establishment of a settlement at Soda Springs in 1870 with Philemon C. Merrill as presiding elder. Expanding their influence throughout the southeastern corner of Idaho, Church members also moved into what is now called Gem Valley in the early 1870s.

Significant numbers of Native Americans living in southern Idaho joined the Church in the 1870s and 1880s. Shoshone Chief Sagwitch was baptized on 5 May 1873 near Bear River City, Utah, by George W. Hill. More than 100 of Sagwitch's tribe were also baptized the same day. Chief Pocatello, accompanied by his band, traveled to Salt Lake City in 1875. There, he was baptized on 5 May by Hiram W. Mikesell. Several hundred of Chief Pocatello's tribe were subsequently baptized in the Bear River near Corinne, Utah.

During the 1870s and early 1880s many Latter-day Saints in Idaho worked as contractors and employees of the Utah and Northern Railroad during its construction that linked Salt Lake City with Helena and other mining cities of western Montana. The availability of arable land in Idaho, coupled with the railroad extension into the Snake River Valley, served as a pressure release valve for the burgeoning younger generations in Utah looking to establish themselves on fertile farmlands. Church members constructed large scale irrigation canals to open immense tracts of agricultural land.

Settlers in the Worm Creek (later Preston) area, a few miles north of Franklin, were organized as a ward in 1879. Also, that year a group of Latter-day Saints from Tooele County, Utah, settled in Goose Creek Valley in present day Cassia County. The townsite of Oakley became the region's initial central settlement. A ward was established there in 1882, and Cassia Stake was organized on 19 November 1887 with Horton D. Haight as president.

Amos R. Wright, appointed as a missionary to Native Americans, traveled frequently between his Bennington home and the Wind River Reservation in neighboring Wyoming. On 25 September 1880, Wright baptized Shoshone Chief Washakie. The baptism was performed at night to avoid detection by antagonistic reservation officials. Wright also baptized about 310 other Native Americans on the reservation during September and October of that year. Chief Washakie had become an early and friendly associate of Church leaders after the saints arrived in Utah.

In 1882, Cache Stake President William B. Preston in Logan, Utah, supervised the colonization of the Snake River Valley. The far flung Bannock Ward centered in Rexburg was organized as Bannock Stake on 4 February 1884 with Thomas E. Ricks as president. A few months later on 1 June the Oneida Stake was organized in Franklin with William D. Hendricks as president.

During the mid to late 1880s, territorial Marshal Fred T. Dubois and deputies spearheaded pursuit and prosecution of polygamists in Idaho. Dubois later became an Idaho congressman and senator. In his senatorial role he championed the unsuccessful effort in 1904 to bar Elder Reed Smoot of the Quorum of the Twelve from being seated as U.S. senator from Utah.

In 1884, the Idaho Territorial Legislature enacted an "Anti-Mormon Test Oath." It barred not only practicing polygamists but anyone who believed in a religion advocating the doctrine of plural marriage from voting, holding public office, serving on juries, or teaching in or administering public schools. The "Test Oath" was enforced rigidly during the election of 1886. Mormons, comprising one-fourth of the territory's population, were prevented from voting.

During the election of 1888, hundreds of Latter-day Saint men in Idaho, with approval from Church leaders, temporarily "withdrew" their membership in the Church in order to vote and thus challenge the legality and enforcement of the "Test Oath." Most of the Latter-day Saint voters were arrested and their votes negated. The U.S. Supreme Court ruled on 3 February 1890 that the "Test Oath" was indeed constitutional. It became part of the state's constitution when Idaho was admitted to the Union the following July. Active enforcement of the "Test Oath" essentially ended after the election of 1892. Attempts to repeal it, however, were unsuccessful until some ninety years later in 1982.

During the troubled 1880s four Church-sponsored academies were founded in Idaho: Fielding in Paris, Oneida Stake in Preston, Cassia Stake in Oakley, and Fremont Stake (later Ricks College) in Rexburg. Also built during this era was the Bear Lake Stake Tabernacle in Paris, generally recognized as one of the finest examples of Idaho architecture. Work on the building, designed by Joseph Don Carlos Young, son of Brigham Young, began in 1884 and was dedicated in 1889. The Saints in the railroad center of Pocatello were organized as a branch in May 1888.

In 1896, Elder Edward Stevenson, one of the first seven presidents of the Seventy, and Matthias F. Cowley, a counselor in the Oneida Stake presidency, were appointed to travel through the northwestern states to locate Church members residing there and establish branches and a mission. As a result, the Montana Mission was established with Phineas Tempest as president. He served under the direction of Bannock Stake president Thomas E. Ricks.

On 26 July 1897, the Northwestern States Mission was organized with Oneida Stake President George C. Parkinson called to serve a dual role as mission president. Six missionaries from Oneida Stake were assigned to begin missionary work in the newly created mission that included Oregon, Washington, and part of Idaho. In 1898, the Montana and Northwestern States missions were consolidated with Franklin S. Bramwell as president.

Latter-day Saints began settling on farms in the Payette Valley in 1900. A branch was organized in Emmett the following year.

The Church's presence in Idaho's capital city was initiated on 18 January 1903 by several Latter-day Saint legislators who requested that Church authorities in Salt Lake City send missionaries to Boise. Joshua H. Paul and Melvin J. Ballard were sent from headquarters to survey the situation. They established a branch a few weeks later on 8 February with Ezra J. Merrill as presiding elder. The Boise Stake was organized 10 years later in 1913.

The construction of the U.S. Reclamation Service's Minidoka Dam in 1905 attracted substantial numbers of Latter-day Saints to farm lands at Heyburn, Acequia, Paul, and Rupert. Wards were soon organized there under the direction of Boise Stake officials. Other irrigation and railroad projects farther west along the Snake River attracted LDS settlers. Branches were organized in Kimberly in 1905 and Twin Falls in 1908. A ward was also established in Burley in 1906. That year Idaho's first General Authority, Charles H. Hart, a native of Bloomington, was called to serve as one of the First Seven Presidents of the Seventy.

The LDS Hospital built in Idaho Falls was dedicated by President Heber J. Grant on 22 October 1923. By 1925 the LDS population of the state numbered 79,887, the largest concentration of Saints living outside Utah.

The Church's first institute of religion was established at the University of Idaho in Moscow in 1926. A building to accommodate the institute's students and staff was constructed in 1928. By 1930, there were 25 stakes in Idaho with membership numbering around 90,000. In 1935, Church officials offered to transfer Ricks Academy to the state of Idaho as a junior college, but the state Legislature turned down the offer in 1937. That year Albert E. Bowen, a native of Henderson Creek, near Malad City, was ordained a member of the Quorum of the Twelve. He was followed into the Quorum in subsequent years by other Idaho natives: Harold B. Lee (1941), Ezra Taft Benson (1943), Matthew Cowley (1945), Howard W. Hunter (1959), and David B. Haight (1976).

Idaho's first temple was built on the banks of the Snake River in Idaho Falls. It was dedicated by President George Albert Smith on 23 September 1945. In 1957, and again in 1958, the Church announced plans to move Ricks College to Idaho Falls. The decision was ultimately reversed, and a major expansion of the college was announced in 1961.

The Idaho Pocatello Mission was created on 1 July 1974 with Ernest Eberhard, Jr. as president. In 1979, the mission's name was changed to the Idaho Boise Mission. On 1 July 1991, the Idaho Pocatello Mission was re-established with Wayne W. Probst as president.

On 5 June 1976, the Teton Dam burst unexpectedly and sent devastating flood waters through the Wilford/Sugar City/Rexburg area. About 40,000 people, mostly Church members, were directly affected by the devastation. Homes, personal property, and agricultural lands were destroyed. A massive relief effort was quickly organized among Church members from stakes in Idaho and neighboring states. President Spencer W. Kimball visited Rexburg a few days later on 13 June and spoke to about 8,000 members at Ricks College. His remarks infused the community with optimism and hope.

Idaho's second temple, in Boise, was dedicated on 25-30 May 1984 by President Gordon B. Hinckley of the First Presidency. The temple was enlarged in 1987 and rededicated in May of that year by President James E. Faust of the Quorum of the Twelve.

On 21 June 2000, President Hinckley announced that Ricks College would become a four-year university and be renamed Brigham Young University-Idaho. At the time of the announcement enrollment at Ricks was 8,628 students.

The First Presidency announced the creation of the Idaho Area on 16 June 2001. The new area was formed from the North America Northwest Area and included central and southern Idaho and portions of Oregon and Wyoming. The state is currently divided among three areas: North America Northwest, Utah North, and Idaho. Two missions encompass most of the state: Idaho Boise and Idaho Pocatello. Parts of the southeastern corner of the state are included in the Utah Ogden Mission while sections of the north are affiliated with the Washington Spokane Mission.

Private historic preservation efforts in 2003 were successful in saving the main LDS Oneida Stake Academy building in Preston from demolition. Church presidents Harold B. Lee and Ezra Taft Benson received much of their formal education there. The building, designed by Joseph Don Carlos Young, son of Brigham Young, was dedicated on 28 July 1895 and is one of the last of its kind still standing. It was moved in December 2003 a few blocks north to Benson Park. The Church provided a permanent site at the park for its relocation and donated a large sum toward the building's restoration as a community cultural center.

A letter from the First Presidency on 12 December 2003 announced that a temple would be built in Rexburg, and in general conference 20 October 2004 President Hinckley announced that Idaho's fourth temple would be built in Twin Falls. In August 2004, the Church was considering plans to restore the original Bear Lake Stake Tabernacle in Paris.

Three Church presidents were born and reared in Idaho: Harold B. Lee (Clifton), Ezra Taft Benson (Whitney), and Howard W. Hunter (Boise). President Benson died 30 May 1994 and was buried in Whitney.

In 2002, membership reached 360,204. In 2004, membership was 376,661.

Some 1,000 local members of the Church gathered April 15, 2006, for the groundbreaking of the Twin Falls Idaho Temple.

Sources: Leonard J. Arrington, History of Idaho, 1994; Merrill D. Beal, A History of Southeastern Idaho, 1942; David L. Bigler, Fort Limhi: The Mormon Adventure in Oregon Territory, 1855-1858, 2003; Scott R. Christensen, Sagwitch: Shoshone Chieftain, Mormon Elder, 1822-1887, 1999; Andrew Jenson, Encyclopedic History of the Church, 1941; Brigham D. Madsen, Chief Pocatello, the "White Plume," 1986; Merle W. Wells, Anti-Mormonism in Idaho, 1872-1892, 1978; Manuscript histories of Franklin Ward and Bannock, Bear Lake, Blaine, Boise, Cache, Cassia, Fremont, Malad, Oneida, Pocatello, and Portneuf stakes, Church Archives; David Croft, "Idaho Members Fight Flood," Church News, 12 June 1976; Dell Van Orden, "Flood Victims Get New Hope," Church News, 19 June 1976; Arnold Irvine, "Idaho Vote Spells Finish to Old Feud," Church News, 13 November 1982; Julie Dockstader Heaps, "Old Academy Rolls into History," Church News, 13 December 2003; "First Presidency Letter to Leaders," Church News, 27 December 2003; Julie Dockstader Heaps, "New Temple in Idaho," Church News, 27 December 2003; Amos R. Wright, Record book: Indians baptized, confirmed, etc. [July 1877- October 1880], LDS Church Archives. This document is an enclosure to a letter dated 18 November 1880 that Wright sent to LDS Church president John Taylor; "Idaho's fourth temple," Church News, 22 April 2006.

Stakes — 121
(Listed alphabetically by area As of Oct. 1, 2011.)

No.	Name	Organized	First President
Idaho Area — 106			
170	*American Falls Idaho		
	‡American Falls	1 Feb 1948	George R. Woolley
343	Ammon Idaho	27 Apr 2003	
	*Idaho Falls Idaho Ammon		

	‡Ammon	26 Nov 1961	Harold W. Davis
2612a	Ammon Idaho Foothills	27 April 2003	Douglas R. Wheeler
2811	Ammon Idaho North	15 Nov 2008	Franklin Dennis Stevens
1481	Arimo Idaho	17 Jun 1984	Douglas Sorensen
695	Ashton Idaho	18 May 1975	Horace E. Hess
52	*Blackfoot Idaho		
	‡Blackfoot	31 Jan 1904	Elias S. Kimball
1391	Blackfoot Idaho East	12 Dec 1982	Franklin D. Transtrum
914	Blackfoot Idaho Northwest	30 Apr 1978	Reijo Laverne Marcum
214	*Blackfoot Idaho South		
	*Blackfoot South	1 Mar 1970	
	‡South Blackfoot	20 Jun 1954	Lawrence T. Lambert
504	*Blackfoot Idaho West		
	‡Blackfoot West	1 Mar 1970	Alan F. Larsen
66	*Boise Idaho		
	‡Boise	3 Nov 1913	Heber Q. Hale
1460	Boise Idaho Central	5 Feb 1984	R. Clair Miles
1041	Boise Idaho East	10 Jun 1979	Cecil Frank Olsen
409	*Boise Idaho North		
	*Boise North Jan 1966		
	‡North Boise	26 Sep 1965	L. Aldin Porter
701	Boise Idaho South	17 Aug 1975	Grant Ruel Ipsen
1856	Boise State University	24 Apr 1992	Robert Reed Boren
218	*Boise Idaho West		
	*Boise West	29 May 1970	
	‡West Boise	7 Nov 1954	David Keith Ricks
77	*Burley Idaho		
	‡Burley	27 Jul 1919	David R. Langlois
1421	Burley Idaho West	22 May 1983	Walter Ray Petersen
405	*BYU-Idaho 1st	10 Aug 2001	
	*Ricks College 1st	7 Nov 1989	
	*Rexburg Idaho College 1st		
	*Ricks College 1st	1 Jun 1969	
	‡Ricks College	7 May 1965	J. Wendell Stucki
480	*BYU-Idaho 2nd	10 Aug 2001	
	*Ricks College 2nd	7 Nov 1989	
	*Rexburg Idaho College 2nd		
	‡Ricks College 2nd	27 Apr 1969	Loren Homer Grover
690	*BYU-Idaho 3rd	10 Aug 2001	
	*Ricks College 3rd	7 Nov 1989	
	‡Rexburg Idaho College 3rd	13 Apr 1975	Ray Wendell Rigby
1689	*BYU-Idaho 4th	10 Aug 2001	
	*Ricks College 4th	7 Nov 1989	
	‡Rexburg Idaho College 4th	6 Mar 1988	Jay Lufkin Risenmay
1836	*BYU-Idaho 5th	10 Aug 2001	
	Ricks College 5th	8 Dec 1991	R. Brent Kinghorn
2454	*BYU-Idaho 6th	10 Aug 2001	
	Ricks College 6th	19 Apr 1998	Jud Earl Miller
2613	BYU Idaho 7th	12 Oct 2003	Bradley D. Foster
2672	BYU Idaho 8th	27 Feb 2005	Jay Martin Harris
2805d	BYU Idaho 9th (student married)	24 Aug 2008	Terry W. Call
564	*Caldwell Idaho		
	‡Caldwell	30 Jan 1972	Talmadge C. Blacker
1446	Caldwell Idaho North	9 Oct 1983	Gerald Leland Jensen
78	*Carey Idaho	31 Oct 1977	
	*Richfield Idaho		
	‡Blaine	3 Aug 1919	William Lennox Adamson
960	*Chubbuck Idaho	8 Sep 1987	
	‡Pocatello Idaho Chubbuck	17 Sep 1978	Errol Smith Phippen
69	*Declo Idaho		
	*Cassia East	15 Jun 1969	
	‡Raft River	27 Apr 1915	John A. Elison
50	*Driggs Idaho		
	‡Teton (Wyoming, Idaho)	2 Sep 1901	Don Carlos Driggs
1840	Eagle Idaho	12 Jan 1992	Gary Wayne Walker
661	Emmett Idaho	22 Sep 1974	David Lee Morton
1147	Filer Idaho	15 Jun 1980	Karl E. Nelson
655	Firth Idaho	8 Sep 1974	Dale Lavar Christensen
36	*Idaho Falls Idaho		
	*Idaho Falls	16 Aug 1925	
	‡Bingham	9 Jun 1895	James E. Steele
825	Idaho Falls Idaho Ammon West	1 May 1977	Boyd Rencher Thomas
1448	Idaho Falls Idaho Central	16 Oct 1983	Paul Roger DeMordaunt

1665	Idaho Falls Idaho Eagle Rock	13 Dec 1987	Michael D. Crapo
285	*Idaho Falls Idaho East		
	*Idaho Falls East	29 May 1970	
	‡East Idaho Falls	7 Jun 1959	Charles P. Birzee
1149	Idaho Falls Idaho Lincoln	22 Jun 1980	Cleon Y. Olson
112	*Idaho Falls Idaho North		
	*Idaho Falls North	29 May 1970	
	‡North Idaho Falls	12 May 1935	David Smith
157	*Idaho Falls Idaho South		
	*Idaho Falls South	29 May 1970	
	‡South Idaho Falls	30 Jun 1946	Cecil E. Hart
2183	Idaho Falls Idaho Taylor Mountain	17 Mar 1996	J Rodney Hayes
602	*Idaho Falls Idaho West		
	‡Idaho Falls West	4 Mar 1973	Terry L. Crapo
607	*Iona Idaho		
	‡Iona	15 Apr 1973	Joseph Dudley Tucker
192	*Jerome Idaho		
	‡Gooding	9 Mar 1952	Ross C. Lee
1015	Kimberly Idaho	15 Apr 1979	David LaVere Carter
2029	Kuna Idaho	26 Feb 1995	Kenneth Arthur Roetto
2825	Kuna Idaho East	19 Apr 2009	Grant H. Francis
72	*McCammon Idaho *Arimo Idaho	19 Feb 1983	
	‡Portneuf	15 Aug 1915	George T. Hyde
1125	Menan Idaho	30 Mar 1980	Garth Victor Hall
580	*Meridian Idaho		
	‡Meridian	11 Jun 1972	J. Richard Clarke
2714	Meridian Idaho Amity	19 Mar 2006	Clair Arvid Waite
847	Meridian Idaho East	12 Jun 1977	Leonard E. Graham Jr.
2586	Meridian Idaho North	21 Jan 2001	Ronald Lee Clark
2706	Meridian Idaho Paramount	5 Feb 2006	Glen Patterson Olsen
1401	Meridian Idaho South	20 Feb 1983	Wenden Wayne Waite
2299	Meridian Idaho West	12 Jan 1997	Loun G. Easthope
2755	Middleton Idaho	3 Mar 2007	Zachary F. Evans
79	*Moore Idaho		
	‡Lost River	18 Aug 1919	William N. Patten
641	Mountain Home Idaho	19 May 1974	Kenneth Herbert Johns
125	*Nampa Idaho		
	‡Nampa	27 Nov 1938	Peter E. Johnson
2589	Nampa Idaho East	25 Feb 2001	Norman Larry Holm
2660	Nampa Idaho North	7 Nov 2004	Robert Allen Buchanan
874	Nampa Idaho South	30 Oct 1977	Dean Ezra Beus
32	*Oakley Idaho		
	‡Cassia (Idaho, Utah)	19 Nov 1887	Horton D. Haight
587	*Paul Idaho		
	‡Minidoka West	24 Sep 1972	Keith C. Merrill Jr.
278	*Pocatello Idaho		
	‡Pocatello	19 Apr 1959	Roland K. Hart
40	*Pocatello Idaho Alameda *Pocatello Idaho East	17 Jun 1984	
	*Pocatello East	29 May 1970	
	*East Pocatello	19 Apr 1959	
	‡Pocatello	7 Aug 1898	William C. Parkinson
1484	Pocatello Idaho Central	17 Jun 1984	Thomas William Ranstrom
971	*Pocatello Idaho East	17 Jun 1984	
	‡Pocatello South	22 Oct 1978	John Burl McNabb
377	*Pocatello Idaho Highland *Pocatello Idaho Alameda	17 Jun 1984	
	‡Alameda	12 May 1963	Homer S. Satterfield
207	*Pocatello Idaho North		
	*Pocatello North	29 May 1970	
	‡North Pocatello	21 Jun 1953	Jared O. Anderson
1444	Pocatello Idaho Tyhee	25 Sep 1983	Eugene Lester Hancock
406	*Pocatello Idaho University 1st		
	‡Idaho State University	9 May 1965	Robert E. Thompson
2458	Pocatello Idaho University 2nd	3 May 1998	Earl L. Christison III
149	*Pocatello Idaho West		
	*Pocatello West	29 May 1970	
	‡West Pocatello	6 May 1945	Twayne Austin
28	*Rexburg Idaho		
	*Rexburg	23 Jun 1935	
	*Fremont	6 Aug 1898	
	‡Bannock	4 Feb 1884	Thomas E. Ricks
1369	Rexburg Idaho Center	24 Oct 1982	Ronald Curtis Martin

697	Rexburg Idaho East	1 Jun 1975	Keith Lester Peterson
2810	Rexburg Idaho Henry's Fork	1 Nov 2008	Robert D. Marcum
153	*Rexburg Idaho North		
	*Rexburg North	29 May 1970	
	‡North Rexburg	28 Oct 1945	Orval O. Mortensen
2270	Rexburg Idaho South	17 Nov 1996	Garth S. Olsen
2936	Rexburg Idaho YSA 4th	21 Aug 2011	Edwin A. Sexton
56	*Rigby Idaho		
	‡Rigby	3 Feb 1908	Don Carlos Walker
158	*Rigby Idaho East		
	*Rigby East	29 May 1970	
	‡East Rigby	7 Jul 1946	James E. Ririe
2866	Rigby Idaho South	13 Dec 2009	William L. Follett
1140	Ririe Idaho	25 May 1980	Arlo J. Moss
606	*Roberts Idaho		
	‡Jefferson	25 Mar 1973	Edwin Cutler Adamson
91	*Rupert Idaho		
	‡Minidoka	11 May 1924	Richard C. May
1476	Rupert Idaho West	3 Jun 1984	Carl B. Garner
60	*Saint Anthony Idaho		
	‡Yellowstone	10 Jan 1909	Daniel G. Miller
211	*Salmon Idaho		
	‡Salmon River	18 Oct 1953	Earl Stokes
67	*Shelley Idaho		
	‡Shelley	16 Aug 1914	Joseph H. Dye
1180	Shelley Idaho South	14 Sep 1980	Kenneth P. Fielding
1129	Sugar City Idaho	4 May 1980	Ferron W. Sonderegger
2935	Star Idaho	14 Aug 2011	Kenneth J. Firmage
76	*Twin Falls Idaho		
	‡Twin Falls	26 Jul 1919	Lawrence Gomer Kirkman
2807	Twin Falls Idaho South	14 Sept 2008	Reed Juan Harris
490	*Twin Falls Idaho West		
	‡Twin Falls West	17 Aug 1969	Joel A. Tate
1156	Ucon Idaho	29 Jun 1980	Joseph Dudley Tucker
126	*Weiser Idaho		
	‡Weiser	27 Nov 1938	Scott B. Brown
1005	Wendell Idaho	25 Feb 1979	Orlo William Stevens

North America Northwest Area — 6

359	*Coeur d'Alene Idaho		
	‡Coeur d'Alene	14 Oct 1962	Gerald E. Browning
2511	Hayden Lake Idaho	7 Feb 1999	Ronald Bruce McIntire
268	*Lewiston Idaho		
	‡Lewiston (Idaho, Wash.)	19 Oct 1958	Golden Romney
638	Moscow Idaho	23 June 2004	
	*Pullman Washington	5 May 1974	John Leo Schwendiman
2553	Moscow Idaho University Stake	23 Apr 2000	Jack Evan McPhie
952	Sandpoint Idaho	20 Aug 1978	Richard William Goldsberry

Utah North Area — 9

1419	*Franklin Idaho	17 Nov 1985	
	‡Preston Idaho East	15 May 1983	Eudean Hawkins Gunnell
39	*Grace Idaho		
	‡Bannock	25 Jul 1898	Lewis S. Pond
32a	*Malad Idaho		
	‡Malad (Idaho, Utah)	12 Feb 1888	Oliver C. Hoskins
75	*Montpelier Idaho		
	‡Montpelier (Idaho, Wyoming)	23 Dec 1917	Edward C. Rich
1020	Montpelier Idaho South	22 Apr 1979	Leonard H. Matthews
8a	*Paris Idaho		
	‡Bear Lake (Idaho, Utah)	20 Jun 1869	David P. Kimball
29	*Preston Idaho North		
	‡Oneida	1 Jun 1884	William D. Hendricks
81	*Preston Idaho South		
	‡Franklin	6 Jun 1920	Samuel W. Parkinson
73	*Soda Springs Idaho		
	‡Idaho	19 Nov 1916	Nelson J. Hogan

Stakes discontinued

70	Curlew (Idaho, Utah)	17 May 1915	Jonathan C. Cutler
	Discontinued 11 Feb 1940 †Malad (32), Pocatello (40)		
1273	Soda Springs Idaho North	31 May 1981	Cleston Murrie Godfrey
	Discontinued 27 Apr 1986 †Montpelier Idaho (75), Soda Springs Idaho (73)		

(111) IDAHO BOISE MISSION
1111 So. Cole Rd.
Boise, ID 83705

(264) IDAHO POCATELLO MISSION
1246 N. Yellowstone Ave., Ste F-3
Pocatello, ID 83201

Illinois

Jan. 1, 2011: Est. population, 12,902,000; Members, 55,750; Stakes, 12; Wards, 94; Branches, 34; Missions, 2; Temples, 2; Percent LDS, 0.43, or one in 234.

In December 1830, Oliver Cowdery, Parley P. Pratt, Peter Whitmer Jr., Ziba Peterson and Frederick G. Williams, passed through Illinois on a mission to the Native Americans. A snowstorm compelled them to stop 20 miles outside St. Louis, where they stayed to preach for several days. In succeeding years, more missionaries passed through Illinois and a few branches were established prior to 1839. In 1834 and 1838 respectively, Zion's Camp and the Kirtland Camp also passed through southern Illinois, en route from Kirtland, Ohio, to Missouri.

When the saints were expelled from Missouri in 1838, many found refuge in Illinois. Quincy, Springfield and other locations generally received them on friendly terms. Temporary stakes were established in Mount Hope, Freedom, Geneva and other locations in Adams County during 1839-1841, as the scattered saints continued to gather. Israel Barlow found his way to Commerce, where he laid the groundwork for the Church to purchase 660 acres of property that later became Nauvoo. As members poured in, the swampy land was drained and buildings were erected. Converts from Canada and Europe arrived by the thousands. The city of Nauvoo received a charter from the state of Illinois in 1840. Settlers built music and cultural halls, schools, stores, mills, and meeting halls. At its peak, Nauvoo's approximate population was 15,000. Although the city was the central gathering place, Joseph Smith planned a network of outlying settlements, foreshadowing the colonization of the West by Brigham Young. These included Ramus, Lima, Quincy, LaHarpe, Green Plains, Plymoth, and Yelrome.

During the peaceful Nauvoo years, Joseph Smith wrote the Articles of Faith, translated the Book of Abraham, and introduced the temple ceremonies. The Female Relief Society, the first Church auxiliary, was organized for the purpose of assisting the poor on 17 March 1842, with Emma Smith as president. In 1840, on a high bluff overlooking the city, a site was selected for the Nauvoo Temple. Portions of the temple were dedicated and used as soon as completed, beginning with the baptismal font in 1841. The building was not completely finished until after the saints left Nauvoo, but approximately 6,000 received temple ordinances between 10 December 1845 and 7 February 1846. A public dedication of the building was held on 1 May 1846. The temple was later destroyed by arson and a tornado.

The relative peace of Nauvoo did not last long. In 1844, Joseph and Hyrum Smith were arrested and taken to jail in nearby Carthage, where they were killed by a mob on 27 June. Following the Prophet's death, the question of succession resulted in many schismatic groups. Two of the most prominent were lead by Sidney Rigdon and James J. Strang, who led their followers to new communities out of state. The majority of the members remained in Illinois for a time and chose to follow the leadership of Brigham Young and the Quorum of the Twelve. However, soon the saints in Nauvoo and surrounding communities were driven by mobs from their homes. In early 1846, starting in the blistery cold of 4 February, they crossed the Mississippi River and traveled across Iowa to establish a temporary residence at Winter Quarters, Neb., some 300 miles away.

Although some members stayed behind, Church membership in Illinois was limited for a time following the saints' migration west. Missionaries traveling in the Eastern States Mission labored in Illinois in the 1850s, visiting old branches, assisting emigrants, and preaching to new congregations. Missionary visits to Illinois increased in the 1870s. Most converts, however, migrated west. Illinois was later included in the Northwestern States Mission when that mission was created in spring 1878. In 1889, the name was changed to the Northern States Mission and headquarters were established in Chicago. By 1890, the mission extended into 22 states and Canada.

Following the conversion of Scandinavian settlers in Minnesota and other nearby states, Christian D. Fjeldsted found success among the Scandinavians in Chicago in 1895-1896. The Church continued to grow and by 1930, three conferences had been organized in Illinois. The Chicago Stake was organized in 1936, the first in Illinois following the Nauvoo era.

In June 1933, when the Century of Progress World's Fair was held in Chicago, the Church sponsored an exhibit in the Hall of Religions, featuring sculptures by Avard T. Fairbanks and two stained glass windows depicting the history of the Church. Missionaries were on hand to answer questions and distribute tracts, and the Chicago Mormon Choir performed every Sunday. The exhibit remained open through October 1934 and drew an estimated 10,000 people per day.

In July 1973, Illinois was separated from the Northern States Mission, and the following year it was renamed the Illinois Chicago Mission. The Nauvoo Stake, organized by Elder Ezra Taft Benson of the Quorum of the Twelve in 1979, was the 1,000th stake organized in the Church. The Illinois Peoria Mission was created from the Illinois Chicago Mission and the Missouri St. Louis Mission in 1983. In 1985, the Chicago Illinois Temple was dedicated. An addition was completed in 1989.

Illinois has been an area of historical interest for many Church members. As early as the 1930s individual Church members began acquiring property in Nauvoo and the vicinity. In 1936, Mission President Bryant S. Hinckley made arrangements to restore the Carthage Jail and establish a Bureau of Information. In 1954, Dr. J. LeRoy Kimball purchased the Nauvoo home of his great-grandfather, Heber C. Kimball, leading to the establishment of the Nauvoo Restoration, Inc., on 27 July 1962. By 1990, the Church had purchased some 1,000 acres and restored 17 homes and buildings. The pioneer cemetery in Nauvoo, where many of its 1840 inhabitants are buried, was acquired and the visitors center was remodeled.

In June 1994, the Church commemorated the 150th anniversary of the martyrdom of the Prophet Joseph Smith. Presidents Howard W. Hunter and Gordon B. Hinckley, and Elder M. Russell Ballard of the Quorum of the Twelve spoke at three meetings in connection with the observance.

Since 1994, BYU has offered a semester in Nauvoo to study American and Church History. In September 1999, the Joseph Smith Academy was opened across the street from the temple block to accommodate student housing and classrooms.

At general conference on 4 April 1999, President Gordon B. Hinckley announced that the Nauvoo Temple would be rebuilt on the original temple site. The new temple closely duplicates the original building, with painstaking attention to craftsmanship and quality. Over 330,000 toured the temple from 1 May to 22 June 2002 during the open house. President Hinckley dedicated the new temple on 27 June 2002 in 13 sessions broadcast in 72 countries around the world. The day after the temple was dedicated, the Mormon Tabernacle Choir presented a benefit concert in Quincy, Illinois, in remembrance of the kind reception the refugee Saints found in 1839 as they were driven from their homes in Missouri. The concert in the Morrison Theater raised $75,000 for the Quincy Area Community Foundation, a public charity.

On 24 March 2004, the Illinois House of Representatives endorsed a resolution expressing regret for the 1846 forced expulsion from Nauvoo. Presidents Thomas S. Monson and James E. Faust were present at a press conference on 7 April to accept the resolution and thank the people of Illinois for their kindness.

In 2002, membership reached 49,972.

Sources: "BYU Announces Nauvoo Study Center," Ensign, July 1999; "Chicago Temple Dedicated," Ensign, October 1985; "Close Successful Work at Fair," Church News, 27 October 1934; "Commemoration of the Martyrdom of Joseph and Hyrum Smith," Ensign, September 1994; Elizabeth Lilenquist, "State of Illinois Expresses Regret for Expulsion of Saints," Church News, April 2004; "Fair Exhibit Viewed Daily by Thousands," Church News, 12 August 1933; "Nauvoo Illinois Temple Dedicated," Church News, September 2002; "New Nauvoo Stake – Number 1,000 - Marks Growth of the Church," Church News, April 1979; Andrew Jenson. Encyclopedic History of the Church, 1941; Andrew Jenson. LDS Biographical Encyclopedia, 1939; Don L. Searle. "Nauvoo: A Temple Reborn," Ensign, July 2002; Glen M. Leonard. Nauvoo: A Place of Peace, A People of Promise, 2002; Gordon A. Buchmiller, " 'Dr. Nauvoo' Honored in S. L.," Church News, April 4, 1981; James L. Kimball. "J. LeRoy Kimball, Nauvoo Restoration Pioneer: A Tribute," BYU Studies, Winter/Spring 1992; Journal History, Church History Library; Northern States Mission, Manuscript history and historical reports 1878-1990, Peoria Mission, Manuscript history and historical reports, Church Archives; Parley P. Pratt. Autobiography of Parley P. Pratt, edited by Scott Proctor, 2000; R. Scott Lloyd. "Era of Restoration Ends in Nauvoo," Church News, October 6, 1990; Victor H. Ludlow (ed.). Encyclopedia of Mormonism, 1990.

Stakes — 12
(Listed alphabetically as of Oct. 1, 2011.)

No.	Name	Organized	First President
North America Central Area			
1672	*Buffalo Grove Illinois	21 May 1991	
	‡Long Grove Illinois	24 Jan 1988	William David Johnston
370	*Champaign Illinois		
	‡Illinois	17 Feb 1963	Ross A. Kelly
2433	Chicago Illinois	25 Jan 1998	A. Clair Jensen
2112	Joliet Illinois	22 Oct 1995	Douglas J. Fredin
368	*Naperville Illinois		
	‡Chicago South (Ill., Ind.)	3 Feb 1963	Lysle R. Cahoon
1000	Nauvoo Illinois	18 Feb 1979	Gene Lee Roy Mann
749	*O'Fallon Illinois	1 Jun 1993	
	‡Fairview Heights Illinois	14 Mar 1976	John Odeen Anderson
1163	Peoria Illinois	3 Aug 1980	Clive Edwin Ashton
1334	Rockford Illinois	11 Apr 1982	Brent L. Horsley
1094	Schaumburg Illinois	20 Jan 1980	Owen D. West Jr.
2280	Springfield Illinois	24 Nov 1996	Alonzo J. Mackelprang
118	*Wilmette Illinois		
	‡Chicago (Ill., Ind., Wis.)	29 Nov 1936	William A. Matheson
Stakes discontinued			
4	Crooked Creek [Ramus] Discontinued 4 Dec 1841	4 Jul 1840	Joel Hills Johnson
8	Freedom Discontinued 24 May 1841	27 Oct 1840	Henry W. Miller
9	Geneva Discontinued 24 May 1841	1 Nov 1840	William Bosley
5	Lima Discontinued 1845	22 Oct 1840	Isaac Morley
7	Mount Hope Discontinued 24 May 1841	27 Oct 1840	Abel Lamb
2a	Nauvoo Discontinued 1846	5 Oct 1839	William Marks
6	Quincy Discontinued 24 May 1841	25 Oct 1840	Daniel Stanton
10	Springfield Discontinued 24 May 1841	5 Nov 1840	Edwin P. Merriam

Missions —2
(As of Oct. 1, 2011; shown with historical number. See MISSIONS.)

(313) ILLINOIS CHICAGO
1319 Butterfield Road Ste 522
Downers Grove, IL 60515

(334) ILLINOIS NAUVOO MISSION
Main and Young Sts., P.O. Box 215
Nauvoo, IL 62354

Indiana

Jan. 1, 2011: Est. population, 6,377,000; Members 41,290; Stakes 11; Wards, 68; Branches 31; Missions 1; Percent LDS, 0.6, or one in 157.

Missionaries Samuel H. Smith and Reynolds Cahoon preached in the cities of Unionville, Madison and Vienna during the summer of 1831. Other missionaries came shortly thereafter, including Parley P. and Orson Pratt. The first branches were organized in September 1831, and the first conference was held on 29 November 1831. In 1832, when Joseph Smith and Newel K. Whitney were traveling between Vincennes and New Albany, Newel K. Whitney broke his leg in a carriage accident. Joseph Smith spent four weeks in Greenville taking care of Whitney until they could continue their journey to Kirtland.

In 1834, Zion's Camp crossed Indiana on its way to Missouri. Although trouble was predicted by their enemies, members of the group passed through Indiana peacefully. In 1838, the Kirtland Camp, a group of seventies, and poorer people who had been left behind in Kirtland, also crossed Indiana.

Many early saints were from Indiana, including Elder David W. Patten of the Quorum of the Twelve. Between 1831 and 1843, missionaries baptized many and branches were established in more than 30 counties. However, with the Church's exodus in 1846 from Nauvoo, Ill., little work was done in the area until later in the century.

In 1876, missionaries John Morgan and Joseph Standing preached in Indiana with limited success. Morgan was a native of the state, and later became Southern States Mission president. By 1882, one missionary reported 24 members in the state when Indiana became part of the Northwestern States Mission, which had been organized in 1878. The name was changed to the Northern States Mission in 1889. In 1898, Greene County members and missionaries built the first chapel in the state, which was used until 1923. Ten years later, 31 members of the Linton Branch in Greene County made a cross country trip to the Logan Temple to receive their temple blessings, a significant sacrifice of the Indiana saints.

Among early converts after the turn of the century were Edward and Anna Faulting of Indianapolis, in whose home meetings were held until 1910. At that time, a home was rented for Church services. Membership grew from 13 people to 10 families by 1913. The Indianapolis branch was organized that year with John L. Thomas as president. The branch met in rented halls until a meetinghouse was erected in 1927 and dedicated by President Heber J. Grant. In 1939, a second branch was organized in Indianapolis. Other branches in the state created as early as 1919 were in Linton, Peru and Evansville, and three years later in Terra Haute.

The first stake in Indiana, the Indianapolis Stake, was organized by Elder Spencer W. Kimball of the Quorum of the Twelve on 17 May 1959 with Philip F. Low as president. The stake included 2,162 members, two wards in Indianapolis and other wards in Bloomington, Columbus, Muncie, Purdue and Richmond, and branches in Kokomo, Anderson and Connersville.

The Great Lakes Mission, created in 1949 from the Northern States Mission, was renamed the Indiana Indianapolis Mission in 1974. Indiana members have supported the Louisville Kentucky Temple since its dedication in 2000. Curtis Ault, from Bloomington, Indiana, was called as the first temple president.

In 2002, there were 35,638 members. In 2005, membership reached 38,987.

Site for the Indianapolis Indiana Temple was announced Jan. 24, 2011. The 50-acre site is located on farmland in the city of Carmel.

Sources: Andrew Jenson, Encyclopedic History of the Church, 1941; Ellen Cox Clayton, Memories of Yesterday in Indiana, 1978; Charles N. Joray, Wending Our Way: A History of Mormonism in Kokomo and Howard County, 1846-1999, 1999; Martha Peterson Taysom, "Glory Is A-Comin' Soon:" A History of Mormonism in Indiana, 1998; Arthur M. Richardson, The Life and Ministry of John Morgan, 1965; "Indianapolis Stake Carved from Mission," Church News, May 23, 1959; "Zions Camp, Across Swamplands," Church News, 5 September 1970, "Zions Camp, the First Prairie," Church News, 12 September 1970; Indiana temple to be built in Indianapolis area, Church News, Jan. 29, 2011.

Stakes — 11
(Listed alphabetically as of Oct. 1, 2011.)

No.	Name	Organized	First President
North America East Area — 9			
1078	Bloomington Indiana	4 Nov 1979	Hollis Ralph Johnson
712	Evansville Indiana	19 Oct 1975	Frank R. Fults Jr.
352	*Fort Wayne Indiana		
	‡Fort Wayne (Indiana, Ohio)	4 Mar 1962	Howard W. Thompson
283	*Indianapolis Indiana		
	‡Indianapolis	17 May 1959	Phillip F. Low
624a	*Indianapolis Indiana North		
	‡Indianapolis North	19 Aug 1973	David Val Glover
2781	Indianapolis Indiana West	11 Nov 2007	William Garn Cowley
1417	Lafayette Indiana	15 May 1983	Koy Eldridge Miskin
2159	Muncie Indiana	4 Feb 1996	Michael W. Ellis
1368	New Albany Indiana	24 Oct 1982	Henry Harvey Griffith
873	South Bend Indiana	30 Oct 1977	Kenneth Bryan Fugal
North America Central Area — 1			
646	*Valparaiso Indiana		
	‡Chicago Heights Illinois	2 Jun 1974	Robert E. Nichols

Mission — 1
(As of Oct. 1, 2011; shown with historical number. See MISSIONS.)
(46) INDIANA INDIANAPOLIS MISSION
3333 Founders Rd., Ste 101
Indianapolis, IN 46268

Iowa

Jan. 1, 2011: Est. population, 3,003,000; Members, 24,614; Stakes 7; Wards 37; Branches 32; Missions, 1; Percent LDS, 0.8, or one in 128.

Following the expulsion of the Church from Missouri in 1838, Iowa Gov. Robert Lucas expressed sympathy for their plight and offered them refuge. Although Joseph Smith instead chose to go to what became Nauvoo, Ill., members also settled across the Mississippi River in Lee County, Iowa, in the cities of Montrose, Augusta, Keokuk, Nashville, and surrounding areas. They also established new settlements in Ambrosia and Zarahemla. In 1839, a stake was organized in Lee County, but it was changed to a branch three years later in 1842.

When the saints were driven from Nauvoo in February 1846, they crossed southern Iowa. Although the exodus occurred in three stages, it took the first company, of which Brigham Young was the leader, 108 days to travel 320 miles due to the rain and mud. En route, they planted grain and established Garden Grove, which today remains a farming community. Farther west, the refugees again farmed at a place they called Mount Pisgah. During the first year, the population of Mount Pisgah reached 2,000. The mortality rate there was very high due to the arduous conditions of the journey. The Mount Pisgah cemetery still remains with a monument erected in 1888. Another significant campsite was Locust Creek, where William Clayton penned "Come, Come Ye Saints."

The emigrating saints reached the eastern bluffs of the Missouri River on 14 June 1846 and established Kanesville, later called Council Bluffs. It was there on 13 July 1846 that nearly 500 men from the "Camp of Israel" were mustered in for military service into the Mormon Battalion. Thereafter, most of the saints moved across the Missouri River where they established Winter Quarters, Neb. In 1848, the U. S. government required the Mormons to move off Indian territory, so those not moving on to the Salt Lake Valley moved back across the river into Iowa. They repopulated Kanesville and established approximately 40 other nearby settlements. All temporary settlements were virtually abandoned in 1852 when Brigham Young hastened the migration to Salt Lake.

After returning to Winter Quarters in the fall of 1847, Brigham Young was formally sustained as president of the Church on 27 December in a log tabernacle in Kanesville. Three weeks earlier on 5 December, the Quorum of the Twelve had reorganized the First Presidency. The same month, President Young issued a general epistle calling upon members all over the world to gather in the Great Basin of the Rocky Mountains.

It was also at Kanesville that Oliver Cowdery, who had helped establish the restored gospel but later became estranged from the Church, rejoined the Saints. At a special conference 21 October 1848, he humbly asked for rebaptism, having earlier been excommunicated. He was rebaptized on 5 November by Orson Hyde and intended to join the migration to the Salt Lake Valley the following season. However, failing health prevented him from making the journey, and he died in Richmond, Mo., in 1850.

After 1848, Kanesville became an important staging area for thousands of Mormon and non-Mormon overland travelers. Many emigrants stopped in the Kanesville area to earn money and prepare for the long trip to Utah. Elders traveling east on missions also stopped in Kanesville. Emigrating saints stopping in southern Iowa built schools, hotels, mills, meeting halls, and a courthouse. By 1850, Kanesville had 350 homes, and Pottawattamie County was the sixth most-populated in Iowa. During 1853, pioneer companies continued to leave from Iowa, many outfitting in Keokuk. In 1856-1857, many handcart pioneers started their trek to the West from Iowa City, then the terminus of the railroad.

A few missionaries passed through southern Iowa during the 1850s and 1860s visiting isolated members in these areas on their way to the Eastern States. The first missionaries mentioned by name to serve in Iowa were Israel Evans and Nymphus C. Murdock, who arrived in 1869. Missionary visits increased in frequency during the 1870s. A branch was established in Keokuk in 1875 and in Council Bluffs in 1878. Iowa became part of the Northwestern States Mission at its organization in 1878. Between 1887 and 1896, headquarters of the mission were located in Council Bluffs. In 1889, the mission name was changed to the Northern States Mission. At that time the Iowa Conference included the states of Iowa, Nebraska, Kansas, Wisconsin, and Minnesota. By 1930, Iowa had branches in Ames, Boone, Sioux City, and Davenport.

In July 1946, President George Albert Smith led a party along the Mormon Pioneer Trail stopping at historic sites and centennial celebrations along the way.

Iowa remained in the Northern States Mission until 1960 when it was transferred to the Central States Mission. In 1954, Elder Hugh B. Brown, then Assistant to the Twelve, dedicated chapels for branches in Des Moines and Cedar Rapids. The first permanent stake in Iowa, the Cedar Rapids Stake, was created in 1966. The Des Moines Stake followed in 1970. For a short time, Iowa became part of the Missouri Independence Mission, until it was reassigned to the Iowa Des Moines Mission in 1976.

During the summer of 1993, Iowa experienced severe flooding along the Mississippi River. Iowa saints responded quickly by helping to place sandbags around homes and businesses. Stakes and wards were able to meet the needs of their members and to assist their neighbors as water supplies were shut off and many homes were evacuated.

Beginning in the late 1970s, appreciation for the contributions of the early Iowa Saints increased as local members cooperated with other Iowa residents to preserve early Church historic sites and the Mormon Trail. Elder Mark E. Petersen of the Quorum of the Twelve dedicated a monument to the handcart pioneers in Iowa City on 1 August 1980. A decade later, a marker commemorating the hymn "Come, Come Ye Saints" was dedicated at Locust Creek Campsite #2 in July 1990. Efforts at restoration and remembrance culminated in 1996 at the sesquicentennial observation of the Iowa portion of the saints' journey from Nauvoo to Council Bluffs. The celebration included an Iowa Mormon Trails History Symposium, a re-enactment of the exodus from Nauvoo, a Grand Encampment near Council Bluffs, a re-enactment of the Mormon Battalion mustering, and two wagon trains and one handcart company tracing the path of the Mormon Trail through Iowa. President Gordon B. Hinckley spoke at a devotional during the Grand Encampment and dedicated the reconstructed Kanesville Tabernacle. The tabernacle is now owned and operated by the Church, and in 2003, a bronze statue of Brigham Young and the newly reorganized First Presidency was placed outside the building.

In 2002, membership reached 19,298. In 2005, membership reached 22,105.

Sources: Andrew Jenson, Encyclopedic History of the Church of Jesus Christ of Latter-day Saints, 1941; Daniel H. Ludlow (ed.). Encyclopedia of Mormonism, 1990; Dell Van Orden. "Mormon Battalion Mustering," Church News, 20 July 1996; Dell Van Orden. "Tabernacle of Log Replicated, Dedicated," Church News, 20 July 1996; "Devotional Honors Epic Pioneer Saga," Church News, 20 July 1996; "Elder Hugh B. Brown Dedicates 6 Chapels," Church News, 5 June 1954; Greg Hill, "Members Quick to Respond in Midwest Floods," Church News, 17 July 1993; Henry A. Smith, "President's Party Ends Pioneer Trail Journey," Church News, 27 July 1947; "Handcart Camp Dedicated in Iowa as Historic Site," Church News, 9 August 1980; Journal History, Church History Library; Kevin Stoker, "Prophet Visits Area of Father's Mission," Church News, 17 October 1987; "Members Help Provide Relief in Flood-Ravaged Iowa," Church News, 7 August 1993; Miriam Beck, "Two Monuments Memorialize Pioneer Legacy," Church News, 19 July 1997; R. Scott Lloyd. "150 Years Ago Converts Camped at Keokuk," Church News, 7 June 2003; R. Scott Lloyd. "Bronze Sculpture Honors 1847 Leaders," Church News, 27 September 2003; R. Scott Lloyd. "Iowans Honor Saints' Trek Across 12 of Their Counties," Church News, 30 March 1996; R. Scott Lloyd. R. Scott Lloyd. "Wagon Trains Re-enact Crossing," Church News, 13 July 1996; "Saints' Crossing of State Remembered," Church News, 11 May 1996; Susan Easton Black and William G. Hartley (eds.). The Iowa Mormon Trail, 1997; "Trails Group Plans to Rebuild Church's 1847 Log Tabernacle," Church News, 18 December 1993; William G. Hartley. "Pushing on to Zion," Ensign, August 2002.

No.	Name	Organized	First President
North America Central Area			
2053	Ames Iowa	21 May 1995	Robert Blaine Schafer
419	Cedar Rapids Iowa		
	‡Cedar Rapids (Iowa, Illinois)	29 May 1966	Richard F. Hagland
2525	Council Bluffs Iowa	25 Apr 1999	Maury Wintle Schooff
902	Davenport Iowa	9 Apr 1978	James Earl Campbell
525	*Des Moines Iowa		
	‡Des Moines	6 Sep 1970	Donald G. Woolley
2595	Iowa City Iowa	10 Jun 2001	Cordell E. Jeppsen
2157	Sioux City Iowa	21 Jan 1996	David W. Roper
		Stakes discontinued	
3a	Iowa [Zarahemla]	5 Oct 1839	John Smith
	Discontinued 6 Jan 1842		

Mission — 1
(As of Oct. 1, 2011; shown with historical number. See MISSIONS.)

(140) IOWA DES MOINES MISSION
8515 Douglas Ave., Ste.19
Des Moines, IA 50322

Kansas

Jan. 1, 2011: Est. population, 2,802,000; Members, 34,190; Stakes, 7; Wards, 53; Branches, 21; Percent LDS, 1.2, or one in 85.

In October 1830 Oliver Cowdery, Parley P. Pratt, Ziba Peterson, and Peter Whitmer Jr. were sent from New York on a mission to the Lamanites. Along the way they preached to two eastern tribes and enjoyed success at Kirtland, Ohio. Passing through Jackson County, Mo., they entered the area that is now Kansas. There they visited the Delaware tribe and introduced them to the Book of Mormon and the restored gospel. As the tribe grew more interested in the missionaries' message, government representatives and ministers from other denominations pressed the elders to leave Indian Territory and they returned to New York in the spring of 1831.

In May 1840, Jonathan Dunham returned as a missionary to the area previously visited by Pratt and the others to preach again to the tribes that had been settled there. Dunham remained only a brief time, being pressed as were others before him by government agents to leave, before moving on to visit tribes in the East.

The next time Latter-day Saints passed through Kansas was in 1846 as a company of Mississippi emigrants traveled through the northeast corner of the territory toward a planned rendevous with Brigham Young's pioneer company on the Platte River. In August of that year, the Mormon Battalion left Council Bluffs and marched south to Fort Leavenworth, where they were outfitted for their trek to California. After leaving the fort, they traveled the length of modern-day Kansas to Bent's fort and then south to Santa Fe. The following year, a contingent of battalion men returned to Kansas as General Stephen W. Kearney's escort from California to Fort Leavenworth.

In 1853, a company of English converts, led by Sylvester H. Earl, assembled in the Atchison, Kan., area to prepare for their journey to the Salt Lake Valley. The following year, emigrating companies outfitted at Westport, Mo., then crossed into Kansas Territory and traveled by way of Fort Leavenworth to the main trail on the Platte River. During 1855 and 1856, some companies assembled at a place called Mormon Grove, a little west of Atchison, to prepare for the trip west. Ground was broken and crops were planted and some of the emigrants remained there as long as two years. During the time that the area was used as an outfitting station, the camp suffered a cholera attack and more than 40 died. They are buried at the site. On 29 August 1855, a branch of the Church was established at Mormon Grove, with Jens Madsen as president. After the 1856 season, Mormon Grove was abandoned and companies were again outfitted at locations in western Missouri, with many traveling through northeastern Kansas en route to Salt Lake City.

On 26 June 1855, the Church sent missionaries to the Indian Territory to carry the gospel to the tribes located there. Five elders entered the territory after stopping at Fort Leavenworth and Mormon Grove. They spent most of their time with the Cherokee and other tribes in the Oklahoma area. By the spring of 1860, all of the missionaries had returned to Utah and it was not until March of 1877 that two elders, John Hubbard and Matthew Dalton, passed through Kansas with the assignment to reopen the mission to the Native Americans. In September of that year, Hubbard died while working with the Wichita tribe. After Dalton buried him in what is now northern Oklahoma, he returned to Utah, arriving on 3 November 1877.

In 1882, Joseph F. Doxey reported missionary work being done in Kansas by himself and two companions. They had some success and established a branch of the Church at Meridian, Kan., which survived only a short while, until branch members were forced by local opposition to leave the area.

After the followers of William Bickerton, leader of a small group that left the Church following the death of Joseph Smith, settled in the St. John area of central Kansas, they were contacted by representatives from the Northern States Mission. Because the Northern States missionaries were having some success working with the group, it was suggested that Kansas be transferred from the Southern States Mission, which had not sent missionaries into the area, to the Northern States Mission to enable that mission to continue the work at St. John. With the approval of the First Presidency, the change was made in April of 1887 and Kansas remained a part of that mission until 1 March 1895, when it was transferred to the Indian Territory Mission. In the meantime, a meetinghouse was built and dedicated in 1895 at St. John, and the mission headquarters was established there. On 29 March 1898, because of the addition of other states to the mission, it was renamed the Southwestern States Mission.

In the early part of 1900, missionaries began working in Jay, eventually organizing a branch there in March of 1901. The branch continued until 1914, when the meetinghouse was sold and branch headquarters moved to Leavenworth. Also in 1900, the mission headquarters was transferred from St. John, Kan., to Kansas City, Mo. As mission boundaries shifted over the next few years to include states outside the Indian Territory, the mission's name no longer reflected its name, so on 4 April 1904 it was renamed the Central States Mission.

During the early decades of the 20th century, the Church continued to grow in Kansas as branches were established in Topeka on 29 June 1913 and Wichita on 23 June 1918. The Topeka Branch began as a dependent branch and became independent in 1926. In 1920, branch members in Wichita completed a chapel of their own. Several General Authorities toured the mission during these years. Among them were Elder James E. Talmage of the Quorum of the Twelve, who spoke at Wichita and St. John, Kan., in December of 1919, and President J. Reuben Clark Jr., first counselor in the First Presidency, who visited in March of 1936.

The Topeka Branch became a ward in the new Kansas City Missouri Stake on 21 October 1956. Then on 24 June 1962, the Wichita Stake, the first with headquarters in Kansas, was established. In 1970, the mission, again experiencing boundary changes, was renamed the Kansas-Missouri Mission. The name was changed to Missouri Independence Mission in June of 1974. Also in 1974, the Church purchased a large home near the Kansas State University campus in Manhattan and established the first institute of religion in the state. The Church had grown enough in Topeka for a stake to be organized there on 29 February 1976.

To help celebrate the Church's connection with Kansas in the early years, on 3 August 1996 more than 500 men and boys from six stakes in the area gathered with families and dignitaries at Fort Leavenworth to re-enact some of the experiences of the Mormon Battalion as it stopped there to prepare for its mission.

In 2002, membership reached 29,122. In 2005, membership reached 30,990.

Sources: Andrew Jenson, Encyclopedic History of the Church of Jesus Christ of Latter-day Saints, 1941; Church of Jesus Christ of Latter-day Saints, History of the Church of Jesus Christ of Latter-day Saints, 1973; Leonard J. Arrington, "Mississippi Mormons," Ensign, June 1977; Brigham H. Roberts, The Mormon Battalion: Its History and Achievements, 1919; Sylvester H. Earl, Biographical sketch, BYU L. Tom Perry Special Collections; Jerome Jacobs, Papers, 1974- 1985, Church Archives; Stanley B. Kimball, Discovering Mormon Trails, 1979; "Mormon Grove," Church News, 20 August 1977; Missouri Independence Mission manuscript history and historical reports, Church Archives; Colly Creek Ward, History, Church Archives; Northern States Mission, Manuscript history and historical reports, Church Archives; Jay Branch, General minutes, Church Archives; Leavenworth Branch, Manuscript history and historical reports, Church Archives; "Martin V. Witbeck, Former Utahn, Called to Preside Over New Unit," Church News, 27 October 1956; "Estate Home now Building for Institute," Church News, 7 September 1974; "Battalion Commemorated at Historic Military Post," Church News, 10 August 1996. Jonathan Dunham, Diaries, Church Archives.

Stakes — 7
(Listed alphabetically as of Oct. 1, 2011.)

No.	Name	Organized	First President
North America Central Area			
2442	Derby Kansas	8 Mar 1998	Brent Edward Nelsen
2613c	Garden City Kansas	18 May 2003	Robert E. Seger
1994	Lenexa Kansas	16 Oct 1994	Donald D. Deshler
1610	Olathe Kansas	19 Oct 1986	Clifton D. Boyack Jr.
1696	Salina Kansas	29 May 1988	Thomas R. Coleman
747	Topeka Kansas	29 Feb 1976	Vahl W. Bodily
355	*Wichita Kansas		
	‡Wichita (Kansas, Oklahoma)	24 Jun 1962	Lee R. Meador

Kentucky

Jan. 1, 2011: Est. population, 4,269,000; Members 32,261; Stakes 7; Wards 42; Branches 34; Missions, 1; Temples, 1; LDS, 0.73, or one in 138.

The first missionaries known to have visited Kentucky were Samuel H. Smith and Reynolds Cahoon. They passed through the northern part of Kentucky in late June 1831 on their way to Missouri. It is unlikely they preached there. About the same time, Joseph Smith and several others, traveling by steamer on the Ohio River, stopped at Louisville for three days. Because of his desire to preach wherever he could, the Prophet Joseph was likely the first to preach in Kentucky, though no record of converts exists.

After this beginning, missionary work was initiated in Ballard, Carlisle, McCracken, Graves, Calloway, Jefferson, Boone, Kenton, and Campbell counties, and a few branches were organized. The first branch organized was at Drury Creek in Campbell County. It was established in April 1834 by Robert Culbertson. In April 1835, Wilford Woodruff and Warren Parrish crossed into Kentucky from Tennessee, and found that several branches had been formed by earlier missionaries in the region. Among those baptized in Kentucky at this time was Abraham O. Smoot. Prior to returning to Kirtland, Parrish ordained Woodruff an elder on 28 June 1835 at the Eagle Creek Branch. From 23 July 1835 into 1836, Woodruff labored alone in Tennessee and Kentucky. In 1835, James Emmett and Peter Dustin baptized 22 people including Benjamin and David Lewis.

The first conference of the Church in Kentucky was held 26 February 1836, at the home of Lewis Clapp in Calloway County. The first company of Kentucky members to gather with the saints in Missouri left on 19 September 1836. This started what became a 50-year movement of saints from the Southern States area. Missionary work continued until the end of 1839, then began again in 1842. In July 1843, Brigham Young and Wilford Woodruff visited Kentucky enroute to the East. Converts were still being baptized a year later when the Prophet Joseph Smith was martyred and missionaries were called back to Illinois.

No other missionary work was done until September 1868 when Jesse W. Crosby Jr. and Owen Dix worked in Kentucky with limited success. On 9 October 1876, Kentucky became part of the newly organized Southern States Mission. Persecution dogged missionaries and members through the 1880s, but by the mid-1890s, toleration of the Church and its members improved, perhaps, in part, because the Church announced that it was discontinuing the practice of plural marriage. By 1900, there were about 1,700 members of the Church in Kentucky.

Kentucky became part of the Middle States Mission on 28 June 1902. When that mission was closed on 7 August 1903, Kentucky returned to the Southern States Mission.

On 27 November 1906, Elders George Albert Smith of the Quorum of the Twelve with Brigham H. Roberts, of the Seventy, visited Louisville while on a tour of the Kentucky Conference. In 1907, M. P. Stinson and Kossnth Dyal visited the tiny community of Jonah, several miles east of Lebanon, and baptized Alfred Crews and his wife, Fannie. In late 1908 or early 1909, the Jonah Fork Branch of the Kentucky Conference was organized. One of the first Church buildings in Kentucky was completed at Jonah and dedicated in 1910.

With the advent of the automobile and improved roads, Bradfordsville, six miles west of Jonah and seven or eight miles south of Lebanon, became the gathering place for Saints from the surrounding communities. As missionary activity in the region continued, meetings were held in homes and the outdoors into the 1930s. One annual tradition was a July 4th fish fry, attended by up to 200 people, including many non-members of the Church. Fiddle and banjo music accompanied the meal, which was followed by preaching by the elders.

Joseph Fielding Smith of the Quorum of the Twelve toured the mission and spoke in Richardsville, Madisonville and Louisville on 7, 8, and 10 November 1929, respectively. President Heber J. Grant visited the mission in 1934, speaking in Louisville on 21 January and Winchester on 22 January.

On 1 January 1929, Kentucky was placed in the jurisdiction of the East Central States Mission with headquarters in Louisville. The mission name was changed to the Kentucky Louisville Mission on 20 June 1974.

Membership in the state in 1930 was 2,879 in the Kentucky and East Kentucky districts, with a total of six branches that had meetinghouses: Grant's Leek, Kentenia, Martin, Owingsville, Louisville, and Larkin.

George Albert Smith of the Quorum of the Twelve visited Louisville Kentucky on 28 November 1929. On 22 June 1941, Joseph Fielding Smith of the Quorum of the Twelve visited Kentucky while on a tour of the East Central States Mission. In October 1949, Harold B. Lee of the Quorum of the Twelve visited Kentucky while on a tour of the mission. Membership continued to grow and many meetinghouses were built during the 1950s and 1960s.

On 17 January 1971, the Louisville Stake, the first in Kentucky, was formed with wards in Fort Knox, Louisville, and New Albany, and branches in Lebanon, Salem, and Sulphur Well.

In 1990, Dan Kelly was elected state senator, the first Latter-day Saint to be elected to a state office.

The Louisville Kentucky Temple was dedicated 19 March 2000 by President Thomas S. Monson, first counselor in the First Presidency.

In 2002, membership reached 25,049. In 2005, membership reached 29,328.

Sources: Andrew Jenson, Encyclopedic History of the Church, 1941; LaMar C. Berrett, History of the Southern States Mission, thesis 1960; Ronald G. Watt, "His First Fruits," Church News, 30 January 1971; Mike Cannon, "My Old Kentucky Home," Church News, 27 August 1977; Southern States Mission, Manuscript history and historical report, Church Archives.

Stakes — 6
(Listed alphabetically as of Oct. 1, 2011.)

No.	Name	Organized	First President
	North America East Area		
2873	Crestwood Kentucky	21 Mar 2010	Albert A. Day II
926	Hopkinsville Kentucky	21 May 1978	Robert Laurence Fears
571	*Lexington Kentucky		
	‡Lexington	23 Apr 1972	Philip M. Moody
540	*Louisville Kentucky		
	‡Louisville	17 Jan 1971	Henry H. Griffith
2621	Lexington Kentucky North	23 Nov 2003	Robert William Hymas
2253	Paducah Kentucky	29 Oct 1996	Larry Wayne Watkins

Mission — 1
(As of Oct. 1, 2011; shown with historical number. See MISSIONS.)

(29) KENTUCKY LOUISVILLE MISSION
1325 Eastern Pkwy.
Louisville, KY 40204

Louisiana

Jan. 1, 2011: Est. population, 4,411,000; Members 28,567; Stakes 6; Wards 32; Branches 19; Missions, 1; Temples, 1; Percent LDS, 0.63, or one in 160.

On 4 January 1841, the Prophet Joseph Smith received a letter from Elam Ludington and Eli G. Terrill of New Orleans who requested an elder to assist the members of the Church who were living there. "Send us Peter, or an Apostle to preach unto us Jesus," they wrote, and enclosed $10 to help defray expenses. The group may have been among those from the sailing ship Isaac Newton, which arrived from London on 21 December 1840 — the first vessel to carry saints to New Orleans,

Harrison Sagers was sent to New Orleans, arriving there on 28 March 1841. He preached to large crowds but was troubled by mobs, and was once protected from a mob by a group of courageous women who circled him in his defense. He baptized several people. More missionaries were sent from Nauvoo to assist Sagers.

By November 1841, New Orleans became the principal port of arrival for Latter-day Saints from Europe. There were 17,463 who immigrated via the Gulf of Mexico port through the years. The New Orleans and Lafayette branch functioned in New Orleans from 1844 to 1855, when New York became the port of arrival for the Church immigrants due to outbreaks of major epidemics.

There was no other known missionary work done in Louisiana until 16 February 1896 when missionaries were assigned to the Louisiana Conference, which was part of the Southern States Mission. Joseph A. Cornwall arrived in Louisiana on 10 September of that year. By the end of 1897, he and his companions had baptized their first converts. The Red Rock Branch was organized on 12 March 1899. That year, 24 missionaries labored in Louisiana. A sawmill owner, John R. Jones, befriended the missionaries and protected them from opposition. Alexander Colman Wagley, first president of the Red Rock Branch, was baptized on 4 September 1898. By 16 June 1899, David A. Broadbent, president of the Louisiana District from 1898 to 1899, reported that 110 people had been baptized.

In October 1899, a mob threatened a missionary under the medical care of Jane Holt Clark, a midwife. She confronted the mob with a shotgun and said, "I brought a good many of you into the world and I can take you out again just as easily." The mob dispersed.

A wagon train of members from Pride traveled to Corleyville, where they settled, organized a branch on 12 November 1916, and erected a meetinghouse about 1920. The Many Branch was organized by June 1935 and a meetinghouse was built by 6 December 1941.

Missionaries labored in New Orleans for 20 years before a branch was again organized in the city. Howard and Marian Bennion arrived in New Orleans in the 1920s and a branch was organized in their apartment in 1924. The branch struggled in the early 1930s, but members joined in the missionary work and contacting via radio, newspapers, and street meetings, they helped the branch grow. About 100 people celebrated the New Orleans Branch centennial in 1944. In 1948, the branch had grown to 300 members, due in part to an influx of Latter-day Saint servicemen who came during World War II. A meetinghouse was begun in January 1951 and dedicated on 16 November 1952. That same year, meetinghouses were dedicated in Hammond, Williamson, and Lake Charles. The New Orleans Stake, the first in the state, was organized on 19 June 1955 by Harold B. Lee and Mark E. Petersen of the Quorum of the Twelve.

Since World War II, Louisiana has been included in the Texas-Louisiana, the Gulf States, and the Louisiana Shreveport missions. The Louisiana Baton Rouge Mission was organized in 1975.

President Spencer W. Kimball visited Baton Rouge on 15 May 1977 and spoke to 12,000 people from the surrounding regions. A temple in Baton Rouge was dedicated 16 July 2000 by President Gordon B. Hinckley.

President Hinckley spoke to 5,000 members in the University of New Orleans Lakefront Arena on 2 March 2003, as part of a two-day tour of members in Southern states.

In 2002, membership reached 24,732. In 2005, membership reached 26,240.

Sources: Andrew Jenson, Encyclopedic History of the Church,1941; J. Malan Heslop, "Boats on the Mississippi are Still Reminder of Part of LDS History," Church News, 24 December 1977; Carol Ann Wagley Burnham, "From Red Rock to Denham Springs," Ensign, April 1983; "Branch Notes 100th Anniversary," Church News, 22 January 1944; Sarah Jane Weaver, "Baton Rouge Temple: 'A House of Refuge,'" Church News, 22 July 2000; Greg Hill, "5,000 Flock to Arena to Hear Church President," Church News, 8 March 2003, Southern States Mission, Manuscript history and historical reports, Church Archives.

Stakes — 6
(Listed alphabetically as of Oct. 1, 2011.)

No.	Name	Organized	First President
	North America Southeast Area		
954	Alexandria Louisiana	27 Aug 1978	Jeffie Jackson Horn
476	*Baton Rouge Louisiana		
	‡Baton Rouge	26 Jan 1969	Harmon Cutler
1254	Denham Springs Louisiana	19 Apr 1981	Stephen H. Cutler
1550	Monroe Louisiana	18 Aug 1985	John Robert Falk
221	*New Orleans Louisiana		
	‡New Orleans	19 Jun 1955	Clive M. Larson
254	*Shreveport Louisiana		
	‡Shreveport (Louisiana, Texas)	26 Jan 1958	J. Milton Belisle
		Stakes discontinued	
1575	Slidell Louisiana	17 Nov 1985	Joseph T. Kuchin
	Discontinued 2 Jun 2007		

Mission — 1
(As of Oct. 1, 2011; shown with historical number. See MISSIONS.)

(31) LOUISIANA BATON ROUGE MISSION
12025 Justice Ave.
Baton Rouge, LA 70816

Maine

Jan. 1, 2011: Est. population, 1,317,000; Members 10,684; Stakes 2; Wards 16; Branches 12; Percent LDS, 0.8, or one in 127.

On 19 September 1832, Orson Hyde and Samuel H. Smith, the first Latter-day Saint missionaries to visit several of the New England states, crossed the Piscataqua River in a canoe from New Hampshire into Maine. During the next several weeks they visited house to house, primarily in the Saco-Biddeford area, and established a branch. Timothy Smith was the first Maine resident baptized, on 31 October. Several converts had been members of the Cochranites, a Protestant group that believed in the need for a living prophet. A branch was established farther north in Farmington by June 1834, and the next year several members of the newly established Quorum of the Twelve met there to organize the Maine Conference, which consisted of four branches and about 100 members.

In August 1837, Wilford Woodruff and Jonathan H. Hale came to Maine to preach in the Fox Islands (present-day North Haven and Vinalhaven), where they established branches on North Fox and South Fox islands and converted more than 100 people. During his time in the islands, Woodruff also briefly visited Bangor and other mainland communities. In August 1838, during his second mission to the Fox Islands, Woodruff received a letter informing him that he had been called as a member of the Twelve and should return to Church headquarters in Missouri. He took with him 53 converts from Maine.

Although 500 Maine residents were baptized by 1844, thanks to the gathering to Kirtland, Ohio, and other Church centers farther west, most Latter-day Saints left the state. There were at least 14 branches in Maine before the Prophet's martyrdom, but by April 1843, only four branches and 128 members were reported.

E. B. Tripp, sent from Utah in 1855 to visit the remaining Latter-day Saints, organized branches at Mexico and Newry among those still faithful to the Church. When Maine native Perrigrine Sessions made a similar visit in 1869, he found about 20 members in the Mexico area "scattered and like sheep without a shepherd," and brought several of them to Utah. They were one of the first groups of Latter-day Saints to make the overland journey entirely by rail.

Eastern States Mission President John G. McQuarrie wrote in 1904 that the northeastern United States was "practically abandoned [as far as missionary work] until 1893 when President Woodruff sent a few Elders ... to try to locate and revive the scattered Saints." McQuarrie reported that the number of elders assigned to his mission had increased and its territory was now divided into conferences. He reported that until 1901 most of the work was done in "country districts" and converts were scattered, which led to a decision to centralize the work in the area's principal cities.

This policy proved difficult to apply in Maine, where even today Portland, the state's largest city, only has a population of 65,000 and 75 percent of Maine residents live in towns with fewer than 10,000 inhabitants. For decades missionaries were assigned to Portland and Bangor and spent the colder months working there while visiting nearby towns or venturing into northern Maine during the summer.

The New England Conference of the Eastern States Mission was divided in 1909 to form conferences in Maine, New Hampshire and Vermont. The missionaries of that era found little success in Maine, as evidenced by the report that they visited 18,000 homes during 1909 and only baptized 10 people. Growth continued to be slow for years to come. The eight missionaries assigned to Maine were transferred to the Canadian Mission in September 1925, with the state becoming part of the newly organized New England Mission in September 1937, when Portland was the only branch in Maine.

Among Maine's pioneer members in the 20th century were Percy and Anne Lane, who were contacted on their farm near Augusta, the state capital, in 1912. Anne and her oldest child were baptized in July 1913 and her husband and other family members later. The first Sunday School was held in the Lane home, and eventually a branch was organized, which was known in sequence as the Ferrin, Litchfield, Farmingdale, and eventually Augusta Branch as it changed meeting places.

A similar process took place at Bangor, where the William G. Bunker family was baptized in 1911 and the William L. Small family of East Bucksport joined the Church in October 1912. Although others were baptized in Bangor, the branch remained small because so many converts moved west. Typical of this was the 1927 move of the entire Relief Society presidency and their families to Utah and California, representing nearly half the branch's families. In 1931, the average sacrament meeting attendance was 11. Later that year the branch was closed and no further sacrament meetings were held for five years. Even when the branch reopened, only two families attended.

Following World War II, the Church in Maine began to be established on a more solid footing. In April 1948, Bangor for the first time had a branch presidency made up of local men, as opposed to missionaries — although some were military personnel from the West stationed at a nearby Air Force base. By 1950, there were 401 Latter-day Saints in Maine, with branches in Litchfield, Bangor, and Portland, but two-thirds of the members lived too far away to be part of organized branches. During the following decade the first LDS meetinghouses were built in Portland and Bangor, both of them dedicated in May 1957. By 1960, as the number of Latter-day Saints in what had before been "outlying areas" began to grow, Church membership nearly quadrupled, with 11 branches functioning.

Further growth came during the 1960s as new approaches to missionary work were developed. One outstanding example took place in Litchfield, where branch president George McLaughlin prayed for inspiration about the growth of his small congregation and began to call "proselyting families" who worked with investigators, with new converts in turn becoming proselyting families. The first year more than 450 people joined the Church, with nearly 200 more being baptized the following year. President McLaughlin left his counselors to run the branch while he devoted his time to training the converts to become strong members of the Church. Additional growth in Maine came with the arrival of Latter-day Saints from the West, including military personnel and faculty and students at various colleges and universities.

With the Church growing and more local converts remaining in the state, a milestone was reached in June 1968 when Elder Harold B. Lee of the Quorum of the Twelve created the Maine Stake. The new stake had 2,200 members and included wards in Bangor, Dover, Augusta, Portland, and Skowhegan, with branches at Ellsworth, Auburn, Farmington, Rockland, and South Paris. All of Maine except the Sanford Branch at the southern extreme of the state and the Caribou and Springfield branches at its northern tip were part of the stake — and Sanford in 1970 became part of the Merrimack Stake headquartered in nearby New Hampshire.

The Church in Maine is made up of small numbers of Latter-day Saints spread over large distances, with a given ward or branch including numerous towns besides the one where the meetinghouse is located. Many times in the past several decades Church units have been divided or had their boundaries realigned to lessen travel distances. In the process, the Maine Stake (renamed the Augusta Maine Stake in 1974) was divided in 1981 to form the Portland Maine Stake and again in 1986 to form the Bangor Maine Stake (which also took in the Caribou Maine District in the far northern part of the state). In 1990, a major realignment took place, with the headquarters of the stake in Portland being transferred to Exeter, N.H., while Caribou and other units in northern Maine were moved to the Saint John New Brunswick Stake, headquartered across the international border in Canada.

In 2002, membership reached 9,304. In 2005, membership reached 9,807.

Sources: Andrew Jenson, "Maine Conference," Encyclopedic History of the Church, 1941; Richard S. Williams, "The Missionary Movements of the LDS Church in New England, 1830-1850," thesis, 1969; Paul E. Damron, The Narrative of the Saints in Maine from 1831 to the 1990s, Church History Library; Donald Q. Cannon, "Wilford Woodruff's Mission to the Fox Islands," in Donald Q. Cannon, ed., Regional Studies in Latter-day Saint History: New England, 1988; John G. McQuarrie, "Eastern States Mission," Millennial Star, 24 February 1904 (quote is from page 113); "Those Who Went Before: Pioneer Members in East and South Recall Rich Past," Church News, 20 July 1991; Viola M. Hawkins, History of the Bangor Ward (1832-1970), 1994; Douglas Jacobsen, "Portland Saints Are Beacons to Maine Neighbors," Ensign, July 1986; "Roadside Prayer Leads to Conversion of Many in Maine," Church News, 17 May 2003; "2 Stakes Organized," Church News, 29 June 1968.

Stakes — 2
(Listed alphabetically as of Oct. 1, 2011.)

No.	Name	Organized	First President
North America Northeast Area			
461	*Augusta Maine		
	‡Maine	23 Jun 1968	Olie W. Ross
1595	Bangor Maine	20 Apr 1986	Paul Herald Risk II

Maryland

Jan. 1, 2011: Est. population, 5,634,000; Members, 40,854; Stakes, 8; Wards, 65; Branches, 13; Missions, 2; Temples, 1; Percent LDS, 0.7, or one in 144.

Jedediah M. Grant, Erastus Snow, William Bosley, and John F. Wakefield began missionary work in Maryland in 1837. Snow and Bosley worked in Washington County, where they organized a branch. Elder Snow also reported preaching in Greencastle, Pa., and baptized more than a dozen people in the village of Leitersburg, Md., just south of the Pennsylvania state line. John Murdock was the first missionary in eastern Maryland, arriving in Baltimore in 1841.

An LDS newspaper, the Mormon Expositor, was begun in 1842 in Baltimore but was soon discontinued. In 1844, both the Whig and Democratic national political conventions were held in Baltimore. At that time Heber C. Kimball and Lyman Wight of the Quorum of the Twelve traveled there to persuade delegates to support Joseph Smith's candidacy for the presidency of the United States. While in Baltimore, they received definite word of the Prophet's martyrdom, having earlier heard rumors about his murder.

Following the removal of the Church from Nauvoo to the Great Basin, little missionary work was done in Maryland during the remainder of the 19th century. Occasionally Latter-day Saints studied there, including future apostles James E. Talmage (1883-1884) and Joseph F. Merrill (1896-1899) at Baltimore's Johns Hopkins University. Elder Merrill's stay followed the re-establishment of missionary work in the area, under the direction of the Eastern States Mission in New York City, and he and his wife served in Maryland's largest city as local missionaries.

The Maryland Conference (as mission districts were then known) was organized in June 1899. When the first conference was held in Baltimore in 1901, there were no Latter-day Saints living there except a few Utah students. A Sunday School was organized not many years later, and missionary work was extended to Havre de Grace, Frederick, and Salisbury. By 1920 missionaries were also working in Annapolis, the state capital. The first branch was organized in Baltimore in April 1923 and an existing church was purchased as a meeting place. That structure was sold to raise funds to buy a building site, which was selected in 1934 by President Heber J. Grant, who returned to Baltimore a year later to dedicate the meetinghouse on Mayfield Avenue.

By the 1930s, as the federal government's New Deal programs brought numerous Latter-day Saints to Washington, D. C., in search of employment, the nation's capital became the focal point for the Church in central Maryland and northern Virginia. A small branch functioned briefly in Capitol Heights, Md., toward the end of World War I, but it was in 1938 that the first permanent outpost of the District of Columbia Church was established in Maryland at Chevy Chase. Later that year, the Capitol District was organized, including the Washington Branch, the Chevy Chase, Baltimore, and Greenbelt branches in Maryland, the Arlington Branch in Virginia, and the Fairview Branch in Pennsylvania. In June 1940, those branches became part of the new Washington Stake.

As the growing population of Washington spilled into the Maryland countryside, over the next several decades, farming communities were transformed into suburbs that extended ever further beyond the limits of the District of Columbia. During the 1950s, as increasing numbers of Latter-day Saints came to the area to work, teach or study at local schools and settled in suburban Maryland, additional wards were established at College Park and Silver Spring, the Baltimore Ward was divided, and a branch was established at Annapolis.

The College Park Ward was typical of others in the area, initially extending across many small communities but then shrinking in size as the LDS populations of those other towns grew and new wards were created. With similar growth following in the next decade, the first Maryland stake was created in 1970, with headquarters at Silver Spring, and later in the 1970s additional stakes were created at Baltimore and Suitland. Maryland's Church membership stood at nearly 18,000 by 1980.

As the Church expanded in the suburbs surrounding Washington, social and economic conditions deteriorated in the inner city. This led Church leaders in Salt Lake City to select Maryland as the site for several important developments in the metropolitan area. In 1960, the Eastern Atlantic States Mission was created, with headquarters in Bethesda, which increased the number of missionaries in the area. The mission became the Delaware-Maryland Mission in 1970 and was renamed the Washington D. C. Mission in 1974, but the headquarters remained in Bethesda.

More significantly, when the First Presidency announced the Washington Temple in 1968, the site selected was in Kensington, Md., where the temple was completed and dedicated in November 1974 and a major LDS visitors center was built in 1976.

In recent years, many new wards and branches and additional stakes have been created in Maryland. A substantial share of the state's LDS population has been quite transient, with students leaving as they complete their schooling and others drawn away by employment or military transfers. In some areas ward and branch boundaries have been frequently realigned, not only to accommodate changes in numbers but also to better meet the needs of local members and congregations. This has especially been the case in Baltimore, where local Church leaders have reached out to inner-city residents, whether Latter-day Saints or potential investigators.

Meanwhile, a handful of Maryland LDS congregations have functioned outside the Washington-Baltimore corridor, some of them for more than 40 years. In 2004, these included the Oakland Branch of the Clarksburg West Virginia Stake and five wards of the Martinsburg West Virginia Stake in the western part of the state, as well as the Salisbury Ward and two branches of the Wilmington Delaware Stake on the eastern shore of Chesapeake Bay.

Membership was 38,517 in 2003. In 2005, membership reached 38,439.

Sources: Andrew Jenson, "Maryland Conference," Encyclopedic History of the Church, 1941; Julian C. Lowe and Florian H. Thayn, History of the Mormons in the Greater Washington Area: Members of the Church of Jesus Christ of Latter-day Saints in the Washington, D. C. Area, 1839-1991, 1991; College Park Ward, 1979; Afton Hepworth Hobbs, Reflections on the Salisbury Branch: A history of the early growth of The Church of Jesus Christ of Latter-day Saints on the lower Delmarva Peninsula, 1989; Susan Buhler Taber, Mormon Lives: A Year in the Elkton Ward, 1993; Frederick Ward (1947-1997): In Commemoration of The Pioneer Sesquicentennial Celebration and of the 50th Anniversary of the Founding of the Frederick Branch, 1997; A History of The Baltimore Stake of The Church of Jesus Christ of Latter-day Saints, 1974-1999, 2003.

(298) MARYLAND BALTIMORE MISSION
4785 Dorsey Hall Drive, Ste 105
Ellicott City, MD 21042-7728

Massachusetts

Jan. 1, 2011: Est. population, 6,498,000; Members, 24,965; Stakes, 4; Wards, 38; Branches, 13; Missions, 1; Temples, 1; Percent LDS, 0.38, or one in 265.

At a conference in Amherst, Ohio, in January 1832, Samuel H. Smith and Orson Hyde were called to serve missions in the northeastern United States. The two reached Boston in June and within a month had baptized seven and were preaching in nearby Lynn. By the time they returned to Kirtland at the end of 1832, there were branches in Boston and New Rowley. During that time Joseph Smith had made a brief visit to Albany, New York City, and Boston in company with Newel K. Whitney.

During the 1830s, Massachusetts was an important destination for missionaries from Kirtland and other Church centers further west, and several branches were established. Following the organization of the Quorum of the Twelve in 1835, the apostles visited the eastern branches. During this trip they grouped branches into geographically defined "conferences" (in later years known as districts), the first time this had been done in the Church. In August 1835, they were in Bradford to organize the Massachusetts Conference, which covered the entire state.

In 1836, Joseph Smith traveled to Salem, Mass. — not far from his family's ancestral home in Topsfield — with his brother Hyrum, Sidney Rigdon and Oliver Cowdery, spending a month in the town Joseph visited as a child recuperating from leg surgery. The Prophet and his companions came at the urging of Jonathan Burgess, who claimed to know the whereabouts of a buried treasure, the recovery of which would help the young Church meet its expenses. Two days after their arrival, Joseph received a revelation (D&C 111) assuring him that the Lord was pleased with their journey, "notwithstanding your follies," and that "there are more treasures than one for you in this city." After Burgess failed to locate the promised money, the word treasures was taken to mean potential converts, and missionaries in succeeding years frequently visited Salem, partly in response to the 1836 revelation. By May 1842, there was a branch of about 90 in the town.

Eight members of the Twelve conducted a three-day conference in Boston in September, and seven of them were again in Boston the following year to promote Joseph Smith's candidacy for the presidency of the United States. In April 1844, the Prophet reported the Lord's instruction that "wherever the Elders of Israel shall build up churches ... throughout the States, there shall be a stake of Zion. In the great cities, as Boston, New York, &c., there shall be stakes."

In 1845, Jedediah M. Grant wrote that Boston had more Latter-day Saints than any other eastern city — somewhere between 300 and 400. Those numbers declined in succeeding years as Brigham Young directed members to join with the body of the saints in the Midwest, and later in Utah. When William I. Appleby, presiding in the eastern states, came to Boston in 1847, he visited the four branches in the area, reported the Boston saints had not met for some time, and found only 30 "true hearted" saints. In 1849, President Young advised Wilford Woodruff to gather the saints to Utah the following year, and when he left Boston in March 1850, 100 local members accompanied him. Over the next four decades, Church activity in Massachusetts was minimal.

The first Latter-day Saints to return to Massachusetts were not missionaries but young people from Utah studying at one of the many schools in the Boston area. In the early 1890s, when future apostle John A. Widtsoe was at Harvard, there were at least 16 other Latter-day Saint students in Cambridge.

As part of the general expansion of LDS missionary work at the end of the 19th century, the Eastern States Mission was re-established in 1893, with headquarters in New York. Missionaries sought to locate old members but could only find the remnant of one branch and 55 Latter-day Saints in the mission's several states. By 1900, there were eight conferences in the mission, including the New England Conference with headquarters at Boston, and 975 members of the Church. There was just one branch in Massachusetts and an average of eight missionaries in all of New England. During the early years of the 20th century there was considerable opposition to Latter-day Saint missionaries in Massachusetts and elsewhere in New England, some of it due to the Smoot hearings in Washington, D.C. These hearings were aimed to deny Reed Smoot of the Quorum of the Twelve his seat in the U. S. Senate.

When a Mutual Improvement Association was established in Boston in 1908, it only had 25 members. A branch was organized in nearby Lynn in December 1909, meeting in the hall from which the group had been "driven" some 12 years earlier. By 1917, when the United States entered World War I, conditions were improving throughout the mission, with increasing numbers of street meetings, more favorable newspaper articles, and new branches in Worcester and elsewhere in Massachusetts.

By 1930, there were five branches in the state and 350 members of the Church. The Massachusetts branches were small and all met in a succession of rented facilities.

In 1930, the Boston Branch rented a building across the Charles River in Cambridge, the home of the Latter-day Saint students from the West who were so important a part of the branch's membership. Naomi B. Cranney, who arrived in Cambridge that year with her husband, a student at Harvard Business College, reported that there were only 10 permanent member families, the other members of the branch all being students who left the area at the end of every school year.

In 1937, the New England States Mission was created, with headquarters in Cambridge and responsibility for six states and Canada's Maritime provinces. Mission president Levi Edgar Young, a member of the First Council of the Seventy, bought part of poet Henry Wadsworth Longfellow's estate in 1941, including a thirty-room mansion used as a mission home, with the house next door being purchased as a meeting place for the Cambridge Branch. President David O. McKay dedicated the new facilities in 1943. President Young's hope for a chapel on the site was realized when a modern structure was built to house the Cambridge Branch, the offices of the New England Mission, and eventually the Cambridge Institute of Religion. President McKay returned in 1956 to dedicate what quickly became the hub of LDS activity in Massachusetts.

In the meantime, Elder S. Dilworth Young of the Seventy who served as New England States Mission president (1947-1951) emphasized "country work," in which elders traveled during the summer without purse or scrip. This effort brought spiritual growth to the missionaries but converts often lived too far away from branch centers to attend meetings regularly.

By the end of 1950, there were 637 members in the seven branches in Massachusetts, but another 200 were not part of any organized branch. One happy result of the country program was the 1949 baptism of Chandler and Edith Abbott in Foxboro, south of Boston, which led to other conversions and the organization of the Foxboro Branch in 1950.

During the 1950s, the Cambridge Branch membership doubled and new branches were established at Fort Devens, Georgetown, Billerica, and South Weymouth. The Boston District was divided and a new district established at Providence, R.I., that included Massachusetts south of Boston. Meetinghouses were constructed in several branches during the late 1950s and early 1960s and proved helpful in missionary work.

By 1962, the Church in eastern Massachusetts had grown to the point that President Henry D. Moyle of the First Presidency, assisted by Elders Harold B. Lee and Gordon B. Hinckley of the Quorum of the Twelve, organized the Boston Stake, with five wards (Billerica, Cambridge, Lynn, South Weymouth, and Weston) and three branches (Fort Devens, Foxboro, and Georgetown).

During the 1960s, helped by referrals from the Mormon Pavilion at the 1964-1965 New York World's Fair, membership in Massachusetts more than doubled to 5,253, divided between sixteen wards and branches. The average size of LDS congregations grew from 91 in 1950 to 183 in 1960 and 328 in 1970. In 1966, during the mission presidency of Elder Boyd K. Packer, the Massachusetts and Rhode Island branches of the Providence District were incorporated into the Boston Stake. The western Massachusetts branches of Springfield, Amherst, and Pittsfield became part of the Hartford (Connecticut) Stake the same year, while Billerica, Fort Devens, and Georgetown, north of Boston, were moved to the new Merrimack (New Hampshire) Stake in March 1970.

A demographic study commissioned by Boston Stake President L. Tom Perry in the early 1970s showed the growth of the Church to be in the suburbs west of Cambridge, rather than in more ethnically diverse inner-city Boston, echoing a pattern observed in other metropolitan areas along the Eastern Seaboard. Thus, when a stake center was constructed in the late 1960s, it was built in suburban Weston. During this period, there was not only an increase in the number of LDS students at Boston-area universities and colleges but also an influx of young single men and women coming to the area to work or serve in the military, leading to the 1967 creation of the University Ward for students and singles and the division of that ward just a year later to form the University 2nd Ward.

In 1977, the Boston stake was divided to form the Providence Rhode Island Stake, which took in all of Rhode Island and southeastern Massachusetts. Four years later the new stake was itself divided to form the Hingham Massachusetts Stake, made up of the Massachusetts units south of Boston and a ward in Newport, R.I. Also in 1981, some of the Massachusetts units of the Nashua New Hampshire Stake were transferred to the new Exeter New Hampshire Stake. In 1987, the Springfield Massachusetts Stake was created, covering all of western Massachusetts and drawing in the Pittsfield Branch from the Albany New York Stake and the Worcester Ward from the stake in Boston.

In recent years expansion of the Church in the greater Boston area has largely come from efforts to bring the gospel to the inner city. The Boston Branch was established in 1984 as the Church's first urban outpost in the area.

In the process, the number of wards and branches increased from eight in 1980 to 26 in mid-2004, leading to the division of the stake in 1998 to create the Cambridge Massachusetts Stake. In 2004, the two stakes included two student wards and two young single adult wards in Cambridge, four Spanish wards and branches, one Portuguese branch, one Haitian-Creole branch, and two wards with substantial numbers of members whose primary language was other than English.

Fueled by growth among ethnic groups, there was an increase in Massachusetts from 21 wards and branches in 1980 to 51 in 2004. During this same period the number of Latter-day Saints in the state tripled.

In recent years, the visibility of the Church in Massachusetts has also increased dramatically. In August 1984, the meetinghouse being built for the suburban Belmont and Arlington wards was severely damaged by fire. During the rebuilding process, there was a great outpouring of concern and support from the local community, with other churches inviting the Belmont Ward to share their facilities. A decade later, in 1994, Latter-day Saints were again in the news when Republican Mitt Romney, former bishop of the Belmont Ward and former president of the Boston Massachusetts Stake, made an unsuccessful bid for a U.S. Senate seat. The following year President Gordon B. Hinckley announced a temple would be built adjacent to the stake center in Belmont, which gave rise to a long legal battle with local residents who were reluctant to have another Church facility in their neighborhood.

When the Boston Massachusetts Temple was dedicated in October 2000 (after some 83,000 people attended its open house), court cases were still pending in relation to a state law regarding the construction of religious buildings and the height of the temple's steeple. A U.S. Supreme Court decision settled the first case in January 2001, while a Massachusetts Supreme Court ruling four months later paved the way for completing the temple's steeple and placing a statue of the Angel Moroni atop the temple in September 2001. The following year, Mitt Romney, a Republican, was elected governor of predominantly Democratic Massachusetts, with public awareness of his religious affiliation continuing to be high as he responded to the state Supreme Court's ruling that same-gender marriages must be allowed in Massachusetts.

Sources: Andrew Jenson, "Massachusetts Conference," Encyclopedic History of the Church, 1941; Richard S. Williams, "The Missionary Movements of the LDS Church in New England, 1830-1850," thesis, 1969; LaMar C. Berrett, Sacred Places: New England and Canada, 1999; Betsey E. Williams, "History of the Mormon Church on the North Shore," 1972, Church History Library; Joseph Smith, History of the Church, 1:295, 6:319; Richard O. Cowan, "Yankee Saints: The Church in New England During the Twentieth Century," and Alan K. Parrish, "Harvard and the Gospel, An Informal History," both in Donald Q. Cannon, ed., Regional Studies in Latter-day Saint Church History, 1988; J.D. Williams, "Highlights in the History of the Church of Jesus Christ of Latter-day Saints in the Boston Area," 1955, Church History Library; "Those Who Went Before: Pioneer Members in East and South Recall Rich Past," Church News, 20 July 1991; New England Mission and Cambridge Branch Chapel Building, 1956; "Church Organizes 345th Stake in Boston," Church News, 26 May 1962; Paul James Toscano, "The Boston Saints," Ensign, February 1973; Janet Peterson, "Belmont's Blessing in Disguise," Ensign, April 1987; Sheridan R. Sheffield, "Boston: Gospel Rolls Forward in One of Nation's Oldest Cities," Church News, 28 September 1991; Larry A. Hiller, "The Brotherhood-Sisterhood Thing," New Era, June 1992; Don R. Brugger, "Climate for Change," Ensign, September 1993; Mark Small, "Stake Is Growing in History-rich Area," Church News, 20 June 1998; Tammy Adams, "Fabric of Faith," Church News, 25 October 2003; Jack Thomas, "LDS Spires Are Point of Friction in New England," reprinted from Boston Globe in Deseret News, 7 December 1996; Carey Goldberg, "Boston Temple Is Rising Despite Constitutional Suit," New York Times News Service story in Deseret News, 31 December 1999; "High Court Rules in Favor of Steeple for Boston Temple," Church News, 19 May 2001; Christopher B. Daly, "Religion Resurrected as Political Issue: Beliefs Come into Question in Massachusetts Senate Race," Washington Post, 10 September 1994; Michael Paulson, "Election 2002 / Religion, Heritage: Romney Win Seen as Sign of Acceptance of Mormons," Boston Globe, 9 November 2002; General mission annual reports and stake statistical recaps, 1940-1980, Church Archives.

Stakes — 4
(Listed alphabetically as of Oct. 1, 2011.)

No.	Name	Organized	First President
	North America Northeast Area		
354	*Boston Massachusetts		
	‡Boston (Mass., N.H., R.I.)	20 May 1962	Wilbur W. Cox
2497	Cambridge Massachusetts	18 Oct 1998	Lloyd S. Baird
1287	Hingham Massachusetts	30 Aug 1981	Brent W. Lambert
1646	Springfield Massachusetts	28 Jun 1987	David O. Sutton

Mission — 1
(As of Oct. 1, 2011; shown with historical number. See MISSIONS.)

(35) MASSACHUSETTS BOSTON MISSION
385 Concord Ave., Suite 100
Belmont, MA 02478

Michigan

Jan. 1, 2011: Est. population, 10,003,000; Members, 42,319; Stakes, 8; Wards, 66; Branches, 30; Missions, 2; Districts, 1; Temples, 1; Percent LDS, 0.4, or one in 235.

Visiting her relatives in Pontiac, Lucy Mack Smith, mother of Joseph Smith, arrived in Michigan in the spring of 1831. Accompanying her was her niece, Almira Mack, a native of Pontiac. She had been baptized in New York in 1830 and became Michigan's first Church member. They visited Lucy Mack Smith's sister-in-law, Temperance Mack, widow of Colonel Stephen Mack, considered the founder of Pontiac. Preaching in Pontiac, Lucy warned an unfriendly pastor that one third of his flock would soon be members of the Church, including the deacon. After she returned to Kirtland, Ohio, the Prophet Joseph Smith sent Jared Carter and Joseph Wood to Pontiac where they arrived 7 January 1833, and baptized 22 people from the pastor's congregation, including the deacon, Samuel Bent.

In 1834, Joseph Smith visited Pontiac and preached for two weeks with his brother Hyrum, Oliver Cowdery, David Whitmer, Martin Harris, Frederick G. Williams, and Robert Orton. Parley P. and Orson Pratt visited Detroit en route to England in the fall of 1839 where they preached to crowded houses. Parley Pratt published a pamphlet there, History of the Late Persecution by the State of Missouri upon the Mormons.

By the early 1840s, more than 25 branches were located in Oakland, Lapeer, Wayne, Livingston, Washtenaw and Lenawee counties. Converts from Jared Carter's efforts of 1833 continued to spread the gospel to much of western Michigan. On 12 January 1844, Mephibosheth Serrine reported that in the previous six months, more than 100 converts had left to gather in Nauvoo. Visiting Church authorities created more branches in June 1844. With the martyrdom of Joseph and Hyrum Smith on 27 June of that year, many members accepted the leadership of Brigham Young and joined the westward movement. Apostate James J. Strang claimed to be the successor of the Prophet and attracted a group who later settled on Beaver Island in Lake Michigan before disbanding. Other splinter groups resided in Michigan as well. Because of the antagonism of these groups and the eruption of the Civil War, missionaries were not sent to Michigan again until the 1870s.

On 4 May 1876, William M. Palmer received a letter from Brigham Young calling him to serve a mission in Michigan. During the next two years Palmer organized branches in the cities of Sylvester, Millbrook and Westville despite serious persecution. In May 1877, additional elders including Cyrus H. Wheelock labored in Michigan and surrounding states in what became the Northwestern States Mission. From 1880 to 1882 William Palmer was called on a second mission to Michigan and supervised the Michigan Conference. For the rest of the 19th century many converts migrated steadily to Utah, and missionary efforts practically ceased in Michigan by the end of the 1880s and during the 1890s. In 1891, there were 47 members in the state.

During the first decade of the 20th century, the Church began to form branches and groups in Flint, Grand Rapids, Detroit, Schoolcraft, Battle Creek and Vermontville. In 1913, the Church sent the Arthur Snow family from Utah to Michigan in order to manage the Church's salt mine business in Detroit. The Snows and the Archie Alger families became the nucleus of the Detroit membership. Two years later, Northern States Mission president German E. Ellsworth organized the Detroit Branch on 21 April 1915 with Alger as president. By 1930, membership in the East Michigan and West Michigan districts, created that year, had a combined membership of 972.

The first meetinghouse in Detroit was dedicated in December 1928. By 1945, some 7,183 members resided in branches in Detroit, Ann Arbor, Battle Creek, Grand Rapids, Jackson, Muskegon, Flint, Lansing, Pontiac, and Saginaw. Michigan's first stake was created on 9 November 1952, in Detroit, with George W. Romney as president. The Great Lakes Mission was created in 1949, and the Indiana-Michigan Mission in 1970. In 1973, the Michigan Mission (changed later to Michigan Lansing) was created. The Michigan Dearborn (later renamed Michigan Detroit) Mission was created in 1978. President Spencer W. Kimball spoke to 14,500 Saints from Michigan and parts of Indiana, Ohio, and Pennsylvania at an area conference in Ann Arbor, on 20 September 1980.

Due to the Detroit race riots in the late 1960s and the segregation that existed in the city, the Church did not make inroads into the inner city until missionaries were sent in 1987. Under the direction of the Bloomfield Hills and Westland stakes, seven branches that served African-Americans and Hispanics were created between 1989 and 1995. From 1991 to 1995, the Detroit Ward encompassed part of the east side of Detroit. During this time, James Edwards was called as the first African American bishop to serve in Michigan. In 1995, the Detroit Ward was divided into seven small branches. Two years later, the Detroit District was formed and Gordon W. Creer from the Bloomfield Hills Stake became president. By 2000, the branches were consolidated to five, and Haitian-born Lamenais Louis was called as district president.

On 26 July 1995, longtime national and Church leader and Michigan's most prominent citizen in the 1960s, George W. Romney, died. He served as governor of Michigan from 1962 until he resigned in 1969 to join President Richard Nixon's cabinet as secretary of Housing and Urban Development. He also was a candidate for president of the United States in 1968.

A temple in the Detroit suburb of Bloomfield Hills was dedicated on 23 October 1999. The roadway in front of the temple was originally built by the Prophet Joseph Smith's uncle, Stephen Mack, who had figured prominently in the early history of the Detroit area.

In 2002, membership reached 39,839. In 2005, membership reached 42,409.

Sources: Hilda Faulkner Browne, The Michigan Mormons, 1832-1952, 1985; John and Audrey Cumming, "The Saints Come to Michigan," Michigan History, March 1965; John Cumming "The Mormon Era in Detroit," Detroit Historical Society Bulletin, March 1968; Andrew Jenson, Encyclopedic History of the Church, 1941; Jonathan W. Snow, Papers, 1949-1993, Church Archives; Frank C. Davis, "LDS Influence Felt in Much of Michigan History," Church News, 15 November 1980; "Longtime National Figure George W. Romney Dies," Church News, 29 July 1995; Greg Hill, "A Temple in Their Midst," Church News, 30 October 1999.

Stakes — 8
(Listed alphabetically as of Oct. 1, 2011.)

No.	Name	Organized	First President
North America Northeast Area			
854	Ann Arbor Michigan	14 Aug 1977	Duane Marvin Laws
197	*Bloomfield Hills Michigan		
	‡Detroit (Michigan, Ohio, Canada)	9 Nov 1952	George W. Romney
940	Grand Blanc Michigan	11 Jun 1978	Trent Pickett Kitley
684	Grand Rapids Michigan	2 Mar 1975	Glenn Goodwin
1091	Kalamazoo Michigan	9 Dec 1979	Donald Lee Lykins
349	*Lansing Michigan		
	‡Lansing	18 Feb 1962	Sylvan H. Wittwer
469	*Midland Michigan		
	‡Mid-Michigan	1 Dec 1968	E. Richard Packham
474	*Westland Michigan	14 Aug 1978	
	*Dearborn Michigan		
	‡Dearborn (Michigan)	12 Jan 1969	Carl S. Hawkins

Missions — 2
(As of Oct. 1, 2011; shown with historical number. See MISSIONS.)

(164) MICHIGAN DETROIT MISSION
33505 State St., Suite 101
Farmington, MI 48335

(104) MICHIGAN LANSING MISSION
1500 Abbott Rd., Suite 110
East Lansing, MI 48823

Minnesota

Jan. 1, 2011: Est. population, 5,220,000; Members, 30,603; Stakes, 8; Wards, 54; Branches, 26; Missions, 1; Temples, 1; Percent LDS, 0.57, or one in 174.

Though missionary work spread through neighboring states during the 1830s and 1840s, it appears the first elder to preach in Minnesota was Ralph Joung, who in 1854, "preached at Spring Grove," according to a Minnesota county newspaper.

In 1857, missionaries baptized Minnesota settlers Robert and Sarah Pope in Morristown, along with Edwin Theodore Pope and his wife, whose name was not recorded. These converts soon gathered with the saints in Utah. The next missionary to Minnesota was Silas Hoyt in September 1868 and two years later Ariah C. Brower and Eli Whipple worked in Minnesota and adjoining states.

Minnesota had a high percentage of Scandinavian immigrants in the 1870s, so in 1875 Bengt P. Wulffenstein, who spoke Swedish, German and Danish began a systematic and successful effort to teach the many Scandinavians in the state. That same year, Wulffenstein organized Minnesota's first branch, a small group of converts in Freeborn County. By 1877, five more branches were organized in the cities of Princeton, Monticello, Farmersville, Burns and Isanti, and by February 1882, Minnesota had 74 members.

The town of Monticello became a center for the work as Deborah Houghton Riggs, the wife of its founder, Ashley C. Riggs, joined the Church. The Riggs family helped support the elders, boarded them, and because of the family's prominence deflected criticism of the elders and the Church. By the end of the 1870s and early 1880s, groups of Latter-day Saints began to migrate to Utah including a group of 70 from Monticello. In 1886, about 227 members belonged to the Minnesota Conference, which also included Wisconsin, the Dakotas and Iowa.

By the turn of the 20th century, most Minnesota converts had left for Zion. The handful who remained worked to build the Church. Minnesota Conference headquarters were established in Minneapolis in 1900 and on 20 May a Sunday School was organized in Minneapolis and another was organized in St. Paul on 5 August. The Sunday Schools were combined in 1902. The new unit had an average attendance of 50. Mission president German E. Ellsworth served from 1904-1919, and under his leadership, the first Church-owned building in Minnesota was purchased on 9 May 1914 for the St. Paul Branch.

A baptismal font was installed in its basement for baptismal services for converts from the entire state. By 1919, membership had increased to 4,000 in 30 branches. A meetinghouse was dedicated in Minneapolis on 26 October 1924 by President Heber J. Grant and Elder George Albert Smith of the Quorum of the Twelve. By 1930, there were three districts in the state: the North, South and Lake.

The Minnesota Stake, the first in the state, was organized in Minneapolis on 29 November 1960 with six wards and five branches, and a membership of 2,600. When the name of the Minnesota Stake was changed to the Minneapolis Minnesota Stake in 1974, it had 4,936 members. Two years later, the St. Paul Stake was created. The Minnesota-Manitoba Mission was created in 1970. Boundary changes occurred creating the Minnesota-Wisconsin Mission in 1973. Three years later the Minnesota Minneapolis Mission was created.

A temple was dedicated in St. Paul on 9 January 2000.

Membership reached 26,333 in 2003. In 2005, membership reached 28,042.

Sources: Andrew Jenson, Encyclopedic History of the Church, 1941; Fayone B. Willes, Minnesota Mormons, a History of the Minneapolis Minnesota Stake, 1990; The Church in Minnesota, unpublished, Church Archives; "Minneapolis Stake Organized in North Central States," Church News, 3 December 1960; "5 More Temples for Canada, U.S.," Church News, 15 August 1998; Janet Kruckenberg, "First Temple in the Year 2000," Church News, 15 January 2000.

Stakes — 8
(Listed alphabetically as of Oct. 1, 2011.)

No.	Name	Organized	First President
North America Central Area			
1562	Anoka Minnesota	20 Oct 1985	Lyle T Cottle
2192	Burnsville Minnesota	28 Apr 1996	Matthew Artell Smith
1939	Duluth Minnesota	9 May 1993	John G. Hancock
317	*Minneapolis Minnesota		
	‡Minnesota (Minn., Wis.)	29 Nov 1960	Delbert F. Wright
2588	Oakdale Minnesota	4 Feb 2001	Evan Anthony Ballard
910	Rochester Minnesota	30 Apr 1978	Lee McNeal Johnson
2826	St. Cloud Minnesota	3 May 2009	Randal Guy Baker
744	St. Paul Minnesota	15 Feb 1976	Thomas Albert Holt

Mission — 1
(As of Oct. 1, 2011; shown with historical number. See MISSIONS.)

(26a) MINNESOTA MINNEAPOLIS MISSION
5931 West 96th St.
Bloomington, MN 55438

Mississippi

Jan. 1, 2011: Est. population, 2,939,000; Members, 21,217; Stakes, 4; Wards, 29; Branches, 14; Missions, 1; Percent LDS, 0.7, or one in 141.

Missionary work in Mississippi began when John D. Hunter and Benjamin L. Clapp arrived in Tishomingo County in 1839. Hunter reported on 26 December 1839 that they had baptized six people. In 1840, Norvel M. Head visited Tishomengo and baptized seven people. Daniel Tyler and R. D. Sheldon began work in Copiah on 1 December 1841 and baptized five people. Escaping persecution, a group of 80 to 90 members in 40 wagons arrived in Nauvoo from Mississippi in April 1842. A small branch was organized in Monroe County in 1843 where other converts, including plantation owner James M. Flake, were converted and baptized by Benjamin L.Clapp. Several other branches were created and membership continued to increase.

On 8 April 1846, a company of emigrants left Monroe County expecting to join the main body of saints in Winter Quarters that was then planning to travel to the Rocky Mountains. Instead, the Mississippi Saints became the first group of Mormons to cross the plains, wintering with fur trappers in Pueblo, Colo., that same year. These members were the first to establish a religious colony in the West since the Spanish priests of 1769. They later founded the second colony in the Salt Lake Valley at Cottonwood (once called the Mississippi Ward) and Holladay. They also helped found San Bernardino, Calif., and years later were involved in other colonies along the Little Colorado in Arizona. One of the children of these early pioneers from Mississippi was Alice Rowan, who taught school in Riverside, Calif. She was among the first African-American women to teach at a public school in the nation.

Missionary work continued in Mississippi until the Civil War. It resumed in 1877 with the arrival of W. H. Crawford and others. On 27 July of that year the Baldwin Branch was organized. In 1880, enemies of the Church tried, but failed, to enlist the governor's help in forcing missionaries to leave the state.

Opposition increased and missionaries were often persecuted. Alma P. Richards was murdered on 3 August 1888, though a church investigation committee concluded the motive likely was robbery, not religious persecution.

By 1930, the Mississippi Conference had a membership of 2,170 in the Darburn and Red Star branches and the Sunday Schools in Bay St. Louis, Meadville, Raytown, Red Hill, Sarah, and Smithville. New buildings were completed for the Senatobia, McNeill, and Jackson branches in 1943, and in Biloxi in 1954.

The first two stakes in Mississippi were created in 1965. The Jackson Stake was created on 2 May and had wards in Jackson, Meridian, Natchez, Columbus, Vicksburg, and Red Star and a branch in Greenville. The second stake in Hattisburg, organized 27 June, had wards in Biloxi, Columbia, Gulfport, Hattiesburg, Liberty, and Pascagoula, along with the Bayou La Croix, Darburn, Laurel, McNeill, Sant Hill and Seminary branches.

In May 1996, members in Monroe County honored early pioneers from Mississippi, known as the Mississippi saints, by dedicating a monument at Mormon Springs where many of the early converts were baptized. Also during that year, a program was held commemorating the temporary colony in Pueblo, Colo., established by the Mississippi saints.

President Gordon B. Hinckley spoke to 6,000 members in rural Southhaven, who had assembled from the tri-state area of

Mississippi, Tennessee and Arkansas on 1 March 2003. With no assignments for that weekend, President Hinckley said he wished to visit an area where he had never been.

In 2002, membership reached 18,408. In 2005, membership reached 19,747.

Sources: Andrew Jenson, Encyclopedic History of the Church, 1941; "Anniversary Noted for Old Backwoods Chapel," Church News, 9 August 1958; LaMar C. Berrett, History of the Southern States Mission 1831-1861, thesis 1960; "Gulf States Get New Stake," Church News, 8 May 1965; DeVon H. Nish, A Brief History of the Southern States Mission for One Hundred Years, 1830-1930, 1966; Mary Elizabeth Stovall, "Orthodoxy Versus Nonconformity: The Mormon Experience in Tennessee and Mississippi, 1875-1905,", research paper, 1976; Leonard Arrington, "Mississippi Mormons," Ensign, June 1977; "Mississippi Saints Headed West in 1846," Church News, 13 July 1996; Greg Hill, "Mississippi Visit Among Tri-state Area Faithful," Church News, 8 March 2003; Southern States Mission, Manuscript history and historical report, Church Archives.

Stakes — 4
(Listed alphabetically as of Oct. 1, 2011.)

No.	Name	Organized	First President
North America Southeast Area			
1364	Gulfport Mississippi	10 Oct 1982	John Sibbald Scott II
408	*Hattiesburg Mississippi		
	‡Hattiesburg	27 Jun 1965	Edwin White
404	*Jackson Mississippi		
	‡Jackson	2 May 1965	Neil J. Ferrell
1801	Tupelo Mississippi	9 Jun 1991	Thomas Evan Nebeker

Mission — 1
(As of Oct. 1, 2011; shown with historical number. See MISSIONS.)

(171) MISSISSIPPI JACKSON MISSION
681 Towne Center Blvd. Ste. C
Riegeland, MS 39157-4903

Missouri

Jan. 1, 2011: Est. population, 5,912,000; Members, 66,071; Stakes, 14; Wards, 108; Branches, 37; Missions, 2; Temples, 1, announced, 1; Percent LDS, 1.1, or one in 93.

Oliver Cowdery, Parley P. Pratt, Peter Whitmer Jr., Ziba Peterson, and Frederick G. Williams arrived in Missouri early in 1831 on a mission to the Native Americans. Peterson and Whitmer remained in Independence, where they were employed as tailors, while the others preached to Delaware and Shawnee Indians in the adjacent Indian Territory. In June 1831, 13 sets of missionaries were called to attend a conference in Missouri and preach along the way. During the same time, a branch of the Church in Colesville, N.Y., was asked to immigrate to Missouri and settled in Kaw Township. In July, Joseph Smith and several elders traveled to Independence, where the prophet received a revelation (D&C 57) indicating that Zion, the New Jerusalem, would be built there.

This revelation led to an immediate influx of members. Edward Partridge was appointed Bishop of Zion and administered to the temporal needs of the incoming saints. In 1832, Sidney Gilbert established a store and W. W. Phelps set up a printing office, from which he published The Evening and The Morning Star and later the Book of Commandments.

By June 1833, there were 1,200 members in 10 branches in Jackson County. Some, however, were ill prepared for settling on the frontier and were disobedient to Church counsel. These difficulties added to the challenge of dealing with the old Missouri settlers, who became alarmed at the increasing number of Latter-day Saints and their different economic, political, and spiritual lifestyle. In July 1833, over 400 Missourians gathered at the Jackson County courthouse to demand removal of the Mormon settlers. When the Mormons refused to leave, the Church's printing press was destroyed and Church leaders and outlying settlements were attacked by mobs. The saints' efforts to seek protection through the courts failed. Finally, on 5 November 1833, the saints were disarmed and mobs drove them from Jackson County.

Joseph Smith and about 200 men, called Zion's Camp, arrived from Kirtland, Ohio, to protect the Missouri members in 1834. A violent storm prevented confrontation and the group was subsequently disbanded at the Prophet's direction.

The Jackson County refugees found safety in Clay County for two years and then, amid growing adversity, moved to the western uninhabited Caldwell and Daviess counties. Throughout 1836 and 1837, Church members continued to gather and establish settlements in Caldwell County. In the fall of 1837, Far West had more than 100 homes, hotels, a printing house, and a school. Joseph Smith moved Church headquarters to Far West in 1838, where a temple site was selected and dedicated. Cornerstones were placed on 4 July 1838. Adam-ondi- Ahman was one of the outlying settlements in Daviess County. It was revealed to Joseph Smith on 19 May 1838, that this location was where Adam would "come to visit his people," as spoken by Daniel (D&C 116).

Apostasy and dissention fueled internal Church problems in 1838. Several prominent leaders were excommunicated. In two speeches during June and July, Sidney Rigdon declaimed the saints' independence from "mobocracy" and called for apostates and dissenters to leave the Mormon community. These speeches incited Missourians. Throughout the fall hostilities escalated and in October Apostle David W. Patten of the Quorum of the Twelve and two other saints were killed in the Battle of Crooked River. Gov. Lilburn W. Boggs, who refused to aid the saints or quell violence, signed an order authorizing the expulsion and extermination of all Mormons. A militia attacked the Church's Haun's Mill settlement killing 17 men and boys. On 31 October, the state militia laid siege to Far West, and several prominent Church leaders were arrested. Joseph Smith was sentenced to death. However, his life was spared when Brig. Gen. A. W. Doniphan refused to carry out the execution. Instead, Joseph Smith was incarcerated for five months in Liberty Jail as he awaited trial. After the Mormon militia surrendered, the Missouri militia plundered Far West and drove out the saints. Thousands of displaced Missouri Mormons found refuge in Illinois, where they later established Nauvoo. In the extremity of his suffering in Liberty Jail, sometimes called the Temple Prison, the Prophet sorrowed for the plight of the saints whom he dearly loved. In his anguish, the Lord comforted him with some of the sublimest prose in scripture in Doctrine and Covenants 121.

Some members found shelter in the more tolerant city of St. Louis, and in 1844, a branch was organized there. Shiploads of Latter-day Saint immigrants used St. Louis as a port of debarkation, or passed through on their way to Council Bluffs. Part of one such company obtained passage on the steamship Saluda. On 9 April 1852, the ship's boiler exploded outside Lexington, Miss., killing approximately 100 passengers. The citizens of Lexington came to the relief of the victims, providing medical care, replacing clothing, burying the dead, and adopting the orphaned. By 1849, a conference was formed in St. Louis with 3,000-4,000 members. The St. Louis Stake was organized in 1854, but was discontinued in 1858 after Brigham Young called all members to Utah.

Missionary work thereafter was sporadic until later in the century. Originally part of the Northern States Mission, Missouri was incorporated into the Southwestern States Mission in 1900, which became the Central States Mission in 1904. That year, Utah entered an exhibit at the World's Fair in St. Louis, which became the focal point of missionary efforts. In 1911, the first branch was organized in Independence, and in 1914 President Joseph F. Smith dedicated a meetinghouse there.

Five new chapels were dedicated between 1926 and 1927. By 1930, branches functioned in Independence, Joplin, Kansas City, St. Louis, Sedalia, St. Joseph, Springfield, and Webb City. In 1939, the mission had over 6,000 members and averaged 200 baptisms per year. President George Albert Smith visited Missouri in 1949 and dedicated meetinghouses in Kansas City and St. Louis. Stakes in those areas followed in 1956 and 1958, respectively. In 1977, the second Missouri mission was created with headquarters in St. Louis. President Gordon B. Hinckley visited St. Louis to conduct his first regional conference as president of the Church in April 1995. He returned on 1 June 1997 to dedicate the St. Louis Temple.

During the early 1900s interest in Church-related historic sites in Missouri was revived. In June 1939 Wilford Wood, in behalf of the Church, purchased the old Liberty Jail where Joseph Smith and others were incarcerated during the winter of 1838-1839. Restoration of the building began in 1945 and on 15 September 1963 it was dedicated by Elder Joseph Fielding Smith. Wood also assisted in the purchase of 30 acres of ground at Adam-ondi-Ahman. Today, there is a visitors center in Independence and a monument at Far West.

In the early part of the 20th century, Church leaders began building friendships with leaders of the Reorganized Church of Jesus Christ of Latter Day Saints, now the Community of Christ. In June 1940, President George Albert Smith paid a visit to Frederick M., Israel A., and Elbert A. Smith. During that visit leaders of both churches foresaw a time of good will coming between the two churches. In 1992, the Mormon Tabernacle Choir performed in the RLDS Church's auditorium.

Over the years, public feeling toward the Church in Missouri has improved. In the 1930s, musical groups comprised of Church missionaries were invited to broadcast performances over local radio stations. In more recent years, the Church sponsored an annual summer pageant, "A Frontier Story, 1833," depicting the early history of the Church in Missouri, which ran between 1985 and 1997. An exhibit at Missouri's capital, Jefferson City, titled "Mormon Experience in Missouri," was shown during the summer of 1998. The extermination order issued by Gov. Boggs in 1838 was eventually rescinded by Governor Christopher S. Bond on 25 June 1976.

In 2002, membership reached 54,761. In 2005, membership reached 59,377.

Sources: Andrew Jenson. Encyclopedic History of the Church, 1941; "Church Dedicates its 50th Temple," Church News, 7 June 1997; "Church Now Owns Liberty Jail Site," Church News, 22 July 1939; Daniel H. Ludlow (ed.). Encyclopedia of Mormonism, 1991; "Exhibit Forges New Link with Missouri," Ensign, July 1998; "Independence Pageant 'A Frontier Story' Has Been Canceled," Church News 19 April 1997; Jay M. Todd, "Another Smashing Tabernacle Choir Tour," Ensign, October 1992; Leland Homer Gentry. A History of the Latter-day Saints in Northern Missouri from 1836 to 1839, 2000; "New Drama Urges: 'Love as He Loved,'" Church News, 30 June 1985; "Pageant Attracts Record Numbers," Church News, 4 July 1987; Parley P. Pratt. Autobiography of Parley P. Pratt, revised by Scott Facer Proctor and Maurine Jensen Proctor, 2000; R. Scott Lloyd, "Church Succors Tornado Victims," Church News, 17 May 2003; Stephen C. LeSueur. The 1838 Mormon War in Missouri, 1987; William G. Hartley and Fred E. Woods, Explosion of the Steamboat Saluda, 2002.

Stakes — 14
(Listed alphabetically as of Oct. 1, 2011.)

No.	Name	Organized	First President
North America Central Area — 9			
1563	Cape Girardeau Missouri	20 Oct 1985	David E. Payne
511	*Columbia Missouri		
	‡Columbia	19 Apr 1970	Samuel D. Richards
544	*Independence Missouri		
	‡Independence	25 Mar 1971	Melvin James Bennion
234	*Kansas City Missouri		
	‡Kansas City		
	(Missouri, Kansas)	21 Oct 1956	Martin V. Witbeck
1071	Liberty Missouri	14 Oct 1979	Dell Earl Johnsen
2323	Platte City Missouri	9 Mar 1997	Ronald Blaine Stapley
265	*St. Louis Missouri		
	‡St. Louis (Missouri, Illinois)	1 Jun 1958	Roy W. Oscarson
634	St. Louis Missouri North	15 Mar 1987	Neal C. Lewis
1118	St. Louis Missouri South	16 Mar 1980	Verner Lorenzo Stromberg Jr.
North America Southwest Area — 5			
859	Joplin Missouri	28 Aug 1977	Kenneth Rae Martin
2356	St. Robert Missouri	18 May 1997	Gary Wayne Pulsipher
610	*Springfield Missouri		
	‡Ozark	29 Apr 1973	Carroll S. Claybrook
2052	Springfield Missouri South	21 May 1995	Robert Charles Brusman
2665	Warrensburg Missouri	5 Dec 2004	Randy Lee Phillips
	Stakes discontinued		
2	Clay-Caldwell	3 Jul 1834	David Whitmer
	Discontinued 1839		
3	Adam-Ondi-Ahman	28 Jun 1838	John Smith
	Discontinued Nov 1838		
6a	St. Louis	4 Nov 1854	Milo Andrus
	Discontinued 1858, reinstated as 265		

(14b) MISSOURI INDEPENDENCE MISSION
517 West Walnut
Independence, MO 64050

(153) MISSOURI ST. LOUIS MISSION
745 Craig Road, Suite 306
Creve Coeur, MO 63141

Montana

Jan. 1, 2011: Est. population, 968,000; Members, 46,484; Stakes, 11; Wards, 78; Branches, 42; Missions, 1; Temples, 1; Percent LDS, 4.7, or one in 21.

The first members of the Church visited the area in November of 1855 when a delegation from Fort Lemhi in Idaho traveled to the Bitteroot Valley to negotiate with a Mr. McArthur for possible purchase of Fort Hall (also in Idaho) by the Church.

In 1856, Utah Church member E. W. VanEtten began hauling freight between Salt Lake City and mining and logging camps in Montana. That same year, Minnie Miller, another Latter-day Saint, moved to Jocko, Mont., with her husband to help manage the Indian Agency there.

After gold was discovered in Montana in 1862, increasing demand for food and supplies in the mining towns drew other Latter-day Saints into the freighting business along the "Montana Trail" between that territory and Utah. During the last few decades of the 19th century, small numbers of Church members moved into Montana, seeking work in the mines and on the ranches.

Other ties with Utah included a Western Union telegraph line between Salt Lake City and Virginia City, Mont., and the Utah and Northern Railroad line from northern Utah through southeastern Idaho and western Montana. This narrow-gauge railroad was built by the Church as far as Franklin, Idaho, then extended into Montana by Jay Gould and the Union Pacific.

During the 1880s, Montana political leaders outlawed plural marriage in the territory and attempted to keep the few members of the Church there from voting. By the 1890s, relations were better and in 1895 the first branch of the Church was established at Lima by President Thomas E. Ricks of the Bannock Stake, headquartered in Rexburg, Idaho. The following year, Elder Edward Stevenson of the Seventy and Matthias F. Cowley of the Oneida Stake presidency, headquartered in Preston, Idaho, visited LDS families and congregations in Montana and, under the direction of the First Presidency, organized the Montana Mission, as well as several branches of the Church. During that trip they also had a cordial meeting with Montana Gov. John E. Rickards, who proved to be friendly to the Church.

In April 1898, the Montana Mission was absorbed into the Northwestern States Mission, which had been established the previous year. In 1925, Montana was shifted to the North Central States Mission. Then in 1950, it was included in the West Central States Mission.

By the end of the 1920s, the Church had grown to 10 branches and a membership of 1,181, with meetinghouses in Anaconda, Butte, Allendale, Dillon, Great Falls and Sun River. Membership increased to 5,210 in 1940, and 6,416 in 1950.

On 28 June 1953, the first stake in Montana was created in Butte. Additional stakes were organized in Great Falls and Missoula on June 16, 1957. By 1960, membership increased to 23,890. The Montana-Wyoming Mission was established in June of 1970 to oversee the work in those two states. Its name was changed to the Billings Montana Mission four years later and, with some modification of boundaries, continues as such to the present.

In 1980, membership was 30,784, and in 1990, 34,401.

On 28 March 1998, ground was broken at Billings for a temple. A little less than two years later, on 20 November 1999, the Billings Montana Temple was dedicated. Montana's LDS population was 39,842 that year, and 41,259 in 2002. In 2005, membership reached 43,878.

Sources: "Montana History," website (http://travel.state.mt.us/tripplanner/thingstodo/history.htm). Cornelius, Don, Mormonism in Montana, 1847-1898, 1962. "Montana's Gold West Country," website (http://www.experiencegoldwest.com/). Montana Mission, Manuscript history, Church Archives. Jenson, Andrew, Encyclopedic History of the Church of Jesus Christ of Latter-day Saints, 1941. "Utah Railroads," Daughters of Utah Pioneers, Our Pioneer Heritage, v. 10. Lima Branch, Butte Stake, Manuscript history and historical reports, Church Archives. Cook, Tom, "Thumbnail History of Montana Governors," website (http://www.state.mt.us/gov2/formergov/). Local Unit History File, Church Archives. Lima Branch, Manuscript history and historical reports, Church Archives. "News of the Church," Ensign, May 1998, p. 119. "News of the Church," Ensign, February 2000, p. 74; Brian Q. Cannon. "Mormonism in Montana." Montana: The Magazine of Western History, 56 (Spring 2006): 2.19.

Stakes — 11
(Listed alphabetically as of Oct. 1, 2011.)

No.	Name	Organized	First President
North America Central Area			
369	*Billings Montana		
	‡Billings (Montana, Wyoming)	10 Feb 1963	Howard C. Anderson
849	Billings Montana East	12 Jun 1977	Wynn J. Ferrell
1066	Bozeman Montana	16 Sep 1979	Frank Wilbert Coil
208	*Butte Montana		
	‡Butte	28 Jun 1953	Edgar T. Henderson
2349	Glendive Montana	4 May 1997	Larry Norman Wolf
244	*Great Falls Montana		
	‡Great Falls	16 Jun 1957	Victor Bowen
976	Great Falls Montana East	5 Nov 1978	Howard Merle Hennebry
464	*Helena Montana		
	‡Helena	8 Sep 1968	Ronald Rex Dalley
535	*Kalispell Montana		
	‡Kalispell	20 Nov 1970	Roy K. Deming
243	*Missoula Montana		
	‡Missoula	16 Jun 1957	Grant K. Patten
1074	Stevensville Montana	21 Oct 1979	Robert H. Sangster

Mission — 1

(As of Oct. 1, 2011; shown with historical number. See MISSIONS.)

(43a) MONTANA BILLINGS MISSION
1848 Rimrock Road
Billings, MT 59102

Nebraska

Jan. 1, 2011: Est. population, 1,783,000; Members, 23,133; Stakes, 4; Wards, 41; Branches, 20; Missions, 1; Temples, 1; Percent LDS, 1.3, or one in 80.

After the Latter-day Saints were driven from Nauvoo, Ill., in February 1846, they spent the rest of that winter and most of the following summer struggling to cross Iowa. Because it was too late to travel to the Rocky Mountains by the time they reached the Missouri River, they stopped there and established several temporary settlements. In August, approximately 2,500 saints set up camp at a place called Cutler's Park on the west side of the Missouri in what is now Nebraska. This settlement lasted only a few months until the camp moved to the higher ground nearby that became known as Winter Quarters. Approximately 8,000 Latter-day Saints settled there between the fall of 1846 and the spring of 1848, when those who were not yet ready to go west moved back across the river to Kanesville, Iowa, and Winter Quarters reverted to the Omaha tribe.

Another temporary settlement was established in northern Nebraska when a group of saints led by Newell Knight spent the winter with the Ponca tribe near the mouth of the Niobrara River. Knight and some others died during the winter and were buried at Niobrara. The survivors remained with the Poncas through the winter of 1846-47 and then returned to Winter Quarters to prepare for the westward trek.

In April 1847, the first pioneer company, led by Brigham Young and several of the apostles, started for the Great Basin, traveling across Nebraska along the Platte River. During the summer of 1847, another larger company followed. Brigham Young and several others returned in the fall of 1847 for their families who had remained at Winter Quarters.

During 1853 and 1854 the Florence Land Company was organized by a group of businessmen in nearby Council Bluffs to re-establish a settlement on the site of Winter Quarters. When Nebraska was opened for settlement in 1854, Florence began to grow and during the latter years of the decade and on into the 1860s, it served as a major outfitting post for Mormon emigrating companies. In order to provide provisions for migrating companies as they traveled, Genoa, Neb., also known as the Nebraska Mission, one of several planned provisioning settlements, was established along the trail in 1857. Two years later, when the Pawnee Reservation was defined, it included the settlement, and the Genoa residents had to abandon the improvements they had made, including crops in the field. This effectively ended the attempt to establish such settlements on the Nebraska portion of the trail.

In 1864, because of opposition in the major river ports, the Church moved its outfitting post for emigrants to the hamlet of Wyoming, Nebraska, a few miles upriver from Nebraska City. This place served for two years until the Union Pacific Railroad pushed beyond the Missouri in 1866. During 1867, migrating saints traveled across Nebraska by train to the station at North Platte before beginning their trek. By the spring of 1868 the railroad was completed into Wyoming and the Mormon Trail through Nebraska fell into disuse.

After 1868, there was little or no Church activity in Nebraska until 1876, when James Little served a short-term mission there. He had the specific intention of finding a family that had converted to the Reorganized Church of Jesus Christ of Latter Day Saints and convincing them to return to the Utah Church. With his success and the family's emigration, he left the state and continued his mission elsewhere. The following spring, Ferdinand Hintze and Anders Frandsen reported 11 baptisms and the establishment of a branch in Fremont. At that time, Nebraska was part of the Northwestern States Mission. It was later renamed the Northern States Mission. Missionaries continued to work in Nebraska with little success, as only sporadic reports were entered in mission logs during the 1880s. Finally, by July 1896, the Church had grown sufficiently for the Nebraska Conference to be organized. Three years later, on 20 August 1899, Elder Matthias F. Cowley of the Quorum of the Twelve visited the conference and spoke to the members and missionaries in a meeting at Omaha. By 1900, a branch had been established in Omaha. In November of that year, Nebraska was transferred to the Colorado Mission. In 1907, that mission became the Western States Mission.

In 1908, descendants of Newell Knight erected a monument near the mouth of the Niobrara River to memorialize their ancestor and the others in the Ponca camp who perished during the winter of 1846-47.

The Church continued to grow slowly in Nebraska during the first half of the 20th century. In 1916, a Sunday School was established in Lincoln, then expanded to a branch on 9 May 1925. In April 1931, another Sunday School was started at Alliance in the western part of the state. In 1935, President Heber J. Grant visited Omaha to negotiate a 50-year lease on the Winter Quarters cemetery. The same year, the Eastern Nebraska District was divided and the Lincoln District was created. In December 1950, the Winter Quarters District, which presided over the other districts in the eastern half of Nebraska, was transferred to the Northern States Mission. By this time, branches existed in Omaha, Lincoln, North Platte, Bridgeport, Scottsbluff, and Grand Island, with Sunday Schools in several other towns.

A large contingent of General Authorities, including the First Presidency, visited Omaha in May 1953 to dedicate the new Mormon Pioneer Memorial Bridge. During the 1950s, growth in the Church in eastern Nebraska made possible the creation of the Winter Quarters Stake, the first in the state, on 11 December 1960. The stake included wards and branches in Omaha, Bellevue, Lincoln, Fremont, Grand Island, Kearney and Hastings. It was later renamed the Omaha Nebraska Stake. Additional units established since then are the Lincoln Nebraska (1974), Omaha Nebraska Papillion (1986), and Kearney Nebraska (1991) stakes. On 1 July 1993, Nebraska was removed from the Missouri Independence Mission and the Nebraska Omaha Mission was established.

On 18 April 1997, the Mormon Trail Center at Historic Winter Quarters was dedicated by President Gordon B. Hinckley. The following day he bade goodbye to the sesquicentennial commemorative wagon train. It left Omaha on the 21 April to re-enact the 1847 pioneer trek from that place to the Salt Lake Valley. On 1 April 1999, the city of Omaha deeded the old Winter Quarters Cemetery to the Church.

One of the most important events for the Nebraska saints took place on 22 April 2001, when the new Winter Quarters Temple was dedicated on property adjacent to the cemetery. At the same time, the cemetery property was rededicated as part of the temple grounds.

Work to commemorate Nebraska's place in the westward migration continued into 2004, as the first of 11 roadside exhibits across the state describing the Mormon Pioneer Trail were dedicated early in the summer. The finished project included the exhibits, plus 16 generic trail markers, thus completing the marking of the Mormon Trail from Nauvoo to Salt Lake City.

In 2002, membership reached 19,762. In 2005, membership reached 21,405.

Sources: Andrew Jenson, Encyclopedic History of the Church of Jesus Christ of Latter-day Saints, 1941; "Early Nebraska Settlement Memorialized," Ensign, October 1997; Edwin Fry, "The Mormon Winter Camp on the Niobrara," Nebraska History, Vol. 5 No. 1, January-March 1922; William G. Hartley, "On the Trail in January," Ensign, January 1997; Richard E. Bennett, "Winter Quarters: Church Headquarters, 1846-1848," Ensign, September 1997; William G. Cutler, History of the State of Nebraska, 1882; Walter H. Rowley, Omaha's First Century, 1954; Andrew Jenson, "Latter-day Saints Emigration from Wyoming, Nebraska 1864-1866," Nebraska History, vol. 17, 1936; Henry James Hudson, "Henry James Hudson and the Genoa Settlement," Nebraska History, September 1960; James A. Little, Diaries and autobiography, BYU, L. Tom Perry Special Collections; Northern States Mission, Manuscript history and historical reports, Church Archives; Nebraska Conference, Manuscript history and historical reports, Church Archives; Colorado Mission, Manuscript history and historical reports, Church Archives; Edwin Fry, "The Mormon Winter Camp on the Niobrara," Nebraska History, Vol. 5 No. 1, January- March 1922; Ellen Elizabeth McKinnon, Lincoln Legacy, 1979; Western States Mission, Manuscript history and historical reports, Church Archives; Winter Quarters District, Manuscript history and historical reports, Church Archives; Fontenelle Branch, Manuscript history and historical reports, Church Archives; Fremont Branch, Manuscript history and historical reports, Church Archives; Nebraska Game and Parks Commission, Mormon Island State Recreation Area; "Nauvoo, Illinois and Omaha, Nebraska," Ensign, July 1997; LaRene Gaunt and Jennifer Ballard, "Letting the World Know," Ensign, October 1997; "Winter Quarters Cemetery now Owned by the Church," Church News, 19 April 1999; "Newest Temple Stands on Sanctified Soil," Church News, 28 April 2001; "Wayside Exhibits Installed Along Historic Pioneer Trail," Church News, 31 July 2004.

Stakes — 4
(Listed alphabetically as of Oct. 1, 2011.)

No.	Name	Organized	First President
North America Central Area			
1803	Kearney Nebraska	16 Jun 1991	Arthur Haymore Taylor
663	*Lincoln Nebraska 2 Nov 1986		
	‡Bellevue Nebraska	27 Oct 1974	Leonard Leroy Gregory
318	*Omaha Nebraska		
	‡Winter Quarters	11 Dec 1960	William D. Hardy
	(Nebraska, Iowa)		
161	*Omaha Nebraska Papillion 3 Dec 1996		
	‡Papillion Nebraska	2 Nov 1986	Wayne Leon Mangelson

Mission — 1
(As of Oct. 1, 2011; shown with historical number. See MISSIONS.)

(289) NEBRASKA OMAHA MISSION
11930 Arbor Street, Suite 203
Omaha, NE 68144-2998

Nevada

Jan. 1, 2011: Est. population, 2,600,000; Members, 175,149; Stakes, 35; Wards, 293; Branches, 30; Missions, 2; Temples, 2; Percent LDS, 6.7, or one in 15.

Two years after the arrival of the Mormon pioneers in the Salt Lake Valley, Church leaders petitioned the U.S. government for recognition as a state or for territorial status. The State of Deseret, as envisioned by Church leaders, took in most of Nevada. On 9 September 1850, U.S. President Millard Fillmore signed an act creating the Utah Territory, much smaller than the state of Deseret, but still encompassing most of present-day Nevada. Nevada was part of the Utah Territory until it became its own territory in 1861.

Samuel Brannan and two traveling companions became the first Latter-day Saints to set foot in what is now Nevada as they left Yerba Buena, now San Francisco, Calif., to intercept Brigham Young's party on its way to the Salt Lake Valley in 1847.

The early history of the Church in Nevada is one of colonization efforts, some of which were abandoned, while others flourished and exist today. In 1850, there were 13 Church members, mostly Mormon Battalion veterans who had been in California, joined 65 non-LDS overlanders and crossed Nevada from Utah on their way to California. Seven men dropped out of the party near what is now Genoa in the Carson Valley and founded a trading post. The men traded profitably with those coming to the California gold fields during the summer of 1850, but sold out and returned to Utah. A year later, John Reese, a Salt Lake City merchant, came with a group that had provisions in 13 wagons and established a trading post that became known as Mormon Station, located two miles south of the original trading post. The station also became a profitable trading post and the site of Nevada's first permanent settlement.

Sensing that the Carson Valley could become an important outpost in the Utah Territory, Brigham Young organized the Carson Valley Mission and sent Orson Hyde of the Quorum of the Twelve to Genoa to act as probate judge for Carson County, Utah Territory, in May 1855. Elder Hyde was to organize the territory, establish a mission among the local Indians, provide a way station for Mormon emigrants, and conduct court business. Over the next two years many Mormon colonists were called to settle there. The Carson Valley Stake was organized in 1856, the first in Nevada, with branches in Carson Valley, Eagle Valley and Washoe Valley. However, the following year, with the approach of Johnston's Army to Salt Lake City, the colony was abandoned and the stake dissolved.

Also in 1855, a group of 30 men was sent to establish an Indian mission at the Meadows in southern Nevada at what is now Las Vegas. The party, under the direction of William Bringhurst, arrived on 15 June 1855 and soon built a fort. It was an important way station on the route between Salt Lake City and San Bernardino, Calif., another Mormon settlement. These missionaries discovered lead nearby and made friendships with the many Indians who lived on the Muddy River, a fertile area in a valley to the northwest.

In 1856, Brigham Young sent another group of missionaries to the Las Vegas area to mine the lead discovered the year before. Both missions were closed because of the advance of Johnston's Army. The abandoned fort was then named Fort Baker, placed on U.S. Army maps, and served strategic purposes during the Civil War, helping to secure the Southwest for the Union.

Today, the Old Fort is the oldest surviving Anglo-American building in Nevada and is a designated historic site located in what is now called the Old Las Vegas Mormon State Historic Park.

The oldest permanent Mormon settlement in Nevada is Panaca. On 6 May 1864, Mormon settlers, under the direction of Francis C. Lee, arrived at the site, which at that time was still in Utah Territory, and established a colony. The Lee party made a settlement that included a schoolhouse and a branch of Zion's Cooperative Mercantile Institution. The Panaca Ward was organized on 12 August 1865 and was made part of the St. George Stake. The Panaca Nevada Stake was created on 29 January 1995.

The Muddy River area north of Las Vegas was settled in May 1865 under the direction of Joseph Warren Foote. Brigham Young wanted to have the gospel preached to the local Indians and also hoped cotton would grow there for the mills built near St. George. The colonists surveyed a town site, naming it St. Thomas (a town now covered by Lake Mead), after Thomas S. Smith, who had also been called by Young to the Muddy Mission. By 1869, there were additional settlements in St. Joseph, Overton, West Point and Junction City. The mission was abandoned in 1871 when this western part of the Utah Territory was made part of Nevada, and Nevada officials demanded back taxes. However, some Latter-day Saints returned to the Moapa Valley in the 1880s. A branch was organized at Overton in 1883, and it became headquarters of Nevada's first permanent stake, the Moapa Stake, in June 1912.

In the early 20th century, particularly following the post-World War I economic crisis in the United States, Church members in Utah migrated to areas where they could find work. Many settled in Nevada.

Completion of the railroad from Salt Lake City to Los Angeles in 1905 began steady growth in Nevada. The first Sunday School in Las Vegas was organized by Newell Leavitt in 1914. It became a ward in 1925. Construction of the Hoover Dam in the 1930s brought another influx of people seeking to better themselves economically. The Las Vegas Stake was created in 1954.

Church members also moved to the counties in northern Nevada, particularly in the areas around Elko and Ely. The short-lived community of Metropolis was founded in 1911 and had a ward until 1949. It was populated mostly by Church members from Ogden, Utah, and southern Alberta, Canada, who came to the township as farmers. The Nevada Stake, headquartered in Ely, was organized in 1926, and by 1930, it had a membership of over 2,000. The Nevada Stake was divided and the Humbolt Stake was organized in 1942.

Nevada was made part of the California Mission in 1898. It was transferred to the Arizona Mission in 1969. On 1 July 1975 the Nevada Las Vegas Mission was organized. Twenty-two years later, in 1997, the mission was divided and the Nevada Las Vegas West Mission was created.

The steady growth of the Church in southern Nevada led to the creation of many stakes in the Las Vegas area. A temple was dedicated there on 16 December 1989 by President Gordon B. Hinckley as "an oasis of peace and life and light, in contrast with the clamor and evil and darkness of the world." A second temple in Nevada was built in Reno and dedicated by President Thomas S. Monson on Easter Sunday, 23 April 2000.

Membership was 163,187 in 2003.

Nearly 3,000 people gathered at the Old Las Vegas Mormon Fort State Park in Las Vagas, Nev., June 11, 2005, to celebrate the 150th anniversary of the establishment of the historic fort and to dedicate a new visitors center.

The Old Mormon Fort was created June 15, 1855, at the request of President Brigham Young as a way station between Salt Lake City and the Mormon settlement of San Bernardino, Calif., and as a mission to the Native Americans in the Las Vegas Valley. It was the first non-native settlement in the Las Vegas area.

In 2005, membership reached 167,822.

Sources: Jeffery O. Johnson, "Deseret, State of," Encyclopedia of Mormonism, v. 1, 1992; James R. Hinds, One Hundred and Twenty-five Years at Las Vegas' Old Fort, [ca. 1992]; Panaca Ward, Manuscript history and historical reports, Church Archives; Panaca Nevada Stake, Manuscript history and historical reports, Church Archives; Andrew Jenson, Encyclopedic History of the Church, 1941; Leonard J. Arrington, The Mormons in Nevada, 1979; Marjorie H. Holbrook, History of Metropolis, Nevada, 1986; John L. Hart, "Las Vegas Temple 'A Crowning Jewel,'" Church News, 23 December 1989; Julie A. Dockstader, "Easter Day Dedication Brings Hope," Church News, 29 April 2000; "Old Las Vegas fort attracts 3,000 for celebration," Church News, 18 June 2005.

Stakes — 35
(Listed alphabetically as of Oct. 1, 2011.)

No.	Name	Organized	First President
	North America Southwest Area		
906	Carson City Nevada	9 Apr 1978	Edgar Gilbert Carlson
143	*Elko Nevada East 19 Mar 1995		
	*Elko Nevada		
	‡Humboldt	31 May 1942	Rodney S. Williams
2038	Elko Nevada West	19 Mar 1995	Kurt Glenn Alleman
96	*Ely Nevada		
	‡Nevada	19 Sep 1926	Carl K. Conrad
500	*Fallon Nevada		
	‡Fallon	18 Jan 1970	G. Verl Hendrix
1650	Fallon Nevada South	30 Aug 1987	Robert Floyd Weed
2613	Henderson Nevada Anthem	21 Apr 2002	Ivan M. Holland
605	*Henderson Nevada Black		
	Mountain	10 Mar 1992	
	*Henderson Nevada West		
	‡Lake Mead West	11 Mar 1973	Joseph Dee Reese
2801	Henderson Nevada Eldorado	26 Apr 2008	Russell Timothy Peterson
228	Henderson Nevada Lake Mead	2 Mar 1993	
	*Henderson Nevada		
	‡Lake Mead		

	(Nevada, Arizona, Calif.)	19 Aug 1956	James I. Gibson
216	*Las Vegas Nevada		
	‡Las Vegas	10 Oct 1954	Thomas Gay Myers
451	*Las Vegas Nevada Central		
	‡Las Vegas Central	18 Feb 1968	Samuel M. Davis
915	Las Vegas Nevada East	30 Apr 1978	Kendall E. Jones
2818	Las Vegas Nevada Elkhorn Springs	7 Dec 2008	Mark E. Waite
1519	Las Vegas Nevada Green Valley	3 Mar 1985	Roger Lee Hunt
2609c	Las Vegas Nevada Highland Hills	9 Dec 2001	Todd L. Moody
1542	Las Vegas Nevada Lakes	23 Jun 1985	Dennis E. Simmons
1775	Las Vegas Nevada Lone Mountain	4 Nov 1990	Scott Keith Higginson
1406	*Las Vegas Meadows 4 Nov 1990		
	‡Las Vegas Nevada West	20 Mar 1983	Terry Dale Rogers
401	*Las Vegas Nevada Paradise	30 Apr 1978	
	*Las Vegas Nevada East		
	‡Las Vegas East	24 Jan 1965	Rulon A. Earl
855	Las Vegas Nevada Redrock	14 Aug 1977	E. LeGrande Bindrup
1776	Las Vegas Nevada Sandstone	4 Nov 1990	Keith R. Edwards
509	*Las Vegas Nevada South		
	‡Las Vegas South	29 Mar 1970	Erval L. Bindrup
2726	Las Vegas Nevada Spring Mountain	25 June 2006	Robert L. Christiansen
1576	Las Vegas Nevada Sunrise	17 Nov 1985	Norman Wellington Gates
2137	Las Vegas Nevada Tule Springs	3 Dec 1995	Scott Keith Higginson
1777	Las Vegas Nevada Warm Springs	4 Nov 1990	Roger Lee Hunt
64	*Logandale Nevada		
	‡Moapa	9 Jun 1912	Willard L. Jones
1974	Mesquite Nevada	13 Feb 1994	Elwin J. Whipple
308	*North Las Vegas Nevada		
	‡Las Vegas North	6 Nov 1960	William L. Taylor
2019	Panaca Nevada	29 Jan 1995	Robert Jay Matthews
135	*Reno Nevada		
	‡Reno (Nevada, California)	9 Feb 1941	Nathan T. Hurst
635	Reno Nevada North	24 Mar 1974	Wilford Darrell Foote
339	*Sparks Nevada		
	‡Reno North (Nevada, California)	22 Oct 1961	Vern Waldo
1296	Winnemucca Nevada	11 Oct 1981	Kenneth H. Lords

Stakes discontinued

7a	Carson Valley	4 Oct 1856	Orson Hyde
	Discontinued 1858		

Mission — 2
(As of Oct. 1, 2011; shown with historical number. See MISSIONS.)

(127) NEVADA LAS VEGAS MISSION
3127 E Warm Springs, Ste 200
Las Vegas, NV 89120-3134

(314) NEVADA LAS VEGAS WEST
7656 W Sahara Ave., Ste. 140
Las Vegas, NV 89117

New Hampshire

Jan. 1, 2011: Est. population, 1,316,000; Members, 8,231; Stakes, 3; Wards, 16; Branches, 5; Missions, 1; Percent LDS, 0.62, or one in 162.

Orson Pratt and Lyman E. Johnson were the first Latter-day Saints to visit New Hampshire. They preached in Bath in the northwestern part of the state in the spring of 1832, baptizing 15 — among them future apostle Amasa M. Lyman — and organized New Hampshire's first branch. Orson Hyde and Samuel H. Smith, who had also been called from Kirtland, Ohio, to missions in the eastern states, arrived in southern New Hampshire in September 1832 and preached in Dover and Portsmouth. Pratt and Johnson returned to New Hampshire on a second mission in March 1833 and appointed several local members to serve as missionaries.

During succeeding years, numerous missionaries worked in New Hampshire and other branches were organized, but from the beginning the state's Latter-day Saints were encouraged to gather to Kirtland, Ohio, and later, to centers farther west. After 1850, few Church members remained in New Hampshire and there was only limited contact with the Church until the Eastern States Mission was re-opened in 1893.

In February 1909, the New Hampshire Conference was organized and 12 elders were assigned to the state. Before the year ended, they were working in Manchester, Nashua, and Laconia while some of them were traveling in other areas without purse or scrip. Some interest was shown, but in 1919, the missionary serving as president of the Maine Conference, which then included New Hampshire, wrote to the Improvement Era that the two states "in the past have been considered the most impregnable, when it comes to teaching the plan of life and salvation, of all the states in our country," though he saw evidence that the situation was beginning to improve.

In January 1928, New Hampshire was transferred to the Canadian Mission and then in October 1937 became part of the newly established New England Mission. Three years later, the six elders and two sister missionaries assigned to New Hampshire were working in the state's two largest cities, Manchester and Nashua, as well as the smaller town of Keene, and reported there were 43 members of the Church in the state.

The Church continued to grow slowly and members often had to travel long distances to attend meetings. In 1950, the lone branch in New Hampshire, located at Concord, the state capital, had only 24 members, but nearly four times as many Latter-day Saints lived elsewhere in the state and did not belong to organized branches. Church membership increased fourfold during the 1950s and nearly tripled during the 1960s. This was a period when the Latter-day Saints were engaged in accumulating building funds and meetinghouses were constructed in Concord, Portsmouth, Laconia and elsewhere. Membership doubled again during the 1970s. By 1980, the number of Church units in the state had increased to 13, each of them covering several towns.

In response to such growth, in March 1970 Elder Mark E. Petersen of the Quorum of the Twelve organized the Merrimack Stake. The new stake had 2,471 members in the Keene, Laconia, Manchester and Portsmouth wards and the Concord Branch in New Hampshire, as well as in three units in northern Massachusetts and the Sanford Branch in southern Maine. The stake's headquarters were moved from Manchester to Nashua in 1980, and in September of the following year the stake had grown sufficiently that it was divided to create two new stakes at Concord and Portland, Maine.

In July 1987, the New Hampshire Manchester Mission was created, covering not only New Hampshire but also Vermont and Maine.

In November 1990, Richard N. Swett, a convert who was an active member of the Concord 2nd Ward, became the first Latter-day Saint to be elected to Congress from the northeastern part of the United States. He served two terms as a Democratic member of the House of Representatives, 1991-1995, and subsequently served as U. S. ambassador to Denmark, 1998-2001.

In 2004, the Nashua New Hampshire Stake included three units in northern Massachusetts, while the Exeter New Hampshire Stake (originally the Portland Maine Stake but realigned and renamed in 1990) included three units in northern Massachusetts and one in southern Maine. Most of New Hampshire belonged to the Concord New Hampshire Stake, except for small portions of the state that were part of the Montpelier Vermont and Springfield Massachusetts stakes. Because of its unusual geography, the stake at Exeter had the unique distinction of having a stake presidency whose members resided in three different states.

In 2002, membership reached 7,825. In 2005, membership reached 8,215.

Sources: Andrew Jenson, "New Hampshire Conference," Encyclopedic History of the Church, 1941; New Hampshire District, Manuscript history and historical reports, Church Archives; Richard S. Williams, "The Missionary Movements of the LDS Church in New England, 1830-1850," thesis, 1969; Richard O. Cowan, "Yankee Saints: The Church in New England During the Twentieth Century," in Donald Q. Cannon, ed., Regional Studies in Latter-day Saint Church History: New England, 1988; Liahona: The Elders' Journal, 6:979, 1122, 1264-65, and 7:341, 371; Improvement Era, March 1919, p. 454; "4 New Stakes Are Organized," Church News, 4 April 1970; Sheridan R. Sheffield, "Congressman Looks to Values for Strength," Church News, 2 February 1991; J Malan Heslop, "She Helped Nurture Fledgling Church during Life of Service," Church News, 23 January 1993.

Stakes — 3
(Listed alphabetically as of Oct. 1, 2011.)

No.	Name	Organized	First President
North America Northeast Area			
1289	Concord New Hampshire	6 Sep 1981	John Tucker Hills
1290	*Exeter New Hampshire		
	‡Portland Maine	6 Sep 1981	J. Barton Seymour
507	*Nashua New Hampshire	9 May 1980	
	*Manchester New Hampshire		
	‡Merrimack	22 Mar 1970	William A. Fresh

Mission — 1
(As of Oct. 1, 2011; shown with historical number. See MISSIONS.)

(195) NEW HAMPSHIRE MANCHESTER
6 Bedford Farms
Bedford, NH 03110-6532

New Jersey
Jan. 1, 2011: Est. population, 8,683,000; Members, 31,673; Stakes, 5; Wards, 36; Branches, 23; Districts, 1; Missions, 2; Percent LDS, 0.36, or one in 281.

The first missionaries to visit New Jersey, Lyman E. Johnson and Orson Pratt, arrived in 1832 in response to the Lord's command to preach in the "eastern countries" (D&C 75:14). While traveling through Ohio, Pennsylvania, and New Jersey, they baptized more than 100. Parley P. Pratt of the Quorum of the Twelve began missionary work in New York City and northern New Jersey in 1837. Benjamin Winchester and Jedediah M. Grant preached the same year in southern New Jersey and eastern Pennsylvania and baptized 12 in the Hornerstown-New Egypt area. The Toms River Branch was organized in 1838 and met in a small building constructed by the members. While traveling to Washington, D.C., Joseph Smith visited one of the New Jersey branches in December 1839. The next year the Times and Seasons, published at Nauvoo, Ill., reported that "in New Jersey eight or 10 are baptized each week."

By 1848, there were 21 organized branches with other Church members living in outlying areas — in spite of the fact that many converts had responded to the November 1845 directive that Latter-day Saints along the Eastern Seaboard prepare to move to the Rocky Mountains. Some New Jersey members were among those who sailed to California on the ship Brooklyn in 1846.

Occasional missionary work was done in New Jersey during the 1850s, and branches were still functioning at Hornerstown and Toms River in 1857. There was a branch in 1867 at Newark, but during the next quarter century there is no record of Church activity in New Jersey. When the Eastern States Mission was re-established in 1893, its records listed only 55 Latter-day Saints in all of New York, New Jersey and Pennsylvania.

Church activity was slow to resume in New Jersey. A branch was organized in Newark by 1920 and meetings were held there and in nearby Hoboken. Both places were home to numerous Latter-day Saints who emigrated from Germany, Scandinavia and especially the Netherlands after World War I. Much of the work of the Hoboken Branch was conducted in Dutch, since many immigrants found work in the New York metropolitan area and remained there.

The Church in northern New Jersey developed from the nucleus of European immigrants and Latter- day Saints from Utah and elsewhere in the West who came to New York City in search of employment. In 1932, the growing Newark Branch moved to a refurbished clubhouse in suburban East Orange. Two years later, the branch became the East Orange Ward of the New York Stake, the first stake on the eastern seaboard. With more Latter-day Saints arriving from the West to work or study in New York City, dependent branches were organized in Union City, Hackensack and North Jersey, none of which survived.

By 1940, there were approximately 400 members of the East Orange Ward. Another 100 Latter-day Saints belonged to the New Jersey District of the Eastern States Mission, made up of branches at New Brunswick and Trenton and "outlying" Church members in other communities.

Efforts were likewise made to launch Church work in southern New Jersey, with a Sunday School organized in 1909 at Camden, across the Delaware River from Philadelphia, Pa., and again in 1915 and 1916. Nothing more happened in the area until 1949 when a Sunday School was organized for the dozen active New Jersey members of the Philadelphia Branch within traveling distance of Camden. The first permanent branch in southern New Jersey was organized there in March 1950. By the end of that year, the Camden Branch listed 94 on its rolls, while the ward in East Orange had more than 500 members and the New Jersey District included branches at Metuchen and Monmouth, as well as 30 members who lived too far away to attend either of those branches.

The small groups of saints on the outskirts of the New York and Philadelphia metropolitan areas grew considerably during the 1950s, primarily because of the influx of members from other states. During this decade, the first Church-built meetinghouses were erected in New Jersey. Members of the East Orange Ward led the way in this regard, constructing a building at Short Hills between 1952 and 1955 that for many years was the focal point of LDS activity in northern New Jersey.

By the late 1950s, there were some 2,400 New Jersey members in the stake and the adjacent mission district, with another 2,800 Latter-day Saints in New York and neighboring Connecticut. When the stake president, a New Jersey resident who well-knew how much time and expense were involved in traveling to Manhattan for stake meetings, urged Church leaders in Salt Lake City to divide the New York Stake along the Hudson River, the First Presidency responded favorably. In February 1960, the New Jersey Stake was created, which included the New Brunswick, Trenton, Montclair, North Jersey and Short Hills wards and the Lakehurst and Monmouth branches.

Similar growth took place in the southern part of the state. The Camden Branch purchased a building site in suburban Audubon, with good access via public transportation for members traveling from several nearby communities. The branch moved into its new building in 1955. The Camden Branch, along with other units in the East Penn District, became part of the Philadelphia Stake in October 1960, at which time the branch became the Audubon Ward, with a group of saints meeting some 50 miles away at Bridgeton looking to the new ward for leadership and support.

Church membership in New Jersey more than tripled during the 1950s, rising from just over 800 to nearly 3,000. The following decade saw another doubling of the state's LDS population, thanks in part to the 1964-1965 New York World's Fair where more than five million visitors toured the LDS pavilion to watch the film "Man's Search for Happiness." The increased visibility generated by the fair brought converts to every Church unit in the greater New York area. The New Jersey Stake was divided in 1967, and seven years later those portions of the Philadelphia Stake outside Pennsylvania became the Wilmington Delaware Stake, which was divided in 1979 to form a stake based solely in southern New Jersey. The LDS population of the state grew from 6,600 in 1970 to 8,400 in 1980.

To this point, Latter-day Saints in New Jersey primarily resided in the suburbs ringing the metropolitan areas, whose white residents had by then abandoned the city centers to African-American migrants from the American South and Hispanics from Puerto Rico and elsewhere in Latin America. Following the priesthood revelation of 1978, Church members and leaders responded to the ethnic diversity of the inner cities, which were also home to recent immigrants from Europe, Africa and Asia. A decade later there were Spanish-language branches in Jersey City, Newark, Paterson and Dover. By 2004, a third of New Jersey's 63 wards and branches were Hispanic units, with a Portuguese branch in Newark and a Korean branch in nearby Englewood. There were another nine Church units in the state that included at least some Latter-day Saints whose primary language was other than English. Part of the Caldwell New Jersey Stake in 1999 became a mission district made up of Spanish and other inner-city branches in Paterson and Passaic, following a brief experiment along the same lines a few years earlier in Camden.

In 2002, membership reached 29,227 members organized in five stakes. In 2005, membership reached 30,080.

Sources: Andrew Jenson, "New Jersey," Encyclopedic History of the Church, 1941; General mission annual reports and stake statistical recaps, 1940-1980, Church Archives; Charles E. Hughes, G. Wesley Johnson, and Marian A. Johnson, The Mormons in Northern New Jersey, 1994; Ronald Bulkley, "The Church of Jesus Christ of Latter-day Saints in Southern New Jersey," 1980- 1981, Church Archives; "New Stake Created by Division of New York," Church News, 5 March 1960; Orson Scott Card, "Neighborliness: Daines Style," Ensign, April 1977; "New Jersey Church members celebrate 150 years," Church News, 17 September 1988; Clawson Cannon, "Gospel fosters unity, peace in inner city," Church News, 28 December 1996; Directory of General Authorities and Officers, 2004.

Stakes — 5
(Listed alphabetically as of Oct. 1, 2011.)

No.	Name	Organized	First President
	North America Northeast Area		
1252	Caldwell New Jersey	12 Apr 1981	Weldon Courtney McGregor
1084	*Cherry Hill New Jersey	23 Sep 1986	
	‡Pitman New Jersey	18 Nov 1979	Victor Warren Hammond
429	*East Brunswick New Jersey		
	‡New Jersey Central		
	(N.J., Penn.)	26 Mar 1967	Robert H. Daines
292	*Morristown New Jersey	26 Feb 1976	
		*Caldwell New Jersey	
	‡New Jersey	28 Feb 1960	George H. Mortimer
2235	Scotch Plains New Jersey	15 Sep 1996	Andrew Kim Smith

Missions — 1
(As of Oct. 1, 2011; shown with historical number. See MISSIONS.)

(202) NEW JERSEY MORRISTOWN
1719 Rte 10, Ste. 309
Parsippany, NJ 07054-4507

New Mexico

Jan. 1, 2011: Est. population, 1,984,000; Members, 67,637; Stakes, 13; Wards, 89; Branches, 46; Missions, 2; Temples, 1; Percent LDS, 3.3, or one in 31.

In 1831, just one year after the organization of the Church, Oliver Cowdery preached to Indians in Missouri and reported to Joseph Smith the existence of a civilized "Navashoes" (Navajo) tribe living 300 miles west of Santa Fe. Church leaders discussed sending a delegation to Santa Fe in 1844 to begin exploration for a possible colonization site.

In 1846, the Mormon Battalion crossed into what is now New Mexico during its march to the Pacific Coast from Fort Leavenworth, Kan. The first of the battalion arrived at Wagon Mound on 3 October 1846 and Santa Fe on 9 October 1846.

Missionary work among New Mexico's Native Americans began as early as the 1860s when Jacob Hamblin and James S. Brown labored in the Southwest, including areas now in New Mexico. In 1875, missionaries Ammon M. Tenney and Robert H. Smith began working among Native Americans in the state. After much fruitless effort with the Isleta, Laguna, and Acoma tribes, they began teaching the Zuni people on the Little Colorado River. There they baptized more than 100.

In 1876, Lorenzo H. Hatch, William McAllister and John Maughan received mission assignments to continue the work among the Zuni. They established a colony in the nearby Savoia Valley, allowing them to teach the gospel and farming skills to the Zuni. A number of converts from Arkansas soon joined them. In 1878, a second settlement, Savoietta, was established several miles from the first. Irrigation problems, food shortages, and a smallpox epidemic ravaged both the Mormon settlements and nearby Zuni pueblos. Savoia and Savoietta were abandoned because of the difficulties, but by 1882, a new settlement called Navajo was established near Savoietta. On 8 April 1883, the Navajo Ward was created with 91 members including 10 Navajos. The community was later renamed Ramah and the ward name was changed to Ramah Ward in 1886.

In 1878, Jeremiah Hatch, Lorenzo H. Hatch, Benjamin Boyce and their families arrived in New Mexico, purchasing ranches on the San Juan River. Other Mormon settlers followed and the new community was named Burnham in honor of the presiding elder, Luther L. Burnham. The Burnham Ward was formed in 1883. Because the community became known for its high quality fruits it was later renamed Fruitland. Some of the families who settled at Fruitland had earlier been part of the Hole-In-The-Rock expedition sent to settle extreme southeastern Utah.

Wilford Woodruff established the Indian Mission in October 1879 with Ammon Tenney as president. Missionaries labored among the Pueblo and Navajo peoples of New Mexico and Arizona. The mission met with success until the late 1880s when government agents forbade the Church from further missionary activities among Native Americans.

In 1881, Church authorities encouraged Latter-day Saints to settle the Gila Valley. Within three years a small but thriving community was established there. Other settlements were soon established in Bluewater, Hammond, Beulah, Carson and Pleasanton.

In 1883, brothers William, John and Melvin Swapp, along with other Latter-day Saints, purchased a large land claim in Luna Valley, Socorro County. They established a settlement there, building a fort for protection against hostile Indians and cattle barons. A branch was established there in 1883. It later became the Luna Ward.

Most of the Mormon settlements in New Mexico absorbed refugees from the Latter-day Saint colonies in northern Mexico who fled from the violence of the Mexican Revolution of 1912.

In May 1912, the Young Stake, New Mexico's first, was created from a division of the San Juan Stake. It was headquartered in Fruitland and included the Burnham, Hammond, Kline, Mancos, and Red Mesa wards. Other New Mexican wards and branches were under jurisdiction of border stakes in Arizona and Utah.

By 1930, membership in New Mexico was 1,643.

The Albuquerque Stake was created on 27 October 1957. Steady growth necessitated creation of another stake in Albuquerque in 1966, and creation of stakes in Las Cruces, Gallup, Farmington and Roswell followed in the 1970s. The New Mexico Albuquerque Mission was organized in 1975. Significant growth in the 1980s required creation of additional stakes for Santa Fe, Grants, Albuquerque, Kirtland, Bloomfield, and Silver City.

In the 1980s, Santa Fe New Mexico Stake President H. Vern Payne also served as chief justice of the New Mexico Supreme Court. In September 1996, more than 700 Church members in New Mexico joined with government officials in rededicating a monument built to honor members of the Mormon Battalion, who had passed through the state 150 years earlier.

A temple in Albuquerque, the first in New Mexico, was dedicated 5 March 2000.

In 2002, membership reached 58,751. In 2005, membership reached 62,572.

Sources: Andrew Jenson, Encyclopedic History of the Church, 1941; Lyle K. and Wilma H. Porter, A History of the Church of Jesus Christ of Latter-day Saints in New Mexico, 1876-1989, 1997; Gary Tietjen, Mormon Pioneers in New Mexico, 1980; Robert Thomas Devitt, "New Mexico and the Mormons," Southwest Heritage, Spring 1976; Luna Ward, Do You Remember Luna? 100 Years of Pioneer History, 1983; "Cultural Diversity is Melting into LDS Unity," Church News, 24 July 1983; Holly Traver, "Ground Broken for Temple in New Mexico," Church News, 27 June 1998; Sarah Jane Weaver, "Temple Melding Members of Three Cultures," Church News, 11 March 2000.

Stakes — 13
(Listed alphabetically as of Oct. 1, 2011.)

No.	Name	Organized	First President
North America Southwest Area			
250	*Albuquerque New Mexico		
	‡Albuquerque	27 Oct 1957	William J. Wilson
422	*Albuquerque New Mexico East		
	‡Albuquerque East	25 Sep 1966	George Van Lemmon
2556b	Albuquerque New Mexico West	21 May 2000	Lane S. Sego
742	*Bloomfield New Mexico	19 Sep 1982	
	‡Farmington New Mexico East	1 Feb 1976	Marlo L. Webb
63	*Farmington New Mexico		
	‡Young (N.M., Colo.)	21 May 1912	David Halls
687	Gallup New Mexico	16 Mar 1975	Donald C. Tanner
1363	Kirtland New Mexico	19 Sep 1982	John Scot Fishburn

654	Las Cruces New Mexico	25 Aug 1974	Harold A. Daw
1353	*Los Lunas New Mexico		
	‡Albuquerque New Mexico South	20 Jun 1982	Ivan Gary Waddoups
2767	Rio Rancho New Mexico	16 Jun 2007	Jared P. Rounsville
816	Roswell New Mexico	13 Mar 1977	J. Allen Levie
1219	Santa Fe New Mexico	4 Jan 1981	H. Vern Payne
1409	Silver City New Mexico	17 Apr 1983	Hal Butler Keeler
		Discontinued Stakes	
1298	Grants New Mexico	18 Oct 1981	Elbert Leon Roundy
	Discontinued 1 Mar 2009		

Mission — 1
(As of Oct. 1, 2011; shown with historical number. See MISSIONS.)

(128) NEW MEXICO ALBUQUERQUE MISSION
4400 Presidential Dr. NE, Suite E
Albuquerque, NM 87109

NEW MEXICO FARMINGTON MISSION
400 W Apache St.
Farmington, NM 87401

New York

Jan. 1, 2011: Est. population, 19,490,000; Members, 78,031; Stakes, 14; Wards, 88; Branches, 63; Districts, 3; Missions, 4; Temples, 2; Percent LDS, 0.4, or one in 257.

The stage was set for New York's role in the Restoration when Joseph and Lucy Mack Smith moved from Vermont to the Palmyra-Manchester area in 1816. Their son Joseph, dismayed by the competing claims of revivalist preachers, sought divine direction in the spring of 1820 and experienced the First Vision in the Sacred Grove on the Smith farm. Three years later, he was visited by Moroni, who told him of gold plates buried in the nearby Hill Cumorah. After obtaining the plates in 1827, Joseph translated most of the unsealed portion at the Whitmer home in Fayette, N.Y. He completed the translation in 1829, then arranged for E. B. Grandin to print the Book of Mormon at Palmyra. The first edition was completed March 1830. (In the meantime, Martin Harris, seeking verification of Joseph Smith's claims, in 1828 took handwritten extracts from the plates to scholars Charles Anthon and Samuel L. Mitchill in New York City.) The Church of Christ, as it was then known, was organized in the Whitmer home on 6 April 1830. In addition, 25 of the revelations later published in the Doctrine and Covenants were received in New York.

The initial missionary work took place in New York, with the Prophet's younger brother Samuel being the first preacher of the restored gospel. Within a year more than 100 had been baptized in the state. When Joseph moved the Church's headquarters to Kirtland, Ohio, in 1831, most of the New York members followed him. Missionaries crisscrossed the state during the next decade and a half, preaching to relatives and acquaintances and in public gatherings. Late in 1832, Joseph Smith himself paid a brief visit to Albany, New York City, and Boston in company with Newel K. Whitney. Many small branches were organized in New York, but time and again Church members left for Kirtland or other gathering places further west.

In July 1837, Parley P. Pratt of the Quorum of the Twelve arrived in New York City. After publishing 4,000 copies of "The Voice of Warning," one of the most influential tracts of the early Church, Elder Pratt spent six months preaching with very little result — leading him to reflect, "Of all the places in which the English language is spoken, I found the City of New York to be the most difficult as to access to the minds or attention of the people." During this period, Pratt baptized six and organized a branch that met in an upstairs room on Goerck Street in lower Manhattan. The discouraged apostle was ready to leave the city when a revelation told him to remain in New York because, "the Lord had many people in that city." Within three weeks, Pratt and companion Elijah Fordham had established 15 meeting places, all of them "filled to overflowing." As they baptized "almost daily," additional branches were organized in Brooklyn and elsewhere on Long Island, at Sing Sing [Ossining], and in northern New Jersey.

In May 1839, the Prophet appointed John P. Greene as the first president of the Eastern States Mission. During the next several years, with missionary work concentrated in the British Isles, only a limited number of elders were assigned to America's Eastern Seaboard, focusing their efforts on the nation's largest cities — New York, Philadelphia and Boston. During his last general conference in April 1844, Joseph Smith reported the Lord's instruction that "wherever the Elders of Israel shall build up churches . . . throughout the States, there shall be a stake of Zion. In the great cities, as Boston, New York, &c., there shall be stakes."

New York City became the principal port of entry for Latter-day Saint emigration from Europe, with the first company of 41 arriving from Liverpool, England, on the Britannia in July 1840. Over the next half century, dozens of companies arrived on ships chartered in Liverpool and were sent on to Nauvoo and later to Utah by Church emigration agents in New York. By 1890, when travel facilities improved to the point that emigration arrangements could be left to individuals, some 50,000 Latter-day Saints had first set foot on American soil in New York City.

New York was also the point of departure for the ship Brooklyn, carrying the first group of 235 Latter-day Saints bound for California, under the direction of Samuel Brannan, leaving in February 1846 for what was then Mexican territory.

Beginning in 1844 an LDS newspaper, The Prophet, was published in New York until the group that sailed on the Brooklyn took the Church's press with them. Subsequently, when John Taylor of the Quorum of the Twelve was called to head Church efforts in the eastern states in 1855, another weekly paper, The Mormon, was also printed for a time in New York City.

The 1857 outbreak of the Utah War led to the withdrawal of missionaries from the Eastern Seaboard and the suspension of the Church's European emigration program. A new emigration agent was sent from Salt Lake City when peace was achieved and Church-sponsored ships again began to dock in New York City. There was little missionary activity in the state during the next three decades. Most Latter-day Saint emigrants from Europe proceeded directly to Utah, although a few stayed in the New York City area to finance travel to the West.

When New York became part of the Northern States Mission in 1889, missionaries sought to determine whether any Latter-day Saints still lived in the area. Only 55 were located, with enough in western Long Island that a branch was organized at Oceanside in 1890. Job Pingree was sent to New York City in 1893 to re-open the Eastern States Mission. By 1900, eight conferences (including Brooklyn and New York) had been established in the several states that made up the mission and there were 975 members of the Church.

Over the course of the next half century, Church growth in New York was slow but steady. By 1930, there were 11 branches and 1,500 Latter-day Saints in the state, about two-thirds of them in New York City.

The number of members outside the New York metropolitan area doubled during the following decade — but even so, Rochester, the largest of the 22 branches in upstate New York, had only 83 members in 1940, while many branches were much smaller and nearly a third of the saints were "outlying" members who lived too far away to belong to an organized branch. Nonetheless, this represented considerable progress in Rochester, since the first 20th-century Latter-day Saints, a family of Dutch converts from Europe, the Willemstyns, had only arrived there in 1912, with a branch not being organized until 10 years later. Similarly, in Binghamton near the Pennsylvania state line, a branch was established in the early 1920s made up of a mix of Latter-day Saint emigrants from Europe and local people. Branches located in upstate cities where there were major universities or companies doing business on a nationwide basis attracted a growing number of Church members from Utah and elsewhere, especially after World War II. Such people, given their broader experience with the Church, often provided leadership in New York branches.

General Church leaders' interest in the area's history contributed to the growth of one branch in western New York. In 1907, Elder George Albert Smith of the Quorum of the Twelve purchased the Joseph Smith Sr. farm property in Manchester. Eight years later, President Joseph F. Smith called Utah residents Willard W. and Rebecca P. Bean to oversee the farm and re-establish a Latter-day Saint presence in the Palmyra area. During the next quarter century, the Beans helped break down prejudice and improve the Church's image in Palmyra, as well as assisting in the conversion of local residents. In 1925, a branch was organized that 15 years later had 50 members. In the meantime, Bean was instrumental in helping the Church purchase the Hill Cumorah (1923 and 1928), the Peter Whitmer farm at nearby Fayette (1926), and the Martin Harris farm north of Palmyra (1937). A monument to the Angel Moroni erected atop the hill was dedicated by President Heber J. Grant in July 1935.

Beginning in 1928 an annual Book of Mormon pageant was held at the Smith farm. In 1937, the pageant was moved to the Hill Cumorah and missionary Harold I. Hansen was appointed its director, an assignment he filled for the next 40 years. In 1937, over 13,000 people attended the pageant's opening night, with Newsweek reporting that 100,000 people attended the pageant in 1948.

During the 1950s and 1960s, the many small upstate branches continued to grow, leading to the January 1962 organization of the Cumorah Stake that included much of western New York. Subsequent growth in membership resulted in divisions to form stakes based in Rochester, Buffalo, and Palmyra. Further east the Susquehanna and Hudson River stakes were created in 1969 and have since developed into the Albany, Ithaca (subsequently Owego), Syracuse, and Utica stakes. The southwestern corner of the state in 1986 became part of the Erie Pennsylvania Stake. In northern New York, branches that were once part of the Montpelier Vermont Stake and Canadian stakes in Ottawa and Montreal were transferred in the year 2000 to the new Potsdam New York District. By 2004, the Church in upstate New York had grown from the 15 congregations operating in 1950 to 77 wards and branches.

The continuing importance of upstate New York in the life of the Church was highlighted by two late-20th-century events. In April 1980, part of conference was broadcast via satellite from the reconstructed Whitmer home in Fayette where the Church had been organized 150 years earlier. And on the 170th anniversary of the Church, in April 2000, the Palmyra New York Temple, overlooking the Sacred Grove and other historic sites, was dedicated by President Gordon B. Hinckley. The dedication was broadcast to 1,300 stake centers and other Church facilities.

The growth of the Church in the New York City metropolitan area during the past 75 years has been equally dramatic. With Latter-day Saints coming to New York from the West to study or accept employment and many LDS emigrants arriving from Europe after World War I, an impressive meetinghouse was built in Brooklyn in 1918, with headquarters for the Eastern States Mission being constructed on an adjoining lot. By 1930, the local district included branches in Brooklyn, Manhattan, and Oceanside, N.Y., as well as across the Hudson River in Newark and Union City, N. J., with a membership of 1,262.

Four years later the New York Stake was created by President Heber J. Grant. The new stake was the first 20th-century stake east of the Rocky Mountains and only the third stake outside the areas of LDS settlement in the West. In many ways it was viewed as a test of how the growing Church might function in the major urban centers of the nation. Besides wards and branches in three of the city's five boroughs (Manhattan, Brooklyn, and Queens), the stake included the New Jersey suburbs across the Hudson and suburban Westchester County, N.Y. While there was little increase in membership during the 1940s, the next decade saw a near doubling of the stake's population, much of it centered in the Long Island, Westchester, and northern New Jersey suburbs, where meetinghouses were built for several wards. Growth across the Hudson was sufficient that in 1960 the three wards there were joined with several branches from the Eastern States Mission to form the New Jersey Stake — at which time portions of southwestern Connecticut were incorporated into the New York Stake.

Further growth was spurred by the LDS pavilion at the 1964-1965 New York World's Fair. The full-time missionary tour guides secured nearly a million referrals and distributed five million tracts and pamphlets. When the fair ended the pavilion was dismantled and used to construct a meetinghouse at nearby Plainview. As a result of the fair, there were thousands of baptisms in the area, making possible the creation of the Long Island Stake.

Another significant development in the New York metropolitan area started about the time of the world's fair. With Church growth centering in the suburbs, coupled with the deterioration of many inner-city areas, missionary work had long since ceased in Manhattan. In April 1963, mission president Wilburn C. West assigned six elders to work with the island's seven million residents, with the missionary force growing to 40 by the next summer. One result was the establishment of a Spanish-speaking branch in Manhattan, with missionary work soon spreading to Hispanic neighborhoods in Brooklyn and the Bronx.

Efforts to reach out to the metropolitan area's racially and ethnically diverse population were further stimulated by the 1978 revelation that extended the priesthood to all worthy males, regardless of race. President Spencer W. Kimball challenged local Church leaders to teach the gospel in the various languages spoken in major urban centers. By the end of

1980, the New York and Plainview stakes included four Spanish wards and branches, a Chinese branch, and a Korean branch. A decade later the number of Spanish units in the area's three stakes had grown to nine. In 1991, districts were organized in Brooklyn and Queens to better accommodate inner-city Church growth in those boroughs, with another district being organized in the Bronx four years later. By 2004, the Brooklyn district had become a stake and the Bronx district had been incorporated into the new Westchester New York Stake, while three districts were functioning in Queens and elsewhere in the western portion of Long Island.

In 2004, the seven stakes and three districts that resulted from the original New York Stake included 75 wards and branches within the boundaries of New York state, of which 24 were Spanish units, while two more operated in Chinese and one in Korean. An additional 14 wards and branches included substantial numbers of Latter-day Saints whose principal language was other than English. Local estimates indicated that between 40 and 50 percent of the Church membership in the area was Hispanic. While the majority of them were baptized in the New York metropolitan area, an important percentage had come from the Caribbean and Central and South America after joining the Church in their homelands.

As the number of Latter-day Saints in the metropolitan area increased, places were needed for the many new congregations to meet. In 1971, the Church purchased property on Columbus Avenue near Lincoln Center on which a multi-story building was constructed as the home to several wards, besides serving as a visitors center and mission headquarters. Following the May 1975 dedication of this facility by President Spencer W. Kimball, many additional meetinghouses were built in the area, making a total of 19 buildings available by 1994, with another dozen being constructed in the next five years, and six more by 2004.

With most New York City Church members being migrants, whether from predominantly Latter-day Saint areas of the western United States or a host of other countries, local leaders at the start of the 21st century were cautiously optimistic that a higher percentage of their people would become permanent residents of the metropolitan area. Such hopes were encouraged by President Gordon B. Hinckley's March 2002 announcement that a temple would be housed in the Church facility at Lincoln Center. Following extensive remodeling and an open house attended by more than 53,000, the Manhattan New York Temple was dedicated June 13, 2004 by President Gordon B. Hinckley, the 119th operating temple in the Church.

In 2002, membership in the greater New York area reached 67,207. In 2004, membership reached 69,882.

Following a two-day open house in November 2005, a 33,000-square-foot meetinghouse on 128th and Lenox Avenue in Harlem was dedicated on 4 December 2005. The stately red brick facility will meet the needs of the growing two wards in Harlem, and has been the means of uniting members with residents of Harlem who perceived the Church as white dominated. The new meetinghouse drew media attention along the east coast as a sign of an American curch growing among all races.

In 2005, membership reached 71,560.

Sources: Andrew Jenson, "Eastern States Mission" and "New York," Encyclopedic History of the Church, 1941; Richard L. Bushman, Joseph Smith and the Beginnings of Mormonism, 1984; Larry C. Porter, A Study of the Origins of The Church of Jesus Christ of Latter-day Saints in the States of New York and Pennsylvania, 1816-1831, dissertation, 1971 (published 2000); Joseph Smith, History of the Church, 1:295, 6:319; Parley P. Pratt, Autobiography of Parley P. Pratt, 1874; David F. Boone, "Palmyra Revisited: The New York Mission of Willard W. and Rebecca P. Bean, 1915-1939," Mary Jane Woodger, "Harold and the Hill: Harold I. Hansen and the Hill Cumorah Pageant, 1937-1977," and Veneese C. Nelson, "The Palmyra Temple: A Significant Link to LDS Church History," all in Alexander L. Baugh and Andrew H. Hedges, eds., Regional Studies in Latter-day Saint History: New York-Pennsylvania, 2002; Horace H. Christensen, "History of The Church of Jesus Christ of Latter-day Saints in the Binghamton, New York Area, 1825 through 1979," Church History Library; Charles J. Ingerson, "Seventy Years of Mormonism in Northwestern Monroe County (The Rochester II Ward), 1910-1980," Church History Library; William L. Woolf, "The Church in New York City," Improvement Era, December 1938; Joan Lemanczyk and Claire Wendt, Beginnings and New Beginnings: A Short History of the Church of Jesus Christ of Latter-day Saints on Long Island, 1981; Heidi Woldrop, "New York LDS Blend in Language Melting Pot," Church News, 23 December 1984; Brent L. Top, "Legacy of the Mormon Pavilion," Ensign, October 1989; Glen Nelson, "Brooklyn's Window on the World," Ensign, June 1990; Mike Cannon, "Diversity of Saints Find Unity in Gospel in New York City," Church News, 27 August 1994; James W. Lucas, "Mormons in New York City," in Tony Carnes and Anna Karpathakis, eds., New York Glory: Religions in the City, 2001; Don Searle, "Church Blossoms in the Big Apple," Ensign, June 2004; Shaun D. Stahle, "'Not That We're Back, It's That We're Still Here'" and "Manhattan Temple Ready for Dedication June 13," both in Church News, 12 June 2004; Carrie Moore, "Members Come to N. Y. — to Stay," Deseret Morning News, 12 June 2004; Shaun D. Stahle, "Miracle in Manhattan: Temple Dedicated in New York," Church News, 19 June 2004; Shaun Stahle, "Harlem meetinghouse," Church News, 26 November 2005.

Stakes — 14
(Listed alphabetically as of Oct. 1, 2011.)

No.	Name	Organized	First President
North America Northeast Area			
485	*Albany New York		
	‡Hudson River	8 Jun 1969	Thomas Lorin Hicken
2501	Brooklyn New York	22 Nov 1998	Alejandro Ernesto Soffiantini
657	Buffalo New York	15 Sep 1974	Ronald Glen Vincent
1592	*Jamestown New York	16 May 1995	
	‡Erie Pennsylvania	23 Mar 1986	Philip Dale Baker
2315	Newburgh New York	2 Mar 1997	Gary R. Ricks Jr.
110	*New York New York		
	‡New York (N.Y., Connecticut)	9 Dec 1934	Fred G. Taylor
483	*Owego New York	9 Oct 1990	
	*Ithaca New York		
	‡Susquehanna	25 May 1969	Harold R. Capener
1543	*Palmyra New York	27 Oct 2002	
	Rochester New York Palmyra	30 Jun 1985	Kay R. Whitmore
439	*Plainview New York		
	‡Long Island	20 Aug 1967	Gordon E. Crandall
2663	Queens New York	31 Oct 2004	David Lee Duffy
346	*Rochester New York		
	‡Cumorah	21 Jan 1962	Bryant W. Rossiter
711	Syracuse New York	19 Oct 1975	George Dale Weight
2152	Utica New York	14 Jan 1996	Dallas Williams Jones
2409	Westchester New York	9 Nov 1997	Douglas Romney Jackson
909	*Yorktown New York	28 Aug 1978	
	‡Kitchiwan New York	30 Apr 1978	Victor B. Jex
	Stakes discontinued		
1574	New York New York East	17 Nov 1985	Mark Eliot Butler
	Discontinued 19 May 1991		

(290) NEW YORK NEW YORK NORTH MISSION
700 White Plains Road, Ste. 315
Scarsdale, NY 10583

(2) NEW YORK NEW YORK SOUTH MISSION
85-69 60th Dr.
Elmhurst, Queens, NY 11373

(77)NEW YORK ROCHESTER MISSION
P.O. Box 2000P.O. Box 149
Fairport, NY 14450-7802

(299) NEW YORK UTICA MISSION

Whitesboro, NY 13492-0149

North Carolina

Jan. 1, 2011: Est. population, 9,222,000; Members, 76,865; Stakes, 16; Wards, 114; Branches, 40; Missions, 2; Temples,1; Percent LDS, 0.8, or one in 124.

The first known missionary to enter North Carolina was Jedediah M. Grant. On 18 May 1838, he reported that he had preached for six months in Stokes, Surrey and Rockingham counties and baptized four people. By 4 February 1840, Grant's brother, Joshua Grant Jr., and Francis G. Bishop joined him. They baptized another six or eight people. Missionaries also began work in other parts of the state. Before Jedediah Grant left, on 12 July 1845, he had organized a conference of 200 members in seven branches.

Following the exodus of the main body of the Church from Nauvoo in 1846, little work was done in North Carolina until March 1868 when a Southern convert, Henry G. Boyle, reported that he had held 40 public meetings, baptized 30 members and organized the Surrey County Branch. This branch (soon changed to Pilot Mountain) was dissolved by 1870 following the migration to the West of most branch members.

The Southern States Mission was created on 9 October 1876 to include North Carolina. The Pilot Mountain Branch was reorganized on 30 April 1876. The Mount Airy Branch was organized on 28 July 1879 and the Burke County Branch followed on 13 December 1885. Continuation of these branches was sporadic, as converts migrated to the West. Membership in 1894 was 128, with 35 leaving during the previous three years. About 1,000 people from surrounding areas attended a conference held in Radford Cross Roads on 21 November 1897. After 1895, members were encouraged to remain in North Carolina.

Anti-Mormon sentiment in North Carolina was occasionally strong. On 16 January 1906, a newly completed meetinghouse on Harker's Island was burned, and the missionaries were driven out by a mob. The meetinghouse was replaced in 1936. Occasional mobs gathered in various other locations, but after the turn of the century, public attitudes generally improved and missionaries were offered more freedom to preach.

On 14 May 1921, Andrew Jenson, visiting as assistant Church historian, reported in the Deseret News that there were three branches and 15 Sunday Schools in North Carolina. Meetinghouses were built in Mount Airy, Hampstad, Union Ridge, Wilmington, Goldsboro and Gilreath by 1930. Membership in the state then was 2,725.

Elder Joseph Fielding Smith of the Quorum of the Twelve visited Goldsboro, attending district conference on 3 November 1929. On 18 November 1932, Elder David O. McKay of the Quorum of the Twelve toured the East Central States Mission, visiting North Carolina.

North Carolina was divided into the East and West districts on 17 April 1935. James L. Bennett Sr., the first local member to serve as district president, was sustained on 26 March 1939. The Central District was created 11 July 1948. A large building program was started in 1947 and 16 meetinghouses were subsequently constructed.

On 27 August 1961, the North Carolina Stake, the first in the state, was created in Kinston from the East District. The Central District was organized into the Greensboro Stake on 13 September 1961.

The Raleigh North Carolina Temple was dedicated by President Gordon B. Hinckley on 18 December 1999 in the suburban community of Apex.

In 2002, membership reached 60,984. In 2005, membership reached 68,398.

Sources: Andrew Jenson, Encyclopedic History of the Church, 1941; Wallace R. Draughon, History of The Church of Jesus Christ of Latter-day Saints in North Carolina, 1974; R. Scott Lloyd, "A Christmastime 'Offering' to the Lord," Church News, 25 December 1999; Southern States Mission, Manuscript history and historical report, Church Archives.

Stakes — 16
(Listed alphabetically as of Oct. 1, 2011.)

No.	Name	Organized	First President
North America East Area			
2615	Apex North Carolina	19 Oct 2003	Harry John Maxwell Jr.
1086	Asheville North Carolina	25 Nov 1979	Luther Andrew Goad
1606	Charlotte North Carolina Central	21 Sep 1986	Kenneth Larson
591	*Charlotte North Carolina South	21 Sep 1986	
	*Charlotte North Carolina		
	‡Charlotte	19 Nov 1972	Byron Cole Williams
1637	Durham North Carolina	3 May 1987	James L. Bennett Jr.
698	Fayetteville North Carolina	8 Jun 1975	Leland Reid Fillmore
2652	Fayetteville North Carolina West	19 Sep 2004	Edward E. Brock Jr.
2725	Gastonia North Carolina	4 Jun 2006	Benjamin C. Poole
1344	Goldsboro North Carolina	30 May 1982	James William Dixon
335	*Greensboro North Carolina		
	‡Greensboro	13 Sep 1961	Eugene A. Gulledge
1371	Hickory North Carolina	31 Oct 1982	Gordon M. Thornton

2888	High Point North Carolina	21 Nov 2010	Joseph T. Baughan
332	*Kinston North Carolina		
	‡North Carolina	27 Aug 1961	Cecil E. Reese
363	*Raleigh North Carolina		
	‡Raleigh	9 Dec 1962	William V. Bartholomew
574	*Wilmington North Carolina		
	‡Wilmington	21 May 1972	Dean Bevin Powell Jr.
881	*Winston-Salem North Carolina	25 Nov 1979	
	‡Statesville North Carolina	20 Nov 1977	Michael Stephen Bullock

Missions — 2

(As of Oct. 1, 2011; shown with historical number. See MISSIONS.)

(105) NORTH CAROLINA CHARLOTTE MISSION
6425 Idlewild Rd., Suite 104
Charlotte, NC 28212

(186) NORTH CAROLINA RALEIGH MISSION
6508 Falls of Neuse, Suite 100
Raleigh, NC 27615-6845

North Dakota

Jan. 1, 2011: Est. population, 642,000; Members, 6,930; Stakes, 2; Wards, 7; Branches, 9; Temples, 1; Percent LDS, 0.96, or one in 105.

The first missionaries began working in North Dakota in the summer of 1884. They returned to the area most summers thereafter. By 1898, the work in North Dakota showed enough promise that Northern States Mission leaders established the North Dakota Conference. When the conference president finished his mission the following spring, the conference was discontinued because of lack of success. This proved to be a temporary setback and missionary work among the North Dakotans was soon resumed.

On 1 November 1900, responsibility for doing missionary work in North and South Dakota was transferred from the Northern States Mission to the Colorado Mission, later renamed the Western States Mission. During this period, both North and South Dakota were administered by the South Dakota Conference, but in 1917, the conference was divided and the North Dakota Conference was reestablished.

In September of 1914, missionaries held a meeting with 108 members of the Gros Ventre tribe on the Berthold Reservation. At that meeting they baptized six. By 1920, membership on the reservation had grown sufficiently that a branch was established at Sully Lake and a meetinghouse was built. The first fast and testimony meeting was held in the new meetinghouse on 4 January 1920 and the building was dedicated on 20 June of the same year.

The first Church unit in North Dakota not on a reservation was a Sunday School, which soon grew into a branch, established in 1923 at Grand Forks in the northeastern part of the state. That year branch members, assisted by missionaries and some who were investigating the Church, began the construction of a meetinghouse.

Responsibility for missionary work in North Dakota was transferred again in August 1925 to the new North Central States Mission. The change caused a temporary reduction in the number of missionaries and it wasn't until 1930 that they were able to return to the Berthold Reservation. The Church grew slowly in North Dakota before and during World War II. Sunday Schools were established at Williston in 1936 and Fargo in 1941, while the Grand Forks Branch was discontinued about 1937. In 1943 and 1944 respectively, the East North Dakota and West North Dakota districts were closed and all missionary activity ceased until after the war.

By April of 1947, both districts had been re-established and missionaries were returning to the area. On 1 February 1948, a sacrament meeting was again held in Grand Forks, the first time in many years. In November 1949, the branch was re-established and a new meetinghouse begun. It was dedicated on 20 August 1950. Meanwhile a Relief Society was started at Fargo on 3 July 1949. A third district was established in North Dakota in January 1951 when the East North Dakota District was divided into the Dakota and Red River districts. The former was centered in Grand Forks and the latter in Fargo. The western portion of the state remained in the West North Dakota District, where on 22 August 1954 the Bismarck Branch was established.

A major administrative change took place on 8 April 1964 when the Northern Indian Mission was created to oversee Church activities on the Indian reservations in the Dakotas, as well as several surrounding states. Thus the work on and off the reservations in North Dakota was administered by two separate missions. This situation persisted for nearly a decade. In 1970 the North Central States Mission was renamed the Manitoba-Minnesota Mission. That year the Standing Rock District of the Northern Indian Mission was created to oversee many of the branches and groups on the North Dakota reservations. Then in 1973 the Dakota-Manitoba Mission was established, composed of part of the discontinued Northern Indian Mission and parts of other missions in the area, including the Manitoba-Minnesota Mission. This brought all of the branches in North Dakota under one head again. In 1974 the mission was renamed the South Dakota Rapid City Mission.

As the Church in North Dakota grew during the 1970s, districts at Minot and Fargo were created from the earlier West North Dakota and Dakota mission districts, with the intention of preparing the Saints for the establishment of stakes. On 7 August 1977, the first stake in the state was organized in Fargo, making every state in the United States with a stake within its boundaries. Nearly 20 years later, on 22 September 1996, the Bismarck North Dakota Stake was created.

In September 1999, President Gordon B. Hinckley visited North Dakota for the first time and on 19 Sept., he dedicated the Bismarck North Dakota Temple, the 61st operating temple in the Church and the first in the Dakotas.

In 2002, membership reached 5,181. In 2005, membership reached 5,669.

Sources: Northern States Mission, Manuscript history and historical reports, Church Archives; Western States Mission, Manuscript history and historical reports, Church Archives; North Central States Mission, Manuscript history and historical reports, Church Archives; East North Dakota District, General minutes, Church Archives; West Minnesota District, Historical record, 1940 Oct.-1959 Nov., Church Archives; Bismarck Branch, General minutes, Church Archives; Fargo Ward, Manuscript history and historical reports, Church Archives; Northern Indian Mission, Manuscript history and historical reports, Church Archives; "New Mission Offers Opportunities," Church News, 2 February 1974; "50th U. S. State Gets Stake," Church News, 13 August 1977; Bismarck North Dakota District, Annual historical reports; Bismarck North Dakota Stake, Annual historical reports; "Shortening the Vast Distances," Church News, 25 September 1999.

No.	Name	Organized	First President
	North America Central Area		
2243	Bismarck North Dakota	22 Sep 1996	Richard A. Adsero
852	Fargo North Dakota	7 Aug 1977	John R. Price

Ohio

Jan. 1, 2011: Est. population, 11,486,000; Members, 58,436; Stakes, 13; Wards, 96; Branches, 32; Missions, 2; Temples, 1; Percent LDS, 0.5, or one in 211.

In October 1830, one month after being baptized in New York, Parley P. Pratt began his first missionary journey, accompanied by Oliver Cowdery, Peter Whitmer Jr., and Ziba Peterson. They traveled to Ohio to preach to the Native Americans. On their way the missionaries taught the gospel to Sidney Rigdon, a Reformed Baptist minister, and his congregation in Mentor, near Kirtland. Within a few weeks 127 people were baptized, including Rigdon and Frederick G. Williams, and a nucleus for the Church was established in Kirtland. The missionaries later preached to Wyandot Indians in Sandusky, Ohio, and to Delaware Indians in Missouri.

In December 1830, Joseph Smith received a revelation instructing the Church to gather in Ohio (D&C 37). He traveled to Kirtland in February where he and his wife Emma lived for a time with Newel K. Whitney. Kirtland served as Church headquarters from 1831 to 1838. The first stake of the Church was created there in 1834.

Sixty-five of the revelations published in the Doctrine and Covenants were received in Ohio. The growing number of Latter-day Saints, especially in Ohio and Missouri, also led to important organizational developments in the Church. The First Presidency was organized in Kirtland in March 1832, followed by the Kirtland High Council, February 1834; the Quorum of the Twelve Apostles, February 1835; and the First Council of the Seventy, also in February 1835.

Lorenzo Snow, president of the Church from 1898 to 1901, was born in Mantua, Ohio, in 1814, attended Oberlin College, and was baptized in Kirtland in June 1836. He embarked on his first mission in the spring of 1837. Many of the Church's new converts were dispatched from Ohio as missionaries to different parts of the United States, Canada and Great Britain.

An important part of the legacy of the early Church in northeastern Ohio was the construction of the Kirtland Temple. Construction began 5 June 1833 and the finished structure was dedicated by the Prophet Joseph Smith on 27 March 1836. The temple was the site of several heavenly manifestations, including a visit of the Savior and the restoration of priesthood keys by Moses, Elias and Elijah (D&C 110).

The Church established a printing press in Kirtland in December 1833, from which issued the Evening and Morning Star (renamed in 1834 to the Latter Day Saints' Messenger and Advocate and in 1837 to the Elders' Journal) and other important publications. The second edition of the Book of Mormon was printed in Kirtland in 1837.

Kirtland had about 2,500 inhabitants in 1836, half of which were Latter-day Saints, and the Church population was growing. Joseph Smith and others established the Kirtland Safety Society Anti-banking Company in January 1837. A financial panic swept the nation within months and the Kirtland Safety Society failed, closing in November 1837.

The failure fostered ill-will against Joseph Smith and other Latter-day Saints. Several Church members became disaffected in the wake of the bank disaster and anti-Mormons resented the growing political influence of Mormons in Kirtland. Matters came to a head in January 1838 when Joseph Smith and other Church leaders fled Kirtland for Missouri to escape mob violence. That same month the Church printing office in Kirtland was destroyed by arson. In the ensuing months many Latter-day Saints moved from Ohio to Missouri, including a group of 500 that left Kirtland in July under the direction of the First Council of the Seventy in a planned migration called the Kirtland Camp.

Between 1838 and 1839 the approximate number of Latter-day Saints in Kirtland dropped from 2,000 to 100. Latter-day Saint numbers in Ohio remained relatively small for over a century thereafter, though there was a slight resurgence in Kirtland in the early 1840s. The Kirtland Temple was used by different groups until 1879, when a court granted ownership of the edifice to the Reorganized Church of Jesus Christ of Latter Day Saints.

Missionaries occasionally visited Ohio but it was not part of an organized mission until the late 1870s. Thereafter missionary work was directed by the Northwestern States Mission (renamed Northern States Mission in 1889), 1878-1899; Southern States Mission, 1899-1926; Northern States Mission, 1926-1949; Great Lakes Mission, 1949-1967; and Ohio Mission beginning in 1967 (renamed Columbus Ohio Mission in 1974). Additional missions were organized with headquarters in Cleveland (1977) and Cincinnati (1998). Stakes were organized in Cincinnati (1958), Cleveland (1961) and Columbus (1962). The Columbus Ohio Temple was dedicated 4 Sept. 1999.

Full-time missionaries returned to Kirtland in 1977, the same year the Kirtland Ward was created. In 1979, the Church acquired the Newel K. Whitney store, which became a well-visited historic site. Another important project was the renovation of the John Johnson home in Hiram, which was dedicated 28 Oct. 2001 by President Gordon B. Hinckley.

In April 2000, the Church announced plans for six historic structures in Kirtland, including construction of a replica of the John Johnson Inn and a new visitors center resembling a 19th-century gristmill used by Samuel Whitney, restoration of the Newel K. Whitney home, and replicas of a tannery, an ashery, and a school house.

President Hinckley visited Kirtland 17-18 May 2003 to dedicate the six structures as part of the Ohio Bicentennial celebration. "There is something unique and wonderful about what happened here," he said. "Nothing like it has occurred anywhere else in the history of the Church, either before or since."

Membership was 51,406 in 2003. In 2005, membership reached 55,128.

Sources: Milton V. Backman Jr., The Heavens Resound: A History of the Latter-day Saints in Ohio, 1830- 1838, 1983; Autobiography of Parley P. Pratt, 1985; "Kirtland, Ohio," 1894, in Historian's Office letterpress copybook, [ca. 1880-1900], 249, Church Archives; Andrew Jenson, manuscript history of the Church in Ohio, [n.d.], Church Archives; Eliza R. Snow, Biography and Family Record of Lorenzo Snow, 1884; Marvin S. Hill, C. Keith Rooker, and Larry T. Wimmer, The Kirtland Economy Revisited: A Market Critique of Sectarian Economics, 1977; Andrew Jenson, Encyclopedic History of the Church, 1941; Illinois Chicago Mission (Northern States Mission), manuscript history, Church Archives; Shaun D. Stahle, "Plans Announced to Renovate Six Major Kirtland Structures," Church News, 29 April 2000; Shaun D. Stahle, "John Johnson Home Will Have Place in History," Church News, 3 November 2001; Shaun D. Stahle, "Something Unique About Historic Kirtland," Church News, 24 May 2003.

No.	Name	Organized	First President
North America East Area			
696	Akron Ohio	25 May 1975	Carmen J. Libutti
270	*Cincinnati Ohio		
	‡Cincinnati (Ohio, Kentucky)	23 Nov 1958	Thomas Blair Evans
1523	Cincinnati Ohio North	17 Mar 1985	William B. Wallis
2628	Cincinnati Ohio East	15 Feb 2004	Keith Alan Jensen
336	*Cleveland Ohio		
	‡Cleveland (Ohio, Penn.)	20 Sep 1961	E. Doyle Robison
351	*Columbus Ohio		
	‡Columbus	25 Feb 1962	James L. Mortensen
793	Columbus Ohio East	28 Nov 1976	Paul Frank Eastman
1609	Columbus Ohio North	19 Oct 1986	D. Richard McFerson
2661	Columbus Ohio South	14 Nov 2004	Steven Matley Wood
516	*Dayton Ohio		
	‡Dayton	24 May 1970	Joseph M. McPhie
1029	Dayton Ohio East	27 May 1979	Melvin Elwin Gourdin
1447	Kirtland Ohio	16 Oct 1983	Zane F. Lee
1204	Toledo Ohio	2 Nov 1980	Ronald Rufus Burke
2751	Youngstown Ohio	17 Feb 2007	James S. Kirk
	Stakes discontinued		
1	Kirtland	17 Feb 1834	Joseph Smith Jr.

Discontinued 24 May 1841 (Reinstated as No. 1447)

Missions — 2

(As of Oct. 1, 2011; shown with historical number. See MISSIONS.)

(77a) OHIO COLUMBUS MISSION
19 Clairedan Dr.
Powell, OH 43065

(154) OHIO CLEVELAND MISSION
23550 Center Ridge Rd., Ste 102
West Lake, OH 44145

Oklahoma

Jan. 1, 2011: Est. population, 3,643,000; Members, 43,033; Stakes, 7; Wards, 58; Branches, 25; Missions, 2; Temples,1; Percent LDS, 1.1, or one in 88.

In the late 1840s, George Miller, a former bishop who had delayed going to the West, traveled from Winter Quarters, Neb., to visit his son in Texas. He and two other members of the Church with him, Joseph Kilting and Richard Hewitt, worked for a time in the Cherokee Nation in the borders of present-day Oklahoma. They arrived in Tahlequah on 9 July 1847. They taught others about the Church, but antagonism forced Miller to leave in December. Hewitt and Kilting remained to work.

In 1855, Orson Spencer and James McGaw visited the Indian Territory from St. Louis, Mo., and on 8 April, five more missionaries were sent from Salt Lake City and four from St. Louis. The Indian Territory Mission was created and placed under the leadership of Miller on 26 June of that year. The missionaries met and re-converted followers of Lyman Wight. One of these was Jacob Croft, who had met missionaries earlier and started for Utah, but met an apostate group that told the Croft party untruths about conditions there. The discouraged Croft party settled in Indian Territory and built a gristmill.

As early as July 1855, missionaries preached to about 400 Indians, and the Cherokee Branch was started at Croft's Spavinaw Creek mill. This became mission headquarters. Croft later led a party of 56, including other former followers of Wight and some re-converted "Strangites" (followers of James J. Strang) to Utah.

Later in the year, missionaries were sent from St. Louis to southern portions of the Cherokee Nation. In 1856, the Princess Creek Branch was organized. The Lehi and Nephi branches were organized in 1858.

Illness was a problem in the mission for many years. At least four missionaries died including Orson Spencer.

In 1858-1859, the remaining members migrated to Utah. By 1860, all the missionaries but John A. Richards, who had married an Indian wife, returned to Utah and the mission was discontinued. Disorder brought on by the Civil War ended what was left of the Church in the Indian Territory. Members and leaders were scattered.

When Matthew Dalton and John Hubbard returned to begin missionary work in 1877, they found John Richards was still faithful, and they received assistance from him. Elder Hubbard died later that year and the mission was closed. In 1883, Matthew Dalton and Elder George Teasdale of the Quorum of the Twelve reorganized the mission. Tracts in the Cherokee language were printed.

Andrew Kimball, father of President Spencer W. Kimball, presided over the mission in 1885. Although he contracted malaria, he carried on the work and was assisted by John Richards, and later by additional full-time missionaries. In 1892, the first meetinghouse was built in Manard. Another was built in Massey.

On 29 March 1898, Oklahoma became part of the Southwestern States Mission, and on 4 April 1904 it was included in the Central States Mission. On 7 November 1911, a branch was established at Gore, with 113 members but was later dissolved. It was not until 1 May 1960 when the branch was again organized in Gore. A Sunday School that began in Bartlesville in 1924 became a branch on 13 October 1945. Membership increased slowly as many converts moved to Utah.

Membership increased in the 1950s and 1960s. Two stakes were created, the Tulsa Stake on 1 May 1960 and the Oklahoma City Stake on 23 October 1960. Additional stakes followed in 1970s and the 1980s. The Oklahoma Mission was created on 10 June 1970. It was renamed the Oklahoma Tulsa Mission in 1974. A second mission in Oklahoma, headquartered in Oklahoma City, was created in 1990.

The Latter-day Saint community reached out to those in need after a bomb destroyed the nine-story Alfred P. Murrah Federal Building in downtown Oklahoma City on 19 April 1995.

The Oklahoma City Temple, the Church's 95th temple in operation, was dedicated on 30 July 2000 by President James E. Faust of the First Presidency.

In 2002, membership reached 35,369. In 2005, membership reached 38,772.

Sources: Lynetta K. Bingham, et. al., A History of the Church of Jesus Christ of Latter-day Saints in Eastern Oklahoma from Oklahoma and Indian Territories to 1980, 1980; Central States Mission, Manuscript history and historical reports; Oklahoma Mission, Manuscript history and historical reports; Indian Mission, Manuscript history and historical reports.

Stakes — 7
(Listed alphabetically as of Oct. 1, 2011.)

No.	Name	Organized	First President
North America Southwest Area			
777	Lawton Oklahoma	31 Oct 1976	Ralph E. Siebach
531	*Norman Oklahoma		
	‡Oklahoma South	18 Oct 1970	H. Aldridge Gillespie
305	*Oklahoma City Oklahoma		
	‡Oklahoma	23 Oct 1960	James A. Cullimore
1381	Oklahoma City Oklahoma South	14 Nov 1982	Lawrence Andrew Jackson
1277	Stillwater Oklahoma	14 Jun 1981	C. Jay Murray
298	*Tulsa Oklahoma		
	‡Tulsa (Okla., Ark., Kan.)	1 May 1960	Robert N. Sears
912	Tulsa Oklahoma East	30 Apr 1978	Raleigh L. Huntsman
	Stakes discontinued		
1418	Muskogee Oklahoma	15 May 1983	Samuel J. Hughes
	Discontinued 11 Aug 1991		

Missions — 2
(As of Oct. 1, 2011; shown with historical number. See MISSIONS.)

(248) OKLAHOMA OKLAHOMA CITY MISSION
416 SW 79th St Ste 210
Oklahoma City, OK 73139-8121

(88) OKLAHOMA TULSA MISSION
5215 East 71st St., Suite 300
Tulsa, OK 74136

Oregon

Jan. 1, 2011: Est. population, 3,790,000; Members, 147,965; Stakes, 36; Wards, 253; Branches, 51; Missions, 2; Temples, 2; Percent LDS, 3.8, or one in 26.

In 1838 Joseph Smith visited Washington, D.C., where on one occasion Sen. Henry Clay suggested that the Prophet take the Mormons to the Oregon Territory. Oregon was one of several locations he considered for possible settlement after difficulties in Illinois in the early 1840s. At the time, Oregon was claimed by both Great Britain and the United States. As early as 25 September 1850, R. Boyd Stewart was called to serve in Oregon, but there is no record of his efforts. Additional missionaries served in 1854 and later, but were called back with their converts at the coming of Johnston's Army to Utah in 1857.

During the 1860s, Latter-day Saints found work as loggers in Oregon. A few settled, but a significant Latter-day Saint presence did not occur until 1887 when businessmen from Utah, David Eccles and Charles Nibley (joined in 1889 by John Stoddard) built a lumber mill on the North Powder River near Baker, Ore., and persuaded Latter-day Saint families to migrate there. The Baker Branch, placed under the Oneida Stake in Idaho, was organized by Elder Franklin D. Richards of the Quorum of the Twelve on 23 July 1893. He prophesied, "There will be stakes of Zion organized in Oregon ... and I would not be surprised if a Temple should be erected."

In 1896, Edward Stevenson and Mathias F. Cowley traveled via train, boat and wagon to survey the situation of the scattered saints in the Northwest. This led to the organization of the Northwestern States Mission on 26 July 1897, under the direction of Oneida Stake President George C. Parkinson. Mission headquarters were established in Portland. (The first Northwestern States Mission was organized in 1878 and had headquarters in Chicago.) Early convert Jens (James) Westergaard became the first branch president in Portland after his baptism in 1898. Mission headquarters were moved to Baker City in 1898 and back to Portland in 1902.

Around the turn of the 20th century, there was another Latter-day Saint movement to Oregon when ranches in eastern and southern Oregon were purchased and divided into sugar beet farms. By 9 June 1901, enough members had migrated that the Union Stake was created in LaGrande. Two years later the six original wards had increased to 13. Completion of the Oregon Shortline Railroad led more members to migrate to the Northwest.

Both World War I and World War II defense industry efforts brought more members of the Church to Oregon. In 1929, a meetinghouse was completed in Portland. By 1930, membership in the state was 3,226, with wards in Baker, Imbler, LaGrande (two), Mt. Glen, and Union. Mission branches also functioned in Bend, Eugene, Klamath Falls, Medford, Portland, Hood River and Salem.

Another stake was organized in Portland on 26 June 1938. Many members also moved into Oregon in the post-World War II boom and four more stakes were created in the 1950s. When the Klamath Falls Stake was divided on 23 August 1964, the Medford Stake became the Church's 400th stake.

Around 1961, the Church purchased property near Portland for a proposed junior college. However, the location was later selected as the site for the Portland Oregon Temple, which was dedicated 19 August 1989. More than 300,000 people toured the temple open house. A second mission was created in the state with headquarters in Eugene on 1 July 1990. A second temple in Oregon, located in Medford, was dedicated 16 April 2000.

Gordon H. Smith, a Latter-day Saint, was elected to the U.S. Senate in 1996 and won re-election in 2002. Smith is Republican and his fellow senior senator, Ron Wyden, is Jewish and a Democrat. Instead of becoming rivals, the two have forged a friendship holding weekly luncheons and joint town hall meetings in Oregon.

In 2002, membership reached 139,507. In 2005, membership reached 142,545.

Sources: Joseph Smith, Documentary History of the Church, 1951; Andrew Jenson, "Oregon," Encyclopedic History of the Church of Jesus Christ of Latter-day Saints, 1941; Kenneth G. Dull, Mormon Migration to Oregon's Grande Ronde Valley: A Portent of Future Mormon Expansion, thesis, 1981; Bruce D. Blumel, "Enterprising beet farmers," Church News, 14 January 1978; Leonard J. Arrington, "History of the Church in the Pacific Northwest," Task Papers in LDS History, No. 18 Church Archives; Dale Z. Kirby, History of the Church of Jesus Christ of Latter-day Saints in Oregon, The First Fifty Years, 1990; Central Point Oregon Stake, A History of The Church of Jesus Christ of Latter-day Saints in Southern Oregon, 1914-1997, 1997; Kent Larsen, "Oregon's Smith-Wyden Political Friendship Celebrates 100th Weekly Luncheon," Mormon News, 17 September 2000.

Stakes — 36
(Listed alphabetically as of Oct. 1, 2011.)

No.	Name	Organized	First President
North America Northwest Area — 33			
386	*Beaverton Oregon		
	‡Portland West (Oregon)	10 Nov 1963	C. Carlile Carlson
2124	Beaverton Oregon West	12 Nov 1995	William Stanley Richardson
472	*Bend Oregon		
	‡Bend	15 Dec 1968	Norman K. Whitney
1373	Cedar Mill Oregon	31 Oct 1982	Edgar Lee Stone
1325a	Central Point Oregon	7 Mar 1982	Michael T. Robinson
493	*Coos Bay Oregon		
	‡Oregon West	12 Sep 1969	Edward Harold Sypher
385	*Corvallis Oregon		
	‡Corvallis	3 Nov 1963	Hugh F. Webb
1410	Eugene Oregon Santa Clara	17 Apr 1983	Terrel B. Williams
767	Eugene Oregon	15 Aug 2004	
	‡Eugene Oregon West	12 Sep 1976	Robert W. Hill
2763	Forest Grove Oregon	19 May 2007	Brad C Richardson
779	Grants Pass Oregon	31 Oct 1976	Darwin Jay Wright
643	Gresham Oregon	26 May 1974	Wilford Smith Stevenson Jr.
1365	Gresham Oregon South	10 Oct 1982	Max B. Holbrook
1200	Hermiston Oregon	26 Oct 1980	Allen D. Alder
710	Hillsboro Oregon	12 Oct 1975	H. Keith Buhler
743	*Keizer Oregon	4 Apr 1984	
	*Salem Oregon Keizer	25 Oct 1981	
	‡Salem Oregon North	8 Feb 1976	Jay Gerald Nelson
205	*Klamath Falls Oregon		
	‡Klamath (Oregon, California)	22 Mar 1953	Carroll William Smith
1469	Lake Oswego Oregon	29 Apr 1984	Thomas Dean Cottle
1102	Lebanon Oregon	3 Feb 1980	Henry Boyd Walthuis
1300	McMinnville Oregon	25 Oct 1981	Thomas Babb III
400	*Medford Oregon		
	‡Medford (Oregon, California)	23 Aug 1964	Dennis R. Hassell
999	Milwaukie Oregon	11 Feb 1979	Thomas Dean Cottle
1171	*Monmouth Oregon	21 May 1996	
	*Dallas Oregon	25 Sep 1990	
	‡Salem Oregon East	24 Aug 1980	William Paul Hyde
563	*Oregon City Oregon		
	‡Oregon City	16 Jan 1972	James Hayward Bean
123	*Portland Oregon		
	‡Portland	26 Jun 1938	Monte L. Bean
190	*Portland Oregon East		
	‡Columbia River (Ore., Wash.)	2 Dec 1951	R. Spencer Papworth
1852	Ranier Oregon	8 Mar 1992	Marion Royal Johnstun
1239	*Redmond Oregon	18 Feb 1986	
	‡Prineville Oregon	1 Mar 1981	Heber D. Perrett
830	Roseburg Oregon	15 May 1977	Gary Richards Lowe
321	*Salem Oregon		
	‡Salem	22 Jan 1961	Hugh F. Webb
191	Springfield Oregon	15 Aug 2004	Corwin G. Lewis
	*Eugene Oregon		
	‡Willamette	2 Dec 1951	Ralph B. Lake
850	The Dalles Oregon	26 Jun 1977	Wayne B. Bush
1895	Tualatin Oregon	16 Aug 1992	Paul Walker Roberts
Idaho Area — 3			
49	*La Grande Oregon		
	‡Union	9 Jun 1901	Franklin S. Bramwell
176	*Nyssa Oregon		
	‡Nyssa (Oregon, Idaho)	8 Jan 1950	Arvel L. Child
1504	Ontario Oregon	18 Nov 1984	Reed Neils Dame

Missions — 2
(As of Oct. 1, 2011; shown with historical number. See MISSIONS.)

(249) OREGON EUGENE MISSION
55 W 29th Ave, Ste A
Eugene, OR 97405

(18) OREGON PORTLAND MISSION
13635 NW Cornell Rd., Suite 100
Portland, OR 97229

Pennsylvania

Jan. 1, 2011: Est. population, 12,448,000; Members, 49,743; Stakes, 10; Wards, 75; Branches, 32; Missions, 2; Districts, 1; Temples, 0, announced, 1; Percent LDS, 0.4, or one in 257.

Northeastern Pennsylvania was the site of some of the most transcendent events of the early Restoration. Joseph Smith and his wife Emma spent most of the time between December 1827 and August 1830 living in Harmony (present-day Oakland). While there the Prophet translated the bulk of the Book of Mormon, with Emma, Martin Harris, and Oliver Cowdery as scribes. On 15 May 1829, Joseph and Oliver were ordained to the Aaronic Priesthood by John the Baptist on the banks of the Susquehanna River, after which he directed the two to immerse each other in the first authorized baptisms of this dispensation. Shortly thereafter, Peter, James, and John appeared to Joseph and Oliver in the same vicinity and conferred upon them the Melchizedek Priesthood. In addition, 15 of the revelations in the Doctrine and Covenants were received while the Smiths lived in Harmony.

After the 1831 establishment of Church headquarters at Kirtland, Ohio, northern Pennsylvania was frequented by missionaries traveling to their former homes farther east and preaching along the way. More than 140 people were baptized in Erie County during the early 1830s. Alpheus Gifford established branches in Rutland and Columbia, from which local Latter-day Saints preached northward into New York, some of them assisting in the conversion of the Brigham Young and Heber C. Kimball families. Young's brother Phinehas, en route to Missouri during the winter of 1832-1833, organized the first branch in southwestern Pennsylvania at Pittsburgh, with more than 100 converts within a few years.

The Church was established in Philadelphia in 1839 by brothers Samuel and Lewis James and Benjamin Winchester, with more than 450 members in the city and adjoining counties by October 1840. By that time Joseph Smith, Sidney Rigdon, and most of the Twelve had visited the Philadelphia area.

During the 1830s, at least 13 branches were established in the state, the bulk of them in sparsely-settled rural areas. Most of these branches eventually ceased to function as converts gathered with the saints in Ohio and Missouri and missionaries shifted their attention to other places. During the Nauvoo era, with missionary work concentrated in the British Isles, fewer elders visited the eastern states, focusing their efforts on the nation's largest cities — New York, Philadelphia and Boston.

After Sidney Rigdon's 1844 break with the Prophet, he returned to Pittsburgh, the area of his birth, where he persuaded many of the saints in southwestern Pennsylvania to join him. When he established a new gathering place farther east in Franklin County, one of his followers, William Bickerton, founded a new splinter group (Bickertonites) that attracted many of the saints who remained in the Pittsburgh area.

Membership in the Philadelphia Branch generally remained loyal to the Twelve in Nauvoo, although apostate James J. Strang appealed to enough to organize a branch of his church in the city in 1846. Out of the ever-shifting balance of conversions, departures for Nauvoo, and European Latter-day Saints spending time in the area before traveling further west, Philadelphia's LDS branch had a membership of more than 300 during much of the 1840s. After the relocation of the Church to the Great Basin in 1847, the number of Latter-day Saints in Philadelphia fell to about 150 and missionaries only occasionally visited the area. This situation was temporarily reversed from 1855 to 1857, when John Taylor of the Quorum of the Twelve presided over the re-established Eastern States Mission, with headquarters in New York City, and selected Philadelphia as one of the American ports of entry for LDS emigrants arriving from Europe. But Church activity was once again suspended when the elders were called home at the outbreak of the Utah War.

During the next 35 years, missionaries occasionally visited Pennsylvania. Two of them baptized Catherine W. Rock and her sons Andrew and Alexander in 1869 in Franklin County, near the settlement Sidney Rigdon had established more than 20 years earlier. In 1882, another pair of missionaries from the West baptized Emanuel Rock, the father in that family, and appointed him president of what was soon known as the Fairview Branch. Members of the branch built a stone meetinghouse at Waynesboro in 1904, the first LDS building erected in Pennsylvania.

Meanwhile, in the Pittsburgh area, George Barnes and others who left the Bickertonite group in 1873 met regularly in the village of New England to study the Book of Mormon and Doctrine and Covenants. They wrote to a friend in Utah requesting a visit from LDS missionaries, and late in 1885 two elders serving in the Northern States Mission were sent to them, finding three branches "waiting for word from Utah." The Pennsylvanians accepted the authority of the missionaries but wondered whether their earlier baptisms were valid. This was settled in December 1885 when the First Presidency advised those interested in the Church to be baptized again. In May 1886, branches were organized at Little Redstone and New England.

Occasionally, other elders from the Northern States Mission labored in Pennsylvania, with two of them arriving in Fulton County's Buck Valley in December 1887 to hold meetings. Their first baptisms were performed in April 1889 and soon others joined the Church, holding meetings in the homes of saints and outdoors in groves of trees. The Buck Valley Branch was organized in 1896 and has functioned continuously since that time, currently as the Hancock (Maryland) Ward.

When the Eastern States Mission was re-established in 1893, its records listed only 55 Latter-day Saints in New York, New Jersey and Pennsylvania. Four years later, western Pennsylvania, Maryland and part of West Virginia were transferred from the Northern States Mission to the new mission. By 1900, its eight conferences — including the Eastern Pennsylvania Conference, with headquarters in Philadelphia, and the Western Pennsylvania Conference, with headquarters in Pittsburgh — had a total membership of 975.

Church growth has been continuous in Pennsylvania during the last 100 years, although everywhere in the state it began slowly and continued slowly for many years. By 1940, the state's 15 branches were home to nearly 900 Latter-day Saints, with about 450 more not being part of organized branches. By 1960, Church membership in Pennsylvania had more than tripled to 4,600 in 28 wards and branches. Another doubling took place in the following decade, and the number of Latter-day Saints in the state nearly doubled again during the 1970s, rising to 18,000 in 79 wards and branches — all but nine were included in Pennsylvania's seven stakes. Not only were there many more Church units in the state, but they were also larger and more mature, the average number of members per unit having risen from 61 in 1940 to 228 in 1980.

As one illustration of these growth patterns, the Philadelphia Branch for many years included Latter-day Saints living in northern Delaware, southern New Jersey, and elsewhere in eastern Pennsylvania. In 1945, the first local district president was called, and soon groups of outlying members were organized into additional branches, including Allentown, Germantown, and Chester in Pennsylvania and Camden across the Delaware River in New Jersey.

As membership growth continued and leadership skills increased, the Philadelphia Stake was organized in October 1960, including six wards and branches in southeastern Pennsylvania (with 1,100 members) and other units in New Jersey, Delaware, and Maryland. Fourteen years later the stake had grown to the point that it was divided and all the units outside Pennsylvania became part of the Wilmington Delaware Stake. By 1980, the Philadelphia Pennsylvania Stake's membership was approaching 3,000.

Similarly, a branch was established in Pittsburgh by the early part of the 20th century — in addition to the New England Branch (soon renamed the Wilson Branch) several miles out of the city — with many members being baptized in other outlying areas. Sunday Schools and other Church meetings under the direction of missionaries were held in members' homes in places such as Carmichaels, California, Redstone, Waynesburg, Johnstown and Butler.

The Pittsburgh Branch bought a frame structure from another church, which was dedicated by President Heber J. Grant in September 1929, when the branch had about 100 members. By 1950, there were nearly 800 members in the West Penn District, with branches in Pittsburgh, Punxsutawney, Washington and Wilson, but the scattered nature of the Church membership is evident from the fact that nearly half the district's Latter-day Saints were identified as "outlying" members who lived too far away to attend Church services regularly.

In 1965, the Pittsburgh and Wilson branches were realigned to form four branches in the greater Pittsburgh area. Four years later the Pittsburgh Stake was organized, with four wards in the city and its suburbs and additional units in nearby Pennsylvania communities. By 1970, the stake membership was nearly 2,700. Ten years later, after a division of the original stake, Church membership in southwestern Pennsylvania had risen to 4,500.

Church growth followed similar patterns in many other Pennsylvania communities. Typical was the experience of Reading, the state's fifth-largest city, where Reading native George Yeager, who married a Latter-day Saint while traveling in the West, brought his family to Reading in 1920. They were joined six years later by G. Albin Schelin, a Utah native who married a Philadelphia girl while studying there. For several years the two families attended Church services in Philadelphia, 65 miles away, but then began holding cottage meetings and Sunday School in their homes in the early 1930s. As they helped the missionaries bring others into the Church, a local hall was rented and in 1939 the Reading Branch was organized. The first phase of what eventually became a larger branch meetinghouse was built in 1959-1960 and Reading became a branch in the Philadelphia Stake in 1960. After growing to ward status in 1966, Reading became part of the Gettysburg Stake in 1970 and the Harrisburg Pennsylvania Stake in 1979. With 600 members, the ward was divided in 1981, and a year later the Reading Pennsylvania Stake was organized, taking in an area nearly 100 miles long and 60 miles wide that previously had been part of the Harrisburg, Scranton and Philadelphia stakes. The majority of the Latter-day Saints in the new stake were Pennsylvania natives.

In the late 1970s, the Philadelphia Stake was composed of five wards, all of them located in the city's suburbs. In 1980, the Church began a return to inner-city Philadelphia, with both the Metro Branch and the Philadelphia Spanish Branch being organized that year.

While much of Pennsylvania in the early 21st century is made up of small ethnically homogeneous cities and towns and rural areas, the highly urbanized southeastern corner of the state is characterized by the ethnic and racial diversity typical of other metropolitan areas on the Eastern Seaboard.

By 2004, the three stakes in southeastern Pennsylvania (Philadelphia, Valley Forge, and Reading) included among their 27 units one Spanish ward and 12 other English wards and branches that were home to substantial numbers of Latter-day Saints whose primary languages were Spanish, Portuguese, Korean, Cambodian or Vietnamese.

Membership was 41,188 in 2003. In 2005, membership reached 44,855.

Sources: Andrew Jenson, "Eastern States Mission" and "Pennsylvania," Encyclopedic History of the Church, 1941; Larry C. Porter, A Study of the Origins of The Church of Jesus Christ of Latter- day Saints in the States of New York and Pennsylvania, 1816-1831, dissertation, 1971 (published, 2000); V. Alan Curtis, "Missionary Activities and Church Organizations in Pennsylvania, 1830- 1840," thesis, 1976; Paul Zilch Rosenbaum, "The Church of Jesus Christ of Latter-day Saints in Pennsylvania (1830-1854)," thesis, 1982; Warren M. Avey, History of The Church of Jesus Christ of Latter-day Saints at Fairview, Franklin County, Penna., 1965, Church Archives; Lynn Matthews Anderson, From These Hills and Valleys: A Brief History of The Church of Jesus Christ of Latter- day Saints in Southwestern Pennsylvania, 1986 (the quote about "waiting for word from Utah" is from page 58); William L. Hendershot, A Brief History of the Buck Valley Branch of the Church of Jesus Christ of Latter-day Saints, 1948, Church Archives; Joseph E. Jorgensen, History of Philadelphia Branch Relief Society, circa 1938, Church Archives; Ronald Bulkley, The Church in Southern New Jersey, 1980-1981, Church Archives; Peter M. Bowman, Donald F. Crego, and William F. Byers, A History of the Church of Jesus Christ of Latter-day Saints in the Reading Pennsylvania Area, 1985.

Stakes — 10
(Listed alphabetically as of Oct. 1, 2011.)

No.	Name	Organized	First President
	North America Northeast Area		
946	*Altoona Pennsylvania	31 Oct 1982	
	‡State College Pennsylvania	23 Jul 1978	Robert Armstrong Wood Sr.
1047	Harrisburg Pennsylvania	12 Aug 1979	Charles A. Cooper
304	*Philadelphia Pennsylvania		
	‡Philadelphia (Penn., Del., Md., N.J.)	16 Oct 1960	Bryant F. West
481	*Pittsburgh Pennsylvania		
	‡Pittsburgh	11 May 1969	William P. Cook
985	*Pittsburgh Pennsylvania North	18 Feb 1992	
	‡Pittsburgh Pennsylvania East	26 Nov 1978	Garth Harrison Ladle
1372	Reading Pennsylvania	31 Oct 1982	Hugh G. Daubek
1044	Scranton Pennsylvania	2 Aug 1979	Frederick Adelman Alderks
2512	Valley Forge Pennsylvania	14 Feb 1999	Robert Blaine Smith
2337	Williamsport Pennsylvania	13 Apr 1997	Russell James Stankiewicz
510	*York Pennsylvania	12 Aug 1979	
	*Gettysburg Pennsylvania		
	‡Gettysburg (Pennsylvania)	19 Apr 1970	Laurence L. Yager

(129) PENNSYLVANIA PITTSBURGH MISSION
2589 Washington Road, Ste. 410
Pittsburgh, PA 15241-2596

(156) PENNSYLVANIA PHILADELPHIA MISSION
1974 Sproul Rd Ste 206
Bromall, PA 19008

Rhode Island

Jan. 1, 2011: Est. population, 1,051,000; Members, 3,833; Wards, 6; Percent LDS, 0.35, or one in 287.

Orson Hyde and Samuel H. Smith, the first Latter-day Saint missionaries to visit several of the New England states, arrived in the capital city of Providence on 13 July 1832. They baptized two members before persecutors and threats of violence drove them away 12 days later. At a conference held in Newry, Maine, in August 1836, Brigham Young reported that nine members belonged to Rhode Island's lone branch. By 1844, another branch had been organized at Newport and had 21 members.

Following the 1844 martyrdom of Joseph Smith, much of the missionary activity in New England was devoted to preparing the area's Latter-day Saints to join with the body of the Church in the Midwest and later in Utah. A few members remained in Rhode Island and were occasionally visited by missionaries. The Providence Branch was again organized in June 1857 with Miner G. Atwood as president, but it was soon closed. Another brief attempt at re-establishing the branch took place in 1873.

Eastern States Mission President John G. McQuarrie wrote in 1904 that the northeastern United States was "practically abandoned [as far as missionary work] until 1893 when President [Wilford] Woodruff sent a few Elders . . . to try to locate and revive the scattered Saints." Missionaries were assigned to Providence as early as August 1896, with a branch being organized about three years later.

The area was visited off and on by elders until the spring of 1908, when four missionaries were assigned to Providence and vicinity. By August, they were holding street meetings, had rented a hall, and reported there were 14 members of the Church. The following month a branch was once more organized. In February 1909, at a meeting of the New England Conference of the Eastern States Mission, new conferences were created in New Hampshire, Rhode Island, and Vermont, with six elders assigned to Rhode Island.

Church growth continued to be slow. When Latter-day Saint Oscar E. Johnson was transferred to Providence in February 1937 by his employer, he found the branch had been closed for about 10 years because of poor attendance. After attending the New Bedford Branch in Massachusetts with his family for several months, he was appointed president of the Providence Branch in September 1937 and reported there were about 50 members of the Church in the area. This time the organization prospered enough to remain open indefinitely. The branch met for some time in the homes of members, until a building previously used as a library was purchased, the facility being dedicated by Elder John A. Widtsoe of the Quorum of the Twelve in June 1944. By that time, a second branch had been functioning in Newport for three months.

Over the next 30 years, Providence and Newport were Rhode Island's only branches, even though their combined membership increased nearly eight-fold from 1950 until 1970. A new meetinghouse was built at Warwick on the southern edge of the Providence metropolitan area in the early 1960s, and ground was broken in 1967 for a building at Newport.

In the mid-20th century, the Rhode Island branches were frequently associated with the Church in eastern Massachusetts. During the 1950s, the Atlantic District (with headquarters in Boston) was divided and the Providence District was organized, including Rhode Island and Massachusetts south of Boston. In 1966, the units in the Providence District were incorporated into the Boston Stake. In March 1977, the Boston and Hartford stakes were divided to create the Providence Rhode Island Stake, which included 2,953 Latter-day Saints living in three units in Rhode Island and six wards and branches in Massachusetts and Connecticut. In 1981, the stake was divided to form the Hingham Massachusetts Stake — which included all the parent stake's Massachusetts units plus the ward at Newport, R.I., — and another Connecticut unit was added to the Providence stake.

In 1981, a branch was organized at Warwick for Spanish-speaking Latter-day Saints living in the Providence area. During the early 1990s, Laotian and Cambodian groups also functioned in the Providence Ward. In 1997, to better reflect the demographics of the Providence metropolitan area, the Spanish branch at Warwick became an English-speaking ward — which continued to meet in the building constructed in the mid-1960s — while the Providence Ward became a Spanish-speaking branch holding its meetings at a new inner-city location. In 2004, even though the stake continued to be called the Providence Rhode Island Stake, its headquarters were at Mystic, Conn.

Membership in Rhode Island in 1974 was 799; increasing to 1,052 in 1980; and to 1,701 in 1990.

In 2002, membership reached 3,475. In 2005, membership reached 3,560.

Sources: Andrew Jenson, "Rhode Island," Encyclopedic History of the Church, 1941; Richard S. Williams, "The Missionary Movements of the LDS Church in New England, 1830-1850," thesis, 1969; Eastern States Mission, Manuscript history and historical reports, 1873, Church Archives; John G. McQuarrie, "Eastern States Mission," Millennial Star, 24 February 1904; Journal History, 10 August 1896, Church Archives; Liahona: The Elders' Journal, 6:318-19, 558, 979, 1098; Oscar E. Johnson, History of the Providence, Rhode Island Branch, Church Archives; "Branch Saints Enjoy Own Chapel," Church News, 31 March 1945; Providence and Newport ward, Manuscript histories and historical reports, Church Archives; "7 Stakes Change; 1st for Rhode Island," Church News, 26 March 1977; Carole Woodbury, "Unified Diversity in Providence Rhode Island Stake," Ensign, October 1993.

Stake — 1
(Listed alphabetically as of Oct. 1, 2011.)

No.	Name	Organized	First President
North America Northeast Area			
818	Providence Rhode Island	20 Mar 1977	Morgan W. Lewis Jr.

South Carolina

Jan. 1, 2011: Est. population, 4,480,000; Members, 36,947; Stakes, 6; Wards, 49; Branches, 13; Missions, 1; Temples, 1; Percent LDS, 0.8, or one in 125.

Missionary work in the Southern States began as early as 1831. The first member of the Church in South Carolina is believed to have been Emmanual Masters Murphy who was baptized in Tennessee in 1836. When Lysander M. Davis arrived in South Carolina about 1 November 1839, he found the Murphys had people prepared for baptism. Seven of these were baptized.

Opposition arose and Davis was briefly jailed. Murphy reportedly later visited Joseph Smith in Carthage Jail shortly before the Prophet's martyrdom. The Prophet reminded him of the prophecy that war would soon begin in South Carolina and exhorted Murphy to warn the people of his home state.

Abraham O. Smoot preached in Charleston and upstate South Carolina, having been called on 16 August 1841, but he failed to gain any converts. However, an unidentified missionary traveled to Charleston earlier that year and baptized three ministers and eight others. Another missionary, John Eldredge, preached in South Carolina in 1842-43.

No other known missionary work was done in the state until the 1870s. The South Carolina Conference was organized on 31 March 1882. Some of the earliest branches were established at King's Mountain beginning 3 March 1882 and among the Catawba Indian community beginning 31 July 1885. Conference headquarters were established at the plantation of John Black, a man who remained unbaptized in order to provide refuge to the Church. Many converts, including Indians, moved onto his plantation to escape persecution. The Catawbas also shielded missionaries from persecutors. Most of the Catawbas joined the Church and remained faithful in South Carolina.

On 9 April 1950, Samuel Taylor Blue, also known as Chief Blue of the Catawba Tribe, spoke in general conference. He had been baptized on 7 May 1897 in South Carolina.

Missionaries braved many adversities while serving in South Carolina including jailing, disease and frequent exposure to the elements. They walked hundreds of miles, often missing meals, and endured other privations, but they continued to find converts and organize branches. There were 2,238 converts baptized throughout the South, from 1880 to 1888, and 1,169 moved to Utah.

Progress and persecution continued in the 1890s. Mobs often gathered to punish and banish missionaries. Branches organized included Society Hill, Columbia, Charleston and Fairfield. About 350 members attended a conference in Society Hill in 1897. However, as converts migrated to the West, branches dwindled and some were reorganized later with new converts.

The conference included six branches (four with meetinghouses) and 10 Sunday Schools. In the 1930s, mission president LeGrand Richards introduced "systematic teaching," a forerunner of today's missionary discussions. By 1937, membership in the entire Southern States Mission had increased to 18,000.

South Carolina's first stake was created in Columbia on 19 October 1947. It included the entire state with wards in Columbia, Greenville, Charleston, Gaffney, Hartsville, Ridgeway and Spartanburg, and branches in Augusta (Georgia), Sumter, Society Hill, Winnsboro and Darlington. Membership totaled 1,869 members.

Additional stakes were organized South Carolina West in 1963, South Carolina East in 1968 and Charleston in 1972. The South Carolina Columbia Mission was organized from the Georgia Atlanta Mission July 1, 1975.

A temple built in Columbia was dedicated on 16 October 1999 by President Gordon B. Hinckley.

In 2002, membership reached 28,605.

Sources: Andrew Jenson, Encyclopedic History of the Church, 1941; Edward R. Bass, Comp., Columbia South Carolina Stake Fortieth Anniversary, Oct. 19, 1947 to 1987, 1987; LaMar C. Berrett, History of the Southern States Mission 1831-1861, thesis 1960; DeVon H. Nish, Brief History of the Southern States Mission for One Hundred Years, 1830-1930, 1966; "Stake Birthday Notes Growth of Church in South Carolina," Church News, 9 December 1972; Ted S. Anderson, Southern States Mission and the Administration of Ben E. Rich, 1898-1908, thesis 1976; Richard L. Jensen, "Persecutor Converted," Church News, 4 February 1978; R. Scott Lloyd, "New Temple in a 'Place of History,'" Church News, 23 October 1999; Southern States Mission, Manuscript history and historical reports, Church Archives.

Stakes — 6

(Listed alphabetically as of Oct. 1, 2011.)

No.	Name	Organized	First President
North America Southeast Area			
584	*Charleston South Carolina		
	‡Charleston	20 Aug 1972	Fred Ittner Harley
169	*Columbia South Carolina		
	‡South Carolina (S.C., Georgia)	19 Oct 1947	W. Wallace McBride
454	*Florence South Carolina	5 Feb 1978	
	*Columbia South Carolina East		
	‡South Carolina East	21 Apr 1968	Clyde Elmer Black Sr.
	(South Carolina)		
366	*Greenville South Carolina		
	*Greenville	19 Nov 1972	
2620	Greenville South Carolina East	16 Nov 2003	George Earl Sanders
	‡South Carolina West	27 Jan 1963	Ivan A. Larsen
	(S.C., N.C.)		
2610c	West Columbia South Carolina	3 Feb 2002	John R. Jensen

Mission — 1

(As of Oct. 1, 2011; shown with historical number. See MISSIONS.)

(130) SOUTH CAROLINA COLUMBIA MISSION
1345 Garner Lane, Suite #307
Columbia, SC 29210-8362

South Dakota

Jan. 1, 2011: Est. population, 804,000; Members, 9,812; Stakes, 2; Wards, 10; Branches, 23; Missions, 1; Districts, 1; Percent LDS, 1.2, or one in 84.

In 1845, shortly after the martyrdom of Joseph and Hyrum Smith, James Emmett, without authorization from Church leaders in Nauvoo, led a group of saints into what is now South Dakota. They stopped at a fur trader fort on the Vermillion River where they settled and began farming. They also attempted to do missionary work among the Sioux and befriended them, but the threat of attack was constant. The colony was nearly attacked when Emmett unwisely interfered in a horse-trading deal between the Indians and traders and an argument ensued. Because of complaints about Emmett's leadership by members of the group, Brigham Young sent representatives to the settlement to investigate. Sometime after these representatives had returned to Nauvoo and reported on their visit to Fort Vermillion, James Emmett also traveled to Nauvoo and became reconciled with Church leaders. The Vermillion saints left the South Dakota area the following spring, in compliance with Brigham Young's request that they join the main westward migration. The Church did not return to the area for nearly 40 years.

In May of 1883, the Dakota Territory was added to the jurisdiction of the Northern States Mission and missionaries were sent into the southeastern part of the territory. On 5 July 1898, the Dakota Conference had progressed enough to divide it into North and South Dakota conferences. Less than two years later, in November 1900, the Dakotas were attached to the Colorado Mission, which was later renamed the Western States Mission.

The first Church unit in South Dakota since the abandonment of the Fort Vermillion Settlement was a Sunday School in Lead, organized on 1 November 1920. Four years later, in October 1924, a branch was established in Rapid City. By this time regular meetings were also being held at nearby Hot Springs and by 1928, at Belle Fourche. In August of 1925, most of South Dakota, with the exception of the Black Hills area, was assigned to the new North Central States Mission. In the new mission, South Dakota was initially included with North Dakota in one district. The work in the area, though slow, resulted by 1930 in the creation of a separate South Dakota District and a Sunday School in Sioux Falls.

Not until 1948 were any further units organized in South Dakota. That year a Sunday School was established in Huron and a branch was organized in Gettysburg. The following year the Sioux Falls saints were organized into a branch. In 1950, a conference was held at Pierre and a Sunday School was organized in Mitchell. At the beginning of 1951, the South Dakota District was divided, creating the Sioux District in the southeastern part of the state. A branch was organized in Mitchell and a new meetinghouse was dedicated in Sioux Falls in 1951. Progress continued during the 1950s, with the dedication of a meetinghouse in Gettysburg in 1952, the establishment of branches in Aberdeen and Pierre in 1953, and the creation of a branch in Lead in 1955.

Meanwhile, on 11 November 1950, the Black Hills District was detached from the Western States Mission and included in the new West Central States Mission. Further fragmentation of the area occurred when the work on the reservations was assigned to the new Northern Indian Mission on 1 May 1964. With this reorganization, the work progressed enough that in 1970 the Standing Rock District was established on the reservation, and in 1972, the first stake in South Dakota was organized at Rapid City. The missionary work in South Dakota, split between three missions for so many years, was consolidated under the Dakota-Manitoba Mission in 1973. This mission was renamed the South Dakota Rapid City Mission a year later. Before the decade was over, South Dakota had its second stake, established in Sioux Falls on 18 November 1979.

The number of new converts to the Church in South Dakota was smaller during the 1990s than it had been, but the saints have become stronger through their support of each other in the scattered stakes, wards, and branches of this sparsely populated area. They have also strengthened each other and their non-LDS friends through participation in humanitarian efforts when called upon, such as the support given to the victims of widespread flooding in the Sioux Falls area in June of 1993.

In 2002, membership reached 8,370.

Sources: Richard Bennett, "Mormon Renegade James Emmett at the Vermillion, 1846," South Dakota History, Fall 1985; Northern States Mission, Manuscript history and historical reports, Church Archives; Western States Mission, Manuscript history and historical reports, Church Archives; North Central States Mission, Manuscript history and historical reports, Church Archives; "Sioux Falls: A Secret Treasure," Ensign, January 1991; West Central States Mission, Manuscript history and historical reports, Church Archives; Sioux Falls Branch, Manuscript history and historical reports, Church Archives; Lead Branch, General minutes, Church Archives; Northern Indian Mission, Manuscript history and historical reports, Church Archives; Fargo Ward, Manuscript history and historical reports, Church Archives; "Stake Proves a Real Asset to Mission," Church News, 2 February 1974; "New Mission Offers Opportunities," Church News, 2 February 1974; Belle Fourche Branch, General minutes, Church Archives; Belle Fourche Branch, Manuscript history and historical reports, Church Archives; "Flooding in Midwest Doesn't Let Up," Church News, 31 July 1993; "Midwestern U. S. Saints Rally Against Flood Damage," Ensign, October 1993; "The Church in the Dakotas," Church News, 30 November 1996.

Stakes — 2
(Listed alphabetically as of Oct. 1, 2011.)

No.	Name	Organized	First President
North America Central Area			
592	*Rapid City South Dakota		
	‡Rapid City	10 Dec 1972	Briant LeRoy Davis
1085	Sioux Falls South Dakota	18 Nov 1979	Russell Lloyd Harward

Mission — 1
(As of Oct. 1, 2011; shown with historical number. See MISSIONS.)

(78) SOUTH DAKOTA RAPID CITY MISSION
2525 W Main, Suite 311
Rapid City, SD 57702

Tennessee

Jan. 1, 2011: Est. population, 6,215,000; Members, 45,574; Stakes, 10; Wards, 69; Branches, 29; Missions, 2; Temples 2; Percent LDS, 0.7, or one in 144.

David W. Patten and Warren Parrish arrived in Tennessee shortly before 11 October 1834 and soon baptized 31 people; organizing a branch by the end of the year. These efforts were in Henry, Benton and Humphreys counties. In 1835, Parrish worked alone after Patten returned to Kirtland, Ohio.

On 27 March 1835, Wilford Woodruff, then a priest, came to assist Parrish. When Warren Parrish was called as a Seventy in July 1835, he ordained Woodruff an elder and placed him in charge of the work in Tennessee. Woodruff was assisted by Abraham O. Smoot and Benjamin L. Clapp. By February 1836 there were about 100 members in seven branches. By 1839, 12 branches existed in the state and by 1846, missionaries had preached in 26 counties. Following the exodus to the West, little work was done in Tennessee. Missionaries visited the state in 1857 to call the saints to gather in the West.

In 1870, Hayden Church resumed work in Tennessee. The Southern States Mission was formally organized in 1875 with headquarters in Nashville. They were moved to Chattanooga in 1882 and remained there until 1919. Henry G. Boyle established a branch at Shady Grove in 1875. Mob activity increased significantly in 1879. Some converts in the South left their homes and migrated to the West in 1883. In 1884, members were fired upon in separate incidents. The worst massacre of Church members in the South occurred on 10 August 1884 when a mob shot to death missionaries William S. Berry and John H. Gibbs and local members Martin Condor and John Riley Hudson during Church services near Cane Creek in Lewis County. Mission president Brigham H. Roberts donned a disguise, traveled to the tense area and retrieved the bodies of the slain missionaries. In 1888, a group of 177 saints left Chattanooga for Colorado and Utah.

By the 1890s, public opinion became more tolerant. The oldest existing meetinghouse in the Southeast was dedicated in Northcutts' Cove on 24 October 1909 by Charles A. Callis. Ten years later branches were listed in Chattanooga and Memphis. On 16 November 1925, a chapel in Memphis was dedicated by Elder George F. Richards of the Quorum of the Twelve. By 1930, about 2,832 members lived in the Middle and East Tennessee districts. At the end of the World War II, many branches were meeting in rented halls. In 1946, the First Presidency approved a new meetinghouse design and in the next few years land was purchased and construction started on meetinghouses throughout parts of Tennessee including the cities of Memphis, Knoxville, Kingsport and Altamont. The 1950s, brought additional growth from the migration of Saints from westward states coming to study and work in Tennessee.

On 18 April 1965, the Memphis Stake, Tennessee's first, with Richard Stoddard as president, was created by Elder Howard W. Hunter of the Quorum of the Twelve. The Memphis Stake included two wards in Memphis and another in Jackson, plus wards in Mississippi and Arkansas. The Tennessee Nashville Mission was created in 1975, and in 1993, the Tennessee Knoxville Mission was organized. More than 6,500 people attended a meeting where President Gordon B. Hinckley spoke in the Knoxville Civic Coliseum on 15-16 March 1997.

On 12 November 1994, a letter sent to priesthood leaders announced plans to build a temple in Nashville. However, after three unsuccessful years of trying to gain approvals, Church leaders announced on 25 April 1998, they would move ahead with plans to build a temple somewhere else in the Nashville area, and said the temple would be substantially smaller in size. That fall, on 17 September 1998, the First Presidency announced that a second temple would be built in Tennessee, this one in Memphis. This temple, in the suburb of Bartlett, was dedicated 23 April 2000. The next month, on 21 May 2000, the Nashville Tennessee Temple, in the suburb of Franklin, was dedicated.

Membership reached 34,265 in 2003. In 2005, membership reached 38,842.

Sources: Southern States Mission directories, 1919-1935, Church Archives; Andrew Jenson, Encyclopedic History of the Church, 1941; Lamar C. Berrett, History of the Southern States Mission, thesis, 1960; Mary Elizabeth Stovall, Orthodoxy Versus Nonconformity: The Mormon Experience in Tennessee and Mississippi, 1875-1905, 1976 research paper, Church Library; Southern States Mission, Manuscript history and historical reports, Church Archives; East Central State Mission, Manuscript history and historical reports, Church Archives; "Memphis Stake Is Organized," Church News, 24 April 1965; "Eight Missions to be Organized," Church News, 22 March 1975; "Historic Tennessee Chapel Rededicated," Church News, 9 November 1986; R. Scott Lloyd, "Chattanooga: LDS in Tennessee Build on a Firm Foundation," Church News, 25 May 1991; "We Expect Great Things of Our People," Church News, 22 March 1997; "New Plans Announced for Nashville Temple," Church News, 25 April 1998; "5 New Temples in U.S., Mexico Announced," Church News, 24 October 1998; Gerry Avant, "Remembering Roots at Memphis Dedication," Church News, 29 April 2000; R. Scott Lloyd, "Second Temple Adds to Tennessee Peace," Church News, 27 May 2000.

Stakes — 10

(Listed alphabetically as of Oct. 1, 2011.)

No.	Name	Organized	First President
North America East Area — 8			
927	Chattanooga Tennessee	21 May 1978	Earl Eugene Callens Jr.
1089	Franklin Tennessee	2 Dec 1979	Buryl Gene McClurg
1093	Kingsport Tennessee	13 Jan 1980	William Keith Clay
581	*Knoxville Tennessee		
	‡Knoxville	25 Jun 1972	Eugene H. Perkins
2269	Knoxville Tennessee Cumberland	17 Nov 1996	Richard Edwin Riggs
2765	Madison Tennessee	9 Jun 2007	Brent J. Ostermiller
1810	McMinnville Tennessee	18 Aug 1991	Gary Wayne Bradford
537	*Nashville Tennessee		
	‡Nashville	6 Dec 1970	Robert N. Brady
North America Southeast Area — 2			
403	*Memphis Tennessee		
	‡Memphis	18 Apr 1965	Richard Stoddard
1179	Memphis Tennessee North	14 Sep 1980	Edward Victor Martin

Missions — 2

(As of Oct. 1, 2011; shown with historical number. See MISSIONS.)

(294) TENNESSEE KNOXVILLE MISSION
11312 Station West Dr
Farragut, TN 37922

(131) TENNESSEE NASHVILLE MISSION
105 W. Park Dr., Ste 190
Brentwood, TN 37027

Texas

Jan. 1, 2011: Est. population, 24,327,000; Members, 296,141; Stakes, 56; Wards, 451; Branches, 126; Districts, 3; Missions, 8; Temples, 4; Percent LDS, 1.1, or one in 87.

In 1844, because of increased persecution in and around Nauvoo, Joseph Smith realized that he would have to relocate the Church outside the borders of the United States. He considered the Republic of Texas, a place where the Church members would be able to practice their religion in peace. The Prophet began to negotiate with Sam Houston, the president of the Texas Republic, for the southern and western portions of Texas as a future Latter-day Saint nation. On 14 March 1844, Joseph Smith sent Lucien Woodworth to Austin, Texas, to meet with Houston.

In May, Woodworth returned to Nauvoo and reported the progress he had made. Not much is known about the exact nature of the negotiations between Houston and Woodworth, but reports indicate that plans were made for the Church to purchase large tracts of land. A three man commission comprised of Woodworth, George Miller and Almon Babbitt was organized to lead the final negotiations. Assuming the negotiations would be successful, Joseph Smith asked that Lyman Wight, who was a member of the Quorum of the Twelve, and George Miller prepare to lead a group of settlers to Texas. The official negotiations ended with the death of Joseph Smith in June 1844.

Though Brigham Young relocated the Church in the Great Basin, he allowed Wight to take a group of 150 to Texas. They arrived north of present-day Dallas on 10 November 1845. Wight and the colonists eventually settled near a German colony called Fredricksburg and founded a town named Zodiac.

In 1848, Brigham Young sent Preston Thomas and William Martindale to invite Wight and the colonists to join the Church in the Salt Lake Valley. However, Wight declined the offer and was excommunicated from the Church. Although he was no longer a member of the Church, Wight and his followers pioneered settlements in five Texas counties and generally left a good reputation for Mormons in the area.

In addition to trying to reclaim the Church members who followed Wight, Brigham Young also sent several missionaries to preach in Texas in the 1850s. Those who joined the Church were encouraged to gather with the Latter-day Saints in the Utah Territory. On 25 December 1855, a conference (district) was established in Texas. Nearly 1,000 converts from Texas immigrated to the Great Basin prior to the Civil War.

Missionary work resumed in Texas in 1875, nearly 10 years after the Civil War. In 1893, another Texas Conference was organized. A.C. Dalley, president of the Texas Conference, reported that there were 64 Latter-day Saints in Texas at the end of 1896.

The Latter-day Saint population in Texas increased dramatically when Church members began to gather in Mormon enclaves within the Lone Star State. Converts living in the South endured ostracism and oc-casional physical violence because of their membership in the Church. In the early 1890s, President James G. Duffin of the Southwestern States Mission sug-gested to Church leaders that they establish a gathering place for Southern Church members. His suggestion was accepted and bran-ches were organized in Missouri, Kansas and Texas. Included in the Texas colonies were Odom Settlement (also known as Odomville) near Spurger, Williamson Settlement near Evadale, Jozye (also known as Little Utah), and Poynor.

One of the most successful and long-lived colonies was located at Kelsey. It was founded by brothers John and James Edgar in December 1898. By the fall of 1901, nine Latter-day Saint families settled the area. The following year Elder Abraham O. Woodruff of the Quorum of the Twelve visited the site and assisted in laying out the town. On 4 August 1901, a Sunday School was organized. By the end of the month, a meetinghouse had been built, and by the end of 1901 a branch had been organized.

Missionaries in the southern states encouraged converts to gather to Kelsey. By 1906, there were approximately 400 Latter-day Saints living in the township. A school had been built and was staffed by missionaries. An article that appeared in the 5 February 1910 Deseret News reported that Kelsey was "one of the largest branches outside the stakes of Zion." Later that year, the colony was divided and the settlement of Enoch was founded and a branch was organized there.

The population of Kelsey reached its peak of about 750 inhabitants in 1923, the same year the local railroad line closed down, isolating the town and causing the settlement to slowly decline. In 1943, the Church-sponsored school was closed. In 1958, the congregations in Kelsey and Enoch were combined with the Gilmer Ward.

Until the first decade of the 20th century, nearly all Church activity in Texas occurred in rural settings. In 1913, Harriett M. Knight, a widow with five children, moved from Kelsey to Dallas, where there was no organized branch. One other Latter-day Saint, Eliza E. Davis, was living in Dallas, having moved there in 1908. Over time, other Latter-day Saints moved to Dallas. Missionaries occasionally visited these urban Church members, but it was not until 1916 that a home Sunday School was organized in Dallas. Sometime between 1918 and 1921 the Dallas Branch was organized.

Church members also began to move to other urban areas. By 1918, Latter-day Saints were living in Ft. Worth, Houston and San Antonio. However, Dallas was the first urban branch in Texas to have its own meetinghouse. In 1927, the Dallas Latter-day Saints moved into a vacant building formerly used by another denomination. In 1943, the North Central Texas District was organized with 500 members. A new meetinghouse was built in Dallas in the early 1950s and dedicated by President David O. McKay on 26 April 1953. Upon seeing the full chapel and overflow area, he felt Dallas was ready for a stake. On 19 October 1953, Elder Mark E. Petersen of the Quorum of the Twelve organized the Dallas Stake, with Ervin W. Atkerson as president.

The first branch in Houston was organized on 5 December 1921. The first official Church-owned meetinghouse was a home willed to the Church by Mrs. Gussie Farmer. The house was quickly remodeled and dedicated on 19 November 1933. A stake was created in Houston on 11 October 1953 with Jack B. Trunnell as president.

The city of El Paso has played an important role in the establishment of the Church in Mexico and the American Southwest. In 1876, Daniel W. Jones led a company of missionaries there, where they prepared to begin missionary work in Mexico. The missionaries stayed in El Paso for several weeks, where they studied Spanish and conducted missionary work, though no conversions were recorded.

At the end of the 19th century, and the beginning of the 20th, a few Latter-day Saint families from the Mormon colonies in

Mexico relocated to El Paso and Ciudad Juarez, just across the river from El Paso. In 1909, a branch was organized for Church members living in El Paso and Ciudad Juarez. In July 1912, nearly 3,000 saints fled their homes in Mexico because of a revolution and made their way to El Paso, where they received assistance from local residents before leaving to settle elsewhere.

A ward was organized in El Paso, the first in Texas, on 11 October 1918. It was originally part of the Juarez (Mexico) Stake, but was later transferred to the St. Joseph (Arizona) Stake. Headquarters of the Mexican Mission was located in El Paso from 1919 to 1929. The first stake in Texas, the El Paso Stake, was organized on 21 September 1952 with Edward V. Turley Sr. as president.

Responsibility for Texas has been shared by several different missions. The state was originally in the Southern States Mission. In 1897, it was transferred to the Indian Territory Mission, which later changed its name to the Southwestern States Mission and, in 1904, to the Central States Mission. Texas remained in the Central States Mission until the Texas Mission was organized in 1931. Texas and Louisiana were combined to form the Texas-Louisiana Mission in 1945. Texas was part of the Gulf States Mission from 1955 to 1960. In 1961, a new Texas Mission was organized, which in 1974 became the Texas Dallas Mission. As the Church grew, other missions in Texas were organized. The Texas Lubbock Mission, the eighth mission with headquarters in Texas and covering western Texas and eastern New Mexico, was announced by the First Presidency on 9 March 2002.

Four temples have been built in Texas in 20 years. The Dallas Texas Temple was dedicated on 19 October 1984. At that time the temple district included 46 stakes and 120,000 members. A temple in Houston was dedicated on 26 August 2000. The Lubbock Texas Temple was dedicated on 21 April 2002.

Membership in 2002 reached 231,173; and 237,931 in 2003.

President Gordon B. Hinckley dedicated the San Antonio Texas Temple May 22, 2005, the fourth temple in the Lone Star State, and the 120th operating temple in the Church. Some 65,000 people visited the 16,800-square-foot edifice during the open house.

Sources: Michael Scott Van Wagenen, The Texas Republic and the Mormon Kingdom of God, 2002; B. H. Roberts, Comprehensive History of the Church, v.2, 1912; Southern States Mission, Manuscript history and historical reports, Church Archives; Bonnie Donetta Means Durning, A History of the Mormon Church in Texas, 1843-1906, thesis, 1964; James Clyde Vandygriff, The Beginnings of Kelsey, Texas: a Southern Gathering Place for the Saints, research paper, 1972, Church History Library; Vera Lavina Winget Richards, Historical Information on the Church in Texas, 1984, Church Archives; The House of the Lord, http://www.lds.org/temples/home/0,11273,1896-1,00.html, 22 July 2004; Andrew Jenson, Encyclopedic History of the Church, 1941; El Paso Branch, Manuscript history and historical reports, Church Archives; El Paso Stake, Manuscript history and historical reports, Church Archives; Clinton A. Hawkins, A Talk on Mormon History of Texas and Houston, 1992, Church Archives; Gary E. Holt, LDS Church History in Texas, 1994, Church Archives; Shaun D. Stahle, "Seven New Missions Created," Church News, 9 March 2002; "A temple on a hill," Church News, 28 May 2005.

Stakes — 56
(Listed alphabetically as of Oct. 1, 2011.)

No.	Name	Organized	First President
North America Southwest Area			
1262	Abilene Texas	3 May 1981	William E. Seegmiller
2772	Allen Texas	25 Aug 2007	Gordon Kurt Wright
1272	Amarillo Texas	31 May 1981	Donald Eugene Pinnell
1594	Arlington Texas	13 Apr 1986	Richard S. Pickering
626	Austin Texas	14 Oct 1973	Amos Luther Wright
1835	Austin Texas Oak Hills	1 Dec 1991	Gary Scott Robinson
1818	Bay City Texas	13 Oct 1991	Joseph Nathanial Cannon Jr.
333	*Beaumont Texas		
	‡Beaumont (Texas, Louisiana)	3 Sep 1961	Alden C. Stout
2608c	Carrollton Texas	9 Dec 2001	Jonathan C. Roberts
1076	*College Station Texas	10 Oct 1989	
	‡Conroe Texas	28 Oct 1979	Nylen Lee Allphin Jr.
2338	Colleyville Texas	13 Apr 1997	Randy J. Vest
398	*Corpus Christi Texas		
	‡Corpus Christi	31 May 1964	Clarence Cottam
1451	Cypress Texas	6 Nov 1983	Bruce A. Nelson
210	*Dallas Texas		
	‡Dallas	18 Oct 1953	Ervin W. Atkerson
828	Dallas Texas East	15 May 1977	Arthur Eugene Gabriel
1860	Denton Texas	3 May 1992	James Boyd Martino
194	*El Paso Texas		
	‡El Paso (Texas, New Mexico)	21 Sep 1952	Edward V. Turley Sr.
1359	El Paso Texas Mount Franklin	29 Aug 1982	Gerald Merrell Pratt
443	*Fort Worth Texas		
	‡Fort Worth (Texas)	24 Sep 1967	John Kelly Jr.
843	Friendswood Texas	29 May 1977	Newell Kenneth Hill
2803	Frisco Texas	4 May 2008	Jonathan Clifford Roberts
1394	Gilmer Texas	16 Jan 1983	Von Webber Freeman
1247	Harlingen Texas	22 Mar 1981	Leonard Moore
209	*Houston Texas (Spanish)		
	‡Houston (Texas, Louisiana)	11 Oct 1953	Jack Byron Trunnell
456	*Houston Texas East		
	‡Houston East (Texas)	5 May 1968	Martell A. Belnap
733	Houston Texas North	16 Nov 1975	Harold Elison DeLaMare
1211	Houston Texas South	30 Nov 1980	Leo C. Smith
2702	Houston Texas West (Spanish)	8 Jan 2006	Sergio Enriquez Perez G.
784	*Hurst Texas	12 Apr 1981	
	‡Fort Worth Texas North	14 Nov 1976	Richard W. Ragsdale
1834	Katy Texas	1 Dec 1991	Collins Wise Steward
986	Killeen Texas	26 Nov 1978	Stephen Brian Hutchings
1337	Kingwood Texas	18 Apr 1982	Robert Lee Ezell
2616	Klein Texas	2 Nov 2003	Paul Kent Oscarson
2802	Kyle Texas	4 May 2008	Charles Terry Allen

No.	Stake	Date	President
1253	Lewisville Texas	12 Apr 1981	Richard W. Ragsdale
2861	League City Texas	25 Oct 2009	Weldon J. Reeves
496	*Longview Texas		
	‡Texas East	9 Nov 1969	Gerald C.F. Knackstedt
446	*Lubbock Texas		
	‡Texas North	26 Nov 1967	Franklin S. Gonzalez
692	McAllen Texas	4 May 1975	Daniel Birch Larsen
2806c	McAllen Texas West	7 Sept 2008	Laren Brice Chandler
1991	McKinney Texas	11 Sep 1994	Robert C. Packard
471	*Odessa Texas		
	‡Texas West	15 Dec 1968	Roland Lamar Hamblin
1360	Orange Texas	29 Aug 1982	Bernard E. Packard
616	*Plano Texas	12 Apr 1981	
	*Dallas Texas North		
	‡Dallas North	27 May 1973	Ivan Leslie Hobson Jr.
1396	Richardson Texas	30 Jan 1983	Larry Wayne Gibbons
2719	Richmond Texas	7 May 2005	John David Oldroyd
2531	Round Rock Texas	6 Jun 1999	Howard J. Nicholas
252	*San Antonio Texas		
	‡San Antonio	19 Jan 1958	Roland C. Bremer
758	San Antonio Texas East	30 May 1976	Archie M. Brugger
2791	San Anonio Texas Hill Country	27 Jan 2008	Jeffrey Duane Foote
2401	San Antonio Texas North	19 Oct 1997	Frank J. Dittmar
1426	San Antonio Texas West	5 Jun 1983	Jan M. Sterneckert
2862	Spring Texas	8 Nov 2009	Randy C. Tolman
2668	Tyler Texas	23 Jan 2005	Evan Grover Nielsen
2884	Waco Texas	17 Oct 2010	Blake R. Christensen
2718	Weatherford Texas	30 Apr 2006	Cary Randal Reeves

Missions — 8

(As of Oct. 1, 2011; shown with historical number. See MISSIONS.)

(60) TEXAS DALLAS MISSION
13747 Montfort Drive, Ste.120
Dallas, TX 75240-4454

(189) TEXAS FORT WORTH MISSION
1331 Airport Freeway, Ste. 305
Euless, TX 76040

(142) TEXAS HOUSTON MISSION
16623 Hafer Road
Houston, TX 77090-4401

(233) TEXAS SAN ANTONIO MISSION
404 E. Ramsey Rd., Ste. 105
San Antonio, TX 78216-4665

(254) TEXAS HOUSTON EAST MISSION
2815 W Lake Houston Pky, Ste. 109
Kingwood, TX 77339

(316) TEXAS HOUSTON SOUTH MISSION
4627 Austin Pky.
Sugar Land, TX 77479-2146

(224) TEXAS MC ALLEN MISSION
200 W La Vista Ave
McAllen, TX 78501-2131

(334a) TEXAS LUBBOCK MISSION
5214 68th St Ste 202
Lubbock, TX 79424-1523

Utah

Jan. 1, 2011: Est. population, 2,737,000; Members, 1,910,343; Stakes, 546; Wards, 4,479; Branches, 355; Missions, 6; Districts, 1; Temples 11, under construction or announced, 2; Percent LDS, 68, or one in 1.47.

Elder Orson Pratt of the Quorum of the Twelve and Erastus Snow were the first Latter-day Saints to enter the Great Basin, arriving in what is now Salt Lake City on 21 July 1847. They were followed by the advance party that included President Brigham Young. On 24 July, Brigham Young and the rest of the group of 148 saints arrived and on 28 July, President Young selected the site where the Salt Lake Temple would be built. Within a month, the city had been surveyed, 80 acres of land had been planted, 29 log houses had been built, nearby valleys had been explored, a bowery and adobe fort had been constructed, and trade shops had been started. Other pioneer companies followed, starting a flood of immigration into the Great Basin that continued through the turn of the 20th century and afterward.

On 26 September 1847, Perregrine Sessions established a settlement in Bountiful. Nearby Farmington was founded the same year by Hector C. Haight. In 1848, James Brown built Brown's Fort in what is now Ogden. Centerville was established in 1848, as were many Salt Lake-area settlements, such as East Millcreek and Sugar House. About 4,500 people were residing in the Salt Lake Valley before the harsh winter of 1848. Because of the difficult circumstances, many subsisted on sego lily roots and boiled rawhide.

On 3 October 1847, the Salt Lake Stake, the first in the territory, was created. Wards were not organized within the stake until 22 February 1849, when the stake was divided into 19 wards.

Provo was founded in 1849, along with Kaysville, Granger, Tooele and Manti. By 1850, Iron City in southern Utah and 28 other settlements had been started.

Education was important to the saints who settled in Utah, and as a consequence, the University of Deseret, now the

University of Utah, was established on 28 February 1850. Academies were founded in most of the stakes within the state. Most significant was the Brigham Young Academy, founded in 1876. It became Brigham Young University, the Church's flagship institution of higher education. On 15 June 1850, the first issue of the Church owned Deseret News was published. The paper continues to this day.

Before 1900, about 500 settlements had been founded within the state and in the adjoining states of Idaho, Nevada, California, Arizona, New Mexico, Colorado, and Wyoming. At least 236 parties or companies of pioneers representing many nations of the world crossed the plains in various wagon companies. Many were assisted by the Church's Perpetual Emigrating Fund, a program designed to loan the resources necessary for Latter-day Saints to come to Utah. An estimated 60,000 Mormon pioneers crossed the plains before the completion of trans-continental the railroad in 1869. Of these, approximately 3,000 came with handcart companies from 1856-60. The Willie and Martin handcart companies of 1856 met with tragedy in Wyoming in an unseasonably early winter. Two-hundred died from exposure and starvation. About 875 were rescued through heroic efforts of the saints in Utah.

Members generally got along well with the Indians, and the most prominent local leader, Ute Chief Walker, was friendly and was baptized in 1850, though he led a brief resistance movement in 1853. Members traded with Indians and shared food with them, and the Indians helped members survive. Indian farms were established in the 1850s, but troubles between the Mormons and the government discouraged most of the Indians.

On 14 February 1853, ground was broken for the Salt Lake Temple. Stone for the temple was hauled from the quarry by ox-drawn wagons until 1873 when a railroad spur between Little Cottonwood Canyon and the temple site was completed.

In 1857, responding to false reports of insurrection, President James Buchanan sent an army under command of Colonel Albert Sidney Johnston to put down an alleged rebellion and install a new governor in place of Brigham Young and put in place a federal judge from the East. In Utah, members considered it another act of persecution and prepared to protect themselves. If attacked, the saints were prepared to burn their homes to the ground, leaving their persecutors nothing but "scorched earth."

However, partly through intercession of friends of the Church, particularly Colonel Thomas L. Kane, war was averted and Johnston's Army passed peacefully through Salt Lake City and established a camp at the south of Salt Lake in Utah Valley. At the height of the war-time hysteria, a group of 120 members of the Baker-Fancher Wagon Train, most of them from Arkansas, were killed in 1857 at Mountain Meadows by a group of local Latter-day Saints and Indians.

Difficulties between federal appointees and citizens continued until Utah was granted statehood in 1896. A major obstacle to statehood was the practice of plural marriage, which ended when the Manifesto was issued by President Wilford Woodruff on 24 September 1890.

On 6 April 1893, the Salt Lake Temple — the largest in the Church — was dedicated. It has become the most recognized worldwide symbol of the Church. Before the completion of the Salt Lake Temple, three other temples were dedicated in St. George, 1877; Logan, 1884; and Manti, 1888.

The domed Tabernacle, was built from 1863-1867 and was dedicated in 1875. It is among the largest timber-roofed buildings in the world and is the home of the weekly broadcast of the Music and the Spoken Word program, which celebrated 75 years of continuous broadcasting in 2003-2004. This is the longest broadcast program in the United States.

During the pioneer period, and shortly after the turn of the century, many of the larger outlying communities also erected tabernacles and meetinghouses built for large gatherings.

The Church's LDS Hospital opened in Salt Lake City in 1905. Primary Children's Hospital opened in 1911. Subsequent hospitals were added over time and when the Church sold the hospitals to private interests in 1974, there were 15 hospitals in the system.

The first seminary program in the Church was started in Salt Lake City in 1912 when 70 teenagers, all members of the Granite Stake, began gathering for daily religious instruction in a small red brick building near Granite High School. By 1918, seminaries had been established in Brigham City, Mt. Pleasant, American Fork, Lehi, and Blanding. Granite Stake is also credited with starting the family home evening program, begun by stake President Frank Y. Taylor and adopted Churchwide in 1915.

During the Depression of the 1930s, the Church founded Deseret Industries in Salt Lake City, an organization devoted to rendering assistance to those in need. There are now a total of 49 Deseret Industries stores in Utah, Idaho, Nevada, Arizona, California, Washington, and Oregon.

At the beginning of the 20th century, more than half the new stakes being created were in Utah. By 1992, about one stake in five was in Utah.

On 1 July 1975, the Utah Salt Lake City Mission, the first in the state, was organized. Previously, full-time missionaries worked in parts of Utah under the leadership of missions headquartered in other states.

On 26 October 1978, the Missionary Training Center in Provo, previously the Language Training Mission, began training all missionaries.

In the 1970s and 1980s, three other temples were erected and dedicated, in Ogden and Provo in 1972, and South Jordan (Jordan River Temple) in 1981. These were followed by the Bountiful Utah Temple in 1995, and the Mount Timpanogos Utah Temple in American Fork in 1996. In 1997, the Vernal Utah Temple was dedicated. It was the first temple constructed from an existing building, the Uintah Stake Tabernacle. The first small temple was dedicated in Monticello, Utah, on 26 July 1998.

On 21 May 1994, Cove Fort, originally built in 1867 under the direction of Ira N. Hinckley, was dedicated by his grandson, President Gordon B. Hinckley. The fort has become one of the most popular tourist sites in the state. Temple Square in Salt Lake City is visited annually by nearly 5 million people and ranks among the top tourist attractions in the nation.

In 1997, during the celebration of the sesquicentennial of the arrival of the 1847 pioneers, a wagon train re-enacted the original trek. The wagon train was greeted in Salt Lake City on 22 July by an estimated 50,000 people, including all three members of the First Presidency.

On 11 September 1999, President Hinckley spoke to 1,000 people and dedicated a monument memorializing the victims of the Mountain Meadows Massacre.

In October 1999, the last general conference in the Tabernacle on Temple Square was held, ending an era of holding conferences there that dated back to 1867. Six months later, on 1-2 April 2000, the first general conference in the 21,000-seat Conference Center was held. Granite for the exterior of the building came from the same area in Little Cottonwood Canyon as the Salt Lake Temple more than 100 years earlier. The Conference Center was dedicated at the 170th Semiannual General Conference on 8 October 2000 by President Hinckley.

An estimated worldwide audience of 3.5 billion watched as the 2002 Winter Games were hosted by Salt Lake City. Many Latter-day Saints worked as volunteers for the games.

The winter home of President Brigham Young in St. George was rededicated in May 2003, after an extensive project strengthened its structure by reinforcing walls and roof and returning it to its original color.

The Church's interest in maintaining a pleasant environment around Temple Square is reflected in the completion of the Main Street Plaza in 2000 and the purchase for remodeling of the Crossroads Mall immediately south of Temple Square in 2003.

In 2002, membership in Utah reached 1,678,941.

At general conference on 2 October 2004, President Hinckley announced that a third temple would be built in Salt Lake County. The location was later announced to be the Draper City area in the southeast corner.

President Gordon B. Hinckley met with 5,700 members from four stakes in the St. George area in southern Utah who were victims of massive flooding in January that washed away 22 homes and severely damaged another 76, leaving an estimated $7-8 million in mortage debt. Gathered in a hastily prepared meeting Feb. 26, 2005, in the Burns Arena, President Hinckley offered solice and a blessing, commending the members for their faith in the face of "some serious problems."

Construction of a new Church History Library was announced April 20, 2005. The five-story building was to be located in downtown Salt Lake City on the northeast corner of North Temple and Main Street. Plans called for the new building to incorporate updated technology and significantly increase archival storage capacity to preserve Church records. Current collections include 3.5 million manuscripts and 100,000 photographs.

Membership was 1,702,807 in 2003.

President Thomas S. Monson presided over all 12 sessions of the Draper Utah Temple dedication held March 20-22, 2009. "There is nothing like the dedication of a temple to bring out the best in people," he said. The Draper temple, the 129th operating temple in the Church, became the third temple in the Salt Lake Valley. The temple is surrounded by a high density of membership.

Only months later, on Aug. 21, 2009, President Monson celebrated his 82nd birthday by dedicating the Oquirrh Mountain Utah Temple in nine sessions over three days. The Oquirrh temple became the fourth in the Salt Lake Valley, the 13th in Utah and the130th in the Church. The temple is located in an area of rapid growth.

The historic Provo Tabernacle was destroyed by a four-alarm fire Dec. 17, 2010, that began when a high-energy stage light was carelessly placed on wood. President Thomas S. Monson announced in October 2011 General Conference that the historic edifice would be restored to its original beauty and redesigned as a temple.

Sources: S. George Ellsworth, Utah's Heritage, 1972; Richard D. Poll, general editor, Utah's History, 1978; Melvin S. Bashore. Pioneer Companies that Crossed the Plains, 1988; Andrew Jenson, Encyclopedic History of the Church, 1941; John L. Hart, "Let the Book of the Past be Closed," Church News, 18 September 1999; Andrew Jenson, Church Chronology, 1914; 2004 Church Almanac; James E. Talmage, The House of the Lord, 1976; Deseret Industries website, www.srbug.com/utah/deseret/htm; Through Our Eyes, 150 Year History as Seen Through the Eyes of the Writers and Editors of the Deseret News, 1999; "Despite flood waters faith still intact," Church News, 5 March 2005; "New, five-story Church History library to be built at headquarters," Church News, 23 April 2005; "Salt Lake Valley's fourth temple opens," Church News, 29 August 2009.

Stakes — 551
(Listed alphabetically as of Oct. 1, 2011.)

No.	Name	Organized	First President
Utah North Area — 143			
918	Benson Utah	7 May 1978	Dale Morgan Rindlisbacher
193	*Bountiful Utah		
	‡Bountiful	23 Mar 1952	Thomas Amby Briggs
2912	Bountiful Utah YSA	1 May 2011	Jacob L. Boyer
539	*Bountiful Utah Central		
	‡Bountiful Center	10 Jan 1971	Steven S. Davis
383	*Bountiful Utah East		
	‡Bountiful East	29 Sep 1963	Rendell N. Mabey
546	*Bountiful Utah Heights		
	‡Bountiful Heights	16 May 1971	Jesse Earl Godfrey
1127	Bountiful Utah Mueller Park	27 Apr 1980	Duane Bowring Welling
260	*Bountiful Utah North		
	‡Bountiful North	20 Apr 1958	Henry E. Peterson
1206	Bountiful Utah North Canyon	9 Nov 1980	Robert Heiner Garff
71	*Bountiful Utah Orchard		
	*Davis South	29 May 1970	
	‡South Davis	20 Jun 1915	James H. Robinson
262	*Bountiful Utah South		
	‡Bountiful South	20 Apr 1958	Ward C. Holbrook
1269	Bountiful Utah Stone Creek	24 May 1981	Richard S. Lemon
501	*Bountiful Utah Val Verda		
	‡Val Verda	25 Jan 1970	Milton W. Russon
382	*Brigham City Utah		
	‡Brigham City	22 Sep 1963	Lawrence C. Taylor
148	*Brigham City Utah Box Elder		
	*Box Elder	30 Aug 1959	
	‡South Box Elder	12 Nov 1944	Abel S. Rich
147a	*Brigham City Utah North		
	*Box Elder North	29 May 1970	
	‡North Box Elder	12 Nov 1944	John P. Lillywhite
375	*Brigham City Utah South		
	*Box Elder South	29 May 1970	
	‡South Box Elder	28 Apr 1963	LeGrande Tea

1242	Brigham City Utah West	8 Mar 1981	Lowell Sherratt Jr.
575	*Centerville Utah		
	‡Centerville	21 May 1972	Joseph A. Kjar
1798	Centerville Utah Canyon View	12 May 1991	Bruce Garrett Pitt
1335	Centerville Utah North	11 Apr 1982	Richard C. Edgley
903	Centerville Utah South	9 Apr 1978	Robert A. Trump
277	*Clearfield Utah		
	‡Clearfield	12 Apr 1959	George Smith Haslam
966	Clearfield Utah North	8 Oct 1978	Alfred Clyde Van Wagenen
2308	Clearfield Utah South	9 Feb 1997	Phillip Michael Hardison
728	Clinton Utah	9 Nov 1975	Albert DeMar Mitchell
1467	Clinton Utah North	15 Apr 1984	Jay Barr Snelgrove
2909	Clinton Utah West	10 Apr 2011	Robert A. Reed
152	*Farmington Utah		
	‡Davis	14 Oct 1945	Leroy H. Duncan
1342	Farmington Utah North	16 May 1982	Richard J. White
1769	Farmington Utah Oakridge	19 Aug 1990	Jerry L. King
1750	Farmington Utah South	13 May 1990	John Leon Sorenson
2579	Farr West Utah	3 Dec 2000	Steven Merrill Petersen
2836	Farr West Utah Poplar	14 Jun 2009	John Lee Watson
1531	Fielding Utah	12 May 1985	Mark H. Jensen
1568	Fruit Heights Utah	27 Oct 1985	Newell John Law
59	*Garland Utah		
	‡Bear River	11 Oct 1908	Milton H. Welling
1494	Harrisville Utah	23 Sep 1984	Robert Lynn Nielsen
141	*Hooper Utah		
	‡Lakeview	22 Mar 1942	John Child
924	Huntsville Utah	14 May 1978	Marlin K. Jensen
1559	Hyde Park Utah	22 Sep 1985	Vincent Eugene Erickson
46	*Hyrum Utah		
	‡Hyrum	30 Apr 1901	William C. Parkinson
1046	Hyrum Utah North	5 Aug 1979	J. Spencer Ward
1635	Kanesville Utah	19 Apr 1987	Roland B. Hadley
350	*Kaysville Utah		
	‡Kaysville	18 Feb 1962	Alan B. Blood
2101	Kaysville Utah Central	24 Sep 1995	Wesley H. Wilcox
1027	Kaysville Utah Crestwood	13 May 1979	Wallace Eldean Holliday
568	*Kaysville Utah East		
	‡Kaysville East	27 Feb 1972	Lawrence E. Welling
2617	Kaysville Utah Haight Creek	2 Nov 2003	Scott Richard Crapo
1010	Kaysville Utah South	11 Mar 1979	Newell John Law
2710	Kaysville Utah West	4 Mar 2006	Justin Tyler Brown
203	*Layton Utah		
	‡Layton	25 Jan 1953	I. Haven Barlow
2609b	Layton Utah Creekside	20 April 2003	Steven L. Hatch
449	*Layton Utah East		
	‡Layton East	4 Feb 1968	Robert F. Bitner
957	Layton Utah Holmes Creek	3 Sep 1978	K. Roger Bean
2062	Layton Utah Kays Creek	11 Jun 1995	Stephen George Handy
2196	Layton Utah Layton Hills	19 May 1996	S. Clair Bankhead
2910	Layton Utah Legacy	17 April 2011	Daren Gayle Stevenson
1529	Layton Utah North	5 May 1985	Lorin Winslow Hurst Jr.
1657	Layton Utah Northridge	11 Oct 1987	Samuel Clair Bankhead
1629	Layton Utah South	8 Feb 1987	William C. Barney Jr.
1948	Layton Utah Valley View	27 Jun 1993	Floyd Stenquist
858	Layton Utah West	21 Aug 1977	William C. Barney Jr.
2913	Layton Utah YSA	1 May 2011	C. Vance Downs
80	*Logan Utah		
	‡Logan	4 Jun 1920	Oliver H. Budge
13	*Logan Utah Cache		
	‡Cache	21 May 1877	Moses Thatcher
1422	Logan Utah Cache West	22 May 1983	Miles Peter Jensen
1241	Logan Utah Central	8 Mar 1981	Thad August Carlson
164	*Logan Utah East		
	*Cache East	29 May 1970	
	‡East Cache	2 Feb 1947	J. Howard Maughan
160	*Logan Utah Mount Logan		
	‡Mount Logan	17 Nov 1946	A. George Raymond
1347	Logan Utah South	6 Jun 1982	Ronald Skeen Peterson
259	*Logan Utah University 1st		
	‡Utah State University	13 Apr 1958	Reed Bullen
427	*Logan Utah University 2nd		
	‡Utah State University 2nd	12 Feb 1967	Reynold K. Watkins
785	Logan Utah University 3rd	14 Nov 1976	LaGrande C. Larsen
1719	Logan Utah University 4th	7 May 1989	Russell Miles Warren
2069	Logan Utah University 5th	25 Jun 1995	Bartell Cowley Jensen
2488	*Logan Utah University 6th	11 Sep 1998	
	*Logan University 6th	2 Aug 1998	Hyrum Grant Vest Jr.
2519	Logan Utah University 7th	21 Mar 1999	Steven Lee Stowers
2646	Logan Utah University 8th	22 Aug 2004	Byron Robert Burnham
2416	Mendon Utah	23 Nov 1997	Edwin Hyrum Jenson
16	*Morgan Utah		

	‡Morgan	1 Jul 1877	Willard G. Smith
1240	Morgan Utah North	8 Mar 1981	Robert Warner Poll
2644	Nibley Utah	20 June 2004	Ronald Dale Bliesner
528	*North Logan Utah		
	‡Cache North	11 Oct 1970	Charles L. Hyde
2244	North Logan Utah Green Canyon	22 Sep 1996	Jerry Allen Wilson
146	*North Ogden Utah		
	‡Ben Lomond	21 Nov 1943	William Arthur Budge
956	North Ogden Utah Ben Lomond	27 Aug 1978	Calvin J. Heiner
1804	North Ogden Utah Coldwater	23 Jun 1991	Eugene Jensen Low
2566	North Ogden Utah East	13 Aug 2000	Carl L. Grunander
1016	North Salt Lake Utah	15 Apr 1979	Clare Anderson Jones
2864	North Salt Lake Utah Legacy	15 Nov 2009	Ronald B. Gordon Jr.
1333	*North Salt Lake Utah Parkway	14 Nov 1999	
	‡Woods Cross Utah East	21 Mar 1982	Wayne A. Beers
57	*Ogden Utah		
	‡Ogden	19 Jul 1908	Thomas B. Evans
998	Ogden Utah Burch Creek	4 Feb 1979	J. Kirk Moyes
199	*Ogden Utah East		
	*Ogden East	29 May 1970	
	‡East Ogden	23 Nov 1952	Scott B. Price
198	*Ogden Utah Lorin Farr		
	‡Lorin Farr	16 Nov 1952	Elton W. Wardle
140	*Ogden Utah Mound Fort	23 Sep 1984	
	*Ogden Utah Farr West		
	‡Farr West	18 Jan 1942	Wilmer J. Maw
1157	Ogden Utah Mount Lewis	29 Jun 1980	Kenneth J. Alford
314	*Ogden Utah North		
	‡Ben Lomond South	20 Nov 1960	Robert M. Yorgason
2652	Ogden Utah Pleasant Valley	10 Oct 2004	Michael Vincent Houtz
458	*Ogden Utah University Stake	18 Oct 1998	
	*Weber State University Stake	21 Aug 1990	
	*Ogden Utah College		
	‡Weber State College	12 May 1968	E. LaMar Buckner
2619	Ogden Utah University 2nd	9 Nov 2003	George Blake Wahlen
520a	*Ogden Utah Weber		
	‡Weber	16 Aug 1970	Nathan C. Tanner
272	*Ogden Utah Weber Heights		
	‡Weber Heights	30 Nov 1958	Keith W. Wilcox
58	*Ogden Utah Weber North		
	*Weber North	29 May 1970	
	‡North Weber	19 Jul 1908	James Wotherspoon
1191	*Ogden Utah West	23 Nov 1993	
	‡Ogden Utah Weber South	12 Oct 1980	Allan T. Clarke
2798	Perry Utah	13 Apr 2008	Bruce O. Tams
876	Plain City Utah	30 Oct 1977	Kent W. Calvert
559	*Pleasant View Utah		
	‡Ben Lomond West	21 Nov 1971	Jay Herbert Rhees
2808	Pleasant View Utah South	19 Oct 2008	Kevin Brent Keller
561	*Providence Utah		
	‡Providence	12 Dec 1971	Asa L. Beecher
1351	Providence Utah South	13 Jun 1982	Lanny J. Nalder
2880	Providence Utah YSA	29 Aug 2010	
47	*Richmond Utah		
	‡Benson	1 May 1901	William H. Lewis
201	*Riverdale Utah		
	*Ogden Utah Riverdale	14 Mar 1995	
	‡Riverdale	30 Nov 1952	Rudolph L. VanKampen
2865	River Heights Utah	15 Nov 2009	William B. Cook
328	*Roy Utah		
	‡Roy	26 Mar 1961	Henry Adolph Matis
1485	Roy Utah Central	24 Jun 1984	Mark Lee Angus
2567	Roy Utah Midland	13 Aug 2000	Grant L. Morgan
438	*Roy Utah North		
	‡Roy North	11 Jun 1967	Walter D. Bingham
1673	Roy Utah South	24 Jan 1988	Alonzo C Heiner
942	Roy Utah West	11 Jun 1978	Lewis R. Child
119	*Smithfield Utah		
	‡Smithfield	9 Jan 1938	Alfred W. Chambers
1384	Smithfield Utah North	21 Nov 1982	W. Noble Erickson
2877	Smithfield Utah South	2 May 2010	Douglas A. Nielson
2881	Smithfield Utah YSA	29 Aug 2010	
139	*South Ogden Utah		
	‡South Ogden	7 Dec 1941	William J. Critchlow
1705	South Weber Utah	27 Nov 1988	LeRoy Horace Poll
424	*Sunset Utah		
	‡Sunset	11 Dec 1966	John L. Nicholas
70a	*Syracuse Utah		
	*Davis North	29 May 1970	
	‡North Davis	20 Jun 1915	Henry H. Blood
2658	Syracuse Utah Bluff	31 Oct 2004	David Lawrence Cook Jr.
2758	Syracuse Utah Legacy Park	10 Mar 2007	Lyle R. Elmore
1858	Syracuse Utah South	26 Apr 1992	Wesley Miller White

2555	Syracuse Utah West	30 Apr 2000	David Lawrence Cook Jr.
2917	Syracuse Utah Lake View YSA	1 May 2011	Robert W. Ferrell
173	*Tremonton Utah		
	*Bear River South	29 May 1970	
	‡South Bear River	1 May 1949	Clifton G.M. Kerr
1004	Tremonton Utah South	25 Feb 1979	Boyd Lee Cullimore
2879	Tremonton Utah West	15 Aug 2010	Chris W. Thurgood
371	*Washington Terrace Utah		
	‡Washington Terrace	24 Feb 1963	Ernest B. Wheeler
798	*Washington Terrace Utah South	3 Dec 1996	
	Ogden Utah Terrace View	12 Dec 1976	Leo Neeley Harris
2805c	Washington Utah East	22 June 2008	Randon Brant Jones
1043	Wellsville Utah	17 Jun 1979	Donald Joseph Jeppesen Jr.
578	*West Bountiful Utah	9 Oct 1984	
	*Bountiful Utah West		
	‡Bountiful West	11 Jun 1972	Clarence D. Samuelson
2885	West Haven Utah	17 Oct 2010	Jeffrey J. Charlesworth
1128	West Point Utah	27 Apr 1980	Vern L. Thurgood
2604	West Point Utah Lakeside	9 Sep 2001	Allen James Bennett
1506	Willard Utah	25 Nov 1984	Robert Kent Lund
498	*Woods Cross Utah		
	‡Woods Cross	4 Jan 1970	D. Hatch Howard
2608a	Woods Cross Utah North	28 Oct 2001	Brent B. Cleverly

Stakes discontinued

20	Box Elder	19 Aug 1877	Oliver G. Snow
	Discontinued 12 Nov 1944		
	†North Box Elder (147), South Box Elder (148)		
14	Davis	17 Jun 1877	William R. Smith
	Discontinued 20 Jun 1915 †North Davis (70), South Davis (71)		
2b	Weber	26 Jan 1851	Lorin Farr
	Discontinued 14 Jun 1970 †Mount Ogden (87)		
87	*Ogden Utah Mount Ogden		
	‡Mount Ogden	21 May 1922	Robert I. Burton
	Discontinued	10 Oct 2004	
1133	Ogden Utah Canyon View	18 May 1980	Luan Holly Ferrin
	Discontinued	17 Oct 2004	

Utah Salt Lake City Area — 187

664	Bennion Utah	27 Oct 1974	John Labrum
1459	Bennion Utah East	29 Jan 1984	Jack L. Green
1482	*Bennion Heights Utah	28 Aug 1988	
	‡Bennion Utah Central	17 Jun 1984	Glen A.Weight
875	Bennion Utah West	30 Oct 1977	Glen A. Weight
1521	Bluffdale Utah	10 Mar 1985	Michael Van Jeppson
18	*Coalville Utah		
	‡Summit	9 Jul 1877	William W. Cluff
142	*Draper Utah		
	‡Mount Jordan	3 May 1942	Stanley A. Rasmussen
2913	Draper Utah YSA	1 May 2011	Stephen L. Olsen
2422	Draper Utah Corner Canyon	7 Dec 1997	Brent Reynolds Bonham
2273	Draper Utah Crescent View	17 Nov 1996	Craig Eugene Middleton
1319	*Draper Utah Eastridge	25 Aug 1991	
	‡Draper Utah North	6 Dec 1981	Richard D. Alsop
2717	Draper Utah Mountain Point	30 Apr 2006	Curtis Eugene Morgan
2611b	Draper Utah River View	27 April 2003	Craig Eugene Middleton
2605b	Draper Utah South Mountain	10 Nov 2002	Rodolfo C. Franco
2647	Fort Herriman Utah	27 June 2004	James William Nielsen
147	*Grantsville Utah		
	‡Grantsville	16 Jan 1944	Paul E. Wrathall
1069	Grantsville Utah West	23 Sep 1979	Don Henning Johnson
2486	Herriman Utah	28 Jun 1998	Carmen Ray Freeman
2705	Herriman Utah Rose Canyon	28 Jan 2006	Russell Jeremy Davey
2704	Herriman Utah South	28 Jan 2006	David Christian Roth
2604d	Herriman Utah West	26 Jan 2003	Lindsay A. Thomas
106	*Kamas Utah		
	*Summit South	29 May 1970	
	‡South Summit	8 Jul 1934	Zach J. Oblad
255	*Kearns Utah		
	‡Kearns	2 Feb 1958	Merrill A. Nelson
1055	Kearns Utah Central	26 Aug 1979	Garth D. Mecham
990	Kearns Utah East	10 Dec 1978	Earl M. Monson
653	Kearns Utah South	25 Aug 1974	Garth D. Mecham
1462	Kearns Utah West	12 Feb 1984	Rodney W. Bushman
1258	Kearns Utah Western Hills	26 Apr 1981	Clarence Myron White
90	*Magna Utah		
	‡Oquirrh	3 Jun 1923	George A. Little
1013	Magna Utah Central	8 Apr 1979	Charles Robert Canfield
410	*Magna Utah East		
	‡Oquirrh East	17 Oct 1965	William B. Martin
1510	Magna Utah South	20 Jan 1985	Hendrick Dorenbosch
246	*Midvale Utah		
	‡Midvale	30 Jun 1957	Reed H. Beckstead

457	*Midvale Utah East		
	*Midvale East	29 May 1970	
	‡East Midvale	5 May 1968	R. Kent King
1561	Midvale Utah North	13 Oct 1985	Grant Leon Pullan
96a	*Midvale Utah Union Fort		
	*Midvale Utah Fort Union		
	*Fort Union	17 Jun 1973	
	*Jordan East	9 May 1970	
	‡East Jordan	8 May 1927	Heber J. Burgon
2509	Midvale Utah Union Park	24 Jan 1999	David D. Cerva
183	*Murray Utah		
	‡Murray	11 Feb 1951	Oral J. Wilkinson
2914	Murray Utah YSA	1 May 2011	Craig P. Burton
543	*Murray Utah Little Cottonwood	8 Jan 1989	
	*Murray Utah East		
	‡Little Cottonwood	21 Feb 1971	James S. McCloy
1009	Murray Utah North	11 Mar 1979	John Mace Johnson
1849	Murray Utah Parkway	1 Mar 1992	Dan Alan Anderson
240	*Murray Utah South		
	‡Murray South	28 Apr 1957	Donald W. Challis
468	*Murray Utah West		
	‡Murray West	24 Nov 1968	Robert H.M. Killpack
1520	Park City Utah	10 Mar 1985	B. Douglas Glad
303	*Riverton Utah		
	‡Riverton	18 Sep 1960	J. Harold Berrett
2573	Riverton Utah Central	17 Sep 2000	William Charles Mills
2564	Riverton Utah Copperview	25 Jun 2000	Ronald L. Larsen
2898	Riverton Utah Harvest Park	23 Jan 2011	Dean B. Ellis
1067	Riverton Utah North	23 Sep 1979	Keith LeRoy Bergstrom
2262	Riverton Utah South	3 Nov 1996	David Blaine Brown
1843	Riverton Utah Summerhill	19 Jan 1992	L. Chad Campbell
	Riverton Utah YSA	1 May 2011	Walter J. Plumb, III
1a	Salt Lake	3 Oct 1847	John Smith
576	*Salt Lake Big Cottonwood		
	‡Big Cottonwood	28 May 1972	Robert B. Barker
115	*Salt Lake Bonneville		
	‡Bonneville	27 Oct 1935	Joseph L. Wirthlin
603	*Salt Lake Brighton		
	‡Butler South	4 Mar 1973	Alvin Don Nydegger
361	*Salt Lake Butler		
	‡Butler	18 Nov 1962	James C. Taylor
418	*Salt Lake Butler West		
	‡Butler West	8 May 1966	Sherman M. Crump
204	*Salt Lake Cannon		
	‡Cannon	1 Mar 1953	Fred H. Peck
237	*Salt Lake Canyon Rim		
	‡Canyon Rim	28 Oct 1956	Verl F. Scott
291	*Salt Lake Central		
	‡University West	7 Feb 1960	Lemonte Peterson
133	*Salt Lake Cottonwood		
	*Cottonwood	11 Feb 1951	
	‡Big Cottonwood	20 Oct 1940	Irvin T. Nelson
936	Salt Lake Cottonwood Heights	28 May 1978	R. Gordon Porter
150	*Salt Lake East Mill Creek		
	‡East Millcreek	17 Jun 1945	L.B. Gunderson
996	Salt Lake East Millcreek North	28 Jan 1979	Joel R. Garrett
129a	*Salt Lake Emigration		
	‡Emigration	10 Mar 1940	George A. Christensen
55	*Salt Lake Ensign		
	‡Ensign	1 Apr 1904	Richard W. Young
249	*Salt Lake Foothill		
	‡Monument Park West	29 Sep 1957	Frank Carl Berg
266	*Salt Lake Granger		
	‡Granger	8 Jun 1958	Wm. Grant Bangerter
491	*Salt Lake Granger East		
	‡Granger East	24 Aug 1969	David D. Lingard
324	*Salt Lake Granger North		
	‡Granger North	26 Feb 1961	Frankland J. Kennard
764	Salt Lake Granger South	22 Aug 1976	Gordon W. Evans
497	*Salt Lake Granger West		
	‡Granger West	4 Jan 1970	Dwayne T. Johnson
42	*Salt Lake Granite		
	‡Granite	28 Jan 1900	Frank Y. Taylor
1457	Salt Lake Granite Park	4 Dec 1983	Robert T. Fitt
92	*Salt Lake Grant		
	‡Grant	25 May 1924	Joseph J. Daynes
114	*Salt Lake Highland		
	‡Highland	8 Sep 1935	Marvin O. Ashton
154	*Salt Lake Hillside		
	‡Hillside	13 Jan 1946	Casper Hugh Parker
227	*Salt Lake Holladay		
	‡Holladay	18 Mar 1956	G. Carlos Smith Jr.
891	Salt Lake Holladay North	12 Feb 1978	John A. Larsen

460	*Salt Lake Holladay South		
	‡Holladay South	16 Jun 1968	Marvin L. Pugh
390	*Salt Lake Hunter		
	‡Hunter	5 Jan 1964	E. Verne Breeze
982	Salt Lake Hunter Central	19 Nov 1978	Evans T. Doxey
1533	Salt Lake Hunter Copperhill	12 May 1985	Stanley Martin Kimball
839	Salt Lake Hunter East	22 May 1977	Merrill Dimick
1539	Salt Lake Hunter South	9 Jun 1985	Morris L. Terry
582	*Salt Lake Hunter West		
	‡Hunter West	13 Aug 1972	Evans T. Doxey
863	Salt Lake Jordan	9 Oct 1977	Robert B. Arnold
162	*Salt Lake Jordan North		
	*Jordan North	29 May 1970	
	‡North Jordan	12 Jan 1947	John D. Hill
53	*Salt Lake Liberty		
	‡Liberty	26 Feb 1904	Hugh J. Cannon
2298	Salt Lake Little Cottonwood	5 Jan 1997	John L. Halverson
68	*Salt Lake Millcreek		
	*Millcreek	11 Feb 1951	
	‡Cottonwood	29 Nov 1914	Uriah G. Miller
187	*Salt Lake Monument Park		
	‡Monument Park	24 Jun 1951	George L. Nelson
1832	Salt Lake Monument Park North	24 Nov 1991	B. Lloyd Poelman
393	*Salt Lake Mount Olympus		
	‡Mount Olympus	12 Apr 1964	Orin R. Woodbury
904	Salt Lake Mount Olympus North	9 Apr 1978	William Schaubel Partridge
267	*Salt Lake Olympus		
	‡Olympus	29 Jun 1958	Heber E. Peterson
145	*Salt Lake Park		
	‡Park	24 Oct 1943	J. Percy Goddard
273	*Salt Lake Parleys		
	‡Parleys	7 Dec 1958	Walter J. Eldredge Jr.
54	*Salt Lake Pioneer		
	‡Pioneer	24 Mar 1904	William McLachlan
	Salt Lake Pioneer YSA	5 May 2011	Richard B. Kinnersley
130	*Salt Lake Riverside		
	‡Riverside	24 Mar 1940	John B. Matheson
222a	*Salt Lake Rose Park		
	‡Rose Park	9 Oct 1955	Joseph F. Steenblik
412	*Salt Lake Rose Park North		
	‡Rose Park North	28 Nov 1965	Joseph L. Lundstrom
345	*Salt Lake South Cottonwood		
	‡South Cottonwood	10 Dec 1961	James S. McCloy
144	*Salt Lake Sugar House		
	‡Sugar House	16 May 1943	Thomas M. Wheeler
178	*Salt Lake University 1st		
	*University 1st	30 Apr 1967	
	‡University	12 Feb 1950	J. Quayle Ward
433	*Salt Lake University 2nd		
	‡University 2nd	30 Apr 1967	Oscar W. McConkie Jr.
1488	Salt Lake University 3rd	19 Aug 1984	James S. Jardine
1934	Salt Lake University 5th	18 Apr 1993	Kem C. Gardner
2466	Salt Lake University 6th	17 May 1998	Harold Roger Boyer
2769	Salt Lake University 7th	23 Jun 2007	Walter J. Plumb
236	*Salt Lake Valley View		
	‡Valley View	28 Oct 1956	Lamont B. Gundersen
1928	Salt Lake Utah (Tongan)	28 Mar 1993	Pita Masaku Kinikini
2603a	Salt Lake Utah South (Tongan)	9 Sep 2001	Molitika Paongo Va'ivaka
1111	Salt Lake Wasatch	24 Feb 1980	Richard G. Peterson
105	*Salt Lake Wells		
	‡Wells	31 Dec 1933	Thomas E. Towler
182	*Salt Lake Wilford		
	‡Wilford	11 Feb 1951	George Z. Aposhian
274	*Salt Lake Winder		
	‡Winder	25 Jan 1959	M. Elmer Christensen
706	Salt Lake Winder West	21 Sep 1975	Wayne O. Ursenbach
2916	Sandy Utah YSA	1 May 2011	Dean R. Burgess
1489	Sandy Utah Alta View	19 Aug 1984	G. Scott Dean
611	*Sandy Utah Canyon View	31 Jul 1990	
	*Sandy Utah North		
	‡Sandy North (Utah)	29 Apr 1973	Eugene D. Tenney
955	Sandy Utah Central	27 Aug 1978	Charles Alma Jones
968	Sandy Utah Cottonwood Creek	15 Oct 1978	John Robert Ruppel
627	*Sandy Utah Crescent		
	‡Crescent Utah	21 Oct 1973	Allen Eugene Hilton
1110	Sandy Utah Crescent North	24 Feb 1980	Gerald Leigh Gunnell
1639	Sandy Utah Crescent Park	17 May 1987	Brad Jensen Sheppard
981	Sandy Utah Crescent South	19 Nov 1978	Marlin Alma Fairbourn
775	Sandy Utah Crescent Ridge		
	Sandy Utah Crescent West	24 Oct 1976	John Burton Anderson
365	*Sandy Utah East		
	‡Sandy East	13 Jan 1963	Orren J. Greenwood
972	Sandy Utah Granite	22 Oct 1978	William Stanley Bush

1367	Sandy Utah Granite South	17 Oct 1982	Charles Winston Dahlquist II
1612	Sandy Utah Granite View	26 Oct 1986	Alan Snelgrove Layton
1812	Sandy Utah Hidden Valley	25 Aug 1991	Mark James Pendleton
811	Sandy Utah Hillcrest	13 Feb 1977	Arnold Christensen
2339	Sandy Utah Lone Peak	13 Apr 1997	Byron Dale Jorgenson
1278	*Sandy Utah Midvalley	9 Oct 1988	
	‡Midvale Utah Fort Union South	14 Jun 1981	Kenneth William Kraudy
	Union South		
276	*Sandy Utah Mount Jordan	11 Aug 1998	
	*Sandy Utah		
	‡Sandy	12 Apr 1959	Stanley A. Rasmussen
579	*Sandy Utah West		
	‡Sandy West	11 Jun 1972	Reed Neff Brown
623	*Sandy Utah Willow Creek		
	‡Willow Creek	17 Jun 1973	Wayne E. Saunders
482	*South Jordan Utah		
	*South Jordan	30 Nov 1970	
	*Jordan South	29 May 1970	
	‡South Jordan	18 May 1969	Theron B. Hutchings
2708	South Jordan Utah Day Break	4 Mar 2006	John Noel Ivor McCorquindale
2612	South Jordan Utah Country Crossing	14 Sept 2003	Fred P. Burton
2087	South Jordan Utah Country Park	13 Aug 1995	Calvin H. Newbold
2809	South Jordan Utah Founders Park	18 Oct 2008	Michael Wade Cottle
1192	*South Jordan Utah Glenmoor	19 Sep 1993	
	‡South Jordan Utah West	12 Oct 1980	Calvin George Osborne
2532	South Jordan Utah Highland	13 Jun 1999	Roger Glen Christensen
1956	South Jordan Utah Parkway	19 Sep 1993	Roger Glen Christensen
1491	*South Jordan Utah River	18 Dec 1990	
	‡South Jordan Utah East	9 Sep 1984	Charles Elmo Turner
2128	South Jordan Utah River Ridge	19 Nov 1995	William H. Webb
138	*South Salt Lake	13 May 1979	
	*Salt Lake South		
	‡South Salt Lake	2 Sep 1941	Axel J. Andresen
2514	Stansbury Park Utah	21 Feb 1999	Douglas Brent Rose
2750	Stansbury Park Utah South	17 Feb 2007	Chad W Allred
217	*Taylorsville Utah		
	‡Taylorsville	10 Oct 1954	Wayne C. Player
598	*Taylorsville Utah Central		
	‡Taylorsville Central	4 Feb 1973	Richard A. Barker
629	Taylorsville Utah North	28 Oct 1973	LeVere Elihu Brady
1473	Taylorsville Utah North Central	13 May 1984	Floyd Keith Rupp
1461	Taylorsville Utah South	5 Feb 1984	Clinton D. Topham
809	*Taylorsville Utah Valley Park	4 Dec 1988	
	‡Taylorsville Utah West Central	6 Feb 1977	Floyd Keith Rupp
411	*Taylorsville Utah West		
	‡Taylorsville West	31 Oct 1965	Richard A. Barker
2918	Taylorsville Utah YSA	1 May 2011	Peter F. Evans
15	*Tooele Utah		
	‡Tooele	24 Jun 1877	Francis M. Lyman
2536	Tooele Utah East	15 Aug 1999	Kim Albert Halladay
206	*Tooele Utah North		
	*Tooele North	29 May 1970	
	‡North Tooele	29 Mar 1953	Orland T. Barrus
2651	Tooele Utah Valley View	12 Sep 2004	David Bruce Hall Jr.
928	Tooele Utah South	21 May 1978	Joel James Dunn
97	*West Jordan Utah		
	‡West Jordan	8 May 1927	Joseph M. Holt
1511	*West Jordan Utah Bingham Creek	29 Nov 1988	
	‡West Jordan Southeast	27 Jan 1985	Frederick James Haydock
2633	West Jordan Utah Cobble Creek	2 May 2004	Craig Edward Judd
2475	West Jordan Utah Copper Hills	7 Jun 1998	David Russell Murray
735	West Jordan Utah East	30 Nov 1975	Dale P. Bateman
929	*West Jordan Utah Heritage	9 Oct 1990	
	‡West Jordan Utah West	21 May 1978	Robert B. Rowley
2155	West Jordan Utah Jordan Oaks	14 Jan 1996	Jerrald M. Jensen
1099	*West Jordan Utah Mountain Shadows	6 Dec 1994	
	‡West Jordan Utah Central	27 Jan 1980	M. Curtis Jewkes
614	*West Jordan Utah Mountain View	21 Feb 1989	
	*West Jordan Utah South		
	‡Jordan River	20 May 1973	Max Curtis Jewkes
1311	West Jordan Utah Oquirrh	22 Nov 1981	Johannes Gerald Erkelens
2778	West Jordan Utah Oquirrh Point	21 Oct 2007	Troy D. Virgin
2647	West Jordan Utah Park	22 Aug 2004	Scott Blaine Linnel
1686	West Jordan Utah Prairie	7 Feb 1988	J. Kim Christensen
1443	West Jordan Utah River	18 Sep 1983	Dennis Arthur Hope
2496	West Jordan Utah River Oaks	20 Sep 1998	Martin Dean Hill
2703	West Jordan Utah Sunset Ridge	14 Jan 2006	Ivin Samuel Murphy
1509	West Jordan Utah Welby	20 Jan 1985	Russell Jean Abney
1512	*West Jordan Utah Westbrook	16 May 1989	
	‡West Jordan Utah North	3 Feb 1985	Henry Keonaona Chai II
2557	West Jordan Utah Westland	21 May 2000	Stephen Brown Allen
2919	West Jordan Utah YSA	1 May 2011	Richard W. Moffat
636	*West Valley Utah	17 Jan 1989	

	‡Salt Lake Granger Central	31 Mar 1974	Norman H. Bangerter
		Stakes discontinued	
1857	Salt Lake University 4th	15 Aug 2004	
1607	Salt Lake Eagle Gate	26 Aug 2003	
256	*Kearns Utah North		
	Discontinued 3 Feb 2002		
	‡Kearns North	2 Feb 1958	Volma W. Heaton
41	Jordan	21 Jan 1900	Orrin P. Miller
	Discontinued 8 May 1927 †East Jordan (96), West Jordan (97)		
275	*Salt Lake Granite Park		
	Discontinued 31 May 1979 †South Salt Lake (138)		
	‡Granite Park	22 Feb 1959	Rolf Christiansen
155	*Salt Lake Temple View		
	Discontinued 24 June 1979 †Salt Lake Wells (105), Salt Lake Liberty (53)		
	*Temple View	14 Apr 1946	
	‡Temple	13 Jan 1946	Adiel F. Stewart
	Draper Utah South Mountain	10 Nov 02	

Utah South Area — 221

44	*Alpine Utah		
	‡Alpine	13 Jan 1901	Stephen L. Chipman
2928	Alpine Utah YSA	5 Jun 2011	William B. Woahn
2206	Alpine Utah North	23 Jun 1996	Terry L. Brown
2616	Alpine Utah West	1 June 2003	Conrad Arthur Gottfredson
1526	Altamont Utah	21 Apr 1985	Everett Dee Roberts
376	*American Fork Utah		
	‡American Fork	12 May 1963	Stanley D. Roberts
2042	American Fork Utah Central	23 Apr 1995	Paul Joseph Rasband
1022	American Fork Utah East	29 Apr 1979	Dale Orville Gunther
2154	American Fork Utah Hillcrest	14 Jan 1996	Craig B. Terry
624	*American Fork Utah North		
	‡American Fork North	17 Jun 1973	Leland Forbes Priday
1218	American Fork Utah West	14 Dec 1980	Brent Lindsay Milne
7b	*Beaver Utah		
	‡Beaver	12 Mar 1869	John R. Murdock
897	Blanding Utah	5 Mar 1978	Fred Eugene Halliday
1283	Blanding Utah West	12 Jul 1981	Preston Gardner Nielson
1690	Bloomington Utah	6 Mar 1988	Steven Howard Peterson
225	*Brigham Young University 1st		
	‡Brigham Young University	8 Jan 1956	Antone K. Romney
295	Brigham Young University 2nd	17 Apr 1960	Bryan W. Belnap
296	Brigham Young University 3rd	17 Apr 1960	William Noble Waite
395	Brigham Young University 4th	3 May 1964	William R. Siddoway
396	Brigham Young University 5th	3 May 1964	A. Harold Goodman
397	Brigham Young University 6th	3 May 1964	Wayne B. Hales
431	Brigham Young University 7th	30 Apr 1967	Dean A. Peterson
432	Brigham Young University 8th	30 Apr 1967	David H. Yarn
478	Brigham Young University 9th	27 Apr 1969	Carl D. Jones
479	Brigham Young University 10th	27 Apr 1969	Ivan J. Barrett
688	Brigham Young University 11th	13 Apr 1975	Gregory E. Austin
689	Brigham Young University 12th	13 Apr 1975	Charles Verl Clark
973	Brigham Young University 13th	29 Oct 1978	Leo Preston Vernon
974	Brigham Young University 14th	29 Oct 1978	Curtis Nicholas VanAlfen
1605	Brigham Young University 15th	31 Aug 1986	H. Donl Peterson
1688	Brigham Young University 16th	21 Feb 1988	Donald J Butler
1722	Brigham Young University 17th	21 May 1989	Stanley Armond Taylor
1889	Brigham Young University 18th	28 Jun 1992	Clark D. Webb Jr.
2489	Brigham Young University 19th	9 Aug 1998	Thomas Edwin Myers
2535	Brigham Young University 20th	15 Aug 1999	Ed Jolley Pinegar
2543	Brigham Young University 21st	6 Feb 2000	James M. Harper
2645	Brigham Young University 22nd	27 June 2004	Vernon McKay Henshaw
23	*Castle Dale Utah		
	‡Emery	Aug 1880	Christen G. Larsen
413	*Cedar City University 1st	30 Apr 1995	
	*Southern Utah University	13 Dec 1990	
	*Cedar City Utah College		
	*Southern Utah State College	12 Oct 1969	
	‡College of Southern Utah	6 Jan 1966	Robert B. White Jr.
2045	Cedar City University 2nd	30 Apr 1995	Warren Morrill Woolsey
2520	Cedar City University 3rd	21 Mar 1999	Russell Grant Bulloch
172	*Cedar City Utah		
	‡Cedar	2 May 1948	David L. Sargent
2170	Cedar City Utah Canyon View	18 Feb 1996	Robert Browning Platt
2796	Cedar City Utah Cross Hollow	16 Mar 2008	Gregory James Powell
901	Cedar City Utah North	19 Mar 1978	Robert L. Blattner
316	*Cedar City Utah West		
	‡Cedar West	27 Nov 1960	Franklin D. Day
2582	Cedar Hills Utah	7 Jan 2001	Reed Stark Swenson
2691	Cedar Hill Utah West	6 Nov 2005	Richard Max Noble
65	*Delta Utah		
	‡Deseret	11 Aug 1912	Alonzo A. Hinckley

1068	Delta Utah West	23 Sep 1979	Glen Wilford Swalberg
62	*Duchesne Utah		
	‡Duchesne	14 Sep 1910	William H. Smart
2546	Eagle Mountain Utah	27 Feb 2000	Carl B. Faulkner
2674	Eagle Mountain Utah East	13 Mar 2005	R. Scott Buys
2875	Eagle Mountain Utah North	25 April 2010	Michael A. Kidd
2607	Eagle Mountain Utah West	22 Sep 2002	Dee Harold Draper
1564	Enoch Utah	20 Oct 1985	Robert Louis Blattner
2932	Enoch Utah West	19 June 2011	Calvin J. Rollins
134	*Enterprise Utah		
	‡Uvada (Utah, Nevada)	15 Dec 1940	Daniel J. Ronnow
1524	Ephraim Utah	24 Mar 1985	Joseph C. Nielsen
1525	*Ephraim Utah College 1st	25 Jun 1999	
	*Snow College Utah 1st	28 Apr 1996	
	‡Snow College Utah	24 Mar 1985	Allen P. Jacobson
2193	*Ephraim Utah College 2nd	25 Jun 1999	
	Snow College Utah 2nd	28 Apr 1996	Richard Wheeler
83	*Escalante Utah		
	‡Garfield	29 Aug 1920	Charles E. Rowan Jr.
1336	Ferron Utah	11 Apr 1982	Jerry D Mangum
6b	*Fillmore Utah		
	‡Millard	9 Mar 1869	Thomas Callister
2523	Goshen Utah	18 Apr 1999	David Byron Allen
89	*Gunnison Utah		
	‡Gunnison	6 May 1923	Allen E. Park
19	*Heber City Utah		
	‡Wasatch	15 Jul 1877	Abraham Hatch
649	Heber City Utah East	16 Jun 1974	Robert F. Clyde
2626	Heber City Utah North	18 Jan 2004	Jay Charles Niederhauser
1170	Helper Utah	24 Aug 1980	Robert E. Olsen
1167	Highland Utah	10 Aug 1980	Merlin B. Larson
1827	Highland Utah East	10 Nov 1991	Stephen Mark Studdert
2680	Highland Utah South	15 May 2005	A. Lynn Scoresby
2609a	Highland Utah West	11 Nov 2001	Larry M. Gibson
871	Huntington Utah	23 Oct 1977	Ira Wallace Hatch
104	*Hurricane Utah		
	‡Zion Park	8 Dec 1929	Claudius Hirschi
2180	Hurricane Utah West	10 Mar 1996	Scott W. Colton
2165	Ivins Utah	11 Feb 1996	Bruce Lynn Gubler
11	*Kanab Utah		
	‡Kanab (Utah, Arizona)	18 Apr 1877	L. John Nuttall
1638	*Kanab Utah Kaibab 20	Aug 1991	
	‡Kanab Utah South	3 May 1987	Nils G. Bayles
1294	*La Verkin Utah	30 Nov 1984	
	‡Hurricane Utah North	11 Oct 1981	Floyd Leon Lewis
100	*Lehi Utah		
	‡Lehi	1 Jul 1928	Anchor C. Schow
2912	Lehi Utah YSA	24 Apr 2011	Robert F. Elzey
2876	Lehi Utah Cedar Hollow	2 May 2010	Kenneth S. Raines
2556	Lehi Utah East	7 May 2000	Douglas C. Muir
2731	Lehi Utah Gateway	9 Sep 2006	Melvyn Frank Gurney
2608e	Lehi Utah Jordan River	16 Mar 2003	W. Kirk Evans
637	Lehi Utah North	5 May 1974	Francis Russell Hakes
2169	Lehi Utah South	18 Feb 1996	James Earl Smith
2730	Lehi Utah Traverse Mountain	9 Sep 2006	Christopher S. Yadon
1416	Lehi Utah West	8 May 1983	Boyd Sabey Stewart
2794	Lehi Utah Willow Park	17 Feb 2008	Douglas James Wilcox
1392	Lindon Utah	12 Dec 1982	Noel Thomas Greenwood
2603	Lindon Utah Central	17 Aug 2002	David P. Harding
2091	Lindon Utah West	20 Aug 1995	James La Verle Hacking
34	*Loa Utah		
	‡Wayne	27 May 1893	Willis E. Robison
43	*Manti Utah		
	*Sanpete South	29 May 1970	
	‡South Sanpete	9 Dec 1900	Canute Peterson
714	Mapleton Utah	19 Oct 1975	Jay M. Smith Jr.
2371	Mapleton Utah North	8 Jun 1997	Kenneth Harold Jones
1407	Midway Utah	27 Mar 1983	Wayne Watkins Probst
2543	Milford Utah	30 Jan 2000	Gary M. Jensen
553	*Moab Utah		
	‡Moab	19 Sep 1971	Leland D. Teeples
85	*Monroe Utah		
	*Sevier South	29 May 1970	
	‡South Sevier	30 Jan 1921	John E. Magleby
27	*Monticello Utah		
	‡San Juan (Utah, Colorado)	23 Sep 1883	Platte D. Lyman
102	*Moroni Utah		
	‡Moroni	16 Jun 1929	James Louis Nielsen
42a	*Mount Pleasant Utah		
	*Sanpete North	29 May 1970	
	‡North Sanpete	9 Dec 1900	Christian N. Lund
2330	Mount Pleasant Utah North	16 Mar 1997	Warren Lynn Benincosa

5b	*Nephi Utah		
	*Juab 1871		
	‡Nephi	20 Sep 1868	Jacob G. Bigler
1538	Nephi Utah North	9 Jun 1985	James Randy McKnight
166	Orem Utah		
	‡Orem	13 Apr 1947	Walter R. Holdaway
1668	Orem Utah Aspen	10 Jan 1988	Ross Steve Wolfley
1518	*Orem Utah Canyon View	1 Mar 1988	
	‡Orem Utah Northeast	3 Mar 1985	Jerry C. Washburn
2230	Orem Utah Cascade	8 Sep 1996	Richard Bryant Brady
271	*Orem Utah Cherry Hill	15 Apr 1988	
	*Orem Utah Sharon West		
	*Sharon West	29 May 1970	
	‡West Sharon	30 Nov 1958	Clyde M. Lunceford
1490	*Orem Utah College 1st	24 Jun 2001	
	*Orem Utah College	25 Jun 1999	
	*Orem Utah Student	8 Jan 1991	
	Orem Utah College	26 Aug 1984	Charles E. Peterson
2596	Orem Utah College 2nd		
2646	Orem Utah College 3rd	27 June 2004	William Steve Albrecht
751	Orem Utah East	21 Mar 1976	Mirl Blake Hymas
251	*Orem Utah Geneva Heights	5 Apr 1988	
	*Orem Utah West		
	‡Orem West	3 Nov 1957	Edward C. Bunker
2272	Orem Utah Heatheridge	17 Nov 1996	Wayne Thomas Watson
1581	*Orem Utah Hillcrest	27 Nov 1988	
	‡Orem Utah Sharon South	1 Dec 1985	Wynn Howard Hemmert
867	*Orem Utah Lakeridge	1 Mar 1988	
	‡Orem Utah South Central	16 Oct 1977	Gordon Max Thomas
2204	Orem Utah Lakeridge North	23 Jun 1996	Spencer Floyd Mack
1184	Orem Utah Lakeview	28 Sep 1980	Merrill Gappmayer
533	*Orem Utah North		
	‡Orem North	1 Nov 1970	Eli Karl Clayson
1682	Orem Utah Northridge	31 Jan 1988	Larry V. Perkins
1176	Orem Utah Park	7 Sep 1980	Richard S. Johns
103	*Orem Utah Sharon		
	‡Sharon	15 Sep 1929	Arthur V. Watkins
812	*Orem Utah Sharon Park	20 Dec 1988	
	‡Orem Utah Central	13 Feb 1977	Clifton M. Pyne
862	*Orem Utah Suncrest	1 Mar 1988	
	‡Utah West Central	18 Sep 1977	James Edwin Mangum
554	*Orem Utah Sunset Heights	19 Apr 1988	
	*Orem Utah South		
	‡Orem South	19 Sep 1971	Richard P. Shumway
1048	Orem Utah Timpview	12 Aug 1979	Carl Crawford
905	Orem Utah Windsor	9 Apr 1978	Dennis LeRoy Hill
12	*Panguitch Utah		
	‡Panguitch	23 Apr 1877	James Henrie
5a	*Parowan Utah		
	‡Parowan	May 1852	John C.L. Smith
		13 Jan 1901	Jonathan S. Page Jr.
45	*Payson Utah	25 Mar 1997	
	*Payson Utah Nebo	18 Mar 1997	
	‡Nebo	13 Jan 1901	Jonathan S. Page Jr.
2614	Payson Utah East	19 May 2002	Logan Neal Nilsson
2805a	Payson Utah Mount Nebo	18 May 2008	Rodney H. Newman
634	*Payson Utah Mountain View	9 Aug 1994	
	‡Payson Utah East	24 Mar 1974	David R. Mangelson
1297	*Payson Utah South	25 Mar 1997	
	*Payson Utah Mount Loafer	18 Mar 1997	
	‡Payson Utah South	18 Oct 1981	Joe Lynn Spencer
1310	*Payson Utah West	25 Mar 1997	
	*Payson Utah Spring Creek	18 Mar 1997	
	‡Payson Utah West	22 Nov 1981	Gerald M. Finch
529	*Pleasant Grove Utah		
	‡Pleasant Grove	11 Oct 1970	Leon R. Walker
894	Pleasant Grove Utah East	26 Feb 1978	Evan Mack Palmer
2551	Pleasant Grove Utah Garden	9 Apr 2000	Rex Lewis Barrington
1958	Pleasant Grove Utah Grove Creek	24 Oct 1993	David Wesley Dickerson
1124	Pleasant Grove Utah Manila	23 Mar 1980	Grant Kay Fugal
2749	Pleasant Grove Utah Mount Mahogan	10 Feb 2007	David A. Miles
2426	Pleasant Grove Utah North Field	11 Jan 1998	Daniel Boyd Fugal
101	*Pleasant Grove Utah Timpanogos		
	‡Timpanogos	1 Jul 1928	Wilford W. Warnick
2829	Pleasant Grove Utah West	17 May 2009	Jon Ross Bratt
61	*Price Utah		
	‡Carbon	8 May 1910	Gustave A. Iverson
2247	Price Utah College	13 Oct 1996	Michael A. Harrison
151	*Price Utah North		
	*Carbon North	29 May 1970	
	‡North Carbon	24 Jun 1945	Cecil Broadbent
127	*Provo Utah		
	‡Provo	19 Feb 1939	Charles E. Rowan Jr.

1437	Provo Utah Bonneville	28 Aug 1983	Norman Dean Anderson
3b	*Provo Utah Central		
	*Utah 1855		
	‡Provo	19 Mar 1851	Isaac Higbee
165	*Provo Utah East		
	*Provo East	29 May 1970	
	‡East Provo	13 Apr 1947	Golden Le Grand Woolf
541	*Provo Utah Edgemont		
	‡Edgemont	17 Jan 1971	Richard A. Call
1692	Provo Utah Edgemont North	20 Mar 1988	Clayton S. Huber
899	Provo Utah Edgemont South	19 Mar 1978	Keith Hale Hoopes
1209	Provo Utah Grandview	23 Nov 1980	Laren R. Robison
2271	Provo Utah Grandview East	17 Nov 1996	John Melvin Beck Jr.
547	*Provo Utah Grandview South	13 June 2000	
	*Provo Utah North		
	‡Provo North	30 May 1971	Wayne Alvin Mineer
2187	Provo Utah North Park	21 Apr 1996	Brent A. Gines
821	Provo Utah Oak Hills	10 Apr 1977	John R. Christiansen
2681	Provo Utah Parkway	15 May 2005	Patrick Wade Shumway
200	*Provo Utah Sharon East		
	*Sharon East	29 May 1970	
	‡East Sharon	23 Nov 1952	Henry D. Taylor
1090	Provo Utah South	2 Dec 1979	Moorlan Wayne Snow
1424	Provo Utah Sunset	29 May 1983	Glen Howard Snyder
2734	Provo Utah Wasatch (Tongan)	6 Oct 2006	Semisi Folau Makai
167	*Provo Utah West		
	*Utah West	29 May 1970	
	‡West Utah	4 May 1947	J. Earl Lewis
10a	*Richfield Utah		
	‡Sevier	24 May 1874	Joseph A. Young
848	Richfield Utah East	12 Jun 1977	Warren T. Harward
82	*Roosevelt Utah		
	‡Roosevelt	26 Jun 1920	William H. Smart
1458	Roosevelt Utah East	11 Dec 1983	Earl V. Allred
685	Roosevelt Utah West	2 Mar 1975	Alvin Leonard Bellon
9a	*St. George Utah		
	‡St. George (Utah, Arizona)	7 Nov 1869	Joseph W. Young
1623	*St. George Utah		
	Bloomington Hills	20 Nov 1994	
	Bloomington Hills Utah	4 Jan 1987	James Grey Larkin
759	*Saint George Utah College 1st	25 June 1998	
	‡St. George Utah College	30 May 1976	Peter A. Nyberg
2492	Saint George Utah College 2nd	16 Aug 1998	Charles Jeffrey Morby
322	*St. George Utah East		
	‡St. George East	5 Feb 1961	Rudger C. Atkin
1813	St. George Utah Green Valley	25 Aug 1991	La Rell David Muir
2688	St. George Utah Little Valley	28 Aug. 2005	Marshall R. Topham
1999	St. George Utah Morningside	20 Nov 1994	James Grey Larkin
1625	*St. George Utah Pine View	12 Dec 1989	
	‡Washington Utah West	18 Jan 1987	H. Carlyle Stirling
2737	St. George Utah Red Cliffs	28 Oct 2006	R. Daren Barney
1814	*St. George Utah Snow Canyon	9 Mar 1999	
	St. George Utah Dixie Downs	25 Aug 1991	Thomas Randy Judd
2605c	St. George Utah Sunset	26 Sep 2002	Lon E. Henderson
895	St. George Utah West	5 Mar 1978	Dale Gubler
2565	St. George Utah Washington Fields	25 Jun 2000	Terry L. Wade
686	*Salem Utah	8 Dec 1976	
	‡Spanish Fork Utah Salem	9 Mar 1975	Kent Blaine Hansen
2205	Salem Utah West	23 Jun 1996	Stanley W. Green
84	*Salina Utah		
	*Sevier North	29 May 1970	
	‡North Sevier	30 Jan 1921	Moroni Lazenby
1361	Santa Clara Utah	29 Aug 1982	Dale Gubler
74	*Santaquin Utah		
	*Santaquin-Tintic	2 Apr 1939	
	‡Tintic	22 Apr 1917	Erastus Franklin Birch
2676	Santaquin Utah North	17 Apr 2005	Chad Alvin Rowley
2270	Saratoga Springs Utah	16 sep 2001	Chad R. Wilkinson
2650	Saratoga Springs Utah North	12 Sep 2004	Samuel Ray Delis
2823	Saratoga Springs Utah South	22 Mar 2009	Ronald Buford Edwards
233	*Spanish Fork Utah		
	‡Spanish Fork	30 Sep 1956	Joseph Y. Toronto
2649	Spanish Fork Utah Canyon Ridge	12 Sep 2004	Lawrence Ralph Duffin
2602	Spanish Fork Utah Canyon View	9 Sep 2001	Brent Richard Butler
2179	Spanish Fork Utah East	10 Mar 1996	Allen Dredge Ward
2884	Spanish Fork Utah Maple Mountain	12 Sep 2010	
94	*Spanish Fork Utah Palmyra		
	‡Palmyra	23 Nov 1924	Henry A. Gardner
1115	Spanish Fork Utah South	9 Mar 1980	Wilbur Angus Stephenson
2869	Spanish Fork Utah River	23 Jan 2010	Christian D. Raleigh
900	Spanish Fork Utah West	19 Mar 1978	Clair O. Anderson
235	*Springville Utah		
	‡Springville	21 Oct 1956	Leo A. Crandall

2885	Springville Dry Creek	12 Sep 2010	
1483	Springville Utah Hobble Creek	17 Jun 1984	Donald Blaine Hadley
2584	Springville Utah Hobble		
	Creek West	21 Jan 2001	Larry Mark Brewer
93	*Springville Utah Kolob		
	‡Kolob	23 Nov 1924	George R. Maycock
705	*Springville Utah Spring Creek	21 Jun 1988	
	‡Springville Utah North	31 Aug 1975	F. Calvin Packard
2311	Springville Utah Spring Creek South	23 Feb 1997	Don D. Bloxham
2648	Springville Utah West	29 Aug 2004	Kelly Royal Norman
239	*Vernal Utah Ashley		
	‡Ashley	2 Dec 1956	William Budge Wallis
1434	Vernal Utah Glines	19 Jun 1983	Gayle F. McKeachnie
913	Vernal Utah Maeser	30 Apr 1978	Venil P. Johnson
30	*Vernal Utah Uintah	10 Jun 1986	
	*Vernal Utah		
	‡Uintah	11 Jul 1886	Samuel R. Bennion
991	Washington Utah	7 Jan 1979	Lorel Wynn Turek
2368	Washington Utah Buena Vista	1 Jun 1997	Leo G.Richardson
2805	Washington Utah East	21 Jun 2008	Randon Brant Jones
1193	Wellington Utah	12 Oct 1980	Charles V. Bradshaw

Stakes discontinued

122	Moon Lake	24 Apr 1938	Edwin L. Murphy

Discontinued 10 Nov 1957 †Duchesne (62)

17	Sanpete	4 Jul 1877	Canute Peterson

Discontinued 9 Dec 1900 †North Sanpete (42), South Sanpete (43)

Missions — 7
(As of Oct. 1, 2011; shown with historical number. See MISSIONS.)

(132) UTAH OGDEN MISSION
2133 Washington Blvd
Ogden, UT 84401

(222) UTAH PROVO MISSION
2520 N. University Ave., Ste. 100
Provo, UT 84604-3877

(187) UTAH SALT LAKE CITY MISSION
3487 S 1300 E.
Salt Lake City, UT 84106

(331) UTAH SALT LAKE CITY SOUTH MISSION
8060 S 615 E
Sandy, UT 84070

(304) UTAH SLC TEMPLE SQUARE MISSION
50 E. North Temple St.
Salt Lake City, UT 84150-1006

MISSIONARY TRAINING CENTER
2005 North 900 East
Provo, UT 84604

UTAH ST. GEORGE MISSION
107 So. 1470 East Ste 304
St. George, Utah 84790

Vermont

Jan. 1, 2011: Est. population, 621,000; Members, 4,384; Stakes, 1; Wards, 7; Branches, 5; Percent LDS, 0.7, or one in 144.

Joseph Smith Sr. and Lucy Mack met and courted in Tunbridge, Vt. After their marriage they lived on several Vermont farms and were renting from Lucy's father when their son Joseph was born at Sharon in 1805. Other early Church leaders born in Vermont include Oliver Cowdery and five members of the original Quorum of the Twelve — Brigham Young, Heber C. Kimball, Luke S. and Lyman E. Johnson and William Smith.

The first Latter-day Saint to visit Vermont was Jared Carter, who in October 1831, returned to his hometown of Benson to preach to relatives and other members of a Free Will Baptist congregation. Twenty-seven members of the group were baptized and a branch organized before Carter's mission ended in January 1832. Later that year, he preached in several other communities on both sides of the Green Mountains and baptized over 100 more. Also during 1832-1833, Orson Pratt and Lyman Johnson visited numerous Vermont towns and baptized more than 40 people.

By July 1835, when several members of the Quorum of the Twelve met at St. Johnsbury to organize the Vermont Conference, there were about 150 members in good standing in the state with branches at St. Johnsbury, Danville, Charleston, Andover and Benson. During the next 10 years, numerous missionaries worked in Vermont and other branches were organized. But from the beginning the state's Latter-day Saints were encouraged to gather to Kirtland, Ohio, and later centers farther west. After 1850, few Church members remained in the state and there was only limited contact with the Church until the Eastern States Mission was re-opened in 1893.

Junius F. Wells came from Utah in 1894 to visit Joseph Smith's birthplace. After viewing the ruins of the farmhouse, Wells felt moved to say, "Sometime we ought to mark this place with a monument to the faith of our people in Joseph Smith." In the spring of 1905, he returned to Vermont on assignment from the First Presidency to buy the site and in July, after suggesting the idea to President Joseph F. Smith, was commissioned to erect a monument there. President Smith, with one of his counselors, five members of the Twelve, and others came to dedicate the monument on 23 December 1905, the centennial of the Prophet's birth. By that time, a "Memorial Cottage" had been built, and in years to come, in one of the Church's earliest experiences with a visitors center, missionary couples welcomed visitors and made friends with area residents.

In July 1909, the Vermont Conference was organized and 16 elders were assigned to the state. A year later, a Sunday School was organized in Barre and eventually a branch, which was closed in 1921 after all but one of its families moved to Utah. In that year, the eight elders and two sister missionaries in Vermont were assigned to Bennington, Rutland, Montpelier and White River Junction, visited people in many other communities, and reported there were about 60 Church members in the state.

In late 1927, the Vermont Conference was transferred to the Canadian Mission, and in October 1937, became part of the newly-established New England States Mission. Three years later, the 10 missionaries assigned to Vermont were living in Burlington, Barre, and Rutland. Church membership had doubled to 120. By 1950, there were branches at Burlington and South Royalton, but half the Latter- day Saints in Vermont were not members of organized branches.

By 1970, there were half a dozen branches, most of which were raising funds to build meetinghouses. A new residence was built at the Joseph Smith Memorial, along with a separate bureau of information. After those facilities were dedicated in 1961, a meetinghouse was also built there for the South Royalton Branch. Other branches subsequently found building sites and raised sufficient money to begin constructing their own meetinghouses.

By April 1976, there were enough members of the Church that the Montpelier Vermont Stake was organized by Elder Boyd K. Packer of the Quorum of the Twelve, who a decade earlier had presided over Vermont as president of the New England States Mission. The new stake had 2,116 members and included the Burlington, Montpelier, Lyndon, and South Royalton wards and the Middlebury and Rutland branches in Vermont, as well as a ward in New Hampshire and another in New York. By 2004, the stake included 10 units in northern Vermont and a branch just over the New York state line in Westport. The southern portion of the state was divided between the Albany New York, Concord New Hampshire, and Springfield Massachusetts stakes.

Latter-day Saints in Vermont tend to identify closely with early Church history, in part because of renewed emphasis in recent years on the Joseph Smith Memorial. In December 1988, to give added prominence to the site, an annual Christmas lighting program was begun, while in June 1998, a lodge, covered pavilion, 15 log cabins, and other facilities were dedicated as a place for Latter-day Saints from across the United States to stay while visiting the site, as well as for priesthood leadership meetings, youth conferences, and other activities sponsored by Church units in New England and eastern Canada.

In 2002, membership reached 4,091.

President Gordon B. Hinckley lead a Churchwide celebration 23 December 2005 on the 200th anniversary of the Prophet Joseph Smith's birth by visiting the Prophet's birth place in Sharon where he and Elder M. Russell Ballard addressed the Church in a broadcast. "I feel as if I am straddling the centuries," he said. "Two hundred years ago, on this very day, in this very place, there was born a child who was prophetically named Joseph, after the name of his father."

Sources: Andrew Jenson, "Vermont Conference," Encyclopedic History of the Church, 1941; "Family Faced Struggles," Church News, 12 December 1992; Vermont District and South Royalton Ward, Manuscript histories and historical reports, Church Archives; Eric Barnouw, "The Benson Exodus of 1833: Mormon Converts and the Westward Movement, Vermont History, Summer 1986; Richard S. Williams, "The Missionary Movements of the LDS Church in New England, 1830-1850," thesis, 1969; Richard O. Cowan, "Yankee Saints: The Church in New England During the Twentieth Century," in Donald Q. Cannon, ed., Regional Studies in Latter-day Saint Church History: New England, 1988; Darel P. Bartschi, "The Joseph Smith Memorial: A 1905 Tribute to the Prophet and His Work," Ensign, February 1988; Proceedings at the Dedication of the Joseph Smith Memorial Monument, 1906, and Dedicatory Services for the Director's Residence and Bureau of Information at the Joseph Smith Birthplace, 1961, both in Church History Library; "1st Stake Formed in State of Vermont," Church News, 24 April 1976; Sheridan R. Sheffield, "Vermont: Members Reflect Spirit of Pioneers in State Rich in Church History" and "Joseph Smith Memorial Serves As Focal Point for The Church," both in Church News, 21 December 1991; Elder and Sister Wayne Bell, "Prophet's Birthplace All Aglow As Lights Go on for First Time," Church News, 24 December 1988; Linda S. Miller, "Camping Facilities Built at Birthplace of Joseph Smith," Church News, 25 July 1998; Gerry Avant, "Joseph, the Seer," Church News, 31 December 2005.

Stake — 1
(Listed alphabetically as of Oct. 1, 2011.)

No.	Name	Organized	First President
North America Northeast Area			
753	Montpelier Vermont	11 Apr 1976	C. Lynn Fife

Virginia

Jan. 1, 2011: Est. population, 7,769,000; Members, 89,297; Stakes, 19; Wards, 153; Branches, 42; Missions, 2; Percent LDS, 1.1, or one in 92.

The first Latter-day Saints to set foot in Virginia were Luke S. Johnson and William E. McLellin, who were sent to the "south countries" to preach the gospel in January 1832. Jedediah M. Grant is likely the first missionary to preach and baptize in an area that is now part of Virginia. He reported that in 1839 and 1840 he worked in the southwestern Virginia counties of Grayson, Patrick, Smyth, Washington and Wythe. Joshua Grant, Jedediah's brother reported 25 baptisms in Rich Valley, Smyth County, and that that there were 80 Latter-day Saints scattered throughout the county. Missionaries laboring in Tazewell County reported that there were 175 Church members by February 1843.

In September 1843, Jedediah M. Grant was appointed to preside over the Virginia Conference — as mission districts were then known. Four branches of the Church were mentioned: Little Nauvoo, Wythe County; Burke's Garden, Tazewell County; Rich Valley, Smyth County; and a Patrick County branch. At this same time several of the early Virginia Latter-day Saints began to gather with the Church in Nauvoo.

Following the death of Joseph Smith, and because of the increasing persecution in Nauvoo, a circular letter was issued by the Quorum of the Twelve calling missionaries home and local men were appointed to lead the congregations. Again, many Virginia converts moved to Nauvoo and prepared to move west.

While the Church moved to Utah, little missionary work was done in Virginia. In 1855 one missionary, Absalom M. Young, preached and cared for Church members in Virginia and North Carolina. In 1857 missionary David O. Rideout reported that "'Mormonism' is spreading in this country [Tazewell County] fast amidst great persecution." He reported being tarred and feathered while attempting to spread the gospel. Missionary work stopped at the outset of the Civil War in 1861 and did not resume until the Reconstruction era.

Between 1865 and 1874, a few missionaries preached in the American South. In the late 1860s two missionaries, Henry G. Boyle and Howard K. Coray, canvassed rural areas along the North Carolina-Virginia border and baptized 200 converts. However, missionary work became more organized after 1875 when the Church formally established the Southern States Mission with Henry G. Boyle, an 1843 convert from Virginia, as president.

Missionaries serving in Virginia during this time usually traveled without "purse or scrip," meaning that they had to rely on the hospitality of the local people for food and lodging. Missionaries often found it easier to live this principle in the rural areas rather than in the cities because of the hospitality of the country people, resulting in a predominantly rural membership. J. Golden Kimball, later called as president of the Southern States Mission from 1891 to 1894 and to the First Council of the Seventy in 1886, served in the Southern States Mission from 1883 to 1885 and labored in several rural Virginia counties.

In 1902, the First Presidency divided the Southern States Mission. Virginia was briefly placed in the Middle States Mission until the next year when it was returned to the Southern States Mission because of the sudden death the Southern States Mission President Ephraim H. Nye, who served from 1902 to 1903. Before he died in 1903, Nye assigned missionaries to work in cities. The change required some reduction in traveling without purse or scrip. By 1919, branches or Sunday Schools existed in Danville, Petersburg, Portsmouth and Richmond.

In 1928, the East Central States Mission was created, which included Virginia. And in 1947, the Central Atlantic States Mission was organized with headquarters in Roanoke, Virginia. In 1970, this mission was renamed the North Carolina-Virginia Mission. It was renamed the Virginia Mission in 1973, and the following year it became the Virginia Roanoke Mission. The Virginia Richmond Mission was created in 1992.

Following World War I and during the Depression many Latter-day Saints moved east to work in government positions in Washington D.C. In 1933, President Heber J. Grant dedicated the Washington D.C. Chapel, which became a focus of missionary work. By 1937, there were 1,800 members of the Church in the Washington area. A branch in what became the Capitol District was organized in Arlington, Va., in 1938. On 30 June 1940 the Washington Stake was organized with Ezra Taft Benson as president. It included parts of northern Virginia and the Arlington Branch became the first ward in Virginia. In October 1945, the branch in Richmond, which was transferred to the Washington Stake, became the Richmond Ward.

The Church in central and southern Virginia grew in the post-World War II era as the result of increased missionary work. On 30 June 1957, at a conference held in Portsmouth presided over by Elder Harold B. Lee of the Quorum of the Twelve, the Virginia Stake was organized with Cashell Donahoe Sr. as president, the first stake with all but one ward in Virginia. In March 1963, the Potomac Stake was organized. It took in the wards in Washington, northern Virginia, and southeastern Maryland. By December 2003, there were 17 stakes in Virginia.

In the 1960s and 1970s many urban families in America moved to the suburbs. Ethnic populations moved into inner city areas. Foreign language-speaking missionaries were called to serve in American inner cities. As the result, groups and branches holding worship services in foreign languages were formed. In 1984, the Mekong Branch of the McLean Virginia Stake was organized to meet the needs of Cambodian and Laotian Latter-day Saints. A year earlier the Dulles Branch, also called the Asian Branch, was formed in the Oakton Virginia Stake. As of June 2004, there were also seven Spanish-speaking units — three branches and four wards — in Virginia.

The growth of the Church in central Virginia was greatly accelerated by the creation of Southern Virginia College, located in Buena Vista, which was founded to fulfill the spiritual, intellectual and social potential of Latter-day Saint students, though the college is not owned or operated by the Church. The college, then known as Bowling Green Female Seminary, was ready to close its doors in 1996 when a group of LDS educators and businessmen reorganized it to become an institution serving the Latter-day Saint community. The influx of staff, students and faculty led to the organization of the Buena Vista Virginia Stake in June 1999, consisting of two branches and 10 wards, four of which are student wards.

Membership was 75,907 in 2003. In 2005, membership reached 80,592.

Sources: Journal History of the Church, 31 January 1832, Church Archives; Virginia District, Manuscript history and historical reports, Church Archives; LaMar C. Berrett, History of the Southern States Mission, 1831-1861, thesis 1960; Heather M. Seferovich, History of the LDS Southern States Mission, 1875-1898, thesis 1996; J. Golden Kimball, Journals, Church Archives; Ted S. Anderson, The Southern States Mission and the Administration of Ben E. Rich, 1898- 1908, thesis 1976; Richmond Virginia Stake, Manuscript history and historical reports, Church Archives; Julian C. Lowe and Florian H. Thayn, History of the Mormons in the Greater Washington Area: Members of the Church of Jesus Christ of Latter-day Saints in the Washington D.C. Area, 1839-1991, 1991; Southern Virginia College: General Information, 2 February 2001; O. Kendall White Jr., "Overt and Covert Politics: The Mormon Church's Anti-ERA Campaign in Virginia," The Virginia Social Sciences Journal, vol. 18 (winter 1983), 11-16.

Stakes — 19
(Listed alphabetically as of Oct. 1, 2011.)

No.	Name	Organized	First President
	North America East Area		
512	*Annandale Virginia		
	‡Mount Vernon	26 Apr 1970	Allen Claire Rozsa
2018	*Ashburn Virginia	29 Apr 2001	
	Warrenton Virginia	29 Jan 1995	Richard L. Brown
2530	Buena Vista Virginia	6 Jun 1999	Edwin Allen Sexton
740	*Centreville Virginia	29 Jan 1995	
	‡Fairfax Virginia	1 Feb 1976	Ed Mordue Hayward
1671	Chesapeake Virginia	17 Jan 1988	Joseph Craig Merrell
1198	Fredericksburg Virginia	26 Oct 1980	Douglas Lynn Marker
1325	McLean Virginia	14 Feb 1982	Earl John Roueche
1583	Mount Vernon Virginia	5 Jan 1986	Keith Alan Gulledge
846	Newport News Virginia	12 Jun 1977	Kirk Thomas Waldron
372	*Oakton Virginia		
	‡Potomac (Virginia, D.C., Md.)	3 Mar 1963	Miller F. Shurtleff
922	Pembroke Virginia	6 Jun 1999	
	*New River Virginia	24 Oct 1989	
	*Bluefield Virginia	14 May 1978	Norman Perry Tyler Jr.
245	*Richmond Virginia		
	‡Virginia (Va., N. C.)	30 Jun 1957	Cashell Donahoe Sr.
1450	Richmond Virginia Chesterfield	30 Oct 1983	John Leonard Ruckart Jr.
2699	Richmond Virginia Midlothian	4 Dec 2005	Michael Stanley Waters

499	*Roanoke Virginia		
	‡Roanoke	11 Jan 1970	Russell B. Maddock
392	*Virginia Beach Virginia	21 Jun 1994	
	*Norfolk Virginia		
	‡Norfolk (Virginia,		
	North Carolina)	12 Apr 1964	Walter H. Hick
934	*Waynesboro Virginia	16 Dec 1982	
	‡Charlottesville Virginia	28 May 1978	Wilford John Teerlink
837	Winchester Virginia	22 May 1977	Harold S. Harrison
2635	Woodbridge Virginia	16 May 2004	Grant Edward Lattin

Mission — 1

(As of Oct. 1, 2011; shown with historical number. See MISSIONS.)
Washington D.C. missions, though headquarters are located in Virginia and Maryland,
are listed under District of Columbia.

(42) VIRGINIA RICHMOND MISSION
9327 Midlothian Tpk, Suite 1-B
Richmond, VA 23235

Washington

Jan. 1, 2011: Est. population, 6,550,000; Members, 267,927; Stakes, 55; Wards, 459; Branches, 63; Missions, 5; Temples, 3; Percent LDS, 3.9, or one in 25.

In 1852, John Bozarth, a Church member who had lived in Nauvoo, Ill., settled on the Lewis River in Washington Territory. In 1854 four missionaries serving in California, John Hughes, Clark Faben, Alfred Bybee, and Silas Harris, were sent to labor in the Washington and Oregon territories. Hughes found the Bozarth family and other "lost Mormons" and organized a branch, but generally a spirit of intense persecution impeded the work. In 1857 David M. Stuart, Silas G. Higgins, Lorenzo F. Harmon, and John H. Winslow were sent to Oregon. During that time, Stuart reorganized the Lewis River Branch, ordaining John Bozarth an elder and "teacher of the branch." Among those who came forth to renew their covenants and to be rebaptized was Louisa A. John. Despite persecution, Louisa was faithful throughout her life. When she died in 1911, animosity against the Church was still so pronounced that her grave was dedicated secretly at night near Woodland, Wash.

Many Church members worked on the construction of the Northern Pacific and Oregon Short Line railroads in the 1880s and a few later moved into the Northwest. In 1896 a mission effort was organized under the direction of George C. Parkinson, president of the Oneida Stake in southeastern Idaho. Elder Edward Stevenson of the First Council of the Seventy was called to visit the states of Montana, Oregon, and Washington, and also the northern part of Idaho and start a mission. He took with him Matthias F. Cowley (later called as an apostle on 7 October 1897) and together they set out from Salt Lake City on 4 June 1896. After traveling through Montana, they took up missionary labors in Spokane, Wash., on 31 August 1896. They also worked in Palouse and Walla Walla before returning to Salt Lake City.

A second Northwestern States Mission was created under the direction of the Oneida Stake presidency on 26 July 1897 (the first Northwestern States Mission, created in 1878, had its headquarters in Chicago, Ill.). Of the initial six missionaries called, Gaston L. Braley and James R. Smurthwaite were sent to Walla Walla. The mission was initially comprised of the Oregon, Washington, and Idaho conferences. Mission President Franklin S. Bramwell established mission headquarters in Baker, Ore., in 1898, (later the mission was moved to Le Grande on 5 June 1900). By 1900, Washington had two conferences, the Eastern (Spokane) and Western (Tacoma) Washington conferences. In 1902, Nephi Pratt was called to be mission president. He established mission headquarters in Spokane on 14 May 1902. He later moved mission headquarters in Portland, Ore., on 1 January 1905.

While always endeavoring to preach and baptize new converts, missionaries also sought out scattered Church members, soliciting Church members in Utah to furnish them with addresses of relatives and friends living in Washington. The first branch in Washington was organized in Tacoma on 24 December 1899 with 21 members. A branch was organized in Seattle on 14 December 1902. A Sunday School was organized in Spokane on 9 September 1906 and a branch was organized 10 years later on 12 March 1916. In Walla Walla, where missionary work first began, a branch was not organized until 14 November 1927.

In 1930, membership in the state was 1,855 in eight branches, with chapels in Everett, Spokane, Seattle, and Olympia. The Seattle Stake, the first in Washington, was created on 31 July 1938. In 1940 membership in the state reached 5,000, and during World War II a great influx of members came to Washington to work in defense industries.

The completion of the Grand Coulee Dam on the Columbia River in the early 1940s opened the way for additional farming in the Columbia River Basin, and many members flocked to the state to farm. By 1960 membership had increased to 11,000. The Pacific Northwest Mission was created from the Northwestern States Mission in 1968, and was renamed the Washington Mission in 1970 and the Washington Seattle Mission in 1974. The Washington Spokane Mission was created on 1 July 1978 and the Washington Tacoma Mission was created on 1 July 1990. The Seattle Temple was dedicated by President Spencer W. Kimball on 17 November 1980. In 1992, Washington became the fifth state in the United States with at least 50 stakes. The Spokane Washington Temple, located in the Spokane suburb of Opportunity, was dedicated by President Gordon B. Hinckley on 21 August 1999. The Columbia River Washington Temple, located in Richland, was dedicated by President Hinckley on 18 November 2001.

The Washington Everett Mission was created on 1 July 2001 and the Washington Kennewick Mission was created on 1 July 2002, bringing the total number of missions in the state to five.

Membership was 240,593 in 2003.

Sources: Andrew Jenson, "Washington," Encyclopedic History of the Church of Jesus Christ of Latter-day Saints, 1941; Leonard J. Arrington, "History of the Church in the Pacific Northwest," Task Papers in LDS History, No. 18.; Lois Kullberg, "Louisa John, LDS Pioneer of the Pacific Northwest," unpublished manuscript, 2002, Church Archives; Kullberg, "Saints to the Columbia," L-K Publications, 2002; North American Northwest Area annual history and historical reports, Church

Stakes — 55
(Listed alphabetically as of Oct. 1, 2011.)

No.	Name	Organized	First President
North America Northwest Area			
2886	Arlington Washington	24 Oct 2010	Ronald J. Southworth
1388	Auburn Washington	28 Nov 1982	Alan Warner Bolles
388	*Bellevue Washington		
	‡Seattle East	1 Dec 1963	Raymond W. Eldredge
1244	Bellevue Washington South	Dec 2006	
	‡Renton Washington North	15 Mar 1981	Denzel Nolan Wiser
1266	Bellingham Washington	10 May 1981	Eugene Clifford Hatch
1312	Bothell Washington	22 Nov 1981	Arnold R. Parrott
299	*Bremerton Washington		
	‡Puget Sound	19 Jun 1960	Herbert S. Anderson
958	Centralia Washington	10 Sep 1978	Frank Edward Berrett
1299	Colville Washington	18 Oct 1981	Garnett Russell Port
1438	Elma Washington	28 Aug 1983	Lou Elwin Green
1148	Ephrata Washington	15 Jun 1980	Robert A. Hammond
532	*Everett Washington		
	‡Cascade South	25 Oct 1970	Wesley K. Duce
883	Federal Way Washington	20 Nov 1977	Jack Lynn Smith
	Gig Harbor Washington	11 Feb 2006	Karl J. Fields
2614a	Graham Washington	18 May 2003	Brian Lloyd McCoy
776	Kennewick Washington	24 Oct 1976	Elton Elias Hunt
1374	Kennewick Washington East	31 Oct 1982	Donald LeRoy Brunson
1495	Kent Washington	14 Oct 1984	Owen Edvin Jensen
1855	Kirkland Washington	19 Apr 1992	Robert Gideon Condie
2397	Lacey Washington	14 Sep 1997	Ralph W. Smith Jr.
1565	Lakewood Washington	20 Oct 1985	James Rolland Ely
599	*Longview Washington		
	‡Columbia River West	4 Feb 1973	Walter Lee Robinson
925	Lynnwood Washington	14 May 1978	Robert C. Barnard
2448	Maple Valley Washington	22 Mar 1998	Larry J. Thomas
1251	Marysville Washington	29 Mar 1981	Verle George Call
213	*Moses Lake Washington		
	‡Grand Coulee	18 Apr 1954	Elmo J. Bergeson
379	*Mount Vernon Washington		
	‡Cascade	30 Jun 1963	Robert E. Jones
440	*Olympia Washington		
	‡Olympia	27 Aug 1967	Herbert S. Anderson
1049	Othello Washington	12 Aug 1979	Jay L. Christensen
437	*Pasco Washington		
	‡Pasco (Washington, Oregon)	21 May 1967	David K. Barber
2900	Pasco Washington North	20 Feb 2011	D. Ross Montierth
1848	Port Angeles Washington	23 Feb 1992	Richard Ernest Shaw
542	*Puyallup Washington		
	‡Mount Rainier	17 Jan 1971	Owen H. Dickson
1389	Puyallup Washington South	28 Nov 1982	Dennis Tripp Sampson
844	Redmond Washington	29 May 1977	Arnold R. Parrott
514	*Renton Washington		
	‡Renton	3 May 1970	Harris A. Mortensen
180	*Richland Washington		
	‡Richland		
	(Washington, Oregon)	25 Jun 1950	James V. Thompson
124	*Seattle Washington		
	‡Seattle	31 Jul 1938	Alex Brown
242	*Seattle Washington North		
	*Seattle North	29 May 1970	
	‡North Seattle	19 May 1957	Wilford H. Payne
1496	Seattle Washington Shoreline	14 Oct 1984	Brent Isaac Nash
1023	*Selah Washington	31 Aug 1982	
	‡Yakima Washington North	29 Apr 1979	Robert Atwood Hague
1057	Silverdale Washington	26 Aug 1979	David Junior Jones
1890	Snohomish Washington	28 Jun 1992	Craig L. Morrison
168	*Spokane Washington		
	‡Spokane	29 Jun 1947	Albert I. Morgan
556	*Spokane Washington East		
	‡Spokane East	17 Oct 1971	James B. Cox
992	Spokane Washington North	7 Jan 1979	Dwaine E. Nelson
2594	Spokane Washington Valley	3 Jun 2001	Gary Fail Ely
1841	Spokane Washington West	12 Jan 1992	Elroy C. McDermott
195	*Tacoma Washington		
	‡Tacoma	28 Sep 1952	Elvin E. Evans
389	*Vancouver Washington		
	*Columbia River North	29 May 1970	
	‡North Columbia	1 Dec 1963	Wallace V. Teuscher
2467	Vancouver Washington East	17 May 1998	Thomas H. Jensen
1570	Vancouver Washington North	3 Nov 1985	Bruce A. Schreiner
979	Vancouver Washington West	5 Nov 1978	Earl Clifford Jorgensen
1011	Walla Walla Washington	11 Mar 1979	David L. Hafen

426	*Wenatchee Washington	7 Dec 1978	
	*Quincy Washington		
	‡Grand Coulee North	29 Jan 1967	Leslie H. Boyce
284	*Yakima Washington		
	‡Yakima	24 May 1959	F. Edgar Johnson
		Stakes discontinued	
1052	Tacoma Washington South	19 Aug 1979	James Rolland Ely
	Discontinued 2006		

Missions — 5
(As of Oct. 1, 2011; shown with historical number. See MISSIONS.)

(333b) WASHINGTON EVERETT MISSION
16124 35th Ave. SE (POB 13390)
Mill Creek, WA 98012-1390

(335a) WASHINGTON KENNEWICK MISSION
8656 Gage Blvd Ste 205
KENNEWICK, WA 99336

(78a) WASHINGTON SEATTLE MISSION
13353 Bel-Red Rd. Ste 103
Bellevue, WA 98005-2329

(166) WASHINGTON SPOKANE MISSION
820 S. Pines Rd Ste 101
Spokane, WA 99206-5420

(255) WASHINGTON TACOMA MISSION
4007-D Bridgeport Way W.
University Place, WA 98466-4330

West Virginia

Jan. 1, 2011: Est. population, 1,815,000; Members, 16,710; Stakes, 4; Wards, 26; Branches, 12; Missions, 1; Percent LDS, 0.9, or one in 109.

Luke S. Johnson and William W. McLellin were sent to what is now West Virginia by Joseph Smith on 25 January 1832. They preached in Cabell County, just over the Ohio River from Ohio on the western tip of West Virginia. The Prophet Joseph Smith visited Wheeling on 4 April 1832 and purchased paper for the Church's press that was then located in Jackson County, Mo. The paper was used to publish the Book of Commandments. That same year, Elder Amasa M. Lyman of the Quorum of the Twelve and an Elder Johnson baptized 40 converts in West Virginia. By 17 October 1836, Lorenzo D. Barnes reported that he and Samuel James had baptized enough converts to start a branch in Shinnston. Elder George A. Smith of the Quorum of the Twelve taught in a grammar school at, or near Shinnston, that had 75 members.

One convert was Bathsheba Wilson Bigler, who later became the wife of Apostle George A. Smith. She was baptized 21 August 1837, along with a number of other family members including her parents, brothers and sisters. She migrated to join the main body of saints shortly after baptism. She served as Relief Society general president from 1901-1910. Others immigrated to join with the saints, and the branches were discontinued. Missionary work did not resume until 28 December 1867.

Laboring in Logan County in June 1884, Andrew W. Spence and an Elder Vickers were served with a warrant for suspicion of being part of a band of robbers. The pair opened their satchels and not only convinced the officers that they were innocent, but also distributed tracts that opened the way for the missionaries to teach at the courthouse. From this opening, a branch of 26 members was organized. The West Virginia Conference was organized on 18 September 1886. A year later, missionaries from the Northern States Mission searched out and taught "Bickertonites," (see Pennsylvania history) but failed to make any headway among them.

West Virginia was placed in the Eastern States Mission on 14 March 1897. It became part of the Middle States Mission on 22 May 1902, but was reunited with the Eastern States Mission on 18 June 1903.

By 1906, George D. Ward and companion completed a small chapel for the Franklin Branch. One of the early converts in this branch was William Perry Hartman. Nearly 100 of his descendants joined the Church. Three branches were later organized because of his family's influence.

The West Virginia Conference was divided and the West Virginia North and South Conferences were created on 31 December 1930. The North conference had 888 members and the South conference had 1,397 for a statewide total of 2,285.

On 18 October 1942, Elder George Albert Smith of the Quorum of the Twelve was present at the Huntington Branch Chapel dedication. On 15 October 1949, Elder Harold B. Lee of Quorum of the Twelve visited West Virginia while on a tour of the East Central States Mission.

Membership grew slowly in West Virginia and during the 1950s and 1960s. Numerous branch chapels were built throughout West Virginia as the Church expanded its building program worldwide.

The first stake in West Virginia was created on 23 August 1970 in Charleston with a membership of 3,966. Units in West Virginia included the Asheland, Charleston, Charleston 2nd, Huntington, and Parkersburg Wards and the Beckley, Logan, Portsmouth, Ripley, Point Pleasant, and Webster Spring branches. The West Virginia Charleston Mission was organized on 1 July 1980. Additional stakes were created in Fairmont on 6 May 1979 and Huntington in 1982.

In 2002, membership reached 12,764, and 12,907 in 2003.

Sources: Andrew Jenson, Encyclopedic History of the Church, 1941; Lorenzo D. Barnes, Reminiscences and diaries, 1834-1839, Church Archives; Bathsheba Wilson Bigler Smith, Autobiography, Church Archives; Southern States Mission, Manuscript history and historical reports, Church Archives; Eastern States Mission, Manuscript history and historical reports, Church Archives; Northern States Mission, Manuscript history and historical report, Church Archives; Lisle G. Brown, "West Virginia and Mormonism's Rarest Book," West Virginia History, January/April 1978; Richard L. Jensen, "'Bell-Snickeled' Builders," Church News, 1 April 1978; Mike Cannon, "West Virginia," Church News, 2 October 1989.

No.	Name	Organized	First President
North America East Area			
522	*Charleston West Virginia		
	‡West Virginia (W. Va., Ky.)	23 Aug 1970	David L. Atkinson
1025	*Clarksburg West Virginia	7 Mar 2004	
	Fairmont West Virginia	6 May 1979	David Glenn Williams
1375	*Huntington West Virginia	23 Nov 2003	
	*Owingsville Kentucky	3 May 1995	
	Huntington West Virginia	7 Nov 1982	Grant Earl Jenson
2629	Martinsburg West Virginia	29 Feb 2004	Steven Charles Grow

Mission — 1

(As of Oct. 1, 2011; shown with historical number. See MISSIONS.)

(188) WEST VIRGINIA CHARLESTON MISSION
888 Oakwood Rd, Ste. 310
Charleston, WV 25314

Wisconsin

Jan. 1, 2011: Est. population, 5,628,000; Members, 24,496; Stakes, 6; Wards, 42; Branches, 27; Missions, 1; Percent LDS, 0.43, or one in 234.

In 1835, three years after joining the Church in New York, Moses Smith moved to Racine County, Wis., and is known as the first settler of Burlington, a city about 40 miles southwest of Milwaukee. Many of his family also moved from New York to Burlington and established Wisconsin's first Latter-day Saint congregation in 1837. The branch wrote a letter to Church leaders in Kirtland, Ohio, asking them to send missionaries to the state. Receiving no response, Moses and Aaron Smith traveled to Kirtland, and met with Joseph Smith, Sr., who recommended that both men be called as presiding elders over the Church in Wisconsin.

In 1841, Joseph Smith sent 14 members to the Black River Valley in Wisconsin Territory to obtain lumber from the pine forests to be used in the construction of the temple and other buildings in Nauvoo. Workers in this "pinery expedition" floated logs some 600 miles from Church-operated sawmills in Wisconsin to Nauvoo. The group grew to about 150 members and supplied the wood for the temple through 1844 when the group disbanded.

Besides the early labors of the Smiths, missionary Elisha H. Groves was called to Wisconsin in 1840 but only preached as far as northwestern Illinois. In 1841, Amasa Lyman and William O. Clark labored in Lafayette County and baptized several individuals including Albert Carrington, future member of the Quorum of the Twelve. The combined efforts of missionaries produced seven Mormon branches in the southern part of the state by 1844.

Following Joseph Smith's death in 1844, James J. Strang, a Wisconsin member and brother-in-law of Moses Smith, claimed to be the successor of the Prophet. Moses Smith eventually sympathized with Strang, and members from branches throughout Wisconsin became the core of Strang's splinter group until he was shot by a disgruntled follower in 1856. Many of Strang's followers helped form the Reorganized Church in 1860. Until Oliver Cowdery left to join the saints at Winter Quarters in 1848, he also resided in Wisconsin and practiced law and ran for political office.

After the 1846 exodus from Nauvoo, the second half of the 19th century saw some missionaries preaching in Wisconsin, followed by the few converts immigrating to Utah. It was not until the Wisconsin Conference of the Northern States Mission was organized in 1896 that the numbers of missionaries began to grow. The Church in Wisconsin expanded rapidly within the next four years, with branches being organized in Fond du Lac, Milwaukee and La Crosse. Christopher Leonard Rueckert, a former missionary in Wisconsin, was assigned by the Church in 1903 to return to Milwaukee with his family and head the new branch. On 23 March 1907, a branch chapel was dedicated. Rueckert oversaw the growth of the Church in Milwaukee from 1904 to 1914, when he died unexpectedly.

During the Depression, the saints in Milwaukee built and paid for a new building which President Heber J. Grant and Elder Rudger Clawson of the Quorum of the Twelve dedicated in 1933. When the Chicago Stake in Illinois was organized in 1936, the Milwaukee Ward was created and included in that stake. This ward was divided in 1958 and the Milwaukee Stake was created in 1963 with Demitt C. Smith as president.

During the 1930s and 1940s, membership grew in Wisconsin through the migration of Latter-day Saints seeking educational and business pursuits particularly in Madison and the larger cities. Growth also occurred through missionary work which expanded on 1 July 1978 with the formation of the Wisconsin Milwaukee Mission. In 1992, the Wisconsin Mormon Sesquicentennial was celebrated, which included a historically focused musical composition by Crawford Gates performed on July 25 by the Milwaukee Symphony Orchestra and the Mormon Tabernacle Choir.

In 2002, membership reached 21,018.

Sources: Andrew Jenson, Encyclopedic History of the Church, 1941; David L. Clark, And They Came Singing: Mormons in Wisconsin, Church Archives; Jill Murvay Derr, "The Pinery Expedition," Church News, 8 April 1978; R. Scott Lloyd, "Mormons in Milwaukee," Church News, 5 December 1998.

Stakes — 6

(Listed alphabetically as of Oct. 1, 2011.)

No.	Name	Organized	First President
North America Central Area			
1597	Appleton Wisconsin	11 May 1986	Nevin Richard Limburg
2335	Green Bay Wisconsin	23 Mar 1997	Ronald S. Godfrey
702	*Madison Wisconsin	11 Apr 1982	
	‡Beloit Wisconsin	24 Aug 1975	Arval Lewis Erikson
2612	Milwaukee Wisconsin North	14 Apr 2002	Walter Lamar Barlow

367	*Milwaukee Wisconsin South	14 Apr 2002	
	*Milwaukee Wisconsin		
	‡Milwaukee	3 Feb 1963	DeWitt C. Smith
2261	Wausau Wisconsin	3 Nov 1996	Robert Thomas Growcock

Mission — 1

(As of Oct. 1, 2011; shown with historical number. See MISSIONS.)

(167) WISCONSIN MILWAUKEE MISSION
5651 Broad St.
Greendale, WI 53129-1889

Wyoming

Jan. 1, 2011: Est. population, 533,000; Members, 63,069; Stakes, 16; Wards, 133; Branches, 21; Percent LDS, 11.5, or one in 9.

Among the earliest Latter-day Saints to enter Wyoming was a group of Mississippi converts immigrating to the West in 1846. They hoped to join the saints en route to the Great Basin and stopped a few miles below Fort Laramie, Wyo., in July 1846. While there, they learned that the vanguard company had decided to winter in Nebraska. The Mississippians left Wyoming for Pueblo, Colo. Some from the group joined Brigham Young's pioneer wagon train the next year that entered Wyoming on 31 May 1847. The Mississippi emigrants included members of the Mormon Battalion sick detachment as well. On 28 June 1847, the combined company under Brigham Young met famed mountain man Jim Bridger in southwestern Wyoming, who gave them a generally optimistic appraisal of the Great Basin area. Brigham Young directed the construction of ferries on the Platte and Green rivers and assigned men to remain there and run them. By the end of 1847, over 2,000 Mormons had crossed Wyoming into Utah.

The Church established a colony near Fort Bridger in 1853, named Fort Supply. It was Wyoming's first non-military agrarian settlement and provided supplies for emigrant companies traveling from the East. The colony was abandoned and burned at the advance of Johnston's Army in 1857. Fort Bridger, purchased by the Church in 1855, was partially burned at the same time.

The Oregon, California, and Mormon trails crossed through the middle of the state so most Mormon companies traveled through Wyoming as part of their westward migration. The majority of these groups made the trip without incident, but the Willie and Martin handcart companies of 1856 were trapped in early winter snows before reaching South Pass, Wyo., and about 200 of the 1,075 in the two companies died of starvation and exposure. The rest were saved by rescue parties from Utah. Some of the rescuers, under the leadership of Dan Jones, remained at Martin's Cove through the winter of 1856-1857 to protect emigrant goods left behind. They occupied the abandoned Fort Seminoe. Brigham Young later purchased the site in behalf of the Church. In 2003, the Church constructed a facsimile of Fort Seminoe at its site near Devil's Gate.

In 1862, President Abraham Lincoln asked Brigham Young to station men along the emigrant road to protect the telegraph lines and mail routes on the plains during the Civil War. Young complied by sending 120 Mormons to live at various sites in Wyoming until they were relieved by federal troops.

In the early 1850s, Brigham Young, as Church president and superintendent of Indian Affairs of Utah Territory, befriended Eastern Shoshone Chieftain Washakie. The federal government placed Washakie's people on the Wind River Reservation in west central Wyoming in 1868 and forbade missionary efforts there by the Mormons. Even so, missionary work was done, and in September and October 1880, there were 310 members of the tribe baptized, including Chief Washakie who was baptized by Amos R. Wright on 25 September 1880.

Church leaders Moses Thatcher and William Preston began seeking areas in 1877 for Mormon colonization and traveled to investigate the Salt River Valley of western Wyoming. They found it to be a promising location and in 1878, the valley was dedicated for Mormon settlement by Brigham Young Jr. Its name was soon changed to Star Valley. The first Latter-day Saint settlers came from the Bear Lake Valley in Idaho Territory. They stayed through the winter of 1879-80 near what is now Auburn, Wyo. In the 1880s, the settlements of Grover, Afton, Freedom, Smoot, Thayne, Bedford, and Fairview were established. Wyoming's first stake was organized in Star Valley on 13 August 1892. Even today, the region is composed primarily of Latter-day Saints.

In 1893, a settlement was begun in a corner of the Big Horn Basin of north central Wyoming. Mormons relocating from Uintah County, Utah, under direction of Elder Abraham O. Woodruff of the Quorum of the Twelve created an irrigation system and established the town of Burlington. In 1900, Wyoming Gov. DeForest Richards petitioned President Lorenzo Snow for help in settling a much larger area of the Big Horn country. In response, Mormon communities were established in Byron, Cowley, Penrose, Owen, and Lovell. The Big Horn Stake comprised of these communities was organized on 26 May 1901.

Increasing Latter-day Saint populations in the areas of Fort Bridger, Kemmerer, Evanston, and Rock Springs caused the First Presidency to authorize creation of the Woodruff Stake on 6 June 1898. It encompassed Wyoming's southwest corner and the northeastern corner of Utah including Randolph and Woodruff, and was headquartered initially in Evanston. On 18 July 1926, the Woodruff Stake was divided and the Lyman Stake was organized.

The worldwide outbreak of the Spanish Influenza in 1918 caused the cessation of missionary work in some Wyoming communities for several months. A thriving congregation in Hanna, Wyo., was hit especially hard by the disease and several of the most active members died. A missionary sent from Cheyenne to nurse the sick members also contracted the disease but survived.

President Heber J. Grant dedicated an institute of religion building on the campus of the University of Wyoming at Laramie in 1936. It was the third such program instituted in the Church.

In the late 1940s, Church leaders in Cody hired Mormon architect Douglas W. Burton to design a new building for their congregation. At the same time, they contracted with world-renowned artist Edward T. Grigware, who had retired to Cody, to produce a mural for the new building's foyer that would depict the history of the Church. The building was completed in

1949 and the mural in 1951. The artwork remains in place in the foyer of the functioning meetinghouse. It is considered Grigware's masterpiece and that portion of the building housing the mural continues to generate interest as the Church's Cody Murals Visitors Center.

Steady growth of the Church in Wyoming characterized the period of the 1930s to the 1980s. Cheyenne's increasing Mormon population during that time justified creation of the Cheyenne Stake in June 1959. Creation of the Casper and Wind River stakes followed in 1962. During the 1970s and 1980s, a total of eight stakes were organized.

Wyoming's statehood centennial in 1990 gave numerous opportunities to highlight the significant contributions of Latter-day Saints in the state. As part of the year-long celebration, the University of Wyoming prepared an exhibit on the history of the Church at the Wyoming American Heritage Center. Mormon sculptor and Wyoming native Peter M. Fillerup cast a 14-foot high bronze of a cowboy on the famous bucking bronco "Steamboat." The artwork was the only sculpture officially sanctioned by the Wyoming Centennial Commission.

In 1992, as part of Riverton Wyoming Stake's "Second Rescue" program, three monuments were erected in west central Wyoming in memory of the Willie and Martin handcart companies. The monuments were dedicated 15 August 1992 by President Gordon B. Hinckley, then first counselor in the First Presidency. Members of the stake also researched family histories and performed temple ordinances for those handcart pioneers whose work had not previously been completed. The Church later purchased the site surrounding a monument at the mouth of Sweetwater Canyon where 21 people perished in one night. It was dedicated in 1994 by President Hinckley.

The portion of the Mormon Trail running through Wyoming was highlighted by the Sesquicentennial Mormon Trail Wagon Train Re-enactment group in 1997. Members and non-members participated in and welcomed the train as it traveled through the state. On 3 May 1997, President Hinckley dedicated a new visitors center at Martin's Cove in central Wyoming in memory of the Willie and Martin companies. The wagon train's travel through Wyoming also provided an opportunity on 5 July 1997 to re-enact the 1858 raid by Lot Smith and the Mormon militia on Johnston's army. President Hinckley dedicated historical markers at that site. Also in 1997, the surviving fragment of a wall built by Mormons at Fort Bridger was repaired and dedicated.

A proposal to sell Martin's Cove to the Church was approved by a vote of the U.S. House of Representatives early in October 2002. The bill, while supported by Church members in Wyoming, was hotly contested by Wyoming's Congressional delegation following public hearings at which many local residents opposed the sale. Although the Church considers the site sacred and has built walking paths to it from adjacent Church property, Congress failed to pass the legislation. The Church later signed a 25-year Bureau of Land Management lease to manage the site.

Membership in 2003 was 55,540. In 2005, membership reached 57,217.

A temple was announced for Star Valley by President Thomas S. Monson on 1 October 2011, the first temple in Wyoming.

Sources: Andrew Jenson, *Encyclopedic History of the Church*, 1941; Daniel H. Ludlow, ed., "Pioneer Settlements in Wyoming," *Encyclopedia of Mormonism*, v. 4, 1992; Arnold K. Garr, Donald Q. Cannon, and Richard O. Cowan, eds., Lowell A. Bangerter, "Wyoming," and Jay G. Burrup, "Chief Washakie," *Encyclopedia of Latter-day Saint History*, 2000; Western States Mission, Manuscript history and historical reports, Church Archives; Lee Roland Call, Star Valley and Its Communities, 1970; Rosa Vida Bischoff Black, Lovell: Our Pioneer Heritage, 1984; Frederick R. Gowans and Eugene E. Campbell, Fort Supply: Brigham Young's Green River Experiment, 1976; Mae Urbanek, Wyoming Place Names, 1988; Cody Ward, The Cody Mural: A Pictorial History of Mormonism, 1957; "Centennials Preserving Heritage: Mormon Settlers helped to Make Wyoming a State," *Church News*, 26 May 1990; R. Scott Lloyd, "University of Wyoming Exhibit Spotlights LDS Pioneer Heritage," *Church News*, 15 December 1990; Julie A. Dockstader, "Wyoming's 'Untamable Spirit' Captured," *Church News*, 22 December 1990; Dell Van Orden, "'Second Rescue' of Handcart Pioneers," *Church News*, 22 August 1992; Julie A. Dockstader, "Project Stands As Reminder of Legacy," *Church News*, 30 July 1994; Dell Van Orden, "'Hallowed Ground Made Sacred,'" *Church News*, 10 May 1997; Twila Van Leer, "Simpson's Hollow Events Recalled," *Church News*, 12 July 1997; "Lot Smith Descendants Honor Ancestor's Role," *Church News*, 12 July 1997; Twila Van Leer, "Portion of Wall At Fort Bridger Reminder of Era," *Church News*, 19 July 1997; Greg Hill, "A Day To Remember in Wyoming," *Church News*, 19 May 2001; Greg Hill, "Temple Work Opened Way for Projects," *Church News*, 19 May 2001.

Stakes — 16
(Listed alphabetically as of Oct. 1, 2011.)

No.	Name	Organized	First President
North America Central Area — 8			
357	*Casper Wyoming		
	‡Casper	14 Oct 1962	W. Reed Green
286	*Cheyenne Wyoming		
	‡Cheyenne (Wyo., Colo.)	21 Jun 1959	Archie R. Boyack
593	*Cody Wyoming		
	‡Cody	7 Jan 1973	Parley J. Livingston
1158	Gillette Wyoming	29 Jun 1980	Marion A. Dalene
1420	Laramie Wyoming	15 May 1983	Philip Munro Hoyt
48	*Lovell Wyoming		
	‡Big Horn	26 May 1901	Byron Sessions
358	*Riverton Wyoming		
	‡Wind River	14 Oct 1962	J. Rex Kocherhans
1194	Worland Wyoming	12 Oct 1980	David Harris Asay
Utah North Area — 2			
33	*Afton Wyoming		
	‡Star Valley	14 Aug 1892	George Osmond
975	Thayne Wyoming	29 Oct 1978	Marlow C. Bateman
Utah Salt Lake City Area — 6			
38	*Evanston Wyoming		
	‡Woodruff (Wyoming, Utah)	5 Jun 1898	John M. Baxter
1493	Evanston Wyoming South	23 Sep 1984	Harold Sidney Stock
660	Green River Wyoming	23 Sep 1984	Ronald Clyde Walker
708	Kemmerer Wyoming	12 Oct 1975	Merrill R. Anderson
790	Lyman Wyoming	21 Nov 1976	Ronald C. Walker
95	*Rock Springs Wyoming		
	‡Lyman (Wyoming, Utah)	18 Jul 1926	H. Melvin Rollins

WORLDWIDE CHURCH

Territories or possessions are listed under the name of the administering country.

Numbers preceding stakes and missions are their chronological numbers assigned at the time of creation. A letter means number was used previously. Re-use of the number corresponds with another stake being discontinued. Populations are rounded estimates.

* Name changed 14 Jan 1974 unless another date indicates otherwise

‡Original name

†Transferred to

ALBANIA

Jan. 1, 2011: Est. population, 3,639,000; Members, 1,984; Branches, 11; Districts, 1; Missions, 1; Percent LDS, .05 or one in 2,545; Europe Area.

Albania, governed by a young democracy, is a small mountainous country in southeastern Europe's Balkan Peninsula. It is 70 percent Sunni Muslim, with 20 percent Greek Orthodox and 10 percent Roman Catholic. The official language is Albanian.

There was no known Church activity in Albania until April 1991 when Elders Dallin H. Oaks and Hans B. Ringger visited the country. In October, Elder Hans B. Ringger and Austria Vienna Mission President Kenneth D. Reber visited with Albanian officials and agreed to send humanitarian aid to Albania. Missionaries Theron G. Sommerfeldt and George Niedens arrived a week later but were there only a short time. Full-time humanitarian missionary couples Thales and Charone Smith and Randolyn and Melvin Brady followed in February 1992, and in June, four full-time elders Matthew Wirthlin, Mark Slaybaugh, Paul McAllister, and Beau Jarvis were transferred there from other European missions. On 25 July 1992, Blendi Kokona became the first convert baptized in Albania.

In conjunction with a visit to Albania in August 1993 by Pope John Paul II, Mother Teresa visited an orphanage where Sister Charone Smith, a humanitarian missionary, was working. She presented Sister Smith with a silver medallion of Mother Teresa's order. That same month, Church activity in Albania came under supervision of the Switzerland Zurich Mission.

In 1994, the Provo Missionary Training Center began teaching the Albanian language. Prior to that time, missionaries learned the language in the field. In June 1995, responsibility for Albania was transferred to the Greece Athens Mission, where it remained until the creation of the Albania Tirana Mission on 1 July 1996. Missionaries were evacuated in March 1997 due to civil unrest. They returned to the mission throughout the summer of 1997, the last arriving in September. Another brief evacuation occurred in August-September 1998.

In November 1999 the Albanian translation of the Book of Mormon was received in the mission. The first seminary class in Albania was held on 24 February 2000 and the first institute class was held 24 March 2000.

Membership in 2003 was 1,285. In 2005, membership reached 1,498.

Sources: United States Department of State, The World Factbook, cia.gov/cia/publications/factbook..; Mehr, Kahlile, Mormon Missionaries Enter Eastern Europe, 2002; Donald Q. Cannon, and Richard O. Cowan, Unto Every Nation: Gospel Light Reaches Every Land, 2003. Albania Tirana Mission, Annual history, Church Archives.

(308) ALBANIA TIRANA MISSION
PO Box 2984, Rr. Qemal Stafa
Vila 1 (Perballe Postes nr. 22)
Tirana, Albania

AMERICAN SAMOA

Jan. 1, 2011: Est. population, 65,600; Members, 15,159; Stakes, 4; Wards, 31; Branches, 6; Percent LDS, 22.5 or one in 4.5; Pacific Area, Samoa Apia Mission.

Located in the South Pacific, American Samoa is a U.S. territory. The people are Protestant, 50 percent; LDS, 22 percent; and Roman Catholic, 20 percent.

On 24 January 1863, two missionaries from Hawaii arrived in Samoa. Kimo Pelia and Samuela Manoa had been sent by an apostate leader, Walter Murray Gibson. The pair labored faithfully for nearly 20 years without the knowledge or support of the Church. The number of baptisms performed by them was never recorded but ranged between 50 and 200.

After learning of Manoa's presence in Samoa, Joseph H. Dean was set apart by Hawaiian Mission president William King to begin missionary work in Samoa. Dean arrived in Aunu'u (now part of American Samoa) with his wife, Florence, on 21 June 1888. The Deans found that Pelia had died but Manoa was still very supportive and was rebaptized and reordained by Dean on 25 June. The same day, Dean baptized a woman named Malaea, who is considered his first Samoan convert. Dean remained in Aunu'u, but made infrequent trips to the island of Tutuila, and within four months 40 others had joined the Church (mostly on Aunu'u). C. K. Kapule, a Hawaiian whom Dean had asked to join him before he left Hawaii for Samoa, arrived on 13 August 1888. They traveled to Tutuila between 27-30 August 1888. During that time Dean baptized Lealao, the first known male baptized on Tutuila.

Missionary work began in earnest on Tutuila after William O. Lee, Edward J. Wood, and Adelbert Beasley arrived in October 1888. The first branch on Tutuila was started in Pago Pago on 27 May 1893, and before the turn of the 20th century, 12 branches had been organized, despite the difficulties caused by internal political conflicts between the German and U.S. governments. In 1899, the Samoan islands were divided between Germany and the United States. Western Samoa, which consists primarily of the islands of Upolu and Savai'i, became a German colony and Eastern Samoa (American Samoa) became a U.S. territory, of which Tutuila is the primary island. A Latter-day Saint village with a school and a supporting 360 acre plantation was founded at Mapusaga on 10 May 1903. Schools were started in a number of branches on Tutuila between 1900 and 1940. The most typical meetinghouse used during this period were large Samoan fales, an oval shaped thatched roof structure supported with pillars along the outer edge, with no walls.

Missionaries were recalled from American Samoa in 1940 prior to World War II, and local members assumed leadership of the branches. Only the mission president and his wife, Wilford W. and Hannahbel Emery, remained at the mission headquarters in Pesaga, Western Samoa. At the time Church membership in all of American Samoa numbered 650, with nine branches located at Tula, Alao, Aua, Pago Pago, Nu'uuli, Tafuga, Faleniu, Amaluia, and Mapusaga. The Mapasaga school had an enrollment of 112 students.

Mission president John Q. Adams was finally able to visit Tutuila in May 1944. The Church's lease to the village and school property had expired in 1943, but he was able to purchase the property as well as renew the lease for the 360 acre plantation.

Missionaries returned in 1946 and the mission re-established a school on the Mapusaga plantation property and in 1953 negotiated to purchase the plantation land. Mapusaga High School began its first classes on 19 September 1960. In 1965, the U.S. government built a new high school in Pago Pago large enough to accommodate students attending Mapusaga High School. However, almost half the students attending Mapusaga were from Western Samoa. The government eventually allowed Western Samoan children to attend Pago Pago High School, and in 1974, the Church closed Mapusaga High School and leased it to the government as a community college. The Pago Pago Stake, the first in American Samoa, was created on 15 June 1969 with Patrick Peters as president.

In February 1976, 11 General Authorities, including Presidents Spencer W. Kimball and N. Eldon Tanner, visited American and Western Samoa, holding area conferences in Pago Pago on 15 February. The Pago Pago Samoa West Stake was created on 24 August 1980.

In 1989, Eni F. [Hunkin Jr.] Faleomavaega, former lieutenant governor of American Samoa, became a non-voting member of 101st U.S. Congress, the first Samoan Latter-day Saint member elected to this office. President Gordon B. Hinckley was welcomed by a proclamation from the governor during a visit to American Samoa on 13 October 1997, where he addressed 7,900 people, the largest crowd ever assembled in the newly opened Veteran's Memorial Stadium in Pago Pago. President Hinckley returned to American Samoa during a six-nation tour of Asia and the South Pacific in 2000 and spoke again in Veteran's Memorial Stadium in American Samoa to 7,000 people on 17 June. Before the meeting, he was greeted by the governor, Tauese P. Sunia, and other political dignitaries.

In 2002, membership reached 13,406.

Sources: Andrew Jenson, "Samoa," Encyclopedic History of the Church of Jesus Christ of Latter-day Saints, 1941; R. Lanier Britsch, Unto the Islands of the Sea, 1986; R. Carl Harris, Samoa Apia Mission History, 1888-1983, 1983; Jennie and John Hart, R. Carl Harris, The Expanded Samoan Mission History, 1888-1900, v. 1, 1988; Excerpts taken from the report of the Governor, American Samoa, Church schools in Samoa, 1940, Church Archives; J. M. Heslop, "Conferences Begin in the South Pacific," Church News, 21 February 1976; Gerry Avant, "Prophet Goes to Islands of Pacific," Church News, 25 October 1997; Samoan Mission, Manuscript history and historical reports, Church Archives.

Stakes — 4
(Listed alphabetically as of Oct. 1, 2011.)

No.	Name	Organized	First President
	Pacific Area		
488	*Pago Pago Samoa		
	‡Pago Pago	15 Jun 1969	Patrick Peters
1972	Pago Pago Samoa Central	6 Feb 1994	Beaver T. Ho Ching
2324	Pago Pago Samoa Mapusaga	9 Mar 1997	Eugene Reid
1169	Pago Pago Samoa West	24 Aug 1980	William T. Geleai

ANDORRA

Jan. 1, 2011: Est. Population: 83,800; Members, 69; Branches, 1; Percent LDS, .07, or one in 1,445; Europe Area; Spain Barcelona Mission.

A parliamentary democracy in the high Pyrenees mountains on the border between France and Spain, Andorra. Its people speak Catalan and French and Spanish.

In 1991, there were five members living in Andorra. The first to be baptized in Andorra was Marlize Gomez Lima on April 11, 1992. The Andorra Branch was created in August 1993, and the first branch presidents were Javier Ortega and Jose Luis Bota, who did not live in the branch boundaries. Previously members traveled 84 miles to Lerida, Spain, to attend meetings.

In that same year, religious freedom was granted and the Church applied for official recognition. In 1994 the branch received its own meetinghouse. Previously, meetings were held in private homes. Javier Agulced Jerez, was baptized with his wife and two daughters in March 1998 and became the first branch president to live in the branch.

Source: Spain Barcelona Mission Annual history, Church Archives. Correspondence from the Spain Barcelona Mission, 4 October 1998, Church News resource files.

ANGOLA

Jan. 1, 2011: Est. population, 12,799,000; Members, 932; Branch 3; Percent LDS, .005, or one in 19,782; Africa Southeast Area.

The Church in Angola became established in three ways: Angolans in Angola somehow obtained Church literature and made contact with Church headquarters; Angolans living abroad were baptized and returned to their country; and American Latter-day Saints working in Angola introduced the gospel to a few of the local population.

In the mid-1970s and throughout the 1980s, people living in Angola came across Church literature and were converted. They wrote the International Mission asking that the Church come to their country. Among these was Dompetelo Paulo Rossi who was converted by reading Joseph Smith's Testimony.

Angolans living abroad, particularly in Portugal, France and the German Democratic Republic, (East Germany) in the 1980s met missionaries, were taught the gospel and baptized. Olivio Gomes Manuel joined the Church in Portugal where he was playing on the national basketball team. After joining the Church, he felt impressed to serve a mission, though it meant sacrificing a lucrative basketball career. He served in the Portugal Lisbon South Mission from 1990-1992, perhaps the first Angolan native to be a full-time missionary.

Wolfgang Paul, president of the German Democratic Republic Dresden Mission, reported that shortly after his arrival in March 1989, missionaries began to teach and baptize Africans, including Angolans. These Africans had gone to East Germany to study or to work as interns with East German companies. From May to December 1989, approximately 25 African men were baptized. Following the unification of the two German nations, many Angolans return to their homes because the agreement with the previous government was not accepted by the Federal Republic of Germany.

Once President Paul knew that their return was inevitable, all were called together in the spring of 1991 for a training seminar to prepare them to return to their homelands where there were no branches. They were taught the principles of the gospel, especially about the power of the priesthood. They were made aware which authority they did and did not hold, since they were all bearers of the Aaronic Priesthood. Their names were then sent to the Africa Area office, where they were placed in a file for future contacts when the Church was established in Angola.

In the mid-1980s, A. Edward Carlson Jr., a Church member from Utah, was working in Angola. He passed out 60 copies of the Book of Mormon. Some who received the gospel formed small study groups. Carlson requested permission to baptize a few of these people, but was told to wait because the government of Angola prevented the free exercise of religion.

Elder Earl C. Tingey, a Seventy and counselor in the Africa Area Presidency, flew to the city of Luanda in March 1992 to lay foundation for establishment of Church in Angola. Elder Tingey was the first General Authority to visit that country. Upon his arrival, he advertised his visit in a newspaper and on the radio, inviting any Latter-day Saints or interested friends to attend Sunday worship services. Approximately 40 attended the Sunday meeting. Papers for registering the Church were filed in August 1992. On 15 October 1992, the registration of the Church in Angola was published in the official paper Diario Da Republica.

Nearly four years later, in June 1996, Elder J. Richard Clarke, president of the Africa Area, and his counselor, Elder James O. Mason, visited Luande to assess the activities of the Church members who had been meeting there. Elders Clarke and Mason met with the U.S. Ambassador and Dr. Francisco A. Correira Losboa Santos, the director of the National Institute of Religious Affairs. Sensing the faith and testimonies of the Angolan Latter-day Saints, Elder Clarke organized the Luanda Branch on 9 June, the first Portuguese-speaking branch organized in Africa. Vuamina Tshaka Mbenza, who had been baptized and given the Melchizedek Priesthood in France, was called as branch president. The branch was under direct supervision of the Area Presidency in Johannesburg, South Africa. The creation of the branch was no indication that the Church was ready to start missionary work in Angola. The country was still in the midst of a civil war.

Outbreaks of war in the late 1990s prevented contact between the Area Presidency and the Angolan Church members for nearly two years. Finally, in May 1999, Elder Ray H. Wood of the Africa Southeast Area Presidency was able to visit and preside at branch a conference in Luanda. At that time, the branch had 107 members with 60 percent attendance at meetings. A baptism had occurred just three weeks prior to Elder Wood's visit. The conference was attended by 150 people.

There were no missionaries in Angola in 2000. In 2001 there was also a small group of foreign Latter-day Saints working for oil companies meeting in Cabinda, Angola.

In 2002, there were 563 members, and 596 in 2003.

On Oct. 20, 2010, Elder D. Todd Christofferson gathered with a small group of members under a several hundred year old baobab tree situated on a hill overlooking the Atlantic Ocean to one side and the capital city of Luanda to the other to bless the country and open the land to missionary work. In the prayer he called to mind the approximately 250 hundreds years of slave trade and the 25-year-old civil war that had ended a decade earlier. He blessed the members and missionaries, though small in number, to be shining lights and guidance to the nation.

Sources: Lisa A. Johnson, "The Secret of His Success," The New Era, May 1992; C.I. Rex Van Collier, "First Branch Formed in Angola after Years of Strife," Church News, 7 September 1996; Jerry R. and Marie J. Mills, Oral History, conducted by Mark L. Grover, 1986, Church Archives; Richard F. Armstrong, Interview, 2001, Church Archives; Wolfgang Paul, Dictation, 2001, Church Archives; Apostles bless two African nations, Church News, Nov. 6, 2010.

ANTIGUA AND BARBUDA

Jan. 1, 2011: Est. population, 85,600; Members, 189 ; Branches, 1;
Percent LDS, .2, or one in 473; Caribbean Area; West Indies Mission.

These eastern Caribbean islands are a constitutional monarchy with a British type of parliament. The population speaks English and is mostly members of the Church of England.

Missionary work began in St. John's, Antigua, on 29 May 1984 when President Kenneth Zabriskie of the West Indies Mission visited the prime minister of Antigua and received permission for missionaries to come to the island. The first missionaries, Ralph and Aileen Tate arrived on 28 July 1984. They were followed in late August by Elders Gill W. Halford, Jay R. Schroeder, Carl Read, and Russell T. Hansen. The first person baptized was Evelyn Shaw on 15 September 1984. Elder Vaughn J. Featherstone of the Seventy visited the island on 26 September 1984 during a tour of the West Indies

Mission. Rex B. Blake, while serving a mission with his wife, Ruth, became the first president of the St. John's Branch, when it was organized 6 January 1985.

Romell Tiwari became the first native branch president in 1993. He and his wife, Indranie, were also the first Antiguan couple sealed on 21 July 1992 in the Salt Lake Temple. Clyton Peters and Kevin Moore were two missionaries called from Antigua in March 1999 to serve in the West Indies Mission. Branch members come from many nations including Guyana, Dominica, and Barbados. Elder Gene R. Cook of the Seventy visited Antigua 25 May 2003 and shared a message encouraging branches in the islands of the sea to follow a simplified program. The branch meets in a rented facility and has 129 members. There are no members currently on the island of Barbuda.

Sources: Kenneth L. Zabriskie, History of the West Indies Mission [ca. 1989], Church Archives; Donald E. Giddings, phone conversation, 5 May 2004.

ARGENTINA

Jan. 1, 2011: Est. population, 40,913,000; Members, 389,393; Stakes, 70; Wards, 481; Branches, 360; Missions, 10; Districts, 37; Temples, 1, announced, 1; Percent LDS, .91, or one in 110; South America South Area.

Located on South America's eastern coast, the Republic of Argentina has a Spanish-speaking population that is 92 percent Roman Catholic, 2 percent Protestant, and 2 percent Jewish.

Latter-day Saints Wilhelm Friedrichs and Emil Hoppe and their families emigrated from Germany to Buenos Aires in the early 1920s, fleeing the economic uncertainties of postwar Europe. Friedrichs soon began publishing gospel messages in local newspapers and in 1924 asked the First Presidency to send missionaries to work among the Germans of Argentina.

Elders Melvin J. Ballard of the Quorum of the Twelve and Rulon S. Wells (who spoke German) and Rey L. Pratt (who spoke Spanish) of the First Council of the Seventy arrived in Buenos Aires on 6 December 1925 to begin missionary work in South America. Six days later the first latter-day baptisms on that continent were performed in the Río de la Plata for German immigrants Anna Kullick and her brother Ernst Biebersdorf, their respective spouses, and two young women.

On Christmas Day, Elder Ballard dedicated South America for the preaching of the gospel, prophesying that "the work will go forth slowly just as the oak grows from an acorn . . . [but] the South American Mission will become a power in the Church." During the next six months, the three General Authorities rented a building in which to hold meetings and distributed thousands of flyers announcing those meetings.

In July 1926, K. B. Reinhold Stoof arrived to replace Elder Ballard as president of the South American Mission, and young elders from the United States soon began to arrive. During the nine years that President Stoof and his family resided in Argentina, missionaries established branches in Buenos Aires and other nearby cities and also launched the preaching of the gospel among the German immigrants of southern Brazil.

When the mission was divided in 1935 to form the Argentine and Brazilian missions, missionary work in Argentina was confined to Buenos Aires, home to some 200 members of the Church. By that time converts had been made among working-class immigrants from a dozen European countries who were living on the outskirts of Buenos Aires. With the exception of one German branch in Buenos Aires, missionary work and church meetings were conducted in Spanish.

The first LDS chapel was dedicated in the Liniers area of Buenos Aires in April 1938, and branches were established in other major cities such as Quilmes, La Plata, Rosario, Bahía Blanca, Córdoba and Mendoza. World War II interrupted missionary work, but the mission president and the local Saints kept the Church alive until missionaries could once more return to Argentina. By 1949 Church membership had reached 1,000 but the missionaries continued to provide much of the leadership for the 27 branches.

Following the Korean War, with an increased number of missionaries available, new fields of labor were opened, leading to the establishment of the North Argentine Mission in 1962. Membership growth accelerated as local leaders were called and missionaries could devote more of their time to teaching others. In addition, missionary work was launched in neighboring Chile in 1956, with those efforts being supervised by the Argentine Mission during the next three years. By the end of 1960 there were over 4,000 Latter-day Saints in Argentina.

The increasing maturity of the Church was marked in November 1966 by the organization of the first stake in Argentina (which was also the first Spanish-speaking stake in South America and only the second such stake in the Church), with 20 more stakes being established by the end of 1980. By that time, there were five missions (two in Buenos Aires and others headquartered in Córdoba, Rosario, and Bahía Blanca) and nearly 50,000 Latter-day Saints in Argentina.

Argentina hosted two area conferences attended by President Spencer W. Kimball and other General Authorities in March 1975 and October 1978. Further progress came in 1986 with the dedication of the Buenos Aires Argentina Temple. Since 1984 Buenos Aires has been the headquarters of the South America South Area.

By December 2000, when the Argentine Saints celebrated the 75th anniversary of the arrival of LDS missionaries in South America, their country was home to 300,000 members, many of them representing the second and third generations of their families in the Church.

In recent times of high unemployment and political and social upheaval, Argentine Latter-day Saints have drawn upon the strength that comes from Church membership. Church leaders have prepared their people for such challenges by reemphasizing the basic principles of tithing, fast offerings and financial self-sufficiency. Many members planted vegetable gardens and learned to make or recondition clothing. But the Argentine Saints, showing the resilience that comes with their faith, have also reached out to the larger society in which they live, giving many thousands of hours of humanitarian and community service to those around them.

In 2003, membership reached 330,349. In 2005, membership reached 348,396.

Sources: "Argentina" in Countries of the World and Their Leaders Yearbook 2004; "South American Mission" in Andrew Jenson, Encyclopedic History of the Church (1941); Frederick S. and Frederick G. Williams, From Acorn to Oak Tree: A Personal History of the Establishment and First Quarter Century Development of the South American Missions (1987); Néstor Curbelo, Historia de los Mormones en Argentina: Relatos de Pioneros (2000); Stanley E. Bellamy, "La Misión Argentina Cumple Treinta Años," Liahona, December 1955; J. M. Heslop, "Argentina Conference

— A Great Experience," Church News, 15 March 1975; Dell Van Orden, "Emotions swell as meetings end," Church News, 11 November 1978; "Groundbreaking for 4th temple in South America," Church News, 1 May 1983; John L. Hart, "Prophecy is fulfilled: two temples are dedicated in South America," Church News, 19 January 1986; Jason N. Swensen, "Church marks 75 years in South America," Church News, November 2000; Néstor Curbelo, "Day of service now tradition in South America," Church News, 17 October 1998; Néstor Curbelo, "Hope amid uncertainty," Church News, 2 February 2002; Néstor Curbelo, "Feeding hungry children," Church News, 20 July 2002; Néstor Curbelo, "34,000 clean up cities of 3 nations," Church News, 8 November 2003

Stakes — 71
(Listed alphabetically as of Oct. 1, 2011.)

No.	Name	Organized	First President
	South America South Area		
1097	Bahia Blanca Argentina	23 Jan 1980	Daniel Humberto Fucci
2117	Bahia Blanca Argentina Villa Mitre	5 Nov 1995	Jorge Horacio Cizek
2172	Bariloche Argentina	25 Feb 1996	Miguel Angel Reginato
2259	Buenos Aires Argentina Adrogue	3 Nov 1996	Enrique Manuel Garcia
1797	*Buenos Aires Argentina Aldo Bonzi	2 Jun 1996	
	‡Buenos Aires Argentina Ezeiza	12 May 1991	Carlos Ernesto Aguero
2239	Buenos Aires Argentina Avellaneda	22 Sep 1996	Oscar Altera
920	Buenos Aires Argentina Banfield	14 May 1978	Heber Omar Diaz
1992	Buenos Aires Argentina Belgrano	18 Sep 1994	Nestor Esteban Curbelo
1143	Buenos Aires Argentina Castelar	8 Jun 1980	Jorge H. Michalek
2502	Buenos Aires Argentina Congreso	6 Dec 1998	Oscar Alberto Ormeno
2295	Buenos Aires Argentina Escobar	15 Dec 1996	Andres Bernardo Martin
2200	Buenos Aires Argentina Gonzalez Catan	2 Jun 1996	Pedro Emilio Ayala
423	*Buenos Aires Argentina Liniers	10 Dec 1998	
	*Buenos Aires Argentina East		
	‡Buenos Aires	20 Nov 1966	Angel Abrea
1178	Buenos Aires Argentina Litoral	12 Sep 1980	Jorge Fernandez
2605b	Buenos Aries Argentina Longchamps	1 Dec 2002	Ernesto Alejandro Jimenez
2276	Buenos Aires Argentina Marcos Paz	24 Nov 1996	Ismael Hector Segovia
950	Buenos Aires Argentina Merlo	13 Aug 1978	Enrique Alfredo Ibarra
1824	Buenos Aires Argentina Monte Grande	10 Nov 1991	Hugo Vicente Riccinti
1405	Buenos Aires Argentina Moreno	20 Mar 1983	Carlos Domingo Marapodi
995	Buenos Aires Argentina North	28 Jan 1979	Tomas Federico Lindheimer
2935	Buenos Aires Argentina Ramos Mejia	21 Aug 2011	Rodrigo Carlos Canga
1946	Buenos Aires Argentina Sarmiento	27 Jun 1993	Carlos Antonio Moure
639	Buenos Aires Argentina West	12 May 1974	May Hugo Angel Catron
1975	Comodoro Rivadavia Argentina	20 Feb 1994	Jorge Esteban Detlefsen
2662	Cordoba Argentina East	21 Nov 2004	Juan Carlos Machado
1021	Cordoba Argentina North	29 Apr 1979	Juan Aldo L.
1959a	Cordoba Argentina Sierras	7 Nov 1993	Roberto Jose Echegaray
569	*Cordoba Argentina South	20 Jun 1996	
	*Cordoba Argentina ‡Cordoba	28 Feb 1972	Arturo Palmieri
2228	Cordoba Argentina West	8 Sep 1996	Ruben B. Luis Spitale
1951	Florencio Varela Argentina	22 Aug 1993	Jorge Luis del Castillo
2639	Formosa Argentina	30 May 2004	Carlos Ruben Zayas
2059	General Roca Argentina	4 Jun 1995	Ruben Sabatino Tidei
1036	Godoy Cruz Argentina	6 Jun 1979	Salvador Molt'o
1978	Guaymallen Argentina	17 Apr 1994	Angel Licursi
1642	Jujuy Argentina	7 Jun 1987	Pedro Horacio Velazquez
1207	La Plata Argentina	23 Nov 1980	Hector Alejandro Olaiz
2284	La Plata Argentina Villa Elvira	1 Dec 1996	Angel Daniel Gatica
2654	La Rioja Argentina	17 Oct 2004	Hugo Manuel Pavon
2058	Maipu de Cuyo Argentina	4 Jun 1995	Luis Wachman
997	Mar del Plata Argentina	31 Jan 1979	Hector Luis Catron
2049	Mar del Plata Argentina North	21 May 1995	Eduardo Bautista Ferrari
570	*Mendoza Argentina ‡Mendoza	1 Mar 1972	Mario A. Rastelli
1918	Neuquen Argentina	20 Dec 1992	Ruben Sabatino Tidei
2210	Neuquen Argentina West	7 Jul 1996	Sergio Marcelo Redaelli
2610b	Parana Argentina	16 Dec 2002	Juan Jose Resanovich
2460	Pergamino Argentina	10 May 1998	Daniel Oscar Banuls
1902	Posadas Argentina	20 Sep 1992	Manuel Aristides Franco
694	Quilmes Argentina	15 May 1975	Hugo Nestor Salvioli
1237	Resistencia Argentina	17 Feb 1981	Leopoldo Oscar Fuentes
2266	Resistencia Argentina South	17 Nov 1996	Oscar Daniel Fernandez
2160	Rio Cuarto Argentina	11 Feb 1996	Esteban Eliseo Colaberardino
636a	Rosario Argentina	5 May 1974	Hugo Ruben Gazzoni
1177	Rosario Argentina North	10 Sep 1980	Daniel Arnoldo Moreno

2055	Rosario Argentina West	28 May 1995	Esteban Gabriel Resek
1260	Salta Argentina	29 Apr 1981	Victor Hugo Machado
2104	Salta Argentina West	15 Oct 1995	Angel Eleodoro Caceres
2166	San Juan Argentina Chimbas	18 Feb 1996	Ruben Dario Romeu
1871	San Juan Argentina Nuevo Cuyo	24 May 1992	Jorge Eduardo Chacon
2624	San Luis Argentina	14 Dec 2003	Daniel Alfredo Mitillo
1001	San Nicolas Argentina	22 Feb 1979	Deolindo Antonio Resek
2023	San Rafael Argentina	19 Feb 1995	Armando Hector Scorziello
1161	Santa Fe Argentina	20 Jul 1980	Raimundo Eduardo Rippstein
2085	Santa Fe Argentina North	13 Aug 1995	Pedro Manuel Zapata
2252	Santa Rosa Argentina	20 Oct 1996	Nicholas Arturo Paradiso
1945	Santiago Del Estero Argentina	20 Jun 1993	Jose Badami
1727	*Trelew Argentina North	8 Dec 1996	
	‡Trelew Argentina	11 Jun 1989	Oscar Daniel Filipponi
2288	Trelew Argentina South	8 Dec 1996	Juan Carlos Pino
1095	Tucuman Argentina	21 Jan 1980	Ronaldo Juan Walker
2004	Tucuman Argentina West	18 Dec 1994	Ricardo Ismael Rodriguez
2208	Zapala Argentina	30 Jun 1996	Humberto Nakad Saade
2385	Zarate Argentina	27 Jul 1997	Jose A. Gutierrez
		Stakes discontinued	
1250	Parana Argentina	29 Mar 1981	Carlos Arturo Sosa
	Discontinued 15 Apr 1990		
1096	San Juan Argentina	22 Jan 1980	Ricardo N. Ontiveros
	Discontinued 30 Jul 1989 †Argentina Cordoba Mission		

Missions — 10
(As of Oct. 1, 2011; shown with historical number. See MISSIONS.)

(180) ARG. BAHIA BLANCA MISSION
Calle San Andres 133
8000 Bahia Blanca, Buenos Aires
Argentina

(32) ARGENTINA BUENOS AIRES NORTH MISSION
Gral. Lavalle 1828
1646 San Fernando
Buenos Aires, Argentina

(112) ARG. BUENOS AIRES SOUTH MISSION
Quintana 447
1846 Adrogue
Buenos Aires, Argentina

(269) ARGENTINA BUENOS AIRES WEST MISSION
Ballesteros 1076
1706 Haedo
Buenos Aires, Argentina

(73) ARGENTINA CORDOBA MISSION
Gay Lussac 5270,
Villa Belgrano
5009 Cordoba, Argentina

(228) ARGENTINA MENDOZA MISSION
Cabildo Abierto 161
5501 Godoy Cruz
Mendoza, Argentina

(230) ARGENTINA NEUQUEN MISSION
Zapla 24
8300 Neuquen
Argentina

(229) ARGENTINA RESISTENCIA MISSION
Avenida Rivadavia 323
H3500AKE Resistencia
Chaco, Argentina

(100) ARGENTINA ROSARIO MISSION
Blvd Argentino 7935
2000 Rosario, Santa Fe
Argentina

(206) ARGENTINA SALTA MISSION
Los Eucaliptus 75
4400 Salta
Argentina

ARMENIA

Jan. 1, 2011: Est. population, 2,967,000; Members, 2,888; Branches, 15; Districts 2; Missions, 1; percent LDS: .09 or 1 in 1,080; Europe East Area; Armenia Yerevan Mission.

The gospel has been preached among Armenians living outside of their homeland since the 1880s. In December 1884, Jacob Spori and George C. Naegle were appointed to serve in Constantinople, Turkey, and began to preach to the community of Armenians there. Mr. Vartooguian and three members of his family were baptized on 4 January 1885, the first Armenians to join the Church.

As the Ottoman Empire began to decline, ethnic hatred and acts of violence against Armenians increased. In May 1909, Thomas P. Page attempted to purchase a tract of land in Syria for the Armenian Church members to colonize. This colony, however, never materialized because the Turkish Mission was closed that same year due to political instability in Turkey.

A little over a decade later, in 1921, Elder David O. McKay of the Quorum of the Twelve reported visiting the Armenian Latter-day Saints who were spread across the Near East, having been driven from their homes because of continuing violence and persecution. Church members in the United States held a fast to benefit Church members in need, including Armenians. A portion of the $115,000 collected from the fast offerings was given to Armenian Latter-day Saints by J. Wilford Booth. Booth was president of the Turkish Mission, which was responsible for missionary work in the Near East.

A branch of 59 Armenians was functioning in Aleppo, Syria, in 1946. Many of these people had been assisted by the Church in moving from Aintab, Turkey, where there had been severe persecution, to Aleppo. These Saints were forced to leave Syria between 1947 and 1950 because of threats against Armenians. Some went to Armenia, then a part of the Soviet Union, others to Beirut, Lebanon, and eventually to the United States. Those who went to the Soviet Union lost contact with the Church. In December 1950, the Near East Mission was closed at the request of the First Presidency. President Badwagan Piranian, and his wife Bertha, were transferred to the California Mission to labor among Armenians there.

In the late 1980s, Beverly Campbell, working for the Church's public communications office in Washington, D.C., began to establish contact with Soviet Ambassador Yuri Dubinin and his wife, Liana, who is Armenian. The Dubinins were hosted at various LDS functions in the Washington, D.C., area.

On 7 December 1988, portions of Armenia were devastated by an earthquake. Approximately 50,000 people died and half a million became homeless. One week later, Elder Russell M. Nelson of the Quorum of the Twelve met with Ambassador and Mrs. Dubinin in Washington, D.C., to convey the condolences of the Church. Elder Nelson presented the Ambassador with a check for $100,000.

In response to the earthquake, Utah industrialist and Church leader Jon M. Huntsman, working with American philanthropist Armand Hammer, began a relief effort to benefit survivors. They founded the American-Armenian Bridge of Friendship, an organization that helped in the rebuilding effort. On 8 August 1989, Huntsman, Hammer, and Elder Russell M. Nelson, of the Quorum of the Twelve, participated in a document-signing ceremony in Moscow pledging assistance.

Jon Huntsman established a concrete plant in Yerevan in late 1991. It produced reinforced concrete plank used to build homes and apartment buildings. The plant was staffed with LDS humanitarian service couples who had expertise in seismic engineering and plant operations. The first Church-service couples arrived in November 1991.

The humanitarian effort was headed by David M. Horne. Aside from operating the plant, Horne was involved in managing shipments of food and supplies. In light of these efforts, the Church was registered in Armenia on 22 December 1995. The assignment for Horne and his wife, Jeanne, lasted from July 1989 to January 1996. Horne died 21 January 1996 from wounds suffered in an explosion of a kerosene heater in his Yerevan apartment.

Elders Dallin H. Oaks and Russell M. Nelson visited Yerevan in June 1991. In Haghtanak Park, Elder Oaks blessed the land and people of Armenia.

Mikhail Oskar Belousov was baptized in Yerevan on 24 March 1992, the first man to join the Church in Armenia. Nara Sarkissian, the first woman to join the Church in Armenia, was baptized on 4 April 1992.

In November 1993, Armenia was assigned to the Bulgaria Sofia Mission. In July 1994, responsibility for Armenia shifted to the Russia Moscow Mission. The first two young missionaries, Dallas V. Woolf and Cade L. Rindfleisch, went to Yerevan from the mission in January 1995. Armenia was transferred to the Russia Rostov Mission in January 1997. Finally, the Armenia Yerevan Mission was organized on 1 July 1999, with Robert H. Sangster as president.

The Yerevan Branch was organized on 20 January 1994. Prior to this, there were groups of Latter-day Saints who met with the humanitarian missionary couples in their apartments for worship services. On 16 July 1995, the Yerevan Armenia District was organized. Elder Robert F. Orton, a counselor in Europe East Area Presidency, dedicated Armenia's first meetinghouse, located in Yerevan, on 2 February 2002.

In January 2001, Artur Minasyan, the first Armenian missionary called to serve in Armenia began his mission. And later that year, in March, the translation of the Book of Mormon into Eastern Armenian was published. These books were distributed in May 2001, which coincided with the 1700th anniversary of Christianity in Armenia. The Book of Mormon had been translated by Nishan K. Sherinian into Western Armenian, which is spoken by Armenians who were living outside of Armenia. It was published in 1937.

The dedication of the Nauvoo Temple on 30 June 2002 was the first Church event broadcast via satellite into Armenia. Six months later, Armenian Church members and their guests enjoyed the broadcast of the First Presidency Christmas devotional.

In 2003, there were 1,537 members.

Elder M. Russell Ballard of the Quorum of the Twelve visited Armenian President Robert Kocharian in the palace in Yerevan in August 2006 as part of a 12-day European mission tour. Elder Earl C. Tingey of the Presidency of the Seventy and Elder Jon M. Huntsman, Area Seventy, accompanied. The Armenian president is a longtime friend of Elder Huntsman following years of contributions to rebuild the country following the 1988 earthquake.

Sources: Armenia Yerevan Mission Annual History, Church Archives; David M. Horne interview, Church Archives; Turkish Mission Manuscript History, Church Archives; Journal History of the Church, 26 May 1909 and 30 December 1909, Church History Library; "Church Section," p. 3, Deseret News, 30 April 1952; Mary Ouzounian Journal [ca. 1978-1991], p. 78, Church Archives; "Church Joining in Effort to Help Armenia Rebuild," Ensign, October 1989, 7; "Church Will Help Armenian Homeless," Church News, 19 August 1989, 3; "Church Gives $100,000 for Relief Efforts in Quake-Stricken Armenia," Church News, 17 December 1988, 5; "'97th translation, Armenians receive Book of Mormon," Church News, 5 May 2001; Shaun Stahle, "Dispelling notions," Church News, 16 September 2006.

Mission — 1

(As of Oct. 1, 2011; shown with historical number. See MISSIONS.)

(332) Armenia Yerevan Mission
Vratsakan #5
Yerevan 0051
Armenia

AUSTRALIA

Jan. 1, 2011: Est. population, 21,262,000; Members, 129,744; Stakes, 33; Wards, 203; Branches, 81; Missions, 7; Districts, 10; Temples, 5; Percent LDS, 0.58, or 1 LDS in 172; Pacific Area.

In the southwest South Pacific, the island-continent of Australia is a democratic federal state in the British commonwealth. Australia's population speaks English, and is 26 percent Anglican, 25 percent Protestant, and 25 percent Roman Catholic.

In 1840, William Barratt, 17, was called from England to serve a mission in Australia. He found circumstances difficult, but baptized Robert Beauchamp who later became an influential mission president in Australia. Then next missionary was Andrew Anderson who had been baptized by Orson Pratt in Scotland. Before he emigrated to Australia, he was given license to preach there. He and his family arrived in 1842. By the end of 1844, he organized a branch of 11 members in the private township of Montefiores, some 220 miles northwest of Sydney.

John Murdock and Charles Wandell arrived from Utah 31 October 1851 in Sydney, and established mission headquarters there. They published tracts, began preaching and found a few converts among a people very distracted by a gold rush. A year later, 47 members were in the mission when Murdock left because of ill health. On 6 April 1853, Wandell left with a company of Saints. A few days later, another 10 missionaries arrived under the direction of Augustus Farnham.

At least nine companies emigrated from Australia to Utah in the 1800s. The most serious ship accident among all the LDS emigrating companies occurred 3 October 1855, when the bark Julia Ann, carrying 28 Saints emigrating to Utah from Australia, broke up on shoals near the Scilly Islands. Five people were drowned in the mishap.

When word of the Utah War arrived in Australia in late December 1857, all missionaries returned to Utah. From then until 1875 only a few American missionaries were sent to Australia. Moreover, with greater successes in New Zealand, efforts of the Australasian Mission were focused there and in 1880 mission headquarters were moved to Auckland. After 1875 efforts in Australia were renewed and on 1 January 1898, the Australasian Mission was divided, forming the Australian and New Zealand Missions. At the time, membership in Australia was about 200.

Missionaries arrived in Perth, Western Australia, in 1888. The first LDS meetinghouse in the country was completed in Brisbane in 1904. Emigrating members continually depleted numbers and upset the Australian government, who in 1917 limited the number of missionaries who could enter Australia and in 1918 forbade "emigration propaganda."

Meetinghouses were dedicated in Melbourne in 1922, Adelaide in 1923, Sydney in 1924, and Perth and Hobart in 1925. World War II brought the evacuation of missionaries and slowed the work. Furthermore, shipping difficulties began immediately after the war and hindered the return of missionaries.

The South Australian Mission was created in 1955, with headquarters in Melbourne, and David O. McKay authorized the construction of new meetinghouses that same year.

Australia's first stake was organized in Sydney 27 March 1960. Additional missions were created in 1958 (Adelaide), 1973 (Brisbane), and 1975 (Perth), 1993 (Sydney North) and 1998 (Melbourne West). The Sydney Australia Temple, dedicated 1984, was Australia's first temple. Additional temples have been dedicated in Adelaide, Melbourne, Perth, and Brisbane.

Members assisted as volunteers with the 2000 Summer Olympic Games.

On 28 March 2003, Elder Kenneth Johnson presented 100,000 Australian Dollars to the Farmhand Foundation for drought relief.

In 2003, membership reached 106,930. In 2005, membership reached 111,098. In 2009, membership reached 123,650.

On 1 July 2010, the Australia Sydney North Mission was combined with the Australia Sndney South Mission to form the Australia Sydney Mission. The Australia Melbourne West Mission was combined with the Australia Melbourne East Mission to form the Australia Melbourne Mission.

Sources: United States Department of State, The World Factbook, cia.gov/cia/publications/factbook.; Andrew Jenson, Encyclopedic History of the Church, 1941; Australasian Mission, Manuscript history, Church Archives; Church Public Affairs, press release, 28 Mar. 2003; Marjorie Newton, Southern Cross Saints, 1991; John Douglas Hawkes, A History of the Church of Jesus Christ of Latter-Day Saints in Australia to 1900, thesis, 1965. "Saints Shine in Perth, Western Australia's 'City of Lights,'" Ensign, October 1988; Australian Mission, Manuscript history and historical reports, Church Archives; and Christopher K. Bigelow, "Australia: Coming Out of Obscurity," Ensign, December 1998.

Stakes — 33
(Listed alphabetically as of Oct. 1, 2011.)

No.	Name	Organized	First President
	Pacific Area		
2129	Adelaide Australia Firle	26 Nov 1995	Philip F. Howes
414	*Adelaide Australia Marion	6 Jan 1982	
	*Adelaide Australia Payneham	23 Apr 1978	
	*Adelaide Australia		
	‡Adelaide	23 Feb 1966	Dudley Russell Tredrea
907	Adelaide Australia Modbury	23 Apr 1978	Douglas E. Hann
306	*Brisbane Australia		
	‡Brisbane	23 Oct 1960	William E. Waters
2776	Brisbane Australia Centenary	15 Sep 2007	James Francis O'Reilly
2605	Brisbane Australia Logan	22 Sep 2002	Robert Gordon
1684	Brisbane Australia North	7 Feb 1988	Douglas Walter Hill
2022	Canberra Australia	19 Feb 1995	Peter John Moir
2141	Devonport Australia	10 Dec 1995	John Robert Hargreaves
892	*Eight Mile Plains Australia	10Dec 1995	
	‡Brisbane Australia South	19 Feb 1978	John D. Jeffrey
2140	Gold Coast Australia	10 Dec 1995	Robert Gordon
860	Hobart Tasmania Australia	14 Sep 1977	John Douglas Jury
1279	*Ipswich Australia	6 May 1986	
	‡Brisbane Australia West	21 Jun 1981	John D. Jeffrey
	Launceton Tasmania		
2498	Liverpool Australia	25 Oct 1998	Maa Junior Maa
1988	*Macarthur Australia Stake	25 Oct 1998	
	Sydney Australia Campbelltown	28 Aug 1994	Ma'a Ma'a Jr.
551	*Melbourne Australia Braeside	5 Apr 1994	
	*Melbourne Australia Dandenong	18 Mar 1986	
	*Melbourne Australia Moorabbin		
	‡Melbourne South	22 Aug 1971	Bruce James Opie

1175	*Melbourne Australia Deer Park	18 Mar 1986	
	*Melbourne Australia		
	‡Fairfield West	7 Sep 1980	Edward Anderson
307	*Melbourne Australia Heidelberg	2 Jul 1995	
	*Melbourne Australia Fairfield		
	‡Melbourne	30 Oct 1960	Boyd C. Bott
1617	*Melbourne Australia Maroondah	2 Jul 1995	
	‡Melbourne Australia Waverly	7 Dec 1986	Ian Frank Davenport
2070	Melbourne Australia Pakenham	2 Jul 1995	J. Murray Lobley
2478	*Melbourne Australia Wyndham	16 Oct 2002	
	Melbourne Australia West	21 Jun 1998	Russell Bruce John Bielenberg
2264a	Nambour Australia	17 Nov 1996	Michael Douglas Keily
1106	*Newcastle Australia	15 Jul 1986	
	‡Sydney Australia Newcastle	15 Feb 1980	Peter R. Barr
2450	Penrith Australia	19 Apr 1998	Jeffrey D. Cummings
447	*Perth Australia Dianella	6 Jul 1980	
	*Perth Australia		
	‡Perth	28 Nov 1967	Donald W. Cummings
2292	Perth Australia Rockingham	15 Dec 1996	Adrian Shane Palm
1159	Perth Australia Southern River	6 Jul 1980	Roy B. Webb
2033	Perth Australia Warwick	12 Mar 1995	Peter Fletcher Meurs
293	*Sydney Australia Greenwich		
	‡Sydney	27 Mar 1960	Dell C. Hunt
1105	Sydney Australia Hebersham	15 Feb 1980	Peter J. Moir
2303	Sydney Australia Hyde Park	2 Feb 1997	Patrick R. Ormond Jr.
435	*Sydney Australia Mortdale	2 Jun 1992	
	*Mortdale Australia	31 Mar 1992	
	*Sydney Australia Mortdale	15 Feb 1980	
	*Sydney Australia South		
	‡Sydney South	14 May 1967	John Daniel Parker
495	*Sydney Australia Parramatta	2 Jun 1992	
	*Parramatta Australia	31 Mar 1992	
	*Sydney Australia Parramatta	15 Feb 1980	
	*Parramatta Australia		
	‡Parramatta (Australia)	2 Nov 1969	Stanley Owen Gray

Missions — 5

(As of Oct. 1, 2011; shown with historical number. See MISSIONS.)

(82) AUSTRALIA ADELAIDE MISSION
P.O. Box 97
Marden, South Australia 5070
Australia

(106) AUSTRALIA BRISBANE MISSION
P.O. Box 348
Hamilton, Brisbane
QLD 4007, Australia

(43c) AUSTRALIA MELBOURNE MISSION
628 Canterbury Road
Vermont, VIC 3133
Australia

(10) AUSTRALIA SYDNEY MISSION
2 Breakwell Street
Mortdale, NSW 2223
Australia

(117) AUSTRALIA PERTH MISSION
P.O. Box 185
Tuart Hill, WA 6939
Australia

AUSTRIA

Jan. 1, 2011: Est. population, 8,210,000; Members, 4,294; Stakes, 2; Wards, 12; Branches, 5; Percent LDS, .05, or one in 1,948; Europe Area; Alpine German-speaking Mission.

Austria, a parliamentary democracy located in south-central Europe, is 98 percent German-speaking. Some 78 percent of the people are Roman Catholic, 5 percent are protestant with 17 percent comprising Muslim and other faiths.

The first Latter-day Saint to visit Austria was Orson Hyde who passed briefly through Vienna on his way to Palestine in 1841.

Orson Pratt and William W. Riter arrived in Austria on 18 January 1865. They remained there until September when they were banished and returned to London reporting that missionary work would be difficult because of exising laws. The first Austrian convert, Joseph A. Oheim, was baptized on 22 January 1870, in Munich, Germany, by Karl G. Maeser. The first convert in Austria was Paul Haslinger, who was baptized on 25 November 1883. Thomas Biesinger and Paul E. B. Hammer arrived in Vienna in November 1883 and baptized a few converts. Fearing arrest, Biesinger went to Prague and Hammer left Austria a few months later.

In 1899, an Austrian convert, Martin Ganglmayer came to Haag am Hausruck and met Johann Huber, who was baptized on 27 April 1900 in Munich. Through Huber's influence, several others were baptized in Haag am Hausruck, and by 1902 a branch was established there.

In 1903, missionaries returned to Vienna as well as in several other cities. In 1909, Royal Eccles formed a branch in Vienna which was closed by police in January 1914.

Because of World War I missionaries were evacuated and many local members enlisted for military service leaving the branches with few members. Consequently, Church activity for those years diminished dramatically. Missionaries returned in 1920 and reorganized the branches. The years between World Wars I and II marked an era of dramatic growth for the Church in Austria as the Church enjoyed full religious freedom and missionaries found people more receptive to their message.

Missionaries were withdrawn again during World War II and local members carried on. Full-time missionary work resumed in 1946 when Ezra Taft Benson established the Austrian District. The Austrian government officially recognized the Church in 1955. In 1960 the Austrian Mission was created. During the 1960s many meetinghouses were built and dedicated to hold the growing branches. In 1965, the centennial of the Church in Austria was celebrated.

In the 1970s, Austria became the center for fledgling Church work in Eastern European countries, including Czechoslovakia and Hungary and particularly, Yugoslavia. It was in Vienna in 1974 where missionaries first worked among Yugoslavian guest workers. A Yugoslavian Sunday school was formed in January 1975. To accommodate the large number of international workers in Austria, the Vienna International Branch, now the Vienna 4th Ward, was formed in March 1975. Austrians celebrated the founding of the first stake in Vienna on 20 April 1980.

In the late 1980s and early 1990s, the Austria Vienna East Mission supervised developing areas in Eastern Europe. During the subsequent difficult economic times in various countries, including the conflict in the former Yugoslavia, members donated food and clothing for relief.

The Church's 2,300th stake was created in Salzburg 19 January 1997. The Austria Vienna Mission was consolidated on 1 July 2002, with the Germany Munich Mission to form the Germany Munich/Austria Mission.

Elder L. Tom Perry of the Quorum of the Twelve, serving as president of the Europe Central Area, joined with members in Vienna to commemorate 50 years of religious freedom in the country and official recognition of the Church granted on 27 September 1955. Elder Perry's two-day visit, May 6-8, 2005, included meeting Dr. Heinz Fischer, president of Austria, in the famed Hofburg Palace.

Membership in 2003 reached 4,038.

Sources: Andrew Jenson, Encyclopedic History of the Church, 1941; Donald Q. Cannon and Richard O. Cowan, Unto Every Nation: Gospel Light Reaches Every Land, 2003; Austrian Mission, Manuscript history and historical reports, Church Archives; Vienna International Branch, A Short History of the Vienna International Branch, Church Archives; "Meets president," Church News, 21 May 2005.

Stakes — 2
(Listed alphabetically as of Oct. 1, 2011.)

No.	Name	Organized	First President
Europe Area			
2300	Salzburg Austria	19 Jan 1997	Gerold Roth
1126	Vienna Austria	20 Apr 1980	Johann Anton Wondra

BAHAMAS

Jan. 1, 2011: Est. population, 309,000; Members, 917; Branches, 3;
Percent LDS, .26, or one in 381; Caribbean Area; Florida Ft. Lauderdale Mission.

A Caribbean commonwealth, the Bahamas is made up of nearly 700 islands. Its English-speaking population includes Baptist, 29 percent; Anglican, 23 percent; and Roman Catholic, 22 percent. A sizable portion of the population are Creole-speakers from Haiti.

In the late 1960s and 1970s LDS families from America held their own Church services while living in the Bahamas during work assignments. In the summer of 1979 two LDS families, Larry and Margery McCombs and Albert and Karen Ballard, moved to Nassau and suggested to Florida Fort Lauderdale Mission president Richard L. Millett that missionaries might be welcome in the Bahamas.

The next mission president Glen E. Stringham sent four missionaries to Naussau and two missionaries to Freeport in November 1979. The elders only stayed for a few months because their visas were not renewed by the government. President Stringham met with government officials, including the Christian Council, who expressed concerns about the Church's intentions to convert people throughout the island. Full-time young missionaries were not permitted to return until March 1985. However, missionary couple Thomas E. and Donna Bauman, arrived in 1982 and did medical volunteer work, strengthened the branch, and were followed by other couples.

Alexandre Paul, consul general from Haiti to the Bahamas, and his wife Helene were baptized on 6 January 1980. The Nassau Branch was organized in February 1981, with recently returned missionary Chris Ballard as president. Over the years membership in the Church has come primarily from the Haitian and Bahamian population in the country. In May 1982 Antoine Ferrier a Haitian became the first local branch president, a calling he held for eight years. His wife Leona, was called at the same time to serve as the first local Relief Society president. Some 48 investigators and members attended the first branch conference on 12 September 1981.

In June 1986 the Soldier Road Branch was formed for Creole-speaking Haitian members. The first meetinghouse in the Bahamas was dedicated on 8 May 1988. The Soldier Road and Nassau Branches were combined in 1998 and the New Providence Branch was created with meetings in English and translation in Haitian-Creole. An expansion was made to the chapel and was dedicated for the New Providence branch on 24 September 2000. Though a branch had been formed in 1979 in Freeport on the Grand Bahama Island, it was later discontinued in 1982 due to a reduction in membership. In May 2000 there were enough members to form the Grand Bahama Branch.

On 20 November 1997 Elder Neal A. Maxwell of the Quorum of the Twelve visited Nassau and blessed the land. One family he visited with was the Adolfo and Elizabeth Rabasto family, a Filipino family who moved to the island of Exuma in

August 2000 where he is a physician. As of 2004 they were the only Church members on the island and hold their own Sunday meetings and seminary for their teenage children.

In 1987 Bahamian Edward R. Smith decided to take free Creole classes given by his friend Antoine Ferrier in the Soldier Road meetinghouse in Nassau, which led to Smith's baptism in April 1988. He later served as branch president from 1990 to 1998. Smith was called as the first native district president in June 2003, less than a year after the New Providence Bahamas District was formed on 15 September 2002.

Sources: Margery McCombs, Telephone conversation, 15 June 2004; "First Dedication Nears," Church News, 19 March 1988; Florida Fort Lauderdale, Mission Manuscript history and historical reports, Church Archives; Joe and Julia Todd, Electronic mail, 19 May 2004; Joe and Julia Todd, Telephone conversation, 7 June 2004.

BANGLADESH

Jan. 1, 2011: Est. population, 156,051,000; Members, fewer than 100; Branches, 1; Asia Area; Singapore Mission.

Located on the northern coast of the Bay of Bengal, the People's Republic of Bangladesh is a parliamentary republic and member of the commonwealth of nations. Its people are 83 percent Muslim and 16 percent Hindi.

During the late 1970s and early 1980s, a few individual Bengalis joined the Church in other countries. One of these, Reza Chowdhury, served as a full-time missionary in Washington, D.C., from 1980 to 1982. In 1985, 1,000 copies of selections from the Book of Mormon were printed in the Bengali language.

During 1985 and 1986, Kenneth and Beatrice Nielsen, a Latter-day Saint couple, lived and worked in Bangladesh for the Canadian government. They were followed by other Latter-day Saint couples, and Church meetings were held in Dhaka. In 1986, Bono Barua and his family, as well as Roseline Gomes, all of whom were introduced to the Church by Kenneth and Beatrice Nielsen, became the first converts to the Church in Bangladesh.

Small numbers of Church members, mostly from other countries, continued to meet in Dhaka, and on 14 March 1992 the Dhaka Bangladesh Branch was organized with Vern M. Lindsay as president. Between 1992 and 1998, the branch averaged between 30 and 40 members. Membership shrank as non-Bengali members were assigned to work elsewhere. In 2001, it was reported that there was a small group of about two local families in Dhaka.

Sources: Lyn R. Jacobs, Mormon Non-English Scriptures, Hymnals, & Periodicals, 1830-1986: A Descriptive Bibliography, 1986; "Expatriate Serves Mission," Church News, 15 May 1993; "Welcome Mat Is Out in Several Countries," Church News, 19 June 1993; Singapore Mission, Manuscript history and historical reports, Church Archives.

BARBADOS

Jan. 1, 2011: Est. population, 284,000; Members, 733; Branches, 4; Districts 1; Percent LDS, 0.21, or one in 45; Caribbean Area; West Indies Mission.

A Caribbean independent sovereign state of Great Britain, English-speaking Barbados is made up of one island where about 70 percent are Anglican.

In January 1853, six elders arrived in Jamaica on a mission to the West Indies. During a meeting Alfred B. Lambson and Jesse Turpin determined to go to Barbados. After purchasing tickets for their passage, the two elders were removed from the boat by a British government official who did not want Mormon American missionaries traveling to additional islands in the British Empire. The six elders soon returned to the United States unable to preach anywhere else in the West Indies.

A ship carrying Elder Melvin J. Ballard of the Quorum of the Twelve stopped for one day in Barbados on 20 November 1925. Elder Ballard continued to Argentina where he dedicated South America. During World War II an LDS serviceman, Clinton E. Weil, was stationed in Barbados and married a local woman. After the war he returned to Barbados and lived there from 1957-1958. He held his own Church services with his 4- year-old son and upon leaving the country donated the Book of Mormon and other Church books to a library in Bridgetown.

Greg Young, a Latter-day Saint from the United States, had family members who operated a hotel in Barbados. During the Christmas holidays he visited Barbados and shared the gospel with a friend John Naime. On 16 April 1978, Young baptized John, June, Norman, and Gema Naime, the first converts in the country. John and Norman were then ordained priests and upon John Naime's request, he was ordained an elder on the same day as his baptism.

President Richard L. Millett of the Florida Fort Lauderdale Mission met the Naimes after they visited Salt Lake City in 1978. In September 1979, President Millett sent Brent Hintze and Kent Bunker to begin missionary work. The first branch in Barbados was the Christ Church Branch, created on 20 October 1979. It was followed by the organization of the Black Rock Branch on 24 August 1983. The Oistins Branch was created 19 February 1985.

On 13 March 1988, Elder Marvin J. Ashton of the Quorum of the Twelve blessed the islands of the West Indies. On the same day, he also dedicated the Christ Church Branch building, and Elder Rex D. Pinegar of the Seventy dedicated the Black Rock Branch building. The Christ Church Barbados District was organized 16 June 2002 with John Naime as president. The district is comprised of three branches.

In 2003, there were 601 members.

Sources: George A. Smith, Rise, Progress, Travels, 1872; Aaron F. Farr, diary, 1853, Church Archives; Melvin J. Ballard, Letter to Martha J. Ballard, 20-30 November 1925, Church Archives; Clinton E. Weil, Letter, 10 August 1981, Church Archives; Richard L. Millett, History of the Church in the Caribbean, 1977-1980; Puerto Rico San Juan Mission, Manuscript history and historical reports, Church Archives; West Indies Mission, Manuscript history and historical reports, Church Archives; John Rappleye, interview with John Naime, 1987, Church Archives.

BELGIUM

Jan. 1, 2011: Est. population, 10,414,000; Members, 6,019; Stakes, 2; Wards, 9; Branches, 8; Missions, 1; Percent LDS, .06, or one in 1,723; Europe Area.

In 1861 Louis Bertrand, president of the French Mission, sent Gustave Chaprix to Brussels to preach the gospel. It is not known how long he stayed in the area, and no success was recorded. Several years later on 23 August 1868, President Albert Carrington of the Swiss and German Mission sent Octave Ursenbach to Belgium. He worked in Antwerp and Liège. After several weeks, Ursenbach wrote three times to the Swiss German Mission stating that the peoples' hearts were closed and not yet prepared for the gospel. He asked permission to return to Switzerland. Two months later, on 30 October, he was given permission to return. He left the same day.

The first missionary to enjoy success in Belgium was Mischa Markow, a Serb converted in Constantinople in 1887. He arrived in Antwerp and baptized Henrietta Esselmann, her four children, and Karl Beckhaus. Henrietta was the first known convert to join the Church in Belgium. Markow wrote to the Swiss and German Mission of his success with the Germanic people and requested that they again try sending missionaries to the area.

The Swiss and German Mission sent missionaries Jacob Grimm, Theodore Brandley, and an Elder Taylor to the Antwerp area in 1889. Within two months, and with the help of the Esselmann family, the missionaries baptized 80 people. Three years later, in 1892, the Esselmanns emigrated to the Salt Lake Valley.

The missionaries of the Swiss and German Mission who were assigned to Belgium had constant difficulties with the French language. As a result, in 1891, the Belgian Branches were moved to the Netherlands Mission under President Timothy Metz. The mission then became known as the Netherlands Belgium Mission for a time. On 31 January 1892, small branches were created in Brussels, with Priest Casper Kuhlmann as president; Liège, with J.H. Bergmann as presiding officer; and Antwerp, with Frederick Peiper as president. Pieper later served as a missionary and mission president from 1896 to 1897 and was the son of Henrietta Esselmann, the first person baptized in Belgium. During this period, almost all of the converts were migrants from Germany. Meetings in both Liège and Brussels were held in German. The Antwerp Branch consisted of German and Dutch Saints that had moved there from Holland.

In 1896, Jean-Baptiste Ripplinger and Frederick Pieper had particular success among the Baptists in the Liège region. The Baptist pastors in the area became concerned and sent a representative to deliver a sermon against the Church. Ripplinger and Pieper attended the meeting and the congregation insisted that they be allowed to respond to the pastor's charges. After a heated discussion, the pastor rose to leave, but he was restrained until the missionaries were able to conclude their message. Following this experience, over a hundred people asked to learn more about the Church.

The curiosity of the Belgian people continued to grow with the opposition. By August 1897, it was necessary to rent a larger meeting hall in Liège and sometimes issue admission tickets to accommodate those that wished to attend. In spite of the large number who gathered to hear the sermons, the work progressed slowly and baptisms remained low.

On 1 November 1897, Belgium was divided into two conferences or districts: Liège and Brussels. The Liège District consisted of eastern Belgium, which included only the Liège and Seraing Branches. The Seraing Branch was organized sometime between 1892 and 1897. The Brussels District included the non-French speaking branches in the western portion of the country. The districts remained separate until 31 December 1904 when the Brussels District was again attached to the Liège District. The Verviers Branch was organized in 1905.

The French Mission was reorganized on 15 October 1912, having been officially closed in 1864. Branches in Liège, Seraing, Verviers, and Brussels became part of the French Mission. The remaining non-French speaking branches to the north remained part of the Netherlands Mission under the direction of President Edgar B. Brossard. Two years later, in August of 1914, France went to war with Germany, missionaries were forced to leave the country, and the French Mission was closed again. The Liège District once again reverted back to the Netherlands Mission. Because no missionaries from Holland were allowed inside Belgium, Church affairs were left to local members. It wasn't until 10 December 1919 that a Latter-day Saint missionary was again sent to Belgium. Alvin Smith Nelson, of the Netherlands Mission was assigned to resume the work in Belgium. He was shortly thereafter called as president of the Liège District.

On 1 December 1923, the country was again split into the Brussels District, which consisted of the Flemish-speaking region, and the Liège District, which consisted of the French-speaking region. This was done on 24 February 1924 in preparation for the reorganization of the French Mission. Headquarters were in Geneva and Russell H. Blood was president. At this time, the Liège District was again removed from the Netherlands Mission and renamed the Belgian District. It was then added to the French Mission. The Brussels District remained a part of the Netherlands Mission.

The first meetinghouses to be built in the French Mission were located in Belgium. French Mission President Ernest C. Rossiter was made aware that members in the Liège and Seraing branches were being forced to meet in locations not completely appropriate to Sunday services. He made a request to Church headquarters and obtained approval to construct the meetinghouses. On 8 November 1931, Elder John A. Widtsoe of the Quorum of the Twelve Apostles dedicated both meetinghouses. Four years later, in December 1935, a baptismal font was constructed in the basement of the Liège chapel. It is thought to be the first Latter-day Saint baptismal font in Europe.

French Mission headquarters were moved from Geneva to Paris on 1 October 1930. In 1936, they were moved from Paris to Liège because it was reported that 95 percent of all converts in the mission were in Belgium.

During this same year, the American-Mormon Sporting Club was organized. Missionaries at the time were encouraged to participate in choirs, sports teams and other recreational activities as a way to contact people interested in the gospel. In June 1936, this team defeated the Belgian national champion basketball team to become the "unofficial" Belgian champions. This event drew much attention to the Church through various favorable articles in local newspapers.

President Heber J. Grant arrived in Herstal to dedicate a meetinghouse in June 1937. Missionaries and the mission president and his family were evacuated September- October 1939. Gaston Chappuis supervised the mission until August 1940 when the mission was left under the leadership of Leon Fariger. As a result of the war, missionary work in Belgium came to a standstill until President James L. Barker arrived in November 1945 to reopen the French Mission, moving the headquarters back to Paris.

On 30 November 1947, the first major thrust at missionary work was made in Flanders or the Flemish-speaking areas in the 20th century. Cornelius Zappy, president of the Netherlands Mission, sent four missionaries to Antwerp: Hendrik Landwaard, Jacob van Goor, Marion T. Millett, and Lothar Nestman. Two months later on 25 January 1948 the first public Church meeting was held and on 18 April 1948 and eight people were baptized. Over the next several years branches were opened in Antwerp, Brussels, Ghent, and Mechelen.

On 15 October 1950, the Belgian District within the French Mission was divided. It became the Liège District, which included the Belgian branches of Liège, Verviers, Seraing, and Herstal; and the Brussels District, including the Belgian branches of Brussels, Charleroi, Namur, Mons, and the French branch of Lille.

In July 1960, the Church implemented a meetinghouse construction program in Europe. Three meetinghouses were built using this system: Brussels, first used in June 1965; Liège, dedicated December 1965; and Charleroi, dedicated March of 1966. The chapel in Brussels was later destroyed by fire in the summer of 1971 and was quickly rebuilt and the Seraing meetinghouse was first used on 3 July of that same year.

Meanwhile, Max L. Pinegar, who served as president of the Netherlands Mission from 1971-1974, greatly increased the work in Flanders. While traveling through northern Belgium, he received the impression that the time had come for a greatly increased missionary effort among the Flemish people. Very little work had been done by the Netherlands in this area prior to this time. During his tenure he visited government officials and obtained help lifting visa restrictions on missionaries. Within two years, the number of missionaries in the Flanders area increased from 10 to more than 50 and missionaries were allowed to spend the full two years within the country. The mission quickly established a missionary program in eight different cities. Progress in Flanders prompted the division of the Netherland Amsterdam Mission, and the Belgium Antwerp Mission was created on 16 July 1975 with Larry Hyde Brim as president. It consisted of all Flemish-speaking people previously served by the Netherlands Amsterdam Mission (the name having been changed from the Netherlands Mission to Netherlands Amsterdam Mission in 1974) and the northern portion of the Belgium Brussels Mission. This area reverted back and forth between the Netherlands Amsterdam Mission and the Belgium Antwerp Mission twice until 1994 when it was again consolidated with the Netherlands Amsterdam Mission.

Over the past four decades, mission boundaries and names in the southern part of the country continued to evolve as well to accommodate the growth of the Church in France and southern Belgium. On 15 January 1961, the French East Mission was organized from the southern portion of France. Two years later on 1 October 1963 the Brussels Branch was moved to the Liège District in the French Mission, creating the Liège-Brussels District, and the mission name was changed to the Franco-Belgium Mission. (This mission was later renamed the France-Belgium Mission in June 1970 and the Belgium Brussels Mission in 1974).

The Brussels Stake, the first in Belgium, was organized on 20 February 1977 with Joseph Scheen as president. On 16 October 1994, the Antwerp Belgium Stake was also organized with Johan A. Buysse as president. By 2002, there were 5,979 members scattered across the country throughout both the French and Flemish regions. In July of that year the two halves of the country were again united under the same mission for the first time in almost 100 years. The Belgium Brussels Mission and the Netherlands Amsterdam Mission were consolidated to form the Belgium Brussels/Netherlands Mission.

In 2003, membership reached 6,030.

Sources: Mehr, Kahlile B. Mormon Missionaries Enter Eastern Europe. Provo, Utah: BYU Press, 2002; Swiss and German Mission, Manuscript History and Historical Reports, Church Archives; French Mission; Manuscript History and Historical Reports; Swiss Italian and German Mission, Manuscript History and Historical Reports, Church Archives; Kahn, Marcel, History of the Liège District 1889-1997, Church History Library; Chard, Gary R., A History of the French Mission of the Church of Jesus Christ of Latter-day Saints 1850-1960, Thesis, Utah State University, 1965; Netherlands Amsterdam Mission, Manuscript History and Historical Reports, Church Archives; Belgium Antwerp Mission, Manuscript History and Historical Reports, Church Archives.

Stakes — 2
(Listed alphabetically As of Oct. 1, 2011.)

No.	Name	Organized	First President
Europe Area			
1993	Antwerp Belgium	16 Oct 1994	Johan A. Buysse
813	Brussels Belgium	20 Feb 1977	Joseph Scheen

Mission — 1
(As of Oct. 1, 2011; shown with historical number. See MISSIONS.)

(76) BELGIUM BRUSSELS/NETHERLANDS MISSION
87, Blvd. Brand Whitlock
B -1200 Brussels, Belgium

BELIZE
Jan. 1, 2011: Est. population, 308,000; Members, 3,852; Districts, 2; Branches, 11; Percent LDS, 1.1, or one in 90; Central America Area; Honduras San Pedro Sula Mission.

Located on the eastern coast of Central America, Belize, formerly known as British Honduras, has a parliamentary government and a population that speaks English, Spanish, and Creole. Belize received independence from Great Britain in 1981.

Missionary work began in Belize on 5 May 1980 when President Samuel Flores of the Honduras Tegucigalpa Mission and missionary Robert Henke arrived, followed by 10 additional missionaries the next day. The Belize City Branch was organized with missionary Merlin Mikkelson as president, and the first meeting was held 11 May. Ernesto Alay, the first member in Belize, was baptized on 1 June 1980.

The Belize District was organized on 17 April 1983 with Harold Smith as president. Meetinghouses were completed in Orange Walk in August 1987 and in San Ignacio ththe following month. By 1987 Church membership in the Belize District numbered approximately 1,000. The Honduras Tegucigalpa Mission was divided on 1 July 1990 and Belize was placed in the new Honduras San Pedro Sula Mission. Hilberto Cassanova was the first missionary called from Belize. He served in the

Honduras Tegucigalpa Misssion from 1987-1989.

In 1997, President Gordon B. Hinckley became the first Church president to visit Belize, speaking to approximately 1,200 members in Belize City on 13 November. It was the largest gathering of members in the country to date.

In 2003, membership reached 2,827.

Sources: Honduras Tegulcigalpa Mission, Annual historical reports, Church Archives; Donald Q. Cannon and Richard O. Cowan, Unto Every Nation: Gospel Light Reaches Every Land, 2003; Belize City Branch, photographs, 1980, Church Archives; "Growth Leads to Four New Missions, Two in Mexico, Two in Central America Reflect Continuing Missionary Success," Church News, 2 February1990; Correspondence from Ralph D. and Dawnetta A. Erickson, 30 November 1994; "Mexico's President Welcomes Prophet," Church News, 22 November 1997, John L. Hart,"Belize: 'Great Manifestations of Faith,'" Church News, 7 February 1998.

BENIN

Jan. 1, 2011: Est. population, 8,792,000; Members, 229; Branches 1; Missions 1; Percent LDS, .003, or one in 351,680; Africa West Area.

In 1998 Claude P. Toze, a citizen of Benin, met Mathias Eguko, a Nigerian member of the Church living in the capital of Cotonou. Eguko shared with Toze the missionary discussions and a copy of the Book of Mormon in French. Sacrament meetings were first held at Eguko's home and later at the home of Bryan Ermatinger, an employee of the United States Embassy. In the meantime, war erupted in the Democratic Republic of the Congo in August 1998 and all non-Congolese missionaries were evacuated from that country. Among the evacuated was a missionary couple, Normand and Sharon Langevin. They were re-assigned to neighboring Benin for one month in September 1998. It was here that the Langevins taught the final discussions to and baptized Claude P. Toze on 4 October 1998. Toze was the first citizen of Benin to be baptized.

The First Presidency and Quorum of the Twelve assigned Benin to the Ivory Coast Abidjan Mission on 21 January 1999. Demoine A. and Joyce Findlay were the first of several missionary couples assigned to support Church members in both Togo and Benin and work for legalization of the Church in those two countries. They lived in Togo and periodically visited Benin.

On 23 January 2001, Verne and Kathleen Davis become the first missionary couple assigned to live in Benin full time. They continued the work begun previously by the Findlays to gain legalization of the Church in Benin, and they also gave support to Church members meeting in the capital of Cotonou.

The BYU Singers toured Benin in May 2001 and were so impressed with the members that they donated blue ties and blue dresses to be worn when legal recognition came. On 7 March 2003, after years of working with government officials, the Church finally received legal recognition. That Sunday the blue ties and dresses were worn in celebration. The following month four young missionaries, Reid Schellhous, Brandon J. Smith, Jean-Boscoh Kouassi, and Ambroise Gbahouo, were assigned to Benin.

Membership on Jan. 1, 2011, was 201. The Benin Cotonou Mission was created by the division of the Ivory Coast Abidjan Mission on July 1, 2011. The mission is comprised of the countries of Benin and Togo.

Sources: Ivory Coast Abidjan Mission, Manuscript history and historical reports, Church Archives; "Sunday School Group in Benin Prepares Way for Legal Status," Church News, 31 May 2003; "Ties, dresses help celebrate legal recognition," Church News, 21 June 2003; Claude P. Toze as told to Peggy Proctor, "First Member in Benin Africa," Meridian Magazine, 21 Dec 2003; Verne and Kathleen Davis, Telephone conversation, 7 May 2004.

Mission — 1
(As of Oct. 1, 2011; shown with historical number. See MISSIONS.)

BENIN COTONOU MISSION
Quartier Cadjehoud #1158
Block F
Contonou, Benin

BOLIVIA

Jan. 1, 2011: Est. population, 9,775,000; Members, 172,640; Stakes, 24; Wards, 172; Branches, 81; Missions, 3; Districts, 10; Temples, 1; Percent LDS, 1.7, or one in 60.; South America Northwest Area.

Bolivia, located in central South America, is a republic with a population that speaks Spanish, Quechua, and Aymara.

Andes Mission President Vernon Sharp and his wife, Fawn, traveled to La Paz in 1961 to investigate the possibility of bringing missionaries into Bolivia. Norval Jesperson, a member, who, in 1962 became director of the American-Bolivian Center in Cochabamba, introduced to the Gospel to a number of Bolivians. As a result, Maria Van Gemerfen, became the first Bolivian to be baptized. In 1963, Jesperson, along with two other Church members, Duane Wilcox and Dube Thomas, who lived in La Paz, helped the Church gain legal status. Andes Mission President Sterling Nicolaysen arrived in Bolivia on 20 October 1964 and met with the Duane Wilcox family in La Paz and the Newell Judkins family in Cochabamba to find suitable locations to hold Church meetings. The first branch meeting in Cochabamba was held 22 November 1964 with 19 people in attendance. Missionaries arrived from the Andes Mission on 24 November 1964. Missionaries baptized Victor Walter Vallejos at Cochabamba just before Christmas in 1964.

The first Bolivian to serve a mission was Desiderio Arce Cano. While pursuing a singing career in Argentina, he was called on 25 April 1967 to return to his native land. The first missionary called from Bolivia was Carlos Pedraja. He was baptized 30 May 1965, and called to the Andes South Mission in 1968, and later served as stake and mission president, and director of seminaries and institutes in Bolivia. Martha Taborga Coca de Oruro received her missionary call to Ecuador on 31 August 1970, the first sister missionary called from Bolivia. Early Church member and leader Jorge Leano Rodriguez became the first Bolivian mission president. He was called on 16 June 1987 as president of the Colombia Cali Mission. In 1995, he was called as president of the Lima Peru Temple.

Elder Spencer W. Kimball and Andes Mission President J. Avril Jesperson met with Bolivian President René Barrientos Ortuño on 6 September 1966. They explained the Church's plan to create the Andes South Mission, headquartered in La Paz, and also invited him to visit the Church headquarters in Salt Lake City, which he subsequently did two years later. The Andes South Mission later became the Bolivia La Paz Mission. In 1968, there were about 350 members in Bolivia. That number increased to 9,700 by 1977. The Bolivia Santa Cruz Mission was organized in 1977, and was renamed the Bolivia Cochabamba Mission in 1982. The Santa Cruz Bolivia Stake, the first in Bolivia, was organized 14 January 1979. More than 4,300 members attended an area conference in La Paz on 3 March 1977, with President Spencer W. Kimball, who also met with the head of state, President Hugo Bonzer Suarez.

At the close of the 1980s, some political extremists carried out random attacks on Church meetinghouses and tragically assassinated missionaries Jeffrey Ball and Todd Wilson in La Paz on 24 May 1989. During this period Bolivian members became more united and many of the youth committed themselves to serve full-time missions. Despite the opposition, Church growth continued, and in 1991, there were more than 4,000 baptisms in Bolivia. On 15 January 1995, workers completed the construction of the 100th meetinghouse in Bolivia, the first having been built by local Church members in Quiriza in 1969.

The Cochabamba Bolivia Temple was dedicated by President Gordon B . Hinckley on 30 April 2000, following a five-day open house in which 65,570 people visited. By the year 2000, there were 118,000 members of the Church in Bolivia.

In 2002, membership reached 133,170.

Sources: Carlos Pedraja, Historia de la Iglesia en Bolivia, 2001; Sistema Educativa de la Iglesia, La Historia de la Iglesia en Bolivia, 1964-1985; Andes Mission, Manuscript history, Church Archives; Andes Mission history [ca. 1960-1962], Church Archives; Dell Van Orden, "Love, Respect and Emotion End Area Conference Series," Church News, 12 March 1977; "Some Missionaries in Bolivia, Peru Are 'Redeployed,'" Church News, 15 July 1989; Allen Litster, "Pioneering in the Andes," Ensign, January 1997; "The Church in Bolivia, Colombia, Ecuador, Peru, and Venezuela," Ensign, January 1997; "President Hinckley Visits South America, Florida, Washington, D.C.," Ensign, February 1997.

Stakes — 24
(Listed alphabetically as of Oct. 1, 2011.)

No.	Name	Organized	First President
South America West Area			
1465	Cochabamba Bolivia Cobija	19 Feb 1984	Guillermo Rivero Paz Soldan
2143	Cochabamba Bolivia Jaihuayco	10 Dec 1995	Ivan Jorge Gutierrez
1940	Cochabamba Bolivia Los Alamos	16 May 1993	Jose Ruben Rivero Zeballos
1062	*Cochabamba Bolivia Universidad	19 Feb 1984	
	‡Cochabamba Bolivia	11 Sep 1979	Carlos L. Pedraja
1831	El Alto Bolivia	24 Nov 1991	Edmundo Chavez Vasquez
2763	El Alto Bolivia Los Andes	9 Jun 2007	Javier Lazo Mamani
1227	*El Alto Bolivia Satelite	6 Mar 1992	
	‡La Paz Bolivia El Alto	18 Jan 1981	Victor Hugo Saravia R.
2207	La Paz Bolivia Alto San Pedro	30 Jun 1996	Juan Carlos Mogrovejo Rocabado
1112	*La Paz Bolivia Constitucion	18 Jan 1981	
	‡La Paz Bolivia West	24 Feb 1980	Victor Hugo Saravia R.
1007	*La Paz Bolivia Miraflores	18 Jan 1981	
	‡La Paz Bolivia	11 Mar 1979	Jorge Leano
1670	La Paz Bolivia Sopocachi	17 Jan 1988	Eduardo Gabarret I.
2120	Montero Bolivia	12 Nov 1995	Hugo Walter Sandoval Pinto
1213	Oruro Bolivia	1 Dec 1980	J. Adrian Velasco C.
2063	Potosi Bolivia	18 Jun 1995	Edgar Medardo Lopez Loayza
993	*Santa Cruz Bolivia Canoto	15 Feb 1981	
	‡Santa Cruz Bolivia	14 Jan 1979	Noriharu Ishigaki Haraguichi
2434	Santa Cruz Bolivia El Bajio	1 Feb 1998	Jose Martin Tellez T.
1782	Santa Cruz Bolivia Equipetrol	2 Dec 1990	Antonio Rolando Oyola
2601	Santa Cruz Bolivia La Merced	9 Sep 2001	Ricardo Villarroel Suarez
2735	Santa Cruz Bolivia La Pampa	14 Oct 2006	Alcides Carlos Sabath Flores
1235	Santa Cruz Bolivia Paraiso	15 Feb 1981	Erwin Birnbaumer
1981	Santa Cruz Bolivia Piray	19 June 1994	Rolando A. Oyola Suarez
2191	Sucre Bolivia	28 Apr 1996	Esteban Portillo Rios
2184	Tarija Bolivia	24 Mar 1996	Juan Garcia Vargas
2611	Trinidad Bolivia	27 April 2003	Jorge Romero Soria
Discontinued			
2277	Oruro Bolivia Agua de Castilla	24 Nov 1996	Johnny Chambi Joaniquina

Discontinued 19 Aug 2001

Missions — 3
(As of Oct. 1, 2011; shown with historical number. See MISSIONS.)

(150) BOLIVIA COCHABAMBA MISSION
Casilla de Correo 1375
Cochabamba, Bolivia

(75a) BOLIVIA LA PAZ MISSION
Av. 20 de Octubre #2550
La Paz, Bolivia

(320) BOLIVIA SANTA CRUZ MISSION
C/ Saavedra esq. Cochabamba
Torres Cainco, Biq Empresarial, Piso 9,
Santa Cruz, Bolivia

BOTSWANA

Jan. 1, 2011: Est. population, 1,991,000; Members, 1,331; Wards, 2; Branches, 2; Percent LDS, .065, or one in 1,526; Africa Southeast Area; South Africa Johannesburg Mission.

Botswana, previously known as Bechuanaland, became independent from Britain on 30 September 1966. Located in south-central Africa, it is bordered by Namibia, Zimbabwe, and South Africa. The official language is English, with Setswana also spoken. Fifty percent of the people are Christian, while 50 percent follow tribal beliefs.

In June 1975, Lawrence C. and Hazel Parker arrived in Botswana where he worked as an agricultural adviser and teacher. By 1977 Latter-day Saints Blaine and Grace McClellan were also living there. A branch in Gaborone was created in 1983.

Missionaries Karl and Marjorie Jenkins were sent to Botswana in 1990 with the assignment to locate Latter-day Saints who had joined abroad that were now residing in Botswana. The first missionaries assigned to work full-time in Botswana, Bruce and Patricia Midge, arrived in June 1990. Members living in Botswana at the time included Peace Corps workers, Patricia Lutz and Javotte Pickering, and the Maurice Mzwinila and Anthony Mogare families, who had joined the Church while studying in the United States.

In March 1992, the branch was divided to form the Gaborone West and Gaborone Broadhurst branches. An additional branch was created at Lobatse on 28 October 1992. The Gaborone Botswana District was created at that same time with Kwasi Agyare Dwomoh as president. It continued until 12 July 1995 when it was dissolved. At that time the Gaborone West and Gaborone Broadhurst branches became wards and along with the Lobatse Branch they were incorporated into the Roodepoort South Africa Stake.

The Gaborone Botswana District was organized on 1 March 1992. Elder Richard G. Scott of the Quorum of Twelve visited Botswana on the following 21 August. On 19 January 1997 the Gaborone Branch meetinghouse was dedicated. The first full-time missionary from Botswana, Yakale Million Moroka, served in the South Africa Cape Town Mission from March 1999 to March 2001.

Sources: Borgna Brunner, "Countries of the World, Botswana," Time Almanac 2003; South Africa Mission, Manuscript history and reports, Church Archives; South Africa Johannesburg Mission, Manuscript history and historical reports, Church Archives.

BRAZIL

Jan. 1, 2011: Est. population, 198,739,000; Members, 1,138,740; Stakes, 239; Wards, 1,457; Branches, 468; Missions, 27; Districts, 49; Temples, 5, under construction, 2; Percent LDS, .53, or one in 187; Brazil Area.

Brazil, a federal republic with a Portuguese-speaking population, covers almost half the continent of South America.

The first known Church member in Brazil was Max Richard Zapf, who was baptized in Germany in August 1908 and emigrated to Brazil in 1913. After many years with no Church contact, Max Zapf and his family learned that Augusta Kuhlmann Lippelt and her four children, who had also joined the Church in Germany before immigrating to Brazil in 1923, were living in the small southern Brazilian town of Ipomeia. Augusta's husband Roberto, although not a member when he moved his family to Brazil, was baptized several years later. The Zapf family soon relocated to be with their new friends, the Lippelt family. These two families represented the beginning of the Church's permanent presence in Brazil.

The first missionaries were William Fred Heinz and Emil A. J. Schindler, accompanied by President Rheinold Stoof of the South American Mission in Buenos Aires, Argentina. President Stoof first visited Brazil in 1927, and returned with the elders to begin missionary work among German-speaking people in September 1928. Bertha Sell and her children, Theodore, Alice, Seigfried, and Adell, were the first converts, baptized 14 April 1929. A branch was organized in Joinville on 6 July 1930 and the first Church-owned meetinghouse in South America was dedicated 25 October 1931, in Joinville.

A mission was created and headquartered in São Paulo, Brazil, on 25 May 1935. At first, missionaries taught only in German. However, a Portuguese edition of the Book of Mormon was published in 1939. Missionaries began teaching in Portuguese partly because the government, worried about the perceived growth of pro-Nazi sentiment among Brazil's large German population, issued decrees which severely restricted the use of languages other than Portuguese. By 1940, there were fewer than 200 members in the country. In 1941, the Church began to remove all North American missionaries from Brazil as a result of World War II, which slowed Church growth. They did not return in appreciable numbers until 1946.

In 1954, President David O. McKay became the first Church president to visit Brazil. At the end of the 1950s, membership totaled 3,700 and by the time the São Paulo Temple was dedicated in 1978 it had reached 54,000. After 1978, in part due to the revelation extending priesthood to all worthy males, Church growth became extraordinary. By 1990, membership exceeded 300,000 and as the 1990s ended, membership totaled more than 700,000.

By 2002, membership reached 842,296.

The Brazil Area was created in August 1987 and divided in August of 1998 to form the Brazil North and South areas. On 2 February 1986, with the creation of the Campinas Brazil Castelo Stake, Brazil became the third country outside the United States to have 50 stakes. When the São Leopoldo Brazil Stake was created 5 December 1993, Brazil reached 100 stakes, the second country outside the United States to do so. Elder Helio A. Camargo, who served in the Seventy from 1985-1990, was the first Brazilian to serve as a General Authority. Other Brazilians called as General Authorities as members of the Seventy include Helvecio Martins, Claudio R.M. Costa, and Athos M. Amorim.

In October 1993, construction began on the the the Church's second largest Missionary Training Center in São Paulo. The seven-story building, capable of accommodating 750 missionaries, was dedicated 18 May 1997 by Elder Russell M. Nelson of the Quorum of the Twelve. In October 1998, North American missionaries called to Brazil began receiving nearly half of their training at the Brazilian Missionary Training Center. The program to send North American missionaries to Brazil for four weeks of training enabled them to be immersed in the Brazilian culture and Portuguese language in a controlled environment.

The program was so successful that in April 2000 the first 22 North American missionaries were sent to Brazil for their full eight weeks of training. The group was the first of four pilot groups to enter the Brazilian center during the summer of 2000 to be entirely trained in another language at a missionary training center in another country. The pilot training program ended in August 2000 and afterward, an average of 33 North American missionaries began their full training in the Brazil center each week.

The São Paulo Stake, the first in South America, was organized on 1 May 1966. Ten years later, Brazil had 10 stakes, and a temple had been announced for São Paulo. President Spencer W. Kimball presided over a cornerstone ceremony for the temple on 9 March1977. The Temple was dedicated 30 October 1978. President Gordon B. Hinckley dedicated the Recife Temple on 15 December 2000. While President James E. Faust, second counselor in the First Presidency attended the groundbreaking of the Porto Alegre Temple, he also was made an honorary citizen of São Paulo, in recognition of his lifelong ties to that city and to Brazil. President Hinckley dedicated the Porto Alegre Temple on 17 December 2000 and the Campinas Temple on 17 May 2002. A fifth temple in Curitiba is currently under construction.

Brazilian Latter-day Saints have been very active in humanitarian efforts and community service projects which have received nationwide recognition and appreciation. Marco Maciel, vice president of Brazil, thanked the Church for its service in 2001 and the Church, represented by its service organization, "Helping Hands," received national recognition on 9 November 2002, as one of the most important volunteer organizations in Brazil.

Elder Russell M. Nelson of the Quorum of the Twelve presided over the groundbreaking of the fifth temple to be built in Brazil, located in Curitiba, on 10 March 2005. It was dedicated on June 1, 2008, by President Thomas S. Monson.

Ground was broken for the Manaus Brazil on June 20, 2008 by Elder Charles Didier of the Seventy and president of the Brazil Area. Plans for the Fortaleza Brazil were announced on Oct. 3, 2009.

Membership reached 866,988 in 2003. In 2005, membership reached 928,926. By the beginning of the 2010, membership was 1,060,556 divided among 233 stakes.

Sources: Frederick S. Williams and Frederick G. Williams, From Acorn to Oak Tree, 1987; Mark L. Grover, "Mormonism in Brazil: Religion and Dependency in Latin America," (PhD diss., 1985); Marcus Martins, "The Oak Tree Revisited: Brazilian LDS Leaders' Insights on the Growth of the Church in Brazil," (PhD diss., 1996); Donald Q. Cannon and Richard O. Cowan, Unto Every Nation: Gospel Light Reaches Every Land, 2003; [Dedication Ceremony, Brazil Missionary Training Center], 18 May 1997, LDS Church Archives; Deseret News, 14 November 1935; Rulon S. Howells, "Brazil, A new frontier for the Restored Gospel," Improvement Era, May 1936 and September 1938; "Brazilian Missions," Improvement Era, May 1963; Shaun D. Stahle, "Missionaries receive full training in Brazil," Church News, 12 August 2000; Fernando Assis and Nestor Curbelo, "Brazilian temples complete historic year of dedication," Church News, 23 December 2000; Fernando Assis, "Hands that help," Church News, 3 November 2001; Fernando Assis, "30,000 serving brighten face of entire nation," Church News, 5 October 2002; Ground broken for temple in Curitiba," Church News, 19 March 2005.

Stakes — 242
(Listed alphabetically As of Oct. 1, 2011.)

No.	Name	Organized	First President
	Brazil Area		
1292	Alegrete Brazil	20 Sep 1981	Waldomiro Siegfried Radtke
2883	Alphaville Brazil	17 Oct 2011	Paulo Cesar Ferrao de Amorim
2887	Alvarenga Brazil	24 Oct 2011	Alexandre Rostirolla da Fonseca
2066	Americana Brazil	25 Jun 1995	Donizetti de Paul Tavares
2383	Anapolis Brazil	29 Jun 1997	Cassio Barbosa Piazzarola
2078	*Aracaju Brazi North	27 Feb 2000	
	‡Aracaju Brazil Cidade Nova	23 Jul 1995	Raulino Gairao LIma Jr.
1851	*Aracaju Brazil South	27 Feb 2000	
	*Aracaju Brazil Bela Vista	23 Jul 1995	
	‡Aracaju Brazil	8 Mar 1992	Manuel Durval Andrade Neto
1886	Aracatuba Brazil	14 June 1992	Paulo Henrique Itinose
2100	Arapiraca Brazil	17 Sep 1995	Antonio de A. de Banos
970	Araraquara Brazil	22 Oct 1978	Marcio Rodrigues Galhardo
2860	Arsenal Brazil	18 Oct 2009	
1959	Bage Brazil	31 Oct 1993	Cecer R. Loureiro Dutra
2402	Barueri Brazil	26 Oct 1997	Marcos Antony Aidukaitis
1893	Bauru Brazil	2 Aug 1992	Lazaro Beteto
1837	Belem Brazil	29 Dec 1991	Luiz Carlos Silva De Franca
2067	Belem Brazil Cabanagem	25 Jun 1995	Jaime Carneiro Costa
2381	Belem Brazil Cidade Nova	22 Jun 1997	Wenceslau W. da C. Coelho
2896	Belem Brazil Entroncamento	12 Dec 2010	Leonelson de Jesus Gatinho Castro
2897	Belem Brazil Icoaraci	12 Dec 2010	Rubens Dario de Castro Souza
1234	*Belo Horizonte Brazil	6 Mar 1990	
	*Belo Horizonte Brazil De Siao	10 Jan 1989	
	‡Belo Horizonte Brazil	15 Feb 1981	Ernani Teixeira
2819	Belo Horizonte Brazil East	15 Feb 2009	Edison Luiz Schuck da Rocha
2570	Belo Horizonte Brazil Pampulha	3 Sep 2000	Rodrigo de Lima e Myrra
1963a	Belo Horizonte Brazil West	12 Dec 1993	Rodrigo de Lima e Myrra
2074	Birigui Brazil	9 Jul 1995	Sebastiao Henrique Neto
1189	Brasilia Brazil	12 Oct 1980	Daniel Alberta da Gloria
1393	*Brasilia Brazil Alvorada	22 Mar 1983	

	‡Alvorada Brazil	9 Jan 1983	Manoel Francisco Clavery G.
2731	Brasília Brazil Ceilândia	17 Sep 2006	Marlon Silva dos Santos
2418	Brasilia Brazil North	30 Nov 1997	Joao A. Machado de Lima
2147	Brasilia Brazil Taguatinga	17 Dec 1995	Jose Claudio de Almeida
2766	Caico Brazil	17 Jun 2007	Cláudio Vale de Araújo
2599	Camacari Brazil	5 Aug 2001	Carlos Simpaio Costa
2821	Camacari Brazil Central	8 Mar 2009	Jesse de Oliveira e Sa
1984	Camaragibe Brazil	24 Jul 1994	Altair Roque da Silva
1442	Campina Grande Brazil	18 Sep 1983	Jose Francisco Barbosa
2712	Campina Grande Brazil Liberdade	12 Mar 2006	José Freire Dias Filho
2689	Campinas Brazil Campos Eliseos	30 Oct 2005	Alexandre Luis Casarini Tavares
1586	Campinas Brazil Castelo	2 Feb 1986	S. Lourenco de Oliveira
1897	Campinas Brazil Flamboyant	23 Aug 1992	Luiz Antonio Cairo
621	*Campinas Brazil		
	‡Campinas	9 Jun 1973	Nelson de Genaro
1805	Campo Grande Brazil	30 Jun 1991	Ricardo Kasimerczak
2412	Campos Brazil	23 Nov 1997	Jarbas Pereira de Souza Filho
1962	Canoas Brazil	5 Dec 1993	Raul Anibal Proenca Krieger
2813	Canoas Brazil North	30 Nov 2008	Pedro Alberto Machado Da Silva
2672	Cariacica Brazil	13 Mar 2005	Ailton Aguirres
2341	Cascavel Brazil	20 Apr 1997	Luiz C. Bernardino da Silva
2889	Castanhal Brazil	28 Nov 2010	José Maria Soares Belo
2782	Caucaia Brazil	18 Nov 2007	Benedito S. de Oliveira
1963	Caxias Do Sul Brazil	5 Dec 1993	Alvacir Luiz Siedschlag
1942	Contagem Brazil	6 June 1993	Evandro Chevitarese Parada
2628	Cruz Alta Brazil	29 Feb 2004	Clademir Elton Trage
2032	Cuiaba Brazil	5 Mar 1995	Ildemar Ferreira Vilas Boas
2827	Cuiaba Brazil Industriario	3 May 2009	Ivanecir da Silva Barboza
2446	Curitiba Brazil Boa Vista	22 Mar 1998	Jarbas F. Souza
1243	*Curitiba Brazil Boqueirao	14 Mar 1989	
	‡Curitiba Brazil East	15 Mar 1981	Francisco Reguim
1468	Curitiba Brazil Iguacu	29 Apr 1984	Waldemar de Lima
2770	Curitiba Brazil Jardim do Sol	11 Aug 2007	Sandro Roberto Machado Fagundes
2438	Curitiba Brazil Luz	15 Feb 1998	Luiz Antonio Cruzato
1974a	Curitiba Brazil Novo Mundo	29 Feb 1994	Valdemiro Skraba
893	*Curitiba Brazil Portao	14 Mar 1989	
	‡Curitiba Brazil South	26 Feb 1978	Albina Bruno Schmeil
1302	*Curitiba Brazil Sao Lourenco		
	‡Curitiba Brazil Bacacheri	1 Nov 1981	Casemiro Antunes Gomes
552	*Curitiba Brazil		
	‡Curitiba	12 Dec 1971	Jason Garcia Souza
2073	Curitiba Brazil Taruma	9 Jul 1995	Ildefonso de C. Dues Neto
2249	Diadema Brazil	20 Oct 1996	Adelson de Paula Parrella
2231	Feira de Santana Brazil	15 Sep 1996	Vaguiner Cruciol Tobias
2600a	Feira de Santana Brazil Kalilandia	5 Aug 2001	Roque Alvim Freitas
1569	Florianopolis Brazil	3 Nov 1985	Cesar A. Seiguer Milder
1284	Fortaleza Brazil	19 Jul 1981	Orville Wayne Day Jr.
2894	Fortaleza Brazil Benfica	12 Dec 2010	Gleydson Ferreira Cintra
2733	Fortaleza Brazil Bom Jardim	17 Sep 2006	Helder Ferreira de Andrade
1828	Fortaleza Brazil Bom Sucesso	17 Nov 1991	Manoel A. De Carvalho Filho
2849	Fortaleza Brazil Castelao	28 June 2009	Francisco de Assis Souza dos Reis
1935	Fortaleza Brazil Ceara	2 May 1993	Jose Vieira de Matos Filho
2689	Fortaleza Brazil East	4 Sept 2005	Fabio H. Correia
2816	Fortaleza Brazil East Messejana	8 Dec 2008	Annysteyne Maia Chaves
2380	Fortaleza Brazil Litoral	22 Jun 1997	Miguel Alves dos Santos
1454	Fortaleza Brazil Montese	13 Nov 1983	Fernando J. Duarte D.
2386	Fortaleza Brazil South	17 Aug 1997	David Garcia Fernandes
1578	Fortaleza Brazil West	24 Nov 1985	Antenor Silva Junior
1952	Franca Brazil	5 Sep 1993	Donizete Pugliesi Braz
2048	Garanhuns Brazil	21 May 1995	Jose C. Furtado Campos
1641	Goiania Brazil	24 May 1987	Antonio Casado Rodriguez
2294	Goiania Brazil East	15 Dec 1996	Jose Renato Ungarelli
2142	Gravatai Brazil	10 Dec 1995	Fabiano Ribeiro Barreto
2310	Guaratingueta Brazil	23 Feb 1997	Pedro G. L. de C. Bruno
2221	Guaruja Brazil	18 Aug 1996	Carlos Roberto Couto E. Silva
2746	Hortolândia Brazil	27 Jan 2006	David Kuceki
2814	Imperatriz Brasil	30 Nov 2008	Glaucio Nascimento Lopes
2256	Itabuna Brazil	27 Oct 1996	Jose M. Sepulveda da Costa
2480	Itatiba Brazil	21 June 1998	Eliseli Colleoni
2342	Itu Brazil	20 Apr 1997	Valoir Teixeira Arantes
1891	*Jaboatao Brazil dos Guararapes	15 May 1994	
	‡Recife Brazil Jaboatao	26 Jul 1992	Jose Antonia da Silva

1979	Jaboatao Brazil Litoral	15 May 1994	Domingos Savio Linhares
1185	Joao Pessoa Brazil	2 Oct 1980	Jose Francisco Barbosa
1896	Joao Pessoa Brazil Rangel	23 Aug 1992	Israel Vilar Neto
2768	Joao Pessoa Brazil Torre	23 Jun 2007	Francisco Ronaldo de Castro Sousa
1338	Joinville Brazil	21 Apr 1982	Heins Dorival Halter
2275	Juiz De Fora Brazil	24 Nov 1996	Eraldo Luis dos Santos
1833	Jundiai Brazil	1 Dec 1991	Domingos Fatobene Jr.
2685	Jundiai Brazil Represa	19 June 2005	Luiz A. Pinto
2257	Lages Brazil	27 Oct 1996	Sebastiao C. de Lima Dias
1821	Livramento Brazil	27 Oct 1991	Clademir Elton Trage
1080	Londrina Brazil	11 Nov 1979	Carlos Roberto Moeller
2251	Londrina Brazil Tiradentes	20 Oct 1996	Amancio Marques do Santos
2890	Macae Brazil	4 Dec 2010	Wagner Destro
1322	Maceio Brazil	21 Jan 1982	Abelardo Rodrigues Camara
1923	Maceio Brazil Litoral	7 Feb 1993	Gilberto C. da Silva Moraes
2030	Maceio Brazil Pajucara	5 Mar 1995	Jose Domingues Silva
2787	Maceio Brazil Tabuleiro	9 Dec 2007	Alvis Costa Ponde
1700	Manaus Brazil	16 Oct 1988	Eduardo A. Soares C.
2116	Manaus Brazil Cidade Nova	5 Nov 1995	Walter Braga De Souza
2707	Manaus Brazil Mindu	5 Mar 2006	Raimundo R. Lima
2760	Manaus Brazil Ponta Negra	5 May 2007	Luiz Carlos Dorneles Queiroz
2447	Manaus Brazil Rio Amazonas	22 Mar 1998	Jose A. Viana Guimaraes
1941	Manaus Brazil Rio Negro	30 May 1993	Divino Presenca
2697	Manaus Brazil Samauma	27 Nov 2005	Kennedy Fonseca Canuto
2319	Manaus Brazil Solimoes	9 Mar 1997	Jose A. Viana Guimaraes
2145	Maracanau Brazil	17 Dec 1995	Raimundo Vieira de Oliveira
1449	Marilia Brazil	23 Oct 1983	Wilson de Souza Novelli
2095	Maringa Brazil	27 Aug 1995	Dirceu Freire
2664	Maua Brazil	28 Nov 2004	Marcos A. Santos
2065	Mogi Mirim Brazil	25 Jun 1995	Milton Cenko
2744	Mossoro Brazil	10 Dec 2006	Nipson Torres de Araújo
1894	Natal Brazil	16 Aug 1992	Ricardo Gueiros
2742	Natal Brazil Pajucara	3 Dec 2006	Edelson Silvestre de Lima
2741	Natal Brazil Ponta Negra	25 Nov 2006	João Fernando Henriques Pinheiro
2470	Natal Brazil Potengi	31 May 1998	Jorge Borges DeLira
769	*Niteroi Brazil	14 Oct 2001	
	‡Rio de Janeiro Brazil Niteroi	19 Sep 1976	Joao Eduardo Kemeny
2325	Nova Iguacu Brazil	16 Mar 1997	Carlos M. Figueireda Patriota
987	Novo Hamburgo Brazil	3 Dec 1978	Paulo R. Grahl
1282	Olinda Brazil	12 Jul 1981	Reinhold Kraft
2020	*Olinda Brazil Paulista	22 Aug 1995	
	‡Paulista Brazil	5 Feb 1995	Reginaldo de Morais Junior
1932	Osasco Brazil	18 Apr 1993	Marcos Anthony Aidu Kaitis
2893	Pacajus Brazil	12 Dec 2010	Sergio Ricardo Castro Guimarães
2785	Palmas Brazil	2 Dec 2007	Tobias Ferreira Leal
2471	Paranagua Brazil	31 May 1998	
1604	Passo Fundo Brazil	10 Aug 1986	Helio Rodrigues Severo
1658	Pelotas Brazil	18 Oct 1987	Marco Antonio Rais
2080	Pelotas Brazil North	23 Jul 1995	Victor A. Asconavieta da Silva
2479	Petrolina Brazil	21 June 1998	Nilo Manuel de Sa
1377	Petropolis Brazil	14 Nov 1982	Antonio Jose Mendoza
2786	Pinhais Brazil	9 Dec 2007	Imar B. Pires
2012	Piracicaba Brazil	22 Jan 1995	Marcos T. Michailuca Nolli
1182	*Ponta Grossa Brazil	30 Nov 1997	
	*Ponta Grossa Brazil Parana	7 Apr 1992	
	‡Ponta Grossa Parana Brazil	22 Sep 1980	Silvina Mendes de Jesus
2419	Ponta Grossa Brazil Campos Gerais	30 Nov 1997	Gilberto P. Lucas de Farias
2423	Ponta Pora Brazil	14 Dec 1997	Rubens Paim Quadros
601	Porto Alegre Brazil	13 Feb 1973	Miguell Sorrentino
1858	Porto Alegre Brazil Moinhos de Vento	3 May 1992	Claudio Weihert
1256	Porto Alegre Brazil North	21 Apr 1981	Silvio Geschwandtner
1793	Porto Alegre Brazil Partenon	5 May 1991	Ulisses Pereira Filho
2283	Porto Alegre Brazil South	1 Dec 1996	Hilario Olmar da Silva
2287	Porto Velho Brazil	22 Nov 1996	Jose S. Paulino de Lacerda
2436	Praia Grande Brazil	8 Feb 1998	Fernando da Silva E Souza
1201	Recife Brazil	31 Oct 1980	Iraja Bandeira Soares
1332	*Recife Brazil Boa Viagem	26 Jul 1992	
	*Boa Viagem Brazil	21 Mar 1982	Iraja Bandeira Soares
2728	Recife Brazil Casa Amarela	3 Sep 2006	Ednei Vieira de Moura
2379	Recife Brazil Caxanga	22 Jun 1997	Altair Rogue da Silva
2135	Recife Brazil Imbiribeira	3 Dec 1995	Marcone Magalhaes Santos
1811	*Recife Brazil Jardim Sao Paulo	10 May 1994	

	‡Recife Brazil Southwest	25 Aug 1991	Herbert Otto Homolka
1916a	Ribeiro Pires Brazil	13 Dec 1992	Guilherme Tell Peixoto
1645	*Ribeirao Preto East	9 Dec 2001	
	‡Ribeirao Preto Brazil	28 Jun 1987	Moises Barreiro Damasceno
1888	Ribeiro Preto West	9 Dec 2001	
	‡Ribeirao Preto Brazil Centro	21 Jun 1992	Augusto Martinez Perez
2136	Rio Branco Brazil	3 Dec 1995	Tarciso Barboza Friere
1135	Rio Claro Brazil	21 May 1980	Marcio Rodriques Galhardo
2079	Rio Grande Brazil	23 Jul 1995	Carlos W. Ramires de Oliveira
589	*Rio de Janeiro Brazil		
	‡Rio de Janeiro	22 Oct 1972	Veledmar Cury
1028	Rio de Janeiro Brazil Andarai	20 May 1979	Nelson Gennari
2293	Rio de Janeiro Brazil	15 Dec 1996	Jackson Alves do Santos
	‡Campo Grande		
2930	Rio de Janeiro Brazil Engenho de Dentro	19 Jun 2011	Leonardo Ovidio de Melo Ferreira
2676	Rio De Janeiro Brazil Itaguai	20 March 2005	Altino Carlos de Oliveira Rosa
2445	Rio De Janeiro Brazil Jacarepagua	22 Mar 1998	Claudio Jose Hottum Da Silva
1378	Rio de Janeiro Brazil Madureira	14 Nov 1982	Atilio Pinto Maio
1862	Salvador Brazil	10 May 1992	Carlos Shunji Obata
2709	Salvador Brazil Imbui	4 Mar 2006	Mario Cesar da Silva Cunha
2604	Salvadore Brazil Libertad	15 Sep 2002	Heitmar Maturino Guaka
1934a	Salvador Brazil North	2 May 1993	Sandro Silva Quatel
1922	Santa Maria Brazil	31 Jan 1993	Aires Luciano
2227	Santa Rita Brazil	1 Sep 1996	Jose Joel Alves Fernandes
1136	Santo Andre Brazil	23 May 1980	Ademar Leal
620	*Santos Brazil		
	‡Santos	8 Jun 1973	Jose Gonzalez Lopes
2491	Sao Bernardo Brazil Rudge Ramos	16 Aug 1998	Valdir Antunes
523	*Sao Bernardo Brazil	23 May 1980	
	*Sao Paulo Brazil South		
	‡Sao Paulo South	6 Sep 1970	Saul Messias de Oliveira
1909a	Sao Carlos Brazil	15 Nov 1992	Justino Carlos Archiza Peres
2081	Sao Joao da Boa Vista Brazil	30 Jul 1995	Izaias Pivato Nogueira
1965	Sao Jose Brazil	19 Dec 1993	Jose Jorge Cordeiro Campos
1917	Sao Jose do Rio Preto Brazil	13 Dec 1992	Guilherme Tell Peixoto
1516	Sao Jose dos Campos Brazil	3 Mar 1985	Eric Brito Correa
2396	Sao Jose dos Pinhais Brazil	14 Sep 1997	Nata Cruciol Tobias
1961	Sao Leopoldo Brazil	5 Dec 1993	Valmir Severo Dutra
2071	Sao Luis Brazil	2 Jul 1995	Jose Benicio Pereira
417	*Sao Paulo Brazil		
	‡Sao Paulo	1 May 1966	Walter Spat
1846	Sao Paulo Brazil Campo Limpo	9 Feb 1992	Dejanir Hadleck de Castro
2717	Sao Paulo Brazil Casa Grande	8 Dec 2008	Antonio dos Sontos Maia
2757	Sao Paulo Brazil Cumbica	10 Mar 2007	José Luís da Silva
2756	Sao Paulo Brazil Embu	3 Mar 2007	Eduardo Vicente Thomazini
2911	Sao Paulo Brazil Ferriera	17 Apr 2011	Ricardo Cerqueira Leite
2369	Sao Paulo Brazil Grajau	8 Jun 1997	Dario Marcolino dos Santos
2367	Sao Paulo Brazil Guarapiranga	1 Jun 1997	Caio Bezerra da Silva
1868	Sao Paulo Brazil Guarulhos	24 May 1992	Gilmar Silva Diasta
1536	Sao Paulo Brazil Interlagos	26 May 1985	Walter Guedes de Queiroz
1137	Sao Paulo Brazil Ipiranga	25 May 1980	Demar Staniscia
2764	Sao Paulo Brazil Itaqua	9 Jun 2007	Carlos Eduardo dos Santos
1869	Sao Paulo Brazil Itaquera	24 May 1992	Vanderlei Zanchetta
2198	Sao Paulo Brazil Jacana	2 Jun 1996	Jorge Luiz de Oliveira
2812	Sao Paulo Brazil Jaragua	23 Nov 2008	Anisio Alves de Sousa
2775	Sao Paulo Brazil Jardim da Saude	15 Sep 2007	Oswaldo de Almeida Pastore
1870	Sao Paulo Brazil Mogi Das Cruzes	24 May 1992	Gilberto Vicente da Silva
815	Sao Paulo Brazil North	20 Feb 1977	Jorge Flavio de Moraes
2395	Sao Paulo Brazil Parque Bristol	14 Sep 1997	Ricardo Vieira
2318	Sao Paulo Brazil Parque Pinheiros	9 Mar 1997	Mario Helio Emerick
467	*Sao Paulo Brazil Penha	24 May 1992	
	*Sao Paulo Brazil East		
	‡Sao Paulo East	24 Nov 1968	Helio da Rocha Camargo
1138	Sao Paulo Brazil Perdizes	25 May 1980	Oswaldo Silva Camargo
1913	Sao Paulo Brazil Piratininga	6 Dec 1992	Luiz Carlos Coronetti
2359	Sao Paulo Brazil Pirituba	25 May 1997	Pedro Pereira do Santos
2076	*Sao Paulo Brazil Raposo Taveres	14 Jan 1997	
	‡Sao Paulo Brazil Cotia	16 Jul 1995	Ulisses Soares
1082	Sao Paulo Brazil Santo Amaro	12 Nov 1979	Wilson Sanchez Netto
1823	Sao Paulo Brazil Sao Miguel Paulista	10 Nov 1991	Gilberto V. Da Silva
1441	Sao Paulo Brazil Taboao	18 Sep 1983	Octavio Baptists de Carvalho
622	*Sao Paulo Brazil West		

	‡Sao Paulo West	10 Jun 1973	Jose Benjamin Puerta
1291	Sao Vicente Brazil	20 Sep 1981	Vicente Verta Jr.
2748	Sao Vicente Brazil Serra do Mar	11 Feb 2007	Luiz Fernando Tavares
2882	Santarém Brazil Pará	12 Sep 2010	
2462	Sete Lagoas Brazil	17 May 1998	Edson D. Goncalves Ribeiro
2727	Sobral Brazil	6 Aug 2006	Jose Silvestre Guimaraes Coelho
989	Sorocaba Brazil	10 Dec 1978	Nelson de Genaro
1892	Sorocaba Brazil Barcelona	26 Jul 1992	Mauro Junot De Maria
2653	Sorocaba Brazil Santana	17 Oct 2004	Carlos Alberto de Genaro
2146	Sorocaba Brazil Trujillo	17 Dec 1995	Valdimir Fernandes Tasso
2899	Sumaré Brazil	23 Jan 2011	David Kuceki
1960a	Teresina Brazil	28 Nov 1993	Alexandre J. Gomes da Cruz
2715	Teresina Brazil Horto	23 April 2006	Manoel Gonçalo do Nascimento Santiago
2441	Teresopolis Brazil	8 Mar 1998	Valter Queiroz Pinheiro
1966	Tubarao Brazil	19 Dec 1993	Gelson Januario
2490	Uberaba Brazil	16 Aug 1998	Jorge Ribeiro Barbosa
2017	Uberlandia Brazil	29 Jan 1995	Raimundo Walter Tavares A.
1912	Uruguaiana Brazil	29 Nov 1992	Saul E. Seiguer Milder
2250	Vale do Itajai Brazil	20 Oct 1996	Joni Luiz Koch
2094	Vila Velha Brazil	27 Aug 1995	Washington Luiz Lima
1630	Vitoria Brazil	15 Feb 1987	Pedro J. da Cruz Penha
2375	Vitoria da Conquista Brazil	15 Jun 1997	Octavio Santos Sousa Neto
2366	Volta Redonda Brazil	1 Jun 1997	Paulo da Silva Santos

Stakes discontinued

1030	Curitiba Brazil North	27 May 1979	Alfredo Heliton de Lemos
	Discontinued 30 Apr 1989 †Curitiba Brazil Iguacu (No. 1468)		
2077	Aracaju Brazil America	23 Jul 1995	Valdeilson de Oliveira
	Discontinued 27 Feb 2000		
1964	Monte Cristo Brazil	19 Dec 1993	Adelson de Paula Parrella
	Discontinued 9 Dec 2001		
1953	Ribeirao Preto Brazil Ipiranga	5 Sep 1993	Jose Alberto Borges da Silva
	Discontinued 9 Dec 2001		
1954	Ribeirao Preto Brazil Quintino	5 Sep 1993	Euclides Jose Maggio
	Discontinued 9 Dec 2001		
2031	Rosario Do Sul Brazil	5 Mar 1995	Jean Jaques
	Discontinued 4 Nov 2001		
1921	Sao Paulo Brazil Vila Sabrina	24 Jan 1993	Jose Olimpio Fabrizio

Discontinued 18 Nov 2001

Missions — 27
(As of Oct. 1, 2011; shown with historical number. See MISSIONS.)

(294a) BRAZIL BELEM MISSION
Avenida Nazare, 532 Sala 412
Royal Trade Center
66035-170 Belem - PA, Brazil

(213) BRAZIL BELO HORIZONTE MISSION
R. Sao Paulo, 1781, 10 Andar
Edif. 17 de Maio, Sala 1001Barrio Lourdes
30170-132 Belo Horizonte - MG, Brazil

BRAZIL TERESINA MISSION
Rua Tersandro Paz, N° 2129,
Salas 105-108 Centro
64001-380 Teresina - PI, Brazil

(185a) BRAZIL BRASILIA MISSION
SHIN CA 05 salas 304/307
LOTE B1
71503-505 Brasilia DF, Brazil

(190) BRAZIL CAMPINAS MISSION
Rua 10 de Setembro, N. 38
Cambui
13023-100 Campinas - SP, Brazil

(181) BRAZIL CURITIBA MISSION
Caixa Postal 9501
Portao
80613-991 Curitiba - PR, Brazil

(281) BRAZIL FLORIANOPOLIS MISSION
R. Feliciano Nunes Pires, 42 Centro
88015-220 Florianopolis - SC
Brazi

(200) BRAZIL FORTALEZA MISSION
Caixa Postal 72800
ACF Rui Barbosa,
60150-973 Fortaleza - CE , Brazil

(321) BRAZIL GOIANIA MISSION
Rua 18, No. 110, Salas 1105 a 1107
Ed. Business Center, Setor Oeste
74120-080 Goiania - GO, Brazil

(322) BRAZIL JOAO PESSOA MISSION
Rua Jose Mariz, 515
Tambauzinho
58042-020 Joao Pessoa - PB, Brazil

(302a) BRAZIL LONDRINA MISSION
Rua Higienopolis, 1100, Sala 61
Centro - Parana
86020-911 Londrina - PR, Brazil

(102) BRAZIL MACEIO MISSION
Av. Dom Antonio Brandao 333/402
Ed. Work Center/Farol
57021-190 Maceio - AL, Brazil

(233) BRAZIL MANAUS MISSION
Rua Loris Cordovil, 1066 Alvorada 1

(256a) BRAZIL PORTO ALEGRE NORTH MISSION
Rua Visconde de Madae 245

69042-010 Manaus - AM
Brazil

(48) BRAZIL PORTO ALEGRE SOUTH MISSION
Av. Princesa Isabel,
342-B Santana
90620-970 Porto Alegre - RS, Brazil

(279) BRAZIL RIBEIRÁO PRETO MISSION
Rua Cerqueira Cesar, 481 sala 606 Centro
14010-130 Ribeirao Preto - SP, Brazil

(280) BRAZIL VITORIA MISSION
Rua João Baptista Parra,
633 Salas 1501/1502
Edf. Enseada Office, Enseada Do Suá
29052-123 Vitória - ES, Brazil

(296) BRAZIL SALVADOR SOUTH MISSION
R. Desembargador Plinio Guyerreiro 429
Apt. 601 Edificio Le Corbusier, Horto Florestal
40295-150Salvador - BA, Brazil

(257) BRAZIL SAO PAULO EAST MISSION
Rua Caa-Acu, 229
Belenzinho
03171-020 - Sao Paulo - SP, Brazil

(101) BRAZIL SAO PAULO NORTH MISSION
Caixa Postal 26095
05513-970 Sao Paulo - SP, Brazil

BRAZIL CUIABA MISSION
Av. Hist Rubens de Mendonca,
1673 Bosque da Saude Consil
78050-000 Cuiaba - MT, Brazil

B. Cristo Redentor
Porto Alegre - RS, 91350-290, Brazil

(167a) BRAZIL RECIFE MISSION
Rua Sáo Francisco 110 sala 102
52010-020 Paissandu
Recife - PE, Brazil

(80) BRAZIL RIO DE JANEIRO MISSION
Av. das Americas, 1155, salas 502/503
Barra da Tijuca, 22631-000 Rio de Janeiro - RJ, Brazil

(234) BRAZIL SALVADOR MISSION
Caixa Postal 6946
Pituba 41811-970 Salvador - BA,
Brazil

(323) BRAZIL SANTA MARIA MISSION
Rua Alberto Pascualine, 121 sala 403 Centro
97015-970 Santa Maria - RS
Brazil

(258) BRAZIL SAO PAULO INTERLAGOS MISSION
Rua Euzebio de Souza
121 Jardim Londrina
05638-100 Sáo Paulo - SP, Brazil

(102) BRAZIL SAO PAULO SOUTH MISSION
R. Dr. Luiz da Rocha Miranda, 159 8 Andar
Parque Jabaquara
04311-990 Sao Paulo - SP, Brazil

BULGARIA

Jan. 1, 2011: Est. population, 7,205,000; Members, 2,206; Branches, 13; Missions, 1; Districts, 2; persent LDS, .03, or one in 3,392; Europe East Area.

Located on the eastern Balkan peninsula on the Black Sea, Bulgaria has a population, with an Orthodox background in religion, that speaks Bulgarian, Turkish and Greek.

Hungarian-born Mischa Markow was a prominent early missionary to the Balkans. While working in Constantinople, he met Argir Dimitrov, a Bulgarian who was investigating the Church. Markow invited Dimitrov to join him in proselyting in Romania. While there, Dimitrov was converted and was baptized by Markow on 30 July 1899. Dimitrov was likely the first Bulgarian convert, and certainly the first Bulgarian missionary.

Markow visited Bulgaria in the summer of 1900 where he registered with the police and received permission to preach. Several ministers allowed him to address their congregations. Soon he was challenged by a Protestant minister who paid for newspaper ads warning people not to attend Markow's scheduled lectures. The result was overflow meetings and enthusiastic interest. A group of clergymen soon became alarmed at Markow's popularity. They had him arrested on charges that he falsified his registration form by listing himself as a minister of the Church of Jesus Christ of Latter-day Saints rather than as a Mormon minister. Despite many appeals, Markow was banished from the country.

The first-known translation of the Book of Mormon into Bulgarian was a manuscript prepared by Bulgarian Latter-day Saint Evangeline Kokotanova Coy in the 1930s. She also prepared complete translations of the Doctrine and Covenants and Pearl of Great Price. In the early 1970s, Julia Caswell produced a manuscript translation as well. In 1980, the Church printed selections from the Book of Mormon in Bulgarian. It could not be made available to people in Bulgaria because of government policies against religious texts, but was utilized by Bulgarian speakers in other countries. A small number of Bulgarians living outside their country joined the Church during this era. The complete translation of the Book of Mormon was first published in February 1999.

Elder Russell M. Nelson of the Quorum of the Twelve and Elder Hans B. Ringger of the Seventy visited Bulgarian leaders in October 1988 hoping for an opportunity to become established there. Their efforts did not meet with success because government policies did not allow the establishment of new religious groups. Elders Nelson and Ringger returned on 13 February 1990 after the fall of the Communist regime and were cordially greeted by officials of the new government.

On 12 September 1990, six missionaries under direction of the Austria Vienna East Mission entered the country. They were Morris and Annetta Mower, Delbert and Marilyn Fowler, Judy Gubler, and Rose Marie Daigle. The Mowers worked in Sofia, the Fowlers in Pravets, and Sisters Gubler and Daigle at the Bulgarian National School of Language in Smolyan. All six missionaries taught English classes.

They were joined on 13 November 1990 by Elders Jon Trent Warner and David Garner who had worked in Yugoslavia, and Elders Christian Elggren and Timothy Kuta who were transferred from the Germany Frankfurt Mission. These elders also helped teach English classes and took part in other charitable endeavors until changes in the law allowed them to proselyte.

The first LDS meeting in Bulgaria was held 1 October 1990. It was a fireside where Austria Vienna East Mission President Dennis B. Neuenschwander spoke. It was held in the Mower's small apartment at Tsar Asen 22a in Sofia. The first church service was held 7 October 1990, also at the Mower's apartment. The first official meeting place for the Church was a rented hall at Parchevich 49 in Sofia.

On 24 November 1990, Emil and Diana Christov with their two sons Rumen and Evgeny, and Ventsislav and Mirela Lazarov were baptized, the first-known baptisms in Bulgaria.

On 1 July 1991 the Bulgaria Sofia Mission was created with Bulgarian native Kiril P. Kiriakov as president. Kiriakov, his wife, Nevenka, and their children Julia and Peter had departed Communist Bulgaria, moving to Algeria on a government appointment in 1963, then fleeing to France in June 1965 where they received political asylum. While in Rennes, France, they met the missionaries and were baptized in June 1966, and emigrated to the United States in 1969. That same year, Kiril Kiriakov received his patriarchal blessing which promised that he would preach the gospel to his people in Bulgaria. The declaration seemed impossible at the time, but was fulfilled in April 1991 when the call to serve was extended by Thomas S. Monson.

Also on 1 July 1991, the first two Bulgarian Church units were created, the Mladost and Sofia Central branches, both in Sofia. Nine days later, on 10 July 1991, the Church was formally recognized by the Bulgarian government.

In November 1992, Bulgarian converts Ivan D. Djambov and Lubomir Z. Traykov began service as the first post-Communism Bulgarian missionaries. Elder Djambov served in the Germany Hamburg Mission and Elder Traykov in the Ukraine Kiev Mission.

In 1993, pediatricians, ophthalmologists, audiologists and others working through the Europe Area Presidency and Church Humanitarian Services went to Bulgaria to help train doctors and nurses to improve health care of children. Other LDS volunteers served in hospitals and educational institutions. Also, through Church Humanitarian Services, educators traveled to Bulgaria to strengthen special education programs, and two Bulgarian school administrators were brought to Utah and Idaho for a tour of training facilities. Elder M. Russell Ballard of the Quorum of the Twelve and Elder Dennis B. Neuenschwander of the Seventy visited Church humanitarian projects in Sofia during May 1993.

Rapid growth of Church membership in the capital city of Sofia necessitated creation of six more branches between November 1991 and March 1993. During the same period, the Plovdiv Branch in the city of Plovdiv was created on 8 November 1992. Beginning in the mid 1990s, branches were begun in other Bulgarian cities including Burgas, Varna, Shumen, Ruse, Veliko Turnovo, Blagoevgrad and Dobrich.

During August 1995, 39 Bulgarians participated in an excursion to the Freiberg Germany Temple. Other temple excursions occurred in 1995 and 1996. By October 1996, 138 Bulgarians had received the ordinances of the temple.

In 1999, the first youth conference in Bulgaria was held in Batak, where 106 youth attended workshops and meetings and participated in games and a talent show. Membership in 1999 was 1,367.

The first Church-built structure in Bulgaria, a building that included a meetinghouse, offices for the Bulgaria Sofia Mission, and a home for the mission president and his wife, was dedicated in Sofia on 18 June 2000, by Europe East Area president Charles Didier of the Seventy. The day before, ground was broken for a second meetinghouse in Bulgaria in Plovdiv.

By mid-year 2000, 20 missionaries from Bulgaria were serving in Russia, England, France and other areas of the world.

By 2002, membership reached 1,927.

Sources: Bulgaria Sofia Mission, Annual historical reports, 1993-2001, and Mission files, 1981-1993, Church Archives; Nevenka L. Kiriakov, My Life Story, 2004, Church Archives; Kahlile B. Mehr, "Keeping Promises: the LDS Church Enters Bulgaria, 1990-1994," BYU Studies 36; Lyn Jacobs, Mormon non-English Scriptures, Hymnals, and Periodicals, 1830-1986, 1986; "Mischa Markow: Missionary to the Balkans," Ensign, June 1980; "First Meetinghouse Dedicated in Bulgaria," Ensign, October 2000; "LDS Bulgarians Come Together for Historic Dedication," Church News, 8 July 2000.

Mission — 1
(As of Oct. 1, 2011; shown with historical number. See MISSIONS.)

(259) BULGARIA SOFIA MISSION
Ul. Marin Drinov No. 21
1504 Sofia
Bulgaria

BURUNDI

Jan. 1, 2011: Est. population, 10,216,000; Africa Southeast Area; DR Congo Kinshasa Mission.

Burundi, formerly known as Urundi, became independent from Belgium on 1 July 1962. Located in east-central Africa bordered by Tanzania, Republic of the Congo, and Rwanda. The official languages are Kirundi and French, with Swahili also spoken, and 67 percent of the people are Christian, while 23 percent follow tribal beliefs, and 10 percent are Muslim.

In 1984, Egide Nzojibwami and his wife, Beatrice, were baptized in Liege, Belgium, while pursuing studies in that country. Soon thereafter, they returned to Burundi. They conducted a Sunday School and other meetings in their home in Bujumbura, although the Church wasn't officially established.

In 1992, Elder Earl C. Tingey of the Seventy traveled to Burundi and met with a representative of the government. The official initially denied the application for recognition, but after Elder Tingey read a list of values from For the Strength of Youth pamphlet, the official was so impressed that he asked for copies to distribute to members of his own church. About a month later, the Church received official recognition from the government.

With official recognition in place, Homer M. LeBaron, president of the Zaire Kinshasa Mission, met with the Nzojibwami family and arranged for the organization of a branch in the capital city of Bujumbura, on 29 November 1992, with Egide

Nzojibwami as president. The first branch meeting was held two days later with 39 attending. The first convert in Burundi, Bosco Nikondeha, was baptized 6 December 1992.

Soon after the branch was organized, missionaries from the Ivory Coast Abidjan Mission were assigned to the country. They were Francois Boue, Felix Gnamba, Aime Cesar Kipre, and Bassin Kouhon.

There was a coup in October 1993. In 1996, the constitution was suspended. The branch was discontinued shortly thereafter and missionaries were withdrawn from the country.

In December 2009, Michael Headlee, president of the DR Congo mission, visited Burundi, accompanied by Eustache Ilunga, a stake president from Kinshasa. They found many people who wanted the true gospel. He felt it was time to reintroduce the Church in Burundi.

On 1 July 2010, the DRC Lubumbashi Mission was created with Gary L. Packer as mission president. Burundi was included in this new mission. An exploratory visit and conference was held in Burundi August 12-19, 2010. President Packer, along with President Eustache Ilunga, Elder Brent Jameson and Elder Craig R. Frogley, attended the conference and visited several pastors who had written to the Church for information. Twenty-eight interested people and members attended the conference.

On 22 September 2010, missionary couples Brent and Lorraine Jameson and Craig and Janet Frogley arrived in Burundi from the DR Congo. They were soon followed by eight missionaries; Elders Moussele Fridorin Aristide, Mpoyi Bukasa Jean Paul, Tshituka Job Lafuluaba, Moussa Kadiata Christopher, Kintembila Nzuzi Jonathan, Kizimbou Guy Alain, Diazola Mbambukula Junior, and N'gondo Nkombo Clerk Gilson.

There were 72 people in the first sacrament meeting. Baptisms began almost immediately. Alice Malabi and her brother Alain were baptized on 24 October 2010, the first baptisms after reopening the country. They were the children of Veronique and Kyubi Malabi who had joined the church earlier in Ivory Coast and moved to Burundi. By the end of 2010, the branch had 39 members including two former pastors who had earlier shown interest in the church.

On 19 October 2010, Elder Jeffery R. Holland of the Quorum of the Twelve visited Burundi and blessed the land. He was accompanied by Elder Stephen E. Snow of the Seventy. Afterward, Elders Holland and Snow met with 90 friends and members, some coming from eastern Congo 120 miles away.

On 9 January 2011, the Bujumbura Branch was created with more than 90 in attendance.

Sources: "Branch Flourishing in Burundi," Church News, 21 August 1993; Ivory Coast Abidjan Mission, Manuscript history and historical reports, Church Archives; "Burundi," The World Fact Book, http://www.cia.gov/cia/publications/factbook/geos/by.html, 1 June 2004; Earl C. Tingey, "Establishing Eternal Patterns," Church News, 5 May 2002; Apostles bless two African nations, Church News, Nov. 6, 2010.

CAMBODIA
(Kampuchea)
Jan. 1, 2011: Est. population, 14,494,000; Members, 10,530; Branches, 24; Districts, 5; Missions, 1; Percent LDS, .06 or one in 1,733; Asia Area.

During the late 1960s and early 1970s, several Latter-day Saints were in Cambodia on assignments with the U.S. military. Small groups of members held Church services in Phnom Penh, but there were no reports of any Cambodian convertions.

In 1982, Book of Mormon selections, translated by Anh Tran, were published in the Khmer language to meet the needs of a growing number of Cambodians who had moved to the United States, Canada, and other countries in the wake instability in their homeland.

In April 1993, Elder and Sister John K. Carmack of the Asia Area Presidency, President and Sister Larry R. White of the Thailand Bangkok Mission, and Vichit Ith, a Church member living in Bangkok, traveled to Phnom Penh and visited with a representative of the government's foreign ministry to discuss the possibility of the Church performing humanitarian service in Cambodia. He informed them that Cambodia enjoyed religious freedom.

The Cambodian government officially recognized the Church on 26 February 1994, largely due to the efforts of Vichit Ith, who served from 1993 to 1997 as an economic advisor to the prime minister, Prince Ranariddh.

On 22 March 1994, Donald and Scharlene Dobson arrived in Phnom Penh as humanitarian missionaries. Pahl Mao was baptized on 9 May, the first convert baptized in Cambodia. Another missionary couple, Ronald and Dawn Oswald, arrived on 27 May. The first young elders arrived in Cambodia on 8 August: Richard W. Henderson, John T. Smith, Jamie T. Hipwell, and Brian W. Strong. All four were transferred from Cambodian-speaking assignments in the United States. By year's end, 27 converts had been baptized.

The Phnom Penh Branch was organized on 19 September 1994 with Shigiyuki Oya, a Japanese member, as branch president. In June 1995, the branch began meeting in two groups, one for Khmer (Cambodian) speakers and the other for Vietnamese speakers. In November, the original Phnom Penh Branch was split to form three branches. The Phnom Penh Cambodia District was organized on 21 January 1996. Two months later, Ohm Borin became the first local member called to serve as a branch president.

On 28 May 1996, President Gordon B. Hinckley, Elder Joseph B. Wirthlin, Elder John H. Groberg and their wives visited Phnom Penh. President Hinckley spoke at a fireside in the Cambodiana Hotel attended by 439 people, an impressive number considering Church membership totalled 285.

Cambodia was part of the Asia Area Mission until 1995, when it was assigned to the Thailand Bangkok Mission. On 1 July 1997, the Cambodia Phnom Penh Mission was organized with Leland D. White as president. Four days later, a military coup began in Phnom Penh. All 22 missionaries were evacuated to Bangkok, Thailand, on 10-11 July, where they remained until 29 August, when political conditions were stable enough for their return.

Over the next several years the Church experienced remarkable growth. At the end of 1998, there were approximately 800 members in Cambodia and over 6,000 by early 2004. Missionaries worked only in Phnom Penh until March 2000, when four elders were sent to Kampong Cham, where they organized a branch in April. The Battambang Branch was formed in December 2003. On 25 January 2004, Bishop Richard C. Edgley dedicated the Cambodia District Center in

Phnom Penh, the first Church-constructed meetinghouse in the country.

In September 1999, Elder Cree-L Kofford and President and Sister Leland D. White were given an audience with King Norodom Sihanouk and his wife at the Royal Palace in Phnom Penh. The king and queen extended the same privilege to a Church delegation in May 2002. Among the gifts that mission President John P. Colton presented to the king was a copy of the newly completed (late 2001) Khmer translation of the Book of Mormon.

On 25 January 2004, Bishop Richard C. Edgley of the Presiding Bishopric dedicated the first meetinghouse in the country. Despite years of strife and conflict, Bishop Edgley noted how peaceful and happy they were, with "faith as strong as any people on the earth."

In 2003, there were 6,089 members. In 2005, membership reached 7,465.

Sources: R. Lanier Britsch, From the East: The History of the Latter-day Saints in Asia, 1851- 1996, 1998; Cambodia Phnom Penh Mission, Manuscript history and historical reports, Church Archives; Shaun D. Stahle, "Emerging Church in Cambodia," Church News, 14 February 2004; Leland D. and Joyce B. White, "Gospel Gains Foothold in Cambodia," Ensign, January 1997.

Mission — 1
(As of Oct. 1, 2011; shown with historical number. See MISSIONS.)

(318) CAMBODIA PHNOM PENH MISSION
PO Box 165, #2B St. 222
Phnom Penh, Cambodia

CAMEROON
Jan. 1, 2011: Est. population, 18,879,000; Members, 1,003; Branches 5; LDS, 1 in 25,968; or .004 percent; Africa Southeast Area; DR Congo Kinshasa Mission.

Cameroon, a Central African nation on the Gulf of Guinea, is bordered by Nigeria, Chad, the Central African Republic, the Republic of Congo, Equatorial Guinea, and Gabon. It became independent from France on 1 January 1960. The official languages are English and French, while 24 African languages are also spoken. Forty percent of the people are Christian, 20 percent Muslim, and 40 percent follow tribal beliefs.

There were members of the Church living in Cameroon as early as 1974. On 21 July 1974, the first sacrament meeting was held in Yaounde. Attending were Ellsworth A. Cragholm, Lynn Cragholm, and her daughter Doree Taylor.

Lucas and Marva Atem, citizens of Cameroon, were baptized in October 1979 in Leeds, England, and returned to Cameroon in 1981. Louis Joseph Beyina was baptized in 1982 in Milan, Italy, and returned to Cameroon soon after. In March 1984, there were six known members of the Church living in Cameroon. They were Louis Joseph Beyina, Etoundi Adalbert Abah, and Paul S. and Gertrud Carpenter, and their children, Christian and Susanne. Carpenter baptized his daughter, Susanne, in Yaounde on 19 March 1984, the first known baptism performed in Cameroon.

The first missionaries to work in Cameroon, Paul D. and Arlene Payne, were assigned there from Nigeria for three weeks in September 1991 to locate members. Two missionary couples were assigned to serve full-time in the country in 1992. They were Gerard and Georgette Gagne of Montreal, Quebec, and Ken and Bea Nielsen from Calgary, Alberta, Canada. On 9 May 1992, Moses Ako Agbortabot was baptized by Gerard Gagne, the first known native baptism in Cameroon.

The Cameroon Yaounde Mission was created on 1 July 1992, mission headquarters were moved to Abidjan, Ivory Coast, on 18 May 1993. Cameroon president Paul Biya approved the Church's request for legal recognition on 9 September 1993. Up to that time about 30 people had been baptized, and another 60 investigators were attending Sunday meetings. On 5 July 1994, Missionaries were temporarily withdrawn from Cameroon due to a war between Nigeria and Cameroon.

The seminary program was introduced in 1995. The Douala Group was organized on 5 August 1996 with R. Bongongui Yondo Ernest as group leader. Cameroon became part of the Ivory Coast Abidjan Mission on 1 January 2003, and was reorganized from the Ivory Coast Abidjan Mission to the Ghana Cape Coast Mission on 1 July 2005, then to the DR Congo Kinshasa Mission by 1 July 2006.

Elder Jeffrey R. Holland of the Quorum of the Twelve blessed the country on 20 August 2009.

In 2005, membership reached 374.

Sources: "Legal status in Cameroon," Church News, 22 January 1994; Ivory Coast Abidjan Mission, Manuscript history and historical reports, Church Archives; Borgna Brunner, "Countries of the world, Cameroon ," Time Almanac 2004; Robert and Beverly Mercer, Interview, 1994, Church Archives.

CANADA

Jan. 1, 2011: Est. population, 33,487,000; Members, 182,415; Stakes, 47; Wards, 325; Branches, 155; Missions, 8; Districts, 5; Temples, 7; Percent LDS, .53, or one in 189.

At the northern end of North America, Canada is a confederation with a parliamentary democracy. It includes 10 provinces and three territories. Its population speaks English and French, and is Roman Catholic, 46 percent; and Protestant, 41 percent. In 2005, membership reached 166,442.

ALBERTA

Jan. 1, 2011: Est. population, 3,257,000; Members, 76,669; Stakes, 22; Wards, 173; Branches, 33; Missions, 2; Temples, 2; Percent LDS, 2.3, or one in 44.; North America Central Area.

The first known Latter-day Saints to enter what is now Alberta were Simeon F. Allen and his son Heber S. Allen of Hyrum, Utah, who contracted work in 1883 on the Canadian Pacific Railroad between Medicine Hat and Calgary. They were joined by other saints from Utah working on the contract.

A few years later in 1886, Cache Stake President Charles O. Card received permission from Church President John Taylor to investigate colonizing opportunities in southwestern Canada. At that time prosecution of polygamists in the Intermountain West was oppressing many saints' families, and Church officials sought to establish colonies outside the U.S. where these families could seek refuge to maintain their cohesiveness and economic stability. Card, accompanied by James W. Hendricks and Isaac E. D. Zundel, traveled to British Columbia in late September 1886. Unsuccessful in locating land there that was both arable and not already leased as ranches, the trio traveled eastward to Calgary. A Montana mountaineer had previously informed them of expansive buffalo plains south of that city. At present-day Stand Off the three men decided to establish a colony. They went back to Utah with plans to return to Stand Off the following year with a group of Saints ready to colonize new settlements.

Upon return to Alberta in April 1887, Card found that the land near Stand Off had been leased by others and was unavailable. A few days later while exploring land farther south near Lee's Creek, Card and companions met E. N. Barker and Herbert Donovan who described land at the edge of the Blood Indian Reserve that was available for settlement. The entourage investigated the land and decided to establish the new colony there. Saints from Utah began arriving in early May and June. The settlement and ward were first known as Card but later changed to Cardston.

The ward was organized on 7 October 1888 as part of the Cache Stake headquartered in Logan, Utah; John A. Woolf was called to serve as the first bishop.

In November 1888, Charles O. Card and Elders Francis M. Lyman and John W. Taylor of the Quorum of the Twelve visited Prime Minister John A. Macdonald in Ottawa. The trio presented a petition asking for government assistance for the newly established colony at Cardston. The petition requested help obtaining land for town sites, securing mineral, timber, and water rights, purchasing farm and grazing lands at a reduced rate, and establishing a post office. In addition, the petition requested transportation aid for immigrants, reduction of custom duties on imported goods, animals, and machinery and permission to practice plural marriage. Most of the requests were denied. Church President Wilford Woodruff and counselors George Q. Cannon and Joseph F. Smith visited the saints in Alberta in October and November 1889.

By October 1894, more than 674 members were living in the Cardston area. The Alberta Stake was organized the following year on 9 June with Charles O. Card as president.

During the 16 years following Cardston's establishment as the central LDS ecclesiastical center, migrating saints from Utah settled the communities of Taylorville, Kimball, Aetna, Woolford, Beazer, Leavitt, Mountain View, Caldwell, Orton, Frankburg, Magrath, Welling, Raymond, Stirling, Barnwell, and Taber. The construction of large irrigation canals was initiated in 1898 by a joint venture between the Alberta Railway and Irrigation Company and the Church. The company provided the capital investment and the Church supplied construction crews and teams. Laborers were paid in both cash and land/water rights. The irrigation projects were extremely vital to successful farming in the area. A large number of members from Utah and Idaho were attracted to the area with promises of agricultural development related to the irrigation projects. Church authorities issued calls to many families to migrate to southern Alberta. Many of them began arriving in April 1899.

Charles A. Magrath, president of the Alberta Irrigation Company, distributed seed to the Saints and encouraged them to begin growing sugar beets around 1899-1900. Three years later Jesse Knight and his sons, businessmen from Utah, built the Knight Sugar Factory in Raymond. In subsequent years the sugar beet industry shifted toward the Barnwell-Taber area.

The Alberta Stake was divided on 30 August 1903 to form the Taylor Stake with Heber S. Allen as president. The new stake included the wards in Magrath, Raymond, and Stirling.

In 1906 through the efforts of Alberta Stake president Edward J. Wood, the Church finalized purchase of the 66,500 acre Cochrane Ranch located a few miles north of Cardston. Resulting from this purchase came the last two LDS-established com-munities of Glenwood (1908) and Hillspring (1910).

The cornerstone for Alberta Stake's Tabernacle in Cardston was laid in August 1908. The building was dedicated on 5 August 1917 by Elder Hyrum M. Smith of the Quorum of the Twelve. A Church Academy was established in Raymond in 1908 as a joint educational venture bet-ween the Alberta and Taylor stakes. It was originally named Taylor Academy and opened in 1910, but later it was renamed Knight Academy in honor of the con-tributions of Jesse Knight and his family.

A temple in Cardston was announced in 1912, but not completed until 1923. It was one of the first temples whose architect-ural style departed from a traditional tower design. The temple was dedicated on 26-29 August 1923 by President Heber J. Grant. At the time, members numbered around 8,000. Edward J. Wood was appointed as temple president and served concurrently for many years as Alberta Stake president. The temple was rededicated in 1962 and 1991 after extensive renovations.

On 10 November 1921, the Lethbridge Stake was organized with Hugh B. Brown as president. He later served as a member of the Quorum of Twelve and counselor in the First Presidency.

The first known saints to live in Alberta's capital city Edmonton were Robert J. and Fannie Gordon and their family. They moved there in 1914. Latter-day Saint university students in Edmonton began associating and meeting together as a group around 1931. The first recorded official meeting of members occurred on 26 February 1933 at the home of Alfred and Mabel Strate. Two years later, a branch was organized with Strate as president. He was followed in 1939 by Nathan E. Tanner, later a member of the Quorum of the Twelve and counselor in the First Presidency. In 1941, the Western Canadian Mission was organized with Walter E. Miller as president. Mission headquarters were established in Edmonton. In 1960, the Alaskan-Canadian Mission was organized from a division of the Western Canadian Mission.

The first stake in Calgary was organized in 1953, followed seven years later in 1960 with a stake in Edmonton. Efforts at missionary work among the Indians living on the Blood Reserve immediately north of Cardston were sporadic until 1949 when Golden Buchanan, coordinator of the Church's Indian Relations Committee came to Cardston to organize the missionary work among the tribe. A separate branch was established there in 1964 with James Blackmore as president.

During the 20th Century three Latter-day Saints were elected to Parliament, all hailing from Alberta. John H. Blackmore served from 1935-1958 and Solon Low from 1945-1958. Both were leaders of the Social Credit Party. Grant Hill served from 1993 to 2004. Elder N. Eldon Tanner, later of the Quorum of Twelve and member of the First Presidency, was appointed speaker of the Alberta Legislature in 1935, and later Minister of Lands and Forests. In 1970, Church membership in Alberta stood at about 28,000.

The Church held a special fast in the U.S. and Canada in January 1985 to raise funds to alleviate famine in Ethiopia. The saints in Canada, with membership concentrated in Alberta, raised nearly $250,000. Tax laws prohibited the transfer of the funds to headquarters in the U.S., so the amount was donated to the Canadian Red Cross. Both the Alberta and Canadian governments matched the donations by Church members and the final total of $1 million was sent to Ethiopia. The Canadian Red Cross recognized the Church at a special banquet in Calgary for donating the largest amount in its history.

From 1988-1991, the Alberta Temple was closed for renovation and restoration. An open house was held for 10 days prior to rededication on 22-24 June 1991. About 40 members of the Alberta Provincial Legislature and provincial Premier Donald Getty toured the temple along with over 100,000 other visitors.

In July 1997, the Historic Sites and Monuments Board of Canada recognized the LDS-founded town of Stirling as a National Historic Site. The designation identified Stirling as "the best surviving example of a Mormon agricultural village."

The Canada Edmonton Mission was organized on 1 July 1998. During a six-province tour of Canada in July-August of that year, President Gordon B. Hinckley visited the members in Edmonton and Lethbridge on 2 August. Also, that summer, a group of Church members and others interested in historical re-enactment, began a 735 mile wagon trek from Preston, Idaho, to Cardston to memorialize the early pioneers who settled Alberta. The caravan of 14 wagons and 90 people left Preston on 10 August and arrived in Cardston on 28 September.

The Edmonton Temple was dedicated on 11-12 December 1999 by President Gordon B. Hinckley. It was one of the first smaller scale temples constructed by the Church. At the time of dedication, Church membership in Alberta numbered about 63,000. The first Church Educational System satellite fireside broadcast hosted outside the United States was held in Calgary on 7 May 2000. Elder Dallin H. Oaks of the Quorum of the Twelve addressed the worldwide audience.

In 2001, Church member Greg Melchin of Calgary was appointed to the Alberta provincial cabinet to serve as Minister of Revenue. He had served previously in the Legislative Assembly since 1997.

Members in Alberta have diligently helped with community and Church humanitarian projects. In 2001, members of the Calgary East Stake made 132 bed quilts for the newly renovated Drop In Centre for homeless people. Five other stakes in the Calgary area committed to continue that project. In 2004, the young men and women of the Lethbridge West Stake assisted in Operation Mercury Hope, a humanitarian effort started by Cpl. Russell Storring of the Canadian Armed Forces. The project aids children in orphanages in developing countries where Canadian forces are stationed. The Lethbridge youth sorted, folded and boxed large quantities of goods donated to the project.

Alberta is included in the North America Central Area. Two missions headquartered in Calgary and Edmonton encompass the province. General Authorities from Alberta include: Presidents Hugh B. Brown and N. Eldon Tanner of the Quorum of the Twelve and the First Presidency, Presiding Bishop Victor L. Brown, and Elders William H. Bennett, Teddy E. Brewerton, Alexander B. Morrison, Lowell D. Wood, and Merlin R. Lybbert of the Seventy. Former Young Women General President Ardeth Kapp and Relief Society General President Elaine Jack were born in Alberta.

In 2002, membership reached 67,394; and 68,586 in 2003.

Sources: Alberta, Taylor, and Lethbridge stakes, Manuscript histories and historical reports, Church Archives; Andrew Jenson, Encyclopedic History of the Church, 1941; Lethbridge Stake, A History of the Church in Canada, 1968; Brigham Y. Card, et. al, The Mormon Presence in Canada, 1990; Donald G. Godfrey and Brigham Y. Card, The Diaries of Charles Ora Card: The Canadian Years, 1886-1903; Dennis A. Wright, et al., Regional Studies in LDS Church History: Western Canada, 2000; Robert M. Graham, "The Mormon Cultural Landscape at Stirling Agricultural Village, Alberta" APT Bulletin, The Journal of Preservation Technology, 32:2-3 (2001), 47-56; "Hundreds Greet Wagon Train in Cardston," Church News, 3 October 1998; "Day of Miracles Has Not Ceased," Church News, 13 May 2000; "Bedding Given to Homeless Shelter," Church News, 6 October 2001; "Latter-day Saints Serve in Alberta Cabinet," Ensign, October 2001; "Operation Mercury Hope," Church News, 12 June 2004.

Stakes — 22

(Listed alphabetically As of Oct. 1, 2011.)

No.	Name	Organized	First President
North America Central Area			
211a	*Calgary Alberta		
	‡Calgary	15 Nov 1953	N. Eldon Tanner
1924	Calgary Alberta East	14 Feb 1993	Geoffrey Bryan Grunewald
2540	Calgary Alberta Foothills	5 Dec 1999	John N. Craig
416	*Calgary Alberta North		
	‡Calgary North	17 Apr 1966	Gerald E. Melchin
1101	Calgary Alberta South	3 Feb 1980	Clarence Lee Robertson
1031	Calgary Alberta West	27 May 1979	Lynn Albert Rosenvall

35	*Cardston Alberta		
	‡Alberta	9 Jun 1895	Charles O. Card
1455	Cardston Alberta West	13 Nov 1983	Brent L. Nielson
655	*Edmonton Alberta Bonnie Doon	6 Nov 1983	
	‡Edmonton Alberta East	3 Nov 1974	Bryant L. Stringham
1453	Edmonton Alberta Millwoods	6 Nov 1983	Kenneth O. Higginbotham
2605	Edmonton Alberta North	9 Sep 2001	Brent Allan Purnell
312	*Edmonton Alberta Riverbend	6 Nov 1983	
	*Edmonton Alberta		
	‡Edmonton	15 Nov 1960	Leroy Rollins
1560	Fort Macleod Alberta	29 Sep 1985	Heber James Beazer
2449	Grande Prairie Alberta	12 Apr 1998	Lenard R. Shaw
189	*Lethbridge Alberta		
	*Lethbridge	15 Nov 1953	
	‡East Lethbridge	28 Oct 1951	Grant G. Woolley
667	Lethbridge Alberta East	24 Nov 1974	Bryce C. Stringham
2405	Lethbridge Alberta West	26 Oct 1997	David Paul Koegler
1199	Magrath Alberta	26 Oct 1980	James Dickson Bridge
1998	Medicine Hat Alberta	20 Nov 1994	Robert Albin Gehmlich
51	*Raymond Alberta		
	‡Taylor	30 Aug 1903	Heber S. Allen
1350	Red Deer Alberta	13 Jun 1982	Dennis William Guenther
302	*Taber Alberta		
	‡Taber	11 Sep 1960	Ray B. Evenson
	Stakes discontinued		
86	Lethbridge	10 Nov 1921	Hugh B. Brown

Discontinued 15 Nov 1953 †Calgary (No. 211a), Lethbridge (No. 189)

Missions — 2

(As of Oct. 1, 2011; shown with historical number. See MISSIONS.)

(36a) CANADA CALGARY MISSION
7044 Farrell Road SE
Calgary, Alberta T2H 0T2
Canada

(325) CANADA EDMONTON MISSION
8925 51st Avenue, Suite 305
Edmonton, Alberta T6E 5J3
Canada

BRITISH COLUMBIA

Jan. 1, 2011: Est. population, 4,254,000; Members, 29,273; Stakes, 8; Wards, 49; Branches, 29; Missions, 1; Districts, 1; Percent LDS, .67, or one in 151; North America Northwest Area.

Vancouver Island was one of several locations Brigham Young considered as a western settlement site for the Saints. In a letter to the members published on 1 November 1845, he mentioned the island as "one of many good locations for settlement on the Pacific." The letter sparked a petition by members in England that was submitted to Queen Victoria seeking support for the Mormons in settling the island. However, the petition was ignored, and no Latter-day Saint immigrants settled there until 1875. That year, Church member William and Maria Judson Copley and their three children settled at Shawigan. For the next 15 years they were the only members there. The first convert on the island was Anthony Maitland Stenhouse, a member of the legislative assembly of British Columbia who chose to resign from the assembly and be baptized in 1887. He became a vigorous defender of the faith, living in Cardston, Alberta, and eventually returning to his homeland of Great Britain. How Stenhouse came to join the Church is not known.

In 1886, Charles O. Card, president of the Cache Stake in Logan, Utah, James W. Hendricks, and Isaac E.D. Zundall went to British Columbia looking for a site for colonization. On 3 October of that year they held a sacrament meeting, likely the first in the province. On 15 March 1902, British Columbia came under the stewardship of the Northwestern States Mission. Seven missionaries, led by mission President Nephi Pratt, arrived in Victoria on 13 May 1903 and the Victoria Conference was organized the next day. Their first converts were members of the Copley family. Clara Copley was baptized on 10 July 1904 and Merian Copley on 6 August 1904. A Sunday School was organized, but was later dissolved when several families moved away. Melvin Oxspring moved his family from Vancouver to Victoria in 1937, contacted the Northwestern States Mission president, and subsequently had missionaries assigned to Victoria. A Sunday School was organized on 17 October 1937. There were not enough members in Victoria to form a branch until World War II brought more Latter-day Saints to the area. A dependent branch was organized in 1942 with Robert Gerber as president. It became an independent branch on 11 August 1946 with Rex Nielson as president. A second group began meeting in Nanaimo in 1946, and a branch was created there on 5 May 1948 with Samuel Dyson as president.

The first known members of the Church in the city of Vancouver were Edward Neill and his wife, who had joined the Church in Brisbane, Australia, and moved to Vancouver in 1903. The Vancouver Branch was organized on 12 February 1911 with Neill as president. In 1925, the branch purchased a building to serve as a chapel. The Vancouver Branch became a ward and was included in the newly created Seattle Stake on 31 July 1938. The northern portion of British Columbia became part of the Western Canadian Mission in 1941. The first meetinghouse to be built in British Columbia was in Creston. It was used for the first time on 2 May 1948. When the Vancouver District was created the following June, it included Vancouver, New Westminster, and Vancouver Island and the area was transferred to the Western Canadian Mission.

A new meetinghouse was dedicated in Vancouver on 1 August 1954. The Vancouver District was divided and the Victoria District was created on 2 August 1959, taking in all Church members living on Vancouver Island. The first stake in British Columbia was created on 21 November 1960 when the Vancouver District became the Vancouver Stake with wards in Vancouver (two), North Shore, New Westminster, Fleetwood, Richmond, White Rock, Langley, and Chilliwack. A growth spurt during the late 1960s and early 1970s came when a number of Latter-day Saint professors were hired at the University of Victoria, as well as others who came to this area. The second stake in British Columbia, the Victoria British Columbia Stake, was created on 9 February 1975 with wards in Victoria (two), Colwood, and Nanaimo and branches in Courtenay, Duncan, Port Alberni, Sidney, and Powell River.

The Canada Vancouver Mission was organized on 20 June 1974, an outgrowth of the Alaska-Canada Mission that had been created in 1960. Missionary work outside of Vancouver and Victoria expanded as the number of missionaries increased over the years, including missionary work in the native American preserves. In 1980, the Prince George District and the Terrace British Columbia District, were created in northern British Columbia to accommodate growth in membership. President Gordon B. Hinckley spoke to about 2,000 members during a visit to Victoria on 31 July 1998, and the next day to 6,000 in Vancouver and 1,600 in Prince George.

In 2002, membership reached 27,984.

The Vancouver British Columbia Temple, located in Langley, 30 miles east of Vancouver, was dedicated 2 May 2010. It became the seventh operating temple in Canada, and the 131st temple in the Church.

Sources: Lethbridge Alberta Stake, A History of the Mormon Church in Canada, 1968; Times and Seasons, 1 November 1845; Northwestern States Mission, Manuscript history and historical reports, Church Archives; Western Canadian Mission, Manuscript history and historical reports, Church Archives; Seattle Stake, Manuscript history and historical reports, Church Archives; New Westminster Ward, Manuscript history and historical reports, Church Archives; Vancouver Stake, Meetinghouse dedication program, 1967, Church Archives; Robert J. McCue, "The Church of Jesus Christ of Latter-day Saints and Vancouver Island: The Establishment and Growth of the Mormon Community," BC Studies, Summer, 1979; Giles H. Florence Jr., "No One Is an Island," Ensign, August 1990; Julie A. Dockstader, "LDS Roots Run Deep in Community," Church News, 22 August 1998; Canada Vancouver Mission, Manuscript History and historical reports, Church Archives; Donald G. Godfrey, and Brigham Y. Card, eds, Diaries of Charles Ora Card: the Canadian Years 1886-1903, 1993.

Stakes — 7
(Listed alphabetically As of Oct. 1, 2011.)

No.	Name	Organized	First President
North America Northwest Area — 7			
1980	Abbottsford British Columbia	12 Jun 1994	Andrew Howard Rattray
2406	Nanaimo British Columbia	26 Oct 1997	William Bert Nilsson
1905	Prince George British Columbia	26 Sep 1992	A. Brice Gurney
1014	*Surrey British Columbia	12 Jun 1994	
	‡Vancouver B.C. South	8 Apr 1979	Richard Bulpitt
315	*Vancouver British Columbia		
	‡Vancouver	21 Nov 1960	Ernest E. Jensen
709	Vernon British Columbia	12 Oct 1975	James Ronald Burnham
679	Victoria British Columbia	9 Feb 1975	Howard Lowell Biddulph
North America Central Area - 1			
994	Cranbrook British Columbia	14 Jan 1979	Brian James Erickson

Mission — 1
(As of Oct. 1, 2011; shown with historical number. See MISSIONS.)

(58) CANADA VANCOUVER MISSION
PO Box 149
Point Roberts, WA 98281

MANITOBA

Jan. 1, 2011: Est. population, 1,177,000; Members, 4,600; Stakes, 1; Wards, 7; Branches, 5; Missions, 1; Percent LDS, .4, or one in 260; North America Central Area.

The earliest known missionary work in Manitoba was done by Theodore Brandley who in company with Samuel Witmore, left Richfield, Utah, on 5 May 1884 to fill a mission. They were to preach to the Mennonites scattered in the northern United States and Manitoba, near what is now Winnipeg. There is no record of baptisms from their work. Brandley received an honorable release and returned home to Richfield on 22 October 1885.

The next missionary effort occurred on 29 November 1896 when President Charles O. Card of the Alberta Stake wrote to John Sherman, a Church member who migrated to Souris from Alberta. President Card asked Sherman if he should send missionaries. The response was positive and President Card called Neils Hansen to begin missionary work in Manitoba on 5 December 1896. On 23 January 1897, Hansen, along with missionaries William S. Baxter, J. G. Stuart, Alonzo G. Baker, Frank May, Alva M. Merkley, and Edward Leavitt prepared to depart for Brandon, Souris, and Winnipeg from Cardston, Alberta. Several converts migrated to Alberta to join the larger group of Saints.

On 20 July 1889, Manitoba was assigned to the Northern States Mission until 1 July 1919 when the Canadian Mission was organized and Manitoba was transferred to the new mission. The Manitoba conference was organized by 5 March 1901. In June 1906, the missionaries in Winnipeg began selling copies of the Book of Mormon. In August, when city officials insisted they pay a vendors license fee, the missionaries gave the books away, accepting any donations. A year later their efforts bore fruit, and five in the province were baptized. Many of the converts later moved to Latter-day Saint centers in other areas.

On 23 May 1909, the Winnipeg Sunday School was organized with 37 members. A year later a branch was organized in Winnipeg on 9 May 1910. A chapel was built and dedicated on 30 August 1914. When the branch was later reorganized on 26 March 1922, the first local member to serve as Winnipeg Branch President was Stanley N. Roberts.

Membership in the district in 1930 was 197, and included the Winnipeg Branch and the Bergland Branch. The branches had their chapel dedicated on 20 November 1925, the same day the branch was organized. The Brandon Branch was created on 3 July 1955, and a second branch in Winnipeg was created on 22 October 1961. Other branches were organized in Portage La Prairie, for U.S. Air Force personnel on 28 March 1954, Kenora by 24 March 1957, and Thompson on 5 January 1969.

On 20 March 1926, Elder Joseph Fielding Smith of the Quorum of the Twelve Apostles visited Winnipeg for two days, and two years later, on 15 June 1928, Elder David O. McKay of the Quorum of the Twelve Apostles also visited.

The Canada Winnipeg Mission was created on 1 March 1976 with about 4,200 members in four districts, including those in Saskatchewan and western Ontario. The Winnipeg Manitoba Stake was created 12 November 1978 by Elder L. Tom Perry of the Quorum of the Twelve. A new stake center was dedicated on November 1988, and stake membership reached 2,500.

At one of the largest gatherings ever in Manitoba on 4 August 1998, President Gordon B. Hinckley, accompanied by President Boyd K. Packer, acting president of the Quorum of the Twelve, spoke to about 1,500 members of the Winnipeg Stake and Fort Francis Ontario District.

Sources: Andrew Jenson, Encyclopedic History of the Church, 1941; Andrew Jensen, Biographical Encyclopedia, 1971; Melvin S. Tagg, A History of the Mormon Church in Canada, 1963; Hal Pruden, Mormons in Manitoba, 1988; Anna Brandley Ostlund, My Father, Theodore Brandley, 1961; Northern States Mission, Manuscript history and historical reports; Alberta Canada Stake, Manuscript history and historical reports; North Central States Mission, Manuscript history and historical reports.

Stake — 1
(Listed alphabetically As of Oct. 1, 2011.)

No.	Name	Organized	First President
North America Central Area			
980	Winnipeg Manitoba	12 Nov 1978	Lorne Leslie Clapson

Mission — 1
(As of Oct. 1, 2011; shown with historical number. See MISSIONS.)

(136) CANADA WINNIPEG MISSION
1661 Portage Avenue, #306
Winnipeg, Manitoba R3J 3T7
Canada

NEW BRUNSWICK

Jan. 1, 2011: Est. population, 752,800; Members, 2,944; Stakes, 1; Wards, 5; Branches, 1; Percent LDS, .4, or one in 256; North America Northeast Area; Canada Halifax Mission.

Missionary work in the Maritime provinces began in 1833 when Lyman E. Johnson and James Heriot began proselyting in Nova Scotia and New Brunswick. Elder Johnson preached in Saint John, New Brunswick, in the spring of 1836 and later in Sackville, where he baptized 18 people and organized the first branch in the Maritimes.

Among those baptized in Sackville was Marriner W. Merrill, who later preached extensively in Canada and eventually became a member of the Quorum of the Twelve.

In 1920, a branch was organized in Saint John, New Brunswick. The branch was discontinued, and then reorganized and has been continuous since 1948. A meetinghouse was completed in 1954. The Fredericton Branch was organized in 1940, later discontinued and started again in 1957, and completed a meetinghouse in 1963. The Moncton Branch, created in 1966, included the Sackville area where the first branch of the Church in the Maritimes was created. Membership in this branch reached 160 in 1974. The Saint John New Brunswick Stake was created in 1988. Growth of the Church in the Maritimes has fluctuated over time, but the work of missionaries and members pushed efforts along in the 1990s. Membership in 1990 was 2,100. New Brunswick is in the temple district of the Halifax Nova Scotia Temple which was dedicated 14 November 1999.

In 2003, there were 2,272 members.

Sources: Encyclopedic History of the Church, by Andrew Jenson; A History of the Mormon Church in Canada, published in 1968 by the Lethbridge Alberta Stake under the direction of Dr. Melvin S. Tagg; Jack E. Jarrard, "Portrait of a New Mission," Church News, September 22, 1973; Eleanor Knowles, "The Saints in Canada's Maritime Provinces," Ensign, June 1974; "LDS in Canada — Growth through faithfulness," Church News, Oct. 23, 1983; Sheridan R. Sheffield, "Maritime provinces," Church News, October 24, 1992; Church News, May 23, 1998, Nov. 20, 1999.

Stake — 1
(Listed alphabetically As of Oct. 1, 2011.)

No.	Name	Organized	First President
North America Northeast Area			
1698	Saint John New Brunswick	26 Jun 1988	Blaine E. Hatt

NEWFOUNDLAND AND LABRADOR

Jan. 1, 2011: Est. population, 515,000; Members, 731; Branches, 3; Percent LDS, .13 or one in 762; North America Northeast Area; Canada Halifax Mission.

The First Presidency authorized S. Dilworth Young, president of the New England Mission on 2 July 1948, to commence missionary work in Newfoundland. Young sent a letter shortly thereafter, instructing Curtis Page and John M. Scowcroft to report to Newfoundland. In another letter dated 10 August 1948 from the First Presidency to President Young reported that no record of any previous mission work can be found for Newfoundland.

The missionaries began their work and made contact with Walter Newman and Wallace Smith a soldier from Ogden, Utah.

Pres. Young with Elder Milton R. Hunter of the First Council of the Seventy, flew to Newfoundland on 6 July 1949. In a meeting on 7 July 1949 attended by the missionaries, Pres. Young and Elder Hunter the Newfoundland District was organized with Elder Harold Daw as president. The first baptism in Newfoundland was Lavina Webber Mercer. She was baptized 13 August 1950 by L. Dale Hanks.

Elder Spencer W. Kimball of the Quorum of the Twelve visited Newfoundland on 28 May 1960 with President John E. Carr of the New England Mission while on a tour of the mission.

The St John's Branch in Newfoundland was created 7 February 1957 with 47 members under the Canada Halifax Mission. In 10 years, the branch grew to 92 members. The name changed to St. John's Newfoundland Branch on 1 December 1976. By 1988, there were 550 members in the three branches, St John's, Corner Brook organized on 19 March 1978 and Gander organized on 1 June 1981.

In 2002, membership reached 597; and 623 in 2003.

Sources: Andrew Jensen, Encyclopedic History of the Church, 1941; Melvin S. Tagg, A History of the Mormon Church in Canada, 1968; Eleanor Knowles, "The Saints in Canada's Maritime Provinces," Ensign, June 1974; New England Mission, Manuscript history and historical reports, Church Archives; Canadian Mission, Manuscript history and historical reports, Church Archives; Newfoundland District, Manuscript history and historical reports, Church Archives.

NOVA SCOTIA

Jan. 1 2011: Est. population, 938,000; Members, 4,886; Stakes, 1; Wards, 6; Branches, 12; Missions, 1; District 1; Temples, 1; Percent LDS, .5, or one in 195; North America Northeast Area.

Lyman E. Johnson and James Heriot began missionary work in the Maritime Provinces. They arrived in Nova Scotia in 1833. Benjamin Brown and Jesse W. Crosby left Nauvoo on 30 July 1843 for Nova Scotia. On 18 September 1843, a conference was held under the direction of district President Robert Dixon. By 14 November 1843, the Halifax Branch was created. On 5 April 1844, another conference was held at Preston, with members attending from Halifax branch as well as Preston and Onslow, Popes Harbour and Sheet Harbor.

Persecution followed the members and most left for the West. One group of 50, most of the Halifax Branch, traveled with their branch president, John A. Jost, aboard the ship Barque Halifax. The ship left Nova Scotia on 12 May 1855 and took the members on the first leg of their journey around Cape Horn to San Francisco. This exodus ended organized branches in the Maritimes until work resumed under President Nephi Jensen with the organization of the Canadian Mission on 1 July 1919.

When missionary work resumed, elders presided over groups in Halifax, Windsor, Glace Bay, Sydney, Kentville and New Glasgow. The Halifax Branch was organized on 6 July 1947 by then Mission President S. Dilworth Young. On 25 June 1958, Elder Mark E. Petersen of the Quorum of the Twelve and former missionary to Nova Scotia in 1920, participated in the ground breaking ceremony for a new meetinghouse in Halifax. The building was completed in January 1959. The New Glasgow Branch was organized on 9 June 1961 and the following day, the Sydney Branch was organized.

In 1959, converts were baptized in Bridgewater, and by 14 June 1961, it was organized as a branch. By 1967, the Bridgewater Branch had 135 members. A meetinghouse was begun July 1965 and dedicated in 1967. Membership in Nova Scotia was the most rapidly growing in Canada. With 250 members in 1972, it increased more than 800 percent in 10 years, reaching 2,331.

The Dartmouth Nova Scotia Stake was created on 12 May 1985. The Dartmouth/Halifax area in Nova Scotia continues to serve as the center of Church activity in the Maritimes.

President Gordon B. Hinckley visited Halifax on 12 February 1998 and spoke to some 2,000 members who had come from throughout the Maritime provinces.

The Halifax Nova Scotia Temple, located in the city of Dartmouth across the harbor from Halifax, was dedicated by President Hinckley on 14 November 1999.

Sources: Andrew Jenson, Encyclopedic History of the Church, 1941; Melvin S. Tagg, A History of the Mormon Church in Canada, 1968; Eleanor Knowles, "The Saints in Canada's Maritime Provinces," Ensign, June 1974; New England Mission, Manuscript history and historical reports, Church Archives; Canadian Mission, Manuscript history and historical reports, Church Archives; Journal History, Church Library.

Stake — 1

(Listed alphabetically As of Oct. 1, 2011.)

No.	Name	Organized	First President
North America Northeast Area			
1530	Dartmouth Nova Scotia	12 May 1985	Terry Lee Livingstone

(107) CANADA HALIFAX MISSION
202 Brownlow Ave., Unit F, Bldg F
Dartmouth, Nova Scotia B3B 1T5
Canada

ONTARIO

Jan. 1, 2011: Est. population, 12,541,000; Members, 45,969; Stakes, 9; Wards, 59; Branches, 41; Missions, 2; Districts, 2; Temples, 1; Percent LDS, .36, or one in 275; North America Northeast Area.

Seeking ways to finance the publication of the Book of Mormon, the first members of the Church to enter Canada were Hiram Page and Oliver Cowdery, who crossed the border from New York in the winter of 1829-30, even before the Church was organized. It is unknown if they did any missionary work. In 1830, Phineas H. Young, brother of Brigham Young, traveled to Earnestown, Upper Canada, now Ontario. Though not yet baptized, Young, a Methodist minister, preached about the Book of Mormon.

Joseph Smith Sr. and Don Carlos Smith entered Canada briefly in September 1830, visiting a few villages north of the St. Lawrence River. Early in June 1832 Phineas H. Young returned to Canada, this time as an ordained elder in the company of his brother Joseph, Elial Strong and Eleazer Miller. By December 1832, Brigham Young, in company with his brother Joseph, joined their brother Phineas to preach in Canada near Earnestown and Loughborough townships. Before the last of these missionaries left Canada, at least four branches had been organized. Missionaries organized a district in Toronto that was placed under the direction of John Taylor. Other missionaries soon followed, including Joseph Smith, who traveled to Mount Pleasant, Ontario, on 26 October 1833. He baptized 12 people and later visited Toronto in August 1837.

Two of the most successful missionaries were John E. Page and Parley P. Pratt. Page baptized almost a thousand converts and Pratt converted future Church leaders John Taylor (who later became president of the Church), Isaac Russell, John Snider, John Goodson, and Joseph Fielding. These last four helped start the highly successful work in Great Britain.

Between 1830 and 1850, an estimated 2,500 Canadians, mostly from Ontario, joined the Church. Most of these who remained faithful gathered with the Saints in the Great Basin. By 14 January 1861, there were only 74 Church members in Ontario.

Little work took place in eastern Canada until the Canadian Mission was re-opened on 22 April 1919 with conferences in Toronto, established 22 July 1919 and Ottawa, on 22 January 1920. President Heber J. Grant visited the Canadian Mission home in Toronto on 4 November 1919. Branches were organized in Toronto and Hamilton by December 1919. Other branches were organized in Kitchener, 1923; Ottawa, 1926; and St. Catherine's, 1933. The Oshawa Branch began on September 1947 after functioning off and on as a Sunday School since 1944. Membership in all of eastern Canada reached 1,974 in 1950.

The first meetinghouse in eastern Canada was dedicated by President Heber J. Grant in Toronto on 25 June 1939. The first stake in eastern Canada was organized on 14 August 1960, also in Toronto, while President Thomas S. Monson, was mission president. In attendance at the conference when the stake was created were 2,249 members, which constituted 92 percent of the new stake's membership. The Toronto Canada Temple was dedicated on 25 August 1990.

On 1 July 1993, Toronto's second mission, Canada Toronto East, was created. Because of the cosmopolitan makeup of the area, missionaries encounter people from upwards of 100 nations in the Toronto area. From Toronto, efforts to improve the image of the Church through the media led to a prime-time television series, "For All Seasons," across Canada in 1994, showcasing Latter-day Saint programs.

On 22 June 1986, President Thomas S. Monson of the First Presidency and Elder M. Russell Ballard of the Quorum of the Twelve created the Kitchener Ontario Stake, the 1,600th stake in the Church. They returned on 5 May 1996 to create the Sudbury Ontario Stake. President Monson and Elder Ballard had previously presided over Canadian missions.

On 9 August 1997, President Thomas S. Monson dedicated a marker placed in Bath, Ontario, by the Napanee Branch in honor of the founding of the first branch in Canada.

President Gordon B. Hinckley, accompanied by President Boyd K. Packer, acting president of the Quorum of the Twelve, visited Sudbury, on 5 August 1998. There President Hinckley spoke to 850 members. Later, in Hamilton, on 8 August, President Hinckley spoke to 12,000 people.

In commemoration of the 40th anniversary of the creation of the Toronto Canada Stake and the 10th anniversary of the Toronto temple, President Monson returned to Ontario on 19 August 2000 to dedicate a historical monument commemorating the contributions of early missionaries and members who served and lived in Upper Canada.

The Greater Toronto Public Affairs Council of the Church presented the first Canadian Family Values Awards on 17 January 2003, to Mayor Hazel McCallion, a 20-year mayor; Father Thomas Rosica, a Catholic priest; and Dolina Smith, an anti-pornography and abuse activist.

In 2003, there were 43,189 members.

Sources: Andrew Jenson, Encyclopedic History of the Church, 1941; Melvin S. Tagg, A History of the Mormon Church in Canada, 1968; Richard E. Bennett, "Canada: From Struggling Seed, the Church has Risen to Branching Maple," Ensign, September 1988; Richard Robertson, "Toronto, a Growing Light in the East," Ensign, September 1988; Dell Van Orden, "Our Treasure, a New Temple is Dedicated" and "Past Legacy Builds Today's Faith," Church News, 1 September 1990; William B. Smart, "Church Begins Series on TV Across Canada," Church News, 5 February 1994; Gerry Avant, "LDS Stalwarts in Upper Canada are Remembered," Church News, 26 August 2000; John Farrington, "Family Values Honored in Canada," Church News, 8 February 2003; Canadian Mission, Church Archives; Journal History, Church Library.

CANADA TORONTO MISSION
197 County Court Blvd Ste 203
Brampton, ON L6W 4P6
Canada

PRINCE EDWARD ISLAND

Jan. 1, 2011: Est. population, 138,000; Members, 440; Branches, 3;
Percent LDS, .3, or one in 337; North America Northeast Area; Canada Halifax Mission.

The first missionary to preach in the province was John Skerry who came to Prince Edward Island in 1845 from Halifax. After baptizing about 12 individuals, Skerry organized branches in Bedeque and Charlottetown. By March 1846 there were about 21 members on the island.

Apostle Wilford Woodruff visited the Bedeque Branch on 31 July 1849 while visiting missionaries and members in eastern New England and Canada. He wrote in his diary that he "found 22 members and 4 Priest[s] in the Bedeque Branch" and "there is also 4 Saints in Charlottetown." William Maxfield, presided over the Bedeque Branch. Maxfield left Prince Edward Island for Utah in June 1850 along with his extended family, totaling 31 members. The branches were disbanded by the early 1850's when all members immigrated to Utah.

The next recorded missionary work began on 14 September 1942 when George R. Hawkes and C. Elmer Clark labored there for four days. They reported to the New England States Mission President William H. Reeder, Jr., that "many fine contacts were made and the missionaries received great joy from their work." On 15 November 1942, Reeder sent elders to investigate the possibility of assigning missionaries regularly to the island. On 10 April 1943, M. Dee Smith and Arthur D. Browne were sent to begin working in Summerside. The first convert was Irene Wyand, baptized 7 November 1943. She later left the Island and became an educator in Ontario.

During World War II pilots assigned to the Canadian Air Force or the British Royal Air Force joined the missionaries at Sunday School services on the island.

In 1964, Ralph and Gerda Waugh, recent converts from New York, returned to Prince Edward Island where Ralph was born. They contacted another member, Kay Callaghan and began meeting on Sunday in their home in Summerside. Elder Boyd K. Packer, then an Assistant to the Twelve and president of the New England States Mission, visited the Waugh home with missionaries in July 1966. About two weeks later full-time missionaries were transferred to the island and missionaries have been there since. Later that same year the Sunday School in Summerside was made dependent on the Moncton Branch, New Brunswick.

Ralph Waugh became the first president of the Summerside Branch on 21 December 1969. In 1974, the branch was divided and the Charlottetown Branch was formed on 28 September. The Prince Edward Island District was organized on 13 April 1980 with A. Michael Shumate as president. Gordon B. Hinckley, a member of the Quorum of the Twelve, with his wife Marjorie, visited the island on 21 September 1980, along with the Canada-Halifax Mission president James A. Kenning.

The Church continued to grow on the island and by 1982, Prince Edward Island District had branches in Montague, Summerside and Charlottetown. The island's first meetinghouse was completed in Summerside on 18 June 1983. A meetinghouse in Charlottetown was completed on 14 July 1984. The Montague Branch was formed 20 July 1981 and a meetinghouse was completed there in June 1988. The three branches became part of the Saint John New Brunswick Stake on 26 July 1988.

On 12 February 1998, many members from Prince Edward Island journeyed to Halifax, Nova Scotia, to see President Gordon B. Hinckley as he addressed members from throughout the Maritime provinces. On 14 November 1999, President Hinckley dedicated the Halifax Nova Scotia Temple. In 2002, membership reached 374; and 382 in 2003.

Sources: Andrew Jenson, Encyclopedic History of the Church, 1941; Melvin S. Tagg, A History of the Mormon Church in Canada, 1968; Ralph Waugh, A History of the Church: Prince Edward Island, 1997; Scott G. Kenney, ed., Wilford Woodruff Journals, 1833-1898, 1982; Eleanor Knowles, "The Saints in Canada's Maritime Provinces," Ensign, June 1974; Sheridan R. Sheffield, Prince Edward Island: Members Find Peace in 'Little Land' Where 'You Find Your Soul,'" Church News, 10 July 1993; Sheridan R, Sheffield, "Maritime Provinces: Members' Commitment to Gospel Keeps Church Growing," Church News, 24 October 1992; New England Mission, Manuscript history and historical reports, Church Archives; Canadian Mission, Manuscript history and historical report, Church Archives, Prince Edward Island District, Manuscript history and historical report, Church Archives.

QUEBEC

Jan. 1, 2011: Est. population, 7,598,000; Members, 10,956; Stakes, 3; Wards, 18; Branches, 17; Missions, 1; Districts, 1; Temples, 1; Percent LDS, 0.13, or one in 743; North America Northeast Area.

Early missionaries in the 1830s frequently traveled through Lower Canada, as the province of Quebec was then called, but found little success. However, in the summer of 1836, Hazen Aldrich and Winslow Farr labored in Stanstead County, and baptized 11 people. Twenty-three members in the area departed for Nauvoo on 20 July 1837.

Converts also migrated from the community of Eardley, north of Ottawa. By the early 1850s, most members had gone to Utah. After the 1850s, there were no known Latter-day Saints in Quebec until the Canadian Mission was re-opened on 22 April 1919 with Nephi Jensen president. By 30 July 1921, an English- speaking branch began meeting in Montreal. A meetinghouse for this branch was purchased and dedicated on 25 June1942 by Elder Joseph Fielding Smith of the Quorum of the Twelve Apostles.

On 20 April 1961, mission President Thomas S. Monson sent two French-speaking missionaries into the area around Montreal. By 18 June, four additional French-speaking missionaries joined them. The missionaries found investigators who joined the Church and established a base that attracted Latter-day Saint French-speaking immigrants. From this effort, missionaries entered Quebec City where a branch was started on 6 April 1969. The Quebec Mission (later changed to the Canada Montreal Mission) was created on 18 March 1972, and by 1974, a French-speaking district was created.

By 1987, membership among the French-speaking people was 2,753, about 65 percent of the total membership in the province. These converts tended to stay in Quebec instead of moving to Utah as many of their English-speaking counterparts did.

The Montreal Quebec Stake, considered the first French-speaking stake in North America, was created on 18 June 1978. On 22 July 1980, the English-speaking Montreal Quebec Mount Royale Stake was created from the Ottawa Ontario Stake. In addition, many Hispanics immigrated to Montreal, and by 2000, there were two Spanish-speaking wards in the city.

President Gordon B. Hinckley addressed 3,000 members in Montreal on 6 August 1998, and announced a temple to be built in the city. The Montreal Canada Temple, the sixth in Canada, was dedicated 4 June 2000.

In 2003, there were 9,349 members.

Sources: Andrew Jenson, Encyclopedic History of the Church, 1941: Melvin S. Tagg, A History of the Mormon Church in Canada, 1968; Richard E. Bennett, "Canada: From Struggling Seed, the Church has Risen to Branching Maple," Ensign, September 1988; Marueen Ursenbach Beecher, "Converts in Quebec," Church News, 24 June 1978; Canadian Mission, Manuscript history and historical reports, Church Archives; Journal History, Church Library.

Stakes — 3
(Listed alphabetically As of Oct. 1, 2011.)

No.	Name	Organized	First President
North America Northeast Area			
2720	Longueuil Quebec	7 May 2006	Pierre-Paul Morin
943	Montreal Quebec	18 Jun 1978	Gerard C. Pelchat
1160	Montreal Quebec Mount Royal	6 Jul 1980	Ian Gillespie Wilson

Mission — 1
(As of Oct. 1, 2011; shown with historical number. See MISSIONS.)

(99a) CANADA MONTREAL MISSION
1320 Blvd Graham, Suite 110
Ville Mont-Royal, Quebec H3P 3C8, Canada

SASKATCHEWAN

Jan. 1, 2011: Est. population, 994,000; Members, 5,554; Stakes, 2; Wards, 8; Branches, 9; Temples, 1; percent LDS, .54, or one in 186; Canada Winnipeg Mission; North America Central Area.

Around the early 1920s a few Latter-day Saints moved to Saskatchewan, mostly from Alberta and settled in Saskatoon, Regina, and other communities. About that same time, G. Gordon Whyte of Moose Jaw acquired a copy of the Book of Mormon, accepted it as being true and requested baptism. He was baptized on 17 August 1923 in Moose Jaw. He is the first known convert in the province. That same year, Whyte and Northern States Mission president John G. Allred, held a street meeting in Regina.

The first missionaries sent to work in Saskatchewan in the summer of 1925 were Raymond L. Allen and Alma Ward. They were assigned by the North Central States Mission to work in Saskatoon and Leo E. Nelson and Theodore Reynolds who were assigned to work in Regina. The North Saskatchewan and South Saskatchewan districts were organized on 6 August of that year. On 30 May 1927 the North Saskatchewan District was dissolved and recombined with the South Saskatchewan District to form the Saskatchewan District.

A Sunday School was organized on 8 May 1927 in Regina with Gordon Whyte as superintendent. It became a branch on 27 May 1934 also with Whyte as president. That year, Latter-day Saint farmers in southern Alberta and their neighbors donated two boxcars of vegetables and food to families in Saskatchewan suffering from the effects of a severe drought. Among those receiving the aid were 20 families in the Regina Branch. A meetinghouse was dedicated for the Regina Branch in 1939.

The Saskatchewan District was incorporated into the Western Canadian Mission on 6 December 1942. This was done in part because it was easier for Church members to pay tithing to mission headquarters in Edmonton. Progress in the area proved difficult during World War II as most missionaries were drafted into the military. This left local members to handle the missionary effort. Full-time sister missionaries, however, were assigned to work in Regina on 6 December 1943.

On 3 September 1961 the North Saskatchewan District was organized. Seminary classes were held in the Saskatoon Branch on 27 September 1965. An Indian seminary program also began in 1965 with children on the Piapot, Carry-the-Kettle and Cowesses reserves east of Regina.

The first known meetinghouse built by the Church was dedicated in Regina on 19 May 1967. The first stake in Saskatchewan was created in Saskatoon on 5 November 1978, from a consolidation of the Regina and Saskatoon districts. The stake then covered the entire province of Saskatchewan and parts of Alberta and Manitoba.

The Regina Saskatchewan Temple was dedicated on 14 November 1999, by President Boyd K. Packer, acting President of the Quorum of the Twelve Apostles. Two years later, the Regina Saskatchewan Stake was organized on 27 October 2001.

In 2002, membership reached 4,826; and 4,833 in 2003.

Sources: Andrew Jenson, Encyclopedic History of the Church, 1941; North Central States Mission, Manuscript history and historical reports, Church Archives; Wilbur Gordon Hackney, History of the Western Canadian Mission, thesis, 1950; Carol Cornwall Madsen "The Christian Way," Church News, 1 July 1978; "Pres. Hunter Returns from Mission Tour, Church News, 5 July 1950; "3 New Stakes Formed in U.S., Canada, 3 Others Reorganized," Church News, 18 November 1978; Liahona, 28 July 1925; Melvin S. Tagg, A History of the Church of Jesus Christ of Latter-day Saints in Canada, 1830-1963, thesis, 1963; Melvin S. Tagg, A History of the Mormon Church in Canada, 1968; Western Canadian Mission, History, 1941-1948, Church Archives; Regina Saskatchewan District, Manuscript history, Church Archives; Saskatoon Branch, Manuscript history and historical reports, Church Archives; Saskatchewan Stake, Manuscript history and historical reports, 1986.

Stakes — 2
(As of Oct. 1, 2011.)

No.	Name	Organized	First President
North America Central Area			
2607	Regina Saskatchewan	27 Oct 2001	E. Gregg Wood
978	Saskatoon Saskatchewan	5 Nov 1978	Noel W. Burt

NORTHWEST TERRITORIES & NUNAVUT

Jan. 1, 2011: Est. population, 71,800; Members, 128; Branches, 1; percent LDS, .2, or one in 488; North America Central Area; Canada Edmonton Mission.

Although the Northwest Territories had been nominally under the jurisdiction of the Western Canadian Mission since 1947, the first branch of the Church in the area was not established until 1963. As Church members moved to Inuvik on the Mackenzie River delta, where the Canadian Armed Forces maintained a small military base, the Latter-day Saint population grew enough for the establishment of a Sunday School and then a dependent branch that year. In 1967 the branch had grown large enough to achieve independent status. This small branch continued until 1973, when the declining Church population at Inuvik no longer justified its existence. In the southern part of the territory, the Mackenzie Branch was established on 18 June 1967 to serve the needs of members scattered through several small communities from Hay River, Northwest Territories on the north to High Level, Alberta on the south. This branch was also discontinued after about two years.

In October 1967, the Mackenzie Zone was created to oversee the work in the northern part of the mission, including the Northwest Territories. In June 1970, the mission was renamed the Alberta- Saskatchewan Mission, then changed again in 1974 to the Canada Calgary Mission, but through both changes it retained responsibility for the Northwest Territories. In 1998, the Canada Edmonton Mission was created from a division of the Canada Calgary Mission and given jurisdiction over the Northwest Territories.

A more permanent center of Church population in the Northwest Territories appeared at Yellowknife, a gold-mining settlement that had grown gradually since the 1930s on the north shore of Great Slave Lake. It was incorporated as a city in 1970 and missionaries were stationed there about that time. Some were also stationed during part of the 1970s at Hay River on the opposite shore of the lake. Thereafter, missionaries were sent to the Yellowknife area during the summer months. On 15 May 1983, the Yellowknife Branch was established to provide Church programs for members living throughout the Northwest Territories and in the recently established Nunavut Territory.

Sources: Western Canadian Mission, Manuscript history and historical reports, Church Archives; Western Canadian Mission, Mission president's files, 1964-1967, Church Archives; Western Canadian Mission, Scrapbook, 1955-1970, Church Archives; Canada Calgary Mission, Manuscript history and historical reports, Church Archives; Lane Johnson, "A Dominion of Saints," Ensign, September 1988; Lethbridge Alberta Stake, A History of the Mormon Church in Canada, 1968; "Largest Branch in the World," Ensign, September 1988.

YUKON TERRITORY

Jan. 1, 2011: Est. population, 31,998; Members, 265; Branch, 1; percent LDS, .77, or one in 129; North America Northwest Area; Alaska Anchorage Mission.

Lying in the northwest corner of Canada's continental mainland, isolated by rugged mountains, the Yukon Territory shares a common border and many characteristics with its American neighbor, Alaska.

Government employment, military assignment, and work in the mines brought some of the earliest Latter-day Saints to Whitehorse, the territory's capital and largest city. Two of these were Norman J. Drayton and Robert M. McDonald and their families. The Draytons arrived in 1952 and the McDonalds in 1957. Jack Forbush and his companion, who were serving in the Western Canadian Mission, organized a Sunday School in Whitehorse on 1 February 1959 with Norman Drayton as superintendent. The first Relief Society meeting was held on 23 May 1959. Thereafter, missionaries irregularly visited Whitehorse.

An independent branch in Whitehorse consisting of the Drayton, Bailey, Sutherland, and Symchych families was created on 15 October 1963 with Norman Drayton as president. Meetings were first held in members' homes, then in rented facilities. The branch was initially part of the Southeast Alaska District of the Alaskan-Canadian Mission.

The first missionaries assigned to work full-time in Whitehorse were Grant W. Andrus and Fred W. Albertson. They arrived in April 1967 and remained until July. During this time they attempted to contact every home in Whitehorse. They baptized one person, Frances P. Foisy. On 24-25 July 1968 LeGrand Richards of the Quorum of the Twelve visited the branch and witnessed the baptism of four people. A meetinghouse was finished in 1981. It has since been enlarged.

The Yukon Interior Branch of the Alaska Anchorage Mission was created in 1979 to administer to scattered members (65 total as of June 2004) living mainly along the Yukon River. The Whitehorse Branch takes in the rest of the territory.

In 2003, there were 241 members.

Sources: History of the Church in Canada project files, Church Archives; Patricia B. Jasper, A Gathering of Saints in Alaska, 1999; Lethbridge Alberta Stake, A History of the Mormon Church in Canada, 1968; Whitehorse Branch, Manuscript history and historical records, Church Archives; Canada Vancouver Mission, Annual history and historical reports, Church Archives.

CAPE VERDE

Jan. 1, 2011: Est. population, 429,000; Members, 7,456; Mission, 1; Districts, 3; Branches, 18; percent LDS, 1.6 or one in 62; Europe Area.

The Republic of Cape Verde is composed of 10 main islands in two volcanic archipelagos located 385 miles west of Senegal off the African Coast. Most of the indigenous peoples are descendants of African slaves brought there by Portuguese traders in the 1400s. They speak Crioulo and Portuguese, and most are associated with the Roman Catholic or Church of the Nazarene faiths.

Spain Las Palmas Mission President Marion K. Hamblin visited Cape Verde in November 1988 to explore the possibilities of sending missionaries there. He sent Christopher Lee and Kenneth C. Margetts there in January 1989. They began their labors on Santiago Island. The first convert baptized was Lino Paulo. The Praia Branch in the capital city of Praia was organized on 27 June 1989. At the time, there were approximately 25 members. Lee and Margetts were forced to leave the country in July 1989 because the government refused to renew their visas. Missionaries were allowed to return within a few months.

The Cape Verde ambassador to the United States attended the Christmas lighting ceremony of the Washington D.C. Temple in 1993. In September 1994, Elder Dallin H. Oaks of the Quorum of the Twelve visited the islands. While there, he was invited to see the president of the Republic of Cape Verde Antonio Mascarenhas and Praia Mayor Jacinto Santos. He described the missionary program and explained Church's doctrines.

By September 1994, there were 50 Cape Verdeans who had been called to serve full-time missions, most working in Portugal, and 48 missionaries from the Portugal Lisbon South Mission were working in Cape Verde.

On a return trip from Africa, President Gordon B. Hinckley stopped in Cape Verde on 22 February 1998 where he spoke to 780 members. At that time Cape Verde included three districts and 18 branches.

The First Presidency on 9 March 2002 announced creation of the Cape Verde Praia Mission from the Portugal Lisbon South Mission. At the time of the creation, it included the Fogo Cape Verde, Mindelo Cape Verde, and Praia Cape Verde districts.

In January 2004, President Hinckley stopped on Cape Verde's Sal Island for refueling. While there, he met with members of the Sal Branch.

Membership in 2003 was 5,975.

Sources: Praia Cape Verde District, Manuscript history and historical reports, Church Archives; Cape Verde Praia Mission, Historical reports, 2002, Church Archives; Kenneth C. Margetts, Spain Las Palmas Mission Papers, 1987-1989, Church Archives; Arnold K. Garr, Donald Q. Cannon, and Richard O. Cowan, Encyclopedia of Latter-day Saint History, 2000; Jocelyn Mann Denyer, "Temple Grounds Aglow for Holidays," Deseret News, 11 December 1993; "Home Emphasized on Island Visits: Meetings at Stops in Caribbean, Cape Verde," Deseret Morning News, 24 January 2004; "Diversity of Land, People and Climate," Church News, 7 December 1991; "Republic of Cape Verde Dedicated by Apostle," Church News, 24 September 1994; Shaun D. Stahle, "Spirit of President Hinckley's Visits Lingers," Church News, 7 March 1998; "Many Nations Represented at Ceremonies," Church News, 12 December 1998; Shaun D. Stahle, "Seven New Missions Created," Church News, 9 March 2002; "Stake Alignment in Newly Organized Missions," Church News, 16 March 2002.

Mission — 1
(As of Oct. 1, 2011; shown with historical number. See MISSIONS.)
(330a) CAPE VERDE PRAIA MISSION
Palmarejo, Praia
Ihla de Santiago, Rep. Cabo Verde, West Africa

CENTRAL AFRICAN REPUBLIC

Jan. 1, 2011: Est. population, 4,511,000; Members, 427; Branches, 1; Percent LDS, .009, or one in 11,478; Africa Southeast Area; Ghana Cape Coast Mission.

The Central African Republic, previously known as Ubangi-Shari, became independent from France on 13 August 1960. It is a landlocked country bordered by Cameroon, Chad, Sudan, Democratic Republic of the Congo, and Republic of Congo. French is the official language with Arabic and local dialects also spoken. Fifty percent of the people are Christian, while 50 percent follow Muslim, and tribal beliefs.

The first known Church member living in Central African Republic was Carol Forrest of the U.S. Peace Corps. A returned missionary, she arrived in June 1991. She shared the gospel with many of her associates and in September 1991, was set apart as a district missionary. Elder J. Ballard Washburn of the Seventy and counselor in the Africa Area presidency, and Robert L. Mercer, president of the Cameroon Yaounde Mission, visited Forrest and a group of investigators in September 1992.

Elder Washburn visited Central African Republic from 16-21 September 1992. On 19 September, 20 people were baptized, and on 20 September, two branches were organized. Celestin N'Gakondou was called as president of the Bangui 1st Branch, and Gaspard Lapet was called to preside over the Bangui 2nd Branch.

The first full-time missionaries, Raymond and Christianne Fourtina, from Bordeaux, France, arrived in January 1993. In July of that year, the Church received legal recognition. The seminary program was introduced in 1995. The Central African Republic was moved to the Ivory Coast Abidjan Mission on 1 January 2003, and then reorganized as part of the Ghana Cape Coast Mission on 1 July 2005.

Membership was 118 in 2003.

Sources: Mary Mostert, "Medical Officer Ministers to Souls," Church News, 5 December 1992; Borgna Brunner, "Countries of the World, Central African Republic," Time Almanac 2003; Ivory Coast Abidjan Mission, Manuscript history and historical reports, Church Archives; Robert Lee Mercer, Interview, 1994, Church Archives.

CHILE

Jan. 1, 2011: Est. population, 16,602,000; Members, 563,689; Stakes, 74; Wards, 421; Branches, 199; Missions, 9; Districts, 23; Temples, 1; Percent LDS, 3.3 or one in 30; Chile Area.

Located on the west coast of South America, the Republic of Chile has a Spanish-speaking population that is 72 percent Roman Catholic and 12 percent Protestant.

The earliest LDS visitors to Chilean national territory were the passengers of the ship Brooklyn, en route from New York City to California, who landed on Juan Fernández Island in May 1846 to replenish supplies, after failing to land at Valparaíso because of a storm.

Parley P. Pratt of the Quorum of the Twelve, in company with his wife Phebe and Rufus C. Allen, spent five months at Valparaíso and Quillota investigating conditions, 1851-1852, but Elder Pratt decided against establishing a permanent mission in Chile. Instead, he recommended to Brigham Young that the Book of Mormon be translated into Spanish for future use in Latin America.

Seventy years later, assistant Church Historian Andrew Jenson visited Antofagasta, Valparaíso, Viña del Mar, and Santiago, March-April 1923, and reported to Church leaders that South America was "a field ready for the harvest."

Although there was no known organized Church activity in Chile, missionaries stationed in Argentina made occasional brief visits from the mid-1920s until the early 1950s (including an attempt to establish missionary work in the southern logging village of Futaleafú) and U.S. Latter-day Saints worked for mining companies in northern Chile.

Former Argentine missionary Billie F. Fotheringham and his family were sent to Santiago in 1952 by his employer. At the urging of Fotheringham, Church President David O. McKay, Sister McKay, and their son Robert visited Santiago in February 1954 to assess the prospects for sending missionaries to Chile.

The First Presidency authorized the Argentine Mission to send missionaries to Chile in May 1955, but it was not until June 1956 that Verle M. Allred and Joseph C. Bentley arrived in Santiago to begin missionary work there. Henry D. Moyle of the Quorum of the Twelve joined them in July 1956 and established the Santiago Branch (soon renamed the Ñuñoa Branch), with Fotheringham as the first branch president. In organizing the branch Elder Moyle stated, "These people will accept the Gospel rapidly and . . . soon there will be a mission here with at least 10 branches." On 25 November 1956, Ricardo S. García, Isidro and Graciela Saldaña, and others were the first group baptized in Chile.

During the next three years, missionaries from Argentina established additional branches in the nation's largest population centers — Santiago, Concepción, and Valparaíso-Viña del Mar — the Church was legally incorporated in Chile, and the first Church property was purchased in Santiago. In May 1958, Opal M. Atwood and Hope C. Kohler were the first sister missionaries assigned to Chile. In February 1959, Spencer W. Kimball of the Quorum of the Twelve visited Chile and stressed the need for developing local leadership. Also in 1959, Ricardo S. García became the first Chilean Latter-day Saint to receive the Melchizedek Priesthood and Ruth I. Peters, María Cristina Donoso, and Guillermo Núñez were the first Chileans called to full-time missionary service. In May 1960, Carlos A. Cifuentes was the first Chilean called as a branch president; both his counselors and the branch clerk were also Chileans. In February 1963, Cifuentes was also the first local member called as a district president and in March 1965 became the first Chilean called to be counselor to a mission president.

In October 1959, Chile, along with Peru, became part of the new Andes Mission with headquarters in Lima. Two years later, on 8 October 1961, the Chilean Mission was organized, with 12 branches and 1,136 members.

During the next decade, branches were established in the balance of Chile's largest cities and towns, Church schools were established in Santiago and elsewhere, meetinghouse construction began, initially through the building missionary program, local Latter-day Saints gained leadership experience and the northernmost part of the country, including branches in Arica and Iquiqu), which had remained during most of the 1960s in the Andes Mission and its successors, was incorporated into the Chilean Mission.

In the early 1970s, the Church in Chile weathered the political and economic turmoil associated with the presidency of Marxist Salvador Allende and the September 1973 military coup that brought Augusto Pinochet to power. Many Chileans, among them some Latter-day Saints, migrated to countries such as Argentina, Venezuela, Australia, Canada and the United States.

During the 1970s and early 1980s, the Church in Chile was transformed from being mission-oriented to a stake-oriented organization — the first stake was organized in Santiago in November 1972 by Elder Gordon B. Hinckley, then of the Quorum of the Twelve, with the national Church membership standing at 20,000 at the end of that year, the seminary and institute programs were established (1972) and the Church schools were closed (1981), an LDS distribution center was established, the meetinghouse construction program accelerated, additional missions were created for a total of five by the end of 1979. Many young Chilean Latter-day Saints served full-time missions and prepared for future Church leadership. President Spencer W. Kimball and other General Authorities conducted an area conference in Santiago, February-March 1977, the Chile Missionary Training Center was established in 1981, and the Santiago Chile Temple was dedicated in 1983.

In the final years of the Pinochet era, before democratic rule returned to the nation, nearly 400 bombings and acts of vandalism and arson were committed against LDS meetinghouses, which were viewed by political extremists as symbols of U.S. influence in Chile.

In 1980, the Chile Area was organized and an area temporal affairs office was established in Santiago. In 1984, Chile became part of the South America South Area with headquarters in Buenos Aires. Twelve years later, with Church membership growing rapidly, the Chile Area was re-established in August 1996 with a full Area presidency.

By the end of the 1980s there were 51 stakes in Chile, nearly 400 meetinghouses had been built by the Church, and Chile's LDS membership was approaching 300,000. After a three-year hiatus during which no new stakes were created, an increase in the number of convert baptisms, which surpassed 36,000 in 1996, prompted Church leaders to divide many stakes and wards into smaller units to stimulate leadership development and membership activity, with 65 more stakes being created between August 1992 and November 1998, bringing the total in Chile to 116.

In August 1999, President Boyd K. Packer and Elder Dallin H. Oaks of the Quorum of the Twelve visited Chile to assess conditions in the Church. In an effort to strengthen Church units, between April 2000 and August 2003 hundreds of wards and branches were discontinued and 41 stakes were merged with other stakes or returned to district status.

In August 2002, the First Presidency assigned two members of the Quorum of the Twelve to serve as presidents of international areas, Elder Jeffrey R. Holland being appointed president of the Chile Area. During the next two years, Elder Holland and his counselors worked to strengthen Church members and train local leaders to serve more effectively as shepherds for a rapidly-growing Latter-day Saint membership.

In 2003, membership reached 530,739. In 2004, membership was 534,754.

President Gordon B. Hinckley rededicated the Santiago Chile Temple March 12, 2006, an edifice he dedicated 22 years earlier. This was his first public appearance after cancer surgery weeks before. At 95 years old and after major surgery, his vigor amazed many. The temple had been closed 14 months to be refurbished and renovated.

Sources: "Chile," Countries of the World and Their Leaders Yearbook 2004; Rodolfo A. Acevedo, Los Mormones en Chile: 30 años de la Iglesia de Jesucristo de los Santos de los Ultimos Días, 1956-1986, 1991; Parley P. Pratt, Autobiography of Parley Parker Pratt, 1874; Andrew Jenson, Autobiography of Andrew Jenson, Assistant Historian of The Church of Jesus Christ of Latter-day Saints, 1938; Argentine Mission manuscript history and historical reports, 1935-1960, Church Archives; A. Delbert Palmer, "Establishing the L.D.S. Church in Chile," 1979; Dale Zabriskie, "First Converts Baptized at Santiago," Church News, 16 February 1957; Michael R. Morris, "Chile's Fruitful Vineyard." Ensign, December 1995; Andes Mission manuscript history and historical reports, 1959-1963, Church Archives; Chilean Mission manuscript history and historical reports, 1961-1975, Church Archives; Dell Van Orden, "Love, respect and emotion end area conference series," Church News, 12 March 1977; John L. Hart, "Temple dedicated in an oasis of calm," Church News, 25 September 1983; Michael Phillips, "Amid Bombs, LDS Church Reshaping Its Image in Chile," Salt Lake Tribune, 20 April 1992; "New Chile Area Announced" Church News, 15 June 1996; "President Packer, Elder Oaks greeted by Chilean leaders" Church News, 11 September 1999; Carrie A. Moore, "2 apostles assigned to live outside U.S.," Deseret News, 10 April 2002; Jason Swensen, "Prophet rededicates Chile temple," Church News, 18 March 2006.

Stakes — 74
(Listed alphabetically As of Oct. 1, 2011.)

No.	Name	Organized	First President
Chile Area			
2005	Angol Chile	18 Dec 1994	Juan Carlos Morales Vasquez
1165	Antofagasta Chile	10 Aug 1980	Octavio Araya Y.
1955	Antofagasta Chile La Portada	5 Sep 1993	Miguel A. Gonzalez Romero
1100	Arica Chile Costanera	29 Jan 1980	Jose Ulloa C.
2035	Arica Chile Los Olivos	11 Mar 1995	Arnando Ernesto Perez M.
1522	Calama Chile	17 Mar 1985	Ivan Gonzalez Castillo
1398	Chillan Chile	13 Feb 1983	Sergio Rios S.
2278	Chillan Chile Nuble	24 Nov 1996	Carlos C. Ortiz Rubilar
808	Concepcion Chile	30 Jan 1977	Claudio Signorelli G.
1075	*Concepcion Chile Andalien	25 June 1998	
	‡Andalien	28 Oct 1979	Pedro E. Arias
2006	*Concepcion Chile Chiguayante	24 Jun 1997	
	‡Chiguayante Chile	18 Dec 1994	Carlos Andres Puig Iguat
1929	Copiapo Chile	11 Apr 1993	Sergio Orlando Mora Oviedo
1264	Curico Chile	10 May 1981	Jose Luis Ferreira P.
1931	El Belloto Chile	11 Apr 1993	Hugo L. Garrido Gonzalez
1621	Iquique Chile	14 Dec 1986	Nelson C. Mondaca I.
1702	La Serena Chile	23 Oct 1988	Ricardo Thomas Rubina
1949	Los Andes Chile	4 Jul 1993	Vicente E. Zuniga Figueroa
1599	*Los Angeles Chile North	1 Dec 1996	
	‡Los Angeles Chile	1 Jun 1986	Mario Carlos Escobar
2285	Los Angeles Chile South	1 Dec 1996	Mario A. Gutierrez Castillo
1267	Osorno Chile	17 May 1981	Raul Hernan Paredes P.
2362	Osorno Chile Rahue	25 May 1997	Jose Luis Valderas Saldivia
1320	*Penaflor Chile	18 Jul 1993	
	*Santiago Chile Penaflor	10 Apr 1990	
	‡Penaflor Chile	10 Dec 1981	Sergio Venegas Pacheo
1268	Penco Chile	24 May 1981	Abel Poblete Flores
1339	Puerto Montt Chile	25 Apr 1982	Juan Carlos Lopez L.
1478	Punta Arenas Chile	10 Jun 1984	Luis Elqueda C.
1275	Quillota Chile	7 Jun 1981	Maximo Ananias Iribarren I.
791	Quilpue Chile	28 Nov 1976	Eduardo Lamartine A.
1285	Rancagua Chile	26 Aug 1981	Hector Verdugo Radrigan
1930	Rancagua Chile Tupahue	11 Apr 1993	Juan Carlos Fredes Duran

1731	San Antonio Chile	2 Jul 1989	Sergio Enrique Gonzalez S.
1286	San Pedro Chile	30 Aug 1981	Juan Cuevas I.
2089	Santiago Chile Alicahue	20 Aug 1995	Patricio R. Ortega H.
1038	Santiago Chile Cinco de Abril	10 Jun 1979	Poblibio Gonzalez Gutierrez
1077	Santiago Chile Conchali	4 Nov 1979	Juan Castro Duque
2036	Santiago Chile Cordillera	19 Mar 1995	Jorge Andres Pedero
1216	Santiago Chile El Bosque	14 Dec 1980	Eduardo Ayala Aburto
2289	Santiago Chile Gabriela	8 Dec 1996	Rene Esteban del Pino Carcia
1933	Santiago Chile Gran Avenida	18 Apr 1993	Andres Maja Basaez
590	*Santiago Chile Huelen	15 Dec 2001	
	*Santiago Chile Quinta Normal	10 Jan 1980	
	*Santiago Chile Providencia	18 Apr 1976	
	*Santiago Chile ‡Santiago (Chile)	19 Nov 1972	Carlos A. Cifuentes
1024	Santiago Chile Independencia	6 May 1979	Wilfredo Lopez G.
1902	Santiago Chile Javiera Carrera	20 Sep 1992	Patricio LaTorre Orellana
2075	Santiago Chile La Bandera	9 Jul 1995	Felix Reinaldo Cofre Quezada
672	*Santiago Chile La Cisterna	18 Apr 1976	
	‡Santiago Chile South	8 Dec 1974	Eduardo Ayala
1039	Santiago Chile La Florida	10 Jun 1979	Carlos G. Zuniga Campusano
1947	Santiago Chile La Reina	27 June 1993	Santiago Vicente Vera Barrera
2090	Santiago Chile Las Araucarias	20 Aug 1995	Luis Enrique Moya Basaez
1402	Santiago Chile Las Condes	12 Mar 1983	E. Gustavo Flores Carrasco
2082	Santiago Chile Los Cerrillos	30 Jul 1995	Renato Alejandro Ruz Leon
1915	Santiago Chile Maipu	6 Dec 1992	Julio Cesar Valdivia Marin
792	Santiago Chile Nunoa	28 Nov 1976	Gustavo Alberto Barrios C.
2126	Santiago Chile Ochagavia	19 Nov 1995	Gerardo Gabezas Leyton
1919	Santiago Chile O'Higgins	20 Dec 1992	Victor A. Cifuentes Droguett
2500	Santiago Chile Olimpo	22 Nov 1998	Alberto Octavio Gonzalez G.
1548	Santiago Chile Puente Alto	18 Aug 1985	Jorge A. Pedrero Martinez
1205	*Santiago Chile Quilicura	13 Dec 1988	
	‡Santiago Chile Huechuraba	9 Nov 1980	Juan Humberto Body B.
1492	Santiago Chile Renca	16 Sep 1984	Eduardo Cabezas O.
754	Santiago Chile Republica	18 Apr 1976	Julio Jaramillo
1003	Santiago Chile San Bernardo	25 Feb 1979	Hugo Balmaceda
1549	Santiago Chile San Miguel	18 Aug 1985	Hector G. Carvajal Arenas
1403	*Santiago Chile San Pablo	15 Dec 2001	
	Santiago Chile Pudahuel	13 Mar 1983	Enrique Espinoza
1927	Santiago Chile Vicuna Mackenna	21 Mar 1993	Jorge A. Pedrero Martinez
1379	*Santiago Chile Zapadores	13 Dec 1988	
	‡Santiago Chile Las Canteras	14 Nov 1982	Juan Castro Duque
1083	Talca Chile	8 Jun 2003	
	*Talca Chile Lircay	11 Jun 1995	
	‡Talca Chile	17 Nov 1979	Emilio Diaz
866	Talcahuano Chile North	3 Aug 2003	
	Talcahuano Chile	16 Oct 1977	Claudio Daniel Signorelli G.
1146	Talcahuano Chile South	3 Aug 2003	
	*Talcahuano Chile Hualpen	7 May 1995	
	*Hualpen Chile	26 Jul 1988	
	‡Talcahuano Chile Hualpen	15 Jun 1980	Fernando Aguilar
2133	Temuco Chile Cautin	26 Nov 1995	Hector L.F. Sandoval
1245	*Temuco Chile Nielol	26 Nov. 1995	
	‡Temuco Chile	18 Mar 1981	Eleazar F. Magnere D.
1667	Valdivia Chile	10 Jan 1988	Armando Ambrosio Linco P.
2413	Valdivia Chile Calle Calle	23 Nov 1997	Jaime Enrique Gonzalez Caro
882	Valparaiso Chile	20 Nov 1977	Abel Correa Lopez
1037	Villa Alemana Chile	8 Jun 1979	Eduardo Adrian LaMartine
2212	Villa Alemana Chile West	14 Jul 1996	M. Gonzalo Sepulveda Moya
671	Vina del Mar Chile	5 Dec 1974	Jose Leyton
1499	*Vina del Mar Achupallas	25 Jun 1998	
	‡Achupallas Chile	28 Oct 1984	Luis Alino Pereira P.
		Stakes discontinued	
1501	*Antofagasta Chile Caliche	24 June 1997	
	‡Caliche Chile	4 Nov 1984	Ricardo Manuel Palma F.
	Discontinued 15 Jun 2003		
1598	Arica Chile El Morro	18 May 1986	Sergio Alberto Funes
	Discontinued 15 Jun 2003		
2026	Buin Chile	26 Feb 1995	Jorge H. Herrera
	Discontinued 28 Jul 2002		
2463	*Concepcion Chile Baquedano	25 Jun 1998	
	‡Andalien Chile Baquedano	17 May 1998	Hernan D. Ferreira P.
	Discontinued 10 Nov 2002		
2481	Concepcion Chile Hualqui	21 Jun 1998	Carlos Andres Puig Iguat
	Discontinued 15 Jun 2003		
1960b	Coquimbo Chile	5 Dec 1993	Marco Oyarzun Vera
	Discontinued 1 Dec 2002		
2348	Copiapo Chile East	4 May 1997	Leonardo Esteban Lufi Mazuela
	Discontinued 9 Jun 2002		
2334	Coronel Chile	23 Mar 1997	Juan Bautista Pereira A.
	Discontinued 17 Nov 2002		
2167	Coyhaique Chile	18 Feb 1996	Feberico Sanchez G.

	Discontinued 17 Aug 2003		
2400	Curico Chile Rauqucn	12 Oct 1997	Nelson Adolfo Vasquez Carrasco
	Discontinued 3 Nov 2002		
2320	Iquique Chile South	9 Mar 1997	Ruperto Arnoldo Reyes Tello
	Discontinued 16 Oct 2005		
2196a	La Union Chile	26 May 1996	Lautaro Roberto Sanchez Cerda
	Discontinued 23 Feb 2003		
2313	Lebu Chile	23 Feb 1997	
	Discontinued 8 Dec 2002		
1694	Linares Chile	24 Apr 1988	Alberto Ariosto Alveal V.
	Discontinued 24 Nov 2002		
1950	Melipilla Chile	18 Jul 1993	Natanael Toro Navarrete
	Discontinued 8 Dec 2002		
1976	Ovalle Chile	20 Feb 1994	Wilson B. Nunez Castillo
	Discontinued 24 Nov 2002		
2353	Quilpue Chile Marga Marga	18 May 1997	Ivan Robinson Letelier C.
	Discontinued 29 Jun 2003		
2321	Puerto Varas Chile	9 Mar 1997	Gerardo J. Wilhelm Kretschmar
	Discontinued 10 Mar 2002		
2290	Santa Cruz Chile	8 Dec 1996	Rodolfo E. Herrera Mejias
	Discontinued 26 May 2002		
2384	San Felipe Chile	6 Jul 1997	Alejandro E. Asete Figueroa
	Discontinued 7 Jul 2002		
1703	San Fernando Chile	30 Oct 1988	Jose Luis Ferreira P.
	Discontinued 30 Jun 2002		
1960	Santiago Chile Cerro Navia	7 Nov 1993	Juan David Huaiguinir Castro
	Discontinued 15 Dec 2001		
2410	Santiago Chile Estacion Central	16 Nov 1997	Cesar Manuel Escobar Perez
	Discontinued 10n Nov 2002		
2352	Santiago Chile Fermin Vivaceta	8 May 1997	Leopoldo S. Parra Suco
	Discontinued 26 May 2002		
1995	Santiago Chile Jose Miguel Carrera	6 Nov 1994	Patricio G. Latorre O.
	Discontinued 23 Apr 2000		
1899	Santiago Chile La Granja	30 Aug 1992	Arturo del C. Jorquera M.
	Discontinued 24 Aug 2003		
2178	Santiago Chile Lo Prado	10 Mar 1996	Raul Alfredo Dote
	Discontinued 15 Dec 2001		
2086	Santiago Chile Lo Blanco	13 Aug 1995	Eric A. Nunez Yevenes
	Discontinued 3 Nov 2002		
2024	Santiago Chile Lo Espejo	19 Feb 1995	David Ormeno Parra
	Discontinued 31 Aug 2003		
2121	Santiago Chile Los Manantiales	12 Nov 1995	Luis A. Inostroza Gomez
	Discontinued 15 Dec 2001		
2487	Santiago Chile Penalolen	26 Jul 1998	Santiago V. Vera Barrera
	Discontinued 11 Aug 2002		
2345	Santiago Chile Progreso	27 Apr 1997	Patricio Latorre O.
	Discontinued 31 Aug 2003		
2451	Santiago Chile San Joaquin	19 Apr 1998	Nicanor Teuquil A.
	Discontinued 16 Jun 2002		
2421	Talagante Chile	7 Dec 1997	Juan Carlos Mena Carreno
	Discontinued 10 Nov 2002		
2060	Talca Chile El Mirador	11 Jun 1995	Gaston A. Rocha Fernandez
	Discontinued 8 Jun 2003		
2047	Talcahuano Chile Colon	7 May 1995	Daniel Marcelo Canoles M.
	Discontinued 3 Aug 2003		
2014	Valparaiso Chile Oriente	22 Jan 1995	Sergio Ignacio Padovani T.
	Discontinued 9 Jun 2002		
2013	Valparaiso Chile Playa Ancha	22 Jan 1995	Bernardo Felix Gallegos B.
	Discontinued 9 Jun 2002		
1230	Valparaiso Chile South	1 Feb 1981	Juan Rios R.
	Discontinued 9 Jun 2002		
2016	Vina del Mar Chile Agua Santa	22 Jan 1995	Dinar Michael Reyes Barbe
	Discontinued 24 Nov 2002		
2015	Vina del Mar Chile Forestal	22 Jan 1995	Edgardo Ramon Salina H.
	Discontinued 4 May 2003		
1967	*Vina Del Mar Chile Miraflores		
	‡Miraflores Chile	19 Dec 1993	Jorge Bernardo Toro
	Discontinued 3 Nov 2002		

Easter Island

It is unclear exactly how members of the Church came to Easter Island or who they were, but on 1 July 1981 a branch was created to serve the Latter-day Saints living there. The new branch was under the direction of the Chile Vina Del Mar Mission. Over the years missionaries have been assigned on an irregular basis to work on the island.

On 4-7 March 1987, Elders Ted E. Brewerton and J. Thomas Fyans of the First Quorum of the Seventy visited the branch and met with the members of the Church.

Responsibility for the branch was transferred to the Chile Santiago East Mission on 1 July 1997 and to the Chile Area Presidency on 20 August 1999. On 1 January 2002, stewardship was transferred to the Chile Santiago North Mission.

In 2003, the Church's Polynesian Cultural Center in Hawaii opened an exhibit, "The Island of Rapa Nui, the Center of the World," about the culture of Easter Island and its famous mysterious statues.

Elder Jeffrey R. Holland of the Quorum of the Twelve Apostles visited the island, 22 February 2004. He was the first Apostle to ever visit there. While there Elder Holland met with branch members and Don Pedro Evans, mayor of Hanga Roa.

Sources: Jason Swensen, "Remote Island Part of the Gospel Community, Apostle Says Easter Island Saints can Enjoy Blessings and Companionship of Church," Church News, 6 March 2004; Carma Wadley, "A 'Dot' in the Pacific: 'Small but Happy' Branch is on Easter Island," Church News, 30 January 1988; "Church to Create Eight New Missions," Church News, 1 March 1997; Polynesian Cultural Center website, http://www.polynesia.com/islands/rapanui.html; 20 August 2004.

Missions — 9
(As of Oct. 1, 2011; shown with historical number. See MISSIONS.)

(214) CHILE ANTOFAGASTA MISSION
Sucre 220, Oficina 504
Edificio Bulnes
Antofagasta, II Region, Chile

(119) CHILE CONCEPCION MISSION
O'Higgins 940, Oficina 502
Concepcion
Chile

(151) CHILE OSORNO MISSION
Mackenna 987, Piso 3, Oficina 32,
Conchali, Region Metropolitana
Santiago, Chile

(311) CHILE SANTIAGO EAST MISSION
Pedro de Valdivia 1423
Providencia
Santiago 29, Chile

(148) CHILE SANTIAGO NORTH MISSION
Forestal 2680, #32
Conchali
Santiago, Chile

CHILE RANCAGUA MISSION
German Riesco 230 Suite 703
Rancagua, Chile

(303) CHILE SANTIAGO WEST MISSION
1423 Pedro de Valdivia
Providencia
Santiago, Chile

(168) CHILE VINA DEL MAR MISSION
4 Norte 1112
Vina del Mar,
Chile

(337a) CHILE CONCEPCION SOUTH MISSION
O'Higgins 940 Oficina 503
Concepcion, Chile

CHINA

Encompassing most of east Asia, the People's Republic of China has a population that speaks Mandarin Chinese, Yue, Wu Minbei, Minnan, and Xiang. The population includes atheists, and traditional Confucians, Buddhists, and Taoists.

Brigham Young discussed the possibility of sending missionaries to China as early as 1849, and by late 1852 three brethren, Hosea Stout, James Lewis, and Chapman Duncan, had accepted calls to serve there. They sailed from San Francisco on 9 March 1853 and arrived in Hong Kong on 28 April. A civil war, the Tai-ping Rebellion, was then underway in China's interior, making it unsafe for the elders to labor beyond Hong Kong. They also struggled to learn the language. The trio barely only had means to sustain themselves and could not afford language tutors. Negative articles in the press and a chilly reception from the small English-speaking population also impeded their efforts. The missionaries sailed from Hong Kong on 22 June 1853, less than two months after their arrival. The Church made no further efforts to do missionary work in China during the 19th Century.

In 1910, Alma O. Taylor, president of the Japan Mission, was assigned to visit China to investigate the prospect of again sending missionaries. He and Frederick A. Caine visited and observed conditions in Beijing, Shanghai, and other places. Taylor recommended against engaging in missionary activity at that time because of unstable political conditions, which culminated a short time later in the collapse of the Ching Dynasty.

David O. McKay and Hugh J. Cannon visited China in January 1921 as part of a world tour. In 1949, President McKay, then serving in the First Presidency, called Hilton A. Robertson to open the Chinese Mission. Hong Kong was chosen as mission headquarters because it was under British control and less likely to be affected by a civil war between nationalist and communist forces on the mainland. On 6 February 1951, missionaries were removed from Hong Kong because of the Korean War and the threat of a communist takeover in Hong Kong. (See Hong Kong for further details about the Church there.)

The Church had very little formal contact with the People's Republic of China until the late 1970s. On 29 September 1978, in a talk focused on spreading the gospel to all parts of the world, President Spencer W. Kimball said, "Nearly one billion of our Father's children live in China . . . Six hundred and sixty million of them speak Mandarin Chinese. How many of us speak Mandarin Chinese?" He continued, "If we could only make a small beginning in every nation, soon the converts among each kindred and tongue could step forth as lights to their own people."

In 1979, under the leadership of Deng Xiaoping, China made itself more accessible to foreigners. In July of that year a Brigham Young University performing group, the Young Ambassadors, toured the country. Their successful tour paved the way for visits by other BYU performing groups, including the Folk Dance Ensemble, Lamanite Generation, Ballroom Dance Company, Chamber Orchestra, and Wind Symphony. At least one group from the Polynesian Cultural Center also performed in China.

Beginning in the 1980s the Church hosted delegations of Chinese officials at Church facilities in Salt Lake City and Provo, Utah; Laie, Hawaii; and Washington D.C. Prominent Chinese visitors to the Polynesian Cultural Center have included Vice

Premier Geng Biao (1980), Premier Zhao Ziyang (1984), President Li Xiannan (1985), and Vice Premier Li Lanqing (1994).

Several members of the First Presidency and Quorum of the Twelve have visited China. On 27 September 1985, Elder Russell M. Nelson was named as the first-ever honorary professor of Shandong Medical College in recognition of his work there in 1980 and 1984. President Gordon B. Hinckley became the first president of the Church to visit Mainland China when he was hosted at a cultural exchange in Shenzhen on 28 May 1996. His party toured the Chinese Folk Villages (patterned after the Polynesian Cultural Center) and other attractions.

A handful of BYU professors, their spouses, and others, began teaching English to students at Chinese universities and other educational institutions in the early 1980s. In 1988, the David M. Kennedy Center for International Studies at Brigham Young University, under the direction of Ray C. Hillam, formed the China Teachers Program to facilitate placement of Latter-day Saint teachers throughout China. In 1989, the first group of 21 teachers arrived there. Since 1995, an average of over 60 teachers have participated in the program each year. Teachers were assigned in 2003 to universities in Beijing, Tianjin, Shanghai, Guangzhou, Qingdao, Jinan, Nanjing, and Xi'an.

In 1976, Lucille (Lu) Sargent moved to Beijing as a secretary with the U.S. representative office. In the ensuing years other Church members working in business, education, and government, moved to Beijing and other major cities. In addition, several hundred Chinese citizens joined the Church while pursuing business or educational opportunities in other countries. Small Church branches were organized in Beijing and Xi'an in 1986. There are also branches in Guangzhou, Shanghai, and Tianjin, with smaller groups in other places. People living in China on foreign passports are allowed to hold religious meetings but Chinese are not permitted to attend.

David Hsiao Hsin Chen, a professor at BYU-Hawaii, was set apart in 1990 as a traveling elder to visit China several times a year to look after the needs of Church members. He died in 1993. In 1997, Chia Chu-jen, a Canadian businessman working in Beijing, was called to serve as an Area Authority, the first resident of China to be called to that position.

Except for Hong Kong and Macau, the Church is not allowed to do missionary work in the People's Republic of China. On 12 March 1991 Elder Dallin H. Oaks, speaking at a BYU devotional, addressed the question of when China will be open for missionary work: "I state my belief that China is already 'open' – it is we who are closed. . . . We must understand their way of thinking, . . . observe their laws, and follow their example of patience. We must deserve to be their friends. . . . our Father in Heaven . . . will bring His purposes to pass in that great nation 'in his own time, and in his own way, and according to his own will'" (D&C 88:68).

Sources: China Mission, Manuscript history and historical reports, Church Archives; Donald Q. Cannon and Richard O. Cowan, Unto Every Nation: Gospel Light Reaches Every Land, 2003; "Polynesians Win Hearts in China," Ensign, January 1991; Malan R. Jackson, One Hundred Years on the Periphery: The Church in China, 1852-1955, 2001; The Church in China: Culture Text, 1980s; R. Lanier Britsch, From the East: The History of the Latter-day Saints in Asia, 1851-1996, 1998; Spencer W. Kimball, "'The Uttermost Parts of the Earth,'" Ensign, July 1979; Telephone conversation with David M. Kennedy Center for International Studies at Brigham Young University, 12 July 2004; "Elders Maxwell, Nelson Welcomed in China," Church News, 29 April 1995; "Elder Nelson is Named Honorary Professor by Chinese Medical College," Church News, 29 September 1985; Gerry Avant, "President Hinckley Visits China," Church News, 1 June 1996.

HONG KONG

Jan. 1, 2011: Est. population, 7,055,000; Members, 24,425; Stakes, 4; Wards, 23; Missions, 1; Districts, 1; Branches, 9; Temples, 1; percent LDS, .33, or one in 304; Asia Area.

At the mouth of the Canton River on the southern coast of mainland China, Hong Kong was a British Crown Colony, acquired in 1841. It reverted to China in 1997. Its people speak Cantonese and English and are mostly Buddhists and Taoists, although small groups of Christians, Hindus, and Jews also live in Hong Kong.

(See China for information about Church activity in Hong Kong before 1949.) In 1949, President David O. McKay of the First Presidency called Hilton A. Robertson to begin work in the Chinese Mission. On 14 July 1949 Hilton and Hazel Robertson, Henry and Sai Lang Aki, and Matthew and Elva Cowley, visited Victoria Peak, where Elder Cowley, of the Quorum of the Twelve, prayed that the way would be opened for the introduction of the gospel into Mainland China.

The first young full-time elders, H. Grant Heaton and William K. Paalani, arrived in Hong Kong on 25 February 1950. Elder James Kam Hoon Yuen, of Chinese ancestry, arrived on 3 May. Aided by private teachers, the missionaries spent most of their time studying the language. On 31 December 1950, three sisters, Nora, Beatrice, and Rose Koot, were baptized, the first Chinese to join the Church in Hong Kong.

On 6 February 1951, the Church withdrew its missionaries from Hong Kong because of the Korean War and the buildup of Chinese troops along the China/Hong Kong border. At that point nine missionaries had served and 14 converts had been baptized in the Chinese Mission. Mission headquarters were temporarily moved to Honolulu and then to San Francisco before the mission officially closed in February 1953.

In May 1955, H. Grant Heaton, age 26, was called to reopen the mission in Hong Kong. The Heatons, accompanied by several missionaries and President and Sister Joseph Fielding Smith, arrived in Hong Kong in August. The mission, renamed the Southern Far East Mission, opened with eight young missionaries. Two of them were assigned to learn Mandarin and the others were to learn Cantonese. Initially, the mission was also responsible for Taiwan, the Philippines, and Guam.

The North Point Branch was organized 23 October 1955 and on 17 November two additional branches were formed in Tsim Sha Tsui and Sham Shui Po. In December, President Heaton successfully negotiated the purchase of a home in Kowloon Tong, which was remodeled and served as the mission home beginning in June 1956.

Mr. and Mrs. Leslie Dickman were the first people baptized in the Southern Far East Mission, on 26 April 1956. Eleven Chinese were baptized on 31 May. On 17 February 1957, Lee Nai Ken, having joined the Church in Hong Kong in June 1956, became the first local member to serve there as a full-time missionary. On 26 May Sister Nora Koot, one of the first converts in Hong Kong, was also set apart as a full-time missionary.

President Heaton had difficulty finding suitable properties for meetinghouses. He decided to purchase the top floors of apartment buildings and have them remodeled to contain chapels, classrooms, and missionary apartments. The roofs of the buildings served as recreation areas. Following this plan, in 1957 the Church purchased building spaces in Tsim Sha Tsui, Sham Shui Po, and Happy Valley (Causeway Bay). In December they bought a complete four-story building in Tsuen

Wan. A small chapel was built at Tiu King Ling between March and June 1959, the first Church-built chapel in Asia since the 1850s.

By the end of 1957, there were 400 members in Hong Kong and the work was accelerated. There were more people who wanted to hear the gospel than there were missionaries to teach. Interested people were actually placed on waiting lists. The missionaries baptized 904 people during 1958. Active missionary work was suspended during January and February 1959 so that more attention could be given to strengthening newly-baptized Church members. In September 1959, there were over 1600 members in 14 branches.

In March 1959, the mission began publishing a monthly magazine, Voice of the Saints, containing translated versions of General Authorities' talks and writings and items of local interest. In September 1957, a committee was organized to translate the Book of Mormon into Chinese. Varying translation styles and President Heaton's release as president in September 1959 hindered the completion of the work. The Chinese Book of Mormon was finally published in Taiwan in 1965. The Chinese Doctrine and Covenants was published in 1974.

In April 1960, Elder Gordon B. Hinckley of the Quorum of the Twelve was appointed to supervise the Asian missions and served in that role until 1968. In May 1960, he and mission president Robert S. Taylor inspected a mansion that was originally built in 1914, Kom Tong Hall, which the Church subsequently leased. The building was remodeled to include a chapel, classrooms and administrative offices, and was used for more than 40 years.

In 2004, in anticipation of a new Church facility to be built in Wan Chai, and as a goodwill gesture, the Church sold Kom Tong Hall at less-than-market value to the city of Hong Kong so that the city could convert it to a museum.

The Hong Kong District was organized in August 1964 with Loh Ying Hwa as president. One year later, in October 1965, the district was split and the Kowloon District was formed. In 1967, Hong Kong felt ripple effects of the cultural revolution in China in the form of riots, bomb threats and political instability. The Church reassigned 60 missionaries who had been serving there to other missions. A large number of Church members emigrated from Hong Kong in the late 1960s and the two member districts were consolidated into one.

The Southern Far East Mission was renamed the Hong Kong-Taiwan Mission in 1969. The mission was divided in 1971 and the Hong Kong Mission was born. In 1977, President David H. H. Chen became the first Chinese member to preside over the mission. When the British returned control of Hong Kong to the People's Republic of China in 1997, the mission was renamed the China Hong Kong Mission.

President Spencer W. Kimball presided over area conferences in Hong Kong in August 1975 and October 1980. The Hong Kong Stake was formed on 25 April 1976 with Sheldon Shiu-Tat Poon as president. When a second stake was formed in 1980 Church membership stood at over 9,000. In 1986, the Asia Area headquarters moved from Tokyo to Hong Kong. Elder Tai Kwok Yuen became the first Chinese to serve as a General Authority when he was called to the Second Quorum of the Seventy in June 1992.

In July 1992, President Gordon B. Hinckley visited Hong Kong to inspect potential temple sites. After one particularly long day he went to bed feeling tired and discouraged. He awoke in the middle of the night with a clear impression about where and how the temple should be built. He sketched a rough plan for a building that would serve multiple purposes, to be built on the site where the mission home and office had stood since 1956. Speaking at the temple dedication in May 1996 he said, "If ever in my life I felt the inspiration of the Lord, it was with this building."

Church membership passed the 20,000 milestone in 1999. In May 1998, the Asia Area Presidency created the Hong Kong International District to serve the needs of Church members who do not speak Cantonese. Branches hold services in either Mandarin or English, and one is comprised primarily of Filipino members. Beginning in 1996, the Church sponsored an annual three-on-three basketball tournament in Hong Kong. Two thousand players, 95 percent of whom were not LDS, participated in the event in 2002.

Asia Area president John K. Carmack noted at temple groundbreaking ceremonies on 22 January 1994 that he was repeatedly asked, "'What is going to happen after 1997 [when Hong Kong reverted to China]?' ... part of the answer is that we are building a temple that will serve China for a long time and that is a statement of our faith and confidence in the future."

In April 1997, President James E. Faust, Elder Russell M. Nelson and other Church leaders met with the chief executive of the Hong Kong Special Administrative Region of the People's Republic of China, who assured them that Hong Kong residents would continue to enjoy religious freedom after 1 July, when control of Hong Kong reverted from Great Britain to China. A Church member observed in 2000, "Our day-to-day freedoms and movements have not changed at all since the 1997 handover."

In 2003, there were 21,529 members.

President Hinckley dedicated a new Church Administration Building in the Wan Chai district on 2 August 2005, which included offices, chapels and classrooms. The new building replaces a building President Hinckley purchased for the Church in 1960, the famed Kom Tong Hall. It was sold to the government in 2004.

Sources: R. Lanier Britsch, From the East: The History of the Latter-day Saints in Asia, 1851- 1996, 1998; China Mission, Manuscript history and historical reports, Church Archives; Nora Siu Yuen Koot, Reminiscence, circa 1995, Church Archives; Donald Q. Cannon and Richard O. Cowan, Unto Every Nation: Gospel Light Reaches Every Land, 2003; Southern Far East Mission, Manuscript history and historical reports, Church Archives; Sarah Jane Weaver, "Hong Kong Hall Preserved by Church," Church News, 17 April 2004; W. Brent Hardy, A brief summary of significant events and accomplishments, Southern Far East Mission, 1968-1971, [2002], Church Archives; Hong Kong Mission, Manuscript history and historical reports, Church Archives; "Hong Kong Region Leader Greets LDS," Church News, 3 May 1997; Anita Louise Hummel, "Hong Kong and the LDS Community," The International Society Newsletter, 2000; "2,000 Participate in Basketball Tournament," Church News, 26 October 2002' "Hong Kong, Most significant experience," Church News, 6 August 2005.

Stakes — 5
(Listed alphabetically As of Oct. 1, 2011.)

No.	Name	Organized	First President
Asia Area			
756	*Hong Kong Island	29 May 1980	
	‡Hong Kong	25 Apr 1976	Shiu-Tat Sheldon Poon

1977	Hong Kong Kowloon West	20 Mar 1994	Poon Yin Sang Peter
1503	Hong Kong New Territories	11 Nov 1984	Johnson Ma
1502	*Hong Kong Tolo Harbour	20 Mar 1994	
	*Hong Kong Kowloon North	11 Nov 1984	Fu Man Yau
		Stakes discontinued	
1141	Hong Kong Kowloon East	20 Mar 1994	
	*Hong Kong Kowloon	11 Nov 1984	
	‡Kowloon Hong Kong	29 May 1980	Patrick Chung-hei Wong
	Discontinued 20 Aug 2006		

Mission — 1

(As of Oct. 1, 2011; shown with historical number. See MISSIONS.)

(44a) CHINA HONG KONG MISSION
2 Cornwall Street,
Kowloon Tong, Kowloon,
Hong Kong

MACAU

Jan. 1, 2011: Est. population, 560,000; Members, 673; Branches, 2, Percent LDS, .22, or one in 444.

In June 1950 Hilton A. Robertson and Henry Aki of the Chinese Mission, headquartered in Hong Kong, visited Macau to explore the prospects for initiating missionary work in the Portuguese colony. They found that the Catholic Church was the only Christian religion operating there and decided that it was not the right time to try to establish a Latter-day Saint presence.

President Jay A. Quealy of the Southern Far East Mission and Elder Gordon B. Hinckley of the Council of the Twelve made a similar visit in April 1964. A short time later, on 2 July, the first two missionaries, Darryl Thomander and Gilbert Montano, arrived. Steven Lau was the first person baptized in the colony on 21 August 1964. Three more people were baptized one week later, and the missionaries started holding Sunday School and priesthood meetings.

Church meetings were suspended in December 1964 because the Church lacked a license from the Portuguese government to conduct religious activities. Legal recognition had still not been granted in September 1965, at which time the missionaries were banned from proselyting. It is not clear whether or not a branch was formally organized in Macau during the 1960s, but historical reports refer to full-time missionaries serving as branch presidents during 1965 and 1966. No branch historical records are extant for the remainder of the decade.

Four full-time missionaries returned to Macau on 6 September 1976 after a constitutional amendment had been passed allowing religions to hold meetings, teach, and preach. One year later the Hong Kong Mission reported that the work in Macau was developing quickly, with 300-400 percent attendance at Church meetings. The Macau Branch was organized on 1 January 1977. In early 1984, Hung Wo Loi became the first Macau resident to serve as branch president. In 1993 there were 640 Church members in Macau.

The Macau Branch was divided in May 1998. Cantonese-speaking members attended the 1st Branch and English speakers attended the 2nd Branch. The Macau 3rd Branch was organized in March 2001 to serve the needs of Mandarin speakers. Macau reverted from Portuguese to Chinese control on 20 December 1999 but continued to enjoy religious freedom, much the same as Hong Kong.

In 2004, there were 1,067 members. In 2005, membership was 1,125. In 2006, membership reached 1,158.

Sources: "Macau: Historical Setting," workmall.com/wfb2001/macau/macau_history, cited 19 July 2004; Chinese Mission, Manuscript history and historical reports, Church Archives; Southern Far East Mission, Manuscript history and historical reports, Church Archives; Macau Branch, Manuscript history and historical reports, Church Archives; Hong Kong Mission, Manuscript history and historical reports, Church Archives; "Elders Now Preach in Macau, a Portuguese Colony in China," Church News, 4 December 1976; "Hung Wo Loi: Finding Truth on the China-Macau Border," Ensign, June 1987; "Church Progress in Asia," Ensign, September 1993.

COLOMBIA

Jan. 1, 2011: Est. population, 45,644,000; Members, 172,534; Stakes, 28; Wards, 175; Branches, 97; Missions, 4; Districts, 12; Temples, 1; percent LDS, .36, or one in 279; South America Northwest Area.

Located in the northwest corner of South America, Colombia is a republic.

Andes Mission president J. Vernon Sharp and his wife, Fawn, visited Bogota in 1960 to assess prospects for missionary work. However, active efforts did not begin until early 1966, when approximately 45 members, mostly North Americans, were meeting in branches in Bogota and Cali. Two missionaries, Randall Harmsen and Jerry Broome of the Andes Mission, were assigned to Bogota in May of that year. They soon rented the former residence of a military general for the first Church meetinghouse. Among the first converts in Bogota was Antonio Vela. Aura Ivars was the first convert in Cali. A government resolution on 6 December 1966 gave the Church legal status. The Colombia-Venezuela Mission was created in 1968. By 1971, there were 27 branches established in 10 cities, and the mission was divided, with the new Colombian Mission headquartered in Bogota. In 1975, the Colombia Cali Mission was created and the Colombia Barranquilla Mission was formed in 1988. Seminaries and institutes were begun in 1972, and by 1976, there were 900 students taking part in the educational programs.

President Spencer W. Kimball visited Colombia and spoke to a gathering of 4,600 at an area conference on 5 March 1977.

That year, the first stake in Colombia was created in Bogota on 23 January. Two years later, Elder Ezra Taft Benson, then of the Quorum of the Twelve Apostles, visited Colombia in January 1979.

In September 1989, internal political difficulties led to a temporary withdrawal of North American missionaries. In the 1980s and early 1990s, extremists occasionally committed acts of violence against Church facilities. Despite these problems, missionary work continued to progress. Membership in Colombia by 1999 had reached 129,105. The first General Authority from Colombia was Julio Davila, who was called to the Second Quorum of the Seventy in 1991.

A temple was announced for Colombia on 7 April 1984, and a site for the temple was announced in 1988. However, construction was delayed pending government approvals. Following countrywide fasts of Latter-day Saints, government approval was received and the long-awaited construction of the Bogota Colombia Temple began in the late spring of 1995. President Gordon B. Hinckley visited Bogota 8 November 1996, spoke to 7,100 members, and toured the temple construction project while there. After 15 years, the temple was dedicated on 24 April 1999, in what President Hinckley called "the greatest event in the history of Colombia."

Earlier that year, on 25 January 1999, a devastating earthquake struck the mountain community of Armenia, Colombia, and the Church responded immediately with relief supplies. The day after the earthquake which killed 920 people including three Church members, a truck from the stakes in Bogota arrived in Armenia with food, clothing, and water. Two trucks arrived later from Cali and another from the two stakes in Medellin and nearby districts.

In 2002, membership reached 139,351, and 146,302 in 2004.

The warm relationship between the Church and this South American country was highlighted 2 December 2005 when the Colombian Congress honored the Church for its humanitarian service that has bettered the lives Colombians in need. Elder Claudio R. M. Costa of the Seventy accepted the congressional commendation.

A temple was announced to be built in Barranquilla by President Thomas S. Monson on 1 October 2011.

Sources: Andes Mission, Manuscript history and historical reports, Church Archives; Colombian Mission, Manuscript history and historical reports, Church Archives; Gordon Irving, "Colombia: A Background Paper," Church Archives; Sistema Educativa de La Iglesia, Historia de la Iglesia en Colombia, 1986; Bombing of the El Prado Ward meetinghouse, January 1994, Church Archives; Donald Q. Cannon and Richard O. Cowan, Unto Every Nation: Gospel Light Reaches Every Land, 2003; Jack E. Jarrard, "Church in Colombia Moving Ahead," Church News, 1 February 1969; Colleen J. Heniger, "The Saints in Colombia," Ensign, October, 1976; "Colombia," Ensign, February 1977; Dell Van Orden, "Love, Respect and Emotion End Area Conference Series," Church News, 12 March 1977; "9 Missions Created, World Total Now 221," Church News, 19 March 1988; "Work Begins on Colombia Temple," Church News, 3 June 1995; "Prophet Visits South America," Church News, 16 November 1996; "Hundreds of LDS Affected by Earthquake, Church News, 6 February 1999; John L. Hart, "Greatest Event in History of Colombia," Church News, 1 May 1999; Jason Swensen, "Colombian Congress honors LDS humanitarian service," Church News, 10 December 2005.

Stakes — 29

(Listed alphabetically As of Oct. 1, 2011.)

No.	Name	Organized	First President
South America North Area			
1537	*Barranquilla Colombia El Carmen	30 May 1992	
	‡Barranquilla Colombia	30 May 1985	Libardo Rodriguez
1879	Barranquilla Colombia Hipodromo	31 May 1992	Donaldo A. Osorio P.
1880	Barranquilla Colombia Paraiso	31 May 1992	Jose Peralbo Aparicio
805	Bogota Colombia	23 Jan 1977	Julio E. Davila P.
1113	Bogota Colombia Ciudad Jardin	2 Mar 1980	Miguel Oswaldo Porras
1659	Bogota Colombia El Dorado	18 Oct 1987	Humberto Lopez S.
2326	Bogota Colombia El Salitre	16 Mar 1997	Orlando Moscoso P.
2336	Bogota Colombia Granada	13 Apr 1997	Hector Hernandez Malaver
1008	Bogota Colombia Kennedy	11 Mar 1979	Miguel A. Vargas
2327	Bogota Colombia Suba	16 Mar 1997	Juan Alfonso Cerquera
2382	Bogota Colombia Tunjuelito	22 Jun 1997	David Fabian Saavedra L.
1308	Bucaramanga Colombia	22 Nov 1981	Horacio Julio Insignarez
2666	Bucaramanga Colombia Terrazas	16 Jan 2005	Nelson Ardila Vasquez
937	Cali Colombia	10 Jun 1978	Luis Alfonso Rios
1054	Cali Colombia Americas	24 Aug 1979	Libber A. Montoya O.
2306	Cali Colombia Versalles	9 Feb 1997	Arnold Porras Martinez
2377	Cartagena Colombia	15 Jun 1997	Rafael A. Ulloque Barrios
2613a	Cartagena Colombia Los Alpes	18 May 2003	Jairo de Jesus Bardi Lopez
2698	Cucuta Colombia	4 Dec 2005	Javier Orlando Manosalva A.
2845	Duitama Columbia	28 Jun 2009	Jairo Alonso Morales Correa
1697	Medellin Colombia	5 Jun 1988	Arnold Porras Martinez
2213	Medellin Colombia Belen	14 Jul 1996	Harold Cristian Cruz Arango
2738	Monteria Colombia	5 Nov 2006	Efrain Ernesto Chavez Cabrales
2363	Neiva Colombia	25 May 1997	Carlos Julio Cubillos Mora
2161	Pasto Colombia	11 Feb 1996	Jose L.Santacruz Fernandez
1968	Pereira Colombia	19 Dec 1993	Jose Luis Gonzalez
2606b	Soacha Colombia	16 Mar 2003	Walter Ciro Caldero R.
2739	Valledupar Colombia	12 Nov 2006	Climaco G. Barragan Romero
Stakes discontinued			
1878	Barranquilla Colombia Cevillar	31 May 1992	Carlos M. Lopez M.
	Discontinued 1 Nov 1998		
2391	Cali Colombia Jardin	7 Sep 1997	Nestor Antonio Lopez
	Discontinued 29 June 2008		
2245	Ibague Colombia	13 Oct 1996	Cesar Hernando Bravo Parra
	Discontinued 21 May 2000		

Missions — 4

(As of Oct. 1, 2011; shown with historical number. See MISSIONS.)

(215) COLOMBIA BARRANQUILLA MISSION
Apartado Aereo 50710
Calle 82 No. 55-20, Apto 2
Barranquilla Atlantico, Colombia

(79a) COLOMBIA BOGOTA NORTH MISSION
Apartado Aereo 90746
Sante fe de Bogota 8, D.C.
Colombia

(270) COLOMBIA BOGOTA SOUTH MISSION
Apartado Aereo 77604
Santa Fe de Bogota DC
Colombia

(120) COLOMBIA CALI MISSION
Apartado Aereo 4892
Cali, Valle
Colombia

DEMOCRATIC REPUBLIC OF THE CONGO

Jan. 1, 2011: Est. population, 68,692,000; Members, 27,058; Stakes, 7; Wards, 55; Districts, 5; Branches, 39; Missions, 2; Percent LDS, .03, or one member in 3,289; Africa Southeast Area.

The Democratic Republic of the Congo, previously known as the Belgian Congo is in west-central Africa, and is bordered by the Republic of Congo, Angola, Burundi, Central African Republic, Rwanda, Sudan, Tanzania, Uganda, Zambia, and the Atlantic Ocean. The country became independent from Belgium on 30 June 1960. Its name was changed to Zaire in 1971, and then to the Democratic Republic of the Congo in 1997. It's sometimes called Congo-Kinshasa, after its capital, to distinguish it from the Republic of Congo. More than 75 languages and dialects are spoken, including the official language, French. Seventy percent of the people are Christian, while 10 percent are Muslim.

There was a Church member in the Democratic Republic of the Congo as early as 1969. On 12 July 1969, Dan Leonard Ecklund of the Congo was baptized at Salisbury, Southern Rhodesia. One of the first known converts from Zaire was Jean-Jacques Tamba-Tamba who was baptized on 10 July 1977 in Brussels, Belgium, where he was attending school. He returned to Zaire three months after his baptism.

Another early convert was Nkitabungi Mbuyi who was baptized on 19 July 1980 in Brussels, Belgium. He served in the England Birmingham Mission from 1982 to 1983 and returned to Zaire in March 1984. He began correspondence with Church headquarters hoping to establish the Church in his country. Senior missionaries, R. Bay and Jean Hutchings arrived on 11 February 1986. Two days later, on 13 February 1986 the Church received legal recognition. On 23 February 1986, the first meeting of the Church was held in the home of Nkitabungi's parents. The first baptisms in Zaire were on 1 June 1986, they were Banza Mucioko Jr. and Banza Philippe, sons of Banza Mucioko Wa Mutumbo. Banza Mucioko Jr.was baptized in Switzerland on 2 October 1979. The Church purchased a villa and remodeled it into a meetinghouse in September 1986. On 11 September, the Kinshasa Branch was organized with Michael C. Bowcutt, as president.

R. Bay Hutchings reported in November 1986 that some groups being taught numbered more than 150 and more than 12 were baptized per week. The Zaire Kinshasa Mission was organized on 1 July 1987 with R. Bay Hutchings as president. In July 1987, membership reached 300. Elders Marvin J. Ashton, of the Quorum of the Twelve and Alexander B. Morrison, of the Seventy visited on 30 August 1987. On 18 September 1988, the Kinshasa District was organized. The first citizens of Zaire to serve as missionaries in Zaire were called in early 1991. They were Banza Mucioko Jr., Diamany Ngalamulume, Mutombo Nkadi Thomas, and Maly-malu Kanda.

Following riots and civil unrest in Kinshasa during September and October 1991, the mission headquarters were moved to Brazzaville, Republic of Congo, and some missionaries were assigned to other missions in November of that same year. Violence continued in the area and spread to Brazzaville. On 23 June 1993, unrest escalated and missionaries were moved to the Ivory Coast. They were able to return to Brazzaville on 3 September 1993. On 23 December 1993, the mission was closed. Missionaries were transferred to the Ivory Coast Abidjan Mission. The mission was re-opened in late 1994, and in May 1995, the mission and temporal office returned to Kinshasa.

The Kinshasa Zaire Stake was organized on 3 November 1996. Less than a year later, on 12 August 1997, the mission name was changed to Democratic Republic of the Congo Kinshasa Mission. The following month, the Lubumbashi Democratic Republic of the Congo Stake was created on 7 September 1997. In January 2001, there was more upheaval in the country and missionaries were evacuated to Ghana where they remained for three weeks before receiving clearance to return to Kinshasa.

In 2002, membership reached 13,637, and 14,991 in 2003. In 2005, membership reached 17,074. In 2010 membership was 23,615 with seven stakes.

The DR Congo Lubumbashi Mission was created 1 July 2010 by the division of the DR Congo Kinshasa Mission.

President Thomas S. Monson announced 1 October 2001 that a temple will be built in Kinshasa.

Sources: Kuteka Kamulete, "From Zaire to the Lord's House," Liahona, August 1997; Nkitabungi Mbuyi, History of the Church of Jesus Christ of Latter-day Saints in Kinshasa/Democratic Republic of the Congo, November 2002, Church Archives; Democratic Republic of the Congo Kinshasa Mission, Manuscript history and historical reports, Church Archives. New Missions, *Church News*, 13 Feb. 2010.

Stakes — 11

(Listed alphabetically As of Oct. 1, 2011.)

No.	Name	Organized	First President
2922	Kananga DR Congo	21 May 2011	Bakajika Christophe Kawaya
2822	Katuba DR Congo	15 Mar 2009	
2258	*Kinshasa DR Congo	12 Aug 1997	
	‡Kinshasa Zaire	3 Nov 1996	Mulielegwa Musithi
2797	Kinshasa DR Congo	13 Apr 2008	Sylvain Wily Nyembive-Mutambaie
2851	Kinshasa DR Congo Kimbanseke	23 Aug 2009	
2527	Kinshasa DR Congo Masina	2 May 1999	Kola Kapumba Tusey
2797	Kinshasa DR Congo Mont Ngafula	12 Apr 2008	Sylvain W. Nyembwe-Mutambaie

2618	Kinshasa DR Congo Ngaliema	9 Nov 2003	Wa Musithi Jaques Muliele
2822	Katuba DR Congo	15 Mar 2009	Mingotyi Francois Mukubu
2390	Lubumbashi DR Congo	7 Sep 1997	Nzembelenge Kefa Milambo
2934	Luputa DR Congo	26 Jun 2011	Sabwe Binene

Mission — 2

(As of Oct. 1, 2011; shown with historical number. See MISSIONS.)

(198) DR CONGO KINSHASA MISSION
Immeuble Gulf 6347
Avenue de la Justice
Zone de la Gombe, Kinshasa
Democratic Republic of Congo

DR CONGO LUBUMBASHI MISSION
Ave M'Siri 1891
Lubumbashi
Democratic Republic of Congo

REPUBLIC OF THE CONGO

Jan. 1, 2011: Est. population, 4,013,000; Members 4,799; Stakes 1; Wards 8; Branches 7; Percent LDS, .1, or one member in 957; Africa Southeast Area; DR Republic of Congo Mission.

The Republic of Congo, previously known as French Equatorial Africa, became independent from France on 15 August 1960. Located in west-central Africa on the equator, it is bordered by Angola, Cameroon, Central African Republic, the Democratic Republic of the Congo, and Gabon. French is the official language, while local dia-lects are also spoken. Fifty percent of the people are Christian, while 48 percent follow tribal beliefs and 2 per-cent are Muslim.

In 1971, there were around 10 members of the Church scattered throughout the country. Twenty years later, on 20 January 1991, the Zaire Kinshasa Mission President Scott H. Taggart traveled to the capital city of Brazzaville to begin missionary work there. They met with the Massamba-Sita family and President Taggart set apart Hyacinthe Massamba-Sita as lead elder in Brazzaville and gave him permission to hold sacrament meetings. Senior missionary couple, George Leland and Emily Burningham arrived a few months later.

The Zaire Kinshasa Mission headquarters were moved to Brazzaville because of civil unrest in Kinshasa, Zaire, during September and October 1991. The mission headquarters returned to Zaire in November 1991. A month later, on 23 December, the government of the Republic of the Congo granted legal recognition to the Church.. The Brazzaville Republic of Congo District was organized on 23 February 1992.

Elder Richard G. Scott became the first member of the Quorum of the Twelve and first General Authority to visit the Republic of Congo on 24 August 1992.

On 29 December 1993, the Zaire Kinshasa Mission, which included the Republic of Congo, was closed because of wars in the region. It was re-opened in late 1994.

On 19 October 2003, the Brazzaville Republic of Congo Stake was created with Jean Patrice Milembolo as president. Membership was 3,262 in 2003.

Sources: "Congo Grants Formal Status to the Church," Church News, 28 December 1991; Borgna Brunner, "Countries of the world, Republic Congo, People's of the," Time Almanac 2004; Democratic Republic of the Congo Kinshasa Mission, Manuscript history and historical reports, Church Archives.

Stakes — 1

(Listed alphabetically As of Oct. 1, 2011.)

No.	Name	Organized	First President
Africa Southeast Area			
2614	Brazzaville Republic of Congo	19 Oct 2003	Jean Patrice Milembolo

COOK ISLANDS

(RAROTONGA)

Jan. 1, 2011: Est. population, 11,870; Members, 1,853; Districts, 1; Branches, 5; Percent LDS, 6.5, or one in 15; Pacific Area; Tahiti Papeete Mission.

Located in the South Pacific, about 400 miles southwest of French Polynesia, the Cook Islands are self-governing, and 75 percent of the population are Protestants. The islands, 13 of which are inhabited, maintain close ties with New Zealand.

On 11 May 1843, Joseph Smith called Addison Pratt on a mission to the Pacific Islands. Pratt was joined by Noah Rogers, Benjamin F. Grouard and Knowlton F. Hanks. In the course of their missionary work, Rogers briefly visited Mangaia of the Cook Islands in May 1845. Sidney A. Hanks, a missionary who arrived later, preached on Tongareva (also called Penrhyn or the present-day Maori name of Mangarongaro) in 1857. The next missionary visit to the Cook Islands wasn't until 1899 when Osborne J. P. Widtsoe and Mervin W. Davis arrived in Rarotonga on 23 May.

However, with no converts after numerous attempts to establish the Church, missionaries were withdrawn in November 1903. There was no known missionary work done there for the next 40 years. During World War II, Matthew Cowley, then president of the New Zealand Mission, assigned Fritz Bunge-Kruger, a New Zealander who had lived in Avarua on Rarotonga from 1940-1942, to help establish the Church on the Cook Islands. He returned to Rarotonga with his wife Maudina. Their first converts were Samuel Glassie and his family, who were baptized on 12 May 1942.

Trevor and Mildred Hamon arrived on Rarotonga on 12 September 1946 and were later joined by Donlon DeLaMar on 8 January 1947 and John L. Sorenson on 9 April 1947. A branch was created on 6 October 1946 at Mauri Enua. Meetings were also held in Avarua.

Matthew Cowley was the first General Authority to visit the Cook Islands on 28 June-2 July 1947. The islands had been part of the New Zealand Mission from 1942 until 17 July 1954 when they became part of the Samoan Mission. President David O. McKay made a one-hour visit with Church members of Cook Islands on 17 January 1955 when his plane made a refueling stop at Aitutaki on his way to Tahiti.

Although a number of meetinghouses had been built in the Cook Islands, they were mostly native hut-like structures. The use of labor missionaries in building more permanent structures commenced in 1955 with a meetinghouse built in Avatiu that was dedicated on 25 November 1955. A meetinghouse was also built in Aitutaki and was dedicated on 18 October 1958. The Rarotonga Mission was organized by Elder John Longden, Assistant to the Quorum of the Twelve, with Joseph R. Reeder as president on 20 November 1960. Mission headquarters were established in Avarua. The new mission had six branches. During the six years that followed, two branches were added; a 38-acre farm was leased; meetinghouses were built at Arorangi, Titikaveka, and Ngatangii; a monthly bulletin was published; and the Book of Mormon was translated into Cook Islands Maori and published in 1966. On 17 April 1966, the Rarotonga Mission was discontinued. That same day the Cook Islands Rarotonga District was created covering the same territory as the mission. It came under the direction of the New Zealand Mission and later the New Zealand North Mission.

The islands became part of the Fiji Mission in 1971, the Tahiti Papeete Mission in 1975, the New Zealand Auckland Mission in 1981, and the Tahiti Papeete Mission again in 2005. President Spencer W. Kimball visited Rarotonga in February 1981 during his trip to the South Pacific and held a short service with members in an airport hangar.

In 1990, the Cook Islands issued a series of postage stamps featuring the first missionaries of various denominations to the islands. The LDS stamp featured a rendition of Osborne J. P. Widtsoe in the foreground and a drawing of an LDS meetinghouse in the background. In September 1996, Church members celebrated the 50th anniversary of the Church in the Cook Islands. During the four-day celebration, members participated in dances, exhibits, sporting events, district conference, and a special fireside. In 2001, the Church distributed more than 3,000 dental care kits to school children of Rarotonga. The effort to improve the children's dental hygiene was begun by Richard Anderson, a dentist serving a mission in the Cook Islands.

In 2002, membership reached 1,369.

Sources: R. Lanier Britsch, Unto the Islands of the Sea, 1986; Dell Van Orden, "New Day Dawns for Temples in Pacific," Church News, 28 February 1981; "Island Stamp Honors LDS Elder," Church News, 23 June 1990; John L. Hart, "He Kept His Promise to Repay the Lord," Church News, 29 August 1992; "Anniversary Marks Progress in Country," Church News, 23 November 1996; "Toothbrushes Bring Smiles to Faces of School Children on Cook Island," Church News, 1 December 2001; "Cook Islands: A Legacy of Faith," Church News, 6 September 2003; New Zealand Auckland Mission, Cook Islands missionary history, 1990, Church Archives; Rarotonga Mission, Manuscript history and historical reports, Church Archives.

COSTA RICA

Jan. 1, 2011: Est. population, 4,254,000; Members, 38,337; Stakes, 5; Wards, 44; Branches, 33; Missions, 1; Districts, 5; Temples, 1; percent LDS, .86, or one in 116; Central America Area.

A Central American democratic republic, Costa Rica has a population that speaks Spanish.

While working for the U.S. government on assignment in Costa Rica, three Church members, Gardner Hale Russell and Clark and Adrienne Falls, held the first sacrament meetings in Costa Rica in 1944. Although no members were baptized during their stay in Costa Rica, Russell noted that they made "many friends who knew of and appreciated the Church." Two years later Costa Rica became part of the Mexican Mission on 8 July 1946. The first two missionaries, Robert B. Miller and David D. Lingard, arrived in Costa Rica on 6 September 1946.

They had an opportunity to visit with Costa Rica's president, Teodoro Picado Michalsky, and present him with a copy of the Book of Mormon. In 1947, Uriel Quesada became the first Costa Rican to be baptized. Due to political unrest, the missionaries left in 1948, but David D. Lingard and Jack M. Farnsworth returned in July 1949. The first conference in Costa Rica was held 7 June 1950, about 70 attended. A branch was organized 25 August 1950. Property for a meetinghouse was purchased in 1951.

During the 1950s, the Church in Costa Rica grew slowly. The Central American Mission was formed from the Mexican Mission on 16 November 1952. When the Guatemala-El Salvador Mission was created in 1965, it included Costa Rica. The first district conference was held in August 1968, with 296 people in attendance. Six years later, the Costa Rica Mission was organized on 20 June 1974.

Costa Rica's first stake, the San Jose Costa Rica Stake, was created on 20 January 1977. A month later, President Spencer W. Kimball spoke at an area conference in San Jose that was part of his seven-nation Latin America tour. At that time, there were 3,800 members in the country. By 1986, Costa Rica had 7,100 members. Eight years later the number reached 25,000.

President Gordon B. Hinckley visited Costa Rica on 20 January 1997 where he met with Costa Rican President Jose Maria Figueres in San Jose. In 1999, Church membership surpassed 30,000 members. The San Jose Costa Rica Temple was dedicated by President James E. Faust on 4 June 2000.

In 2002, membership reached 32,563.

Sources: Costa Rica San Jose Mission, Manuscript history and historical reports, Church Archives; Clarice Tetz, History of the Costa Rica Mission, 1943-1995, Church Archives; Gardner Hale Russell, One Small Rough Stone, [n.d.]; San Jose Branch, Manuscript history and historical reports, Church Archives; Arthur V. Kocherhans, "Church Branch in Costa Rica," Church News, 28 December 1949; "An Outpouring of Love for Prophet," Church News, 1 February 1997; Jason Swensen, "A New Landmark in Shining Seas," Church News 10 June 2000.

Stakes — 5
(Listed alphabetically As of Oct. 1, 2011.)

No.	Name	Organized	First President
Central America Area			
1783	*Alajuela Costa Rica	20 Jun 1995	
	‡San Jose Costa Rica Alajuela	9 Dec 1990	Milton Perez Ruiz

1826	San Jose Costa Rica La Paz	10 Nov 1991	Max Enrique Urena Fallas
917	San Jose Costa Rica La Sabana	7 May 1978	Jorge Arturo Solano Castillo
803	*San Jose Costa Rica Los Yoses	10 Nov 1991	
	‡San Jose Costa Rica	20 Jan 1977	Manuel Najera G.
2524	San Jose Costa Rica Toyopan	25 Apr 1999	Rodrigo Bernal Soto Bolanos

Mission — 1
(As of Oct. 1, 2011; shown with historical number. See MISSIONS.)

(43b) COSTA RICA SAN JOSE MISSION
Apartado Postal 2339-1000
San Jose, Costa Rica, C.A.

CROATIA

Jan. 1, 2011: Est. Population, 4,489,000; Members 532; Branches 6; Districts 1; Percent LDS, .01, or one member in 8,750; Europe Area.

Located on the Balkan Peninsula in southeast Europe, Croatia is a republic made up of what was a northern internal division of Yugoslavia, where Croatian is spoken.

Due to political restrictions, no missionary work was done in Croatia until 1966 when Tomislav Zidar wrote to the Church requesting information. He had found a tract of "Joseph Smith Tells His Own Story" inside a newspaper.

In response to Zidar's letter, J. Peter Loscher, president of the Austrian Mission and his assistant Ralph V. Benson, traveled to Zagreb, Yugoslavia, to meet with Zidar. On 12 July 1966 he was baptized by Benson in the Sava River.

In 1971, Kresimir Cosic, a basketball player recruited to play for Brigham Young University, was baptized in Provo, Utah. Because of his popularity he became the Church's most powerful influence in Croatia until his death from leukemia on 25 May 1995. During his summer break from school in 1972, Cosic returned to his home in Zadar where he shared his new-found faith. He found a few converts and on 11 September 1972 the first sacrament meeting was held in Zadar.

In November of 1974 missionaries from the Austria Vienna Mission, at the suggestion of Elder Neal A. Maxwell, Assistant to the Quorum of the Twelve, began to conduct missionary work among Serbo-Croatian guest workers in Vienna. A Serbo-Croatian Sunday school was established in Vienna in March 1975. The work was sufficiently successful that six missionaries who had been trained in Serbo-Croatian at the Language Training Mission arrived on 7 May 1975 to work in Vienna.

Missionaries Kirk Barrus and Michael Meyer were sent from the Austria Vienna Mission to Zadar on 1 February 1978. Other missionaries soon followed to work there and in other cities. Missionaries continued to work throughout the 1980s under the jurisdiction of the Austria Vienna Mission. Though not allowed to actively work as traditional missionaries, they were permitted to speak about the Church if they were first asked by a potential investigator.

Church registration was granted in 1985 after the first meetinghouse in Zagreb was dedicated in November of that year by Elder Thomas S. Monson of the Quorum of the Twelve.

In July 1987 the Austria Vienna East Mission was created and responsibility for Croatia was transferred to that mission.

Responsibility for Yugoslavia returned to the Austria Vienna Mission on 22 March 1991. In June of that year, when Croatia and neighboring Slovenia declared independence from Yugoslavia, missionaries were evacuated due to the ensuing war. They returned in February 1992.

Following the dissolution of Yugoslavia, Kresimir Cosic, because of his relationship with the United States, and because of the respect held for him within the country, was appointed deputy ambassador to the United States from Croatia in 1992.

July 1996 marked the creation of the Austria Vienna South Mission with Johann Wondra as president. The mission was responsible for supervising the nations of the former Yugoslavia including Croatia. In June of 1999 the mission offices were transferred from Vienna, Austria, to Ljubljana, Slovenia, and the name of the mission was changed to the Slovenia Ljubljana Mission. The name was changed again in January 2003, to the Croatia Zagreb Mission.

In 2003, membership reached 375. In 2008, membership was 513.

More than 120 people attended a groundbreaking ceremony 14 April 2007 for the first LDS meetinghouse in Croatia located in Zagreb. The meetinghouse was dedicated 24 May 2009.

Sources: Kahlile B. Mehr, Mormon Missionaries Enter Eastern Europe, 2002; Zagreb Croatia District, Annual historical report, Church Archives; Croatia Zagreb Mission, Annual historical report, Church Archives; Donald Q. Cannon and Richard O. Cowan, Unto Every Nation: Gospel Light Reaches Every Land, 2003; Arnold K. Garr, Donald Q. Cannon, and Richard O. Cowan, eds., "Croatia," Encyclopedia of Latter-Day Saint History, 2000; "Former Y. Basketball Star is Deputy Ambassador," Church News, 26 September 1992.

Mission — 1
(As of Oct. 1, 2011; shown with historical number. See MISSIONS.)

(309) CROATIA ZAGREB MISSION
Molekova Ul. 3
1211 Ljubljana - Smartno, Slovenia

CYPRUS

Jan. 1, 2011: Est. population, 796,000; Members, 381; Branches, 4; District, 1; Percent LDS, .04, or one member in 2,362; Europe Area; Greece Athens Mission.

Located in the Mediterranean Sea off the Turkish coast, the republic has groups speaking Greek and Turkish, and follow the Greek Orthodox and Muslim religions. The island has biblical significance as the birthplace of Barnabas, a companion of the Apostle Paul, and as a refuge place for persecuted saints in the early Church.

In 1960, Britain granted Cyprus its independence. Disagreements and violence between the country's Greek and Turkish citizens led to a coup in 1974 and the invasion of Cyprus by Turkey which took possession of the northern third of the island. A guarded wall, the "green line," has separated the Greek and Turkish sections of the country since that time. The Church does not have a presence in Turkish Cyprus.

By 1961, the Nicosia Cyprus Group was functioning as part of the East Mediterranean District of the French Mission. The 20 members were servicemen and their families stationed at the British Akrotiri Sovereign Base. The group was discontinued in 1969 after transfer of LDS servicemen from the base.

On 6 May 1971 Switzerland Mission President M. Elmer Christensen visited southern Cyprus and re-established the Nicosia Cyprus Group. This group held regular meetings for eight Latter-day Saints and participated in interdenominational protestant meetings, some of which were under the direction of LDS leaders.

In 1972, Linda Mylona, a Latter-day Saint originally from Ayrshire, Scotland, moved to Nicosia, Cyprus with her non-member Greek husband and four sons. As the only permanent resident of the island who was a member of the Church, she sought out and fellowshipped other Latter-day Saints. In the decade that followed, several other members, including Avelina Marvilla from the Philippines, emigrated to Cyprus adding strength to the fledgling congregation.

In 1987, Elders James O. and Evelyn H. Henrie became the first missionaries to work in Cyprus.

On 10 September 1989, 28 members gathered at the Henrie home in Nicosia to witness the creation of the Nicosia Cyprus Branch under direction of Austria Vienna East Mission President Dennis B. Neuenschwander. James O. Henrie was set apart as branch president. Linda Mylona was set apart as Relief Society president.

In August 1990, Robert L. and Melpha L. Kane were assigned to labor in Cyprus. After working there for over a year, immigration officials who were concerned about the establishment of the Church in their country insisted that they leave. Although the Kanes were forced to finish their mission elsewhere, another couple, David and Ruth I. Ririe were allowed to take their place, serving from 1990-1992. Through the 1990s a number of missionaries were detained and questioned by the police and their passports and other papers were often taken. Eventually as the Church became better-understood, these occurrences of legal trouble lessened and the Cypriot constitution which grants broad religious freedoms to individuals and churches became an aid to the establishment and defense of the Church.

In July 1990, Cyprus came under the direction of the newly-created Greece Athens Mission. That same month Elders Buce L. Alder and Ryan L. Risenmay began working in Nicosia, the first young missionaries to be assigned to Cyprus.

By 1991, the Nicosia Branch had 29 members along with four elders serving in Cyprus and one missionary couple.

On 29 February 1992, Georgia Philippou, a 67-year-old Greek Cypriot was baptized by Elder Blaine F. Steele, becoming the first Cypriot member. Five weeks later Maria Zenieri, also a Greek Cypriot, became the second native convert to be baptized. A few years later, Sister Zenieri visited Church headquarters in Salt Lake City. Her visit coincided with that of the Cypriot Ambassador to the United States and she was able to act as a Cypriot Latter-day Saint hostess during a banquet the Church provided in his honor.

In April 1993, branch members living in Limassol began meeting at the home of Kenneth and Catherine Clulow, British saints permanently settled in Cyprus. On 30 July 1994, a meetinghouse was rented and the Limassol Branch was established with Clulow as branch president.

On 14 September 1993, Elder Joseph B. Wirthlin of the Quorum of the Twelve and Elder Hans B. Ringger of the Seventy and their wives visited Cyprus.

In 1997, there were 90 members of the Church in Cyprus meeting in branches in Nicosia and Limassol and another group of seven saints in Larnaca. In 2003, there 202 members.

Sources: Greece Athens Mission, Historical files, Church Archives; Cyprus Group, History, Church Archives; "A Church for All Lands: Cyprus Nicosia Group," Church News, 21 October 1978; Joan Farbus, "Report from Cyprus," Ensign, December 1981.

CZECH REPUBLIC

Jan. 1, 2011: Est. population, 10,212,000; Members, 2,282; Branches, 14; Missions, 1; Districts, 2; Percent LDS, .02, or one member in 4,879; Europe Area.

In east-central Europe, the Czech Republic's people speak Czech and Slovak, both of which are official languages. Some 65 percent of the population is Roman Catholic.

Thomas Biesinger, was the first missionary to enter what was then Austria. He arrived in Prague on 26 February 1884. He labored there for less than a month when he was arrested for preaching and held for two months before he was brought to trial. He served another month in prison before he was released, but before his departure in June 1884 he baptized and confirmed Anthon Just. No other missionary work was done for some time, although in 1919 Frantika Brodil, who was baptized in Vienna in 1913, moved back to Prague with her two daughters.

At the age of 84 Thomas Biesinger returned to Prague where on 2 February 1928 he petitioned authorities for permission to preach and on 7 March of that year permission was granted. The Czechoslovak Mission was organized 24 July 1929 with Arthur Gaeth as president.

The Book of Mormon was translated into Czech in 1933. A shortage of missionaries during the Great Depression slowed the work. Missionaries were evacuated in September 1938 because of a political crisis that ceded some of Czechoslovakia's border lands to Germany. Missionaries returned in December of that year and were not evacuated during the 15 March 1939 occupation by Germany.

However, in August 1939, missionaries left prior to the beginning of World War II. The mission was left under the direction of a young convert, Josef Roubicek. During the war, he kept the Saints together, added 28 members, and published a mission circular letter.

Missionary work resumed in June of 1946 and continued until 6 April 1950, when the mission was closed. During that time the communist government increased legal restrictions against the Church and other religions, culminating with the arrest and imprisonment of two LDS missionaries for nearly a month between January and February 1950. Latter-day Saints had little contact with the outside world until 1964 and 1965 when several Church leaders visited including Austrian

Mission President J. Peter Loscher and former Czechoslovak mission president Wallace F. Toronto.

The Czechoslovakia District was organized on 3 February 1982. Local missionaries began having success in the 1980s. After the democratization of the nation in 1989-90, the first full-time missionaries arrived 2 May 1990. About that time, the Church applied for recognition. According to President Thomas S. Monson, then second counselor in the First Presidency, "The government leaders had said to us, 'Don't send an American, a German, or a Swiss. Send us a Czech.' " Eventhough acknowledging that he was a Church leader during the prohibition of religion was tantamount to imprisonment, Jiri Snederfler, Czechoslovakia district president, and later the first Czech president to preside over a temple (Freiberg Germany), answered the call and faced the risk as he applied for government recognition.

Snederfler met with Deputy Prime Minister Josef Hromadka in Prague on 6 February 1990 and recognition, first granted to the Church in 1928, was officially renewed on 21 February 1990. The Czechoslovakia Prague Mission was reorganized 1 July 1990, with Richard W. Winder as president. Soon Czechs began to receive greater exposure to the Church. The Tabernacle Choir performed in Prague in 1991 and in 1993, Czech broadcasters visited Salt Lake City and televised a nationwide feature on the Church.

In April 1993 the mission name was changed to the Czech Prague Mission. The first meetinghouse built by the Church in the Czech Republic was dedicated in Brno on 11 November 2001.

In 2003, membership reached 1,877. Elder Dieter F. Uchtdorf, born in Ostrava, Moravia, was called to the Quorum of the Twelve Apostles on 7 October 2004.

Sources: Thomas Biesinger, Experiences of missionary life, 24 July 1929, Church Archives; Austrian Mission, Manuscript history and historical reports, Church Archives; Gaeth, Arthur, Relating Czechoslovak Mission history, 2 October 1981, Church Archives; Czechoslovak Mission, Manuscript history and historical reports, Church Archives; Martha Sharp Toronto Anderson, A Cherry Tree Behind the Iron Curtain, 1977; "First Czech Meetinghouse Dedicated," Church News, February 2002, 79.

Mission — 1
(As of Oct. 1, 2011; shown with historical number. See MISSIONS.)

(236) CZECH PRAGUE MISSION
Milady Horakove 85/95
170 00 PRAGUE 7 - Holesovice,
Czech Republic

DENMARK

Jan. 1, 2011: Est. population, 5,500,000; Members, 4,378; Stakes, 2; Wards, 13; Branches, 10; Missions, 1; Temples, 1; Percent LDS, .08 , or one in 1,261; Europe Area.

Located in northern Europe on the Baltic Sea, Denmark is a constitutional monarchy with a population that speaks Danish, Faroese, and Greenlandic (an Inuit dialect). The people are 95 percent Evangelical Lutherans, 2.5 percent Protestant and Roman Catholic, 2 percent Muslim, and one half-percent other including LDS.

At the October 1849 general conference, Apostle Erastus Snow was assigned to establish the Church in Scandinavia, and Peter O. Hansen was called to serve as a missionary to Denmark. Hansen, a native of Copenhagen, was one of the first Danes to accept the gospel, having received baptism while temporarily living in Boston in 1844. Once converted, Hansen moved to Nauvoo, then migrated with the Saints to the Great Salt Lake Valley in 1847. There, he completed the Danish translation of the Book of Mormon he had begun at Nauvoo in 1845.

When it was announced that Elder Snow and Hansen would work in Scandinavia, John E. Forsgren, a Swedish convert, petitioned and was granted an opportunity to also be called to the work. The three men left Utah in October 1849, arriving in Copenhagen the following spring.

Within two months, the elders had established the headquarters of a mission in Copenhagen. The first baptisms took place on 12 August 1850 in the Oeresund near Copenhagen. The group of converts included eight men and seven women, with Ole C. U. Moenster being the first. The first branch was organized in Copenhagen on 15 September 1850. George P. Dykes established a second branch in Aalborg on 25 November 1850. By April 1851, the Aalborg branch contained 91 members.

The Book of Mormon translation prepared by Peter O. Hansen was published in January 1851, the first non-English language into which the book was published.

Although the Danish Parliament passed laws guaranteeing religious freedoms as part of the new constitution in 1849, early missionaries and members faced significant threats, opposition, and harassment from civil authorities and citizens. In Aalborg in 1851, a mob vandalized the hall where the Saints were meeting, and persecutions against Mormon children at school became so severe that in April of that year a Mormon-sponsored school, the first established in continental Europe, began in Aalborg.

Despite opposition, conferences (districts) were established in November 1851 in Copenhagen, Aalborg, and Fredericia to accommodate the rapidly-multiplying branches. The first converts to emigrate to Utah left Denmark on 31 January 1852. Of about 26,000 Danes converted during this early period, 13,984 of them emigrated to the United States by 1930.

The missionary work in Denmark functioned under the jurisdiction of the Scandinavian Mission until 1905 when it was renamed the Danish-Norwegian Mission. On 1 April 1920, the Danish Mission was organized. During World War II all missionaries from the United States were withdrawn, but work continued through the service of local Danish missionaries. A number of members emigrated to the United States at the end of the war.

Between 1966 and 1974, convert baptisms varied from 50 to 200 each year. By 1971, Church membership in Denmark totaled 4,193 people in three districts.

The Copenhagen Denmark Stake, the first in Denmark and in all of Scandinavia, was created on 16 June 1974. On 25 January 1975, a Danish government committee classified the Church as a Christian religion, opening the way for the Church to enjoy the privileges of other Christian organizations in Denmark.

President Spencer W. Kimball spoke to 3,800 members at an area conference in Copenhagen in August 1976. Richard Swett, a Church member and two-term Congressman, was sworn-in as U.S. ambassador to Denmark on 5 September 1998.

It was announced on 17 March 1999 that, for only the second time in the history of the Church, an existing building would be remodeled to become a temple. The historic Copenhagen Branch Chapel on Priorvej Street built by the Church in 1930 would become the Copenhagen Denmark Temple. The neo-classical chapel was originally dedicated by Elder John A. Widtsoe of the Quorum of the Twelve on 14 June 1931. The completed Copenhagen Denmark Temple was dedicated on 23 May 2004 by President Gordon B. Hinckley.

The 150th anniversary of the Church in Scandinavia was celebrated in Denmark during the first week of July 2000, with a series of firesides, dances, reunions, and the presentation of two statues. The first statue, unveiled on 4 July in Denmark's only national park in the hills of Rebild, is titled "The Family," and symbolizes a Mormon family as they prepare to make the voyage to Utah in the 19th century. The second statue titled "Kristina" was unveiled on 6 July near the Copenhagen harbor where it represents early Saints who boarded sailing ships for the journey to America.

The 19th Century gathering of European converts to Zion and the sesquicentennial of the first converts emigrating from Scandinavia in January 1852 was commemorated in August 2001 in five European countries. Beginning in Denmark, eight tall sailing ships, under the sponsorship of Sea Trek Foundation, a private venture, left from the western seacoast town of Esbjerg on 7 August 2001.

In 2002, membership reached 4,457; and 4,427 in 2004.

Sources: Andrew Jenson, Encyclopedic History of the Church, 1941; Gerald Myron Haslam, Clash of Cultures: The Norwegian Experience with Mormonism, 1842-1920, 1984; Arnold K. Garr, Donald Q. Cannon, and Richard O. Cowan, eds., Encyclopedia of Latter-day Saint History, 2000; Scandinavian Mission, Manuscript history and historical reports, Church Archives; Denmark Copenhagen Mission, Manuscript history and historical reports, Church Archives; Lyn R. Jacobs, Mormon non-English scriptures, hymnals, and periodicals, 1830-1986, 1986; "The Saints in Scandinavia," Ensign, July 1974; John L. Hart, "Prophet Visits 5 European Countries, Asks Saints to Keep Commandments," Church News, 22 June 1996; "Statesman Sworn in as Ambassador to Denmark," Church News, 5 September 1998; "Danish Chapel Will Become New Temple," Church News, 29 May 1999; Ford Stevenson, "Church Marks 150 Years in Scandinavia," Church News, 15 July 2000; R. Scott Lloyd, "Epic Atlantic Voyage," Church News, 4 August 2001; R. Scott Lloyd, "Sea Trek's Tall Ships Embark from Denmark," Church News, 11 August 2001; R. Scott Lloyd, "Sea Trekkers Make Connections in Denmark," Church News, 11 August 2001; "Denmark Crowned with Statue," Church News, 23 August 2003.

Stakes — 2

(Listed alphabetically as of Oct. 1, 2011.)

No.	Name	Organized	First President
Europe Area			
945	Aarhus Denmark	2 Jul 1978	Knud Bent Andersen
648	Copenhagen Denmark	16 Jun 1974	Johan Helge Benthin

Mission — 1

(As of Oct. 1, 2011; shown with historical number. See MISSIONS.)

(23b) DENMARK COPENHAGEN MISSION
Borups Alle 128, 1, tv
DK-2000 Frederiksberg, Denmark

GREENLAND

Jan. 1, 2011: Est. population, 53,375; Members, 14; Branches, 1; Percent LDS, .04, or one member in 2,320; North America Northeast Area; Denmark Copenhagen Mission.

This very large island, slightly larger than Mexico, in the North Atlantic between Canada and Iceland is a province of Denmark under home rule. Greenland has a parliamentary government with a population that speaks Danish and Greenlandic, and most are members of the Evangelical Lutheran Church.

During World War II a servicemen's group was organized to support men serving in the 30th Weather Reconnaissance Squadron. In 1952 or 1953, another LDS servicemen's group was organized at Thule Air Force Base. Sometime in the 1960s or 70s, the group was organized as a branch, but it was discontinued in 1989, and reverted to group status. Greenland has, over time, been supervised by the Massachusetts Boston Mission, the International Mission and the Denmark Copenhagen Mission. As of 1998 a Church group of Danish natives comprised of the of Kim Hvistendahl family and one other member was meeting weekly in Nuuk, under the direction of the Denmark Copenhagen Mission president.

Sources: Correspondence from Kim Hvistendahl, 13 May 1998, Church News resource files; Servicemen's Group (30th Weather Reconnaissance Squadron : Greenland), Meeting minutes and attendance records, 1944, Church Archives; Servicemen's Group (Thule Air Force Base: Greenland), Meeting minutes and attendance records, 1959, Church Archives; Local unit history file, Church Archives; Arnold K Garr, Donald, Q. Cannon, and Richard O. Cowan, eds., Encyclopedia of Latter-day Saint History, 2000, 446; Thule Air Base Servicemen's Group, General minutes, Church Archives.

DOMINICAN REPUBLIC

Jan. 1, 2011: Est. population, 9,650,000; Members, 118,557; Stakes, 18; Wards, 118; Branches, 83; Missions, 3; Districts, 10; Temples, 1; percent LDS, 1.1, or one in 88; Caribbean Area.

On the island of Hispaniola, Dominican Republic is about the size of Vermont and New Hampshire combined, but has nearly five times their combined populations. The Dominican Republic is a representative democracy. Its population speaks Spanish and is mostly Roman Catholic.

In the 1960s and 1970s, a few Latter-day Saint families from the United States came to the country on business and held their own Church services. In 1978, the Amparo and Rappleye families moved from the United States and began holding Church services under the direction of the Florida Fort Lauderdale Mission. Eddie and Mercedes Amparo were native Dominicans baptized in the United States. They returned to their homeland in 1978. The Amparos soon met another

Latter-day Saint family, John and Nancy Rappleye. John Rappleye befriended, Rodolfo Bodden, who was also a boyhood friend of Eddie Amparo. The Bodden family was baptized in August 1978, the first to join the Church on Dominican Republic soil.

Florida Fort Lauderdale Mission President Richard L. Millett sent missionaries in 1978, including John and Ada Davis. On 7 December 1978, Elder M. Russell Ballard of the Quorum of the Seventy visited and blessed the land. The first branch was organized 12 September 1978 in Santo Domingo. The Church grew rapidly and on 1 January 1981, the Dominican Republic Santo Domingo Mission was organized with John A. Davis as president. At that time, membership was 2,500.

Another highlight came two months later on 8-9 March 1981 when President Spencer W. Kimball addressed the Saints, including another late night discourse to Saints from Puerto Plata whose bus had broken down causing them to arrive after the meeting concluded.

Membership increases have been rapid in the country. In 1979, 354 people were baptized. By 1986, membership reached 11,000. The first stake was created in Santo Domingo on 23 March 1986. The following year, the second mission was organized in Santiago when membership was about 13,000. A third mission was created on 1 July 1991 with the division of the Santo Domingo mission. A missionary training center for the Caribbean was dedicated in Santo Domingo on 13 April 1998. Stakes have also grown quickly with the second stake organized 16 October 1988, and a third on 5 November 1989.

Membership in 1990 was 31,000. The Santo Domingo Dominican Republic Temple was dedicated 17 September 2000 by President Gordon B. Hinckley. In 2002, membership reached 84,754. By 2004, 12 stakes and 11 districts covered the country.

Sources: William B. Smart, "2 Families Bring gospel to a Nation," Church News, 11 July 1981; Jason Swensen, "Dominican Republic: Land of Believers," Church News; 13 January 2001; "Mission Created in Dominican Republic," Church News, 6 December 1980; Gerry Avant, "History is Made: Prophet Visits Caribbean Islands, Church News, 21 March 1981; "Dominican Growth: From Zero to Thousands Since 1978," Ensign, January 1987; Spencer W. Kimball, "Rendering Service to Others," Ensign, May 1981; Elizabeth and Jed VanDenBerghe, "Dominican Republic: A Second Decade for Dominican Saints," Ensign, October 1990; "Ground Broken for Caribbean's First Temple," 24 August 1996, Church News; Jason Swensen, "Caribbean's First Temple Prompts Rejoicing," Church News, 23 September 2000.

Stakes — 22
(Listed alphabetically as of Oct. 1, 2011.)

No.	Name	Organized	First President
Caribbean Area			
2700	La Romana Dominican Republic	11 Dec 2005	Tomas Familia Muñoz
2480	La Vega Dominican Republic	21 Jun 1998	Juan E. Almonte
2672	Los Alcarrizos Dominican Republic	13 March 2005	Wilson Sigfrido Segura
2931	Navarrete Dominican Republic	19 Jun 2011	Florentino Garcia López
2670	Puerto Plata Dominican Republic	13 Feb 2005	Edward Nixon Reynoso Crespo
2360	San Cristobal Dominican Republic	25 May 1997	Juan Paciano Felipe
1800	San Francisco de Macoris Dominican Republic	26 May 1991	Eric Edison Olivero P.
2722	Santiago Dominican Republic East	21 May 2006	Jorge S. Domínguez
2009	Santiago Dominican Republic North	8 Jan 1995	Roberto Antonio Rodriguez
1786	*Santiago Dominican Republic South	8 Jan 1995	
	Santiago Dominican Republic	17 Feb 1991	Ramon Matias Lantigua
1593	Santo Domingo Dominican Republic	23 Mar 1986	Jose Delio Ceveno
2799	Santo Domingo Dominican Republic Hainamosa	13 Apr 2008	Florentino Alcantara
1906	Santo Domingo Dominican Republic Independencia	18 Oct 1992	Felix Sequi-Martinez
2800	Santo Domingo Dominican Republic Las Americas	13 Apr 2008	Victor de la Cruz
1593	Santo Domingo Dominican Republic Las Caboas	2 Nov 2003	Ruddy Emilio Monegro Gomez
2806b	Santo Domingo Dominican Republic Los Restauradores	31 Aug 2008	Paulino Agame Martinez
1735a	*Santo Domingo Dominican Republic Oriental	2 Feb 1992	
	*Oriental Dominican Republic	29 Oct 1991	
	*Santo Domingo Dominican Republic Oriental	24 Sep 1991	
	‡Santo Domingo Dominican Republic East	5 Nov 1989	Pedro Arturo Abreu C.
1844	Santo Domingo Dominican Republic Ozama	2 Feb 1992	Jose Andres Taveras Arias
1701	*Santo Domingo Dominican Republic San Geronimo	18 Oct 1992	
	‡San Geronimo Dominican Republic	16 Oct 1988	Victor Alejandro Navarro M.
2182	Santo Domingo Dominican Republic Villa Mella	17 Mar 1996	Domingo Antonio Aybar A.

(196) DOMINICAN REPUBLIC SANTIAGO
Av. Estrella Sadhala
Plaza Alejo 2-B
Santiago, Dominican Republic

(259) DOMINICAN REPUBLIC SANTO DOMINGO EAST
Avenida Bolivar #45 (con Dr. Delgado)
Gazcue
Santo Domingo, Dominican Republic

(188a) D.R. SANTO DOMINGO WEST MISSION
C/Hatey #73
Los Caciazgos
Santo Domingo, Dominican Republic

ECUADOR

Jan. 1, 2009: Est. population, 14,573,000; Members, 195,941; Stakes, 34; Wards, 224; Branches, 76; Missions, 3; Districts, 9; Temples, 1; Percent LDS, 1.3, or one in 78; South America Northwest Area.

Located on the equator on the Pacific Coast side of South America, the Republic of Ecuador is divided into three zones by two ranges of Andes mountains. Its population speaks Spanish or Quechua.

A telephone call from Elder Spencer W. Kimball, then of the Quorum of the Twelve, to President J. Averil Jesperson of the Andes Mission in Lima, Peru, on 22 September 1965, directed the beginning of missionary work in Ecuador. Four missionaries, Craig Carpenter, Bryant R. Gold, Joel Lindon Robinson, and Paul O. Allen, were sent to Quito, and on 9 October, Elder Kimball visited the city. Less than a month after Elder Kimball's visit, nine people were baptized on 31 October 1965 in Alangasi de la Merced, located about 50 miles southeast of Quito.

Missionary work progressed rapidly. In the city of Guayaquil missionary work began on 28 January 1966. When the Ecuador Mission, headquartered in Quito, was created on 1 August 1970, membership was 1,000. Ecuador's first stake was organized in Guayaquil 4 June 1978 under the leadership of President Lorenzo Garaycoa. A second mission in the country was organized in Guayaquil on 1 July 1978. Some early missionary efforts were conducted among the Otavalo Indians near Quito, among whom the first all-Lamanite stake in South America was organized in 1981. In 1989, the headquarters for the South America North Area was moved from Lima, Peru, to Quito, Ecuador.

Membership in 1999 approached 150,000 in 32 stakes.

Although the construction of a temple for Guayaquil was announced in March 1982, it was not finished and dedicated until 1 August 1999. On 11 August 1997, President Gordon B. Hinckley became the first Church President to visit Ecuador. He toured the temple under construction and in two meetings, described to 15,000 Ecuadoran Church members how he had been impressed to find the site several years earlier. At a regional conference on 31 July 1999 President Hinckley spoke to nearly 22,000 members and told them, in contemplation of the temple dedication the following day, "This is a day to be remembered by Latter-day Saints for many years to come."

In 2002, membership reached 156,988, and 161,396 in 2003.

Sources: Andes Mission manuscript history and historical reports, Church Archives; Donald Q. Cannon and Richard O. Cowan, Unto Every Nation: Gospel Light Reaches Every Land, 2003; "Ecuador," Ensign, February 1977; "Language No Barrier," Church News, 11 November 1978; Gerry Avant, "Tip Your Panama Hat, This is Ecuador," Church News, 14 February 1981; "Ecuador's First Stake Formed in Guayaquil," Church News, 8 July 1978; Elayne Wells, "In the Andes, Lehi's Children Grow Strong in the Gospel," Church News, 17 February 1990; "Temples in Latin America," Church News, 25 June1994, "Ecuador Receives 1st Visit from a President of Church," Church News, 23 August 1997; "'A Wondrous Day' at Dedication of Guayaquil Temple," Church News, 7 August 1999; John L. Hart, "Burst of Zeal Opens Work in Ecuador," Church News, 6 November 1999.

Stakes — 34
(Listed alphabetically as of Oct. 1, 2011.)

No.	Name	Organized	First President
South America North Area			
2144	Ambato Ecuador	10 Dec 1995	Jorge Humberto Verde
2679	Babahoyo Ecuador	15 May 2005	Byron W. Manzo Castillo
2414	Cuenca Ecuador	23 Nov 1997	Wilson Arcesio Pulla Quito
1882	Duran Ecuador North	31 May 1992	Mark Roy Kent
1883	Duran Ecuador South	31 May 1992	Jimmy Winston Olvera
2110	Esmeraldas Ecuador	22 Oct 1995	Jorge Miguel Arroyo Jacombe
2162	Guayaquil Ecuador Alborada	11 Feb 1996	Henry Alejandro Mora
1808	Guayaquil Ecuador Centenario	18 Aug 1991	Luis Guillermo Granja G.
1809	Guayaquil Ecuador East	18 Aug 1991	Jimmy Winston Olvera C.
2163	Guayaquil Ecuador El Cisne	11 Feb 1996	Melvin Merchan
939	*Guayaquil Ecuador El Salado	11 Feb 1996	
	*Guayaquil Ecuador West	22 Mar 1987	
	‡Guayaquil Ecuador	4 Jun 1978	Lorenzo Garaycoa
1716a	*Guayaquil Ecuador		
	Garcia Moreno	11 Feb 1996	
	‡Guayaquil Ecuador Central	30 Apr 1989	Gonzalo Eduardo Alvarado R.
1916	Guayaquil Ecuador Huancavilca	6 Dec 1992	Jose Eladio Paredes Garcia
2773	Guayaquil Ecuador La Pradera	1 Sep 2007	Jorge Amaro Garcia Tapia
2370	Guayaquil Ecuador Pascuales	8 Jun 1997	Luis Fernando Ramirez C.
1117	*Guayaquil Ecuador Prosperina	11 Feb 1996	

	‡Guayaquil Ecuador North	22 Mar 1987	
	‡Guayaquil Ecuador Febres Cordero	16 Mar 1980	Douglas Alarcon Arboleda
2394	Guayaquil Ecuador Puerto Liza	7 Sep 1997	Luis E. Romo Martinez
1006	*Guayaquil Ecuador South	22 Mar 1987	
	‡Guayaquil Ecuador Centenario	4 Mar 1979	Vincente de la Cuadra S.
2641	Libertad Ecuador	13 June 2004	Washington Manuel Cedeno Guale
2831	Los Chillos Ecuador	31 May 2009	Julio Anibal Angulo De la Cruz
1853	Machala Ecuador	22 Mar 1992	Manuel Andres Galan Pereira
2173	Manta Ecuador	25 Feb 1996	Wilson Marino Chinga H.
1796	Milagro Ecuador	5 May 1991	Alberto W. Guillen Fuentes
1316	Otavalo Ecuador	6 Dec 1981	Luis Alfonso Morales C.
2301	Otavalo Ecuador Imbabura	19 Jan 1997	Juan J. Munoz Otavalo
1224	Portoviejo Ecuador	13 Jan 1981	Jorge Vicente Salazar H.
1259	*Quevedo Ecuador North	18 May 2003	
	*Quevedo Ecuador Bellavista	7 Sep 1997	
	‡Quevedo Ecuador	27 Apr 1981	Pedro Jose Cantos J.
2392	*Quevedo Ecuador South	18 May 2003	
	‡Quevedo Ecuador Guayacan	7 Sep 1997	Jose Meliton Vera Lopez
2453	Quito Ecuador Calderon	19 Apr 1998	Jorge Gonzalo Montoya
2050	Quito Ecuador Chillogallo	21 May 1995	Eduardo Calderon Poveda
1053	*Quito Ecuador		
	*Quito Ecuador Colon	15 Jan 1981	
	‡Quito Ecuador	22 Aug 1979	Ernesto Franco
2431	Quito Ecuador La Ofelia	25 Jan 1998	Olvin Enrique Mora B.
1225	Quito Ecuador Santa Ana	15 Jan 1981	Cesar Hugh Cacuango C.
2096	Santo Domingo Ecuador	3 Sep 1995	Wilson Alcides Echanique Cueve

Stakes discontinued

1839	Quito Ecuador Inaquito Discontinued 9 Jun 2002	12 Jan 1992	Horacio Araya Olivares
2393	Quevedo Ecuador San Camilo Discontinued 18 May 2003	7 Sep 1997	Angel Cristobal Garcia M.
2279	Esmeraldas Ecuador San Rafael Discontinued 14 Mar 1999	24 Nov 1996	Cesar O. Intriago Argandena
1116	Guayaquil Ecuador Duran Discontinued 22 Mar 1987 †Guayaquil Ecuador West (939), Guayaquil Ecuador South (1006), Guayaquil Ecuador North (1117)	16 Mar 1980	Lorenzo Augusto Garaycoa
1221	Guayaquil Ecuador Kennedy 22 Mar 1987 †Guayaquil Ecuador West (939), Guayaquil Ecuador South (1006), Guayaquil Ecuador North (1117)	11 Jan 1981	Fausto Montalvan Morla

Missions — 3
(As of Oct. 1, 2011; shown with historical number. See MISSIONS.)

(261) ECUADOR GUAYAQUIL NORTH MISSION
Casilla de Correo 16160
Guayaquil, Ecuador

(160) ECUADOR GUAYAQUIL SOUTH MISSION
Casilla 09-06-286
Guayaquil, Ecuador

(93) ECUADOR QUITO MISSION
Casilla de Correo 17-03-078
Quito, Ecuador

Galapagos Islands

A branch of the Church was organized in the Galapagos Islands in 1998. It is administered as part of the Ecuador Guayaquil South Mission. Meetings are held on the island of San Cristobal, one of several islands that comprise the Galapagos.

In 2002 and 2003, the Academy of LDS dentists, in conjunction with the Charity Anywhere Foundation, conducted service expeditions to the Galapagos to help residents who needed restorative dentistry.

Sources: www.academyofldsdentists.com

EL SALVADOR

Jan. 1, 2011: Est. population, 7,185,000; Members, 109,118; Stakes, 17; Wards, 115; Branches, 46; Missions, 2; Districts, 2; Temples, 2; Percent LDS, 1.4, or one in 70; Central America Area.

El Salvador, in Central America, is a republic with a Spanish, and some Nahuatl-speaking population.

On 20 August 1948, President Arwell L. Pierce of the Mexican Mission visited El Salvador and explored the possibility of sending missionaries to the country. On 26 May 1949, he assigned missionaries Glenn Whipple Skousen and Omer Farnsworth to the country to begin missionary work. A conference was held at San Salvador on 16 February 1951, attended by Elder Albert E. Bowen of the Quorum of the Twelve. There were 63 people present. A short time later, on 2 March 1951, Ana Villasenor became the first person baptized in the country. Eleven others were also baptized that day.

In 1952, Elder Spencer W. Kimball of the Quorum of the Twelve visited the country and offered a prayer of peace and prosperity upon the nation. The country was transferred from the Mexican Mission on 16 November 1952 to the new Central America Mission. The new mission was created the same day. The San Salvador District was organized in January 1965 and was soon followed by the Guatemala-El Salvador Mission. Membership then numbered 4,200. The district was organized as the San Salvador Stake on 3 June 1973. The El Salvador San Salvador Mission was organized on 1 July 1976. At that time the nation had 4,745 members. Ten years later in 1986, membership had climbed to 15,100, and the number of stakes had increased to six. In 1990, the El Salvador San Salvador East Mission was created and membership in the country was 38,000. President Gordon B. Hinckley visited San Salvador on 23 January 1997 and spoke to approximately 10,000 members.

In January 2001, an earthquake rocked El Salvador, killing hundreds of people including 15 Church members. Four weeks later, a second quake hit the country. The Church sent 1.1 million pounds of relief supplies.

El Salvador was one of three Central American countries where the Church, in partnership with California philanthropist and Wheelchair Foundation founder Kenneth Behring, donated 500 wheelchairs in 2001 via the country's First Lady charitable organization. The ceremony in El Salvador, where wheelchairs were presented to the first group of recipients, was attended by El Salvador's first lady, Lourdes Maria Rodriguez.

In 2002, membership reached 90,926.

Elder Spencer V. Jones of the Seventy and president of the Church's Central America Area met with Salvadoran President Elias Antonio Saca at the presidential palace on Feb. 10, 2006. Their hourlong meeting marked the first time a Salvadoran president had met with a delegation from the Church.

The San Salvador El Salvador Temple was dedicated 21 August 2011, by President Thomas S. Monson as the 135th temple in the Church, serving a membership of approximately 110,000 in more than 160 congregations at the time of dedication.

Sources: Central American Mission, Manuscript history and historical reports, Church Archives; El Salvador San Salvador Mission, Manuscript history and historical reports, Church Archives; El Salvador District, Manuscript history and historical reports, Church Archives; Donald Q. Cannon and Richard O. Cowan, Unto Every Nation: Gospel Light Reaches Every Land, 2003; "Growth Leads to Four New Missions, Two in Mexico, Two in Central America Reflect Continuing Missionary Success," Church News, 3 February 1990; "An Outpouring of Love for Prophet: Pres. Hinckley Addresses 88,000 in Central America,"Church News 1 February 1997; Neil Newell, "Earthquake Devastates El Salvador,"Church News, 20 January 2001; Jason Swensen, "Church Sends More Supplies to Distressed Salvadorans,"Church News, 27 January 2001; "Church Aids Quake Victims in El Salvador, India," Ensign, April 2001; "Wheelchairs Given to Central American Nations," Church News, 27 October 2001; "Salvadoran president meets with Church delegation," Church News, 4 March 2006.

Stakes — 18

(Listed alphabetically as of Oct. 1, 2011.)

No.	Name	Organized	First President
Central America Area			
1817	Ahuachapan El Salvador	22 Sep 1991	Juan Antonio Merlos V.
2254	Apopa El Salvador	20 Oct 1996	Julio Alberto Reyes Vargas
2219	Atiquizaya El Salvador	11 Aug 1996	Jose Salvador Molina Linares
2114	Chalchuapa El Salvador	20 Oct 1995	Jose Salvador Molina
2122	Juayua El Salvador	12 Nov 1995	Oswaldo Rodriguez Villata
2839	Paraiso El Salvador	14 June 2009	Rene Armando Sanchez Martinez
1223	San Miguel El Salvador	11 Jan 1981	Carlos Antonio Hernandez
618	*San Salvador El Salvador		
	‡San Salvador (El Salvador)	3 Jun 1973	Mario Edmundo Scheel
1035	San Salvador El Salvador Cuzcatlan	3 Jun 1979	Franklin Henriquez Melgar
741	*San Salvador El Salvador Ilopango	3 Jun 1979	
	‡San Salvador El Salvador East	1 Feb 1976	Alfonso Octavio Diaz
2111	San Salvador El Salvador La Libertad	22 Oct 1995	H. Edgardo Alvarado Renderos
2241	San Salvador El Salvador Layco	22 Sep 1996	E. Leonardo Rivera Herrera
1745a	San Salvador El Salvador Los Heroes	8 Apr 1990	Cristobal A. Hernandez
1744	San Salvador El Salvador Soyapango	8 Apr 1990	Rene Francisco Esquivel G.
1217	Santa Ana El Salvador Modelo	14 Dec 1980	Jorge Alberta Benitez M.
1088	*Santa Ana El Salvador Molino	14 Dec 1980	
	‡Santa Ana El Salvador	2 Dec 1979	Elmer Barrientos
1816	Sonsonate El Salvador	22 Sep 1991	Rolando Arturo Rosales H.
2929	Sonzacate El Salvador	12 Jun 2011	Alvaro R. Cantarero Zelaya

(137a) EL SALVADOR
SAN SALVADOR EAST MISSION
Apartado Postal 3362
San Salvador, El Salvador, C.A.

(181a) EL SALVADOR
SAN SALVADOR WEST MISSION
Boulevard El Hipodromo #537
Colonia San Benito, San Salvador, El Salvador, C.A.

ENGLAND
(See United Kingdom)

EQUATORIAL GUINEA

Jan. 1, 2011: Est. population, 633,000; Members, 339; percent LDS; .05or one in 1,867; Africa Southeast Area.

Equatorial Guinea, previously known as Spanish Guinea, became independent from Spain on 12 October 1968. Located on the coast of Western Africa, near the equator, it's bordered by the Bight of Biafra, Cameroon, and Gabon. The people are predominantly Christian, while others follow pagan practices. The official languages are Spanish and French, with pidgin English, Fang, Bubi, and Ibo also spoken.

Few members live in the country, but occasionally Latter-day Saints have served there in behalf of the United Nations and other humanitarian agencies over the past decades. In March 1980, there was one known member of the Church in the country, Matias Mba Nlutumo, who had been baptized in the Spain Barcelona Mission.

Equatorial Guinea was included in the Ivory Coast Abidjan Mission when the mission was created on 1 February 1992, but by July 2005, it was no longer associated with a mission.

Sources: "News of the Church," Ensign, June 1992; "Three Areas to be Realigned Aug. 15," Church News, 14 June 2003.

ESTONIA

Jan. 1, 2011: Est. population, 1,299,000; Members, 1,043; Districts, 1; Branches, 5; Percent LDS, .07, or one in 1,341; Europe East Area; Baltic Mission.

Estonia, located on the Baltic Sea, is a parliamentary republic made up of various ethnic groups: Estonian 65.3 percent, Russian 28.1 percent, Ukrainian 2.5 percent, Belarusian 1.5 percent, Finn 1 percent, other 1.6 percent (1998). Major religions in Estonia include Evangelical Lutheran, Russian Orthodox, Estonian Orthodox, Baptist, Methodist, Seventh-Day Adventist, Roman Catholic, Pentecostal, Word of Life, and Jewish. The official language is Estonian, but Russian, Ukrainian, and Finnish are also spoken.

In the late 1980s missionaries serving in the Finland Helsinki Mission began to contact Soviet citizens who were visiting Finland. Also, Finnish Latter-day Saints started traveling to Estonia, then part of the Soviet Union, where they began to spread the gospel. Tallinn, Estonia's capital, was one of these initial contact points.

Valttari Rödsä, a native of Tallinn, was baptized in Finland on 16 July 1989 by Wade Ashworth. On 8 December 1989 Finland Helsinki Mission president Steven R. Mecham, his wife Donna, and missionaries Kevin Dexter and David Reagan visited Rödsä in Tallinn. He introduced the missionaries to a group of his family and friends, one of whom, Jaanus Silla, would become one of the first missionaries to be called from the Soviet Union.

The first branch organized in the former Soviet Union was in Tallinn on 28 January 1990, presided over by a Finnish missionary, Hari Aho. Peep Kivit later became the first native branch president. In September 1991, two more branches in Tallinn were organized, one Estonian speaking, the other Russian speaking. The two Estonian branches were combined in the summer of 1997.

To nurture the first Soviet converts, President Mecham organized the Baltic District in January 1990 and called Finnish couples to serve as missionaries to visit Church members in Leningrad and Vyborg, Soviet Union and Tallinn, Estonia, which was still part of the Soviet Union at the time. Jussi Kemppainen, a Finn, served as Baltic District president.

Later that year on 1 July the Finland Helsinki East Mission was officially established with Gary L. Browning as president. This mission was given specific responsibility for missionary work in the USSR, which included Estonia. After September 1991, once Estonia had gained its independence, the Church experienced an increase in growth. That month the city of Tartu was opened for missionary work and two more branches in Tallinn were organized, one was Estonian speaking, the other was Russian. Later, in 1997, the two Estonian branches were combined to consolidate strength.

On 2 February 1992 the Russia St. Petersburg Mission was organized with Charles H. Creel as president. This mission was responsible for Estonia, as well as the other Baltic nations until the Latvia Riga Mission was created on 1 July 1993 encompassing Latvia, Lithuania, and Estonia, under mission president Robert W. Blair. On 16 April 1996 mission headquarters were transferred and the name changed to the Lithuania Vilnius Mission, then changed back to the Latvia Riga Mission on 13 December 2001, and finally it was changed to the Baltic Mission on 1 July 2002.

The Church received government recognition in Estonia on 2 July 1990. However, new Estonian laws passed in 1993 required that the Church be re-registered. In 1994, through the efforts of Jussi Kemppainen and senior missionary James Ames, the Church fulfilled its registration requirements. A few years later, on 21 December 1997 the Tallinn Estonia District was organized.

The first meetinghouse in the Baltic nations was dedicated in Tallinn on 7 November 1999 by Area Authority Seventy Johann A. Wondra. The Book of Mormon in Estonian was published in January 2000.

In 2003, membership reached 625.

Sources: Jaanus Silla Oral History, Church Archives; Kahlile Mehr, Mormon Missionaries Enter Eastern Europe, 2002; "Eight new missions announced," Church News, March 6, 1993; "Focusing on LDS pioneers in Russia," Church News, 8 November 1997; "Seven new missions created," Church News, March 9, 2002; Gary L. Browning, Russia and the Restored Gospel, 1997; Baltic Mission annual history, Church Archives.

ETHIOPIA

Jan. 1, 2011: Est. population, 85,237,000; Members, 1,125; Districts, 1: Branches, 4; Africa Southeast Area; Kenya Nairobi Mission; percent LDS, .001, or 1 in 100,515.

In east central Africa, Ethiopia has a population that speaks Amharic, English, Orominga and Tigrigna and who are primarily Ethiopian Orthodox, Islam, and animist (a belief of conscious life within objects).

From the 1950s-1970s, small groups of foreign Latter-day Saints met in Addis Ababa and Asmara. These Church members and their families worked in Ethiopia in embassies, the U.S. military, and other humanitarian organizations. They held Church meetings in their homes and reported to the Swiss Mission or the International Mission.

In 1974, the Ethiopian government was overthrown and a military committee known as the Dergue assumed leadership. The Dergue, which had overtly anti-church policies, lasted until 1991. During this time, famine struck parts of Ethiopia. In January 1985, the Church held a fast and donated a portion of the money for Ethiopian famine relief. Elder M. Russell Ballard, then a Seventy, and Glenn L. Pace, then managing director of the Welfare Services Department, visited Ethiopia to oversee the Church's donation.

In 1991, Elder Richard P. Lindsay, first president of the Africa Area, began to correspond with Ethiopians who had in various ways heard about the Church. In the summer of 1991, Robert and Gloria DeWitt, Latter-day Saints from America, moved to Addis Ababa, where they worked in the U.S. Embassy. They began to hold church meetings in their home. Also in 1991, Jonas Yirgu Belay, an Ethiopian native, was baptized in Germany. Belay wrote to the DeWitts and told them he was returning to Ethiopia. Shortly after his arrival, he met with the DeWitts for Church services and brought members of his family and friends to the meetings. By spring 1992, 12 people were attending meetings at the DeWitt home.

In August 1992, Elder Lindsay and his counselor in the Area Presidency, Elder J Ballard Washburn, traveled to Ethiopia to locate members and look into possibilities to establish the Church. They met with the DeWitt family and called Robert DeWitt as presiding elder. Shortly thereafter, Ethiopia became part of the Kenya Nairobi Mission.

A. Eugene and L. Ruth Hilton, the first LDS missionaries to serve in Ethiopia, arrived in Addis Ababa in January 1993. The Church was officially recognized in Ethiopia on 16 September 1993. The first branch in Ethiopia was organized on 5 January 1994 with Denisa Girma as president. Girma had been baptized while attending Ricks College in Idaho in 1973. Girma's counselors were Haile Mariam Yadessa and Hine Hasenu.

When the Addis Ababa Branch was organized, the branch moved from the DeWitts' home into the International Community School in southwest Addis Ababa. The first meetinghouse in Ethiopia, built in Addis Ababa, was dedicated on 30 November 2003.

The Book of Mormon was translated into Amharic by Tigist Negash and published in 2000.

In 2001, the Ethiopian government did not renew missionary visas and all non-Ethiopian Christian missionaries had to leave once their visas expired. By August of 2001, no full-time missionaries were serving in Ethiopia. However, local member missionaries continued to bring people into the Church. In September of that year, mission president Raymond Botterell reported that 12 people had been baptized by local "district missionaries."

The Church shipped 6,000 tons of food to famine-stricken areas of Ethiopia in 2003. At the end of the year, there were three branches in Ethiopia: Megenagna and Bekulobet branches in Addis Ababa, and the Debre Zeit Branch.

Membership was 564 in 2003.

Sources: Kenya Nairobi Mission, Annual histories, Church Archives; Kenya Nairobi Mission history, 1998, Church Archives; "First meetinghouse in east African nation," Church News, 20 December 2003; Gloria Robertson DeWitt, Experiences in Ethiopia, Church Archives; BYU NewsNet Website, 12 Oct 2000; Ethiopia Ministry of Internal Affairs, Certificate of Registration, 1993, Church Archives; Kirk T. Waldron Oral History, 1998-2001, Church Archives; "Ethiopian aid," Church News, 15 March 2003; "Severe drought continues to plague Ethiopia," Church News, 14 June 2003; Allen Eugene Hilton interview, 1994, Church Archives.

FIJI

Jan. 1, 2011: Est. population, 944,000; Members, 15,897; Stakes, 4; Wards, 25; Branches, 21; Missions, 1; Districts, 1; Temples, 1; Percent LDS, 1.6 or one in 62; Pacific Area.

Located in western South Pacific, the republic of Fiji has a population that speaks English, Hindustani, and Fijian. The archipelago has 322 islands, of which 106 are inhabited. Between 1874 and 1970 Fiji was a British colony. It gained independence on 10 October 1970.

The first known Latter-day Saint in Fiji was Mele Vea Ashley and her family, who joined the Church in Tonga and moved to Fiji in 1924. There are no records of missionary activity in Fiji prior to the 1950s. Fiji was officially assigned to the New Zealand Mission in 1953, but no missionaries were ever sent. In the 1950s, the Ashley family was joined by the Cecil B. Smith family. Together they held Church meetings in Suva.

On 21 May 1954 the area was reassigned to the Samoan Mission. Mission president Howard B. Stone sent Boyd L. Harris and Sheldon L. Abbott to begin working in Suva. They arrived on 3 September 1954. Missionaries were limited by the multiple languages spoken in Fiji and by a limit of two missionary visas.

Between 22-24 January 1955 President David O. McKay had a layover in Suva during a tour of the South Pacific. On this segment of his trip he was accompanied by President Stone. He met with the missionaries, and attended Sunday services. Twenty-eight people attended that day. The Suva Branch was organized on 7 October 1956 with John A. Bigelow as president. The Fiji District was created in 1957 with missionary Cornell A. Grover as president. Fiji was placed in the Tonga Mission on 15 January 1958. The Tongan mission president regularly passed through Fiji in his travels and new missionaries assigned to Tonga always passed through Fiji. When President McKay dedicated the Suva Branch meetinghouse on 4 May 1958, over 300 were in attendance. Afterwards, the quota of missionaries was increased by six and missionary work began in Lomaloma in the Lau Island group on 18 February 1959 and in Lautoka, Fiji's second largest town, on 9 October 1959.

Gideon Dolo was the first Fijian to serve a mission. He began his service in February 1959 and served locally. Missionary work was begun in other villages during the 1960s and membership gradually increased. Educational efforts were also strengthened. In 1969, a Church primary school was begun with classes held in the Suva Branch meetinghouse. In 1973, it had more than 100 students.

The Fiji Mission (later renamed the Fiji Suva Mission) was created on 23 July 1971, with Sherman A. Lindholm as president. The Fiji District was divided on 8 October 1972 to form the Suva and Vualiku districts.

President Spencer W. Kimball presided over the Fiji Area conference held in the Suva Civic Center on 23 February 1976. Later that year, the Church's Fiji Technical College began holding classes on 10 July 1976. The first copies of the Book of Mormon in Fijian arrived on 29 October 1980. The two districts in Suva were combined into one on 14 March 1982 and the Suva Fiji Stake was organized on 12 June 1983. A milestone was reached on 15 June 1997 when the 100th stake in the Pacific, the Suva Fiji North Stake, was organized.

On 15 October 1997, President Gordon B. Hinckley visited Fiji and spoke to 10,000 people in the National Stadium in Suva. In May 2000, because of political unrest, all missionaries serving in or near the city were transferred to the west side of the island. Later, because of continuing civil unrest, missionaries and mission leaders who were not Fijian citizens were temporarily relocated to New Zealand, leaving missionaries native to Fiji to continue the work. Only a small service was held when the Suva Fiji Temple was dedicated on 18 June 2000. On 21 May 2001, President Hinckley, while returning home from Australia, made a return visit to Fiji. With only 12 hours' notice, 900 Latter-day Saints throughout the island packed a stake center for a 40-minute meeting.

On 21 October 2001, the prime minister of Fiji, Laisania Qarase and his wife, Lemba, attended the Suva Fiji Stake Conference, and expressed appreciation for the good work the Church is doing for the people of Fiji. With a grant from Church Humanitarian Services, members in the Nausori Fiji Stake built a greenhouse where seedlings could grow without being destroyed by rains or the sun. By July 2002, members were enjoying nutritious food and selling the extra.

In 2002, membership reached 13,228 among four stakes; and 13,563 in 2003.

Members observed the Church's golden jubilee with a three-day celebration of culture, service and spirituality 10-12 December 2004 in a festive atmosphere that penetrated the islands and villages for several months. Bearing signs designating the five decades of missionary work in Fiji, returned missionaries and those serving at the time in the Suva Jiji Mission marched onto the field at the Fiji National Outdoor Stadium carrying a mission flag and a national flag, creating an emotional scene for many.

Sources: R. Lanier Britsch, Unto the Isles of the Sea, 1986; Fiji Suva Mission, Annual history and historical reports, Church Archives; Sarah J. Weaver, "Pacific Area Reaches Milestone with 100th Stake," Church News, 19 July 1997; Richard Hunter and Alan Wakely, "Fortress of Faith Prompts Brotherhood and Tears," Church News, 24 June 2000; Alan Wakely and Richard Hunter, "Gospel Shines in Faces of Members in Fiji," Church News, 26 May 2001; Neil K. Newell, "Church Farm in Fiji Offers Hope," Church News, 8 February 2003; "50 years in Fiji," Church News, 18 December 2004.

Stakes — 4
(Listed alphabetically as of Oct. 1, 2011.)

No.	Name	Organized	First President
Pacific Area			
2216	Lautoka Fiji	11 Aug 1996	Jone Sovasova
2040	*Nausori	15 Jun 1997	
	‡Nasinu Fiji	16 Apr 1995	Vilikesa Ravia
1428	Suva Fiji	12 Jun 1983	Inosi Naga
2372	Suva Fiji North	15 Jun 1997	Josefa N.T. Sokia

Mission — 1
(As of Oct. 1, 2011; shown with historical number. See MISSIONS.)

(99) FIJI SUVA MISSION
GPO Box 215
Suva, Fiji Islands

ROTUMA

An isolated 18-square-mile volcanic island, located some 440 miles north of Suva, Fiji, Rotuma has been politically a part of Fiji since 1881, but its 2,000 residents have maintained their Polynesian culture and distinct language.

The first native Rotuman to be baptized was Metuisela Sheffet, who joined the Church in 1961 while living in Fiji. After other Rotumans left the island, joined the Church, and returned to Rotuma, the Oinafa Branch was created in October 1996.

In June 2002, Church Humanitarian Services donated needed medical supplies to the Rotuma hospital in a ceremony attended by all the Rotuman village chiefs, hospital personnel, and many island residents. The supplies were donated to the chairman of the Council of Chiefs by the two missionaries serving on the island, Ben Wanamaker and Adam Chase. Due to scarcity of flights and long boat travel, Latter-day Saints on the island have little direct contact with the outer world.

Sources: R. Lanier Britsch, Metuisela F. Sheffet, interview, 1974, Church Archives; "Medical supplies donated to Rotuma," Church News, 17 August 2002; Fiji Suva Mission, Annual history and historical reports, Church Archives.

FINLAND

Jan. 1, 2011: Est. population, 5,250,000; Members, 4,629; Stakes, 2; Wards, 15; Branches, 15; Missions, 1; Districts, 2; Temples, 1; Percent LDS, .09 or one in 1,154; Europe Area.

Located in northern Europe, the Republic of Finland has a population that speaks Finnish and Swedish, and 83.6 percent are Lutherans.

The first known Finnish native to join the Church was Gustaf Wallgren who was baptized 30 Oct. 1860 in Sweden. He left Sweden to work in Finland in 1861. It is not known if he baptized anyone, although he did report sharing his newfound faith with others. The first missionaries were Swedish brothers Carl A. and John E. Sundstrom. They preached in Vaasa and performed the first baptisms in the country: Johanna Berg and Johanna Sundstrom on 5 May 1876. During the first decade in Finland, the missionaries worked among Swedish-speaking Finns, and by 1886 had baptized 25 people. In the mid 1880s the Finnish government tightened restrictions on religious freedom, and little work was done there with the exception of periodic visits from leaders headquartered in Sweden. In 1903, Elder Francis M. Lyman of the Quorum of the Twelve visited Finland and blessed the land. In 1905 Finland came under the stewardship of the Swedish Mission.

Efforts were made to establish branches in several areas, but none were permanent until Anders and Lovis Stromberg were converted in 1910 in Larsmo. A permanent branch was eventually established there. As late as 1941, all Church members in Finland had their records in Larsmo. With the commencement of World War I all ties between the Larsmo branch and the mission were severed. In 1922, a Finnish law was passed allowing full religious freedom. Still, missionaries did not visit the branch until the 1930s. The beginning of World War II effectively halted missionary work. During the war, packages of food and clothing sent by members in Sweden helped sustain members in Finland. On 11 August 1945 the Larsmo Branch was reorganized. In 1946, seven missionaries from Sweden were sent to Finland.

During his 1946 trip to Europe, Elder Ezra Taft Benson then of the Quorum of the Twelve, visited Finland and blessed the land. Up to this time, missionary work was focused only on the Swedish minority that lived in Finland, but that changed with the arrival in Finland of Mark E. Anderson on 3 November 1946. He had been given the assignment to learn Finnish and preach among the Finnish-speaking majority. Other missionaries assigned to learn Finnish were soon to follow.

On 1 September 1947 the Finnish Mission was officially organized with Henry A. Matis, an American with Finnish roots, as president. Membership in Finland was 129 when Matis arrived. During the seven years that he served, the Church gained legal status (1 July 1948), began microfilming Finnish Church records (December 1948-November 1955) and translated and published the Book of Mormon in Finnish (December 1954). English lessons and basketball became effective missionary tools during those years. During the 1952 Olympic Games in Helsinki, President Matis served as liaison for the United States Olympic Committee and missionaries served as interpreters for the various U.S. teams.

Between 1955 and 1958 several plays were staged under the direction of Fred Adams, who went on to found the Utah Shakespearean Festival in Cedar City, Utah. The first meetinghouse specifically built for Church services was dedicated in Hämeenlinna on 20 Dec. 1959. The first temple trip to Switzerland for Finnish-speaking Latter-day Saints was made in June 1960 when the temple ceremony in Finnish became available.

In August 1976, President Spencer W. Kimball spoke to nearly 2,000 members at an area conference in Helsinki. The next year, the Helsinki Stake, was organized on 16 Oct. 1977.

Finnish members were the first to introduce the gospel to Estonia and parts of Russia (see Estonia history). The Helsinki East Mission was created in 1990 to serve members in Leningrad and other areas in the Soviet Union. It was discontinued with the creation of the Russia missions in 1991, although Finnish leaders were among those called to serve in Russia.

Nearly half the members in Finland attended the commemoration of the 50th anniversary of the Finnish Mission, held in September of 1997. Among them was 92-year-old Henry A. Matis.

In general conference on 2 April 2000, President Gordon B. Hinckley announced that a temple would be built in Helsinki, and ground was broken for the temple in the Helsinki suburb of Espoo, 29 March 2003. Two former missionaries have returned to Finland as U.S. ambassadors, Mark A. Austad, who served as ambassador 1975-1977, and Keith Nyborg who served 1981-1986.

The president of the Republic of Finland, Tarja Halonen, visited Salt Lake City, Utah, during the 2002 Winter Olympics. While there she met with President Gordon B. Hinckley at a private reception prior to the official Olympic Banquet of Finland that featured a 100-voice men's choir of missionaries who had served in Finland.

The Helsinki Finland Temple was dedicated 22 October 2006 in four sessions by President Gordon B. Hinckley, his 95th dedication or rededication of the Church's then 124 temples. The temple district spanned 12 time zones, including most of Russia, to be the largest temple district of the time. Proceedings of the dedication were broadcast by satellite to 62 sites throughout eastern Europe to an estimated 15,000 members.

Sources: Arnold K Garr, Donald, Q. Cannon, and Richard O. Cowan, eds., Encyclopedia of Latter-day Saint History, 2000, 376-377; Finnish Mission Society, Suomi Calls, 1957; Kati Hietala, "Finland's Temple Groundbreaking: Hundreds gather at traditional site for beautiful ceremony," Church News, 5 April 2003; Finland Helsinki Mission (Finnish Mission), Manuscript history and historical reports, Church Archives; Henry A. Matis Family Society, Muistamme, 1997; "Six Temples Announced," Church News, 8 April 2000; Shaun Stahle, Temple dedicated in Helsinki, Finland, Church News, 28 October 2006.

Stakes — 2

(Listed alphabetically as of Oct. 1, 2011.)

No.	Name	Organized	First President
Europe Area			
865	Helsinki Finland	16 Oct 1977	Kari Juhani Aslak Haikkola
1408	Tampere Finland	17 Apr 1983	Kari Juhani Aslak Haikkola

Mission — 1

(As of Oct. 1, 2011; shown with historical number. See MISSIONS.)

FRANCE

Jan. 1, 2011: Est. population, 64,058,000; Members, 35,960; Stakes, 9; Wards, 57; Branches, 54; Missions, 2; Districts, 2; Percent LDS, .05, or one in 1,835; Europe Area.

In western Europe, France has a population that speaks French, and includes minorities who speak Breton, Alsatian, German, Flemish, Italian, Basque, and Catalan. The population of France is mostly Roman Catholic.

The first mention of France in the history of the Church is a report of a council meeting held at Nauvoo, Illinois, 6 May 1844, when it was voted to send Almon W. Babbit there on a mission. For reasons unknown, Babbitt never went. In a general conference of the British Mission held in Manchester, England on 14 August 1848, it was resolved that William Howells of Wales would be sent to France and Brittany to preach the gospel.

The French Mission was organized on 18 June 1849, and a month later, Howells arrived in Le Havre, France. He experienced some frustration, but on 30 July 1849, baptized Augustus Saint d'Anna, a "single, intelligent young man." A month later Howells traveled to St. Malo, where, later that same year, he baptized a man named Pebble and a young woman named Anna Browse. Browse had been ill for years and her friends feared that her baptism in the icy waters of the bay would end her life, but her illness left after she emerged from the waters and her health was restored.

In February 1850, Howells traveled to Boulogne and distributed tracts with greater success. The Boulogne-sur-Mer Branch was organized with six members on 6 April 1850. On 18 June of the same year Elder John Taylor of the Quorum of the Twelve and Curtis E. Bolton arrived in Boulogne, accompanied by Howells. John Pack and two Englishmen called by Taylor to assist in the work joined them a few days later. Over a period of a few weeks, Taylor held several public meetings and debates with little success before traveling to Paris.

While in Paris, the missionaries devoted their time to translating Mormon literature into French and writing new tracts. They continued to preach the gospel, but due to the difficulty with the language, the work progressed slowly. However, by November 1850 there were a few people desiring baptism, so on 8 December 1850 a branch was organized in Paris.

In December 1851, John Taylor appointed Curtis E. Bolton as president of the French Mission. By this time there had been four branches established: Paris, Le Grande Luce, Le Havre and Boulogne-sur-Mer. Opposition and government restrictions due to the unsettled state of political affairs under Napoleon III slowed progress. The government prohibited the gathering of any more than 20 people, making it difficult for the missionaries to hold meetings. Church members were also prohibited from publishing materials expounding Mormon doctrine. John Taylor was forced to leave the country when he defied the printing ban in 1851 with a tract entitled, "The Kingdom of God." In 1852, the French translation of the Book of Mormon was completed, but members were blocked by law from distributing it.

The work continued very slowly over the next several years. In 1859, Louis Adolphe Bertrand, a member of the original Paris Branch, was called to preside over the mission, but in 1864, Betrand left France, bound for Utah. The Emperor would not allow Mormonism in France and the mission was officially closed with Bertrand's departure. After the mission's closure, several attempts were made to re-establish missionaries in the country, but none met with lasting success until the French Mission was re-organized in 1912.

In spite of the mission closure, in 1890 a unique group of Latter-day Saint missionaries arrived in France. In the spring of that year John Hafen wrote a letter to the First Presidency requesting that he and two other aspiring artists be allowed to go to Paris to pursue their training in the arts. They wished to gain the skill necessary to paint the murals inside the nearly completed Salt Lake Temple. Their request was granted and on 3 June 1890 Hafen, Lorus Pratt, and John B. Fairbanks were called as "art missionaries." They arrived in Paris on 24 July of that year and were later joined by Edwin Evans and Herman Haag. They studied at the Julian Academy. They returned home in 1892 and immediately made plans to complete the murals in the garden and world rooms of the temple. The murals were completed, just in time for the dedication of the temple on 6 April 1893.

A meeting was held in Lille on 27 June 1909 by the missionaries of the French Conference. It was attended by approximately 50 members. It was the first meeting held by the Church within French boundaries since the religious expulsion of the 1860s.

On 15 October 1912, the French Mission was re-organized with Edgar Brossard as president. The mission, much larger in area this time, included French-speaking sections in western Switzerland and southern Belgium. Only two years later, with the threat of World War I, all missionaries were withdrawn. After the war in November of 1919, Elder George Albert Smith of the Quorum of the Twelve visited France to meet with the Saints. Not until 24 February 1924 was the French Mission formally re-organized with Russell H. Blood as president. It was headquartered in Geneva, Switzerland.

Missionaries worked hard to build the Church's image by getting involved in the communities. Some helped by singing in groups while others played on successful basketball teams. Two new branches were established in Lille and Blois on 5 August 1930. The Mission headquarters were moved from Geneva to Paris on 1 October of that year, and then from Paris to Liege, Belgium, in 1936 because the majority of the converts were being found in the Belgian District. From 1932 to 1936, branch after branch was closed because fewer missionaries could serve due to the Great Depression. Golden L. Woolf, mission president at the time, made an appeal to local members to share the gospel in their own country. Many volunteered their time to keep the work progressing. Members were encouraged by an increase in the arrival of American missionaries in late 1936 and a visit by President Heber J. Grant in June of 1937.

In 1939, at the onset of World War II, missionaries and mission President Joseph E. Evans were evacuated. This left a local leader, Leon Fargier, as the sole, active priesthood holder in France. With the approval of priesthood leaders, Fargier almost single-handedly conducted the affairs of the Church in France during the war. On foot or bicycle he traveled around the country to members' homes, often across enemy lines, to administer the sacrament, bless, baptize, confirm, confer the priesthood and simply administer to the needs of the Saints.

After World War II, missionary worked resumed. Elder Ezra Taft Benson of the Quorum of the Twelve arrived in April of 1946 to tour the French Mission and assess the condition of the members and the country. One month later, James L. Barker arrived to re-open the mission and re-establish its headquarters in Paris. Over the next several years, missionaries continued to arrive as did thousands of cases of food, clothing and bedding. These supplies were shipped from Salt Lake City to support members and missionaries suffering because of the economic crisis following the war. Many branches were re-opened, while new ones were organized, including Belfort, Toulouse, Lille, and Cannes.

On 13 July 1952, a mission-wide conference was held and was attended by President David O. McKay, who was en route to Switzerland to announce a temple in that country. Three months later, on 9 October 1952, the Church was granted status by the French Government as "Une Association Etranger" (A Foreign Society).

As of 1 January 1947, when missionary work resumed after the war, there were 13 active branches in the mission, 754 members and 13 missionaries.

The late 1950s proved to be especially challenging for the French Mission. It was soon discovered that a group of missionaries was studying questionable doctrine rather than teaching the fundamental elements of the gospel. A growing number of missionaries began to foster beliefs contrary to the teachings of the Church. When mission President Milton Christensen became aware of the apostasy within the mission, he notified the First Presidency. Interviews were held with the missionaries involved to discover their convictions. Nine were excommunicated and left the mission.

In the years following the excommunications, Edgar Brossard served as mission president and under his leadership, the mission reached the high point of its history. In January of 1960, in anticipation of the new year, mission leadership set a goal of 400 baptisms, more than twice that of prior years. By June the goal had been surpassed and was revised to 800. Total baptisms reached more than 900 that year.

In June 1960, a building project was announced for the construction of chapels in Europe through the use of "labor missionaries." The Bordeaux Chapel was dedicated by Elder Howard W. Hunter of the Quorum of the Twelve on 10 December 1965. Less than a year later, on 23 October 1966, the first Latter-day Saint meetinghouse in the Paris area was dedicated. In the next decade, land was purchased and chapels were completed in Sceaux, Nogent, Nantes, Paris, Epinay, Rennes, Brest, Le Mans and Angouleme.

In 1961, the French-East Mission, later named the Switzerland Geneva Mission was organized. It covered eastern France and the French- Speaking portion of Switzerland. It was followed in 1963 by the formation of the Franco-Belgian Mission, later named the Belgium Brussels Mission. This mission covered northern Franch and the French-speaking portion of Belgium. In 1970, the name of the French Mission was changed to the France Mission, and in 1974 to the France Paris Mission. The France Toulouse Mission was created from portions of the France Paris and Switzerland Geneva Missions.

The Paris France Stake, the first stake in France, was created 16 November 1975. There were 28,454 members organized into seven stakes by 1996. President Spencer W. Kimball spoke to 4,200 members at an area conference in Paris in 1976.

The France Bordeaux Mission was created in 1989, and the France Marseille Mission was created 1 July 1991. They were later consolidated into the France Toulouse and France Paris Missions in 2001.

President Gordon B. Hinckley visited and spoke in Versailles and Paris on 4 June 1998, and again on 28 May 2004, as part of a European tour. Speaking of temples, he encouraged the French members to be patient, and told them that they were "worthy of the richest blessings of the Church" and was confident that "sometime in the future a beautiful house of the Lord [would] grace this land."

By 2002, membership reached 31,971; and 32,353 in 2003.

President Thomas S. Monson confirmed in the October 2001 general conference that a temple will be built in Paris.

Sources: "Moments in History," Church News, 31 July 1971; "The Church in Europe," Ensign, August 1973; J. Malan Heslop. "Church's Second Generation Growth is Strong in France," Church News, 1 December 1973; John L. Hart, "New Missions Are Evidence of Church's Dynamic Growth," Church News, 25 February 1989; Alain Marie, "Leon Fargier: His Faith Wouldn't Go Underground," Ensign, September 1991; "New Areas Created in Asia, Europe," Church News, 7 September 1991; "You Are Worthy of the Richest Blessings: A Temple Will be Built in France, Says President Hinckley" Church News, 5 June 2004; William Howell, Millennial Star, 1 September 1849, William Howell, Millennial Star, 1 October 1849; William Howell, Millennial Star, 1 January 1850; William Howell, Millennial Star, 15 March 1850; William Howell, Millennial Star, 15 May 1850; Curtis E. Bolton, Journal, Church Archives; France Paris Mission, Manuscript history and historical reports, Church Archives; Gary Ray Chard, A History of the French Mission of the Church of Jesus Christ of Latter-day Saints 1850-1960, 1965; Linda Jones Gibb, "The Paris Art Mission," Pioneer, January/February 1994.

Stakes — 9
(Listed alphabetically as of Oct. 1, 2011.)

No.	Name	Organized	First President
Europe Area			
2623	Angers France	14 Dec 2003	Alain Charles Roger Marie
1867	Bordeaux France	24 May 1992	Jacquie Simonet
1669	Lille France	17 Jan 1988	Dominique Degrave
1772	Lyon France	9 Sep 1990	Pierre-Marie Brenders
1413	Nancy France	24 Apr 1983	John Keith Bishop
1130	Nice France	14 May 1980	Joseph Michel Paya
731	Paris France	16 Nov 1975	Gerard Giraud-Carrier
1850	Paris France East	8 Mar 1992	Dominique Calmels
2606	Toulouse France	22 Sep 2002	John Paul Guerinot

Missions — 2
(As of Oct. 1, 2011; shown with historical number. See MISSIONS.)

(6) FRANCE PARIS MISSION	(262) FRANCE LYON MISSION
23, rue du Onze Novembre	8, Chemin William Barbey
78110 Le Vesinet	1292 Chambesy (GE)
France	Switzerland

FRENCH GUIANA

Jan. 1, 2011: Est. population, 195,000; Members, 368; Branches, 3; Percent LDS, .16, or one in 637; Caribbean Area; West Indies Mission.

French Guiana is an overseas department of France located in northern South America.

Charles Fortin, a native of French Guiana, was baptized in France and returned to his homeland in 1980. Rosiette Fauvette, also baptized in France, returned to French Guiana on 8 July 1981. She attended Sunday meetings at Fortin's home in Cayenne. Charles Fortin introduced the Church to many people before his death in April 1986. By then, several other members were attending services, including Gerard Charpentier, who later became the first branch president in Kourou. Meetings were then held in the home of the Masinski family until January 1987 when they were moved to Rosiette Fauvette's home in Kourou. In August 1987, the Francois Pratique family moved from France to Cayenne and began attending meetings.

Elder Charles Didier of the Seventy visited on 4 March 1988 and organized a group. On 5 November 1988, Serge and Christie Bonnoit of France became the first converts in French Guiana. On 25 May 1989, the Kourou Branch was formed and in August, the Cayenne Branch was created with Francois Pratique as president.

In July 1989, the first missionary couple Wilbur and Jacqueline Wortham arrived in the country. They were followed in November 1989 by A. Edward and Louise P. Schmidt. The newly organized branch in Cayenne had about 23 members. On 27 February 1990, Elder M. Russell Ballard of the Quorum of the Twelve blessed the land and with Elder Charles A. Didier of the Seventy visited branch members in both Cayenne and Kourou.

The Church has grown slowly in French Guiana due to members immigrating to France and lack of sustained priesthood leadership. A chapel was constructed in Cayenne and was dedicated on 18 March 1999 by West Indies Mission president Kenneth J. Mason.

Membership in 2002 was 251.

Source: Rosiette Fauvette, Reminiscence, Church Archives; Jacqueline Wortham, Our Mission in French Guiana, Church Archives; A. Edward and Louise P. Schmidt, Interview, 14 October 2003, Church Archives; "Services in 3 South American Nations and Island Republic," Church News, 10 March 1990; West Indies Mission, Manuscript history and historical reports, Church Archives.

FRENCH POLYNESIA

(Tahiti)

Jan. 1, 2011: Est. population, 287,000; Members, 21,245; Stakes, 6; Wards,53; Branches, 29; Missions, 1; Districts, 3; Temples, 1; Percent LDS, 7.1, or one in 14; Pacific Area.

Located in the South Pacific midway between South America and Australia, the French Polynesia archipelago is a French overseas territory. Tahiti's population speaks French and Tahitian. Most of the French speaking Polynesians are Protestants.

On 11 May 1843, Joseph Smith called Addison Pratt to serve a mission to the Pacific Islands. Pratt was joined by Noah Rogers, Benjamin F. Grouard, and Knowlton F. Hanks. Hanks died during the voyage and the three remaining missionaries first arrived at Tubuai in the Society Islands on 30 April 1844. Pratt remained on the island of Tubuai and Rogers and Grouard continued to Tahiti, arriving on 14 May. Pratt had been to Hawaii as a young man and knew some Hawaiian words that were cognate with the Tahitian language. This helped him make an initial favorable impression with the natives. The first convert on Tubuai was Ambrose Alexander, a non-native shipbuilder, who was baptized on 15 June 1844 and became the first person to join the Church in the Pacific Islands. Ten more joined five weeks later (five Europeans and five natives) and the Tubuai Branch was organized on 28 July.

Grouard and Rogers, in the course of trying to learn Tahitian, taught the gospel to the few Europeans and Americans on the island. The first converts on the island of Tahiti were Mr. and Mrs. Seth George Lincoln, friends made during the missionaries' voyage. The two missionaries separated in October 1844 and began visiting other islands. Rogers experienced little success and returned to the United States in late 1845. Grouard visited the Tuamotu Islands and experienced some success, though at great personal sacrifice and effort. He was later joined by Pratt, and their converts numbered in the hundreds. Pratt returned to the United States in 1848, but came back to Tahiti with his family in 1850. This promising start for the Church was halted when French government restrictions led to the mission being closed in May 1852.

The work was resumed in 1892 by missionaries Joseph W. Damron and William A. Seegmiller, who found that most of the early members had fallen away. They started branches again among those who had remained stalwart, and built meetinghouses that helped speed the work. The largest branch was on Tuamotu and was headquarters for the missionaries. A language-learning program was begun in 1898, and the Tahitian Book of Mormon was finished on 7 July 1899 but was not published until 1904. After the turn of the century, there was a gradual trend toward centralization of the Church in Papeete, the main port of call for sailing vessels. In October 1906, the missionaries completed a new mission home and meeting hall. Having new headquarters did much to elevate the Church in the eyes of missionaries, members, and nonmembers alike.

Elder David O. McKay of the Quorum of the Twelve and his traveling companion, Hugh J. Cannon, visited Papeete on 11 April 1921. Elder Rufus K. Hardy of the First Council of the Seventy visited Tahiti in May-June 1939 and encouraged the calling of local Saints to be branch leaders to free the missionaries to do more work among the people and to expand their effors to the outlying islands. Tahiti was never attacked during World War II, but all foreign missionaries were recalled. Ernest C. Rossiter and his wife, Venus arrived in 1941 and presided over the Church during the war. Local members were called to act in the supervisory positions previously held by foreign elders. Foreign missionaries returned to Tahiti in June 1946. A large meetinghouse and mission home was built in Papeete and dedicated by Elder Matthew Cowley of the

Quorum of the Twelve on 22 January 1950. The meetinghouse later served as the first stake center in Tahiti. That same year, the Church bought an 82-foot two-masted schooner in San Pedro, California. It arrived in Papeete on 8 April 1950. The ship was rechristened the Paraita (or the "Pratt") after the Tahitian name of Addison Pratt. The Paraita was used to transport missionaries, members, and the mission president from island to island. It was eventually sold in July 1961.

Missionary work among the French-speaking people of the islands began in 1955 and a French-speaking branch was organized on 13 October 1957. Completion of the New Zealand Temple in 1958 was a blessing for the Tahitian Saints, who proved to be faithful attenders. On 23 May 1963, in the worst-recorded sea disaster for Latter-day Saint members in the South Pacific, 15 members of the Maupiti Branch, about 160 miles northwest of Tahiti, lost their lives when the boat in which they were returning from a meetinghouse dedication sank on the Maupiti reef. Elder Gordon B. Hinckley, then of the Quorum of the Twelve, visited the bereaved branch members to offer solace and comfort.

In 1964, the Church constructed an elementary school in Tahiti, and on 14 May 1972 the Tahiti Stake was organized, the first in Tahiti. The new stake consisted of all the former branches on Tahiti and Moorea. On 1-2 March 1976, Presidents Spencer W. Kimball and N. Eldon Tanner, along with nine other General Authorities, met in Papeete for an area conference. The Papeete Tahiti Temple was dedicated by President Gordon B. Hinckley, then a counselor in the First Presidency, on 27 October 1983. The Pirae Tahiti Stake, Tahiti's second stake, was created in 1982, and the Paea Tahiti Stake, its third, in 1990. In 1991, Saints in Takaroa in the Tuamotu islands observed the 100th anniversary of a meetinghouse built by early members, the oldest in the South Pacific. The imposing building took 20 years to complete.

In 1994, members celebrated the 150th anniversary of the missionaries arriving in their islands. Closer relations with other religions resulted as Elder Russell M. Nelson of the Quorum of the Twelve was formally introduced to the territory's president and full cabinet. President Gaston Flosse and other top government leaders attended several events. President Gordon B. Hinckley was welcomed to French Polynesia by President Flosse on 15 October 1997.

On 11 January 2000, President Gaston Flosse, of the Territory of French Polynesia, Vice President Edward Fritche and 15 government ministers attended a dinner at the mission home in Papeete, hosted by Mission President Ralph T. Andersen and local stake and district presidents. When a new administration building of the French Polynesia presidency was inaugurated in 2000, a 400-voice Latter-day Saint regional choir, composed of members from the five stakes in Papeete, sung at the ceremonies that were part of a weeklong 16th anniversary celebration of the autonomy of the French Polynesia Territory.

Following the 11 September 2001 terrorists attacks on America, Latter-day Saints in French Polynesia joined 3,000 others, including Tahiti President Gaston Flosse, in a memorial service in Papeete for the victims. As part of the service, all American missionaries were asked to go to the podium and sing the American national anthem. Afterwards, President Flosse and other government officials went to the podium and shook hands with the missionaries, symbolically showing their love and solidarity to the American people.

A lease was granted to the Church in June 2002 for property near the University of French Polynesia campus on which to build an institute building. On 27 July 2003, a 400-voice choir of Church members of five stakes sang before a gathering of 30,000 people who gathered to welcome French President Jacques Chirac to Tahiti.

Members held a three-day celebration 8-10 October 2005 in Papeete to commemorate the 160-year anniversary of the arrival of the first missionaries. An evening program included a 500-voice choir performing musical numbers in Tahitian and French to a congregation of about 3,000, with proceedings broadcast to a larger television audience. Also part of the program, a large replica of the whaling ship Timoleon seemed to sail across the stage carrying the first three missionaries to arrive.

MARQUESAS ISLANDS

The Marquesas Islands are approximately 1,000 miles northeast of Tahiti and are among the largest island groups of French Polynesia. The islands were first visited by Elders Edgar L. Cropper and Eli Horton in 1899. They arrived on 30 May and found the inhabitants already committed to either the Roman Catholic or Protestant religions. Subsequent missionaries also had no success and the last missionaries left in July 1904. Tahitian Mission president Kendal Young attempted to establish missionary work in the Marquesas Islands in 1961, but again the missionaries were not successful.

Other missionaries were sent in the 1980s and again had no success. Rudolphe Etienne and Marie Hana Teura Tua served on the island of Hiva Oa in the Marquesas Islands in 1989 and were able to teach and baptize four large families on 12 October 1991, including Robert O'Conner who became the first branch president on the islands. His wife, Ziella Vivish O'Conner, is a native Tahitian and he is a Marquesian. She had joined the Church in her youth and was the only known member when the Tuas arrived. The first meetinghouse in the Marquesas Islands was dedicated on 11 May 1998.

Sources: Andrew Jenson, Encyclopedic History of the Church, 1941; R. Lanier Britsch, Unto the Islands of the Sea, 1986; Yves R. Perrin, L'Histoire de l'Eglise Mormone en Polynesie Francaise de 1844 a 1982, 1982; Tahitian Mission, Manuscript history and historical reports, Church Archives; Kathleen C. Perrin, "Link to the Past, Hope for Future," Church News, 9 February 1991; Kathleen C. Perrin, "150th Year of Church in Tahiti," Church News, 7 May 1994; John L. Hart, "LDS Note 150 Years in French Polynesia," Church News, 14 May 1994; John L. Hart, "Sesquicentennial: 'Spiritual Feast,'" Church News, 21 May 1994; John L. Hart, "Tireless Couple Influenced Many Lives, Church News, 18 February 1995; Gerry Avant, "Prophet Goes to Islands of the Pacific,"Church News, 25 October 1997; "French Polynesian President Meets with Church Leaders," Church News, 26 February 2000; "Choir Sings at Inauguration," Church News, 2 December 2000; "A Common Prayer for Peace," Church News, 27 October 2001.

Stakes — 7
(Listed alphabetically as of Oct. 1, 2011.)

No.	Name	Organized	First President
Pacific Area			
573	*Arue Tahiti	28 May 1995	
	*Papeete Tahiti		
	‡Tahiti	14 May 1972	Raituia Tehina Tapu
2398	Faaa Tahiti	21 Sep 1997	Benajmin Tauraa Sinjoux

1747	Paea Tahiti	15 Apr 1990	Jean Alexis Tefan
2054	*Papeari Tahiti	21 Sep 1997	
2915	Punaauia Tahiti	1 May 2011	Ahyn Claude Nauta
1355	*Papeete Tahiti		
	‡Pirae Tahiti	20 Jun 1982	Lysis G. Terooatea
1962a	*Raromatai Tahiti 7 Jan 1994		
	‡Uturoa Tahiti Raiatea	5 Dec 1993	Michel Just Doucet

Mission — 1

(As of Oct. 1, 2011; shown with historical number. See MISSIONS.)

(3) TAHITI PAPEETE MISSION
B.P. 93
Papeete, Tahiti
French Polynesia

GUADELOUPE
Jan. 1, 2011: Est. population, 449,000; Members, 423; Branches, 4; District 1; Percent LDS, .09, or one in 1,172; Caribbean Area; West Indies Mission.

The Caribbean Island of Guadeloupe is a department of France.

Among the first converts in Guadeloupe was the Claire Dinane family. Dinane came into contact with the Church because of his duties as a customs officer where he met Latter-day Saints. His family soon moved, but a nucleus of members had joined the Church through contact with Dinane. The Guadeloupe Branch was organized 10 June 1982, but was discontinued several months later due to the apostasy of a member of the Church.

In June 1984, West Indies Mission President Kenneth Zabriskie sent French-speaking missionaries to Guadeloupe who had been transferred from French-speaking missions in Europe. Through their efforts the Grande-Terre Branch was organized by Elder Ronald E. Poelman of the Seventy on 24 August 1984. The branch was strengthened by Dusan Kolvic, a Yugoslavian refugee who learned of the Church in France, but was not baptized. Kolvic's work as a policeman for the French government required a transfer to Guadeloupe, and one evening he was dispatched to arrest a drunkard who was attacking two missionaries. Kolvic later joined the Church and served as branch president from 1986-1988. Because of Guadeloupe's connection to France, there have been several members from France, who have lived on the island for a few years and brought valuable experience to the Church there. Michel Menardin served as a branch president in Angouleme, France, before moving to Guadeloupe. He was called again as a branch president in 1995.

The first missionary from Guadeloupe was Claude Gamiette who served a mission in Florida from 1991-1993. He has also served as a branch president in Basse-Terre, and in 2004, was called as a counselor in the West Indies Mission presidency. On 19 April 1998, West Indies Mission President Kenneth J. Mason dedicated the first meetinghouse in Guadeloupe at Basse-Terre. Four years later, on 12 May 2002, the Basse-Terre Guadeloupe District was organized with Jean Bernard Otto as president. By 2010, there where nine branches in the district, with five in Guadeloupe, two in Martinique, and one each in St. Martin and Bonaire.

Sources: Kenneth L. Zabriskie, History of the West Indies Mission, [ca. 1989], Church Archives; Kenneth L. Zabriskie interview, 2003, Church Archives; West Indies Mission, Manuscript history and historical reports, Church Archives; Elden L. Wood, Autobiography, 1994, Church Archives; Hendrik Dorenbosch, Telephone conversation, 21 June 2004.

MARTINIQUE
Jan. 1, 2011: Est. population, 433,000; Members, 203; Branches, 2; Percent LDS, .04 or one in 2,328; Caribbean Area; West Indies Mission.

The Caribbean island of Martinique is a department of France and is the northernmost of the Windward Islands.

Andre Condoris, a young man baptized in France while serving in the military, returned to his homeland on 9 August 1980 and was the first known convert from the country. In July 1983, West Indies Mission President Kenneth Zabriskie visited Andre Condoris and Joell Joseph- Agathe, who had also been baptized in France. The two members welcomed missionaries Mark Richards, Stan Jones, and David Simons on 4 May 1984, and held the first meeting on May 6. One month later Elder Ronald E. Poelman of the Seventy visited and a few months later Elder Vaughn J. Featherstone of the Seventy visited. The Martinique Branch was organized 10 October 1985. The work has been slow in the country partly due to opportunities for members to immigrate to France. Since 1997, Paul Colombe Caussier has been Martinique's branch president.

Sources: Kenneth L. Zabriskie, History of the West Indies Mission, [ca. 1989], Church Archives; Kenneth L. Zabriskie interview, 2003, Church Archives.

NEW CALEDONIA
Jan. 1, 2011: Est. population, 227,000; Members, 1,949; Branches, 8; Districts, 1; Percent LDS, .83, or one in 121; Pacific Area; Fiji Suva Mission.

An overseas territory of France, New Caledonia is a group of islands in the South Pacific east of Australia. New Caledonia is the largest of the islands (about the size of New Jersey).

The first Latter-day Saints in New Caledonia were servicemen stationed there during World War II. Servicemen's groups held meetings in Noumea beginning in 1943. The last group was disbanded in 1946. There is no known Church activity in New Caledonia from 1946 until the 1950s when a few Tahitian members migrated there to work in a nickel smelter. They were organized into the Noumea Branch on 21 October 1961 with Teahumanu Manoi as president. The branch became part of the French Polynesian Mission. Manoi later became the first president of the New Caledonia District.

Missionary work was delayed for many years because of visa restrictions. On 15 July 1968, the first two missionaries arrived, Harold and Jeannine Richards, and their daughter, Jacquelina. Restrictions on additional missionaries delayed James A. Tatton and Lyle W. Parker from entering until January 1969.

Harold Richards negotiated the purchase of property for the Noumea Branch meetinghouse. It was dedicated on 24 December 1972. In June 1975, New Caledonia and the Noumea Branch were transferred to the Fiji Suva Mission. The Noumea Branch was divided on 16 May 1976 and the meetinghouse was enlarged. The Tontouta Branch was organized from the Noumea 2nd Branch on 18 June 1978.

In February 1982, the government lifted its quota on the number of missionaries of French citizenship who could serve in that country and granted permission for four non-French missionaries to enter. With more missionaries Church membership doubled by 1992. In 2001, membership was 1,571. President Gordon B. Hinckley visited Noumea on 17 June 2000 as part of a six-nation tour of Asia and the South Pacific. About 1,000 members crowded into the local meetinghouse to hear the Church leader, and many more gathered outside in tents, where the proceedings of the meeting were relayed via video feed.

In 2002, membership reached 1,631.

Sources: Servicemen's Group (398th Army Service Forces Band), Meeting minutes and attendance records, 1943-1944, Church Archives; Servicemen's Group (New Caledonia), Meeting minutes and attendance records, 1944-1946, Church Archives; R. Lanier Britsch, Unto the Islands of the Sea, 1986; Fiji Suva Mission, Manuscript history and historical reports, Church Archives; Noumea New Caledonia District, Manuscript history and historical reports, Church Archives; Wilford and Ruth Smith, Our Fiji Suva Mission, 1981-1984, 1985; "We Have Been on a Long Journey," Church News, 1 July 2000.

RÉUNION

Jan. 1, 2011: Est. population, 777,000; Members, 851; Districts, 1; Branches, 4; Percent LDS, .1, or one in 985; Africa Southeast Area; Madagascar Antananarivo Mission.

Réunion is a volcanic island in the Indian Ocean, east of Madagascar. Réunion became an overseas department of France in 1947. Eighty-six percent of the people are Christian, while the rest of the population are Hindu, Muslim, and Buddhist. French is the official language, while Creole is widely spoken.

The first known members of the Church to live in Réunion were Alain and Danielle Chion-Hock, who were baptized in Montpellier, France, on 19 April 1969. They returned to Réunion in 1969. Shortly thereafter, he Chion-Hocks began holding sacrament meetings under the direction of the International Mission. On 3 July 1977, their daughter Catherine, became the first to be baptized on Réunion. Over time, other Latter-day Saints, mostly from France, moved to Reunion and joined the group. They subsequently made a request to the International Mission that missionaries be sent to the island.

In October 1979, missionaries Joseph and Ruth Edmunds arrived. That was followed by the organization of The St. Denis Branch on 30 December 1979, with Alain Chion-Hock as president. The same day Alain Chion-Hock's sister, Rose Thia Soui Tchong and her two sons, Richard and Jacquy, were baptized, the first convert baptisms in Reunion. On 29 April 1981, Elder Carlos E. Asay of the First Quorum of Seventy and president of the International Mission became the first General to visit the island.

During her missionary service with her husband, Edward, between 1982 and 1984, Louise P. Schmidt introduced the seminary and institute curriculum to the area.

On 11 August 1982, the Mascarene Island District was created. It was renamed the St. Denis Reunion District in 1997. In 1984, the St. Pierre Branch was organized, followed in 1985 by the organization of the St. Paul Branch.

On 20 January 1984, Christopher B. Munday, Richard Fourtina, Alain Jacky Gathercole, and Rene Leon Ernest Montulet, arrived on Réunion as the first young missionaries. Nelly Lycurgue, the first missionary called from Réunion, served in the France Paris Mission from July 1985 to January 1987. In 1986, Réunion Island became part of the South Africa Johannesburg Mission, and on 1 July 1988 it became part of the Mascarene Islands Mission. Elder Marvin J. Ashton became the first member of the Quorum of the Twelve to visit the island on 23 November 1988.

On 1 July 1998, Réunion was placed in the newly created Madagascar Antananarivo Mission.

Sources: Alain Chion-Hock, "A Short History of the Beginnings of the Church of Jesus Christ of Latter-day Saints on La Réunion, 1969-1981," Church Archives; Alain Chion-Hock, "Speech given by Alain Chion-Hock at the Sons of Utah Pioneers, Mills Chapter meeting, National Headquarters, Sons of Utah Pioneers, Salt Lake City, Utah, 12 April 2004, (Translation by Vard Lott); Borgna Brunner, "Countries of the World, Réunion," Time Almanac 2004; Louise P. Schmidt, Conversation, 29 April 2004.

GABON

Jan. 1, 2011: Est. population, 1,515,000; Members, fewer than 100; Africa Southeast Area; DR Congo Kinshasa Mission.

Gabon, in western Africa, borders the Atlantic Ocean, Republic of the Congo, Cameroon, and Equatorial Guinea. It became independent from France on 19 August 1960. The people are predominantly Christian, while less than 1 percent are Muslim. The official language is French, with Fang, Myene, Bateke, Bapounou/Eschira, Bandjabi also spoken.

The first records showing Church activity in Gabon indicate that three Church members met together in Libreville, in the early 1980s, for Sunday School meetings. They were Jacqueline Poulette Augustin Demolombe, from France, Ron Mortensen, an employee of the American Embassy, and Mbanzabugabo Celestin. Celestin was born in Gabon and baptized in Germany on 7 November 1980.

Jerome Obounou-Mbogo, a Gabonese diplomat, visited Utah in August 1990 and met with Elders Neal A. Maxwell of the Quorum of the Twelve and Richard P. Lindsay of the Second Quorum of Seventy. Jean Mickouma, a member of the Church from Gabon, accompanied Obounou to Salt Lake City. Mickouma joined the Church several years earlier while working in Washington, D.C.

The Church received permission to enter the country in 1992. Gabon was assigned to the Africa West Area on 15 August 1998. On 15 August 2003, it was transferred to the Africa Southeast Area. There are no branches or missions. Few members live in the country, but occasionally members have served there in behalf of the United Nations and other humanitarian agencies over the past decades.

Sources: "African Dignitary Visits Church Headquarter," Church News, 25 August 1990; "7 New Missions Created; Total Now 275," Church News, 29, February 1992; "Three Areas to be Realigned Aug. 15," Church News, 14 June 2003.

GEORGIA

Jan. 1, 2011: Est. population, 4,616,000; Members, 208; Branches,2;
Percent LDS, .003, or one in 36,635; Europe East Area; Armenia Yerevan Mission.

Georgia, which had been a republic in the Soviet Union, became an independent nation on 9 April 1991. Following the demise of the Soviet Union, a few Georgians were able to go abroad and some joined the Church.

Roman and Nana Amirkhanashvili were baptized in Hanover, Germany, on June 1996. Shortly after their baptisms, they returned to Georgia. An American couple, John and Rebecca Dockery, who were working at the U.S. Embassy in Tbilisi, met with the Amirkhanashvilis for Sunday worship services until returning to the United States in June 1998. The Amirkhanashvilis eventually immigrated to the United States. However, Latter-day Saint involvement in Georgia goes back to the late 1980s.

Doris S. Platt, a Latter-day Saint living in Sandy, Utah, befriended a Georgian woman, Maya Kavtaradze, who was visiting Utah in 1987. The following year, with the help of her Georgian friend, Platt and her twin daughters were able to travel to Georgia. Platt began to visit regularly and stay for extended periods of time. While in Georgia, she taught English at the Foreign Language Institute in Tbilisi.

While visiting Georgia in 1992, Platt became aware of the country's meager and outdated firefighting equipment. She returned to Utah and was able to arrange for the donation of two retired fire trucks that were still in good working condition. National television broadcasts showed the fire engines, with the Salt Lake City emblem still on the doors, responding to a bombing near Georgian President Eduard Shevardnadze's car in 1995.

Over the years, Platt arranged for several more humanitarian shipments to Georgia, and for her work she was asked to be a special advisor to President Eduard Shevardnadze. Platt began to work with local humanitarian societies, including Georgian Women for Peace and Life, which was headed by Nanuli Shevardnadze, the president's wife. Platt also contacted the Church Welfare Services Department to see about humanitarian assistance being sent to Georgia. The Church responded by sending in several shipping containers of clothing, food, and medical supplies.

In March 1999, Elder Jeffrey R. Holland of the Quorum of the Twelve, accompanied by Elder Charles A. Didier, president of the Europe East Area, and their wives, visited Tbilisi. At a historical site Elder Holland blessed the land. Later that afternoon, Elders Holland and Didier, their wives, and Doris Platt visited with Mrs. Shevardnadze and discussed humanitarian aid issues.

In June 1999, Phillip and Betty Reber, a missionary couple serving in the Russia Rostov na Donu Mission, were assigned as the first missionaries to serve in Georgia. They could not proselyte but served as humanitarian missionaries, answering questions about the Church when asked. They worked through the Georgian Women for Peace and Life organization to relieve suffering through the donation of clothing, food, and medical supplies. They also taught English lessons.

While the Rebers were in Georgia, they met Vazha Natroshvili, a Georgian who had been baptized in Holland some years before. They began holding sacrament and Sunday School meetings in their home. People asked the Rebers why they were in Georgia, which gave the couple an opportunity to talk about the Church. Vazha accompanied the Rebers as they would teach missionary discussions. Since the Church was not registered in Georgia, the first converts, the Mamasakhlisi family and an Armenian, Hike Bagdasaryan, were baptized in Yerevan, Armenia, the closest mission location, on 25 September 1999.

The Rebers were replaced by two missionary couples, Ray and June Kemp, and Brent and Jean McGhie. They were assigned to teach English and also oversee humanitarian projects sponsored by LDS Charities.

On 1 July 1999 Georgia became part of the newly-organized Armenia Yerevan Mission. On 23 September 2001, Robert Beckstrand, president of the Armenia Yerevan Mission, organized the Tbilisi Group. Less than a year later, on 9 June 2002, Elder Robert F. Orton, a member of the Seventy and counselor in the Europe East Area Presidency, organized the Tbilisi Branch, with LDS missionary David Jankowski as president and Vazha Natroshvili as a counselor.

At the end of 2003, there were more than 60 Latter-day Saints in Georgia. Two humanitarian missionary couples were working in and around Tbilisi. Converts were now allowed to be baptized in Georgia and a portable baptismal font was taken to Tbilisi for that purpose. The first baptisms in Georgia were performed on 29 September 2003.

Sources: Doris S. Platt, Interview, Church Archives; Joyce Wilson, Draft newspaper article, 9 June 2002, Church Archives; Armenia Yerevan Mission, Annual historical reports, Church Archives; Blaine R. Wilson, Hello from T'blisi, Church Archives.

GERMANY

Jan. 1, 2011: Est. population, 82,330,000; Members, 38,257; Stakes, 14; Wards, 89; Branches, 84; Missions, 3; Districts, 3; Temples, 2; Percent LDS, .05 or one in 2,193; Europe Area.

A central European nation divided following World War II and united in October 1990, Germany is predominantly Catholic in the south and Protestant in the north. Prior to the unification of Germany in 1870 under Prussian Chancellor, Otto von Bismarck, there were a multitude of smaller Germanic states in what comprises the Germany of today.

Probably the first German convert was Jacob Zundel who joined the Church in Kirtland, Ohio, in 1836. The first Latter-day Saint to go to Germany was James Howard, a British convert working there in 1840. He tried to preach but was unsuccessful due to local restrictions. Elder Orson Hyde spent 10 months in Germany in 1841-42, but was unsuccessful in preaching, although he did study German and oversaw the translation of a tract into German. In Nauvoo prior to the death of Joseph Smith, there were sufficient German converts to justify the creation of a German Branch with Daniel Carn (later changed to Garn) as president.

Several other short-lived and poorly documented attempts to preach the gospel were probably made in Germany before George P. Dykes arrived in 1851. He went from the Scandinavian mission to Schleswig-Holstein, an area then under Danish rule. He baptized what were likely the first two converts in Germany on 15 September 1851. Elder John Taylor, assigned to France, went to Hamburg in October 1851, where he joined Dykes and supervised translation of the Book of Mormon into German. It was published in May 1852.

The first mission president, Daniel Carn arrived in Hamburg on 3 April 1852. By August he had baptized 12 and organized the Hamburg Branch. Pres. Carn was exiled by the Hamburg government without any legal cause, but continued to supervise the German Saints from Denmark. Five additional missionaries from the United States arrived on 25 May 1852, the same day as Pres. Carn's exile. Within four months, however, they went to England, discouraged by being constantly harassed by the police.

Orson Spencer and Jacob Houtz were sent to Prussia after King Frederick William IV sought information about the Church through intermediaries in Washington. Houtz and Spencer arrived on 27 January 1853 to learn that Prussian officials had taken sufficient interest in the Church to have monitored their trek nearly the entire way from Salt Lake City. They did not meet with the king, but did gain the audience of the minister of religion. Discouraged by the meeting, they reported that conditions in Prussia were even more adverse to missionary work than in the Hamburg area.

The first converts to emigrate left Germany on 13 August 1852. In 1854, apostates and police halted missionary work by imprisoning and exiling the elders. Most of the local faithful converts emigrated and the branch in Hamburg was dissolved.

The most prominent convert of this period was Karl G. Maeser, who was attracted to the Church by an anti-Mormon tract. He wrote to Church leaders with questions about the gospel and in response, William Budge was sent to Maeser's home in Dresden. Maeser and several relatives and associates were baptized. On 21 October 1855, the Dresden Branch was established with Maeser as president. The branch lasted until 1857, when public opposition prompted many members to emigrate, including Maeser. He later became president of Brigham Young Academy in Provo, Utah.

Southern Germany's first branch was organized in Karlsruhe in 1860, under the jurisdiction of the Swiss, Italian and German Mission. Active missionary work was also begun in that region, in part, because of greater religious tolerance found there compared to many other German states. The mission was boosted in 1867 by the return of Karl G. Maeser as a missionary. The mission was renamed the Swiss and German mission on 1 January 1868. Elder Maeser became president of the mission in June of that year. More than 600 people joined the Church in the next three years. The first issue of Der Stern was published 1 January 1869, with Maeser as editor.

In 1871 with the unification of the German states under Bismark, religious freedom was guaranteed. However, officials used the Church's practice of plural marriage as a reason to continue persecution and arrest of missionaries even after the Church discontinued the practice in 1890. This persecution continued until the end of World War I.

Nevertheless, work had progressed sufficiently in Germany that by 1898 branches had been established in Saargemuend, Frankfurt-am-Main, Leipzig, Hamburg, and Cologne, and the German Mission was created with headquarters in Hamburg. Persecution, however, increased to the extent that in 1904 the mission was recombined with the Swiss Mission to recreate the Swiss and German Mission with mission headquarters in Switzerland.

The first Church president to visit Germany was Joseph F. Smith who spoke at a meeting in the Berlin Branch on 12 August 1906. After World War I began in August 1914, nearly 200 missionaries left some 60 branches in Switzerland and Germany. Despite the war, most branches remained intact and the mission was never closed. Hyrum W. Valentine and his successor, Angus J. Cannon presided over the mission from its headquarters in Basel, Switzerland. In August 1919, Cannon was able to visit the members living in Germany and found them in need of hunger relief. As a result, he was commissioned by the First Presidency to purchase $200,000 worth of supplies from the United States military in France for the German members.

The first missionaries to return after World War I arrived on 15 April 1921. They found a government considerably more tolerant of religious freedom and a people more receptive to the gospel message. The years 1921-1925 marked the greatest growth the Church has ever experienced in Germany. In 1925, the mission was divided with 6,125 members in the newly created German-Austrian Mission and 5,305 members in the Swiss-German Mission. In 1928, the first meetinghouse constructed in Germany was dedicated in Selbongen.

The advent of National Socialism (Nazism) brought new restrictions to the Church including limitations on missionary work, prohibition of the Boy Scout program and restrictions on the use of certain curriculum. The Church, however, progressed during the Nazi era and the East German Mission, Germany's third, was formed 31 December 1937.

In light of Germany's contention with its neighbors over the Czech Sudetenlands, on 16 September 1938, the First Presidency directed all missionaries to be evacuated from Germany and move to neutral countries. Missionaries returned after the crisis subsided, but were evacuated for the duration of World War II beginning on 24 August 1939.

By the end of World War II, more than 600 German Saints had been killed, 2,500 were missing, and 80 percent were homeless. Relief efforts by the Church, first supervised by Elder Ezra Taft Benson, then of the Quorum of the Twelve, helped sustain German members for several years. Management of the relief effort was transferred from Elder Benson to mission president Walter Stover, who arrived in Berlin on 26 November 1946. Late in 1949, Pres. Stover wrote to the First Presidency stating that the more serious part of the crisis was over and no more welfare relief would be needed for the German Saints.

Missionaries returned in 1947 to find Germany divided between West Germany and East Germany. A primary motive in the first half of the 20th century for Latter-day Saints to emigrate to the United States was their desire to enjoy the full blessings of Church membership. With the dedication of the Swiss Temple on 11 September 1955, those blessings became available to Latter-day Saints in Europe. In the fall of 1961 three stakes were created in Berlin, Stuttgart and Hamburg.

A large proportion of Latter-day Saints found themselves living behind the Iron Curtain in East Germany and isolated from their fellow Church members. However, in the late 1960s, more regular visits began from Church Authorities, particularly Elder Thomas S. Monson of the Quorum of the Twelve. On 14 June 1969, a mission was created with headquarters in Dresden, East Germany, with Henry Burkhardt as president. On 29 August 1982, the Freiberg German Democratic Republic Stake was created, and on 19 June 1985, the Freiberg Germany Temple was dedicated, the only temple constructed in a communist bloc country.

A temple in Frankfurt, West Germany, was dedicated 28 August 1987. Following the publicity of the dedication, missionary work increased in the late 1980s.

Missionaries were given permission from the government both to leave and enter East Germany on 28 October 1988. On 30 March 1989, the first missionaries called to serve in East Germany entered that country. Their East German counterparts arrived on 28 May 1989 at the Provo Missionary Training Center.

Barriers separating East and West Germany fell 9 November 1989, and the two countries were reunified on 3 October 1990. With the end of the Cold War, many American military personnel were withdrawn in the early 1990s and the military stakes were reduced from four to one, with the Nuremberg Germany Servicemen's Stake being converted to a German-speaking stake.

The Freiberg Germany Temple was renovated and enlarged to roughly double the size of the original temple. It was rededicated 7 September 2002.

Elder Dieter F. Uchtdorf of the Presidency of the Seventy presented German President Johannes Rau with a three-volume history of his family and his wife's family in the Palace Bellevue in Berlin. The half-hour presentation was made in a private meeting 18 December 2002.

In 2003, membership reached 36,721. In 2005, membership reached 37,149.

Sources: Andrew Jenson, Encyclopedic History of the Church, 1941; Gilbert Scharffs, History of the Church of Jesus Christ of Latter-day Saints in Germany Between 1840 and 1968, Thesis, 1969; "Elder Uchtdorf meets with German president," Church News, 14 September 2002, 2004 Church Almanac; Jeffery L. Anderson, Mormons and Germany, 1914-1913: A history of the Church of Jesus Christ of Latter-day Saints in Germany and its relationship with the German Governments from World War I to the Rise of Hitler, Thesis, 1991; Justus Ernst, Highlights from the German-speaking L.D.S. Missions, 1836-1940, Church Archives; Albert Riedel, Geschichte der deutschsprachigen Missionen der Kirche Jesu Christi der Heiligen der Letzten Tage, 1971; Thomas S. Monson, Faith Rewarded, 1996; "Dedicatory Prayer Excerpts, 'Thou Hast Reached Down in Mercy," Church News, 14 September 2002.

Stakes — 14

(Listed alphabetically as of Oct. 1, 2011.)

No.	Name	Organized	First President
	Europe Area		
334	*Berlin Germany		
	‡Berlin	10 Sep 1961	Rudi Seehagen
768	Dortmund Germany	19 Sep 1976	Klaus Fritz K. Hasse
1358	*Dresden Germany	21 Oct 1990	
	‡Freiberg German D. R.	29 Aug 1982	Frank Herbert Apel
577	*Dusseldorf Germany		
	‡Duesseldorf	4 Jun 1972	Klaus Fritz K. Hasse
766	Frankfurt Germany	12 Sep 1976	Magnus R. Meiser
342	*Hamburg Germany		
	‡Hamburg	12 Nov 1961	Michael Panitsch
845	*Hannover Germany	4 Nov 1996	
	*Hanover Germany	25 Jan 1993	
	‡Hannover Germany	12 Jun 1977	Michael Schulze
466	*Kaiserslautern Germany Military		
	‡Servicemen Stake Europe		
	(W. Germany)	30 Oct 1968	Herbert B. Spencer
1475	*Leipzig Germany	21 Oct 1990	
	‡Leipzig German		
	Democratic Republic	3 Jun 1984	Hermann M. Schutze
1324	Mannheim Germany	7 Feb 1982	Baldur H.H. Stoltenberg
870	Munich Germany	23 Oct 1977	August Schubert
1305	*Neumuenster Germany	9 Apr 1985	
	‡Hamburg Germany North	8 Nov 1981	Karl-Heinz Danklefsen
1651	*Nürnberg Germany	4 Nov 1996	
	*Nurenberg Germany	22 Apr 1995	
	*Nuremberg Germany	3 Feb 1994	
	Nuerenberg Germany Servicemen	6 Sep 1987	Jon Paul Baker
340	*Stuttgart Germany		
	‡Stuttgart	26 Oct 1961	Hermann Moessner

824	Frankfurt Germany Servicemen	1 May 1977	Kenneth Alvin Nessen
	Discontinued 20 Feb 1994		
765	Stuttgart Germany Servicemen	12 Sep 1976	Gary K. Spencer
	Discontinued 15 Nov 1992		

Stakes discontinued

Missions — 3

(As of Oct. 1, 2011; shown with historical number. See MISSIONS.)

(263) GERMANY BERLIN MISSION
Zerbster Str. 42
12209 Berlin
Germany

(35a) GERMANY FRANKFURT MISSION
Corneliusstrasse 18
60325 Frankfurt am Main
Germany

(49) ALPINE GERMAN-SPEAKING MISSION
Lommel Strasse, 7
81479 Munich
Germany

GHANA

Jan. 1, 2011: Est. population, 23,832,000; Members, 45,094; Stakes, 7; Wards, 58; Branches, 63; Missions, 2; Districts, 6; Temples, 1; percent LDS, .16, or one in 623; Africa West Area.

Ghana is located on the south central west coast of Africa and has constitutional democracy. The official language is English, but tribal languages are common. The ethnic make-up of Ghana is diverse: black African 98.5 percent (major tribes — Akan 44 percent, Moshi-Dagomba 16 percent, Ewe 13 percent, Ga 8 percent, Gurma 3 percent, Yoruba 1 percent), European and other 1.5 percent (1998). The major religions include indigenous beliefs 21 percent, Muslim 16 percent, Christian 63 percent.

In the early 1960s, R.A.F. Mensah obtained a copy of the Book of Mormon, read it, and was converted. In February 1964 he introduced his friend Joseph William Billy Johnson to the Book of Mormon. Mensah and Johnson began to organize unofficial LDS congregations as best they knew from the minimal Church literature that they had. They actively participated in missionary work and prayed for the day when the Church would send missionaries to West Africa.

In August 1978, two months after the revelation extended the priesthood to all worthy males, Merrill J. Bateman (now of the Seventy) and Edwin Q. "Ted" Cannon were sent by the Church to West Africa on a fact-finding trip. Three months later, on 8 Nov. 1978, Cannon, with his wife, Janath, and Rendell N. and Rachel Mabey arrived in Nigeria as Church representatives. They entered Ghana 9 Dec. 1978, and, on Dec. 12, baptized Mensah, Johnson, and 123 others who had been prepared by Mensah and Johnson and taught by the Mabeys and Cannons.

The Africa West Mission was organized on 1 July 1980. It included Ghana and Nigeria, with Bryan Espenschied as president. The Ghana Accra Mission was organized 1 July 1985 with Miles H. Cunningham as president.

Elder David B. Haight of the Quorum of the Twelve became the first apostle to visit Ghana on 4 June 1983. During his visit, he met with Church members and missionaries and blessed the land.

The government expelled the missionaries and forbade Church operations on 14 June 1989, including missionary work and Sunday meetings. This time of trial became known among the Ghanaian Latter-day Saints as "The Freeze." Members were permitted, however, to hold services in the privacy of their homes. Faithful Latter-day Saints demonstrated to the Ghanaian government that Church members were good citizens and loyal to their country, and in November 1990, the government permitted Church activities to resume. The government expressed satisfaction that the Church taught members to be obedient to government laws and promoted racial harmony.

On 21 April 1991, five months after "The Freeze," the first two stakes were organized in Ghana with Emmanuel Ohene Opare as the president of the Accra Ghana Stake and Kweku Prah Ghartey as president of the Cape Coast Ghana Stake.

President Gordon B. Hinckley, then a member of the First Presidency, visited Ghana for the first time in May 1993. Less than two years later, on 1 Jan. 1995, the first young North American missionaries arrived in Ghana: Tyson P. Newmann, Tad R. Raban, and Daniel J. Graham. In July 1995, Preston and Barbra Brooksby of Salt Lake City, Utah, were called as the first family history missionaries to serve in West Africa. They were headquartered in Accra.

A gathering of 6,000 members welcomed President Gordon B. Hinckley on 16 Feb. 1998, the first visit of a Church president to West Africa. During the visit, President Hinckley announced that the first temple in West Africa would be built in Ghana. He also met with Ghana President John A. Kufuor.

Ground was broken for the temple on 16 Nov. 2001. Elder Russell M. Nelson of the Quorum of the Twelve presided at the event. Many current and former members of government attended the groundbreaking ceremony. On the same day, Elder Nelson visited with Ghana President John Ageykum Kufuor. The meeting was covered by numerous television and newspaper reporters. President Kufuor said to Elder Nelson that the Church was "a part of Ghana."

The first missionary training center in Africa was built in Tema, Ghana, and dedicated on 17 May 2002. It serves missionaries from the Democratic Republic of the Congo, Ivory Coast, Nigeria, Uganda and Togo.

On 17 Sept. 2002, President Kufuor met with the First Presidency during a visit to Salt Lake City and expressed appreciation for the Church's humanitarian and religious contributions to his country. In the past 15 years, the Church sponsored 142 humanitarian projects in Ghana, valued at $7.5 million.

Emmanuel Ohene Opare was the first Ghanaian called as an Area Authority Seventy during April 1998 General Conference. Another early Ghanaian convert, Dr. Emmanuel Abu Kissi, who operates a clinic in Accra supported by friends of the Church, was called as an Area Authority Seventy at April 2002 General Conference.

Church President Gordon B. Hinckley dedicated the Accra Ghana Temple on 11 Jan. 2004, the first to be built in West

Africa. The Ghana Cape Coast Mission was organized 1 July 2005, and consisted of the English-speaking western portion of Ghana, as well as French-speaking Benin, Togo, Cameroon and Central African Republic. Membership was 23,738 in 2003.

In 2005, membership reached 29,315.

Sources: Janet Brigham, "Nigeria and Ghana," Ensign, February 1980; E. Dale LeBaron, "Pioneers in Africa," Church News, 21 September 1991; Steve Fidel, "Pres. Hinckley announces plans for first temple in West Africa," Deseret News, 16 February 1998; "Meeting Ghana president," Church News, 1 December 2001; Shaun D. Stahle, "First 54 missionaries enter first training center in Africa," Church News, 25 May 2002; Julie Dockstader Heaps, "Saints in West Africa await temples," Church News, 21 September 2002; Church News, March 1, 2003; Ghana Accra Mission, Papers, 1967-1988, Church Archives; Emmanuel A. Kissi, Walking in the Sand, 2004; Rendell N. Mabey, An African Legacy, 1998; James B. Allen, "Would-Be Saints: West Africa before the 1978 Priesthood Revelation," Journal of Mormon History, v. 17, 1991.

Stakes — 8

(Listed alphabetically as of Oct. 1, 2011.)

No.	Name	Organized	First President
Africa West Area			
2407	Accra Ghana Christiansborg	9 Nov 1997	Emmanuel Ohene Opare
1792	*Accra Ghana Lartebiokorshie	9 Nov 1997	
	‡Accra Ghana	21 Apr 1991	Emmanuel Ohene Opare
2768	Accra Ghana McCarthy Hill	16 Jun 2007	Philip K. W. Y. Xaxagbe
2901	Assin Foso Ghana	6 Mar 2011	Abraham Kwaku Fokuo
1791	Cape Coast Ghana	21 Apr 1991	Kweku Prah Ghartey
2499	Kumasi Ghana	22 Nov 1998	Kwaku Annoh
2351	Takoradi Ghana	18 May 1997	Kenneth Kobena Andam
2716	Tema Ghana	23 Apr 2006	Daniel Yirenya-Tawiah

Mission — 2

(As of Oct. 1, 2011; shown with historical number. See MISSIONS.)

(183a) GHANA ACCRA MISSION
P.O. Box 2585 Main
Accra, Ghana

GHANA CAPE COAST MISSION
79 Nkanfoa Rd
Third Ridge, Ghana

GREECE

Jan. 1, 2011: Est. population, 10,737,000; Members, 735; Missions, 1; Branches, 4; Percent LDS, .006, or one in 15,494; Europe Area.

Located on the southern end of the Balkan Peninsula in southeastern Europe, Greece is a presidential parliamentary republic. About 98 percent of the Greek-speaking population belong to the Greek Orthodox Church.

In 1895, Rigas Pofantis and Nicholas Malavetis began a search for gospel truths. After their discovery in 1898 of a newspaper that included an article about Mormonism, they wrote to Church headquarters in Salt Lake City requesting information. As a result, President Ferdinand F. Hintze of the Turkish Mission visited and taught the pair in March 1899. Malavetis died in 1903, but Pofantis wrote again to Church leaders in 1905, this time requesting baptism. He mentioned that he had studied with three other people who were also desirous of baptism, including Malavetis's widow. He had translated into Greek one hundred pages of the Book of Mormon and had also translated and published a Church pamphlet titled "Rays of Living Light."

Turkish Mission President J. Wilford Booth and his wife Mary arrived in Athens on 1 October 1905 to meet with Pofantis and the others. On 6 October 1905, Booth and his wife knelt on Mars Hill, praying that Greece would be receptive to the gospel. In the ocean near Phaleron in the Saronic Gulf on Sunday, 22 October 1905, Booth baptized the first five Greeks: Rigas Pofantis, Andromache Malavetis, George Zdralis, Constantine Theodoseau and John Lazos. They then returned to the Pofantis home on Kaningos Square in Athens where the sacrament was administered there for the first time. On 29 November 1905 a sixth Greek convert, Marie Pechany, was baptized in the Bay of Piraeus.

In March 1906, full-time missionaries were assigned to Greece, the first being Joseph F. Thorup and Bertrand W. Clayton. Over the next three years, several additional converts were baptized and by April 1909, Thorup, working with Pofantis and others, had translated the entire Book of Mormon into Greek. The First Presidency asked him to bring his translation to Salt Lake City for review. It was found to be an excellent translation in a classical Greek style, but was not a high priority for publication due to closure of the work in Greek-speaking areas. Between 1971 and 1979 the translation department of the Church edited Thorup's manuscript to be publication-ready by modernizing its language. Part of Thorup's translation was published as Book of Mormon selections in 1979.

Missionaries continued to teach and baptize in Greece until August 1909 when work in the Turkish Mission was suspended due to continued political unrest in Armenia and Turkey. The Greek saints were placed under the direction of Pofantis.

In September 1921, J. Wilford Booth was appointed to reopen the work in the jurisdiction of the old Turkish Mission. The Armenian Mission was established that month with headquarters in Aleppo, Syria. The meager resources of the mission were, however, expended completely in rescuing Armenian saints in war-torn Aintab, Turkey, so additional resources were not available to reopen the work in Greece.

Brigham Young University President Franklin S. Harris visited the Armenian Mission in 1927 on assignment of the First Presidency. His 10 February 1927 report included the recommendation that elders return to Greece "as soon as practical."

President Booth's unexpected death on 5 December 1928 left the mission without leadership until the appointment of Badwagan Piranian in February 1933. President Piranian and his successor Joseph Jacobs focused on the work in Syria and Lebanon until World War II closed mission activities in 1939. Piranian was appointed in September 1947 to reopen the work as the Palestine-Syrian Mission. Again, the limited availability of missionaries made it impossible to send elders to

Greece.

Although missionary activities were not reinstated for many years, Church leaders directed occasional humanitarian programs that benefitted the Greek people. In November 1947 the Church donated 80,000 pounds of seed wheat to the Greek War Relief Association. After a major earthquake in the Greek Ionian Islands in 1953, the Church participated with the United Churches Ionian Relief Project, providing more assistance to the earthquake survivors than did any other organization or government. As an expression of gratitude, on 29 November 1954, John Tzounis, Greek Consul representing King Paul of the Hellenes, awarded to President David O. McKay the Cross of Commander of the Royal Order of the Phoenix. It was the second- highest honor Greece could bestow upon an individual.

A number of diplomatic exchanges were made in the era of the 1950s to 1980s including visits in 1954 and 1980 from Greek ambassador John Tzounis, a 25 February 1966 visit by ambassador Alexander A. Matsas to David O. McKay; and a February 1969 visit by Greece's Princess Irene and Greek consul general Anthony Protonotarios.

Although active missionary work did not occur in Greece between the 1910s and 1970s, Greek people learned about the Church from servicemen stationed in that region, and while traveling or studying abroad. A number of people of Greek heritage living in Utah were baptized during this period. In Salt Lake City, in 1959, a Hellenic Latter-day Saint Society was formed in Salt Lake City to help Greek members retain their heritage and maintain ties with their homeland.

By 1960, the Athens Greece Group, a Church unit for LDS servicemen, was functioning in Greece. It was replaced by the Athens Branch which was created on 18 June 1967 with Frank K. Swenson as first branch president. At the time of creation, the Athens Branch membership rolls included 80 people: U.S. servicemen, embassy officials, their families, and eight Greeks. By 1975 the branch had about 150 members including more than 13 Greek families.

Increased membership and the establishment of the Church in different parts of Greece led to creation of the Greece Athens Branch on 15 July 1991, the Thessaloniki Branch on 21 January 1992, and the Pireas Branch on 1 September 1992. In 2004, five branches were functioning in Greece: Faliro, Halandri, Thessaloniki, Omonia and Greece Athens Mission.

The Church began sending official representatives to Greece in the mid-1970s. Among the first were James C. and Tena S. Nackos, Angel K. and Mary S. Caras, and Phillip V. and Gwen J. Christensen. It is assumed that the first young elder to work in Greece since 1909 was Clark H. Caras, who arrived in Athens in July 1978.

By the late 1980s, a number of elders and two sisters from the Austria Vienna East Mission were assigned to labor in Greece. The Greece Athens Mission was created from a division of the Austria Vienna East Mission on 1 July 1990. Many of those assigned to serve in Greece were from European Union countries whose citizens had a greater likelihood of obtaining visas to work there.

A trial held on 2-3 June 1991 in Thessaloniki charged four missionaries, J. Darren Burrup, Charles L. Phillips, Karl L. Noyes, and Jed P. Nye, with illegal proselyting. All four were declared innocent. It was the first time that threatened legal action against missionaries was officially prosecuted. This court case was important because it tested the status of the Church in Greece and affirmed the legal rights of Latter-day Saints to do missionary work in the country. Occurrences of police harassment of missionaries lessened after the verdict became known.

The first meetinghouse in Greece was dedicated in Athens 30 May 1999 by Elder Charles Didier of the Seventy as the home for the Halandri, Athinai and Pireas branches. In 2002, there were 591 members.

In 2003, membership reached 598.

Sources: Turkish Mission, "Manuscript history," v. 2; Swiss Mission, "Manuscript history," v. 13-15; Athens Branch directories, July 1967 and July 1975; Lyn R. Jacobs, Mormon non-English scriptures, hymnals, and periodicals, 1830-1986 (Ithaca: The Author, 1986); "The Gospel in Greek," Journal History of the Church, 22 July 1905, 3; [Untitled], Journal History of the Church, 14 April 1909, 7; "Greece's Ambassador arrives in S.L. as guest of Utah Symphony Guild," Journal History of the Church, 24 February 1966, 6; Elder James C. Nackos, "Letter to the editor," Improvement Era, February 1959, 70; "Baptisms in Greece," Deseret Evening News, 25 November 1905; "L.D.S. Church Donates Car of Wheat to Greece," Deseret News, 1 November 1947; "Greek leaders express thanks for Church wheat," Deseret News, 29 November 1947; "Pres. McKay given royal award by king of Greece," Church News, 4 December 1954, 2; "Helenic unit sees show," Church News, 7 November 1964, 13; "This week in Church history: Convert baptized after 10-year wait," Church News, 8 October 1966; Stephen W. Gibson, "Royalty on Temple Square," Church News, 15 February 1969, 15; Maureen Ursenbach Beecher, "Conversion in Athens," Church News, 30 December 1978, 12; "Greek ambassador renews association with Church," Church News, 18 October 1980; "Branch begins in historic city," Church News, 9 May 1992, 12; Meetinghouse is dedicated, first in Greece," Church News, 12 June 1999, 6.

Mission — 1
(As of Oct. 1, 2011; shown with historical number. See MISSIONS.)

(241) GREECE ATHENS MISSION
Panayias Eleftherotrias 9
PO Box 51178
145 63 Kifissia, Athens, Greece

GREENLAND
(See Denmark)

GRENADA
**Jan. 1, 2011: Est. population, 91,000; Members, 230; Branches, 1;
Percent LDS, .2, or one in 511; Caribbean Area; West Indies Mission.**

Composed of three Caribbean mountainous islands, Grenada is an independent state with a parliamentary democracy. Its population is 64 percent Roman Catholic and 22 percent Anglican.

Although members of the Church lived in Grenada while attending medical school in the early 1980s, little permanent missionary work started until after the 1983 coup and subsequent invasion of Grenada by U.S. and United Nations forces.

In 1985, President Kenneth L. Zabriskie of the West Indies Mission met with Ben Jones Deputy Prime Minister. Jones welcomed the opportunity for missionaries to enter the country and said that following the coup, the new prime minister met with local clergy and rededicated the land of Grenada to Jesus Christ. President Zabriskie sent Elders Robert W. Hoffmaster and Leonard G. Gill to Grenada in May 1985. They met with a medical student, Al Nuttal, and his wife, Julie, and their children, who had just moved from St. Lucia.

A branch was established in St. George's on 3 September 1985, but growth of the Church slowed in 1987 when organized anti-Mormon efforts in the press led to senior missionaries being brought to testify in court about Church beliefs.

As a result of missionaries were removed from the island. For several years, missionaries could only stay if they renewed their visas every two weeks. In September 1990, Kelvin Diaz, counselor in the West Indies mission presidency, met with Prime Minister Nicholas Braithwaite whom he had known from their previous service in the Red Cross. President Diaz's friendship with Braithwaite helped open a dialogue and change negative opinions about the Church.

At a critical time following a fire which gutted several government buildings in 1990, three computers were delivered to Prime Minister Braithwaite by senior missionary Dean Sloan in December 1990 on behalf of the Church. Shortly thereafter, the government allowed missionaries to have six-month visas. On 13 May 2001 the St. George's chapel was dedicated by President M. Don Van Noy of the West Indies Mission.

Sources: Kenneth L. Zabriskie, History of the West Indies Mission, [ca. 1989], Church Archives; West Indies Mission, Mission history and historical reports, Church Archives. A. Dean and Darnell Z. Jeffs, interview, 2003, Church Archives; Elden Wood, Autobiography, 1994, Church Archives.

GUAM
(See also Micronesia)

Jan. 1, 2011: Est. population, 178,000; Members, 2,140; Stakes, 1; Wards, 4; Missions, 1; Percent LDS, 1, or one in 95; Asia North Area; Micronesia Guam Mission.

The largest of the Mariana islands in the South Pacific, the self-governing U.S. territory of Guam has a population that is mostly Roman Catholic. Guam became a U.S. possession on 21 June 1898 following the Spanish-American War.

There are no records of missionary activity on Guam or visits by Latter-day Saints prior to World War II. The first known members on Guam came with the U.S. armed forces during the war. Servicemen's groups numbering from 50 to 300 members existed on Guam from 1944- 1945.

Families were able to join their servicemen stationed in Guam as early as 1946 and all of the groups were consolidated into one Guam Servicemen's Group. Membership grew steadily and all auxiliaries were fully organized when the Guam Branch, with Victor Olson as president, was formed under the direction of the Japanese Mission on 9 October 1951. Soon members raised enough money to purchase land and two quonset huts in Anigua to be used for a meetinghouse. Prior to this, meetings were held in military facilities.

The branch was transferred to the Southern Far East Mission when the Japanese Mission was divided in July 1955. The first full time missionaries, Dannie T. Gallego and Paul R. Ray, arrived in January 1957. Elder Mark E. Petersen of the Quorum of the Twelve dedicated the Guam Branch meetinghouse on 18 June 1959. The Guam Branch became part of the Honolulu Stake on 15 October 1959 and missionary work was assumed by branch members called as stake missionaries.

Land for another meetinghouse was purchased in April 1964. On 3 March 1970, the Guam Branch became a ward in the Honolulu Stake and a new meetinghouse in Barrigada was dedicated on 10 March 1970 by Elder Ezra Taft Benson of the Quorum of the Twelve. Full-time missionary work in Guam resumed on 7 July 1970 when Michael D. Corrigan and Vern H. Liljenquist were assigned to work there by Hawaiian Mission president Kenneth W. Gardner. There had been no full-time missionaries in Guam since becoming part of the Honolulu Stake due mostly to distance. Guam is separated from Hawaii by 3,300 miles of ocean. Missionary work expanded at that time to include the native Chararro people besides American servicemen.

The Honolulu Stake was divided on 21 November 1971, and the ward became part of the newly created Kaneohe Stake. The ward was divided in May 1976. The two wards shared the same meetinghouse in Barrigada. The first Chamorro couple to join the Church, Donald and Maria Calvo, were baptized on 21 May 1977. The Agat Branch was created in the southern part of Guam in 1978. In 1979, Herbert J. Leddy, the first missionary of Chamorro lineage, was called to the Tennessee Nashville Mission.

The Micronesia Guam Mission was created on 1 April 1980. In 1989, selections of the Book of Mormon were translated into Chamorro, and that same year, Herbert J. Leddy became the first Chamorro member to be called as district president. The Barrigada Central Branch was created in January 1992 to meet the needs of an influx of Micronesian Church members coming to Guam.

President Gordon B. Hinckley visited Guam on 31 January 2000 while on a tour of Pacific Rim countries. He was welcomed to Agana by Carl Gutierrez, governor of Guam, along with 684 Church members. President Hinckley's address was carried to a meetinghouse on the island of Saipan via telephone connection. He recounted visiting Guam in 1965 with Elder Hugh B. Brown and meeting with only fifteen members at the time.

In 2005, membership was 1,669.

Elder L. Tom Perry of the Quorum of the Twelve created the first stake in Guam on 12 December 2010 called the Barrigada Guam Stake. Growth of the Church came from convert baptisms as members became more active in missionary efforts.

Sources: Servicemen's Group (Orote, Guam), Meeting minutes and attendance records, 1944- 1946, Church Archives; Servicemen's Group (Nob Hill), Meeting minutes and attendance records, 1946, Church Archives; Servicemen's Group (Guam), Meeting minutes and attendance records, 1947-1948, Church Archives; Japanese Mission, Manuscript history and historical reports, Church Archives; Southern Far East Mission, Manuscript history and historical reports, Church Archives; Honolulu Stake, Manuscript history and historical reports, Church Archives; Guam 1st Ward, Manuscript history and historical reports, Church Archives; Kaneohe Hawaii Stake, Manuscript history and historical records; Church Archives; Guam District, Manuscript history and historical reports, Church Archives; Alan E. Muller, "A historical account of The Church of Jesus

Christ of Latter-day Saints on Guam," 1955, Church Archives; Micronesia Guam Mission, A Brief History of the Micronesia-Guam Mission, 1980-1990, Church Archives; R. Lanier Britsch, Unto the Islands of the Sea, 1986; Years of faith and effort, Church News, Jan. 15, 2011.

Stakes — 1
(Listed alphabetically as of Oct. 1, 2011.)

No.	Name	Organized	First President
Asia North Area			
2892	Barrigada Guam	12 Dec 2010	Arthur B. Clark

Mission — 1
(As of Oct. 1, 2011; shown with historical number. See MISSIONS.)

(178) MICRONESIA GUAM MISSION
PO Box 21749 GMF
Barrigada, GU 96921

GUATEMALA

Jan. 1, 2011: Est. population, 13,277,000; Members, 226,027; Stakes, 39; Wards, 235; Branches, 180; Missions, 5; Districts, 19; Temples, 1; Percent LDS, 1.62, or one in 62; Central America Area.

Guatemala is the northernmost isthmus country in Central America. The national language is Spanish, but various Indian dialects are also spoken.

John F. O'Donnal, a member of the Church from the Mormon colonies in Mexico, moved to Central America in 1942 as an agricultural adviser of the U.S. government. In December 1946, he visited Church headquarters and made a personal appeal to President George Albert Smith to open missionary work in Guatemala. President Arwell L. Pierce of the Mexican Mission assigned Seth G. Mattice and Earl E. Hansen to work in Guatemala. They arrived 4 September 1947. John F. O'Donnal was set apart as district president on 12 August 1948 and more than 60 people attended the first meeting in a rented building in Guatemala City two weeks later. President O'Donnal baptized his wife, Carmen, the first convert in Guatemala on 13 November 1948.

Elder Spencer W. Kimball, then a member of the Quorum of the Twelve, visited Guatemala on 16 November 1952 and organized the Central American Mission with headquarters in Guatemala City. The first visit by a Church president took place 13 February 1954 when President David O. McKay visited Guatemala City. By the end of 1956, branches had been established in 15 cities.

Continued Church growth in Central America prompted the division of the Central American Mission and the creation of the Guatemala-El Salvador Mission on 1 August 1965. When the Church received official government recognition on 29 June 1966, there were already 10,000 members. Elder Marion G. Romney of the Quorum of the Twelve Apostles organized the Guatemala City Stake, on 21 May 1967, the first in the country, with Udine Falabella as president. President Spencer W. Kimball presided at the Guatemala Stake conference in September 1971. The stake was divided the following year, and the mission was divided in 1976, creating separate missions in Guatemala and El Salvador.

In 1977, President Spencer W. Kimball again visited Guatemala. On 22 February, he met with Guatemalan President Kjell Eugenio Laugerud-Garcia. He also spoke at an area conference at the National Gymnasium to members from Guatemala and El Salvador, and was given the key to the city from Mayor Leonel Ponciano Leon.

By 1977, the mission had been divided again with the creation of the Guatemala Quetzaltenango Mission, with John F. O'Donnal as president. Four stakes had been established and membership was more than 17,000. President Gordon B. Hinckley dedicated the Guatemala City Temple, 14 December 1984. John F. O'Donnal was called as temple president. At that time, membership was 40,000 in eight stakes and 13 districts. A third mission, the Guatemala City North, was created on 1 January 1988, and a fourth, Guatemala Central, was created on 1 July 1993.

Elder Carlos H. Amado, former temple committee chairman, was called to the Second Quorum of the Seventy on 1 April 1989, becoming the first Guatemalan General Authority. President Boyd K. Packer of the Quorum of the Twelve dedicated a new 36,400-square-foot missionary training center in Guatemala City, not far from the temple on 22 January 1994. President Gordon B. Hinckley visited Guatemala on 26 January 1997, and in two meetings addressed about 20,000 members from 29 stakes and districts.

By 2001, a little more than 50 years after the first missionaries arrived, Church membership in Guatemala exceeded 180,000. By 2002, membership reached 188,531. By 2003, it was 192,207.

For the first time in the history of the Church in Guatemala, more than 4,000 young women gathered for a two-day national LDS girls camp on 27-28 November 2004. More than 90 buses filled with enthusiastic young women arrived at a campground in Santa Catarina Pinula, about 10 miles outside Guatemala City.

In 2003, membership reached 192,207.

Sources: Central American Mission, Manuscript history and historical reports, Church Archives; Guatemala-El Salvador Mission, Manuscript history and historical reports, Church Archives; Guatemala District, Manuscript history and historical reports, Church Archives; Guatemala Branch, Manuscript history; Church Archives; John Forres O'Donnal, Pioneer in Guatemala, The Personal History of John Forres O'Donnal, 1997; Donald Q. Cannon and Richard O. Cowan, Unto Every Nation: Gospel Light Reaches Every Land, 2003; Andrew Jenson, Encyclopedic History of the Church, 1941; "Guatemala Training Center Dedicated," Church News, 12 February 1994, "An Outpouring of Love for Prophet," Church News, 1 February 1997; "Thousands gather," Church News, 4 December 2004; "New missions," Church News, 13 Feb. 2010.

Stakes — 39

(Listed alphabetically as of Oct. 1, 2011.)

No.	Name	Organized	First President
Central America Area			
2843	Amatitlan Guatemala	28 Jun 1998	Vicente Bernardo Rodriguez C.
1611	*Chimaltenango Guatemala Guat. Chimaltenango ‡Guatemala City	22 Mar 1988 26 Oct 1986	Mario Salazar Moran
1738	Coatepeque Guatemala	10 Dec 1989	Ricardo Rolando Morales
2115	Coban Guatemala	29 Oct 1995	Jorge Rafael Cabrera Galindo
436	*Guatemala City Guatemala ‡Guatemala City	21 May 1967	Udine Falabella
2506	Guatemala City Guatemala Alameda	10 Jan 1999	Luis Javier Rabanales
1618	Guatemala City Guatemala Atlantico	7 Dec 1986	Luis Alvarez Ovando
2105	Guatemala City Guatemala Bosques De San Nicolas	15 Oct 1995	Cesar Antonio de Leon
1619	Guatemala City Guatemala Central	7 Dec 1986	Armando G. Diaz L.
1768	Guatemala City Guatemala El Molino	19 Aug 1990	Jose Julio Aguilar
1620	Guatemala City Guatemala Florida	7 Dec 1986	Miguel A. Gomez L.
2510	Guatemala City Guatemala La Esperanza	30 Jan 1999	Erwin Reynaldo Rosales Chigua
1704	Guatemala City Guatemala La Laguna	27 Nov 1988	Carlos Estrado Mouna M.
778	Guatemala City Guatemala Las Victorias	31 Oct 1976	Carlos Enrique Soto D.
1040	Guatemala City Guatemala Mariscal	10 Jun 1979	Samuel Ramirez Abrego
1745	Guatemala City Guatemala Milagro	15 Apr 1990	Victor Manuel Canenguez P.
2106	Guatemala City Guatemala Monserrat	15 Oct 1995	Sam Mino Galvez Orellana
1733	Guatemala City Guatemala Nimajuyu	9 Jul 1989	Rene Humberto Oliva L.
2010	Guatemla City Guatemala Palmita	15 Jan 1995	Carlos Francisco Arredondo C.
699	*Guatemala City Guatemala Utatlan ‡Guatemala City	31 Oct 1976 8 Jun 1975	Mario Antonio Lopez
2043	Guatemala City Guatemala West Guatemala Villa Hermosa	30 Apr 1995	Bruno Emilio Vasquez R.
1982	Huehuetenango Guatemala Calvario	19 Jun1994	Victor M. Rodas Corado
1706	*Huehuetenango Guatemala Zachuteu Huehuetenango Guatemala	19 Jun 1994 4 Dec 1988	Edgar Leonardo Fuentes P.
1937	Jalapa Guatemala	9 May 1993	Luis Daniel Aragon Aquino
1938	Malacatan Guatemala	9 May 1993	Edilzar Joel Barrios Rodriguez
1737	Mazatenango Guatemala	10 Dec 1989	Mario Antonio de Leon S.
2195	Momostenango Guatemala	12 May 1996	Francisco de J. Rosales Santiago
2263	Patzicia Guatemala	10 Nov 1996	Carlos Antonio Guit Ajiquichi
713	Quetzaltenango Guatemala	19 Oct 1975	Jorge Herminio Perez C.
1996	Quetzaltenango Guatemala El Bosque	6 Nov 1994	Melvin Enrique Recinos D.
1497	Quetzaltenango Guatemala West	24 Oct 1984	Amilcar Raul Robles A.
1168	Retalhuleu Guatemala	17 Aug 1980	Manuel Efrain Barrios F.
2514	Retalhuleu Guatemala Las Palmas	28 Feb 1999	Moises Gomez Guzman
1955a	San Felipe Guatemala	19 Sep 1993	Mario A. Monterroso Gonzalez
1498	San Marcos Guatemala	24 Oct 1984	Abraham Raymundo Juarez C.
2469	San Pedro Guatemala	24 May 1998	Arnoldo O. Gonzalez G.
1785	Villa Nueva Guatemla	27 Jan 1991	Luis Gomez Garcia
2153	Zacapa Guatemala	14 Jan 1996	Arnulfo Franco Martinez

Stakes discontinued

No.	Name	Organized	First President
1681	*Escuintla Guatemala 3 Apr 1990 Discontinued 12 Jun 1994 ‡Guatemala City Guatemala Escuintla	31 Jan 1988	Enrique Leveron L.
2484	Guatemala City Guatemala Monte Maria Discontinued 22 June 2008	28 Jun 1998	Gerardo Soto Urbina

2505 Mazatenango Guatemala East   13 Dec 1998   Armando Gonzalez Figueroa
       Discontinued 25 May 2008

Missions — 5
(As of Oct. 1, 2011; shown with historical number. See MISSIONS.)

(287) GUATEMALA GUATEMALA CITY CENTRAL MISSION
Apartado Postal 921-A
Guatemala City, 01909, Zona 9
Guatemala, C.A.

(205a) GUATEMALA GUATEMALA CITY NORTH MISSION
5a Avenida 5-55, Edificio Euro Plaza
15 avo. Nivel, Oficina 1504, Zona 14
Guatemala, Guatemala C.A

(76a) GUATEMALA GUATEMALA CITY SOUTH MISSION
Apartado Postal 340-A
Guatemala City 01909
Guatemala, C.A.

(152) GUATEMALA QUETZALTENANGO MISSION
5a. Calle 14-35, Zona 3
Quetzaltenango, 09001
Guatemala, C.A.

GUATEMALA RETALHULEU MISSION
Barrio Concepión
Boulevard Centenario, Zona 2
Retalhuleu, Guatemala, C.A.

GUYANA

Jan. 1, 2011: Est. population, 772,000; Members, 5,016; Branches, 15; District, 2; percent LDS, .51 or 1 in 196; Caribbean Area; West Indies Mission.

On the north eastern coast of South America, Guyana is a republic in the United Kingdom commonwealth of nations. Its population is 57 percent Christian and 37 percent Hindu, and speaks English and Amerindian dialects.

Senior missionaries Benjamin and Ruth Hudson entered Guyana on 19 August 1988, and held a sacrament meeting in September of that year. Among those who attended was the Majid Abdulla family, who had been baptized previously in Canada. The first convert was Indra Sukhdeo, who was baptized on 23 October 1988, by Majid Abdulla.

The Church gained legal recognition in February 1989, and a small branch with Benjamin Hudson was organized in Georgetown in March. In February 1990, Elder M. Russell Ballard of the Quorum of the Twelve blessed the land and attended services with 45 members and investigators. Kenrick Latchmansingh was called as the first local branch president in 1990.

On 15 September 1992, President Desmond Hoyte, Guyana's head of state, was a special guest at a luncheon hosted by Elder Stephen D. Nadauld of the Seventy and J. Richard Toolson, Trinidad Tobago Mission president.

By late 2002, membership reached 1,251, a ten-fold increase in 10 years, making Guyana the fastest growing area of the West Indies. The first meetinghouse was dedicated on 15 March 2003 in Prashad Nagar. Some 250 members attended the dedication.

The Georgetown Guyana District was organized on 21 December 2003 with Wayne D. Barrow as district president. The district is comprised of three branches in the capitol Georgetown, as well as one in the eastern port city of New Amsterdam, and one in Patentia in western Demerara.

In 2003, membership reached 1,340. In 2005, membership reached 1,845.

Sources: Benjamin and Ruth Hudson, Interview, 2003, Church Archives; John L. Hart, "Taking Root in 'Land of Waters,'" Church News, 18 May 1991; "Guyana Leader Hosted," Church News, 7 November 1992; Wayne Barrow, "Guyana Growing, First Chapel Dedicated," Church News, 19 April 2003; Jacob Swensen, "'Forgotten' Guyana Carving Gospel Mark," Church News, 8 May 2004.

HAITI

Jan. 1, 2011: Est. population, 9,036,000; Members, 16,902; Stakes, 2; Wards, 16; Districts, 2; Branches, 16; Missions, 1; Percent LDS, .17, or one in 583; Caribbean Area.

On the west side of Hispaniola Island in the West Indies, Haiti has a people who speak Haitian Creole and French. About 80 percent are Roman Catholic, and 10 percent are Protestant.

The first member of the Church in Haiti was Alexandre Mourra, a prominent Haitian businessman of Jewish-Arabic descent, who wrote a letter to Florida Ft. Lauderdale Mission President Richard L. Millett requesting a copy of the Book of Mormon. Soon thereafter, Mourra traveled to Florida and was baptized there on 30 June 1977. He was active in sharing the gospel and on 2 July 1978, President Millett and his counselors came to Haiti to preside over the baptism of 22 Haitians at Hatte Marie, near Port-au-Prince. In September of that year, J. Frederic Templeman of the Canadian embassy arrived, and he helped Mourra to further the work. The first four full-time missionaries were transferred from the Paris France mission and sent to Haiti in May 1980 under the direction of Glen E. Stringham of the Florida Fort Lauderdale Mission. The first branch was established that October with Mourra as president. The Haiti District was created in 1982 with Ludner Armand as president. Among many youth who joined the Church was Fritzner Joseph who was baptized in 1979 and two years later served a mission in Puerto Rico. He was the first missionary called from Haiti.

On 17 April 1983, Elder Thomas S. Monson of the Quorum of the Twelve blessed the land. At that time, Haiti had about 500 members of the Church. On 4 August 1984, the Haiti Port-au-Prince Mission was created with James S. Arrigona as president. Foreign missionaries were removed from Haiti because of civil strife on 25 October 1991. In early 1992, Fritzner Joseph was called as the first native mission president to preside over the Haiti Port-au-Prince Mission. He served for more than four-and-a-half years with only local missionaries. Foreign missionaries returned in February 1996. By July 1998, 48 missionaries were serving; by July 2003, there were 130 missionaries about half of whom were Haitians.

The Port-au-Prince stake, the first in Haiti, was organized 20 September 1997 with Reynolds Antoine Saint-Louis as president. Districts were organized in Gonaives on 28 November 1999 and Les Cayes on 22 July 2001. The Port-au-Prince stake was divided on 7 September 2003, creating the Port-au-Prince North stake. Haitian members rejoiced when the Santo Domingo Temple in the Dominican Republic was dedicated on 17 September 2000. The first couple sealed in the temple was Paul Henry and Wildermina Jean-Baptiste of Haiti.

In 2002, membership reached 11,329.

By 2003, there were 14 chapels throughout the country with others in various stages of planning and construction. Foreign missionaries were pulled out of Haiti in February 2004 due to political and civil unrest. On 26 May 2004, after the turmoil subsided, eight missionaries from the United States were sent to the country.

Sources: Richard L. Millett, History of the Church in the Caribbean, 1977-1980, Church Archives; "Haiti Dedicated During Historic Visit," Church News, 22 May 1983; "Two New Missions to be Created in Florida and Haiti," Church News, 22 April 1984, Kenneth L. Zabriskie, History of the West Indies Mission [ca. 1989], Church Archives; Elizabeth and Jed VanDenBerghe, "Haitian Saints See Hope in Gospel," Ensign, March 1991; "Ground Broken for Caribbean's First Temple," Church News, 24 August 1996; Haiti Port-au-Prince Mission, Mission history and historical reports, Church Archives; "Happy in Haiti," Church News, 3 May 2003; Michael Moody, Telephone conversation, 27 May 2004.

Stakes — 2
(Listed alphabetically as of Oct. 1, 2011.)

No.	Name	Organized	President
2399	Port-au-Prince Haiti	21 Sep 1997	Reynolds Antoine Saint-Louis
2610d	Port-Au-Prince Haiti North	7 Sep 2003	Gheuthewannha Ghammald Francillon

Mission — 1
(As of Oct. 1, 2011; shown with historical number. See MISSIONS.)

(180a) HAITI PORT-AU-PRINCE MISSION
Boite Postale 15319
HT 6140 Petion-ville
Haiti, F.W.I.

HONDURAS

Jan. 1, 2011: Est. population, 7,793,000; Members, 142,258; Stakes, 20; Wards, 137; Branches, 82; Missions, 3; Districts, 7; Percent LDS, 1.7 or one in 59; Central America Area.

Located in Central America between Nicaragua and Guatemala, Honduras has a population that speaks Spanish and Indian dialects.

Elder Spencer W. Kimball of the Quorum of the Twelve Apostles, and Central American Mission president Gordon M. Romney, were instrumental in promoting missionary work in Central America. They visited Tegulcigalpa, Honduras, and left a tract and a copy of the Book of Mormon with a hotel waiter, Jose Santos Ortega Flores, on 17 November 1952. Missionary work in Honduras began on 10 December 1952, a month after the Central America Mission was created. On 21 March 1953, the first two missionaries in Honduras, James T. Thorup and George W. Allen, baptized Alicia Castanado, Corina de Bustamante, Mario A. de Chotria, and Carmen B. Corina, as well as Jose Ortega, who first met Elder Kimball and President Romney. The Church organized a branch in Tegucigalpa the day after that first baptismal service. Missionaries began working in San Pedro Sula on 4 October 1954 and a branch was organized there in 1955. The San Pedro Sula District was organized on 4 June 1961.

The first stake in Honduras was created in San Pedro Sula on 10 April 1977. The Honduras Tegucigalpa Mission was created on 1 January 1980, with 6,300 members and only seven years later membership totaled 23,000. The mission was divided 1 July 1990 and the country's ninth stake was created in September 1990. From September 1992 to April 1993, North American missionaries were withdrawn because of threats from extremists groups. Nevertheless, the missionary work continued to grow with non-North American missionaries. By 1995, membership was 65,000, 10 times what it was just 15 years earlier.

The Church responded with extensive food and clothing following the devastation of Hurricane Mitch in November and December of 1998. President Gordon B. Hinckley visited that November, offering words of comfort and encouragement.

Honduras was one of three Central American countries where the Church, in partnership with California philanthropist and Wheelchair Foundation founder Kenneth Behring, donated 500 wheelchairs in 2001 via the country's First Lady charitable organization. The other two countries that also received 500 wheelchairs each were Nicaragua and El Salvador. The ceremony in Honduras, where wheelchairs were presented to the first group of recipients, was attended by Honduran president Carlos Roberto Flores and his wife, Mary Flake de Flores.

In 2002, membership reached 108,217.

The First Presidency announced in a 9 June 2006, letter that a temple will be built in the Honduran capital of Tegucigalpa, the first in Honduras and the fourth in Central America.

Sources: Honduras District, Central American Mission, Manuscript history and historical reports, Church Archives; Honduras Tegucigalpa Mission, Manuscript history and historical reports; Church Archives, Central American Mission, manuscript history and historical reports Church Archives; Donald Q. Cannon and Richard O. Cowan, Unto Every Nation: Gospel Light Reaches Every Land, 2003; "Twenty-three New Stakes: Honduras, Norway, and Venezuela Get First Stake," Church News, July 1977, "Nine Missions Announced, Four Lands Dedicated in the Americas," Church News, May 1990; "Wheelchairs Given to Central American Nations," Church News, 27 October 2001; "Temple to be built in Honduras capital," Church News, 24 June 2006.

Stakes — 21
(Listed alphabetically as of Oct. 1, 2011.)

No.	Name	Organized	President
Central America Area			
2051	Choluteca Honduras	21 May 1995	Edwin Raul Ferman Zelaya
2150	Comayagua Honduras	17 Dec 1995	Carlos Armando Zepeda H.

1383	Comayaguela Honduras	21 Nov 1982	Jorge Alberto Sierra B.
2097	Comayaguela Honduras Country	3 Sep 1995	Carlos Martin Velasquez Aceituno
1990	Comayaguela Honduras Torocagua	4 Sep 1994	Luis Gustavo Duarte Fonseca
2027	Danli Honduras	26 Feb 1995	Rodolfo Diaz Ortiz
1757	El Merendon Honduras	17 Jun 1990	Jose Francisco Funes R.
2061	Fesitranh Honduras	11 June 1995	Victor Guillermo Sierra Barahona
1647	La Ceiba Honduras	28 Jun 1987	Luis Alfredo Salazar V.
1601	La Lima Honduras	22 Jun 1986	Rodolfo Arguello A.
2224	San Pedro Honduras El Progreso	25 Aug 1996	Sami G. Medrano Ramiriz
820	San Pedro Sula Honduras	10 Apr 1977	Samuel Ben-Zion Ventura
2168	Satelite Honduras	18 Feb 1996	Marvin Ivan Gudiel Castillo
947	Tegucigalpa Honduras	30 Jul 1978	Jose Miguel Dominguez C.
1709	Tegucigalpa Honduras Guaymuras	29 Jan 1989	Armando Antonio Sierra
2099	Tegucigalpa Honduras La Esperanza	10 Sep 1995	Jose Benigno Triminio Rodriguez
2922	Tegucigalpa Honduras Loarque	15 May 2011	Daniel David Dominguez Sauceda
1771	*Tegucigapa Honduras Toncontin	4 Sep 1994	
	‡Toncontin Honduras	2 Sep 1990	Ricardo Valladares B.
2197	Tegucigalpa Honduras Uyaca	26 May 1996	Moises Abraham Molina Guillen
1732	Valle de Sula Honduras	2 Jul 1989	Solomon Jaar Welchez
2322	Villa Nueva Honduras	9 Mar 1997	Aaron Fernandez Amaya

Missions — 3
(As of Oct. 1, 2011; shown with historical number. See MISSIONS.)

(312) HONDURAS COMAYAGUELA MISSION
Edificio Plaza America, Contiguo a Sears
3 Nivel
Tegucigalpa, F.M. Honduras

(242) HONDURAS SAN PEDRO SULA MISSION
Apartado Postal 1970
San Pedro Sula, Cortez
Honduras, C.A.

(177) HONDURAS TEGUCIGALPA MISSION
Apartado Postal 556 o 3539
Tegucigalpa MDC,
Honduras, C.A.

HUNGARY

Jan. 1, 2011: Est. population, 9,906,000; Members: 4,738; Stakes 1; Wards 5; Branches, 17; Missions, 1; Districts, 2; Percent LDS, .045, or one in 2,214; Europe Area.

In east central Europe, Hungary has a population that speaks Hungarian (Magyar), and is Roman Catholic, 67 percent, and Protestant, 25 percent.

The first missionary effort into Hungary was made by Thomas Biesinger in 1885. He was there for only about three months and then left having found little success.

Mischa Markow was likely the first Hungarian convert. He joined the Church near Constantinople, Turkey, in 1887. In December 1898 Markow was called to serve a mission to Europe. He taught in Belgrade until he was banished and sent to Bechkeret, Hungary, in June 1899. There, he was again arrested and banished from the country in July 1899 for preaching. He continued his work in neighboring countries, but having had similar difficulties in Romania and Bulgaria, he went to Temesvar, Hungary, (now in Romania) on 3 September 1900. He and his companion, Elder Hyrum Lau, worked there until 1 April 1901 when they were again banished, leaving a behind a branch of 31 converts.

Missionaries continued to work in Hungary and the Church received legal recognition in 1911. However, missionary work among Hungarian-speaking people was not successful, and the area was closed in March 1913.

Political restrictions limited missionary work between 1913 and the late 1980s, but there were a few contacts and converts made — notably through the work of Otto Neu who visited Hungary in 1928 and performed some baptisms. He also visited and baptized several converts in 1966.

In 1961, Austrian Mission president W. Whitney Smith created a Hungarian district devoted to working among Hungarians living in Austria, and on 12-14 June 1965 Austrian Mission president Peter Loscher and mission secretary Siegfried Szoke visited members in Hungary. Loshcher returned 21-25 May 1966 with Ernst Griell and baptized Louis Györkös in the Danube River.

On 18-19 September 1976, President Gustav Salik of the Austria Vienna Mission visited Budapest and established a branch there. Due to government restrictions, however, the branch had to be disbanded. In April 1978, Joseph T. Bentley and his wife, Kathleen began their 18-month service in Hungary, the first missionary couple called to serve there.

The Church received welcome publicity in the 1980s that prompted many Hungarians to seek information about the gospel. In 1982, Hungarian Television broadcast a Tabernacle Choir program and a documentary on Utah and the Church. In 1985, a book titled, "The People of the Golden Plates" was published and in November and December of that year a documentary on the Church ran on Hungarian television.

Hungarian officials were impressed by the temple in Freiberg, East Germany, so late in 1986 they approached the Church to see if missionaries could work in their country. They agreed to allow missionaries so long as they did not proselyte openly.

On 21 April 1987 Elder Russell M. Nelson of the Quorum of the Twelve Apostles and Elder Hans B. Ringger of the First Quorum of the Seventy met with the Secretary of the Office of Religion and Internal Affairs in Budapest. He gave full approval for the building of the Church in Hungary. That same month, the first young elders arrived in Hungary. The next year on 1 June the Church was given full recognition by the government. Missionaries saw so much success in early 1988 that appointments had to be scheduled three weeks in advance. The first meetinghouse was purchased in Budapest in April and dedicated in October of 1989.

The Hungary Budapest Mission was created on 1 June 1990 with James L. Wilde as president. At the time there were about 75 members in one district. The Book of Mormon in Hungarian was published in 1991 and the Doctrine and Covenants in 1995. In 2003, a complex housing the mission office and home, a chapel, CES offices, and classrooms and an activity area was dedicated in Budapest.

In 2003, membership reached 3,829. In 2005, membership reached 4,147.

The first stake in Hungary was created 4 June 2006, in the Tihany Ter meetinghouse by Elder Bruce C. Hafen with Gabor Klinger called as president.

Sources: Kahlile B. Mehr, Mormon Missionaries Enter Eastern Europe, 2002; Austrian Mission (now Austria Vienna Mission), Manuscript history and historical reports, Church Archives; Justus Ernst, Highlights from the German-speaking LDS mission histories, 1836-1960, Church Archives; Albert Riedel, Geschichte der deutschsprachigen Missionen der Kirche Jesu Christi der Heiligen der Letzten Tage, 1971; Hungary Budapest Mission annual historical report, Church Archives; Swiss and German Mission (now Switzerland Zurich Mission), Manuscript history and historical reports, Church Archives.

Stakes — 1
(Listed alphabetically as of Oct. 1, 2011.)

No.	Name	Organized	President
Europe Central Area			
2724	Budapest Hungary	4 Jun 2006	Gabor Klinger

Mission — 1
(As of Oct. 1, 2011; shown with historical number. See MISSIONS.)

(243) HUNGARY BUDAPEST MISSION
Hajoczy Jozsef u. 14
1122 Budapest
Hungary

ICELAND

Jan. 1, 2011: Est. population, 307,000; Members, 246; Branches, 2; Percent LDS, .08, or one in 1,274; Europe Area; Denmark Copenhagen Mission.

Located between Scandinavia and Greenland, the constitutional Republic of Iceland has a people who speak Icelandic and who are 87 percent Evangelical Lutheran, 4 percent other Protestant, 2 percent Roman Catholic, and 7 percent other including LDS.

Icelanders Thorarinn Thorason and Gudmund Gudmundson were baptized in Denmark in 1851. They returned to Iceland that year and began preaching on the Westmann Islands off Iceland's south coast. Even though they experienced significant opposition from priests, civil authorities, and others, a number of people were converted and baptized including Benedikt Hanson and his wife. Unfortunately, Thorason drowned a short time later, and Gudmundson, who had been ordained a teacher, was not authorized to baptize. He continued his work, but it was not until 1853 that Johan P. Lorentzen arrived from Copenhagen to assist him. Lorentzen ordained Gudmundson an Elder and set him apart to preside over a branch organized on the Westmann Islands on 19 June 1853 and also taught and baptized a handful of additional converts. Soon thereafter, nearly all the members immigrated to America.

In 1873, Icelanders Magnus Bjarnason and Loptur Johnson were appointed by the presidency of the Scandinavian Mission to resume the work in Iceland. They returned to the Westmann Islands where they baptized a few more converts and reorganized the branch on 1 May 1874. They were arrested on three occasions for preaching. Each time they were acquitted. Eleven converts immigrated to America in 1874. The work continued in 1875 with the calling of Theodor Didrikson and Samuel Bjarnason as missionaries. While serving, they translated several pamphlets into Icelandic but could not find a printer willing to publish them. Didrikson's Icelandic pamphlet titled "Warning and Voice of Truth" was finally printed in Denmark in 1879.

In April 1880, John Eyvindson and Jacob B. Johnson baptized the first converts in Reykjavik on the Icelandic mainland. When this became known, broad and violent opposition mounted and the elders were assaulted and threatened with stoning. Even so, they were able to baptize 28 people during their labors. Twenty-two of those converts emigrated with them to Utah upon completion of their mission.

Through the 1880s and 1890s, a trickle of converts continued to join the Church and immigrate to the United States. Many of the Icelandic converts settled in Spanish Fork, Utah, an area that became known as "Little Iceland." An Icelandic Mission existed from about 1896 until 1914 when missionary work was discontinued due to the outbreak of war in Europe. Assistant Church historian Andrew Jenson traveled to Iceland in 1911 while serving as president of the Danish-Norwegian Mission. He delivered illustrated lectures about the Church in the capitol city Reykjavik.

For several years after World War I no missionaries worked in Iceland, and only a smattering of converts remained in the country. In 1930, the work was renewed as two missionaries from the Danish Mission were again sent there. After their departure in 1930, missionary work again ceased. The distance from mission headquarters in Copenhagen made it difficult to administratively oversee the work there, and the lack of a membership base made it difficult to host a missionary program where broad and sometimes violent opposition had marked previous attempts. Further, World War II made travel to the island nation more difficult.

Church members visiting Iceland, and Latter-day Saints in military service or stationed at the NATO Keflavik Base informally shared the gospel and held Church meetings from the 1940s on. At Keflavik, a branch was formed with 130 servicemen and their families.

Formal missionary work, under the direction of the Denmark Copenhagen Mission, did not resume until April 1975 when Byron and Melva Geslison were called to work in Iceland. They were accompanied by their twin returned-missionary sons David and Daniel who served as the first two district missionaries in Iceland. A branch was organized at Reykjavik on 8 August 1976 with about 10 members. A year later, it had grown to 40.

The first convert in 1976 after the work was resumed was a widow, Sveinbjorg Gudmundsdottir, who in 1977 was hired as the Church's Icelandic translator. Working with Halldor Hansen, Gudmundsdottir translated the Book of Mormon into Icelandic. It was published in Reykjavik in October 1980. Gudmundsdottir also worked on the translation of the Doctrine and Covenants and Pearl of Great Price. They were published in 1982.

A remodeled building in Reykajvik used for a meetinghouse was dedicated in 1981 by Elder David B. Haight of the Quorum of the Twelve. By 1986, membership had reached 180.

Iceland's president, Olafur Ragnar Grimsson, and his wife, Guorun Katrin Thorbergsdottir, visited Spanish Fork, Utah, on 23-29 July 1997, at the invitation of the Icelandic Association of Utah. While there, they visited Church headquarters. President Grimsson also spoke at a fireside attended by about 2,000 people. Spanish Fork is believed to have the oldest Icelandic community in the United States.

Ground was broken on 6 March 1999 in the Reykjavik suburb of Garoabaer for the first meetinghouse built by the Saints in Iceland. The building is the home of two branches. After the groundbreaking, Elder William Rolfe Kerr, along with Pres. Byron A. Rasmussen of the Denmark Copenhagen Mission and Iceland District President Olafur Einarsson visited Iceland President Grimsson.

On 30 June 2000, a monument, honoring 410 Icelanders who immigrated to America from 1854 to 1914, was dedicated near "Mormon Pond," a tide pool on the coast of the Westmann Islands.

The following week, on 3 July 2000, a museum display devoted to Latter-day Saint Church history focusing on the Mormon emigration from Iceland was opened in the new Icelandic Emigration Center in Hofsos. On 4 July 2000, the newly-constructed LDS meetinghouse was dedicated by Elder Kerr. Iceland's President Grimsson, participated in both events.

President Gordon B. Hinckley stopped in Iceland and met with members in Reykjavik on 11 September 2002, and with Iceland's President Grimsson.

On 25 June 2005, President Grimsson attended a ceremony in Spanish Fork, Utah, honoring the first 16 Icelandic settlers to the area. President Hinckley rededicated a monument originally placed there in the 1930s.

In 2002, membership reached 273.

Sources: Andrew Jenson, Encyclopedic History of the Church, 1941; Denmark Mission, Manuscript history and historical reports, Church Archives; Marius A. Christensen, History of the Danish Mission of the Church of Jesus Christ of Latter-day Saints, 1850-1964," thesis, 1966; Lyn R. Jacobs, Mormon non-English scriptures, hymnals, and periodicals, 1830-1986, 1986; Flint J. Stephens, "Land of Fire and Ice," New Era, December 1981; Janet Thomas," Warm at Heart," New Era, September 1996; Tod R. Harris, "Icelandic Saints' Flame of Faith," Ensign, July 1995; "Hostility Melts in Iceland," Church News, 20 August 1977; Tod Harris, "Gospel Touches Remote Iceland," Church News, 6 August 1994; Greg Hill, "Iceland Day Preserves Settlers' Heritage," Church News, 12 August 1995; Gerry Avant, "Iceland President Visits Utah," Church News, 2 August 1997; "Ground Broken for First Meetinghouse in Iceland," Church News, 27 March 1999; "A Monument At 'Mormon Pond," Church News, 15 July 2000; "Iceland Visit: Light, Warm," Church News, 21 September 2002; "Icelandic Pioneers Honored by Memorial," Church News, 2 July 2005.

INDIA

Jan. 1, 2011: Est. population, 1,166,079,000; Members, 9,188; Missions, 2; Districts, 6; Branches, 36; percent LDS, .0006, or one in 153,918; Asia Area.

Occupying the Indian subcontinent in south Asia, India is a federal republic with a population that speaks 16 languages including the official language, Hindi, and associate official, English, and is 83 percent Hindu; 11 percent Muslim; 3 percent Christian; and 2 percent Sikh.

In 1849, two British, Thomas Metcalf and William A. Sheppard, wrote to the British Mission from India requesting information about the Church. At about the same time two recently baptized Mormon sailors, George Barber and Benjamin Richey, arrived in Calcutta, where they shared their limited gospel knowledge. Upon returning to England, Barber and Richey asked that missionaries be sent to Calcutta to teach and baptize several interested people.

Missionary Joseph Richards arrived in Calcutta in June 1851. He performed the first Latter-day Saint baptisms in India and organized a branch. William Willes replaced Richards in Calcutta later that year and Hugh Findlay began missionary work in Bombay. By May 1852, there were 189 baptized members in Calcutta, comprised of a few European converts and many local farmers. A short time later in August, James P. Meik was installed as branch president in Calcutta. Over the next several months Meik built a small chapel, the first Church building in Asia. Findlay had little success in Bombay, but by September, had established a small branch of 12 members in Poona, where he also built a small chapel.

In a special conference held August 1852 in Salt Lake City, Brigham Young called 108 missionaries to serve throughout the world, nine of them in India: Richard Ballantyne, William F. Carter, William Fotheringham, Nathaniel V. Jones, Truman Leonard, A. Milton Musser, Robert Owens, Robert Skelton, and Samuel A. Woolley. They arrived in Calcutta on 25 April 1853 and found that the branch had largely disintegrated, with no more than eight members still active. On 29 April, they held a Church conference and appointed Nathaniel V. Jones as president of the East India Mission and the Calcutta Branch. The other elders were assigned to labor in Calcutta, Chinsura, Dinapore, and Madras. Other missionaries who had accompanied the group to India, departed for Burma, Siam, and Ceylon.

The missionaries quickly discovered that the British and Europeans who lived in India "were aristocratic and cared little for spiritual things," and the Indians, influenced by proselyting tactics of other Christian faiths, anticipated some economic reward for joining the Church. Few people were baptized and the number of missionaries dropped after July 1854. Robert Skelton, who in May 1856 was the last missionary to leave, estimated that there were 61 members in India and Burma at the time of his departure. James P. Meik presided over the Church in India from the time the missionaries left until 1869, when he immigrated to Utah.

William Willes, Henry F. McCune, Milson R. Pratt, and George H. Booth arrived in Calcutta on 1 August 1884 to re-establish the East India Mission. They had little success. Willes, Pratt, and Booth subsequently labored in Rangoon, Burma, where they organized a branch. They returned to Calcutta for a short time and left India in June 1885.

John H. Cooper, who was baptized in Burma in 1884 and later emigrated to Utah, returned as a missionary in 1902-03. He labored in Rangoon, Calcutta, and Karachi, where he baptized members of the Robert Marshall family and a few others and organized a branch of 17 people. Marshall had received Church literature from Truman Leonard, one of the 1850s missionaries, and requested that the Church send someone to baptize him. Cooper returned again to India in 1914. He baptized Nazam Khan, a former preacher, in Lahore, who accompanied him to preach in several villages. Cooper baptized more than 40 people and established a branch in the Punjab.

David O. McKay became the first General Authority to visit India when he passed through Delhi and Bombay in 1921. Between 1944 and 1946, several Latter-day Saints were stationed in India with the U.S. military and met together in small groups to hold religious services.

In 1954, Paul Thiruthuvadoss of Madukkarai read a Church tract and began corresponding with presidents of the Southern Far East Mission and other Church leaders. He also started teaching the gospel in Coimbatore. In 1957, he requested baptism. He and three others were baptized on 7 February 1965. At that time Jay A. Quealy, president of the Southern Far East Mission, assigned two missionaries, Gilbert Montano and John Aki Jr., to teach and baptize Paul's contacts in the vicinity of Coimbatore. The missionaries remained until August. During that time they baptized six people.

A few Church members on work assignments from other countries moved to New Delhi, Bombay, and Madras in the early 1960s and started to hold worship services. They also taught and baptized some of their Indian friends. In 1972, one of these converts, Maureen Das, became the first person called from India to serve a full-time mission when she was assigned to service in the Philippines Mission.

The group in Coimbatore continued to grow. Paul Thiruthuvadoss baptized 18 people on 7 March 1970 and full-time missionaries were again assigned to work in Coimbatore during 1973 and 1974. There were 115 known Church members in India in 1974, most of them in Coimbatore.

Beginning in December 1978, Edwin and Elsie Dharmaraju, who had joined the Church in Western Samoa, served a short-term mission to India. They taught the gospel to several of their relatives and interested friends and organized Church groups in Hyderabad and Vijayawada. Another family, Tagg and Maria Hundrup and their daughter Helen, were assigned to Goa as special representatives for the Church in 1978, primarily to make friends for the Church and nurture local members. During the next 15 years, 120 or more couples served as Church representatives in India.

Missionary work in India was administered by the Southern Far East Mission, 1955-1969; Southeast Asia Mission, 1969-1974; Singapore Mission, 1974-1978 and 1980-1993; International Mission, 1978-1980; and India Bangalore Mission beginning in 1993. The first branches were officially organized in Hyderabad and Coimbatore in 1980, and New Delhi in 1981. During 1984, branches were also formed in Bangalore, Goa, Madras, Manado, and Rajahmundry. The India District was organized in 1981, followed by the India North District in 1985.

Several important Church events transpired in India in 1982. The Church was incorporated as a legal entity, the Book of Mormon was printed in Hindi, Book of Mormon selections were printed in Tamil and Telugu, the Genealogical Society of Utah began microfilming Indian records, and a BYU performing group, the Young Ambassadors, toured the country and gave a special performance for Prime Minister Indira Gandhi. Book of Mormon selections were printed in Bengali in 1985. The complete Book of Mormon was printed in Telugu in 2000.

In 1986, the first Indian missionaries were called to serve in their own country. Natives were allowed to actively proselyte, where foreigners were required to take a passive approach. The Singapore Mission sent six young full-time missionaries to India in January 1992: Ryan Escher, Karl Kirby, Todd Lloyd, Shawn Cook, Bart Sorenson, and Timmy Satot. In January 1993, the Church created the India Bangalore Mission. The first president was Gurcharan S. Gill, a native of Moga, Punjab, who was baptized in California in 1956. Gill was a professor of mathematics at BYU, where he had also served as a stake president. Under his leadership the number of branches in India grew from nine in early 1993 to 21 by mid-1995, with approximately 1,500 members.

In December 1995, the Indian government requested that all of the Church's missionaries who were in the country on tourist visas, leave the country. The Church complied and reassigned 52 missionaries to other missions. The government once more allowed a small number of non-Indian missionaries to enter the country in 1998.

The Diwaliben Mohanlal Mehta Charitable Trust presented the Progress in Religion award to Latter-day Saint Charities in January 2001 in recognition of the Church's work with over 50 organizations in India to provide volunteers, educational materials, clothing, food, equipment, medical supplies, and grants, to organizations in need.

The first Church-built meetinghouse in India was dedicated in Rajahmundry on 2 February 2002. Before the year was over ground was broken for meetinghouses in Bangalore, Hyderabad, and Coimbatore.

In 2003, there were 4,632 members.

On 3 August 2005, President Hinckley met in the Maurya Sheraton Hotel in Delhi with some 600 members of the Church as part of an seven-nation tour of Asia. He left a powerful testimony of the work and a blessing that the members would the necessities of life.

In 2005, membership reached 5,951.

On Nov. 1, 2007, the India New Delhi Mission was organized, the second in the country. It included Pakistan, Nepal, Bhutan and Bangladesh.

Sources: R. Lanier Britsch, From the East: The History of the Latter-day Saints in Asia, 1851- 1996, 1998; East India Mission, Manuscript history and historical reports, Church Archives; Thomas E. Brown, The Church in India, 2003, Church Archives; Southern Far East Mission, Manuscript history and historical reports, Church Archives; Jerry C. Garlock, A history of the Church in India, circa 1955, Church Archives; Dianna J. Greer, "Young Ambassadors 'Unlock Hearts' During Tour of India," Church News, 24 April 1982; Lyn R. Jacobs, Mormon Non- English Scriptures, Hymnals, and Periodicals, 1830-1986: A Descriptive Bibliography, 1986; Singapore Mission. Manuscript history and historical reports, Church Archives; India Bangalore Mission, Manuscript history and historical reports, Church Archives; "India Honors LDS Charities," Church News, 27 January 2001.

(As of Oct. 1, 2011; shown with historical number. See MISSIONS.)

(277) INDIA BANGALORE MISSION
Anjali Plaza, 2nd Floor
493 C.M.H. Road Indiranagar
Bangalore 560 038
India

(348) INDIA NEW DELHI MISSION
B 4/53 ground floor
Safdarjung Enclave
110029 New Delhi
India

INDONESIA

Jan. 1, 2011: Est. population, 240,272,000; Members, 6,683; Missions, 1; Districts, 3; Branches, 21; percent LDS, .0027 or one in 37,584; Asia Area.

An archipelago of more than 13,500 islands, including Java, one of the world's most densely populated areas, Indonesia is a republic whose population speaks Bahasa Indonesia (the official language), Javanese, and up to 100 other Austronesian languages.

In October 1957, a man named Sutrisno (many Indonesians have only one name) became acquainted with Garth N. Jones and George H. Hansen, Latter-day Saints who were living in Yogyakarta. Sutrisno lived with Hansen's family for three years. He later formed friendships with other Church members who were temporarily residing in Indonesia, including Perry Polson, Dennis B. Butler and Ludy M. VanderHoeven. On 1 June 1969 Sutrisno became the first Indonesian to be baptized in his native country.

Elders Ezra Taft Benson of the Quorum of the Twelve, Bruce R. McConkie, then of the Seventy, and other leaders visited Indonesia in October 1969. A short time later, on 5 January 1970, six missionaries from the Southeast Asia Mission arrived in Jakarta to formally initiate missionary work there. They were Frank Willard, Dale Storer, Robert Meier, Ross Marchant, Greg Hawker and Larry Hunt.

The missionaries were met by four Latter-day Saint families who were stationed in Jakarta on work assignments. Several local people assisted the missionaries with legal and other issues, including Ibrahim, an Indonesian businessman who had joined the Church in Holland; Piet Tandiman, an attorney who joined the Church; Siang Sililahih, member of the Department of Religion and Culture who had attended BYU in the 1950s; and Jan Walendouw, who knew of the Church through his business dealings with Church members Peter and Maxine Grimm in the Philippines.

Mission President G. Carlos Smith organized the Jakarta Branch on 15 February 1970 with Dennis B. Butler as president. The missionaries baptized their first two converts on 29 March and the Church was officially recognized by the Republic of Indonesia on 11 August. Before the end of the year missionaries were also working in Bandung and Bogor. Several other cities on the island of Java received missionaries in the next three years: Yogyakarta, Solo, Semarang, Surabaya, and Malang. The Java District was created on 16 November 1972. The country had 770 Church members and six branches at the end of 1974.

In 1975, Tjan Hardjiono and Suharto became the first two Indonesians to serve full-time missions in their homeland. The Indonesia Jakarta Mission was created on 1 July 1975. Hendrik Gout, the first president, was born in Java and joined the Church in 1953 in the Netherlands.

In 1977, the Book of Mormon was printed in the language of Bahasa Indonesia, the Central Java District was created (the second district in the country), the Church opened an elementary school in Jakarta, and welfare services sister missionaries arrived in Indonesia to help Church members and others improve nutrition and avoid disease. A third member district, the East Java District, was organized in February 1978.

In August 1978, Indonesia's Minister of Religion issued Ministerial Decree Number 70. It limited missionary activities of all religions among people of other faiths. Beginning in August 1979, the government refused to renew visas for several missionaries, most of whom were transferred to the Philippines to finish their missions. On 1 September, the leader of the country, President Suharto, requested that all foreign missionaries in Indonesia be gradually replaced by Indonesian nationals. The Indonesia Jakarta Mission was discontinued in December 1980 and missionary efforts were coordinated by the Singapore Mission. The Church's last young non- Indonesian missionaries left the country in August 1981. Leadership responsibility in the country now rested almost entirely on the shoulders of local Church members.

In early 1981, there were 24 Indonesian full-time missionaries serving in their homeland. By the end of 1987, the number had doubled, to 49. The Indonesia Jakarta Mission was re-opened in July 1985 with Effian Kadarusman as president. He served for four years instead of the usual three. When his intended successor encountered visa problems in 1989, the mission was again discontinued and Indonesia again became part of the Singapore Mission. At that time Piet Tandiman began serving as a local full-time counselor to the mission president in Singapore. He was succeeded in this position in 1992 by his son Juswan, who in 1994 was succeeded by Subandriyo. The Indonesia Jakarta Mission was re-opened once more in 1995.

In 1987, the Church closed its elementary school in Jakarta because of high costs, the fact that only a small number of Latter-day Saint children were able to attend, and the feeling that Church funds could be better used in supporting other educational needs in Indonesia. In the mid-1990s, missionaries began working in cities on islands outside of Java, including Sumatra and Sulawesi.

Couple missionaries from other lands began serving in Indonesia during the 1990s. A few young non-Indonesian missionaries were allowed to serve there for five months in 1993. Missionaries from Australia, Canada, Germany, and Great Britain were granted visas in 2001, but were evacuated after the bombing of the World Trade Center in New York City on 11 September.

President Gordon B. Hinckley met with Indonesia's new President Abdurrahman Wahid and members of his cabinet in January 2000 and also held a conference with Church members in Jakarta. Later that year the Church donated rice, hygiene kits, and clothing to assist refugees who were fleeing from violence in East Timor. In April 2003, Subandriyo became the first Indonesian called to serve as an Area Authority Seventy.

In 2002, membership reached 5,604. In 2003, there were 5,720.

Sources: Garth N. Jones, Spreading the gospel in Indonesia: A Jonah and a contagion, 1981, Church Archives; Lorna H. Cook, The Church in the Republic of Indonesia, 1994, Church Archives; R. Lanier Britsch, From the East: The History of the Latter-day Saints in Asia, 1851- 1996, 1998; Southeast Asia Mission, Manuscript history and historical reports, Church Archives; Local unit history file (microfiche), 1983, Church Archives; Singapore Mission, Manuscript history and historical reports, Church Archives; "Indonesian Minister Thanks Church for Aid," Church News, 6 May 2000; "Travels of the Prophet," Church News, 30 December 2000; "2000: 'A Remarkable Year for the Church," Church News, 30 December 2000; "Changes Announced in Leadership Positions," Church News, 5 April 2003.

Stakes — 1
(Listed alphabetically As of Oct. 1, 2011.)

No.	Name	Organized	First President
Asia Area			
2923	Jakarta Indonesia	21 May 2011	Djarot Subiantoro

Mission — 1
(As of Oct. 1, 2011; shown with historical number. See MISSIONS.)

(306) INDONESIA JAKARTA MISSION
Jalan Senopati 115
Kebayoran Baru
Jakarta 12190, Indonesia

IRELAND
(See also Northern Ireland, under United Kingdom)

Jan. 1, 2011: Est. population, 4,203,000; Members, 2,890; Stakes, 1; Wards, 4; Branches, 9; Districts, 1; Percent LDS, .066, or one in 1,516; Europe Area.

The island of Ireland comprises two states, namely, The Republic of Ireland and Northern Ireland, and lies in the Atlantic Ocean west of Great Britain.

The larger of these states is the Republic of Ireland, covering more than three-quarters of the island's 32,000 square miles. It is a parliamentary democracy with two official languages, Irish and English. The Republic, known in the Irish Constitution as "Ireland," is 88 percent Roman Catholic.

Until 1922, the island of Ireland consisted of 32 counties and was part of the United Kingdom, including England, Scotland and Wales. The partition of Ireland took place as a result of the Anglo-Irish Treaty of that year. The treaty allowed for an all-Ireland "Free State" with dominion status and attached to the British Crown, which was conditional on the agreement of six northern counties which had the option of not joining. Northern Ireland, as these counties became known, decided to remain with the United Kingdom.

In the following years, the Free State evolved, leading in 1948 to the formal establishment of a republic.

Though missionary work had been done in what is present-day Northern Ireland since 1840, missionaries did not arrive in what is now the Republic of Ireland until early in June 1850 when John Sunderland arrived in Dublin, the capital city. He established a branch there on 1 September 1850.

A few small branches were established in the Irish midlands including Athlone, Kings County, now Laois, and Gurteen, near Tullamore, and also in the mid-west at Rathkeale, County Limerick, but Dublin was the only branch to retain any continuity during the second half of the 19th century.

Early missionaries remarked that proselyting was slowed by opposition, particularly that of landowners who threatened sharecroppers with expulsion if they welcomed LDS missionaries.

One of the relatively few early members in Ireland was Charles A Callis, born in Dublin in 1865. He was ordained an apostle in 1933 by Heber J Grant and lived until 1947.

Many converts who joined the Church in England during the 1840s and 1850s were Irish – particularly in Lancashire.

By 1863, however, most members in Dublin had either emigrated to the U.S., or lost interest and the branch was dissolved. It was not until 1900 that a branch was again organised in Dublin. It was made up largely of German immigrants, many of whom were pork butchers.

Missionaries continued to serve in Ireland during World War I, but by the end of the conflict, there were only two serving in the entire country. Of significant influence in Ireland was Benjamin Birchill, who had traveled to Utah in 1890 as a Methodist minister to labor among the Latter-day Saints. Impressed by what he saw there, he was baptised in January 1893. He later returned to Ireland where he served as president of the Irish District between 1919 and 1937, spending many hours and much of his own money visiting members throughout the island.

On 30 September 1923, in partial response to the partition of Ireland, both the Free State and Ulster Conferences were formed to administer the Church in their respective areas. They were merged again on 31 March 1935 to form the Irish District.

A prominent Latter-day Saint who was an international soccer player in the 1920s and 1930s was Fred Horlacher. In 1936, Fred Horlacher and Harold B Mogerley were the first missionaries called from Ireland to serve outside the country. They were soon followed by the first sisters to leave on missions, Gertrude S Horlacher and Laura Dimler. All were descendants of the German immigrants of earlier years.

World War II brought the evacuation of missionaries from Ireland. They did not return until 11 September 1946.

On 9 August 1953, President David O McKay became the first prophet to visit, spending one day in Dublin where he spoke to a gathering of members.

The dedication of the London Temple on 7th September 1958 meant that Irish Latter-day Saints had the opportunity to partake of all the blessings of the gospel.

In January 1961, Ireland became part of the Scottish-Irish Mission with Bernard B. Brockbank as president. Elder Brockbank encouraged the creation of a separate mission for Ireland. On 8 July 1962, the Irish Mission was formed with Steven R. Covey as president. Headquarters were in Belfast, Northern Ireland.

This led to a growth in the missionary work in the Republic. At that time, there was one small branch in Dublin, under the Presidency of William R. Lynn who served continuously from 1947 to 1971. His wife, Maureen Mogerley, was of German ancestry. She had been a missionary in London during the war when Elder Hugh B. Brown was mission president.

By the end of 1964, there were also branches in Cork and Limerick. In December of that year, President and Sister Covey had met with Eamon de Valera, President of Ireland, and had presented him with several Church books.

On 14 July 1976, Northern Ireland became part of the Scotland Glasgow Mission. The Ireland Dublin Mission, covering the Republic, was created with headquarters in Dublin. When the Glasgow Mission was discontinued in 1981, the Ireland Dublin Mission had responsibility for the entire island.

On 23 October 1985, Church leaders and members traveled from the Republic to Loughbrickland in County Down, Northern Ireland where, along with fellow members from the North, witnessed the dedication of Ireland for the preaching of the gospel by Elder Neal A Maxwell of the Council of the Twelve.

Less than a month earlier, on 27 September 1985, the Dublin District eas divided and the Munster, later Cork, District created.

Indicative of the growing strength of the Church, President Van F. Dunn noted in 1994 that seven missionaries from both parts of Ireland were serving at the same time in the England London South Mission.

On 12 March 1995, the Dublin Ireland Stake was created with Liam Gallagher as president.

In September of that year, President Gordon B. Hinckley visited Ireland, the first serving prophet to visit since President David O. McKay in 1953.

After its dedication on 7 June 1998, Ireland became part of the Preston England Temple district.

While much of the membership is found in the large population centers such as Dublin, Cork and Limerick, there are increasing numbers in smaller cities and towns around the state.

Membership in 1990 was 1,800, increasing to 2,341 in 1999, and 2,375 in 2001.

In 2005, membership reached 5,956.

The Ireland Dublin Mission was combined with the Scotland Edinburg Mission on 1 July 2010. The resulting mission was the Scotland/Ireland Mission headquartered in Edinburgh.

Sources: Encyclopedic History of the Church, by Andrew Jenson; "Emerald Isle Hosts Beauty, Friendliness," by Gerry Avant, Church News, Feb. 25, 1978; "The Saints in Ireland," by Orson Scott Card, Ensign, Feb. 1978; Church News, July 6, 1974, Dec. 1, 1985; "Markers tell where history was made," by Dell Van Orden and Gerry Avant, Church News, Aug. 1, 1987, and Church News, Aug. 8, 1987; Church News, Aug. 27, 1994; "Visit to Ireland caps 'whirlwind trip' " by Mike Cannon, Church News, Sept. 9, 1995.

Stakes — 1
(Listed alphabetically As of Oct. 1, 2011.)

No.	Name	Organized	First President
Europe West Area			
2034	Dublin Ireland	12 Mar 1995	Liam Gallagher

ITALY

Jan. 1, 2011: Est. population, 58,126,000; Members, 23,976; Stakes, 7; Wards, 37; Branches, 56; Missions, 2; Districts, 5; Temples, 1 announced; Percent LDS, .039, or one in 2,540; Europe Area.

In southern Europe, jutting into the Mediterranean Sea, the boot-shaped Republic of Italy has a population that speaks Italian and is nearly all Roman Catholic.

An early missionary area for the Apostles Peter and Paul, the first proselyting efforts in this dispensation began under the direction of Elder Lorenzo Snow of the Quorum of the Twelve Apostles. Arriving in Genova on the 25 June 1850, Elder Snow and his two companions, Thomas B. H. Stenhouse and Joseph Toronto, proceeded to the valleys of the Piedmont mountains in northeast Italy. Laboring among the Waldenses, a protestant religious group of French origin living in the area, the missionaries participated in the healing of three-year old Joseph Guy, opening the door for their missionary efforts. High in the Italian Alps above the city of La Tour (now known as Torre Pellice), Elder Snow dedicated the country for the preaching of the gospel on 19 September 1850, renaming the location Mount Brigham.

Missionary work progressed with Elder Snow baptizing the first convert, Jean Antoine Bosc (also spelled Bose, Bos, and Box), at La Tour on 27 October 1850. The same year he also published the missionary tract, The Voice of Joseph, and two years later, the Book of Mormon in Italian. The missionaries organized three branches of the Church in the Piedmont area, Angrogne, St. Germain, and St. Bartholomew, baptizing a total of 221 people in the region between 1850 and 1854.

Local opposition to the new faith and encouragement from Utah to gather west caused many of these early converts to immigrate to America. Conversions slowing, the missionaries shifted their efforts to Switzerland. By 1862, all active proselyting in the country stopped, with the mission officially closed in 1867. Daniel B. Hill Richards, serving in the Swiss mission, tried to re-open the work in 1900, but was refused legal permission.

A Church presence, brought by foreign servicemen, finally returned to Italy during World War II. Five LDS chaplains served nearly 2,000 LDS military personnel in the region during the mid-1940s, organizing branches, performing ordinances, counseling and corresponding with family and friends. From that time onward there has been a continued LDS military presence in the country.

Following the war, a permanent presence among Italians was established by the first converts. Vincenzo di Francesca, his story later portrayed in the 1987 Church film How Rare a Possession: The Book of Mormon, became the first modern Italian convert when he was baptized off the coast of Sicily by President Samuel E. Bringhurst of the Swiss-Austrian Mission on 18 January 1951.

Other native Italians, like Pietro and Felicita Snaidero, found the Church while living in France, Germany or Switzerland during the 1950s. Taught the gospel by Italian speaking missionaries, these early converts returned to Italy and joined LDS servicemen stationed in the country in organizing the first branch in Naples on 28 April 1963 under the direction of the Swiss Mission. By 1964, when the Church republished the Book of Mormon in Italian, Church records showed 229 Latter-day Saints living in Italy. Among them were recent converts Leopoldo and Maria Larcher, who later served in their native Italy as mission president and regional representative.

The presence of these early members led Elder Ezra Taft Benson of the Quorum of the Twelve Apostles to seek and receive permission from the Italian government for missionaries to enter the country. Missionary work formally began again in Italy on 27 February 1965 when President John M. Russon sent 20 Italian speaking missionaries from the Swiss Mission to the newly created Italian zone. Laboring in Turin, Milan, Brescia, Verona, Vicenza, Pordenone, Como and Varese, these elders prepared the way for the creation of the Italian Mission formed on 2 August 1966 by Ezra Taft Benson. Three months later, on 10 November, Elder Benson returned to Torre Pellice and Mount Brigham and blessed the country.

With the formal organization of the mission, the Church grew in Italy. Five years after the mission was formed, it was split into the Italy North and Italy South Missions on 11 July 1971. A mission in Padova was opened in 1975 (closed and opened several times in later years). Also a mission was opened in Catania in 1977. Total Church membership passed 7,000 in 1978.

Highlighting this decade of growth were visits by President Harold B. Lee in September of 1972 and President Spencer W. Kimball later in August of 1977. These visits marked the first to Italy by presidents of the Church since the Apostle Peter in the first Century.

As the Church grew in Italy, so did its priesthood organization. The first stake was formed in Milan on 7 June 1981 with Mario Vaira as president. A second, the Venice Italy Stake, was created on 15 September 1985 with Claudio E. Luttmann as president. More recently, the Puglia Stake was organized on 9 March 1997 with Giovanni Carlo DiCarlo as president. Membership continued to grow, rising to over 14,000 by 1990.

As membership increased, so did public notoriety. After years of lobbying, the Church gained legal status in the country when Italian President Oscar Luigi Scalfaro signed the legislation on 22 February 1993. The act allowed the Church to formally own property and its ministers to perform government-recognized marriages.

In 1999, Elder Dieter F. Uchtdorf, president of the Europe West Area, met with President Scalfaro, thanking him and presenting him with a leather-bound copy of the Book of Mormon and a porcelain statue of a family. BYU and Ricks College groups (now BYU-Idaho) have also visited the area, performing to national audiences. They also participated with local members in commemorating the Pioneer sesquicentennial in July of 1997 by parading handcarts around the historic streets of Rome. The Mormon Tabernacle Choir visited in June of 1998, performing in Turin and later in Rome. Beginning in 2000, periodic national television programs have focused attention on the Church and its organizations, including programs on doctrine as well as the Primary and family history programs.

In 2005, membership reached 21,791.

On 1 July 2010, the Italy Catania Mission was combined with the Italy Rome and the Italy Milan missions.

Sources: Lorenzo Snow, The Italian Mission, 1851; Daniel B. Hill Richards, Ten Years Continuous Labor as Missionary for the Church of Jesus Christ of Latter-day Saints, 1902; Joseph Toronto: Italian Pioneer and Patriarch, 1983; Michael D. Homer, "Gli Italiani e I Mormoni," Renovatio, January-March, 1991; Leavitt Christensen, History of the LDS Church in Italy, Swiss Mission for the Years 1962, 63, 64, 65, and 66, Church Archives; Ralph Layton Cottrell, A History of the Discontinued Mediterranean Missions of the Church of Jesus Christ of Latter-day Saints, 1963; Richard T. Maher, For God and Country: Mormon Chaplains During World War II, 1975; Italy Rome Mission History, manuscript history and historical reports, Church Archives; Quarterly historical report of the Italian Mission, manuscript and historical reports, Church Archives; Quarterly historical report of the European Mission, manuscript and historical reports, Church Archives; John Duns, Jr. Interview, 1975, Church Archives; Leopoldo Larcher Interviews, 1991, 1999, Church Archives; Leavitt Christensen interview, 1993, Church Archives; James R. Christianson, "Early Missionary Work in Italy and Switzerland," Ensign, August 1982; Don L. Searle, "Buon Giorno!," Ensign, July 1989; "News of the Church," Ensign, August 2002; "Missionary Work Resumed in Italy After Lapse of Century," Church News, 20 March 1965; "Milestone Reached in Italy; Church Gains Legal Status," Church News, 12 June 1993; Maurine Jensen Proctor, "Overcoming Odds, Wagons Trek Down Streets of Rome," Church News, 19 July 1997; Gerry Avant, "Concert is Artistic Treasure in Rome's Cultural Landscape," Church News, 27 June 1998; "Italian President Greets Leaders," Church News, 9 January 1999; "Missionary Referrals Increase Following Church Programs Aired on Italian Television," Church News, 29 July 2000; New missions, Church News, 13 Feb. 2010.

Stakes —7
(Listed alphabetically As of Oct. 1, 2011.)

No.	Name	Organized	First President
Europe Area			
2762	Alessandria Italy	9 Jun 2007	Maurizio Maria Salvatore Bellomo
1274	Milan Italy	7 Jun 1981	Mario Vaira
2878	Palermo Italy	26 June 2010	Ernesto Nudo
2317	Puglia Italy	9 Mar 1997	Giovanni Carlo DiCarlo
2683	Rome Italy	22 May 2005	Massimo De Feo
1556	Venice Italy	15 Sep 1985	Claudio E. Luttmann
2795	Verona Italy	2 Mar 2008	Massimo Botta

Missions — 2
(As of Oct. 1, 2011; shown with historical number. See MISSIONS.)

(7) ITALY ROME MISSION	(98) ITALY MILAN MISSION
C.P. 11/282 Montesacro	Via Gramsci 13/4
00141 Rome, Italy	20090 Opera (MI), Italy

IVORY COAST
(CÔTE D'IVOIRE)

Jan. 1, 2011: Est. population, 20,617,000; Members, 15,638; Stakes, 4; Wards, 30; Missions, 1; Branches, 14; Percent LDS, .06, or one in 1,557; Africa West Area.

Located on the Gulf of Guinea on the west coast of Africa next to Ghana, Ivory Coast has a population that speaks tribal languages and French, and belongs to tribal religions and Islam.

In the 1970s and early 1980s, isolated LDS families lived and worked in Ivory Coast as diplomats, Peace Corps, or in the oil and sugar industries. They maintained contact with Church headquarters through the International Mission. Cherry and Barnard Silver, who worked in Ferkessedougou, held meetings in their home from 1974 to 1976.

Records indicate that a few Ivorians in the 1980s heard about the gospel and wrote to Church headquarters requesting that missionaries be sent and that the Church be established in Ivory Coast. Leaders in Salt Lake City responded by sending literature.

During the 1980s, Ivorians living in Europe joined the Church and eventually moved back to Ivory Coast. While in Germany, Philippe Assard, a native Ivorian studying engineering, and his German wife, Annelies, were converted and baptized in 1980. Assard was later called to serve on the high council of the Düsseldorf Germany Stake, preparation for later leadership callings in Ivory Coast. Before returning to his homeland in 1986, Elder Russell C. Taylor, first counselor in the Europe Area Presidency, gave Assard a list of members living in Ivory Coast and asked him to find them.

Lucien and Agathe Affoue joined the Church in 1980 in Lyon, France, where he was a student. In 1984, the Affoues returned to Ivory Coast. They were disappointed to discover that they were the only Latter-day Saints living there at that time. A couple of years later they rejoiced when the Assard family wrote them and invited them to Sunday worship services in the Assard's backyard. In October 1988, the Affoue family moved from Abidjan to Bouake, where they were instrumental in establishing a branch.

On 4 September 1987, Elder Marvin J. Ashton of the Quorum of the Twelve visited Ivory Coast. He met with local members, including Terry Broadhead, who worked at the U.S. Embassy. Elder Ashton called Broadhead to serve as group leader. Soon, the small group began to meet in a rented facility near the Broadhead home.

Cherry and Barnard Silver returned to Ivory Coast in April 1988 as the first missionaries. They were only able to serve nine months because of terrorist threats against U.S. citizens. In January 1989, the Silvers were reassigned to Zaire, where they completed their mission. Also in January 1989, Terry Broadhead was released as group leader and Philippe Assard was called as the first Ivorian branch president.

In April 1989, Robert M. and Lola Mae Walker, who were serving in the Ghana Accra Mission, were assigned as lead missionary couple in Ivory Coast. With the presence of missionaries, the Church began to grow. On 3 September 1989, the Abidjan Branch was divided and the Cocody Branch was organized. On that same day the Abidjan District was organized with Douglas Arnold, an employee of the U.S. State Department, as president. Two years later, in January 1991, Philippe Assard was called as first Ivorian district president, and on 19 April the Church received legal recognition in Ivory Coast.

Ivory Coast was transferred from the Ghana Accra Mission to the Cameroon Yaounde Mission on 30 June 1992. The mission consisted of Ivory Coast, Republic of Central Africa, and Cameroon. This mission was originally envisioned to be the center for missionary work in French-speaking Africa.

However, the focus shifted to building up Ivory Coast as a center of strength before moving into the other countries, that meant that missionary couples serving in Cameroon and Republic of Central Africa were transferred to Ivory Coast. Members in Cameroon and Republic of Central Africa were cared for by periodic visits from the mission president in Ivory Coast. In May 1993, the Cameroon Yaounde Mission was moved and renamed the Ivory Coast Abidjan Mission.

As the Church continued to grow, permanent meetinghouses were built. In February 1996, the first stone was set for the Yopougon meetinghouse. A year and a half later, on 18 August 1997, the meetinghouse was dedicated. At that same meeting the Abidjan Ivory Coast Stake was organized with Philippe Assard as president. Three years later, on 27 August, the Abidjan Stake was divided and the Abobo Stake was created, the 22nd stake in West Africa.

In 1990, local records indicate a membership of 350. In 1995, membership was 2,800. In 1999, it was 5,402. In 2001, membership was 6,893. In 2002, it grew to 7,840.

On 1 July 2005, four countries of the Ivory Coast Abidjan Mission, Benin, Togo, Cameroon and Central African Republic, were reorganized to become part of the Ghana Cape Coast Mission.

Membership in 2003 was 8,456.

Sources: Robert L. and Beverly K. Mercer, Interview, 1994, Church Archives; Philippe Assard, Interview, 1999, Church Archives; Lola Mae Hoover Walker, "Brief Overview of Church Growth in Ivory Coast," 1990, Church Archives; Ivory Coast Abidjan Mission, Annual historical reports, Church Archives; "Ivory Coast Grants Recognition of the Church," Ensign, August 1991; Hermine Horman, "Gospel Flourishes in Ivory Coast," Ensign, September 1995; Chirley Roundy Arnold, "Legal Recognition Granted to Church in Ivory Coast," Church News, 25 May 1991; Robert L. Mercer, "Pioneers in Ivory Coast," Ensign, September 1997.

Stakes—4
(Listed alphabetically As of Oct. 1, 2011.)

No.	Name	Organized	First President
2387	Abidjan Ivory Coast	17 Aug 1997	Cyr Philippe Assard
2870	Abidjan Ivory Coast Niangon	7 Feb 2010	
2569	Abobo Ivory Coast	27 Aug 2000	Kalogo Norbert Ounleu
2728	Cocody Ivory Coast	26 Aug 2006	Zahui Dominique Dekaye

Mission — 1
(As of Oct. 1, 2011; shown with historical number. See MISSIONS.)

(271) IVORY COAST ABIDJAN MISSION
06 B.P. 1077
Abidjan 06
Cote d'Ivoire
Ivory Coast, West Africa

JAMAICA

Jan. 1, 2011: Est. population, 2,826,000; Members, 5,721; Districts, 2; Branches, 20; Missions, 1; percent LDS, .21, or one in 472; Caribbean Area.

Located in the West Indies, south of Cuba, Jamaica is an independent state where English and Jamaican Creole are spoken, and 70 percent of the people are Protestants.

The first LDS elder called to Jamaica was Harrison Sagers in 1841, but it is unclear if he ever left Nauvoo and arrived in Jamaica. Twelve years later, James Brown, Aaron F. Farr, Alfred B. Lambson, Darwin C. Richardson, Elijah Thomas, and Jesse Turpin arrived to preach the gospel. They preached in Kingston, Linstead, Spanish Town and near Falmouth. They baptized an English widow, Eliza Kay and her two grandsons near Salisbury and an unknown person in Kingston. Due to resistance from government officials, the elders had few opportunities to preach, and after they were shot at and threatened by mob violence, all but Elder Richardson left about four weeks after their arrival. Elder Richardson followed shortly thereafter upon completing his assignment to ordain Eliza Kay's grandsons to the priesthood.

Little transpired from then until 1969 when two American LDS families, the John L. Whitfields and Jay P. Bills families, came to Jamaica to work for an alumina plant. The two families began holding meetings in Mandeville, and the Mandeville Branch was created 22 March 1970. The Bills also found a Jamaican member, Iris M. Blair, who began attending their meetings. She had joined the Church in 1967 outside of Jamaica and had returned to her homeland. Church member Paul Schmeil introduced the gospel to a Jamaican co-worker, Victor E. Nugent, in 1973.

The first native converts in Jamaica were the Victor and Verna Nugent family baptized 20 January 1974. As new converts, the Nugents remained faithful when the branch's priesthood leaders moved away. They introduced the gospel to the Errol and Josephine Tucker family in February 1978. The two families became the branch's nucleus.

Amos Chin joined the Church while living in Montreal, Canada, in 1976. He returned to Kingston and in 1978 became the first Jamaican missionary. Chin served in the Florida Ft. Lauderdale Mission and was sent with five others in November 1978 to begin missionary work in Jamaica following President Spencer W. Kimball's June 1978 revelation on the priesthood. The elders were assisted by senior missionaries Rolla "Mac" and Nellie McBride, who served for six months in 1979.

Victor E. Nugent was the first native elder and first Jamaican branch and district president. The first district was organized in Kingston on 4 February 1983 and a second district was formed four years later in Mandeville. Elder M. Russell Ballard, then of the Seventy, visited Jamaica on 5 December, 1978, and in April 1983 Elder Thomas S. Monson of the Quorum of the Twelve was the first apostle to visit the island.

The Jamaica Kingston Mission was organized in 1985 with Richard L. Brough as president. From 1985 to 1988 the Church was persecuted greatly in the press. The period of persecution resulted in greater interest in the Church and membership grew from 520 in 1985 to 2100 in 1989.

President Gordon B. Hinckley, en route to two temple dedications in South America, made a stopover in Kingston 15 May 2002 where he addressed 2,000 people at a fireside. Later that year, in October, the Montego Bay and Linstead districts were organized. All four districts celebrated the 25th anniversary of the Church in Jamaica from 5-7 December 2003 which included the participation of Elder H. Aldridge Gillespie of the Seventy, former mission presidents, and pioneer members Victor and Verna Nugent and Josephine Tucker.

In 2003, there were 5,113 members. In 2005, membership reached 5,499.

Sources: Ella Sagers Swanson, The Sagers Clan, 1980, pg. 55-59; Millennial Star, 2 April 1853; Aaron F. Farr, diary, 1853, Church Archives; Norman B. Manley, Jesse Turpin Pioneer, 1998; Journal History, 11 February 1853; George A. Smith, Rise, Progress, Travels, 1872; Edwin O. Haroldsen, "Jamaica Branch Sees Chain of Baptisms," Church News, 28 August 1976; Jay and Shirley Bills interview, Church Archives; Victor E. Nugent interview, 28 January 2003, Church Archives; Amos B. Chin interview, 16 January 2003, Church Archives; Nellie McBride interview, 13 December 2002, Church Archives; Jamaica news clippings, 1980-2003, Church Archives; Church Almanac, 1991-1992; Greg Hill, "2,000 meet in Jamaica," Church News, 1 June, 2002; Rodney and Geneva Showalter and Sharol Moore, "Joy in Jamaica," Church News, 20 December 2003.

Mission — 1

(As of Oct. 1, 2011; shown with historical number. See MISSIONS.)

(186a) JAMAICA KINGSTON MISSION
36 1/2-38 Red Hills Road
Kingston 10, Jamaica
West Indies

JAPAN

Jan. 1, 2011: Est. population, 127,079,000; Members, 125,107; Stakes, 28; Wards, 160; Branches, 126; Missions, 6; Districts, 15; Temples, 2, one announced in Sapporo; Percent LDS, .1, or one in 1,031; Asia North Area.

The history of the Church in Japan dates back to the turn of the 20th Century when Elder Heber J. Grant of the Quorum of the Twelve and missionaries Horace S. Ensign, Louis A. Kelsch and Alma O. Taylor arrived on 12 August 1901.

Under Elder Grant's direction, the first Church mission in Asia was established with headquarters in Tokyo. The first baptism was 8 March 1902 when Elder Grant baptized Hajime Nakazawa, a former Shinto priest. A second baptism came two days later when Saburo Kikuchi was baptized.

Alma Taylor began translating the Book of Mormon into Japanese in 1904, and continued that work for more than five years while he served as president of the Japanese Mission. The book was printed in October 1909.

Missionary work came to a halt on 7 August 1924 when President Heber J. Grant, then president of the Church, closed the mission to await a more "favorable time." Mission President Hilton A. Robertson and the remaining missionaries sailed on that date for the United States. Brother Fujiya Nara was one of the converts who saw the missionaries off. In 1927, Nara was appointed presiding elder by the First Presidency over the small group that remained. He published a newsletter, "Shuro" (Palm) and for a time and held meetings with the remaining Japanese members.

The Japanese-Central Pacific Mission, was opened in 24 February 1937 with headquarters in Honolulu, Hawaii, with Hilton A. Robertson as president. On 22 October 1947, Edward L. Clissold was called to preside over the Japanese Mission, and on 6 March 1948, was given permission to return to Japan to do missionary work. He found a group of about 50 meeting with Fujiya each Sunday. The first five missionaries arrived in Japan on 26 June 1948. They were: Harrison Theodore Price, Paul C. Andrus, Wayne McDaniel, Koji Okauchi and Raymond C. Price.

Latter-day Saint servicemen had prepared the way by baptizing Tatsui Sato on 7 July 1946. His wife Chiyo, and son Yasuo, were also baptized. Sister Sato was baptized by Elder Boyd K. Packer, later of the Quorum of the Twelve, who was in military service in Japan at the time.

Tatsui Sato re-translated the Book of Mormon, the Doctrine and Covenants, the Pearl of Great Price, and other important works. The Japanese Mission was divided on 28 July 1955 to form the Northern Far East and the Southern Far East missions. On 1 September 1968, the renamed Japan Mission was organized with Walter R. Bills as president.

The first meetinghouse in Asia, housing the Tokyo North Branch, was dedicated by Elder Gordon B. Hinckley, then of the Quorum of the Twelve, on 26 April 1964.

Hawaii native, Adney Y. Komatsu was called as mission president in 1965, the first mission president of Japanese ancestry. Ten years later, on 4 April 1975, he was called to be the first general authority of Japanese ancestry. Elder Yoshihiko Kikuchi was the first native Japanese general authority. He was called to the first Quorum of the Seventy on 1 October 1977.

The first stake of the Church in Asia, the Tokyo Stake, was organized on 15 March 1970. The Japan Nagoya Mission was formed from the Japan Mission and the Japan Central Mission in 1973.

The Tokyo Temple, the first temple in Asia and the first in a non-Christian country, was dedicated on 27 October 1980, in what was described by President Spencer W. Kimball as "the most significant and important event in the history of Asia."

Following the dedication, President Kimball participated in Area conferences on 30-31October in Tokyo and on 1 November in Osaka. On 1 September 1992, the Asia North Area was created and it's offices were established in Tokyo.

The Church provided extensive assistance after a major earthquake devastated the Kobe/Osaka area in the predawn hours of 17 January 1995. The Kobe Ward meetinghouse and adjoining Japan Kobe Mission Home were used as shelters for members and others. One member of the Church died in the earthquake and 35 Latter-day Saint families were homeless.

President Hinckley spoke at six meetings in Japan during an extended visit to Asia on 17-21 May 1996. It was the first visit of a Church president to Japan in 16 years. He spoke to members and missionaries in Tokyo, Osaka, Fukuoka and Naha, Okinawa. He also met with the U.S. ambassador to Japan, Walter Mondale, and the media. The Fukuoka Japan Temple was dedicated on 11 June 2000 by President Gordon B. Hinckley.

The first Latino branch of the Church in Japan, the Kouga Branch, was created on 7 January 2001, in the southeast corner of the Shiga Prefecture, approximately one hour from Kyoto and Nagoya.

The 100th anniversary of the dedication of Japan for missionary work was commemorated 1 September 2001, with the unveiling of two bronze monuments in Yokohama, not far from the site where the first four missionaries to Japan began their work on 1 September 1901. The Yokohama commemoration was part of a series of centennial activities that took place throughout Japan during 2001.

By 2002, membership reached 118,508. In 2003, there were 119,267.

In July 2007, the boundaries of the Hiroshima, Nagoya and Tokyo missions were realigned.

The Sapporo Japan Temple was announced 3 October 2009 in general conference.

In the wake of a record 9.0 magnitude earthquake and tsunami that devasted northern Japan on 11 March 2011, the Church relocated nearly 200 missionaries and pledged support, including food, supplies and fishing gear. When Presiding Bishop H. David Burton visited the devastation on June 15, 2011, he noted how had seen many disaster sites around the world, but he'd "never seen anything like this." Inaddition to relief supplies, he commited funds to each of the three prefectures, with more funds to assist with education and employment needs. Plans also include new technology to restore fields damaged by sea water. During an informal ceremony with local fishermen, Bishop Burton pledged an ice maker, a refrigerator, a cooler truck and other supplies to help restore the fishing industry.

Sources: Andrew Jenson, Encyclopedic History of the Church, 1941; R. Lanier Britsch, From the East, The History of the Latter-Day Saints in Asia, 1851-1996, 1998; Dell Van Orden, "Dedication of Temple Called Historic Event," and "Tremendous' Future for Church in Japan," Church News, 8 November 1980; Terry G. Nelson, A History of the Church in Japan from 1948 to 1980, 1986; Yukikon Konn, "Fujiya Nara, Twice a Pioneer," Ensign, April 1993; Church responds in Japan, Church News, March 19, 2011; Church leaders visit Japan, Church News, June 18, 2011.

Stakes — 29
(Listed alphabetically As of Oct. 1, 2011.)

No.	Name	Organized	First President
Asia North Area			
1901	Abiko Japan	13 Sep 1992	Shigejiro Akamatsu
2493	Asahikawa Japan	20 Sep 1998	Katsuo Fuji
1121	*Chiba Japan	2 Feb 2003	
	Tokyo Japan East	23 Mar 1980	Ryotaro Kanzaki
2455	*Fujisawa Japan	2 Feb 2003	
	Yokohama Japan South	19 Apr 1998	Seiji Saijo

1018	Fukuoka Japan	20 Apr 1979	Yoshizawa Toshiro
2508	Ginowan Japan	24 Jan 1999	Yoshitaka Asato
1271	Hiroshima Japan	31 May 1981	Satoshi Nishihara
2547	Kanazawa Japan	5 Mar 2000	Motokazu Arata
1120	Kobe Japan	19 Mar 1980	Keiichi Mizuno
2350	Kumamoto Japan	18 May 1997	Mitsunori Sumiya
1874	*Kyoto Japan	25 Apr 1993	
	‡Kyoto Japan North	31 May 1992	Katsuichiro Fukuyama
1197	Machida Japan	26 Oct 1980	Koichi Aoyagi
1329	Musashino Japan	2 Feb 2003	
	Tokyo Japan West	21 Mar 1982	Koichi Aoyagi
919	Nagoya Japan	10 May 1978	Masaru Tsuchida
1195	*Naha Japan	24 Jan 1999	
	Naha Okinawa Japan	23 Oct 1980	Kensei Nagamine
1404	Okayama Japan	20 Mar 1983	Akira Watanabe
2498a	Okazaki Japan	8 Nov 1998	Toshihide Tsukahara
586	*Osaka Japan		
	‡Osaka (Japan)	12 Sep 1972	Noboru Kamio
872	Osaka Japan North	30 Oct 1977	Noboru Kamio
1328	Osaka Japan Sakai	17 Mar 1982	Hiroshi Takayoshi
869	*Saitama Japan	2 Feb 2003	
	Tokyo Japan North	23 Oct 1977	Ryo Okamoto
949	Sapporo Japan	13 Aug 1978	Seiji Katanuma
1154	Sapporo Japan West	29 Jun 1980	Bin Kikuchi
1202	Sendai Japan	2 Nov 1980	Shigenori Funayama
1255	Shizuoka Japan	21 Apr 1981	Tadachika Seno
1164	Takasaki Japan	10 Aug 1980	Masataka Kitamura
505	*Tokyo Japan		
	‡Tokyo	15 Mar 1970	Kenji Tanaka
2615	Tokyo Japan South (English)	1 June 2003	Lee Alford Daniels
662	Yokohama Japan	27 Oct 1974	Hitoshi Kashikura

Stakes discontinued

1270	Tokyo Japan South	30 May 1981	Kazutoshi Ono
	Discontinued	2 Feb 2003	
1875	Kyoto Japan South	31 May 1992	Kenichiro Kimura
	Discontinued	25 Apr 1993	
1257	Takamatsu Japan	23 Apr 1981	Takejiro Kanzaki
	Discontinued	2 June 1991	
1873	Osaka Japan East	31 May 1992	Ryochi Tanaka
	Discontinued	23 Sep 2001	
1203	Nagoya Japan West	2 Nov 1980	Take Shi Nakamura
	Discontinued	26 Feb 2006	

Missions — 6

(As of Oct. 1, 2011; shown with historical number. See MISSIONS.)

(91) JAPAN FUKUOKA MISSION
9-16 Hirao-josuimachi
Chuo-ku,
Fukuoka-shi, Fukuoka 810-0029
Japan

JAPAN TOKYO MISSION
4-25-12 Nishi Ochiai
Shinjuku-ku
Tokyo 161-0031
Japan

(108) JAPAN NAGOYA MISSION
1-304 Itakadai
Meito-ku, Nagoya-shi 465-0028
Japan

(90) JAPAN SAPPORO MISSION
24-1-25 Kita 2jo-nishi,
Chuo-ku, Sapporo-Shi,
Hokkaido 064-0822
Japan

(109a) JAPAN SENDAI MISSION
3-1-5 Yagiyama Minami
Taihaku-ku
Sendai-Shi, Miyagi-ken 982-0807
Japan

JAPAN KOBE MISSION
4-6-28 Shinoharahonmachi
Nada-ku
Kobe-shi, Hyogo 657-0067
Japan

OKINAWA

Latter-day Saint servicemen were the first Church members on Okinawa. They arrived during the closing days of World War II. As early as 29 April 1945, Ray H. Zenger, leader of the Latter- day Saints Servicemen's Group 10th U.S. Army, was holding meetings on Okinawa. On 23 June 1951, Okinawa was added to the Japanese Mission under President Vinal G. Mauss. Elder Harold B. Lee of the Quorum of the Twelve visited servicemen stationed there on 19-20 September 1954. He was accompanied by Japanese Mission President Hilton A. Robertson. Later, in July 1955, Elder Joseph Fielding Smith, president of the Quorum of the Twelve, also in company with President Robertson, visited servicemen in Okinawa.

By 28 July 1955, newly assigned Northern Far East Mission president Paul C. Andrus was charged with the responsibility to begin missionary work on Okinawa. In 1955, serviceman Ralph Bird was temporarily assigned to Okinawa from Guam. While exploring the island, he went to a home and decided to ask the homeowners if he could take a photograph of their house. When the woman of the house, Nakamura Nobo, answered the door she found an American who could speak Japanese. When asked how he learned to speak Japanese so well, Bird responded that he had been a missionary for the Mormon Church in Japan. She invited him into her home and asked him to teach her the gospel. On 25 December 1955, Nakamura Nobu, along with her daughter Ayako and another woman named Tamanaha Kunike, were baptized in the East China Sea.

The first missionaries assigned to work there full-time, Sam K. Shimabukuro and Clarence LeRoy B. Anderson, arrived on Okinawa 17 April 1956. By 1961, there were two branches, Naha and Kadena, and one servicemen's group meeting on Okinawa. On 11 June 1960, Elder Gordon B. Hinckley, Assistant to the Twelve, visited Okinawa while on a tour of Asia.

In July 1966, the Naha Branch had completed construction of a meetinghouse. Ten years prior, on 25 January 1956, the servicemen had purchased property for a meetinghouse. They moved an old, unused quonset hut to the property to hold their meetings. The Naha Okinawa Ward was organized on 26 April 1979 as part of the Ginowan Japan Stake.

The Japan Okinawa Mission was organized on 1 July 1990. On 20 May 1996, President Gordon B. Hinckley visited Okinawa while on a tour of the Far East. On 30 June 1996, the Japan Okinawa Mission was closed and Okinawa was included in the Japan Fukuoka Mission.

Sources: R. Lanier Britsch, From the East: The History of the Latter-day Saints in Asia, 1851- 1996, 1998; Japanese Mission Manuscript history and historical reports; Okinawa Japan Military District, Annual historical reports; Japan Fukuoka Mission, Manuscript history and historical reports; and Japan Kobe Mission, Manuscript history and historical reports.

KAZAKHSTAN

Jan. 1, 2011: Est. population, 15,399,000; Members, 162; Branches, 1; Percent LDS, .0009, or one member in 114,067; Europe East Area.

In geographical size, Kazakhstan, a republic of the former the Soviet Union, is the ninth largest country in the world. The vast country in central Asia extends from the southern border of Russia on the north to the Himalayan Mountains on the south. Its diverse population consists of Kazakh 53.4 percent, Russian 30 percent, Ukrainian 3.7 percent, Uzbek 2.5 percent, German 2.4 percent, Uighur 1.4 percent, other 6.6 percent (1999 census). Major religious denominations include Muslim 47 percent, Russian Orthodox 44 percent, Protestant 2 percent, other 7 percent. Languages spoken include Kazakh, which is the state language and Russian, which has been designated the "language of interethnic communication." Kazakhstan has a republican form of government.

The first Latter-day Saints to live in Kazakhstan were Russell and Margaret Backus, Americans working in Almaty, who began having sacrament meetings in their apartment in late 1997. In 1998, other LDS families moved to Almaty and provided the nucleus around which the Church began to grow. In July 1999, Paul B. Pieper, an American working as a contractor for governments in Central Asia and stationed in Almaty, was called as group leader.

The Kabdegaliev family, who joined the Church in Ukraine in the early 1990s, moved to Astana in September 1999. Zhastalop Kabdegaliev had served as a branch president in Ukraine. The first Church conference in Kazakhstan was held in October 1999, which was preceded by an open house in Almaty. Brother Kabdegaliev conducted the conference in Russian.

The first baptism in Kazakhstan was on 7 November 1999. A woman named Jazigul Tugelbaeva learned of the Church from American Church members living in Almaty.

The Church received official recognition from the government of Kazakhstan on 19 December 2000. Later, on 2 February 2001, Elder Wayne M. Hancock of the Seventy and president of the Europe East Area met with government officials in Astana to express appreciation for the recognition. During Elder Hancock's visit, the first Melchizedek Priesthood ordinations were performed and the first temple recommends were issued to local members, which in 2001 numbered about 40 in Almaty and 25 in Astana.

Seven months after the government recognition, the first branch of the Church in the country was created in Almaty on 29 July 2001 by Elder Douglas L. Callister of the Seventy and president of the Europe East Area. Paul B. Pieper was called as the branch president, with Averroes Utamagambetov as first counselor and Nurlan Kadyrbekov as second counselor. Because there were no full-time missionaries serving in Kazakhstan when the branch was organized, Kazakhstani members were responsible for teaching and fellowshipping those interested in the Church.

On 25 August 2003, Elder Russell M. Nelson became the first member of the Quorum of the Twelve to visit the country. He visited government officials, was interviewed by Yuzhnaya Stalitsa television and met with members of the Almaty Branch in a fireside. Members living in remote cities traveled 13 hours by bus to attend the fireside. The meeting was the largest gathering of members since the Church received recognition three years earlier. The next morning, Elder Nelson and his entourage gathered in a quiet grove in the shadow of the snowcapped peaks of the Tien Shan Mountains. With the view of the city Almaty spread before them, he blessed the land.

Barry A. and Tamara H. Baker were the first missionaries called to Kazakhstan. Representing LDS Charities, the Bakers undertook projects in hospitals and orphanages, provided aid to victims of the May 2003 earthquake in the Jambul region of Kazakhstan, and also worked with other humanitarian organizations.

In 2002, membership was less than 100 members.

Sources: "Kazakhstan recognizes Church," Church News, 17 February 2001; "First LDS Branch Created in Kazakhstan," Church News, 11 August 2001; "Elder Nelson visits Kazakhstan," Church News, 13 September 2003; Barry and Tamara Baker interview, 3 November 2003, Church Archives.

KENYA

Jan. 1, 2011: Est. population, 39,003,000; Members, 10,270; Stakes, 1; Wards, 5; Missions, 1; Districts, 31; Branches, 30; Percent LDS, .02, or one member in 4,634; Africa Southeast Area.

American Church members and their families working in Kenya in the 1970s held Church services in their own homes. They formed small branches, one in Nairobi and one in Nakuru, that reported to the International Mission.

Elizaphan Osaka and his wife, Ebisiba, and their two oldest children, Margaret and Jairo, were baptized on 21 October 1979, the first Kenyans to be baptized in their country. The Osakas lived in the small town of Kenyenya, which is about 200 miles from Nairobi. Boyd V. Whipple, president of the Nairobi Branch, regularly visited the Osakas and welcomed them to their home when the Osakas traveled to Nairobi. Working with the approval of President Whipple, Osaka held meetings to teach the gospel in four villages. However, due to the remoteness of these villages and the lack of missionaries, nothing became of Osaka's efforts.

The first missionaries to serve in Kenya were Elders L. Farrell and Blanche M. McGhie. They arrived in Nairobi in September 1980 with the charge to teach the gospel, associate with civic and government leaders, strengthen the Latter-day Saints, and to explore the possibility of registering the Church in Kenya. Missionary work progressed slowly in the 1980s, in part, because the Church was not registered as a legal entity in Kenya, and also because only one missionary couple was sent at a time into the country. By 1985, there were 62 Latter-day Saints in Nairobi.

For nearly 12 years Church representatives tried to obtain legal recognition in Kenya. In 1989, because the Church was not registered, the Africa Area Presidency decided to withdraw missionary couples. This absence lasted nearly two years. On 5 February 1991, Joseph W. Sitati, who had joined the Church in 1985 and had been designated as "lead elder" in Kenya by the Area Presidency, was invited to meet with Kenya's President Daniel arap Moi.

Sitati explained to the president why he thought the Church should be granted legal status. On 25 February, Sitati and a few other Church members met with Kenya's attorney general, who reported, "The President is very pleased with you." The attorney general then pulled from his desk a certificate of registration. As a legally recognized organization, the Church could purchase property for meetinghouses and dramatically expand the missionary effort.

After receiving legal recognition, the Church began to grow more rapidly. The Kenya Nairobi Mission was organized in July 1991 with Larry King Brown as president. The mission included Kenya, Tanzania, Uganda and later Ethiopia. More than 30 full-time missionaries serving in Kenya freely preached the gospel and baptized converts. At the end of 1991, there were 333 Church members in Kenya. The first meetinghouse in the country, built for the Langata Branch in Nairobi, was completed in July 1994. By the end of 1994, Church membership had grown to 1,836.

The Church in Kenya was also established in a rural and remote area of the country known as Chyulu. In 1979, Gideon Kasue was working at Hunters Lodge where he met American Church member Dennis Child who was working at the Kiboko Range Research Station for the Kenyan Ministry of Livestock Development. The Child family befriended the Kasue family and shared the Book of Mormon with them. Gideon's sons, Nickson and Benson, traveled to Nairobi in 1985, where they were baptized. In 1986, the Kasue brothers were called as the first two Kenyans to serve missions: Benson went to the California Los Angeles Mission and Nickson served in the Washington D.C. North Mission.

In 1980, Julius Kasue, another of Gideon's sons, was introduced to the gospel in the Child home. Julius then returned to his home in the Chyulu area, where he organized Sunday School groups and taught from Church literature that had been given to him. The missionaries asked Julius to stop conducting Sunday School classes because he did not have the priesthood. Julius waited patiently for nearly five years to be baptized. This happened in February 1986. Following this event, a small branch was organized and meetings were held at Gideon Kasue's home.

In spite of Chyulu's remoteness, the gospel found fertile soil and the Church began to grow. In times of famine, the Church literally saved the lives of many Chyulu inhabitants by shipping food. Wells were dug and Church members were taught farming techniques that would lead to self sufficiency. By January 1993 the Chyulu Kenya District had been organized. Mission records indicate that in April 1998 there were nearly 600 Latter-day Saints living in the Chyulu region.

Three new meetinghouses were dedicated in the Chyulu District on 2-3 November 2002 by Elder Robert C. Oaks of the Seventy and Africa Southeast Area president. At the time, there were 1,300 Church members in the district. The dedications exemplify the phenomenal growth of the Church in the bush area of Kenya between Nairobi and Mombasa.

President Gordon B. Hinckley visited Nairobi on 17 February 1998. He spoke to about 900 members who had gathered from Kenya, Uganda, Tanzania, Ethiopia and Somalia and promised them the work would continue to grow in eastern Africa and that a temple would one day be built in Kenya if the Latter-day Saints continued to "walk in faith and patience." President Hinckley was the first Church president to visit eastern Africa.

The Nairobi Kenya Stake, the first in Kenya, was organized on 9 September 2001 with Joseph W. Sitati as president. At April 2004 General Conference, Joseph W. Sitati was called as an Area Authority Seventy, the first from East Africa.

Membership reached 6,285 in 2003.

On 1 July 2005, the four countries comprising the Kenya Nairobi Mission, namely, Ethiopia, Kenya, Uganda and Tanzania, were reorganized to include Kenya and Tanzania.

On 4 August 2005, President Hinckley met in the Grand Regancy Hotel in Nairobi with some 800 members of the Church as part of an seven-nation tour of Asia. Members came from as far as Dar-es-Salaam, Tanzania and Kampala, Uganda.

Sources: E. Dale LeBaron, "Pioneering in Chyulu, Kenya," Ensign February 2001; Lowell W. Dobson, Chyulu Branch History, Church Archives; Kenya Nairobi Mission history, Church Archives; John L. Hart, "This Work Will Grow and Grow in this Land," Church News, 28 February 1998; Gerald W. Jensen and Carolyn Jensen, "First Stake in Kenya Created," Church News, 29 September 2001; "New Meetinghouses Foster Goodwill," Church News, 7 December 2002; "Visiting Far Corner," Church News, 13 August 2005.

(Listed alphabetically as of Oct. 1, 2011.)

No.	Name	Organized	First President
2600b	Nairobi Kenya Stake	9 Sep 2001	Joseph Wafula Sitati

Mission — 1
(As of Oct. 1, 2011; shown with historical number. See MISSIONS.)

(265) KENYA NAIROBI MISSION
Upper Hill Road
Next to Citigroup
PO Box 46162-00100
Nairobi, Kenya

KIRIBATI

Jan. 1, 2011: Est. population, 113,000; Members, 14,927; Stakes, 2; Wards, 11; Districts, 0; Branches, 14; Percent LDS, 11.9, or one in 8; Pacific Area; Marshall Islands Majuro Mission.

Kiribati, formerly known as the Gilbert Islands, is made up of 36 Micronesian islands in the mid-Pacific where the equator and international dateline meet. It is a republic that became independent in 1979, with Tarawa as its capital. The islands' population speaks Gilbertese and English. About half of the population is Protestant and half is Roman Catholic.

There are no records of missionary activity or visits by any Latter-day Saint members prior to 1972 when the Church was first introduced to Kiribati. During that year, Waitea Abiuta, a school teacher and headmaster of Auriaria Kokoi Ataria School (A.K.A.S.), a small secondary school, asked to have graduates from his school attend the Church-owned Liahona High School in Tonga. Fiji Mission President Ebbie L. Davis visited Kiribati in September 1972 and recommended that 12 students be enrolled on a trial basis. Twelve more were enrolled the following year. By the end of 1976, 60 Gilbertese students had been enrolled at Liahona High School. All of these students were non-Latter-day Saints when they arrived in Tonga; however, all but a few joined the Church. Six of these former students were later called to serve in the Fiji Suva Mission and assigned to labor in their native Kiribati, arriving in Tarawa on 19 October 1975. These six missionaries were Tarate Timea, Abakite Tuneti, Tekaibeti Taratake, Teema Bentitai, Bename Taawai, and Taaiti Natanga.

Among those who joined the Church shortly after the missionaries arrived were Waitea Abuita and several of the staff and students of the school. Waitea Abuita was sustained as president of the Tarawa Branch (later renamed the Eita Branch) when it was organized on 24 January 1976. His school's association with the Church brought some opposition and enrollment at A.K.A.S. declined. In August 1976, Grant and Pat Howlett, Latter-day Saint educators at Liahona High School, were called to teach at the A.K.A.S. Through their efforts, enrollment increased and government relations improved. The Church later purchased the school and named it Moroni Community School (later renamed Moroni High School) and other teachers arrived from Tonga as enrollment continued to increase.

In 1984, the student body reached 240. Many of its teachers are graduates of BYU-Hawaii. In 1994, Teatao Teanaki, president of the Republic of Kiribati, was the main speaker at the graduation ceremonies at Moroni High School. In 1999, the new president of the Republic, Teburoro Tito, visited Moroni High School and spoke to students, commenting on the spirit of cooperation among Church members and the rapid growth of the Church in Kiribati. Moroni High School has been the largest single contributor to that growth.

Kiribati was assigned to the Micronesia Guam Mission when that mission was created on 1 April 1980. The Tarawa Branch meetinghouse was completed in 1981, but meetings were not held in the chapel until February 1982. The Tarawa District was organized in October 1985 and included the Alieu, Abaiang, and Eita branches. When the Micronesia-Guam Mission was divided on 1 July 1986, Kiribati was reassigned to the Fiji Suva Mission. Selections of the Book of Mormon were translated into Gilbertese in 1988. Missionary work and conversions increased thereafter and by 1993, attendance at district conferences was over 1,000. The Tarawa Kiribati Stake was created on 11 August 1996 with Atunibeia Motee as president.

Seminary began on Kiribati in March 1997. On 26 January 2000, President Gordon B. Hinckley, on a tour of Pacific Rim countries, stopped at Tarawa. Among those who greeted President Hinckley was Kataotika Teeke, Minister of Environment and Social Development, who represented the president of Kiribati. Minister Teeke expressed appreciation for Moroni High School and for the humanitarian aid the island nation has received from the Church.

In 2002, membership reached 10,019.

On 1 July 2006, Kiribati became part of the Marshall Islands Majuro Mission which was organized from the Fiji Suva Mission.

Sources: R. Lanier Britsch, Unto the Isles of the Sea, 1986; William W. Cannon, Beachheads in Micronesia, 1997; Fiji Suva Mission, Manuscript history and historical reports, Church Archives; Micronesia Guam Mission, Manuscript history and historical reports, Church Archives; "President Speaks at Ceremony," Church News, 5 February 1994; Dell Van Orden, "Elder Perry Creates First Kiribati Stake, Dedicates Islands," Church News, 21 September 1996; "Pres. Hinckley Completes Tour in Pacific Rim, Church News, 12 February 2000.

Stakes — 2
(Listed alphabetically as of Oct. 1, 2011.)

No.	Name	Organized	First President
	Pacific Islands Area		
2215	Tarawa Kiribati	8 Aug 1996	Atunibeia Mote
2747	Tarawa Kiribati East	27 Jan 2007	Iotua Bareeta Tune

KOREA
(See Republic of Korea)

LAOS

On 28 August 1852, Elam Luddington and Levi Savage were called to serve in the Kingdom of Siam. At that time, Siam governed the area of present-day Laos. Elders Chauncey West and Benjamin F. Dewey were also called to serve in Siam at about the same time.

Savage and Luddington traveled in the spring of 1854 from India to Burma and stayed there for some time. Luddington continued to Bangkok and arrived there on 6 April 1854. Though he likely did not travel to the area known today as Laos, he did write a letter at the request of the Siamese minister of foreign affairs to "His Most Gracious Majesty Phrabat Somdet Pra Chom Klaw Chao Yu Hua, Sovereign of Laos," telling him in the letter "something about the gold plates." Luddington stayed in Bangkok for several months and baptized James Trail, the skipper of the ship on which he had arrived.

In 1945, the nation of Laos was formed, having declared its independence from France.

There is no other known record of a Latter-day Saint presence in Laos until the mid-1960s, when a group was formed to serve American Latter-day Saints living in Vientiane. From then until the mid-1970s, missionaries serving in Thailand occasionally visited to renew their Thai visas. They often met with the local Church members. Church leaders also occasionally visited. By 1970, the group in Vientiane also had a small "Chinese division" that met on a regular basis.

On 20 March 1971, Latda Phornnikhom became the first known native Laotian to join the Church. She was baptized by Elders Rodger D. Garner and Clifford W. Martell.

In 1975, President Paul D. Morris of the Thailand Bangkok Mission challenged Church members living in Laos to submit papers to the government requesting official recognition. The papers were submitted but before they could be approved, the political situation in Laos deteriorated and the non-Laotian Church members left the country.

From that time into the 1980s, many refugees who left Laos came in contact with the Church and were baptized. Several Laotian and Hmong branches were formed outside of Laos during this time.

On 24 September 1982, selections of the Book of Mormon were published in Lao. On 4 August 1983, selections of the Book of Mormon were published in Hmong. A complete Book of Mormon in Hmong was published in 2000.

From 7-9 September 1993, Elder John K. Carmack visited Vientiane to explore the possibility of sending Church humanitarian missionaries to Laos. He was followed on 3-4 February 1994 by Elder Kwok Yuen Tai and President Larry R. White of the Thailand Bangkok Mission who met with Laotian government officials. They arranged to have the Church ship rice to Laos to aid in drought relief. Later that year, 40 tons of rice and 328 bales of clothing from Church storehouses arrived in Laos.

In November 1995, Leland and Joyce White were assigned by Elder Hugh W. Pinnock to serve up to four weeks in Vientiane to cultivate local government contacts. Humanitarian missionaries Ralph D. and Gale L. Steiner arrived in Vientiane on 22 December 1995 on a 30-day tourist visa, one day before the Whites left the country. The Steiners arranged to teach English to a few government officials, which led to them acquiring six-month visas. Numerous humanitarian missionaries followed, with an average between eight and 14 missionaries serving at any given time over the next few years.

Toukta Sonevilay Phongsavanh was baptized 28 April 1996 in the Mekong River by D. Justin Thorp, just outside of Nong Khai, Thailand. She had traveled there from Laos for her baptism. She had been taught the gospel in Nong Khai because at the time missionaries were not permitted to teach in Laos.

On 1 July 1997 responsibility for the development of the Church in Laos was transferred from the Thailand Bangkok Mission to the newly formed Cambodia Phnom Mission. Laos returned to the Thailand Bangkok Mission on 1 June 2004. Shortly thereafter, a proselyting district was formed across the border from Vientiane in Nong Khai, Thailand.

The group in Vientiane was likely formed into a branch sometime between 2000-2004.

LATVIA

Jan. 1, 2011: Est. population, 2,231,500; Members, 1,102; Mission, 1; Districts, 1; Branches, 7; Percent LDS, .04 , or one in 2,426; Europe East Area.

Latvia, located on the Baltic Sea, is a parliamentary democracy. Its major religions are Lutheran, Orthodox, Roman Catholic. The official language is Latvian, though Russian is spoken widely.

Mischa Markow was the first to preach in what is presently Latvia. Markow registered with the district court in October 1903 and then preached to Germans in the city of Riga, which was then part of the Russian Empire.

However, when he was summoned to court and asked to explain what he was doing in Riga, he chose to comply with instructions from President Francis M. Lyman of the European Mission and leave the country, rather than face the possibility of exile in Siberia. No missionary work was done in Latvia because of religious intolerance, world wars, and Soviet occupation until after 1991 when Latvia gained its independence from the Soviet Union.

Recent missionary work in Latvia began on 17 June 1992 with the arrival of four missionaries serving under the direction of the Russia St. Petersburg Mission President Charles H. Creel: Dale Franklin, Dennon Ison, Matthew H. Lyman, and Michael G. Van Patten. They were followed on June 30 by a missionary couple, Boris A. and Liselotte Schiel. Boris Schiel was a native Latvian who left Latvia during World War II, and joined the Church in Germany in 1954, and moved to America.

The first convert in Latvia, Gunars Kavals, was baptized on 25 July 1992. Prior to this, a Latvian couple living and studying in Moscow, Russia, Gvido and Velga Senkans, joined the Church. Shortly thereafter, they returned to Latvia to help build the

Church in their native land.

In March 1993 Latvia was visited by Elder James E. Faust of the Quorum of the Twelve. During that visit, Elder Faust said in a missionary meeting, "I prophesy, in your lifetime, you will see several stakes organized in the country of Latvia under the Latvian leadership. You are pioneers; you can tell your children about it."

The Latvia Riga Mission, created on 1 July 1993, included Latvia, Lithuania, and Estonia and later for a brief time, Belarus. The first mission president was Robert W. Blair. On 16 April 1996, the mission office was transferred and the name changed to the Lithuania Vilnius Mission. The mission was changed back to the Latvia Riga Mission on 13 December 2001 and was then changed to the Baltic Mission on 1 July 2002. The mission is headquartered in Riga, Latvia.

Missionaries began to learn Latvian in the Provo Missionary Training Center on 15 July 1993. Prior to this time, they were trained in Russian and learned Latvian in the country.

The first branch in Latvia was organized in Riga on 30 May 1993 with Olegs Siropjatovs as branch president. A short time later, on 3 October 1993 the branch was divided and Russian and Latvian-speaking branches were organized. Gvido Senkans was called as first president of the Latvian-speaking branch.

Missionaries were sent to the city of Liepaja on 10 April 1997, and on 23 February 2001 missionaries were sent to work in Daugavpils.

On 8 October 1993 the application for the registration of the Church in Latvia was rejected. Branch registration was postponed for three years until 28 February 1996 when the branches in Riga were officially registered. This was followed by the organization of the Riga Latvia District on 25 January 1998.

Translation of Church literature and the Church name began in 1992. Gvido Senkans, Viesturs Tivums, Zigfrids and Rasma Liepa, and Zane Eglaja were the translation team of the Book of Mormon, which was delivered to missionaries and Church members in February 2001.

In 2003, membership reached 692.

Sources: Mischa Markow's missionary journal, edited by Matthew K. Heiss and published in Kahlile Mehr, Mormon Missionaries Enter Eastern Europe, 2002; "I feel that my soul is not empty," Church News, 16 November 1991; "Eight new missions announced," Church News, 6 March 1993; "4 European lands dedicated," Church News, 12 June 1993; "Seven new missions created" Church News, 9 March 2002; Correspondence from the Lithuania Vilnius Mission in Church News files; Baltic Mission Manuscript History and historical reports, Church Archives.

LESOTHO

Jan. 1, 2011: Est. population, 2,131,000; Members, 747; Branches, 2;
Percent LDS .028, or one in 3,516; Africa Southeast Area; Bedfordview South Africa Stake.

Lesotho, previously known as Basutoland, became independent from Britain on 4 October 1966. It's a landlocked country surrounded by South Africa. The people are predominantly Christian, while others follow tribal beliefs. The official language is English, while Sesotho, Zulu, and Xhosa are also spoken.

The first known baptisms were Norman and Irene Halse. They were baptized while visiting Cape Town on 5 February 1931. The first baptism to take place in Basutoland was the Halses' daughter, Norma Renee. This baptism took place on 17 January 1937. This baptism was performed in conjunction with a visit from South African Mission President LeGrand P. Backman. No other visitors representing the Church came until the arrival of June B. Sharp who visited on 29 September 1948.

Scattered Latter-day Saints from the United States lived in Lesotho during the 1970s and 1980s, who were working for humanitarian agencies. In July 1988, South Africa Johannesburg Mission president, Richard J. Snow, organized the Maseru Branch with Garry Massey as president.

The Church received legal recognition on 6 July 1989, and the first missionaries, Marc Modersitzki and Bradley Saunderson arrived in September 1989. They baptized Paul Khobutle and Lawrence van Tonder on 17 December 1989. Elder Neal A. Maxwell became the first member of the Quorum of the Twelve to visit Lesotho on 22 February 1990.

The seminary program was introduced in late 1991. The first full-time missionary from Lesotho, Ts'ooane Patrick Molapo, baptized in 1990, served in the Durban South Africa Mission from 1993-1995.

A branch was created on 4 July 1993 at Mazenod. It functioned for a short time before being discontinued because facilities for meetings were not available. The Maseru Branch eventually purchased and remodeled a home as a meetinghouse. The first meeting held there was 2 January 1994.

In 2002, membership reached 485.

Sources: Record of members, Church Archives; Evan P. Wright, "A History of the South African Mission, 1852-1970"; Cumorah's Southern Cross, Church Library; "Missionaries Serving in Tiny African Kingdom," Church News, 2 December 1989; "'New Day Dawning' in 2 Small African Mountain Kingdoms," Church News, 10 March 1990; "Gospel Pioneers Still Making Inroads on Diverse Continent," Church News, 26 January 1991; South African Mission, Manuscript history and historical reports, Church Archives.

LIBERIA

Jan. 1, 2011: Population, 3,442,000; Members, 5,447; Branches, 13; Districts, 2;
Percent LDS, .15 or 1 LDS in 683; Africa West Area.

Records in the Church Archives indicate that a small group of foreign Latter-day Saints was meeting in Monrovia in the mid-1970s. Every month they reported their sacrament meeting attendance, which sometimes was as high as five, to the International Mission.

In the early 1980s, two small branches were formed, one in Monrovia and the other at Cuttington University College, also in Monrovia, to meet the needs of foreign Church members working in Liberia. The International Mission did not encourage these members to do any missionary work because the Church had not yet expanded into Liberia.

In 1985, Edwin C. Shipp, a tour guide on Temple Square, noticed two Africans in the Visitors' Center. They were both police chiefs from Liberia visiting Salt Lake City for a convention. He felt a desire to talk with them and get their addresses. A short time later he wrote a follow-up note thanking them for their visit. Upon his return to Liberia, one of the men, Kadalah K. Kromah, gave Shipp's address to Joe C. Jarwhel, who was operating a school for underprivileged children. Jarwhel wrote Shipp asking for information about the Church. Shipp referred the letter to the International Mission because Liberia was not yet part of any mission. Elder John K. Carmack, president of the International Mission, sent Jarwhel a copy of the Book of Mormon. In a later letter, Jarwhel informed Elder Carmack that he was using the Book of Mormon to teach his pupils and their parents.

Meanwhile, Thomas Peihopa, a Church member from New Zealand, arrived in Monrovia to work in April 1985, and while looking for a school, met Jarwhel. Jarwhel introduced Peihopa to some of his friends, one of whom was John Tarsnoh, who, in February 1986, had organized a Sunday School known as The Temple of Christ's Church, and who was teaching Church doctrines as best he knew. Peihopa attended and began to teach this group the gospel. Toby Wleboe Tweh, the future first stake president in Liberia, was a member of this Sunday school

Elder Marvin J. Ashton of the Quorum of the Twelve visited Church members in Monrovia and blessed the land on 2 September 1987.

Previous to this, on 3 July 1987, the first LDS missionary couple, J. Duffy and Jacelyn Palmer, arrived in Liberia. Philander and Juanita Smartt joined the Palmers in August. John Tarsnoh was baptized on 22 August 1987. A week later, 47 people were baptized, many from the Tarsnoh congregation. The Congo Town Branch, with U.S. citizen Steven Wolf as president, and New Kru Town Branch, with Thomas Peihopa as president, were organized on 23 August 1987.

In February 1988 Joseph Forkpah was called as the first Liberian branch president. A month later, on 13 March, he became the first Liberian to receive the Melchizedek Priesthood. On 1 March 1988 the Liberia Monrovia Mission was organized with J. Duffy Palmer as president.

Throughout most of the 1990s, Liberia suffered from civil war, which disrupted missionary work and progress of the Church. On 8 May 1990, missionaries serving in Liberia were transferred to Sierra Leone because of civil strife. In April 1991, the mission in Liberia was closed due to civil war and responsibility for the Church transferred to the Ghana Accra Mission. Da Tarr, first counselor in Monrovia District, was left in charge. Of the 1,200 Latter-day Saints, 400 remained in Liberia, 400 fled to other countries, and 400 were missing. Missionaries did not return to Monrovia until 10 March 1999.

On 4 July 1999, the districts in Monrovia were combined in preparation for organization of the first stake, the Monrovia Liberia Stake, on 11 June 2000 with Toby Wleboe Tweh as president.

In 2001, membership was 3,394, which increased to 3,871 in 2002.

Sources: Miles Cunningham Oral History, 17 September 1993, Church Archives; Correspondence from James C. Palmer, Bill K. Jarkloh, Da A. Tarr, June 1994, and from Richard Woolley, 17 August 1998 in Church News files; Harvey Dean Brown papers, Church Archives; Harvey D. Brown, oral history, March 1999, Church Archives; The Ghana Accra Mission, "The Church in Liberia," Church Archives.

Stakes discontinued

2562	Monrovia Liberia	11 Jun 2000	Toby Wleboe Tweh Sr.
	Discontinued	2 Jun 2007	

LIECHTENSTEIN

Jan. 1, 2011: Est. population, 34,700; Members, fewer than 100; Europe Area.

Liechtenstein is a small country located between Switzerland and Austria. It is governed by a constitutional monarchy and a democratic parliament. Religious freedom is granted to all citizens. Religious distribution is Roman Catholic 76.2 percent, Protestant 7 percent, and other 16.8 percent.

Only a handful of Latter-day Saints reside in Liechtenstein. Those Saints living in northern Liechtenstein attend the ward in Dornbirn, Austria, and those living in southern Liechtenstein attend the ward in Chur, Switzerland. The country is administered by the Zurich Switzerland Stake and is within the boundaries of the Switzerland Zurich Mission. Missionaries have never been assigned there, though they have occasionally visited investigators and members.

In January 2004, Bishop Andreas Viussa of the Dornbirn Ward met with the Prince Hans Adam and discussed principles of the gospel. The prince spoke kindly of the Church and its members.

Sources: Ernst Griell, Interview, Church Archives. Telephone conversation with Andreas Viussa, 25 May 2004; Telephone conversation with Neil M. Hahl, 25 May 2004.

LITHUANIA

Jan. 1, 2011: Est. Population, 3,555,000; Members, 894; Districts, 1; Branches, 5;
Percent LDS, .024, or one in 4,197; Europe East Area; Baltic States Mission.

Lithuania, located on the Baltic Sea, is a parliamentary democracy made up of various ethnic groups. Based on the 2001 census, the major religions in Lithuania include Roman Catholics (79 percent) and the Orthodox Church (4 percent). An estimated 9.4 percent of the population does not identify with any religious denomination.

One of the first Lithuanian converts was Irute Meskiene of Vilnius. She heard the gospel preached in Szeged, Hungary, and was baptized there in 1988.

Robert and Ruth Rees were called to Lithuania as missionaries in October 1992. They labored as humanitarian (teaching) missionaries in Kaunus, where they taught English, consulted with the Ministry of Education and worked with the media to have Church-produced programs broadcast on Lithuanian television.

On 21 December 1992, the first four young missionaries were sent from the Russia St. Petersburg Mission to work in the city of Vilnius: Neil Checketts, Greg Lorenzon, Spencer Glende and Jason Swenson.

On 11 July 1993, the city of Kaunas was opened by Shane Allred, Brandon Rohrer, John Dobbs and Jason Riggs. On 17 December 1995, Arunas Tankus became the first native branch president in Kaunas. Missionaries were sent to a third city, Klaipeda, on 3 December 1995. Before World War II, Klaipeda was the German city of Memel and once had a branch of German-speaking Latter-day Saints. The Klaipeda Branch was organized on 9 June 1996. In December 2001, the city of Siauliai was opened.

Elder M. Russell Ballard of the Quorum of the Twelve visited Lithuania in May 1993. The country had been suffering from a drought. He left a blessing that there would be moisture for Lithuania. Not two days passed before rain fell.

The Latvia Riga Mission, created on 1 July 1993, included Latvia, Lithuania and Estonia. The first mission president was Robert W. Blair. On 16 April 1996, the mission office was transferred and the name changed to the Lithuania Vilnius Mission. The mission resumed its earlier name of the Latvia Riga Mission on 13 December 2001, and was then changed to the Baltic Mission on 1 July 2002. It is now headquartered in Riga, Latvia.

In July 1993, missionaries in Vilnius began to study Lithuanian. Prior to this time, the missionaries had spoken Russian.

In late 1993 and 1994, Lithuanian television presented Church-produced programs and also focused on missionaries and their work. In November 1994, Marek Vasilkov of Vilnius became the first native Lithuanian to be called on a mission. He served in the Utah Salt Lake City Mission. In 1995, the Church was registered in Vilnius and Kaunas. The Vilnius Lithuania District was organized on 18 January 1998. Seminary and institute began in the late 1990s.

In January 2001, copies of the first Lithuanian translation of the Book of Mormon were delivered. Membership was 640 in 2001, and 735 in 2002. In 2005, membership reached 791.

Source: "4 European lands dedicated," Church News, 12 June 1993; Correspondence from Robert A. Rees and Gabriele Sirtl, Church News files, 2 May 1994; Correspondence from Nathaniel Currey, Lithuania Vilnius Mission, Church News files; "Church Education," Church News, 17 August 2002; Baltic Mission, Manuscript history and historical reports, Church Archives; Kahlile Mehr, Mormon Missionaries Enter Eastern Europe, 2002; and Internet site on 15 March 2004, U.S. Department of State, International Religious Freedom Report, 2003, http://www.state.gov/g/drl/rls/irf/2003/24419.htm (accessed 26 April 2004).

Mission — 1
(As of Oct. 1, 2011; shown with historical number. See MISSIONS.)

(288) BALTIC STATES MISSION
A/D 3016
LT-2026 Vilnius, Lithuania

LUXEMBOURG
Jan. 1, 2011: Est. population, 492,000; Members, 296; Ward, 1;
Percent LDS, .06, or one in 1,697; Europe Area; Belgium Brussels/Netherlands Mission.

Located in western Europe, the Grand Duchy of Luxembourg's population speaks French, German, and Luxembourger. The people are 97 percent Roman Catholic.

On 23 October 1963, Joseph T. Edmunds, president of the recently formed Franco-Belgian Mission met with officials in Luxembourg who granted permission for missionaries to work there. Missionaries arrived on the following 16 November and immediately began their labors. They were Lynn Farnsworth, Robert Weeks, Raymond Ridge, Clarence Hawes, Russell Minson, LeRoy Billings, Lynn Martin and Guy Frost. On 3 February 1964, Cecile J. Franck became the first known convert baptized in Luxembourg.

A branch was formed in the mid-1960s, and in 1965 Sunday meetings were conducted in the Hotel Kons. The branch remained small and struggled until it was discontinued in 1971.

A branch was again organized 15 November 1988 from the Thionville (France) Branch. In 1994, the branch came under the jurisdiction of the newly created Metz France District, and on 10 April 2003, it became part of the Nancy France Stake.

In 2003, membership reached 194. In 2005, membership was 252.

Sources: Belgium Brussels/Netherlands Mission, manuscript history and historical reports, Church Archives; Local Unit History File, Church Archives; "From Around the World," Church News, 9 July 1994.

MADAGASCAR
Jan. 1, 2011: Est. population, 20,654,000; Members 6,736; Stakes 1; Wards 12; Branches 16;
Missions 1; Percent LDS, .023, or one in 4,331; Africa Southeast Area.

Madagascar, previously known as Malagasy Republic, became independent from France on 26 June 1960. It is in the Indian Ocean east of Mozambique and is the world's fourth largest island. It's people speak Malagasy and French. Fifty-two percent of the people follow traditional beliefs, while 41 percent are Christian, and 7 percent are Muslim.

The first member of the Church in Madagascar was Saholivololona Rabevazaha Andriantseheno, who was baptized on 3 June 1982 in Italy where she was a student. She soon returned to Madagascar where she was the only known member in the country for several years. Razanapanala Ramianadrisoa was baptized on 1 November 1986 in France where he was a student. When he returned to Madagascar in 1988, he began teaching the gospel in his home. As a result, Jean-Claude Rafenonirina was baptized on 9 November 1988, the first person to join the Church in Madagascar. The Antananarivo Branch was organized on 23 September 1990 with Ramianadrisoa as president.

The first missionaries to serve in Madagascar were Fred L. and Eileen Forsgren, who arrived on 3 March 1991. On 7 June

1991, Elder Richard P. Lindsay of the Second Quorum of Seventy and Africa Area president became the first General Authority to visit Madagascar. He met with Antananarivo Branch members and presented the prime minister, Victor Ramahatra, with a copy of the Book of Mormon. The second missionary couple to serve in Madagascar, Marvyn and LaVeeta Hogenson, arrived in May 1991, the same month the first young missionaries, Jason Tarbet and Jeffry Gifford, arrived. The Church received legal status on 13 July 1993.

The Hogensons returned for a second mission and served from December 1993 to August 1994. During this period, the seminary program and the auxiliaries were introduced. The first missionary called from Madagascar was Rondro Mbolatiana Razafiarison, she served in the South Africa Johannesburg Mission from 1995 to 1997.

The Madagascar Antananarivo Mission was created from a division of the South Africa Durban and South Africa Johannesburg Missions on 1 July 1998. The first meetinghouse in Madagascar was dedicated in the capital city of Antananarivo on 9 May 1999.

The Malagasy translation of the Book of Mormon was published in February 2000. A Malagasy issue of the international magazine, Liahona, first appeared in April 2000. Six months later, the Antananarivo Madagascar Stake was created on 17 September 2000 with Dominique Andriamanantoa as president.

In December 2001, violence erupted, followed by a declaration of martial law. On 18 April 2002, mission president, John R. Hill, had all 54 missionaries who were not citizens of Madagascar evacuated from the country. A welfare system was put into place to help the members affected by the crisis. Mission personnel and missionaries returned in July 2002.

In 2001, membership was 2,428.

Sources "Gospel Pioneers Still Making Inroads on Diverse Continent," Church News, 26 January 1991; Marvyn and La Veeta Hogenson, "Rich Harvest of Souls on Island of Madagascar," Church News, 4 February 1995; Borgna Brunner, "Countries of the world, Madagascar," Time Almanac 2004; South Africa Durban Mission, Manuscript history and historical reports, Church Archives. Stephen T. Case, "Unity Amid Diversity, the Durban South Africa Stake," South Africa Country Web Site: http://www.lds.co.za/Artview.asp?ObjectID=238, accessed 23 June 2004.

Stake — 2
(Listed alphabetically as of Oct. 1, 2011.)

No.	Name	Organized	First President
2572	Antananarivo Madagascar	17 Sep 2000	Dominique L. Andriamanantoa
2903	Antananarivo Madagascar Ivandry	13 Mar 2011	Tahina-Elisoa Rakotoson

Mission — 1
(As of Oct. 1, 2011; shown with historical number. See MISSIONS.)

(327) MADAGASCAR ANTANANARIVO MISSION
B.P. 5094
Antananarivo 101
Madagascar

MALAWI
Jan. 1, 2011: Est. population, 14,269,000; Members, 925; Branches, 3; Percent LDS, .005 or 1 LDS in 19,230; Africa Southeast Area; Zambia Lusaka Mission.

The first known Latter-day Saint to live and work in Malawi was Dr. Donal A. Brody. In 1953, while in London, Brody befriended a physician from Malawi, Hastings Kamuzu Banda. Banda became prime minister in 1964 and the founding president of Malawi in 1966. In 1969, Brody was asked to be a business and economic advisor to President Banda, and served in that capacity. He lived in Malawi, from 1969 to 1977. Thereafter, he returned annually until Dr. Banda's passing in 1997. Brody served a total of 31 years as Honorary Consul General.

In 1978, shortly after the revelation extending the priesthood to all worthy males, missionaries in Toulouse, France, taught McDunstan A. Minikwa, a native of Malawi. Minikwa was converted, but returned to Malawi without being baptized, telling the missionaries he wanted to be baptized after the Church was established in Malawi. A year later, however, Minikwa was once again in France and sought out the missionaries. He was baptized in Tarbes, France, on 10 July 1979, the first Malawian to be baptized.

In the late 1970s and throughout the 1980s, Malawians, who were either living abroad and had met the missionaries or had somehow found Church literature in Malawi, began to write Church headquarters asking that the Church be established in their country. The presidency of the International Mission, which had jurisdiction over nations with no official Church presence, corresponded with these people and sent Church literature.

One such person was McFarlane N. Phiri. While visiting a friend in Mzuzu in 1978, Phiri noticed James E. Talmage's Articles of Faith on a bookshelf. Phiri's friend, who was not LDS, said he could have the book. Phiri read the book, was converted, and began corresponding with the International Mission and later with the Area Presidency in England. Phiri moved to Sitima Village and began to teach his family and friends about the Church.

In January 1991, Elder Richard P. Lindsay, of the Second Quorum of the Seventy and Africa Area president, went to Lilongwe, Malawi, and met with American Latter-day Saints working in the country. He set apart Jerry Mills as lead elder. The first baptism in Malawi was performed at the U.S. Ambassador's residence, where Mills baptized his daughter. In July 1991, Phiri traveled 100 miles by bus to meet Elder Lindsay.

After waiting 14 years, missionaries serving in Zimbabwe, Brian and Betty Peedle, drove to Sitima Village in July 1992, where they taught and baptized Phiri and 32 others, the first convert baptisms in Malawi.

Following these baptisms, missionary couples traveled to Malawi from Zimbabwe for about a year. Soon thereafter, unrest in neighboring countries prevented the missionaries from going there. The Church gained legal recognition in Malawi on 25 April 1995 and Malawi was assigned to the Zimbabwe Harare Mission. James Palmer, an LDS diplomat stationed at the U.S. Embassy in Lilongwe, was the presiding elder in 1997 and often traveled to Sitima to teach and assist the people.

In 1999, Elder Dennis E. Simmons of the Seventy and president of the Africa Southeast Area, accompanied by President Frank Bagley of the Zimbabwe Harare Mission, visited the Sitima members. After observing their faithfulness, Elder Simmons organized the Sitima Village Branch on 23 May 1999 with Phiri as branch president.

In September 1999, Dan and Berylene Frampton, who were serving in the Zimbabwe Harare Mission, were sent to Malawi as the first missionary couple to live there. They lived in Blantyre. Though Sitima Village was several hours away, they regularly visited President Phiri and the branch. Within a year, membership of the branch increased to about 200. "We baptized more than 20 each week for four weeks," said Elder Frampton. They were assisted by Malawians Leonard and Mary Nchika, who had joined the Church in Zimbabwe, but moved back to Blantyre. The Sitima Village Branch met at President Phiri's home under a bowery. A second branch was organized in the country on 30 July 2000 in Blantyre.

In 2001, membership was 326. In 2002, membership reached 377. By Jan. 1, 2011, membership was 798.

Malawi became part of the Zambia Lusaka Mission on July 1, 2011, when the Zimbabwe Harare Mission was divided from Zambia and Malawi to create its own mission.

Sources: Donal A. Brody, Telephone conversation, 11 May 2004; Brian and Betty Peedle, Interview, June 2000, Church Archives; McFarlane N. Phiri, Interview, May 2000, Church Archives; James Palmer, Interview, October 2000, Church Archives; McFarlane N. Phiri Autobiographical Sketch, 2000, Church Archives; Dan and Berylene Frampton, Interview, May 2000, Church Archives; John L. Hart, "Village Branch is a Testimony of Enduring Faith," 18 November 2000 Church News; "New Boundaries," 19 February 2011, Church News.

MALAYSIA

Jan. 1, 2011: Est. population, 25,716,000; Members, 7,314; Districts, 6; Branches, 28; Percent LDS, .02, or one in 4,555; Asia Area; Singapore Mission.

On the southeast tip of Asia and the northern half of the island of Borneo, Malaysia is a federal parliamentary democracy with a constitutional monarch. Its people speak Malay, Chinese, English, and Indian languages, and practice primarily Muslim, Hindu, Buddhist, Confucian, Taoist, and local religions.

In February 1854, Elam Luddington, a Latter-day Saint missionary, preached for about five days on Prince of Wales Island, later renamed Penang. There were no other known Latter-day Saints in Malaysia until the 1960s, when Church members from Australia and the U.S. moved there on military or work assignments and began holding worship services in small groups. G. Carlos Smith of the Southeast Asia Mission organized the Penang Group with David K. Smith as leader on 16 May 1971. A second Church group was formed in Kuala Lumpur on 17 June 1973. The first conference of Church members in Malaysia was held the next month, on 28 July, in Penang.

A few Malaysians were baptized in other parts of the world during the 1970s who later became Church leaders in Malaysia: Ivan B. Ho in Taiwan, 1970; Jacob Kong in England, 1977; and Chong Sun Fu in Australia, 1979. See Ba Thee became the first Malaysian baptized in his own country on 26 July 1971. Two local members, Derrick Ho and Chan Wai Leong, were set apart in early 1976 as full-time missionaries to serve in Kuala Lumpur, where they remained for a few months.

The Church was incorporated in Malaysia on 19 October 1977. The Penang Group was dissolved sometime between 1976 and 1978 because most of its Australian and American members had moved from the area.

On 23 June 1978 Werner and Mercedes Kiepe arrived in Kuala Lumpur to serve as special representatives of the International Mission. In February 1980, J. Talmage Jones of the Singapore Mission organized the Malaysia District with J. Floyd Stoker as president. Jones also restarted the Penang Branch. The Ipoh Branch was created in 1981.

Church representatives from outside Malaysia have had difficulty obtaining visas to stay in the country for more than a few months at a time. In 1980, two young men who had joined the Church abroad, David Soon Ewe Seang and Chong Sun Fu, wrote to the mission president in Singapore expressing a desire to serve missions in their homeland. They began their service in June 1981. Other young Malaysian Latter-day Saints have followed their example.

Ivan B. Ho was sustained as the first local branch president in Kuala Lumpur on 3 January 1983 and as the first local president of the Malaysia District on 1 December 1986. Malaysia was part of the Southeast Asia Mission, 1971-1974; Singapore Mission, 1974-1978; International Mission, 1978-1980; and the Singapore Mission, beginning again in 1980.

The Church's efforts in the nation focused almost exclusively in West Malaysia before February 1985, when William and Blanch Dalby were sent to Kuching, East Malaysia. They and their successors, Manahi and Hineapa Paewai, made friends in Kuching and visited with isolated Church members in Miri, Kota Kinabalu, and Brunei, a small coastal country located in the middle of East Malaysia. After the Paewais concluded their service no further missionaries were assigned to East Malaysia for another eight years.

Jacob Kong was one of the handful of Church members whom the missionary couples met in East Malaysia in 1985. Kong joined the Church in England in 1977 and had taught school in Singapore before returning to Miri, East Malaysia, in 1984. He later moved to Kuching. When missionaries finally returned to Kuching in August 1993, Jacob Kong was set apart as group leader. He became the first president of the Kuching Branch on 18 June 1995.

Missionaries began serving elsewhere in East Malaysia during 1995 and 1996, including Kota Kinabalu in June 1995, Sibu in January 1996, and Miri in March 1996. The Kota Kinabalu East Malaysia District was organized on 4 May 1997. By the end of 1998, there were six branches each in West Malaysia and East Malaysia.

On 30 October 1990, King Syed Putra Jamallail, who served as Malaysia's head of state from 1961 to 1965, visited the Polynesian Cultural Center with members of his family. Several Church leaders in Malaysia were privileged to have dinner with King Tuanku Ja'afar and Queen Tuanku Najiha in the Royal Palace in Kuala Lumpur on 28 September 1994. The event was arranged by Church members Vincent and Sandra Gordacan, personal friends of the king and queen.

In 2003, there were 2,237 members.

The first meetinghouse constructed by the Church in Malaysia was dedicated by Elder Daryl H. Garn of the Seventy on 19 March 2006 in Miri, Sarawak. Members of the Miri Branch were assigned to the meetinghouse.

Sources: R. Lanier Britsch, From the East: The History of the Latter-day Saints in Asia, 1851- 1996, 1998; Southeast Asia Mission, Manuscript history and historical reports, Church Archives; Anthony T. K. Lim, Church history in Malaysia, 2003, Church Archives; Singapore Mission,

Manuscript history and historical Reports, Church Archives; Mike Foley, "Malaysian King Is Met with Royal 'Aloha,'" Church News, 3 November 1990; http://tourmalaysia.tripod.com/pst_kings.htm, cited 30 July 2004; "Members Dine with Royalty," Church News, 17 December 1994; "Meetinghouse for Malaysia," Church News, 15 April 2006.

MALTA

Jan. 1, 2011: Est. population, 405,000; Members, 146; Branches, 1; Percent LDS, .03, or one in 3,068; Europe Area; Italy Catania Mission.

Located in the Mediterranean Sea, Malta is a republic with a population that speaks Maltese and English, and is mostly Roman Catholic.

On 26 February 1852, Apostle Lorenzo Snow and Jabez Woodard arrived on Malta and began to preach the gospel. Elder Snow departed for Gibraltar on 16 May 1852, leaving Woodard and James F. Bell to carry on the work. Shortly thereafter, Ferndinanda Seiapati and Jean Alais Frouche were the first people baptized on the island. Thomas Obray arrived on 30 May 1852 having been appointed to succeed Woodard as mission president. The following 20 June a branch was organized. Most of the converts were British military personnel. Opposition surfaced, however, and many converts were threatened by military officials with loss of rank or punishment for their involvement in the Church. Many remained faithful, but others fell away.

In 1854, many branch members left Malta to serve in the Crimean War. Four mobile branches were organized to serve the members at war from the original branch in Malta. By 1856, however, the main branch was dissolved.

Sources: Andrew Jenson, Encyclopedic History of the Church, 1941; Malta Mission, Manuscript history and historical reports, Church Archives; "French, Italian, German, and Malta Missions," Millennial Star, 14:603; Deseret News, 10 October 1854; Malta Branch, Sunday School minutes, Church Archives; Italy Catania Mission, Manuscript history and historical reports, Church Archives; JoAn B. Bitton, Personal account of the island of Malta, 1976, 1993, Church Archives; Malta Branch, General minutes, Church Archives.

MARSHALL ISLANDS

Jan. 1, 2011: Est. population, 64,500; Members, 5,093; Stakes, 1; Wards, 6; Districts, 1; Branches, 6; Mission, 1; Percent LDS, 7, or one in 14; Pacific Area; Marshall Islands Majuro Mission.

The Marshall Islands are made up of two atoll chains in the Pacific. Kwajalein is the largest atoll and Majuro is the capital island. The Marshalls became a trusteeship of the United States in 1947 and self-governing republic in 1979.

There are no records of missionary activity in the Marshall Islands or visits by Latter-day Saint members prior to World War II. The first known Latter-day Saints in the Marshall Islands came as members of the armed forces during World War II. Missionary work in this island group began on the Majuro Atoll in 1977 under the direction of the Hawaii Honolulu Mission. The Marshall Islands became part of the Micronesia Guam Mission on 1 April 1980.

MAJURO

The first missionaries to the Majuro Atoll were William Wardel and Steven Cooper, who arrived on 3 February 1977. Eldred Fewkes, a Church member who had come to Majuro for work, arranged to hold meetings in the Seventh-Day Adventists' church until another location could be secured. He was the group's initial leader. Misao Lokeijak, who had been introduced to the Church earlier in Hawaii, was baptized on 23 April 1977. By the end of that year there were 27 converts on the island. Victor and Beatrice Merrill, the first missionary couple to serve in the Marshall Islands, arrived in Majuro on 11 March 1978. Misao Lokeijak was called to be the first native branch president on 11 May 1978. By the end of 1979, there were 177 members on the atoll. A seminary program was started with the 1980-1981 school years. A second branch was formed at Rita in July 1982 and the Majuro Branch was renamed the Laura Branch. Orlo Hall, who served with his wife Meinel as a missionary couple, was assigned by mission president Joseph B. Keeler to organize the Majuro District. They arrived in October 1984. Hall was set apart as district president on 30 December 1984. Shortly before their arrival, construction of meetinghouses for the Laura and Rita branches had begun in September. The meetinghouses were dedicated on 13-14 January 1986, respectively. Church membership has steadily increased and the Majuro District now includes the Ajeltake, Delap, Jenrok, Laura, Long Island Majuro, Rita, and Uliga branches.

On 1 July 2006, the Marshall Islands Majuro Mission was organized from the Micronesia Guam Mission with an estimated 12,704 members in the mission.

CHRISTMAS ISLAND

Jan. 1, 2011: Est. population, 1,508; Members, 117; Branches, 1; percentage of LDS, 7.7 or one in 13; Pacific Area; Marshall Islands Majuro Mission.

Situated among the Line Islands in the South Pacific, Christmas Island, a 140-square mile atoll, is a part of the Republic of Kiribati with a population that speaks Gilbertese and English. It is about 2,000 miles from Tarawa.

The first branch on Christmas Island was organized by Pres. H. Ross Workman of the Hawaii Honolulu Mission on May 23, 1999, in the village of London. Located some 1,500 miles south of Hawaii, Christmas Island previously was in the Fiji Suva Mission, but was transferred to the Hawaii mission in 1998.

The first president of the branch was Timei Kaitaua, who, early in 1999, had contacted Pres. Workman about the possibility of a branch on Christmas Island.

Most of the 117 members of the branch were converted elsewhere, many attending Moroni High School on Tarawa, the capital of the Republic of Kiribati, and/or BYU Hawaii, and then either returning or moving to Christmas Island for one reason or another.

During a brief stop June 19, 2003, President Hinckley addressed members on the island and promised "marvelous things will happen" if they are true to their faith. "You will raise missionaries who will go out among the islands of the Pacific and teach the gospel," he said. "You will enjoy greater comfort and all of the good things of life if you will live the gospel." President Hinckley walked near many well-dressed youth who wore white shirts and ties and had bare feet.

On 1 July 2006, Christmas Island became part of the Marshall Islands Majuro Mission.

Source: Julie A. Dockstader, "New branch created on Pacific isle," Church News, 3 July 1999.

Stake — 1
(Listed alphabetically as of Oct. 1, 2011.)

No.	Name	Organized	First President
2837	Majuro Marshall Islands	14 Jun 2009	Arlington Tibon

Mission — 1
(As of Oct. 1, 2011; shown with historical number. See MISSIONS.)

MARSHALL ISLANDS MISSION
Eletutu Weto
Delap Island, Majuro Atoll
Marshall Islands

KWAJALEIN/EBEYE

The Kwajalein Island Branch was organized in 1978, made up entirely of U.S. citizens serving in the military or as civil service personnel (the entire island is essentially a U.S. Army installation). A servicemen's group had existed on Kwajalein prior to a branch being created. The most populous island of the Kwajalein Atoll is Ebeye. Kepiloni Foliaki and Michael Steele began missionary work on Ebeye on 16 May 1989 and baptized Mary Kekuhuna on 11 June 1989. The Ebeye Branch was organized in June 1990 with Renoun Sylvester as president. The Kwajalein District was organized on 12 May 1991 with John Haldeman as president. Bruce Saunders and Joel Robison began missionary work on the neighboring island of Lae on 27 December 1991 and a branch was organized on 10 August 1992.

That same year the Ebeye Branch Relief Society began a project to pick up litter to beautify their island. After the sisters had done this a few times, the queen of the island, First Lady Emlain Kabua, joined them. On 7 November 1998, after years of negotiations, mayoral approval was granted and an agreement was reached for the Ebeye Branch to lease space for a chapel to be constructed in a storm shelter the branch had been meeting in for years. Because building space was limited on the island, the Church agreed to share in the cost for a school addition to be constructed at the other end of the shelter. During the remodeling of the shelter, the Ebeye 2nd Branch was organized on 22 October 2000. The two branches celebrated the dedication of the chapel portion of the building on 18 March 2001. The Lae Branch held their first conference on 12 May 2003, even though the branch had been organized since 1992. The 40 branch members invited their non-member friends and family to attend. In all, 110 people were in attendance out of a total island population of 400. The Kwajalein District now includes the Kwajalein, Ebeye 1st, Ebeye 2nd, and Lae branches.

Source: Micronesia Guam Mission, Brief History of the Micronesia-Guam Mission, 1980-1990, 1990, Church Archives; Hawaii Honolulu Mission, Annual histories and historical reports, Church Archives; Majuro Branch, Historical reports, Church Archives; Majuro District, Historical reports, Church Archives; Kwajalein Branch, Historical reports, Church Archives; Kwajalein District, Historical reports, Church Archives; Lae Branch conference report, Church Archives.

MAURITIUS

Mauritius located east of Madagascar. The official languages are English, and French, while Creole, Hindi, Urdu, Hakka, and Bojpoori are also spoken. Fifty-two percent of the people are Hindu, while 28.3 percent are Christian, 16.6 percent Muslim, and 3.1 percent follow other beliefs.

George Kershaw, a Latter-day Saint from South Africa, served as a missionary for two months in Mauritius in 1856. His only known converts were an army private and several members of the crew of the ship on which he arrived.

In recent years, the first known Mauritian to be baptized was Sylvie Babajee who joined the Church outside the country on 5 June 1966. Mauritius and the Mascarenes Islands came under the direction of the International Mission in 1979. The first baptisms on Mauritius were for Rowan Sanjay Narraidoo, Harold Clément Désiré Essoo, Alain Kheeroo, Jocelyn Rudy (Ruddy) Lenette, Jayprakash (Vyas) Mohabeer, and Gérard Gabriel Goder who joined the Church on 27 November 1981.

Preston and Isabelle Gledhill, arrived on 29 December 1980, the first full-time missionaries assigned to work on the island. The Mauritius Branch was organized on 25 February 1982 with Don Norton as president. Senior missionary couple, Edward A. and Louise P. Schmidt, served a teaching mission to Mauritius from 1984 to 1986. It was during this time that Sister Schmidt introduced the seminary and institute curriculum to the island. On 1 July 1985, the parliament of Mauritius passed a bill granting the Church legal recognition.

Several months later, on 24 October 1985, Richard A. Clawson and Blake C. Rick arrived on Mauritius as the first young missionaries to serve there. Between 1984 and 1987, missionaries were called to the Mascarene Islands from French-speaking missions in Europe.

In 1986, Mauritius was transferred from the International Mission to become part of the South Africa Johannesburg Mission. On 1 July 1988 the Mascarene Islands Mission was created. Elder Marvin J. Ashton of the Council of the Twelve visited the island on 22 November 1988. On 1 July 1998, Mauritius was placed in the newly created Madagascar Antananarivo Mission.

In 2004, there were 361 members organized in two branches. In 2005, membership was 358. In 2011 there were 406 members organized in two branches.

Sources: Hal H. Hunter, The history of the Church of Jesus Christ of Latter-day Saints in the Mascarene Islands, 1987, Church Archives; Madagascar Antananarivo Mission, Manuscript history and historical reports, Church Archives; Borgna Brunner, "Countries of the World," Mauritius," Time Almanac 2004; Louise P. Schmidt, Conversation, 29 April 2004.

MEXICO

Jan. 1, 2011: Est. population, 111,212,000; Members, 1,234,545; Stakes, 221; Wards, 1,544; Branches, 465; Missions, 23; Districts, 34; Temples, 12; Percent LDS, 1, or one in 96; Mexico Area.

Located in southern North America, Mexico is a federal republic with a Spanish-speaking population.

In 1874, just prior to the first missionaries arriving in Mexico and at the request of Brigham Young, Meliton Trejo and Daniel W. Jones printed "Trozos Selectos del Libro de Mormon [Short Selections from the Book of Mormon]." In 1875, seven missionaries were sent to Mexico. On the way they preached to Native Americans and sent a favorable report to Church headquarters that led to the founding of Mesa, Ariz. Rebuffed in Mexico at first, the missionaries divided into two groups. The first, Daniel W. Jones, James Z. Stewart, Helaman Pratt, Anthony W. Ivins and Wiley Jones, traveled to Chihuahua, where they were well-received. They scouted settlement sites and mailed pamphlets containing translated sections of the Book of Mormon to 500 influential leaders throughout Mexico. They found many listeners among the mountain villages and among the natives, but made no converts. Meliton Trejo, with possibly two missionary companions, traveled to Hermosillo, Sonora, where they baptized the first five members in Mexico.

Dr. Plotino C. Rhodakanaty of Mexico City received a tract from the original Jones expedition and began corresponding with Meliton Trejo and the First Presidency. Rhodakanaty represented a group of 20 investigators and asked for missionaries to baptize them. Apostle Moses Thatcher, Meliton Trejo, and James Z. Stewart traveled to Mexico City, where on 20 November 1879, they baptized Rhodakanaty and Silviano Arteaga and organized a branch with Rhodakanaty as president. By 1880, more literature had been translated into Spanish. Missionaries left Mexico City and found converts in the small rural town of Ozumba. Additional missionaries arrived and despite setbacks, the work moved forward in the states of Hidalgo, Mexico, and Morelos. In 1885, Meliton Trejo and James Z. Stewart completed the translation of the Book of Mormon into Spanish.

In 1885, a group of nearly 400 colonists from Utah, fleeing prosecution in the United States for practicing plural marriage, arrived at the Casas Grandes River in the state of Chihuahua and acquired property. Soon these and other Latter-day Saints arriving from Utah and Arizona founded several small colonies including Juarez, Dublan, Diaz, Pacheco, Garcia, and Chuichupa in Chihuahua, and Oaxaca and Morelos in Sonora. Mexico's first stake, the Juarez Stake, was created in 1895. It primarily represented these English-speaking colonists.

On 8 June 1901, the Mexican Mission was reopened with Ammon M. Tenney as mission president. Visiting branches near Mexico City, Tenney found the early members still faithful. Branches were re-organized and by 1911, membership in central Mexico reached 1,000.

The Mexican Revolution, which began in 1910 and continued for almost a decade, halted much of the Church's progress. The Latter-day Saints in the Juarez Stake left Mexico in 1912 to avoid the conflict and members in central Mexico were left without leaders and were abused by conflicting armies. Two local Church leaders, Rafael Monroy and Vicente Morales, were executed.

When mission President Rey L. Pratt returned to central Mexico in November 1917, he found many members who had remained faithful throughout the period of the revolution. Work again progressed, but the nationalism generated by the revolution resulted in the expulsion in 1926 of all foreign clergy – including Latter-day Saint missionaries — by Mexican authorities. Local Mexican Church leaders maintained stability and expanded the work, calling six local missionaries in 1930. However, in 1936, a group called the Third Convention, influenced by the wave of nationalism that continued to sweep through Mexico even after the revolution, broke away from the Church for a period. They were reunited with the Church through the able leadership of Mexican Mission President Arwell Pierce. In 1946, President George Albert Smith visited members of the Church, who numbered more than 5,300.

The Mexican Mission was divided on 10 June 1956 and the Northern Mexico Mission was created. The Mexico Stake was created on 3 December 1961, the first Spanish-speaking stake in the Church. Six years later, Agricol Lozano became the first local stake president in Mexico. Church membership in Mexico at that time was about 25,000.

Although the Juarez Stake Academy had served the educational needs of Church members in the colonies for decades, other Church schools were established beginning in 1959. The most significant was the large preparatory school, Benemerito in Mexico City. It was started in 1963.

In the late 1960s, membership began to expand rapidly. By 1972, it reached 100,000. In February 1977, President Spencer W. Kimball spoke at area conferences in Monterrey and Mexico City. Nearly 25,000 members, the largest congregation ever to attend an area conference during the 10 years they were held from 1971-80, participated in the Mexico City conference. While in Mexico City, President Kimball visited with President Jose Lopez Portillo at the national palace.

The Mexico City Temple was dedicated on 2 December 1983. Mexico was the first country outside the United States to have 100 stakes. When the 100th stake was created at Tecalco 25 July 1989, membership in Mexico was estimated to be more than half a million. In 1992, Mexico became the first nation outside the United States to be divided into two areas, Mexico North and Mexico South.

Elder Waldo Call was called to the Seventy in 1985 from the original Mexican colonies, the first Mexican General Authority. He was followed in 1989 by Elder Horacio Tenorio, the first of Mexican ancestry to be called as a General

Authority.

A historic event occurred on 29 June 1993 when the Mexican government formally registered the Church, allowing it to own property. The recognition was granted at a ceremony presided over by Patrocinio Gonzalez Garrido, Secretary of Government. Agricol Lozano, the Church's legal counsel in Mexico, was instrumental in gaining official recognition for the Church. The effort was under the direction of Elders F. Burton Howard and Angel Abrea of the Seventy, presidents of the Mexico North and Mexico South areas.

President Howard W. Hunter visited Mexico to create the Church's 2,000th stake, the Mexico City Contreras Stake, on 11 December 1994. President Gordon B. Hinckley visited Veracruz in January 1996 for a regional conference and spoke to 9,000 members. He visited the Mormon colonies on 5 June 1997 and spoke at the centennial observance of the Juarez Academy. Returning to El Paso, Texas, to catch a flight back to Salt Lake City, President Hinckley conceived the plan for the small temple design that he announced at general conference in October 1997 that ushered in an era of unprecedented temple building.

President Hinckley returned to Mexico in November 1997 and spoke to 54,000 members in Mexico City, Puebla, Villahermosa, Cancun, and Merida. During the trip, he met with Mexican President Dr. Ernesto Zedillo and foreign minister Jose Angel Gurria. President Hinckley once again went to Mexico in March 1998, and visited the cities of Hermosillo, Ciudad Obregon, Culiacan, Guadalajara, Torreon, Leon, Ciudad Victoria, Monterrey, Chihuahua, and Ciudad Juarez in northern Mexico.

After the announcement of small temples, the Church began to construct several temples in Mexico. The temple in Colonia Juarez was dedicated on 6 March 1999. The year 2000 was a milestone year for temple dedications in Mexico with eight dedicated, including Ciudad Juarez, Hermosillo, Oaxaca, Tuxtla Gutierrez, Tampico, Villahermosa, Merida, and Veracruz. The Guadalajara temple was dedicated by President Hinckley on 29 April 2001.

The Monterrey Mexico Temple was dedicated by President Hinckley on 28 April 2002. The temple was the last of the announced temple construction projects in Mexico, capping an unprecedented three-year period in which 11 temples in the country were built and dedicated. "The temples not only have established the presence of the Church in Mexico, but also have established the presence of the Church in the hearts of the members," said Elder Lynn A. Mickelsen of the Seventy.

Mexico's 19th mission, the Mexico Mexico City West Mission, was announced in 2001. The 100th anniversary of the re-opening of missionary work in Mexico was celebrated in June 2001 in cities throughout the country.

President Hinckley, along with Elder Henry B. Eyring of the Quorum of the Twelve, met with Mexician President Vicente Fox in Mexico City on 29 April 2002. During their 30-minute meeting, President Hinckley and the Mexican president discussed the Church's effort to improve the lives of Mexican members and others. President Hinckley explained the Church's Perpetual Education Fund and an instructional welding program funded by the Church at the Technological University of Santa Catarina in Monterrey. President Hinckley presented President Fox with a donation from the Church Humanitarian Fund, earmarked for a charitable organization championed by Mexican First Lady Marta Sahagun de Fox.

The Church, in partnership with philanthropist Kenneth E. Behring and his Wheelchair Foundation, donated 1,000 wheelchairs on 10 December 2002 to Mexico's National Center for Rehabilitation for use by the disabled in Mexico. Bishop Richard C. Edgley, first counselor in the Presiding Bishopric, represented the Church in ceremonies with Mexican President Fox.

In 2002, membership reached 952,947.

A historic milestone occurred in July 2004 when Church membership in Mexico reached 1 million members. In 2005, membership reached 1,043,718.

About 3,000 members and friends attended events in Tecalco on April 6-9, 2006, to commemorate the 125th anniversary of the dedication of Mexico for the preaching of the gospel, as well as the 130th anniversary of the coming of the first missionaries to Mexico.

Two missions were created on 1 July 2010; the Mexico Mexico City Northwest Mission and the Mexico Villahermosa Mission, bringing the total of missions to 23.

Sources: Agricol Lozano, "Historia Del Mormonismo en Mexico, 1980; F. Lamond Tullis, Mormons in Mexico: The Dynamics of Faith and Culture, 1987; F. Lamond Tullis, "Los Primeros: Mexico's Pioneer Saints," Ensign, July 1997; Thomas Cottam Romney, The Mormon Colonies in Mexico, 1938; Alonzo Taylor, Record of the Exodus of the Mormon Colonies from Mexico in 1912, 1970; Karl E. Young, Ordeal in Mexico, 1968; Mark L. Grover, "Execution in Mexico: The Deaths of Rafael Monroy and Vicente Morales," BYU Studies, 1996; Donald Q. Cannon and Richard O. Cowan, Unto Every Nation: Gospel Light Reaches Every Land, 2003; Dell Van Orden, "Emotional Farewell in Mexico,"Church News, 19 February 1977; Dell Van Orden, "Prophet Meets Latin Leaders," Church News, 5 March 1977; "Mexico Formally Registers Church," Church News, 17 July 1993; Jason Swensen, "New Temples in Mexico Are Making Eternal Impact in Thousands of Lives," Church News, 12 August 2000; Jason Swensen "Patience Rewarded in Monterrey," Church News, 11 May 2002; "President Hinckley Meets With Mexican Leader," Church News, 11 May 2002; John L. Hart, "Temple Work Increasing in Mexico," Church News, 18 May 2002; John L. Hart, "125 Years of Converts in Mexico," Church News, 3 August 2002; Jason Swensen, "Hundreds Receive Gift of Mobility, Independence," Church News, 21 December 2002; Jason Swensen, "Broadening Horizons in Northern Mexico," Church News, 25 January 2003; "A Million in Mexico on Aug. 1, After 128 Years," Church News, 10 July 2004; "125 years in Mexico," Church News, 15 April 2006; "New missions," Church News, 13 Feb. 2010.

Stakes — 222
(Listed alphabetically as of Oct. 1, 2011.)

No.	Name	Organized	First President
735	Acapulco Mexico	24 Sep 1989	Francisco Javier Torres G.
2574	Acapulco Mexico Costa Azul	15 Oct 2000	Joel Martinez Cano
2328	Acayucan Mexico	16 Mar 1997	Leonardo Hoyes Montiel
1640	Aguascalientes Mexico	17 May 1987	Jose Luis Rios A.
2472	Aguascalientes Mexico Jardines	31 May 1998	Daniel Cordova Esparza
2485	Amecameca Mexico	28 Jun 1998	Cuauhtemoc Sanchez Pineda
2683	Apodaca Mexico	22 May 2005	Joel Martinez Ortega
1971	Atlixco Mexico	16 Jan 1994	Hector Garcia Ceballos
2753	Atotonilco Mexico	24 Feb 2007	Javier Tovar Baltazar
2833	Cabo San Lucas Mexico	7 June 2009	Ezequiel Fernando Ramirez Quinones

1474	Campeche Mexico	27 May 1984	Gabriel Francisco Ramos G.
2056	Cancun Mexico	28 May 1995	Victor Sebastian Roca Gomez
2456	Cancun Mexico Kabah	26 Apr 1998	Victor S. Roca Gomez
2682	Cancun Mexico Kukulcan	15 May 2005	Gabriel Serna Poot
2343	Cardenas Mexico	20 Apr 1997	Raymundo Morales Barrera
941	Celaya Mexico	11 Jun 1978	Armando Gaona
722	Chalco Mexico	9 Nov 1975	Ruben Valenzuela G.
2636	Chalco Mexico Solidaridad	23 May 2004	Carlos Roberto Rivero Rodriguez
1822	Chetumal Mexico	27 Oct 1991	Raul Gaspar Rodriguez F.
2612b	Chiautempan Mexico	17 Aug 2003	Samuel Ahuacatitan Farias
782	Chihuahua Mexico	13 Nov 1976	Gustavo Ulises Cortez S.
1633	*Chihuahua Mexico Chuviscar	14 Nov 1989	
	‡Chihuahua Mexico East	1 Mar 1987	Humberto Enrique Serna G.
1736a	Chihuahua Mexico Tecnologico	26 Nov 1989	Arturo Galindo Rubalcava
2364	Chilpancingo Mexico	25 May 1997	Jesus Antonio Torrijos Acevedo
1109	Ciudad Juarez Mexico East	24 Feb 1980	Armando Arzate Saldana
2264	Ciudad Juarez Mexico La Cuesta	10 Nov 1996	Jesus Octavio Seanez Flores
1699	Ciudad Juarez Mexico North	9 Oct 1988	Luis Carlos Gomez M.
783	*Ciudad Juarez Mexico South	9 Oct 1988	
	‡Ciudad Juarez Mexico	14 Nov 1976	Sergio Armando de la Mora M.
1301	*Ciudad Mante Mexico	25 Jan 1982	
	‡Mante Mexico	1 Nov 1981	Humberto Noriega F.
772	Ciudad Obregon Mexico	10 Oct 1976	Jorge Mendez I.
1712	Ciudad Obregon Mexico Nainari	19 Feb 1989	Jesus Angulo Montoya
1500	Ciudad Obregon Mexico Yaqui	28 Oct 1984	Jorge Mendez Ibarra
2576	Ciudad Valles Mexico	12 Nov 2000	Ricardo Baez Trejo
797	Ciudad Victoria Mexico	12 Dec 1976	Jesus Martinez T.
2815	Coacalco Mexico	29 Nov 2008	
1043a	Coatzacoalcos Mexico	1 Jul 1979	Raymundo Madris Carbajal
1766	Coatzacoalcos Mexico Puerto	29 Jul 1990	Raul Munoz Z.
2830	Colima Mexico	24 May 2009	Oscar Manuel Molina Rodriguez
1742	Colonia Dublan Mexico	25 Feb 1990	Carl L. Call
37	*Colonia Juarez Mexico		
	‡Juarez	9 Dec 1895	Anthony W. Ivins
721	Cuautla Mexico	9 Nov 1975	Juan Angel Alvaradejo
1983	*Cuautla Mexico Palmas	23 Jan 1996	
	‡Cuautla Mexico Aguahedionda	19 Jun 1994	Luis F. Rodriguez Trejo
2526	Cuautla Mexico Zapata	25 Apr 1999	Hugo Alberto Sanchez Morales
1427	Cuernavaca Mexico	5 Jun 1983	Sergio Rojas Espinoza
2518	*Cuernavaca Mexico Civac Civac	21 Nov 2001	
838	Culiacan Mexico	21 Mar 1999	Saul Figueroa Lopez
		22 May 1977	Federico Fragoza Diaz
1710	Culiacan Mexico Humaya	12 Feb 1989	Jose Exaltacion Astorga E.
1644	Culiacan Mexico Tamazula	21 Jun 1987	Rosario Lobo
1707	Delicias Mexico	18 Dec 1988	Sergio Trejo L.
1228	Durango Mexico	21 Jan 1981	Ernesto Padilla Lozano
2057	Durango Mexico Del Valle	28 May 1995	Miguel Angel Martinez Macias
1761	*Ensenada Mexico	8 Aug 1990	
	‡Tijuana Mexico Ensenada	24 Jun 1990	Jose Pedroza A.
2606b	Fresnillo Mexico	23 Sep 2001	Noel A. Mora Ruiz
2835	Galeana Mexico	7 Jun 2009	Oscar Armando Aguilar Torres
935	Gomez Palacio Mexico	28 May 1978	Ruben Martinez A.
1749	Gomez Palacio Mexico La Laguna	6 May 1990	Magdaleno Sanchez S.
1183	Guadalajara Mexico Independencia	27 Sep 1980	Felipe Covarrubias S.
2842	Guacamayas Mexico	21 June 2009	Adrian Trevino Vazquez
2474	Guadalajara Mexico Lomas	7 Jun 1998	Sergio Miguel Anaya
2495	Guadalajara Mexico Mirador	20 Sep 1998	Jose Romero Gutierrez
2457	Guadalajara Mexico Moctezuma	3 May 1998	Americo Garcia Soto
1753	Guadalajara Mexico Reforma	3 Jun 1990	Jose Saavedra T.
2482	Guadalajara Mexico Tlaquepaque	21 Jun 1998	Rogelio Martinez
683	*Guadalajara Mexico Union	28 Sep 1980	
	‡Guadalajara Mexico	23 Feb 1975	Emilio Garcia L.
2044	Guadalajara Mexico Victoria	30 Apr 1995	Luis Ruben Castrejon Bonilla
1779	Guaymas Mexico	18 Nov 1990	Ruben A. Palestino
771	Hermosillo Mexico	8 Oct 1976	Hector Ceballos L.
1636	Hermosillo Mexico Pitic	26 Apr 1987	Carlos Pineda O.
2107	Iguala Mexico	15 Oct 1995	Alberto Saucedo Roa
1232	*Irapuato Mexico	24 Mar 1992	
	‡Leon Mexico	8 Feb 1981	Armando Gaona J.
1589	Jalapa Mexico	2 Mar 1986	Jorge Sanchez
1764	Juchitan Mexico	22 Jul 1990	Gerardo Castellanos A.

2415	Juchitan Mexico Las Flores	23 Nov 1997	Wilfrido Orozco Ramirez
1734b	*La Paz Mexico	30 Jan 1990	
	‡Finisterra Mexico	10 Sep 1989	Antonio Aguilar V.
2220	Leon Mexico	11 Aug 1996	Alberto Galo de Jesus Romo Gonzalez
1139	Los Mochis Mexico	25 May 1980	Victor Manuel Soto
1714	Los Mochis Mexico El Fuerte	5 Mar 1989	Ezequiel Fernando Ramirez Q.
795	Madero Mexico	11 Dec 1976	Gabriel Raymundo Saldivar F.
2590	Madero Mexico Ampliacion	4 Mar 2001	Jorge Luis Saldivar Balboa
2905	Martinez de la Torre Mexico	13 Mar 2011	Francisco Octavio Morales Ontiveros
1131	Matamoros Mexico	18 May 1980	Luciano Ramirez
1718	Mazatlan Mexico	7 May 1989	Jose Alberto Holcombe I.
2611	Mazatlan Mexico West	14 Apr 2002	Alfonso Filippine Aguayo
804	Merida Mexico	22 Jan 1977	Abel R. Ordaz R.
2694	Merida Mexico Brisas	20 Nov 2005	Gabriel de Jesus Palma
1728	Merida Mexico Centro	11 Jun 1989	Joaquin Eduardo Carrillo V.
2690	Merida Mexico Chuburna	18 Sep 2005	Armando Carreon Rivera
1754	Merida Mexico Itzimna	10 Jun 1990	Mauro Jose Luis Gil P.
923	Merida Mexico Lakin	14 May 1978	Benigno Pena Pech
2696	Metepec Mexico	27 Nov 2005	Francisco J. Bravo Vélez
819	Mexicali Mexico	20 Mar 1977	Eduardo Del Rio P.
1626	Mexicali Mexico Los Piños	18 Jan 1987	Jose de Jesus Ruelas U.
1603	Mexico City Mexico Anahuac	29 Jun 1986	Luis Manuel Angel B.
617	*Mexico City Mexico Aragon		
	‡Mexico City Aragon	27 May 1973	Agricol Lozano H.
658	Mexico City Mexico Arbolillo	15 Sep 1974	Guillermo Torres
1317	Mexico City Mexico Azteca	6 Dec 1981	Juan Alberto Ramos B.
719	Mexico City Mexico Camarones	8 Nov 1975	Jorge Rojas O.
2420	Mexico City Mexico Centenario	30 Nov 1997	Dominguez G. D. Rodriguez I.
1357	Mexico City Mexico Chapultepec	27 Jun 1982	Jose Ismael Ruiz G.
716a	Mexico City Mexico Churubusco	8 Nov 1975	Juan Casanova C.
2000	Mexico City Mexico Contreras	11 Dec 1994	Victor Manuel Salinas G.
1752	Mexico City Mexico Cuautepec	20 May 1990	Salvador Aguirre Osorio
1763	Mexico City Mexico Cuautitlan	8 Jul 1990	Victor M. Cardenas L.
2740	Mexico City Mexico Culhuacan	11 Nov 2006	Ricardo Flores Alvarez
1759	Mexico City Mexico Culturas	17 Jun 1990	Octavio Saul Morales A.
1663	Mexico City Mexico Ecatepec	6 Dec 1987	Juan Manuel Rodriguez C.
718	Mexico City Mexico Ermita	8 Nov 1975	Aurelio Valdespino O.
723	Mexico City Mexico Industrial	9 Nov 1975	Juan Roberto Alva
2659	Mexico City Mexico Ixtapaluca	7 Nov 2004	Gustavo Ramos Landaverde
2403	Mexico City Mexico Iztapalapa	26 Oct 1997	Daniel Delgado Rios
1760	Mexico City Mexico La Perla	24 Jun 1990	Pedro Espinosa C.
965	Mexico City Mexico Lindavista	8 Oct 1978	Fernando R. Dorantes T.
2522	Mexico City Mexico Lomas Verdes	18 Apr 1999	Omar Villalobos Saunders
2267	Mexico City Mexico Los Reyes	17 Nov 1996	I. Pedro Espinosa Cruz
1070	*Mexico City Mexico Meyehualco	11 Dec 1994	
	*Mexico City Mexico Iztapalapa	14 Oct 1979	Aurelio Valdespino
726	Mexico City Mexico Moctezuma	9 Nov 1975	Filiberto Ledezma M.
727	Mexico City Mexico Netzahualcoyotl	9 Nov 1975	Jaime Garay M.
1433	Mexico City Mexico Oriental	19 Jun 1983	Felipe Gerardo Ramirez N.
2404	Mexico City Mexico Pantitlan	26 Oct 1997	Luis R. Rosales Gonzalez
2608d	Mexico City Mexico Paraiso	13 Jan 2002	Gilberto Lule Cervantes
2307	Mexico City Mexico Prados	9 Feb 1997	Guillermo Velasco Coronado
717a	Mexico City Mexico Tacubaya	8 Nov 1975	Roman Gomez I.
2286	Mexico City Mexico Tecamac	1 Dec 1996	Francisco C. Salazar Sanchez
2602a	Mexico City Mexico Tenayo	24 Nov 2002	Francisco Javier Hernandez
2477	Mexico City Tepalcapa	14 Jun 1998	Rafael Eduardo Ramos R.
720	*Mexico City Mexico Tlalnepantla	10 Oct 1978	
	‡Mexico City Mexico Satelite	9 Nov 1975	Horacio Tenorio O.
1356	Mexico City Mexico Tlalpan	27 Jun 1982	Jose Alberto Rasales G.
1579	Mexico City Mexico Valle Dorado	28 Nov 1985	Arturo Lopez G.
1980	Mexico City Mexico Vergel	15 May 1994	Ernesto Rosas Vazquez
724	Mexico City Mexico Villa de las Flores	9 Nov 1975	Juan Manuel Cedeno R.
2357	Mexico City Mexico Xalostoc	18 May 1997	Jose Luis Escobar Maya
715a	Mexico City Mexico Zarahemla	8 Nov 1975	Bonaerges Rubalcava E.
829	Minatitlan Mexico	15 May 1977	Ignacio Cruz S.
2329	Minatitlan Mexico Tecnologico	16 Mar 1997	Gabriel Garcia Gomez
644	Monclova Mexico	26 May 1974	Francisco Aragon Garza
2621	Monclova Mexico East	30 Nov 2003	Benito Martinez Mendez
774	Monterrey Mexico Anahuac	17 Oct 1976	Lehi Gracia L.
2571	Monterrey Mexico Andalucia	3 Sep 2000	Francisco Rivera Davila
572	*Monterrey Mexico Libertad	17 Oct 1976	
	*Monterrey Mexico East		

	‡Monterrey East	7 May 1972	Jose Humberto Gonzalez
1765	Monterrey Mexico Los Angeles	22 Jul 1990	Carlos Charles Plata
508	*Monterrey Mexico Mitras	8 Jun 1980	
	*Monterrey Mexico		
	‡Monterrey	22 Mar 1970	Guillermo G. Garza
1114	Monterrey Mexico Moderna	9 Mar 1980	Mauro Garcia Herrera
1144	Monterrey Mexico Morelos	8 Jun 1980	Carlos R. Merino D.
908	Monterrey Mexico Paraiso	23 Apr 1978	Alfredo Gallegos L.
773	Monterrey Mexico Roma	16 Oct 1976	Jose Humberto Gonzalez G.
1615	Monterrey Mexico Valle Verde	2 Nov 1986	Jose F. Torres M.
2425	Morelia Mexico	4 Jan 1998	Juan Alberto Gonzalez S.
2843	Morelia Mexico Aeropuerto	21 June 2009	Rodolfo Sifuentes Castilla
2443	Nuevo Laredo Mexico	15 Mar 1998	Santiago Vazquez Davalos
1280	*Oaxaca Mexico Amapolis	19 Sep 2000	
	Oaxaca Mexico	21 Jun 1981	M. Ociel Bengoa Vargas
2575	Oaxaca Mexico Atoyac	12 Nov 2000	Hermengildo Escobar Sampablo
2209	Oaxaca Mexico Mitla	30 Jun 1996	Jose Luis Alonso Trejo
1685	Oaxaca Mexico Monte Alban	7 Feb 1988	Valentin Cruz B.
801	Orizaba Mexico	16 Jan 1977	Humberto Sanchez R.
1466	*Pachuca Mexico	13 Nov 1990	
	‡Mexico City	18 Mar 1984	Alejandro Chavez Rodriguez
	Mexico Pachuca		
2158	Pachuca Mexico Centro	28 Jan 1996	Ismael Mendoza Regino
2805b	Pachuca Mexico South	15 June 2008	Jose Raul Serrano Cruz
1716	Papantla Mexico	23 Apr 1989	Antonio Casino C.
857	Piedras Negras Mexico	21 Aug 1977	Fidencio Guzman Lugo
730	Poza Rica Mexico	13 Nov 1975	Jose Luis Pichardo M.
799	Poza Rica Mexico Palmas	15 Jan 1977	Angel Valle G.
2225	Puebla Mexico Amalucan	25 Aug 1996	Jose Manuel de la Rosa Rojas
898	*Puebla Mexico Cholula	25 Sep 1997	
	Puebla Mexico Popocateptl	12 Mar 1978	Zeferino Tlatelpa
1293	Puebla Mexico Fuertes	11 Oct 1981	Francisco Pineda Salazar
2424	Puebla Mexico La Libertad	14 Dec 1997	Zeniff Mejia Mora
680	Puebla Mexico La Paz	16 Feb 1975	Santiago Mejia M.
2543	Puebla Mexico Mayorazgo	27 Feb 2000	Edgar Flores P.
1758	Puebla Mexico Nealtican	17 Jun 1990	Marcelino Osorio P.
681	Puebla Mexico Valsequillo	16 Feb 1975	Ramiro Goana M.
2677	Puerto Vallarta Mexico	24 Apr 2005	Gonzalo Rodriguez M.
2037	Queretaro Mexico	19 Mar 1995	Glendon Lyons Castillo
2550	Queretaro Mexico Los Arcos	12 Mar 2000	Jose Cruz Pineda C.
1132	Reynosa Mexico	18 May 1980	Noe Flores Silva
2607c	Reynosa Mexico East	16 Mar 2003	Pedro Zamora V.
2021	Salina Cruz Mexico	5 Feb 1995	Jose Ceferino Castillo Cupil
1767	Saltillo Mexico Miravalle	12 Aug 1990	Edmundo Rodriguez Pena
1155	Saltillo Mexico Republica	29 Jun 1980	Roberto Teodoro Guzman R.
2759	San Cristobal Mexico	14 Apr 2007	Indalecio Tomas Morales
1231	San Luis Potosi Mexico	1 Feb 1981	Guillermo G. Soubervielle R.
2214	*San Luis Potosi Benito Juarez	27 Aug 1996	
2846	San Luis Rio Colorado Mexico	28 June 2009	Eduardo Coronado de los Reyes
	Benito Juarez Mexico	4 Aug 1996	Victor Joaquin Herrejon Faburrieta
2268	San Nicolas Mexico	17 Nov 1996	Abelardo Morales Mendez
567	*Tampico Mexico	27 Feb 1972	Guillermo Garmendia
	‡Tampico	12 Nov 1995	Luis Eduardo de Leon de Leon
2123	Tampico Mexico Bosque	26 Nov 2000	Manuel Acosta Mar
2577	Tampico Mexico Chairel	20 Aug 1978	Jorge David Arrevilla M.
951	Tapachula Mexico	8 Jul 1990	Guillermo Sanchez R.
1762	Tapachula Mexico Izapa	25 Jun 1989	Felipe Hernandez L.
1730	Tecalco Mexico	18 Apr 1999	Demesio de Jesus Rueda J.
2521	Tehuacan Mexico	15 Dec 1996	Jose A. Prida Herrma
2296	Tepic Mexico	7 Mar 1999	Alejandro Perez Alvarez
2516	Teziutlan Mexico	12 Jan 2003	Ricardo Salomon Morales
2603d	Tierra Blanca Mexico	23 May 1976	Carlos Mendez S.
757	Tijuana Mexico	14 Jan 2001	David Zamarrip Navarro
2583	Tijuana Mexico Central	13 March 2005	Jose Alberto Fernandez Hernandez
2673	Tijuana Mexico Florido	13 Oct 1996	Jorge Mendez Ibarra
2248	Tijuana Mexico Insurgentes	15 Apr 1986	
1587	*Tijuana Mexico La Mesa	9 Feb 1986	Angel Luevano Cordova
	‡La Mesa Mexico	11 Mar 2001	Luis Sergio Hernandez Gallo
2991	Tijuana Mexico Otay	1 Mar 1998	Samuel Ayala P.
2439	Tizimin Mexico	11 Feb 1996	Mosiah Saul Delgado Gonzalez
2164	Tlaxcala Mexico	17 Nov 1991	Gilberto Lopez D'Antin
1829	Toluca Mexico		

781	Torreon Mexico	12 Nov 1976	David Limon Miranda
1532	Torreon Mexico Jardin	12 May 1985	Rafael Leon Miranda
1736	Torreon Mexico Reforma	15 Oct 1989	Miguel Angel Rivera C.
725	Tula Mexico	9 Nov 1975	Silvino Mera U.
2871	Tulancingo Mexico	14 Feb 2010	
2848	Tuxpan Mexico	28 Jun 2009	Fernando Ramos Godinez
1943	Tuxtepec Mexico	6 Jun 1993	Marcelo Valis Medina
1174	Tuxtla Gutierrez Mexico	31 Aug 1980	Enrique Sanchez Casillas
2028	Tuxtla Gutierrez Mexico Grijalva	26 Feb 1995	Moises Ulloa Solis
2775	Tuxtla Gutierrez Mexico Mactumatza	1 Sep 2007	Julio Cesar Pineda Franco
2834	Uruapan Mexico	7 June 2009	Juan Carlos Tulais Juarez
628	*Valle Hermoso Mexico		
	‡Valle Hermoso	28 Oct 1973	Benjamin Morales
1653	Valle del Mezquital Mexico	13 Sep 1987	Joel Gandara Salazar
700	Veracruz Mexico	15 Jun 1975	Leon Lopez Alavez
1751	Veracruz Mexico Mocambo	20 May 1990	Fernando Lagunez V.
800	Veracruz Mexico Reforma	16 Jan 1977	Leon Lopez A.
2119	Veracruz Mexico Villa Rica	5 Nov 1995	Marco A. Carrillo Bogard
1166	Villahermosa Mexico	10 Aug 1980	Jose Luis Madrigal N.
1746	*Villahermosa Mexico Gaviotas	5 Oct 1993	
	‡Villahermosa Mexico	15 Apr 1990	Joaquin Gonzalez L.
	Las Gaviotas		
2553	Zacatecas Mexico	16 Apr 2000	Jesus Antonio Madera L.
2242	Zamora Mexico	22 Sep 1996	Juan Lopez Tejeda

Stakes discontinued

344	‡Mexico City Mexico		

Discontinued 8 Nov 1975 †Mexico City Mexico Churubusco (716a), Mexico
City Mexico, Tacubaya (717a), Mexico City Mexico Ermita (718), Mexico City
Mexico Chapultepec (No. 1357)

	*Mexico City	May 1967	
	‡Mexico	3 Dec 1961	Harold Brown
534	*Mexico City Mexico East	15 Nov 1970	Agricol Lozano

Discontinued 8 Nov 1975 †Chalco Mexico (No. 722), Mexico City Mexico
Villa de las Flores (No. 724), Mexico City Mexico Moctezuma
(726), Mexico City, Mexico Netzahualcoyotl (727)

	‡Mexico City Mexico East		
434	*Mexico City Mexico North		
	‡Mexico City North	7 May 1967	Agricol Lozano

Discontinued 8 Nov 1975 †Tampico Mexico (No. 567), Mexico City
Mexico Camarones (No. 719), Mexico City Mexico Satelite (No. 720)

2515	Tuxtla Gutierrez Mexico Centro	28 Feb 1999	Mario Alberto Morales Z.
	Discontinued 20 Feb 2005		
2581	Monterrey Mexico Modelo	10 Dec 2000	Rene Arenas Santana
	Discontinued	17 Apr 2005	

Missions — 24
(As of Oct. 1, 2011; shown with historical number. See MISSIONS.)

(208) MEXICO CHIHUAHUA MISSION
Calle Ojinaga 2210 A
Antes Morelos
Colonia Cuauhtemoc
31020 Chihuahua, Mexico

(201) MEXICO CULIACAN MISSION
Rio Choiz 888
Colonia Rosales
80230 Culiacan, Sinaloa
Mexico

(125) MEXICO GUADALAJARA MISSION
Apartado Postal 51-74
Colonia Las Aguilas,
45081 Zopapan, Jalisco, Mexico

(56) MEXICO HERMOSILLO MISSION
Apartado Postal 557
83000 Hermosillo, Sonora
Mexico

(222a) MEXICO LEON MISSION
Apartado Postal 1-1125
37000 Leon, Guanajuato
Mexico

(126) MEXICO MERIDA MISSION
Calle 45 #527 Q y Calle 70
Colonia Centro
97000 Merida, Yucatan, Mexico

45) MEXICO MONTERREY EAST MISSION
Cerralvo 134
Colonia Libertad
67130 Cd. Guadalupe, Nuevo Leon
Mexico

(276) MEXICO MONTERREY WEST MISSION
Calle Chiapas #2202
Colonia Roma Sur
64700 Monterrey, Nuevo Leon
Mexico

(193) MEXICO MEXICO CITY EAST MISSION
Fuente de Piramide # 1 Piso 1
Lomas de Tecamachalco Naucalpan
53950 Estado de Mexico
Mexico

(163) MEXICO MEXICO CITY NORTH MISSION
Apartado Postal #98
54740 Cuautitlan Izcalli
Estado de Mexico
Mexico

(10a) MEXICO MEXICO CITY SOUTH MISSION
Av. del Taller # 540
Col. Jardin Balbuena
Delegacion Venustiano Carranza
15900 DF Mexico

(332b) MEXICO MEXICO CITY WEST MISSION
Sierra de Las Vertientes #310
Col. Lomas de Chapultepec
Del. Miguel Hidalgo
11010 DF Mexico

(246) MEXICO OAXACA MISSION
Huerta de los Olivos #100
Fracc. Trinidad de las Huertas
68120 Oaxaca
Mexico

(217) MEXICO PUEBLA MISSION
Calle 25 Sur # 907
Col. La Paz
72160 Puebla
Mexico

(218) MEXICO TAMPICO MISSION
Apartado Postal 241
Cd. Madero, Tamaulipas 89460
Mexico

(247) MEXICO TIJUANA MISSION
Sonora #3805 Local 7 y 8
Fracc. Chapultepec Campestre
22420 Tijuana, Baja, Mexico

(81) MEXICO TORREON MISSION
Apartado Postal 792
29000 Torreon, Coahuila
Mexico

(209) MEXICO TUXTLA GUTIERREZ MISSION
Apartado 278
29000 Tuxtla Gutierrez, Chiapas CP
Mexico

(75) MEXICO VERACRUZ MISSION
Apartado Postal 103
91700 Veracruz, Veracruz
Mexico

MEXICO CUERNAVACA MISSION
Avenida Paimira #35
Fracc. Villas de Arco
Colonia Palmira
62490 Cuernavaca, Morelos Mexico

MEXICO GUADALAJARA EAST
Calle Aguamarina #3292
Colonia Residencial Victoria
45089 Zapopan, Jalisco, Mexico

MEXICO MEXICO CITY NORTHWEST MISSION
Cienfuegos #689 piso 7
Lomas de Tecamachalco
07300 Ciudad de Mexico, Distrito

MEXICO VILLAHERMOSA MISSION
Calle Vias #104
86095 Villahermosa, Tabasco
Mexico

MEXICO MEXICO CITY SOUTHEAST
Av. del Taller No. 540
Delegacion Venustiano Carranza
C.P. 15900, Distrito Federal, Mexico

MICRONESIA

Jan. 1, 2011: Est. population, 107,500; Members, 4,193; Districts, 4; Branches, 20; Percent LDS, 3.5, or one in 28; Asia North Area; Micronesia Guam Mission.

Extending along the 1,800-mile Caroline Islands archipelago in the Pacific east of the Philippines, the Federated States of Micronesia have a culturally diverse population that speaks eight island dialects.

Until the 1950s missionary work in the Pacific was limited to the peoples of Polynesia and Australia. This part of the Pacific was first assigned to the Japanese Mission, then the Northern Far East, then the Southern Far East, and finally the Hawaii Honolulu Mission. In January 1975, President Robert E. Crandall of the Hawaii Honolulu Mission sent Callis Carleton and Jeffery Frame to Saipan, headquarters of the U.S. Trust Territory, in the Mariana Islands. This was the first missionary venture into Micronesia proper. Missionary work first began on Pohnpei in 1976, Chuuk and Yap in 1977, and Kosrae in 1985. Micronesia came under the Micronesia Guam Mission when the mission was created on 1 April 1980. Translation of The Book of Mormon in Trukese and Pohnpeian was completed in 1987. The first visit by a General Authority to Micronesia was John H. Groberg, Pacific Area executive administrator, who visited the fledgling branches in Yap and Pohnpei in January 1978.

Between 1976 and 1995 Church membership grew from a single person, Ohren R. Ohry of Pohnpei, to 2,467. At that time there were 839 members in Pohnpei, 1,122 in Chuuk, 308 in Yap, and 198 in Kosrae. In 1998 and 2000 LDS Charities sent shipments of education and medical supplies to support the hospitals on the islands of Yap, Chuuk, and Pohnpei.

On 1 July 2006, the Marshall Islands were divided from the Micronesia Guam Mission to form the Marshall Islands Majuro Mission.

POHNPEI

Missionary work began in Phonpei on 23 October 1976, when George L. Mortensen and Aldric L. Porter (Hawaii Honolulu Mission) arrived in the city of Kolonia. Missionaries were sent at the request of Ohren R. Ohry, who had joined the Church in August 1976 while attending BYU- Hawaii. Two more missionaries were assigned to Pohnpei, Brian D. Tate and Chris Harrison, who arrived on 13 January 1977. The first baptisms on the island were on 5 March 1977 when Ohry's wife, Rihne, other family members, and Siesero Salomon were baptized in the village of Mand. Naped S. Elias and his family along with Perden Samson were baptized in Kolonia a week later on 12 March 1977. The Mand and Kolonia Pohnpei branches were created shortly thereafter, first with missionaries as branch presidents, then with native leaders–Naped Elias as president of the Kolonia Branch and Johnny Bridge as president of the Mand Branch. The branches were initially in the Guam District. A third branch was created in Sapwalap (it became an independent branch in December 1977) and three meetinghouses were built between October 1980 and September 1981 in Sapwalap, Mand, and Kolonia. The Truk-Pohnpei District was created on 31 May 1981. The district was divided on 22 November 1985 and the Truk and Pohnpei districts were created. There are now four branches in Pohnpei, the fourth being in Sekere.

CHUUK

The first missionaries in Chuuk (formerly Truk), Donald M. Baldwin and Torlik Tima (Hawaii Honolulu Mission), arrived on 7 July 1977. They baptized T. M. Conrad Mailo and his wife, Nisor Cerly David, on 22 October 1977. The Truk Branch (later Mwan Branch) was created on 26 July 1979. By 1980 ,membership reached 170, and on 31 May 1981 the Truk-Pohnpei District was created. The first meetinghouse on Chuuk was dedicated on 24 April 1983. The Truk- Pohnpei District was divided in 1985 and the Truk (later renamed the Namoneau Chuuk District) and Pohnpei districts were created. There are now nine branches in Chuuk.

YAP

The Church came to Yap in 1977, when Charles Keliikipi, under contract to organize a police department on the island, arrived with his wife Odetta and their six children. The first missionaries, David S. Ige and Douglas Andrews, arrived on 14 November 1977. The first native Yapese to be baptized was Antonia Siso Isao on 18 March 1978. Afterwards several families joined the Church. A scouting program was initiated in June 1978, attracting 60 Boy Scouts and 15 Cub Scouts. Seven of the Boy Scouts were later baptized. The Yap Branch (later renamed Colonia Branch) was created on 26 July 1979 and a meetinghouse was completed on 13 January 1981. The Thos Branch was created in 1986. Seminary and institute classes were inaugurated on 9 September 1981. The Kosrae Micronesia and Yap Mirconesia districts were created on 14 and 18 March 1990 respectively. There are only the two branches in Yap, Colonia and Thol.

KOSRAE

Kosrae is the most religious of the Micronesia islands. About 95 percent of its inhabitants are Congregationalists. Work in Kosrae began in 1985 when Elders Matterson Ramon and Ioichey Diapulos, both natives of Pohnpei, arrived on 26 March. Within days of their arrival, they gave the radio station a news release introducing themselves and their mission. Less than two weeks later the missionaries received a letter from the Kosraean legislature asking them to stop missionary work. Despite little success, they worked hard to break down public opinion against the Church. The first Kosraen to be baptized was Isidro Abraham on 26 April 1986. The Lelu Branch was organized on 18 June 1986. A second branch was created in Utwe in 1988. The Kosrae Micronesia District was created on 14 March 1990. There are only the two branches in Kosrae, in Lelu and Utwa.

Sources: "Temple Moments–'Best part of life,'" Church News, 26 August 2000; R. Lanier Britsch, Unto the Isles of the Sea, 1986; Micronesia Guam Mission, Brief History of the Micronesia-Guam Mission, 1990, Church Archives; William W. Cannon, Beachheads in Micronesia, 1997; Yap Branch, Historical reports, Church Archives; Hawaii Honolulu Mission, Manuscript history and historical reports, Church Archives; David M. Walden, The LDS Church on Ponape, 1979, Church Archives; Micronesia Guam Mission, Manuscript history and historical reports, Church Archives; Namoneas Chuuk District, Manuscript history and historical reports, Church Archives; Kosrae District, Manuscript history and historical reports, Church Archives; Yap District, Manuscript history and historical reports, Church Archives.

MOLDOVA

Jan. 1, 2011: Est. population, 4,321,000; Members, 321; District, 1; Branches, 2; Percent LDS, .006, or one in 15,161; Europe Area;

Moldova, formerly a republic in the Soviet Union, became an independent nation in 1991. Following the Soviet Union's demise, Moldovans were able to travel abroad. A few joined the Church.

Vitalii Volosin met missionaries in Moscow, Russia, while on a business trip. He was given a Book of Mormon. Upon his return to Moldova, he read it and wanted to be baptized. He discovered that the nearest missionaries were in Russia, so he traveled there to be baptized in June 1995. Contact between the American Latter-day Saints in Chisinau and Volosin, who lived in Balti, was established with the help of the Area Presidency. Volosin traveled two hours to Chisinau as often as he could to participate in worship services with other Church members.

Sylvia Vacarciuc was baptized on 3 April 1994 in Odessa, Ukraine. On 20 November 1995 she was set apart as a missionary, the first Moldovan to serve. She was called to the Russia St. Petersburg Mission. Lilia Carasciuc, while studying in southern California in 1996, met Latter- day Saints and was converted to the Church. She was baptized in May 1997, shortly before returning to Moldova.

The American Latter-day Saints who were meeting together moved to Moldova to work. In September 1995, Paul and Betty Morris arrived in Chisinau, where Paul worked in the U.S. Embassy. In June of that year, John Nielson, a private contractor doing development work, arrived in Moldova. And in May 1996, Janet Jasen, a nurse with the Peace Corps, began her tour in Chisinau. These four Latter-day Saints met each week.

On 11 September 1997, Elder Charles A. Didier, a member of the Seventy and president of the Europe East Area, and Romania Bucharest Mission president, Robert F. Orton, traveled to Chisinau and met with Moldovan and American Latter-day Saints and friends. This was the first visit of a General Authority to that country. The meeting was held in the Morris home. It was announced that the first branch was shortly to be organized and missionaries were to be assigned to labor in Moldova, under the auspices of the Romania Bucharest Mission.

Five weeks after that visit, on 18 October 1997, Elders Brett M. Williams and Frederick D. Wadsworth, missionaries serving in Romania, were sent to Chisinau to begin missionary work. At that time, missionaries could not wear name tags or openly proselyte; rather, they provided service and taught people who had been referred to them by Church members or waited for people to ask them about the Church. On 11 November of that same year, five people were baptized in the bathtub of the Morris home, the first baptisms in Moldova. On that same day, a branch was organized with Paul Morris as president.

After missionaries arrived, with the small membership growing, the branch was moved into rented facilities, the Artists Union Hall in Chisinau in November 1997. A year later, on 30 November 1998, Ion Virlan was called as the first native branch president in Moldova.

On 23 December 1998, the first complete translation of the Book of Mormon in Romanian arrived. This "special Christmas gift" was a blessing to the majority of members in Moldova who could now read the Book of Mormon in their native language.

In 2003, membership reached 218.

Sources: Ukraine Kiev Mission, Annual historical reports, Church Archives; Romania Bucharest Mission, Annual historical reports, Church Archives; Sylvia Vacarciuc, Interview, Church Archives; Janet Jasen, Interview, Church Archives; Brett M. Williams, Papers, Church Archives; Frederick Wadsworth, Interview, Church Archives; Lilia Carasciuc, Interview, Church Archives.

MONGOLIA

Jan. 1, 2011: Est. population, 3,041,000; Members, 9,896; Missions, 1; Stakes, 1; Wards, 6; Districts, 2; Branches, 17; Percent LDS, .28, or one in 360, Asia Area.

Mongolia is located in east central Asia between Russia and China, and has a parliamentary type of government. Its religious composition: Tibetan Buddhist Lamaism 96 percent, Muslim (primarily in the southwest), Shamanism, and Christian 4 percent (1998).

In 1984, Monte J. Brough, who would later be called to the Seventy, traveled to Mongolia on a hunting trip. During his visit, he developed a love for the Mongolian people. Eight years later, in May 1992, Elders Merlin Lybbert and Monte Brough, members of the Asia Area presidency, traveled to Mongolia to explore the possibility of the Church providing humanitarian aid. Prior to this trip, the Mongolian ambassador to United States had traveled to Brigham Young University, which had paved the way for Elders Lybbert and Brough by providing positive contact with the Mongolian government.

After several months of negotiation, permission was granted to send six missionary couples to assist the country's higher education program and to teach others about the Church. The first couple, Kenneth H. and Donna Beesley, arrived on 16 September 1992. Kenneth Beesley, former president of LDS Business College, was designated as lead elder. The first sacrament meeting was held on 20 September 1992 in the Beesley's apartment. The five other missionary couples to follow were Royce P. and Mary Jane Flandro, Richard G. and Anna M. Harper, Stanley B. and Marjorie Smith, C. DuWayne and Alice C. Schmidt, and Gary and Barbara L. Carlson.

The first six young elders arrived in Mongolia in August 1993: Bart J. Birch, Duane L. Blanchard, Brett A. Hansen, Jared K. Meier, Curtis D. Mortensen and Bradley J. Pierson. The first four sisters arrived in March 1996: Natalie Romrell, Katherine Sego, Sheryl E. Mott and Marcie L. Wellman.

The first Mongolian converts, students of the missionary couples, were Lamjav Purevsuren and Tsendkhuu Bat-Ulzii. They were baptized on 6 February 1993. The Ulaanbaatar Branch was organized in September 1993.

Other cities were later opened to missionaries and branches were organized in Erdenet, Darkhan, Gorodok, Hovd, Baganoor, Sukhbaatar and Saynshand.

The Mongolia Ulaanbaatar Mission was officially established on 1 July 1995. The first mission president, Richard E. Cook, and his wife were serving as missionaries in Mongolia when he was called as mission president. President Cook would later be called to the Seventy and serve in the Asia Area presidency. Before the establishment of the mission, Mongolia was overseen by the Asia Area presidency.

On April 15, 1993, Elder Neal A. Maxwell of the Quorum of the Twelve and Elder Kwok Yuen Tai of the Seventy visited Mongolia. Fifty government officials attended a reception that evening hosted by the Church. On 24 October 1994, the Church was registered with the Mongolian government. The first native Mongolians received mission calls on 11 April 1995: Sister Magsar Batchimeg (Utah Salt Lake City Temple Square Mission) and Sister Urtnasan Soyolmaa (Utah Provo Mission).

The Ulaanbaatar Mongolia District was organized on 15 September 1996 with Togtokh Enkhtuvshin as president. Seminary and institute classes began in 1996. The translation of the Book of Mormon into Mongolian was completed and distributed to Church members in late 2001.

Also during 1996 Church-sponsored humanitarian projects included the support of the Mongolian Scout Association, training of professional accountants, cold weather housing, teaching English, and relief for victims of grass fires.

On 12 June 1997 Elder Joseph B. Wirthlin of the Quorum of the Twelve visited with Dr. R. Gonchigdorj, chairman of parliament. Mr. Gonchigdorj, who had visited Utah in 1995, thanked Elder Wirthlin for the humanitarian assistance the Church had provided Mongolia.

On 6 June 1999 a building in Ulaanbaatar, widely known as the "Children's Cinema," was dedicated by Elder Richard E. Cook as the first LDS meetinghouse in Mongolia. In 1999, membership in Mongolia was 1,850 in nine branches.

In June 2001 the Darkhan meetinghouse was dedicated by Elder Richard E. Cook, the first Church-built meetinghouse in Mongolia. In the fall of 2000 the Church began construction of the Bayanzurkh Church Center, a five-story Church building to house the mission home and office, service center, meetinghouse and CES offices.

Mongolian government leaders made an appeal in 2000 for international assistance, after a severe winter, followed by the worst drought in 60 years. In response, the Church sent three shipping containers of clothing and quilts, in addition to 8,000 food boxes.

Membership in 2002 was 4,358 organized in two districts and 21 branches. In 2003, there were 5,455.

In 2005, membership reached 6,735.

Source: Mary Nielsen Cook, "A Mighty Change in Mongolia," Ensign, June 1996; "News of the Church," Ensign, Nov. 1992 and May 1999; Kwok Yuen Tai, "Go Ye Therefore, and Teach All Nations," Ensign, Oct. 1995; Church News articles, 19 June 1993 "Mongolia dedicated for preaching of the gospel," 19 September 1992, "Six missionary couples to help with Mongolia's higher education," 22 February 1997, "Testimonies burn brightly: Mongolia," 3 July 1999, "Well-known building is first meetinghouse in Mongolia"; Mongolia Ulaanbaatar Mission website as of 2 August 2000; R. Lanier Britsch, From the East; Mongolia Ulaanbaatar Mission history, Church Archives.

Stakes — 1
(Listed alphabetically as of Oct. 1, 2011.)

No.	Name	Organized	First President
2832	Ulaanbaatar Mongolia West	7 June 2009	Odgerel Ochirjav

Mission — 1
(As of Oct. 1, 2011; shown with historical number. See MISSIONS.)

(307) MONGOLIA ULAANBAATAR MISSION
UB 49 Box 242, Ulaanbaatar 210349, Mongolia

MOZAMBIQUE

Jan. 1, 2011: Est. population, 21,669,000; Members, 5,392, Mission, 1; Districts 2; Branches, 18; Percentage LDS, .02, or one LDS in 4,467; Africa Southeast Area; Mozambique Maputo Mission.

A country on the southeast coast of Africa, Mozambique covers 309,496 square miles. Almost all are Africans and speak one of the Bantu languages, though the country's official language is Portuguese. About 55 percent of the people practice tribal African religions. About 30 percent are Christians, mostly Roman Catholics, and Muslims.

The Church was established in Mozambique at two separate locations, first in the city of Beira, which spilled over to the village of Marromeu, then in the capital city of Maputo.

Mozambique was a Portuguese colony until the latter part of the 20th Century. In 1975, Mozambique became an independent nation, adopting a Marxist-Leninist form of socialism and forming strong political ties with the Soviet Union and its Eastern Bloc satellites. Mozambique was invited to send young students to Eastern Bloc nations and Cuba for training.

In 1982, 13-year-old Chico Mapenda left his hometown of Beira, Mozambique, to study in the German Democratic Republic. In 1989, while looking for a branch of his church, Mapenda met the missionaries, who gave him a Book of Mormon in Portuguese. He was baptized on 14 January 1990.

Shortly after Mapenda's baptism, East and West Germany were reunited and many of the foreigners in the former German Democratic Republic had to return to their homelands. Mapenda returned to Mozambique that same year.

Soon after arriving in his homeland, Mapenda began to share his new religion with his family and friends, including his father-in-law, Francisco Dique Sousa. Mapenda's brother, Gimo, who was working as a minister in a Protestant congregation, was one of Chico's earliest followers. The Mapenda brothers began to organize small groups of unbaptized "Latter-day Saints." The brothers served as traveling ministers for these congregations. Chico held the Aaronic Priesthood. Gimo hadn't even been baptized.

In November 1991 Elder Earl C. Tingey of the Seventy and a member of the Africa Area Presidency visited Mozambique and reported that Chico was leading and teaching groups of up to 150 people. Five years later, in June 1996, Elder James O. Mason, also a member of the Africa Area Presidency, visited Beira and organized the Beira Group and authorized the first baptisms. Gimo Mapenda was finally baptized.

John and Jan Hunter, a missionary couple serving in Mutare, Zimbabwe, were assigned to visit Beira to care for these new converts. On 1 September 1996, the Beira Group was transferred from the Zimbabwe Harare Mission to the South Africa Johannesburg Mission.

Finally, on 30 January 1999, nine years after Chico Mapenda was baptized, the Beira Branch was organized with Augusto Cherequejanhe as branch president. He had been introduced to the Church in 1992 by his father-in-law Francisco Dique Sousa.

Sousa was so enthusiastic about the gospel that he organized congregations of unbaptized "Latter-day Saints" in his village of Marromeu. In May 2000, the first missionaries, Andre Kemmeny, James Dewey, Petros Dlamini and Travis Williams, from the South Africa Johannesburg Mission traveled to Marromeu and in four days taught 69 first discussions. People waited all day outside of the huts where the missionaries were teaching to hear the first discussion. A month later, missionaries returned to that village and in three and a half days taught 21 second through fourth discussions. A month later, the first baptisms occurred in Marromeu with 25 people being baptized. In October, 30 more people were baptized. The Marromeu Branch was organized on 21 October 2000 with Francisco Dique Sousa as branch president.

Over a year after the Beira Branch was organized, on 3 March 2000, missionaries were transferred to Beira and began to teach the gospel. Missionary work went well in Beira. A little over three years after the arrival of the first missionaries, on 13 April 2003, about 650 members gathered for the creation of the Beira Mozambique District, the first in the country. Augusto Cherequejanhe was called as president and Chico Mapenda as a counselor.

In the mid-1990s the Church was established in Maputo. In February 1995, Elder James O. Mason of the Seventy traveled there and formed a group with Samo P. Goncalves as leader. Like many of the early Mozambican Church members, Goncalves had joined the Church while living abroad. He had been baptized in Viseu, Portugal, in 1992. Through the efforts of Elder Mason, Goncalves, and Church attorneys Hugh M. Matheson and H. Thomas Kay, the Church obtained legal recognition in Mozambique in February 1996. Later that year, on 8 September, Elder Mason organized the Maputo Branch with Goncalves as the first branch president.

In June 1999, the first senior missionary couple, Ray and Judy Caldwell, and young missionaries Patrick J. Tedjamulia and Chimbinja J. Valente from the South Africa Johannesburg Mission arrived in Maputo to begin missionary work in Mozambique.

In October 1999 Elder Richard G. Scott of the Quorum of the Twelve visited Maputo. In a park near the sea he blessed the land. Jorge Mounga, the first Mozambican missionary, began to serve in December 1999. On 17 February 2001, an open house was held in the newly-reconstructed Maputo meetinghouse.

The people of Mozambique benefited from Church humanitarian aid. A deadly drought, the worst in 100 years, caused great suffering in Mozambique and neighboring countries. In 1992, the Church shipped 1 million pounds of food and relief items for victims of the drought in this area.

Membership in 2003 reached 1,976 organized in nine branches.

The Mozambique Maputo Mission, the 339th mission of the Church, was organized in January 2005. It had been one of four countries comprising the expansive South Africa Johannesburg Mission. Since the first baptisms in 1996, the number of missionaries has steadily grown to about 30 at the time the mission was organized. The mission also included the other Portuguese-speaking country of Angola, located on the west coast, opposite Mozambique.

Membership in 2003 was 1,976. In 2005, membership reached 3,472.

Sources: Chico Mapenda papers, Church Archives; "Interview between Sofia Abrantes and Xico Mapenda," June 1999, in E. Dale LeBaron Mozambique research file, 1995-2000, Church Archives; Ferron and Peggy Orton, "Spreading the Gospel in Africa," Church News, 17 May 2003, 14; "New mission, Miracle in Mozambique," Church News, 8 January 2005.

Mission — 1
(As of Oct. 1, 2011; shown with historical number. See MISSIONS.)

MOZAMBIQUE MAPUTO MISSION
Caixa Postal 1166
Correio Central, Maputo, Mozambique

NAMIBIA
Jan. 1, 2011: Est. population, 2,109,000; Members, 686; Branches, 2;
percent LDS .027, or one in 3,753; Africa Southeast Area; South Africa Cape Town Mission.

The Republic of Namibia is located in southwest Africa. It's bordered by South Africa to the south, Botswana to the east, and Angola and Zambia to the north. It became an independent nation on 20 March 1990. It has a population that speaks Afrikaans, English, and indigenous languages. Namibians are 50 percent Lutheran and 30 percent other Christian.

On 7 September 1924, Lawrence and Maud Ratcliff, his sister, Audrey Ratcliff, and his step-children, Bertram Joseph and Norah Cecelia Glynn, joined the Church in South Africa. Soon after the family emigrated to Karibib, Southwest Africa (now Namibia) for work. On 24 July 1927, the Karibib Branch was organized with Lawrence Ratcliff as presiding elder. The first converts in the country were Johannes Andries Cloete and Martha Vermeulen Cloete who were baptized on 11 March 1928 at Karibib by Lawrence C. Ratcliff. The Ratcliffs eventually left Karibib for Utah.

Howard C. Badger, South African Mission president, brought missionaries Russell V. Harper, Michael Cates, and C. (Cecil) Eric Johnson to Windhoek on 25 February 1969. Dennis R. Saunders was transferred from Durban, South Africa to Windhoek on 29 February 1969.

The Windhoek Branch was organized on 19 Dec 1983 with Dieter Greiner as president. A year later the Windhoek Branch was transferred from the South Africa Johannesburg Mission to the South Africa Cape Town Mission.

In February 1990, missionary couple Melvin and June Mabey were transferred from the South Africa Cape Town Mission to Windhoek and were designated lead couple in Namibia. On 5 March, four missionaries were transferred from the South Africa Cape Town Mission to Namibia. The Church was registered 11 May 1990. A. Eugene and L. Ruth Hilton, who arrived on 30 May 1990, were the first missionary couple called to work full-time in Namibia. The Windhoek District was organized in October 1991, with Elder A. Eugene Hilton as president. However, the district was dissolved in February 1992.

In August 1992, Andre Van der Merwe, the first missionary called from Namibia, began serving in the South Africa Johannesburg Mission. Elder Russell M. Nelson became the first member of the Quorum of the Twelve to visit Namibia in August 1992. The seminary program began in late 1994.

The Windhoek Branch meetinghouse, the first and only one in Namibia, was dedicated 6 July 1997 by Elder James O. Mason, of the Africa Area presidency.

Membership in 2001 was 312. It reached 336 in 2002.

Sources: Evan P. Wright, History of the South African Mission, period II, 1903-1944, Church History Library; Melvin Pack Mabey, Journal, Church Archives; Mark Newman and Greg Hagen,"Gospel Springs Forth in Harsh Desert Land of New Africa Nation," Church News, 5 October 1991; Mary Mostert and Gerry Avant, "Prayers of Dedication Offered on 4 Nations in Central, Southern Africa,"Church News, 26 September, 1992; Telephone conversation with Scott W. Colton, 13 April 2004; Record of members, Church Archives; South African Mission, Manuscript history and historical reports, Church Archives; South Africa Cape Town Mission, Manuscript history and historical reports, Church Archives.

NAURU
Jan. 1, 2011: Est. population, 14,000; Members, less than 100; Branches, 1; Percent LDS, .77,
or one in 130.; Pacific Islands Area; Marshall Islands Majuro Mission.

Nauru is an island of 8.2 square miles in the west Pacific Ocean just south of the Equator and near the Solomon Islands. Four-fifths of its residents are Christian, most belong to the Nauruan Protestant Church.

There are no records of missionary work or visits by Latter-day Saints to Nauru prior to the island being assigned to the Micronesia Guam Mission when the mission was created on 1 April 1980.

It is presumed that sometime in the early 1980s, Church members from Kiribati began moving to Nauru for employment and initially met for Church services in homes. Micronesia Guam Mission President Joseph B. Keeler visited Nauru in April 1984. During that time the Nauru Branch was organized with 16 members. The branch was later transferred to the Fiji Suva Mission on 1 July 1986. Church membership has increased and declined according to the demand and export of the island's chief economic product, phosphate rock. Due to restrictions on missionary work, only temporary visits by Church representatives are allowed. Raymond and Lorraine Schmedes were the first missionary couple to make periodic visits from Tarawa, Kiribati, to Nauru beginning in 1998. They helped establish a Relief Society and Primary and also began a seminary program. The Nauru Branch had 128 members in February 1999 when it was made part of the Tarawa Gilbert Islands District.

Sources: Micronesia Guam Mission, Annual history and historical reports, Church Archives; Fiji Suva Mission, Annual history and historical reports, Church Archives.

On 1 July 2006, Nauru was divided from the Fiji Suva Mission to become part of the newly organized Marshall Islands Majuro Mission.

NEPAL

Jan. 1, 2011: Est. population, 28,563,000 Members, fewer than 100; branches, 1; Asia Area.

A few Latter-day Saints from other countries lived in Nepal beginning about the mid-1970s and were at various times organized into Church groups. During the 1970s and 1980s, a handful of Nepalese joined the Church in the U.S., Hong Kong, England, and Nepal. Three Nepalese Church members lived in Kathmandu in 1985. The Church received public exposure in Nepal in 1980 and 1986 through performances of the Young Ambassadors, a BYU entertainment group.

Elders John K. Carmack and Kwok Yuen Tai of the Asia Area presidency visited Kathmandu in February 1993 and organized a group with Madhav Kumar Rimal, who was baptized in 1982, as leader. In early 1994, President Gurcharan S. Gill of the India Bangalore Mission rented an apartment in Kathmandu where missionaries could stay while they renewed visas enabling them to return to India. He recommended that a missionary couple be assigned to Kathmandu.

Robert and Linda Houghton were the first missionary couple to arrive on 2 June 1994. Nepal became part of the India Bangalore Mission on 25 August of that year and President Gill organized the Kathmandu Branch the following 25 October with Dirk Richards as president. The first young full-time missionaries, David Pitcher and Joshua Chiles, arrived on 1 December 1994.

In July 1995, there were nearly 50 Church members in Nepal. Missionaries were subsequently disallowed from actively seeking converts there. Senior missionary couples continued to serve in humanitarian projects and give support to local Latter-day Saints.

The first Kathmandu Branch conference was held in March 1996. At that time, Panna Lal Khadgi, thought to be the first Nepalese baptized in his homeland, was sustained as branch president. Dilip Shrestha became the first Nepalese to serve a full-time mission when he was called to the India Bangalore Mission in 1997.

The Kathmandu Branch held its first youth conference on 6-7 July 2003, attended by seven Church youth and 14 investigators. An article that appeared in the New Era magazine that same month noted, "Once converted, Nepali people can teach each other, and these young people have not been afraid to speak about their new faith."

Sources: R. Lanier Britsch, From the East: The History of the Latter-day Saints in Asia, 1851- 1996, 1998; India Bangalore Mission, Manuscript history and historical reports, Church Archives; David Jardine, "The India Bangalore Mission: A Season of Change and Blessings" 2000; Fay Klingler, "Himalayan Setting for Edification, Service: Members, Investigators Mingle During Nepal's First Church Youth Conference," Church News, 19 July 2003; Lynne S. Topham, "Light in the Land of Mystery," New Era, July 2003.

NETHERLANDS

Jan. 1, 2011: Est. population, 16,716,000; Members, 9,052; Stakes, 3; Wards, 20; Branches, 13; Temples, 1; Percent LDS, .05, or one in 1,919; Europe Area.

In northwest Europe on the North Sea, The Netherlands, also known as Holland, is a constitutional monarchy with a Dutch- and Frisian-speaking population that is 31 percent Roman Catholic, 21 percent Protestant, 4 percent Muslim, 3 percent other, and 40 percent unaffiliated.

In June 1841, when Elder Orson Hyde was en route to Palestine, he spent more than a week in Rotterdam. While there, he engaged in gospel discussions with a leading Jewish Rabbi.

Paul Augustus Schettler and A. Wiegers van der Woude were set apart in the spring of 1861 to preach the gospel in the Netherlands. Van der Woude, a native of Holland, had been baptized in Cardiff, Wales, in 1852. He was possibly the first Dutchman to receive the gospel. The two arrived at Rotterdam on 5 August 1861. Van der Woude traveled to his home town of Friesland where he shared the gospel with relatives and on 1 October 1861 baptized three people including two cousins. These were the first known baptisms of Dutch people in the Netherlands. Schettler traveled to Amsterdam and on 23 December 1861 baptized three people. The two missionaries concentrated their labors in Amsterdam and soon had 14 converts. Early in 1862, they organized the first branch of the Church there. In 1863, missionary work and baptisms extended to Gorinchem, Leeuwarden, Rotterdam, Werkendam, and Heukelom.

The first company of 61 Dutch converts immigrated to Utah in the summer of 1864, and on 1 November 1864 the work in the Netherlands, which had been under the direction of the Swiss and German Mission, was placed under the newly-formed Netherlands Mission. By 22 October 1865, when the first conference meeting in the Netherlands was held in Gorinchem, there were three branches in Holland, namely, Amsterdam, Rotterdam, and Gorinchem.

The first two Dutch-language tracts were published in June 1866. During the 1860s and 1870s, the progress of the Church was slowed through organized opposition by mobs, ecclesiastical representatives, and the press. Missionaries also struggled with the languages spoken in the Netherlands, and by the lack of Church publications in Dutch.

In 1884, Heilige Lofzangen, the first Dutch language hymnal was published, and in 1889 John W. F. Volker completed a translation of the Book of Mormon. It was published in Amsterdam in 1890. In 1896, Dutch-speaking Saints received the first issues of De Ster, the first Church periodical in their language. The first Dutch Doctrine and Covenants was printed in Rotterdam in 1908 and was followed in 1911 by the Pearl of Great Price.

The Netherlands Mission purchased its first building, Excelsior Hall, in Rotterdam in 1908.

Because of the mobilization of military forces at the beginning of World War I, most American missionaries were withdrawn from Holland in 1914. Although 54 elders were released and reassigned to U.S. missions, a force of nine elders remained in Holland under the direction of mission President LeGrand Richards. Local Dutch leaders assumed full responsibility for the branches and districts. Holland remained neutral during the war, but placed restrictions on the number of missionaries who could serve primarily because of war-time food shortages. During the war years, 393 Dutch saints, including many local leaders immigrated to the United States. During the same period, 579 converts joined, largely due to a corps of Dutch women who served as district missionaries.

After the war, restrictions were lifted and missionaries were allowed to return. From 1921 to 1929, missionaries baptized 1,712 converts. From 1930 to 1945, however, the work made very little progress because of a severe economic depression and another world war.

In 1937, ground was broken at Rotterdam for the first Church-built chapel in the Netherlands. The building was dedicated on 3 April 1938 as the home of the Overmass Branch.

Missionaries were evacuated from Germany and other European countries in 1939 because of World War II. Thirteen of those serving in the West German Mission traveled first to Holland where they were hosted by the Netherlands Mission and the Dutch people. By late 1939, all missionaries and the mission president had departed, leaving responsibility for the 16 branches in Holland to a mission presidency made up of local Dutch leaders.

Germany invaded the Netherlands in 1940, killing more than 30,000 Netherlanders and destroying cities, including over one square mile of downtown Rotterdam. Excelsior Hall, home of the Rotterdam North Branch, was destroyed and many members were left homeless. The mission presidency raised $3,962 to be distributed among poor and displaced members. Under Nazi occupation all Church meetings were initially cancelled, but permission was obtained in 1941 to resume meetings although under surveillance of the German government.

Nazi occupation of the Netherlands ended in 1945, and on 28 February 1946, Cornelius Zappey, the newly appointed Netherlands Mission President, arrived in Rotterdam. Missionaries from America were not allowed to enter Holland because of the rigorous food rationing program in place. They were finally admitted in April 1946. President Zappey obtained the use of a large warehouse in Rotterdam and received Church shipments of food and clothing. After distribution of goods to members, additional shipments were distributed to the general public through the Dutch Red Cross. One of the great sacrifices of this time was the shipment of 70 tons of potatoes grown by the Dutch Saints to the Latter-day Saints in Germany. Later, an additional 90 tons of potatoes and 60 tons of herring were sent to Germany.

President David O. McKay met with Queen Juliana in the royal palace in 1953. An exchange of letters followed and the Queen accepted a specially-bound copy of the Book of Mormon from President McKay.

Official recognition of the Church was granted in August 1955, after nearly 20 years of petitioning. Legal recognition gave the Church rights to hold property and be exempt from taxation. It also meant that missionaries experienced less conflict with legal authorities while engaging in missionary work.

The Rotterdam South Ward meetinghouse was constructed and dedicated in 1955. On 12 March 1961, the Holland Stake in The Hague was organized with J. Paul Jongkees as president. This occurred 100 years after the beginning of missionary work in the Netherlands and marked the creation of the first stake on the European continent and the first non-English-speaking stake in the Church.

In the early 1960s, a major Church building program was instigated in western Europe. By 1966, there were 38 buildings in use as branch and ward meetinghouses.

During the first 100 years of the Church in The Netherlands, some 4,500 missionaries served there, and more than 14,000 people were baptized. A large percentage of those converts immigrated to the United States. However, after more temples were constructed in Europe, fewer members emigrated, and today, there are many second-, third-, and even fourth-generation members. Elder Jacob de Jager, who served in the Seventy, was the first General Authority born in Holland.

The Netherlands Amsterdam Mission was consolidated on 1 July 2002 with the Belgium Brussels Mission to form the Belgium Brussels/Netherlands Mission.

The Hague Netherlands Temple, the eighth in Europe, was dedicated 8 September 2002 by Gordon B. Hinckley. Dutch laws prohibit the construction of buildings that are closed to the public but the government granted an exemption for the temple

Membership reached 7,899 in 2002; and 8,006 in 2003. In 2005, membership reached 8,286.

Sources: Andrew Jenson, Encyclopedic History of the Church, 1941; "Netherlands," Ensign, August, 1973; Keith C. Warner, "History of the Netherlands Mission 1861-1966," thesis, 1967; Arnold K. Garr, Donald Q. Cannon, and Richard O. Cowan, eds., Encyclopedia of Latter-day Saint History, 2000; Lyn R. Jacobs, Mormon non-English scriptures, hymnals, and periodicals, 1830-1986, 1986; Hoyt W. Brewster, Jr., "Netherlands Awaits First Stake in Foreign Language," Church News, 11 March 1961; "1000 Members Witness Organization of Holland Stake," Church News, 25 March 1961; Dell Van Orden, "Visits Bless Lands of World," Church News, 14 August 1976; "Holland Stake Was a First 25 Years Ago," Church News, 9 March 1986; "Love of God Stressed in First Holland Regional Meet," Church News, 24 June 1984; "Members in Netherlands Gather Food," Church News, 17 March 1990; "Netherlands Cities Honor Church Member for Service," Church News, 20 November 1993; "Strengthening Youth Their Goal," Church News, 29 July 1995; "Netherlands Temple Announced," Church News, 28 August 1999; "Pylons Mark Progress of Temple," Church News, 27 January 2001; Shaun D. Stahle, "Seven New Missions Created," Church News, 9 March 2002; "Open House Dates Announced for Freiburg, The Hague Temples, Church News, 11 May 2002; O. Jay and Jeanette Call, "Netherlands: Pres. Hinckley Dedicates New Temple in The Hague," and "A New Day in This Great Nation," Church News, 14 September 2002.

(Listed alphabetically as of Oct. 1, 2011.)

No.	Name	Organized	First President
Europe Area			
1720	Apeldoorn Netherlands	14 May 1989	Max Henning Van Der Put
933	*Rotterdam Netherlands	16 Oct 1994	
	Utrecht Netherlands	28 May 1978	Eugene M. Engelbert
326	*The Hague Netherlands	12 Aug 1976	
	*The Hague Holland		
	‡Holland	12 Mar 1961	Johan Paul Jongkees

ARUBA

**Jan. 1, 2011; Est. population, 103,000; Members, 489; Branches, 2;
Percent LDS, .44, or one in 225; North America Southeast Area; Venezuela Caracas Mission.**

An autonomous member of The Netherlands, Aruba is a flat, riverless island with wide beaches covering about 75 square miles. It is located in the Caribbean Sea, 18 miles off the coast of Venezuela. Its citizens speak Dutch, English, Spanish and the local Papiamento.

Missionaries Clay Jorgensen and Julio Gonzalez were sent to Aruba on 20 January 1987 from the Venezuela Caracas Mission. When they arrived Jose Gonzalez was the only member on the island. He had joined the Church in Venezuela and had come to work in Curacao. The missionaries began meetings with Gonzalez, which provided the nucleus that led to the formation of the Aruba Branch. Selections of the Book of Mormon were translated into Papiamento in 1987. The San Nicolas Branch was formed on 18 June 1991.

Church President Gordon B. Hinckley and Elder Dallin H. Oaks of the Quorum of the Twelve visited Aruba on 16 March 2001 while on their way to dedicate the temple in Uruguay. They met in the Aruba San Nicolas Branch meetinghouse with about 180 Latter-day Saints. This is believed to be the first time a Church president had visited the island. Since 2003 all Church meetings have been taught in Papiamento instead of Spanish or English.

Elder Claudio R. M. Costa of the Seventy organized the Oranjestad Aruba District on 2 May 2004 with native Roland A. Odor as district president. The Santa Cruz Branch was created on the same day through a division of the Oranjestad Branch.

Sources: Venezuela Caracas Mission, Manuscript history; "Book of Mormon Now in 80 Languages," Ensign, March 1988; Jason Swensen, "Prophet Teaches, Motivates Caribbean Islanders," Church News, 24 March 2001; Allan J. Webb, Telephone conversation, 1 July 2004; Ingrid and Roland Odor, Telephone conversation, 2 July 2004; Clay Jorgensen, Telephone conversation, 6 July 2004.

NETHERLANDS ANTILLES

**Jan. 1, 2011: Est. population, 227,000; Members, 847; Branches, 3; percent LDS, .39,
or one in 255; North America Southeast Area; West Indies Mission.**

Made up of two groups of islands in the Caribbean, the Netherlands Antilles are considered part of The Netherlands. Its citizens speak Dutch, English, Spanish and the local Papiamento.

Ingeborg Zielinski went to school in the Netherlands and joined the Church there in October 1970. She returned to Curacao in the Netherlands Antilles in September 1971. Over the next few years, she met with a few Latter-day Saints that temporarily lived in or visited the country.

In 1973, Zielinski was crowned Miss Curacao. She hosted hourly radio programs and taught the family home evening program and other gospel subjects, which were well received across the island, though she used a non-denominational approach to her show. She was the most well-known member of the Church on the island. She married and moved to the United States in 1982.

Missionary work was opened and closed on Curacao in 1978-1979 by the Venezuela Caracas Mission following many requests for missionaries by Zielinski. The Curacao Branch was created on 31 October 1979. Though missionaries had visited for a couple weeks at a time since 1972, it was not until mission president Wesley W. Craig, Jr. sent missionaries in 1982 and decided that meetings should be conducted in the local language of Papiamento that the Church began to progress among natives. A meetinghouse was dedicated in August 1988.

Elder Walter F. Gonzalez of the Seventy organized the Curacao Netherlands Antilles District on 9 May 2004 with Gary A. Pedersen as president. On the same day the Curacao Branch was divided into two branches.

Bonaire, which is part of Netherlands Antilles, had 79 members in 2004. The first branch was organized on 13 September 1990.

Membership in Netherlands Antilles in 2002 was 342.

Sources: Venezuela Caracas Mission, Manuscript history; "Book of Mormon now in 80 Languages," Ensign, March 1988; Allan J. Webb, Telephone conversation, 1 July 2004.

ST. MAARTEN

**Jan. 1, 2011: Est. population, 30,000; Members, 159; Branches, 1;
Percent LDS, .67, or one in 149; North America Southeast Area; West Indies Mission.**

The Clair Dinane family was baptized on Guadeloupe in 1980 and moved to St. Maarten on 1 December 1982. They held meetings with Utah natives Stirling and Mary Jane Wadley until the Wadley's returned to the United States, and then the Dinanes held meetings by themselves or with other visiting American families. On 16 January 1984 Kenneth Zabriskie president of the West Indies Mission organized the St. Maarten Branch and called Clair Dinane as president. In 1984, Thad Ariens and Victor Quarty were the first missionaries to arrive. They taught in English on an island jointly administered between the Dutch and French governments. Robert Salomons arrived on the Dutch side of the island on 14 April 1985 and was called as first counselor to Clair Dinane in May 1985. Later that year, the Salomons began holding meetings in Dutch with the help of missionaries that arrived on 11 August 1985.

The St. Maarten and Marigot branches were combined to form the Phillipsburg Branch in August 1992 with Arnold Blazek as president. Property was purchased for a chapel in January 1992. Elder Gene R. Cook of the Seventy visited on 7 January 2002 and met with members of the branch.

Sources: France Toulouse Mission, Manuscript history and historical reports, Church Archives; Kenneth L. Zabriskie, History of the West Indies Mission [ca. 1989], Church Archives; West Indies Mission, Mission history and historical reports, Church Archives.

NEW CALEDONIA
(See FRANCE)

NEW ZEALAND
Jan. 1, 2011: Est. population, 4,213,000; Members, 104,115; Stakes, 25; Wards, 154; Branches, 53; Missions, 2; Districts, 3; Temples, 1; Percent LDS, 2.36, or one in 42; Pacific Area.

Located between the South Pacific Ocean and the Tasman Sea, New Zealand includes two major islands, North Island and South Island, and a number of smaller islands. Its government is a parliamentary democracy. The population is 24 percent Anglican, 18 percent Presbyterian, 15 percent Roman Catholic, 3 percent other Protestant, 2 percent LDS, 2 percent Baptist, and 33 percent other or unaffiliated. New Zealand has two official languages, English and Maori.

Augustus Farnham, president of the Australasian Mission headquartered in Australia, accompanied by William Cooke and Thomas Holder, arrived in New Zealand on 27 October 1854. They preached for two months with little success in Auckland, Wellington, and Nelson. They focused their missionary labors on the European population because they could not speak Maori. Farnham returned to Australia in December 1854, leaving Cooke and Holder to continue the work. In March 1855, they baptized 10 people, and in April organized New Zealand's first branch at Karori (near Wellington). From 1854 to 1897, missionary work in New Zealand was conducted under the direction of the Australasian (also called Australian) Mission, though little work was done in New Zealand until 1866.

In 1867, Carl C. Amussen, a Danish immigrant and jeweler in Utah, was called to serve in the Australasian Mission. While in New Zealand, Amussen taught and baptized brothers William and James Burnett on 6 March 1867 at Kaiapoi near Christchurch on South Island. When Amussen left New Zealand in June 1867, he placed William Burnett in charge of the Kaiapoi congregation which consisted of seven members.

During 1870, Australasian Mission President Robert Beauchamp visited the Saints in New Zealand. He assigned William Burnett to serve as president of the New Zealand Conference and appointed Henry Allington to preside over the Karori Branch. By July 1870, there were 41 New Zealanders on the conferences membership rolls, but that number was reduced in December 1871 when a group of 11 saints sailed from New Zealand to Utah. Another immigrant group followed in April 1872 under direction of Henry Allington.

In 1871, persecutions began to mount as the Church became better known. At one point the issue was brought before the Colonial Parliament. Neither restrictions nor punitive actions were taken against the Church due to "insufficient evidence of malfeasance."

A group of five elders arrived from Utah in December 1875. They served in the Wellington area until their release in 1877. In November 1879, New Zealand was divided into three conferences; Auckland, Canterbury, and Otago. By the end of 1880, branches were established at Christchurch, Prebbleton, Alford Forest, Auckland, Napier, Norsewood, and Timaru. Also in 1880, headquarters for the Australasian Mission were moved from Sydney, Australia, to Auckland, New Zealand.

In 1872, James Burnett reported working among the Maori in the Canterbury region. Language and cultural barriers limited his success, and the first known Maori baptism occurred not in New Zealand, but in Honolulu, Hawaii, in 1874.

On 6 March 1881, Mission President William M. Bromley visited the Maori settlement at Orakei near Auckland on the North Island. There he met with chieftain Paora Tuhare of the Ngati-Paoa tribe and received permission to preach the gospel to the Maori and to seek an audience with their Maori prophet Te Whiti and King Tauhio. Soon afterwards, Bromley appointed John S. Ferris to work on the coast of the Bay of Plenty, John P. Sorensen was assigned to work in the villages near New Plymouth, and Thomas L. Cox and his wife worked near Cambridge.

Prior to the arrival of the missionaries, at least five Maori leaders, some of whom were Tohungas (spiritual leaders) and others who were tribal wise men, had told of a "true religion" that would come. Many Maori beliefs were similar to those taught by the missionaries. This made the conversion process much easier. The first conversions came in the Waikato region, but others soon followed. On 18 October 1881, Ngataki, an advisor to King Tauhio, was the first known Maori baptized in New Zealand.

On 25 February 1883, a branch was established in the Waotu settlement with Hari T. Katera as branch president. The work progressed rapidly and by 1885 there were 1,038 of the 1,238 New Zealand members were Maoris. Two years later, in 1887, natives comprised 2,243 of the 2,573 members in New Zealand.

In 1887, Ezra F. Richards and Sonda Sanders began translating the Book of Mormon into Maori. They were assisted by Henare Potae, Te Pirihe Tutekohi, and James Jury. The translation was published in April 1889.

In 1897, the Australasian Mission was dissolved. It was replaced by the Australian and New Zealand missions. The change became final on 1 January 1898. At the time, the LDS population in New Zealand was 4,000, and 90 percent were Maori.

In 1907, the New Zealand Mission began publishing a semi-monthly magazine titled Elder's Messenger, printed in both English and Maori. The title was later Te Karere (The Messenger). In 1908, New Zealand Mission President Rufus K. Hardy began publishing a Maori translation of the Doctrine and Covenants in serialized form in issues of Te Karere.

On 4-6 April 1913, the Maori Agricultural College was dedicated. It operated until 1931 when it was damaged beyond repair by an earthquake.

Matthew Cowley served as a missionary in New Zealand from 1914 to 1919. During that time, he re-translated the Book of Mormon into Maori for publication in 1918. He also helped to prepare complete translations of the Doctrine and Covenants and Pearl of Great Price which were published as a single volume in 1919. From 1938 to 1945, he served as New Zealand mission president, and from 1945 to 1953 as a member of the Quorum of the Twelve and as the supervising General Authority for New Zealand.

On 21 April 1921, Elder David O. McKay of the Quorum of the Twelve arrived in Wellington on an official visit to the New Zealand Mission. Elder McKay visited government officials, hoping to improve the quality of relations between the Church and the country's representatives. In the following week, a six-day conference was convened.

As part of an effort to create missionary opportunities among New Zealand's caucasian population, the mission president in 1937 arranged sports leagues in conjunction with the YMCA. Basketball, baseball, and softball were organized, coached, and refereed by full-time missionaries. Additionally, beginning in 1939, MIA programs were broadcast on radio stations.

In November 1939, the Church sponsored a major exhibit at the New Zealand Centenary Exhibition in Wellington. By April 1940, there were 6,000 people who had signed the visitor book, and 22,000 tracts and 9,000 Articles of Faith cards had been distributed.

The First Presidency sent a cable on 14 October 1940 specifying that because of World War II all American missionaries in the South Pacific should return to the United States as soon as possible. Five days later, the Mariposa set sail for America carrying New Zealand's missionary force. District and branch presidencies were reorganized with local leaders, but Matthew Cowley remained as mission president. At that time there were 8,250 members in New Zealand in 13 districts. Elder Cowley conducted a subscription campaign for Te Karere, and used the magazine to communicate with members.

During February 1946, American missionaries were allowed to return to New Zealand.

David O. McKay dedicated the New Zealand Temple on 20 April 1958 and the Church College of New Zealand on 26 April. The following month, the first stake in New Zealand was created in Auckland on 18 May. In August 1958, the New Zealand Mission was divided and the New Zealand South Mission was added. Membership at the time was 17,000, but grew to 26,000 during the next eight years as 200 missionaries canvassed the country and convert numbers doubled. It was necessary to create additional stakes in Hamilton and Hawkes Bay in 1960, Wellington in 1965, another in Hamilton in 1967, and in Auckland in 1968.

During 1968-1970 a seminary program was established in New Zealand. About 13,000 members attended an area conference in Temple View in 1976, at which President Spencer W. Kimball spoke. Three years later, President Kimball addressed 11,600 in area conferences in Auckland and Wellington held on 24-25 and 27 November 1979.

In 1987, Elder Douglas J. Martin, a former stake president from Hamilton, was called to the Seventy. President Gordon B. Hinckley spoke at a regional conference in Hamilton 10-11 May 1997, and spoke to 10,000 members in Auckland on 11 May.

In August 2001, missionaries serving at the Hamilton New Zealand Temple Visitors Center began traveling to wards and stakes on the North and South islands presenting firesides and concerts. By year-end 2000, more than 12,000 people had attended the programs, with 6,800 of them requesting missionaries. In addition, New Zealand Public Radio asked the temple visitors center to produce a radio program. A radio series was designed similar to the weekly Mormon Tabernacle Choir broadcasts.

The prime minister of New Zealand, Helen Clark, was a special guest during the annual Christmas Light Display and Concert at the temple visitors center on 21 December 2001.

In 2003, record numbers of members from Christchurch welcomed President Gordon B. Hinckley on 17 June, the first Church president to visit and speak. In 2003, the Church had grown to the sixth largest religion in New Zealand with 93,840 members residing in 25 stakes.

In October 2004, more than 4,000 members and friends gathered in Hamilton to celebrate 150 years of the Church in New Zealand by attending a pageant chronicling the history and people who built the Church since missionaries arrived in 1854.

In 2003, membership reached 93,840.

Sources: Rangianewa Baillie Parker, Kia Ngawari Trust history, 2003, Church Archives; Brian W. Hunt, Zion in New Zealand: A History of the Church of Jesus Christ of Latter-day Saints in New Zealand, 1854-1977, 1977; Brian W. Hunt, The Maori Agricultural College, 1969; Andrew Jenson, Encyclopedic History of the Church, 1941; Lyn R. Jacobs, Mormon non-English scriptures, hymnals, and periodicals, 1830-1986, 1986; Mervyn Dykes, "The Church in New Zealand," Ensign, February 1976; Clyde P. Larsen, "Three Days with Missionaries in the New Zealand Bush," Church News, 9 May 1936; "Remarkable Career Closes for Oldest LDS Maori, Church News, 18 January 1964; "Pres. Hinckley Visits New Zealand," Church News, 17 May 1997; "Hearts Were Touched," Church News, 20 December 1997; Peti Transfield, "Celebrating 40 Years of Church Education in New Zealand," Church News, 30 May 1998; Pat Malouf, "Celebrating Anniversary of New Zealand's First Stake," Church News, 18 July 1998; "Sharing Gospel in New Ways in New Zealand," Church News, 27 October 2001; Marilynn Leonard, "Prime Minister Turns On Lights On New Zealand Temple Grounds," Church News, 29 December 2001; John L. Hart, "A City's First Visit by Church President," Church News, 28 June 2003; John L. Hart, "Steadfast in Faith, From One Era to Next," Church News, 26 July 2003; "Pageant reflects heritage," Church News, 2 October 2004.

Stakes — 25
(Listed alphabetically as of Oct. 1, 2011.)

No.	Name	Organized	First President
Pacific Area			
630	Auckland New Zealand Harbour	4 Nov 1973	Kenneth M. Palmer
1304	Auckland New Zealand Henderson	8 Nov 1981	Alan Robert Patterson
861	Auckland New Zealand Manukau	18 Sep 1977	Oscar Westerlund

455	*Auckland New Zealand Manurewa		
	‡Auckland South	5 May 1968	Geoffrey R. Garlick
264	*Auckland New Zealand Mount Roskill		
	‡Auckland	18 May 1958	George R. Biesinger
1973	Auckland New Zealand Panmure	13 Feb 1994	Stephen Aubrey Keung
2222	Auckland New Zealand Papakura	25 Aug 1996	Moses Christopher Armstrong
2223	Auckland New Zealand Papatoetoe	25 Aug 1996	Ephraim Cooper
1664	Auckland New Zealand Tamaki	13 Dec 1987	Clark W. Palmerston Larkins
2305	Auckland New Zealand Waterview	9 Feb 1997	Panama Leauanae
953	Christchurch New Zealand	27 Aug 1978	Bardia Pine Taiapa
1104	Gisborne New Zealand	14 Feb 1980	William Pakimana Taurima
310	*Hamilton New Zealand		
	‡Hamilton	13 Nov 1960	Wendell H. Wiser
2001	Hamilton New Zealand Glenview	18 Dec 1994	Richard Saxon Ball
313	*Hastings New Zealand		
	‡Hawkes Bay	20 Nov 1960	Joseph Alvin Higbee
2103	Hastings N.Z. Flaxmere	15 Oct 1995	Lawrence Victor Maxwell
475	*Kaikohe New Zealand		
	‡New Zealand North	19 Jan 1969	Stanley J. Hay
	(New Zealand)		
1012	Palmerston North New Zealand	18 Mar 1979	James Dunlop
2302	Porirua New Zealand	26 Jan 1997	Michael John Fermanis
884	Rotorua New Zealand	27 Nov 1977	Paul Robert Thomas
2304	Tauranga New Zealand	9 Feb 1997	Robert Solomon
445	*Temple View New Zealand		
	‡Hamilton South	19 Nov 1967	Harry S. Peckham
853	Upper Hutt New Zealand	14 Aug 1977	Trevor A. Beatson
407	*Wellington New Zealand		
	‡Wellington	12 May 1965	Keith A. Harrison
2002	Whangarei New Zealand	18 Dec 1994	Hira Paea Nepia Christy

Missions — 2

(As of Oct. 1, 2011; shown with historical number. See MISSIONS.)

(20) NEW ZEALAND AUCKLAND MISSION
7A Auburn Street
Takapuna, North Shore 0622
New Zealand

(143) NEW ZEALAND WELLINGTON MISSION
6 Hagley Street
Porirua 5022
New Zealand

NICARAGUA

Jan. 1, 2011: Est. population, 5,891,000; Members, 71,888; Stakes, 9; Wards, 58; Missions, 2; Districts, 7; Branches, 45; percent LDS, 1, or one in 92; Central America Area.

Located in Central America, the Republic of Nicaragua has a Spanish-speaking population.

Elder Spencer W. Kimball, then of the Quorum of the Twelve, organized the Central American Mission in 1952. Two missionaries from that mission, Elders Manuel Arias and Archie R. Mortensen, entered Nicaragua in 1953. They encountered difficulties at first, but on 11 April 1954 they baptized Jose D. Guzman. Other conversions followed. The Nicaraguan District was organized in 1959. The Managua Stake was organized on 22 March 1981, discontinued in October 1989, and re-organized on 21 June1998.

Church growth in Nicaragua was impeded for a number of years because of natural disasters and political unrest. A major earthquake in 1972 severely damaged Church meetinghouses in the capital of Managua. Missionary work was interrupted in September 1978 because of internal political conflicts which erupted into a civil war. Full-time missionaries were withdrawn in May 1980. Work continued under local missionaries, and full-time work resumed in the late 1980s. During the periods when few outside leaders entered the country, the local members continued faithfully despite serious difficulties, including the appropriation of two meetinghouses as schools and recruitment centers for one of the warring factions. In the summer of 1987, members of the Managua Stake received government permission and traveled by bus to the Guatemala City Temple to do temple work.

When political circumstances stabilized, the Nicaragua Managua Mission was organized on 15 October1989, with Church membership in Nicaragua at 3,453. President Gordon B. Hinckley visited Nicaragua on 21 January 1997 and spoke to approximately 2,400 members. This was the first visit to Nicaragua of a Church president since David O. McKay visited in 1954.

Nicaragua was one of three Central American countries where the Church, in partnership with California philanthropist and Wheelchair Foundation founder Kenneth Behring, donated 500 wheelchairs in 2001 via the country's First Lady charitable organization. The ceremony in Nicaragua, where wheelchairs were presented to the first group of recipients, was attended by Nicaraguan President Arnoldo Aleman and his wife, Maria.

In 2002, membership reached 41,224. In 2005, membership reached 52,184.

Sources: Clarice Tetz, History of the Costa Rica Mission, 1943-1995, Church Archives; Donald Q. Cannon and Richard O. Cowan, Unto Every Nation: Gospel Light Reaches Every Land, 2003; Costa Rica San Jose Mission photograph album, Church Archives; Managua Nicaragua District, Manuscript history and historical reports, Church Archives; "LDS Scene," Ensign, November, 1978; "Church Continues to Progress in Nicaragua," Ensign, February 1979; William Hale Kehr, "A Prayer Answered," Church News, 19 May 1979; Gerry Avant, "Nicaraguans Eager to Learn, Improve Lives Through Gospel," Church News, 22 November 1980; "Church Denies Sandinista Charges in Nicaragua," Ensign, October 1982; "Wheelchairs Given to Latin American Countries," Church News, 27 October 2001.

Stakes — 9
(Listed alphabetically as of Oct. 1, 2011.)

No.	Name	Organized	First President
2563	Chinandega Nicaragua	25 Jun 2000	Jose Ernesto Maravilla
2838	Chinandega Nicaragua West	14 Jun 2009	Jose Ernesto Maravilla
2634	Jinotepe Nicaragua	9 May 2004	Moises Antonio Campos Obando
2754	Leon Nicaragua	24 Feb 2007	Rogelio Hurtado E.
2481	Managua Nicaragua	21 Jun 1998	Pedro Jose aviles Zapata
2678	Managua Nicaragua Bello Horizonte	8 May 2005	Ronald J. Baquedano
2638	Managua Nicaragua Villa Flor	30 May 2004	Francisco Ricardo Silva Mendoza
2669	Managua Nicaragua Universitaria	30 Jan 2005	Pio Agustin Quintero
2671	Masaya Nicaragua	20 Feb 2005	José B. Contreras Rosales
	Stakes discontinued		
1246	Managua Nicaragua	22 Mar 1981	Jose R. Armando Garcia A.

Discontinued 15 Oct 1989 †Nicaragua Managua Mission

Mission — 2
(As of Oct. 1, 2011; shown with historical number. See MISSIONS.)

(227) NICARAGUA MANAGUA SOUTH MISSION
Apartado Postal 3527
Managua, Nicaragua C.A.

NICARAGUA MANAGUA NORTH MISSION
Frente Al Club Terraza, Villa Fontana
Nival #3
Managua, Nicaragua C.A.

NIGERIA

Jan. 1, 2011: Est. population, 149,229,000; Members, 98,359; Stakes, 16; Wards, 139; Districts, 21; Branches, 160; Missions, 4; temples, 1; percent LDS, .06, or one in 1,689; Africa West Area.

The gospel began to take root in Nigeria two decades before it was formally preached in the country. Letters came to Church headquarters from Nigerians inquiring about the Church as early as 1946. From the late 1950s on, some Nigerians learned about the Church through magazine articles and Church literature. Groups of people began meeting unofficially in the Church's name. These groups had boards of directors, formalized constitutions and rules, and were legally registered with the government.

In 1960, the First Presidency asked Glen G. Fisher, returning president of the South African Mission, and Marvin R. Jones, a young missionary called to serve in South Africa, to visit Nigeria. Fisher reported to the First Presidency that he met with several groups that had obtained Church literature, believed the doctrine and organized themselves as best as they could, and looked to Church headquarters for help. He said that the Church had been invited to establish the work in Nigeria and believed that an organization could be set up, even without the priesthood, the people would be blessed.

In 1959, LaMar S. Williams, an employee in the Church Missionary Department, was assigned to answer correspondence received from West Africa. In October 1961, Williams made the first of three trips to Nigeria to visit those people with whom he had corresponded and to check on the feasibility of establishing a mission. His positive reports and the many letters from Nigeria sent to Church headquarters prompted a decision to begin missionary work.

On 21 November 1962, Williams was set apart as the first presiding elder over Nigeria by Church President David O. McKay. In December 1962, Elder N. Eldon Tanner, a newly called member of the Quorum of the Twelve, traveled to Lagos, Nigeria, to inquire about the possibility of obtaining visas for missionaries, the first General Authority to set foot on Nigerian soil.

After a prolonged struggle to obtain Nigerian visas and the uncertainties about organizing the Church in Africa without most of the local male members holding the priesthood, Williams was finally able to begin his mission. In Enugu, Nigeria, on 6 November 1965, his visa was extended for 90 days and arrangements were made to have the Church officially registered in Nigeria. The same day, however, the First Presidency directed Williams to discontinue negotiations in Nigeria and return home immediately.

Williams did not record any reasons explaining the reversal of the First Presidency decision, but two months later, in January 1966, a violent military coup ignited the Biafran War, a bloody civil conflict in Nigeria. For the next 13 years no attempts were made to establish the Church in Nigeria.

About this time in 1966, Anthony O. Obinna, who was living in eastern Nigeria, had a dream in which someone gave him a copy of the Reader's Digest. Four years later, in 1970, during the civil war, Obinna dreamed about the Reader's Digest again. He began searching for a copy of the magazine. The one he finally found contained a picture of the Salt Lake Temple in an advertisement. Obinna felt prompted to write to the Church, which began an eight-year correspondence.

After he received Church literature from the International Mission, Obinna wanted to share his new-found faith with his neighbors, family and friends. He built an extra room on his house which he would use as a chapel. This and other small groups of prospective Latter-day Saints waited patiently for the first missionaries.

There were a few foreign Latter-day Saints living in Nigeria between the end of the Biafrian War in 1970 and the arrival of the first missionaries in late 1978. Records indicate that they were holding Sunday worship services in their homes in the mid-1970s.

There were also a few Nigerians who had joined the Church while living abroad and had returned. Ime O. Eduok went to California in 1968 to further his studies. An LDS friend invited Eduok and his wife to Church. In September 1970, the Eduoks were baptized in Inglewood, Calif. They returned to Nigeria in 1973. Back in Calabar, Nigeria, they began to associate with American Latter-day Saints, who were working there. Eduok was also able to locate Obinna and others.

The revelation granting the priesthood to all worthy males, announced in June 1978, allowed the successful beginning of missionary work in Nigeria. In August of that year, Merrill Bateman and Edwin Q. Cannon were sent to Nigeria on a fact-finding trip. They visited foreign Latter-day Saints and Nigerians who had been writing to the Church for 20 years. In November of that year the first missionary couples, Rendell N. and Rachel W. Mabey and Edwin Q. and Janath R. Cannon, were sent to Nigeria and Ghana. They soon located and taught the gospel to people who had been meeting in the Church's name.

The first person to be baptized in Nigeria was Anthony Obinna on 21 November 1978. The Aboh Branch, the first in Nigeria, was created the same day with Obinna as president. He remained faithful throughout his life. He and his wife traveled to the Logan Temple in Utah where they were sealed in January 1989. He died in 1995.

The organization of administrative units became necessary as more Nigerians joined the Church. In January 1979, Mabey and Cannon organized the Cross River State District in Calabar, the first district in Nigeria, with Ime O. Eduok as president. The Africa West Mission was organized on 1 July 1980 with Bryan Espenschied as president. It included both Nigeria and Ghana. The mission name was changed to the Nigeria Lagos Mission on 1 July 1985. The mission was divided on 1 July 1988 to create the Nigeria Aba Mission. The Jos and Ilorin missions, with local African mission presidents, Ato K. Dadson and John A. Ehanire, respectively, were organized on 1 July 1992, but discontinued a year later due, in part, to religious intolerance and violence in these regions. On 9 March 2002, the First Presidency announced the Nigeria Uyo and Nigeria Ibadan missions, bringing the total number of missions in the country to four. By 2004, there were five missions in Nigeria.

The Church has grown rapidly in Nigeria. Less than 10 years after the Church's establishment in the country, membership approached 10,000 in 1987. Elder Neal A. Maxwell of the Quorum of the Twelve organized the Aba Nigeria Stake on 15 May 1988, the first in West Africa, with David Eka as president. (Eka was later called as a Regional Representative in 1990 and Area Authority Seventy in 1997.) By 1994, Nigeria had three stakes and 12 districts. In 1999, membership in Nigeria was 42,746, the most of any African country.

President Gordon B. Hinckley visited Nigeria in February 1998, the first Church president to set foot on Nigerian soil. He addressed 1,150 priesthood leaders and more than 12,000 members in a regional conference in Port Harcourt. He also visited Aba, where members lined the streets to welcome him. While speaking to members in Ghana on the same trip, President Hinckley announced that a temple would be built in Accra, more accessible to the Nigerians. Two years later in general conference on 2 April 2000, President Hinckley announced that a temple would be built in Aba. Ground was broken for the temple on 23 February 2002 by Elder Bruce H. Stucki of the Seventy. That year membership reached 60,087 with 14 stakes.

Membership in 2003 was 64,151. In 2005, membership was 74,055.

On 7 August 2005, President Hinckley returned to Nigeria to dedicate the Aba temple on a warm, humid day where 7,415 gathered from throughout Nigeria. During that weekend, activities related to the dedication carried the theme: "A Day of Rejoicing," a fitting description for members who seemed hardly able to contain their joy. In the dedicatory prayer, President Hinckley called the temple a "thing of beauty," which would help heal the land.

There were more than 68,000 members in 2004, and an estimated 70,000 by time of the dedication.

Sources: Charles A. Agu, "The constitution and bye-laws [sic]...," [no date], Church History Library; "Mormons: The Black Saints of Nigeria," Time, 18 June 1965; James B. Allen "Would- Be Saints: West Africa Before 1978," Journal of Mormon History, vol. 17, 1991; Anthonia Nwachukwu, Interview, 1999, Church Archives; Ime Eduok, Interview, 1999, Church Archives; Rendell N. Mabey, An African Legacy, 1998; Glen G. Fisher, Report, 1960, Church Archives; Nyla B. Williams, "Life history of LaMar Stevenson Williams, [1983], Church Archives; Marvin R. Jones, Papers, 1961-1962, Church Archives; Ime O. Eduok, History, 2001; Church Archives; Edwin Q. Cannon, Correspondence, 1972-1980, Church Archives; Julie Dockstader Heaps, "Saints in West Africa Await Temples," Church News, 1 March 2003; "Nigeria Marks Twin Milestones," Church News, 21 May 1988; Richard G. Hinckley, Interview, 1998, Church Archives.

Stakes — 17
(Listed alphabetically as of Oct. 1, 2011)

No.	Name	Organized	First President
Africa West Area			
1695	Aba Nigeria	15 May 1988	David William Eka
2743	Aba Nigeria Ogbor Hill	2 Dec 2006	Robert Okoronkwo Johnson
1957	*Benin City Nigeria East	2 Mar 1997	
	Benin City Nigeria	24 Oct 1993	Alexander Afamefuna Odume
2774	Benin City Nigeria New Benin	1 Sep 2007	Olusegun Frederick Akinbo
2314	Benin City Nigeria South	2 Mar 1997	Godpower Etinosa Uwadiae
2604b	Calabar Nigeria	1 Dec 2002	Christopher Nchor Odock
2211	*Eket Nigeria	31 Dec 1996	
	Qua River Nigeria	14 Jul 1996	Udo David Umoh
2237	Etinan Nigeria	22 Sep 1996	Emmanuel Sunday Ekaete
2534	Ikot Akpaden Nigeria	27 Jun 1999	Idem Adiaha Etuk
2309	Lagos Nigeria	23 Feb 1997	Adesina Joshua Olukanni
2921	Lagos Nigeria South	15 May 2011	Umana Effiong Umana
2672	Lagos Nigeria West	20 Feb 2005	Olusegun Charles Oyewole
2538	Nsit Ubium Nigeria	19 Sep 1999	Etim Thomas Ekong
2476	Owerri Nigeria	14 Jun 1998	Stephen Chukwuma Ejielo
1781	Port Harcourt Nigeria	25 Nov 1990	Ephriam Sobere Etete
2615b	Port Harcourt Nigeria West	6 July 2003	Onwudiwe Christian Obinna
2610a	Uyo Nigeria	9 Dec 2001	C. Christian Nwobi
	Discontinued stakes		
2238	Umuahia Nigeria	22 Sep 1996	Godwin E. Woko
	Discontinued	23 Oct 2005	

(275) NIGERIA ENUGU MISSION
315/32 Umuoji Str. Independence Layout
P.O. Box 4133
New Haven
Enugu, Nigeria

(179) NIGERIA LAGOS MISSION
6, Gbemi Oluwa Close
Off Sule Abuka Crescent, off Ophebi Road,
Ikeja, Lagos State,
Nigeria

(221) NIGERIA PORT HARCOURT MISSION
#4 Estate Road, Rumuogba
Port Harcourt
Rivers, Nigeria

NIGERIA CALABAR MISSION
#20 MCC Road, opp. Mirage Hotel
Calabar
Cross River, Nigeria

NIUE

Jan. 1, 2011: Est. population, 1,398; Members, 284; Districts, 0; Branches, 2; Percent LDS, 19.1, or one in 5; Pacific Area; Tonga Nuku'alofa Mission.

Niue, located in the South Pacific about 300 miles south of the Samoan Islands, is a self- governing island nation under New Zealand protection. Most residents speak Niuean and belong to the London Missionary Society religion.

The first known Latter-day Saints in Niue were Fritz Bunge-Kruger and his family from Samoa, who arrived in 1952. He was set apart to do missionary work on Niue before arriving by New Zealand Mission President Gordon C. Young. He operated a traveling movie business and went about the island showing movies in all the villages, and then, with the contacts he made, started a home Sunday School. Attendance soon grew to 80 and services were moved to a local dance hall. At Kruger's recommendation, full-time missionaries were sent to the island from the New Zealand Mission. Robert M. Goodman and Wallace L. Barrett arrived on 10 May 1952. The first baptisms took place on 14 August when 26 people were baptized and a branch of the Church was organized in Alofi. Other baptismal services followed, and a total of 65 were baptized the first year.

The Niue Island District (later renamed Niue District) was created in June 1954 with branches in Alofi, Liku, and Makefu and became part of the Tongan Mission. Work commenced on the Alofi meetinghouse on 12 February 1955, with a handful of members raising money and doing much of the building themselves. They were also assisted by labor missionaries. The building was completed in 1958. Meetinghouses were completed in Avatele, Mutalau, and Lakepa in 1959. In the 1960s, there was steady growth in Church membership and Church program development, especially in Primary and MIA. N. Feki Po'uha, a native of Tonga, was sustained as the first non-missionary district president on 12 April 1964. Due to transportation problems and in order to provide closer leadership support and training, the Niue District became part of the Samoan Mission on 1 February 1968, the Fiji Mission on 23 July 1971 when that mission was created. The Niue District reverted back to the Tonga Nuku'alofa Mission on 31 May 1975. Translated selections of the Book of Mormon in Niuean were first published in 1981 and revised in 1983.

Despite early opposition and persecution of Church members, and emigration of many Niuean Latter-day Saints to New Zealand, Church membership in 1999 was 14 percent of the island population. Moreover, Church members are now found in prominent government positions in Niue, many of which are children of earlier converts. Veve Jacobsen was a member of the National Assembly and Minister of Health and Education (1993-1999). Lagavalu Haioti is presently a senior magistrate of the court, responsible for 50 land commissioner judges and six justices of the peace. Latter-day Saint Youth are also represented on Niue's National Youth Council.

When super tropical cyclone Heta devastated the government offices on the island of Niue on 6 January 2004, the vital records of the country fell victim to the storm's incredible forces. In the village of Alofi, powerful waves whipped by 180 mph winds literally washed 70 homes and businesses into the sea from a cliff 90 feet above the South Pacific Ocean. In a ceremony held at the Auckland City Library on 25 February 2004, Elder Spencer J. Condie, second counselor in the Pacific Islands Area Presidency, presented 28 rolls of microfilm as a gift to the people and government of Niue from the Church. The vital records were captured on microfilm when the Genealogical Society of Utah contracted with the Niuean government to photograph and preserve the records in February 1994.

In 2003, membership was 252.

Sources: Robert M. Goodman, Niue of Polynesia, 2002; Relva R. Price, History of the Church in Niue, 1973, Church Archives; R. Lanier Britsch, Unto the Islands of the Sea, 1986; Douglas W. Banks, "Church Grows Prominent on Coral Atoll of Pacific," Church News, 18 September 1999; New Zealand Mission, Nuie Island reports, 1952-1954, Church Archives; Tongan Mission, Manuscript history and historical reports, Church Archives; "Priceless National Records Saved by Microfilm Efforts," www.lds.org/newsroom/showrelease/0,15503,4044-1-19551,00.html, accessed 24 August 2004.

NORTHERN IRELAND
(See United Kingdom)

NORTHERN MARIANA ISLANDS

Jan. 1, 2011: Est. population, 89,000; Members, 632; Branches, 1; Percent LDS, .85, or one in 118; Asia North Area; Micronesia Guam Mission.

The Commonwealth of the Northern Mariana Islands forms a chain of 14 volcanic islands. The three major inhabited islands are Saipan, Tinian, and Rota. The islands first came under Spanish rule (until 1899), German (until 1914), and then

Japan (until 1945).

Until the 1950s, missionary work in the Pacific was limited to the peoples of Polynesia and Australia. This part of the Pacific was first assigned to the Japanese Mission, then the Northern Far East, then the Southern Far East, and then the Hawaii Honolulu Mission. In February 1975, President Robert E. Crandall of the Hawaii Honolulu Mission sent Callis Carleton and Jeffery Frame to Saipan. This was the first missionary venture into Micronesia proper. The Commonwealth of the Northern Mariana Islands came under the Micronesia Guam Mission when the mission was created on 1 April 1980.

Membership in 2003 was 888.

SAIPAN

Among the first Church members to Saipan were American servicemen in 1944 during World War II, including L. Tom Perry, later a member of the Quorum of the Twelve. Latter-day Saint servicemen even built a chapel on Saipan that was dedicated on 9 September 1945. As the headquarters of the U.S. Trust Territory, there remained a small U.S. military presence on the island after the war and a servicemen's group existed off and on, but full-time missionaries had never visited the island until 1975.

Missionary work began when Callis Carleton and Jeffery Frame arrived in Saipan on 4 February 1975 and were welcomed by a few Latter-day Saint servicemen. The first convert in Saipan was Juanita Augustine, from Palau, who was baptized on 19 July 1975. Alfred Gonzalez, a Church member from Hawaii, arrived on 16 July 1975 to become construction manager of the new airport. He brought his family the following October. He helped form a dependent branch and utilized a small vacant quonset hut that had been abandoned in the jungle and used it for a meetinghouse. After outgrowning this building, meetings were held in the missionaries' kitchen and living room. Sunday School classes were held outside under the coconut trees.

Through the efforts of Alfred Gonzalez and his family, Brad T. Nago and his wife, Jean, were converted and baptized on 24 January 1976. Nago became the branch president when the Gonzalez family moved away. An independent branch was created in August 1979 with Nago as branch president. At the time the Micronesia Guam Mission was created in 1980, the Saipan Branch had 85 members. It became part of the Guam District on 18 April 1982. A meetinghouse was dedicated on 19 June 1983. It was later expanded and rededicated on 15 August 1988.

President Gordon B. Hinckley and Elder Joseph B. Wirthlin visited briefly with 10 missionaries and met with about 60 of Saipan's 300 members during a refueling stop en route home from Asia on 1 June 1996. When President Hinckley visited Guam on 31 January 2000, while on a tour of Pacific Rim countries, his address was carried to the Saipan Branch meetinghouse via a telephone connection.

ROTA AND TINIAN

In June 1977, Donald Baldwin and Alfred B. Stratton, missionaries assigned to Saipan, visited Rota where there were a small number of Church members temporarily working. Stephen Jones and Kamealoha Kaniho were assigned to begin missionary work on Rota and arrived on 5 September 1986. Since then, missionaries have made infrequent visits to the island. Members on Rota are assigned to the Saipan Branch.

It was on Tinian that the first atomic bombs were loaded for their ultimate destinations of Hiroshima and Nagasaki to end World War II. No doubt Latter-day Saint serviceman were also on this island during the war. There are, however, no records of servicemen groups or later LDS missionary work on Tinian until Henry Van Den Hazel, Stephen Sua-Filo, and A. Vern and Eathel M. Busby left from Saipan and spent a day of tracting on the island in July 1978. A few Church members later moved to the island and in March 1990 the San Jose Branch was organized with Cezar Penaflor as president, becoming part of the Guam District. Missionary work was resumed on Tinian on 14 August 1992 by James Adamson and Ryan C. McCune; however, the branch was discontinued in 1997 as some members moved away. As with Rota, missionaries have since made infrequent visits to the island with few Church members living there. Their memberships are also with the Saipan Branch.

Sources: Alan E. Muller, A Historical Account of The Church of Jesus Christ of Latter-day Saints on Guam, 1955, Church Archives; Micronesia Guam Mission, Brief History of the Micronesia-Guam Mission, 1990; Guam District, Manuscript history and historical reports, Church Archives; "Final Stop: 'Just One More Meeting' in Saipan," Church News, 8 June 1996.

NORWAY

Jan. 1, 2011: Est. population, 4,661,000; Members, 4,361; Stakes, 1; Wards, 7; Branches, 16; Missions, 1; Districts, 1; percent LDS, .09, or one in 1,119; Europe Area.

In western Scandinavia, on the Norwegian Sea, the kingdom of Norway is a hereditary constitutional monarchy. Its people speak Norwegian with a small Lappish minority speaking Sámi. The majority of the people are Evangelical Lutheran (86 percent). The remainder are Roman Catholic, Protestant or other faiths.

Missionary work among Norwegians began in the Fox River settlements of La Salle County, Illinois, in March 1842. Missionary George Parker Dykes, traveling from Nauvoo, met with great success there, baptizing dozens of Norwegians and establishing the La Salle Branch. Included in the harvest were Canute Peterson who would later serve as president of Sanpete Stake in Utah, Christian Hyer who would preside over the Richmond, Utah, Cooperative Mercantile Institution, and Shure Olson who helped build the Salt Lake Tabernacle organ.

Missionary efforts in Norway grew out of the work begun in Denmark. In 1849, Apostle Erastus Snow was asked to open a mission in Scandinavia. To accomplish this goal, Peter O. Hansen was called to work in Denmark and John E. Forsgren in Sweden. Stopping in England en route to Copenhagen early in 1850, Elder Snow met George Parker Dykes who was working as a missionary there. Elder Snow knew of Dykes' earlier experiences with the Norwegians in Illinois and of his language abilities and asked him to accompany the group to Copenhagen.

Dykes was assigned to work in Aalborg, Denmark. In April 1851, he preached to a large group there, including Svend Larsen, a Norwegian ship captain who expressed interest in the gospel and purchased several tracts. Four months later, after a long meeting with Erastus Snow, Larsen was converted and, in September 1851, traveled in company with missionary Hans F. Petersen to Larsen's hometown of Risoer, Norway. There, engaging in the first official missionary activities in Norway, they distributed tracts and held gospel discussions until Petersen was found to be without a valid passport and was forced to leave the country. The two returned to Aalborg, Denmark, where Svend Larsen was baptized on 23 September 1851, the first resident Norwegian to join the Church. In October, he returned with missionaries Hans F. Petersen and Johan August Aahmanson to continue the work. John Olsen and Peter Adamsen were the first to be baptized in Norway on 26 November 1851.

Branches were organized at Risoer on 16 July 1852 and at Fredrikstad on 25 July 1852. By June 1852, missionaries had also begun to labor in Brevik, forming the core of the Brevik (later Christiania and then Oslo) Conference which was established on 14 August 1852. On 8 December 1853, the Brevik Branch was formed, followed by the Christiania Branch on 29 September 1854. There were 309 people baptized in Norway from 1851-1854.

Although the Norwegian constitution granted religious liberties to non-Lutheran religions, Mormon missionaries and converts encountered strong opposition, occasional acts of mob violence, and numerous legal challenges. On 4 November 1853, the Norwegian Supreme Court ruled that Mormonism was a non-Christian faith and, therefore, did not enjoy protection under an 1845 statute called the Dissenter Law which protected minority Christian religions from prosecution. For many years this decision hampered the work in Norway. Even so, 7,907 Norwegians joined the Church in the period of 1851 to 1919, with 3,292 of that number immigrating to the United States. Elder John A. Widtsoe, who served in the Quorum of the Twelve from 1921-1952, was born in Norway and was among the Norwegian converts during this period.

Growth of the Church in Norway necessitated division of the Christiania Conference on 8 May 1899 to become the Christiania, Bergen, and Trondheim conferences. Church units in Norway remained part of the Scandinavian Mission until July 1905 when the Danish-Norwegian Mission was organized. Norway was separated from Denmark to form the Norwegian Mission on 1 April 1920.

The first Church-owned meetinghouse and mission office was built in Oslo by members in 1871. It was torn down and rebuilt in 1903.

Until 1950, members and missionaries in Norway used the Danish translation of the Book of Mormon. That year, a Norwegian translation was published, and Norwegian translations of the Doctrine and Covenants and the Pearl of Great Price followed in 1954 and 1955, respectively.

Norway's only stake was created in Oslo on 22 May 1977. In 1988, the Church was registered for the first time with the Norwegian government.

Norwegian Latter-day Saints knighted by the king include John Langeland (1983) and Erlend D. Peterson (1997). Other prominent Norwegian Latter-day Saints include concert pianist Grant Johannessen and sculptor Thorleif Knaphus.

In 2002, membership reached 4,102.

Sources: Andrew Jenson, Encyclopedic History of the Church, 1941; Gerald Myron Haslam, Clash of Cultures: The Norwegian Experience with Mormonism, 1842-1920, 1984; Arnold K. Garr, Donald Q. Cannon, and Richard O. Cowan, eds., Encyclopedia of Latter-day Saint History, 2000, Erlend D. Peterson, s.v. "Norway"; Norway Oslo Mission, Manuscript history and historical reports, 1920-1977, Church Archives; Lyn R. Jacobs, Mormon non-English scriptures, hymnals, and periodicals, 1830-1986, 1986; Curtis B. Hunsaker, History of the Norwegian Mission from 1851-1960, thesis, 1965; "The Saints in Scandinavia," Ensign, July 1974; Harold Ecker, "Norway Saints Note Anniversary," Church News, 19 July 1950; A. Dennis Mead, "Beyond the Arctic Circle," Church News, 17 January 1959; "First Stakes for Norway, Venezuela" Church News, 11 June 1977; John L. Hart, "To be a Mormon Here, You Need a Testimony," Church News, 16 January 1988; R. Scott Lloyd, "'Field is White' in Norway's Arctic Region," Church News, 16 March 1991; John Floisand, "Inner Peace can Come in Time of War," Church News, 26 February 1994; R. Scott Lloyd, "Leaving an Impact in Scandinavia," Church News, 18 August 2001.

Stake — 1
(Listed alphabetically as of Oct. 1, 2011.)

No.	Name	Organized	First President
Europe Central Area			
835	Oslo Norway	22 May 1977	Osvald Bjareng

Mission — 1
(As of Oct. 1, 2011; shown with historical number. See MISSIONS.)

(24) NORWAY OSLO MISSION
Postboks 94
1306 BPT, Norway

PALAU (BELAU)

Jan. 1, 2011: Est. Population, 20,800; Members, 443; Branch, 1; Percent LDS, 2, or one in 49; Asia North Area, Micronesia Guam Mission.

Palau is a republic in the West Pacific Ocean whose residents speak English and Palauan and are mostly Roman Catholic and Protestant.

There are no records of missionary activity in this 100-plus island group or visits by Latter-day Saints prior to World War II. The first known Latter-day Saints on Palau came as members of the armed forces during the war. There were no other Latter-day Saints on Palau until Heber Butler, a counselor in the Hawaii Honolulu Mission presidency, visited Palau on 15 October 1977 to investigate the potential for missionary work.

Full-time missionary work began when Ron Brown and Stanton Akana arrived on 5 July 1978. Their missionary activities were initially restricted by the Palauan government to the islands of Koror, Arakabesan, Malakal, and Airai. The first to be baptized in Palau were Thaem and Marina Oei and eight of their nine children on 15 September 1978. On 1 December

1978, the Sakuma family was baptized, the first native Palauans, to join. The Palau Branch, later renamed the Meyungs Branch, became part of the Micronesia Guam Mission on 1 April 1980.

Another early convert was Vincent (Ben) Roberto, who was baptized on 19 December 1980 and later served as the first native branch president. By the end of 1981, there were 59 members in Palau. The Airai Branch was created on 27 September 1987 with Bing de Leon as president. The Meyungs Branch was divided and the Koror Topside Branch was created on 18 December 1988 with Walter Mauiur as president. The Koror Central Branch was created on 12 March 1989 bringing the total to four branches with 208 members. The Koror Palau District was organized two weeks later on 26 March with Walter Mauiur as president. The district was later discontinued and the branches reported to the mission. A meetinghouse was dedicated in Meyungs on 20 May 1990. The meetinghouse was later torn down after the branch was dissolved to give greater strength to the Koror Topside Branch.

There is a fluctuating population on Palau, in and around Meyungs, comprised mostly of workers from mainland China. Missionary efforts among them began with Kenneth and Margaret Styles, a missionary couple who served in Palau from 1990 to 1991. Donglong Liu and his wife Mei Li were baptized by Kenneth Styles on 5 August 1990. Liu was the first president of the Chinese Branch. It was later discontinued when many of its members returned to China. On 11 November 1991, Rebluud Kesolei, the first Palauan missionary, was set apart to serve in the Micronesia Guam Mission. Today there is only the Koror Topside Branch in Palau.

Source: Hawaii Honolulu Mission, Manuscript history and historical reports, Church Archives; Koror Palau District, Manuscript history and historical reports, Church Archives; Palau Branch, Manuscript history and historical reports, Church Archives; Micronesia Guam Mission, Manuscript history and historical reports, Church Archives; Micronesia Guam Mission, A Brief History of the Micronesia-Guam Mission, 1980-1990, 1990, Church Archives; William W. Cannon, Beachheads in Micronesia, 1997.

PANAMA

Jan. 1, 2011: Est. population, 3,360,000; Members, 46,425; Stakes, 8; Wards, 42; Branches, 36; Missions, 1; Districts, 5; Temples, 1; Percent LDS,1.3, or one in 77; Central America Area.

Located in southern Central America, the Republic of Panama has a population that speaks Spanish and some English.

In February 1940, Church member Otto L. Hunsaker was sent by his employer to work in Panama. He wrote to the First Presidency in September 1940 and again in March 1941 requesting that the Church organize a branch in the Canal Zone. Elder Antoine R. Ivins visited Panama and organized the Canal Zone Branch on 18 May 1941, with Otto L. Hunsaker as president. Most of the branch members were serving in the U.S. military. The branch met at a Jewish meeting hall that also served as a U.S.O. center, provided to the Church at no cost by local Rabbis, who said Brigham Young had provided Utah Jews with a meeting house and a cemetery when Jewish settlers first arrived in Utah. The branch reached a membership of 100 in its first year. Initially, the Canal Zone Branch was part of the Mexican Mission until the Central American Mission was created in November 1952. The first missionaries to Panama were Carl Guthrie and William Parker, who arrived in August 1953.

Servicemen, including Eran A. Call, later a member of the Second Quorum of the Seventy, and Ladd Black, taught some of the San Blas Indians in 1953 who were employed at the U. S. military base. They also taught the San Blas chief, Iguanigdipipi, who gave permission for his people to join the Church. The first of these baptized was his son-in-law, Jose Coleman. He was interviewed for baptism by President David O. McKay, who had stopped in Panama on 13 February 1954 while returning from a three-continent tour. Coleman was baptized on 18 April 1954. The first known native convert was José D. Guzman who was baptized on week earlier on 11 April 1954. In 1961, Elder Marion G. Romney presented a copy of the Book of Mormon to the president of the republic, Roberto F. Chiari. Because the Panamanian government did not recognize the Church until 1965, missionary work was limited until that time.

In 1965, Central America Mission president Ted E. Brewerton visited the San Blas islands and started full-time missionary work. Because the people there had traditions that corresponded closely with Book of Mormon events, many joined the Church. The first meetinghouse, completed in April 1970, was built on the island of Ustopo. The Panama Stake, the first in the country, was created on 11 November 1979, with Nelson L. Altamirano as president.

The Panama Panama City Mission was created on 1 July 1989. At the time, approximately 10,400 members lived in Panama. Most North American missionaries were withdrawn from the country in 1988 because of increasing political difficulties, but local leaders and missionaries continued the work.

President Gordon B. Hinckley visited Panama on 20 January 1997 and spoke in Panama City to 3,000 members. The prophet again visited Panama 18 December 2000, as he returned from dedicating two temples in Brazil. He addressed 5,000 members at a meeting in a downtown convention center in Panama City and told them the day would come when a temple would be built in Panama if members proved worthy. A temple was announced for Panama City on 13 September 2002.

In 2002, membership reached 39,559. By 2004, membership was 40,356 in seven stakes.

On 20 October 2005, ground was broken for the Panama City Panama Temple on a beautiful hillside in the suburb of Villa Cardenas. Elder Spencer V. Jones of the Seventy and president of the Central America Area presided at the ceremony and offered the dedicatory prayer.

The Panama City temple was dedicated by President Thomas S. Monson on 10 August 2008.

On 11 August 2008, President Thomas S. Monson visited Panama's President Martin Torrijos and his wife, First Lady Vivian Fernandez de Torrijos. The occasion marked the first time a Church president had met with a Panamanian president.

Membership by January 2010 reached 43,703.

Sources: Hunsaker family papers,1940-1999, Church Archives; Panama City Branch, Manuscript history and historical reports, Church Archives; Central American Mission, Manuscript history and historical reports, Church Archives; [Canal Zone Branch], photograph, 17 May 1942, Church Archives; "Canal Zone Branch Notes Anniversary," Church News 27 June 1942; Central American Mission, scrapbook, 1966-1970, Church Archives; "Elder Romney Sets Busy Schedule in Canal Zone," Church News, 2 December 1961; Ronald K. Esplin, "San Blas Indians," Church News, 2 June 1979; "Panama Gains First Stake from Costa Rica Mission," Church News, 25 April 1970; "New Missions," Church News, 25 February 1989; "An Outpouring of Love for Prophet: Pres. Hinckley Addresses 88,000 in Central America," Church News, 1 February 1997; "Travels of the Prophet," Church News, 30 December 2000; "Two New Temples Announced," Church News, 14 September 2002.

(Listed alphabetically as of Oct. 1, 2011.)

No.	Name	Organized	First President
Central America Area			
2711	Arraijan Panama	12 Mar 2006	Jose Rafael Martinez H.
2118	Colon Panama	5 Nov 1995	Eugenio Antonio Rodriguez Jacclos
1634a	David Panama	19 Apr 1987	Manuel Salvador Arauz
1734	*La Chorrera Panama	5 Nov 1995	
	*Bella Vista Panama	25 Jan 1993	
	‡Bellavista Panama	23 Jul 1989	Gustavo Brandaris Vergara
1081	Panama City Panama	11 Nov 1979	Nelson Altamirano Lopez
2464	San Isidro Panama	17 May 1998	Juan Bautista Reyes Ortega
1596	San Miguelito Panama	20 Apr 1986	Domingo Estribi
2465	Tocumen Panama	17 May 1998	Eliezar Navarro O.

Missions — 1

(As of Oct. 1, 2011; shown with historical number. See MISSIONS.)

(226) PANAMA PANAMA CITY MISSION
Entrega General
Estafeta Paitilla,
Panama

PAPUA NEW GUINEA

Jan. 1, 2011: Est. population, 6,057,000; Membership 18,336; Stakes, 1; Wards 5; Districts 9; Branches, 60; Missions, 1; percent LDS, .28, or one in 363; Pacific Area.

Located on the eastern half of the island of New Guinea in the Coral Sea and spreading across hundreds of smaller islands, Papua New Guinea is a constitutional monarchy with a parliamentary democracy. Its populations speaks Motu, Pidgin English, English, and approximately 713 other village languages. The nation's residents are 42 percent Protestant, 22 percent Roman Catholic, 34 percent indigenous faiths, and 2 percent other Christian denominations including LDS.

During World War II, a number of Latter-day Saints serving in the United States military were stationed in Papua New Guinea. At least two servicemen groups conducted regular Church services on the island from 1944-1945. At the conclusion of the war, the servicemen were transferred to other assignments and there is no record of any other organized Latter-day Saint activity in Papua New Guinea in the following three decades until after the revelation extending the priesthood to all worthy male members.

In 1979, Australia Brisbane Mission President Keith W. Hubbard visited Papua New Guinea. He found that there were a few Papuans who had received the gospel while living outside their country along with a number of Australians who had relocated to Papua New Guinea for employment. On 10 October 1979, he organized the Port Moresby Branch with Athol W. Pike as president.

Australia Brisbane Mission President Dennis D. Flake assigned the first missionaries, L. Douglas and Eva Johnson, to work in Papua New Guinea beginning in August 1980. The following 19 October, the first Papuans to receive the gospel in their own country, Maria Biai, Komara Nana, Sarah Nana, and Rhoda Baka were baptized. Douglas L. and Nita B. Campbell succeeded the Johnsons in November 1980, and during their service, property was obtained for a missionary residence and meetinghouse. On 4 January 1981, the Lae Branch was organized with Kelvin Horsford as president.

On 29 August 1982, Robert Goisisi and Johnson Auda were set apart as the first Papuans to serve as full-time missionaries. By October 1982, membership in Papua New Guinea had reached 475. Many of those converts had heard of the Church by word of mouth and contacted the missionaries to learn more.

By mid-year 1983, nine branches had been organized: Port Moresby, Lae, Arawa, Rabaul, Korobosea, Tokarara, Girabu, Konedobu, and Mt. Hagen. In 1984, the first meetinghouse in Papua New Guinea was completed in Port Moresby.

By March 1987, there were 1,450 members. Many more contacts were made in remote villages. Residents of the Daru Village asked for missionaries, who arrived in July 1990. Just three months later, the Daru Branch had 160 members. During this short time, two full-time missionaries, Brian J. Mott and Benjamin R. Lish were involved in the conversion of approximately 100 people. By 1989 twelve Papuans were serving as full-time missionaries.

The Papua New Guinea Port Moresby Mission was created in February 1992 with Joseph J. Grigg as president. Elder V. Dallas Merrell of the Seventy created the Papua New Guinea Port Moresby Stake, the first stake on the island, on 21 October 1995.

A plan was implemented by the Church in 2001 to help Papuans become more self-reliant in a region of the country that suffers from high unemployment and high illiteracy. Church Humanitarian funds also helped members develop water sources and sanitation systems and provided medical supplies, textbooks, desks, and repairs to school buildings. Members also learned to grow gardens. In a country suffering an economic crisis, these efforts proved to be "remarkable and dramatic" according to Elder John M. Madsen of the Area Presidency.

In 2003, there were 12,668 members. In 2005, membership reached 14,850.

Sources: Servicemen's Group (Army Post Office 43: New Guinea), Minutes, 1944, Church Archives; Servicemen's Group (Army Post Office 322: New Guinea), Minutes, 1944-1945, Church Archives; Australia Brisbane Mission, Manuscript history and historical reports, Church Archives; Papua New Guinea Port Moresby Mission, Manuscript history and historical reports, Church Archives; Carol West, "New Guinea: Light and Truth Pouring Into Nation 10 Years Following Church's Arrival," Church News, 16 September 1989; "Literacy Opened 'Whole New World' For Her," Church News, 6 February 1993; "Faith Leads To First Papua New Guinea Stake," Church News, 11 November 1995.

No.	Name	Organized	First President
Australia/New Zealand Area			
2109	Port Moresby Papua New Guinea	22 Oct 1995	Valba Rome
2925	Daru Papua New Guinea	29 May 2011	Tom Songoro

Mission — 1
(As of Oct. 1, 2011; shown with historical number. See MISSIONS.)

(275) PAPUA NEW GUINEA PORT MORESBY MISSION
P.O. Box 6947
Boroko, NCD.
Papua New Guinea

PARAGUAY

Jan. 1, 2011: Est. population, 6,996,000; Members, 80,788; Stakes, 10; Wards, 63; Branches, 86; Missions, 2; Districts, 11; Temples, 1; percent LDS, 1, or one in 94; South America South Area.

Residents of the Republic of Paraguay in central South America speak Spanish, Guaraní and Portuguese. They are 98 percent Roman Catholic.

Argentine Mission president Frederick S. Williams and his traveling companion, Edgar B. Mitchell, were the first Latter-day Saints known to visit Paraguay, spending a few days in the capital city of Asunción in November 1939. Williams hoped that someday the gospel would be extended to Paraguay, which was fulfilled some 10 years later while he was serving as president of the Uruguayan Mission.

The door to Paraguay was opened by Samuel J. Skousen, a former Argentine missionary, who in 1946 arrived in Asunción to work for the U.S. government. While stationed earlier in Brazil, Skousen had met Paraguayan Carlos Alberto Rodríguez and his wife Mafalda, who returned to Paraguay about the same time Skousen arrived there. When his friends asked for baptism, permission was requested from the First Presidency, and in August 1948, Brother Rodríguez was baptized by Skousen, who a month earlier had been set apart as president of the Asunción Branch.

President Williams visited Skousen and other Latter-day Saints in February 1949, shortly before Skousen left Paraguay for another assignment, and met with several government leaders. Later that year, the First Presidency granted permission to send missionaries to Paraguay, which resulted in Williams and his wife and missionary Wilford M. Farnsworth traveling to Asunción in January 1950. There they met with Paraguayan officials to seek authorization to begin missionary work in the capital city.

Williams was delighted when permanent permission was granted not just to work in Asunción but in the whole country. He left Elder Farnsworth in Paraguay, where he was soon joined by missionaries Keith J. Morris, Norval C. Jesperson and Daryl L. Anderson.

Missionary work proceeded slowly, with the next baptism not taking place for another year, when Clara G. de Krisch was baptized in January 1951. Paraguay remained under the jurisdiction of the Uruguayan Mission for more than a quarter century, with the efforts of the relatively few missionaries sent there confined entirely to Asunción. At one point in the early 1950s, consideration was even given to closing the work. Two new branches were created in Asunción in 1955, but 15 years later there were only 714 Church members in the city.

Beginning in the early 1970s, new attention was given to Paraguay, with the mission president in Montevideo sending missionaries to open the cities of Fernando de la Mora, Coronel Oviedo, Paraguarí, San Lorenzo, Villarrica and Pedro Juan Caballero. By the end of 1975, there were 10 branches in the country and approximately 1,700 members. With such renewed evidence of Church growth, the First Presidency created the Paraguay Asunción Mission in July 1977, and 19 months later the first stake was organized.

As missionary work was extended to additional cities and towns, the elders came in contact with some of Paraguay's rural Indian peoples. A notable success came in 1980 when Walter Flores, a Nivaclé Indian who had joined the Church in Asunción, prepared the way for missionaries to baptize some 200 members of his tribe who had recently established an agricultural colony in Mistolar, the branch there growing to 400 by 1990.

The pace of missionary work has quickened in recent years, with new areas being opened and Church membership increasing from about 12,000 members in 1990 to over 20,000 in 1995, and more than 50,000 in 2001. With more Latter-day Saints living in many wards, branches, stakes and districts, the construction of a temple was announced in April 2000, to be built on the site where the country's first LDS meetinghouse was constructed in 1964. The Asunción Paraguay Temple was dedicated by President Gordon B. Hinckley in May 2002. With its dedication, every Spanish-speaking country in South America now had an operating temple.

In 2003, membership reached 55,813. In 2005, membership reached 61,308.

Sources: "Paraguay" in Countries of the World and Their Leaders Yearbook 2004; Frederick S. and Frederick G. Williams, From Acorn to Oak Tree: A Personal History of the Establishment and First Quarter Century Development of the South American Missions (1987); Néstor Curbelo, Historia de los Santos de los Últimos Días en Paraguay : Relatos de Pioneros (2003); Gordon Irving, "Paraguay: A Preliminary Background Paper" (Historical Department, 1976); "Branch thrives in jungle," Church News, 27 November 1983; Néstor Curbelo, "Chulupi colony, Mistolar, thrives deep in interior," Church News, 2 June 1990; Néstor Curbelo, "'Heart' of South America opening to gospel," Church News, 27 May 1995; "'May This Temple Stand As a Crowning Jewel to Thy Work in This Nation,'" Church News, 25 May 2002

Stakes — 10
(Listed alphabetically as of Oct. 1, 2011.)

No.	Name	Organized	First President
South America South Area			
1002	Asuncion Paraguay	25 Feb 1979	Carlos Ramon Espinola
1911	Asuncion Paraguay North	22 Nov 1992	Gregorio Figueredo Servian
2655	Capiata Paraguay	31 Oct 2004	Daniel Antero Monzon Jara
2199	Ciudad Del Este Paraguay	2 Jun 1996	Juan Ramon Ocampos Gonzalez
1142	Fernando de la Mora Paraguay	1 Jun 1980	Guillermo M. Riveros A.
2376	Fernando De La Mora Paraguay South	15 Jun 1997	Humberto Canete Castorino
2588	Luque Paraguay	11 Feb 2001	Jorge Daniel Colina Araujo
2736	Luque Paraguay South	21 Oct 2006	David J. Riveros Florentin
2686	Nemby Paraguay	24 July 2005	Victor Dario Benitez G.
1997	San Lorenzo Paraguay	20 Nov 1994	Jorge Daniel Colina

Missions — 2
(As of Oct. 1, 2011; shown with historical number. See MISSIONS.)

(155) PARAGUAY ASUNCION MISSION
Casilla de Correo 818

Asuncion, Paraguay

(329) PARAGUAY ASUNCION NORTH MISSION
Casilla de Correo 1871

Asuncion 1831, Paraguay

PERU

Jan. 1, 2011: Est. population, 29,547,000; Members, 493,563; Stakes, 94; Wards, 596; Branches, 180; Missions, 9; Districts, 24; Temples, 1; Percent LDS, 1.6, or one in 64; South America Northwest Area.

Located on the Pacific Coast side of South America, Peru is a constitutional republic with a population that speaks Spanish, Quechua and Aymara.

Prior to 1956, Latter-day Saint families living in Peru held group meetings, but no organized missionary work was done. A Peruvian copper mine owned by Alfred W. McCune, a Church member from Salt Lake City, also brought a few members to Peru. Frederick S. Williams, a former mission president in Argentina and Uruguay, moved to Peru with his family on 1 January 1956 and soon contacted Church headquarters for permission to organize a branch and begin missionary work.

A branch in Lima was organized on 8 July 1956 by Elder Henry D. Moyle of the Quorum of the Twelve. Four missionaries, Darwin Thomas, Edward T. Hall, Donald L. Hokanson and Shirrel M. Plowman, arrived on 7 August 1956. A building for branch meetings was purchased the following November. Missionaries were sent to Arequipa later in the year. The Andes Mission, headquartered in Lima, was established on 1 November 1959. At the time, there were five branches and 300 members.

The mission was divided on 1 October 1961. When the first stake was organized in Lima on 22 February 1970, with Roberto Vidal, an early convert, as president membership was 10,771. That same year the mission was divided and renamed the Peru Mission.

Growth continued as local leaders assumed priesthood leadership. At a two-day area conference in Lima on 26-27 February 1977, presided over by President Spencer W. Kimball, 7,900 attended. Four years later in 1981, President Kimball announced a temple for Lima, which was completed and dedicated on 10 January 1986. Twelve years, later on 3 September 1998, a new mission training center, with capacity for 150 missionaries and room for expansion, was dedicated by Elder Russell M. Nelson of the Quorum of the Twelve.

Just 32 years after missionary work started in Peru, seven stakes in Lima were created the weekend of 30-31 January 1988 by Elder M. Russell Ballard of the Quorum of the Twelve. Lima then had the second largest number of stakes of any metropolitan area outside the United States. Although Peru experienced political instability, the Church continued to grow, even after extremist groups murdered three Peruvian missionaries, Christian Ugarte and Manuel Hidalgo in August 1990 and Oscar Zapata in March 1991.

In July 1993, the Peru Chiclayo Mission was created, which included the highland Andes bordering Ecuador. Seven additional stakes were created from October 1992 to October 1994; and 18 stakes were created from October 1994 to October 1996. President Gordon B. Hinckley visited Lima on 8-9 November 1996 and spoke to some 35,000 people. A new area, the South America West Area, was created 15 August 1998, comprising only Peru and Bolivia, with headquarters in Lima.

A massive earthquake shook much of southern Peru on 23 June 2001, killing a young LDS girl and seriously injuring four other Church members. More than 130 member homes were destroyed and another 175 were severely damaged in the quake. One meetinghouse was reported severely damaged. The Church sent 110,000 pounds of food, blankets, hygiene kits and first aid supplies in relief aid to victims in Moquegua and neighboring towns.

In 2002, there were 368,568 members in 80 stakes and 512 wards. In 2005, membership reached 416,060.

On 1 July 2010, two missions were created, bringing the total number of missions to nine. The Peru Cusco and Peru Lima West missions were created from an realignment of the Peru Arequipa, Peru Lima Central, Peru Lima East, Peru Lima North and Peru Lima South missions.

The Peru Chiclayo Mission was created on 1 July 2011 from a division of the Peru Piura and Trujillo missions to become the 10th mission.

Membership was 480,816 on 1 Jan. 2010.

Sources: Andes Mission history, [1960-1962], Church Archives; Andes Mission, Manuscript history and historical reports, Church Archives; Peru Branch, Manuscript history and historical reports, Church Archives; Manuel Sanchez, Relatos de la Historia de la Iglesia en El Valle del Mantaro, 1990, Church Archives; Donald Q. Cannon and Richard O. Cowan, Unto Every Nation: Gospel Light Reaches Every Land, 2003; Frederick S. Williams and Frederick G. Williams, From Acorn to Oak Tree, 1987; Gordon Irving, "Peru: A Background Paper," Church Archives; "Peru," Ensign, February 1977; Lee Warnick, "Resourceful People of Lima Making Church 'Blossom,'" Church News, 6 February 1988; "Shooting Claims Peruvian LDS Missionary," Deseret News, 14 March 1991; Lee Davidson, "Were Terrorist Attacks Related to the Gulf War," Deseret News, 26 March 1991; "Prophet Visits South America," Church News, 16 November 1996; "5 New Areas Announced Worldwide," Church News, 4 July 1998; "New Training Center Dedicated in Peru, Leaders Asked to Raise Worthy Generation" Church News, 12 September 1998; Jason Swensen, "Church Assists Peruvian Quake Victims," Church News, 7 July 2001; "New missions," Church News, 13 February 2010.

Stakes — 96
(Listed alphabetically as of Oct. 1, 2011.)

No.	Name	Organized	First President
	South America West Area		
1815	Arequipa Peru Central	15 Sep 1991	Cesar Leoncio Gamarra G.
2361	Arequipa Peru Hunter	25 May 1997	Alberto Enrique Mansilla Luque
1540	Arequipa Peru Manuel Prado	20 Jun 1985	Efrain Jorge Rodriguez M.
1985	Arequipa Peru Selva Alegre	24 Jul 1994	Elias A. Rebaza Rado
1108	*Arequipa Peru Umacollo	20 Jun 1985	
	‡Arequipa Peru	21 Feb 1980	Victor H. Gamero
2312	Arequipa Peru Zamacola	23 Feb 1997	Federico A. Rosas Molina
2189	Ayacucho Peru	21 Apr 1996	Job Edwin Quintanilla Pretel
2246	Cajamarca Peru	13 Oct 1996	German Maximo
2933	Casa Grande Peru	26 Jun 2011	Lázaro M. Neira Briceño
2156	Cerro de Pasco Peru	21 Jan 1996	Bernardo Cristocal Santiago
1145	Chiclayo Peru	8 Jun 1980	Jorge Humberto del Carpio M.
1567	Chiclayo Peru Central	27 Oct 1985	Franklin D. Orroyo S.
1820	*Chiclayo Peru El Dorado	29 Oct 1995	
	‡Chiclayo Peru North	20 Oct 1991	Javier Delgado Torres
2260	Chiclayo Peru La Victoria	3 Nov 1996	Erasmo Delgado Rivera
2113	Chiclayo Peru Latina	29 Oct 1995	Oswaldo Tello Mier y Teran
1122	Chimbote Peru	23 Mar 1980	Carlos Santos Lopez O.
2820	Chimbote Peru Buenos Aries	22 Feb 2009	Alfonso Anibal Granados Aguirre
1790	Chimbote Peru South	17 Mar 1991	Julio Arturo Leiva P.
2867	Chincha Peru	13 Dec 2010	
1527	Cusco Peru	28 Apr 1985	Jose U. Coacalla
1910	Cusco Peru Inti Raymi	15 Nov 1992	Miguel A. Vallenas Frisancho
1725	Huacho Peru	4 Jun 1989	Carlos Manuel Zapata P.
1471	Huancayo Peru	6 May 1984	Moises Sanchez T.
1756	Huanuco Peru	17 Jun 1990	Raul Rodriguez S.
2148	Huanuco Peru Amarilis	17 Dec 1995	Jesus Antonio Epinoza Solorzano
2936	Huaraz Peru	11 Sept 2011	Roger Zavaleta Muñoz
1739	Ica Peru	17 Dec 1989	Alexander Alfonso Nunez T.
2041	Ilo Peru	23 April 1995	Miguel Fernando Neyra M.
1162	Iquitos Peru	3 Aug 1980	Carlos Rojas Romero
2132	Iquitos Peru Nueve de Octubre	26 Nov 1995	Johnny Padilla Bustos
1864	Iquitos Peru Punchana	23 May 1992	Alfonso Frederico Rojas R.
2779	Jaen Peru	4 Nov 2007	S. Guillermo Sanchez Caseaneda
2007	Juliaca Peru	18 Dec 1994	Jesus Mario Barreda Ponze
2771	La Merced Peru	25 Aug 2007	Elferh David Diaz Gamero
1924a	Lima Peru Bayovar	7 Mar 1993	Augusto R. Ordinola Salva
1063	Lima Peru Callao	16 Sep 1979	Manuel Paredes
2355	Lima Peru Campoy	18 May 1997	Carlos Roberto Cabrera Rondon
1743	*Lima Peru Canto Grande	7 Mar 1993	
	‡Canto Grande Peru	18 Mar 1990	Augusto Ordinalo S.
2181	Lima Peru Carabayllo	17 Mar 1996	Johnny Enrique Tunque Carrasco
789	Lima Peru Central	21 Nov 1976	Oscar H. Aguayo U.
1679	Lima Peru Chorrillos	31 Jan 1988	Israel Antonio Gonzalez B.
1794	Lima Peru Chosica	5 May 1991	Ricardo Enrique Lazo T.
1675	Lima Peru Comas	31 Jan 1988	Grover Pinto R.
2824	Lima Peru Condevilla	19 Apr 2009	Richard Manolo Vasquez Anaya
1680	Lima Peru El Olivar	31 Jan 1988	Antero Miguel Sanchez M.
2611c	Lima Peru El Trebol	7 Sep 2003	Richard Manolo Vasquez
788	*Lima Peru Independencia		
2841	Lima Peru La Libertad	21 Jun 2009	Martin Isidoro Waitong Campos
2297	Lima Peru La Molina	5 Jan 1997	Abel T. Gonzales Rebaza
1677	Lima Peru Las Flores	31 Jan 1988	Miguel Fernando Rojas A.
1674	Lima Peru Las Palmeras	31 Jan 1988	Albina Isidro Chagua C.
503	*Lima Peru Limatambo	22 Feb 1970	
	*Lima Peru		
	‡Lima	22 Feb 1970	Roberto Vidal
2858	Lima Peru Los Olivos	20 Sep 2009	Angel Herberth Alarcon Villar
670	*Lima Peru Magdalena	21 Nov 1976	

	‡Lima Peru West	1 Dec 1974	Manuel Paredes L.
1678	Lima Peru Maranga	31 Jan 1988	Benedicto S. Pacheco M.
1486	Lima Peru Palao	1 Jul 1984	Rene Loli
2604e	Lima Peru Puente Piedra	16 Feb 2003	Carlos Francio Solis R.
2201	Lima Peru Rimac	16 Jun 1996	Gustavo Guillermo Andrade Brouseet
1439	Lima Peru San Felipe	11 Sep 1983	Mauro Luis Artica Q.
2185	Lima Peru San Gabriel	24 Mar 1996	Juan Carlos Mercado Briceno
1064	Lima Peru San Juan	16 Sep 1979	Jorge Salazar
1440	Lima Peru San Luis	11 Sep 1983	Philippe J. Kradolfer
1065	Lima Peru San Martin	16 Sep 1979	Rene Loli
2149	Lima Peru Santa Anita	17 Dec 1995	Jose Humberto Naupori Velez
2378	Lima Peru Santa Isabel	15 Jun 1997	Gerardo R. Jillar Quevedo
2186	Lima Peru Surco	24 Mar 1996	Alejandro Julian Llanos Morales
1795	Lima Peru Tahuantinsuyo	5 May 1991	Albino Isidro Chagua C.
1553	Lima Peru Villa Maria	25 Aug 1985	Juan Maguina Colquis
1881	Lima Peru Villa Salvador	31 May 1992	Victor Nicolas Anicama
1676	Lima Peru Vitarte	31 Jan 1988	Luis E. Stiglich S.
2859	Lima Peru Prolima	20 Sep 2009	Juan Carlos Guevara Rivas
1734a	Mantaro Peru	30 Jul 1989	Manuel Moises Sanchez T.
2008	Moquegua Peru	18 Dec 1994	Claudio Luis Zeballos Flores
1925	Pisco Peru	13 Mar 1993	Marcelo P. Munante Salguero
1755	Piura Peru Castilla	17 Jun 1990	Oscar Alfredo Galvez C.
1400	*Piura Peru Central	10 Mar 1996	
	‡Piura Peru	16 Feb 1983	Pedro Puertas Rojas
2177	Piura Peru Miraflores	10 Mar 1996	Jose Alberta Castillo Saldarriaga
2784	Pomalca Peru	2 Dec 2007	Mercedes Edgardo Clavo Chero
1961a	Pucallpa Peru	5 Dec 1993	Ferrando Vela Lopez
2130	Puno Peru Bellavista	26 Nov 1995	Pedro Tito Huanca
1872	*Puno Peru Central	10 Mar 1998	
	*Puno Peru Titicaca	26 Nov 1995	
	‡Puno Peru	28 May 1992	Adan Bravo Mathens
2745	Sicuani Peru	9 Dec 2006	Alfonso Rios Calle
2788	Sullana Peru	9 Dec 2007	Jose F. Alvarado Arambulo
1399	Tacna Peru	13 Feb 1983	Abraham La Torre Parades
2233	Tacna Peru Alameda	15 Sep 1996	Roger Valdivia
1914	Tacna Peru Arias Araguez	6 Dec 1992	Derliz Guzman Tejadi
1987	Trujillo Peru Central	14 Aug 1994	Pedro Gerardo Rodriguez H.
1802	Trujillo Peru East	16 Jun 1991	Raymundo Aponte Garcia
2428	Trujillo Peru Esperanza	18 Jan 1998	Laureano Gaspar Arrellano L.
2429	Trujillo Peru Laureles	18 Jan 1998	Luis Yvan Sanchez
1487	Trujillo Peru Palermo	12 Aug 1984	Jose Neyra
2452	Trujillo Peru Porvenir	19 Apr 1998	Wilson Americo Moreno U.
887	*Trujillo Pero Primavera	23 Feb 1998	
	*Trujillo Peru North	19 Aug 1984	
	Trujillo Peru	22 Jan 1978	Teofilo Puertas Vega
2780	Tumbes Peru	4 Nov. 2007	Victor A. Pereyra Talledo
2229	Ventanilla Peru	8 Sep 1996	Luis Arnaldo Alvarado Zegarra

Stakes discontinued

2131	Iquitos Peru Mi Peru Discontinued 21 Jun 1998	26 Nov 1995	Roger Braga Llerena
1541	Iquitos Peru Sachachorro Discontinued 21 Jun 1998	23 Jun 1985	Jorge Diaz Suarez
2354	Lima Peru Las Violetas	18 May 1997	Elras Humberto Alcantara
	Lima Peru Lamanita Discontinued 27 Apr 2003	21 Nov 1976	Rafael de la Cruz
2234	Tacna Peru Los Angeles Discontinued 6 Feb 2000	15 Sep 1996	Rolando Melchor
1860	Chincha Peru Discontinued	8 May 1992 26 Sep 1999	Alfonso Eduardo Ormeno Villa

Missions — 10

(As of Oct. 1, 2011; shown with historical number. See MISSIONS.)

(165) PERU AREQUIPA MISSION
Casilla de Correo 1884
Arequipa, Peru

(291) PERU PIURA MISSION
Los Naranjos Mz H, Lt 4,
Urb. Los Geranios
Piura, Peru

(302) PERU LIMA CENTRAL MISSION
Ave Joge Basadre 592,
Oficina 604-B,
San Isidro, Lima 27, Peru

(210) PERU LIMA EAST MISSION
Casilla Los Agrologos 368
Urbanizacio Las Acacias De Monterrico
La Molina, Lima 12, Peru

(149) PERU LIMA NORTH MISSION
Carlos Salaverry 3664
Urb. Panamericana, Los Olivos
Llima, Peru

(50) PERU LIMA SOUTH MISSION
Ave Jorge Basadre 592, Oficina 604-A
Edifico Torre Azul
San Isidro
Lima 27, Peru

(184a) PERU TRUJILLO MISSION
Avenida Larco 849 Piso 3
Urb. La Merced
Trujillo, La Libertad, Peru

PERU CUSCO MISSION
Jeron Ricardo Palma
Manzana A. Lote 24 to Piso
Urb. Santa Monica, Cusco, Peru

PERU LIMA WEST MISSION
Ave Carlos Salaverry 3664
Los Olivos
Lima 39, Peru

PERU CHICLAYO MISSION
Calle Maria Izaga #690
Chiclayo
Lambayeque, Peru

PHILIPPINES

Jan. 1, 2011: Est. population, 97,977,000; Members, 645,776; Stakes, 80; Wards, 500; Branches, 600; Missions, 16; Districts, 85; Temples, 2; percent LDS, .63, or one in 159; Philippines Area.

A large archipelago off the southeast coast of Asia, the Republic of the Philippines has a population of more than 70 million, speaking mainly English and Tagalog, along with seven other major dialects. More than 80 percent of the population is Catholic, due to a long period of Spanish rule, with the remainder being predominantly Protestant and Muslim.

The first attempt to introduce the Church in the Philippines was made in 1898 during the Spanish-American War by Willard Call and George Seaman, American servicemen from Utah, who had been set apart as missionaries prior to their departure. As opportunity arose, they preached the gospel, but with no apparent success. Following World War II, Maxine Grimm, who came to the Philippines with the Red Cross in 1945, introduced the gospel to Aneleta Pabilona Fajardo, who was baptized in 1945. She was the first Filipino to join the Church in the islands.

In 1953, during the Korean War, the Luzon Servicemen's District was organized under the direction of the Japanese Mission to accommodate the needs of Latter-day Saint servicemen stationed in the Philippines. The district became part of the new Southern Far East Mission, established under the direction of Joseph Fielding Smith in August of 1955. While in the area, President Smith also visited the Philippines. Although legal questions delayed the official assignment of missionaries to the country, some work was begun by LDS servicemen, in particular Kendall B. Schaefermeyer, a returned missionary serving in the U.S. Navy. By October of 1957 he had baptized four Filipino investigators and was teaching the gospel to more than 20 others.

During 1960, Elder Gordon B. Hinckley, Assistant to the Twelve, and Elder Ezra Taft Benson of the Quorum of the Twelve visited the Philippines, focusing primarily on the work of the LDS servicemen's groups, but returning with encouraging reports of the prospects for missionary work among the Filipinos. The following year, on 23 January 1961, Southern Far East Mission President Robert S. Taylor was finally able to submit paperwork for the official registration of the Church in the Philippines.

Then on 28 April 1961, Elder Gordon B. Hinckley returned to the islands and met with a small group of servicemen, American residents, and Filipino members and officially opened the islands for missionary work. The first American missionaries, Ray Goodson, Harry Murray, Kent Lowe and Nestor Ledesma arrived in Manila less than two months later. Among the first of their converts were members of the Jose Gutierez Sr. family. By year's end, six others had accepted the gospel. By 1967, the work had progressed to the point where the Philippine Mission was organized, with Paul S. Rose as president.

The Church in the Philippines grew rapidly, with the first stake being established in Manila on 20 May 1973. In 1974 the mission was divided, creating the Philippines Manila Mission and the Philippines Cebu City Mission. Church President Spencer W. Kimball presided over area conferences in Manila in 1975 and 1980.

During his 1980 visit he also met briefly with Philippines President Ferdinand E. Marcos at the presidential palace. In 1983, the Church opened a missionary training center in the Philippines and the following year dedicated the Manila Philippines Temple. In 1987, the Philippines/Micronesia Area was established with headquarters in Manila.

Augusto A. Lim, the first Filipino General Authority, was called to the Second Quorum of Seventy in June of 1992. In 1996, President Hinckley returned for a visit with the saints in the Philippines, this time as president of the Church. His Philippines stop was part of an eight-nation tour.

In 2005, membership reached 553,121.

The Cebu City Philippines Temple was dedicated on June 13 in three dedicatory sessions by President Thomas S. Monson. For some, the boat ride to attend a temple was reduced from 30 hours to 11. The Cebu City temple became the second temple in the Philippines, with approximately 200,000 members in the temple district.

In 2009, there were 614, 585 members.

On 1 July 2010, the Philippines Iloilo Mission was created from a division of the Philippines Bacolod Mission to form the countries 16th mission.

The Cebu City Philippines Temple was dedicated on 29 August 2010, the second in the Philippines. Proceedings of the dedication were broadcast to 164 stake and district meetinghouses.

Sources: Southern Far East Mission, Manuscript history and historical reports, Church Archives. Philippines Manila Mission, Manuscript history and historical reports, Church Archives; Japanese Mission, Manuscript history and historical reports, Church Archives; Luzon District,

Southern Far East Mission, A history of the Church of Jesus Christ of Latter-day Saints in the Philippines, 1965; R. Lanier Britsch, "Faithful, Good, Virtuous, True: Pioneers in the Philippines," Liahona, February 1998, 41; Spencer W. Kimball, "A Report of My Stewardship," Ensign, May 1981, 5; Francis M. Orquiola, "Gospel Flourishes in Soil of Filipino Faith," Ensign, September 1984, 78; Francis M. Orquiola, "Temple Dedication Rewards Faith of Filipino Saints," Ensign, November 1984, 106. "Four New Areas to be Organized in August," Ensign, July 1987 July, 74; "Cebu temple dedicated," Church News, 19 June 2010, "New missions," Church News, 13 Feb., 2010.

Stakes — 80
(Listed alphabetically as of Oct. 1, 2011.)

No.	Name	Organized	First President
Philippines Area			
1226	Angeles Philippines	18 Jan 1981	Orlando D. Aquilar
2388	Antipolo Philippines	31 Aug 1997	Arnulfo T. Roda
1281	Bacolod Philippines	5 Jul 1981	Remus G. Villarete
1323	Bacolod Philippines North	7 Feb 1982	Rufino Alvarez Villaneuva Jr.
2559	Bacolod Philippines South	4 Jun 2000	Avelino N. Santillan
2609c	Bago Philippines	13 Jan 2002	Danilo C. Delos Santos
1573	Baguio Philippines	17 Nov 1985	Carlos F. Chavez
1806	Balanga Philippines	7 Jul 1991	Torbio Nuguid Santos
2331	Batac Philippines	23 Mar 1997	Nathaniel Oasan Berroidan
2374	Bayambang Philippines	15 Jun 1997	Jose Mirafelix Balajadia
1788	Binalbagan Philippines	3 Mar 1991	Jose Vicente Pioquinto
1711	Butuan Philippines	19 Feb 1989	Henry Ferrer Acebedo
1340	Cabanatuan Philippines	9 May 1982	Arsenio A. Pacaduan
1884	Cabuyao Philippines	7 June 1992	Tomas S. Merdegia Jr.
1572	Cadiz Philippines	10 Nov 1985	Carmelino M. Cawit
1535	Cagayan De Oro Philippines	26 May 1985	Loreto Balanta Libid
1748	Cagayan de Oro Philippines East	6 May 1990	Danilo D. De La Vega
2528	Cagayan de Oro Philippines West	16 May 1999	Harry Waga Tenestrante
2427	Cainta Philippines	18 Jan 1998	Ramon De La Cruz Rodriguez
1238	*Caloocan Philippines		
	*Kalookan Philippines	17 Feb 1996	
	‡Caloocan Philippines	22 Feb 1981	Godofredo Hilario Esguerra
2804a	Catarman Philippines	10 May 2008	Jemmy Dumdum Pedrola
1545	Cavite Philippines	24 Oct 1989	Charles W. Brooks
	‡Makiling Philippines	18 Aug 1985	Jose Trinidad Aguilar
1220	Cebu City Philippines	11 Jan 1981	Jacob Torres Lopez
2568	Cebu Philippines Central	27 Aug 2000	Paul Johnson Reyes Codina
2538a	Cebu Philippines Liloan	17 Oct 1999	Allen Sagario Velasco
2554	Daet Philippines	30 Apr 2000	Aquilino Zapanta Aloc
1229	Dagupan Philippines	25 Jan 1981	Bernardo G. Reamon
2504	Dasmarinas Philippines	13 Dec 1998	Remegio Evangelista Meim Jr.
1307	Davao Philippines	15 Nov 1981	George S. Lavarino
1544	Davao Philippines Buhangin	18 Aug 1985	Patrick Hartford M. Clair
1876	Digos Philippines	31 May 1992	Paul Farinas Bunoan
2561	Fairview Philippines	11 Jun 2000	Raul Antonio V. Jose
2461	Gapan Philippines	17 May 1998	Roger Young Salvador
2084	General Santos Philippines	6 Aug 1995	Fabian L. Simamban
2558	Goa Philippines	28 May 2000	Edgar Pia Pesimo Sr.
2580	Ilagan Philippines	10 Dec 2000	Honorato Tagao Macaballug
1908	Iligan Philippines	18 Oct 1992	William C. Garife
1508	Iloilo Philippines	20 Jan 1985	Hannibal Delgado D.
2316	Iloilo Philippines North	9 Mar 1997	Eusebio B. Sollesta
2548	Kalibo Philippines	5 Mar 2000	Winston Bantigue Del Rosario
1715	Laoag Philippines	23 Apr 1989	Jose Miguel Tumaneng
1555	Las Pinas Philippines	15 Sep 1985	Delfin T. Justiniano
1551	Legazpi Philippines	19 Aug 1985	Jose P. Leveriza
1557	Lingayen Philippines	22 Sep 1985	Oberlito R. Cantillo
2597	Lipa Philippines	1 Jul 2001	Joselito S. Geling
2605e	Lopez Philippines	16 Mar 2003	Librado A. Azares Sr.
2503	Lucena Philippines	13 Dec 1998	David D. Sanglap
841	Makati Philippines	29 May 1977	Ruben Moscaira Lancanienta
2924	Makati Philippines East	21 May 2011	David Rusia Alicando
1726	Malolos Philippines	11 Jun 1989	Rogelio C. Coronel
1735b	Mandaue Philippines	19 Nov 1989	Cesar Abina Perez Jr.
613	*Manila Philippines		
	‡Manila	20 May 1973	Augusto Alandy Lim
1210	Marikina Philippines	30 Nov 1980	Augusto Alandy Lim
2560	Montalban Philippines	4 Jun 2000	Hernelio Alos Baradi
1546	Naga Philippines	18 Aug 1985	Avelino S. Babia Sr.
2332	Narvacan Philippines	23 Mar 1997	William R. Beralta Sr.
2389	Novaliches Philippines	7 Sep 1997	Bartolme M. Baldenor
2533	Ormoc Philippines	27 Jun 1999	Reynaldo Saligo Delante Sr.
2340	Oroquieta Philippines	20 Apr 1997	Arturo Bugas Macalisang
2891	Paniqui Philippines	12 Dec 2010	Petronilo C. Nadado

1309	Paranaque Philippines	22 Nov 1981	Ruben M. Lacanienta
2430	Pasay Philippines	25 Jan 1998	Eleazer Salipot Collado
1554	Pasig Philippines	15 Sep 1985	Macario Molina Yasona Jr.
842	Quezon City Philippines	29 May 1977	Augusto Alandy Lim
2417	Quezon City Phillippines South	30 Nov 1997	Manuel Mendoza Agustin
2176	Rosales Philippines	10 Mar 1996	Emmanuel Vallejos Damasco
2549	Roxas Philippines	12 Mar 2000	Francisco D. Dariagan
1315	San Fernando La Union Philippines	6 Dec 1981	Angel B. Salanga Jr.
2459	San Jose Philippines	10 May 1998	Gavino Penales Apao Jr.
1552	San Pablo Philippines	20 Aug 1985	Cleofas S. Canoy
1875	Santa Cruz Philippines	31 May 1992	Rolando Pramis Nueva
2609	Santa Ignacia Philippines	2 Dec 2001	Joselito Y. Velasco
2444	Santiago Philippines	22 Mar 1998	Efren M. Lamoglia
2847	Sagay Philippines	28 Jun 2009	Diovalre Ofianga Pastones
2762	Tacloban Philippines	12 May 2007	Artemio A. Cabanag
1330	*Talisay Philippines	10 Aug 1989	
	‡Cebu City Philippines South	21 Mar 1982	Bienvenido Pangilinan Flores
1321	Tarlac Philippines	13 Dec 1981	Mario de Jesus
1721	Tuguegarao Philippines	21 May 1989	Quirino Sumabat Donato
1558	Urdaneta Philippines	22 Sep 1985	Felino Caparas Ocampo
2435	Valenzuela Philippines	8 Feb 1998	Godofredo Hilario Esguerra
1571	Zamboanga Philippines	10 Nov 1985	Catalino A. Dugupan Sr.

Stakes discontinued

1547	La Carlota Philippines Discontinued 4 Jul 2004	18 Aug 1985	Antonio V. Custodio
2537	Agoo Philippines Discontinued 22 Feb 2004	22 Aug 1999	Ricardo Castillo Lopez
2411	*Bauang Phillippines	22 Aug 1999	
	‡Aringay Philippines Discontinued 30 Nov 2003	23 Nov 1997	Buenaventura Soriano Obscena
1807	Camiling Philippines Discontinued 3 Aug 2003	14 Jul 1991	Celso Arenzana Nicolas
1877	Kidapawan Philippines Discontinued 19 Feb 1995	31 May 1992	Rodolfo Bergado Estrella
1789	*Mangaldan Philippines	22 Aug 1999	
	‡San Fabian Philippines Discontinued 17 Aug 2003	17 Mar 1991	Loreto D. Querimit
1577	Munoz Philippines Discontinued 31 May 1992	24 Nov 1985	Juanito Wytangooy Tanedo
1713	Olongapo Philippines Discontinued 5 Sep 1993	5 Mar 1989	Richard Noboru Kivabu
1780	Ozamiz Philippines Discontinued 7 Nov 1993	25 Nov 1990	Wilfredo Tumampos Romero
2592	Burgos Philippines Discontinued 22 May 2005	20 May 2001	Rogelio Sumaoang Martin

Missions — 17

(As of Oct. 1, 2011; shown with historical number. See MISSIONS.)

(268) PHILIPPINES ANGELES MISSION
1827 Gumain Street
Redwood Villas
Clark Field, Pampanga 2009
Philippines

(110) PHILIPPINES BACOLOD MISSION
P.O. Box 660, Bacolod City
6100 Negros Occidental
Philippines

(172) PHILIPPINES BAGUIO MISSION
P.O. Box 380
2600 Baguio City, Benguet
Philippines

(211) PHILIPPINES CAGAYAN DE ORO MISSION
PO Box 0400
Cagayan de Oro City 9000
Misamis Oriental, Philippines

(194) PHILIPPINES CEBU MISSION
P.O. Box 338
Cebu City 6000, Philippines

(157) PHILIPPINES DAVAO MISSION
P.O. Box 80741
8000 Davao City, Philippines

(256) PHILIPPINES CAUAYAN MISSION
Burgos Street
Cauayan
Isabela, Philippines

(76b) PHILIPPINES MANILA MISSION
P.O. Box 1997
Makati Central Post Office
Makati City, Metro Manila 1200, Philippines

(223) PHILIPPINES NAGA MISSION
P.O. Box 8857
Camarines Sur
4400 Naga City, Philippines

(219) PHLIPPINES OLONGAPO MISSION
National Highway, Mangan-Vaca
2209 Subic, Zambales
Philippines

(192) PHILIPPINES QUEZON CITY MISSION
Ortigas Center PO Box 1505
Emeral Avenue
1600 Pasig, Metro Manila, Philippines

PHILIPPINES TACLOBAN MISSION
P.O. Box 69
6500 Leyte, Tacloban City,
Philippines

PHILIPPINES BUTUAN
LDS Chapel
Montilla Blvd, Butuan City
8600 Agusan del Norte, Philippines

(250) PHILIPPINES SAN PABLO MISSION
P.O. Box 38
San Pablo City, Laguna
4000 Philippines

PHILIPPINES QUEZON CITY NORTH MISSION
Almar Road, Camarin
Novaliches
Quezon, Philippines

PHILIPPINES LAOAG MISSION
#50 Suba Road
Makati Central Post Office
Metro Manila 1200, Philippines

PHILIPPINES ILOILO MISSION
Osmena St.
Arevalo
5000 Iloilo, Philippines

POLAND

Jan. 1, 2011: Est. population, 38,483,000; Members, 1,648; Missions, 1; Districts, 2; Branches, 13; Percent LDS, .004 or one in 24,796; Europe Area.

On the Baltic Sea in east central Europe, Poland has a population that speaks Polish, and is mostly Roman Catholic.

At the close of World War II many Latter-day Saints in branches of the Church in Eastern Germany found themselves within the borders of the newly redefined Poland. Many ethnic Germans were driven out of Poland by the new government but some remained including members of the Selbongen Branch, a group of Latter-day Saints who had pooled their own money and constructed a meetinghouse that was dedicated in 1929 by John A. Widtsoe. Under the new government the town of Selbongen was given the Polish name of Zelwagi.

Elder Ezra Taft Benson, then a member of the Quorum of the Twelve, was the first priesthood leader to visit Zelwagi after the war. Upon his arrival, more than 100 members and friends gathered in a quickly convened meeting to receive his counsel.

On 7 December 1948 government officials forbade public meetings in German and the meetings at Zelwagi were discontinued, but just before Christmas of 1950 permission was granted from the government so long as the meetings were in Polish. The branch continued until 1971 when the last branch president emigrated and deeded the meetinghouse to the government. The meeting-house still stands, but is no longer used for LDS functions.

Polish Latter-day Saints had intermittent Church visitors beginning in the late 1950s. Richard Ranglach, counselor in the North German Mission, was the first to visit in 1957. On 24 September 1962, William S. Erekson, president of the Swiss Mission, and his wife Jenne visited and brought Church manuals and other materials to the Latter-day Saints. Rendell Mabey visited on 3 September 1966 and organized a branch in Debnica Kaszub. He returned on 13-18 September 1967 with Elder Howard W. Hunter of the Quorum of the Twelve Apostles. In 1975 and 1976, David M. Kennedy visited leaders in Poland several times culminating with the Church receiving recognition by the Polish Government on 30 May 1977. This recognition allowed the Church to own property and answer questions about the Church but not to actively proselyte. This prompted a visit to Poland on 22-24 August of that year by President Spencer W. Kimball.

The first missionary couple to serve in Poland, Matthew and Marian Ciembronówicz, arrived in 1977. In 1978, the Church purchased a small apartment and converted it to an information center that was manned by numerous missionary couples throughout the 1980s.

The first young missionaries, Elders Matthew Binns and Stephen Thomas, arrived in January 1988. Urzula Adamska, the first Polish missionary, was called in 1989.

The Poland Warsaw Mission was created 1 July 1990 with Walter Whipple as president. A meetinghouse constructed in Warsaw was dedicated 22 June 1991. Seminary and institute classes were introduced in 1995.

On 19 December 2000, the Church gave to Polish officials the famed Potocki Archive, which contains the history of a powerful Polish family. The records are considered a national treasure. The Church had purchased the collection from a Swiss document dealer in 1985 and housed it at Brigham Young University.

In 2002, membership reached 1,296.

Sources: Swiss Mission, Manuscript history and historical reports, Church Archives; "New Branch Organized in Red Poland," Church News, 1 October 1966; Gilbert Scharffs, "The Branch that Wouldn't Die," Ensign, 1971; Douglas F. Tobler, "Polish Treasure Donated to National Archives," Church News, 13 January 2001; Werner R. H. Ranglach, Geschichte unserer Bruder und Schwestern in Polen, Ungarn, Tschechslowakei, 1960, Church Archives; Justus Ernst, Highlights of the German-speaking mission histories, Church Archives; Kahlile Mehr, Mormon Missionaries Enter Eastern Europe, 2002; Arnold Garr, Donald Q. Cannon, and Richard O. Cowan, eds., Encyclopedia of Latter-day Saint History, 2000; Poland Warsaw Mission, Manuscript history and historical reports, Church Archives.

Mission — 1
(As of Oct. 1, 2011; shown with historical number. See MISSIONS.)

(252) POLAND WARSAW MISSION
ul. Polczynnka 50 m 5
PL-01-337 Warsaw, Poland

PORTUGAL

Jan. 1, 2011: Est. population, 10,708,000; Members, 39,031; Stakes, 6; Wards, 33; Branches, 35; Missions, 2; Districts, 4; percent LDS, .36, or one in 280; Europe Area.

At the southwest corner of Europe, the Republic of Portugal is a parliamentary democracy. Its population is 97 percent Roman Catholic.

The earliest known members of the Church to live in Portugal were Latter-day Saints serving in the U.S. military beginning about 1954. A few Latter-day Saints serving in the military lived there through the 1960s and 1970s.

In April 1974, a bloodless coup resulted in a change in the Portuguese government. Shortly thereafter, David M. Kennedy, ambassador at large for the Church went to Portugal to determine if missionaries could be sent there. Portuguese government officials gave their permission within an hour.

In November 1974, the Portugal Lisbon Mission was formed with W. Grant Bangerter as president. He was joined by four missionaries who had been transferred from other missions in Brazil. They were Elders Werner de Carmargo from the Rio de Janeiro Mission, Dale Earl Thompson, and Paulo Marcello Perisse, from the São Paulo North Mission, and W. Shane Topham, of the São Paulo South Mission. Four more joined them in December and many others soon followed. The first converts in the mission were Maria De Lourdes Dias Prista and Maria José Dias Prita on 4 March 1975.

The Church experienced rapid growth in Portugal. The first thousand converts were made by July 1978. The Lisbon Portugal Stake, the first in the country, was created on 10 July 1981. The Portugal Porto Mission was formed from the Portugal Lisbon Mission in July 1987. The Lisbon mission was further divided in 1989 to create the Lisbon North and Lisbon South missions.

In 1999, there were 35,248 members in Portugal.

Much of the Portugal Lisbon North Mission was combined with the Portugal Lisbon South Mission on 1 July 2002 to create the Portugal Lisbon Mission, the original name of the first mission in Portugal. A smaller portion of the former Lisbon North mission, which was one of five missions in Europe that was consolidated in 2002, was placed in the Portugal Porto Mission.

By 2003, membership reached 37,170, making it the largest congregation of members in a European country. In 2005, membership reached 37,812.

The Portugal Porto Mission was consolidated with the Lisbon mission on 1 July 2011.

Sources: Missionary Training Center, Culture for Missionaries: Portugal, 1984; "Discovering Gospel Riches in Portugal," by Don L. Searle, Ensign, October 1987; Donald Q. Cannon and Richard O. Cowan, Unto Every Nation: Gospel Light Reaches Every Land, 2003; Lisbon Portugal Mission, Manuscript history and historical reports, Church Archives; Record of members, Portugal, Church Archives.

Stakes — 6
(Listed alphabetically as of Oct. 1, 2011.)

No.	Name	Organized	First President
Europe Area			
2610e	Coimbra Portugal	14 Apr 2002	Joaquim Teixeira da Silva
1276	Lisbon Portugal	10 Jun 1981	Jose Manuel da Costa Santos
1729	Lisbon Portugal Oeiras	25 Jun 1989	Vitor Manuel Pereira M.
1613	*Porto Portugal North	5 Nov 2000	
	Porto Portugal	2 Nov 1986	Alcino Pereira Da Silva
1723	*Porto Portugal 5 Nov 2000		
	*Porto Portugal South	10 Nov 1998	
	*Matosinhos Portugal	28 May 1989	Alexandre Rocha Benidio
1652	Setubal Portugal	6 Sep 1987	Octavio Da Silva Melo

Missions — 1
(As of Oct. 1, 2011; shown with historical number. See MISSIONS.)

(115) PORTUGAL LISBON MISSION
Rua Jorge Barradas 14C
1500 Lisbon
Portugal

AZORES AND MADEIRA ISLANDS

The Azores Islands, located 800 miles off the coast of Portugal in the North Atlantic, includes nine main islands that are populated. Both archipelagos are Portuguese territories where Portuguese is spoken.

The earliest known Latter-day Saints living on the island were members of the U.S. military assigned to Lajes Air Field about 1954. By 1958, a servicemen's group was functioning, and on 1 October 1967, the group was disbanded and the Lajes Branch was organized. The following 9 October Maria Morgado was baptized on the island by members of the branch. She is the first known native to be baptized on Portuguese soil.

On 16 July 1978, President Allen K. Coryell of the Portugal Lisbon Mission traveled to the Azores to see if missionaries could begin work there. Two missionaries, Alice R. Kuster and Steven M. Sims were called on 6 September 1979 to go to the island.

The first Portuguese branch was organized in Angra on 5 March 1980. The Terceira Portugal District was created on 16

September 1982 to administer the branches on the islands.

Sources: Record of Members, Portugal, Church Archives; Servicemen's Group (France), Record of members, Church Archives; Ljaes Azores Servicemen's Branch, Manuscript history and historical reports, Church Archives; Lisbon Portugal Mission, Manuscript history and historical reports.

PUERTO RICO

Jan. 1, 2011: Est. population, 3,971,000; Members, 20,785; Stakes, 5; Wards, 27; Branches, 14; Missions, 1; percent LDS, .51, or one in 198; Caribbean Area.

The easternmost island of the Greater Antilles in the east Caribbean Sea, Puerto Rico is a U.S. commonwealth with a population that speaks Spanish. Most of the people are Roman Catholic.

In 1945, returned missionaries from the Argentine Mission, Donald Brown and Bryon C. Wheeler, began working in Puerto Rico and were the first known Church members to live in the country and hold their own Sunday School services.

Gardner H. Russell began holding Church meetings with his family and LDS servicemen at Guajataca in 1951, and later in San Juan. For the first few years, those who attended the meetings were LDS servicemen. Later, other members moved to Puerto Rico, including Morris Burk, Sr. and Heber Haws, whose wives were Puerto Rican. On 7 October 1959, these spouses Cristina Burk and Irma Haws, and Cristina's son Morris, became the first native Puerto Ricans baptized in the country.

Florida Mission President Ned Winder visited Puerto Rico in October 1963 on a routine visit and felt inspired to send missionaries. As a result, in January 1964, Verl Tolbert and Dwight K. Hunter were sent to Puerto Rico. They visited several branches in the Caribbean District, which had been organized earlier for military personnel. Elder Tolbert baptized Becky Fraticelli who, with others, became part of an increasing group of young Puerto Ricans in the Church.

The next Florida Mission president, Glen L. Rudd, sent Spanish-speaking missionaries Steven Johnson and Craig Van Tassell to the island in May 1969. The first Spanish-speaking branch was organized in 1970. On March 8 of that year the first meetinghouse in the Caribbean District of the Florida Mission was dedicated in San Juan by Elder Sterling W. Sill of the First Quorum of the Seventy. On October 17 home seminary was started. The Spanish branch became an independent branch a year later. Members' spirits were lifted 8 March 1981 by a visit from President Spencer W. Kimball, the first president of the Church to visit there.

The Puerto Rico San Juan Mission was created 1 July 1979 with a membership of 1,892. The first stake was created in San Juan on 14 December 1980 by Ezra Taft Benson, then president of the Quorum of the Twelve. New stakes were also created in 1982, 1984 and 1985. President Benson visited again on 12 April 1987. By this time membership had increased to more than 12,000.

However, primarily due to the continual emigration of members to the United States, in December 1993 the four stakes were discontinued and eight districts were formed by Elder L. Tom Perry of the Quorum of the Twelve. Between 1996 and 1998 the four stakes were reinstated. There are currently four districts in operation as well.

Beginning in 1991 Jose O. Moreno spent 10 years coordinating the microfilming of genealogical records from the government and local churches throughout Puerto Rico for the Genealogical Society of Utah. En route to Brazil to dedicate two temples, President Gordon B. Hinckley stopped in Puerto Rico on 13 December 2000, his first visit ever to the "enchanted island." He addressed a member meeting in Roberto Clemente Coliseum in San Juan.

The Puerto Rico San Juan East Mission was created on 1 July 2007 from a division of Puerto Rico San Juan and West Indies missions. On 1 July 2010, the East mission was divided among Dominican Republic Santo Domingo East Mission, Puerto Rico San Juan West Mission and the West Indies Mission. The name of the Puerto Rico San Juan West Mission was changed to the Puerto Rico San Juan Mission.

Sources: Maria Wheeler phone conversation, 12 April 2004; Richard L. Millett, History of the Church in the Caribbean, 1977-1980; Delbert Goates, "Puerto Rico organizes two branches," Church News, 25 June 1955; Florida Mission Manuscript history and historical reports, Church Archives; Morris and Cristina Burk interview, 9 March 2004, Church Archives; Gordon Irving, "Caribbean beginnings," Church News, 22 April 1978; "First Puerto Rican stake organized," Church News, 27 December 1980; Gerry Avant, "History is made: Prophet visits Caribbean islands," Church News, 21 March 1981; Gerry Avant, "President Benson visits Puerto Rico," 18 April 1987; Virgil N. Kovalenko, Development of LDS Church presence in Caribbean nations, 1993, Church Archives; Jose O. Moreno interview, 10 March 2004, Church Archives; Jerry D. Fisher, "Prophet's spirit, counsel, bless Puerto Rico, Church News, 23 December 2000; New missions, Church News, 13 Feb. 2010.

Stakes — 5
(Listed alphabetically as of Oct. 1, 2011.)

No.	Name	Organized	First President
Caribbean Area			
2707	Caguas Puerto Rico	26 Feb 2006	Jose Manuel Santos G.
2217	Mayaguez Puerto Rico	11 Aug 1996	Tomas Olmo
	Reinstated from No. 1580		
2240	Ponce Puerto Rico	22 Sep 1996	Rafael Ortiz
	Reinstated from No. 1349		
2347	San Juan Puerto Rico	4 May 1997	William A. Burk
	Reinstated from No. 1215		
2473	Toa Baja Puerto Rico	7 Jun 1998	Jorge Miguel Alvarado
		Stakes discontinued	
1480	Carolina Puerto Rico	17 Jun 1984	Jesus Nieves
	Discontinued 5 Dec 1993		
1580	Mayaguez Puerto Rico	1 Dec 1985	Heriberto Hernandez Vera
	Discontinued 5 Dec 1993		
1349	Ponce Puerto Rico	13 Jun 1982	Noah Jefferson Burns
	Discontinued 5 Dec 1993		

1215	San Juan Puerto Rico	14 Dec 1980	Herminio De Jesus

Discontinued 5 Dec 1993

Mission — 1
(As of Oct. 1, 2011; shown with historical number. See MISSIONS.)

(157) PUERTO RICO SAN JUAN MISSION
Urb. Jardines de Caparra
500 Calle Marginal Norte
Bayamon, PR 00959, Puerto Rico

REPUBLIC OF KOREA
SOUTH KOREA

Jan. 1, 2011: Est. population, 48,509,000; Members, 84,380; Stakes, 17; Wards, 93; Branches, 46; Missions, 3; Districts, 6; Temples, 1; percent LDS, .17, or one in 597; Asia North Area.

Latter-day Saint servicemen performed the first missionary work during the Korean War, between 1951 and 1953. Among the first Korean members was Ho Jik Kim, converted while earning a doctorate in the United States. He was baptized on 29 September 1951 in the Susquehanna River, near Harmony, Pa. He became an influential leader in the Korean government and paved the way for missionaries to enter Korea. His children, Tai Whan and Young Sook, were among the first four baptized in Korea, on 3 August 1952.

The first missionaries, Richard L. Detton and Don G. Powell, arrived in Korea in April 1956. At that time, membership in Korea was 64. The missionaries focused much of their work among young students.

Originally part of the Northern Far East Mission, the Korean Mission was created on 8 July 1962 with Gail C. Carr, one of the early missionaries to Korea, as president. The new mission had seven branches in Seoul, Pusan and Taegu. The Book of Mormon was printed in Korean in 1967. From 1974 to 1977 a girls choir in an orphanage operated by Latter-day Saint member Whang Keun-Ok was promoted on national media. The first stake in Korea — and the first stake on mainland Asia — was created in Seoul on 8 March 1973. The Church's first visitors' center in Korea was opened on 7 October 1974, in Kwang Ju, the provincial capital in southwestern Korea to introduce the Church to the Korean people.

President Spencer W. Kimball visited Korea on 26 October 1980, and spoke to 6,000 members in two sessions of an area conference. One session was held outdoors with a stiff wind sending the wind chill factor to many degrees below freezing.

The Seoul Korea Temple was dedicated 14 December 1985 by President Gordon B. Hinckley. When the 1988 Summer Olympic Games were held in Korea, the BYU Folk Dancers performed at the opening ceremonies. The ceremony was viewed by an estimated audience of 1 billion worldwide.

Elder In Sang Han, called to the Second Quorum of the Seventy on 1 June 1991, was the first Korean General Authority. In 1992, a record of the testimonies of the early Korean converts was published by Spencer J. and Shirley Palmer. In 1995, the book was published in English.

In May 1996, President Gordon B. Hinckley conducted meetings for members and missionaries in Seoul and Pusan during an extended visit to Asia. He also attended a press conference and luncheon with members of the media in Korea.

Elder Dallin H. Oaks of the Quorum of the Twelve met with South Korean Prime Minister Lee Han-Dong on 28 April 2001 while in Seoul for a regional conference. Elder Oaks presented the prime minister with a copy of the "Proclamation on the Family" and a sculpture of a family.

In 2003, membership reached 75,149.

Members of the Church from across Korea gathered in Olympic Gymnasium No. 1 on 31 July 2005, to join with President Hinckley for a regional conference. He had come as part of the 50th anniversary celebration of the dedication of Korea for the preaching of the gospel. An estimated 10,000 attended.

On 1 July 2010, the Korea Seoul West Mission was combined with the Korea Seoul Mission.

Sources: R. Lanier Britsch, From the East, The History of the Latter-Day Saints in Asia, 1851- 1996, 1998; George W. McCune, A tribute to Brother Tatsui Sato, 1996; John D. Nash, History of the Church in Korea, 1998; Spencer J. Palmer, The Church Encounters Asia, 1970; Dell Van Orden, "Saints Throng to Area Meetings in the Far East," Church News, 1 November 1980; Gerry Avant, "Renewing Ties with Asian Lands, Peoples," Church News, 8 June 1996; Spencer J. Palmer, "Pioneering in South Korea, Ensign, October 1997; "Korean jubilee" Church News, 6 August 2005; "New missions," Church News, 13 Feb. 2010.

Stakes — 17
(Listed alphabetically as of Oct. 1, 2011.)

No.	Name	Organized	First President
Asia North Area			
1865	Anyang Korea	24 May 1992	Young Hwan Lee
1059	*Busan Korea		
	‡Pusan Korea	6 Sep 1979	Chaewhan Chang
1385	*Cheongju Korea	23 Sep 1986	
	‡Seoul Korea Chong Ju	28 Nov 1982	Chung Yul Hwang
1435	*Daegu Korea		
	*Tae Gu Korea	24 Jun 1993	
	*Dae Gu Korea	3 Dec 1990	
	‡Daegu Korea	24 Jun 1983	Chan Tae Kwon
2440	*Daejeon Korea		
	‡Taejeon Korea	8 Mar 1998	Song Yoom-heon
1196	*Gwangju Korea	26 Apr 2002	
	‡Kwang Ju Korea	25 Oct 1980	Bjong Kyu Pak
1306	Inchon Korea	12 Nov 1981	Chea Huo
1596a	Jeonju Korea	27 Apr 1986	Ju In Pak

1382	*Masan Korea	13 Apr 1995	
	‡Pusan Korea West	20 Nov 1982	Gil Whe Do
604	*Seoul Korea		
	‡Seoul	8 Mar 1973	Ho Nam Rhee
1412	Seoul Korea Dongdaemun	24 Apr 1983	Son Wun Ju
1017	Seoul Korea East	18 Apr 1979	Won Yong Ko
1386	Seoul Korea Gangseo	28 Nov 1982	Do Hwan Lee
1060	Seoul Korea North	9 Sep 1979	Moo Kwang Hong
834	*Seoul Korea South		
	‡Seoul Korea West	22 May 1977	Chang Sun Kim
1387	Seoul Korea Yeong Dong	28 Nov 1982	Jae Am Park
1866	Suwon Korea	24 May 1992	Yong Hwan Lee

Missions — 3
(As of Oct. 1, 2011; shown with historical number. See MISSIONS.)

(124) KOREA BUSAN MISSION
Dongnae P.O. Box 73
Busan 607-600,
Korea

(71) KOREA SEOUL MISSION
Kwang Hwa Mun
PO Box 210
Seoul 110-602, Korea

(191) KOREA DAEJON MISSION
Daejon PO Box 38
Daejon 300-600, Korea

ROMANIA

Jan. 1, 2011: Est. population, 22,215,000; Members, 2,905; Missions, 1; Districts, 2; Branches, 17; Percent LDS, .012, or one in 8,120; Europe Area.

Romania is a republic in southeast Europe located on the Black Sea. Its people are Romanian with a Hungarian minority. Most are Romanian Orthodox with a small percentage of Protestant and Roman Catholics.

The first Latter-day Saint to set foot on Romanian soil was Elder Orson Hyde, a member of the Quorum of the Twelve. In 1841, while traveling to Palestine, Hyde took a steamer on the Danube River from Vienna, Austria, to Galati, now Galai, Romania, on his way to the Black Sea. Hyde later wrote, "I am a witness that the gospel has been proclaimed all along the Danube."

Years later Mischa Markow, shortly after his 1 February 1887 baptism in Constantinople, Turkey, went to Romania, where he stayed until January 1888. Markow did not record what he did in Romania during these months. However, the following year he returned and preached the gospel in four cities that are now part of Romania. In July 1899, he worked in Constanta, where he baptized one person. The following month, he preached in Bucharest, where he labored for six months and baptized several people. While in Bucharest Markow was arrested, jailed and eventually banished from the city for preaching the gospel.

In September 1900, Markow began preaching in Temesvár, Hungary, now Timisoara, Romania, where he had his greatest missionary success. There he met a group of Catholics who were seeking spiritual guidance. Markow and his companion, Hyrum M. Lau, baptized nine people from this group on 24 January 1901. On 30 March that same year, the missionaries baptized 12 converts, increasing the Latter-day Saint group to 31 members. The next day, the missionaries left the city on orders of the local supreme court. On his second mission in 1903, Markow worked in Brassó, Hungary, present day Brasov, Romania.

In January 1904, due in part to Markow's success, Hugh J. Cannon, president of the German Mission, created the Austro-Hungarian Conference, that included the branches in Temesvár, Brassó and Vienna, Austria.

Missionary work continued in these cities that would later become part of Romania for the next decade in spite of police harassment and persecution. However, on 5 March 1913, under the direction of European Mission president Rudger Clawson, the conference was closed and missionary work was discontinued in this area. Missionaries in Vienna periodically visited the few Church members in Temesvár and Brassó until World War I.

Between World War I and World War II missionaries visited the few Latter-day Saints who remained in Romania or who moved there after being baptized elsewhere. In 1926, missionaries Thalman Hasler and Obert C. Tanner visited Church members in Brassó and gave them the sacrament, something they had not had for 12 years. President Arthur Gaeth of the Czechoslovak Mission also visited the scattered Latter-day Saints living in Romania in the late 1920s and 1930s. World War II, however, ended contact with these Church members. Missionary work would not resume full force in Romania until 1990.

In 1968, Church member Bud Halderman traveled to Romania as a security guard for a prominent California businessman. While there, Halderman met a young translator, Consuela Icleanu, to whom he gave an English copy of the Book of Mormon. The book sat on Icleanu's bookshelf for more than 20 years until the missionaries arrived at her home. Consuela, her husband George, and their two children were baptized on 29 November 1992. Shortly thereafter, Consuela became part of the team that translated the Book of Mormon into Romanian.

Elder Russell M. Nelson of the Quorum of the Twelve and Elder Hans B. Ringger of the Seventy made their first visit to Bucharest in October 1987. They held preliminary talks with government officials exploring possibilities to place humanitarian missionaries in Romania. Over two years later, in February 1990, Elders Nelson and Ringger, together with Peter Berkhahn, Europe Area director for Temporal Affairs, met again with Romanian officials to make plans for humanitarian relief. While in Bucharest, on 9 February, this small group visited Cismigiu Park, where Elder Nelson felt to bless the country.

The first team of humanitarian missionaries arrived in Romania on 2 September 1990: Beverly Cutler, Virginia Bruse, Harold and Enid Davis, Alvin and Barbara Price, and Reed and Dorothy Fife. The missionaries worked in orphanages and institutions for the disabled. Perhaps the most successful humanitarian effort accomplished by the missionaries was the institution of Special Olympics for disabled children in June 1991, the first ever held in Romania. Handicapped children were often shunned and neglected in communist Romania. The missionaries' efforts to begin the Special Olympics publicized the plight of these children and began to change attitudes towards the disabled.

Romania became part of the Austria Vienna East Mission in 1990, where it remained until the mission was discontinued in 1992. Missionaries serving in Romania then reported to the Hungary Budapest Mission. The Romania Bucharest Mission was created on 1 July 1993 with John R. Morrey as president.

In December 1990 the first young missionaries arrived in Romania: Christopher Jessop, Ryan Osborne, Raymond Van Wagoner, all transferred from the Italy Padova Mission, and Dan Peterson, whose call was changed from Yugoslavia to Romania. The first young sister missionary to serve in Romania was Lanette Payne who arrived in October 1991.

In 1990, Steve and Cheryl Worsley traveled to Romania to adopt children. While in Bucharest they hired a translator and driver, Octavian Vasilescu. On 18 November 1990, the Worsleys and Vasilescu attended worship services. Vasilescu accepted a Book of Mormon from the humanitarian missionary couples and was also impressed by the talk given by Austria Vienna East Mission President Dennis B. Neuenschwander. The Worsleys also invited another of their newly-made friends, Doina Biolaru, to attend Church services. As a result of their experiences, Octavian Vasilescu and Doina Biolaru were baptized on 24 March 1991.

Another significant humanitarian project occurred in August 1991. During the revolution that toppled the communist regime, the Central University Library in Bucharest was burned and many books were lost. Retired Brigham Young University professor George S. Barrus and Elder Russell M. Nelson of the Quorum of the Twelve encouraged BYU students to sponsor a book drive for the library. They collected over 20,000 volumes. These books represented the single largest book donation from the United States.

The first branch in Romania was organized on 28 July 1991 in Bucharest with Octavian Vasilescu as president. With the slow but steady growth of the Church, the branch was divided on 1 September 1992. Work began in a second city, Ploiesti, and shortly thereafter a branch was organized on 15 February 1993. In early 1995 two districts were organized in Bucharest with Octavian Vasilescu and George Icleanu as presidents. Three years later, in February 1998, in order to strengthen the Church members, the two districts were reorganized into the Romania Bucharest District.

In 2002, there were 2,146 members. In 2004, there were two districts in Romania, one in Bucharest and the other in Ploiesti.

Missionary work accelerated and Church members were strengthened when the first complete Romanian translation of the Book of Mormon was released in December 1998 and when the first two meetinghouses were built and dedicated: the Bucharest meetinghouse was completed in December 1999 and the Ploiesti meetinghouse in February 2000. Both were dedicated by Area Authority Seventy Johann A. Wondra in May 2000.

All the cities where Mischa Markow first preached the gospel were once again open for missionary work. On 14 May 1995 a Church meeting was held in Timisoara. Missionary work began there the following February. On 5 June 1995 missionary work began in Brasov. In March 1998 missionaries began to preach in Constanta, where Markow baptized his first Romanian convert. And finally, a branch was organized in Galati in December 2000. This was 159 years after Orson Hyde disembarked in Romania on his way to Palestine.

In 2003, membership reached 2,196. In 2005, membership reached 2,483.

Sources: Myrtle Stevens Hyde, Orson Hyde: The Olive Branch of Israel, 2000; Mischa Markow's missionary journal, edited by Matthew K. Heiss and published in Mormon Missionaries Enter Eastern Europe, Kahlile Mehr, 2002; Helene Bernhardt, History of the saints in Roumania [sic], 1933; Church Archives; Doina Biolaru, Conversion story, 1992, Church Archives; Carmin Clifton, Come Lord, Come, 2002; Consuela Icleanu Interview, 1999, Church Archives; Octavian Vasilescu Interview, 1993, Church Archives; Romania Bucharest Mission Annual historical reports, Church Archives.

Mission — 1
(As of Oct. 1, 2011; shown with historical number. See MISSIONS.)

(292) ROMANIA BUCHAREST MISSION
Sos. Pipera Nr. 41 Et. 7
Sector 2
COD 014254
Bucharest, Romania

RUSSIA

Jan. 1, 2011: Est. population, 140,041,000; Members, 21,023; Missions, 8; Districts, 13; Branches, 116; Percent LDS, .014, or one in 7,021; Europe East Area.

From early in Church history, Russia was considered a prospective mission field. In 1843, Joseph Smith instructed George J. Adams and Orson Hyde to prepare for a mission to Russia. "To that vast empire," the Prophet said, "is attached some of the most important things concerning the advancement and building up of the kingdom of God in the last days." Their missions, however, were never fulfilled because of the martyrdom of Joseph Smith and the departure of the Latter-day Saints from Nauvoo, Ill.

In 1887, Joseph M. Tanner, while serving in the Turkish Mission, reported baptizing Russians living in Jaffa, Palestine. The Russians immigrated to Utah shortly after their conversions.

The first baptisms in Russia occurred in June 1895. August J. Hoglund, a native of Sweden, went to St. Petersburg, where he baptized Johan and Alma Lindelof, who had written to the Scandinavian Mission asking for missionaries. Johan Lindelof's mother had been baptized years earlier in Finland. In 1918, after the Bolshevik Revolution, the Lindelof family was arrested and sentenced to imprisonment and hard labor. Only two of the seven Lindelof children are known to have survived. Two daughters died in exile. The fate of the other three children is unknown.

On 6 August 1903, Elder Francis M. Lyman, president of the European Mission and a member of the Quorum of the Twelve, traveled to St. Petersburg and visited members there. Elder Lyman had hoped to use the Lindelof family as a nucleus around which to build the Church. However, political events surrounding the Bolshevik Revolution prevented the establishment of the Church on Russian soil. Nearly 90 years passed before missionary work could begin in Russia.

On 18 March 1918, Andre K. Anastasion, a native Russian, was baptized in London. He translated a number of Church works into Russian, including the Book of Mormon. The manuscript sat unpublished for many years. Finally, after review and revision, the Russian Book of Mormon was completed and published on 3 June 1981.

Elder Ezra Taft Benson, while serving in the Quorum of the Twelve Apostles and as U.S. Secretary of Agriculture, traveled to the USSR in October 1959. While in Moscow, he visited the Central Baptist Church and delivered a message of peace and hope to a full congregation.

During a visit to the Soviet Union in August 1970, Andre Anastasion, met with a member of the Department of Foreign Affairs, T. B. Makartzev, who told him that if there were 20 members of the Church in Moscow, the Church could secure a place to worship. However, at that time, there were no Latter-day Saints in Russia.

In Washington, D.C., Beverly Campbell, who was working for the Church's office for public communications, began to contact Soviet officials about the possibility of Church authorities visiting the Soviet Union. As a result of her work, Elders Russell M. Nelson and Hans B. Ringger went to Moscow in June 1987. They met with the chairman of the Council of Religious Affairs and with leaders of other denominations.

Campbell extended an invitation to the Soviet Ambassador to the United States, Yuri Dubinin, and his wife, Liana, to visit Utah, which they did on 27-29 April 1990. While at BYU, Ambassador Dubinin was asked if the Church would be allowed in the Soviet Union. Without hesitation, Dubinin answered that it would. This would set the stage for the missionary work that was soon to follow.

During the latter part of 1988, missionaries in the Finland Helsinki Mission began to contact Soviet citizens traveling in Finland. Leena Rihimäkki and her companion, Carina Mahoney, received permission to contact Russians arriving in Helsinki from Leningrad and Moscow. This Russian contacting program proved to be a training ground for the missionaries who would later enter the Soviet Union.

To accommodate Latter-day Saints working in Moscow, a group was organized in February 1989 with Bruce Wheeler as group leader. Olga Smolyanova, a Muscovite, had joined the Church in Italy and later returned to Moscow. Other Russian investigators, who had contact with American Church members living in Moscow, began attending group meetings. On 10 June 1990, Galina Goncharova, who had been contacted by Latter-day Saints in Moscow, was baptized.

In 1989, the Terebenin family, Yuri, Liudmila, and their daughter, Anna, heard about the Church and were baptized during a trip to Budapest, Hungary. They returned to their home in Leningrad and told their friends about their new-found faith. It was in the Terebenins' apartment on 11 February 1990 that the first branch in Russia was organized by Finland Helsinki Mission President Steven R. Mecham.

To nurture the first Russian converts, the Baltic District was organized in January 1990. Five Finnish couples were called to serve as missionaries to visit Church members in Leningrad, Vyborg and Tallinn, Estonia, which was still part of the Soviet Union at the time. Jussi Kemppainen served as Baltic District president. These missionary couples were Jussi and Raija Kemppainen, Aimo and Nellie Jäkkö, Vesa-Pekka and Minna Kirsi, Arto and Katri Lammintaus, and Antti and Leena Riihimäkki Laitinen.

Two missionaries from the Finland Helsinki Mission, David S. Reagan and Kevin A. Dexter, arrived in Leningrad on 26 January 1990. They taught investigators and baptized Anton Skripko on 3 February 1990, the first member baptized in Russia in many years. He later became the first native Russian to fill a full-time mission.

Around this same time, Aimo and Nellie Jäkkö of Lappeenranta, Finland, met Andrei Semionov, a Russian physician from Vyborg, Russia, while on a canoeing trip. The Jäkkös befriended Semionov and introduced him to the Church. Andrei was baptized on 24 February 1990. The Vyborg Branch was organized on 25 March 1990. Semionov was called as the first branch president.

The Finland Helsinki East Mission, which was given specific responsibility for missionary work in the USSR, was officially established on 1 July 1990 with Gary L. Browning as the first mission president. On 3 February 1992, this mission became the Russia Moscow Mission. At that same time, the Russia St. Petersburg Mission was organized. Charles H. Creel, who was serving as a missionary in Kiev, Ukraine, part of the Austria Vienna East Mission, was called to serve as the first mission president.

The first official recognition of the Church in Russia was granted to the branch in Leningrad on 13 September 1990. The Russian Soviet Socialists Republic granted the Church republic-wide recognition on 28 May 1991. The announcement was made by Alexander Rutskoi, then serving as vice president of the republic, at a banquet following the performance of the Mormon Tabernacle Choir at the Bolshoi Theater on 24 June.

After the official recognition was granted, the number of missions in Russia increased dramatically: Russia Samara Mission (July 1993), Russia Novosibirsk and Russia Rostov missions (July 1994), Russia Yekaterinburg Mission (July 1995), Russia Moscow South Mission (1997), and Russia Vladivostok Mission (1999).

In June 1996, the Church received unwelcome publicity when Russian national security advisor Alexander Lebed singled out the LDS Church and called for the outlawing of foreign churches. U.S. President Bill Clinton raised concerns about Lebed's statement with Russian Prime Minister Viktor Chermomyrdin and was assured by the Prime Minister that Russia would maintain religious tolerance. Lebed later apologized for his remarks.

In March 1998, two missionaries serving in the Russia Samara Mission were kidnapped and held for ransom. Four days later, Elders Travis Tuttle and Andrew Probst were released. And in October of that same year, Elder Jose Mackintosh was attacked by a drunk and killed while serving in the city of Ufa, part of the Russia Yekaterinburg Mission. His companion, Bradley Borden, was wounded in the attack but recovered.

On 14 May 1998, a certificate of registration was issued to the Church, allowing the Church to continue to provide humanitarian and missionary work, and have places for its members to meet. The new approval was needed following passage of a law requiring re-registration of religious organizations that were considered foreign to Russia.

On 1 December 2000, offices of the Europe East Area, including the Area presidency, were moved from its location in Frankfurt, Germany, to new facilities in Moscow, making this the first time that general authorities of the Church maintained a permanent residence within the former Soviet Union.

Viacheslav I. Efimov was the first Russian native to be called as a mission president. He served in the Russia Yekaterinburg Mission from 1995 to 1998.

At the last moment, the Russian government granted the Church a license to set up satellite receivers so that Saints in Russia could participate in the dedication of the Nauvoo Temple on 27 June 2002. According to Europe East Area President Douglas L. Callister, "Only the hand of the Lord – intervening in the last crucial moment – could have made the transmission possible to nearly 6,000 members who had gathered in meetinghouses across Eastern Europe."

President Gordon B. Hinckley visited Russia in September 2002, the first Church president to visit the country. He spoke to a gathering of 2,300 members, encouraging them to adhere to the basic principles of the gospel and promising them that if they did so, the Lord would take care of their temporal needs.

In July 2003, about 250 athletes from Utah, most of them members of the Church, participated in the first Moscow-Utah Youth Games held for 17 days. LDS members of the delegation held a special sacrament meeting July 20. The idea for the games developed from a conversation between Utah's Governor Mike Leavitt and Moscow Mayor Yuri Luzhkov during the 2002 Winter Olympics in Salt Lake City.

In 2003, membership reached 17,284.

President Hinckley met with some 200 members in Vladivostok, Russia, 31 July 2005, as part of a seven-nation Asian tour. They met in a large room in the airport during a 45-minute refueling stop. President Hinckley is the first president of the Church to visit Vladivostok, a port city on Russia's east coast that was closed to foreign visitors during the Cold War until 1992.

In 2005, membership reached 18,785.

On June 5, 2011, Elder Russell M. Nelson of the Quorum of the Twelve and Elder Gregory A. Schwitzer of the Seventy and president of the Europe East Area organized the first stake in Russia — nearly 170 years after the Prophet Joseph Smith attempted to send the first missionaries to that country. More than 1,100 members gathered in Moscow's Amber Plaza Auditorium to participate in the creation of the Moscow Russia Stake. Yakov Mikhaylovich Boyko was called as president of the stake that included six wards and three branches. At the time of the creation of the stake there were approximately 21,000 members worshiping in 116 congregations.

Sources: History of the Church of Jesus Christ of Latter-day Saints, 1902-1932, 5:417; Gary Browning, Russia and the Restored Gospel, 1997; Turkish Mission Manuscript History, Church Archives; Kahlile Mehr, "The 1903 Dedication of Russia for Missionary Work," Journal of Mormon History, 1986; "A Church Service in Soviet Russia," US News and World Report, 26 October 1959; Bruce A. Wheeler interview, 16 October 1992, Church Archives; Galina I. Goncharova interview, 13 May 1995, Church Archives; "Reliving 'LDS Question' envoy recalls day Iron Curtain was lifted for Mormons," Salt Lake Tribune, 15 October 1995; "Quick action is sought on missionaries," Deseret News 21 March 1998; "Lebed vows to cleanse Russia of religious 'filth,'" Deseret News, 27 June 1996; "Tough words from Russia countered," 28 June 1996; "Clinton taking offense at remarks against LDS," Deseret News, 30 June 1996; "Lebed sorry for picking on Mormons — sort of," Deseret News, 2 July 1996; "LDS missionary slain in Russia," Deseret News 18 October 1998; "Kidnapped missionaries safe; two arrested.," Church News, 28 March 1998; "Members in Europe East Area view Nauvoo Temple dedication," Church News, 13 July 2002; "Choir leaves trail of joyful tears," Church News, 6 July 1991; "Growth of Church in 'that vast empire,'" Church News, 6 November 1993; "Church formally recognized in Russia," Church News, 23 May 1998; "While Church will feel, mourn loss of missionary," Church News, 24 October 1998; "Soviet envoy's Utah visit is 'historic,'" 5 May 1990; Church News, "History making trip - Church leader in Russia," Church News, 14 September 2002; "Athletes hold services in Moscow," Church News, 26 July 2003; Kahlile Mehr, Mormon Missionaries Enter Eastern Europe, 2002; "1989-90, The Curtain Opens," Ensign, December 1993; Church News, Moscow Russia Stake organized June 5, Jason Swensen, June 11, 2011.

Stakes — 1
(Listed alphabetically as of Oct. 1, 2011.)

No.	Name	Organized	First President
Euorpe East Area			
2926	Moscow Russia	5 June 2011	Yakov Mikhaylovich Boyko

Missions — 8
(As of Oct. 1, 2011; shown with historical number. See MISSIONS.)

(272) RUSSIA MOSCOW MISSION
Galvpochtampt a/ai 257
101000
Moscow, Russia

RUSSIA MOSCOW WEST MISSION
International PO Box 148
131000 Moscow
Russia

(301) RUSSIA NOVOSIBIRSK MISSION
46 Kirova Street
Pochtampt a/ai 146
630102 Novosibirsk oblast'
Russia

(302) RUSSIA ROSTOV NA DONU MISSION
Vtoraya Voladarskaya 64
Rostov-na-Donu
Rostovskaya oblast'
344008 Russia

(293) RUSSIA SAMARA MISSION
Glavpochtampt a/ai 3007
443099 Samara, Russia

(273) RUSSIA ST. PETERSBURG MISSION
Pr Malookhtinshy 16/1 POM 11-H, 12-H
195112 St. Petersburg, Russia

(333) RUSSIA VLADIVOSTOK MISSION
Mordovtseva 3-304
Vladivostok, Primorskly Kray 690000
Russia

(305) RUSSIA YEKATERINBURG MISSION
Glavpochtampt A/YA 250
620151 Yekaterinburg
Russia

ST. KITTS AND NEVIS
(ST. CHRISTOPHER-NEVIS)

Jan. 1, 2011: Est. population, 40,000; Members, 197; Branches, 1; Percent LDS, .41, or one in 247; Caribbean Area; West Indies Mission.

Located in the Eastern Caribbean in the Leeward Islands, St. Kitts and Nevis has a population that speaks English and is mostly Protestant.

In 1983, Pres. Kenneth Zabriskie of the West Indies Mission and his wife, LeOra, were introduced to the deputy prime minister of St. Kitts through a mutual acquaintance, Kutaba Alghanin, who sailed about the Caribbean in his yacht and employed two returned missionaries as tutors to his children.

In July 1984, Elders Douglas Myers and Robert J. Molina arrived on St. Kitts and were soon followed by Reuel and Alice Lambourn on Oct. 20, 1984. They adapted a home into a meetinghouse and the St. Kitts-Nevis Branch was organized on Sept. 10, 1985, with Elder Lambourn as the first president. On Feb. 2, 1985, Dianna Ermintude Johnson was baptized, the first convert on the island. A weekly open house was held on Thursdays where the newly baptized members and investigators could study together.

A local member, Carol Pamela Heather Thomas, became the first missionary from the islands when she was called June 14, 1991, to serve in the New Jersey Morristown Mission. Three other missionaries served from St. Kitts and Nevis in the next two years. In 1994, the branch had about 70 members taking part in all the programs, including seminary. Two choirs regularly participate in the meetings. In February 1995, a small group of Church members went to the government and asked permission to clean up a park in the center of town. This act helped change many people's attitudes about the Church. Terry Lewellyn Hanley became the first native branch president to serve on St. Kitts in early 1996.

Sources: Kenneth and LeOra Zabriskie journals; correspondence from West Indies Mission, 1994; "Caribbean members plan to celebrate achievements of pioneers — those on island and of 1847 trek," Church News, June 22, 1996; Deseret News, Sept. 21, 1998.

ST. LUCIA

Jan. 1, 2011: Est. population, 160,000; Members, 217; Branches, 2; Percent LDS, .1, or one in 964; Caribbean Area.

Anna Clarita Philgence joined the Church in England in July 1982 and soon returned to her homeland, St. Lucia. In August 1983, after learning about Sister Philgence, West Indies Mission President Kenneth Zabriskie visited St. Lucia and met with Sister Philgence and Al and Julie Nuttal, who had transferred from medical school in Grenada to St. Lucia. Zabriskie was accompanied by Elder Ronald E. Poelman of the Seventy. In November 1983 President Zabriskie sent Elders Todd Hardy, Paul Jackson, Jay Schroeder and Marty Harris to begin missionary work. The first baptism in St. Lucia was Caren Cotter on 2 September 1984.

The Castries Branch was organized 21 January 1984 with Michael Choo-Tung as the first president. He had joined the Church in Nova Scotia, Canada. By June 1984, about 40 investigators and members were attending meetings. In the summer of 1984, the first senior missionaries, Vail and Betsy Hatt, arrived. In September 1987, Clarita Philgence and Joseph and Dilcie Clarke from St. Lucia visited Utah to receive their ordinances in the Salt Lake Temple.

During the next few years missionaries began having trouble renewing their visas after anti-Mormon information was spread in the press. In 1986, missionaries Lewis and Jean Call were asked to leave the country by immigration officials in preparation for a visit of Pope John Paul II. Missionaries were not allowed to return following the papal visit.

Local member Joseph Clarke served as branch president until he died in 1993 and then Derrick St. Rose served as group leader when the Castries Branch was discontinued in 1994. Kelvin J. Felix who had joined the Church in England moved to St. Lucia and became branch president on 18 April 2003 when the branch was reorganized.

The Church has petitioned the government for legal recognition since May 2004 so that missionaries could return to the island.

Sources: Kenneth L. Zabriskie, History of the West Indies Mission, [ca. 1989], Church Archives; Kenneth L. Zabriskie interview, 2003, Church Archives; Julie Nuttal phone conversation, 14 May 2004; Elden Wood, Autobiography, 1994, Church Archive; Roy R. Valentine, Journal, 1997, Church Archives; Jean Call phone conversation, 18 May 2004.

ST. VINCENT AND THE GRENADINES

Jan. 1, 2011: Est. population, 104,500; Members, 493; Branches, 2; Percent LDS, .4, or one in 245; Caribbean Area; West Indies Mission.

In the eastern Caribbean and part of the Windward Island chain, the Grenadines are a parliamentary democracy. Most of the population speaks English. Religious adherents are primarily Methodist, Anglican, and Roman Catholic.

Elder Joseph B. Wirthlin, then of the Seventy, visited St. Vincent in January 1980 along with President Richard L. Millett of the Puerto Rico San Juan Mission. Steven B. Wooley and Thomas B. Williams were sent from the mission to begin work in the country in March 1980. Millett visited St. Vincent again the following month. Among those attending the meetings was Ebenezer Joshua, the first chief minister of the country who helped St. Vincent obtain independence from England. Brother Joshua was one of the earliest converts and served in the branch presidency.

The Kingstown Branch was organized 22 October 1980 with Edmund Israel as president. He had also been taught by Elders Wooley and Williams. Missionaries cleared the land for a meetinghouse and a site dedication was held 16 June 1985; a building was subsequently constructed. Sharon Nichols was the first local member called on a full-time mission in 1983.

When Ebeneezer Joshua died in 1991, a crowd of 30,000 to 40,000 people, including top government officials, viewed or attended his televised funeral in the Kingstown meetinghouse. Jay Hughes spoke about Joshua's beliefs and the plan of salvation. In August 1991 Edmund and Evelyn Israel left for the Milwaukee Wisconsin Mission and became the first senior missionaries from St. Vincent. Since 29 January 1995 Verrol W. Young has served as branch president, and St. Vincent has continued to be part of the West Indies Mission.

Sources: Richard L. Millett, History of the Church in the Caribbean, 1977-1980, Church Archives; Kenneth L. Zabriskie, History of the West Indies Mission, [ca. 1989], Church Archives; Puerto Rico San Juan Mission, Mission history and historical reports, Church Archives.

SAMOA

Jan. 1, 2011: Est. population, 220,000; Members, 71,272; Stakes, 16; Wards, 118; Branches, 16; Missions, 1; Temples, 1; Percent LDS, 31, or one in 3; Pacific Area.

Located in the South Pacific, Western Samoa is a parliamentary democracy. The people are Protestant, 45 percent; LDS, 28 percent; and Roman Catholic, 20 percent.

On 24 January 1863, two missionaries from Hawaii arrived in Samoa. Kimo Pelia and Samuela Manoa had been sent by an apostate leader, Walter Murray Gibson. The pair labored faithfully for nearly 20 years without the support of the Church. The number of baptisms performed by them was never recorded (but ranged between 50 and 200). Upon learning of Manoa's presence in Samoa, Joseph H. Dean was set apart by Hawaiian Mission president William King to begin missionary work in Samoa. Dean arrived in Aunu'u (now part of American Samoa) with his wife, Florence, on 21 June 1888. The Deans found that Pelia had died but Manoa was still very supportive and was rebaptized and reordained by Dean on 25 June. The same day, Dean baptized a woman named Malaea, who is considered his first Samoan convert. Dean remained in Aunu'u and within four months 40 others had joined the Church. Missionary work did not expand beyond Aunu'u until more missionaries arrived. A native named Polonga, was called as the first local missionary. Mission headquarters were eventually established on the island of Upolu, were the majority of Samoans lived. In August 1889, Dean purchased property in Fagalii, near the main village of Apia. It became the center of operations for a little more than 10 years. When the Deans left for home on 16 August 1890, there were 13 missionaries and around 80 members of the Church.

The use of lantern slide shows about the Church and a record player were used to attract attention and open the way to teach the gospel in villages that had been closed to missionaries before. Missionaries also helped educate youths in small chapel schools. By 1899, membership in Samoa had grown to 1,139. As Samoans were ordained elders, they were often called to leave their own villages and preside in distant branches, a pattern unique to Samoa that continued into the 1950s. Many local members also served missions and contributed toward the growth of the Church.

At the turn of the century, missionary work was made difficult by internal political conflicts. In 1899, the Samoan islands were divided between Germany and the United States. Western Samoa, consisting primarily of the islands of Upolu and Savai'i, became a German colony. Shortly thereafter, the Germans banned English-language schools, an act that temporarily slowed missionary work. German control ended in 1914. Eastern Samoa became and remains a U.S. territory, of which Tutuila is the primary island. In the early 1900s, President Joseph F. Smith authorized the establishment of Sauniatu, in the mountains near the capital city of Apia, as a refuge for converts expelled from their villages for joining the Church. Today, it encompasses a small LDS primary school and the Sauniatu Agriculture Center, a program designed to promote family self-reliance based on gospel principles and training in agriculture and entrepreneurship. In 1902 mission headquarters were moved from Fagalii to Pesega, on the outskirts of Apia.

By June 1903, the Book of Mormon had been translated into Samoan. By 1920, membership numbered 3,500, about 5 percent of the total population. A visit by Elder David O. McKay, then of the Quorum of the Twelve, in May 1921 had great impact upon the membership. He made a special visit to the Saints at Sauniatu where he offered an apostolic blessing upon the village prior to his departure. Conversions increased afterward and some entire villages joined the Church. Schools were the most important missionary tools of the Church. Foreign missionaries staffed some grades of the central schools, but young graduates of the schools did most of the teaching. Before World War II, almost none of the Samoan teachers had a high-school education. The main Church sponsored schools on Upolu were at Sauniatu and Pesega, and at Vaiola on Savai'i.

The year 1938 marked the 50 anniversary of missionary work in Samoa. Elaborate plans were made to celebrate the jubilee. George Albert Smith of the Council of the Twelve and Rufus K. Hardy of the First Council of Seventy arranged a tour of the South Pacific missions so that they could be in Samoa during the celebration. With war looming in 1939, missionaries from the United States were sent home, the last leaving in November 1940. Only the mission president and his wife, Wilford W. and Hannahbel Emery, remained. Thousands of marines were stationed on Tutuila and Upolu during World War II. As a result of the war, the Samoan priesthood bearers proved not only capable of leading the Church, but enlarging it as well. They were also able to continue the schools, but the Church-owned buildings had fallen into disrepair because of the unavailability of supplies. Missionaries returned to Samoa in 1946.

When President McKay visited Samoa in 1955, Church membership numbered 6,853, despite a growing trend of Samoan Church members to emigrate to Hawaii and New Zealand. His visit to Sauniatu was a spiritual highlight. He told the members they soon would be able to "enter a house of the Lord in some location not far away, and this would be one of the greatest blessings they could obtain." When the New Zealand Temple was dedicated in 1958, 50 Samoan Church members participated in the services.

Membership grew from 7,808 in 1951 to 16,649 by 1961. The growth that came during these years was founded on significant advancements in Church organization and administration, education, and meetinghouse construction. By the mid-1960s more than 50 new concrete-brick chapels had been constructed in Samoa, mostly by labor missionaries. Because transportation facilities were generally poor, it was necessary to construct chapels close enough to the people so that most ward or branch members could walk to meetings. A stake was organized in Apia on 18 March 1962 with Percy J. Rivers as president. By 1974, the country had six stakes and became the first country of the world to be entirely covered by stakes.

In February 1976, 11 General Authorities, including Presidents Spencer W. Kimball and N. Eldon Tanner, visited both

American and Western Samoa, holding as area conference in Pago Pago and Apia. On 15 October 1977, a temple was announced to be built in American Samoa, but it was later determined that it would be better suited if it were built in Apia, Western Samoa. The temple was dedicated on 5 August 1983. At that time, membership had reached an estimated 20,000, about 20 percent of the population of the islands.

Six new stakes were created in Western Samoa between 1994 and 1996. In 1997, the country changed its official name from Western Samoa to Samoa. President Gordon B. Hinckley visited Savai'i on 12 October 1997, where he spoke to 4,000 members and met with Samoa's Prime Minister Tofilau Eti Alesana. He addressed another 10,000 that afternoon in Apia Park on Upolu.

In October 2000, the Prime Minister of Samoa visited the Humanitarian Center in Salt Lake City, Utah, and learned of the contributions of clothing and education and medical supplies the Church has quietly made to help the Samoan people.

In 2000, there was a resurgence among the local community chiefs (matai) in exerting control over land use and title to land, in addition to making the final decision as to which religions would be allowed in the village, even though the Samoan Constitution provides for freedom of religion. The Church was excluded from three villages, including one where the Church had constructed a meetinghouse. A decision in July 2000 by a Samoan Supreme Court Justice ruled that the freedom of religion provisions in the Samoan Constitution does not allow the villages to exclude or limit religious worship. The Church established a Community Leader and Government Relations committee in Samoa to improve relationships and understanding between the Church and the village Matai.

While the Apia Samoa Temple was closed for renovation, a fire engulfed it on the night of 9 July 2003, making this the first time that an operating temple had burned. The First Presidency announced a week later that the temple would be rebuilt using a new temple design.

In 2002, membership reached 61,094; and 62,413 in 2003.

In 2005, membership reached 63,640.

Nearly 1,000 people came from overseas and all parts of Samoa in November 2004 to participate in the 100th anniversary of the establishment of the village called Sauniatu, originally created on 8 November 1904. The celebration honored the early Samoan members who fled here seeking refuge from religious persecution. It is sometimes referred to the "Nauvoo of the South Pacific."

Membership in 2003 was 62,413.

President Hinckley returned to Apia 4 September 2005 to dedicate a new temple rebuilt after the previous temple was destroyed by fire 9 July 2003, during renovation project.

Sources: Andrew Jenson, "Samoa," Encyclopedic History of the Church of Jesus Christ of Latter-day Saints, 1941; R. Lanier Britsch, Unto the Islands of the Sea, 1986; R. Carl Harris, Samoa Apia Mission History, 1888-1983, 1983; Jennie and John Hart, R. Carl Harris, The Expanded Samoan Mission History, 1888-1900, Vol. 1, 1988; Gerry Avant, "Prophet Goes to Islands of Pacific," Church News, 25 October 1997; "One-time Refuge Now is Center of Self-reliance," Church News, 19 February 2000; Samoan Mission, Manuscript history and historical reports, Church Archives; "South Pacific's Nauvoo," Church News, 15 January 2005; "Precious gift returns to Samoa," Church News, 10 September 2005.

Stakes — 16
(Listed alphabetically as of Oct. 1, 2011.)

No.	Name	Organized	First President
Pacific Area			
353	*Apia Samoa		
	‡Apia	18 Mar 1962	Percy John Rivers
2134	Apia Samoa Navu	3 Dec 1995	Tigi Manumaluena
513	*Apia Samoa West		
	‡Apia West	26 Apr 1970	Percy J. Rivers
2138	Fagamalo Samoa	4 Dec 1995	Pama Endemann
2011	Pesega Samoa	22 Jan 1995	Meliula Meafou Fata
538	*Savai'i Samoa		
	‡Savai'i	8 Jan 1971	Amuia W. Hunt
2098	Savai'i Samoa Sagone	10 Sep 1995	Paulo Sofeni Matofai
1366	Savai'i Samoa South	17 Oct 1982	Malina Ropeti Ti'a
619	*Savai'i Samoa West		
	‡Savai'i West	3 Jun 1973	Fa'afoi Tuitama
1045	Upolu Samoa Aleisa	10 June 2000	
	Apia Samoa East	5 Aug 1979	Daniel Afamasaga Betham
868	Upolu Samoa East	23 Oct 1977	Kovana Pauga
2171	Upolu Samoa Faleasi'u	25 Feb 1996	Pouono Lameko
1909	Upolu Samoa North	25 Oct 1992	Sofeni Pilimai
2139	Upolu Samoa Saleilua	5 Dec 1995	Polesi Avauli Salani
645	Upolu Samoa South	1 Jun 1974	William Richard Schwalger
545	*Upolu Samoa West		
	‡Upolu West	25 Apr 1971	Tua'ifaiva O. Aiono

Mission — 1
(As of Oct. 1, 2011; shown with historical number. See MISSIONS.)

(13c) SAMOA APIA MISSION
P.O. Box 1865
Apia, Samoa

SCOTLAND

(See United Kingdom)

SERBIA AND MONTENEGRO

Jan. 1, 2011: Est. population, 10,829,000; Members, 307; District, 1; Branches, 3;
Percent LDS, .0026, or one in 39,094; Europe Area; Bulgaria Sofia Mission.

Located on the Balkan Peninsula in southeast Europe, Serbia is a republic made up of the easternmost internal division of Yugoslavia where Serbian is spoken.

Mischa Markow was the first LDS missionary to work in Serbia. He arrived in Beograd in May 1899. Forces of opposition soon turned against him and Markow was banished to Hungary in June 1899 without baptizing anyone.

The president of the Czechoslovak Mission, Arthur Gaeth, visited Beograd in August 1934, where there were two members of the Church, Sister Evize Vujicic and Brother Mateja Spacek. Records do not indicate how they joined the Church. Gaeth held a sacrament meeting with them and four friends. No further missionary work was done in Yugoslavia until the 1970s.

Following World War II, Yugoslavia became a communist republic under Prime Minister Josip Broz Tito. In 1959, while serving as U.S. Secretary of Agriculture, Elder Ezra Taft Benson of the Quorum of the Twelve toured Yugoslavia and met with Tito.

Tito allowed a freer exchange of people and ideas than most of the countries in the Eastern Bloc. Many Yugoslavs worked in Western Europe where they came in contact with Mormon missionaries. In October 1974, the First Presidency representative David M. Kennedy visited Beograd to seek recognition for the Church. Shortly thereafter, missionaries serving in Austria began a program to teach Yugoslav emigrés working there with the hope of eventually opening missionary work in Yugoslavia.

In anticipation of establishing a mission there, the Church called Gustav Salik as mission president and stationed him in Austria near the Yugoslav border in 1975. Salik spent the next year attempting to open the mission, but could not get the necessary permission to work in the country. In 1977, missionaries entered as students. They wore casual dress but could not proselyte. Though they served mostly in Croatia, they also worked in Beograd.

When the missionaries arrived, they found two members of the Church, Radmila Ranovic, who had been baptized in Switzerland in 1975, and Dusan Tabori, who had also been baptized in Switzerland in 1977. Ranovic began seeking recognition for the Church in Beograd. In December 1980, she was called to serve in the Canada Montreal Mission, the first Serb and the first Eastern European to serve a mission in the 20th Century.

Lee and Marilyn Manwill arrived in Beograd in January 1983, the first missionary couple to serve full time in that city. The first baptisms were in May of that same year. By November 1983, a branch was organized.

In July 1987, Yugoslavia was made part of the Austria Vienna East Mission. On 22 March 1991, responsibility for Yugoslavia was transferred to the Austria Vienna Mission.

In June 1991, Slovenia and Croatia declared independence from Yugoslavia. The threat of civil war caused Church leaders to evacuate all missionaries working in the former Yugoslavia on 1 July 1991.

Four months later, missionaries returned to Beograd. Two months later, the Church purchased a building, the culmination of a five-year effort. On 28 January 1992, the building passed inspection, one of the requirements for an organization's obtaining legal status which meant that Serbia had officially recognized the Church. Missionaries were then granted permanent visas to work in the country. In February 1992, missionaries opened the second Serbian city, Novi Sad.

Cvil war erupted in1992. Because communication was better between Budapest and Beograd, responsibility for Serbia was temporarily transferred to the Hungary Budapest Mission in November 1993.. Shortly thereafter, missionaries were evacuated to other Central European nations due to rising tensions.

By the summer of 1994, Serbia was transferred back to the Austria Vienna Mission. Shortly thereafter, Serbia canceled the visas for foreign missionaries. The last two elders left Serbia in September 1995. During the next year, Austria Vienna Mission President Swen R. Swensen visited the Church members in Serbia each month. The Church also contributed humanitarian assistance during this time. A tenuous peace was achieved in November 1995 and missionaries re-entered Serbia in June 1996.

In July 1996, the Austria Vienna South Mission was organized with Johann A. Wondra as president. The mission had jurisdiction for all nations that were once Yugoslavia. In June 1998, the first official delegation from the Church to travel to Montenegro were Wondra, his wife Ursula, Beograd Branch President Dragomir Savic, and his counselor, Sladan Mihajlovic. They entered Montenegro with the hope of registering the Church. While in Podgorica, the party met with the minister of religion, Slobodan Tomovic, who was positive about allowing the Church to be registered in Montenegro. Their efforts were cut short by a renewed threat of war.

Violence in Kosovo began in 1996. As the violence escalated, missionary work slowed. Missionaries were evacuated from

Serbia to Croatia on 3 October 1998. While in Croatia, a special mission conference was held by President Wondra. It included a day of prayer and fasting for missionary work to resume in Serbia. Three weeks later, on 28 October, missionaries returned to Serbia.

On 17 January 1999, the Beograd Yugoslavia District was formed, the first in Serbia, with Dragomir Savic as president. This time of growth and missionary work was short lived. In March 1999, violence resumed. Missionaries were evacuated from Serbia shortly before the outbreak. In September 2000, responsibility for Serbia was transferred to the Bulgaria Sofia Mission. And in December 2001, after peace was restored, six missionaries re-entered Serbia.

By 2002, there were 213 members organized in three branches and one district.

Sources: "Life and History of Mischa Markow" found in Kahlile Mehr's Mormon Missionaries Enter Eastern Europe, 2002; Czechoslovakian Mission, Manuscript history, Church Archives; Francis M. Gibbons, Ezra Taft Benson: Statesman, Patriot, Prophet of God, 1996; Austria Vienna South Mission, Clippings and reports, Church Archives; James L. Wilde, Interviews, Church Archives, 1994; Bulgaria Sofia Mission, Annual historical reports, Church Archives; Kenneth D. Reber, Interviews, 1994, Church Archives.

SIERRA LEONE

Jan. 1, 2011: Est. population, 6,440,000; Members, 8,907; Districts, 2; Branches, 23; Mission, 1; Percent LDS, .13, or one in 800; Africa West Area; Ghana Accra Mission.

Sierra Leone is located on the west coast of Africa and has a constitutional democracy. The official language is English, but tribal languages are common. The ethnic make-up of Sierra Leone is diverse: 20 native African tribes 90 percent (Temne 30 percent , Mende 30 percent, other 30 percent), Creole 10 percent (descendants of freed Jamaican slaves), refugees from Liberia's recent civil war, small numbers of Europeans, Lebanese, Pakistanis, and Indians. The major religions include Muslim 60 percent, indigenous beliefs 30 percent and Christian 10 percent .

Michael Samura, a native of Sierra Leone, was baptized in Holland in 1981, and shortly thereafter returned to the capital city of Freetown. He wrote to the International Mission requesting that the Church be established there. Though the Church was not yet ready to send in missionaries, the International Mission presidency sent Church literature and encouraged him to live the gospel. Samura began to tell people about his new-found faith. Soon, groups of people interested in the Church were holding informal meetings.

Elizabeth Judith Bangura and Monica Orleans were baptized in Ghana and formed a study group in Freetown in January 1988. Christian L. George was baptized in Germany, given the Melchizedek Priesthood, and had been through the temple. He returned to Sierra Leone and presided over the first approved meeting held on 18 January 1988 at Goderich, a suburb of Freetown. In May 1988 two missionary couples, Claire J. and Iliene M. Fisher and C. Erwin and Colleen Waite, arrived in Sierra Leone. On 11 June 1988 the first 14 converts were baptized in Sierra Leone.

The Goderich Branch, the first branch in the country, was organized on 7 August 1988, with Christian George as president. In May 1989, Elder Richard G. Scott became the first member of the Quorum of the Twelve to visit Sierra Leone. He met with Church members and blessed the land in prayer from the top of Leicester Peak.

The Liberia Monrovia Mission, which included Sierra Leone, was created on 1 March 1988. The first president was J. Duffy Palmer. The mission offices were moved to Freetown in May 1990 because of the unrest in Liberia. Later, as civil war developed, the Liberia Monrovia Mission was discontinued in February 1991, and the area was transferred to the Ghana Accra Mission.

In December 1990, Elder Robert E. Sackley of the Seventy organized the Freetown Sierra Leone District with Michael Samura as president. The Bo Sierra Leone District was organized in July 1991.

In the early 1990s, the Church experimented with home group meetings. Church members living in the same general vicinity met at someone's home for Sunday worship services. These meetings would cut down on expenses that often prohibited people from attending meetings in meetinghouses that were often far from their homes. Once a month, these groups combined for a large branch meeting. In July 1992 the home group meetings were discontinued in Sierra Leone. The local Church members wanted to meet in the larger branches.

In May and August 1992, missionary couples were temporarily removed from Sierra Leone because of civil unrest. By year-end 1993, 89 Sierra Leonians were serving full-time missions, including 41 from the six branches of the Freetown District.

In February 1995 missionaries once again left Sierra Leone and did not return until April 1997. However, the Church members were not left alone during this time. Mission president Larry B. Duke flew to Sierra Leone and visited districts in Wellington, Bo, and Freetown. During this time, missionary work by district missionaries continued and people were baptized.

After being in Sierra Leone for only a month, missionaries were again evacuated by the U.S. military at the end of May 1997 because of riots and chaos that followed a military coup.

In 1999, membership numbered 3,564. In 2001, membership was 4,265, and in 2003, membership was 4,782 in three districts and 16 branches.

Ground was broken for the first meetinghouse in Sierra Leone on 13 October 2004 in a city called Bo. Presiding at the groundbreaking was the Sierra Leone District President Mohamed Turay. He was accompanied by civic leaders and prominent tribal chiefs, who lauded the building as a great asset to the area and a symbol of cooperation and good will between the community and the Church.

The first mission, Sierra Leone Freetown Mission, was organized 1 July 2007. It was created from a division of the Ghana Accra Mission.

Sources: Miles Cunningham oral history, 17 September 1993, Church Archives; Correspondence in Church News office from Christopher N. Chukwurah, Ghana Accra Mission, 14 March 1994; Ghana Accra Mission papers, 1967-1988, Church Archives; Robert B. Tueller, and Verne and Shirley Nelson oral history, 13 March 1998, Church Archives; Church News, 6 November 2004.

Mission — 1
(As of Oct. 1, 2011; shown with historical number. See MISSIONS.)

(347) SIERRA LEONE FREETOWN MISSION
P.O. Box 263
Freetown, Sierra Leone
West Africa

SINGAPORE
Jan. 1, 2011: Est. population, 4,658,000; Members, 3,337; Stakes, 1; Wards, 8; Branches 1; Missions, 1; Percent LDS, .06, or one in 1,612; Asia Area.

On the tip of the Malay Peninsula in southeast Asia, Singapore is a parliamentary democracy. Its population speaks Chinese, Malay, Tamil, and English (all are official languages). The people are Buddhist, Christian, Islam, Taoist, and Hindu.

Elder Gordon B. Hinckley of the Quorum of the Twelve and President Jay A. Quealy of the Southern Far East Mission visited Singapore in May 1963 and found three British Church members residing there. By August 1964, the number had grown to 11, and Quealy organized a group with John Waller as leader. In February 1965, Quealy took two of his missionaries to Singapore, where they held several gospel conversations and determined that it was "an ideal place for the preaching of the gospel."

The first full-time missionaries assigned to Singapore arrived on 19 March 1968: Kim A. Shipley, Joel Richards III, Rhett T. Bake, and Melvin D. Shurtz. The first convert, Alice Tan, was baptized on 4 May. The Church was legally recognized on 12 October and W. Brent Hardy organized the Singapore Branch the next day with John McSweeney as president. By the end of the year 40 converts had joined the Church.

Elder Ezra Taft Benson of the Quorum of the Twelve visited Singapore in 1969. Speaking to a group of Church members on 14 April, he said, "We expect . . . that this may someday become a center from which the gospel can be directed and sent into other countries." The Southeast Asia Mission, headquartered in Singapore, was organized on 1 November 1969 with G. Carlos Smith Jr. as president. In addition to Singapore the new mission was given responsibility for missionary work in Brunei, Burma, Cambodia, India, Indonesia, Laos, Malaysia, Sri Lanka, Thailand, and Vietnam. By the end of 1969, there were 48 missionaries in Singapore.

In early 1970, local newspaper editors and leaders of other Christian faiths leveled attacks against the Church and its missionary methods. In March, the government refused to renew the visas of 29 Latter-day Saint missionaries. They were reassigned to other missions in April. There were only three foreign Latter-day Saint missionaries remaining in Singapore by November. By 1973 ,the Church was allowed to have one foreign missionary in Singapore, plus the mission president and his wife. Local Church members were then largely responsible for the Church's slow-but-steady growth.

In February 1970, the Singapore Branch was divided and the Church purchased a large home to hold meetings and other activities. A meetinghouse and a building for Church administrative offices were subsequently built on this site.

In January 1971, President G. Carlos Smith Jr. called a local member, Teo Thiam Chye, to serve for one year as a full-time missionary in Singapore. Missionaries were called in this manner until 1975, when Roy Thong and Peter Tan became the first local members to receive two-year mission calls. By the end of 1977, there were 12 full-time missionaries serving in Singapore, including 10 Singaporeans, one Malaysian, and one American, in addition to several members who served part-time as district missionaries. On 20 June 1974, the Southeast Asia Mission was renamed the Singapore Mission.

The Singapore District was organized on 17 January 1971 with Soren F. Cox as president. At that time Eddie Chew became the first local member to be sustained as a branch president. He later became the first local Latter-day Saint to preside over the Singapore District, serving from 1973 to 1982. Home-study seminary started in Singapore in 1975, followed by early-morning seminary in 1986 and early-morning institute in 1988.

The Singapore Mission was temporarily dissolved in July 1978. For the next 18 months Winfield Q. Cannon supervised missionary work in Singapore as a counselor to the president of the Indonesia Jakarta Mission. J. Talmage Jones was called to preside over the Singapore Mission when it was reinstated 1 January 1980.

The Church's image in Singapore received a positive boost in June 1980 when performers Donny and Marie Osmond held a concert for 30,000 people in the National Stadium. They also spoke at a fireside sponsored by the Singapore District and attended by 2,200 people, 1,800 of whom were not Church members. The Church also benefitted from the appointment of Jon M. Huntsman Jr., a Latter-day Saint, as U.S. Ambassador to Singapore. He served from September 1992 to June 1993.

On 18 March 1988, Elder M. Russell Ballard of the Council of the Twelve, businessman Jon M. Huntsman Sr., and Utah Sen. Jake Garn met with Singapore's prime minister, Lee Kuan Yew, to discuss government and business issues. Huntsman inquired about the heavy restriction on the number of foreign Latter-day Saint missionaries who were allowed into the country. The number of missionary visas granted subsequently rose to 12.

In October 1993, the Ministry of Community Development invited the Church to participate in a discussion on family values. The next year on 19 June the Church hosted a booth at a National Family Day exhibition. An estimated 10,000 people visited the booth, including Prime Minister Goh Chok Tong and his wife.

Elder Neal A. Maxwell of the Quorum of the Twelve organized the Singapore Singapore Stake, the first in the country, with Leonard Woo as president on 26 February 1995. The new stake had 1,650 members in four wards and two branches. Singapore's ethnic diversity is evidenced by the creation of a Mandarin Branch in 1983, a Philippine Branch in 1993, and the Clementi Branch (for members from other countries) in 1995. President Gordon B. Hinckley spoke to 1,450 Church members in Singapore on 30 January 2000, marking the first visit there by a Church president.

Latter-day Saints in Singapore have been active in community and humanitarian projects. In July 2000, the stake Relief Society arranged for the BYU-Hawaii Concert Choir to perform at the Victoria Concert Hall and gathered personal donations, resulting in a $50,000 gift to the Asian Women Welfare Association Special School for children with multiple disabilities. In March 2001, members donated 400 boxes of clothing, kitchenware, utensils, toys, books, school supplies, shoes and computers, plus $10,000 for the purchase of rice, to Church members and an orphanage in Phnom Penh, Cambodia.

In 2002, membership reached 2,265.

Sources: Southern Far East Mission, Manuscript history and historical reports, Church Archives; R. Lanier Britsch, From the East: The History of the Latter-day Saints in Asia, 1851-1996, 1998; Dale S. Cox, A brief history of the LDS Church in Singapore, 1978, in Southeast Asia Mission manuscript history, Church Archives; Pang Beng Ling, A History of The Church of Jesus Christ of Latter-day Saints in Singapore: Journey to Stakehood, 1964-1997, 1997; Southeast Asia Mission, Manuscript history and historical reports, Church Archives; "Seminary Class Launched," Church News, 9 November 1986; Gerry Avant, "Ambassador's Term Brief, Yet Notable," Church News, 5 June 1993; Richard Tice, "Singapore Saints," Ensign, April 1990; "Prime Minister Visits Booth," Church News, 6 August 1994; "Pres. Hinckley Completes Tour in Pacific Rim," Church News, 12 February 2000; "$50,000 Raised for Singapore Charity," Church News, 22 July 2000; "Sending Gifts to Cambodia," Church News, 28 April 2001.

Stake — 1
(Listed alphabetically as of Oct. 1, 2011.)

No.	Name	Organized	First President
Asia Area			
2025	Singapore Singapore	26 Feb 1995	Woo Hoi Seng Leonard

Mission — 1
(As of Oct. 1, 2011; shown with historical number. See MISSIONS.)

(89) SINGAPORE MISSION
253 Bukit Timah Road, Floor 4
259690, Singapore

SLOVAKIA

**Jan. 1, 2011: Est. Population, 5,463,000; Members, 193; Branches, 4;
Czech Republic Prague Mission; percent LDS, .0025 or 1 LDS in 39,302; Europe Area.**

The Slovak Republic, also known as Slovakia, is located between Poland on the north and Hungary on the south. It includes territory comprising the eastern half of the former state of Czechoslovakia which was split on 1 January 1993, creating the Slovak Republic and the Czech Republic. Slovakia is a parliamentary democracy with a population that speaks Slovak, Czech, and Hungarian. It is 60 percent Roman Catholic, 10 percent atheist, 8 percent Protestant, 4 percent Orthodox, and 16 percent other.

On 24 July 1929, the Czechoslovak Mission was formed with Arthur Gaeth as president. Most missionaries were assigned to labor in Prague and other cities which are now within the Czech Republic.

President Gaeth performed limited missionary work in a portion of Czechoslovakia now within the Slovak Republic, working in Bratislava in 1929. In January 1931, Joseph I. Hart traveled to Bratislava where he taught a family and may have baptized a few converts before his return to Prague.

After the democratization of Czechoslovakia in 1989-1990 following the communist era, missionaries were allowed to return. On 21 February 1990 the new Czech government officially recognized the Church, and on 2 May 1990 the first full-time missionaries arrived. On 1 July 1990, the Czechoslovakia Prague Mission was created with Richard W. Winder as president.

The first known member to live in the area that became the Slovak Republic was Valreie Ruzenia Fantiska Zizkova. She was born to Latter-day Saint parents and was baptized on 20 July 1939, just before the missionaries departed prior to World War II. She regained contact with missionaries for a brief period after the war, and then due to restrictions imposed by the government, again lost contact with the Church. She later married and moved to central Slovakia. It was not until 1992 that she renewed contact with the Church.

Other Slovakians were introduced to the gospel outside their country. Alzbeta Domotorova was baptized in Germany in 1977, and Pavel Pirovits, who had requested political asylum in Germany prior to the fall of the communist regime, also joined the Church in this era. Other influential converts, including Peter Vaclav, had been baptized in March 1991 after having contact with Church members in Moravia. His wife Hanka joined the Church several months later.

The first Church meeting in Slovakia in the 20th century was held in October 1991 at Trencin in the home of the Vaclavs.

David F. Backman and Christopher J. Williams of the Czechoslovakia Prague Mission arrived in Slovakia to work in Trencin on 29 March 1992. Among their earliest converts were Martin and Zuzana Blaskova who were baptized 25 July 1992 at Trencin.

Ten months later, on 24 January 1993, mission President Richard W. Winder directed the formation of the Trencin Branch, the first branch formed in Slovakia. At about the same time, a group of members began meeting in the capital city Bratislava. A second branch was created there on 11 July 1993.

In 1993, Czechoslovak television producer Radim Smetana and reporter Premysl Cech visited Salt Lake City to make a documentary about the Church for broadcast in the Czech and Slovak republics.

On 30 April 1994, a translation team with Marcello de Oliveira as coordinator began translating basic Church materials into Slovak, including the Book of Mormon. In January 1999, the book Gospel Principles and the pamphlet Joseph Smith's Testimony were published in Slovak. They were followed by the publication of a Slovak hymnal in March 1999.

In July 1999, the Slovak Republic president visited a Church meeting place in Bratislava where he received a Czech translation of the Book of Mormon.

In 2002, membership reached 110.

Elder Dieter F. Uchtdorf of the Quorum of the Twelve blessed the land of Slovakia for the preaching of the gospel on May 12, 2006. On a hill overlooking the ancient castle of Tencin, he led a group of 56 members and friends to a clearing among the large trees. Growth has come slowly, said Elder Uchtdor, "but it will grow strong with a firm foundation."

Sources: Andrew Jenson, Encyclopedic History of the Church, 1941; Czechoslovakian Mission, Manuscript history and historical reports, Church Archives; Czechoslovakian Mission, Record of members, 1930-1939, Church Archives; "Czech Broadcasters See Church Close Up," Church News, 22 May 1993; Alysa Hatch, "Church Hosts Picnic for Diplomats, Church News, 15 October 1994; Gloria T. Wilkinson, "Diplomats Welcomed By Elder Maxwell to Festival of Lights," Church News, 10 December 1994; Kathryn Baer Newman, "Foreign Diplomats Enjoy Outing with Western Flavor In Virginia," Church News, 17 October 1998; Sarah Jane Weaver, "Finding Hope In Gospel Message: In Eastern Europe, Seminary, Institute Programs Thriving," Church News, 16 January 1999; "Slovakia dedicated," Church News, 9 Sept. 2006.

SLOVENIA

Jan. 1, 2011: Est. Population, 2,006,000; Members, 385; Missions, 1; Districts, 1; Branches, 4; percent LDS, .019, or one in 5,279; Europe Area.

Located on the Balkan Peninsula in southeast Europe, Slovenia is a republic made up of what was the northernmost internal division of Yugoslavia. The people are nearly all Roman Catholic and speak Slovene and Italian.

By the early 1970s a few Latter-day Saints were living in Yugoslavia, some of whom had joined the Church while working or studying abroad. Few, if any, however, resided in present-day Slovenia.

In 1974 and 1975 Neil D. Schaerrer, president of the Austria Vienna Mission, met with officials in the cities of Ljubljana and Maribor to see if there were a possibility that the Church could be introduced in the region. In 1987 responsibility for the area, then part of Yugoslavia, was transferred to the Austria Vienna East Mission.

In November 1990, Elders Jeffery Moore and Corey Bodily from the Austria Vienna East Mission entered Ljubljana. On 1 March 1991, they were able to secure recognition in the region for the Church. Responsibility for the area was transferred back to the Austria Vienna Mission on 22 March. Elders Moore and Bodily soon met Suzana Klenovek who was baptized on 30 March 1991, becoming the first to join the Church.

On June 28 of that year Slovenia declared independence from Yugoslavia. Elders Moore and Bodily were forced to leave due to the ensuing civil war. Missionaries returned in August.

The Ljubljana Branch was organized on 26 March 1992. The Ljubljana Slovenia District was organized the following 16 August. The organization of the Celje and Maribor branches followed in September.

In August 1995 missionaries serving in neighboring Croatia and Serbia were evacuated from those countries due to war and were reassigned to Slovenia. The Austria Vienna South Mission was organized in July 1996 to supervise the countries comprising the former Yugoslavia including Slovenia. On 15 September of that year the Church was again officially registered in Slovenia.

Leon Bergant, a timed-trial bicycle champion and a promising member of the Slovene National Bike Team, left the team in 1997 to serve a full-time mission in Croatia. Two main newspapers carried major stories about his decision.

Mission headquarters of the Austria Vienna South Mission was moved from Vienna, Austria, to Ljubljana in July 1999 and the name was changed to the Slovenia Ljubljana Mission. In May 2002 the Book of Mormon was published in Slovenian. The mission name was changed to the Croatia Zagreb Mission in January 2003.

Membership in 2002 was 286.

On 14 October 2006 ground was broken in Ljubljana for the first meetinghouse in Slovenia. Members of the Ljubljana, Maribor and Celje branches attended the ceremony. Also attending were Dr. Drago Cepar, director of the Office for Religious Communities of the Republic of Slovenia, and Ljubljana Vice-Mayor Milos Pavlica. Ground was broken by Slovenia/Croatia Mission President Douglas L. Weight, Ljubljana Slovenia District President Matjaz Juhart and Ljubljana Branch President Bogdan Kralj.

Sources:"Bike Champion Gives up Racing to Serve Mission," Church News, 14 February 1998; Austria Vienna Mission, Manuscript history and historical reports, Church Archives; Kahlile B. Mehr, Mormon Missionaries Enter Eastern Europe, 2002; Austria Vienna East Mission, Manuscript history and historical reports, Church Archives; Heidi Hess, "LDS Missionaries Pulled out of Croatia, Serbia," Daily Universe, 9 August 1995; Croatia Zagreb Mission, Manuscript history and historical reports, Church Archives; Ljubljana Slovenia District, Annual history and historical reports, Church Archives.

Mission — 1
(As of Oct. 1, 2011; shown with historical number. See MISSIONS.)

(309) SLOVENIA LJUBLJANA MISSION
Molekova Ul.3
1211 Ljubljana - Smartno
Slovenia

SOLOMON ISLANDS

**Jan. 1, 2011: Est. population: 596,000; Members, 234; Branches, 1;
Percent LDS, .04, or one in 2,423; Papua New Guinea Mission, Pacific Area.**

The Solomon Islands lie in the West Pacific Ocean east of Papua New Guinea. Their people speak English, Melanesian pidgin, Motu, and 120 other tribal languages. The country is a parliamentary democracy. The population is 45 percent Anglican, 18 percent Roman Catholic, 12 percent Methodist/Presbyterian, 9 percent Baptist, 7 percent Seventh-Day Adventist, 5 percent other Christian including Latter-day Saint and 4 percent indigenous faiths.

During the World War II, a number of Latter-day Saints serving in the U.S. military were stationed in the Solomon Islands. At least two servicemen groups conducted regular Church services on Guadalcanal and other of the islands in 1943-1945.

The first natives baptized were Imo Ta'asi, who joined the Church in 1986 at Brigham Young University, and Peter Joseph Salaka, a member of Parliament who had been baptized in England.

The Immigration Department of the Solomon Islands issued a directive on 27 January 1992 forbidding entry of Latter-day Saints into the country. When the first missionary couple was assigned to work there in 1994, they learned of the restriction. After appeal of the immigration directive, the Church was allowed to send representatives. The first missionaries were E. Crawford Jones and his wife, Judith, who arrived at the beginning of 1995. They were soon joined by two young elders, Glenn R. Cockburn and Sa Francis Togia.

The first meeting since World War II was held in Honiara, Guadalcanal, on 5 February 1995 with four in attendance. On 26 April 1995, Papua New Guinea Mission president John Gibson met with Prime Minister Solomon Mamaloni and presented to him a copy of the Book of Mormon.

The first Solomon Islander baptized in the islands was Eddie Misi on 21 May 1995. He later served as first branch president. The Honiara Branch was created on 4 February 1996.

In June 2000, because of political unrest, eight missionaries — six elders and one senior couple — were temporarily relocated from the Solomon Islands and sent to the Australia Brisbane Mission. Missionaries were allowed to return a short time later.

In 2003, membership was 183.

Sources: Servicemen's Group (Guadalcanal) minutes, 1944-1945, Church Archives; Servicemen's Group (Army Service Forces Band: Solomon Islands) minutes, 1943-1944, Church Archives; "The Church in the Pacific," Ensign, February 1998; "Missionary Work Opens," Church News, 15 April 1995; Missionaries Evacuated from Solomon Islands," 17 June 2000.

SOMALIA

**Jan. 1, 2011: Est. population, 9,832,000; Members, fewer than 100;
Africa Southeast Area; Kenya Nairobi Mission.**

Somalia was formed 1 July 1960 by a merger of British Somaliland and Italian Somaliland. It is the easternmost country on the African continent and is bordered by the Gulf of Aden and Indian Ocean, Ethiopia, Djibouti, and Kenya. The majority of the population are Sunni Muslim. The official language is Somali, while Arabic, Italian, and English are also spoken.

In 1983, members of an agricultural development project from Utah State University began work in Somalia. Many of those working on the project were members of the Church. To serve this group, the Mogadishu Branch was formed under the direction of the International Mission. When the project concluded, the branch was dissolved.

Michel Guillas, a French doctor, had begun meeting with missionaries in Geneva, Switzerland, in 1983. That same year he moved to Somalia. He soon met a group of Latter-day Saints who were meeting in a private home. Guillas was baptized in the Indian Ocean on 15 December 1984, the first known convert baptized in Somalia.

Drought and border disputes in Somalia continued through the 1980s and early 1990s. In 1992, the Church sent over 1 million pounds of relief supplies to Somalia and other neighboring countries. The Church also funded several water reclamation projects.

Also in 1992, U.S. Marines were sent to Somalia as part of a United Nations peace keeping force. Latter-day Saints within the contingent requested permission from the Africa Area Presidency to hold Church meetings. In response, the Kenya Nairobi Mission sent manuals and hymn books. As of 2004, there was no official Church group in the country.

Sources: "When Michel Guillas First Received a Book," Church News, 23 December 1989; "Deadly Drought," Church News, 26 September 1992; "Church Sends Aid to Africa," Ensign, November 1992; "Church Sends Assistance to Somalia," Ensign, April 1993.

SOUTH AFRICA

Jan. 1, 2011: Est. population, 49,052,000; Members, 54,996; Stakes, 11; Wards, 72; Branches, 75; Districts, 4; Missions, 3; Temples, 1; percent LDS; .1 or one in 1,020; Africa Southeast Area.

In August 1852, a conference was held in Salt Lake City where Jesse Haven, Leonard I. Smith, and William H. Walker were called to serve missions in the Cape of Good Hope, Africa, a British colony. They arrived in Cape Town on 19 April 1853. A month later, on 23 May, the missionaries ascended The Lion's Head, a mountain near Cape Town, and organized the mission with Haven as president. The first convert, Henry Stringer, was baptized on 15 June 1853.

As people began to join the Church, the missionaries organized branches. The first in Africa was organized on 16 August 1853 at Mowbray, four miles from Cape Town. Three weeks later, on 7 September, a second branch was organized at Newlands, six miles from Cape Town. At that meeting, Thomas Weatherhead was sustained as the first local branch president.

In spite of a good beginning, Church growth slowed due to Latter-day Saints' emigration to Utah. The South African Mission was closed from 1865 to 1903 with no official reasons given by Church authorities.

On 25 July 1903, Latter-day Saint missionaries once again arrived in Cape Town: Warren H. Lyon, who was called to preside over the mission, George A. Simpkins (also spelled Simkins), Thomas L. Griffiths and William R. Smith. They found a few Latter-day Saints who had kept the faith during the long absence of missionaries. The missionaries baptized their first converts on 16 October 1904. In 1905, President Lyon baptized an African named Dunn, whose father was a Scotsman and his mother Zulu. Though Dunn did not stay with the Church, he was most likely the first black African baptized in Africa.

The first person of color in South Africa to join the Church and remain active in the Church was William Paul Daniels who was baptized on 30 May 1915 while visiting family in Utah. Before returning to South Africa, Daniels met twice with Church President Joseph F. Smith, who gave Daniels a blessing that someday, perhaps in the next life, he would hold the priesthood.

After returning to South Africa, Daniels felt uncomfortable meeting with the white Church members because of South Africa's ban on the mixing of the races. The mission president, Don Mack Dalton, assigned missionaries to visit the Daniels' home every Monday night. Daniels died on 13 October 1936, firm in the faith. Alice Daniels Okkers, William P. Daniels' daughter, was alive when the priesthood was granted to all worthy males. She, too, had kept the faith and was present in the Salt Lake Temple when her parents' temple work was performed by former South African Mission president Evan P. Wright in 1980.

Following the re-establishment of the South African Mission in 1903, more missionaries were called to serve in southern Africa. Missionary work expanded throughout the area that is now South Africa, though the missionaries tended to concentrate their efforts in the cities and towns populated by British colonists. Many of the inhabitants of the inland settlements spoke only Afrikaans, an obstacle for the English-speaking missionaries. In his last letter to Church authorities, dated 7 April 1908, returning mission President Ralph A. Badger mentioned the two other obstacles facing missionaries in southern Africa: the issue of race — missionaries were discouraged from teaching blacks about the Church until 1978 — and the immense size of the mission, both of which would concern mission presidents for the next 70 years.

Nicholas G. Smith, later called as an Assistant to the Quorum of the Twelve Apostles in 1941, presided over the South African Mission from 1913 to 1921. When he arrived in Cape Town, there were only 15 missionaries in the field. During World War I, missionaries left South Africa. In October 1916, Smith purchased a villa in Mowbray that he named "Cumorah," which became the mission home and Church headquarters for South Africa.

For the last year and a half of Smith's tenure and the first seven months of his successor, J. Wiley Sessions, the South African Mission president had no missionaries because the government had imposed restrictions on foreign nationals entering the country. President Sessions worked hard to gain permission for missionaries to once again labor in South Africa. With the help of U.S. Sen. Reed Smoot, Sessions was successful. The first missionary, Golden W. Harris, arrived in October 1921. The government, however, established a quota of 25 LDS missionaries in the mission. It eventually rose to 60 missionaries by 1967, but would hinder the progress of the Church until it was lifted in the 1980s.

During President Sessions' administration, a meetinghouse was built in Johannesburg. Much of the funds needed for construction were donated or raised by local Church members. The building was dedicated on 1 February 1925 and named "Ramah." This building served as Church headquarters in South Africa when the mission office was moved from Cape Town to Johannesburg in 1960.

To meet the needs of the Latter-day Saints scattered throughout South Africa, the mission began publishing the "Cumorah Monthly Bulletin" on 15 June 1927. Its name changed briefly to "Cumorah's Southern Cross," and later to "Cumorah's Southern Messenger," a name it retained until publication stopped in 1970.

Richard E. Folland, president of the South African Mission from 1938 to 1944, presided over a total of only 50 missionaries during his entire tenure because of World War II. Soon after his arrival, he noticed that the missionaries were doing most of the administrative and leadership work. One of Folland's first tasks was to help local members assume leadership positions in the branches and districts. On 11 October 1940, because of World War II, all the missionaries were called home. Folland and his family were asked to remain in South Africa. He also installed local officers to take charge of branches.

June B. Sharp arrived in Cape Town in August 1944 as the new president of the mission. Because the war was still raging in Europe and the Pacific, Sharp spent his first two years without any missionaries. He traveled around the country visiting branches and looking for "lost" Church members. On 16 October 1946, missionaries arrived once again in South Africa.

As mentioned earlier, the Afrikaans language was considered one of the obstacles facing missionaries in South Africa. In 1949, mission President Evan P. Wright asked the First Presidency for permission to translate the Book of Mormon into Afrikaans. He estimated Afrikaans was spoken by 68 percent of white South Africans. By 1951, one tract was translated into Afrikaans, laying the groundwork for more Afrikaans translations of Church literature. The Afrikaans translation of the Book of Mormon was introduced to the South African Latter-day Saints on 14 May 1972.

For several decades, members in South Africa wanted to be visited by General Authorities. Their desires were finally realized when David O. McKay, president of the Church, arrived in Cape Town on 9 January 1954, the first General Authority to visit the African continent.

In 1953, there were only two Church-owned buildings in South Africa, Cumorah and Ramah. Leroy H. Duncan, who was mission president from 1953 to 1957, began arranging to have many meetinghouses built. A mission-wide building fund was organized in 1949 and chapels were constructed in Springs in 1954, Port Elizabeth in 1956, and Durban in 1956. The building program continued during the presidency of O. Layton Alldredge, who served from 1960 to 1964. He planned 14 new meetinghouses and remodeled four of the five existing buildings.

Elder Marion G. Romney of the Quorum of the Twelve organized the first stake in South Africa 22 March 1970 with Louis P. Hefer as president. The next landmark event in the history of the Church in South Africa was the 1978 revelation granting the priesthood to all worthy males. The majority population of South Africa was black or "coloured." With the revelation, the gospel could be taught to all citizens of South Africa. Within six years of the revelation, three more stakes were organized: Sandton in 1978, Durban in 1981, and Cape Town in 1984.

Up until 1984 South African Mission presidents presided over the whole of South Africa. With the lifting of the missionary quota, the South African Mission was divided on 1 July 1984, creating the South Africa Johannesburg and South Africa Cape Town missions. The South Africa Durban Mission was created in 1988.

South African Latter-day Saints had to travel to England or the United States to attend the temple, until the Johannesburg South Africa Temple was completed and dedicated on 24 August 1985 by President Gordon B. Hinckley.

In 1990, the Africa Area was organized with Richard P. Lindsay of the Seventy as first Area President. He and his counselors, Robert E. Sackley and J Ballard Washburn, also of the Seventy, moved to Johannesburg to direct the work of the Church throughout Africa, which is the first time General Authorities lived in Africa.

On 4 November 1991, Julia Mavimbella, a member of the Soweto Branch who joined the Church in 1981, became the first black woman elected by the white members of the National Council of Women to that organization. This occurred only two months after the repeal of apartheid.

President Gordon B. Hinckley visited South Africa in February 1998 and held three conferences to meet as many of the South African Latter-day Saints as possible. He met with 5,500 members in Johannesburg, making it the largest gathering of Church members in South Africa. He also visited Church members in Durban and Cape Town.

During 2003, the 35,000 members of the Church in South Africa celebrated 150 years since the first missionaries arrived. A year of activities and service projects began with 91 members of the Cape Town South Africa Stake gathering on Signal Hill on 19 April 2003 on the anniversary.

In 2005, membership reached 42,569.

A temple was announced for Durban, South Africa, by President Thomas S. Monson on 1 October 2011.

Sources: South Africa Mission, Manuscript history and historical reports, Church Archives; Journal History of the Church, 28 August 1852, Church Archives; Evan P. Wright, A History of the South African Mission, 1977; Cumorah Monthly Bulletin; Leroy H. Duncan, President McKay Visits South Africa, 1953-1954, Church Archives; John L. Hart and Steve Fidel, "Members Urged to Build up Homeland," Church News, 28 February 1998; Richard G. Hinckley, Interview, 1998; Church Archives; Julie Dockstader Heaps, "South Africa Celebrates 150 Years," Church News, 6 September 2003.

Stakes — 12
(Listed alphabetically as of Oct. 1, 2011.)

No.	Name	Organized	First President
Africa Southeast Area			
2437	Bedfordview South Africa	15 Feb 1998	Neil P. Fourie
1662	Benoni South Africa	29 Nov 1987	Jan G. Hugo
1470	Cape Town South Africa	6 May 1984	Otto Wilhelm Miessner
2904	Centurion South Africa	13 Mar 2011	Walter Chatora
1314	Durban South Africa	29 Nov 1981	Percy E.A. Winstanley
2610d	East London South Africa	17 Feb 2002	Willem Johan van Heerden
2529	Hillcrest South Africa	16 May 1999	Garith Charles Hill
506	*Johannesburg South Africa		
	‡Transvaal (South Africa)	22 Mar 1970	Louis P. Hefer
2684	Port Elizabeth South Africa	12 June 2005	Leslie Carl Palmer
969	*Pretoria South Africa	29 Nov 1987	
	‡Sandton South Africa	22 Oct 1978	Johannes P. Brummer
2046	Roodepoort South Africa	7 May 1995	Christoffel Golden Jr.
2516a	Soweto South Africa	14 Mar 1999	Robert Eppel

(177a) S. AFRICA CAPE TOWN MISSION
P.O. Box 181
Observatory
7935 Cape Town Pinelands
Republic of South Africa

(216) S. AFRICA DURBAN MISSION
P.O. Box 174
Wandsbeck 3631
Republic of South Africa

(14) SOUTH AFRICA JOHANNESBURG MISSION
Private Bag X 4
Ansfrere 1711
Republic of South Africa

SPAIN

Jan. 1, 2011: Est. population, 40,525,000; Members, 47,337; Stakes, 10; Wards, 67; Branches, 66; Missions, 3; Districts, 6; Temples, 1; percent LDS, 1.1, or one in 915; Europe Area.

Located in southwest Europe, Spain is a constitutional monarchy. Its people speak Spanish, Catalan, Galician, and Basque, and 90 percent are Roman Catholic.

In 1932, missionaries Ray L. Richards and Garland F. Smith traveled from the Swiss and German Mission to Spain to investigate the possibilities of conducting missionary work there. Though no report of their experiences is known, Spain's laws governing religious freedom were restrictive at that time and would have prevented a successful missionary program. That was to remain the case until 1967. In 1952, Juan Ventura learned about the Church "through correspondence in 1949" and was baptized in France in 1952. He married and moved to Salt Lake City, but returned to live in Spain in 1972.

In 1954, Spain and the United States entered into an agreement allowing US military bases to be established in Spain. By 1956, servicemen's groups were meeting at bases throughout Spain, and the first branch was established for servicemen stationed at Torrejon Air Base about 1957. One of the first converts in Spain, Jose Maria Oliveira, was baptized in France on 12 March 1966, because it was illegal for non-state religions to perform ordinances in Spain. Gabriel Diez became the first known native member of the Church to be baptized on Spanish soil on 27 November 1966.

On 28 June 1967, the Spanish Parliament enacted the religious liberty law allowing all Churches the right to function in Spain. Elder Howard W. Hunter of the Quorum of the Twelve visited Spain in April 1967 to explore the possibility of establishing the Church under the new law, and Elder Gordon B. Hinckley of the Quorum of the Twelve traveled to Spain in November of 1967 to review the developments in the Church's efforts to establish itself there.

The Madrid Spanish Speaking Branch was organized 7 January 1968 with David B. Timmins as president. Jose Maria Oliveria became the first native president of the branch later that same year.

The Church became fully recognized on 22 October 1968. Early in June 1969 four missionaries, Clark Hinckley, Jose Louis Barco, Craig Ward, and Robert Hernandez arrived from the North Argentine Mission and began missionary work in Madrid on 6 June 1969.

The Spain Mission (renamed the Spain Madrid Mission in 1974) was officially organized on 1 July 1970 with R. Raymond Barnes as president. That was followed by the organization of the Madrid District on 12 September with Jose Maria Oliveria as president. During this period, many Spanish-speaking Church members from around the world were transferred by their businesses to Spain and this helped to strengthen the new branches.

On 1 July 1976, the Spain Madrid Mission was divided and the Spain Seville and Spain Barcelona Missions were created. The first meetinghouse built by the Church was dedicated on 10 July 1977 in Madrid. Spain's first stake was created in Madrid on 14 March 1982 with Jose Maria Olivera as president.

President Hinckley has met with King Juan Carlos I and Queen Sofia on three occasions. The first meeting was in the Fall of 1978. Then, on 9 March 1992, President Hinckley met with the King and Queen, and presented them with a personalized, leather-bound copy of the Book of Mormon. He also met with the King and Queen on 18 March 1999 and presented them with a figurine of the Christus. The next day, President Hinckley dedicated the Madrid Spain Temple. The complex where the temple is located also houses a missionary training center and Church offices.

Membership in 1999 was 30,439.

On 11 March 2004, terrorist bombs exploded on commuter trains in Madrid. A few Latter-day Saints were injured in the explosions. Many Latter-day Saints attended an ecumenical service on 25 March of that year to memorialize those killed in the attacks.

Membership in 2005 reached 39,784.

On 1 July 2010, the Spain Bilboa Mission was combined with Spain Barcelona, Spain Madrid and Spain Malaga missions.

Sources: Swiss Mission, Manuscript history and historical reports, Church Archives; Betty Ventura, "The Saints in Spain," Ensign, April 1975, 6-11; "Mormons Meet King of Spain," Church News, 14 October 1978; Spain Madrid Mission, history files, Church Archives; Madrid Servicemen's Branch, Manuscript history and historical reports, Church Archives; Michael J. Mitchell, History of the first Church unit in Spain, Church Archives; Jose Maria Oliveria, Interview, 1997, Church Archives; Spain Madrid Mission, History files, Church Archives; French Mission, Manuscript history and historical reports, Church Archives; Spain Madrid Mission, Manuscript history and historical reports, Church Archives; "Church Leaders

Make Courtesy Visit to Spain's King and Queen," Church News, 28 March 1992, 3; "President Hinckley visits King, Queen of Spain," Church News, 20 March 1999, 5; Jason Swenson, "Victims Memorialized: Mission President Offers Prayer in Madrid Service," 24 April 2004; New Missions, Church News, 13 Feb. 2010.

Stakes — 10
(Listed alphabetically as of Oct. 1, 2011.)

No.	Name	Organized	First President
Europe Area			
1370	Barcelona Spain	31 Oct 1982	Jose Lara Straube
2022a	Cadiz Spain	19 Feb 1995	Cristobal Rodriguez Vasquez
2408	Elche Spain	9 Nov 1997	Manuel Parreno Ruiz
2640	Granada Spain	13 June 2004	Rafael Munoz Campos
2365	Hospitalet Spain	1 Jun 1997	Vicenc Lacambra
2507	Madrid Spain East	17 Jan 1999	Jose Leopoldo Reina A.
1327	*Madrid Spain West	17 Jan 1999	
	‡Madrid Spain	14 Mar 1982	Jose Maria Oliveira Aldamiz
1687	Seville Spain	14 Feb 1988	Jesus Manuel Benitez S.
2617	Valencia Spain	8 June 2003	Ramon Bleda Tevar
2854	Vitoria Spain	5 Sept 2009	Saulo G. Franco

Missions —3
(As of Oct. 1, 2011; shown with historical number. See MISSIONS.)

(137) SPAIN BARCELONA MISSION
Calle Calatrava, 10-12, bajos
E - 08017 Barcelona
Spain

(92) SPAIN MADRID MISSION
Avenida de Espana 17
Local 01-1,
Alcobendas 28100, Spain

(141) SPAIN MALAGA MISSION
Paseo Jesus Santos Rein No. 2
Edf. Ofisol 3rd floor D-E
29640 Fuengirola, Malaga
Spain

CANARY ISLANDS
Jan. 1, 2011: Est. population, 1,844,000; Members, 3,500; Districts, 3; Branches, 18; percent LDS, .19, or one in 527; Europe Area; Spain Las Palmas Mission.

The Canary Islands, two provinces of Spain in the South Atlantic off the northwestern coast of Africa, are rugged volcanic mountainous islands with rich soil and long beaches where sand from the western Sahara Desert has drifted. Thirteen islands make up the provinces, seven of which are inhabited: Gran Canaria, Fuerteventura, Lanzarote, Tenerife, La Palma, Gomera, and Hierro.

The first converts baptized in the Canary Islands were Juana Vega Garcia, Francisco Dominguez Peña, his wife, Francisca, and their son, Javier, on 13 June 1979. They were introduced to the Church by Jesus Ramón Gomez Vega, a native of Gran Canaria, who had accepted the gospel while residing in Spain where he was baptized in 1973. He served in the Spain Madrid Mission before returning home to share the gospel with his mother, Juana, and friends, the Peña family.

For the first several months, meetings of the small Church group were held in the Peña home. The first missionaries to the Canary Islands were Elders David L. Gill and Scott C. Jensen of the Spain Seville Mission who arrived 30 September 1979.

The first branch was organized in Las Palmas on 29 January 1980. The first district, Las Palmas Gran Canarias, was organized 2 October 1984, with eight branches. The second district, Santa Cruz de Tenerife Canaria, was organized 8 August 1989, with six branches.

The Spain Las Palmas Mission, headquartered on Gran Canaria Island, was created on 1 July 1988 from portions of the Spain Seville and Portugal Porto missions. Marion K. Hamblin was called as president. In the first year of operation, the mission baptized 1,000 converts, and by 1990 was averaging 80 baptisms per month.

President Gordon B. Hinckley stopped in Las Palmas on 13 February 1998 on his way to Nigeria and spoke to 775 members.

The mission experienced a great loss on 18 January 1999 when full-time missionaries Jaarl M. Papenfuss and Joshua M. Prymak were drowned off the coast of Tenerife. A large wave swept the two missionaries off a cliff and into the ocean. One made it to shore but the other, Elder Prymak, was unable to swim to safety. Elder Papenfuss, who witnessed the scene from a safe position on the shore, attempted to save him, but both perished.

Three tall sailing ships of Sea Trek 2001, re-enacting the Mormon emigration, spent three days in Las Palmas on 6-8 September before embarking across the Atlantic.

Sources: Spain Las Palmas Mission, Annual historical reports, Church Archives; Las Palmas Branch, Annual historical reports, Church Archives; Lewis A. Leake, Canary Islands historical resource file, Church Archives; Maria Torio de Gomez Vega, Los comienzos de la Iglesia de Jesucristo de Los Santos de los Últimos Dias en las Islas Canarias, Church Archives; Las Palmas De Gran Canaria Spain District, Annual historical reports, Church Archives; "President Hinckley Uplifts Members in Nova Scotia, Africa, Northern Mexico," Ensign, May 1998; "9 Missions Created: World Total Now 221," Church News, 19 March 1988; Gospel Takes Wing in Canary Islands," Church News, 10 November 1990; Gerry Avant, "Many are Still Blazing Gospel Trails," Church News, 24 July 1993; "Spirit of President Hinckley's Visits Lingers," Church News, 7 March 1998; "2 Missionaries Drown off the Canary Islands," Church News, 23 January 1999; "Canary Islands to Host Sea Trek 2001 Celebration, Church News, 7 July 2001; Manuel Benitez, "Sea Trek Spirits Remain High," Church News, 8 September 2001.

SRI LANKA

Jan. 1, 2011: Est. population, 21,325,000; Members, 1,294; Branches, 3; Districts, 1;
Percent LDS, .006, or one in 16,699; Asia Area, Singapore Mission.

Sri Lanka, formerly Ceylon, is an island republic located in the Indian Ocean off the coast of India. Sinhala and Tamil are the country's primary languages.

Two Latter-day Saint missionaries, Chauncey W. West and Benjamin F. Dewey, arrived in Ceylon on 26 May 1853. They briefly labored in Galle and Colombo but could find neither a hall in which to preach nor a person to listen to their message, thanks largely to the influence of anti-Mormon tracts and newspaper articles. They remained in the country only a short time before sailing to India.

The Church's next official contact with Sri Lanka (renamed from Ceylon in 1972) was in August 1975, when two missionaries en route home from the Singapore Mission, Matthew A. Hyde and Cyril W. Hill, were assigned to stop in Sri Lanka to explore the prospects for initiating missionary work. They reported favorably.

In 1976, Clarence Long, a Latter-day Saint from Texas, visited Colombo on business and became acquainted with Reginald and Easvary Rasiah and presented them with a Book of Mormon. He later invited their son, Rosignald, to travel to the U.S. to work with him. Rosignald Rasiah was baptized into the Church in Texas on 25 June 1977.

During his visits to Sri Lanka, Long also introduced the Rasiahs to the Bruce Wilson family, Church members from Canada, and to Stanley and Margaret Kimball, who arrived in Colombo in June 1977 to serve as special Church representatives. Reginald and Easvary Rasiah were baptized on 28 August 1977. A few of their family members and others were baptized in ensuing months.

"Our loving Heavenly Father knew the desires of our hearts," said Easvary Rasiah in her history. "He knew that we truly wanted to be in the true church. He knew we were human and [were] scared to change, therefore, he sent our son Rosignald 10,000 miles away to receive the gospel. When we found our son had joined this Church, our hearts and minds were opened to investigate and we found that this was indeed the true Church."

A Church group was formed in October and the Sri Lanka Branch was organized in March 1978 with Reginald Rasiah as president.

The Church was officially registered in Sri Lanka on 2 March 1979. By early 1980, there were 25 Church members, mostly in Colombo, and on 1 July administrative responsibility for the area shifted from the International Mission to the Singapore Mission. Book of Mormon selections were printed in Tamil in 1982 and in Sinhala in 1983.

In June 1981, Milton Rasiah became the first Church member from Sri Lanka to serve a full-time mission when he was assigned to the Philippines. In April 1985, Harold Sandrasagara and Tissa Ferdinando became the first Sri Lankans to serve as full-time missionaries in their own country.

In 1979, the Genealogical Society of Utah started microfilming Sri Lanka's vital records. The Church and the Rotary Club in Colombo worked together to start a program to teach English as a second language in February 1982. The first four teachers were sister missionaries from New Zealand, the Philippines, and the U.S.

Several senior couples served in Sri Lanka beginning in the late 1970s. They did not actively proselyte, but taught those who requested more information about the Church. Missionaries were removed from the country at different times due to civil war. Sri Lanka had one branch and 135 members in 1990. Limited numbers of young foreign missionaries were allowed to serve there beginning about the late 1990s. This led to accelerated Church growth.

A second branch was organized in Colombo in 1998 to serve the needs of Sinhala-speaking members. The Colombo Sri Lanka District was created on 22 October 2000 with Sunil Arscularatne as president. On the same day the district was organized, ground was broken for the first Church-built meetinghouse in Sri Lanka. The completed building was dedicated on 2 December 2001 by Elder John B. Dickson of the Asia Area Presidency. The first branches outside of Colombo were organized in Negombo in October 2000 and in Kandy in June 2002.

In 2003, membership reached 783.

Sources: CultureGrams 2004 World Edition, 2003; R. Lanier Britsch, From the East: The History of the Latter-day Saints in Asia, 1851-1996, 1998; George A. Smith, The Rise, Progress and Travels of the Church, 1872; Easvary Rasiah, We were thirsting for the gospel and Heavenly Father sent it to us, 1998, Church Archives; Georgene Evans, comp., History of the Church of Jesus Christ of Latter-day Saints in Colombo, Sri Lanka, 1986, Church Archives; Lyn R. Jacobs, Mormon Non-English Scriptures, Hymnals, & Periodicals, 1830-1986: A Descriptive Bibliography, 1986; Pang Beng Ling, A History of The Church of Jesus Christ of Latter-day Saints in Singapore: Journey to Stakehood, 1964-1997, 1997; Singapore Mission, Manuscript history and historical reports, Church Archives; Douglas L. Vermillion, "Gospel Splendor in Sri Lanka," Ensign, August 1995; Asia Area news, March 2002, Church Archives.

SURINAME

Jan. 1, 2011: Est. population, 481,000; Members, 1,233; Districts, 1; Branches, 6;
Percent LDS, .22, or one in 455; Caribbean Area; West Indies Mission.

Located on the Atlantic Coast at the top of South America, the Republic of Suriname has a population that speaks Dutch,

Creole, and English. They are Hindu, 27 percent; Muslim, 23 percent; and Christian, 25 percent.

The Jay and Shirley Bills family lived in Suriname from 1969 to 1972 and held their own Church services. Their daughter Lisa Bills was baptized at age 8 on 26 August 1967 in a river outside Paramaribo, the first known baptism in the country.

Former Netherlands Amsterdam Mission President John Limburg and his wife, Beverly, were called by the South America North Area Presidency to begin missionary work in Suriname. Limburg's ties to the country reach to his ancestors, who had been early Dutch colonizers of Suriname. The Limburgs arrived in Paramaribo in October 1988. By the beginning of 1989, approximately 16 people were attending services. On Easter Sunday, 26 March 1989, August Marengo and two sisters, Eleni and Maudi Treonosimitoe, became the first converts baptized.

A month later Iwan Nathaniel and Philly Denswel were baptized. Denswel's extended family lived in Lelydorp, which led the Limburgs to begin holding group meetings there and then sacrament meeting in December 1989. Membership had increased in Paramaribo so that on 22 November 1989 a branch was formally organized. By 1990, attendance at the branch averaged about 100 people. Members' ethnic backgrounds include East Indian, African, Javanese, Creolie, and Amerindian.

Elder M. Russell Ballard of the Quorum of the Twelve visited in February 1990 and offered a blessing for the country. Four men saw in the newspaper an announcement of Elder Ballard's coming to Suriname and attended the meeting. All four joined the Church, including Stanley Cooman, who became the first native branch president. In 1990, Don and Lorna Rapier received copies of pre-recorded radio broadcasts about gospel principles from missionaries in Holland and arranged for broadcasts on a local Dutch-speaking radio program. Irena Manakavera heard one of the broadcasts and was later baptized. She was influential in bringing 28 people into the Church, including several members from a local Carib Indian tribe.

In 2001, there were 495 members in Suriname. The Paramaribo chapel was dedicated on 8 July 2001 and, due to membership growth, the Paramaribo Branch was divided on 1 September 2002 to form the Wanica Branch.

Sources: Jay and Shirley Bills interview, 8 February 2003, Church Archives; Don W. and Lorna N. Rapier interview, 14 August 2003, Church Archives.

SWAZILAND

Jan. 1, 2011: Est. population, 1,124,000; Members, 1,287; Branches, 4; Districts, 1; Percent LDS, .1, or one in 993; Africa Southeast Area; South Africa Johannesburg Mission.

Swaziland is a landlocked country in southern Africa bordered by South Africa and Mozambique. The people speak Siswati and English. Sixty percent are Christian and 10 percent are Muslim, while 30 percent follow tribal beliefs.

The Robert Beckman family, Church members from Montana, lived in Swaziland from 1978 to 1981, the first known Latter-day Saints to live in the country. Robert Dlamini was the first known Swazi to join the Church. He was baptized in 1979 while in Cardiff, Wales. He returned to Swaziland after graduation. A group of non-African Latter-day Saints moved to Swaziland in the mid-1980s. To meet the needs of this group, the Mbabane Branch was organized on 5 November 1985, with George Gardner as president. Two years later, the Church received legal recognition in February 1987. Senior missionary couple Kenneth and Betty Edwards arrived that same year.

The first missionary from Swaziland, Paulo Cipriano Zandamela, a Mozambican, served in the Pennsylvania Philadelphia Mission from 1989 to 1991. Fikile Nolwazi Dlamini was the first native Swazi to serve a mission. She was in the England London Mission from 1989 to 1991. Elder Neal A. Maxwell was the first member of the Quorum of the Twelve to visit the country on 21 February 1990.

The Mbabane Swaziland District was created on 18 January 1991, but it was disbanded when its units were incorporated into the Benoni South Africa Stake on 7 May 1995.

Swaziland's first meetinghouse, built for the Mbabane Branch, was dedicated on 18 July 1993, in a ceremony attended by government representatives and presided over by Elder Richard P. Lindsay of the Seventy.

In 1995, the Swazi units became part of the Durban South Africa Stake and in 1999 they became part of the newly created Hillcrest South Africa Stake.

Membership in 2003 was 886.

Sources: A brief history of the South Africa Durban Mission, 1999, Church Archives; South Africa Mission, Manuscript history and historical reports, Church Archives; South Africa Johannesburg Mission, Manuscript history and historical reports, Church Archives; South Africa Durban Mission, Manuscript history and historical reports, Church Archives; Borgna Brunner, "Countries of the World, Swaziland," Time Almanac 2004.

SWEDEN

Jan. 1, 2011: Est. population, 9,060,000; Members, 9,206; Stakes, 4; Wards, 24; Branches, 16; Missions, 1; Districts, 1; Temples, 1; percent LDS, .10, or one in 1,010; Europe Area.

Located in northern Europe on the east side of the Scandinavian Peninsula, the kingdom of Sweden is a constitutional monarchy. Its population speaks Swedish, Finnish, and Sámi, and is 87 percent Lutheran. Other religions represented include Roman Catholic, Baptist, Muslim, Jewish, Buddhist and Latter-day Saint.

The first missionary to Sweden was John Erik Forsgren, a Swedish seaman who joined the Church in Boston, Mass., in

1843 and then moved to Nauvoo, Ill., to be with the Saints.

At the October 1849 General Conference in Salt Lake City, Utah, Elder Erastus Snow of the Quorum of the Twelve was assigned to establish the Church in Scandinavia, and Peter O. Hansen was called as a missionary to Denmark. When these assignments were announced, Forsgren petitioned for an opportunity to join in the work. He was called to go to Sweden. The three men left Utah in October 1849. Snow and Forsgren arrived in Copenhagen, Denmark, in June 1850. Forsgren continued on to his home town of Gävle, Sweden, where he immediately commenced preaching the gospel. His first convert was his brother Peter Adolf Forsgren who was converted after a priesthood healing of a severe illness. His baptism on 26 July 1850 was the first in Sweden. A few additional converts were baptized before Forsgren was arrested and banished.

In 1853, Anders W. Winberg and others began missionary labors in southern Sweden. On 24 April 1853, the Skönabäck Branch was established. Within a short time, small branches were also established at Malmö, Loma, and Lund. These four branches were organized into the Skåne Conference on 25 June 1854.

From a base of strength in the south, missionary work pushed northward where the Stockholm Branch was organized on 31 December 1854, followed by Göteborg, 5 September 1857, Norrköping, 12 May 1858; and Sundsvall or Norland 12 June 1859.

In 1878, the Book of Mormon was printed in the Swedish language. The translation had been prepared by John C. Sandberg and August W. Carlson. Translations of the Doctrine and Covenants and Pearl of Great Price into Swedish were published in 1888 and 1927, respectively.

In 1904, the Church purchased a large apartment building in Stockholm that provided space for a meetinghouse and offices. It was the first building owned by the Church in Sweden and the only Church-owned property in the country until small meetinghouses were purchased in the 1930s in Göteborg and Vingåker.

In 1905, Sweden was taken from the Scandinavian Mission, and the Swedish Mission was organized with four conferences. From humble beginnings in Sweden, from 1850 to 1930, the centennial year of the Church, 19,147 Swedes joined the Church. Of that number, 8,545 immigrated to the United States to join the Saints in the intermountain west.

In 1904, the First Presidency encouraged members outside of the United States to remain and build the Church where they live. For Swedish Saints, this counsel was personalized in 1910 when Church President Joseph F. Smith, while attending a Church conference in Stockholm, encouraged the members not to immigrate to Utah. Also in 1910, the Swedish government completed a study of Mormon immigration which incorrectly assessed that it was a vehicle of the white slave trade and recommended that Mormon Swedes be barred from immigrating.

Continuing concern about Mormon plural marriage and immigration caused Sweden's two houses of Parliament to address the issue in legislative sessions between 1912 and 1915. Each year from 1912 through 1914 Parliament allocated funds to counter Mormon missionary activities through printing of anti-Mormon publications and in any other ways deemed effective. During this period missionary work was still allowed but missionaries met with significant opposition as anti-Mormon information was widely distributed. The Parliament in 1915 questioned the accuracy of some of the critical reports about the Church and refused to fund further anti-Mormon campaigns.

Sweden was not a participant in World War I, but the effects of the war impacted the Church there. In October 1914, the Swedish Mission sent 37 American elders back to the United States in keeping with instructions from the European Mission. The few remaining missionaries and a number of members filled the leadership positions vacated by missionaries. Theodore Tobiason, for instance, served for a time simultaneously as branch, district, and mission president.

In 1920, Sweden's Department of Foreign Affairs restricted the issuance of visas to Mormon missionaries. Swedish Church members filed an appeal with the king, and on 11 April 1921, the American Minister to Sweden informed the government that the Church was willing to pay expenses of any investigative body the Swedish government might wish to send to Utah. In 1923, the American Consulate petitioned the Royal Minister for Foreign Affairs, this time accusing the Swedish government of discrimination against American citizens based on religious affiliation. He assured them that the Church no longer practiced plural marriage. In June 1924, Sweden relented and began issuing visas to Latter-day Saint missionaries. The effects of an economic depression in the 1920s and of continued anti-Mormon articles published in influential Swedish newspapers caused difficulties for the missionary work in the 1920s-1930s.

In 1936, mission President Gustive O. Larsen initiated a public relations program to correct misconceptions about plural marriage and other issues. He visited with Crown Prince Gustaf Adolf in the Stockholm Castle in March 1938 in connection with the tercentenary of Swedish settlement in America. Newspapers began printing articles that included positive content about Mormon contributions to cultural, financial, and academic fields. During August 1937, President Heber J. Grant held meetings in Stockholm, Göteborg, and Malmö increasing positive exposure and contacts for the Church. Missionaries were organized into exhibition basketball teams and a singing group, "The Harmony Singers," performed for clubs and associations.

Even though Sweden positioned itself as a neutral country during World War II, it nevertheless mobilized for war. All missionaries were evacuated from Sweden in October 1939 and local missionary C. Fritz Johansson was set apart as president. During the war, Swedish Saints sent packages of food and clothing to Saints in Russian-occupied Finland and German-occupied Norway. Member missionaries continued to do missionary work during the war.

By 1946, missionaries from America were again serving in Sweden, which received 66 missionaries that year. Within a few years, the mission had a full complement of about 100 missionaries. Anti-Mormon prejudices were largely forgotten, but missionaries struggled to generate interest in the gospel among a people that was becoming less religiously inclined. Even so, a number of converts were baptized, and growth of the Church justified creation of districts in Lulea and Sundsvall in May 1947 and Gävle and Karlskrona in 1948.

In 1952, Sweden passed a law guaranteeing religious freedoms for all non-state churches. This greatly aided the Church in its efforts to purchase property and meetinghouses. Properties bought previously were held in the name of real estate trusts signed by local members. This development was well timed for the Church in Sweden which purchased, remodeled and dedicated 22 meetinghouses during the 1950s.

Sweden participated in the Building Missionary Program in the early 1960s. In a two-year period, 1963-1965, 25 Swedes were called as building missionaries. During the same period, just 13 were called as proselyting missionaries. It was through this program that the first Latter-day Saint meetinghouse built by the Church was erected in the Stockholm suburb of Gubbängen. During the same period, brick meetinghouses were also built through the program in Göteborg and Malmö.

The Church hosted a Nordic Area conference on 16-18 August 1974 in Stockholm. Increasing Swedish membership necessitated creation of the Stockholm Sweden Stake on 20 April 1975 and the Göteborg Sweden Stake on 20 November 1977. Additional stakes were created in the 1990s in Malmö and Stockholm.

The Stockholm Sweden Temple was dedicated on 2 July 1985 by Gordon B. Hinckley.

On 24 March 1988, President Thomas S. Monson, then second counselor in the First Presidency, took part in Sweden's observance of the 350th anniversary of the first Swedish settlement in the United States. He exchanged greetings with King Carl XVI Gustaf and Queen Silvia. Also taking part in the event was Church-member Gregory J. Newell, U.S. ambassador to Sweden. On 23 August 1995, President Monson hosted King Carl XVI Gustaf and Queen Silvia on a visit to the Stockholm Temple grounds.

The 150th anniversary of the first baptism in Sweden was observed on 25-26 July 2000 in a series of events in Gävle, Sweden. The event received national attention. As a follow-up to that celebration, a monument memorializing John E. Forsgren, the first missionary to Sweden, was dedicated on 26 July 2001 in a city-owned park in Gävle adjacent to the Forsgren family home.

Göteborg, Sweden was one of eight seaports in Europe visited by the Sea Trek 2001 sailing ships that commemorated in August 2001 the 19th century emigration of European converts to Zion.

In 2002, membership reached 8,678.

Sources: Andrew Jenson, Encyclopedic History of the Church, 1941; Gerald Myron Haslam, Clash of Cultures: The Norwegian Experience with Mormonism, 1842-1920, 1984; Arnold K. Garr, Donald Q. Cannon, and Richard O. Cowan, eds., Encyclopedia of Latter-day Saint History, 2000; Lyn R. Jacobs, Mormon non-English scriptures, hymnals, and periodicals, 1830-1986, 1986; A. Dean Wengreen, History of the Church in Sweden 1850-1905, 1968; Carl-Erik Johansson, History of the Swedish Mission of the Church, 1905-1973, 1973; "The Saints in Scandinavia," Ensign, July 1974; John L. Hart, "Sweden: Members Mold Lives to Gospel Ideals, Look to Growth," Church News, 21 November 1987; Gerry Avant, "Royal Couple Visits at Swedish Temple with Pres. Monson," Church News, 2 September 1995; "Sweden Festivities Note 150-Year Anniversary," Church News, 19 August 2000; R. Scott Lloyd, "Sweden's First Missionary Memorialized," Church News, 4 August 2001; David M.W. Pickup, "Zion's Call Answered by 'Torrent' of Saints Crossing Sea," Church News, 4 August 2001; "CD-ROM a Treasury of Scandinavian Family History," Church News, 4 August 2001; David M.W. Pickup, "Largest Family History Exhibition in Sweden," Church News, 18 August 2001.

Stakes — 4
(Listed alphabetically as of Oct. 1, 2011.)

No.	Name	Organized	First President
	Europe Area		
880	*Göteborg Sweden		
	*Goeteborg Sweden	7 Jan 1991	
	‡Goteborg Sweden	20 Nov 1977	Arne Lennart Hedberg
2226	Malmö Sweden	1 Sep 1996	C. Urban Girhammar
691	Stockholm Sweden	20 Apr 1975	Evert W. Perciwall
2088	Stockholm Sweden South	20 Aug 1995	Ulf Arne Gilhammer

Mission — 1
(As of Oct. 1, 2011; shown with historical number. See MISSIONS.)

(145) SWEDEN STOCKHOLM MISSION
Box 2087
S-183 02 Taby, Sweden

SWITZERLAND

Jan. 1, 2011: Est. population, 7,604,000; Members, 8,092; Stakes, 5; Wards, 26; Branches, 10; Missions, 1; Temples, 1; percent LDS, .10, or one in 958; Europe Area.

In central Europe, Switzerland is a federal republic with a population that speaks German, 65 percent; French, 18 percent; Italian, 12 percent; and Romansch, 1 percent. The Swiss people are 49 percent Roman Catholic and 48 percent Protestant.

In September of 1848, a new Swiss law established freedom of religion for all of its citizens. Two years later, T.B.H. Stenhouse, who had been laboring as a missionary in Italy, arrived in Geneva, and began missionary work there in late November or early December of 1850.

In February of 1851 Lorenzo Snow and Stenhouse dedicated Switzerland for the preaching of the gospel. By March of that year, Stenhouse reported having performed several baptisms. By the fall of 1851 Stenhouse expanded his efforts to Lausanne and by the end of the year reported about 20 converts in Geneva and Lausanne. His success was followed by the organization of the Geneva Branch in the Spring of 1852.

It was not until 14 February 1853 that missionaries T.B.H. Stenhouse, Serge Ballif, and Frederick Roulet preached in Basel, Switzerland, the first missionary effort in the German-speaking portion of Switzerland. Subsequent missionary efforts expanded into the German and French-speaking portions of Switzerland thereafter, but the years 1858 through 1868 were met with increased opposition from local government officials.

In 1864, having investigated the accusations against the Church and its doctrine, a Swiss government official declared that Latter- day Saints were in fact, Christians. On 1 January 1868, the Swiss and German mission was formed having changed it's name from the Swiss, German and Italian Mission. It became the Swiss Mission in 1898, only to revert to the Swiss and German Mission in 1904.

In June of 1886 a police chief published a report on the alleged destitute conditions of Swiss Latter-day Saints living in Utah. Over 300 Swiss Latter-day Saints responded with a petition published in the Bern newspaper stating that the claims of the official were untrue. In 1887, however, the Church leaders discontinued encouraging converts to emigrate to Zion, and in 1899 they began actively encouraging Latter-day Saints to remain in their homelands to build up the Church there.

Moreover, on 7 August 1906 President Joseph F. Smith visited Switzerland where he promised that the time would come when the land would be dotted with temples.

The French-speaking portion of Switzerland came under the jurisdiction of the newly created French Mission on 15 October 1912, but it reverted to the Swiss and German Mission in September 1914 with the advent of World War I. Stewardship of the region returned to the French Mission on 23 December 1923.

With the beginning of World War I, missionaries were evacuated and local branches were left to local leaders. Hyrum Valentine continued to supervise the mission from Basel until late 1916 when Angus J. Cannon arrived as his replacement. In 1919, Cannon purchased supplies for relief of the Latter-day Saints who had suffered the ravages of war in Germany. Some supplies were distributed to Swiss Latter-day Saints who had also suffered deprivations during the war.

In November of 1939, as the non-Swiss missionaries and mission presidents evacuated due to World War II, Max Zimmer was left in charge of the German-speaking portion of Switzerland and Robert Simond became responsible for French-speaking Switzerland. The work progressed in spite of the war and in the spring of 1940 a meetinghouse was dedicated in Basel. In 1944, Max Zimmer received permission from the German government to visit LDS servicemen held in German prisoner of war camps.

In March 1946, Ezra Taft Benson of the Quorum of the Twelve Apostles visited Switzerland in an effort to extend welfare relief to war-ravaged Europe. He was followed on 21 June 1946 by the first missionaries to return from Utah.

In the Spring of 1946, Scott Taggart arrived in Switzerland from the United States and replaced Zimmer and Simond as mission president. French-speaking Switzerland was assigned to the Swiss-Austrian Mission. Stewardship for that portion of Switzerland did not return to the French Mission until 1957.

The Swiss Temple built in Zollikofen, Switzerland, was dedicated on 11 September 1955. Swiss Latter-day Saints no longer had to travel to the western United States to participate in temple blessings. The temple also reduced the number of Swiss Latter-day Saints who emigrated to Zion.

On 18 September 1960, the Swiss-Austrian Mission was dissolved and the Swiss Mission (now the Switzerland Zurich Mission) and Austrian missions were formed. Headquarters for the newly formed French-East Mission (now the Switzerland Geneva Mission) were established in Geneva in January 1961. The founding of the Swiss Stake (now the Zurich Switzerland Stake), the first in Switzerland, came on 27 October 1961. Swiss Mission headquarters were moved from Basel to Zurich on 21 December 1962. This move was due in part to the Church gaining permission for the first time to own property in Zurich.

Missionaries began working for the first time in the Italian-Swiss region in June of 1963. This was to be the beginning of the re-introduction of the Church into Italy. By June of 1968, the Italian-speaking portion of Switzerland was transferred to the Italian Mission.

Throughout the 1960s and 1970s, the Swiss Mission was responsible for countries where the Church had not been fully developed. These years also marked extensive construction of meetinghouses under the building missionary program adding further stability to the Church in Switzerland.

The first French-speaking stake in Switzerland was organized in Geneva on 20 June 1982 with Denis Bony as president. The Swiss Temple was rededicated on 23 October 1992 after extensive remodeling. On 26 March 1996, full-time Latter-day Saint missionaries were allowed to remain in Switzerland for the full two years. Prior to that time, their stay had been limited to 18 months.

By 2002, membership reached 7,418.

In 2003, Swiss Latter-day Saints celebrated the 150th anniversary of the beginning of the Church in Switzerland. A video recording of President Gordon B. Hinckley congratulating Swiss members was broadcast to the joy of those attending a gala celebration on July 4.

In 2003, membership reached 7,527. The Switzerland Zurich Mission was combined with the Germany Munich/Austria Mission and portions of the German Frankfurt Mission. The resulting mission was the Alpine German-Speaking Mission headquartered in Munich.

The Switzerland Geneva Mission was consolidated with the France Paris and Toulouse missions on 1 July 2011.

Sources: Andrew Jenson, Encyclopedic History of the Church, 1941; Dale Z. Kirby, History of the Church in Switzerland, thesis, 1971; "A Marvelous Harvest has Occurred in Switzerland," Church News, 19 July 2003; Donald Q. Cannon and Richard O. Cowan, Unto Every Nation: Gospel Light Reaches Every Land, 2003; Highlights from the German-speaking L.D.S. Missions, 1836-1940, Justus Ernst, Church Archives; Chronik der Kirche Jesu Christi der Heiligen der Letzten Tage in der Schweiz 1850 bis 2003; Swiss and German Mission (Switzerland Zurich Mission), Manuscript history and historical reports, Church Archives; Swiss documents relating to Mormons, 1879-1924, 1977, copy in Church Archives, originals in Swiss National Archives. New Missions, Church News, 13 Feb. 2010.

Stakes — 5
(Listed alphabetically as of Oct. 1, 2011.)

No.	Name	Organized	First President
Europe Area			
1261	Bern Switzerland	3 May 1981	Peter Lauener
2761	St. Gallen Switzerland	5 May 2007	Curdin Conrad
341	*Zurich Switzerland ‡Swiss (Switzerland, Germany)	28 Oct 1961	Wilhelm Friedrich Lauener
1352	Geneva Switzerland	20 Jun 1982	Denis Bonny
2687	Lausanne Switzerland	28 Aug 2005	Bernard S. Ochs

TAHITI
(See French Polynesia under FRANCE)

TAIWAN

Jan. 1, 2011: Est. population, 22,974,000; Members, 53,111; Stakes, 11; Wards, 83; Branches, 17; Missions, 2; Districts, 1; Temples, 1; percent LDS, .21, or one in 468; Asia Area.

Located off the southeast coast of China, Taiwan has a population that speaks Mandarin Chinese, and Taiwan and Hakka dialects. They mostly adhere to Buddhism, Taoism, and Confucianism.

In 1955, a convert to the Church, Stanley Simiskey, was stationed in Taipei, Taiwan, with the U.S. military. He found a few other Latter-day Saint servicemen and they began holding Church meetings. Simiskey served as leader of the Church group in Taipei and was on hand in March 1956 to greet President H. Grant Heaton of the Southern Far East Mission, headquartered in Hong Kong, who visited Taiwan to explore the possibility of sending missionaries there.

The first four missionaries arrived on 4 June 1956: Duane W. Degn, Keith A. Madsen, Weldon J. Kitchen, and Melvin C. Fish. Soon a branch was established in Taipei with Simiskey as president. Thomas V. Kintaro Sr., the husband of a Church member, was baptized on 22 July 1956. The first Chinese converts in Taiwan, Ch'iu Hung-hsiang and Tseng I-Chang, were baptized on 27 April 1957. By year's end, more than 50 people had joined the Church. Missionary work was started in Tainan in 1957, and in Taichung in January 1958.

In May 1958, the Chinese and American members in Taipei began holding separate meetings, and in 1959 Liang Jun-shen was called as the first local branch president. By May 1959, there were seven branches in Taiwan. Elder Mark E. Petersen of the Quorum of the Twelve was the first General Authority to visit, holding several meetings between 25 May and 1 June of that year. By September, the missionary force had grown to 46.

Elder Gordon B. Hinckley, then Assistant to the Quorum of the Twelve, visited Taiwan in May 1960, the first of his many visits to that land. In 1961, he worked with others to purchase a piece of land in Taipei. On 2 November 1963, ground was broken on the site for a Latter-day Saint chapel and Elder Hinckley dedicated the completed building on 16 October 1966. A meetinghouse was also constructed in Kaohsiung during the 1960s.

Taiwan was organized into the North, Central, and South districts on 17 November 1964. The presidents were, respectively, Liang Jun-shen, Ung Min-Tsan, and He Shuen-Ding.

In 1957, a committee was appointed in Hong Kong to translate the Book of Mormon into Chinese, but the translation was not completed. Elder Hinckley called Larry K. Browning and Hu Wei-I to start anew on the translation in Taipei in 1963. Browning left Taiwan in September 1964 and Hu finished the initial translation in November. The Chinese Book of Mormon was printed in December 1965.

The Southern Far East Mission was renamed the Hong Kong-Taiwan Mission on 1 November 1969, and on 1 January 1971, the Taiwan Mission was formed with Malan R. Jackson as president. The seminary and institute program was established in Taiwan in September 1973. By 1975, there were 7,000 members in 30 branches and about 200 full-time missionaries.

President Spencer W. Kimball presided at area conferences in Taipei in August 1975 and October 1980. Both meetings were attended by approximately 2,500 Church members and friends. During President Kimball's first visit he also met with Yen Chia-Kan, president of the Republic of China, and during his second stay he met with President Chiang Ching-kuo and Prime Minister Sun Yun-suan. Elder Gordon B. Hinckley created the Taipei Taiwan Stake on 22 April 1976 with Chang I-Ch'ing as president. Chang was later called, in November 1984, to serve as Taiwan's first local regional representative.

The Taiwan Mission was renamed the Taiwan Taipei Mission in 1974 and was divided in July 1976 to form the Taiwan Kaohsiung Mission. The Taiwan Taichung Mission was created in July 1979 and then discontinued in 1982. The next year the headquarters of the Kaohsiung Mission were moved to Taichung. The Taiwan Kaohsiung Mission was re-established in 1998. From about 1979 to the late 1990s, Taiwan saw an average of about 1,000 people join the Church each year.

On 31 March 1982, the Church announced that it would build a temple in Taiwan. It was constructed on the first Church-owned property in Taipei, adjacent to the original meetinghouse. The mission home that had stood on the site since the early 1970s was razed and the Church bought a six-story office building across the street, thereby creating a three-building complex: the temple, a meetinghouse, and administrative offices. The Taipei Taiwan Temple was dedicated by President Gordon B. Hinckley of the First Presidency on 17 November 1984.

The Taiwan track and field team trained at Brigham Young University's athletic facilities in Provo, Utah, in 1984 to prepare for the Los Angeles summer Olympics. The following year the Taiwan government invited 45 members of the BYU track and field team to compete in the National Track and Field Championships at Taitung. BYU was the only foreign team invited. In 1989, the Church and the University of Chinese Culture completed a 10-year joint project to microfilm Chinese family records throughout Taiwan, and in June of that year a week-long genealogical exhibition, attended by 6,000 persons, was held in the new National Center Library in Taipei.

Hsu Shui-The, Taiwan's Minister of Interior, visited with local Church leaders in Taipei on 3 May 1990 as part of an effort to enlist the help of religions to strengthen families. During his visit he quoted from former Church president David O. McKay: "No other success can compensate for failure in the home." The Church subsequently distributed bumper stickers displaying the slogan in Chinese characters in a successful public relations campaign.

Shih-An (Kent) Liang became the first Latter-day Saint in Taiwan called to serve as an Area Authority on 15 August 1995. Church President Gordon B. Hinckley spoke to more than 3,000 Church members and friends in the Taipei International Convention Center on 23 May 1996, 40 years after the arrival of the first missionaries, stating, "The work will prosper in this great land."

In 2002, membership reached 36,598; and 38,731 in 2003.

President Hinckley addressed some 1,200 members prior to dedicating a new Church Administration Building-Taipei on 1 August 2005. Members described the meeting as a time of memories, laughter and tears.

In 2005, membership reached 42,881.

Sources: Gary Williams, Taiwan report, 1957, in Southern Far East Mission historical reports, Church Archives; Southern Far East Mission, Manuscript history and historical reports, Church Archives; R. Lanier Britsch, From the East: The History of the Latter-day Saints in Asia, 1851-1996, 1998; Lyn R. Jacobs, Mormon Non-English Scriptures, Hymnals, & Periodicals, 1830- 1986: A Descriptive Bibliography, 1986; "History of the Church in Hong Kong," Ensign, September 1991; Taiwan Mission, Manuscript history and historical reports, Church Archives; Wang Lu-Pao, Church history in China, 1984-85, Church Archives; Janice Clark, "Taiwan: Steep Peaks and Towering Faith," Ensign, August 1975; Dell Van Orden, "Saints Throng to Area Meetings in the Far East," Church News, 1 November 1980; "At Taiwan National Meet, BYU Track Athletes Win Events, Friends," Church News, 28 April 1985; "Chinese Records Filmed," Church News, 17 June 1989; Paul Hyer, "Chinese Visit Exhibit, Learn of Ancestors," Church News, 17 June 1989; Kellene Ricks, "Official Visits the Church in Taiwan," Church News, 2 June 1990; "The Church in Taiwan–40 Years," Church News, 22 June 1996; "Church Names Area Authorities," Church News, 5 August 1995; "He Bears Testimony, Reaffirms Blessings," Church News, 8 June 1996; "Ties to Taiwan," Church News, 6 August 2005.

Stakes — 11
(Listed alphabetically as of Oct. 1, 2011.)

No.	Name	Organized	First President
Asia Area			
2643	Chung Hsing Taiwan	20 Jun 2004	
2622	Hsin Chu Taiwan	14 Dec 2003	Wei Chin Hong
1303	Kaohsiung Taiwan	6 Nov 1981	Ho Tung Hai
2872	Kaohsiung Taiwan East	28 Feb 2010	Lei Yang
2003	Taichung Taiwan	18 Dec 1994	Chou, Wen Tsung
2759	Taichung Taiwan North	21 Apr 2007	Chang, Jui Sheng
2373	Tainan Taiwan	15 Jun 1997	Hsin-chin Chen
2468	Taipei Taiwan Central	24 May 1998	Shuei-Tyan Konrad Tzeng
1326	Taipei Taiwan East	14 Mar 1982	Yuan-Hu Yen
755	*Taipei Taiwan West	14 Mar 1982	
	‡Taipei Taiwan	22 Apr 1976	I-Ch'ing Chang
2598	Tao Yuan Taiwan Stake	08 Jul 2001	Chen, Cheng Erh Michael

Missions —2
(As of Oct. 1, 2011; shown with historical number. See MISSIONS.)

(146) TAIWAN TAICHUNG MISSION
498-11 Wu Chuan Road
Taichung 404-46
Taiwan, ROC

(94) TAIWAN TAIPEI MISSION
Floor 4, No. 24, Lane 183
Chin Hua Street
Taipei 106, Taiwan ROC

TANZANIA

Jan. 1, 2011: Est. population, 41,049,000; Members, 1,007; District, 1; Branches, 5; Percent LDS, .002 or one in 51,504; Africa Southeast Area; Kenya Nairobi Mission.

On the east coast of Africa, Tanzania is a republic with its people speaking Swahili and English. The people are Muslim, 35 percent; Christian, 30 percent; and the remainder follow tribal beliefs.

In the mid-1970s, expatriate Latter-day Saints moved to Tanzania to work in embassies, humanitarian aid organizations, and on construction projects. They reported to the International Mission, from which they received Church literature and encouragement. Courtney H. Brewer and his family, while living in Tanzania, received permission in 1982 to baptize an

Indian family, Itty Mathew and Grace Sunny Panakkal, who were Brewer's co-workers. This was the first baptism in Tanzania.

The first Church leader to visit Tanzania was Elder J Ballard Washburn, a counselor in the Africa Area Presidency. He went to Dar es Salaam in March 1991. In July 1991 he and H. Thomas Kay, area legal counsel, returned to Tanzania, where they met with government officials to determine the requirements for registering the Church. Legal recognition was approved on 8 October 1992. J. Clifford Wallace, a Latter-day Saint and Chief Judge of the U.S. Court of Appeals in San Diego, Calif., assisted in the process by helping to establish contact with government officials.

Tanzania became part of the Kenya Nairobi Mission when the mission was created in July 1991. The next month, Bruce Wilson and his family from Smith Falls, Ontario, Canada, arrived in Dar es Salaam. The Wilson family began holding meetings in September 1991.

Native Tanzanian Robert Muhile was baptized in Cairo, Egypt, before the arrival of missionaries in Tanzania. After returning to Tanzania, he felt a need to once again partake of the sacrament, so he traveled to Nairobi, Kenya, because he was unaware of the Wilsons holding Church meetings in their home.

On 17 January 1992, following a two-day journey and four days of wandering the streets of Nairobi, Muhile saw a sign for the Church and was soon directed to Lervae and Joyce Cahoon, a missionary couple who had just been informed that they would be the first missionaries to serve in Tanzania. Muhile served as the Cahoons' guide and translator when they arrived in Dar es Salaam in February 1992.

In October 1992 the Dar es Salaam Branch, the first in Tanzania, was created, with Bruce Wilson as president. Robert Muhile was called as Dar es Salaam Branch president on 13 March 1994.

In March 2002, members of the Church in Tanzania made a 68-hour bus trip to the Johannesburg South Africa Temple, a trip that had been in the planning stages since July 2001. During the temple sessions, 27 members received their endowments and 10 couples and 10 families were sealed.

Membership was 639 in 2003. In 2005, it reached 751.

Sources: Kenya Nairobi Mission history, 1998, Church Archives; "Determined to Keep Covenants," Church News, 18 May 2002.

THAILAND

Jan. 1, 2011: Est. population, 65,905,000; Members,16,331; Stakes, 1; Wards, 7; Branches, 30; Districts, 5; Missions, 1; percent LDS, .02, or one in 4,152; Asia Area.

Thailand is a constitutional monarchy located on the Indochinese and Malay Peninsula. The Thai-speaking population is 95 percent Buddhist and 4 percent Muslim.

In October 1853, Brigham Young called four missionaries to preach the gospel in Siam (renamed Thailand in 1939). They labored in India, Ceylon, and Burma, but only one, Elam Luddington, made it to Siam, arriving in Bangkok on 6 April 1854. The next day he preached a public discourse and after the meeting baptized James Trail and his wife. Luddington worked in Bangkok for another four months but had little success. He departed on 12 August 1854.

The Church's next formal activity in Thailand occurred in June 1961 when a few Latter-day Saint families from the U.S. began holding Church meetings in Bangkok. They were organized into a group in early 1962 with Max Berryessa as leader. The escalation of the Vietnam War led to increased numbers of military personnel being stationed in Thailand. Some were Church members. Servicemen's groups were established at U.S. Air Force bases in Udorn, Ubon, Thakli, and Khorat. On 21 January 1966, Jim McElvee, a serviceman, became the first known convert baptized in Thailand since 1854.

President Keith E. Garner of the Southern Far East Mission formed the Thailand District on 27 March 1966 with Stirling Merrill as president. In July, Merrill organized the Bangkok Branch with Gordon M. Flammer as president. Nangnoi Thitapoora was baptized on 11 September 1966. She was the first known Thai to join the Church. In November of that year Elders Gordon B. Hinckley of the Quorum of the Twelve and Marion D. Hanks of the Seventy visited Bangkok and investigated the requirements for registering the Church in Thailand. The Church was officially recognized there on 1 November 1967.

Six full-time proselyting missionaries arrived in Bangkok on 2 February 1968: Peter W. Basker, Craig G. Christensen, L. Carl Hansen, Alan H. Hess, Larry R. White, and Robert W. Winegar. They enrolled in Thai language classes and received further language assistance from Anan Eldredge, a young man who had joined the Church several weeks earlier. The missionaries began actively sharing the gospel on 6 March 1968. They saw the first fruits of their labors on 18 May, when Boonpluke and Rabiap Klaophin, husband and wife, were baptized. The Thai group was organized in Bangkok the next month, on 9 June. Missionaries were sent to Khorat before the end of the year. In January 1969, Anan Eldredge became the first Thai to serve a full-time mission in his native country.

Elder Ezra Taft Benson of the Quorum of the Twelve visited Bangkok on 1 December 1968 and presented a copy of the Book of Mormon to King Bhumibol Adulyadej. In November 1969, Thailand became part of the Southeast Asia Mission, headquartered in Singapore. Missionary work began in Chiang Mai and Khon Kaen in 1970 and in 12 other cities over the next six years.

The Church in Thailand suffered a major setback in July 1972 when two missionaries were arrested for disgracing a Buddha. They were imprisoned for six months.

The Church created the Thailand Mission in August 1973, which was renamed the Thailand Bangkok Mission the following year. Elder David B. Haight, an Assistant to the Twelve, dedicated the first Church-constructed meetinghouse in Bangkok on 28 August 1974, on property that the Church had acquired in 1967. At the time of the dedication there were 395 native members of the Church in Thailand, plus 335 foreign members.

In May 1975, mission President Paul D. Morris organized a missionary performing group in an effort to make the Church more visible. They performed on television, in schools, and at church functions. By the time the group was finally disbanded in July 1979, it had recorded five music albums and given live performances to more than 1 million people, including Queen Sirikit and King Bhumibol. When Queen Sirikit and Princess Chulabhorn visited the United States in 1981, the Church hosted them from 25-28 October, during which time the Tabernacle Choir performed a concert in their honor.

The Book of Mormon was printed in Thai in October 1976. Several people worked on the translation beginning when it was commissioned in late 1969, but Sister Srilaksana Gottsche, a 1968 convert, played a leading role throughout.

In November 1980, 10 welfare services missionaries, headed by Rita M. Edmonds, began serving at a new refugee camp near Phanat Nikhom. They taught western culture and English to Cambodian, Hmong-Yao, Laotian and Vietnamese refugees to help ease their transitions into life in other nations. The missionaries did not teach the gospel except by example. However, a number of refugees sought out the Church after reaching their destinations and were baptized. Missionaries continued to work at the camp until it closed in 1990.

Anan Eldredge became the first Thai to preside over the Thailand Bangkok Mission on 1 July 1988. In a meeting with district and ward leaders in October 1989 he challenged them to prepare to obtain temple blessings for themselves and families at the Manila Philippines Temple in six months. As a result, 201 Thai Saints traveled to the temple in June 1990 to be endowed and sealed as families.

Prior to 1992, missionaries in Thailand were required to leave the country every few months to renew their visas. Beginning in September 1992, the government granted one-year visas to Latter-day Saint missionaries and increased the number of visas issued. This enabled the Church to open several new areas and the number of convert baptisms increased. Elder Neal A. Maxwell of the Quorum of the Twelve and Kwok Yuen Tai of the Asia Area presidency organized the Thailand Bangkok Stake with Thipparat Kitsaward as president on 17-18 June 1995. Church membership passed 6,000 that year.

In July 1997, Latter-day Saint Charities sent 20 missionary sisters and couples to Thailand to assist English teachers in Bangkok schools. Bangkok Gov. Bhichit Rattakul, a non-Mormon graduate of BYU, informed the missionaries, "This is the first time in our history that any of our 429 Bangkok schools will have foreign teachers." BYU-Hawaii made an agreement with the Thai government in 1998 to provide between six-to-eight full four-year scholarships each year to some of Thailand's top high school students.

President Gordon B. and his wife, Marjorie, visited Thailand on 12-13 June 2000 and met with Prime Minister Chuan Leekpai and other government leaders. President Hinckley, in the first visit of a Church president to Thailand, also addressed a meeting of more than 2,600 Church members and friends. He reflected on his earlier visits and said, "Now it's been a long time since I was here and I have seen a miracle, a very real miracle."

In 2003, there were 38,731 members. In 2005, membership reached 14,652.

Sources: CultureGrams 2004 World Edition, 2003; R. Lanier Britsch, From the East: The History of the Latter-day Saints in Asia, 1851-1996, 1998; Siam Mission, Manuscript history and historical reports, Church Archives; Larry R. White, A short history of the Church in Thailand, 1993, Church Archives; Southern Far East Mission, Manuscript history and historical reports, Church Archives; Brief history of Bangkok Branch, 1961-1968, circa 1968, Church Archives; Southeast Asia Mission, Manuscript history and historical reports, Church Archives; "Thailand Chapel is Dedicated," Church News, 19 October 1974; Thailand Bangkok Mission, Manuscript history and historical reports, Church Archives; "Helping Refugees Begin New Life,"Church News, 21 March 1981; "Church Welcomes Thai Royalty," Ensign, January 1982; "Work, Sacrifice, Bring 201 Thais to Manila Temple," Church News, 11 August 1990; "Missionaries Assist English Teachers in Bangkok," Church News, 26 July 1997; "Six BYU-Hawaii Scholarships Available to Thailand Students," Church News, 29 July 2000; "'We Have Been on a Long Journey – But It Was a Great Occasion,'" Church News, 1 July 2000.

Stake — 1
(Listed alphabetically as of Oct. 1, 2011.)

No.	Name	Organized	First President
Asia Area			
2064	Bangkok Thailand	18 Jun 1995	Thipparad Kitsaward

Mission — 1
(As of Oct. 1, 2011; shown with historical number. See MISSIONS.)

(109) THAILAND BANGKOK MISSION
50/829-832 Muang Thong Thani
Chaengwatana Rd., T. Ban Mai, A. Pakkret
Nonthaburi 11120
Thailand

TOGO

Jan. 1, 2011: Est. population, 6,020,000; Members, 1,246; Districts, 1; Branches, 5; Percent LDS, .01; or one in 7,591; Africa West Area.

Togo became an independent nation on 27 April 1960. Twenty-nine percent of the people are Christian, 12 percent Muslim, while the rest of the population are Hindu and Buddhist. French is the official language, while Ewe, Mina, Kabye, and Dagomba are also spoken.

Africa Area President James O. Mason organized the Lomé Togo group on 15 July 1997 with Agnon Améri Didier as presiding elder. There were by this time about 25 Latter-day Saints living there. In October 1998, 12 dancers from Togo joined the Church while at a dance festival in Bountiful, Utah. Due to unrest in the country, they had difficulties returning to their homeland.

On 19 February 1999, Togo came under the Ivory Coast Abidjan Mission. That same month, the first missionary couple, Demoine A. and Joyce Findlay, began missionary work in Togo and on 21 February 1999, the Lomé Branch was organized with Dieudonne Attiogbe as president. In December 1999, Robert C. and Marilyn Witt were transferred to Togo. Part of their assignment was to seek to obtain legal recognition of the Church. Recognition was granted in July 2000. Church Educational System classes began to be taught in the late 1990s.

The first Lomé Branch conference was held 17 December 2000.

Sources: "5 New Areas Announced Worldwide," Church News, 4 July 1998; Sarah Jane Weaver, "Church Education: Students are Real Success of Seminary, Institute," Church News, 17 August 2002; Gerrit and Judy Steenblik, "State of the Mission for the Mission Reunion, April 2003," Ivory Coast Abidjan Mission website, http://www.mission.net/ivory- coast/abidjan/, accessed 30 April 2004; Alumni, Ivory Coast Abidjan Mission website, http://www.mission.net/ivory-coast/abidjan, as of 30 April 2004.

TONGA

Jan. 1, 2011: Est. population, 121,000; Members, 58,805; Stakes, 17; Wards, 129; Districts, 1; Branches, 36; Missions, 1; Temples, 1; percent LDS, 45, or one in 2.2; Pacific Area; Tonga Nuku'Alofa Mission.

In the western South Pacific, the kingdom of Tonga is a constitutional monarchy whose population speaks Tongan and English. Tongans are Free Wesleyan, Latter-day Saints, Roman Catholic, Church of Tonga, and Free Church of Tonga.

The first Latter-day Saint missionaries to Tonga were Brigham Smoot and Alva J. Butler, sent by Samoan Mission President William O. Lee. They arrived on 15 July 1891 and soon met with King Jiaoji (George) Tubou and received permission to preach. They acquired property, erected a mission home and school, and purchased a boat to travel between islands. The first convert was Alipate, who was baptized on 15 July 1892. However, the mission made little progress and was closed in 1897.

Missionary work resumed in 1907 by William O. Facer and Heber J. McKay under the direction of the Samoan Mission. They opened a school in Nieafu on the island of Vava'u, and by 1908, there were 28 day students and 13 night students. Facer later went to Ha'alaufuli where he was successful in organizing a branch with 32 converts. Missionary work opened on the main island of Tongatapu on 17 March 1911, and by December 1912, a meetinghouse and school had been completed and a conference organized. The Tongan Mission was reopened on 11 May 1916 with the arrival of a new mission president, Willard L. Smith.

Tonga became a protectorate of Great Britain following World War I and missionaries experienced problems obtaining visas. Consequently, the number of missionaries in Tonga declined. In 1921, Elder David O. McKay of the Quorum of the Twelve visited Tonga, but was quarantined on a nearby island for 11 days before he was allowed to enter the country. This hindrance was the result of anti-Mormon influences on Tongan government officials, culminating in passage of an exclusion law in June 1922. It prohibited Latter-day Saints from entering Tonga. The continued denial of visas to missionaries led to the calling of locals to do missionary work and serve in positions of leadership. In 1921, Elder David O. McKay of the Quorum of the Twelve visited Tonga, but was quarantined on a nearby island for 11 days before he was allowed to enter the country. This hindrance was the result of anti-Mormon influences on Tongan government officials, culminating in passage of an exclusion law in June 1922. It prohibited Latter-day Saints from entering Tonga. The continued denial of visas to missionaries led to the calling of locals to do missionary work and serve in positions of leadership. The exclusion law was repealed in 1924 due to the efforts of mission president M. Vernon Coombs. Shortly after the law's repeal, Coombs obtained a property lease on which he started a school, called The Makeke school, meaning "arise and awake." It opened in 1926 and became the foundation for an enlarged school system in later years. The use of local missionaries continued through the 1930s and 1940s.

Elder George Albert Smith of the Quorum of the Twelve visited Tonga 10 May-8 June 1938. His encouragement and teaching had an inspiring effect on the missionaries and members resulting in 117 new members being baptized in 1938. The Tongan Mission did not have more than 100 convert baptisms in a given year until 1954.

All foreign missionaries were called home during World War II, but many Latter-day Saint servicemen were stationed on Tongatapu and attended local meetings. After the war, foreign missionaries were once again restricted from entering Tonga, with the exception of the mission president and his family. Publication of the Book of Mormon in 1946 helped strengthen the Church. Membership in Tonga in 1946 was 2,422. Mission presidents called local missionaries in what became one of the most successful local missionary programs in the Church.

Much of the progress on the islands has been through Church schools. The establishing of schools in 1892 and 1908 proved significant, and led to other schools starting. The Makeke School was the principal method of advancing the Church for many years. In 1947, the Church obtained the lease on a 276-acre plantation outside of Nuku'alofa not far from Makeke to build an expanded school campus named "Liahona." Liahona High School opened in 1952. Building the school represented the beginning of the Church's labor missionary program and probably the catalyst for expansion of the Church in Tonga.

There was a great contrast between David O. McKay's visit to Tonga as an apostle in 1921 and his visit as president of the Church in January 1955, when he received a welcome that was ordinarily reserved for royalty and nobles. During his brief stay, President McKay prophetically stated to the Tongan Saints in Vava'u, "Do you know what I saw today, in vision? A temple on one of these islands, where the members of the Church may go and receive the blessings of the temple of God. You are entitled to it." Between 1952 and 1968, the Church in Tonga grew from 3,280 members to almost 12,000, due in part to strong local priesthood leadership in the branches, the reputation of Liahona High School in attracting non-Mormon youth to attend – a high percentage of which eventually joined the Church – and the training of unmarried young Tongans to serve on local missions. The Nuku'alofa Stake, Tonga's first stake, was created on 5 September 1968 with Orson H. White as president. After that, the Church in Tonga was led almost exclusively by local members, including its mission, many of the schools, and the stakes.

President Spencer W. Kimball visited Tonga in February 1976 and spoke to 10,600 members at an area conference in Nuku'alofa. The Tonga Nuku'alofa Temple, located adjacent to Liahona High School, was dedicated 9-11 August 1983. In 1991, Tongan Saints celebrated the centennial of the Church in Tonga that included a dance festival in which 3,000 youths performed for King Taufa'ahau Topou IV. President Gordon B. Hinckley visited Nuku'alofa on 14 October 1997 and spoke to some 11,400 people and met Tonga's King Taufa'ahau Topou IV.

In 2002, membership reached 49,719.

Sources: R. Lanier Britsch, Unto the Islands of the Sea, 1986; David W. Cummings, Mighty Missionary of the Pacific, 1961; "Celebrating 100 Years in Tonga," Church News, 31 August 1991; Gerry Avant, "Prophet Goes to Islands of the Pacific," Church News, 25 October 1997; Tongan Mission, Manuscript history and historical reports, Church Archives; Samoan Mission, Manuscript history and historical reports, Church Archives.

Stakes — 17
(Listed alphabetically as of Oct. 1, 2011.)

No.	Name	Organized	First President
Pacific Area			
2174	Eua Tonga	26 Feb 1996	Tuifio Finau
1430	Ha'apai Tonga	14 Jun 1983	Fanongonongo Vaitai
737	Neiafu Vava'u Tonga	4 Dec 1975	Mosese Hetau Langi

1172	Neiafu Vava'u Tonga North	27 Aug 1980	Mosese Hetau Langi
2092	Neiafu Vava'u Tonga West	27 Aug 1995	Tukia'i Vava'u Havea
463	*Nuku'alofa Tonga		
	‡Nuku'alofa	5 Sep 1968	Orson Hyde White
1986	Nuku'alofa Tonga Central	31 Jul 1994	Filimone Fie'eiki
550	*Nuku'alofa Tonga East		
	‡Nuku'alofa East	21 Jul 1971	Viliami Pele Folau
2175	Nuku'alofa Tonga Ha'akame	10 Mar 1996	Sosaia Lehonitai Mateaki
2083	Nuku'alofa Tonga Halaliku	3 Aug 1995	Staleki Tonga Faemani
2806a	Nuku'alofa Tonga Harbour	22 June 2008	Hakeai Vehekie Piutau
1173	Nuku'alofa Tonga Liahona	31 Aug 1980	Vaikalafi Lutui
2188	Nuku'alofa Tonga Mu'a	21 Apr 1996	J. William Harris
1445	Nuku'alofa Tonga North	9 Oct 1983	Sione Moala Fineanganofa
519	*Nuku'alofa Tonga South		
	‡Nuku'alofa South	26 Jul 1970	Tevita Folau Mahuinga
1431	Nuku'alofa Tonga Vaini	15 Jun 1983	Samuela Iloa
520	*Nuku'alofa Tonga West		
	‡Nuku'alofa West	26 Jul 1970	Orson H. White

Mission — 1

(As of Oct. 1, 2011; shown with historical number. See MISSIONS.)

(22c) TONGA NUKU'ALOFA MISSION
P.O. Box 58
Nuku'Alofa, Tonga

TRINIDAD & TOBAGO

Jan. 1, 2011: Est. population, 1,230,000; Members, 2,885; Stake, 1; Wards, 5; Branches, 6; Missions, 1; percent LDS, .2 or one in 494; Caribbean Area.

Off the east coast of Venezuela in the Caribbean Sea, Trinidad & Tobago is a parliamentary democracy where the people speak English as the official language. The major religions are Roman Catholic, 32 percent; Protestant, 29 percent; and Hindu, 25 percent.

A visit to England by Elizabeth Rogers led to her baptism there in April 1974. When she moved back to Trinidad in 1976, she wrote to President Spencer W. Kimball requesting missionaries. Howard J. Marsh, Venezuela Caracas Mission president, sent missionaries into the country for short periods of time as early as March 1975, but official recognition of the Church was denied and permanent missionary work could not be established for many years.

Among the first converts to the Church were Lucy Payne and the Basil D. and Felicia Borde family baptized in 1977 by missionaries Daniel Rector and Michael Willis. Basil Borde worked as a newspaperman and wrote articles about the Church in order to dispel misconceptions held by public and government officials. During a visit to Trinidad by Elder Gene R. Cook of the Seventy and Venezuela Caracas Mission President Dale E. Miller, the Trinidad Branch was organized on 5 June 1980 in Port of Spain with Errol O. Balfour as branch president.

Trinidad was transferred to the West Indies Mission in September 1983. The first missionaries from the West Indies Mission were Chris Doty, Doug Mathews, Randy Clark and David Roos who helped organize a citywide cross-country race that raised the Church's profile. Missionaries still could not actively preach in the country, so in 1987 Frank Talley, Regional Representative in Puerto Rico, and his wife, Arline, organized a Health Fair in Trinidad to teach hygiene and principles from the Word of Wisdom. The fair resulted in 300 referrals and the baptism of Kelvin Diaz. He was chief executive of the Boy Scouts of Trinidad and head of civil service training for the government. Diaz used his influence with the government in April 1988 for 10 missionaries to enter the country and subsequent missionaries to proselyte in the country.

On 22 February 1990, Elder M. Russell Ballard of the Quorum of the Twelve visited Trinidad along with Elder Charles Didier of the Seventy and blessed the land. The Trinidad Tobago Mission was created on 1 July 1991, but discontinued in 1994, with Trinidad becoming the new headquarters of the West Indies Mission. Growth in Trinidad led to branches developing throughout the island in Port of Spain, San Fernando, Arima, Sangre Grande, Couva and Curepe. The Port of Spain Trinidad District was formed 3 March 1996 with Albert Alleyne as district president.

President Gordon B. Hinckley stopped in Trinidad on 20 May 2002 after dedicating temples in Brazil and Paraguay. He addressed 900 people at a member meeting in the Cascadia Hotel conference center in St. Anns. Also in attendance was Donna Carter, the minister of religions for the government of Trinidad and Tobago. Prior to the meeting, President Hinckley met with the prime minister of the republic, Patrick Manning.

In 2002, there were 1,778 members.

Sources: Jean A. B. Borde, History of the Saints in Trinidad and Tobago, Church Archives; Kenneth L. Zabriskie, History of the West Indies Mission, [ca. 1989], Church Archives; A. Dean and Darnell Z. Jeffs interview, Church Archives; Arnold Irvine, "New Friendship Brings About Major Changes," Church News, 6 March 1983; "2 New Missions in U.S. and West Indies," Church News, 10 July 1983; "Services in 3 South America Nations and Island Republic," Church News, 10 March 1990; "Visit to West Indies Because 'We Love You,'" Church News, 1 June 2002.

Stakes — 1

(Listed alphabetically as of Oct. 1, 2011.)

No.	Name	Organized	First President
	Caribbean Area		
2820	Port of Spain Trinidad	1 Mar 2009	Emrol Ian Gould

(As of Oct. 1, 2011; shown with historical number. See MISSIONS.)

(178a)TRINIDAD &TOBAGO MISSION
#1 Morequito Ave
ValPark Shopping Plaza Bldg 10
PO Box 543
Valsayn, Trinidad, West Indies

TURKEY

**Jan. 1, 2011: Est. population, 76,805,500; Members, 254; Branches, 4;
Percent LDS, .0003, or 1 LDS in 347,536; Europe East Area.**

Located in Southeastern Europe and Southwestern Asia, Turkey was created in 1923 after the Ottoman Empire was dissolved. Turkey is a parliamentary democracy. It is 99.8 percent Muslim and .02 percent other, mostly Christians and Jews. Turkish citizens enjoy religious freedom though there are some restrictions imposed on non-Muslim religious groups.

In early 1884, Hadop T. Vartooguian, an Armenian living in Constantinople wrote to the European Mission asking about the Church. In response, Jacob Spori was sent to Constantinople, arriving 31 December 1884. On 4 January 1885, Vartooguian, his wife, Philimae, and their two children, Sisak Vartoo and Armais, were baptized. Spori went to work sharing the gospel, finding most of his success among non-natives, including Armenians.

The first meeting was held in Vartooguian's apartment on 18 January 1885. Other missionaries soon followed including Joseph M. Tanner who gained an audience with Nunif Pasha, Minister of Public Instruction. Pasa showed a great interest in Tanner's message. Efforts to expand the work beyond Constantinople, particularly to Armenians living in the interior, however, were continually turned down.

One of the converts of the time was Mischa Markow who joined the Church in Constantinople 1 February 1887. Markow became the first to conduct missionary work in many central European countries.

In May of 1888, Ferdinand F. Hintze tried to hold meetings in Turkish, but due to the poor response the meetings were soon discontinued. By August of 1888, Hintze was able to travel to the interior and meet with several Armenians who had requested information about the Church. In Sivas, more than 100 people called at the home of Dekran Shahabian, where Hintze stayed for a few days, to learn more about the Church.

The greatest missionary success occurred at Aintab. Missionaries arrived there in April 1889 and soon thereafter, a branch was established. On 14 November 1895, as unrest commenced between Turks and Armenians, missionaries were evacuated. They returned 1 March 1898. A school was established in the fall of 1898 at Aintab so that Latter-day Saint students could study free from persecution.

The Book of Mormon was translated into Turkish in 1906 and shipped to Constantinople, but it was delayed by customs and did not reach the missionaries serving in Turkey until late 1908. On 28 July 1909, Wilford Booth, president of the Turkish Mission, received word that due to increasing violence in the region, the mission should be closed. Booth and the missionaries left shortly thereafter.

On 7 November 1921, Wilford Booth arrived in Aleppo, Syria, to re-establish the mission. At that time, conflict over the area in and around Aintab prompted Booth to seek the evacuation of Church members and some investigators who still resided in Aintab. Booth was able to negotiate with the French military for nine wagons to evacuate the members from Aintab. Upon their arrival on 16 September 1921 in Aleppo, Syria, the refugees were rebaptized because their membership records had been lost during the years of war and upheaval.

The evacuation of this group marked the end of missionary work in Turkey. (See the Armenia history for additional information regarding Armenians evacuated from Turkey.)

In the 1950s, as U.S. military presence increased in Turkey, Latter-day Saint servicemen began to hold meetings in groups in cities throughout the country including Istanbul, Adna, Izmir, and Ankra. These branches were organized and then closed as U.S. military presence was reduced at the end of the Cold War. A few small units still function in scattered locations. In the 20th and 21st centuries there has been no concerted effort to conduct missionary work among native Turks.

There were 151 members in 2003.

Sources: Rao H. Lindsay, A History of the Missionary Activities of the Church of Jesus Christ of Latter-day Saints in the Near East, 1884-1929, thesis, 1958; Turkish Mission, Manuscript history and historical reports, Church Archives; Kahlile Mehr, Mormon Missionaries Enter Eastern Europe, 2002; Swiss Mission, Manuscript history and historical reports, Church Archives; Reuben Ouzunian, A short history of the Church of Jesus Christ of Latter-day Saints in the Middle East, Church Archives; French Mission, Servicemen's group record of members, 1958-1959, Church Archives; Servicemen's Group (Ankara, Turkey) Primary minutes and attendance record, 1959-1961, Church Archives; Austria Vienna East Mission, Annual history and historical reports, Church Archives.

TUVALU

**Jan. 1, 2011: Est. population, 12,400; Members, 135; Branches, 1;
Percent LDS, 1, or one in 95; Pacific Area; Fiji Suva Mission.**

Tuvalu, pronounced "too-VAH-loo," is an independent constitutional monarchy in the southwest Pacific Ocean. Its nearest neighbors are the Fiji Islands, about 650 miles to the south, and Samoa, about the same distance to the southeast. Ethnic Tuvaluans are Polynesian, and account for 94 percent of the population. Most Tuvaluans are members of the Christian Church of Tuvalu (Ekalesia Kelisiano o Tuvalu).

When Joseph B. Keeler became president of the Micronesia-Guam Mission in July 1983 he found that Tuvalu was part of the mission but there was no record of any members there. While visiting Tarawa in 1983 he became acquainted with two of his missionaries, Teuai Lekasa and Tekafa Tinai, and learned that they were originally from Tuvalu. They had become acquainted with the Church and were baptized while students at Liahona High School in Tonga. They told President Keeler that there were about 25 members of the Church in Funafuti, Tuvalu's main village, all converts from either Liahona or Moroni High School in Fiji.

Keeler was not able to visit Tuvalu until 9 September 1984. He and his wife arrived unannounced, but Tavita Tapu, another Church member who had joined the Church while attending a Church school, worked at the airport and immediately recognized the man dressed in a white shirt and tie and wearing a missionary tag as probably someone from the Church. He helped the Keelers get a room at the only hotel in Funafuti, then he got on his bike and notified all the members he could find. They met with the Keelers at the hotel that same day and held a testimony meeting. President Keeler assigned Glenn and Shirley Cornwall from Murray, Utah, to begin the work of organizing a branch in Tuvalu and registering the Church with the local government. They arrived in March 1985 and held the very first sacrament meeting in their hotel room on 24 March 1985 with seven present. Two sister missionaries, Nolaise Maumau (a native of Tuvalu) and Kalou Tetapo, arrived in April, and were joined by Elders Tevasa and Popeieta Raponi in May.

The Cornwalls began the process of registering the Church (which required completion of a petition with 50 signatures). Ward and Madge Little replaced the Cornwalls on 25 August 1985 and continued with the registration process. The first Primary was organized in October for all of the non-member children attending the branch. The first baptism in Tuvalu was Tepenga Luka, who was baptized in the lagoon on 14 December 1985. Official Church recognition was received on 16 December 1985. Sixty-two members and friends of the Church had signed the petition.

Tavita Tapu, the first to be called to serve a mission from the Funaafuti Tuvalu Branch, began his mission on 12 March 1986 in the Micronesia Guam Mission. Tuvalu was transferred from the Micronesia Guam Mission to the Fiji Suva Mission on 1 July 1986 (the branch is not in any district).

By 2002, the branch had grown to 91 members.

Sources: Madge Little, Tuvalu, 1986, Church Archives; Micronesia Guam Mission, Manuscript history and historical reports, Church Archives; Fiji Suva Mission, Manuscript history and historical reports, Church Archives.

UGANDA

Jan. 1, 2011: Est. population, 32,370,000; Members, 9,024; Stakes, 1; Wards, 6; Mission, 1; Districts, 1; Branches, 12; percent LDS, .02, or one in 4,678; Africa Southeast Area

Records from the South African Mission indicate that Lorel Nicole was baptized in Uganda on 1 July 1969, which is quite possibly the first Latter-day Saint baptism in that country. Non-Ugandan Latter-day Saints living and working there in the early 1970s met in small groups that reported to the Switzerland and International missions.

In the 1980s, several Ugandans living abroad joined the Church, returned to Uganda, and wrote to Salt Lake City wanting to know if the Church was established in Uganda. The International Mission responded with Church literature and encouragement to live the gospel. At this same time, other Ugandans who came across references to the Church also wrote to headquarters wanting information and contact with the Church. Among them was Mugisa James Collins, who had heard about the Church from a pen pal in Denmark.

Charles Osinde, a native Ugandan, joined the Church in 1989 while living in Scotland. Just before Osinde returned to Uganda, the Area Presidency in England gave him a list of seven members and a few investigators and asked that he try to locate them. Osinde found Mugisa James Collins.

In October 1989, Guy and Peggy Denton, Church members from Utah, moved to Uganda to organize agricultural education programs at Makasero University. The Dentons held Church services in their home. In February 1990, Elder Robert E. Sackley, a counselor in the United Kingdom-Ireland-Africa Area Presidency, visited Uganda and began applying for legal recognition of the Church. He located Osinde and introduced him to the Dentons, and they began meeting together on Sundays. A short while later, Collins was taught the gospel by Guy Denton and baptized in Lake Victoria by him, the first native Ugandan to be baptized in the country.

The first full-time missionary couple to be stationed in Uganda, Lark and Arlea Washburn, arrived in Kampala on 8 December 1990. The first Ugandan missionaries, Robert Kagabo and Amos Tumwesigye, began their service in the Kenya Nairobi Mission in December 1992.

The first branch in Uganda was organized on 31 March 1991 in Kampala, with Guy Denton as president, Charles Osinde as first counselor, and Mugisa James Collins as second counselor. A short while later, on 16 February 1992, a district was organized with Guy Denton as president. A second district was organized in Jinja in December 1993.

Uganda became part of the Kenya Nairobi Mission when it was organized 1 July 1991. In October of that year, Elder James E. Faust of the Quorum of the Twelve visited Uganda and blessed the land.

The Church was registered in the cities of Kampala and Jinja on 23 April 1991. On 16 June 1992, the Church received nationwide recognition as a registered religious organization by the National Board for Non-Governmental Organisations.

In 1997, two meetinghouses were constructed in Uganda, one in Jinja and the other in Kampala. The Kololo meetinghouse in Kampala, the first to be completed, was dedicated in September 1997.

In March 1998, missionaries, along with many citizens of Kampala, were invited to participate in a citywide clean up campaign just prior to the visit of U.S. President Bill Clinton. Several missionaries, while helping to cut the grass at the presidential airstrip across the street from the Kololo meetinghouse, were interviewed by Uganda's First Lady, Janet Museveni.

Membership in 2003 was 3,580.

The Uganda Kampala Mission was organized 1 July 2005, and included the countries of Uganda and Ethiopia.

In 2005, membership reached 3,920.

Sources: Cumorah's Southern Messenger, September 1969; Kenya Nairobi Mission history, 1998, Church Archives; Lark and Arlea Washburn oral history, 1997, Church Archives; Lark Washburn papers, 1991, Church Archives.

Stakes — 1
(Listed alphabetically as of Oct. 1, 2011.)

No.	Name	Organized	First President
Africa Southeast Area			
2868	Kampala Uganda	17 Jan 2010	

Missions — 1
(As of Oct. 1, 2011; shown with historical number. See MISSIONS.)

UGANDA KAMPALA MISSION
PO Box 8989
Kampala, Uganda

UKRAINE

Jan. 1, 2011: Est. population, 45,700,000; Members, 10,880; Stakes, 1; Wards, 8; Missions, 3; Districts, 4; Branches, 54; Temples, 1; percent LDS, .02, or one in 4,329; Europe East Area.

The first missionaries to enter Ukraine were Elders Ivan Stratov and Brian Bradbury, both were transferred from the Finland Helsinki East Mission. They were accompanied by President Dennis B. Neuenschwander of the Austria Vienna East Mission. They arrived in Kyiv on 7 October 1990 with a list of Ukrainian referrals. They quickly made enough contacts to gather 17 people for a fireside held in the Writers' Union Hall, where the first sacrament meetings were later held.

Valery Stavichenko, baptized on 25 November 1990 in the icy waters of the Dniper River by Elder Ivan Stratov, was the first Ukrainian to join the Church in Ukraine. Two years later, in November 1992, Stavichenko, his wife Tatyana, and their children traveled to the Freiberg Germany Temple as part of the first temple excursion from Ukraine.

The Kiev Branch was organized on 9 June 1991 with Valery Stavichenko as president. By the end of the month there were 44 members in the branch.

Ukraine remained under the jurisdiction of the Austria Vienna East Mission, with Howard L. Biddulph as president, until February 1992 when the Ukraine Kyiv Mission was organized and the Austria Vienna East Mission was discontinued. A year later, in July 1993, the mission was divided to create the Ukraine Donetsk Mission with Leo Merrill as president.

Prior to this time, an attempt had been made to register the Church in Kiev. By August 1991, no word on the application had been received. Concerned about the delay, Biddulph made it a matter of prayer. On the first Sunday in August, a deputy of the City Soviet (the legislative assembly for Kiev), Viktor Cherinko, attended Church services. Cherinko had heard good things about the Latter-day Saints and wanted to investigate. President Biddulph explained his desire that the Church be registered and Cherinko agreed to help. A few weeks later, Mr. Cherinko introduced a bill to register "The Kyiv Community of The Church of Jesus Christ of Latter-day Saints," which was passed at midnight on 9 September 1991.

Two days later, on 11 September, Elders Boyd K. Packer and Dallin H. Oaks of the Quorum of the Twelve, accompanied by Elder Dennis B. Neuenschwander, newly called to the Seventy, visited Ukraine and met with about 40 people, including members, missionaries and investigators. The following day, Elders Packer, Oaks and Neuenschwander, together with missionaries and Church members, went to a park overlooking the Dniper River and Elder Packer blessed the land.

By April 1994, the Church had grown and branches had been established in several cities. Local members had registered the Church in six Ukrainian cities. Church leaders desired to have national recognition of the Church. Ukrainian law required that the head of the Church's national organization be elected. Aleksander Manzhos was elected to be the Church's representative to the nation. Documents for national registration were filed on 6 April 1994, and two years later registration was granted.

The first meetinghouse was dedicated in Donetsk on 28 June 1998. On 7 September 2001, the first meetinghouse in Kyiv was dedicated. The following day a second meetinghouse in Kyiv was dedicated.

History was made in July 1998 when President Gordon B. Hinckley, at the dedication of the Monticello Utah Temple, announced that a temple was planned for Kiev. This was welcome news to Ukrainian Latter-day Saints. In 2002, there were more than 1,000 temple recommend holders in Ukraine, who had to travel 30 hours one way to get to the nearest temple.

Ukrainian Latter-day Saints Sergie and Laryssa Pankov were called to serve as Church-service missionaries in April 2000. They are thought to be the first native Eastern Europeans to serve as Church-service missionaries. Brother Pankov oversaw missionary housing, while Sister Pankov served in the Ukraine Kiev Mission office. They completed their mission in April 2001.

President Gordon B. Hinckley became the first president of the Church to visit Ukraine in September 2002. He met with about 3,200 Church members in the Palace Ukraine Concert Hall in Kyiv. Members came from across Ukraine, spending, in some cases, the equivalent of a month's income for train tickets. The meeting was the largest assembly of Latter-day Saints in Ukraine history. President Hinckley assured them that they were part of the great nation of God.

Membership in 2002 reached 8,627. In 2003, membership reached 8,984.

The first stake in Eastern Europe was organized in Kyiv by Elder Russell M. Nelson of the Quorum of the Twelve at a special conference held on 30 May 2004. Former district president Vladimir Kanchnko was sustained as president. In his remarks, Elder Nelson, reflecting on the time when he was given responsibility for establishing the Church in Eastern Europe, said, "The Lord had accomplished a miracle."

In 2005, membership reached 9,951.

The Ukraine Dnepropetrovsk Mission was organized July 1, 2007, the third mission in the country.

The Kyiv Ukraine Temple was dedicated on 29 August 2010, the first on former Soviet soil. It became the 134th temple in the Church, and was dedicated 20 years after the first missionaries arrived in 1990.

Sources: Kahlile Mehr, Mormon Missionaries Enter Eastern Europe, 2002; Howard L. Biddulph, The Morning Breaks, 1996; Ukraine Kiev Mission, Annual historical reports, Church Archives; Shaun D. Stahle, "Ukrainian Faith: Gospel Seeds Falling on Rich Soil," Church News, November 2002; Greg Hill, "Anchoring Odessa with Faithful Families," Church News, May 2004; Shaun D. Stahle, "4,000 Gather in Ukraine for Pres. Hinckley," Church News, 21 September 2002; Shaun D. Stahle, "Kiev Members Revere Historic Moment," Church News, 5 June 2004.

Stakes — 1
(Listed alphabetically as of Oct. 1, 2011.)

No.	Name	Organized	First President
Europe East Area			
2637	Kyiv Ukraine	30 May 2004	Vladimir Akimovich Kanchenko

Missions — 3
(As of Oct. 1, 2011; shown with historical number. See MISSIONS.)

(295) UKRAINE DONETSK MISSION
Prospekt Bogdana Khmelnitskogo 67a
83087 Donetsk
Ukraine

(274) UKRAINE KYIV MISSION
vul. Yabluneva 1
s. Sofiivska Borshahivka
Kyevo-Svyatoshinskiy rayon
Kyiv oblast 08131, Ukraine

(345) UKRAINE DNIPROPETROVSK MISSION
27-A Karla Marksa Ave 5th fl
Dnipropetrovsk
49044 Ukraine

UNITED KINGDOM
Jan. 1, 2011: Est. population, 72,848,000; Members, 186,814; Stakes, 45; Wards, 281; Branches, 52; Missions, 6; Temples, 2; percent LDS, .24, or one in 404; Europe Area.

The United Kingdom consists of England, Scotland, Wales, and Northern Ireland, and is located off the northwest coast of Europe. The population speaks English, Welsh, and Gaelic. Most belong to the Church of England or are Roman Catholics.

Sources: Truth Will Prevail, editors V. Ben Bloxham, James R. Moss and Larry C. Porter; A History of the Church in Cambridgeshire, unpublished history by Leonard Reed; Church News, July 6, 1974, Dec. 1, 1985; "Church celebrates its British history," "Markers tell where history was made," both by Dell Van Orden and Gerry Avant, Church News, Aug. 1, 1987, Aug. 8, 1987; Church News, Nov. 24, 1990; "Temples rededicated, lives renewed," by Gerry Avant, Church News, Oct. 31, 1992; "Ground broken for Preston temple," by Bryan J. Grant, Church News, June 18, 1994; "Prophet returns to beloved England" by Mike Cannon, Church News, Sept. 2, 1995; Church News, June 13, 1998, June 20, 1998, June 27, 1998, May 15, 1999, Sept. 11, 1999, April 22, 2000, May 6, 2000, June 16, 2001; "Zion's call answered by 'torrent' of saints crossing sea," by David M.W. Pickup, Church News, Aug. 4, 2001 "Welcomed by city, sailing ships dock in Scottish port," by David M.W. Pickup, Church News, Aug. 25, 2001; "Mayor of Liverpool rolls out red carpet," by David M.W. Pickup, Church News, Aug. 25, 2001; "Portsmouth: Final port before the crossing," by David M.W. Pickup, Church News, Sept. 1, 2001; "20,000 line riverbanks leading to Hull," by John and Shauna Hart, Church News, Sept. 1, 2001; Church News, March 9, 2002.

ENGLAND
Jan. 1, 2011: Est. population, 59,093,000; Members, 145,294; Stakes, 36; Wards, 228; Branches, 30; Missions, 5; Temples, 2; percent LDS, .23, or one in 427.

Just two years after the founding of the Church, missionaries were sent to preach the gospel in Canada. They met with great success and baptized a number of British subjects who then desired that the gospel be preached to their relatives in Great Britain. Consequently, Elder Heber C. Kimball of the Quorum of the Twelve was set apart on 4 June 1837 to open a mission in England. Willard Richards, Joseph Fielding, and Elder Orson Hyde were also called to serve with him. As the group traveled to New York, they were joined by Canadians John Goodson, Isaac Russell, and John Snider.

On 1 July 1837, the seven men set sail for England. They arrived on 19 July 1837 in Liverpool. Two days later they traveled to Preston where Fielding's brother James was pastor of the Vauxhall Chapel. They preached the gospel there the following two Sundays, 23 and 30 July. Just 11 days after their arrival, a baptismal service was held in the nearby River Ribble that was viewed by about 8,000 curious onlookers. Nine converts, all former members of Fielding's church, were baptized by Elder Kimball, the first of whom was George D. Watt. A week later, the number of converts reached 50.

The first branch in England was created in Preston on 6 August 1837. It continues today as the oldest continuously functioning unit in the Church. The first conference in England was held four months later on Christmas Day. Missionaries extended their labors to Alston and Bedford, where branches were soon established, but the greatest work was done in the Preston area. Opposition began to mount through ministers and the press, but within nine months, more than 1,000 had been baptized. During 1837, branches were established at Walkerfold, Ribchester, Thornley, Penwortham, Wrightington, Alston, Barshe Lees and Bedford. During 1838-1839 an additional 21 branches were created.

In 1838, Elders Heber C. Kimball and Orson Hyde returned to Nauvoo, leaving Joseph Fielding in place as president of the mission. Elders Brigham Young, Heber C. Kimball (on his second mission to England), Orson Pratt, Parley P. Pratt, John Taylor, Wilford Woodruff, and George A. Smith arrived in England in 1840.

Wilford Woodruff traveled to the potteries district and established the Church in Hanley. While there he became acquainted with converts William and Ann Benbow. In March 1840, he traveled south in company with William Benbow to the Herefordshire area where he met William's brother John Benbow. The Benbow family was converted after their first visit with Woodruff and told him of their congregation of over 600 people who had formed their own church, the United Brethren. Woodruff preached to members of the United Brethren and in five days baptized 32 people from the congregation. Within 18 days of his arrival at Herefordshire, Woodruff had baptized the two most influential members of the United Brethren, John Benbow and Thomas Kington, and 15 of their preachers. Eventually, all but one of the congregation was converted and baptized, and in 1840 they deeded their Gadfield Elm Chapel to the Church. It was the first building to be owned by the Church in England. Ministers were so concerned about the progress of the Church that they petitioned without success the Archbishop of Canterbury to ask Parliament to ban the Mormons from England.

In 1840, additional members of the Quorum of the Twelve arrived in England. On 14-16 April 1840, they held a meeting of the Quorum, the first such meeting held outside of the United States, and conducted a general conference of the Church. The Apostles grouped the many local congregations into conferences, beginning with the Gadfield Elm Conference organized on 14 June 1840. In 1840, the mission began publication of a periodical, the Millennial Star. During the same year, through the generosity of former United Brethren leaders Benbow and Kington, an edition of the Book of Mormon and a hymnal were prepared for publication. Brigham Young obtained the British copyright for the first European edition of The Book of Mormon. It was published in Liverpool in January 1841. The British Mission was headquartered in Manchester until 1842 when it was moved to Liverpool. It remained there until it was moved in 1929 to Birmingham.

Soon many converts began immigrating to the United States. John Moon brought the first company of 41 converts with him on the ship Britannia in June 1840. Around 800 members left for America during 1840-1841.

Because of the hardships suffered by the first groups of emigrating Latter-day Saints, the Church in Britain established a system of emigration, chartering its own ships for the huge numbers desiring to emigrate. Leaders procured ample provisions for the voyage and set up companies of emigrants presided over by priesthood brethren. The system was enhanced in 1849 when President Brigham Young established the Perpetual Emigrating Fund (PEF), a revolving fund wherein those without means could have their way to Zion paid for by the Church, but were expected to repay the loan once they were settled. The money would then be loaned again to other immigrants needing financial help in order to join the Saints in America.

In 1851, the British Mission published the Pearl of Great Price. It was the first time the texts had been compiled and published together. The volume was canonized as scripture 27 years later.

Out-migration took thousands of members and many of the district and branch leaders from England in the 19th Century creating a shortage of leaders. From the period 1840 to 1868, at least 150 sailing vessels brought tens of thousands of saints from England to the United States.

In the 1880s, former member William Jarman traveled through England with his anti-Mormon lectures and helped to create deep prejudices against the Church. He eventually lost favor after losing several debates to B.H. Roberts. The 1890 manifesto officially renouncing polygamy helped to create a period of relative calm for the Church in England. In June 1894, the First Presidency began to encourage the European Saints to remain and build up the Church in their own countries. Nevertheless, many continued to immigrate to the United States.

In August and September 1906, England received its first visit from a prophet, Joseph F. Smith, who spent several weeks in England and Scotland giving sermons which were later published in the Millenial Star.

From 1910 to 1914, in the wake of the Reed Smoot hearings in the United States Senate during the first decade of the 20th century, a well-organized anti Mormon campaign was mounted by various ministers and former-Mormons. They lectured and published pamphlets accusing the missionary program as being a front to enslave British girls as polygamous wives. Missionaries during this era were often attacked, and one was tarred and feathered. Eventually, British Home Secretary Winston Churchill investigated and then dismissed these accusations as having no basis in fact.

In 1914, England became fully involved in World War I. Missionaries from America continued to staff the mission until the United States involvement in the war began in 1917, effectively eliminating available men to serve. In 1913, the British

Mission had enjoyed a force of 258 missionaries. By 1919, the number had dropped to 31 with just five being Americans. Local missionaries filled the void. In 1919, the Church applied again for missionary visas. The request was denied because politicians prejudiced by the anti-Mormon campaign preceding the war felt that Mormon missionary work was disruptive to English society. Appeals launched through Utah's congressional delegation eventually prevailed and missionaries from America were allowed to return in 1920.

During the early 1930s the British Mission instituted a "chapel-acquisition programme" intended to encourage the construction or acquisition and remodeling of buildings as meetinghouses. Even though the program was launched during an economic depression, branch leaders enthusiastically embraced the challenge and instituted building fund-drives in their branches. By 1935 twelve meetinghouses had been built or acquired and others were underway.

In 1937, Church leaders in Great Britain celebrated the centennial of the Church in the British Isles. During the first one hundred years, 126,593 persons had been baptized, and 52,000 of those had immigrated to the United States. To be part of the observances, President Heber J. Grant, his counselor J. Reuben Clark Jr., and 50 other Church leaders arrived in England during July 1937. During two weeks of festivities, President Grant dedicated chapels in Burnley, Bradford, Rochdale, Merthyr Tydfil, Liverpool, South-west London, and North London, and attended a pageant and Centennial Ball. He also conducted three overflow sessions of conference.

The upheaval of World War II, 1939-1945 disrupted every aspect of life in England including the Church's operations. In September 1939, after England's declaration of war, the American missionaries were evacuated. Mission President Hugh B. Brown followed in January 1940 and British members were appointed to the leadership positions vacated by the missionaries. With great zeal, "home missionary work" was performed by the members and many converts were made during the war. When American leadership resumed in May 1944, with President Brown's return, the number of branches had increased from 68 to 75, although they were later consolidated into 29 units. During January 1946, the first post-war missionaries returned to England.

More than 12,000 members attended the dedication services of the London Temple conducted by President David O. McKay on 7-9 September 1958.

On 17 June 1960, the first stake in England was created in Manchester. The British Mission was divided the same day, creating the North British Mission. An aggressive building program, aided by building missionaries, was responsible for the construction of several meetinghouses in the early 1960s. The Institute of Religion was inaugurated in Britain in 1970.

The first-ever area conference of the Church was held in 1971 in Manchester. Fourteen General Authorities, including President Joseph Fielding Smith, participated in the 27-29 August meetings. After the Church discontinued holding large area conferences and replaced them with more localized regional conferences, the first regional conference of the Church was held in London on 13 October 1983.

Latter-day Saints throughout the British Isles participated in three days of celebration on 24-26 July 1987, in commemoration of the 150th anniversary of the first missionary work in Great Britain. Thirteen General Authorities, including President Ezra Taft Benson and his first counselor, President Gordon B. Hinckley, four apostles, and seven members of the First Quorum of the Seventy participated in the events. Former Prime Minister Edward Heath attended the anniversary dinner in London. The dinner featured a videotaped message from United States President Ronald Reagan.

Conferences were held in six cities in the British Isles and nine public markers were dedicated at various sites of importance to the Church. Five of the markers were dedicated in England: in Avenham Park along the banks of the River Ribble where the first converts were baptized on 30 July 1837; at Benbow Farm in Herefordshire, where Wilford Woodruff baptized 65 in March 1840; at Hungerford, where Apostle James E. Talmage was born; at Hyde Park Chapel in London; and at Albert Dock in Liverpool, where the first missionaries landed and where the first emigrants sailed from on 6 July 1840.

In November 1990, Terry Rooney of the Bradford 2nd Ward, Huddersfield England Stake, became the first Latter-day Saint elected to Parliament.

Natives of England who have been called as General Authorities through the years include John Taylor, president of the Church 1880-87; Elders George Q. Cannon, John R. Winder, George Teasdale, James E. Talmage, John Longden, B. H. Roberts, George Reynolds, Joseph W. McMurrin, and Derek A. Cuthbert. Elder Kenneth Johnson is currently serving in the Seventy.

The London Temple was rededicated on 18 October 1992 by President Gordon B. Hinckley. A second temple, in Preston, England, was dedicated on 7 June 1998 by President Gordon B. Hinckley.

On a trip to England and the Republic of Ireland 24 August-2 September 1995, President Gordon B. Hinckley created the Canterbury England Stake, rededicated the Hyde Park Chapel, and met with members, missionaries, and news media in Liverpool and elsewhere. The Tabernacle Choir performed in Royal Albert Hall in London on 14 June 1998, a performance taped by BBC for rebroadcast in September 1998.

Following a six-year effort, the rebuilt Gadfield Elm Chapel, the oldest LDS meetinghouse in the Church, was rededicated on 23 April 2000, by Elder Jeffrey R. Holland of the Quorum of the Twelve. In 1842, the chapel was sold to assist new British converts immigrating to America, and during the next 152 years the building fell into disrepair. In 1994, a group of members from the Cheltenham England Stake formed a charitable trust to purchase the historic site and restore it. On 26 May 2004, President Gordon B. Hinckley received the title to the meetinghouse on behalf of the Church.

The England Bristol Mission was consolidated with the England Birmingham, England London, and England London South missions on 1 July 2002.

In 2002, membership reached 135,819.

Sources: Andrew Jenson, Encyclopedic History of the Church, 1941; Arnold K. Garr, Donald Q. Cannon, Richard O. Cowan, ed., Encyclopedia of

Latter-day Saint History, 2000; V. Ben Bloxham, James R. Moss, Larry C. Porter, Truth Will Prevail: The Rise of the Church of Jesus Christ of Latter-day Saints in the British Isles, 1837-1987; 1987; James B. Allen, Ronald K. Esplin, David J. Whittaker, Men With a Mission: The Quorum of the Twelve Apostles in the British Isles, 1837-1841, 1992; Europe West Area Public Affairs Council, Exploring Your Heritage: Church Historical Sites in the British Isles, nd.; Derek A. Cuthbert, The Second Century: Latter-day Saints in Great Britain, 1937-1987, 1987; "Gadfield Elm: The Oldest LDS Chapel in Europe," Ensign, October 1986; "English, Irish Members Greet President Hinckley," Ensign, November 1995; Don L. Searle, "The Church in the United Kingdom and Ireland," Ensign, June 1998; "Cradle of the British Mission," Church News, 17 January 1959; Bryan J. Grant, "Church History Exhibit Opens in Britain," Church News, 11 July 1987; Parry D. Sorensen, "Pres. Grant Visited Great Britain for LDS Centennial," Church News, 18 July 1987; Dell Van Orden and Gerry Avant, "Church Celebrates its British History" and "Markers Tell Where History was Made, Church News, 1 August 1987; Dell Van Orden, "Liberty Sparked First in Britain," Church News, 1 August 1987; Gerry Avant, "British Strength Lauded in Birmingham," Church News, 1 August 1987; President Reagan Praises Church's Accomplishments" and "Saga of Church in British Isles Lauded at Anniversary Dinner " and "Scriptures Given to Queen, Prime Minister," Church News, 1 August 1987; Gerry Avant, "Site Acquired for Second Temple in England" and "Thousands Tour London and Swiss Temples," Church News, 24 October 1992; Gerry Avant, "Thousands Gather and Savor Experience of Temple Dedication" and "Temples Rededicated, Lives Renewed," Church News, 31 October 1992; "Oldest LDS Chapel in England Refurbished and Rededicated," Church News, 6 May 2000; Historic Chapel Given to LDS, Church News, 27 May 2004.

Stakes — 36

(Listed alphabetically as of Oct. 1, 2011.)

No.	Name	Organized	First President
Europe Area			
1345	Ashton England	6 Jun 1982	Brian Ashworth
760	*Billingham England	10 Jun 1986	
	‡Hartlepool England	13 Jun 1976	Craig Lithgow Marshall
494	*Birmingham England		
	‡Birmingham	14 Sep 1969	Derek A. Cuthbert
609	*Bristol England		
	‡Bristol	29 Apr 1973	Donald V. Norris
2093	Canterbury England	27 Aug 1995	Christopher Brian Munday
1331	Cheltenham England	21 Mar 1982	Warrick N. Kear
1346	Chester England	6 Jun 1982	Peter Furniss Lee
2693	Chorley England	13 Nov 2005	Malcolm Gordon Beverly
1936	Coventry England	9 May 1993	Thomas William Phillips
856	Crawley England	19 Aug 1977	J.A. Casbon
327	*Huddersfield England		
	‡Leeds	19 Mar 1961	Dennis Livesey
608	*Hull England		
	‡Hull	26 Apr 1973	Ian David Swanney
1423	Ipswich England	29 May 1983	Brian Arthur Frank Watling
780	Leeds England	12 Nov 1976	Douglas Rawson
325	*Leicester England		
	‡Leicester	5 Mar 1961	Derek A. Cuthbert
814	Lichfield England	20 Feb 1977	Robert James Mawle
748	Liverpool England	14 Mar 1976	Michael R. Otterson
928a	*London England Hyde Park	28 May 1978	Vance R. Leavitt
	‡London North	20 Sep 1970	Thomas Hill
929a	London England Wandsworth	28 May 1978	John Dodd
930	Maidstone England	28 May 1978	William J. Jolliffe III
294	*Manchester England		
	‡Manchester	27 Mar 1960	Robert G. Larson
677	Newcastle-Under-Lyme England	17 Jan 1975	James Kenneth Cork
810	Northampton England	13 Feb 1977	Michael J. Wade
549	*Norwich England	28 May 1978	
	*Ipswich England		
	‡East Anglia	20 Jun 1971	Dennis R. Reeves
597	*Nottingham England		
	‡Nottingham	4 Feb 1973	Ernest Hewitt
885	Plymouth England	27 Nov 1977	Leonard Eden
1343	Poole England	23 May 1982	Peter J. Crockford
600	*Portsmouth England	6 Feb 1990	
	*Southampton England		
	‡Southampton	11 Feb 1973	Reginald V. Littlecott
762	Preston England	17 Jun 1976	Eric Cryer
615	*Reading England		
	‡Thames Valley	24 May 1973	Peter B.C. Brighty
666	Romford England	24 Nov 1974	Arthur James Turvey
932	Saint Albans England	28 May 1978	Roland Edward Elvidge
1376	Sheffield England	14 Nov 1982	Kenneth Jones
931	Staines England	28 May 1978	Peter Benjamin C. Brighty
374	*Sunderland England		
	‡Sunderland	17 Mar 1963	Fred W. Oates

2190	Watford England	28 Apr 1996	Michael John Plant
2274	York England	24 Nov 1996	David Clark Thiriot
		Stakes discontinued	
323	*London England		
	‡London	26 Feb 1961	Donald W. Hemingway

Discontinued 28 May 1978 †London England Hyde Park (928a), London

England Wandsworth (929a), Staines England (931)

527   *London England North
Discontinued 28 May 1978 †Saint Albans England (932), Romford

England (666), Staines England (931), London
England Hyde Park (928a)

Missions — 5
(As of Oct. 1, 2011; shown with historical number. See MISSIONS.)

(183) ENGLAND BIRMINGHAM MISSION
187 Penns Lane
Sutton Coldfield
West Midlands B76 1JU England

(1) ENGLAND LONDON MISSION
64-68 Princes Gate
Exhibition Road, South Kensington
London SW7 2PA,
England

(138) ENGLAND MANCHESTER MISSION
Trafalgar House
110 Manchester Road
Altrincham, Cheshire WA14 1NU, England

(52) ENGLAND LEEDS MISSION
Lister House, Lister Hill
Horsforth, Leeds LS18 5AZ
England

(79) ENGLAND LONDON SOUTH MISSION
The London Temple
West Park Road
Newchapel, Surrey RH7 6NB
England

FALKLAND ISLANDS

Jan. 1, 2011: Est. population, 2,967; Members, 10; Branches, 1; Percent LDS, .1or one in 742.

Administered by the United Kingdom, the Falkland Islands gained notoriety in April-June 1982 in a war for the islands between the U.K. and Argentina. The islands are administered by the United Kingdom and are subject to British law.

In 1983 Ann Reid and her children David and Shialee Green traveled from the British Isles to the Falkland Islands. They had gone there to visit the grave of Sister Reid's son, Paul, who was killed during the Falkland Islands war, and decided to remain. They met as a small group with the few members of the Church who were there temporarily with the British military. A branch was created on 22 July 1996 in Port Stanley with Ian Henderson as president. The branch answers directly to the Europe West Area. There have been no known baptisms performed on the island, and missionaries have never visited. Branch members are generally able to attend the London Temple every three years.

Sources: Telephone conversation with Ann Reid, 26 May 2004; Telephone conversation with David Green, 27 May 2004.

NORTHERN IRELAND

Jan. 1, 2011: Est. population, 1,710,000; Members, 5,351; Stakes, 1; Wards, 8; Branches, 3; percent LDS, .30, or one in 326; Europe Area; Ireland Dublin Mission.

Located in the northeast corner of the island, Northern Ireland, consisting of six counties, remained part of the United Kingdom when Ireland was partitioned following the Anglo-Irish Treaty of 1922. The remaining 26 counties of Ireland became the Irish Free State. In 1948, the Free State was formally declared a republic. By 2001, 46 percent were Protestant and 40 percent Catholic.

Throughout the history of the Church on "Emerald Isle," the greatest success has been in this part of Ireland. The majority of Church members are to be found around the capital city of Belfast.

The first known Latter-day Saint to visit Ireland was Reuben Hedlock who arrived on 23 May 1840. He spent three days there.

On 28 July of that year, future Church President John Taylor and two Irish natives, James McGuffie and William Black who had joined the Church earlier in England, arrived by steamer at Warrenpoint, County Down and traveled to Newry, a town 37 miles south of Belfast.

That evening, between 600-700 gathered to hear Elder Taylor preach the restored gospel for the first time in Ireland. The following night another meeting was held but only a few attended.

The next morning, James McGuffie stayed in Newry and Elder Taylor, together with William Black and Thomas Tate, set off northwards in the direction of Lisburn, William Black's home town. They stayed overnight at a townland called Ballymacrattybeg before setting off again, on the morning of 31 July.

As they walked along on that fine summer's morning discussing the gospel, they crossed the brow of a small hill. They saw below them the little freshwater lake close to the village of Loughbrickland.

Thomas Tate, quoting the eunuch's words to Philip (Acts 8:36), said: "See, here is water, what doth hinder me to be baptized?" Thus Thomas Tate became the first person to be baptised in Ireland.

Two months later, Elder Theodore Curtis arrived in Ireland and established a branch of 35 in Hillsborough. Reuben Hedlock returned in October and was the first missionary to preach in Belfast. By may of 1842, David Wilkie reported that there were 71 members in Ireland with branches in Hillsborough and Crawfordsburn.

Famine raged throughout Ireland between 1845 and 1850 and more than a million people starved to death. A million and a half emigrated to America, Britain and Australia. As a consequence, little missionary work was carried out. However, in 1848, the Belfast Conference was established with a number of branches.

With the beginning of the Utah War in 1857, missionaries were called home, not returning until 1861. Missionary success declined in the 1860s and on 25th October 1867, Elder Charles W. Penrose, president of the British Mission, traveled to Belfast to encourage the members to emigrate to Utah.

The next attempt to preach began in May 1884 when Robert Marshall and George Wilson arrived in Belfast. On 20 October, they created a branch in Belfast with 29 members. Between then and the turn of the century, 214 people were baptised in what now constitutes Northern Ireland.

Throughout Europe, the establishment of permanent branches had been hindered by emigration to Utah. In 1907, the Church officially announced that members ought to build up the Church in their own countries rather than come to the Salt Lake Valley. Though growth continued to be slow, this marked the beginning of true permanence for the Church in Ireland.

After the 1922 separation of the southern 26 counties from the United Kingdom, the Ulster Conference was organized in Northern Ireland with a second conference in the Irish Free State. The two conferences were merged again on 31 March 1935.

The first meeting hall owned by the Church was dedicated in Belfast on 8 March 1948. On 8 August 1953, President David O McKay became the first prophet to visit Northern Ireland.

After the creation of the Irish Mission on 8 July 1962 with Stephen R. Covey as president, conversions increased dramatically growing from 600 members to 2,500 members 18 months later. By December 1967, there were 3,500 members in Northern Ireland, and on 9 June 1974, the first stake in Northern Ireland was created with Andrew Renfrew as president.

The 14 July 1976 division of the mission placed Northern Ireland in the Scotland Glasgow Mission. It returned to the jurisdiction of the Ireland Dublin Mission on 28th January 1985.

On 23 October 1985, Elder Neal A. Maxwell of the Quorum of the Twelve visited Ireland, meeting members close to Loughbrickland, the lake in which John Taylor had baptised Thomas Tate in 1840.

In the summer of 1990, special conferences were held in Belfast and Dublin under the direction of Elder Boyd K Packer of the Quorum of the Twelve to celebrate the 150th anniversary of the first baptism in Ireland.

On 1 September 1995, many Latter-day Saints from Northern Ireland traveled to Dublin where they heard President Gordon B. Hinckley speak.

On 7 June 1998, members living in Northern Ireland became part of the Preston England Temple district following the dedication of that temple.

In 2003, there were 5,349 members.

Sources: Andrew Jenson, Encyclopedic History of the Church, 1941; Ireland Dublin Mission, Manuscript history and historical reports, Church Archives; Orson Scott Card, "The Saints in Ireland," Ensign, February 1978; "First Stakes Organized in Ireland and Denmark," Church News, 6 July 1974, 12; Mike Cannon, "Visit to Ireland Caps 'Whirlwind Trip'" Church News, 9 September 1995, 3; Brent A. Barlow, History of the Church of Jesus Christ of Latter-day Saints in Ireland Since 1840, thesis, 1968; "Preston England Temple," Church News, 13 June 1998, 4; British Mission, Manuscript history and historical reports, Church Archives.

Stake — 1
(Listed alphabetically as of Oct. 1, 2011.)

No.	Name	Organized	First President
	Europe Area		
1647	*Belfast Northern Ireland	13 Jan 1987	
	‡Belfast Ireland	9 Jun 1974	Andrew Renfrew

SCOTLAND

Jan. 1, 2011: Est. population, 5,078,000; Members, 26,826; Stakes, 5; Wards, 27; Branches, 13; Missions, 1; percent LDS, .5, or one in 196; Europe Area.

Native Scots Alexander Wright and Samuel Mulliner were converted and baptized while living in Ontario, Canada in the mid-1830s. They were eager to share the gospel with their countrymen and were called as the first missionaries to Scotland, arriving in Glasgow on 20 December 1839. The following day, they traveled to Edinburgh where Mulliner's parents lived. Mulliner taught and baptized Alexander Hay and his wife Jessie in the River Clyde at Bishopton near Paisley on 14 January 1840, likely the first to join the Church in Scotland. Wright traveled to Marnoch where he shared the gospel with his parents and friends. In February, Mulliner and Wright reunited and on 2 February 1840 baptized two young men from Leith.

A hall was rented in Paisley and regular meetings were held. By May 1840, membership had increased to 80. Orson Pratt of the Quorum of the Twelve Apostles arrived and organized a branch at Paisley on 8 May. Pratt and Mulliner then labored in Edinburgh where they baptized a number of converts.

While in Edinburgh, Pratt wrote and published the pamphlet "An Interesting Account of Several Remarkable Visions." It included the first published account of Joseph Smith's first vision, and with the scriptures, became a standard Church publication in Scotland.

In May 1840, missionary Reuben Hedlock began working in Glasgow where he organized a branch on 8 August 1840. By March 1841, when Orson Pratt departed from Scotland, he left George D. Watt in charge. More than 200 had joined the Church in Edinburgh. All the Scottish branches, located in urban centers, were experiencing growth. Efforts were made by missionary Peter McIntyre to preach the gospel among Gaelic tribes in the highlands in 1845, and in 1850, some Gaelic tracts were printed by a press in Inverness, but very few highlanders were willing to be baptized.

In the first 15 months of missionary efforts, 600 Scots were added to the rolls of the Church. By 1850, membership had risen to 3,257 in more than 50 branches, and by 1855, four conferences had been organized.

Membership began a decline after 1851, largely due to the effects of immigration to the United States. The third official Church immigrant company from Great Britain was, in fact, the first immigration of Scottish Latter-day Saints. The company of 50, led by Mulliner and Wright, left Liverpool on board the ship Isaac Newton on 15 October 1840.

From 1850-1899, there were 5,329 of the 7,528 Scottish members, a full 71 percent, who immigrated to America. Even by 1870, membership losses had become so pronounced that the Edinburgh, Glasgow, Dundee and Kilmarnock conferences had been consolidated to the Glasgow Conference that had jurisdiction for all of Scotland.

During the 1850s, just 1,308 converts were baptized. A decline in convert numbers continued in the 1860s and 1870s. In 1873, for example, just 35 people were baptized. In 1897, there were 55 baptisms, but the number included children of members.

From the 1870s-1890s, the Church continued to send a few missionaries to staff the Scottish Conference. One such missionary serving in Scotland in 1897-1899 was David O. McKay. He had little success. While serving in Stirling, he noticed a phrase engraved in stone above the entrance to a house that read: "What e'er thou art, act well thy part." The inspiration he took from this epigram had a great impact on his life, and upon the future of the Church he later directed as president from 1951-1970.

Besides President McKay's family, a number of other prominent Latter-day Saints hailed from Scotland. Among them were Charles W. Nibley, from Huntersfield, who served as Presiding Bishop from 1907-1925 and as second counselor in the First Presidency from 1925-1931; Richard Ballantyne, from Roxburgshire, who established the Sunday School program in Salt Lake City in 1849; John McFarland from Stirling, wrote the words to the hymn "Far, Far, Away on Judea's Plains" and the music for "Dearest Children, God Is Near You;" and Glasgow native Ebenezer Bryce, for whom Bryce Canyon National Park in southern Utah is named.

In 1914, the United Kingdom countries including Scotland became fully involved in World War I. Missionaries from America continued to work in Scotland until the United States became involved in the war beginning in 1917, effectively eliminating available men to serve. In 1913, the British Mission had enjoyed a force of 258 missionaries. By 1919, the number had dropped to 31 with just five being Americans. In 1919, the Church applied again for missionary visas. The request was denied because politicians prejudiced by the anti-Mormon campaign preceding the war felt that Mormon missionary work was disruptive to society. Appeals launched through Utah's congressional delegation eventually prevailed and missionaries from America were allowed to return in 1920.

The upheaval of World War II from 1939-1945 disrupted every aspect of life in Scotland, including the Church's missionary program. In September 1939, after England and its United Kingdom allies, including Scotland, declared war against Germany, American missionaries were evacuated. Mission President Hugh B. Brown followed in January 1940 and local members were appointed to the leadership positions vacated by the missionaries. With great zeal, "home missionary work" was performed by local members and a number of converts were made during the war. During January 1946, the first missionaries returned to Scotland since the war.

Post-war interest in the Church led to greater numbers of converts in the 1940s and 1950s. During June 1952, David O. McKay dedicated the first meetinghouse for the Church in Scotland at Glasgow. Two days later he dedicated another meetinghouse in Edinburgh. As part of a major Church building program in the early 1960s, there were several additional buildings constructed through donated labor by members and building missionaries. In 1961, the British Mission was divided to create the Scottish-Irish Mission. It was re-named the Scottish Mission the following year.

Scotland's first stake was created in Glasgow on 26 August 1962 by President David O. McKay. It was followed by creation of the Dundee Stake in 1975, and the Aberdeen, Edinburgh and Paisley stakes on 12 October 1980.

Members in Scotland participated in the 150th anniversary of the Church in the British Isles in July 1987. Two markers were dedicated on 25 July 1987 by Elder David B. Haight of the Quorum of the Twelve commemorating events in Scotland's Church history. One marker, on the banks of the River Clyde near Glasgow, is where the first converts in Scotland were baptized in January 1840. The second marker in Holyrood Park in Edinburgh denotes where Orson Hyde dedicated

Scotland for the preaching of the gospel in 1840.

The Church in Scotland also celebrated the 150th anniversary of the Glasgow Branch on 21 October 1990.

A historical occasion for Scottish members of the Church occurred on 2 May 2001 when Stephen Kerr, president of the Edinburgh Scotland Stake, was invited to represent the Church before Parliament.

Sea Trek 2001, an epic voyage of eight tall sailing ships commemorating the 19th century gathering of European converts to Zion, made a stopover 18 August 2001, in Greenock, Scotland, on its 59-day voyage from Denmark to America. Some 20,000 people gathered at the Ocean Terminal Port to see two of the ships docked side by side.

In 2002, membership reached 25,622.

Sources: Andrew Jenson, Encyclopedic History of the Church, 1941; Arnold K. Garr, Donald Q. Cannon, Richard O. Cowan, ed., Encyclopedia of Latter-day Saint History, 2000; V. Ben Bloxham, James R. Moss, Larry C. Porter, Truth Will Prevail: The Rise of the Church of Jesus Christ of Latter-day Saints in the British Isles, 1837-1987; 1987; James B. Allen, Ronald K. Esplin, David J. Whittaker, Men With A Mission: The Quorum of the Twelve Apostles in the British Isles, 1837-1841, 1992; Muriel Cuthbert, "Strong Saints in Scotland," Ensign, October 1978; Don L. Searle, "The Church In the United Kingdom and Ireland," Ensign, June 1998; "Steady Growth in Scotland Comes from 'Hard Work,'" Church News, 4 May 1986; Dell Van Orden and Gerry Avant, "Church Celebrates its British History" and "Markers Tell Where History was Made, Church News, 1 August 1987; "Irish, Scots, Welsh Celebrate 150th Year," and "Scottish LDS Urged to Unite, Build Up Church," Church News, 8 August 1987; "150th Year Brings Prestige in Glasgow," Church News, 24 November 1990; "LDS Team Wins Praise, Tournament in Scotland," Church News, 24 April 1993; "Members Boost Retention," Church News, 4 December 1993; "Spotlight on Historic Sites: Scotland Baptisms," Church News, 22 April 2000.

Stakes — 5
(Listed alphabetically as of Oct. 1, 2011.)

No.	Name	Organized	First President
Europe Area			
1186	Aberdeen Scotland	12 Oct 1980	William Albert Wilson
734	Dundee Scotland	23 Nov 1975	John Keogh
1187	Edinburgh Scotland	12 Oct 1980	Alexander Mutter Clark
356	*Glasgow Scotland		
	‡Glasgow	26 Aug 1962	Archibald R. Richardson
1188	Paisley Scotland	12 Oct 1980	Alexander Cumming

Mission — 1
(As of Oct. 1, 2011; shown with historical number. See MISSIONS.)

(61) SCOTLAND IRELAND MISSION
51 Spylaw Road
Edinburgh, EH10 5BP
Scotland

WALES
Jan. 1, 2011: Est. population, 2,952,000; Members, 9,343; Stakes, 3; Wards, 18; Branches, 6; percent LDS, .27, or one in 377; Europe Area; England Leeds Mission.

Henry Royle was the first known missionary to work in Wales. Frederick Cook, a new convert, was assigned to travel with him. They arrived in Wales on 6 October 1840 and met with immediate success in the village of Cloy, now part of Overton, in North Wales. Just three weeks after their arrival, on 30 October 1840, Royle organized the Overton Branch, the first in Wales, at Flintshire with 32 members. Within four more months membership there had risen to 150 even though the missionaries experienced active and angry opposition from ministers and others. Within a few years, most of the early converts from North Wales had immigrated to Nauvoo.

In South Wales, missionary work also began in 1840 as missionaries, including James Palmer and John Needham, introduced the gospel but struggled to find converts. Missionary work in the first 3 years occurred in those Welsh counties bordering England and largely among those who spoke English. Language barriers limited the success of the work in Wales. The work did progress, however, and it was from southern Wales that approximately 80 percent of the converts hailed during the first 15 years of missionary work.

Much of that success was due to work in new fields of labor including the industrial areas of Monmouthshire and Glamorganshire, and a willingness to begin missionary work among Welsh speakers as William Henshaw did in 1843. Soon Welsh-speaking units were formed, beginning with the Pen-y-Darran Branch in Glamorganshire on 25 March 1843. It was followed by the Beaufort, Rumney, Tredagar, Merthyr Tydfil, and Aberdare branches that were organized as the Merthyr Tydfil Conference on 6 April 1844.

On 26 June 1844, Dan Jones, one of the first Welsh converts, who joined the Church while working in the United States, was imprisoned with Joseph Smith in the Carthage Jail. Smith had asked Jones if he was afraid to die. Jones declared that he was not afraid to die for the gospel. Joseph Smith then declared in prophecy: "You will yet see Wales and fulfill the mission appointed you before you die." The next morning Jones left jail to deliver a letter for the prophet. The martyrdom occurred hours later and within a few months, Jones and his wife, Jane, were assigned to labor in Wales. When they arrived in January 1845, there were just under 500 members in the country in small congregations.

Under Jones's direction, the mission began publication in July 1846 of a periodical titled Prophwyd y Jubili ("Prophet of the Jubilee.") In January 1849, it was renamed Udgorn Seion ("Zion's Trumpet.") Jones's brother John, although a minister for another faith, published 45 different Welsh pamphlets authored by Jones. Also in 1846, the first Welsh hymnal was published. It was the first non-English printing of Latter-day Saint hymns.

Under Dan Jones's leadership, the saints in Llanelli built the first Latter-day Saint meetinghouse in Wales in 1849. That same year Jones completed his mission and returned to America as leader of an immigrating company of 330 Welsh converts. At the time of his departure, membership rolls listed 3,603 converts in Wales in 11 conferences. One convert, William Howells, was called to serve from Wales as one of the first missionaries to France in 1849. Another convert, John Parry, immigrated to Utah and established a chorus which eventually became the Mormon Tabernacle Choir.

In 1851, John Davis's Welsh translation of the Doctrine and Covenants was published. It was followed early in 1852 by the Book of Mormon which was distributed bi-weekly in 16 page signatures with issues of the Udgorn Seion. A Welsh translation of the Pearl of Great Price was published at the same time as well as an enlarged songbook containing 575 hymns.

Dan Jones returned again as a missionary to Wales in August 1852. By the end of the year, there were well over 5,000 members in 13 conferences. In April 1856, Jones completed his second mission and again immigrated to Utah with a company of Welsh saints, this time numbering about 560 members including 11 of the 13 conference presidents.

The sudden loss of most of the major leaders in Wales in 1856, coupled with the continuing impact of out-migration to Utah, dramatically reduced Church membership in Wales. Udgorn Seion ceased publication in May 1861, and within a few years, the 13 conferences were condensed to three: Glamorgan, Pembrokeshire, and North Wales. In 1873, the three remaining conferences were consolidated to become the Welsh Conference that covered the entire country. Although missionaries continued to work in Wales through the remainder of the 19th century, they struggled against strong and organized opposition and without the support of a large membership base.

During the first World War, 1914-1918, wartime anxieties increased interest in religion and the Church in the United Kingdom countries, including Wales, experienced growth. Missionaries from America continued to staff the mission until United States involvement in the war in 1917 effectively stopped the flow. By 1919, there were only five American missionaries remaining in the British Mission. Local missionaries filled the void. In 1937, a small chapel was built by the saints in Merthyr Tydfil. It was dedicated by President Heber J. Grant who toured the British Isles on the occasion of the centennial anniversary of the Church in Britain.

By 1930, the Welsh District of the British Mission listed just three branches in Wales with a total membership in the country of 200. The beginning events of World War II caused the evacuation of all missionaries from the United Kingdom including Wales. In September 1939, all but a handful of missionaries returned to the United States. In January 1940, British Mission president Hugh B. Brown and the last three missionaries left Great Britain. It was the first time in 104 years that the Church had not run a mission there.

Increased postwar placement of missionaries in Wales, coupled with missionary efforts by members began to build the Church again, and by 1950, there were 1,500 members in two districts.

In 1962, missionaries began to enjoy greater success in North Wales. Three months after beginning missionary work in the cities of Wrexham and Rhyl, enough converts had been baptized to justify creation of branches in those cities. The branches were not far from where the Church's first branch in Wales had been formed in 1840.

A large meetinghouse was built in Merthyr Tydfil in South Wales in 1963 by local members and building missionaries, the second meetinghouse constructed in Wales in the 20th century. Twelve years later it became home to the Merthyr Tydfil Stake, the first stake in Wales, created on 12 January 1975.

The Cardiff Wales Stake was created on 9 May 1982.

Members in Wales participated in celebrating the 150th anniversary of the Church in the British Isles in July 1987. A conference was held on 26 July in Cardiff, with Elder Russell M. Nelson of the Quorum of the Twelve Apostles participating. In 1990, local members joined with descendants of Welsh immigrants from Utah to celebrate the 150th anniversary of the Church in Wales. Events included a Church historic sites tour and a banquet. Wales House of Commons member Dafydd Ellis Thomas attended.

On 6 March 1993, the Sons of Utah Pioneers sponsored a Welsh Festival in Provo, Utah. As part of the festivities, a portrait of Dan Jones was presented to Gordon B. Hinckley for placement in the Provo Missionary Training Center. In a meeting that followed at the Marriott Center, the Tabernacle Choir sang Welsh hymns and Lord Ellis Thomas, a Welshman who sits in the British House of Lords, addressed the crowd.

Members in Wales are in the Preston England Temple District and many attended the dedication of the Preston temple on 7-10 June 1998.

In 2002, membership reached 7,615.

Sources:Andrew Jenson, Encyclopedic History of the Church, 1941; Arnold K. Garr, Donald Q. Cannon, Richard O. Cowan, ed., Encyclopedia of Latter-day Saint History, 2000; V. Ben Bloxham, James R. Moss, Larry C. Porter, Truth Will Prevail: The Rise of the Church of Jesus Christ of Latter-day Saints in the British Isles, 1837-1987; 1987; James B. Allen, Ronald K. Esplin, David J. Whittaker, Men With A Mission: The Quorum of the Twelve Apostles in the British Isles, 1837-1841, 1992; Europe West Area Public Affairs Council, Exploring Your Heritage: Church Historical Sites in the British Isles, n.d.; James R. Moss, "The Kingdom Builders," Ensign, December 1979; Ronald D. Dennis, "Dan Jones, Welshman, Ensign, April 1987; Don L. Searle, "The Church In the United Kingdom and Ireland," Ensign, June 1998; "2 Branches Organized in North Wales Area, Church News, 3 February 1962; "U.S. Singers Tour Wales," Church News, 19 September 1964; Gerry Avant, "Gospel Enhances Welsh Love of Family, Music and Country," Church News, 25 October 1980; Dell Van Orden, "Cardiff Wales Stake Deals With Challenges," Church News, 15 September 1985; Bert J. Rawlins, "Gospel Spread Quickly in Wales, Church News, 18 July 1987; "Church's Past Prelude to Its 'Glorious' Future," Church News, 8 August 1987; "LDS Sesquicentennial Is Observed In Wales," Church News, 8 September 1990; Mike Cannon, "Festival Celebrates Welsh Heritage," Church News, 13 March 1993.

Stakes — 3

(Listed alphabetically as of Oct. 1, 2011.)

No.	Name	Organized	First President
Europe Area			
1341	Cardiff Wales	9 May 1982	Barry Derek Roy Whittaker
676	Merthyr Tydfil Wales	12 Jan 1975	Ralph Pulman

BERMUDA

Jan. 1, 2011: Est. population, 68,000; Members, 140; Branches, 1;
Percent LDS, .19; or one in 524; North America Northeast Area; New York New York South Mission.

Bermuda, a United Kingdom dependency, consists of 360 small coral islands, 20 of which are inhabited, located 580 miles east of North Carolina. Most residents are Protestant.

Church members serving in the military and their families were the first Latter-day Saints in Bermuda in the early 1950s. On 16 July 1953, a group of servicemens' wives organized a Relief Society under the jurisdiction of the Eastern States Mission on 11 October 1956. In 1959 Elder Harold B. Lee of the Quorum of the Twelve Apostles visited Bermuda and spoke to the Latter-day Saints on the island. Sacrament meetings and Sunday School were held among the military personnel beginning on 8 October 1961.

Missionaries Arthur L. McMullin and his wife, Melba, arrived 19 April 1966, and received government permission to conduct missionary work on 3 May 1966. On the following 31 May, missionaries Kenneth R. French and Curt S. Call arrived. Eastern States Mission president W. Jay Eldredge organized the Bermuda Branch, with about 50 in attendance, on 25 June 1966 and called Rodney S. Gillihan as president. This branch became part of the New York New York Mission in 1974.

Native Bermudians began to join the branch in the 1980s. Vernon Every, converted in 1982, became the first Bermudian to serve in the branch presidency in 1985. In 1993, Bermuda was placed in the New York New York South Mission. Seminary began there in 1994.

As the U.S. military base was phased out in the early 1990s, many families moved away. When the base finally closed in 1995, its closure had minimal impact on the branch, taking only one family. The first Bermudian branch president, Robin Mello-Cann, joined the Church in 1993 and became branch president two years later. That same year Bermudian Amy Trott became the first native missionary to serve from the branch. She served an eighteen month family history mission in Ohio.

Three tall sailing ships of Sea Trek 2001, the commemorative voyage honoring the thousands of Latter-day Saints who immigrated to America from Scandinavia, Continental Europe and the British Isles, arrived in Bermuda on 27 September 2001, after crossing the Atlantic.

Sources: "Branch on Island Supervised from N.Y.," Church News, 14 December 1957; Bermuda Branch, History, 1998, Church Archives; Heidi Waldrop, "Bermuda Branch Sprouts in Gentle Island Climate," Church News, 25 August 1985; "Nine New Missions Created," Church News, 13 March 1993; Sarah Jane Weaver, "Worldwide Seminary," Church News, 31 May 1997; "Bermuda: Small Branch on Small Island," Church News, 29 September 2001.

CAYMAN ISLANDS

Jan. 1, 2011: Est. population, 49,000; Members, 203; Branches, 1;
Percent LDS, .17 or 1 LDS in 579; Caribbean Area; Jamaica Kingston Mission;

Lying south of Cuba, the Cayman Islands are a British dependency, located in the Caribbean Sea some 400 miles south of Florida, with most of the population on the Grand Cayman Island.

In 1970, Joan M. Evans, who was born in the Cayman Islands, joined the Church in Miami, Fla. In 1979, her family returned to her homeland where she operated a motel. She and her family were the only known members of the Church. For years she requested missionaries and was visited by mission presidents once or twice a year.

Church members Harold and Marjorie Booth from then Rhodesia moved to the Cayman Islands in November 1982 where the Booths found employment. They started holding sacrament meetings with the Evans family. He was set apart as branch president on 1 May 1983.

Harold Booth developed a friendship with a Mr. Wilcox who was the islands' chief immigration officer, and who had a brother that was a member of the Church in Rhodesia. In September 1985, Wilcox made arrangements so that missionaries complied with immigration law. Shortly thereafter, Richard Brough, president of the Jamaica Kingston Mission, sent the first missionaries. On 5 June 1989, the Booths retired and moved to South Africa.

Due to Cayman's economic strengths, Church membership in the country changes rapidly and has included people from the United States, Jamaica, Guyana, Canada and the United Kingdom. A philanthropist Church member donated land and money for a chapel to be built, which members moved into on 20 July 2003.

In 2003, there were 113 members.

Sources: Kathleen Jones Brown, Telephone conversation, 12 April 2004; Margene Stringham, Florida!!–But not Forever, 1991; "Cayman Islands Opened," Church News, 24 November 1985; Marjorie Booth and Noel da Silva, telephone conversation, 4 May 2004. Noel da Silva, electronic mail, 23 May 2004; Lowell R. Gerner, telephone conversation, 28 May 2004.

GIBRALTAR

Jan. 1, 2011: Est. population, 28,000; Members, 16; Branches, 1; Cadiz Spain Stake;
Spain Malaga Mission; percent LDS, .11 or 1 LDS in 875.

A British dependency on Spain's southern coast, Gibraltar is a narrow peninsula ending with a cliff nearly a quarter of a mile high.

On 7 March 1853 Edward Stevenson and Nathan Porter arrived at Gibraltar. They began preaching there, but encountered opposition from local government officials. Because Porter could not get permission to stay, he left Gibraltar on 1 April 1853, but Stevenson, a native of Gibraltar remained. On 4 April Stevenson was arrested, but he was soon released because he had almost successfully converted one of his jailors. On 28 July 1853 Stevenson baptized John McCall and Thomas Miller, the first known baptisms performed on Gibraltar. A branch was organized on 23 January 1854, but with the onset of the Crimean War that year, most of the members of the branch left for military duty in Asia. Feeling that his work was done, and being summoned to Portugal to bless a sick Latter-day Saint living there, Stevenson left Gibraltar on 2 December 1854.

No further Church activity is recorded until the 1970s when membership, mostly composed of British military personnel and their families, was sufficient to organize a Sunday School on 7 November 1971. A branch was organized on 27 May 1972 but membership dwindled and the branch was disorganized on 25 April 1976. During that time, the branch was under jurisdiction of missions in England. Another branch was created in 1982 and dissolved in 1984.

A branch was again created on 5 June 1991. On 19 February 1995, Gibraltar became a part of the Cadiz Spain Stake.

Sources: Andrew Jenson, Encyclopedic History of the Church of Jesus Christ of Latter-day Saints, 1941; Gibraltar Mission, Manuscript history, Church Archives; Ralph L. Cottrell, Jr., A History of the Discontinued Mediterranean Missions of the Church of Jesus Christ of Latter-day Saints, thesis, 1963; Donald Q. Cannon and Richard O. Cowan, Unto Every Nation: Gospel Light Reaches Every Land, 2003; Gibraltar Branch, Manuscript history, Church Archives; Local unit history file, Church Archives.

URUGUAY

Jan. 1, 2011: Est. population, 3,494,000; Members, 95,726; Stakes 16; Wards 107; Branches 55; Missions, 2; Districts, 4; Temples, 1; percent LDS, 2.6, or one in 38; South America South Area.

On the eastern coast of South America, the Republic of Uruguay has a Spanish-speaking population that is 52 percent Roman Catholic, 16 percent Protestant, 2 percent Jewish, and 30 percent non-professing or other.

Beginning in the mid-1920s, Montevideo was a frequent stopping point for missionaries traveling by steamship to and from the United States to serve in Argentina. In 1940 Rolf L. Larson of the Argentine Mission became well known in Uruguay as a member of the Argentine all-star team participating in the South American basketball finals, where he was often recognized as an LDS missionary. Shortly thereafter mission president Frederick S. Williams and his secretary visited Montevideo to meet with friends made by Larson.

From 1942 to 1947 various LDS families lived in Montevideo, many of them working for the U.S. government or businesses. In July 1944, President James L. Barker of the Argentine Mission organized a branch in Montevideo for these members, with Fred Williams as branch president. As World War II progressed, many of the Latter-day Saints living in Montevideo returned to the U.S. or were transferred elsewhere and the branch was closed.

With the war over, in August 1946, Williams and other former Argentine missionaries met with Church President George Albert Smith to urge that missionary work be established in additional South American countries. Two months later Williams submitted to the First Presidency a document regarding conditions in various countries, with Uruguay heading the list of places he recommended be opened to proselyting. He heard nothing more about his proposal until April 1947, when President David O. McKay called him as the first president of the Uruguayan Mission.

Williams and his family arrived in Montevideo in August 1947. In October they were joined by Charles C. Janson, who had been serving in the Argentine Mission, and Argentine Latter-day Saint Juan D. Sciorra. Ten days later the first missionaries called to Uruguay from the United States (Wilford M. Farnsworth, Preston J. Bushman Jr., and William N. Jones) joined the small group appointed to launch the new mission.

By February 1948, when Stephen L Richards of the Quorum of the Twelve visited Uruguay, four branches had been organized in Montevideo and a branch had been established in the interior city of Treinta y Tres. The first baptisms took place in November 1948, including Avelino J. and María Esther Rodríguez and Diber Alba Preciozzi in Montevideo and others in Treinta y Tres and Durazno. Local residents Eduarda Argault, Argina Williams, Elsa Vogler, and Juana Gianfelice were the first full-time missionary sisters to serve in Uruguay (1948-1949), with La Von Evans and Mersel M. Day being the first sister missionaries to arrive from the United States (February 1950). Late in 1949 the country of Paraguay was added to the territory of the Uruguayan Mission, a situation that continued for more than 25 years. (Some years later the mission was also given temporary responsibility for beginning missionary efforts in Peru, on South America's west coast, and for a month late in 1956 was assigned similar responsibility for missionary work in Chile.)

Missionary work proceeded slowly, but by the time President Williams was released in 1951, branches had been opened in fourteen of the country's nineteen departmental capitals and total LDS membership stood at approximately five hundred. Ground was broken in January 1953 for the first LDS meetinghouse in Uruguay, built for the Deseret Branch in Montevideo, with President McKay laying the cornerstone for the building in February 1954 and Elder Mark E. Petersen of the Twelve dedicating the building in December of that year. Additional buildings were started for the Rodó Branch in Montevideo and in Treinta y Tres.

To familiarize Uruguayans with the Latter-day Saints, the mission organized the Club Deseret to sponsor athletic activities, especially basketball and softball, as well as a mission choir and other musical groups that performed for the general public. More formal approaches to missionary work were also emphasized and by 1960 Church membership had risen to nearly 3,400. In spite of the growth in numbers, as late as 1959 the majority of the branch presidents and all of the district presidents were missionaries from the United States. When mission president J. Thomas Fyans arrived in 1960, he determined that greater emphasis should be given to training local Latter-day Saints to fill leadership positions. His systematic approach to teaching the principles of lay leadership, "Six Steps to Stakehood," helped to move the Church in Uruguay into a new era and paved the way for increased success in the missionary effort. By 1965 the total Church membership in Uruguay exceeded 11,000.

During the early 1960s, Uruguay became the administrative center for the Church in South America when Elder A. Theodore Tuttle of the First Council of the Seventy was assigned as supervisor of the missions on that continent and took up residence in Montevideo. Following the introduction of the building missionary program in 1961, the Church constructed residences and offices in the Carrasco section of Montevideo for the officers of the South American Building Committee. Under this program, 10 new meetinghouses were completed in Uruguay by 1967.

With the progress of the Church in Montevideo, both in terms of numbers of members and trained leaders, by November 1967 the time had come for a stake to be organized in the Uruguayan capital. At the time there were only two other stakes in South America.

Church growth continued during the years that followed, although the country was plagued for many years by urban guerrillas and soaring inflation. The Montevideo Stake was divided in February 1974, and four stakes were organized in the interior during May 1977. By March 1980, with three more stakes in the capital and four in the interior, all of Uruguay was covered by stakes, although because of the challenges posed by the extensive territories covered by some of the interior stakes, three of them were returned to district status during 1989.

Other milestones in the Church's history in Uruguay include an area conference in Montevideo in October 1978, where President Spencer W. Kimball and other General Authorities addressed some 9,000 Latter-day Saints; the creation of a second mission in Uruguay in July 1997; President Gordon B. Hinckley's visit to Montevideo, where he spoke to some 11,000 Saints in August 1997 in conjunction with the 50th anniversary of the Uruguayan Mission; and the dedication of the Montevideo Uruguay Temple by President Hinckley in March 2001.

Membership reached 80,000 in 2002. In 2005, membership reached 86,943.

Sources: "Uruguay," Countries of the World and Their Leaders Yearbook 2004; Frederick S. and Frederick G. Williams, From Acorn to Oak Tree: A Personal History of the Establishment and First Quarter Century Development of the South American Missions, 1987; Nestor E. Curbelo, Historia de los Santos de los Últimos Días en Uruguay : Relatos de Pioneros, 2002; Gordon Irving, "Uruguay: A Preliminary Background Paper," 1976; Dee F. Green, "La Misión Uruguaya," Liahona, April 1959; Dell Van Orden, "Emotions swell as meetings end," Church News, 11 November 1978; Arnold J. Irvine, "Church makes strides in this small country," Church News, 30 January 1982; John L. Hart, "They had the faith to be first," Church News, 9 November 1986; "Visit is climax to events, greeted with reverence, joy," Church News, 23 August 1997; "Mission created in Uruguay flourishes among a prepared people," Church News, 27 September 1997; Nestor Curbelo, "Dream of many decades now a reality," Church News, 24 March 2001.

Stakes — 16
(Listed alphabetically as of Oct. 1, 2011.)

No.	Name	Organized	First President
	South America South Area		
1123	Artigas Uruguay	23 Mar 1980	Luis Gonzalez
1098	Durazno Uruguay	25 Jan 1980	Luis Alberto Ferrizo
2072	Las Piedras Uruguay	2 Jul 1995	Gustavo Eduardo Sarasua
2232	Maldonado Uruguay	15 Sep 1996	Louise Laurito
1033a	Melo Uruguay	2 June 1979	Santiago Gonzalez
1944	Mercedes Uruguay	20 Jun 1993	Milton Jose Airala Perez
1058	Montevideo Uruguay Cerro	2 Sep 1979	Nester Rivera M.
631	Montevideo Uruguay East	17 Feb 1974	Ariel A. Fedrigotti
2265	Montevideo Uruguay Flores	17 Nov 1996	Miguel H. D'Amore Tavani
1034	Montevideo Uruguay Maronas	3 Jun 1979	Jorge Washington Ventura
890	Montevideo Uruguay North	12 Feb 1978	Ariel Omar Fedrigotti
444	*Montevideo Uruguay West *Montevideo Uruguay ‡Montevideo	17 Feb 1974 12 Nov 1967	Vincente C. Rubio
2344	Paysandu Uruguay	27 Apr 1997	Jorge Bautista Scarpiny Inda
832	Rivera Uruguay	20 May 1977	Ormesindo Correa
1019	Salto Uruguay	22 Apr 1979	Atilio Silveiro
2614b	Tacuarembo Uruguay	22 June 2003	Cesar Gustavo Hernandez Silveira
	Stakes discontinued		
836	Minas Uruguay Discontinued 12 Nov 1989	22 May 1977	Alberto E. Hernandez
833	Paysandu Uruguay Discontinued 22 Oct 1989 †Uruguay Montevideo Mission; Reinstated 27 Apr 1997	21 May 1977	Atilio Silveira
840	Santa Lucia Uruguay Discontinued 20 Aug 1989 †Uruguay Montevideo Mission	23 May 1977	Hector Julio Vigo

Missions — 2
(As of Oct. 1, 2011; shown with historical number. See MISSIONS.)

(40) URUGUAY MONTEVIDEO MISSION
Dalmiro Costa 4635 Bis, Malvin,
11400 Montevideo
Uruguay

(317) URUGUAY MONTEVIDEO WEST
Avenida Italia 2364, Piso 4
11600 Montevideo
Uruguay

VANUATU

Jan. 1, 2011: Est. population, 218,500; Members, 4,354; Districts, 2; Branches, 26; 1.7 percent LDS, or one in 58; Pacific Area; Fiji Suva Mission.

Formerly known as the New Hebrides Islands, Vanuatu is an archipelago of 80 islands in the southwest Pacific that became an independent republic in 1980. This island chain was made popular by the musical, "South Pacific." Vanuatu is populated by mostly Melanesians who speak Bislama, French, and English, and who are mostly Protestants.

Fiji Suva Mission President Ebbie L. Davis organized the Port Vila Branch on 15 July 1973 with Lanipota Fehoko as president. Missionary work began in Vanuatu in 1974 after several Latter-day Saint Tongan families moved there. Elder Hartman Rector Jr., of the Seventy and President Davis visited Port Vila in April 1974 to determine the possibility of assigning full-time missionaries to the island. Elder Rector felt it was essential that the area receive missionaries. Asaeli Mokofisi and Peni Malohifo'ou, two Tongans, began missionary work in Port Vila on 12 January 1975. Over the years, government restrictions on visas slowed the work. Non-native missionaries were expelled from Vanuatu in 1982. The branch was made part of the New Caledonia District in November 1983 to provide closer leadership training.

Between 1987-1989, Fred Massing and Timothy Proveau, both natives of Vanuatu, were the only missionaries on the island. They found success and baptized more than 40 people, including several family members. More missionaries were eventually allowed and Church membership increased. The Port Vila District was created on 19 October 1996 and additional branches were organized in the 1990s on the islands of Efate, Espiritu Santo, Tanna, and Ambae. The Luganville District was organized on 27 September 1998.

On 3 October 1998, Tom and Janet Tarohati, the first couple to be called on a mission from Vanuatu, began their mission in their native land. That same year, a seminary class was organized in each branch and an institute class in each district. At the request of Church members living on the island of Mere Lava, missionaries began visiting that island in 2002. The Church responded with aid via the missionaries in the wake of an earthquake in November 2002.

President Gordon B. Hinckley, in planning a tour of the Pacific Islands, looked on a map of the South Pacific to see where he had never been, and saw Vanuatu. He determined to visit there. He addressed the largest group of members ever known to have assembled in Port Vila when 2,212 members gathered on 19 June 2003. Members filled classrooms, clustered around doorways and on the lawn, and sat outside the chapel where they caught a glimpse of President Hinckley through louvered windows. The full Book of Mormon was published in the Bislama language in July 2004.

In 2005, membership reached 3,057.

Sources: Fiji Suva Mission, Manuscript history and historical reports, Church Archives; "Work Thrives in Earthquake's wake," Church News, 1 February 2003; John Hart, "An Island Welcome, First Trip to Melanesian Isle," Church News, 28 June 2003.

VENEZUELA

Jan. 1, 2011: Est. population: 26,815,000; Members, 150,017; Stakes, 29; Wards, 192; Branches, 82; Missions, 4; Districts, 8; Temples, 1; percent LDS, .5, or one in 186; South America Northwest Area.

On the Caribbean coast of South America, Venezuela is a federal republic where the people speak Spanish and Indian languages.

As early as 1966, a group of members, mostly foreigners working in Venezuela, held Church meetings in the home of Carl C. Wilcox in Caracas. A branch of 45 members was organized by Elder Marion G. Romney of the Quorum of the Twelve Apostles on 2 November 1966 with Carl C. Wilcox as president. Costa Rica Mission President Ted E. Brewerton sent four missionaries, Floyd Baum, Neil Gruwell, David Bell and Fred Podlesny, to Venezuela to begin missionary work. Baum, Bell, Steve Jensen and Stephen Edmunds began work in Maracaibo on 7 July 1967.

Fred Podlesny and David Bell baptized the first convert, Hernan Sepulveda, on 12 February 1967. Though initial converts were few, the Colombia-Venezuela Mission was created in 1968. The first district conference was held on 15 October 1968 with 28 missionaries then serving in Caracas and Maracaibo.

When the Venezuela Mission was created on 1 July 1971, membership had reached 1,259. Under the leadership of President Clark D. Webb, the mission began to average 40 converts per month. The Church Educational System started in Venezuela in 1972 under the direction of Alejandro Portal Campos.In January 1975, President Spencer W. Kimball became the first Church president to visit Venezuela. In 1977, about 4,000 members were organized in 23 branches and five districts. Successive mission presidents emphasized building programs and leadership preparation. The Caracas Venezuela Stake, Venezuela's first, was created on 15 May 1977, followed by the creation of the Maracaibo Venezuela Mission in 1979. Membership that year was 5,000. President Gordon B. Hinckley dedicated the Caracas Venezuela Temple on 20 August 2000.

Local Church leaders urged members to keep their focus on Christ and His teachings during the summer of 2003, a time of turbulent and volatile political divisiveness which caused much suffering due to fuel and food shortages. Despite political troubles, "We are baptizing more than ever," said Elder Claudio R.M. Costa, president of the South America North Area.

Membership in 2002 reached 113,652. In 2005, membership reached 134,597.

Sources: Venezuela Caracas Mission, Manuscript history and historical reports, Church Archives; Church Educational System, La Historia de la Iglesia en Venezuela 1966 a 1986, 1986; Donald Q. Cannon and Richard O. Cowan, Unto Every Nation: Gospel Light Reaches Every Land, 2003; "Venezuela," Ensign, February 1977; "Perseverance Pays," Church News, 10 November 1979; "Rapid Pace Across South America," Church News, 23 August 1997; Jason Swensen, "Venezuelan Saints Rejoicing at New Caracas Temple," Church News 26 August 2000; Jason Swensen, "Church Leaders Work to Buoy Members' Spirits," Church News 25 January 2003.

Stakes — 32
(Listed alphabetically as of Oct. 1, 2011.)

No.	Name	Organized	First President
South America North Area			
1724	Barcelona Venezuela	4 Jun 1989	Angel Luis Fajardo C.
2701	Barinas Venezuela	18 Dec 2005	Alexander Gamez V.
1989	Barquisimeto Venezuela	28 Aug 1994	Julio Ramon Davila Duran
2604c	Barquisimeto Venezuela Obelisco	23 Feb 2003	Wilker Jose Pacheco D.
2924	Cagua Venezuela	29 May 2011	Luis Fernando Silva Flores
827	Caracas Venezuela	15 May 1977	Adolfo F. Mayer G.
2695	Caracas Venezuela Los Teques	20 Nov 2005	Juan Carlos Chacin N.
1887	Caracas Venezuela Palo Verde	14 June 1992	Edgardo Angulo de la Paua
1717	Caracas Venezuela Urdaneta	7 May 1989	Hector Manuel Arraez R.
2607b	Ciudad Bolivar Venezuela	10 Nov. 2002	Hector Luis Arevolo
1787	Ciudad Ojeda Venezuela	24 Feb 1991	Juan Silfrido Carrizo C.
2920	Cumana Venezuela	15 May 2011	Alexander G. Navas A.
2615a	El Tigre Venezuela	29 June 2003	Alfredo Jose Rodriguez Carmona
2783	Guacara Venezuela	18 Nov 2007	Rigoberto Rodriguez Rojas
2608b	Guarenas Venezuela	11Nov 2001	Edgar Lopez Delgado
1585	Guayana Venezuela	15 Jan 1986	Luis A. Aguilar Guevara
1181	Maracaibo Venezuela	15 Sep 1980	Francisco Giminez S.

1862	Maracaibo Venezuela Centro	17 May 1992	Ruben Dario Blanco Valles
1414	Maracaibo Venezuela South	24 Apr 1983	Omar Alvarez
2721	Maracaibo Venezuela West	7 May 2006	Eulogio Jose Quero P.
1774	Maracay Venezuela	4 Nov 1990	Jairo R. Herrera
2608a	Maturin Venezuela	20 Oct 2002	Felix David Hurtado C.
2333	Merida Venezuela	23 Mar 1997	Freddy V. Herrera Molma
2627	Ocumare Del Tuy Venezuela	25 Jan 2004	Angel Maria Leal Hernandez
1885	Puerto La Cruz Venezuela	7 June 1992	Luis Jose Gonzalez
2863	Punto Fijo Venezuela	8 Nov 2009	Pedro Esteban Hernandez Alfonzo
2127	San Cristobal Venezuela	19 Nov 1995	Javier Ibanez Leon
2927	San Cristobal Venezuela Pirineos	5 June 2011	Guillermo Ignacio Guardia Arguello
2874	San Felix Venezuela	27 Jun 2010	Carlos Manuel Acosta Chan
2895	San Francisco Venezuela	12 Dec 2010	Jose Gregorio Cañizales
2125	Valencia Venezuela Candelaria	19 Nov 1995	Gamaliel de Jesus Osorno Flores
1050	*Valencia Venezuela Los Sauces	19 Nov 1995	
	‡Valencia Venezuela	19 Aug 1979	Teodoro Hoffman

Missions — 4
(As of Oct. 1, 2011; shown with historical number. See MISSIONS.)

(303) VENEZUELA BARCELONA MISSION
Av. Intercomunal Jorge Rodriguez
Torre BVC, Piso 5, Oficina 5A
Lecheria Anzoategui, Venezuela

(95) VENEZUELA CARACAS MISSION
Clle La Estancia, Edif. Centro Bonaven
Torre B, Piso 1 Oficina 14 B
Chuao, Amazonas, Venezuela

(174) VENEZUELA MARACAIBO MISSION
Calle 73 Ave 3G No. 3F-87
Edif. El Tama Sector Bella Vista
Maracaibo, Edo. Zulia
Venezuela

(267) VENEZUELA VALENCIA MISSION
Calle 137 Centro Comercial Imperial 2
Urb. Comoruco Sector Los Sauces
Piso 1 Oficina 1-7
Valencia, Carabobo 02001 Venezuela

VIETNAM

Jan. 1, 2011: Est. population, 86,968,000; Members, fewer than 100; Branches, 2; Percent LDS, .0001 or one in 869,680; Asia Area.

There were probably a few Latter-day Saints among the Americans who were sent to South Vietnam in the late 1950s as advisors in the conflict with North Vietnam. A small number of members, mostly U.S. military personnel and their families, began meeting in Saigon in 1962, and on 30 June of that year, President Robert S. Taylor of the Southern Far East Mission organized them into a group with Cecil L. Cavender as leader.

Many Latter-day Saints in Vietnam actively shared the gospel with their associates. Captain John T. Mullenex became the first known convert there on 3 November 1962. Two Vietnamese women, Duong Thuy Van and Nguyen Thi Thuy, were baptized on 3 February 1963. A future Church leader in Vietnam, Nguyen Cao Minh, joined the Church on 14 August 1963 while receiving military training in Biloxi, Mississippi.

Elder Gordon B. Hinckley of the Quorum of the Twelve became the first General Authority to visit Vietnam in May 1963 when he and President Jay A. Quealy of the Southern Far East Mission met with Church members in Saigon. By the end of 1964 there were 140 members in Saigon, 17 of whom were Vietnamese. In August 1963, a small group of servicemen began holding Church meetings on an airbase in Bien Hoa.

In May 1965, President Quealy organized the LDS servicemen in Vietnam into four groups, including the branch in Saigon. He also appointed Harper K. Morris as LDS servicemen's coordinator for South Vietnam and designated the country as a zone of the Southern Far East Mission. In November, the zone was divided into three districts: North, Central, and South, with a president and counselors over each.

Ray A. Young received permission to build a small Latter-day Saint chapel on the Air Force base at Bien Hoa in June 1965. The building was completed by November. At the end of the year, there were an estimated 1,500 LDS military personnel serving in Vietnam from the United States, and meetings were being held in at least 17 locations. Groups were organized wherever three or more members could meet together. The first Latter-day Saint chaplain, Navy Lt. Richard F. Wood, began his tour of duty in Vietnam in February 1966.

In June 1967, the Saigon Branch rented a home that could serve as a chapel. It included a cement enclosure, probably intended as a rain reservoir, that doubled as a baptismal font. The Church was officially recognized by the South Vietnamese government on 26 October 1967. By 1968, at the height of U.S. involvement in the Vietnam War, the Church estimated that there were more than 5,000 Latter-day Saint servicemen in the country, including six chaplains, organized into over 60 groups. About 70 Vietnamese had joined the Church by that time.

Responsibility for Church efforts in Vietnam shifted from the Southern Far East Mission to the Southeast Asia Mission in November 1969. Vietnam became part of the Hong Kong-Taiwan Mission in October 1970 and of the Hong Kong Mission in January 1971.

Cong Nu Tuong-Vy (Sister Vy) was assigned to translate the Book of Mormon into Vietnamese in December 1969. She completed the translation in two years. Book of Mormon selections were published in 1980 and the complete translation was printed on 10 December 1982. Sister Vy, whose whereabouts were unknown for several years after 1975, finally saw a copy of the completed work in 1985.

In November 1991, Elder Merlin R. Lybbert, president of the Asia Area, became the first General Authority to visit Vietnam since the 1970s.

Church affairs in Vietnam were administered by the Thailand Bangkok Mission in the early 1990s and then by the newly-formed Cambodia Phnom Penh Mission beginning on 1 July 1997. In addition to the local Church members who were living in Vietnam, others moved there from abroad during the 1990s. Members of the Asia Area presidency organized branches in Hanoi and Ho Chi Minh City (formerly Saigon) in 1995. Church President Gordon B. Hinckley and other leaders visited with Saints in these two cities on 29 May 1996. He expressed his faith that in "the due time of the Lord, this land will be opened, and many wonderful people will become the beneficiaries of the gospel."

Sources: Richard C. Holloman Jr., The Snap of the Silver Thread: The LDS Church in Vietnam, 1977; Southern Far East Mission, Manuscript history and historical reports, Church Archives; R. Lanier Britsch, From the East: The History of the Latter-day Saints in Asia, 1851-1996, 1998; The Nguyen, "Freedom (A Prisoner of War in Vietnam)," Salt Lake Institute of Religion devotional, 6 November 1987; Southeast Asia Mission, Manuscript history and historical reports, Church Archives; Hong Kong Mission, Manuscript history and historical reports, Church Archives; "BYU Alumni Provide Aid to Vietnam Church Members," BYU Today, February 1986; David L. Hughes, "An End, A Beginning," This People, April 1985; Translation Division, Vietnamese Book of Mormon translation history, 1982, Church Archives; Cong Ton Nu Tuong- Vy, "Out of the Tiger's Den," Ensign, June 1989; Sheridan R. Sheffield, "Church Donates Medical Gift to Vietnam," Church News, 11 January 1992; "Church Hosts Recipients of Microscope," Church News, 27 June 1992; "Couples Enter Vietnam to Teach English," Church News, 30 January 1993; "Pres. Hinckley Dedicates Cambodia: Gives 'Addendum' to Prayer During His Visit to Vietnam," Church News, 8 June 1996.

VIRGIN ISLANDS
(British and U.S.)
Jan. 1, 2011: Est. population,110,000; Members, 712 Branches, 2; percent LDS, .6, or one in 168; Caribbean Area; Puerto Rico San Juan Mission.

The Virgin Islands are made up of three large islands (St. Thomas, St. Croix, and Tortola) and 50 small islands located 70 miles east of Puerto Rico. The majority of residents speak English and have a republican form of government

Beginning in the 1960s, various Latter-day Saint families from the United States lived on St. Thomas. Earl Keele arrived in May 1969 and his wife, Celia, and two children followed in August. The family held a home Sunday School under the jurisdiction of the San Juan Branch in Puerto Rico. In 1970, another family, James and Carolyn Boykin, joined the group. Debra Rybacki met with the family and received permission to be baptized in Brewer's Bay in January 1976. Other families arrived and the St. Thomas Branch was created on 13 December 1977.

The first missionaries, John Sorensen and Dean Blomquist, arrived in June 1978. They baptized a friend of Debra Rybacki, Aubrey Nelthropp, and his wife, Carol, on 16 July 1978. In the early 1980s, the Church designed a prefabricated meetinghouse for use in tropical climates and built a prototype for display purposes. Originally, the building was to be sent to Mexico, but laws in Mexico prevented it, so the meetinghouse was given to St. Thomas. On 21 October 2001, Joseph W. Hodge became the first local branch president. Branches have also been established on St. Croix, Tortola, and since 2003 a group meets in St. John.

The first missionaries to St. Croix were Thomas Williams, Eric Leach, Gregory Collier, and Kurtis Gibbons, who arrived on 28 January 1981. They held meetings in the home of a member, Jack Cluett, with about 15 attending. A branch was organized on 8 February 1981, with Stephen L. Whitmer as the first president. A meetinghouse was later built on the island and dedicated in 1985. Until 1999, branch presidents were natives of the United States. In 1998, Tydel B. John, a local teacher from St. Vincent, joined the Church after serious study about Joseph Smith. He was called as branch president on 21 February 1999. About 60 members attend weekly meetings in St. Croix.

In 1985, a Latter-day Saint woman vacationed on the island of Tortola and met William Osborne, a local doctor. She offered to send him materials about the Church. Osborne read the Church literature and during a business trip in July 1985 to Puerto Rico visited the mission office. Within a few days Osborne was baptized. He was the first member in Tortola. On 8 August 1999, the Tortola Branch was organized.

President Gordon B. Hinckley and Elder Russell M. Nelson of the Quorum of the Twelve made a brief stopover in St. Thomas on 12 January 2004. President Hinckley was returning from dedicating the Accra Ghana Temple and held a member meeting before returning to Salt Lake City. It was the first visit of a Church president to the Virgin Islands.

In 2002, membership reached 427.

Sources: Puerto Rico San Juan Mission, Manuscript history and historical reports, Church Archives; West Indies Mission Manuscript history and historical reports, Church Archives; "Home Emphasized on Island Visits," Church News, 24 January 2004; John K. Baird, Telephone conversation, 14 June 2004; Tydel B. John, Telephone conversation, 17 June 2004.

WALES
(See United Kingdom)

ZAMBIA
Jan. 1, 2011: Est. population, 11,863,000; Members 2,587; District 2; Branches 10; Missions 1; Percent LDS, .019, or one in 5,303; Africa Southeast Area.

Zambia, previously known as Northern Rhodesia, became independent from Britain on 24 October 1964. It is a landlocked country in south-central Africa, surrounded by Angola, Zaire, Tanzania, Malawi, Mozambique, Zimbabwe, Botswana, and Namibia. Most of the population follows Christian beliefs, with smaller numbers who follow indigenous, Hindu, and Muslim beliefs. English is the official language, while Bemba, Kaonda, Lozi, Lunda, Luvale, Nyanja, Tonga, and about 70 other indigenous languages are also spoken.

There were two known members of the Church, Edward L. and Hester Orton, in Northern Rhodesia as early as April

1942. In August 1943, Latter-day Saint Frederick J. Spear, moved with his family to the Copperbelt Region of Northern Rhodesia. They settled in Luanshya. In November 1945, William A. Jubber moved to N'Dola, Northern Rhodesia. The first known baptisms in Northern Rhodesia, Jubber's wife, Johanna and their son, William, were held on 28 September 1947.

By this date a Sunday School group was meeting in the Spear's home. South African Mission President, Evan P. Wright conducted a mission tour of Northern and Southern Rhodesia in April 1950 and on 4 April, he set apart Frederick J. Spear as presiding officer in Northern Rhodesia.

By the end of April 1951, there were 12 known Latter-day Saints living in Northern Rhodesia. In May 1951, the Church received permission for missionaries to work there. Soon thereafter, Dean W. Martin and Murray C. Nichols were transferred to Luanshya, and commenced missionary work. When the missionaries arrived, they found several people already prepared for baptism, having been converted by the Spear family.

N'Dola also received missionaries, Ronald T. Pace and Arthur W. Wiscomb, about this same time. The first convert was Willem Coenraad Fourie who was baptized by Frederick J. Spear on 17 June 1951. The next day, the Luanshya Branch was organized with Frederick J. Spear as president.

On 25 June 1961, the Copperbelt Branch was organized in Kitwe with Leonard L. Clark as president. The branch immediately began to raise the funds necessary to build a chapel. Groundbreaking for the Copperbelt Branch meetinghouse was held on 31 August 1963. Slightly over a year later, on 24 October 1964, Northern Rhodesia declared its independence from Britain and became Zambia. Political unrest followed. Building of the Copperbelt meetinghouse continued despite the political crisis. It was dedicated 16 May 1965. Because of government policies many people, including most of Latter-day Saints, left Zambia in the late 1960s.

By August 1969, missionaries were no longer allowed to work in the country, and by January 1971 most members had moved away. The Copperbelt Branch meetinghouse was sold on 11 October 1972 to the Zambian government for use as a school.

The Zimbabwe Harare Mission was organized on 1 July 1987, and in April 1992 Dean and Ruth Harrison were sent to resume missionary work in Zambia. In July, the Church again received legal recognition.

The Lusaka Branch was organized on 14 July 1992. Elder Russell M. Nelson of the Quorum of Twelve visited Zambia on 20 August 1992. Branches of the Church were organized in three major cities in the Zambian Copperbelt, in Luanshya on 27 October 2002 and in Kitwe and N'Dola on 1 December 2002. That was followed by the formation of the Lusaka Zambia District on 16 February 2003.

Membership was 1,191 in 2003. In 2005, membership reached 1,648. Membership was 2,359 by Jan. 1, 2011.

The Zambia Lusaka Mission was created by the division from the Zimbabwe Harare Mission on July 1, 2011.

Sources: "Branches Organized in Zambia," Church News, 4 January 2003; Evan P. Wright, "A History of the South African Mission, 1852-1970"; Cumorah's Southern Cross, Record of members, Church Archives; South African Mission, Manuscript history and historical reports, Church Archives; Borgna Brunner, "Countries of the world, Zambia," Time Almanac 2004.

Mission — 1
(As of Oct. 1, 2011; shown with historical number. See MISSIONS.)

ZAMBIA LUSAKA MISSION
Plot No. 14038
Katima Mulilo Rd
Lusaka, Zambia

ZIMBABWE

Jan. 1, 2011: Est. population, 11,393,000; Members, 18,549; Stakes, 3; Wards, 18; Districts, 2; Branches, 30; Missions, 1; percent LDS, .15, or one in 661; Africa Southeast Area.

There were Church members in Southern Rhodesia as early as 1925. Peter and Elizabeth DuPlooy, who lived 62 miles out of Salisbury, were baptized on 10 March 1925 while on a visit to South Africa. South African Mission President Samuel Martin made a trip to Southern Rhodesia in July 1927 where he and Marion L. Allred baptized two sons of Walter Taylor Jubber, an early member of the Church who emigrated to Southern Rhodesia from South Africa. During July 1930, South African mission President Don Mack Dalton sent missionaries, George C. Maw, Vern D. Greene, and Bertram C. Cutforth, to begin work in the new Rhodesia District in August 1930. On 30 August 1931, missionaries, A.K. Berry and Thomas Y. Wilson, organized Shangani Branch, with Walter Taylor Jubber as president. By 1935, Dalton stopped sending missionaries to Rhodesia because of the shortage of missionaries and Rhodesia's distance from mission headquarters in Cape Town, South Africa.

Members continued contact through letters written to the South African Mission headquarters that ran news in the mission publication The Southern Cumorah Cross.

It was not until 1 September 1950 that missionaries returned to Southern Rhodesia. Four missionaries, Dale G. Johnson, George L. Albright, Monroe McKay and Tharon Bigler, were transferred to Salisbury, while four other missionaries, Glen L. Hamberlin, Gail Weggeland, Donald Cook, and Dimar Hoggan, went to Bulawayo. On 1 February 1951 the first convert, Hugh Hodgkiss, was baptized.

On 17 April 1951, the missionaries distributed 3,000 handbills, prompting a large crowd to attend an introductory meeting. The Salisbury Branch was organized in September 1951. The first services were held in a preschool building. Ernest Sibanda was the first native Rhodesian baptized in Rhodesia in March 1965. The first known missionary to serve from Rhodesia was Judith Jubber who served in the Netherlands Mission from 1967 to 1969.

Meetinghouses were built and dedicated in Rhodesia in the late 1960s. Elder Mark E. Petersen of the Quorum of the Twelve dedicated the Salisbury Branch meetinghouse on 17 September 1967. Elder Marion G. Romney of the Quorum of the Twelve dedicated the Bulawayo Branch meetinghouse on 3 September 1968.

On 18 April 1980, Britain recognized Rhodesia's independence and the country's name was officially changed to Zimbabwe. On 1 July 1987, the Zimbabwe Harare Mission was organized from the South Africa Johannesburg Mission. In 1988, selections from the Book of Mormon were translated in Shona.

President Gordon B. Hinckley, on a five-country tour of Africa, visited Zimbabwe on 18 February 1998, and spoke to about 1,500 Latter-day Saints. Several government officials, including the Secretary of Defense and the Social Welfare director, attended the meeting in Harare.

On 12 December 1999, the Harare Zimbabwe Stake was organized by Elder Dennis E. Simmons of the Second Quorum of Seventy, with Edward Dube, president.

Membership in 2003 was 12,616, and 14,561 in 2004.

Sources: Evan P. Wright, "A History of the South African Mission, 1852-1970"; Cumorah's Southern Cross, Church Library; South African Mission, Manuscript history and historical reports, Church Archives; Record of members, Church Archives.

Stakes — 4
(Listed alphabetically as of Oct. 1, 2011.)

No.	Name	Organized	First President
2908	Gweru Zimbabwe	20 Mar 2011	Kasnos Paradzai
2541	Harare Zimbabwe	12 Dec 1999	Edward Dube
2804b	Harare Zimbabwe Marimba Park	8 June 2008	Stanley Makaza
2675	Bulawayo Zimbabwe	20 March 2005	Tasara Makasi

Mission — 1
(As of Oct. 1, 2011; shown with historical number. See MISSIONS.)

(204) ZIMBABWE HARARE MISSION
65 Enterprise Road,
Highlands, Harare, Zimbabwe

Editor's note: Information in this section has been gathered from a variety of sources and is believed to be the best available at the time of publication. Corrections, additional information and further country or state histories will be appreciated. Those with comments or information may write to: Church Almanac Histories, P.O. Box 1257, Salt Lake City, UT 84110 or Email ldschurchnews@desnews.com

Index